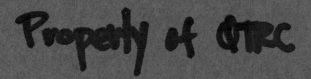

Lesbians and Gay Men Speak Out About Sexual Experiences and Lifestyles

by
Karla Jay
and
Allen Young

RE

WITH THE TECHNICAL
ASSISTANCE OF
Don Barrett

THE
GAY
PORT

SUMMIT BOOKS
NEW YORK

ALSO EDITED BY
KARLA JAY *and* ALLEN YOUNG

Out of the Closets: Voices of Gay Liberation

After You're Out:
Personal Experiences of Gay Men and Lesbian Women

Lavender Culture

BY ALLEN YOUNG

Allen Ginsberg:
Gay Sunshine Interview

Copyright © 1977, 1979 by Karla Jay and Allen Young
All rights reserved
including the right of reproduction
in whole or in part in any form
Published by *Summit Books*
A Simon & Schuster Division of Gulf & Western Corporation
Simon & Schuster Building
Rockefeller Center
1230 Avenue of the Americas
New York, New York 10020

Designed by Stanley S. Drate

Manufactured in the United States of America

Printed and bound by Fairfield Graphics

1 2 3 4 5 6 7 8 9 10

Library of Congress Cataloging in Publication Data

Jay, Karla.
   The gay report : lesbians and gay men speak out about sexual experiences and lifestyles.

   1. Homosexuals—United States. 2. Sexual intercourse—United States. I. Young, Allen,
joint author. II. Title.
HQ76.3.U5J38   301.41'57'0973   78-24056

ISBN 0-671-40013-4

*Dedicated to
all the lesbians and gay men
who participated in this survey*

Acknowledgments

The Gay Report could not have been completed without the assistance of many other people, some of them total strangers whom we shall never meet, some of them the very same people who share our homes and our daily lives with us.

For their assistance in the preparation and distribution of the questionnaires, including the concept, formulation, and content; typography, layout, and printing; and storage, shipping, and distribution, our thanks go to Robert Ames, Buddy Barkerr, Alan Bell, B. Meredith Burke, John C. Burton, Lucy Candib, Robert Chesley, Roan Conrad, M. Louise Crawford, Nancy Cunningham, Cyndy, Andrea Dworkin, Bruce Fitzgerald, Ann Gregory, Barbara Grier, Gerald Hannon, John Paul Hudson, Jonathan Katz, Chuck Keeton, David Krumroy, Julie Lee, J. Lee Lehman, Len Mazza, Brian McNaught, John Mitzel, Daniel Monette, Arthur H. Platt, Mike Richter, June V. Rook, Sheila Rowe, Tony Russo, Lynne D. Shapiro, Ken Sheppard, Mark Silber, Joan Sophie, Ted Steele, John Stoltenberg, David Stryker, Maida Tilchen, Mary Wickensheimer, and employees of Saltus Press, Worcester, Mass., and of the U.S. Postal Service. In fact, the number of people who aided in the distribution runs in the hundreds and our gratitude is warmly extended to these helpful women and men, too numerous to name.

We would like to thank the following periodicals that printed the questionnaire in full or in part: *The Lesbian Tide,* 8706 Cadillac Ave., Los Angeles, Calif. 90034, which has the largest paid readership of any lesbian magazine in the world and prints news, analysis, reviews and in-depth features; *Majority Report,* 74 Grove St., New York, N.Y. 10014, a national feminist publication printing feature stories and news articles; *Blueboy,* 185 N.E. 166 St., Miami, Fla. 33162; *Metro Gay News* (defunct), Detroit, Mich.; *The Gay Alternative* (publication suspended), Syracuse, N.Y., and *Playguy,* Suite 400, 888 Seventh Ave., New York, N.Y. 10019.

An incredibly large amount of raw material came to us, and for helping us deal with it, our special thanks go to Marjory Ackerman, John Cummings, Mgt. Desmond, Denis Helmus, John Kyper, Margaret Jeffries, Bruce McLay, Sonia Roth, Lester Stockman, and Mimi Verlaine, all of whom gave generously of their time.

As a result of his straightforward and unsolicited offer of help, Don Barrett became an important co-worker in this effort, coordinating the computer work and providing invaluable technical assistance, as well as reading the manuscript. The authors wish to thank Don for his work and for his patient understanding even when we lacked technical expertise or wished to do things in an unorthodox manner. Don joins with us in thanking the people who did coding and keypunching: Donna Davis, Sally First, Bill Grainge, Bob Kuhn, Catherine Martin, Tom Morganti, Lincoln Sharpless, Russ Shuman, Marion Tholander, and Nancy Walker.

The conception and realization of *The Gay Report*—and our association with this effort—would not have been possible without the contribution of our literary agents, Berenice Hoffman and Charlotte Sheedy, and the editorial staff of Summit Books: Christine Steinmetz, Jill Bailin, and Jim Silberman. The authors have appreciated not only their ideas and advice and their willingness to work hard to help create *The Gay Report,* but also the human warmth and friendliness that is so welcome in a work relationship.

Finally, the authors wish to extend thanks to each other for the affection and patience that make this collaboration possible, and to the lesbian and gay communities which have given us so much encouragement over the years.

Contents

13

14

15

THE EROTIC IMAGINATION AND MASTURBATION OF GAY MEN

621

16

HANGUPS AND HANDICAPS: THE LESBIAN EXPERIENCE

655

17

ANXIETIES AND AILMENTS: THE GAY MALE EXPERIENCE

18

PREJUDICE AND PRIDE, OPPRESSION AND LIBERATION

19

"What Do You People Do, Anyway?"

"What do you people do, anyway?" This is a real question that is sometimes asked of lesbians and gay men, but the question itself betrays an attitude that is often negative and hostile. The implication is that gay men and lesbians are bizarre, otherworldly creatures. And yet gay people don't think that way about themselves—not any more, as most of the writing in this book will attest.

A more specific question is, "What do lesbians do in bed?" This question contains within it the obvious male prejudice (and vanity) that sex without a penis is somehow unimaginable or at best insignificant. As for gay men, they are often asked, "Who does what to whom?" Or, even more crudely, "Which one of you is 'the woman'?" These questions illustrate the insistence on rigid sex roles that govern most heterosexual relations, as well as ignorance of the many options available to two men involved in an erotic relationship. The questions also reveal the link between the disdain for gay males and the inferior status of women in this culture.

From the Atlantic to the Pacific, from the Arctic Circle to the Gulf of Mexico, in the tiniest hamlets and in the biggest cities, the inhabitants of the United States and Canada include a significant portion of lesbians and gay men, people who are often ignored or persecuted and only rarely appreciated. Reached by means of a widely distributed questionnaire containing more than a hundred questions, 5,000 men and women offer the reader of this book intimate facts and feelings about the homosexual component of their lives. Most of the words in *The Gay Report* have been written by lesbians and gay men from the most diverse backgrounds, who willingly share what is usually considered private and intimate—presumably in the hope that there may be some vital connection between openness and understanding, between honesty and harmony.

In giving the information replying to straight society's dehumanizing, biased, and yes, ignorant questions, the thousands of gay men and lesbians

whose voices are heard in *The Gay Report* discuss their sexuality openly and frankly, often explicitly. To the extent that heterosexual people question homosexuals on the basis of healthy curiosity and an honest quest for understanding, gay people welcome the questions and try to answer them. Straight people looking for easy, consistent, one-dimensional, or comfortable answers about their lives, however, are likely to be frustrated or disappointed as they read this book. In fact, there are no such simple answers, since lesbians and gay men are an extremely varied group of people. It isn't only that gay people don't want to be pigeonholed—they can't be. For gay people, this book functions as a forum for communication. Such sharing of information, whether about sex acts or about surviving as a gay person in a hostile world, is a very useful and important process. A widely distributed book such as this, however, is obviously not merely a vehicle of communication for lesbians and gay men. It is also destined to be a source of solid information for the straight reader.

It is a fact that many straight people despise homosexuals. For some this hatred is based on ignorance, or on their inability to deal with the idea that other people are different. The problem of homophobia, as this anti-gay hatred is called, is very complex and is closely related to the rigid sex-role stereotype system for men and women that is now being attacked and defended so strenuously in our culture. The authors do not pretend that *The Gay Report* will undo centuries of male supremacy, but we hope the human realities presented in it will help erode some of the hatred that surrounds gay people.

The authors also hope that *The Gay Report* will be widely read by heterosexuals in certain institutionalized roles who often touch the lives of gay men and lesbians—and that includes parents, educators, clergy, psychologists, doctors, nurses, police officers, lawyers, and many other social and occupational categories. Of course, many heterosexuals are already the friends of gay people, both personally and politically, and we hope this book will answer some of these friends' questions, satisfying their genuine curiosity and their sincere interest in the lives of lesbians and gay men.

Beyond Sex, but Not Against Sex

Beyond the specifics of sexual acts, there is much in this book about how gay men and lesbians live. For, as with all people, sex is only a part of life. *The Gay Report,* like the questionnaires upon which it was based, focuses on sexual expression, but for gay men and lesbians—as for all people—sexuality cannot be divorced from consciousness. Thus, this report confronts not only the specifics of sexuality, but such issues as social interaction among gay people, relationships with family, the prejudice encountered and how to deal with it, coming to terms with sexuality and personality, and determining how to live one's life. This is a book on lifestyles and consciousness, on politics and economics, on sociology and psychology, as much as it is a book on sex and love.

Gay men and lesbians rightfully resent being dealt with exclusively on the basis of sexuality, as so often is the case. This is one of the reasons so many gay people prefer the words "gay" or "lesbian"—the term "homo-*sex*-ual" focuses on sex. Also, it has been totally abused by some psychiatrists who see gay people as sexual misfits, not people to be respected or learned from for this "difference," but objects to be abused, studied, "cured."

In rejecting this branding as purely sexual creatures, however, gay men and lesbians should not have to retreat from celebrating the sensual and emotional joy shared with a partner during intimate physical contact. For virtually all of the people who replied to the questionnaires we distributed, sex is a form of great pleasure as well as a vital means of communication, loving, and sharing.

Furthermore, at this point in the history of the human species, traditional forms of sexual relations, notably relations between men and women, are undergoing a revolutionary transformation. The women's movement and the gay political movement are involved in bringing the social consequences of sex and gender into the popular consciousness, and this survey is a part of that process.

For lesbians and gay men, lack of basic information is still a very real problem, even as the modern gay liberation movement approaches its tenth birthday and as gay bookshelves grow in size. Most gay people grow up in isolation (perhaps thinking that no one else can possibly be experiencing these feelings) or at least terribly misinformed by the stereotypes and other misinformation one might find in books on psychology and sex.

While movement leaders and a handful of theoreticians occasionally have access to the media, and while television portrays its often distorted characterizations of gay people, there are few opportunities to hear the voices of "ordinary" lesbians and gay men. With few exceptions, gay people have remained the invisible minority. Many Americans state that they do not even know a single gay man or woman, and yet it is generally agreed that about 10% of the population is gay! The anonymous nature of this survey has encouraged many to speak out who otherwise would remain silent, and this process challenges our invisibility to a certain extent, just as a gay person who writes about homosexuality under a pseudonym is expressing himself or herself more than a writer who avoids the subject altogether.

In recent years, a small number of gay activists have written about gay sexuality and gay consciousness in gay publications, but most of these writings have not been made available to a general audience. There are a few books of the "sex manual" type, but these tend to avoid problems and complexities. The view of gay people expressed in this survey, however, is a fresh, new one—from the "grass roots" up.

The need for such a fresh view should be clear. Even in the 1960s and 1970s, as sex-education programs become more common, as some churches liberalize their attitudes toward sex, as parents become more permissive, still for many lesbians and gay men the realities of homosexual life remain

shrouded in negativity. Widespread prejudice against homosexual people continues—prejudice evidenced in a 1977 Gallup poll in which a random sample of the general public agreed that homosexuals are the most discriminated-against group in the United States.

One of the most vicious stereotypes is that of the "child molester," the pervert who hangs out in schoolyards, an image conjured up by Anita Bryant with her "Protect America's Children" crusade. According to Susan Brownmiller, in *Against Our Will: Men, Women and Rape* (New York: Simon and Schuster, 1975, p. 278), "ten girls are molested for every one boy," and 75% of the offenders (97% of whom are male) knew the child. And yet no one condemns all heterosexual males for the actions of a minority.

Those lesbians and gay men who know the stereotypes to be based on falsehood, who would like to put a stop to the epithets and myths, are often the very same people who feel obliged to remain silent in the face of their own oppression. This complicity sometimes takes such extreme forms as laughing at "queer" jokes or even participating in violence against gays. The reason for this "closetry" varies, from subtle ingrained self-contempt to fear of physical abuse or loss of employment; elsewhere in this book gay men and women discuss their experiences and attitudes regarding this secrecy.

Gay people want civil rights, but most also want sexual satisfaction, a goal sometimes shunted aside. The two goals of civil rights and sexual satisfaction are interrelated, as the attaining of the latter is not so likely in an atmosphere of isolation, ignorance, and oppression. In giving so many gay people an opportunity to describe their sexual experiences and feelings, we believe we have encouraged a widespread dialogue, long overdue, about sexual expression and social relations among gay people.

Facilitating communication among gay people is a major function of this book, for despite the existence of a gay subculture or a gay community and a lesbian community, relatively few gay people communicate with other gay people on an intimate level. Many of the feelings and experiences written down in response to our questionnaires were being carefully thought about and expressed verbally by those individuals for the very first time in their lives. People even told us things they never told their lovers, their best friends, or their psychiatrists! It is exceedingly useful for people to share their enthusiasm, revulsion, good experiences and bad ones, anxieties, and also the sheer abandon of sexual pleasure.

For the gay reader of this book, the sexual information may be helpful, but not in the instructional sense of a sex manual. Most sex manuals are compiled by one or two people whose personal experiences and feelings often limit the presentation of information. Our purpose is not instruction, for knowing how to do something is not always the issue, but we do hope that the reader can grow from reading about the various experiences and viewpoints.

We also expect to challenge certain stereotypes and preconceived no-

tions, even those held within the gay community. As compilers, we have resisted the temptation to present the well-scrubbed homosexual man and woman, hollow figures who are exactly like heterosexuals except for sexual proclivities. This image often makes certain "liberal" heterosexuals comfortable, or it fits the needs of some political ideology or movement rhetoric, but it serves to ignore diversity and cover up the life experiences that very often make gay people "different" indeed.

Although *The Gay Report* will not generally make comparisons with heterosexual women and men, we do recognize that the rigid separation of people into "heterosexual" and "homosexual" is unrealistic, even harmful, and many bisexual women and men are included in these pages, helping to show that straight sexuality and gay sexuality are not worlds apart. Since each gay man or lesbian grows up in a predominantly heterosexual and male-chauvinistic environment, the sexual development of human beings is generalized throughout the culture. Gay male attitudes toward male genitals and lesbian attitudes toward the importance of emotion during sex, for example, reflect general ideas and attitudes prevalent in popular heterosexual culture. We know, furthermore, that sadomasochistic relationships exist between heterosexual men and women and that sadomasochism is probably not more pronounced among gay people than among straight people. It has been exasperating for gay people to discover how many straight people assume that what a certain minority does—men dressing in women's clothes, for example—is assumed to be the behavior of all. Thus, it is hoped that this survey will play a role in laying to rest forever numerous unfortunate homophobic and destructive myths about lesbians and gay men.

Why Us?

Karla Jay and Allen Young began working together as a team in the fall of 1970 when each was separately collecting early gay liberation articles for an anthology. When we discovered our similar efforts, we combined them and worked toward a common goal as co-editors, but we had to overcome certain barriers. Our collaboration began at a time when lesbians were separating themselves from gay men in response to widespread anti-woman feelings in the gay male community, feelings that clashed with the lesbian's heightened feminist consciousness. While the separation of lesbians and gay men was a necessary and constructive idea, it also seemed sensible to maintain a vision of a society where men and women could live and work together as equals. We find that we can work together and if our works contain the writings of both lesbians and gay men between the same covers, they are an attempt not at portraying false unity but rather at keeping open lines of communication. Karla communicates primarily with lesbians and Allen with gay men, but each of us also has his or her own contacts and friends of the "other" gender.

One anthology led to another, then a third, and although we made contact with experienced writers whose work appeared regularly in the gay

press, we also discovered the writings of lesbians and gay men expressing themselves as gays in print for the first time. We frequently encouraged the "rank-and-file" gay people we met, people not self-defined as "writers," to put their experiences and feelings down on paper; indeed, some of the essays in our anthologies are a direct result of our exhortations.

The grass-roots expression contained in *The Gay Report* is the logical extension of the anthologizing we have done; the very personal statements that abound in this book are a continuation of the best tradition of radical gay-feminist journalism.

Included in our original proposal for this study was a paragraph entitled "Why us?" In it, we said, "A crucial aspect in all of this is *trust,* for gay people have legitimate reason to fear and distrust straight society in general, and especially those engaged in research. Our experience as gay activists and anthologists as well as our contacts with the gay press and other media means we offer ideal credentials and credibility for proceeding with this project." We also stressed our independence and our commitment to honesty, and our political stance by stating that "the primary goal for gay people is not winning acceptability or tolerance, but rather self-love, overcoming the self-contempt that is the gay person's first enemy." We have kept those principles in mind constantly.

The Questionnaires

We decided to reach out to lesbians and gay men throughout the U.S. and Canada, recognizing that although Canada is a separate nation with a different political structure, the overall milieu for Canadian homosexuals is similar to that for Americans. We also decided at the outset that there should be two separate but interrelated questionnaires, one for lesbians and one for gay men. Each of us independently drew up a list of questions, Karla preparing questions for women, Allen preparing questions for men. The final questionnaires consisted of short-answer questions (mostly of the multiple-choice type) as well as a number of open-ended essay questions. We were convinced that large numbers of gay people would be turned off by the type of questionnaire used by social-science research organizations and pollsters, for although professionals use many valid techniques, they can alienate people with pseudo-scientific jargon and certain techniques such as asking the same question in several different ways in order to discern patterns. We didn't want people to be reminded of the tests they took in school, and we especially didn't want people to think they were being dissected in someone's laboratory. We also knew, in a very practical vein, that a book premised on written self-expression (for that would be the bulk of the book) required essay questions.

When we each had a list of essay questions, we compared them. There was considerable overlapping of questions. Each of us had come up with certain questions that the other had neglected, and we added most of them to each questionnaire. Only questions that were completely a function of

gender—menstruation for women, penis size for men, for example—were separated out. Of course, the questions on sexual acts would be different to reflect anatomy. We felt it was essential for us to recognize at the outset that "homosexuality" is not the same thing for men and for women, but the presence of many parallel questions would allow shared social experiences and problems of the women and the men to emerge clearly. We agreed that no attempt would be made to falsely correlate gay male and lesbian experiences—for example, gay men have more sex partners than lesbians, and misuse of this data could lead us to untrue "findings" about "gay people" generally, or could involve misleading, vague, or highly debatable statements about what behavior is "liberated," "promiscuous," "sexually objectifying," "puritanical," etc.

We then contacted a diverse group of friends and acquaintances—not essentially an activist group—and tried out the questionnaire. They felt that the long-answer format demanded too much, and suggested we replace most of the answers with short-answer or "scaled" questions. The panels also suggested adding several important topics we had omitted. We then decided to put together questionnaires that would combine short-answer questions and essay questions, and we obtained the assistance of people experienced in survey work, such as market researchers. Short-answer responses would contribute to our portrait, but we remained relatively unconcerned about compiling statistics, and we would not nor could not claim that statistics represented all gay people; they represent only those who responded. Our primary focus in preparing the questionnaires was to encourage self-expression in written form. However, we eventually concluded that by presenting an easy-to-do short-answer questionnaire first, we might encourage people to spend the time on the essay questions (where many of the short questions were repeated in different form).

Not every topic could be included in the questionnaires. Thus, there is very little on family background (e.g., "Were your parents separated or divorced during your childhood?"), a subject that has been overemphasized and abused in the traditional psychiatric literature. We felt we would turn people off if they felt we were trying to prove, or even disprove, the shrinks' popularized theories about how gay people get "that way," though some respondents felt we should have asked that very question. We could have asked people about their habits and preferences in such areas as food, arts and entertainment, books and periodicals, sports, home decorations, and dozens of other cultural and lifestyle subjects, but we limited ourselves to only a few such topics. These topics reflect our interest, and there isn't any particular explanation for what we left in and what we left out; perhaps gay men and lesbians will discover and develop means of communicating about all of these subjects in the future.

What sort of language to use in the questionnaire was an issue we confronted early on. Both of us found ourselves feeling most comfortable using a mixture of informal and formal language. For example, we agreed that some men might be more comfortable with the word "penis," while others

would feel that "penis" is only for talking to a doctor while "cock" is for a friend or a lover. The lesbian questionnaire contains somewhat less vulgar or coarse language. This difference results not from a conscious decision but perhaps from the fact that so many of the words relating to female sexuality and anatomy have a tradition of being used by men in a way that connotes humiliation, violence, or degradation, even though some lesbians use these words exuberantly. But in the lesbian questionnaire too, we tried to be forthright and frank in the choice of words, and there was no purposeful intention of a "ladylike" approach. We used a lot of gay slang, too, usually defining it. Though we may have confused a few people with these words, we made many others feel "at home."

A basic language problem involved what words to use for gay men and lesbians. We chose "gay men" and "lesbians" as our primary ones because of a sense we had that they were the most widely acceptable, but we also used the term "homosexual" in many of the questions. See Chapter 18 for more on this word debate.

Anonymity seemed essential to the success of our survey, so we asked people filling out the questionnaire to omit names and addresses. In addition, we did not wish to have in our possession a large list of names and addresses, because given gay people's status as criminals, completely lacking civil rights, such a list could be harmful if it fell in the wrong hands. Nonetheless, some people were adamant about not being anonymous, and gave us their names and addresses, an affirmation of gay freedom. Various comments on the questionnaires are printed in Chapter 19.

The format was a half-tabloid booklet, 8½ × 11 inches, with a glued binding, 16 pages long, printed on newsprint. Our funds were limited, and in order to circulate this large number of questionnaires we required the voluntary help of gay people throughout the U.S. and Canada. From the National Gay Task Force, we purchased a mailing list of more than 1,800 organizations, including gay churches, bookstores, and women's centers. *The Body Politic* and the *Gayellow Pages* provided a similar list of Canadian groups. To these groups, as well as to hundreds of friends, acquaintances, and contacts, we sent questionnaires, a letter explaining our purpose, and a return card to be used for requesting additional copies of the questionnaires. Response was overwhelmingly positive, and shipping out questionnaires was a major time-consuming task for a while. We had to go back to the printer twice to reorder; in all, we printed approximately 50,000 questionnaires for men and 45,000 for women, but this was not our total outreach.

We sent a special mailing to the more than 300 gay periodicals and radio shows listed in the *Gayellow Pages*. We asked them to print the full text of the questionnaires where possible, or at least to report the existence of our survey and to inform readers and listeners that the questionnaires were available by mail from our post-office box. The full text of the female survey was published in two periodicals, *Majority Report* (New York) and the *Lesbian Tide* (Los Angeles), with a combined total circulation of about

40,000. (*Majority Report* is a weekly newspaper circulated to gay and straight women.) The full text of the male questionnaire was published in the *Metro Gay News* (Detroit) and the *Gay Alternative* (Syracuse, N.Y.), with a total circulation of about 20,000. An abridged version with short-answer questions only appeared in *Blueboy* (Miami), with a national circulation of about 225,000, and the essay questions alone appeared in *Playguy* (New York), circulation 90,000.

Fag Rag (Boston) and the *Body Politic* (Toronto) distributed our own printed questionnaires as inserts with all mailed subscriptions. Scores of periodicals and radio stations, too many to be listed here, notified their readers about our efforts and published our address. These periodicals have a combined circulation of over 300,000. In addition, word of our efforts (in ads or articles) was published in a few nongay periodicals, including the *Village Voice, In These Times* (Chicago), and *Together* (New York), now called *Sexology*. In all, we estimated that 400,000 gay men and 100,000 lesbians actually saw our survey, while tens of thousands more were aware of it and had an opportunity to participate by writing in for the questionnaire.

We realized that our initial outreach, through gay groups and periodicals, was to people relatively comfortable with their gay sexuality, but this was by no means a population of gay activists or gay militants, and a significant portion were people who consider themselves to be "in the closet." You don't have to be very far out of the closet to read a gay periodical, to attend Sunday services at a gay church, or to stop in at a women's center, or even to go to a gay bar. Personal acquaintances as well as people we will probably never meet, including a few bartenders, distributed thousands of questionnaires at gay bars in small and large cities.

Employees at all-male movie theaters in Boston and Los Angeles distributed a significant quantity of questionnaires to men who might otherwise never have seen them. We also urged everyone to take extra copies to distribute to friends and acquaintances who do not have contact with the institutions of the gay community, and we know we reached many people in that way. We also dropped them off in therapy centers, sex shops, adult bookstores, regular bookstores, and even some sympathetic restaurants.

Word got out to groups not included in the Task Force list of gay organizations. At their request, a men's masturbation club called J/O Buddies, based in San Francisco, distributed the questionnaire to 250 members. The survey was also publicized through a men's group called TAIL (Total Ass Involvement League) and in a male porno consumer bulletin, the Market Reports Newsletter. A member of the National Socialist League (Nazis) in Los Angeles distributed several hundred. We sent the questionnaire unsolicited to nearly all advertisers in the "Trader Dick" (personal ads) section of a couple of spring issues of *The Advocate,* to the contact list published by *RFD* (a magazine for "country faggots"), and the "contact dykes" of the influential and popular *Lesbian Connection* newsletter based in East Lansing, Mich. One of our friends even gave a few questionnaires out to men cruising in a rest stop on Interstate Highway 91 near Holyoke, Mass.

We personally initiated distribution at two gay conferences in the spring of 1977, the New England Gay Conference in Providence, R.I., and the Southeastern Gay Conference in Chapel Hill, N.C. Questionnaires were shipped to various other spring conferences, including an International Conference of Gay Jews in New York City, a gathering of the National Organization for Women (NOW) in Detroit, and the Conference on Men and Masculinity in Des Moines, Iowa.

Completed questionnaires came from every state in the union, from nearly every province in Canada, and from as far away as Singapore. We were especially pleased to note that the responses proved that there was distribution not only to the big cities traditionally known for gay populations, but also to smaller cities, small towns, and rural areas. After seven months, we allowed the questionnaires to go out of print, and distribution ceased. Eventually, statistical analysis of the data collected in the survey showed that the people participating in the survey were generally representative of the overall adult population of the U.S. and Canada in terms of age, place of residence, and religious background. The two most populous states— California and New York—had the most participants, but every region of the U.S. and Canada was well represented. The average age of both lesbian and gay male participants was around 30, but the age range went from 14 to 82. Every major religious grouping was represented, as well as many smaller ones, from the most open-minded to the most repressive. As anticipated, the educational level of the respondents was unusually high—with more than 60% of both the lesbians and gay men holding at least a college diploma. This factor undoubtedly is related to unrepresentatively low participation by members of racial minorities, by people with lower incomes, and by those in unskilled jobs. The income figures, however, do reflect the disadvantaged economic status of women. Statistical information published in the appendix of this book provides demographic facts about who we did reach (broken down by gender), in some detail.

While satisfied with the range of people reached, we do not claim to have a scientific or representative sample of lesbians and gay men. The questionnaire was printed only in English, so we missed Spanish-speaking and French-speaking people. We also acknowledge that those individuals who occasionally participate in homosexual acts but who are unwilling (even in their own minds) to identify themselves as "gay" or "lesbian" were pretty much eliminated from the survey. (This is not to say that all or even a majority of our respondents are not concerned with secrecy or discretion. Many questionnaires arrived in our mailbox with elaborate wrapping and enough tape to take care of an entire family's Christmas gifts. One came carefully protected by several layers of aluminum foil. While a surprising number of people used envelopes that came from their places of employment and made no effort to cross out the return addresses, there were many who made certain that such return addresses were completely obliterated, and of course many envelopes came with no return address at all. This was

real physical evidence of the fear of discovery so many people wrote about in the essays.)

Teenagers living at home, and others in authoritarian situations, were hard to reach. Several of the gay men were inmates in mental hospitals. We succeeded in communicating with several prisoners, but our questionnaire was formally excluded from federal prisons (though one prisoner offered to distribute them) because of the same directive that has excluded gay periodicals for several years.

Another factor limiting responses is the fact that a 16-page survey is a formidable verbal exercise. So this is a sampling of people who volunteered to spend the time answering so many questions, and presumably a group of people for whom reading and writing come fairly easily. Although most respondents wrote out a few brief comments where requested in the short-answer section, only about one-third of the participants enclosed responses to the essay questions. Most of those who did respond to the essay questions, however, put in incredible amounts of thought and effort. What appears in this book is less than 10% of the written material submitted to us.

Class bias is probably inevitable in a survey of this type that requires a certain educational level, but we could think of only one solution to this problem—lengthy personal interviews—and we did not have the resources for that.

Writing the Book

When we began writing *The Gay Report* at the beginning of 1978, we had 1,900 regular questionnaires from gay men plus 2,500 *Blueboy* questionnaires, and 1,000 questionnaires from lesbians.

With the assistance of Don Barrett, a social-science computer specialist employed by a major Boston-area research contractor and a part-time staff member at Boston's *Gay Community News,* we made arrangements to have the short-answer results tallied by computer. Our emphasis was to be on simple percentages for each question, a choice that was ours, not Don's. We agreed at the outset not to pretend that these percentages represented the practices and views of all gay people—they reflected only our respondents. Excluding any questionnaires from countries other than the U.S. and Canada, we took a subsample of 250 lesbian questionnaires and 419 male questionnaires, since studies have shown such a subsampling technique to be at least 95% valid for a total sample as big as ours. The complete statistical or demographic information was taken from *all* of the questionnaires.

Given the versatility and current achievements of computer science, we did relatively little with the short-answer statistics. From the data, we could have created endless pages of charts and analyses. We were personally not inclined to produce a book filled with statistics and analysis—we were most excited about presenting excerpts from the comments and essays in a balanced, readable format, using the statistics we had in order to provide a

context. We approached this survey as writers and editors, with a commitment to *communication,* not to social science.

As the answers arrived, we realized that the questionnaire was by no means perfect. A few of the short-answer questions were not clear and sometimes people found groups of them difficult to answer. For example, when questioned about frequency of sex acts, people said their experiences differed greatly when they had a lover and when they didn't. By and large, we expected people to answer the questions in terms of their most current attitudes and situations, and we believe that most did interpret the questions in this way.

The questionnaires were divided by gender. We determined that most chapters would be organized by gender, while others would unite a discussion of lesbian and gay male experiences, but always with responses clearly identified as to gender. Karla wrote the chapters exclusively on lesbians, Allen those on gay men.

In addition, we agreed on some guidelines for deciding what to put in the book. We wanted the selection of questions to reflect the patterns of behavior and attitudes given in the short-answer questions. Obviously, then, the book could not overemphasize the unusual (no matter how curious or funny), and we needed to make a balanced presentation of people's preferences, giving the appropriate weight to each preference. But we agreed that those experiences or attitudes that the average lesbian or gay male reader might term unusual, bizarre, politically incorrect, or even "sick" definitely had a place in the book.

Did people just make up answers, going off into fantasies or perhaps just goofing off or even trying to foul up our survey? Two or three questionnaires were so illogical and so obviously inconsistent that we removed them from consideration—but all of these "rejects" had only short-answer responses. Among the essay questions, there were none that struck us as obviously phony. A few were a bit strange, and we did consider having a section in the book called "Believe It or Not" or "No Comment." Ultimately, however, we decided to include such material in the chapter where it seemed to fit, rather than separating out the "bizarre" for special attention. Our feeling was that those who spent the time to answer these questionnaires did not waste their time fabricating false answers. If some did, so be it. Let the reader decide.

No attempt was made to censor anyone's language in the responses. We found that some people wrote about their sexuality in a style that was nearly clinical, while others were very lyrical and romantic; some were frank and direct, and a few were downright coarse. The writing reflected attitudes ranging from exuberant to shy. We wanted the full range to remain for the reader to experience and to enjoy, as we did. We did correct some punctuation, grammar, and sentence structure, for the purpose of clarity, but where so-called "bad grammar" came through as a natural, comfortable way for the person to express himself or herself, we made no changes. Because misspelled words can be distracting, we did correct spelling. We retained

variant spellings of the words "woman" and "women," "womon," and "wimmin," as preferred by some lesbians. And, also for consistency, we adopted our personal preference of lowercase (small) *g* for "gay" and *l* for "lesbian."

In preparing the book we tried most of all not to get bored reading about something as wonderful and exciting as sex. And we tried not to lose our sense of humor. Some of the experiences and comments were quite funny. In some cases, the writer was trying to be funny, and we hope we've passed on a good deal of that intentional humor to the reader, so you can enjoy it as much as we did. In other cases, the humor may not have been intended, but we laughed anyway, always good-naturedly. Although we asked people directly to describe their funniest experiences, many had no response to that question and some replies seemed to reflect a very private moment of mirth that existed only in the past (a bed collapsing in the middle of raucous sex, for example), and it just doesn't evoke the same response from those reading about it now. We can't be sure what there is in this book that will make someone laugh, or for that matter what will make someone sexually aroused or, to the contrary, turned off or even disgusted. We only hope that no one will take one particular passage and use it to "prove" a point, positive or negative, about all lesbians or gay men.

We did have to be aware of our own subjective attitudes. After all, we, Karla and Allen, have our own preferences in sexual acts, attitudes, political views. We filled out questionnaires like the rest of our respondents, and so some of our preferences and views appear, unidentified as such, in this book. Our points of view may be noticeable in the comments presenting the material, though we tried not to be stridently opinionated. Any imbalance apparent in the material itself reflects the overall participants in the survey, not us as individuals. In short, we made every effort to see that the selection and overall presentation of material from the completed questionnaires is fair.

2

The Questionnaires

The full text of both the lesbian and gay-male questionnaires follows. (The explanatory introduction to the questionnaires was the same, and it is accordingly printed only once here.) The page numbers given in parentheses after each question indicate where in *The Gay Report* the reader can find the responses to that question. In some cases, where the question is complex or multifaceted, the page number indicates the first page of an entire chapter or section in which the answers may be found. If no page numbers are given, it is because the authors decided that the data gathered were not significant, interesting or valid enough to include in this book.

Lesbian Questionnaire

In an age of "sexual liberation" and "sexual awareness," lesbians and male homosexuals have often been conveniently forgotten or intentionally left out. Many of us wanted to talk about our experiences, but we didn't have the opportunity, or circumstances kept us silent.

This questionnaire has been prepared by lesbians and gay men as a project in self-awareness for ourselves. It is being distributed throughout the United States and Canada to as many lesbians and gay men as can be reached — literally hundreds of thousands. No survey of this magnitude has ever before been attempted, and it is our hope that the questionnaire will not only provide important information about lesbians and gay men, but also that participating in the survey will be rewarding, educational and fun for all.

A Personal Approach

Our study does not involve a "scientific" approach to homosexuality, but rather a personal one. We are not psychiatrists or social-scientists; we only hope to present an honest portrait of the feelings and practices of the people who answer the questionnaire.

We encourage you to answer the questionnaire regardless of your particular situation or experience, even if you do not usually discuss your sexuality or sex life.

Selected responses to the questions, as well as statistical compilations, are expected to be published in a book in 1978 by Summit Books, a division of Simon and Schuster. The compilers of this survey are Karla Jay and Allen Young, who have previously collaborated in several anthologies of writings by lesbians and gay men, including *Out of the Closets: Voices of Gay Liberation*, *After You're Out*, and *Lavender Culture* (in preparation). In effect, this survey will result in an anthology with thousands of participants. The book will consist primarily of your words.

Separate questionnaires have been prepared for lesbians and gay men, and no attempt will be made to falsely correlate these experiences. Lesbian and gay male response will be identified as such at all times in any publication.

About the Questions

There are two types of questions. The questions at the beginning require multiple choice or short answers. Please write on the questionnaire itself for these. Questions in the second part ask you to tell us about your experiences and feelings. Please type or write on separate sheets of paper for these.

If you like writing only short answers, feel free to do just the short answer questions, but a few of the longer questions may appeal to you also. If you prefer longer responses, you may answer just the **"essay" questions. Statistics are important, but letting us know your personal feelings and experiences is also vital to our survey. Of course we hope you will answer all questions in both parts, but if a question does not interest or apply to you, skip it. Also feel free to answer only those questions on subjects of special interest to you. You may also comment at length about any item in the short questions. In brief, any and all responses are appreciated.**

Replying to this questionnaire may take a few hours, but we think that you will enjoy doing this and that the results of this survey will be extremely valuable to all of us.

Your Answers Are Anonymous

Please do not put your name on the questionnaire. Your answers are anonymous. If you want to be notified of publication, send your name and address in a separate envelope or postal card to our address. Please mail your finished questionnaire and the additional pages to **Survey, Box 98, Orange, Mass. 01364**, as soon as possible.

Please help us distribute this questionnaire. Ask us for more copies to give to your friends and acquaintances; diversity is important. If you wish more copies of the questionnaire, write to the same address. Don't forget to indicate how many copies and specify male or female questionnaire.

Mail to: Survey, Box 98, Orange, MA 01364

Sex

(Unless specified otherwise, all of these questions refer to sex with women.)
1. How important is sex to you (check one)?
☐ very important
☐ somewhat important
☐ neutral
☐ somewhat unimportant
☐ very unimportant
☐ not sure   **(PAGE 162)**

2. Do you feel that you place too much or too little importance on sex?
☐ too much
☐ just right
☐ too little
☐ not sure   **(PAGES 162, 662)**

3. **Do you feel that others place too much or too little importance on sex?**
☐ too much
☐ just right
☐ too little
☐ not sure   **(PAGES 163, 662)**

4. On the average, how often would you like to have sex?
☐ more than once a day
☐ once a day
☐ several times a week
☐ once a week
☐ several times a month
☐ once a month
☐ less frequently than once a month
☐ never
☐ not sure   **(PAGE 161)**

5. On the average, how often do you actually have sex?
☐ more than once a day
☐ once a day
☐ several times a week
☐ once a week
☐ several times a month
☐ once a month
☐ less frequently than once a month
☐ never
☐ not sure   **(PAGE 161)**

Emotion and Love

6. How important is emotional involvement with your partner?
☐ very important
☐ somewhat important
☐ neutral
☐ somewhat unimportant
☐ very unimportant
☐ not sure   **(PAGE 171)**

7. When you have sex, how often does it include emotional involvement?
☐ always
☐ very frequently
☐ somewhat frequently
☐ somewhat infrequently
☐ very infrequently
☐ once
☐ never   **(PAGE 171)**

8. Have you ever been in love?
☐ Yes   ☐ No   ☐ Not sure
If yes, how many times? . . . .
If not sure, how many times? . . . .   **(PAGE 171)**

Specific Sexual Acts

Some of the following questions have "frequency scales." The scales refer to how often, on the average, you engage in or have engaged in certain sexual acts, no matter how often you have sex itself. For example, if you have sex less frequently than once a month but have oral sex (cunnilingus) each time you do have sex, check "always."

	always	very frequently	somewhat frequently	somewhat infrequently	very infrequently	once	never
9. On the average, how often do you engage in each of the following aspects of cunnilingus (oral sex, clitoral or vaginal)? Check one for each item.							
a. doing it to your partner	☐	☐	☐	☐	☐	☐	☐
b. having it done to you	☐	☐	☐	☐	☐	☐	☐
c. you have an orgasm	☐	☐	☐	☐	☐	☐	☐
d. your partner has an orgasm	☐	☐	☐	☐	☐	☐	☐
e. simultaneous ("69")	☐	☐	☐	☐	☐	☐	☐
f. orgasm during "69"	☐	☐	☐	☐	☐	☐	☐

(PAGE 396)

Whether or not you engage in any of the following aspects of oral sex, indicate how you feel about the idea of each of them.

very positive / somewhat positive / neutral / somewhat negative / very negative / not sure

a. doing it to your partner
b. having it done to you
c. you have an orgasm
d. your partner has an orgasm
e. simultaneous ("69")
f. orgasm during "69"

(PAGE 397)

10. How do you feel about the following aspects of female genitals?

very positive / somewhat positive / neutral / somewhat negative / very negative / not sure

a. smell of your own
b. feel of your own
c. appearance of your own
d. smell of others
e. feel of others
f. appearance of others
g. taste of others

(PAGE 418)

11. How often do you engage in any of the following aspects of tribadism (rubbing of genitals against partner)?

always / very frequently / somewhat frequently / somewhat infrequently / very infrequently / once / never

a. lying on top of partner
b. partner lies on top of you
c. rub against each other's thighs
d. you rub on partner's pelvic bone
e. partner rubs on your pelvic bone
f. you rub on partner's pubic bone
g. partner rubs on your pubic bone
h. rub clitoral areas together
i. other (specify)
j. any of these to the point of orgasm

(PAGE 405)

Whether or not you engage in any of the following aspects of tribadism (rubbing), indicate how you feel about the idea of each of them.

very positive / somewhat positive / neutral / somewhat negative / very negative / not sure

a. lying on top of partner
b. partner lies on top of you
c. rub against each other's thighs
d. you rub on partner's pelvic bone
e. partner rubs on your pelvic bone
f. you rub on partner's pubic bone
g. partner rubs on your pubic bone
h. rub clitoral areas together
i. other (specify)
j. any of these to the point of orgasm

(PAGE 406)

12. On the average, how often do your sexual experiences involve any of the following aspects of manual stimulation ("mutual masturbation")?

always / very frequently / somewhat frequently / somewhat infrequently / very infrequently / once / never

a. partner stimulates your clitoris/clitoral area
b. partner stimulates your vaginal area
c. partner stimulates your anus
d. partner stimulates herself
e. you stimulate your partner's clitoris/clitoral area
f. you stimulate your partner's vaginal area
g. you stimulate your partner's anus
h. you stimulate yourself
i. any of these to the point of orgasm

(PAGE 388)

Whether or not you engage in any of the following aspects of mutual stimulation, how do you feel about each of them?

very positive / somewhat positive / neutral / somewhat negative / very negative / not sure

a. partner stimulates your clitoris/clitoral area
b. partner stimulates your vaginal area
c. partner stimulates your anus
d. partner stimulates herself
e. you stimulate your partner's clitoris/clitoral area
f. you stimulate your partner's vaginal area
g. you stimulate your partner's anus
h. you stimulate yourself
i. any of these to the point of orgasm

(PAGE 388)

13. How often do you engage in either of the following aspects of analingus ("rimming" — stimulation of the anus with the lips and tongue)?

always / very frequently / somewhat frequently / somewhat infrequently / very infrequently / once / never

a. rimming your partner
b. being rimmed

(PAGE 519)

Whether or not you engage in analingus, how do you feel about either of these?

very positive / somewhat positive / neutral / somewhat negative / very negative / not sure

a. rimming your partner
b. being rimmed

(PAGE 519)

14. On the average, how often do you engage in the following aspects of kissing?

always / very frequently / somewhat frequently / somewhat infrequently / very infrequently / once / never

a. kiss on lips only
b. get kissed on lips only
c. soul kiss (deep kiss, French kiss)
d. partner soul kisses you
e. you refuse to kiss partner
f. partner refuses to kiss you

(PAGE 411)

Whether or not you engage in the following aspects of kissing, indicate how you feel about the idea of each of them.

very positive / somewhat positive / neutral / somewhat negative / very negative / not sure

a. kiss on lips only
b. get kissed on lips only
c. soul kiss (deep kiss, French kiss)
d. partner soul kisses you
e. you refuse to kiss partner
f. partner refuses to kiss you

(PAGE 411)

15. On the average, how important for your satisfaction is the stimulation of each of the following parts of your body by your partner?

very important / somewhat important / neutral / somewhat unimportant / very unimportant / not sure

a. your clitoris
b. your clitoral area
c. outer vaginal area
d. vagina
e. pubic bone, mons Veneris
f. breasts
g. ears, neck, toes
h. anus
i. other (specify)
Comment:

(PAGE 413)

On the average, how important for your satisfaction is it for you to stimulate each of the following parts of your partner's body?

Headers: very important, somewhat important, neutral, somewhat unimportant, very unimportant, not sure

a. clitoris
b. clitoral area
c. outer vaginal area
d. vagina
e. pubic bone, mons Veneris
f. breasts
g. ears, neck, toes
h. anus
i. other (specify)

Comment:

(PAGE 414)

Other Sexual Styles

16. On the average, during sex with another woman, how often do you use the following items?

Headers: always, very frequently, somewhat frequently, somewhat infrequently, very infrequently, once, never

a. hand-held dildo ("penis imitation")
b. strap-on dildo
c. battery vibrator
d. electric vibrator (cord)
e. oils
f. pornography

(PAGE 543)

Whether or not you use any of the following during sex, indicate how you feel about the idea of each of them.

Headers: very positive, somewhat positive, neutral, somewhat negative, very negative, not sure

a. hand-held dildo ("penis imitation")
b. strap-on dildo
c. battery vibrator
d. electric vibrator (cord)
e. oils
f. pornography

(PAGE 544)

17. On the average, how often do your sexual experiences include the following? (check for each one)

Headers: always, very frequently, somewhat frequently, somewhat infrequently, very infrequently, once, never

a. sado-masochism (S&M)
b. bondage and discipline (B&D)
c. humiliation
d. "talking dirty"
e. fist-fucking
f. clothing fetishes
g. foot fetishism
h. urination ("water sports")
i. defecation ("scat")
j. enemas
k. sex with animals (bestiality)
l. "threesomes"
m. orgies or group sex
n. other (specify)

(PAGE 512)

Whether or not you experience any of the following, indicate how you feel about the idea of each of them.

Headers: very positive, somewhat positive, neutral, somewhat negative, very negative, not sure

a. sado-masochism (S&M)
b. bondage and discipline (B&D)
c. humiliation
d. "talking dirty"
e. fist-fucking
f. clothing fetishes
g. foot fetishism
h. urination ("water sports")

i. defecation ("scat")
j. enemas
k. sex with animals (bestiality)
l. "threesomes"
m. orgies or group sex
n. other (specify)

(PAGE 510)

18. a. Have you ever forced another woman to have sex with you against her will?
☐ Yes   ☐ No
If yes, how many times? .... **(PAGE 541)**
b. Have you ever been forced by another woman to have sex against your will?
☐ Yes   ☐ No
If yes, how many times? .... **(PAGE 541)**

Whether or not you have done either of the following, indicate how you feel about the idea of each of them.

Headers: very positive, somewhat positive, neutral, somewhat negative, very negative, not sure

a. forcing someone to have sex with you
b. being forced to have sex against your will
Brief comment:

(PAGE 542)

19. How often, in connection with attracting sex partners, do you wear any of the following items?

Headers: always, very frequently, somewhat frequently, somewhat infrequently, very infrequently, once, never

a. skirts and/or dresses
b. unisex clothing, blue jeans, etc.
c. drag butch clothing
d. make-up
e. cigars, pipes
f. other (specify)

(PAGE 525)

Whether or not you wear any of the following items, how do you feel about the idea of each of them?

Headers: very positive, somewhat positive, neutral, somewhat negative, very negative, not sure

a. skirts and/or dresses
b. unisex clothing, blue jeans, etc.
c. drag butch clothing
d. make-up
e. cigars, pipes
f. other (specify)
Brief comment or experience:

(PAGE 526)

20. How often do your sex partners wear any of the following items?

Headers: always, very frequently, somewhat frequently, somewhat infrequently, very infrequently, once, never

a. skirts and/or dresses
b. unisex clothing, blue jeans, etc.
c. drag butch clothing
d. make-up
e. cigars, pipes
f. other (specify)

(PAGE 526)

Whether or not your sex partners use the following items, how do you feel about the idea of sex partners who use them?

Headers: very positive, somewhat positive, neutral, somewhat negative, very negative, not sure

a. skirts and/or dresses
b. unisex clothing, blue jeans, etc.
c. drag butch clothing
d. make-up
e. cigars, pipes
f. other (specify)

(PAGE 527)

Age

21. How often do you have sex with women or girls of the following ages? (check for each one)

	always	very frequently	somewhat frequently	somewhat infrequently	very infrequently	once	never
a. 65+	☐	☐	☐	☐	☐	☐	☐
b. 55-64	☐	☐	☐	☐	☐	☐	☐
c. 45-54	☐	☐	☐	☐	☐	☐	☐
d. 35-44	☐	☐	☐	☐	☐	☐	☐
e. 30-34	☐	☐	☐	☐	☐	☐	☐
f. 25-29	☐	☐	☐	☐	☐	☐	☐
g. 20-24	☐	☐	☐	☐	☐	☐	☐
h. 16-19	☐	☐	☐	☐	☐	☐	☐
i. 13-15	☐	☐	☐	☐	☐	☐	☐
j. 9-12	☐	☐	☐	☐	☐	☐	☐
k. under 9	☐	☐	☐	☐	☐	☐	☐

(PAGE 204)

Whether or not you have sex with any of the following age groups, indicate how you feel about the idea of having sex with each of them.

	very positive	somewhat positive	neutral	somewhat negative	very negative	not sure
a. 65+	☐	☐	☐	☐	☐	☐
b. 55-64	☐	☐	☐	☐	☐	☐
c. 45-54	☐	☐	☐	☐	☐	☐
d. 35-44	☐	☐	☐	☐	☐	☐
e. 30-34	☐	☐	☐	☐	☐	☐
f. 25-29	☐	☐	☐	☐	☐	☐
g. 20-24	☐	☐	☐	☐	☐	☐
h. 16-19	☐	☐	☐	☐	☐	☐
i. 13-15	☐	☐	☐	☐	☐	☐
j. 9-12	☐	☐	☐	☐	☐	☐
k. under 9	☐	☐	☐	☐	☐	☐

Brief comment or experience: **(PAGE 205)**

22. How much does what you do to your partner "turn you on"?
☐ quite a lot
☐ some
☐ very little
☐ none at all
☐ not sure   **(PAGE 414)**

23. On the average, during sex, do you feel that you are more physically active than your partner?
☐ much more active
☐ a little more active
☐ the same
☐ a little less active
☐ much less active   **(PAGE 319)**

24. How often do you ask your partner for what you want done to you?
☐ always
☐ very frequently
☐ somewhat frequently
☐ somewhat infrequently
☐ very infrequently
☐ once
☐ never   **(PAGE 661)**

Where Do You Have Sex

25. On the average, how often do you have sex in each of the following places?

	always	very frequently	somewhat frequently	somewhat infrequently	very infrequently	once	never
a. your home	☐	☐	☐	☐	☐	☐	☐
b. your partner's home	☐	☐	☐	☐	☐	☐	☐
c. a friend's home	☐	☐	☐	☐	☐	☐	☐
d. car	☐	☐	☐	☐	☐	☐	☐
e. van or camper	☐	☐	☐	☐	☐	☐	☐
f. tent	☐	☐	☐	☐	☐	☐	☐
g. motel or hotel	☐	☐	☐	☐	☐	☐	☐
h. secluded woods or fields	☐	☐	☐	☐	☐	☐	☐
i. barn or farm building	☐	☐	☐	☐	☐	☐	☐
j. other (specify)	☐	☐	☐	☐	☐	☐	☐

(PAGE 426)

Whether or not you have sex in any of these places, indicate how you feel about the idea of having sex in each of them.

	very positive	somewhat positive	neutral	somewhat negative	very negative	not sure
a. your home	☐	☐	☐	☐	☐	☐
b. your partner's home	☐	☐	☐	☐	☐	☐
c. a friend's home	☐	☐	☐	☐	☐	☐
d. car	☐	☐	☐	☐	☐	☐
e. van or camper	☐	☐	☐	☐	☐	☐
f. tent	☐	☐	☐	☐	☐	☐
g. motel or hotel	☐	☐	☐	☐	☐	☐
h. secluded woods or field	☐	☐	☐	☐	☐	☐
i. barn or farm building	☐	☐	☐	☐	☐	☐
j. other (specify)	☐	☐	☐	☐	☐	☐

(PAGE 427)

26. While having sex, how important is each of the following?

	very important	somewhat important	neutral	somewhat unimportant	very unimportant	not sure
a. privacy	☐	☐	☐	☐	☐	☐
b. lack of privacy	☐	☐	☐	☐	☐	☐

Brief comment or experience: **(PAGE 428)**

27. How often do you spend the whole night with your sex partner?
☐ always
☐ very frequently
☐ somewhat frequently
☐ somewhat infrequently
☐ very infrequently
☐ once
☐ never
Comment on why or why not: **(PAGE 428)**

28. How often has a sexual encounter been terminated because . . .

	always	very frequently	somewhat frequently	somewhat infrequently	very infrequently	once	never
a. you would not perform a particular sexual act your partner wanted	☐	☐	☐	☐	☐	☐	☐
b. your partner would not perform a particular sexual act you wanted	☐	☐	☐	☐	☐	☐	☐

Comment briefly: **(PAGE 540)**

29. How often do you go home to have sex with someone you have just met? How often, when you are going home with someone for the first time, do you determine in advance whether or not you are going to have sex with her?

	always	very frequently	somewhat frequently	somewhat infrequently	very infrequently	once	never
a. go home with stranger	☐	☐	☐	☐	☐	☐	☐
b. determine whether or not sex will take place	☐	☐	☐	☐	☐	☐	☐

(PAGE 226)

Whether or not you do either of the following, how do you feel about each of them?

	very positive	somewhat positive	neutral	somewhat negative	very negative	not sure
a. go home with stranger	☐	☐	☐	☐	☐	☐
b. determine whether or not sex will take place	☐	☐	☐	☐	☐	☐

Brief comment or experience: **(PAGE 227)**

30. How often do you use the following in association with sex?

	always	very frequently	somewhat frequently	somewhat infrequently	very infrequently	once	never
a. alcohol	☐	☐	☐	☐	☐	☐	☐
b. marijuana	☐	☐	☐	☐	☐	☐	☐
c. psychedelics (LSD, mushrooms, mescaline)	☐	☐	☐	☐	☐	☐	☐
d. "uppers" (speed, amphetamine)	☐	☐	☐	☐	☐	☐	☐
e. quaaludes	☐	☐	☐	☐	☐	☐	☐
f. "downers" (barbituates, tranquilizers)	☐	☐	☐	☐	☐	☐	☐
g. heroin	☐	☐	☐	☐	☐	☐	☐
h. cocaine	☐	☐	☐	☐	☐	☐	☐
i. amyl nitrite ("poppers," "aroma")	☐	☐	☐	☐	☐	☐	☐
j. other (specify)	☐	☐	☐	☐	☐	☐	☐

(PAGE 431)

Whether or not you use any of the following, how do you feel about their use in association with sex?

	very positive	somewhat positive	neutral	somewhat negative	very negative	not sure
a. alcohol	☐	☐	☐	☐	☐	☐
b. marijuana	☐	☐	☐	☐	☐	☐
c. psychedelics (LSD, mushrooms, mescaline)	☐	☐	☐	☐	☐	☐
d. "uppers" (speed, amphetamine)	☐	☐	☐	☐	☐	☐
e. quaaludes	☐	☐	☐	☐	☐	☐
f. "downers" (barbituates, tranquilizers)	☐	☐	☐	☐	☐	☐
g. heroin	☐	☐	☐	☐	☐	☐
h. cocaine	☐	☐	☐	☐	☐	☐
i. amyl nitrite ("poppers," "aroma")	☐	☐	☐	☐	☐	☐
j. other (specify)	☐	☐	☐	☐	☐	☐

(PAGE 432)

31. Have you ever refused to have sex with a partner because . . .
a. she used any of these?
☐ Yes   ☐ No
If yes, specify which one(s) . . . .

b. she would not join you in the use of any of these.
☐ Yes   ☐ No
If yes, specify which one(s) . . . .

(PAGE 432)

32. How often have you had the following venereal diseases (VD) or sex-related maladies?

	never	once	twice	three times	more than three times	not sure
a. syphilis ("siff")	☐	☐	☐	☐	☐	☐
b. gonorrhea ("clap")	☐	☐	☐	☐	☐	☐
c. lice ("crabs")	☐	☐	☐	☐	☐	☐
d. scabies	☐	☐	☐	☐	☐	☐
e. other (specify)	☐	☐	☐	☐	☐	☐

(PAGE 671)

How often does the fear of venereal disease influence any of the following?

	always	very frequently	somewhat frequently	somewhat infrequently	very infrequently	once	never
a. your choice of sex partner	☐	☐	☐	☐	☐	☐	☐
b. sexual acts you engage in	☐	☐	☐	☐	☐	☐	☐
c. how often you have sex	☐	☐	☐	☐	☐	☐	☐

Comment:

(PAGE 671)

Fantasies

33. How often do you fantasize?

	always	very frequently	somewhat frequently	somewhat infrequently	very infrequently	once	never
a. during sex with a partner	☐	☐	☐	☐	☐	☐	☐
b. during masturbation	☐	☐	☐	☐	☐	☐	☐

(PAGES 597, 606)

Whether or not you fantasize, how do you feel about the idea of fantasizing . . .

	very positive	somewhat positive	neutral	somewhat negative	very negative	not sure
a. during sex with a partner	☐	☐	☐	☐	☐	☐
b. during masturbation	☐	☐	☐	☐	☐	☐

(PAGES 597, 607)

34. Are you secretive about any specific aspects of your sex life, even though you may be openly lesbian?
☐ Yes   ☐ No
If yes, indicate briefly which aspects you keep secret and why:

Orgasms

35. How important is having orgasms to you?

	very important	somewhat important	neutral	somewhat unimportant	very unimportant	not sure
a. during sex with a partner	☐	☐	☐	☐	☐	☐
b. during masturbation	☐	☐	☐	☐	☐	☐

(PAGES 385, 608)

36. How often do you have an orgasm?

	always	very frequently	somewhat frequently	somewhat infrequently	very infrequently	once	never
a. during sex with a partner	☐	☐	☐	☐	☐	☐	☐
b. during masturbation	☐	☐	☐	☐	☐	☐	☐

(PAGES 386, 608, 656)

How often do you have multiple orgasms?

	always	very frequently	somewhat frequently	somewhat infrequently	very infrequently	once	never
a. during sex with a partner	☐	☐	☐	☐	☐	☐	☐
b. during masturbation	☐	☐	☐	☐	☐	☐	☐

(PAGES 386, 608, 656)

37. How important is it to you whether your partner has orgasm(s) during sex with you?

	very important	somewhat important	neutral	somewhat unimportant	very unimportant	not sure
a. one orgasm	☐	☐	☐	☐	☐	☐
b. multiple orgasms	☐	☐	☐	☐	☐	☐

(PAGE 386)

38. When having sex with a woman, how often do you fake or have you faked orgasm?
☐ always
☐ very frequently
☐ somewhat frequently
☐ somewhat infrequently
☐ very infrequently
☐ once
☐ never

(PAGE 386)

39. On the average, how do you feel about the quality of the sexual experiences you have with women (without reference to how often you have sex)?
☐ completely satisfied
☐ very satisfied
☐ somewhat satisfied
☐ neutral
☐ somewhat dissatisfied
☐ very dissatisfied
☐ completely dissatisfied
☐ not sure

(PAGE 435)

Sex With Men

40. How often have you had or do you have sex with men?

	always	very frequently	somewhat frequently	somewhat infrequently	very infrequently	once	never
a. in the past	☐	☐	☐	☐	☐	☐	☐
b. currently	☐	☐	☐	☐	☐	☐	☐

(PAGE 58)

41. How do you feel about sex with men?

	very positive	somewhat positive	neutral	somewhat negative	very negative	not sure
a. your past experiences	☐	☐	☐	☐	☐	☐
b. your current experiences	☐	☐	☐	☐	☐	☐

(PAGE 59)

42. Have you considered or do you consider yourself bi-sexual?
a. in the past .... ☐ Yes ☐ No
b. in the present .... ☐ Yes ☐ No

(PAGE 64)

Masturbation

43. On the average, how often do you masturbate?
☐ more than once a day
☐ once a day
☐ several times a week
☐ once a week
☐ several times a month
☐ once a month
☐ less frequently than once a month
☐ never
☐ not sure **(PAGE 607)**

How do you feel about masturbation?
☐ very positive
☐ somewhat positive
☐ neutral
☐ somewhat negative
☐ very negative
☐ not sure **(PAGE 617)**

44. How often do you use any of the following in connection with masturbation?

	always	very frequently	somewhat frequently	somewhat infrequently	very infrequently	once	never
a. hand-held dildo	☐	☐	☐	☐	☐	☐	☐
b. strap-on dildo	☐	☐	☐	☐	☐	☐	☐
c. battery vibrator	☐	☐	☐	☐	☐	☐	☐
d. electric vibrator (cord)	☐	☐	☐	☐	☐	☐	☐
e. oils	☐	☐	☐	☐	☐	☐	☐
f. pornography	☐	☐	☐	☐	☐	☐	☐

(PAGE 614)

Affection

45. How often do you engage in physical affection (hugging, cuddling, caressing, kissing) with each of the following?

	always	very frequently	somewhat frequently	somewhat infrequently	very infrequently	once	never
a. lovers	☐	☐	☐	☐	☐	☐	☐
b. sex partners	☐	☐	☐	☐	☐	☐	☐
c. lesbian friends	☐	☐	☐	☐	☐	☐	☐
d. gay male friends	☐	☐	☐	☐	☐	☐	☐
e. straight women	☐	☐	☐	☐	☐	☐	☐
f. men in general	☐	☐	☐	☐	☐	☐	☐
g. parents	☐	☐	☐	☐	☐	☐	☐
h. other relatives	☐	☐	☐	☐	☐	☐	☐
i. children	☐	☐	☐	☐	☐	☐	☐

(PAGE 183)

Whether or not you engage in physical affection with any of the following, indicate how you feel about the idea of physical affection with each of them.

	very positive	somewhat positive	neutral	somewhat negative	very negative	not sure
a. lovers	☐	☐	☐	☐	☐	☐
b. sex partners	☐	☐	☐	☐	☐	☐
c. lesbian friends	☐	☐	☐	☐	☐	☐
d. gay male friends	☐	☐	☐	☐	☐	☐
e. straight women	☐	☐	☐	☐	☐	☐
f. men in general	☐	☐	☐	☐	☐	☐
g. parents	☐	☐	☐	☐	☐	☐
h. other relatives	☐	☐	☐	☐	☐	☐
i. children	☐	☐	☐	☐	☐	☐

(PAGE 184)

Relationships

46. In the past or the present, what is the longest you have been in a relationship with one lesbian lover? Specify length of time . . . . **(PAGE 302)**

Do you now have a lover or "womanfriend" or "girlfriend"? ☐ Yes ☐ No **(PAGE 302)**

How long have you been with your current lover?........ **(PAGE 302)**

On the average, how often do you have sex together?........ **(PAGE 309)**

Do you live together? .... ☐ Yes ☐ No **(PAGE 313)**

Briefly indicate why or why not .... **(PAGE 313)**

47. Do you consider or have you considered yourself "married" to another woman?
☐ Yes ☐ No ☐ Not sure Comment. **(PAGE 316)**

Have you ever had a lesbian marriage ceremony? .... ☐ Yes ☐ No **(PAGE 316)**

Whether or not you are in or have been in a lesbian marriage, what is your attitude toward it?
☐ strongly favor
☐ somewhat favor
☐ neutral
☐ somewhat oppose
☐ strongly oppose
☐ not sure **(PAGE 316)**

48. How often do you "role play" (butch/femme, masculine/feminine, husband/wife, dominant/submissive) in your relationship?

	always	very frequently	somewhat frequently	somewhat infrequently	very infrequently	once	never
a. sexually	☐	☐	☐	☐	☐	☐	☐
b. other than sexually	☐	☐	☐	☐	☐	☐	☐

(PAGE 319)

49. How often do you relate to a certain "type"?
☐ always
☐ very frequently
☐ somewhat frequently
☐ somewhat infrequently
☐ very infrequently
☐ once
☐ never **(PAGE 204)**

50. How important is each of the following, in terms of what you look for or what you avoid, when you seek a sex partner?

	very important	somewhat important	neutral	somewhat unimportant	very unimportant	not sure
a. age	☐	☐	☐	☐	☐	☐
b. height	☐	☐	☐	☐	☐	☐
c. weight	☐	☐	☐	☐	☐	☐
d. build	☐	☐	☐	☐	☐	☐
e. "looks" in general	☐	☐	☐	☐	☐	☐
f. eyes	☐	☐	☐	☐	☐	☐
g. nose	☐	☐	☐	☐	☐	☐
h. lips	☐	☐	☐	☐	☐	☐
i. complexion	☐	☐	☐	☐	☐	☐
j. facial hair	☐	☐	☐	☐	☐	☐
k. head hair	☐	☐	☐	☐	☐	☐
l. body hair	☐	☐	☐	☐	☐	☐
m. breasts	☐	☐	☐	☐	☐	☐
n. legs	☐	☐	☐	☐	☐	☐
o. buttocks (ass)	☐	☐	☐	☐	☐	☐
p. hygiene, cleanliness or lack of it	☐	☐	☐	☐	☐	☐
q. clothing	☐	☐	☐	☐	☐	☐
r. race	☐	☐	☐	☐	☐	☐
s. social class	☐	☐	☐	☐	☐	☐
t. educational level	☐	☐	☐	☐	☐	☐
u. religion or spiritual orientation	☐	☐	☐	☐	☐	☐
v. political views	☐	☐	☐	☐	☐	☐
w. overall personality	☐	☐	☐	☐	☐	☐
x. masculinity/femininity, butch/femme	☐	☐	☐	☐	☐	☐
y. intelligence	☐	☐	☐	☐	☐	☐
z. other (specify)	☐	☐	☐	☐	☐	☐

(PAGES 202, 415)

If you have checked "very important" for any of the above, indicate specifically what things you are looking for or avoiding. (Attach separate piece of paper if you need more room.) ....
....
....
....

How many different sex partners or lovers have you had in the past week? .... In the past month? .... In the past 12 months? .... In your lifetime? ....   **(PAGE 324)**

51. How often do you meet other lesbians in each of the following places?

	always	very frequently	somewhat frequently	somewhat infrequently	very infrequently	once	never
a. bars	☐	☐	☐	☐	☐	☐	☐
b. at work	☐	☐	☐	☐	☐	☐	☐
c. at school	☐	☐	☐	☐	☐	☐	☐
d. neighborhood	☐	☐	☐	☐	☐	☐	☐
e. parties	☐	☐	☐	☐	☐	☐	☐
f. gay dances (mixed men and women), other than bars	☐	☐	☐	☐	☐	☐	☐
g. lesbian or all-women's dances, other than bars	☐	☐	☐	☐	☐	☐	☐
h. social groups	☐	☐	☐	☐	☐	☐	☐
i. political groups	☐	☐	☐	☐	☐	☐	☐
j. through friends	☐	☐	☐	☐	☐	☐	☐
k. gym, "Y," sports	☐	☐	☐	☐	☐	☐	☐
l. church	☐	☐	☐	☐	☐	☐	☐
m. personal ads	☐	☐	☐	☐	☐	☐	☐
n. other (specify)	☐	☐	☐	☐	☐	☐	☐

(PAGE 215)

Whether or not you meet other lesbians in any of these places, indicate how you feel about the idea of meeting lesbians in each of them.

	very positive	somewhat positive	neutral	somewhat negative	very negative	not sure
a. bars	☐	☐	☐	☐	☐	☐
b. at work	☐	☐	☐	☐	☐	☐
c. at school	☐	☐	☐	☐	☐	☐
d. neighborhood	☐	☐	☐	☐	☐	☐
e. parties	☐	☐	☐	☐	☐	☐
f. gay dances (mixed men and women), other than bars	☐	☐	☐	☐	☐	☐
g. lesbian or all-women's dances, other than bars	☐	☐	☐	☐	☐	☐
h. social groups	☐	☐	☐	☐	☐	☐
i. political groups	☐	☐	☐	☐	☐	☐
j. through friends	☐	☐	☐	☐	☐	☐
k. gym, "Y," sports	☐	☐	☐	☐	☐	☐
l. church	☐	☐	☐	☐	☐	☐
m. personal ads	☐	☐	☐	☐	☐	☐
n. other (specify)	☐	☐	☐	☐	☐	☐

(PAGE 216)

52. How active (you do the "picking up") or passive (you get "picked up") are you in seeking a relationship or a sex partner?
☐ very active
☐ somewhat active
☐ equal
☐ somewhat passive
☐ very passive
☐ not sure

(PAGE 220)

53. How often have you paid for sex with a woman?

	always	very frequently	somewhat frequently	somewhat infrequently	very infrequently	once	never
a. with money	☐	☐	☐	☐	☐	☐	☐
b. in other ways (specify)	☐	☐	☐	☐	☐	☐	☐

(PAGE 531)

Whether or not you have paid for sex, how do you feel about the idea of paying for sex

	very positive	somewhat positive	neutral	somewhat negative	very negative	not sure
a. with money	☐	☐	☐	☐	☐	☐
b. in other ways (specify)	☐	☐	☐	☐	☐	☐

Comment: **(PAGE 532)**

54. How often have you been paid for sex?

	always	very frequently	somewhat frequently	somewhat infrequently	very infrequently	once	never
a. with money	☐	☐	☐	☐	☐	☐	☐
b. in other ways (specify)	☐	☐	☐	☐	☐	☐	☐

(PAGE 532)

Whether or not you have been paid for sex with money or in other ways, how do you feel about the idea of receiving money or other benefits for sex?

	very positive	somewhat positive	neutral	somewhat negative	very negative	not sure
a. receiving money	☐	☐	☐	☐	☐	☐
b. receiving other benefits (specify)	☐	☐	☐	☐	☐	☐

Comment: **(PAGE 532)**

Self-Image

55. How do you feel about each of the following aspects of your body?

	very positive	somewhat positive	neutral	somewhat negative	very negative	not sure
a. **height**	☐	☐	☐	☐	☐	☐
b. **weight**	☐	☐	☐	☐	☐	☐
c. **build**	☐	☐	☐	☐	☐	☐
d. "looks" in general	☐	☐	☐	☐	☐	☐
e. how people perceive your age	☐	☐	☐	☐	☐	☐
f. facial hair	☐	☐	☐	☐	☐	☐
g. eyes	☐	☐	☐	☐	☐	☐
h. nose	☐	☐	☐	☐	☐	☐
i. lips	☐	☐	☐	☐	☐	☐
j. complexion	☐	☐	☐	☐	☐	☐
k. head hair	☐	☐	☐	☐	☐	☐
l. body hair	☐	☐	☐	☐	☐	☐
m. breasts	☐	☐	☐	☐	☐	☐
n. legs	☐	☐	☐	☐	☐	☐
o. buttocks (ass)	☐	☐	☐	☐	☐	☐
p. genitals	☐	☐	☐	☐	☐	☐
r. other (specify)	☐	☐	☐	☐	☐	☐

If you have checked "very positive" or "very negative" to any of the above, specify what there is about each thing that you intensely like or dislike. (Attach separate paper if you need more room.) ....
....
....

(PAGES 195, 416, 418)

56. How do you feel about aging?
☐ very positive
☐ somewhat positive
☐ neutral
☐ somewhat negative
☐ very negative
☐ not sure   **(PAGE 205)**

57. In general, how do you feel about the use of the categories or labels masculine/feminine, butch/femme?
☐ very positive
☐ somewhat positive
☐ neutral
☐ somewhat negative
☐ very negative
☐ not sure   **(PAGE 190)**

Coming Out

58. What is your age now? ....

At what age did you first realize that you were a lesbian or somehow sexually "different"? ....   **(PAGE 52)**

At what age did you associate this "difference" with lesbian acts? ....
                                          (PAGE 52)

At what age did you have your first lesbian experience? ....
                                          (PAGE 52)

How many years have you been a "practicing lesbian"? ....
                                          (PAGE 67)

59. At what age did you first tell anyone other than your sexual partners about your lesbianism? ....
                                          (PAGE 67)

Indicate who (relationship) ....
                                          (PAGE 68)

Indicate calendar year ....

If you have told no one, briefly indicate why:

60. How many of the following (if applicable) know about your lesbianism?

	All (Yes)	Most	Some	Only One	None (No)	Not sure
a. lesbian friends	☐	☐	☐	☐	☐	☐
b. gay male friends	☐	☐	☐	☐	☐	☐
c. straight friends	☐	☐	☐	☐	☐	☐
d. neighbors	☐	☐	☐	☐	☐	☐
e. employer	☐	☐	☐	☐	☐	☐
f. teacher	☐	☐	☐	☐	☐	☐
g. co-workers	☐	☐	☐	☐	☐	☐
h. schoolmates	☐	☐	☐	☐	☐	☐
i. your employees	☐	☐	☐	☐	☐	☐
j. mother	☐	☐	☐	☐	☐	☐
k. father	☐	☐	☐	☐	☐	☐
l. sisters and brothers	☐	☐	☐	☐	☐	☐
m. your children	☐	☐	☐	☐	☐	☐
n. other relatives	☐	☐	☐	☐	☐	☐
o. other children	☐	☐	☐	☐	☐	☐

(PAGE 68)

61. How important is it for you to keep your lesbianism a secret from each of the following (see also next question)?

	very important	somewhat important	neutral	somewhat unimportant	very unimportant	not sure
a. lesbian friends	☐	☐	☐	☐	☐	☐
b. gay male friends	☐	☐	☐	☐	☐	☐
c. straight friends	☐	☐	☐	☐	☐	☐
d. neighbors	☐	☐	☐	☐	☐	☐
e. employer	☐	☐	☐	☐	☐	☐
f. teacher	☐	☐	☐	☐	☐	☐
g. co-workers	☐	☐	☐	☐	☐	☐
h. schoolmates	☐	☐	☐	☐	☐	☐
i. your employees	☐	☐	☐	☐	☐	☐
j. mother	☐	☐	☐	☐	☐	☐
k. father	☐	☐	☐	☐	☐	☐
l. sisters and brothers	☐	☐	☐	☐	☐	☐
m. your children	☐	☐	☐	☐	☐	☐
n. other relatives	☐	☐	☐	☐	☐	☐
o. other children	☐	☐	☐	☐	☐	☐

62. How important is it for you to purposely communicate the fact that you are a lesbian to each of the following?

	very important	somewhat important	neutral	somewhat unimportant	very unimportant	not sure
a. lesbian friends	☐	☐	☐	☐	☐	☐
b. gay male friends	☐	☐	☐	☐	☐	☐
c. straight friends	☐	☐	☐	☐	☐	☐
d. neighbors	☐	☐	☐	☐	☐	☐
e. employer	☐	☐	☐	☐	☐	☐
f. teacher	☐	☐	☐	☐	☐	☐
g. co-workers	☐	☐	☐	☐	☐	☐
h. schoolmates	☐	☐	☐	☐	☐	☐
i. your employees	☐	☐	☐	☐	☐	☐
j. mother	☐	☐	☐	☐	☐	☐
k. father	☐	☐	☐	☐	☐	☐
l. sisters and brothers	☐	☐	☐	☐	☐	☐
m. your children	☐	☐	☐	☐	☐	☐
n. other relatives	☐	☐	☐	☐	☐	☐
o. other children	☐	☐	☐	☐	☐	☐

63. Of those who know you are a lesbian, what has been the reaction of each of the following to that fact? (answer for those that are applicable).

	very positive	somewhat positive	neutral	somewhat negative	very negative	not sure
a. lesbian friends	☐	☐	☐	☐	☐	☐
b. gay male friends	☐	☐	☐	☐	☐	☐
c. straight friends	☐	☐	☐	☐	☐	☐
d. neighbors	☐	☐	☐	☐	☐	☐
e. employer	☐	☐	☐	☐	☐	☐
f. teacher	☐	☐	☐	☐	☐	☐
g. co-workers	☐	☐	☐	☐	☐	☐
h. schoolmates	☐	☐	☐	☐	☐	☐
i. your employees	☐	☐	☐	☐	☐	☐
j. mother	☐	☐	☐	☐	☐	☐
k. father	☐	☐	☐	☐	☐	☐
l. sisters and brothers	☐	☐	☐	☐	☐	☐
m. your children	☐	☐	☐	☐	☐	☐
n. other relatives	☐	☐	☐	☐	☐	☐
o. other children	☐	☐	☐	☐	☐	☐

(PAGE 68)

64. How do you feel about people who you perceive to be "in the closet" (secretive)?
☐ very positive
☐ somewhat positive
☐ neutral
☐ somewhat negative
☐ very negative
☐ not sure   **(PAGE 77)**

65. How do you feel about people who you perceive to be "blatantly gay"?

	very positive	somewhat positive	neutral	somewhat negative	very negative	not sure
a. those who are politically outspoken	□	□	□	□	□	□
b. those who physically appear to be "obvious" homosexuals and lesbians	□	□	□	□	□	□

Comment: **(PAGE 77)**

66. Do you feel that most people can tell instantly that you are a lesbian?
□ Yes   □ No   □ Not sure

Briefly comment on your answer.   **(PAGE 188)**

Society

67. Do you ever or have you ever experienced any of the following in connection with your lesbianism?

	quite a lot	some	very little	once	none at all	not sure
a. harassment	□	□	□	□	□	□
b. loss of job	□	□	□	□	□	□
c. forced to move	□	□	□	□	□	□
d. arrest	□	□	□	□	□	□
e. blackmail or threat of blackmail	□	□	□	□	□	□
f. physical abuse	□	□	□	□	□	□
g. verbal abuse, name-calling	□	□	□	□	□	□
h. robbery	□	□	□	□	□	□
i. shakedown	□	□	□	□	□	□
j. shame, guilt	□	□	□	□	□	□
k. fear of discovery	□	□	□	□	□	□
l. other (specify)	□	□				

(PAGE 698)

How do you feel about your experience(s) in therapy?

	very positive	somewhat positive	neutral	somewhat negative	very negative	not sure
a. straight therapist	□	□	□	□	□	□
b. lesbian therapist	□	□	□	□	□	□
c. feminist therapist	□	□	□	□	□	□
d. don't know sexuality of therapist	□	□	□	□	□	□
e. other factor (specify)	□	□	□	□	□	□

(PAGE 723)

68. Have you ever gone to a psychiatrist or psychologist to be "cured" of your lesbianism?
□ Yes   □ No   **(PAGE 722)**

If yes, how long did you spend, or have you spent, in this kind of treatment? ....   **(PAGE 722)**

If you could take a pill to make you straight, would you do it?
□ Yes   □ No   □ Not sure   **(PAGE 772)**

Are you currently seeing a therapist, psychiatrist or psychologist for any reason?
□ Yes   □ No   **(PAGE 722)**

If yes, state briefly what reason.

69. Have you ever attempted or seriously contemplated suicide?
□ Yes   □ No   **(PAGE 728)**

If yes, was this experience related to your lesbianism?
□ Yes   □ No   **(PAGE 728)**

70. How much is your lesbianism something other than a sexual orientation?
□ quite a lot
□ some
□ very little
□ none at all
□ not sure
Comment: **(PAGE 763)**

71. How important are the concepts of lesbian and/or gay community, and lesbian and/or gay culture to you?

	very important	somewhat important	neutral	somewhat unimportant	very unimportant	not sure
a. gay community	□	□	□	□	□	□
b. lesbian community	□	□	□	□	□	□
c. gay culture	□	□	□	□	□	□
d. lesbian culture	□	□	□	□	□	□

(PAGES 219, 763)

72. How often do you socialize with each of the following?

	always	very frequently	somewhat frequently	somewhat infrequently	very infrequently	once	never
a. lesbians	□	□	□	□	□	□	□
b. straight women	□	□	□	□	□	□	□
c. gay men	□	□	□	□	□	□	□
d. straight men	□	□	□	□	□	□	□
e. bi-sexual women	□	□	□	□	□	□	□
f. bi-sexual men	□	□	□	□	□	□	□

(PAGE 219)

73. How do you feel about each of the following?

	very positive	somewhat positive	neutral	somewhat negative	very negative	not sure
a. lesbians	□	□	□	□	□	□
b. straight women	□	□	□	□	□	□
c. gay men	□	□	□	□	□	□
d. straight men	□	□	□	□	□	□
e. bi-sexual women	□	□	□	□	□	□
f. bi-sexual men	□	□	□	□	□	□

(PAGE 219)

74. How much of your time do you spend in each of the following environments?

	quite a lot	some	very little	none at all	not sure
a. lesbians only	□	□	□	□	□
b. women only (lesbians and straight women)	□	□	□	□	□
c. gay only (lesbians and male homosexuals, mixed	□	□	□	□	□
d. mixed straight and gay, men and women ..	□	□	□	□	□

(PAGE 218)

Whether or not you spend time in any of the following environments, how do you feel about each of them?

	very positive	somewhat positive	neutral	somewhat negative	very negative	not sure
a. lesbians only	□	□	□	□	□	□
b. women only (lesbians and straight women)	□	□	□	□	□	□
c. gay only (lesbians and male homosexuals mixed)	□	□	□	□	□	□
d. mixed straight and gay, men and women ..	□	□	□	□	□	□

Comment: **(PAGE 218)**

75. If you are legally married to a man, check any of the following that apply.
□ living with husband, and he knows about my lesbianism
□ living with husband, but he doesn't know about my lesbianism
□ living with husband, and I'm not sure whether or not he knows
□ marriage of convenience (to help me pass for straight)
□ marriage of convenience (for inheritance or gifts, for immigration, etc.)
(PAGE 63)

How do you feel about your marriage?
□ completely satisfied
□ very satisfied
□ somewhat satisfied
□ neutral
□ somewhat dissatisfied
□ very dissatisfied
□ completely dissatisfied
□ not sure
Comment:

76. Are you separated or divorced? (check one, if applicable).
☐ Separated   ☐ Divorced

Was your lesbianism a major factor in your separation or divorce?
☐ Yes   ☐ No   ☐ Not sure   **(PAGE 64)**

Children

77. Do you have children?
☐ Yes   ☐ No   If yes, how many? . . . .   **(PAGE 79)**

Whether or not you have children, what is your attitude, in general, toward children?
☐ very positive
☐ somewhat positive
☐ neutral
☐ somewhat negative
☐ very negative
☐ not sure   **(PAGE 80)**

78. Has custody been an issue for you?
☐ Yes   ☐ No
If yes, comment briefly on your situation.   **(PAGE 80)**

79. Has any aspect of visiting rights been an issue for you?
☐ Yes   ☐ No
If yes, comment briefly on your situation.   **(PAGE 80)**

80. Do you participate in the rearing of children, even though they are not your own biologically?
☐ Yes   ☐ No
If yes, briefly explain this arrangement   **(PAGE 80)**

How do you feel about this arrangement?
☐ completely satisfied
☐ very satisfied
☐ somewhat satisfied
☐ neutral
☐ somewhat dissatisfied
☐ very dissatisfied
☐ completely dissatisfied
☐ not sure   **(PAGE 80)**

81. If you don't have children, how do you feel about being childless?
☐ very positive
☐ somewhat positive
☐ neutral
☐ somewhat negative
☐ very negative
☐ not sure   **(PAGE 80)**

Politics

82. How do you feel about each of the following?

	very positive	somewhat positive	neutral	somewhat negative	very negative	not sure
a. women in dresses and skirts	☐	☐	☐	☐	☐	☐
b. women in blue jeans, unisex, etc.	☐	☐	☐	☐	☐	☐
c. women in drag butch, "very masculine" clothing	☐	☐	☐	☐	☐	☐
d. male transvestites	☐	☐	☐	☐	☐	☐
e. drag shows, entertainment	☐	☐	☐	☐	☐	☐
f. men in colorful, stylish or unisex clothing .	☐	☐	☐	☐	☐	☐
g. men in "butch" clothing, uniforms, etc. . .	☐	☐	☐	☐	☐	☐

83. In general, which word do you consider the most appropriate (best) word to be used for lesbians? (check one).
☐ lesbian
☐ homosexual
☐ female homosexual
☐ gay
☐ gay woman
☐ homophile
☐ other (specify) . . . .
                                              (PAGE 766)

84. How would you describe yourself politically? (check one or more).
☐ Democrat
☐ Republican
☐ independent
☐ conservative
☐ liberal
☐ moderate
☐ radical
☐ apolitical
☐ anarchist
☐ socialist (specify tendency or group, if applicable) . . . .
☐ feminist
☐ women's liberationist
☐ matriarchist
☐ separatist
☐ dyke separatist
☐ "third world" liberationist (specify group, if applicable) . . . .
☐ libertarian
☐ environmentalist
☐ revolutionary
☐ humanist
☐ pacifist
☐ gay liberationist
☐ other (specify) . . . .
                                              (PAGE 731)

85. How do you feel about each of the following?

	very positive	somewhat positive	neutral	somewhat negative	very negative	not sure
a. gay liberation (mixed male and female) . . .	☐	☐	☐	☐	☐	☐
b. lesbian liberation (independent lesbian efforts)	☐	☐	☐	☐	☐	☐

                                              (PAGE 735)

86. In what year did you first hear about any organized efforts for gay liberation or lesbian liberation?
(indicate calendar year) . . . .   **(PAGE 732)**

How did you first hear about such efforts?   **(PAGE 733)**

To what extent, if any, have you become involved with each of the following?	quite a lot	some	very little	none at all	not sure
a) gay liberation ·	☐	☐	☐	☐	☐
b) lesbian liberation ·	☐	☐	☐	☐	☐

                                              (PAGE 734)

87. Do you feel that the repeal of laws against homosexual and lesbian acts and/or the enactment of anti-discrimination legislation in your state, neighboring state (or province), or nationally, will make your life better?
☐ quite a lot
☐ some
☐ very little
☐ none at all
☐ not sure   **(PAGE 733)**

How much have you worked for such reform(s)?
☐ quite a lot
☐ some
☐ very little
☐ none at all
☐ not sure   **(PAGE 733)**

Statistical Information   **(PAGES 805–816)**

The following group of questions is for statistical purposes, to find out more about the kind of people who answer the questionnaire. In no way is this designed to infringe on anyone's anonymity. Of course, you may leave any of these blank.

88. What is your age? . . . .

89. What is your race or ethnic group? . . . .

90. What was your religious upbringing? . . . .

91. What is your present religion or spiritual orientation? . . . .

92. What was your annual income for 1976?
☐ less than $5,000
☐ between $5,000 and $9,999
☐ between $10,000 and $14,999
☐ between $15,000 and $24,999
☐ $25,000 or more
☐ not sure

93. What is your occupation? . . . .
Describe briefly the kind of work you do . . . .
. . . .

94. Indicate your educational level:
☐ some grade school
☐ completed grade school
☐ completed 9, 10, or 11 grades
☐ completed 12 grades
☐ some college
☐ college graduate
☐ some graduate school
☐ graduate degree

95. Do you have brothers and sisters?
How many brothers? . . . .
How many sisters? . . . .

96. Do you have any relatives who are homosexual or lesbian? Indicate
relationship.
. . . .
. . . .
. . . .

97. Where do you live?
Name of state or province . . . .
Name of town or city . . . .
(or nearby town)

98. What sort of a place do you live in?
☐ rural or small town
☐ small city
☐ medium-sized city
☐ large city
☐ major metropolitan center
☐ suburb

99. Where did you get this questionnaire? Please be specific. . . . .
. . . .

Part Two

The following questions ask you in detail about your experiences
and feelings. Please type or write on separate sheets of paper for these.
Remember, we will be delighted if you answer all the questions, but if
a question does not interest or apply to you, skip it. Also feel free to
answer only those questions on subjects of special interest to you.

Sexual Experiences

1. a) Tell us about a very pleasing love-making experience that
you have had with a sex partner or lover. What is it that you
do from beginning to end? How does each thing feel to you?
Please indicate how long it takes; describe movements and
positions used by you and your partner(s). Be precise: try to
include such things as leg positions, body position, movements, and other factors important to you such as roughness
or gentleness, sounds, clothing, lighting, etc. Re-reading
questions 6 through 39 may help you answer this. b) Indicate
your feelings about this experience. c) If you haven't had a
real experience that you consider pleasing, tell us about an
imaginary one but be sure to indicate that it is imaginary.
                                                    (PAGE 385)

2. a) Describe your feelings about the following sex acts.
What do you like about them? How do they feel to you? Feel
free to express strong preferences or passions and to tell about
things you hate or absolutely won't do.
    Cunnilingus (oral sex)
    Tribadism (rubbing of genitals against partner)
    Manual stimulation
    Analingus (rimming)
    Kissing   (PAGE 385)

b) Have your feelings about these acts changed over time and
if so, how?   (PAGE 385)

3. How do you feel about female genitals (their smell, appearance and feel) — your own and others?   (PAGE 418)

4. How do you feel about the size, appearance and feel of
breasts — your own and others?   (PAGE 416)

5. What are your feelings about menstruation? Does it affect
your sex life and if so, how?   (PAGE 418)

6. Tell us about your general feelings and experiences with the
list of practices included in Question 17, Part One. Which
ones do you like or hate, and why?   (PAGE 509)

7. How do you feel about "toys" — dildos, vibrators, oils,
pornography and others? Are they important to your sex life?
                                                     (PAGE 544)

8. Relate any feelings and experiences concerning anxieties,
"hang-ups," compulsions, blocks, repressions, special needs,
handicaps, problems with sexual performance or functioning,
problems with the frequency of sex or the quality or skill of
your sex partners, that you have had in regard to your general
sex life or specific sexual acts.   (PAGE 655)

9. Tell us about the importance of sex in your life. Do you feel
that too much or too little importance is placed on sex by you
or by others, and why do you feel that way?   (PAGE 161)

10. a) What is the importance of emotion to you sexually? Do
you have sex with or without emotional involvement, or
both? b) What is the connection between love and sex?
Comment. c) Have you ever been in love? Can you describe
your feelings of being in love, of being loved? Of not being in
love, or not being loved? Of wanting love, of not wanting
love?   (PAGES 171, 177)

11. Describe your funniest, scariest and/or most unusual
sexual experience with another woman.   (PAGE 597)

12. If you fantasize during sex or masturbation, describe your
most favorite or most common fantasy or fantasies, and your
feelings about them. Be specific as to people, situations,
places, circumstances, etc., whether real or imaginary
(indicate which). If you don't fantasize, what are your
feelings about fantasies?   (PAGE 41)

13. a) Tell us about your childhood "crushes" or sexual feelings directed toward other children or adults. Recall your own
experiences and feelings as a child and people's responses to
those experiences or feelings. b) Regardless of your own
childhood experiences, how do you feel now about childhood
sexuality in general?   (PAGE 607)

14. a) Tell how you masturbate. Be specific. What parts of
your body do you stimulate? With what and how? Indicate
positions, movements and other important aspects such as
lighting, music, pornography. How often do you masturbate?
How long does it take? b) How does masturbation feel to
you? c) How do you feel about masturbation in general, and
how have these feelings changed over time?   (PAGE 607)

Relationships

15. Tell about any present or past relationship with a lover or "womanfriend." a) How often do you have sex? How do you feel about the quality and intensity of your sexual relationship? b) Do you live together? Why or why not? c) Do you have sex outside of that relationship and how does outside sex or the lack of it affect the relationship? Do you have an agreement about "fidelity" or the lack of it? Comment. d) If you don't have a lover, would you like one? Why or why not? e) What do you like or dislike about having a lover and/or being single? **(PAGE 301)**

16. Do you "role-play" (butch/femme, masculine/feminine, husband/wife) in your relationships with other women, sexually as well as other than sexually? If you do, tell about who does what and how you feel about it. What do you like or dislike about role-playing in your relationships or in relationships you observe? **(PAGE 318)**

17. a) Do you have a "type" that you prefer sexually? Tell us about your type. Referring to the list in question 50, tell in detail what attributes are important, whether they are things you look for or things you avoid. b) Do you relate only to that certain type? What happens when you don't find your type? c) Whether or not you have a type, what do you like or dislike about the idea of having a type? d) Tell about the important factors, if any, for you in choosing a sex partner or lover? (Refer to question 50.) **(PAGE 202)**

18. a) Tell about the process of meeting other lesbians. In what ways are you shy and/or outgoing? Insecure and/or self-confident? b) What are your experiences, if any, with making sexual advances toward women when you are not certain they are gay? c) How do you feel about cruising, courtship, one-night stands, "promiscuity," etc. d) How important are the various places where lesbians meet (see list in question 51), regardless of whether or not you use these places? e) Tell about any positive or negative experiences you have had meeting other lesbians. **(PAGE 187)**

Self-Image

19. a) In what ways do you consider yourself "attractive" or "unattractive"? Tell about your feelings and experiences relating to your looks. b) How do you feel others relate to your body or to specific aspects of your body (refer to list in question 55). c) Do you feel you are a sex object? **(PAGE 195)**

20. a) Do you consider yourself masculine ("butch") or feminine ("femme"), or both, or neither? In what ways? b) Which physical characteristics, personality traits, activities, etc., do you identify as masculine or feminine? c) Do you think others identify you as masculine or feminine? d) How do you feel about these categories or labels, and what importance do these categories have to your self-identity? **(PAGE 190)**

21. a) Tell us your experiences with and feelings about your sexual "coming out" and/or "being in the closet." b) At what age and under what circumstances did you first realize that you were a lesbian or somehow sexually "different" from other people? c) At what age and under what circumstances did you have your first lesbian experience, and how did you deal with it? d) Tell us about your sexual evolution from that first experience to now. **(PAGE 51)**

22. a) What has been your experience, if any, with telling other people that you are gay? When did you first tell other people that you are a lesbian and whom did you tell? b) In your daily life now, which people do you tell, how do you tell them, and what has been their response? Refer to question 60.

If any experience was particularly important or interesting, tell about it in detail. c) Indicate your experience with and feelings about keeping your lesbianism secret. What do you like or dislike about being "out of the closet" or "in the closet"? What do you like or dislike about others who are "out of the closet" or "in the closet"? **(PAGE 67)**

23. a) How do you feel now about your lesbianism? b) How have these feelings changed over time? c) What has influenced these feelings and any changes in them? **(PAGE 771)**

You and Society

24. a) How do you feel that you have been oppressed (if at all) as a lesbian? Refer to question 67. b) In what ways has your lesbianism, or the fear of being discovered, been a factor, an aid or a hindrance, in your employment, schooling, housing, social status? c) How has the relationship between your lesbianism and any of these changed over time, and what influenced that change? **(PAGE 697)**

25. a) How would you describe yourself politically? How does your lesbianism interact with your politics, if at all, including any involvement you may have with other political groups or movements (refer to list in question 84)? b) Tell about your experiences with gay liberation and/or lesbian liberation. What have you liked or disliked about such experiences? **(PAGE 731)**

26. How has feminism or the women's movement had an impact on or changed your sexual practices, values or identity? **(PAGE 743)**

27. Please tell us something about the following topics. If you have strong feelings about them, or any interesting experiences, please share them with us.

a. celibacy	**(PAGE 335)**
b. sexual experiences with men, especially as these experiences compare to sex with women	**(PAGES 52, 66)**
c. bi-sexuality	**(PAGE 164)**
d. marriage	**(PAGES 58, 63)**
e. children, being childless	**(PAGE 79)**
f. drugs	**(PAGE 431)**
g. transvestism, cross-dressing	**(PAGE 525)**
h. transsexualism (sex-change surgery)	**(PAGE 529)**
i. therapy	**(PAGE 721)**
j. suicide	**(PAGE 728)**
k. race, class, age differences	**(PAGE 207)**
l. aging	**(PAGE 205)**
m. physical "handicaps"	**(PAGE 667)**
n. pornography	**(PAGES 550, 617)**
o. sexual jealousy	**(PAGE 328)**
p. monogamy	**(PAGE 324)**
q. lovers' quarrels, including violence	**(PAGE 328)**
r. violence in the lesbian community, bars	**(PAGE 328)**
s. sex in prison	**(PAGE 717)**
t. influence of religion on your sexuality	**(PAGE 719)**
u. incest	**(PAGE 537)**
v. residence (gay neighborhood, rural vs. urban, etc.)	**(PAGE 767)**

28. a) What do you think of this questionnaire? b) What in it made you pause and think? Why? Do you feel that we have omitted any important questions? If so, indicate the questions and your answers. c) As a lesbian, is there anything you would like more information on? d) Did answering parts of this questionnaire turn you on? Make you feel good? Feel bad? Feel angry? e) Comment. **(PAGE 787)**

Thank you very much.

Mail to: **Survey, Box 98, Orange, MA 01364**

Gay Male Questionnaire

Sex

(Unless specified otherwise, all of these questions refer to sex with men.)

1. How important is sex to you (check one)?
- [ ] very important
- [ ] somewhat important
- [ ] neutral
- [ ] somewhat unimportant
- [ ] very unimportant
- [ ] not sure **(PAGE 162)**

2. Do you feel that you place too much or too little importance on sex?
- [ ] too much
- [ ] just right
- [ ] too little
- [ ] not sure **(PAGE 162)**

3. Do you feel that others place too much or too little importance on sex?
- [ ] too much
- [ ] just right
- [ ] too little
- [ ] not sure **(PAGE 163)**

4. On the average, how often would you like to have sex?
- [ ] more than once a day
- [ ] once a day
- [ ] several times a week
- [ ] once a week
- [ ] several times a month
- [ ] once a month
- [ ] less frequently than once a month
- [ ] never
- [ ] not sure **(PAGE 161)**

5. On the average, how often do you actually have sex?
- [ ] more than once a day
- [ ] once a day
- [ ] several times a week
- [ ] once a week
- [ ] several times a month
- [ ] once a month
- [ ] less frequently than once a month
- [ ] never
- [ ] not sure **(PAGE 161)**

Emotion and Love

6. How important is emotional involvement with your partner?
- [ ] very important
- [ ] somewhat important
- [ ] neutral
- [ ] somewhat unimportant
- [ ] very unimportant
- [ ] not sure **(PAGE 171)**

7. When you have sex, how often does it include emotional involvement?
- [ ] always
- [ ] very frequently
- [ ] somewhat frequently
- [ ] somewhat infrequently
- [ ] very infrequently
- [ ] once
- [ ] never **(PAGE 171)**

8. Have you ever been in love?
- [ ] Yes   [ ] No   [ ] Not sure

If yes, how many times? _____

If not sure, how many times? _____ **(PAGE 171)**

Specific Sexual Acts

Some of the following questions have "frequency scales." The scales refer to how often, on the average, you engage in or have engaged in certain sexual acts, no matter how often you have sex itself. For example, if you have sex less frequently than once a month but have oral sex (fellatio) each time you do have sex, check "always."

9. On the average, how often do you engage in the following aspects of fellatio (cocksucking or "blow jobs")? Check one for each item.

	always	very frequently	somewhat frequently	somewhat infrequently	very infrequently	once	never
a. sucking your partner's cock							
b. getting your cock sucked							
c. coming in your partner's mouth							
d. partner coming in your mouth							
e. swallowing partner's come							
f. partner swallows your "come"							
g. simultaneous sucking ("69")							
h. simultaneous orgasm during "69"							

(PAGE 456)

Whether or not you engage in any of the following, indicate how you feel about the idea of each of them.

	very positive	somewhat positive	neutral	somewhat negative	very negative	not sure
a. sucking your partner's cock						
b. getting your cock sucked						
c. coming in your partner's mouth						
d. partner coming in your mouth						
e. swallowing partner's come						
f. partner swallows your "come"						
g. simultaneous sucking ("69")						
h. simultaneous orgasm during "69"						

(PAGE 456)

10. How do you feel about the following aspects of male genitals?

	very positive	somewhat positive	neutral	somewhat negative	very negative	not sure
a. smell of your own						
b. feel of your own						
c. appearance of your own						
d. size of your own						
e. smell of others						
f. feel of others						
g. appearance of others						
h. size of others						
i. taste of others						

(PAGE 447)

11. On the average, how often do you engage in the following aspects of anal intercourse (ass-fucking)? Check one for each item.

	always	very frequently	somewhat frequently	somewhat infrequently	very infrequently	once	never
a. fucking your partner							
b. getting fucked							
c. coming inside your partner							
d. partner coming inside you							
e. come while being fucked (without manipulating yourself)							
f. come while being fucked (with manipulation)							

(PAGE 464)

Whether or not you engage in any of the following, indicate how you feel about the idea of each of them.

	very positive	somewhat positive	neutral	somewhat negative	very negative	not sure
a. fucking your partner						
b. getting fucked						
c. coming inside your partner						
d. partner coming inside you						
e. come while being fucked (without manipulating yourself)						
f. come while being fucked (with manipulation)						

(PAGE 464)

12. On the average, how often do you engage in the following aspects of analingus ("rimming" — stimulating the anus with the lips and tongue)?

	always	very frequently	somewhat frequently	somewhat infrequently	very infrequently	once	never
a. rimming your partner	☐	☐	☐	☐	☐	☐	☐
b. being rimmed	☐	☐	☐	☐	☐	☐	☐

(PAGE 490)

Whether or not you engage in any of the following, indicate how you feel about the idea of each of them.

	very positive	somewhat positive	neutral	somewhat negative	very negative	not sure
a. rimming your partner	☐	☐	☐	☐	☐	☐
b. being rimmed	☐	☐	☐	☐	☐	☐

(PAGE 490)

13. On the average, how often do you engage in placing your body against your partner's body so that your penises rub together?

	always	very frequently	somewhat frequently	somewhat infrequently	very infrequently	once	never
a. with you lying on top	☐	☐	☐	☐	☐	☐	☐
b. partner lies on top of you	☐	☐	☐	☐	☐	☐	☐
c. either of these to the point of orgasm	☐	☐	☐	☐	☐	☐	☐

(PAGE 486)

Whether or not you engage in any of the following aspects of rubbing, indicate how you feel about the idea of each of them.

	very positive	somewhat positive	neutral	somewhat negative	very negative	not sure
a. with you lying on top	☐	☐	☐	☐	☐	☐
b. partner lies on top of you	☐	☐	☐	☐	☐	☐
c. either of these to the point of orgasm	☐	☐	☐	☐	☐	☐

(PAGE 486)

14. On the average, how often do your sexual experiences involve the following aspects of manual stimulation ("mutual masturbation," "jerking off")?

	always	very frequently	somewhat frequently	somewhat infrequently	very infrequently	once	never
a. masturbating your partner	☐	☐	☐	☐	☐	☐	☐
b. your partner masturbates you	☐	☐	☐	☐	☐	☐	☐
c. simultaneous masturbation	☐	☐	☐	☐	☐	☐	☐
d. rubbing your cocks together manually	☐	☐	☐	☐	☐	☐	☐
e. you masturbate yourself	☐	☐	☐	☐	☐	☐	☐
f. partner masturbates himself	☐	☐	☐	☐	☐	☐	☐
g. any of these to the point of orgasm	☐	☐	☐	☐	☐	☐	☐

(PAGE 480)

Whether or not you engage in any of the following aspects of manual stimulation, indicate how you feel about the idea of each of them.

	very positive	somewhat positive	neutral	somewhat negative	very negative	not sure
a. masturbating your partner	☐	☐	☐	☐	☐	☐
b. your partner masturbates you	☐	☐	☐	☐	☐	☐
c. simultaneous masturbation	☐	☐	☐	☐	☐	☐
d. rubbing your cocks together manually	☐	☐	☐	☐	☐	☐
e. you masturbate yourself	☐	☐	☐	☐	☐	☐
f. partner masturbates himself	☐	☐	☐	☐	☐	☐
g. any of these to the point of orgasm	☐	☐	☐	☐	☐	☐

(PAGE 481)

15. On the average, how often do you engage in the following aspects of "finger-fucking" — (inserting one or more fingers in the anus)? (Note: "fist-fucking" is covered in another question.)

	always	very frequently	somewhat frequently	somewhat infrequently	very infrequently	once	never
a. you insert finger(s)	☐	☐	☐	☐	☐	☐	☐
b. partner inserts finger(s)	☐	☐	☐	☐	☐	☐	☐
c. you come while being finger-fucked	☐	☐	☐	☐	☐	☐	☐
d. partner comes while you finger-fuck him	☐	☐	☐	☐	☐	☐	☐
e. you touch partner's anus, but don't insert	☐	☐	☐	☐	☐	☐	☐
f. partner touches your anus, but doesn't insert	☐	☐	☐	☐	☐	☐	☐

(PAGE 488)

Whether or not you engage in any of the following aspects of finger-fucking, indicate how you feel about the idea of each of them.

	very positive	somewhat positive	neutral	somewhat negative	very negative	not sure
a. you insert finger(s)	☐	☐	☐	☐	☐	☐
b. partner inserts finger(s)	☐	☐	☐	☐	☐	☐
c. you come while being finger-fucked	☐	☐	☐	☐	☐	☐
d. partner comes while you finger-fuck him	☐	☐	☐	☐	☐	☐
e. you touch partner's anus, but don't insert	☐	☐	☐	☐	☐	☐
f. partner touches your anus, but doesn't insert	☐	☐	☐	☐	☐	☐

(PAGE 489)

16. On the average, how often do you engage in the following aspects of kissing?

	always	very frequently	somewhat frequently	somewhat infrequently	very infrequently	once	never
a. kiss on lips only	☐	☐	☐	☐	☐	☐	☐
b. get kissed on lips only	☐	☐	☐	☐	☐	☐	☐
c. soul kiss (deep kiss, French kiss)	☐	☐	☐	☐	☐	☐	☐
d. partner soul kisses you	☐	☐	☐	☐	☐	☐	☐
e. you refuse to kiss partner	☐	☐	☐	☐	☐	☐	☐
f. partner refuses to kiss you	☐	☐	☐	☐	☐	☐	☐

(PAGE 494)

Whether or not you engage in the following aspects of kissing, indicate how you feel about the idea of each of them.

	very positive	somewhat positive	neutral	somewhat negative	very negative	not sure
a. kiss on lips only	☐	☐	☐	☐	☐	☐
b. get kissed on lips only	☐	☐	☐	☐	☐	☐
c. soul kiss (deep kiss, French kiss)	☐	☐	☐	☐	☐	☐
d. partner soul kisses you	☐	☐	☐	☐	☐	☐
e. you refuse to kiss partner	☐	☐	☐	☐	☐	☐
f. partner refuses to kiss you	☐	☐	☐	☐	☐	☐

(PAGE 494)

17. On the average, how important for your satisfaction is the stimulation of each of the following parts of your body by your partner?

	very important	somewhat important	neutral	somewhat unimportant	very unimportant	not sure
a. penis	☐	☐	☐	☐	☐	☐
b. testicles (balls)	☐	☐	☐	☐	☐	☐
c. anus	☐	☐	☐	☐	☐	☐
d. prostate gland (inside rectum)	☐	☐	☐	☐	☐	☐
e. ass	☐	☐	☐	☐	☐	☐
f. nipples	☐	☐	☐	☐	☐	☐
g. ears, neck, toes	☐	☐	☐	☐	☐	☐
h. other (specify)	☐	☐	☐	☐	☐	☐

Comment

(PAGE 439)

On the average, how important for your satisfaction is it for you to stimulate each of the following parts of your partner's body?

Columns: very important, somewhat important, neutral, somewhat unimportant, very unimportant, not sure

a. penis
b. testicles (balls)
c. anus
d. prostate gland (inside rectum)
e. ass
f. nipples
g. ears, neck, toes
h. other (specify)

Comment

(PAGE 440)

Other Sexual Styles

18. On the average, during sex with another man, how often do you use the following items?

Columns: always, very frequently, somewhat frequently, somewhat infrequently, very infrequently, once, never

a. hand-held dildo (penis imitation)
b. strap-on dildo
c. vibrator
d. accu-jack (masturbation machine)
e. cock ring
f. nipple clamp
g. oils
h. pornography
i. other (specify)

(PAGE 582)

Whether or not you use any of the following during sex, indicate how you feel about the idea of each of them.

Columns: very positive, somewhat positive, neutral, somewhat negative, very negative, not sure

a. hand-held dildo (penis imitation)
b. strap-on dildo
c. vibrator
d. accu-jack (masturbation machine)
e. cock ring
f. nipple clamp
g. oils
h. pornography
i. other (specify)

(PAGE 582)

19. On the average, how often do your sexual experiences include the following? (Check for each one.)

Columns: always, very frequently, somewhat frequently, somewhat infrequently, very infrequently, once, never

a. sado-masochism (S&M)
b. bondage and discipline (B&D)
c. humiliation
d. "talking dirty"
e. jock-straps, underwear
f. boots, leather
g. other clothing fetishes
h. foot fetishism
i. fist-fucking
j. urination ("water sports")
k. defecation ("scat")
l. enemas
m. sex with animals (bestiality)
n. "threesomes"
o. orgies or group sex
p. masturbation during phone call
q. other (specify)

(PAGES 555, 587, 647)

Whether or not you experience any of the following, indicate how you feel about the idea of each of them.

Columns: very positive, somewhat positive, neutral, somewhat negative, very negative, not sure

a. sado-masochism (S&M)
b. bondage and discipline (B&D)
c. humiliation
d. "talking dirty"
e. jock-straps, underwear
f. boots, leather
g. other clothing fetishes
h. foot fetishism
i. fist-fucking
j. urination ("water sports")
k. defecation ("scat")
l. enemas
m. sex with animals (bestiality)
n. "threesomes"
o. orgies or group sex
p. masturbation during phone call
q. other (specify)

(PAGES 555, 587, 647)

20. Have you ever been raped or forced to have sex against your will?
☐ Yes   ☐ No
If yes, how many times? . . . .

Have you ever forced anyone to have sex with you?
☐ Yes   ☐ No
If yes, how many times? . . . .

(PAGE 592)

Whether or not you have done either of the following, indicate how you feel about the idea of each of them.

Columns: very positive, somewhat positive, neutral, somewhat negative, very negative, not sure

a. forcing someone to have sex with you
b. being forced to have sex against your will

Brief comment:

(PAGE 592)

21. How often in connection with attracting sex partners do you wear any of the following items?

Columns: always, very frequently, somewhat frequently, somewhat infrequently, very infrequently, once, never

a. women's clothing
b. make-up
c. jewelry
d. hand-bag, purse, etc.
e. "very masculine" clothing, uniforms
f. colorful, stylish or unisex clothing
g. blue jeans
h. other (specify)

(PAGES 571, 575)

Whether or not you wear any of the following items, how do you feel about the idea of each of them?

Columns: very positive, somewhat positive, neutral, somewhat negative, very negative, not sure

a. women's clothing
b. make-up
c. jewelry
d. hand-bag, purse, etc.
e. "very masculine" clothing, uniforms
f. colorful, stylish or unisex clothing
g. blue jeans
h. other (specify)

Brief comment or experience:

(PAGE 571, 575)

22. How often do you like sex partners who, in connection with sex, wear any of the following items?

	always	very frequently	somewhat frequently	somewhat infrequently	very infrequently	once	never
a. women's clothing	☐	☐	☐	☐	☐	☐	☐
b. make-up	☐	☐	☐	☐	☐	☐	☐
c. jewelry	☐	☐	☐	☐	☐	☐	☐
d. hand-bag, purse, etc.	☐	☐	☐	☐	☐	☐	☐
e. "very masculine" clothing, uniforms	☐	☐	☐	☐	☐	☐	☐
f. colorful, stylish or unisex clothing	☐	☐	☐	☐	☐	☐	☐
g. blue jeans	☐	☐	☐	☐	☐	☐	☐
h. other (specify)	☐	☐	☐	☐	☐	☐	☐

(PAGES 570, 576)

Whether or not your sex partners wear any of the following items, indicate how you feel about sex partners who use each of them.

	very positive	somewhat positive	neutral	somewhat negative	very negative	not sure
a. women's clothing	☐	☐	☐	☐	☐	☐
b. make-up	☐	☐	☐	☐	☐	☐
c. jewelry	☐	☐	☐	☐	☐	☐
d. hand-bag, purse, etc.	☐	☐	☐	☐	☐	☐
e. "very masculine" clothing, uniforms	☐	☐	☐	☐	☐	☐
f. colorful, stylish or unisex clothing	☐	☐	☐	☐	☐	☐
g. blue jeans	☐	☐	☐	☐	☐	☐
h. other (specify)	☐	☐	☐	☐	☐	☐

(PAGES 570, 576)

Age

23. How often do you have sex with men or boys of the following ages? (Check for each one.)

	always	very frequently	somewhat frequently	somewhat infrequently	very infrequently	once	never
a. 65+	☐	☐	☐	☐	☐	☐	☐
b. 55-64	☐	☐	☐	☐	☐	☐	☐
c. 45-54	☐	☐	☐	☐	☐	☐	☐
d. 35-44	☐	☐	☐	☐	☐	☐	☐
e. 30-34	☐	☐	☐	☐	☐	☐	☐
f. 25-29	☐	☐	☐	☐	☐	☐	☐
g. 20-24	☐	☐	☐	☐	☐	☐	☐
h. 16-19	☐	☐	☐	☐	☐	☐	☐
i. 13-15	☐	☐	☐	☐	☐	☐	☐
j. 9-12	☐	☐	☐	☐	☐	☐	☐
k. under 9	☐	☐	☐	☐	☐	☐	☐

(PAGE 275)

Whether or not you have sex with any of the following age groups, indicate how you feel about the idea of having sex with each of them.

	very positive	somewhat positive	neutral	somewhat negative	very negative	not sure
a. 65+	☐	☐	☐	☐	☐	☐
b. 55-64	☐	☐	☐	☐	☐	☐
c. 45-54	☐	☐	☐	☐	☐	☐
d. 35-44	☐	☐	☐	☐	☐	☐
e. 30-34	☐	☐	☐	☐	☐	☐
f. 25-29	☐	☐	☐	☐	☐	☐
g. 20-24	☐	☐	☐	☐	☐	☐
h. 16-19	☐	☐	☐	☐	☐	☐
i. 13-15	☐	☐	☐	☐	☐	☐
j. 9-12	☐	☐	☐	☐	☐	☐
k. under 9	☐	☐	☐	☐	☐	☐

Brief comment or experience:

(PAGE 275)

24. How much does what you do to your partner "turn you on"?
☐ quite a lot
☐ some
☐ very little
☐ none at all
☐ not sure

(PAGE 441)

25. On the average, during sex, do you feel that you are more physically active than your partner?
☐ much more active
☐ a little more active
☐ the same
☐ a little less active
☐ much less active

(PAGE 441)

26. How often do you ask your partner for what you want done to you?
☐ always
☐ very frequently
☐ somewhat frequently
☐ somewhat infrequently
☐ very infrequently
☐ once
☐ never

(PAGE 684)

Where Do You Have Sex?

27. On the average, how often do you have sex in each of the following places?

	always	very frequently	somewhat frequently	somewhat infrequently	very infrequently	once	never
a. your home	☐	☐	☐	☐	☐	☐	☐
b. your partner's home	☐	☐	☐	☐	☐	☐	☐
c. a friend's home	☐	☐	☐	☐	☐	☐	☐
d. gay bath	☐	☐	☐	☐	☐	☐	☐
e. beach	☐	☐	☐	☐	☐	☐	☐
f. park, "bushes"	☐	☐	☐	☐	☐	☐	☐
g. public rest room	☐	☐	☐	☐	☐	☐	☐
h. car	☐	☐	☐	☐	☐	☐	☐
i. van or camper	☐	☐	☐	☐	☐	☐	☐
j. tent	☐	☐	☐	☐	☐	☐	☐
k. motel or hotel	☐	☐	☐	☐	☐	☐	☐
l. bar	☐	☐	☐	☐	☐	☐	☐
m. secluded woods or field	☐	☐	☐	☐	☐	☐	☐
n. barn or farm building	☐	☐	☐	☐	☐	☐	☐
o. peep show, pornographic movie house	☐	☐	☐	☐	☐	☐	☐
p. other (specify)	☐	☐	☐	☐	☐	☐	☐

(PAGE 500)

Whether or not you use any of these places for sex, how do you feel about the idea of having sex in each of these places?

	very positive	somewhat positive	neutral	somewhat negative	very negative	not sure
a. your home	☐	☐	☐	☐	☐	☐
b. your partner's home	☐	☐	☐	☐	☐	☐
c. a friend's home	☐	☐	☐	☐	☐	☐
d. gay bath	☐	☐	☐	☐	☐	☐
e. beach	☐	☐	☐	☐	☐	☐
f. park, "bushes"	☐	☐	☐	☐	☐	☐
g. public rest room	☐	☐	☐	☐	☐	☐
h. car	☐	☐	☐	☐	☐	☐
i. van or camper	☐	☐	☐	☐	☐	☐
j. tent	☐	☐	☐	☐	☐	☐
k. motel or hotel	☐	☐	☐	☐	☐	☐
l. bar	☐	☐	☐	☐	☐	☐
m. secluded woods or field	☐	☐	☐	☐	☐	☐
n. barn or farm building	☐	☐	☐	☐	☐	☐
o. peep show, pornographic movie house	☐	☐	☐	☐	☐	☐
p. other (specify)	☐	☐	☐	☐	☐	☐

(PAGE 500)

28. While having sex, how important is each of the following?

	very important	somewhat important	neutral	somewhat unimportant	very unimportant	not sure
a. privacy	☐	☐	☐	☐	☐	☐
b. lack of privacy	☐	☐	☐	☐	☐	☐
c. danger or possibility of violence	☐	☐	☐	☐	☐	☐

Brief comment or experience:

(PAGE 502)

29. How often do you spend the whole night with your sex partner?
☐ always
☐ very frequently
☐ somewhat frequently
☐ somewhat infrequently
☐ very infrequently
☐ once
☐ never

Comment on why or why not.

(PAGE 508)

30. How often has a sexual encounter been terminated because . . .
a. you would not perform a particular sexual act your partner wanted . . . .
b. your partner would not perform a particular sexual act you wanted . . . .
Comment briefly.   **(PAGE 441)**

Column headers: always, very frequently, somewhat frequently, somewhat infrequently, very infrequently, once, never

31. How often do you go home to have sex with someone you have just met? How often do you determine what is going to happen sexually in advance with someone you have just met by asking him certain questions? How often do you or your partner wear something that indicates you prefer a particular sex act?
a. go home with a stranger . . . .
b. ask questions to plan sex . . . .
c. wear something to plan sex . . . .
(PAGES 251, 574, 683)

Column headers: always, very frequently, somewhat frequently, somewhat infrequently, very infrequently, once, never

Whether or not you do any of the following, how do you feel about the idea of each of them?
a. go home with a stranger . . . .
b. ask questions to plan sex . . . .
c. wear something to plan sex . . . .
Brief comment or experience: **(PAGES 252, 574, 683)**

Column headers: very positive, somewhat positive, neutral, somewhat negative, very negative, not sure

32. How often do you use the following in association with sex?
a. alcohol . . . .
b. marijuana . . . .
c. psychedelics (LSD, mushrooms, mescaline) .
d. "uppers" (speed, amphetamine) . . . .
e. quaaludes . . . .
f. "downers" (barbituates, tranquilizers) . . . .
g. heroin . . . .
h. cocaine . . . .
i. amyl nitrite ("poppers," "aroma") . . . .
j. other (specify) . . . .
(PAGE 496)

Column headers: always, very frequently, somewhat frequently, somewhat infrequently, very infrequently, once, never

Whether or not you use any of the following, how do you feel about their use in association with sex?
a. alcohol . . . .
b. marijuana . . . .
c. psychedelics (LSD, mushrooms, mescaline) .
d. "uppers" (speed, amphetamine) . . . .
e. quaaludes . . . .
f. "downers" (barbituates, tranquilizers) . . . .
g. heroin . . . .
h. cocaine . . . .
i. amyl nitrite ("poppers," "aroma") . . . .
j. other (specify) . . . .
(PAGE 496)

Column headers: very positive, somewhat positive, neutral, somewhat negative, very negative, not sure

33. Have you ever refused to have sex with a partner because...
a. he used any of these?
☐ Yes   ☐ No
If yes, specify which one(s) . . . .
b. he would not join you in the use of any of these.
☐ Yes   ☐ No
If yes, specify which one(s) . . . .
(PAGE 497)

Venereal Disease

34. How often have you had the following venereal diseases (VD) or sex-related maladies?
a. syphilis ("siff") . . . .
b. gonorrhea ("clap," "drip") . . . .
c. warts . . . .
d. herpes . . . .
e. hepatitis (from sex) . . . .
f. non-specific urethritis (NSU) . . . .
g. lice ("crabs") . . . .
h. scabies . . . .
i. other (specify) . . . .
(PAGE 691)

Column headers: never, once, twice, three times, more than three times, not sure

35. How often do you go for VD checkups?
☐ every three months
☐ every six months
☐ once a year
☐ less frequently than once a year
☐ never   **(PAGE 692)**

36. Where do you go for VD checkups?
☐ your regular doctor
☐ other doctor
☐ public clinic
☐ gay clinic
☐ other (specify) _____   **(PAGE 692)**

37. In general, how do you feel about the way you are treated when you have VD check-ups?
☐ very positive
☐ somewhat positive
☐ neutral
☐ somewhat negative
☐ very negative
☐ not sure   **(PAGE 693)**

38. How often does the fear of VD influence any of the following?
a. your choice of sex partner . . . .
b. sexual acts you engage in . . . .
c. how often you have sex . . . .
Comment:
(PAGE 693)

Column headers: always, very frequently, somewhat frequently, somewhat infrequently, very infrequently, once, never

Fantasies

39. How often do you fantasize?
a. during sex with a partner . . . .
b. during masturbation . . . .
(PAGES 621, 623)

Column headers: always, very frequently, somewhat frequently, somewhat infrequently, very infrequently, once, never

Whether or not you fantasize, how do you feel about the idea of fantasizing . . .
a. during sex with a partner . . . .
b. during masturbation . . . .
(PAGES 622, 623)

Column headers: very positive, somewhat positive, neutral, somewhat negative, very negative, not sure

40. Are you secretive about any specific aspects of your sex life, even though you may be openly gay?
☐ Yes   ☐ No
If yes, indicate briefly which aspects you keep secret and why.
(PAGES 595, 650, 681)

Orgasms

41. How important is having orgasms to you?

Scale: very important / somewhat important / neutral / somewhat unimportant / very unimportant / not sure

a. during sex with a partner
b. during masturbation

(PAGES 635, 674)

42. How often do you have one or more orgasms?

Scale: always / very frequently / somewhat frequently / somewhat infrequently / very infrequently / once / never

a. during sex with a partner
b. during masturbation

(PAGES 635, 675)

43. How important is it to you whether your partner has orgasm during sex with you?
☐ very important
☐ somewhat important
☐ neutral
☐ somewhat unimportant
☐ very unimportant
☐ not sure

(PAGE 677)

44. When having sex with a man, how often do you fake or have you faked orgasm?
☐ always
☐ very frequently
☐ somewhat frequently
☐ somewhat infrequently
☐ very infrequently
☐ once
☐ never

(PAGE 676)

45. How often do you experience premature ejaculation ("coming too soon")?
☐ always
☐ very frequently
☐ somewhat frequently
☐ somewhat infrequently
☐ very infrequently
☐ once
☐ never

(PAGE 677)

46. How concerned are you about premature ejaculation...

Scale: very concerned / somewhat concerned / neutral / somewhat unconcerned / very unconcerned / not sure

a. in yourself
b. in your partner

(PAGE 678)

47. On the average, how do you feel about the quality of the sexual experiences you have with men (without reference to how often you have sex)?
☐ completely satisfied
☐ very satisfied
☐ somewhat satisfied
☐ neutral
☐ somewhat dissatisfied
☐ very dissatisfied
☐ completely dissatisfied
☐ not sure

(PAGE 684)

Sex with Women

48. How often have you had or do you have sex with women?

Scale: always / very frequently / somewhat frequently / somewhat infrequently / very infrequently / once / never

a. in the past
b. currently

(PAGE 123)

49. How do you feel about sex with women?

Scale: very positive / somewhat positive / neutral / somewhat negative / very negative / not sure

a. your past experiences
b. your current experiences

(PAGE 124)

50. Have you considered or do you consider yourself bi-sexual?
a. in the past .... ☐ Yes ☐ No
b. currently .... ☐ Yes ☐ No

(PAGE 127)

Masturbation

51. On the average, how often do you masturbate?
☐ more than once a day
☐ once a day
☐ several times a week
☐ once a week
☐ several times a month
☐ once a month
☐ less frequently than once a month
☐ never
☐ not sure

(PAGE 635)

How do you feel about masturbation?
☐ very positive
☐ somewhat positive
☐ neutral
☐ somewhat negative
☐ very negative
☐ not sure

(PAGE 651)

52. How often do you use any of the following in connection with masturbation?

Scale: always / very frequently / somewhat frequently / somewhat infrequently / very infrequently / once / never

a. hand-held dildo
b. strap-on dildo
c. vibrator
d. accu-jack
e. cock ring
f. nipple clamp
g. oils
h. pornography

(PAGE 641)

Affection

53. How often do you engage in physical affection (hugging, cuddling, caressing, kissing) with each of the following?

Scale: always / very frequently / somewhat frequently / somewhat infrequently / very infrequently / once / never

a. lovers
b. sex partners
c. gay friends
d. straight men
e. women
f. parents
g. other relatives
h. children

(PAGES 183, 438)

Whether or not you engage in physical affection with any of the following, indicate how you feel about the idea of physical affection with each of them.

Scale: very positive / somewhat positive / neutral / somewhat negative / very negative / not sure

a. lovers
b. sex partners
c. gay friends
d. straight men
e. women
f. parents
g. other relatives
h. children

(PAGES 184, 439)

Relationships

54. In the past or the present, what is the longest you have been in a relationship with one male lover? Specify length of time . . . . **(PAGE 340)**

Do you now have a lover or "boyfriend"? . . . . ☐ Yes   ☐ No
(PAGE 339)
How long have you been with your current lover? . . . . **(PAGE 340)**

On the average, how often do you have sex together? . . . . **(PAGE 354)**

Do you live together? . . . . ☐ Yes   ☐ No
(PAGE 355)
Briefly indicate why or why not . . . .

55. Do you consider or have you considered yourself "married" to another man? . . . . ☐ Yes   ☐ No   ☐ Not sure
Comment.
Have you ever had a gay marriage ceremony? . . . . ☐ Yes   ☐ No
(PAGE 363)
Whether or not you are in or have been in a gay marriage, what is your attitude toward it?
☐ strongly favor
☐ somewhat favor
☐ neutral
☐ somewhat oppose   **(PAGE 363)**
☐ strongly oppose
☐ not sure

56. How often do you "role play" (butch/femme, masculine/feminine, husband/wife, dominant/submissive) in your relationships?

	always	very frequently	somewhat frequently	somewhat infrequently	very infrequently	once	never
a. sexually	☐	☐	☐	☐	☐	☐	☐
b. other than sexually	☐	☐	☐	☐	☐	☐	☐

(PAGE 365)

Whether or not you role play, how do you feel about it in your own relationship or in relationships you observe?

	very positive	somewhat positive	neutral	somewhat negative	very negative	not sure
a. sexually	☐	☐	☐	☐	☐	☐
b. other than sexually	☐	☐	☐	☐	☐	☐

(PAGE 366)

57. How often do you relate to a certain "type"?
☐ always
☐ very frequently
☐ somewhat frequently
☐ somewhat infrequently
☐ very infrequently
☐ once
☐ never   **(PAGE 265)**

58. How important is each of the following, in terms of what you look for or what you avoid, when you seek a sex partner?

	very important	somewhat important	neutral	somewhat unimportant	very unimportant	not sure
a. age	☐	☐	☐	☐	☐	☐
b. height	☐	☐	☐	☐	☐	☐
c. weight	☐	☐	☐	☐	☐	☐
d. build, physique	☐	☐	☐	☐	☐	☐
e. "looks" in general	☐	☐	☐	☐	☐	☐
f. eyes	☐	☐	☐	☐	☐	☐
g. nose	☐	☐	☐	☐	☐	☐
h. lips	☐	☐	☐	☐	☐	☐
i. complexion	☐	☐	☐	☐	☐	☐
j. facial hair, beard, moustache	☐	☐	☐	☐	☐	☐
k. head hair, baldness	☐	☐	☐	☐	☐	☐
l. body hair	☐	☐	☐	☐	☐	☐
m. buttocks (ass)	☐	☐	☐	☐	☐	☐
n. penis size	☐	☐	☐	☐	☐	☐
o. circumcision	☐	☐	☐	☐	☐	☐
p. hygiene, cleanliness or lack of it	☐	☐	☐	☐	☐	☐
q. clothing	☐	☐	☐	☐	☐	☐
r. race	☐	☐	☐	☐	☐	☐
s. social class	☐	☐	☐	☐	☐	☐
t. educational level	☐	☐	☐	☐	☐	☐
u. religion or spiritual orientation	☐	☐	☐	☐	☐	☐
v. political views	☐	☐	☐	☐	☐	☐
w. overall personality	☐	☐	☐	☐	☐	☐
x. masculinity/femininity, butch/femme	☐	☐	☐	☐	☐	☐
y. intelligence	☐	☐	☐	☐	☐	☐
z. other (specify)	☐	☐	☐	☐	☐	☐

(PAGE 265)

If you have checked "very important" for any of the above, indicate specifically what things you are looking for or avoiding. (Attach separate paper if you need more room.)   **(PAGE 265)**

How many different sex partners or lovers have you had in the past week? . . . . In the past month? . . . . In the past 12 months? . . . . In your lifetime? . . . .
(PAGE 248)

59. How often do you meet other gay men in each of the following places? (This question refers to meeting people, not necessarily having sex. See question 27.)

	always	very frequently	somewhat frequently	somewhat infrequently	very infrequently	once	never
a. bars	☐	☐	☐	☐	☐	☐	☐
b. at work	☐	☐	☐	☐	☐	☐	☐
c. at school	☐	☐	☐	☐	☐	☐	☐
d. neighborhood	☐	☐	☐	☐	☐	☐	☐
e. parties	☐	☐	☐	☐	☐	☐	☐
f. gay dances (other than bars)	☐	☐	☐	☐	☐	☐	☐
g. social groups	☐	☐	☐	☐	☐	☐	☐
h. political groups	☐	☐	☐	☐	☐	☐	☐
i. through friends	☐	☐	☐	☐	☐	☐	☐
j. resorts and beaches	☐	☐	☐	☐	☐	☐	☐
k. gym, "Y," straight health club, sports	☐	☐	☐	☐	☐	☐	☐
l. church	☐	☐	☐	☐	☐	☐	☐
m. personal ads	☐	☐	☐	☐	☐	☐	☐
n. public toilets	☐	☐	☐	☐	☐	☐	☐
o. highway rest stops	☐	☐	☐	☐	☐	☐	☐
p. baths	☐	☐	☐	☐	☐	☐	☐
q. parks	☐	☐	☐	☐	☐	☐	☐
r. streets	☐	☐	☐	☐	☐	☐	☐
s. pornographic movie theaters	☐	☐	☐	☐	☐	☐	☐
t. other (specify)	☐	☐	☐	☐	☐	☐	☐

(PAGE 239)

Whether or not you meet other gay men in any of these places, indicate how you feel about the idea of meeting other gay men in each of them.

	very positive	somewhat positive	neutral	somewhat negative	very negative	not sure
a. bars	☐	☐	☐	☐	☐	☐
b. at work	☐	☐	☐	☐	☐	☐
c. at school	☐	☐	☐	☐	☐	☐
d. neighborhood	☐	☐	☐	☐	☐	☐
e. parties	☐	☐	☐	☐	☐	☐
f. gay dances (other than bars)	☐	☐	☐	☐	☐	☐
g. social groups	☐	☐	☐	☐	☐	☐
h. political groups	☐	☐	☐	☐	☐	☐
i. through friends	☐	☐	☐	☐	☐	☐
j. resorts and beaches	☐	☐	☐	☐	☐	☐
k. gym, "Y," straight health club, sports	☐	☐	☐	☐	☐	☐
l. church	☐	☐	☐	☐	☐	☐
m. personal ads	☐	☐	☐	☐	☐	☐
n. public toilets	☐	☐	☐	☐	☐	☐
o. highway rest stops	☐	☐	☐	☐	☐	☐
p. baths	☐	☐	☐	☐	☐	☐
q. parks	☐	☐	☐	☐	☐	☐
r. streets	☐	☐	☐	☐	☐	☐
s. pornographic movie theaters	☐	☐	☐	☐	☐	☐
t. other (specify)	☐	☐	☐	☐	☐	☐

(PAGE 239)

60. How active (you do the "picking up") or passive (you get "picked up") are you in seeking a relationship or a sex partner?
☐ very active
☐ somewhat active
☐ neutral
☐ somewhat passive
☐ very passive
☐ not sure   **(PAGE 257)**

61. How often have you paid for sex with a man or boy?

	always	very frequently	somewhat frequently	somewhat infrequently	very infrequently	once	never
a. with money	☐	☐	☐	☐	☐	☐	☐
b. in other ways (specify)	☐	☐	☐	☐	☐	☐	☐

(PAGE 259)

Whether or not you have paid for sex, how do you feel about the idea of paying for sex

	very positive	somewhat positive	neutral	somewhat negative	very negative	not sure
a. with money	□	□	□	□	□	□
b. in other ways (specify)	□	□	□	□	□	□

(PAGE 259)

62. How often have you been paid for sex?

	always	very frequently	somewhat frequently	somewhat infrequently	very infrequently	once	never
a. with money	□	□	□	□	□	□	□
b. in other ways (specify)	□	□	□	□	□	□	□

(PAGE 260)

Whether or not you have been paid for sex with money or in other ways, how do you feel about the idea of receiving money or other benefits for sex?

	very positive	somewhat positive	neutral	somewhat negative	very negative	not sure
a. receiving money	□	□	□	□	□	□
b. receiving other benefits (specify)	□	□	□	□	□	□

(PAGE 260)

Self-Image

63. How do you feel about each of the following aspects of your body?

	very positive	somewhat positive	neutral	somewhat negative	very negative	not sure
a. height	□	□	□	□	□	□
b. weight	□	□	□	□	□	□
c. build, physique	□	□	□	□	□	□
d. "looks" in general	□	□	□	□	□	□
e. how people perceive your age	□	□	□	□	□	□
f. facial hair, beard, moustache	□	□	□	□	□	□
g. eyes	□	□	□	□	□	□
h. nose	□	□	□	□	□	□
i. lips	□	□	□	□	□	□
j. complexion	□	□	□	□	□	□
k. head hair, baldness	□	□	□	□	□	□
l. body hair	□	□	□	□	□	□
m. buttocks (ass)	□	□	□	□	□	□
n. penis size	□	□	□	□	□	□
o. circumcision	□	□	□	□	□	□
p. other (specify)	□	□	□	□	□	□

If you have checked "very positive" or "very negative" for any of the above, specify what there is about each thing that you intensely like or dislike. (Attach separate paper if you need more room.)

(PAGE 282)

64. How do you feel about aging?
□ very positive
□ somewhat positive
□ neutral
□ somewhat negative
□ very negative
□ not sure

(PAGE 287)

65. In general, how do you feel about the use of the categories or labels masculine/feminine, butch/femme?
□ very positive
□ somewhat positive
□ neutral
□ somewhat negative
□ very negative
□ not sure

(PAGE 291)

Coming Out

66. What is your age now? . . . .

At what age did you first realize that you were a homosexual or gay or somehow sexually "different"? . . . . **(PAGE 105)**

At what age did you associate this "difference" with homosexual acts? . . . . . **(PAGE 106)**

At what age did you have your first homosexual experience? . . . . **(PAGE 107)**

How many years have you been a "practicing homosexual"? . . **(PAGE 108)**

67. At what age did you first tell anyone other than your sexual partners about your homosexuality? . . . . **(PAGE 146)**

Indicate who (relationship) . . . . **(PAGE 147)**

Indicate calendar year . . . . **(PAGE 147)**

If you have told no one, briefly indicate why. **(PAGE 144)**

68. How many of the following (if applicable) know about your homosexuality?

	All (Yes)	Most	Some	Only One	None (No)	Not sure
a. gay male friends	□	□	□	□	□	□
b. lesbian friends	□	□	□	□	□	□
c. straight friends	□	□	□	□	□	□
d. neighbors	□	□	□	□	□	□
e. employer	□	□	□	□	□	□
f. teacher	□	□	□	□	□	□
g. co-workers	□	□	□	□	□	□
h. schoolmates	□	□	□	□	□	□
i. your employees	□	□	□	□	□	□
j. mother	□	□	□	□	□	□
k. father	□	□	□	□	□	□
l. sisters and brothers	□	□	□	□	□	□
m. your children	□	□	□	□	□	□
n. other relatives	□	□	□	□	□	□
o. other children	□	□	□	□	□	□

(PAGE 141)

69. In general, how important is it for you to keep your homosexuality a secret from each of the following (see also next question)?

	very important	somewhat important	neutral	somewhat unimportant	very unimportant	not sure
a. gay male friends	□	□	□	□	□	□
b. lesbian friends	□	□	□	□	□	□
c. straight friends	□	□	□	□	□	□
d. neighbors	□	□	□	□	□	□
e. employer	□	□	□	□	□	□
f. teacher	□	□	□	□	□	□
g. co-workers	□	□	□	□	□	□
h. schoolmates	□	□	□	□	□	□
i. your employees	□	□	□	□	□	□
j. mother	□	□	□	□	□	□
k. father	□	□	□	□	□	□
l. sisters and brothers	□	□	□	□	□	□
m. your children	□	□	□	□	□	□
n. other relatives	□	□	□	□	□	□
o. other children	□	□	□	□	□	□

(PAGE 142)

70. How important is it for you to purposely communicate the fact that you are gay to each of the following?

	very important	somewhat important	neutral	somewhat unimportant	very unimportant	not sure
a. gay male friends	□	□	□	□	□	□
b. lesbian friends	□	□	□	□	□	□
c. straight friends	□	□	□	□	□	□
d. neighbors	□	□	□	□	□	□
e. employer	□	□	□	□	□	□
f. teacher	□	□	□	□	□	□
g. co-workers	□	□	□	□	□	□
h. schoolmates	□	□	□	□	□	□
i. your employees	□	□	□	□	□	□
j. mother	□	□	□	□	□	□
k. father	□	□	□	□	□	□
l. sisters and brothers	□	□	□	□	□	□
m. your children	□	□	□	□	□	□
n. other relatives	□	□	□	□	□	□
o. other children	□	□	□	□	□	□

(PAGE 142)

71. Of those who know you are gay or homosexual, what has been the reaction of each of the following to that fact? (Answer for those that are applicable.)

	very positive	somewhat positive	neutral	somewhat negative	very negative	not sure
a. gay male friends	□	□	□	□	□	□
b. lesbian friends	□	□	□	□	□	□
c. straight friends	□	□	□	□	□	□
d. neighbors	□	□	□	□	□	□
e. employer	□	□	□	□	□	□
f. teacher	□	□	□	□	□	□
g. co-workers	□	□	□	□	□	□
h. schoolmates	□	□	□	□	□	□
i. your employees	□	□	□	□	□	□
j. mother	□	□	□	□	□	□
k. father	□	□	□	□	□	□
l. sisters and brothers	□	□	□	□	□	□
m. your children	□	□	□	□	□	□
n. other relatives	□	□	□	□	□	□
o. other children	□	□	□	□	□	□

(PAGE 143)

72. How do you feel about people who you perceive to be "in the closet" (secretive)?
□ very positive
□ somewhat positive
□ neutral
□ somewhat negative
□ very negative
□ not sure
(PAGE 156)

73. How to you feel about people who you perceive to be "blatantly gay"?

	very positive	somewhat positive	neutral	somewhat negative	very negative	not sure
a. those who are politically outspoken	□	□	□	□	□	□
b. those who physically appear to be "obvious" homosexuals or lesbians	□	□	□	□	□	□

Comment
(PAGE 157)

74. Do you feel that most people can tell instantly that you are gay?
□ Yes　　□ No　　□ Not sure
Briefly comment on your answer.
(PAGE 139)

Society

75. Do you ever or have you ever experienced any of the following in connection with your homosexuality?

	quite a lot	some	very little	once	none at all	not sure
a. harassment	□	□	□	□	□	□
b. loss of job	□	□	□	□	□	□
c. forced to move	□	□	□	□	□	□
d. arrest	□	□	□	□	□	□
e. blackmail or threat of blackmail	□	□	□	□	□	□
f. physical abuse	□	□	□	□	□	□
g. verbal abuse, name-calling	□	□	□	□	□	□
h. robbery	□	□	□	□	□	□
i. shakedown	□	□	□	□	□	□
j. shame, guilt	□	□	□	□	□	□
k. fear of discovery	□	□	□	□	□	□
l. other (specify)	□	□	□	□	□	□

(PAGE 698)

76. Have you ever gone to a psychiatrist or psychologist to be "cured" of your homosexuality? □ Yes　□ No
(PAGE 722)
If yes, how long did you spend, or have you spent, in this kind of treatment?
(PAGE 722)

If you could take a pill to make you straight, would you do it?
□ Yes　　□ No　　□ Not sure
(PAGE 722)

Are you currently seeing a therapist, psychiatrist or psychologist for any reason? □ Yes　□ No

If yes, state briefly what reason
(PAGE 722)

How do you feel about your experience(s) in therapy?

	very positive	somewhat positive	neutral	somewhat negative	very negative	not sure
a. straight therapist	□	□	□	□	□	□
b. gay therapist	□	□	□	□	□	□
c. don't know sexuality of therapist	□	□	□	□	□	□
d. other factor (specify)	□	□	□	□	□	□

(PAGE 722)

77. Have you ever attempted or seriously contemplated suicide?
□ Yes　　□ No　　　　**(PAGE 728)**

If yes, was this experience related to your homosexuality or gayness?
□ Yes　　□ No　　　　**(PAGE 728)**

78. How much is your homosexuality or gayness something other than a sexual orientation?
□ quite a lot
□ some
□ very little
□ none at all
□ not sure
Comment　　　　　　　　　　　　**(PAGE 763)**

79. How important is the concept of gay community and gay culture to you?

	very important	somewhat important	neutral	somewhat unimportant	very unimportant	not sure
a. gay community	□	□	□	□	□	□
b. gay culture	□	□	□	□	□	□

(PAGE 763)

80. How often do you socialize with each of the following?

	always	very frequently	somewhat frequently	somewhat infrequently	very infrequently	once	never
a. gay men	□	□	□	□	□	□	□
b. heterosexual men	□	□	□	□	□	□	□
c. lesbians	□	□	□	□	□	□	□
d. heterosexual women	□	□	□	□	□	□	□
e. bi-sexual men	□	□	□	□	□	□	□
f. bi-sexual women	□	□	□	□	□	□	□

(PAGE 232)

81. How do you feel about each of the following?

	very positive	somewhat positive	neutral	somewhat negative	very negative	not sure
a. gay men	□	□	□	□	□	□
b. heterosexual men	□	□	□	□	□	□
c. lesbians	□	□	□	□	□	□
d. heterosexual women	□	□	□	□	□	□
e. bi-sexual men	□	□	□	□	□	□
f. bi-sexual women	□	□	□	□	□	□

(PAGE 232)

82. How much of your time do you spend in each of the following environments?

	quite a lot	some	very little	none at all	not sure
a. gay men only	□	□	□	□	□
b. men only (gay and straight mixed)	□	□	□	□	□
c. gay only (lesbians and male homosexuals, mixed)	□	□	□	□	□
d. mixed straight and gay, men and women	□	□	□	□	□

(PAGE 232)

Whether or not you spend time in any of the following environments, how do you feel about each of them?

	very positive	somewhat positive	neutral	somewhat negative	very negative	not sure
a. gay men only	☐	☐	☐	☐	☐	☐
b. men only (gay and straight mixed)	☐	☐	☐	☐	☐	☐
c. gay only (lesbians and male homosexuals mixed)	☐	☐	☐	☐	☐	☐
d. mixed straight and gay, men and women	☐	☐	☐	☐	☐	☐

Comment ....   **(PAGE 232)**

83. If you are legally married to a woman, check any of the following that applies.
☐ living with wife, and she knows about my homosexuality
☐ living with wife, but she doesn't know about my homosexuality
☐ living with wife, and I'm not sure whether or not she knows
☐ marriage of convenience (to help me pass for straight)
☐ marriage of convenience (for inheritance or gifts, for immigration, etc.)

How do you feel about your marriage?
☐ completely satisfied
☐ very satisfied
☐ somewhat satisfied
☐ neutral
☐ somewhat dissatisfied
☐ very dissatisfied
☐ completely dissatisfied
☐ not sure
Comment   **(PAGE 130)**

84. Are you separated or divorced? (check one, if applicable)
☐ Separated   ☐ Divorced   **(PAGE 130)**

Was your homosexuality a major factor in your separation or divorce?
☐ Yes   ☐ No   ☐ Not sure   **(PAGE 130)**

Children

85. Do you have children?
☐ Yes   ☐ No   If yes, how many?........   **(PAGE 133)**

Whether or not you have children, what is your attitude, in general, toward children?
☐ very positive
☐ somewhat positive
☐ neutral
☐ somewhat negative
☐ very negative
☐ not sure   **(PAGE 133)**

86. Has custody been an issue for you?
☐ Yes   ☐ No
If yes, comment briefly on your situation.   **(PAGE 135)**

87. Has any aspect of visiting rights been an issue for you?
☐ Yes   ☐ No
If yes, comment briefly on your situation.   **(PAGE 135)**

88. Do you participate in the rearing of children, even though they are not your own biologically? ....☐ Yes   ☐ No
If yes, briefly explain the arrangement.   **(PAGE 134)**

How do you feel about this arrangement?
☐ completely satisfied
☐ very satisfied
☐ somewhat satisfied
☐ neutral
☐ somewhat dissatisfied
☐ very dissatisfied
☐ completely dissatisfied
☐ not sure   **(PAGE 134)**

89. If you don't have children, how do you feel about being childless?
☐ very positive
☐ somewhat positive
☐ neutral
☐ somewhat negative
☐ very negative
☐ not sure   **(PAGES 134, 137)**

Politics

90. How do you feel about each of the following?

	very positive	somewhat positive	neutral	somewhat negative	very negative	not sure
a. male transvestites (drag queens)	☐	☐	☐	☐	☐	☐
b. drag shows, entertainment	☐	☐	☐	☐	☐	☐
c. men in colorful, stylish or unisex clothing	☐	☐	☐	☐	☐	☐
d. men in "butch" clothing, uniforms, etc.	☐	☐	☐	☐	☐	☐
e. women in "butch" or very masculine clothing	☐	☐	☐	☐	☐	☐
f. women in blue jeans, unisex clothing	☐	☐	☐	☐	☐	☐
g. women in dresses and skirts	☐	☐	☐	☐	☐	☐

(PAGES 377, 577)

91. How often do you camp it up or watch others camp it up?

	always	very frequently	somewhat frequently	somewhat infrequently	very infrequently	once	never
a. camp it up	☐	☐	☐	☐	☐	☐	☐
b. watch others camp it up	☐	☐	☐	☐	☐	☐	☐

(PAGE 375)

Whether or not you camp it up or watch others camp it up, how do you feel about the idea of each of them?

	very positive	somewhat positive	neutral	somewhat negative	very negative	not sure
a. camp it up	☐	☐	☐	☐	☐	☐
b. watch others camp it up	☐	☐	☐	☐	☐	☐

(PAGE 375)

92. In general, which word do you consider the most appropriate (best) word to be used for male homosexuals? (check one)
☐ homosexual
☐ gay man
☐ gay
☐ homophile
☐ other (specify) ....
(PAGE 766)

93. How would you describe yourself politically? (check one or more)
☐ Democrat
☐ Republican
☐ independent
☐ conservative
☐ liberal
☐ moderate
☐ radical
☐ apolitical
☐ anarchist
☐ socialist (specify tendency or group, if applicable) ....
☐ feminist
☐ pacifist
☐ "third world" liberationist (specify group if applicable) ....
☐ libertarian
☐ environmentalist
☐ revolutionary
☐ humanist
☐ gay liberationist
☐ other (specify) ....
(PAGE 731)

94. How do you feel about each of the following?

	very positive	somewhat positive	neutral	somewhat negative	very negative	not sure
a. gay liberation (mixed male and female)	☐	☐	☐	☐	☐	☐
b. lesbian liberation (independent lesbian efforts)	☐	☐	☐	☐	☐	☐

(PAGE 735)

95. In what year did you first hear about any organized efforts for gay liberation? (Indicate calendar year) ....
(PAGE 732)
How did you first hear about such efforts? ....
....
(PAGE 733)

To what extent, if any, have you become involved with gay liberation?
☐ quite a lot
☐ some
☐ very little
☐ none at all
☐ not sure   **(PAGE 734)**

96. Do you feel that the repeal of laws against homosexual and lesbian acts and/or the enactment of anti-discrimination legislation in your state, neighboring state (or province), or nationally, will make your life better?
☐ quite a lot
☐ some
☐ very little
☐ none at all
☐ not sure   **(PAGE 733)**

How much have you worked for such reform(s)?
☐ quite a lot
☐ some
☐ very little
☐ none at all
☐ not sure   **(PAGE 733)**

Statistical Information   **(PAGES 805–816)**

The following group of questions are for statistical purposes, to find out more about the kind of people who answer the questionnaire. In no way is this designed to infringe on anyone's anonymity. Of course, you may leave any of these blank.

97. What is your age?.......

98. What is your race or ethnic group?........

99. What was your religious upbringing?........

100. What is your present religion or spiritual orientation?........

101. What was your annual income for 1976?
☐ less than $5,000
☐ between $5,000 and $9,999
☐ between $10,000 and $14,999
☐ between $15,000 and $24,999
☐ $25,000 or more
☐ not sure

102. What is your occupation? ....
Describe briefly the kind of work you do. ....

103. Indicate your educational level:
☐ some grade school
☐ completed grade school
☐ completed 9, 10, or 11 grades
☐ completed 12 grades
☐ some college
☐ college graduate
☐ some graduate school
☐ graduate degree

104. Do you have brothers and sisters?
How many brothers?........
How many sisters?........

105. Do you have any relatives who are homosexual or lesbian? Indicate relationship.
....
....
....

106. Where do you live?
Name of state or province ....
Name of town or city (or nearby town) ....

107. What sort of a place do you live in?
☐ rural or small town
☐ small city
☐ medium-sized city
☐ large city
☐ major metropolitan center
☐ suburb

108. Where did you get this questionnaire? Please be specific ....
....

Part Two

The following questions ask you in some detail about your experiences and feelings. Please type or write on separate sheets of paper for these. Remember, we will be delighted if you answer all the questions, but if a question does not interest or apply to you, skip it. Also feel free to answer only those questions on subjects of special interest to you.

Sexual Experiences

1. a) Tell us about a very pleasing love-making experience that you have had with a sex partner or lover. What is it that you do from beginning to end? How does each thing feel to you? Please indicate how long it takes; describe movements and positions used by you and your partner(s). Be precise: try to include such things as leg position, body position, movements, and other factors important to you such as roughness or gentleness, sounds, clothing, lighting, etc. Re-reading questions 9 through 47 may help you answer this. b) Indicate your feelings about this experience. c) If you haven't had a *real* experience that you consider pleasing, tell us about an imaginary one but be sure to indicate that it is imaginary.
(PAGE 437)

2. a) Describe your feelings about the following sex acts. What do you like about them? How do they feel to you? Feel free to express strong preferences or passions and to tell about things you hate or absolutely won't do.

Fellatio (Cocksucking, "Blow Jobs")
Manual stimulation
Analingus (rimming)
Rubbing of genitals against partner
Kissing
Anal intercourse
Fingerfucking   **(PAGE 437)**

b) Have your feelings about these acts changed over time, and if so, how?   **(PAGE 437)**

3. How do you feel about male genitals (their size, smell, appearance and feel) — your own and others?   **(PAGE 447)**

4. Tell us about your general feelings and experiences with the list of practices included in Question 19, Part One. Which ones do you like or hate, and why?   **(PAGE 553)**

5. How do you feel about "toys" — dildos, vibrators, oils, pornography and others. (Refer to Question 18.) Are they important to your sex life?   **(PAGE 581)**

6. Relate any feelings and experiences concerning anxieties, "hang-ups", compulsions, blocks, repressions, special needs, handicaps, problems with sexual performance or functioning, problems with the frequency of sex or the quality or skill of your sex partners, that you have had in regard to your general sex life or specific sexual acts.   **(PAGE 673)**

7. Tell us about the importance of sex in your life. Do you feel that too much or too little importance is placed on sex by you or by others, and why do you feel that way?   **(PAGE 161)**

8. a) What is the importance of emotion to you sexually? Do you have sex with or without emotional involvement, or both? b) What is the connection between love and sex? Comment. c) Have you ever been in love? Can you describe your feeling of being in love, of being loved? Of not being in love, and not being loved? Of wanting love, of not wanting love?   **(PAGES 171, 177)**

9. Describe your funniest, scariest and/or most unusual sexual experience with another man or boy. **(PAGE 503)**

10. If you fantasize during sex or masturbation, describe your favorite or most common fantasy or fantasies, and your feelings about them. Be specific as to people, situations, places, circumstances, etc., whether real or imaginary (indicate which). If you don't fantasize, what are your feelings about fantasies? **(PAGE 621)**

11. a) Tell us about your childhood "crushes" or sexual feelings directed toward other children or adults. Recall your own experiences and feelings as a child and people's responses to those experiences or feelings.· b) Regardless of your own childhood experiences, how do you feel now about childhood sexuality in general? Discuss your experiences with and feelings about sex between younger men and/or boys and older men, whether you have such experiences or not.
(PAGE 83)

12. a) Tell how you masturbate. Be specific. What parts of your body do you stimulate? With what and how? Indicate positions, movements and other important aspects such as lighting, music, pornography. How often do you masturbate? How long does it take? b) How does masturbation feel to you? c) How do you feel about masturbation in general, and how have these feelings changed over time? **(PAGE 634)**

Relationships
13. Tell about any present or past relationship with a lover or boyfriend. a) How often do you have sex? How do you feel about the quality and intensity of your sexual relationship? b) Do you live together? Why or why not? c) Do you have sex outside of that relationship and how does outside sex or the lack of it affect the relationship? Do you have an agreement about "fidelity" or the lack of it? Comment. d) If you don't have a lover, would you like one? Why or why not? e) What do you like or dislike about having a lover and/or being single? **(PAGE 339)**

14. Do you "role-play" (butch/femme, masculine/feminine, husband/wife) in your relationships with other men, sexually as well as other than sexually? If you do, tell about who does what and how you feel about it. What do you like or dislike about role-playing in your relationships or in relationships you observe? **(PAGE 365)**

15. a) Do you have a "type" that you prefer sexually? Tell us about your type. Referring to the list in question 58, tell in detail what attributes are important, whether they are things you look for or things you avoid. b) Do you relate only to a certain type? What happens when you don't find your type? c) Whether or not you have a type, what do you like or dislike about the idea of having a type? d) Tell about the important factors, if any, for you in choosing a sex partner or lover? (Refer to question 58) **(PAGE 265)**

16. a) Tell about the process of meeting other men. In what ways are you shy and/or outgoing? Insecure and/or self-confident) b) What are your experiences, if any, with making sexual advances toward men when you are not certain they are gay? Tell your experiences, if any, with "trade" (men who will have sex with you even though they claim to be "straight"). c) How do you feel about cruising, courtship, one-night stands, "promiscuity," "quickie sex," sex for money? How important are the various places where gay men meet (see list in question 59), regardless of whether or not you use these places. Tell about any positive or negative experiences you have had meeting other gay men. **(PAGE 231)**

Self- Image
17. a) In what ways do yo consider yourself "attractive" or "unattractive"? Tell about your feelings and experiences relating to your looks. b)How do you feel others relate to your body or to specific aspects of your body (refer to list in question 63)? c) Do you feel you are a sex object? **(PAGE 282)**

18. Do you consider yourself masculine ("butch") or feminine ("femme"), or both, or neither? In what ways? Which physical characteristics, personality traits, activities, etc., do you identify as masculine or feminine? Do you think others identify you as masculine or feminine and how do you feel about these categories or labels? What importance do these categories have to your self-identity? **(PAGE 291)**

19. a) Tell us your experiences with and feelings about your sexual "coming out" and/or "being in the closet." b) At what age and under what circumstances did you first realize that you were homosexual or gay or somehow sexually "different" from other people? c) At what age and under what circumstances did you have your first homosexual experience, and how did you deal with it? d) Tell us about your sexual evolution from that first experience to now. **(PAGE 105)**

20. a) What has been your experience, if any, with telling people that you are gay? When did you first tell other people that you are gay and who did you tell? b) In your daily life now, which people do you tell, how do you tell them, and what has been their response? (Refer to question 68.) If any experience was particularly important or interesting, tell about it in detail. c) Indicate your experience with and feelings about keeping your homosexuality secret. What do you like or dislike about being "out of the closet" or "in the closet"? What do you like or dislike about others who are "out of the closet" or "in the closet"? **(PAGE 138)**

21. a) How do you feel now about your homosexuality? b) How have these feelings changed over time? c) What has influenced these feelings and any changes in them?
(PAGE 771)

You and Society
22. How do you feel that you have been oppressed (if at all) as a homosexual? (Refer to question 75) In what ways has your homosexuality, or the fear of being discovered, been a factor,· an aid or a hindrance, in your employment, schooling, housing, social status, etc.? How has the relationship between your homosexuality and any of these changed over time, and what influenced that change? **(PAGE 697)**

23. a) How would you describe yourself politically? How does your homosexuality interact with your politics, if at all, including any involvement you may have with other political groups or movements (Refer to list in question 93)? Tell about your experiences with gay liberation; what have you liked or disliked about such experiences? **(PAGE 731)**

24. How has feminism or the women's movement had an impact on or changed your sexual practices, values or identity? **(PAGE 743)**

25. Please tell us something about the following topics. If you have strong feelings about them, or any interesting experiences, please share them with us.

a. celibacy **(PAGE 381)**
b. sexual experiences with women, especially as these experiences compare to sex with men **(PAGES 118, 124)**
c. bi-sexuality **(PAGE 127)**
d. marriage **(PAGES 130, 362)**
e. children, being childless **(PAGE 132)**
f. drugs **(PAGE 496)**
g. transvestism, cross-dressing **(PAGE 575)**
h. transsexualism (sex-change surgery) **(PAGE 575)**
i. therapy **(PAGE 721)**
j. suicide **(PAGE 728)**
k. race, class, age differences **(PAGES 266, 274)**
l. aging **(PAGE 287)**
m. physical "handicaps" **(PAGE 688)**
n. pornography **(PAGE 581)**
o. sexual jealousy

p. monogamy   **(PAGE 357)**
q. lovers' quarrels, including violence   **(PAGE 361)**
r. violence in the gay community, bars   **(PAGE 591)**
s. sex in prison   **(PAGE 717)**
t. influence of religion on your sexuality   **(PAGE 719)**
u. incest   **(PAGE 99)**
v. residence (gay neighborhood, rural vs. urban, etc.)
                                               (PAGE 767)

26. a) What do you think of this questionnaire? b) What in it
made you pause and think? Why? Do you feel that we have
omitted any important questions? If so, indicate the questions
and your answers. c) As a gay man, is there anything you
would like more information on? d) Did answering parts of
this questionnaire turn you on? Make you feel good? Feel
bad? Feel angry? e) Comment.   **(PAGE 787)**

Thank you very much.
     Mail to: **Survey, Box 98, Orange, MA 01364**

3

Lesbians—Growing Up and Coming Out

Same-Sex Childhood Crushes

When the authors received feedback on the questionnaire, a few lesbian and gay male respondents said that one question they thought had been omitted was "Why do you think you became a lesbian?" or "How do you think you became gay?" The authors did not ask such questions because frankly no one has conclusively shown how a person develops or adheres to any sexuality, heterosexuality included! The authors also felt that such a question or questions, which look for the "cause," are in fact dangerous to lesbians and male homosexuals because pinning down the cause also implies that there might be a way to remove the cause or "cure" homosexuality.

The authors did ask several questions, concerning childhood sexuality and coming out, whose wording allowed people, if they wanted, to pin down how, when, and why they became lesbians or gay men.

The first question had to do with *childhood "crushes" or sexual feelings directed toward other children or adults.* The respondents were also asked *to recall their own experiences or feelings as a child and people's responses to those experiences or feelings.*

The questions about childhood sexuality and crushes elicited some of the most enthusiastic responses from lesbians (along with those on pleasing sexuality, coming out sexually, and being openly gay by telling other people). One common denominator of lesbian experience for those who answered the survey seemed to have been childhood crushes on people of the same gender, although a few had crushes on men or boys or had no crushes at all. The object of the crush was most often a teacher, playmate, or neighborhood figure, although sometimes as girls the respondents also had crushes on celebrities. As the reader will note, the stories are often told with great enthusiasm, and most of the memories, although not all, were pleasant and were joyfully remembered. A few, however, felt guilt at the time or had unhappy memories. The heterosexual reader might also remember her or his own childhood crushes and will quickly realize that

many girls and boys have same-gender crushes, no matter what their later sexual preference turns out to be. In some cases the respondent thought these crushes were the "cause" or "first sign" of her own lesbianism. The following are some of the hundreds of lesbian stories of childhood crushes and childhood sexuality received by the authors.*

♀ "I was madly in love with the little girl I used to take naps with when I was about 3. I remember our parents thinking it was 'sweet' that we were such good friends. She moved away when we were about 4. Then when I was 5, I fell madly (and I mean madly—I was a very passionately emotional child!) in love with a girl I went to kindergarten with. I was in love with her until we were about 12, when we had a fight over her friendship with another girl who I was jealous of because of my friend's affection for her. The girl I had a crush on, Cheryl, was studious and feminine, everything I wasn't. My mother approved of our friendship and treated Cheryl like one of the family. I also had a crush on Cheryl's mother, who was an artist. She was very independent. I remember one time watching her lay floor tile in her basement and how it really impressed me that (a) she knew how to do such a 'male' thing and (b) how neatly she cut the tile to fit around the door-jamb trim. I always had sexual fantasies about being her husband and being naked with her and doing whatever they did. I didn't really have any concept of straight sex even though I knew where babies came from. All I know was it was sexy and must feel good. Cheryl's mother loved kids and always had a houseful. She was very indulgent. One time she let us get a mattress out and slide down the stairs all day on it."

♀ "It seems like I always had crushes on my women teachers. I loved little girls more than boys, but I thought it was natural and that boys were harder to love and be loved by and therefore the ultimate challenge—a mysterious sort of thing. In fifth grade (age 10) I had two girl friends with whom I kissed and petted *heavily* during a slumber party. When I was 12, I fell in love with a lifelong friend who was 17. (I hadn't adored her before that. We were just pals.) Looking back I'd say she knew that I loved her because she was always flirting with me and telling me to be sensual and look at girls' bodies as well as boys. All my girl friends had crushes on teachers, but none of them wanted to hug them like I did. I dreamed about women, too, and about my favorite girl friends."

♀ "I had innumerable childhood crushes—for example, camp counselors. Some I just felt for, and others turned me on. I used to watch them undressing when they thought they were well hidden! Then there were my coaches in seventh-ninth grades. I used to 'play' with a chick when I was 7 and 8 years old and would spend the night at her house. We'd get through and the whole room told our tale with the smell. As I grew up, I was quite a girl watcher though very discreet. At about age 10, my brother called me a 'bull dyke,' but I don't think he knew what it meant. He used to call me a

*The symbols ♀ for a lesbian and ♂ for a gay man are used to indicate each time a new person's response begins.

dyke all the time, and I knew it was because I wore jeans and did what the guys did, like play football, basketball, box, wrestle, etc. When I was just 4, I played with army men: Dolls were stupid as far as I was concerned. I used to wish like hell I was a guy 'cuz then people would let me alone. I'd be able to do what I wanted. My best friend (from ages 9-12) and I used to play with each other quite often though she insists today that she's straight and tells me *I'm* sick. Oh, lord . . . At the time, though, we knew it was something to hide.''

♀ "Martha J., Jan and Dana B., the Logan kids, Sue Ellen. I may not remember where my checkbook is day-to-day, but I remember all those little girls by first and last names. Playing with Martha was dressing up in her older sister's dresses and lipstick and going with her dad to take 'the teenagers' to see Elvis in *Blue Hawaii.* We played doctor in a big double bed with flashlights in the night illuminating symptoms—over here, down there. Since playing with your genitals was 'dirty' and punishable with a swat, we probed the pink folds with equally pink pencil erasers. I sniffed those erasers so enthusiastically I'm surprised I didn't suck one up my nose! Jan and Dana and I would crawl around in our bedsheet tents, usually naked, touching, poking, and stroking, hiding from their three brothers. Terry and her sister Jan plus two other girls, Pam and Linda, acted out their fantasies as the Beatles. My role was Jane Asher, Paul's (Terry's) girl friend. One long summer night we five slept in a long line on the floor. I couldn't sleep. My mind was caught up in the pulsing body of Terry next to mine. Unable to resist a moment longer, leaning forward ever so gently, I kissed her. Right on the mouth twice!''

♀ "I was in love with my childhood female friend who I grew up with. We played 'doctor'—I'm totally blocked on the specifics on how beyond it involving lying in the bed. I was in love with my female junior high school classmate. I remember being teased for liking a boy—the teasing made me decide that I didn't really like him. I was in love with my junior high school gym teacher (a woman) (Yes, yes, Meg Christian!)''*

♀ "I was in love with the woman who played tenor sax in the high school band. I deliberately stayed last-chair flute so we could sit next to each other. We went to each other's house every weekend, gave each other backrubs for hours and hours, and spent the night a lot. We often ended up sleeping together because we never would bother to decide who was going to move to the other twin bed. I can't remember fondling her breasts, but I remember that they were very soft. We wrote each other between two and six letters each day and we talked on the phone for hours and hours each evening. I was terrified that this relationship was 'homosexual' and I had a lot of 'proof' in my head that it wasn't, including her having a 'boy friend' and me sleeping with men occasionally. We *never* talked about it—I was so terrified of the thought that it might be homosexual that I stopped myself

*Authors' note: Meg Christian wrote a song, wildly popular among lesbians, about her own crush on a high school gym teacher, called "Ode to a Gym Teacher" on her album *I Know You Know* (Olivia Records).

from thinking about it. I didn't know what 'lesbian' was exactly, but I knew it was awful. I think the first place I knew about lesbianism was from *Everything You Ever Wanted To Know About Sex . . .* (I get *outraged* every time I remember that this was my first source of information about my lesbian sexuality.)''

♀"I had a profound loyalty and strong feeling for (though they really weren't sexual since I was so unaware of my sexuality until my late teens) this one woman all the way through junior high and high school. I simply worshipped her. Every time I saw her in the hallway at school, I would get a twinge in my chest or a lump in my throat. I would take crazy routes between classes just to get a glimpse of her. We sort of knew one another outside of school, also. We did sports together and music, and I don't think she ever really knew how I felt.

"There wasn't too much of a response to me, although once in a while someone from her group (she was two years older than I, though only one class ahead) would make a comment like 'Out of the four of us in this car, one of us is queer.' I remember asking what that meant. And they told me that it was when two women made out in parked cars the way boys and girls did. I couldn't even imagine the latter, so pretty much shrugged off the former as uninteresting. I do remember, though, thinking that I was probably the 'one' . . . but it was a vague and not-too-frightening half-thought.''

♀"I've always had crushes on older women. The first one I remember is my nursery school teacher. I had a crush on my women teachers all through school. (I had a terrible crush on a woman I work with and it went on for about ten months. I got over it after I met my present lover.) When I was about 5, a girl my age who lived down the street used to play 'naughty' with me. We got together just about every day, and we'd take off our clothes and rub together and suck each other's nipples. I think she initiated our play, but I went along, and I think I was more inventive than she. We knew we had to hide what we did, and we never got caught in the act. She's married now, and I feel absolutely no attraction to her whatsoever. She's thin, bordering on scrawny, very ladylike, wears very fashionable clothes, and the last time I talked to her, she was an A-1 'cold bitch.' One time when I was 6, I showed 'mine' to a boy while he showed me 'his.' He seemed ashamed about the whole thing and wouldn't do it again. I guess I was quite curious about sex, especially boys, since I didn't have any brothers.''

♀"I fell in love with a girl when I was 12. She was the same age. I still dream about her even though it has been twelve years since I last saw her and there have been many girls after her (and even one before). Paula and I were inseparable for three years at which time her family moved away. I was crushed more so than I have ever been since. Our parents and friends thought we were strange for spending so much time together. I am inclined to believe that women are born lesbians and only become heterosexual due to social pressures. Probably men are born gay.''

♀"In grade five, I remember having a crush on my music teacher and

wanted to get the best grades so that I could sit in the front row near her desk (I succeeded). It's funny but I met a woman about a year ago who was also in that class (we hadn't seen each other since). We met in a women's bar. She is also gay. She also had a crush on that teacher. I can also remember having a crush on a schoolmate in grade six. We played volleyball together on the same team. We were never overly close friends, as I was aware of my feelings and was afraid of them. My next strong feelings didn't come until grade nine. They all seemed to come at once. I was in love with so many people, but again was frightened of my feelings and never attempted anything. I was more afraid of what my parents would think if they ever found out and also I was thinking that it was just a passing phase (a rather long one at that) and that I'd eventually be interested in men. My only interest in boys was whether they were good tree climbers, baseball players, or snake catchers. I was a 'tomboy' in every respect.''

♀"I was very attracted to my babysitter when I was 3. One incident is one of my earliest memories, and I'm placing the time by the house it happened in. I was sitting on the living-room floor looking at her. She was then about 14 or 15, I think. I remember thinking that she was beautiful and feeling a vague desire.

"I started school at 5 and the first day I met a young womon with the same birthday as me. I decided I was in love with her and that we would get married when we grew up. I did not connect sexual differences with adult gender until I was about nine, and this realization must have come gradually. Actually I think I believed that my cousins' pricks would fall off when they got older. I couldn't imagine a grownup having such a thing. So I thought that at about the age of 12 people got to choose whether they'd be wimmin or men, no matter whether they were girls or boys. So since my cousin was a crybaby, I figured if he went on that way he would probably choose to be a womon. I was a smartass bully, and I sure didn't want to grow up and be oppressed, though of course I did not realize that at the time, but was extremely counterrevolutionary and politically incorrect then. Of course, I was only 5.

"Back to the first grade—in school I drew pictures showing me as an adult in drag. I don't remember any responses to these; probably they didn't understand where my pointed little head was at. Every year after that, I latched onto a young womon in my class. At the same time, the young males would pick on me for their 'girl friend'—that was just silly or annoying. This ended in the fifth grade when I became violently anti-male. I suppose the knowledge of oppression had gotten to me by then.

"I didn't have any knowledge of sex until the sixth grade, so any feelings of desire I had were probably just not understood. I did kiss, hug, and hold hands with these young wimmin, and was never put down for it either. The first day of the sixth grade—September 3, 1963—(I said I was a romantic) when we got to meet the kids we'd be with the whole year, I saw this young womon and was fascinated by her, even at a distance. So I got a seat across the aisle from her. She talked to me—of course, I had been

staring at her. The conversation was about drawing gorillas and skeletons. We were best friends from that minute on. Of course, we started secret clubs, played practical jokes on the boys and the girls we hated, went to each other's houses to play after school, and I started going to her church (same disgusting denomination as mine). We explored all the creepy places in the church and confounded our Sunday school teacher.

"In the seventh grade, since we were so close, we had absolutely no classes together. I was in band, and she was in chorus, and since we were violently anti-athletic, we weren't on teams or anything, not that there were any. We did have PE together, and I am sure poor Ms. T., who had enough crap to cope with anyway, had her mind blown. But she did let us always be in the same group, probably because otherwise we'd have been going from one part of the gym to the other and really wouldn't have done anything. We were thought of as really weird, especially me. I'm sure that the more knowledgeable children called us 'queer,' but I don't remember it.

"The summer after seventh grade, I felt my first real sexual feelings. Karen and I were wrestling. We did a lot of crazy semi-violent things—in my den. One minute we were just wrestling, very roughly, but scuffling would be a more appropriate word really, and the next I was intensely aware of her, the feel of her body and her arms around me. I freaked out, completely, and jumped what must have been 4 feet off her. I often regret this enormously and wonder what my life would have been like if I hadn't. Anyway, we never wrestled again, but we are still friends."

♀"My current lover, M., is my childhood crush I grew up with."

♀"I had overwhelming crushes on adult women, often teachers (often nuns). Those were usually ignored and certainly any underlying or accompanying sexual feelings were ignored by everyone involved. My dreams and fantasies were often, though not always, heterosexual. One day in the eighth grade, we were working at our desks and the nun was walking around the room, answering individual questions. I had been passionately devoted to her all year and indicated that I had a question just to get her to stand by my desk for a few moments. She bent over my desk, and I looked up and her starched head and neck gear bent in such a way that I was looking at a soft little curl at the nape of her neck, and I felt an overwhelming desire to kiss it, and her, all over her body. I wanted to be naked with her. It was a rush of such intense desire that I can feel it yet. I had never felt anything like that before (and not often since). It took me nine years and a lot more crushes before I identified myself to myself as a lesbian."

♀"I remember my first awareness of sexual feelings when I was 11 years old. The source of these feelings was another girl my same age at Campfire Girls on a camping trip. Just holding hands turned me on. I could hardly keep my hands off her. I thought she was magic. I was that naive and we were incredibly happy. I do remember the embarrassed reactions of my mother and a few other people, but we were somewhat oblivious to it all in our innocence. It was not until she had moved away and I had gone on to junior high school that the full realization of what those feelings meant to

other people came crashing down on me. It was at that time I heard the words 'queer' and 'homo' for the first time, and I felt very ashamed and guilty."

♀"Most of my childhood fantasies centered on kissing. I'd mentally line up everyone in the classroom and go down the row kissing each of them, imagining how each of them would kiss, how much time I'd spend with each one, etc. (This was third to sixth grade mostly.) I still get into this fantasy occasionally at meetings when I am bored."

♀"At 7 I fell in love with an 18-year-old female cousin, an emotion which did much to direct the course of my subsequent life. I stayed pretty much in love with her until she died a few years ago, and had frequent dreams of great joy where she would be with me and I was drowning in love. Almost nothing overtly physical occurred even in my dreams, nothing at all in 'real' life. Yet it was a strong, even crucial emotion for me."

♀"Thinking back, I can see that I've always loved women. I saved women's pictures for a scrapbook when I was 8. I played 'movie stars kissing' in the bushes at the same age. I fell asleep with a young teenage babysitter at about 9 and really got close to her breast with my mouth. Another time sitting in the crowded front car seat with my mother's friend, she put her arm on the back of the seat and her breast was against my arm (I was 12). That was good for months of masturbating fantasies."

♀"As a young girl, I was attracted to the same kinds of women I am still attracted to. Before I became a teenager, I was infatuated by some of my girl friends and would attempt to seduce them. At 13, I was sleeping with my best friend and enjoyed holding her close and seeing her naked. My parents and other adults didn't really take much notice. We kept it very quiet. She had older sisters and from their heterosexual behavior we knew that what we were doing was 'different.' Somehow we figured it was all very normal and that we would grow out of it. I did for a couple of years anyway until I'd made sure being with boys was not as interesting."

♀"My girl friends and I used to pretend we were boys and girls and play at fucking a lot."

♀"There was a girl two years younger than me and her sister, two years older. We used to look to see whether the older one had any hairs yet. There was a lot of looking, smelling, exhibitionism. We got caught once, and we had to take castor oil."

♀"I feel my childhood sexuality was pretty well blighted. There was no display of affection at home and no hints of sexuality. When I was 11, I got heavy into 'mutual masturbation' with my best friend. I always instigated, and she always went along, but it always had some kind of 'game' form, like daring each other to touch 'there.' I had also done the same with a younger cousin, and it continued into junior high. In junior high, I had a three-year crush on another cousin which lasted until she totally parted ways with me and broke my heart. I still hurt about that. After that, I got heavy into guys, totally forgetting all the pleasures with women, until I came to my senses again, about eight years later."

Childhood Crushes on the Opposite Sex

Some of the women who answered the questionnaire had had crushes on boys or men.

♀"My childhood crushes were probably nonexistent. My sexual recollections revolve around putting objects in my underpants so I would look like a boy. I wanted to be a boy for a long time. My preadolescent crushes were on boys, but I always felt I was in control, leading them on. Once in puberty, I found that I was not attracted to boys. They were so shallow and horny."

♀"I had very strong love and sexual feelings for a boy when I was 11. I remember when he wouldn't be my boy friend any more I felt so horrible I wished I could have broken my leg instead. It would have hurt less."

♀"When I was a little girl, grade school age, I always had crushes on little boys. I felt like I wanted to take care of them and protect them."

♀"Most of my childhood crushes were on older men. When I was 10, I did have a crush on an older woman, the director of a chorus I sang in."

♀"Well, as a child, I hated most girls, thought they were silly and stuck up, and confided in boys. My first 'crush' was on my seventh grade history teacher, who was a man, and also on my father, who would French-kiss me now and then and tell me sex was beautiful but got upset when he caught me masturbating at 10 years of age, a bit young in his mind. My mother thought I didn't have enough women as idols. I idolized a lot of great male writers, but took no interest in women who were famous. I also had a big crush on one of the rock stars when I was about 11 and used to pretend I was him. This got to be quite an extensive fantasy with myself playing him and one of my girl friends (who was about 7) playing his girl friend. We even had children, and once about five years later, we started to explore each other's bodies. This was my first sexual experience with anyone besides my father's kisses."

♀"I don't remember any sexual crushes as a child, only romantic, emotional ones, all directed toward my peers, male. I exchanged views of sexual organs at 6 with a red-headed boy named Jerry under a boardwalk on a summer vacation. I wasn't impressed. Kissing interested me a great deal more from the age of 8 until 12 and still does! I played 'doctor' with the neighborhood kids (which I considered career-oriented and perfectly normal, for my grandfather was a doctor, and I intended to be one), but I never discussed it with my parents or other adults, any more than I did any other of our games which I considered our business!"

♀"My uncle had a friend who would visit. He had a motorcycle and seemed good-looking to me. I had a crush on him. I don't remember too much, but I think I cried when he got married."

A few lesbian participants had had no childhood crushes.

♀"I don't recall any specific crushes, but I do know that even though my parents were very open about sex, I somehow got the impression that sex was dirty."

♀"I don't remember childhood crushes. I grew up with parents already in their 40s when I was born. Their ideas about sexuality seemed particularly repressive to me, so I probably repressed any sexual feelings I had. I remember being warned about men who 'molest' women and girls and boys. I had no idea what 'molest' meant, but I knew it was incredibly embarrassing for my mother to bring up. I avoided inspiring such feelings, of course."

A few lesbian participants also had very negative memories of childhood crushes and sexuality, often a result of oppression, repression, or guilt.

♀"Most of my crushes were teachers. I would sit at home listening to music and think about them and the futility of the feelings I had for them. I would hate getting a crush on someone (it was always a woman) because it was such an agonizing ordeal. I never admitted to myself that I was a lesbian and that made it all the worse. I kept my crushes very secret and unrequited."

♀"I had a seven-year-long crush on a high school teacher. I had no idea of what my feelings for her were. I saw a psychiatrist because of my vague uneasiness about this, and depression about other things. He suggested I might be a lesbian. All of a sudden everything clicked into place!"

♀"One time my mother found my friend and me in the same bed. We were touching each other's breasts in a sort of game. It was fun. My mother called me out into the hall and smelled my hands. I felt very humiliated and dirty. She did not accuse me of anything or really say what was wrong. She just was angry and told me we had to sleep in different beds. They were always suspicious of my friends having a bad influence on me. After that, when I had friends over, I had to leave my bedroom door open."

♀"My feelings were directed toward girls instead of boys like everyone said they should be. I had no name for my feelings so I decided I was a freak of some kind. During the next couple of years those feelings increased and on a few occasions I made mild advances toward other girls but it seemed as though they thought I was only trying to act silly. I thought I was the only person in the world who possessed these feelings, and it confirmed my belief that I was a freak. I knew absolutely no adult or peer that I could talk to about this. My relationships with everyone became strained, my schoolwork failed badly, and I often considered suicide as an escape from my miserable life."

♀"When I was 14, I was going steady and a *devoted* church member. One night I rededicated my life to Christ and after the church the pastor

told me I would be a good missionary and told me I should come to his house after school to pray about it. I told Mama and she said she was glad. Well, that s.o.b. minister nearly tore my clothes off me as soon as I got there. Then he had one hand in my panties and one hand was holding me down. I screamed and struggled and he had the nerve to say it was God's will. Bullshit. I left in a hurry and told my boy friend. He said I should forget it if nothing other than that happened. After that, I didn't trust a one of them.''

Feelings About Childhood Sexuality

The lesbian respondents were also asked *how they felt about childhood sexuality in general, regardless of their own childhood experiences.* Most of them felt that childhood sexuality was fine if indulged in by two children, but most lesbians objected to sexuality between an adult and a child.

♀"Childhood sexuality should be indulged in by children, as consenting children, to learn about themselves and others. It should never be *forced* on others, and it should never be given the label of shame or guilt by adults. Hopefully, it should lead to constructive questioning by a child of an understanding adult. Also this is not an ideal world. Perhaps it is better if children and adults both keep their sexual experiences in perspective and to themselves. It is better to misunderstand sex than to be misunderstood *for* it! I have earnestly tried to be honest and careful with my own children in this matter, and if anything, have probably been too permissive and open. Only time will be the judge of this.''

♀"I think childhood sexuality should be left to children. Sensual experiences between child and adult should be available to children, such as hugging and kissing and general body contact. I think they need this to develop as loving human beings. One can't expect to be able to give love if one has never gotten it.''

♀"I think it is extremely wrong for an adult womon to seduce an underage one. It is illegal for very good reasons. There is already, I think, too much of a tendency for lesbian relationships to pattern themselves after parental models, without adding the greater inducement of a real generation gap. But I see nothing wrong with young wimmin relating to each other. If I have a daughter, I would be pleased for her to be able to go out with other young dykes before she is adult, and I don't see anything wrong in their making love. I would discourage her from becoming serious about an older womon.''

There was also a general consensus among the respondents who wrote about child sex that children should be given more information about sex and that people should recognize that children are sexual beings.

♀"I think feelings about childhood sexuality are far too repressive in this society. It makes children too inhibited about sexuality as they get older.''

♀"Kids are just miniature people and should be treated as such, with a little bit of consideration for their maturity and judgment."

♀"I don't think sexuality is talked about to children enough. I think sexuality should be acknowledged and masturbation encouraged in children."

♀"I don't think that we give children enough credit, for they know much more than we think. They are exposed to the media—to libraries and to our own conversations. I think they stop touching each other out of fear of our disapproval. They are terribly sensual and we tell them that it is bad."

♀"I think that children have a lot more sexual feelings than they're often considered to have. The hard part is that they don't understand them and are often confused by them."

♀"Childhood sexuality is wonderful. It should not be repressed or feared. I wish that all children could grow up aware and unthreatened by their sexuality, so that when it becomes social and so into focus at puberty, it is not such a savage, cruel, horrible thing. I think this ties in with the importance of teaching children from day one that their bodies are theirs, that they are nice and beautiful. We should also teach them that what they do and feel is okay, whatever shape it has."

♀"I think that kids should be allowed to express their natural affection toward each other whether or not it is sexual. One should not be taught that emotions, physical pleasure, and bodily responses are dirty or shameful. I think a lot of adults' hangups in our society are a result of this early repression."

♀"I firmly believe that children are just as sexual as adults and that most children have great difficulty dealing with these sexual feelings. I think most kids would cope with their feelings a lot better if they were told their feelings are normal and acceptable and if they were given permission to masturbate. I think that most youngsters feel very uptight about masturbating. (I work with teenage girls and this form of sexual activity is harder for them to acknowledge than any other!) And so they carry around a lot of unnecessary guilt about it, rather than seeing it as a natural part of their sexual lives."

♀"I think that most parents raise their kids with a lot of sexual biases, whether it be black, white, Jewish, Catholic, or man/man, woman/woman. They put their sexual fears into their kids and it is not good! My parents raised me not to have sex with anyone. They told me that sex was dirty, and that the body is only pretty in the dark. I really can't say how all other kids are brought up, but I think parents should be more careful with how they bring out the sexual identities in their children."

Coming Out Sexually

After childhood crushes, the next milestone in a lesbian's life is often coming out. Coming out can happen at almost any age. In the subsample,

the youngest lesbian was 14 and the oldest one was 60. The mean age for the subsample (which almost exactly matched the average age for the entire group of lesbians who answered the questionnaire) was 29.6 years of age. The respondents were asked three questions about their age when coming out: (1) *At what age did you first realize that you were a lesbian or somehow sexually different?* (2) *At what age did you associate this "difference" with lesbian acts?* and (3) *At what age did you have your first lesbian experience?* The following table gives their responses broken down by ranges; the oldest and youngest age in each group; and the average age in each group.*

Age Groups	First Realize	Associate Difference	First Experience
1 to 8	7	.5	.5%
9 to 12	13	5.5	6.5
13 to 15	19	17	13
16 to 19	25	32	30
20 to 24	20	25	27
25 to 29	9	10	13
30 +	7	10	10
oldest lesbian	48	49	49 (years)
youngest	3	7	7
average	18	20	21

Next the respondents were asked, *How long have you been a "practicing" lesbian?* The shortest time was less than a year and the longest time was thirty-seven years—the most frequent answers were one year (14% of the subsample) and four years (again, 14% of the subsample). A full 53% of the subsample had been practicing lesbians for five or more years.

Each story of coming out is unique. Coming-out stories are a common topic of conversation among lesbians and a standard topic of discussion in consciousness-raising groups and at lesbian and gay male conferences. After all, coming out, or having a first lesbian sexual experience, is a rite of passage for lesbians. The first sexual experience often tells the woman that she is indeed a lesbian, that this is indeed what she wanted. This experience does not necessarily make someone a lesbian for life, and as many lesbians revealed in their essays, coming out is a process often interrupted by experiences with and sometimes long periods of heterosexuality. Nevertheless, that first lesbian experience is often a meaningful and memorable one. The participants were asked *to elaborate on the questions given above,* and were also asked *to relate experiences with and feelings about "coming out" and "being in the closet."* They were also asked *to tell the circumstances and age at which they realized they were lesbians or somehow sexually "dif-*

---

*In general, the statistics are rounded off to the nearest whole number; therefore, the total percentage may range from 97 to 102.

ferent" and *to tell about their first lesbian experience.* Respondents were then asked *to tell about their sexual evolution from that first experience until now.*

The experiences varied so widely that it was very difficult to categorize them. Here are those answers in which the respondent discusses relationships primarily with other women only.

♀"I was only 'closeted' from the point in my life when I realized that what I was was bad news as far as the rest of society or from when I knew the name for what was 'wrong' with me. I was closeted for only about three years. I came out when I was 21 and published a lesbian story that everyone assumed was autobiographical. Those three years were hellish, like having a Jesus Freak roommate in college who hated queers, and other homophobic roommates. God, how horrible to live one's whole life that way. I feel very good about being 'out,' even with this impending anti-gay holocaust that is supposed to be on the horizon. Well, we'll all go together when we go (sing along, folks!)."

♀"My first experience with a woman was just as I was turning 21. (She took me to my first gay bar, and all the drag queens had me scared shitless.) I don't even remember the first time we made love since we did a lot of romancing and caressing and lying together and whispering, but she wouldn't let me spend the night because her bed was too small (I eventually *insisted* on it, and found out that indeed it *was!*) and it was not until a few months later that I even had an orgasm with her, mainly due to the fact that vaginal stimulation hurt, and I have a very well-hidden clitoris. I still now have a hard time defining 'lovemaking' since a lot of my friends can give very sensual kisses and we caress and hug and *that's* all part of it. What, though, is the definition? There isn't any decisive act, like in intercourse, where he puts it in and that's that. I don't even know if I'm still a 'virgin,' though I don't really care since I see it as a word men use in order to define their property lines.

"I'm still living with that woman with whom I had my first relationship, so I guess I haven't evolved much yet!"

♀"Even when I was in friendships with girls (14-17 years old), and we touched each other's genitals, I thought it was a passing phase. I knew that I was different because I liked less girly hobbies and pastimes. But in high school, I found I was attracted to women. The women I idolized were not very feminine by my acculturated standards—Joan Joyce and Billie Jean King. It was at the end of high school that I knew (admitted) that I actually preferred women. A year later and after some transient relationships at college, I had the pleasure of having my first woman lover. I was 18. That's when I knew that I was a lesbian because we touched for sexual gratification, not only for emotional intimacy. I was very happy with that lifestyle, but for the following two years I was torn with guilt. My Christian conscience would tell me I was doing wrong. My first lover and I broke off because we had lost our emotional closeness and were only lovers (and not friends). I wanted a lover, and a friend. I had a very close friend for over a

year who was not a lover, and I still love her tremendously. But since then I have grown to love my present woman friend. Now I am not only admitting and accepting my lesbianism, I am actually proud of it! I am glad that I am the way I am and I wouldn't change it if I could. So at the age of 20, I can say that I am a lesbian and I'm glad. I am also much more open about sex for I see it as not some dirty animal-like drive for satisfaction, but as a beautiful way to know someone completely. And the neat thing is that I am still growing and expanding. My womanness and her sexuality are being affirmed within me. I am a full woman, with room to grow.''

♀"As early as 13, I knew I was different, because I didn't like boys; that is, I liked boys a lot, but not when they got sexual. I never dated in high school, and I despised girls who did. I thought they were a bunch of brainless twits, throwing their precious lives away.

"I had my first lesbian experience when I was 20. By then I was desperate to affirm my lesbianism, for fear that it wasn't genuine, but only self-delusion. So I semi-seduced a straight woman who thought she might be bisexual. In other words, I took advantage of her doubts to try to settle my own. I pretended to be very worldly and said I would show her how lesbians do it. She didn't know it was my first time too. Afterward, I felt stupid, because she had done a better job at it than me. Anyway, she had an orgasm and I didn't, so I shouldn't feel too guilty about her. Since then, I have had brief affairs, always hoping to find a permanent companion. I've learned a lot—not in terms of techniques (I'm still very unskilled) but in terms of having respect for women and thus, ultimately, for myself.''

♀"I've gone through a long process of falling in love—that is, each time a different type of love, but the unifying element is that I always love women. My first 'love' was for Mrs. P., who was my intelligent, kind, and (I thought at the time) pretty teacher in fifth and sixth grades. She was married to a jock. I remember that once I drew what I felt to be an extremely flattering portrait of dear Mrs. P. and left it on my desk so that she would see it when she walked the aisles, looking over our shoulders. She just took it and said nothing. The school rule was that any 'doodling' that was taken from you was put in your record folder, and I wonder if she knew that I had a crush on her (she must have), and if she was flattered, or just never cared at all, or if she put the picture in my school record, and if it says underneath, 'Caution: Possible Future Lesbian.' Then as feelings became more defined for me, and as they were also becoming more intense, in seventh and eighth grades I had a pretty good crush on a girl, K.D. She was liberal and daring and independent and blond—everything I wanted to be at that age. I worshipped her from afar. In eighth grade, I was trying to look like a member of the Woodstock generation. I wore boots and workshirts and patched jeans. I did dope. That year was a complete horror. 'M. is a lez' started appearing on lavatory walls, and I was quickly losing friends. What the hell was a 'lez' anyway? Well, I looked up the word in an unabridged dictionary, blushed a lot, and never went to the lavatory at

school again that year. Ninth grade: high school, adjustment, more drugs, more (spaced-out) friends. Aimlessness. I idolized the folk singer Melanie. I took up the guitar and told everyone that I was going to be a singer, but it wouldn't have worked out since I'm tone-deaf. I used to fantasize about being 'good friends' with Melanie; I used to kiss her picture goodnight—but I never realized that it was a matter of love or sex. I stopped buying Melanie's albums when she had a baby: I felt betrayed.

"The summer before I entered tenth grade, I was still trying to 'fulfill myself as a woman,' without recognizing my lesbian feelings. I decided that what was wrong with my sex life was that I needed someone I could talk to on an equal footing. I needed an 'older man.' So one fine day I called up a 'man' of 18 (I was 14), and invited him to come pick me up for some dope-smoking and fucking in the woods. He came right over, and we 'balled' (his term—which sort of took some of the wind out of my sails right there). He was kind, patient, handsome, and stoned. When he was pumping away on top of me, I thought vaguely that *this* was terrific proof I wasn't a 'lez.' I never saw the dear boy after that, and I don't feel that he 'used' me or 'defiled' me—he was, as I said, very kind, and I guess that we sort of 'used' each other. Also in the tenth grade I got off dope, began looking toward college again, and fell in love with my English teacher. She was beautiful (really, this time), very intelligent, and very gentle. I knew her for four years, and I watched her grow from dependent wife to independent divorcee, from contented high school teacher to struggling writer. She was a great inspiration for me, and I think that we helped each other grow during that period. I saw my future in her, sort of, and she saw her past reflected in me. I became aware that my feelings for her were too intense to be labeled 'friendship'—I wanted her to love me too. I sent her gifts and once, finally, when I sent her a *very* expensive fur coat (for no special occasion), she guessed what I was feeling for her. She quickly (but civilly) ended the relationship. I was crushed when she made me take back the gift. She was making me take back my love. She too was very upset, and she told me that I was making her feel too 'obligated.'

"Then I had a short 'thing' for this artist friend of mine, but was too hurt by the previous rejection to really approach this new friend. At this point, during my freshman year at college, I began to read gay writers (Rita Mae Brown, Renée Vivien, May Sarton, etc.) and I began to be involved with some gay liberation groups. And now I feel that I've gone beyond accepting my gayness. I even feel *comfortable* with it. And I'm appalled by how ignorant I was, only a year ago, of gay community, gay culture, and gay history."

♀"My first sexual experience with another girl was at 15. I didn't realize I was a lesbian until I was 20. It took a while—intellectually coming out was very hard and traumatic. I used to look at myself in a mirror and cry. I couldn't believe what I was. How could a good girl like me be something as wicked as a lesbian? Once I found the gay bars and the gay community I

found that there were many 'good girl' lesbians. My self-image improved and is improving every year. Sexually coming out was a joy—a discovery of pleasure, a slow exciting mutual exploring of two passionate young girls. I would want it no other way.''

♀''Coming out was a difficult experience for me since I didn't un-derstand the politics of the taboo behind homosexuality. I taught at a university and many of my students reacted strangely (wouldn't look at me or say hi unless I spoke to them first) when they saw me in the women's bar. Now that I'm out of the closet I enjoy more and closer friends (mostly gay), but still have problems with people who don't know I'm a lesbian.

"I didn't consciously know I was a lesbian until age 19 and suspected I was different prior to that because I found male company boring but didn't actually consider myself a lesbian until eleven years later.

"My first experience was with a woman in college and lasted only six months due to guilt on her part, fear on my part, and her decision that she couldn't live a lifestyle that was not socially approved. My second relationship with a woman was when I was 24. It lasted five years. She also felt guilty and very afraid to 'come out.' She decided to become involved with men and had psychiatric help which encouraged her to go straight. My psychiatrist (at the time of our break-up) did not discourage my homosexuality nor did he encourage my going straight. He felt I should further explore my feelings and not feel guilty if my sexual preference was women.

"My third and current relationship with a woman is with a feminist, and my introduction into feminism was through discussions with her and her friends, reading and consciousness-raising. These experiences have resulted in my feeling great about my sexual orientation and have made me un-derstand the futility of my ever trying to lead a straight life. I have no desire to ever have a relationship with a male.''

♀''I was attracted to women since age 10, but it was not until I was 21 that I was 'brought out' by this very sensitive, sensual gay woman I met through a friend. It was not she that came on to me, but the other way around. Afterwards, I felt a sense of relief, having finally released myself from an eleven-year-old repression. I enjoyed making her come. She felt guilty and afraid. She felt she had caused my doom. We are still friends, and she's only just realized that she did the best thing in the world for me.''

♀''Since coming out only a month ago, I have had to do a lot of thinking about my past. I realize now that my sexual orientation was towards women as far back as ages 7–8. I never found men sexually attractive. I saw them more as comrades or friends. I was a 'tomboy' up until age 13. I assumed the male role in most games. I had male toys (guns, trucks, trains) and found nothing odd in this. In my teens, I began to realize that I did feel more attracted to women, but that socially this was not acceptable. I sublimated a lot of these feelings by having a lot of friends, getting involved in various social and church groups. Underneath, though, I have been fairly

restless and unhappy. When I had my first lesbian experience at age 23, I knew that this was really me, and when I came out of the closet last month I felt like I'd finally come home. I went to my first lesbian dance with two friends (one of whom is now my lover) and they said I just fit in like I belonged. Since then I've gone to dances and a meeting of the lesbian organization here. I'm still not completely out to family and straight friends, but by associating with lesbians, this is a big step. I've finally looked in the mirror and said 'I am a lesbian and proud of it!' "

♀"I lived the first eighteen years of my life in a small Texas town and didn't dare come out or talk to anyone although I began to suspect I was different at age 6. I never liked to play with dolls or play little-girl games. I preferred to play football with the boys. It really hit me at age 12. I began to have strong sexual feelings for girls and suspected I was a lesbian. Still I wondered if lesbians really existed at all, since no one spoke of their existence. I suspected that homosexuals in general were mostly fictional and few existed, so few that I might live out my whole life alone, never meeting one, especially since they would also be 'in the closet.' I was very sad and lonesome and wondered why I could not have these feelings for boys. I dared not speak of this to *anyone*. I feared what might happen. I might be branded as a freak—the only one in Texas—locked up or something bad.

"I couldn't wait to go to college in Corpus Christi, Texas. I lived in the dorm and began to party and drink a lot so I wouldn't think about it. I brought booze into the dorm, went to Mexico without permission, caused a disturbance in the dorm. I never got in any real trouble, but in those days things like that were serious. My parents transferred me to a Catholic school, hoping the nuns would lock me up. (We were Protestant.) I was considerably more restricted there, but didn't mind since I met a girl there and we started sleeping in the same bed. I began to sober up since I found something better (her). Anyway she poured the booze in the sink. Neither of us had had a gay experience so we didn't start really getting it on for about three months. We were both 18. I thought how lucky I was to get stuck in that Catholic school. We became best friends as well as lovers and still are very good friends even though we are no longer lovers."

♀"I guess this is the place to write about this. Are you forgetting or ignoring or negating the women who love other women who know they are lesbians but have never had sex with one? Or do you not concern yourself with them? For 5½ years, I was aware of my lesbianism before I took on my first woman lover. I loved, very deeply, certain women before I made love or had sex with one. I had declared my love, my bisexuality, to them—sometimes ignored, sometimes accepted. I had made nonsexual love—sleeping with Bev for five months nightly, sleeping in each other's arms, crying and laughing together, expressing love through a dance of our hands, through dancing together, through massages. With Kathy we bathed and showered together and slept together, kissed often but briefly, and loved and expressed love, but with limits. They were heterosexual or at least

had not recognized their bisexuality and did not wish to be so, although they acknowledged mine. The love was important, terribly important to me. If I wanted it, I could have had a sexual fling with someone else easily, but I wanted to be their first woman lover (sexual) if and when they decided to take one—to be a choice and a joy, as I knew—or rather hoped—it would be. I did *not* want a favor or pity. I wanted similar enjoyment and exploration. So I was a lesbian/virgin. I knew the difference that a sexual love makes. I can see my priorities, but I was a lesbian. I loved women. I desired women. But I was celibate and inexperienced. I was somewhat trapped as I was known among my friends as gay, believed myself to be gay, and yet I was frightened to admit my inexperience to other gay women. I was frightened to be quite that vulnerable.

"When I finally made love to Toni, she had no idea that she was my 'first' so to speak. But she knew I was nervous—actually frightened that I'd make a mistake, hurt her, show my inexperience too much, and that *she'd* get nervous and call it off. For it's a big responsibility to be somebody's 'first'—especially after 5½ years of waiting. I told her later, and she was dumbfounded and admitted that she'd never have considered it if she had known for fear that I might be using her and might be insincere and out for an 'experience,' for fear that I might expect much, much more than she could give, etc. She wasn't my first lesbian experience—but my first lesbian *sexual* experience."

♀"At the time I 'discovered' myself, I did not consider myself sexually different and the word 'lesbian' was not a part of my vocabulary. I do not know if one would classify my very first experience as lesbian or not. A counselor at a camp (I was 19) got in bed with me one night (I was also a counselor) and played around a little. I did not know what to do, or was scared or something, but I did not toss her out. Of course, the camp director found us in the morning—apparently along with a few other staff. Anyway, that was my eighth summer at that camp and my last! That fall, I entered college and became acquainted with a professor. We were both deeply in love for about three years. I managed to get permission to move out of the dorm to an off-campus apartment. Being very poor, I had to earn my board and room somehow, and so it was logical (I guess) for the teacher to help the student. This was her first experience too. Sex was simple, but satisfying. The evolution has not been remarkable—more knowledge in general, and more sophisticated techniques."

Sex with Men

For other women, marriage, or at least sex with men on more than a casual or experimental basis, was part of coming out or happened prior to coming out. The respondents were asked: *How often have you had or do you have sex with men?*

	ALWAYS	VERY FREQUENTLY	SOMEWHAT FREQUENTLY	SOMEWHAT INFREQUENTLY	VERY INFREQUENTLY	ONCE	NEVER
in the past	8	19	21	16	17	3	17%
currently	.5	2	1	3	6.5	4	83

Thus, while almost all lesbians (83%) have had sex with a man at least once in the past, only a small minority currently have sex with men at all. In fact, only 16% of the subsample currently consider themselves bisexual, while 56% considered themselves bisexual in the past. The respondents were also asked: *How do you feel about sex with men?*

	VERY POSITIVE	SOMEWHAT POSITIVE	NEUTRAL	SOMEWHAT NEGATIVE	VERY NEGATIVE	NOT SURE
your past experiences	5	18	21	24	31	1%
your current experiences	12	6	24	14	34	9

One can see that a slight majority (55%) felt negative about past experiences with men with a good number of the lesbians feeling neutral (21%) and only 23% feeling positive. Even among lesbians currently having sex with men, a large 48% felt negative about those experiences and only 18% felt positive. However, due to a wording problem, those 18% may have felt positive about currently having *no* sex with men. Here are some experiences of lesbians who started out married to men or in long-term or serious relationships or at least sexual involvement with men before they became lesbians.

♀"I realized I was different in junior high school, but I denied it all through high school and got married after my freshman year in college. I thought by getting married I would straighten out and no longer have to fight. I was successful until age 27 (I was married at 19) when I had my first real experience with another woman. I was ecstatic and on a high for about

one month, and then I discovered it was just a game with her. She then moved away, and I was devastated. I really believe I nearly had a nervous breakdown. I reacted by retreating into my marriage. My second experience came two years later and to date is the longest relationship I have had. The breakup of this relationship was even worse than the first and was complicated by the fact that we both wanted to remain best friends which we had been up to the start of the sexual involvement. I again responded by retreating into my marriage. But this lasted only until March of 1977, when I realized that I was attracted to another woman again. I related this involvement to a very close lesbian friend, and I knew that there was no turning back this time. This experience proved to be a very bad one for several reasons, but I think it did make me deal with my sexual orientation.

"The most recent relationship for me has been very pleasing up to this point. I have no idea how long it will last, but I could make a long-term commitment to this woman. I have matured in my ideas about what I want and need from a relationship. I want long-term relationships as opposed to affairs. I have an essentially monogamous nature. I want to be able to relate to my partner on levels other than sexual. I have made the decision to stop fighting my sexuality, to get a divorce, and to live the way I want to. I am not 'out' on the job or with my family. I do not want my husband to discover this until after the divorce is final. I can't afford a scene in court."

♀"It feels like I have always been a lesbian even though I didn't know the words. I have always identified with women. I've gotten along best with women, yet been strong and able to play with the boys. I remember being about 11 and reading about homosexual men. And turning the word over and over in my head—really thinking that I had come to some sort of understanding or something. I told my best friend, and she thought it was gross and disgusting. Yet we had played doctor together for years. And this idea of loving someone of the same sex always seemed to be with me. I have a cousin my age, and she started becoming interested in boys. I followed her by oohing and ahing over some guy on the TV and I remember my parents nodding to each other. I felt like it was all a lie. I couldn't have cared less about men. But for all my high school life I dated, always had to follow the crowd, lost my virginity, and thought about getting married, settling down, and becoming a lemming like my parents. It *never* felt right, never was what I really wanted. I was bored with the adolescent fumbling, yet I participated, and at times really got into it.

"Finally I left home and started thinking that I was responsible for me, so I stopped dating completely in college—worked hard on political issues and loved women from a distance. After a few embarrassing attempts I found a woman I could talk to and be frank with and I fell in love for the first time. She was 24 and I was 21. Even after that I was afraid to say I am gay. And slowly, oh so slowly, I unlearned all the trash I had been fed and I read everything that I could get my hands on, and the world got brighter, and one day I was not afraid of anyone, and I said loud and with certainty, *'I am a lesbian!'* And I am proud and I am ready to fight again."

♀"I was fed up with men. I knew I deserved better than they were giving but didn't know how to find it. A woman left her husband to have experience with other women and moved in across the street. She sized me up and pursued me! I held out for two months, but I was so excited I finally did it and loved it. She was a very manipulating person and did some terrible things to me which in the jag of what I was feeling I allowed her to do.

"That whole year I was terrified anyone would find out (and she was too). I fantasized what would happen if my kids knew, my ex-husband knew, neighbors, job, etc. It was terrible and also kept me tied to her for by then I knew I wanted a woman and knew no others.

"After we broke up, I started going to the retreats* where I not only met many wonderful women but started thinking about the politics of it all. I needed politics to alleviate the paranoia, and needed meeting other lesbians to know I was okay. Unfortunately, I didn't find out about lesbianism until I was 41!"

Some lesbians went through periods of lesbianism followed by heterosexuality and then returned to lesbianism or followed other diverse patterns.

♀"At the age of 21 I was in the Air Force and fell in love with a woman. I was dating guys (lots more fellows around and I could go out whenever I wanted to). But I fell in love with a woman. It seemed so right and felt good. She turned me on. I wanted to be with her all the time. I was a student in training, and she was stationed at the base permanently. We had an intense three-week relationship but never slept together. After I was finished with school and left the base, she got together with another woman. They were caught in a compromising situation, and during the investigation my name came up. I was interrogated and had an administrative hearing and was discharged. General discharge! I was so hurt and angry over all the circumstances that I decided to leave women alone. I had some problems but finally got a job. I dated men but thought about women and read all the lesbian books I could. There weren't many in the late '50s. I got married in 1960, had a son in 1961. My husband knew about my Air Force experiences. He admitted to homosexual experiences himself, and we felt we could work things out. We had many ups and downs. I was very unhappy, and he had a lot of sexual hangups and found it hard to express affection. I thought about women a lot but didn't know anything except what I had read about and my short experience in the Air Force. I got crushes on my bowling friends but never did anything about it. They were all married too. In 1965 we moved to the San Francisco Bay Area. In June 1966, I found my Air Force friend's name in the local phone book. I phoned her, and we began seeing each other. She would not have sex with me, but I knew right away I was still in love with her. She would not agree to an affair or help me to

*Authors' note: There are several women's retreats or resorts around the country.

leave my husband. I told my husband, and we were going to try to have a marriage of convenience. He wanted to explore his gay feelings also. I started going to gay bars and met another woman who brought me out (at last). I loved it. We were together for three years. I then got a divorce. My son lives with his father. I didn't have the courage or resources for a court fight. I had seen what the government could do to you in the service. I became active in the Bay Area gay community. I met my present lover at a women's meeting there. We have been together almost seven years. I feel very good to be a lesbian. I have almost nothing to do with men or my Mormon family. I enjoy my life very much.''

♀"As a child I had lots of friends of both sexes and identified well with both. I did well at school and conformed (on the surface anyway). When I was 9, I was sent away to a Roman Catholic convent (I was a Protestant, but anyway I think my mother thought the nuns would teach me how to sew and become a lady—poor deluded soul—they failed on both counts). When I was 12, I developed a very close friendship with a girl my own age (same birthday) at summer camp. It was something *very* important to me, but to her I suppose I was just another friend. Maybe it was because I didn't have any brothers or sisters. It was just a nice feeling to care about somebody *a lot*. She lived in another city so we drifted apart and boys came on the scene for the next few years (for both of us). Still I had a strange feeling from that time on that I was different somehow even though I had lots of dates. The boys never quite managed to allay that inner sensation that I was looking for something they couldn't offer. Through my teenage years of 'trauma and tribulation' (according to Mothers, Inc.), I had several close girl friends, but no 'contact,' until I was 19 or 20 when I was briefly involved with a 'friend' who was similarly inclined. It was a short-lived thing. She wanted to move on (got bored, maybe—who knows, we never talked it out), then another 'relationship'—not really sexual but more affection and enjoyment of one another's company. We're still friends twenty years later. Men were still on the scene. I spent a year studying in Paris and another two at college and had my first teaching job. I *still* had that inner feeling that I was different, but I'd better keep it to myself. Then I met my husband. It was love at first sight. I'd never really planned to get married or even pictured myself as a wife (much less a *mother!*). I was blissfully happy for about six months to a year although even then sex wasn't the greatest. By the second year, I knew I'd been fooling myself. Something was missing. I was pretty sure I knew what it was, but what was I going to do about it—*wait and hope?* It was worth waiting for. My first child, a girl, was 6 months old when I met my match (thirteen years later I can *still* say that!). It was instant electricity for us both. We were skiing when a mutual friend introduced us. I knew instinctively and immediately and didn't fight it. She was more cautious—less trusting of herself (let alone anyone else) and brilliant, funny, lovable, and confused. After six months of fighting it (she *claims* she was seduced methodically and diabolically) we got it together and we've rarely (who can say never?) looked back. Once she got engaged, but it

fizzled out on her part. Then she fell for a married man (fairly recently). That was another rough spot but nothing has ever really changed between us. We're totally ourselves: no games, no lies, no cover-ups even when it hurts. We've shared enough to last three lifetimes, and I'll die with a smile on my face. I think she'd say the same.''

♀"I think 'coming out' is an extremely imprecise term. I've asked at various lesbian rap groups what it means, and it seems to mean entirely different things to different people. I 'came out' in my head when I read *The Well of Loneliness* by Radclyffe Hall when I was 12 and thought to myself that that's the kind of love I wanted to have—a very happy, positive feeling. I 'came out' emotionally from then on—a wild crush on a teacher when I was 16, a very warm attachment to a fellow girl student when I was 16, then wildly falling in love when I was 17. The first time this particular woman kissed me, my eyes immediately flooded over with tears of joy, one of the happiest moments of my life. Does being petted to climax constitute 'coming out?' Then I came out at 18, a reasonably happy experience. Or are you not really 'out' until you first perform cunnilingus? In that case, if that's what counts, then I was 50 before I came out.

"Although I decided I was a lesbian at 12, at 20 I began to doubt that I was. All I'd seen in the gay world up to then was indiscriminate bedding down, and I couldn't play that kind of sexual musical chairs. Sex was never a casual thing for me. I could do without it with great ease but could not pop into bed with different partners every time the music changed, which is what all my friends seemed to be doing. By the age of 25, I decided that I couldn't hack the life. I wanted to love; I wanted a child. So I married to get pregnant—and found it less easy to adjust than I'd thought. I started seeing a psychiatrist to try to overcome my depression, saw him only three times, began pulling out of it, adjusting to marriage. I got pregnant, my husband left me, I had my baby, lived happily in love with my son until he was almost 6, by which time he wanted a 'daddy' and I wanted another baby so I married again, knowing full well that my heterosexual feelings are far less strong than my homosexual ones, but my maternal feelings are strongest of all. My second marriage 'took,' my husband and I have been very happy, but four years ago he began pushing me out the door to go find a woman lover, as he knew how hungrily I longed for one. Now that I've found one we are becoming closer and more committed all time and my husband is very happy for me and very fond of my lover.''

As this last response indicates, some women (7%) who answered this survey were still married. Of those who were married, 2% said they were living with a husband who knew about their lesbianism, less than 1% said they were living with a husband who didn't know about their lesbianism, 1% said that they were living with their husbands but were not sure whether or not he knew. Another 1% said that they had a marriage of convenience (to help pass for straight), and 1.5% said they had a marriage of con-

venience for gifts or for immigration purposes. Of those who were separated or divorced, 58% said lesbianism was a factor in the dissolution of the marriage.

The last respondent despite her two marriages to men, did not identify herself as 'bisexual,' but some women who answered the survey did. The lesbian participants were asked, *Have you considered or do you consider yourself bisexual?*

	YES	NO
in the past	56	44%
currently	16	84

Obviously many women who answered the survey considered themselves bisexual in the past no longer do. Perceiving oneself as bisexual was often a stage of transition between heterosexuality and homosexuality. But others did consider and still consider themselves bisexual. Here are some stories of bisexual or pansexual women and some comments about bisexuality.

♀"From an early age I knew that I was different, but I didn't exactly know how. I enjoyed many things that boys did because they were freer, but I also liked things girls did. My initial sexual orientation was towards men, but I always felt close to women. I fell in love with a girl in college; we used to joke about being lesbians, but we never acted upon it. Three years ago, after a minor breakdown, I realized/discovered the anima of my sexuality. I accepted my attraction for one woman and fell in love with another. When that relationship ended unhappily for both of us (and after a ménage with a man), I entered my first sexual relationship with a woman—an older lesbian.

"At first I was afraid and unnerved by my attraction for her, but then I realized it was something deep and rooted which must express itself. I was afraid of becoming a lesbian, any more outcast than I had already been (as a strange and lonely child, teenager, and young adult). I followed my instincts, and I trusted her and grew to love her. She guided me through that experience, and we're still together after a year and a half. I was 28 then. Since then I've adjusted to the sexuality of my nature, which was always bisexual, although I was too inhibited to act it out until more recently in my life. I feel freer, more in touch with myself. I feel closer to both men and women, more honest and relaxed."

♀"It seems to me that people should be able to love anyone of either sex. Gender does not seem the most important variable to me. I feel pansexual rather than bisexual, heterosexual, or homosexual. There is much evidence to discount my sense of human sexuality and maybe I'll be proved wrong after generations have grown up without the gender-role conditioning a patriarchy imposes. This won't be any time soon."

♀"There is a part of me that likes men, and I'm not out to stifle it. At the moment, for instance, I've been attracting men quite easily, and I've had a few one-night stands with guys. They were all pleasurable experiences,

although nothing I really get off on. But I feel it's good for me to be bisexual; everybody should try both sexes! Why not? We're all human beings. I don't want to close the door to half mankind. I feel it's a gift and a skill to be able to relate to either sex. I don't need a man as badly as I need a woman, but I don't dislike being with a man for one night. I don't think I'll have a long-lasting relationship with a man any more, but who knows? And I fantasize about being in bed with a woman and a man. I've done this three times and it was good, can be even better. But it's sort of using the man as a dildo. The real scene would be between me and her, and he would be an added extra to our pleasure.''

Many lesbians, however, were very hostile to bisexuals and bisexuality. The accusation that bisexuals 'sit on the fence' often came up. Here are some comments.

♀''I feel that for the good of all women and lesbians that bisexuals should renounce men and proclaim themselves lesbians. However, I know that some women still feel a strong sexual urge and love-tie towards some men. I wish these women could realize that if they chose women exclusively the sexual urge towards men would fade and be channeled into women. I think this is only a matter of unlearning and not 'going against nature.' Lesbians that love bisexual women are hurt the worst. Who wants to put energy into a woman that will give it to a man? No matter how much she thinks otherwise, a woman who still fucks men always gives them priority over her sisters. I do believe that bisexuality is a threat to the lesbian movement, but I see no point in persecuting bisexual sisters. They may come around to lesbianism if we can lovingly convince them that we have a better way.''

♀''Bisexuals are a group I tend to stay away from. Of the bisexuals I've known, they all seem to be confused. They change so radically. I would never want a relationship with a bisexual. I am a rather possessive type of person and with the bisexuals I've known they like to play the field.''

♀''There are many true bisexuals, but there are just as many people who call themselves bisexual so they don't have to face their homosexuality.''

♀''I never touch them sexually. I hate fence sitters. Somebody else can deal with the pain if and when they turn straight.''

Other lesbians did not consider themselves bisexual but were more tolerant of those who are.

♀''Bisexuality is a legitimate lifestyle. I do get annoyed that so many homosexuals and heterosexuals put it down. Frequently, I think, it is used as a cop-out for those who are afraid to accept their own homosexuality. Frequently, though, it is a stage in sexual development, a transition from heterosexuality to homosexuality. I think real bisexuality is rare.''

♀"I think bisexuality is a good thing ideally, but I couldn't stand my lover seeing a man."

♀"Probably in some distant utopian future, bisexuality would be the ideal. Right now, though, it would be a difficult course to follow. The straight world considers the bisexual to be just as 'queer' as the rest of us. The gay world, and I too am guilty of this, is distrustful of the bisexual."

♀"Bisexuality is the wave of the future."

The following comments compare sex with women with sex with men.

♀"Only one of the eight or nine experiences with men was somewhat satisfying sexually. Of the 2½ active heterosexual years I achieved only one orgasm. My female lover has never failed to take me there and back. No man ever gave me the sexual rushes that sex can give. I'm not saying every woman I've been to bed with can, but at least women, understanding the female body, understand our need of caress. It has never been a power play with women. Men seemingly want to conquer our bodies. With men sex is lust; with women it's a sensuous experience and very tender."

♀"Sex with men is like experiencing the joy of walking for the first time with one leg."

♀"Men are the most inept sexual alternatives I've experienced. I feel that few if any straight women reach orgasm."

♀"Men are easier to pick up than women."

♀"I have been married for over eighteen years. I would not have believed how much the two experiences differed and how much loving women would mean to me. It was as if eighteen years of heterosexual experiences were canceled out by my one experience with a woman I loved."

♀"I loved fucking men. Sometimes I miss it. Usually I don't think much about it."

♀"My sexual experiences with men weren't all that bad. I didn't know how to make them more the way I wanted and the men were, as men generally are, not much into affection and touching, the two things I love best. Nevertheless, it is not the physical act of sleeping with men that turned me against it, but the psycho-cultural myths that surround it that make any kind of meaningful relationship a hopeless undertaking, as far as I am concerned. There just isn't the possibility for sharing, caring, and equality that there is between women."

♀"The best times I've had with a man don't even compare with the mediocre times with women."

♀"In fucking with a woman there is a feeling of mutual sharing of self, of learning of self, and most important, enjoyment of each other's and one's own body. When I fucked with men, these feelings were never there. It was always that we were just using each other to get off. More often I was being used to get off."

♀"I find that men are genital-oriented whereas women make love with their whole bodies."

♀"Comparing men to women is like comparing buffalo hide to doe skin."

♀"My sexual experiences with men were not that unpleasant; what I disliked was all the posturing and role-playing that went along with it. I could never be myself. I generally like the female body better, however, and have found sex with women to be much more satisfying on many different levels."

♀"It *is* different all right, but not just because of the equipment. Women, on the whole, are more sensitive to one another, more approachable, more physical. Orgasm is not necessarily the end result in lovemaking with women. Lovemaking with women is prolonged. The quality of orgasm is essentially the same for me. I've had great times with both. My sexual experiences with men tended to be more violent, and I took a more active part in that violence. Women like to be held more, touched, caressed, etc."

Telling Other People

After a lesbian has come out, the next step for her very often is to tell other people that she is a lesbian. Some of the responses in the previous section of this chapter specifically mentioned how it felt to tell other people or not to tell other people. Several questions were asked to further investigate this aspect of coming out, since, as several lesbians mentioned, coming out is a verbal as well as a sexual process. The respondents were asked *at what age they first told anyone other than a sex partner that they were lesbians.* The youngest age was 7 and the oldest was 49. The mean age was 23. The lesbians told the following people first:

a friend	51%
gay friend	9
sister	8
straight friend	7
mother	5
parents	4
spouse	4
psychiatrist or other therapist	3
brother	2
father	1
cousin or other relative	1
teacher	1
a member of the clergy	1
son or daughter	1
everyone	1

The respondents were also asked *in what year they had first told someone they were gay.*

1942 to 1959	7%
1960 to 1969	17
1970-1971	14
1972	12
1973	14
1974	11
1975	9
1976	11
1977	5

Respondents were then asked, *How many of the following (if applicable) know about your lesbianism?*

	ALL (YES)	MOST	SOME	ONLY ONE	NONE (NO)	NOT SURE
lesbian friends	89	8	2	.5	1	0%
gay male friends	72	11	7	1	8	2
straight friends	19	32	36	6	6	2
neighbors	6	8	28	2	38	19
employer	12	8	11	2	50	17
teacher	4	7	26	3	47	13
co-workers	12	16	33	6	23	10
schoolmates	4	19	32	4	30	11
your employees	16	5	9	2	59	9
mother	51	0	0	0	38	10
father	41	0	0	0	48	9
sisters and brothers	48	3	6	8	26	11
your children	43	0	2	0	36	19
other relatives	6	7	21	5	42	19
other children	5	4	21	1	54	15

One can easily see from these figures that lesbians and then gay male friends were told most readily. Fathers were less likely to be told than mothers or siblings. Employers and children scored the biggest "no" answers.

Another question asked, *Of those who know you are a lesbian, what has been the reaction of each of the following to that fact? (Answer for those that are applicable.)*

	VERY POSITIVE	SOMEWHAT POSITIVE	NEUTRAL	SOMEWHAT NEGATIVE	VERY NEGATIVE	NOT SURE
lesbian friends	91	6	2	.5	0	1%
gay male friends	78	12	6	.5	3	.5
straight friends	24	41	18	12	3	3
neighbors	7	14	40	10	7	22
employer	15	17	31	9	5	23
teacher	15	25	27	8	4	21
co-workers	18	29	31	10	2	11
schoolmates	16	27	34	8	3	13
your employees	19	15	31	5	3	27
mother	12	15	14	23	25	10
father	5	11	22	16	24	22
sisters and brothers	17	28	22	16	7	10
your children	12	14	24	16	0	35
other relatives	10	10	20	16	10	34
other children	7	11	31	1	4	44

Of course, extensive analyses could be done of these charts, and perhaps in some future work there will be room for more analysis of these and the other data. However, a few interesting observations can be made quickly. Although mothers were more likely to be told of lesbianism than other family members and were told more than any other categories except gay male and lesbian friends, their reactions seem to have been more negative than positive, certainly more negative than sisters and brothers. Perhaps this indicates a "generation gap." In addition, the lesbian respondents seemed generally unsure about the reaction of their own and other children. Another point is that teachers, employers, co-workers, and schoolmates were more positive than neighbors and other children. Perhaps one would rather go to school with a lesbian or work with one than have a lesbian live next door! The following stories confirm these statistics. Here are some experiences of lesbians who received predominantly positive responses.

♀ "When I first realized I wanted more than sex with my current lover, I told my father (my mother is dead), and my daughter—and my best friend, a gay man. At my birthday party, one of my daughter's friends asked, 'Are Elizabeth and your mother dating?' When my daughter said, 'I guess you

could call it that,' her friend said, 'I thought those were dating presents.' The response of my family and friends has all been very similar and very positive. My father doesn't understand, but he accepts and likes my lover very much. Because of Anita Bryant, he allowed himself to be dragged to the Boston Gay Pride Parade in 1977 with Elizabeth's mother. He rode (he's 80); she walked with us.

"At my previous job, where I had worked for fourteen years, I simply started to talk about my current lover and what we'd been doing as I had talked about my men. When I asked to trade weekends to go to the Gay Pride Parade, no one fell over, and their attitude did not noticeably change towards me. In my present work I wear gay buttons, talk about the woman I live with and even asked a couple of my clients who are interested in civil rights to write their representatives for the gay bills. They did it. Our landlord and the other tenants in the house know. Our landlord has gay friends and identified us as a couple when we looked at the house. He has since rented another apartment to a couple of guys and asked us to let any interested gays know that he has some smaller apartments in another building. Our upstairs neighbor knows. Everyone says that all the neighborhood knows and it certainly hasn't made them keep their children at home or ignore us in the street. I get asked to babysit."

♀ "I am only gradually learning to be able to tell other people I am a lesbian. It is much easier, of course, when I am certain that they too are lesbians. My ex-husband took much of my ability to choose the time and circumstances myself out of my hands because he told my parents, my employer, and many of my friends. Much to his surprise and my pleasure, none of them reacted negatively."

♀ "I told my brother first because he was homing in on my honey. He thought it must be April Fool's Day. . . . He got over it and still loves me for myself. Next came Mom, who told Dad. She handles it well. My father will never understand why I can't remarry some wealthy *man* and live happily ever after. I would never jeopardize my job by telling a co-worker—especially after Anita has stirred up the pious."

♀ "I began to tell people I was gay—or more accurately began not to hide it—when I became involved in the gay movement. Before that time I had told some isolated people (not counting other gay friends): a straight woman friend, a guy with whom I was involved, my sisters. Their response was not negative at all, but I'm not sure how seriously they took me. Telling my mother was a direct result of my involvement in the gay movement. The experience with her was very positive and supportive. My father is quite ill, and she requested that I not tell him. I honor this request of hers because I realize he would be terribly upset and would probably take out his feelings on her."

♀ "The first person I told was my psychiatrist—in 1950, four years after my first lesbian experience. He was the only one I told until 1952, when I went to New York after grad school and made other homosexual friends. I

confined my discussions of my homosexuality during those days to other homosexuals only. There seemed to be too much danger in the '50s and early '60s in revealing my lesbianism to others.

"Currently I tell most of my close friends, some of my patients (homosexual and heterosexual—if it is pertinent to their treatment), and, of course, all my friends in the gay community. How I tell them is quite individual, but it usually is done quietly, as a result of friendship, not for shock value. My response so far has been rather positive—and having others know feels good to me—my relationships have improved as a result."

♀"The first person I told that I was a lesbian was my mother, when I fell in love with my present lover. She is a very open-minded woman who has always been politically active in minority rights in our city, especially blacks and gay rights. She was on the school board for eight years, and at that time helped allow entrance of gay speakers into our school system's 'Life Science' classes and also helped the desegregation of our schools. She was very understanding and still is, seeing that my lover lives with my mother, my sister, and me, and sleeps in the same bed as myself!"

♀"The first person I told about my gayness was a fairly close friend, Anne-Marie. She had just said, with an air of fear and shame, 'And I'm not so sure I'm not *gay*.' I laughed and told her that I certainly wouldn't damn her for that since I was gay myself. We were driving along a freeway at night, and I started speeding without realizing it. Anne was humming merrily. We'd each found someone to confide in, at last."

♀"The first person I told was my first lover, after we'd stopped being lovers and were friends. She'd figured I wasn't really gay (she isn't) and was surprised I was. She was supportive and protective of me. She wanted to make sure I didn't get swept away unrealistically. I love that about her and find it very special. I also shared my lesbianism with a group of people (men and women) during a weekend of personal growth via gestalt, experiential learning, etc., after my present relationship was six months old. It was important for me to say in words where I was and to receive feedback from the group. That was one of the richest experiences of my life. Everyone in the groups was positive, supportive, and very much nonthreatening. They asked several questions and seemed to care about me as a person. Their positive response was wonderful and I'll never forget it.

"It's important, however, for me to stay 'in the closet' a propos of work and family. I want to be honest, but not at the price of losing parental support or a meaningful career. Besides, I don't want to lay something on other people that they're not ready or prepared to hear."

♀"The first person that I ever told I was gay was a co-worker about six months ago. I told this woman over the telephone. She was the most understanding woman (straight) that I have ever spoken with. She even told me that on occasion she had been in love with a friend of hers (but from a distance). I still talk with this woman about my sexuality quite often."

Probably just as many women experienced mixed reactions, some positive and some negative. Here are some stories.

♀"Most people I've told I was gay simply accepted it. Some thought I was sick. Others said I needed to find a 'good man' and others, like my folks, accepted it but said, 'Don't advertise it.' Now I only tell people I really want to know. I rarely tell straights if I don't know them well."

"It was important to me that my immediate family know of my gayness. Their response was relatively mild—ranging mostly from unspoken acceptance to mild disbelief. My mother pointed out all the times she'd seen me respond to men, etc. My friends—old, straight friends—were already in the process of withdrawal. This hastened it, I feel. A few straight women friends responded with a confused retreat, screaming. 'I'm not into sex as much as you are.' Translation: 'Don't touch me.' Basically, though, I never tell anyone that I'm a dyke, and I never tell anyone that I'm not. I assume they can know what they want to know and I'm sick of explaining being gay to the 'liberals' and so just let it go."

♀"I usually tell anybody I talk with that I'm gay, if the subjects of love, marriage, sex, or boy friends ever come up. In my job, I do *not* make a public announcement of it, because of my sensitive position vis-à-vis students. I wrote an article in the student newspaper in 1975 supporting gay rights and lifestyle, and my director got some 'flak' to fire me for speaking out, and I didn't even personally 'come out' in the article."

♀"When my friend and I first realized, at 16, that we were in love with each other, something in us or around us told us not to celebrate our happiness with anyone else. When our parents finally suspected what was going on, we told them about our feelings as honestly as we could. My parents were unhappy at first—not because I was a lesbian but because they knew I'd have a harder life because of it. But eventually they realized that, for me, the joy and strength I found were well worth a lifetime of struggle. Now they are very supportive of us and of gay (and other) civil rights. Pam's parents freaked out, especially her mother, and were very restrictive about letting us see each other. We also had told our minister, who was understanding and somewhat conservatively supportive. He helped us to get through the hard times of Pam's parents' irrational fears and accusations, the shrinks, and our gradual realization of what the world had in store for us."

♀"I have lost several longtime friends. We grew up in a small, midwest farming town. Some of my friends still live there. They seem the same as my parents. Going back to visit a few years ago, I told my closest friends. For the most part I was accepted, but in a couple of painful cases, I felt like I should have stayed in the closet. I felt dirty. Why wasn't I like the rest? Why couldn't I accept it and get married and settle down, play cards, and give up all that I had learned? I will never forget those painful moments nor will I ever feel completely comfortable visiting that sleepy little town."

♀"In 1973 I told my mother. I think that may have been a mistake, since her and my relationship was just at that time getting good after years of

power struggles and weirdness. Although she had told me that she had been attracted to women when she was young, and there was a nice bond there temporarily, it deeply affected our relationship after that day and caused some real hostility and awkwardness between us. She simply couldn't believe that her eldest daughter, whom she clearly felt the strongest about of her four daughters, wasn't going to turn out to be a nice, normal heterosexual woman and bring home a nice man. Telling her was a fiasco and caused her to do much talking nasty behind my back to my younger brother, whom she immediately formed a strong alliance with, an alliance of the sort that had been with me before.

"On the other hand, my father, whom I never directly told, but whom my mother obviously told, although he has never said the unspeakable word or anything, has been wonderful about it. He had several gay relationships, not just experiences, before he was married and his older brother is a guilty closet gay, whom he feels very sorry for. He wishes his brother would at least feel good about who he is rather than go to Mass every day out of his guilt. Anyway, my father accepts who I am beautifully, although it's not like we talk about it at any length or anything. He met my lover and her son, was very good to them, and always says hello to them when he calls or writes. I feel very good about that, kind of let alone to be who I am, nurtured in a way."

Some women related stories of mainly negative experiences in telling other people they're lesbians.

♀"At first, I was fairly nonjudicial about who I told I was a lesbian. Once a woman started screaming, 'Don't rape me!' Next, I told a couple of acquaintances and that led to gossip and scandal. Now, I sound people out first. I'm fairly physically obvious, but the verbalization makes me susceptible to a lot of flak."

"My parents and much of my family found out by seeing my picture in a UPI photo in newspapers across the nation. When I admitted that it was me, and yes, I was participating in a gay-rights march like the caption indicated, I got a very sterile, defensive attitude from my father. My mother said 'What have I done wrong?' And my grandmother said, 'It *must* be a hormone imbalance.' She also added prayers to God for my salvation. I got an array of disgust and embarrassment from the other family members. One common reaction was 'You have no right to be proud of that,' and 'Keep it to yourself' or 'You can be cured.' "

♀"When I told my mother, she freaked out and said she wished she were dead. She asked me if I were trying to 'cure' myself (*no!*) and said she needed to stop talking to me. She hasn't talked to me in eight months. That experience has affected me so that I expect other people not to accept me."

♀"I gave up telling co-workers in classified government jobs. I lost two of these jobs and another nongovernment job."

♀"The only people who know I am gay are my friends (close) and my

immediate family. My family reacted with shock, disgust, and worry. They have decided it's just a 'phase.' My friends don't care much, although some guys do. It is upsetting to think of the taboos of sexual preference—that people will dislike or harass because of such a small, personal thing. It always hurts me to lie about it.''

♀ "The few times I've told straight men that I'm gay, their first response is invariably, 'It's nothing a good male fuck can't cure.' ''

♀ "Most people I know either know I'm gay or suspect it. The first person I told (outside of my first lover, of course!) was a friend. Then my first lover's parents found out. Since they are both teachers (one a guidance counselor), I expected a degree of understanding from them. Instead, I met with extreme homophobia. Her father wanted to send her to an institution for aversion therapy, and ordered us to separate immediately. He also wanted me to see a psychiatrist to 'help me adjust to a normal lifestyle.' My response was to contact a gay organization and counselor. Unfortunately, my lover had a great deal of emotional involvement with her family and got really confused. This caused us to split up.''

♀ "I have lost many heterosexual friends since I've told them of my orientation. That's their loss and their problem. It saddens me to see how uptight seemingly sophisticated New York women are about this. I guess they're afraid I'll rape them or try to convert them or perhaps they can't confront their own feelings about loving women.''

♀ "When I told my parents I was gay, I did it in a 'chicken way' and on the spur of the moment. I was in the local mental health center for depression and possible suicide prevention, and I knew that I had to tell them, and I knew that at this time and place my parents wouldn't try to put me down. Also the people at the center helped me straighten out my feelings and realize that what I was doing was normal and healthy. People I share this with (straight people, mostly girls) think I am crazy, that I don't know what I'm doing, and that somebody brainwashed me into this.''

Being In or Out of the Closet

As one can see from the above stories, people were in or out of the closet to varying degrees. Here are some more feelings about being in the closet.

♀"I dislike having to pretend that C. and I are just roommates in discussion with other teachers. Maybe if they like and understand me, their ideas about homosexuality would change. Also, I can't take C. places as my date (faculty parties) or get teased about the fact that I look forward to seeing her.''

♀ "Here in the midwest, it's better not to say anything because the only effect it has on these unintelligent people is negative. However, it would do terrible things to my own self-respect if I were 'in the closet' like most of the gay women around here in Indianapolis. Here for me it's best not to admit it, and yet at the same time not to deny it.''

♀ "We tell no one in our daily life that we are gay. Keeping our lesbianism secret has been the hardest thing we've had to do! I hate living a lie, but there's no other choice. My lover and I are very shy and sensitive, and in the town we live in, there's no acceptance. We live in much isolation, too, and loneliness. I admire others who are open because they are not afraid to face others, and take life's bumps and falls. I wish we could be as strong."

♀ "Because of my job (a teacher no less), I must play it cool. Co-workers and bosses eventually know about my preferences, but I would never tell students."

♀ "I hate being in the closet. It's so boring having people ask if I have a boy friend. I feel like putting the most horrified look possible on my face, and as if I'm deeply insulted exclaim, 'I beg your pardon? I certainly hope not!' If I were sure of a job and safe living conditions, everyone would be fully informed that I am gay. I am seriously contemplating getting a T-shirt with 'Support Gay Liberation' inscribed on it."

♀ "At this point I'm fairly closeted. My parents and sister know. I'm working on a healthy way to let my daughter know (she's 7) and ask questions. She's probably the only reason I wouldn't be a lot more open about it. Maybe someday. . . ."

♀ "Keeping it quiet is important to me only inasmuch as it could seriously upset people I care about, particularly my kids and even my husband. I don't feel I have the right to make the choice of coming out at their expense, but to each his/her own."

♀ "I keep it a secret at school and work (would you believe I'm typing this at work on the boss's typewriter? He's gone for the day!)."

♀ "At times I wish I were not in the closet. There are aspects of my social life which I cannot relate normally to in social conversations because they were gay social activities. So I am limited in the degree to which I can be close to straight friends. On the other hand, I know it will be disturbing to be open about my gayness. As a kid, I fought to be accepted and liked, and I just can't go through that fight any more. I am not a person to want my life to be an open book to everybody, so to be closeted in a sense is not that much pressure. I do not want to put my job on the line or force my family to have to deal with it. My mother had begun to accept the fact that I will not be getting married, most likely, and that's enough struggle for her. I don't care if others are out of the closet. I just feel they should respect the right of others to choose not to be out."

♀ "Being in the closet is really annoying. You always have to be thinking about what this person will think, or if my clothes are too masculine. The thing I hate most about it is having to laugh at nasty cutting jokes about 'fags.' I get these things because I hang around with 16- and 17-year-old guys. To preserve my image I even have to tell these jokes every now and then. I feel like a total hypocrite. There's nothing I like about being in the closet—even the feelings of security are fake."

♀ "I don't really like being in the closet at all, and resent not having told

my parents yet as it keeps one foot stuck in the closet door. I try to be low-key around the apartment, as I can be evicted for lesbianism in this state.''

♀ ''I generally don't tell people. I'm too worried about it getting to my employer. I'm fairly sure my immediate boss knows, or has a good idea that I'm a lesbian, but the YWCA might prove a bit stuffy about having an open lesbian work for them. I also don't want to jeopardize my lover's position. And my family—no way. They are so damn conservative. My mother's uptight enough about me being a 'women's libber.' But I hate the secrecy. They don't know me any more. I'm so different from what they think I am.''

♀ ''My biggest concern about telling straight people who are not in the movement is that they will write me off and dismiss my ideas because I am a lesbian (i.e., man-hater).''

Some people felt that they are half in the closet and half out of the closet. Women in this category often expressed the feeling that they are living in two worlds.

♀ ''The most frustrating thing about being out is having to live in two worlds, the gay and the straight, the disadvantages of living in either of them completely and trying to keep them separate. It's like having to live two lives, and be on guard in one of them. There are times when I want to say I'm gay to a woman, but the fear of rejection is so strong. It's terrible that there is such a stigma in the straight world about being gay. What's even more frustrating is to realize that for all the fears of the straights that we're hideous and perverted, the gay community is as normal, with the same situations and feelings, as the straight world. There shouldn't be such a division.''

♀ ''I feel like I live two lives—one at work (I'm in the education field), school, and at home. At school and work, I have to be 'in the closet' but at home and with women friends I feel free and easy. I'd like to tell the world or be able to walk with a woman and hold and kiss her without people freaking out or without interference with my teaching profession.''

Other women were totally out, or almost totally out.

♀ ''Everybody knows except my grandmothers and other distant relatives. I couldn't hold it in because I feel that people should accept me for what I am. And if they don't accept it, at least I don't have to hide it within. Everybody knows that I am proud of what I am.''

♀ ''For myself, I love being out of the closet and in print and knowing the FBI has me on their list. It's exhilarating after years of such uncertainty! But it's still not easy to be 'out,' so I can't be down on somebody who's closeted. Frankly I can't see how they can stand it!''

♀ ''I resent continually having to come out—having to nip assumptions in the bud in situations I have no investment in, and open myself up for

anxiety about how someone on the bus who's asking me if I've just come from seeing my boy friend (good-natured coots, usually) and whose values have no value to me, will react to a lesbian admission. Not to admit it is a cause for anxiety too, and unauthentic feelings. I lack patience for closeted women, unfairly. Older women, especially have had to create a safe place for themselves. Who can believe that an all-clear has been sounded when Anita Bryant can evoke such homophobic response? Still, I think that closet oppression and misery are worse than open discrimination in which there is at least some dignity.''

♀"I have an incurably big mouth and have always told anyone I became friends with of my lesbian tilt.''

♀"I feel real good about being out of the closet. My lesbianism gives me a lot of strength that I didn't have before. I feel it's unfortunate some people have to be in the closet for financial reasons.''

♀"I *love* to tell men I'm a lesbian! When I hitchhike and they get macho or try to pick me up, I tell them, 'Too bad, buddy, I'm a lesbian.' Or: 'You got the wrong pussy, sweetie! I *love* women!' Or: 'I like men, but I *love* women!' I come off the wall with reality remarks similar to this in every social setting. I love to blow their minds! With women I'm a bit more subtle, a bit more polite about it, but nevertheless, I tell them that yes, there are very feminine, sexy, beautiful women out here who are aggressive, assertive, and like to suck other women and *be* sucked by other women.''

♀"I like being out of the closet as much as I am because I feel a pride in showing my loving and physical affection towards women. I dislike some lesbians' attitudes which feel affected, hostile towards men and/or society, and even look for attention for lack of self-confidence or self-esteem.''

Some of the lesbian respondents, when discussing their own status of being in or out of the closet, also mentioned how they felt about other lesbians who were in the same or a different position. The respondents were asked, *How do you feel about people whom you perceive to be "in the closet" (secretive)?*

very positive	2%
somewhat positive	10
neutral	42
somewhat negative	35
very negative	6
not sure	6

In other words, more people felt distinctly negative than positive, but almost an equal number felt neutral or not sure.

The respondents were also asked, *How do you feel about people whom you perceive to be "blatantly gay"?*

	VERY POSITIVE	SOMEWHAT POSITIVE	NEUTRAL	SOMEWHAT NEGATIVE	VERY NEGATIVE	NOT SURE
those who are politically outspoken	57	25	10	5	1	1%
those who physically appear to be "obvious" homosexuals and lesbians	23	25	24	19	6	4

It is obvious from this last chart that the lesbians in the survey felt much more positively about other gays who are politically outspoken than about those who look blatantly gay ('faggoty' men and 'butchy dykes'). However, only 26% were outright negative to people who look gay and a large 24% were neutral. Here are some comments about others being in the closet, or out of the closet.

♀"I don't like to see people in the closet because I know they're freer being themselves. Pretending is painful, no matter what anyone says. The only thing I dislike about those 'out of the closet' is some of the interminable proselytizing that goes on like ex-smokers or former alcoholics. There's nothing worse than a reformed closet case."

♀"If people need to be in the closet, that's their choice—so long as they don't cop out politically."

♀"I'm sorry that their lives are so insecure that other people might harm them for that so they stay in the closet."

♀"I try to be understanding of each person's process and decisions."

♀"I can understand very well why others may conceal their sexuality from employers or families. A couple of women I know are pretty open and sometimes I feel nervous with them. I'm scared of the hostility toward gays. I don't want it directed at me."

♀"I don't blame anyone for being in the closet, and I congratulate those who can afford to be out. It feels so much better to be out whenever and wherever you can."

♀"I think that being *out* is indeed a luxury, and I admire those who are politically active for gay rights. I am a feminist activist, and get my political fulfillment that way. I would never want to be out on my job. I wouldn't be any effective. I'd be fired undoubtedly. Society is simply not ready yet. I dislike pressure from some of those who are out. They sometimes are not sensitive enough. It's more important to have gay teachers, etc., under cover and working in the system to change sexist, racist, capitalist, classist, homophobic attitudes than to have a bunch of gays unemployed and marching in the streets. No, I didn't march in the Gay Pride March, and

wouldn't take that risk, ever. Job security is important to me. I am definitely angered at times by newly come-out dykes who are overeffusive about loving being a dyke. Such simplistic attitudes bother me a lot.''

♀"I dislike gay people who feel that they're 'gayer' than others because they can be socially visible. If they'd pay me a salary and I'd not have to worry about my job, I'd go out marching too. I'm not *so* into the closet, but enough to get money to feed myself with.''

♀"I do not like the obvious homosexual image (bizarre) as it implies to the heterosexuals that 'this is how homosexuals *all* are.' ''

♀"I say whatever other lesbians and homosexuals do is their own business. Each has her own life to live and the right to live it the way she wants.''

♀"The men and women in drag . . . well, that's fine. Let them do their own thing.''

♀"I don't like nellie faggots, or old-style heavy 'truckdriving type butch dykes.' All other obvious gays are fine.''

♀"I admire those who are publicly outspoken and working for our civil rights.''

♀"We need all the political spokespeople we can get. And there's nothing like 'zapping' the straight world.''

♀"Obvious dykes I like. Obvious men I often don't like—particularly in drag. I think it's often sexist.''

♀"If it's a put-on or a show, then I'm somewhat negative. I have a very positive reaction to physically 'blatant gays' who are honest and sure of themselves. They *de facto* have to be strong people.''

♀"Aside from very tough women and men, it's a good feeling to recognize each other on the street, etc.''

♀"I believe that everyone should stand up for what they believe, whether that means giving a speech or wearing a jockstrap.''

♀"I feel negative about very camp men and butch women, but good about people who clearly affirm their sexual orientation. I have close-cropped hair and feel good about people thinking I am a dyke because of that.''

♀"I admire politically outspoken gays. I would like to be more politically involved/outspoken. As it is, I am more active in writing on bathroom walls.''

♀"I'm flabbergasted to find good straight friends assuming that the people who parade and look outrageous represent *our* majority.''

Children of Lesbians

In deciding whether to come out or stay in the closet, lesbians were often influenced by whether or not they have children. Of the lesbians in the subsample, 18% had children. Those lesbians who had children were positive about them—in fact more positive than those who did not have

children. When asked, *Whether or not you have children, what is your attitude, in general, toward children?* the lesbian mothers were far more enthusiastic.

	VERY POSITIVE	SOMEWHAT POSITIVE	NEUTRAL	SOMEWHAT NEGATIVE	VERY NEGATIVE	NOT SURE
have children	54	37	3	3	0	1%
don't have children	32	27	14	18	8	0

A corresponding question which asked, *If you don't have children, how do you feel about being childless?* backs up these statistics.

very positive	56%
somewhat positive	12
neutral	17
somewhat negative	11
very negative	3
not sure	2

However, 25% of those lesbians who were not biological mothers said that they participated in the rearing of children—presumably their lovers', although a few lesbians stated they are teachers and rear children in an educational sense. 73% of these women were satisfied with their nonbiological mothering arrangement.

In short, those who have children were happy about having them and generally wanted to keep them. However, for 12% of lesbian mothers, custody of the children has been an issue and for 6% visiting rights have been an issue. Many of those who stated that custody and/or visiting rights were not an issue also stated it was because they were secretive about being a lesbian. The following are some comments about custody, visiting rights, and children.

♀ "I lost my children through total surrender papers. No choice at all."

♀ "At one time I had custody. Then I gave custody to my husband. Knowing I was gay, my ex-husband decided I couldn't see my kids, so I kidnapped them until we finally reached an agreement out of court. Now I see them whenever I'm up north, and I call them at least once a month."

♀ "Since I live with friends, and some of them have children, custody has been an issue."

♀ "Visiting rights are a problem as we live in different cities because it means only part-time with our daughter for both of us."

♀"Since parents tend to use children as pawns in their nonsense games, visiting rights being a big one, it has come into my house."

♀"I have a problem. I abused my own children and I'm still trying to work this out with a therapist, but I don't feel that I could raise a child that was not mine."

♀"My daughter is very important to me. I want security and happiness for her. I hope I can provide this atmosphere for her in a gay setting. Obviously there will be problems."

♀"I raised my own children. I wish I had hugged and coddled my kids more. Circumstances and numbers, plus my own needs outside the family, made this almost impossible. However, they were hardly 'deprived,' and feel they had a wonderful childhood, escapades and disasters which they recall with glee. Ultimately all children have to find their own level of spiritual and physical needs anyway. I let them go with joy, and a lot of pain. I try now always to make reunions cheerful, interesting, and free of demands. It works. Consideration and lively, warm interaction has come at last."

Like this last mother, most lesbians, whether out to their children or not, seemed to have positive relationships with them as can be seen in the stories throughout this chapter. In coming out, the women made choices which seemed the most positive and practical (or the least painful) to them at the time. And it is good to end this chapter with the children, because perhaps the gay children of lesbians, and the gay children of nonlesbians (which will probably occur in about equal percentages), will not have to go through the pain of coming out or staying in the closet when they are grown up.

From Childhood to Gay Manhood

Childhood Crushes

Sigmund Freud, the founder of modern psychiatry, said many upsetting things in his day, but perhaps the most upsetting statements of all were those concerning the sexuality of infants and children. While many of Freud's concepts have become widely popularized, even absorbed into establishment thinking, his forthright affirmation of the sexual behavior of the young has been conveniently shunted aside. In most households, sexuality is hidden from children. Most children learn about sex, according to popular expressions, "in the gutter," or "in the locker room," but it is much more likely in fact that children learn about sex in their bedrooms or their own secret places—with other children. The sexual feelings that children have, starting in early childhood if not infancy, can be directed toward adults as well as toward other children. Sometimes, the feelings have a strong emotional component, and are recognized by adults and called "crushes."

The men readily recalled childhood crushes, and a good many of them involved celebrities and other figures known through the mass media of communication:*

⚣"As early as 10 years old, I had crushes on male Western stars. As I look back, I see my reaction to male stars as somewhat different from others my age. Most youngsters want to be like the stars; I wanted to be with the stars, and be cuddled by them."

Among the many stars or hero figures mentioned by the men were the following: Robin Hood, Zorro, Annette Funicello (of the Mickey Mouse Club), Richard Chamberlain, Paul McCartney, George Hamilton, Johnny Carson, Roy Rogers, Dale Evans, Guy Madison, Robert Horton, Peter

*The symbols ⚢ for a lesbian and ⚣ for a gay man are used to indicate each time a new person's response begins.

Brown, Lloyd Bridges, Tarzan, Little Richard, and the Jolly Green Giant. This experience is typical.

⚛ "I was raised in the '30s. We didn't know much about sex then. So, my crushes were just that. I had no idea there was anything sexual about them. I did have crushes on movie actors—most guys drooled over Betty Grable, while I secretly had the hots for Richard Green and Tyrone Power."

Childhood fantasy-world crushes and daydreams for some of the men often lacked a sexual element, especially if the object of the fantasy was unattainable.

⚛ "One of my most unusual fantasies I remember now was at the age of 9 or 10. I would look at the men's underwear section in Ward and Sears magazines, and pray very sincerely and faithfully that God would put these men in a locked room that only I had a key to, and they would obey me like robots."

⚛ "When I was prepuberty I fantasized myself being in an orphanage, or all-boys school and getting into trouble, and receiving caring nurturance from peers."

⚛ "I recall going to Saturday matinees at the movies and enjoying scenes where the hero was shirtless or in swim trunks. For romantic fantasy, I recall paging through *Homes and Gardens* types of magazines and imagining sharing a house with a really gorgeous guy (fictional, not anyone I knew). I have a particular memory of whiling away time this way in a dentist's waiting room."

⚛ "At the age of 7 or so, I began having fantasies of being with naked grown men in an open place, a beach beside a lake. Because at that age, prepuberty, I had no knowledge of sex or sexual organs, my dreams were of excrement, of wallowing in piss and shit among muscular hairy bodies. I can therefore understand the attraction of scat, of places like the now-defunct watering hole in the Village called the Toilet. It is there that grown men reenact childhood fantasies such as I had, I believe."

The bulk of childhood crushes and sexual feelings, however, were very down-to-earth and specific, usually directed toward schoolmates, older boys, or older men. Many of the men reported that even at a young age, these feelings were directed only toward males:

⚛ "I remember that in fifth grade I had a crush on a couple of boys in my class. I didn't know about sex, and I had no instinctual feeling about what it was I wanted to do with these boys, but there was always a general feeling of wanting to share some tender, sweet, caressing experience. I wanted to share with these boys something as warm and loving and tender as what I shared with my pet dog, who would sleep in the bed with me, and lie at my feet on the bed, and who would let me fondle him for hours. There was a boy I met in Boy Scout camp, and I wanted to kiss him. God, there were so many boys in camp on whom I had crushes. Somehow, I must have known that this

was not acceptable, because I can't recall anyone's reactions to those feelings. I must not have shared them with anyone, which indicates that I must have known they were not acceptable.''

♂ "I had a crush on a high school athlete when I was in the eighth grade, and during basketball practice I used to go into the locker room so I could see him emerge from the shower. I was in 'love' with him, talked about him all the time, went out to look at his house, found out about him in every way I could—his birthday, brothers' names, the church they went to, etc. I even stole pictures from his wallet. He must have thought me weird.''

♂ "Around the age of 5, I began to experience an inexplicably strong affinity towards men. A year later, at the age of 6, I literally 'fell in love' with a boy in high school, thus beginning my strong attraction towards older men. When I say I 'fell in love' with him, that's exactly what I mean. Every night I dreamed about this boy and how we kissed each other on the lips. I know that psychologists insist that children feel no romantic attachments towards adults, but I disagree strongly—at least I was an exception. This boy—my first love affair—was a member of the baseball team and every day after school I used to walk past the baseball diamond just to watch him play. I loved the way he looked in his uniform, I loved the way he ran, I loved the way he spoke, and I tried to copy all his mannerisms. One day he and another guy were horsing around and they accidentally ran into me and knocked me to the ground. Even though I was hurt, he picked me up before I could start to cry and he tossed me playfully into the air. Then he hugged me and messed my hair as he repeated, 'Don't cry! Don't cry! Everything is going to be okay.' Those were the most beautiful words I had ever heard. I immediately forgot about my bruises and that night I was very hesitant to take a bath for fear of washing his scent off my body. This silent love affair of mine continued for two years until he graduated from high school and joined the army. The strange thing is that I never told anyone about it. Somehow I knew it was something I was supposed to keep secret. My childhood was pretty 'normal,' except for the one secret which I kept to myself. I knew nothing about homosexuals, and I most certainly had never heard the word. I had heard the word 'queer' directed at certain boys, but I didn't associate it with myself because it was obvious to me that the reason these boys were being labeled 'queer' was due to their effeminacy (I was not an effeminate little boy), and not because they preferred boys sexually. As a matter of fact, I thought I was the only boy in the whole wide world who loved other boys!''

♂ "Perhaps the earliest memory I have of having a 'crush' happened when I was around 11 or 12. My father took me to Princeton University just to show me around (we didn't live far from it). We were walking through the botany building, when we came to these long series of greenhouses. I guess it was all right for people to just walk in and look at the plants, because we did just that. A young (around 25) very good-looking man came up and asked if he could help us. My father said that we were just looking around, and the man offered to give us a tour. He took us around to all the

plants, explaining about them, where they came from, how they were obtained, their various qualities. I remember his telling me to touch the leaves of one plant, and when I did the leaves immediately folded up. He was very intelligent and knowledgeable (at least he seemed so) and he was very friendly towards me all the time. After about an hour, he had shown us everything, and my father thanked him, and we left. For some time after that, I used to fantasize about him, like going out on botany excursions together, or just spending a lot of time with him. One fantasy involved going out in a boat with him, with us changing into our bathing suits together (that was the only way that I would permit myself to fantasize his being naked, because even then I had been thoroughly indoctrinated about the 'evils' of homosexuality).

"I developed similar crushes all throughout adolescence, with camp counselors, teachers, older students. As the people involved had the qualities of strength, honesty, and open affection, I tried to win their approval by returning these qualities."

⚥"I was attracted to a number of boys who matured early physically. I felt very ripped off by them; they would tease me sexually (they were much more sophisticated about sex and I was rather platonic and romantic) and then make fun of me. I loved them and hated them."

⚥ "When I was in the Boy Scouts around age 14, there was a campout with another troop. I met another camper my age with whom I 'fell in love,' although I didn't know what it was. I just wanted to be near him. I had short breath and fast heartbeat etc. We did sleep in the same tent, but nothing sexual happened. In looking back now, I can appreciate it, but then, I was just overcome by the event."

⚥ "My childhood crushes probably started at the age of 8 or 9 when I used to take a friend into the furnace room of my house and we would insert Tinkertoys into our anuses. We had no conception of orgasm. I also dimly remember something about an uncle, especially his feet. Then I always wanted to masturbate with friends, after I learned of this act. People obviously worried when they heard about these feelings. I routinely confessed them to a priest, of course. However, I felt that they were so wrong it didn't matter that they were homosexual. The special wrongness of homosexuality wasn't clear to me until I was in my early teens. At that point I was shocked that my parents, after being so opposed to sexuality in general, now wished to split hairs about some kinds being worse than others. This seemed cynical to me."

⚥ "I remember even at the age of 3 or 4, an attraction to men. Being picked up by my father was very exciting to me. My crushes were with my older brother's friends, who were a couple of years older than myself and were around a lot during my junior high years. I was more aware of the masculinity of their presence and not their genitals."

⚥ "When I was 4 years old, I used to go to the municipal swimming pool. The highlight of the day was the changing; seeing naked men! I wanted so

much to touch or at least talk to the men. I wanted to ask them about their wonderful bodies, and to touch them, for them to touch me.''

⚶ "At age 14 I had a crush (sexual attraction) on my high school English teacher. I masturbated, with his picture in the yearbook as a stimulant. However, I sublimated this physical attraction into a more platonic/religious 'love.' ''

⚶ "I longed for a father as a child. I had one but he was busy making money. So I looked for male companionship in teachers or older boys. The older boys taught me about sex and used me.''

⚶ "My earliest recollection of a childhood crush was of a fourth-grade classmate, who was very good-looking with golden curls and a dimple in his chin. We used to play together, and although we never had a sexual encounter, I knew that I wanted to be with him and would do anything he asked me to do. A few of my male classmates teased me about being Harry's 'girl friend.' He would usually tell them to shut up or he'd shut them up. As he was the most popular boy in class, they usually obeyed him, and kept their distance, at least when he was around.''

⚶ "When I was in high school and junior high I wasn't into sports but I was a manager for several sports and I had 'crushes' on several of the athletes—yet they never knew and I didn't really admit to those feelings myself.''

⚶ "In junior high school, I used to love to go down to the gym at school and watch the basketball players with their shirts off. Later in high school, I never missed a chance to watch the swimmers and tried becoming friends with a few really hunky football players. I was constantly on guard so as not to betray my real feelings to these guys and thus lose their friendship, not to mention the fact that I didn't want them to think I was queer.''

⚶ "When I was 8, I had a crush on a '50s greaser from next door named Ed. I used to sit for hours watching him work on his car. I had frequent sexual fantasies about him, being in the shower with him naked, rubbing my genitals against his, having his penis between my legs. When I was confirmed in the Roman Catholic Church, I took his name as my confirmation name: Edward. No one ever knew. I don't know what their reactions were. When I was a teenager and my parents discovered my gay pornography, I was put through a tortuous route with psychiatrists, etc., for several years until I went to college. I think sexual preference is determined early in childhood, long before adolescence. I have confirmed my experiences then with many other people's—most, whether they realize it or not, were sexually attracted to people of the same sex when they were very young.''

⚶ "I can recall having a crush on a fellow who lived in our mobile home park across the street from us when I was 9 or 10. He was lean and sexy and often was active outdoors without a shirt. On several occasions he responded to my admiring remarks by flexing his muscles and letting me feel them on various parts of his body. In adolescence, still in the closet but having occasional guilt-ridden sexual contacts, I fell in love with my best

friend (that happened to me on more than one occasion before I came out) and wrestled with the burden of hiding that from him while making every opportunity possible to spend time with him.''

↺ "I had a crush on my gym teacher, mainly because he had a big prick. I got as many chances to see it as I could. Nothing else happened, unfortunately.''

↺ "I never really had a crush on anyone till I was 12. That's when my 17-year-old stepbrother came to live with us. He smoked rather openly, got to use the family's Country Squire, and had many girls after him. I would do anything I could to get to see his body but even though he roomed with me, he made sure I didn't get to see him. We didn't get along (mostly because he thought I was a 'sissy'). So finally one night he was bathing so I casually strolled outside and wandered around the side of our ranch-style house to the bathroom windows and was thrilled to discover a space about 1½ " between the curtains and the sill. I had a perfect view of his completely naked body. He was posing before the full-length mirror first from the front, then the side. He was sporting a beautiful erection. He came over to the window and proceeded to soap up his hands then to jack off about a foot from my face. As I watched, he read a *True* magazine and got more and more excited. After a time of intense concentration, he rushed to the stool, where he seemed to piss a little and it shot straight into the air. Well, this was something new and strange to me but it was such a turn-on for me that I rushed to a darkened corner of the yard and rubbed my dick till I shot off (my very first time).''

↺ "I had a continuous series of crushes which were highly sexual, going back to preschool. I have always been a connoisseur of male beauty, usually modified by friendly, outgoing interest in others; the cold ones don't interest me for long. As a child this was true, too, and I could probably name most of the boys I had crushes on, and describe them in loving terms. The feelings themselves were much more loving than overtly sexual—I would dwell on thoughts of the 'crush' as I masturbated, but not on the idea of having sex with them—it would most commonly be a simple facial projection, or the visualization of the whole boy. Many of these crushes were directed at the school's 'hero' types. The feelings were always secret, but of course there were shy attempts to become friends with most, although it was rarely successful: often the object-individual would be a year or two older, and/or deeply into his own social clique which left little room for outsiders. The general pattern continued up into high school, at which point I tended to turn my sights around and discover the younger ones coming along a year or so behind me. I can still go through the old yearbooks and get a real buzz out of looking at the pictures of my favorites.''

Some men recalling their boyhood sexuality remembered crushes on females as well as males, or sexual play involving boys and girls in mixed settings.

⚤ "I guess all my crushes were on girls. I liked a few boys along the way, but never to the extent of girls."

⚤ "I never had sex when I was younger. I did have a crush on my female third-grade teacher. I also had a crush on a girl in my class in fourth grade. I had a crush on my sixth-grade teacher and wanted to go to bed with his younger, better-looking aide."

⚤ "The first crush I can remember more than vaguely was over some musclebound black-haired construction worker who was on the team building a church across the street from where I lived. It was summertime and he was always stripped to the waist. I was around 8 years old at the time, and I think he knew that I was not the average little 8-year-old boy, and I used to bring him peanut-butter sandwiches to prove it. Nothing ever happened, of course, because right up to the age of 12, all I ever did was the usual 'doctor' games with my female friends."

⚤ "My romantic attachments throughout my childhood were for females. I always had romantic crushes for women. I thought I would get married, envelop myself in a consuming love for a female, and produce children out of that love. (I still have similar fantasies.) All the time I had romantic attachments to females, I had physical attractions to men. For years I looked at other men's bodies, particularly their genitals."

⚤ "As a child I had two crushes, one with the girl next door, and another with a girl who lived down the street. When I told my mother she whipped me for being 'dirty.' I never expressed my crush to either of them. In high school, I had a real crush on a boy in my class but, of course, never told him or anyone else. I feel childhood crushes are a normal part of growing up."

⚤ "When I was a kid I wanted to see a woman do a striptease. I also wanted to play with (manipulate) unconscious (but definitely alive) boys and girls. At one point—I don't remember how old—I liked to stick Tinkertoys up my ass."

Two men recalled attachments to little girls whom they later recognized as lesbians:

⚤ "When I was in first grade, I spent as much time as I could with a little girl named Arline C. I considered her to be my girl friend, and everyone used to tease us. We stopped being close, however, though we went through school together and I always knew she was a 'tomboy' and she must have known I was a 'fairy.' We met as adults, now both openly gay, but we didn't have much to say to each other. It was disappointing somehow."

⚤ "I had this crush on this girl in public school and I used to follow her everywhere and offer to carry her books to calculus class (because this was the only class we had together). Well, this infatuation carried on for about six years until I found out about the area homophile association and went to it and saw her there and then since that time we've been the closest of friends and know a lot about each other. Since that time I only dated boys with no particular problems."

There were a few men who reported no childhood crushes or sexual feelings whatsoever:

⚥ "I can't say that I remember my childhood that much. I know that I was often called a sissy and that I didn't like to go to school in grade nine because I would get beaten up. I then went to a seminary where I enjoyed boarding school a lot. I never had sex while in school or college. I don't remember being attracted sexually until I was in my 20s."

⚥ "I have almost no recollection. Can't remember any 'crushes' early on or sexual feelings directed to other kids or adults. This is really a separate issue, i.e., childhood—I have lots of it blocked out because, probably, of its unhappy nature."

⚥ "I can't evoke any sexual memories from early childhood, not even seeing other kids naked. I always hated locker rooms, I suppose because I was ashamed of my scrawny nonathletic body. Though sometimes I'd go swimming with my father and brother and that was pleasant. Sometimes we would shower or bathe together, the three of us. It was a pleasant experience. I never saw my mother naked and definitely felt there must be something disgusting about her body, for why else would she hide it so thoroughly?"

⚥ "I don't now remember that in my childhood I much noticed or responded to attractiveness in either males or females, and I hardly, if at all, thought about sexuality as such. I do remember rather furtively observing the Greek nude statues at the Met and being vaguely disappointed that the cocks were broken off."

Childhood Sexuality

Childhood sexuality is not all feelings and longings. Very often, it is action, some of it occurring at a very young age. Recalling their sexual experiences as little boys, many of the men remembered physical sexual play, often involving "adult" sexual acts beyond realm of exploratory "doctor" games. Such prepuberty experiences involved other little boys much of the time, but sometimes the experiences included older boys and even grown men:

⚥ "My first homosexual experiences, long remembered, enjoyed, and later worried over as I reached the age of first confession, were playing 'Smokehouse' or 'Savages' with a neighbor boy about two years older—I must have been 5 at the time. The games involved grabbing each other's genitals rather roughly and were done in an outbuilding next to the garage with much pleasure on both sides."

⚥ "With my circle of childhood friends, we all played around together. When I was 8, this kid next door, who was 13, caught me in the woods with his younger brother. I thought we were in for it. But for months afterward, the 13-year-old and I would go off in the woods together, or sleep out in a tent, and we'd spend hours feeling, kissing (never on the lips, I remember!),

sucking, until one day I felt guilty about it, like I was going to hell or something, so I broke it off.''

⚭ "I can remember in earliest days being asked by another boy to suck him. Whenever we little boys wrestled, I had a sexual response which sometimes led to boyish sex play and experimentation. By the time I was in the third grade, a friend and I did just about everything. We were fortunate enough to have corn fields nearby that provided the necessary privacy for fellatio, masturbation, and anal intercourse. In fact, my first orgasm came while I was 'in' my friend. What an experience!''

⚭ "I was taught by an older cousin, age 10, to masturbate when I was 8 years old. He and I played with each other well into our teens. From him I learned my favorite position—interfemoral intercourse (between the legs). I loved being fucked that way (and still do) and it is my favorite way of coming. I tried every boy friend I had from third grade on to see whether or not they would jack off with me. Many would, but most would not. Somehow I felt guilty about my sex life from third grade on, but the guilt never slowed me down—until I started seminary at age 21. Then I only masturbated for three years.''

⚭ "I was a very sexual child. I remember masturbating at age 5; I lulled myself to sleep manipulating myself. At age 9, I entered a private school and we all jacked each other off, sucked each other, tried to fuck each other. It was more experimental than sexual. As a child of 7 or 8, I used to get highly stimulated thinking of my parents having sex or anyone else having sex.''

⚭ "During even my earliest childhood years, I can remember being fascinated with the bodies of all the older males (males older than myself) that I came into contact with. Males who had reached the age of puberty held a special interest for me. When the older boys and young men sought a fast blow job, I made myself available (I had a knack for being in the right place at the right times). They all felt that I was too young and too naive to understand exactly what was happening; but I *always knew precisely* what was going on, because they were being manipulated by me to do exactly what *I* wanted in the first place.''

⚭ "As a child I was an adult molester.''

⚭ "I've had sex since I can remember—6 years old and on. Two babysitters played with me and I learned about masturbation from them; I remember I enjoyed their playing with me and my playing with their—to me—enormous penises. Another boy and I had an active sexual life from the time we were about 9 or 10 until we went to different colleges.''

⚭ "I had one sexual experience as a child before I came out. It happened when I was 9 years old and staying overnight with a good friend. We slept in the same bed and talked about sex with girls (what little we knew). Soon he asked me to fuck him. I did not know what he meant, so he said he would do it to me. He unbuttoned my pajamas and his. Then he started kissing my body, starting at my nipples and working his way down to my pants. After

that, he lay carefully on top of me and rubbed his penis against mine. It felt good, although we were not old enough to be able to have orgasms. After five minutes, he got off me and I reciprocated. It was a valuable experience for me in childhood sexuality, and I was glad that it happened."

⚢ "My mother had a young cousin hitchhiking through the western U.S. when I was 9 or 10. We had a meal or two with him and drove him some distance. I remember sitting in the back seat with my hand on his thigh and I knew I loved him."

⚢ "Growing up I think I had an active healthy sex life and it was mainly with boys my own age. We ran around nude in the woods a lot. There was an older guy that used to get me to pay him to let me feel his cock."

The "older guy" referred to in the last quotation would probably qualify in the popular mind as a "child molester." A number of the men recalled incidents where they were "molested," though none of them used the term:

⚢ "When 11 or 12, I was seduced by a man in his 20s living with my parents. It was a little shaky at first, but after it began I realized I liked it. I can still remember his cock, his coming, my inability to put it in my mouth. I still get off on fantasy trips over it. (The man, since married, moved to Cape Cod, has three sons, and is a successful businessman. He writes my father every year. I tell my father to send a very warm special hello back to Dick!)"

⚢ "I lived on a farm. We were trying to harvest some *perfectly* cured hay before the predicted rain next day, so all hands were working by moonlight. I was on front of the haywagon, driving the horse team. I was lying down on my back with my legs bent to the side so that my crotch was exposed. One of the hired hands, a young boy of 19, working near me, came and gently and quietly lay on top of me for just a moment. There was no movement. Just the warmth of our two bodies and his warm breath plus the fullness of his crotch pressed against mine. I was young, perhaps 9 years old, and innocent—but I liked the feelings I got from his body. No words were spoken."

⚢ "I now realize that I had a great many sexual feelings as a child. My earliest recollection of any kind of sexual feeling (I wasn't aware of it at the time but now recognize it as such) was when I was somewhere around 5 or 6 years old. I was outside playing, alone for some reason, when a man of about 20 or so came out to me. He was dressed in an army uniform and his hair was cut fairly short. He began asking me what I was doing, who I was, where I lived, my age, and other questions in a sort of 'small talk' way that made me feel like he was just being a nice person and not a nosy adult. He didn't talk down to me or anything, and was very pleasant. He asked me if I would like to go for a walk with him and, even though I had been told all of the usual stories about strangers, I knew that this man would not harm me. We walked for a few minutes, until we came to a field of high grass. There

were a few boxes that had been thrown away which he flattened out and arranged for us to sit on. He resumed talking in very general terms, about the weather, did I go to school, etc., while he rubbed his crotch.

"Before long whatever he was rubbing in his crotch must have moved because now, he was rubbing a rather long, thick lump along his thigh. After a few more minutes he asked me if I had ever 'seen a man's prick.' I replied that I hadn't and he offered to show me his. Since I didn't know what the word meant, and was curious about what it was he was talking about, I said that I would like to see it. It did not take more than two seconds for him to whip it out and show it to me. I was amazed that his penis was so huge and told him so. He asked if he could see how big mine was. I hesitantly took out mine, which was very hard and felt a little funny. He took it between his thumb and index finger and rubbed it up and down and said, 'Don't worry, someday yours will be as big as mine. Maybe even bigger.' He took my hand and placed it upon his cock near the base. The tips of my fingers felt his pubic hair, and my elbow felt the head of that huge cock bobbing against it. It must have been at least 9 inches long, and I could just barely encircle it using both hands. He asked me if I like licking lollipops, to which I replied yes. And he then asked if I would like to lick his prick as if it were a lollipop. I said yes and he leaned back on his elbows with his cock pointing skyward. I got up onto my knees, bent over, and began licking at the head of his cock. I can still recall the musky odor and salty taste of that beautiful tool. After I worked on him for a few minutes, he offered to lick mine. I lay down and he slid his ass past my head until his face was even with my crotch. He then took my hand and again placed it on his cock and told me to squeeze it as hard as I could. I remember the feel of his warm wet mouth as it encircled my cock and balls and the wonderful feeling of his gentle sucking. I squeezed his cock hard and began moving my hand up and down the way he was when his cock was still in his pants.

"He sat up abruptly and told me to start licking his cock again. 'If you lick it fast enough, it will give you some milk, just like a cow,' he said. Being skeptical, I just had to see this. So I ran my tongue up and down and all around his enormous prick. He pushed my hand away just as a stream of thick white 'milk' spurted out. 'See,' he said, 'would you like to taste it?' I said that it didn't taste like milk and I told him no. He offered to try to make mine give milk but something about what happened had scared me for some reason and I told him I had to go.

"He walked me to the edge of the field and asked if I could find my way home. Since I knew my way, I said yes I could. He said thanks and gave me a quarter, which I thought of refusing ('Don't take money from strangers; they'll make you do bad things'). But I decided to take it, since this man was leaving and he wasn't going to do anything bad to me. He was nice. I took the quarter and we walked off in different directions.

"I never saw him again, even though I went back to the same spot several times. And I didn't have another sexual experience until I was 14. But I remember having a very pleasant feeling about that man. I suppose

that if I told a Freudian analyst about this experience he would say that it caused me to 'become fixated at the latent stage of your psychosexual development' and therefore was the cause of my homosexuality. But I don't believe that is the case. I know now that there were many feelings that I had before this that were indicative of my future sexual needs, as well as many afterward which I doubt very much were influenced by that one isolated incident.

"As for now, I don't want to have sex with young boys, and I don't much care for men who do. I feel that children should be free to experiment with their sexual feelings with other children even up to several years' age difference. And I feel it's okay for a teenaged boy to have sex with a man in his young 20s. But not an adult with a child."

Only a small portion of the men had a sexual experience at such an early age, as prepubescents. Puberty, however, is by definition the time of sexual maturation (the term comes from the hairs that appear at this time in the genital region), and many of the men reported that their first sexual experiences occurred during puberty or adolescence. Again, the experiences occur with peers as well as with older men:

⚥ "Had a real neat relationship with a guy a year older than I when I was 12. We sang in the choir together and had frequent oral sex—choir rehearsals gave us an excuse to be away from our homes for extended periods without raising suspicion. We continued to have sex regularly until I entered the navy in World War II."

⚥ "My gay urges emerged when I was in the seventh grade in school. I seemed to specialize in ministers' sons for some reason. This no doubt reflected a spirit of rebellion. Perhaps it was like farting in church. I started with a Nazarene minister's son, then graduated to a Methodist minister's son (my own church)."

⚥ "When I was very very young I had terrible crushes on older men—in their 20s and 30s. I lived in a small town on the south shore of Long Island out about 65 miles from New York, and let me tell you everybody, and I mean everybody, had active sex together. When I was like 15 I had a thing going with three brothers. They were probably 23, 26, and maybe 30 at the time. We used to go in their car to the docks and they would blow me and I would blow them. We never discussed it as 'gay' or anything but we really did the game. I was always in love with a good-looking older man and the more virile the more I was in love. Many times I would have sex and often with what we would call straight men. And more than often they would do everything. A school principal seduced me when he drove me home from a soccer game while I was still in grammar school. He took me in the woods in his car and told me a dirty joke and then felt me and before we were through we both went down on each other. He had an uncircumcised penis and it had a strong odor and I really didn't like doing him but it was very exciting and I saw him many times. He sent two or three older friends over to me as

time went by. I have no interest in younger children and feel older men should leave them alone to decide their own thing as they will. I do not feel abused by the principal because I already was gay even though I didn't really know what it was all about. I believe everyone finds his thing and no one could influence me either way if I didn't want it myself. Nevertheless, I would not touch a kid or care to in any way.''

⚥ "When I was in seventh grade, in San Diego (Claremont), Calif., I and two friends went into one of the numerous undeveloped canyons. We three stripped and neatly folded/piled our clothes in a hollow niche, inside some trees and bushes. A hill there was known to us as the White Cliffs of Dover. Now totally nude, we three climbed to the hilltop several times, and using cardboard on our bare bottoms, slid down the hill and climbed back up. At one point somebody decided it would be fun to beat the other two back to the clothes and hide them. Troy ran for the clothes and Mike and I gave chase. We caught him in the bushes, and the three of us wrestled each other to the ground, grappling and masturbating each other. We ended up masturbating and sucking each other off. We walked back toward our houses, three abreast, holding hands, until we came to an area where we thought someone might see us. Then we started playing a seventh-grade version of three macho guys. P.S.: Honest to God this is a true story.''

⚥ "I had a crush on my seventh-grade teacher when I was in school and my best friend did too. Ray made it with him a lot of times, and it wasn't his idea either. I mean the teacher seduced him. I was so jealous and frustrated; you wouldn't believe it. This guy was 27 at the time and the real athletic type. Had a wife and three kids, but had a real thing for little-boy chicken. In fact, just chicken in general, because he was making it with this seventh-grade girl in my class, too.''

⚥ "My first sexual experience in the full sense was at 17, with a mature man, a priest, who could understand my conflicts. I needed this experience. As long as homosexuality is prohibited, I think sex between boys and older men will be necessary in order to instruct the boys. Another 17-year-old could not effectively have explained to me that my feelings were all right. I needed to hear this from someone with more authority.''

Pain and violence are prominent in the recollections of some early experiences with sex. When experiences are of this type—rather than the exuberance, even lyricism, of some of the others described above—the impact on the youth can be very negative:

⚥ "When I was 12 I was spending several weeks with my cousin in Beverly Hills. Her girl friend invited us over to go swimming in their pool and it was then that I met the girl friend's 18-year-old brother. From the moment I first saw him I never wanted to leave him. The girls left us in the pool and went shopping. He suggested we lie in the sun and in a few minutes he put his hand inside the leg of my trunks, felt me, and said, 'I like little cocks.' For the next week he had all the little cock he could handle. It wasn't

just sex: he took me places and we did things together, and all the time as much in love as two high school seniors. It all came to a crashing end, however, when he took me hiking in the Santa Monica Mountains. About noon we ate our packed lunches and rested, then he began to undress me (not unusual), but he insisted on fucking me. I had never tried it before, so said okay. When it began to hurt I asked him to stop, but he wouldn't. I started to cry and managed to get away from him and get dressed. As I was crying and pulling on my clothes, I remember saying, 'If you really loved me you wouldn't have hurt me.' I never saw him again after we got home.''

⚥ "My childhood experiences or sexual feelings towards adults mainly aren't what I could say were the best for me, as at the age of 13 years, I was raped and forced into having sex with an older guy. I was also beaten as I was trying to get away from being raped and forced into having sexual attempts with someone I didn't know or want to do it with. And I hated it all. I just hope other small boys don't have the same thing happen to them as I did at age 13. And I still have nightmares about that time and experiences. I also don't think younger homosexual boys should have anything to do with sex. This is how I feel.''

There are times, however, when youthful sexual longings do not lead to overt acts. The result is often frustrating, as the following example indicates:

⚥ "My first childhood crush was on a fellow classmate in high school. It began in my freshman year. He was a farm boy (this took place in Iowa) and I was a city boy (small town of 1,200). At that time, he had a physique that I admired. It showed through his clothing. But there was something unusual about him in his personality. He never played baseball with the guys or participated in any of the activities the guys did. I never heard it in so many words, but it was hinted at that he was gay, because he also played jumprope with the girls during recess. That was okay in my eyes, but it made it more difficult to get close to him.

"In the summer of '63 right after I got my driver's license and before school started in late August or early September, I invited him to go to Cedar Rapids one sunny Sunday afternoon and goof around.

"In the midafternoon on the way back home, he asked me to take off my T-shirt, to get some sun, he said. Out in the country he started to take off his clothes and got down to his shorts. We then pulled off onto a dead-end farm lane and played strip poker.

"The strip poker later continued at my home, where I took some pictures of him in various states of undress, but he wouldn't let me take one of him in the nude.

"Later that year, the weekend of John F. Kennedy's death, which turned into a three-day weekend for school kids, I asked him if he'd like a rubdown with rubbing alcohol, which he accepted. This was the first time in my life (at 16) that I was able to touch and rub another guy, and one that I

admired the most at that time. It was all I could do to muster up enough courage to offer him a rubdown, let alone do anything overtly sexual with him after I got him naked on my bed. I was afraid how he'd react and what he'd say at school, if he wasn't gay. Looking back, after all the massages I gave him, I marvel at my self-control.

"Four years later at college in Iowa City, we returned to his dorm room after swimming. I lay on his bed in my swim trunks. He sat at his desk, with the chair turned to face the bed, with his feet resting on the edge of the bed. The topic of conversation escapes me, but I *pretended* to lapse into a state of sleep. He put his foot on my swim trunks on top of my penis and rubbed it back and forth until I ejaculated. (I don't know whether he knows I came or not; we never talked about it.) At that point I could have come out and probably brought him with me, but never did. He's probably at least bisexual, because four years later he married. The after-swimming scene was the closest I ever came to having a reciprocating sexual encounter with him."

Opinions on Childhood Sexuality

The men were generally very supportive of free expression of childhood sexuality, and many said that good sex education was both desirable and necessary. There were varied perspectives on whether sexual contact with adults was helpful or not:

⚥ "I know from my own experiences that children can have very strong drives at a very early age. It's when you don't let a child express himself sexually that hangups come about. However, I feel, now, that this desire for sexual expression should be given freedom, but channeled so that he expresses it with another of his own, or near own, age. I enjoyed having sex with adults, but never felt as free or as happy as when having sex with boys my own age. You can answer their questions honestly without having to show them how to do it with an adult. Let them enjoy discovery together. In my work I have been approached by boys wanting sex with me, but have turned them down with love. One 10-year-old came into my bathroom one night as I was showering. He slid open the shower door, pulled down his pajamas, and asked if I would like to suck his dick. I told him that I didn't have to do that, that he knew I loved him, and I bent over and kissed his forehead and give his little firm butt a smack with my hand. He pulled up his pajamas, said, 'I love you too,' and went off to bed (probably with another boy, but so what?). Have to admit, though, that I was tempted and have been on more than one occasion."

⚥ "I feel good about childhood sexuality, and ripped off that I grew up in such a repressed time and environment. Today, I feel very good about young children having sex, and I feel good about having sex with young children. Anita Bryant be damned."

⚥ "I've never had sex with a child (since being grown up) and haven't the slightest desire to do so. But I do care about children and don't want any of

them to suffer as I did. It is for this reason that I'm in the gay liberation movement.''

œ "I never had sex with man or woman until I was 21. I spent years alone with my own thoughts of sex with another man. How I wish I had been 'seduced' by somebody sooner than that. I feel very strongly that young gays need more positive and enlightened support. They are often exploited and cast aside by the gay community. Young boys present a very touchy issue to most gays . . . and a thorn in the side of every backslapping liberal. It's Anita Bryant's 'bread and butter' issue.''

œ "I had no overt sexual experience of any kind during my childhood. Indeed, I was not even aware that such a thing as sex existed. My family never talked about it, and neither did the other children I grew up with. I think parents should be completely open with their children about all aspects of human sexuality.''

œ "I believe young boys 13–15 are very sexually oriented, only inhibited by lack of opportunity and fear of rejection or being put off by their peers.''

œ "Forcing a child into sex is completely reprehensible, and should be punished by having Anita Bryant hung around the offender's neck until they are both dead.''

œ "I believe that every child will find his own sexuality in his own way, as I did, no matter what barriers are put up by people like Anita Bryant. Nature will find its own way. I also believe that it's beautiful when children find sexuality among themselves, as I did, even when sexuality is impossible, and only love exists. What else is there that can be more beautiful than that? I realize that there is a lot about the porno business that I don't know. If a boy is employed as a slave, I'm against it. But if he really enjoys his way of making money, I'm all for it.''

œ "The most blatant sign of the utter sickness and depravity of our society is the frantic, almost psychotic, repression of its young people, and nowhere is this repression more apparent than in the area of sexuality. Let me say that it is my belief/opinion that children should be absolutely *free* (notice I didn't say *encouraged*) to experiment among their peers with whatever form of touch-communication that is consonant with basic ideas of respect for other people.''

œ "I believe that the liberation of ideas about children's sexuality will be the major sexual liberation area of the next couple of decades. I think it is about time that children's sexuality was recognized to exist.''

œ "I definitely think that all young guys should be urged to try homosexual sex. This would be a wonderful way for them to satisfy the pent-up sexual drives that are present in most young men.''

œ "Homosexuals who accept positions of teaching or counseling of teenagers should understand that they're in a position of trust, and should be able to control their lust for boys and not molest them sexually.''

œ "I feel very, very strongly that children should be exposed to the

picture of sexuality openly and with a healthy attitude so that they can understand the early feelings they have and so that they can be free of the terrible hangups which spring from the assiduous hiding of all things sexual from the sight of children. I think that children should not have to feel guilty about prepubescent exploration and experimentation, but should be given information and preparation to be able to make sense of it and make sound decisions about it.''

⚢ "Chicken hawks are exploitative. A guy has to be over 18 to have it together well enough to deal with gay sex's volatile emotions.''

⚢ "I would rather see an older person break a child into sex than to see an adult break into mental breakdown the first time they experience sex. Raping children or forcing them is wrong to me.''

⚢ "I would not encourage direct sexual involvement between adult and minor; yet I do not think such involvement should be criminal either.''

⚢ "Laws are made by people, mostly arrogant and wrong-headed people. I'm an unrepentant anarchist, and the law is no more sacred to me than the flag or the President or the Pope. Relations between the ages should be free, as well as between sexes and among the same sex. At any age.''

⚢ "I don't have any recollections of personal childhood sexuality, except for once when I was about 6 or 7. I had an erection while I was taking a bath and I asked my mother if there was something wrong (she's an RN). She told me that it wasn't good and that if it didn't go down, I'd have to wear a gold box to keep my penis in, like some old men. I'm not sure, now, just how much of this I believed, but the subject never came up again, until in high school, when I was lectured on how it was unhealthy to masturbate. (My mother again; my father was too embarrassed.) The discussion arose from soiled sheets. I believe that as children become aware of their own sexuality, of their sexual selves, the knowledge and guidance of others should not be denied them. Sex, even nudity, should not be hidden or secret. It is not dirty, nor should it be treated as such. It can be beautiful. If children can be brought up in a healthy sexual environment, I'm sure there will be less violent sex, rapes, VD, abortions, unwed mothers, child abuse, divorce, etc. Sex entails responsibility and if it's hidden, so is the responsibility.''

Incest

Although incest is one of the strongest taboos of Western culture, it is not really surprising that it exists nonetheless. After all, intimacy and love are first experienced in the family environment, and sex can be an extension of that intimacy and love. Incestuous relations, however, especially between adults and children, can and do have elements of abuse, power-tripping, and even violence. No statistics on incest are forthcoming from the survey, as the question was not presented in the short-answer format, but many of the men had comments and experiences to share. None of the experiences

involved acts of actual father-son incest, but there were a number who reported having incestuous feelings toward their own fathers:

⚤ "I had a desire to cling to my father and enjoyed seeing him in underwear, though it 'disturbed' me. He told me facts of life in seventh grade and all I could think about was being naked with *him* and holding him. I would go into his closet and get his jockstrap. It fascinated me but I didn't know what to do with it."

⚤ "My childhood crushes included almost every man that walked, my father in particular. I can recall being very small and running after him as he went to work, and feeling a sexual response in my groin as I ran."

⚤ "A very dim memory of very early childhood was when I would go to the laundry basket and get out my father's used underwear. I'd put them over my head and be in ecstasy. I was never found out, even though I knew it was 'wrong' somehow. I now have no attraction or repulsion (fetish) for underwear. I wanted to see, touch, and feel my father's body."

Some of the gay men who are fathers describe their sexual feelings and experiences regarding their own offspring; again, none of the men reported having sex with his son, though undoubtedly such relations do occasionally occur:

⚤ "I generally avoid very young men. In relationship to my own son and daughter, I do have sexual feelings, as they do, also. My son used to explore my body when we awoke in the morning and is still remarkably affectionate and caressing. I never follow the erotic potential of those moments. I was in a community in Arizona of feminists and faggots, many of us parents, where we examined the incest taboo. My personal conclusion is that in my life the power of sexuality has been so great that in almost every relationship which is very sexualized my danger instincts go way up. There need to be some places in life which are Highly Safe. When sex is so volatile and children's power compared with adults so fragile, I prefer not to mix the two. I feel like they need a safety zone, and that is what I prefer to be. I do/will encourage them to explore sexually with others when they trust and have sufficient privacy not to have to deal with social attitudes about childhood sexuality. (We cannot ignore that our culture is very hostile to child sex.) But I feel like we can be sensuous and loving without being erotic."

⚤ "When my own son was 15 or 16, he wanted to sleep with me several times, and in a single bed. I avoided the situation completely, horrified at the thought that indeed something of father-son sex might have come out of it. At the same time, I was attracted by the idea of it, if only because I love my son and I would love to be that close to him. But conventional bringing-up forbade me to consider it for a minute. As of today, I'm sorry. I would say that I do approve of boy-man sex *provided* that it is gentle, loving, and always and only considerate of the boy's welfare and development. (My

son, by the way, turned out to be depressingly straight—depressing, in that he seems to be attracted to the dreariest girls.)''

⚥ ''I love my sons but don't want to have sex with them or even with their friends, beautiful as they are.''

One man recalled his involvement with a young boy friend, and the boy friend's gay father—perhaps this qualifies as a kind of father-in-law incest:

⚥ ''In the seventh and eighth grades I met another boy who lived near the grade school. Both parents worked. We went to his house for lunch—and *dessert*! It was wonderful. One day I came over to see him and he wasn't there. His father was. He invited me in and offered me a bottle of pop and a piece of cake. He put on classical music and brought out male/female porno. I was very excited to see the men in the pictures, not the women. Before long, the father and I were in bed. We repeated this many times. I continued still to see my friend, who told me he never did anything with his father, but both knew that both had such interests in having sex with other men. (I was told the mother and sister knew nothing of this.) When I visited my friend in the eighth grade, the father had a night job and was home days, while the mother worked days. After school we'd come to his house and listen to music for a while, then repair to my friend's bedroom. His father always, said, 'Have fun!' as we went down the hall.''

Several of the men reported sexual involvement or feelings with uncles:

⚥ ''I was indoctrinated into actual homosexual activities by an uncle. He was 13 or 14 and I was 5 or 6. We were both nude as I recall. He wanted me to stick my cock up his ass, which I guess I did. I remember asking him to reciprocate and he said he was too large. I have often wondered if this was why I still crave getting fucked.''

⚥ ''As a small child (4–8 years) I had 'crushes' on my two younger uncles (ten years older than I). I enjoyed being with them, touching them, hugging them, bathing with them, kissing them, and they enjoyed me also. As I grew older I continued close relationships with each, but a less sensual one. They both married and have families. We still have warm feelings for each other and care what happens to one another.''

⚥ ''When I was in grade school I had a crush on a buddy of my older brother as well as my father's youngest brother, who was ten years older than I (18 compared to 8), who was the person initiating me into homosexual acts. After all, when you are only 8, a high school senior is a really big deal. My experiences with my uncle continued for several years, as he accompanied my family on our vacation trips, although I am quite sure my parents had no idea of what was going on at the time, nor did my brother or sister.''

⚥ ''Incest—if both partners are of age, then I feel it is all right. If some of my uncles wanted to fuck me, I would be in bed in seconds.''

While a number of lesbians recalled unpleasant experiences involving aggressive sexual behavior by their brothers (see Chapter 12), the men were generally positive about "brotherly love":

♇ "For many years I had a beautiful, passionate, and perfect relationship with my beautiful brother. It *was* wonderful. I thought that was the way brothers were, and still believe they should be . . . in love. Cocksucking, screwing, kissing, tumbling, happy—love. Both of us were married, but we continued. Our love was real. His touch made me quiver. His smile was everything. We traveled together, treasured our moments together. Then distance, the miles, came between us. We learned we were queer—and *bad*. 'It is awful to put your brother's cock in your mouth . . . to hold him . . . to cry with him . . . to smile with him.'

"*They*—society's wonderful gruesome *they*—kept it up and kept it up. Finally he gave in. Bit by bit. Until he wrote the letter: we would *not* be lovers. And he was gone. But I had lived and had known his strength and had held him close and warm on the side of the beautiful Colorado Rockies. I had been there and watched his lovely cock grow, watched his back, his arms, his person strengthen and become a man. We were close as his forehead pounded against my belly, feeling the roughness of his beard, running with him, watching the sweat bead on the back of his neck. Summer would come and go so quickly and we would find one another in passion night after night, time and time again. It was beautiful. You can call me names and decide I'm a 'pervert, a creep, a deviant.' But I'll tell you goddammit, you don't know. It is (was) beautiful. So I'm searching now. Standing there in the bar looking for someone, anyone, like him. A happily married man, a straight, handsome father who will be a brother."

♇ "A few months before my 12th birthday my brother, age 16, offered to jack me off. I said, 'I'm not old enough.' He said, 'Do you have hair down there?' I said, 'Yes.' 'Then let's go inside.' Inside the bunkhouse he said, 'Let's see.' I opened my fly and brought out my penis. He said, 'Take down your pants. It's better when you can see and feel everything.' When I was ready he jacked me off and I had my first orgasm. He jacked me off quite often after that, and then took me in his bed, mounted me belly-to-belly, put his cock between my legs in the crotch, had me hold my legs tight together, and fucked me between the legs. He fucked me that way regularly from then on. One morning I was in bed jacking off when my brother said, 'I've got something better for you.' He had me come over and fuck him between the legs, with my brother two years older than I lying there as an audience. After that my brother and I fucked each other regularly, usually with the middle brother lying in the bed watching. I watched my brothers fuck each other from my bed, but my middle brother and I never got together; actually, he was a smart-ass bastard and we didn't hit it off. My brother left home for a city job at 19 and married at 20. We've never mentioned our teenage affair but feel closer for it. I'm grateful to my brother for what he did to me and for me. He was completely without embarrassment about wanting sex with me. That it was homosexual incest

had no bearing. The emotional exchange between my brother and me during our homosexual relationship made it a rewarding, satisfying love affair.''

⚥ "I came out at 9 with a brother, five years my elder. He and his friends made me their blow boy. But I liked it. It got me attention. I blew them all the time, till my mom found out. They took me to a priest, who told them to beat me soundly, which my father did.''

⚥ "One of my fantasies is that I am half of a set of twins, and my brother is my lover. Were it at all possible, I would not sleep with my actual brother, but that's only because I can't stand him.''

⚥ "I had sex with my two brothers—years ago—wish it hadn't been so *furtive*. I knew two brothers who were lovers for seven years.''

⚥ "If you have a hunky brother and he's willing, why not?''

⚥ "My first homosexual encounter occurred at an early age, about 5 or 6. One day my brother, who was two years older, and I were playing in a field near our farm home. He asked me to lie down in the hayfield and told me he was gonna 'fuck you.' He asked me to pull my pants down and he lay on top of my back and buttocks and put his small penis in my anus. He whispered to me during the encounter, 'Does that feel good?' and it did.''

⚥ "Well, it may have been when I was 3 and my oldest brother was 5 going on 6. We were in our cribs supposed to be having naps. He got into my crib and told me to suck his wee-wee and he'd suck mine. There we were, having our very first 69, and of course our mother found us in this compromising position. She beat us savagely with the back of her hairbrush. I've been gay ever since and this is my earliest sexual memory. I swear it is true. My brother, who has fathered seven beautiful children, has forgotten the incident completely, I'm sure. I am positive he's never had a homosexual experience, probably never even a thought of it, in his adult years. For me it was basic and formative.''

A few of the men reported incestuous experiences or feelings toward females:

⚥ "I have fantasized sex with my mother and if she were alive now I know I would attempt or suggest sex with her. I would love to have sex with one of my sisters but have hesitated.''

⚥ "When I was about 4 my sister, about 8, gave me my first lesson in sex.''

⚥ "I would like one day to have sex with my twin sister.''

Some of the respondents expressed strong disapproval of incest, though opinions on the topic covered a broad spectrum:

⚥ "Incest is something which can only lead to tragedy, in my opinion, particularly in cases of sex between parents and children.''

⚥ "Vice is nice, incest is best? I'm not so sure. I've had sexual relations

for many years with my brother. If anything, it seemed to lessen our respect for each other. It could be that we were pretty fucked up while we were doing it. I think it's pretty normal for brothers to experiment. It can be beautiful. My concept of parenthood includes an inequality or a distance where one person (the parent) has domination over the other (the child). This doesn't seem like a good relationship or background for introducing sex. Maybe I'm old-fashioned.''

⚨ "Although I get highly aroused hearing or thinking of incest, all I can do when contemplating incest within my own family is laugh.''

⚨ "The taboo is strongly implanted in my mind regardless of whether it's gay or straight. I find the concept distasteful.''

⚨ "I really want to become lovers with my nephew (he's now 16 but I've loved him since he was 12). That's the closest family relationship that I could find permissible with incest—parent/child incest is beyond my comprehension.''

⚨ "I would like to try it. I don't see what the problem is. They say the kids come out crazy—I don't know if it's true or not. I do know I could (or could have) dug sleeping with my father and/or brothers. I think it would have brought us closer together.''

⚨ "My views are quite irrational on this; having first had sex with my brother, and knowing of several similar cases, there seems nothing wrong in this. Sometimes while masturbating I fantasize having sex with my own son, so it would seem that my subconscious doesn't reject that form of incest—but I find myself very negative at the thought of brother/sister, father/daughter, or mother/son incest. I would certainly reject any form of violence or coercion to bring about the incestual act. Provided that it is done from free choice, I suppose I'd say, again, to each his own.''

Out of the Closets

"Coming out" is one of those phrases from gay terminology that has made it into the common parlance of the English language. Actually, there's a double meaning to it—on the one hand, it's an abbreviation for "coming out of the closet," on the other, it's a play on high society's debutante balls, at which the young ladies of the wealthy elite "come out" into society. Indeed, old campy gay slang, now less common, includes "debut" (a first gay experience) and "debutante" (someone new to the gay life). A workshop on coming out is often held at gay conferences, rap groups to help those who are just coming out are sponsored by gay community centers, and coming-out stories are an easy, comfortable way for gay men to get to know one another. Just as college students ask, "What's your major?" at mixers, so at gay bars men ask each other, "How long have you been out?" (To the more sophisticated in each setting, of course, the questions are a bit cliché.) "Coming out" is a term embodying many levels of consciousness and action, from self-awareness to sexual activity.

In one of the essay questions, the men were asked several related

questions: *Tell us your experiences with and feelings about your sexual "coming out" and/or "being in the closet." At what age and under what circumstances did you first realize that you were homosexual or gay or somehow sexually "different" from other people? At what age and under what circumstances did you have your first homosexual experience, and how did you deal with it? Tell us about your sexual evolution from that first experience to now.* Several men wrote that we'd have to wait until they wrote their novels. One said, "You are asking for a book. Every gay person could write a book." Fortunately for the authors of this book, quite a few of the men did put their coming-out stories down on paper.

That sense of being "different" is the beginning—and quite a few men said that they did not "realize" that they were gay, but rather than they *always* knew it. Psychologists can and do argue about the age at which perception begins, or about how far back a person can remember.

The men perceived this essential "difference" mostly in their formative years, as can be seen by the following chart. This shows replies to the question *At what age did you first realize you were a homosexual or gay or sexually different?*

1–8	8%
9–12	31
13–15	29
16–19	16
20–30	12
31 +	1

The following are a sampling of these recollections:

♂ "In looking back, I recall at the age of 5 or 6 I went into the apartment of my kid friends who lived downstairs and walked by the open bathroom door where their father was shaving. I noticed his dark, almost black wavy hair and thought it was beautiful. I told my mother so. She scolded me for talking that way about a man. That was my first awakening that there was something taboo about expressing admiration for another male."

♂ "I think I always knew I was 'different.' When I was 14, I heard the word 'homosexual' on TV, found out what it meant, and things clicked. I was a homosexual. I began reading all I could find about it and became depressed. *Boys in the Band* did not help."

♂ "I probably first conceived of myself as different when my sister explained what a 'queer' was to me."

♂ "My first realization of being gay came after my first sexual encounter with a female. For a long time afterward I felt that it held no interest for me but my sexual awareness of other males kept growing. I was 19 years old. I have considered myself gay from that time on."

♂ "I first felt 'different' at age 6, when my mother commented that the woman in an Indian couple at a beach was beautiful—I remember thinking the *man* was far more beautiful."

♉"Though I imagine there were stirrings at a much earlier age, I can remember my first gym class in seventh grade (when I had moved from the grade school to junior high). The sight of naked and near-naked 'men' all around me—showering, dressing, undressing, horsing around, involved in athletic activities—was galvanizing. I sat rooted to the locker-room bench, my eyes must have been in serious danger of falling from my face (and anyone sufficiently 'in the know' could have pegged me instantaneously as eventually to become gay), and just stared at all the bodies around me. Future participation in gym classes saw me carefully capping my wonderment (literally, I had *never* seen a naked male before, other than my younger brother). And my study of my reaction to all those bodies convinced me, without knowing any of the labels which might be put to it, that I was somehow different from most of them. If *I* had not been very different, they all would have been openly staring and admiring each other; if they *were* doing so, it wasn't evident to me."

♉ "I first knew I was gay about age 4 or 5. I was looking through a family, decorating, or women's magazine and saw a picture of what appeared to be a nude man lying on a bare mattress. Some time later that same day, I told my mother I had seen a picture of a naked man in a magazine. She told me that was impossible. I swore I saw it and started leafing through piles of old magazines, looking for the picture, but couldn't find it. My mother insisted it was impossible because 'they only photograph women in the nude.' When I asked her why that was so, she told me it was because women were beautiful and men weren't. It was as if a giant chasm suddenly opened in the floor between us. I guess it's very difficult to be 4 or 5 and know your mother's wrong on a major point. The picture in the magazine, by the way, was a mattress ad. I've seen it since, and it was a definite come-on for housewives. The model had on pajama pants that must have been silk gauze. The late '40s were very hard-sell days."

♉"I realized I was sexually 'different' when all of a sudden the boys in my Boy Scout troop started paying me much more attention when they found out I sucked dick."

As some of the previous quotations indicate, perception of this "difference" is not necessarily linked to sexual acts. The men were asked, *At what age did you associate this "difference" with homosexual acts?* The chart indicates the responses:

2–9	5%
10–12	15
13–15	27
16–19	28
20–30	24
30+	3

The men were also asked, *At what age did you have your first homosexual experience?* The chart below shows the responses, indicating that most men acted on their sexual feelings in puberty and adolescence.

3–9	13%
10–12	13
13–15	24
16–19	22
20–30	22
30 +	2

Many of those first experiences have been covered earlier in this chapter, under "Childhood Sexuality." The following group of "first experiences," some of them taking place past adolescence, illustrate a variety of circumstances under which this important "initiation" can occur. Significantly, a number of men commented that despite negative feelings about their first time, they were able to return to homosexuality and develop positive feelings.

♂"I had my first overt gay experience with a roommate at summer school (age 14). We sucked each other off under the guise of acting out a scene from *Dionysius 69*. I felt frightened and ashamed and refused to speak to him for the rest of the summer."

♂"After struggling with obvious homosexual desires for nearly four years, fantasizing about men, wanting somehow to be 'freed,' I decided to take positive action. I called the Gay Liberation number listed in an underground paper. Two days later I had my first gay experience (with the guy who answered the phone and who later became my first 'lover'), and shortly thereafter I became active in the day-to-day activities of the Louisville Gay Liberation Front. A perfect coming out—into a healthy, liberating environment."

♂"My first homosexual experience was with a total stranger I met in a park. I didn't attach feelings of loving, caring, or being 'gay' to these first homosexual encounters."

♂"I had my first sexual experience with a man at the age of 23. It was around the same time I had my first complete sexual experience with a woman; in other words, I had been a virgin until quite late; and sexuality in general came almost as a surprise to me. I came out by being picked up while I was hitchhiking, and by being given a blow job. I tried to give one to the man who had picked me up, thinking that it was only fair and what he expected; but I gagged and he finished himself off, told me he was straight, and dropped me off at my destination. I don't think that it made an immediate impact on me psychologically, except that I decided that I liked the feeling of it. I hitchhiked in the same place a lot after that; and eventually someone told me the address of a gay bar."

♂"My first homosexual experience occurred exactly three years ago

today (August 3) at a 'Medieval Fair' given outdoors at 22nd and Spruce
streets in Philadelphia. (How's that for details?) The fair had been
recommended by a friend as something I might enjoy (I did). And it just so
happens there was a kissing booth with a sign that said, in front of the
female, 'for straight males and gay females,' and vice versa in front of the
male. Before that day I thought kissing booths were ridiculous. It took me
all day to get up the nerve to express myself but, just before I left, I did. The
male was gorgeous. Okay, so it was one simple kiss. It was the biggest
political statement of my life, and it was my first homosexual experience.''

Sexual evolution from a first experience can and does involve many
twists and turns. The men who responded to the survey were asked, *How
many years have you been a "practicing homosexual?"* As the following
chart indicates—and taking into consideration the ages of the respondents
(see Appendix)—the sample includes novices and veterans.

0–5	31%
6–10	24
11–20	24
21–30	13
30+	7

In the following statements, men describe their sexual evolution, some
with great detail, others only sketchily. The first of these were written by
men whose sexuality is primarily homosexual, that is, men who related
sexually to women only perfunctorily or not at all:

⚭ "Coming out (several stages) has been great. I'm now completely open,
a full-time faggot, as I say. It's just healthy in every way. I've always felt
sexually different, but I was 11 before I knew there was a word for it. I
expected the 'Bambi effect' (where the young males in spring all suddenly
turn their attention away from each other towards females with puffy
cheeks, red lips, batting eyelashes, etc.—where even Bambi and Thumper
don't need each other any more) because I read that homosexuality was a
phase for children to go through. Am still waiting for the Bambi effect.
First experience was when I was about 5, opportunity to play with a
brother's friend's cock—I dealt with it by playing with it, also showing him
mine, hoping he would show interest in it like I had in his, but the fact that
he didn't didn't deter me. Later I learned to feel guilty because of Church,
but that disappeared when I discovered some of my best friends are gay,
also after leaving the long arm of the Church. It cost me family
relations—they haven't rejected me, I just haven't lived near them for over
ten years, but it has been worth it. I'm more of an independent individual
than most are.

"Phase one: childhood sex with other children. Phase two: more child

sex (age 11 or so) but involving cocksucking and some effort at anal intercourse. Phase three: close friends in college came out to me and that led to some heavy sex, kissing, caressing, mutual sucking mainly, which was a whole new world. Phase four: park cruising in Indianapolis and Boston, largely because I feared involvement with bars, etc. would lead to exposure. Phase five: started going to bar, met first 'lover,' lasted six months as such, then continued bar cruising, mostly used bars to see friends, continued park cruising for sex. Phase six: second love, the big one, lasted three years, failed due to lack of communication and job split geographically, during which I continued occasional park cruising and spent a lot of time in the Harvard College library john. Lots of masturbation there, sometimes encounters. Peep holes were the turn-on. Phase seven: moved to small town, got into baths, trips to city regularly spending most of time in baths, met some friends, good sexual acquaintances, had them over to visit, met some people in small town, had some sexual relations with them. Phase eight: became gay and proud, lost guilt, got more sensuous, got more self-esteem and sense of attractiveness, started having more fun. Phase nine: where I am now—liberal, liberated, enjoying sex, hedonistic, outgoing, not selfish, looking for stable but sensible relationship, trying to scope out gay life in the city again and find my places . . . having a good time and looking forward to more.''

♂ "I didn't come out till the age of 38. In retrospect the fact that I waited so long seems fantastic and stupid. By 'come out,' I don't mean only that I told other people; I mean that I was finally able to admit *to myself* that I'm gay. It's not that I didn't have gay sex at an earlier age. I did. From the age of 21 on, I engaged in occasional homosexual acts. In retrospect, I can see that I carefully structured these so that they would be unsatisfying. I did this by keeping these experiences impersonal—pick-ups at the Y and so forth. Also by choosing sex partners who weren't particularly attractive. Thus I was able to tell myself, 'Well, that wasn't very satisfying. I guess I'm not a queer.' When somebody I knew made a pass at me—someone I could have a real relationship with—I always said no. I wanted desperately to say yes but somehow I didn't have the courage. I told myself that if he made a pass at me a second time, I'd say yes. Unfortunately that never happened. I never made a pass at any man till I became involved with the man who became my lover when I was 38."

♂ "I came out at age 20 while in college. I'd be sexually active in the summer away from home and school, but back in the closet during the school year. I would have preferred having more self-confidence at an earlier age to have been able to come out earlier. I'm very out now at age 28 and glad to be gay."

♂ "Being in the closet was a nightmare which lasted about ten years. A homosexual, in our family, was a butt of a joke, or a dangerous pervert lurking in schoolyards in Boston. (There just *weren't* any queers in Maine!) Since my sexual awakening at age 13, I knew I was gay, but I believed the lies, and it was something so evil, so unthinkable that I had to push it to the

back of my head, just not deal with it, and pretend to the world that I was
'normal.' I remember night after night, in bed alone, futilely pleading with
a God that never answered and doesn't exist, 'Why *me*?? Why *me*??' I
remember constantly lying in order to keep a front of heterosexuality
protectively between me and the heterosexual world around me. I remember
talking myself into love with a teenaged woman, but only carrying the
relationship so far in order to avoid anything sexual. Finally, at age 21,
after the army and before college, I lost grasp of the world, plunged into a
depression, and finally lifted myself out of it by coming out. Coming out
was an either/or decision for me: either go insane and live a miserable lie all
my life, or buck the system, outrage those around me, and be honest with
myself. Not having the political analysis nor the support of other gay people
available, it was a difficult decision, but I now know that I made the right
one—the only one.

"I always knew, even before puberty, that I was somehow 'different,'
but I didn't have the words or concepts to define it. As a child, I was the
'bookworm' type and hated sports, playing trucks etc. The things that little
boys do never appealed to me. I remember at age 6, asking my mother if
there was anything 'wrong' with me or if I was a 'sissy.' Sparing my
feelings, she answered in the negative, but I was soon to discover in school
that I was not 'like the other boys.' Luckily, I did have some things going
for me—intelligence and kindness—and made friends easily at that point.
My closest friends were girls, by the way. For a while I thought I wanted to
be a girl, but I realize now that that was because they were gentler, softer,
'nicer,' and they didn't present the threat that the boys did.

"I realized that I was gay at age 12 or 13; while other boys were watching girls, I was watching them. It wasn't the 'stage I was going through' that
I had hoped it was. And because of the homophobic society I learned very
easily to loathe myself.

"I had one homosexual experience while in the army, but that just
confirmed my 'sickness,' which had always been literally unspeakable. I
had never dared to talk with anyone about it. It was always there, just under
the surface, to be avoided like the plague, always burdening me down. After
the service and a bout with the Depression, I happened to stop at a highway
rest area and discovered a new facet. I found that men actually go there to
have sex with one another. Being so hungry to actualize my fantasies that I
had been having for years, I continued visiting them. The experiences I had
satisfied the immediate need, but always left me overwhelmed by guilt and
disgust. They only served to reinforce the idea that I was 'perverted.' The
men I 'met' there did nothing to convince me otherwise. They seemed as
furtive and sick as I felt; and they were somehow fearful that we would
make other-than-physical contact while sucking each other's cocks.

"This went on from January to August when I finally met someone at
the rest area who was an example of a gay man with a healthy self-image.
His example showed me that my life didn't have to be one of guilt, anxiety,
and loneliness, and that homosexuality was not 'abnormal' per se—that

there was more than the heterosexual way of looking at thing. A month after that, in September, I moved away to college, became acquainted with the local gay group, and soon after familiarized myself with gay politics. I came out publicly to my family (with the notable exceptions of my parents) and have been enjoying life ever since.''

⚥ ''First knew I was gay at about 15, but I was so naive that I didn't meet another gay person until I was 25, and I picked him up in church. What a lot of time I wasted! How sad! Today guys are more aware and there are so many ways to meet other gays. It is so much more out in the open today; there is no need for a young gay person to be alone.''

⚥ ''My childhood was quite normal. I went 'steady' with a girl when I was 14 and had the usual crushes and affairs through high school. I was a star athlete in high school and was thought to be very outgoing, but was inwardly very shy. I had absolutely no interest sexually in boys and did not masturbate until I was 16. My first homosexual experience occurred in the navy when I was 19 and I thought that the idea was horrifying. I was an enlisted man, and an officer, who was about 40, started to open my pants. I didn't believe what was happening and I pretended to become ill to end the scene. The incident bothered me very much. In college, after my discharge from the navy, I continued to date girls. But not with a great deal of enthusiasm. At a fraternity party I was cruised by a medical student and although nothing took place, I found the experience stimulating, but my straight upbringing would not allow my inward self to consider a sexual act with a person of my own sex. My total sexual outlet was from masturbation with very little use of fantasy—frequency ten or twelve times per week. Slowly through the years I began buying magazines featuring men and boys in various stages of sexual excitement, and I used these in my own sexual sessions.

''At 40, I became somewhat plastered one night and went to a local steam parlor. I think consciously I went to sober up, but I'm sure deep down I had heard stories about what went on in these places. I am good-looking, very athletic in build, and look ten years younger than I am. Within ten minutes in the steam I was invited to a private room and given a blow job that wouldn't stop. I found it very exciting, but I had deep guilt feelings. I went to these places about every three or four weeks, but could only do it after drinking. It took about a year for me to be able to blow a partner and slowly my feelings of guilt became less painful. I realized that the steam-room routine was totally impersonal and I have stopped using this outlet.

''My entire sexual outlet now is masturbation by a sophisticated vibrator and dildo technique while watching male movies or photographs. The technique is very satisfying, but I would very much like to have a sincere warm body next to me.''

⚥ ''From a scared little queer to a proud individual who follows a gay life style. That has been the progression and I hope it never ceases.''

⚥ ''I always accepted my gay feelings, but felt that I lived in a world

which would call me a 'dirty pervert.' I came out in the furtive dormitory rooms of a New England prep school where 'dirty guy' was the attitude. Then, soon after, in the Merchant Marine where the attitude was very sentimental (lovers were treated with awe and respect, but God help the 'femme' if he was known to 'sleep around'—he quickly became ship's whore and was up for grabs, rape, etc.—but that's another story, and I'd rather not dwell on it).''

♂ ''I was in the closet for 27 years and miserable much of the time, at least a part of me was. I suffered with my secret for years telling no one. Eventually I attempted suicide as my self-image and respect were very low. This was followed by two years of psychotherapy which was helpful in many ways but not positive about my sexuality. I had to get that together myself once I had worked out aspects of my twisted per-sonal/emotional/self-image. Before I came out I recall I was very shy and introverted, afraid that my appearance and behavior would give away the fact that I was homosexual. I first realized my sexual attraction to men early in puberty and thought it merely an aberration that would eventually straighten itself out. My first sexual experience was in secondary school with one of my classmates. Not very satisfying and not repeated. I had a few other sexual experiences subsequently but with great guilt feelings associated. Acquired Edmund Bergler's *Homosexuality: Disease or Way of Life* at the age of 23, which convinced me I was a psycho or a pervert for sure. I figured the only honorable thing to do was total sexual abstention, which I did for years—until the pressure and shame and misery became too great and I tried suicide, which failed. And then I ended up in therapy. That took two years. Then two more years of maintaining and then finally gay liberation arrived and I smashed down the closet doors. Got involved in gay politics for several years with the xenophobia of the newly converted. Subsequently I have mellowed and live my life as I am most comfortable, neither denying nor advertising my gayness—jut being me.''

♂ ''I will discount childhood experiences with boys because the culture I was reared in, the Frontier-Mormon subculture, was so malignantly homophobic that I was isolated nearly from the first. I was sexually aware very young and as I picked up the little bits of information here and there that led me to the knowledge of what I was, I was simultaneously being subjected to a very damaging imprinting as a sissy, queer, and so on. My family nickname was Girly. This grew out of my love of books and drawing pictures and other unacceptable things. By the time I was free of that en-vironment there was no chance of responding normally to another male. When I was 21 years old, a very patient and kind man brought me out with infinite care, and it was wonderful. I was in love with him, and happy to be able to kiss and hold a man. The affair did eventually become sexual and although I tried, I was unable to accept that. I was to need a few more years before I could undo what had been done in those early years. I am now at home with my identity but I wish it had been easier. The pain and fear of that harmful early life led me to alcohol and drugs as a way of getting

through. That's doing it the hard way, and everyone can do without jails and emergency stomach pumps and mental hospitals. I want more than anything for the new generations of homosexuals to miss that.''

♂ "I knew I liked guys before I knew what the word 'faggot' meant or that being gay was supposed to be wrong. I figured I could hide it while in school. The pressure intensified in junior high school. Went on maybe two or three dates to prove myself . . . a fool. My pot-smoking friends from eighth grade turned into redneck monsters in ninth grade. They somehow knew (suspected) I was gay. Had many threats, even on my life. Seriously considered suicide. Then, when I was 15, my mom took me on a trip around the country. I'd never known anything gay, so when I discovered some glory holes in bus stations, I was ecstatic. During that month I did it maybe five times in public toilets. The next fall, in November, I heard about the group Gay Youth of D.C. and went. My parents didn't want me to go to the meetings because if I were to start changing it might 'keep me gay' permanently. I kept going anyway. It took me a long time before I felt right about my gayness. Went to my first disco gay bar in March and freaked out; it was the best time I'd had in years. I started listening to disco music and went to the bars as often as possible, always with the threat of being carded. During the summer of 1976, Gay Youth went up to New York for the Gay Pride Day March. Incredible! I'd never seen so many gay people and decadence. I loved it! It really helped instill some 'gay pride' in me. Went to a back-room bar one night and just observed (fear of VD). The next day I went back . . . couldn't leave New York without tricking once! Things have been pretty steady since then.''

♂ "I think I first realized that I was gay and sexually different when I was in early adolescence. All of the kids in my class at school were awakened to sexual interests, and I was always silent. I knew then that what interested me was not the same. I talked with my older brother and told him that I thought I was interested in sucking penis. He scolded me, saying that I could be putting myself down. I learned not to talk about my feelings with anyone.

"It was at this time, when I was about 12–13 years old, that I had my first sexual experience. Me and another boy would stay in the music room during lunch hour at the junior high school I went to. We would often talk about sex. Finally, we started doing more than talk about it. One day we went back into the practice rooms and we blew each other. He had an older brother as well. His older brother heard about our carryings-on and decided that we should start a sex club. I never showed up. I stopped having sex with this other boy, all because I feared the consequences of my real sexual orientation coming out to my class. I learned that I might be a scapegoat, so I went back deep into my closet. From that time on, I was very much of a loner at school. I did have a few friends here and there, but was very anti-social. I knew exactly what the situation was and only hoped that I could make it through public school. After that I decided that I wouldn't go away to college because I might have to room with someone in a dorm, and they

might pressure me to be heterosexual, or might discover that I wasn't heterosexual. So instead I stayed at home and commuted to the university in the city. It was at this time that I started hustling. I would work in factories during the summer. One summer I worked in the steel mill. There were a number of gays there. I had sex for money on many occasions. The last week I worked there I received more compensation for sex than earnings from the company. I continued this pattern for several years. Finally I came out in 1968. I didn't receive any support for being honest. There were many attempts by my 'friends' to 'straighten' me out. I cannot forget these experiences, the way I was manipulated and discounted. I could write a book about it. I was very much into self-discovery and acceptance at that time. I dropped out of school and became a gay hippie. It was later, when I realized that all of my hippie friends were sexist and homophobic, that I finally rejected that lifestyle. I suffered a nervous breakdown and did not recover until I started to read gay-liberation periodicals. There was a Gay Liberation Front in Detroit; I finally got involved. It was through this involvement that I finally began to put the pieces of my life together. I met my present lover there at one of the rap groups. Those many rap groups were like a therapy for me; without them I doubt that I would have gotten as far as I have.''

⚥ "When I first became aware that I had gay feelings, I did not right off realize that this was a 'no-no.' Somewhere I had stumbled across the word 'homosexual' and realized that it applied to me. When I was about 12, I told my older brother that I thought I was a homosexual, and proceeded to tell him of the various boys and men I was attracted to. His reaction was the predictable horror and revulsion, and that was the first time I heard the words 'fag' and 'queer.' Needless to say I was mortified by his reaction, and from then on realized that I had to be ashamed of my gay feelings, and repress them at all costs. This was a lot harder to do than I had originally thought it would be. I kept getting crushes on older boys and men, I kept fantasizing about men when I did masturbate, and in the junior high and, later, high school gym shower rooms it was all I could do to keep from getting an erection. The only release I allowed myself was an occasional day trip to New York City (about 20 miles to the north). I had discovered earlier the porno book stores in Times Square. When I got so horny that I couldn't stand it, I'd invent some pretext for going to New York, and then at nighttime go from bookstore to bookstore, like a relapsed alcoholic going from bar to bar, only I was getting drunk on pornography. It was such a relief to let down the repressions just that much, and ogle openly naked, beautiful men. I got to be a real aficionado of porno, and learned which magazines had the hunky men (e.g., *Golden Boys*) and which didn't.

"I would never dare buy any porno, for fear that it would be found in my room, and after several hours of this, I would go back to the Port Authority building and catch the last bus home. I would then beat off, with the images of all those beautiful men in my mind. I still look back at those

crummy Times Square porno bookshops with tremendous nostalgia and good feelings.

"All this time that I was haunting the Times Square porno shop, I was still convincing myself that I wasn't gay. I was a repressed, uptight, scared-shitless, miserable kid. The effort it took to hide my feelings of loneliness, self-loathing, bitterness, guilt, and depression was extreme, but I did not want anyone to suspect that I was as fucked up as I was convinced that I was. I spent all my time trying to behave 'normally' and to conform, but the gay feelings would not go away.

"College was more of the same, only things got decidedly worse. I was expected to score with the 'chicks' and my value was judged by how much of a stud I was. I am not bisexual, I am exclusively gay, and thus I was pretty much of a wash-out as a stud. Again, I felt like a reject, and I was usually pretty isolated from others. It was an extremely painful period of my life.

"Then things really started getting serious. I started having fits of depression that were really scary. I have never been suicidal, and even during the bleakest of these depressions I didn't want to 'end it all,' but I really believe that during these spells of depression I was certifiably insane. The self-loathing and despair would turn up in volume to the point where they would completely immobilize me. If I had lived in the Middle Ages during that period of my life, I would have been convinced that I was possessed by a demon. Eventually, the depression would lift and I'd be able to behave in a reasonably normal fashion, but I always knew that another one would be coming. As the depressions got more intense and came more frequently I knew I needed some help. I tried first group therapy and then a shrink provided by the school, but I didn't dare tell anybody even then that I thought I was gay. The group therapy was totally unstructured; one of the members, a chubby, delicate boy eaten up with guilt and self-hatred, confessed that he was gay, and it was like throwing a lamb to a pack of wolves. After what I saw the group do to him, I was damned if I'd bring up my own gay feelings.

"Surprisingly, when things were at their bleakest, I suddenly just got better. Nobody did it for me, I just realized, I guess, that I had a choice of either really going off the deep end or getting my shit together. The periods of depression decreased dramatically in both frequency and intensity, and I began finding it easier to relate to people. I was still insecure and uptight, but at least I was able to get some grip on reality. However, by the time I graduated from college, I had still not had a sexual experience with a man or a woman.

"After school, I became an officer in the navy and was stationed in San Diego. Again, it was made plain to me that homosexuality was not going to be tolerated by any means, and that any queer caught in the act would get his ass kicked out of the service with a dishonorable discharge. The navy was not an enjoyable experience, but it was an improvement over college. I

made some good friends there, and I had my first really serious crush. There was a fellow officer there, named Phil, who was a few years older than I. He was a truly beautiful man, very handsome, with a great build, and an extroverted, dynamic personality. Nobody gave him any shit, and he was always in control. Phil more or less took me under his wing, showed me the ropes, and became a close friend. Sexually, I wanted him more than I had ever wanted anybody else, but he was completely straight, and I kept my gay feelings to myself. We were always just 'buddies,' and if he ever noticed anything more than platonic in my attachment to him, he never let on. Phil did have an ego, and I think it flattered him that I was so obviously enamored with him.

"While in the navy, I found it increasingly hard to ignore my gay feelings. Stationed on board a ship in a contained, compact environment of just men, I found myself getting hornier and hornier. After Phil was released from active duty and went back to Hillsborough (he was also rich), I felt somewhat at a loss, and more vulnerable.

"Finally, one night, while driving down a road by the harbor in San Diego, I noticed a bar a lot of people were streaming into. I don't know how, but I intuitively picked up that it was a gay bar. I filed this away for future reference, but did not act on it at the time.

"Shortly after that, I somehow got my hands on a gay newspaper. I saw advertised a bar in Hollywood where there were nude male go-go dancers. I immediately became interested, and that Saturday I drove the 100 miles up to L.A. and found the bar. It was like Times Square all over again, except that instead of two-dimensional stills, here were live, in-the-flesh men whom I could ogle openly. One dancer in particular was beautiful. He was older, around 35, but he had a body builder's physique and was very masculine. Others in the bar were just watching casually, or ignoring the show and cruising each other. This dancer could tell that my attention was riveted, and he started teasing me, dancing to me, grinding his hips in my direction and shaking his cock at me. I was so horny I was almost sick to my stomach. I drove home that 100 miles at 2:00 a.m. in a cold sweat.

"Next weekend I went to the bar I had noticed along the harbor, called the Club, grimly determined to get it on with a man. After about half an hour there I noticed a man in his middle 30s, not bad-looking, sitting alone, and I deliberately struck up a conversation with him, although I was nervous as hell. Things got rolling, and later a friend of his came up and we all started talking. Eventually, the inevitable proposition came, and scared shitless, I accepted. As I followed them to their house in my car, I was tempted half a dozen times to turn around, but kept on going.

"It turned out to be a pretty lousy introduction into gay sex. Both of these characters regarded me as some little bimbo they could have their way with and and then ignore. I was butt-fucked for the first time, and it was painful as hell. When I tried to carry out what I wanted, I was angrily rebuffed. In the final analysis, they were a couple of card-carrying pricks.

"Somewhat shaken by the experience, I didn't return to the bar, but

just went back to my old abstention. But the old feelings kept coming back and were even harder to deal with. We were overseas when I learned that I was up for an early out. At that moment, I decided, fuck it, I'm going to find some gay men again, and do it right this time. I normally would have been sent back to San Diego, my home port, to be processed out, but I requested Treasure Island, because I knew that San Francisco was where all the action was. Once there, I picked up a gay newspaper, located a nude go-go boy bar (I had had such a turn-on at the one in L.A.), and that night I went there. This time things worked out a little better. I met an attractive guy, who was a dancer there, though he was off that night; and eventually we went home together. I was somewhat fumbling and awkward that night, but we both reached orgasm, and it was a positive experience.

"Of course I had to deal with the old guilt feelings again; I didn't just calmly accept being actively gay. I went down to San Diego again and got a job as a teacher in a navy program (though I was civilian). This time I found out about the bars in San Diego and the other gay meeting places. However, I was still really fucked up in my attitude. I was scared shitless that someone would find out about my being gay, and I went through all these elaborate precautions, including cultivating a girl friend, to cover my tracks. I had always been taught that homosexuals were sick, degraded perverts, and you just don't throw out twenty-two years of indoctrination overnight. I felt contempt for other gays, and contempt for myself. The sex I had was mechanical and furtive. While I looked down on most gays, I felt very isolated and wanted to be accepted and at ease with the gay world. That did not happen while I was in San Diego, and I was just getting more and more depressed with me and my life.

"Finally, through a series of events I won't go through, I got an unexpected job offer in San Francisco. The change was dramatic. I began meeting gays who weren't fucked up or stereotypical, and I began to un-wind a little and make some gay friends. I felt better and better about myself and my gayness, and this just steadily improved. Anita Bryant pushed me into a considerably higher outlook. After the catastrophe in Dade County, I began to be active in the gay movement and join a number of gay organizations. The gay people I met there, men and women both, were intelligent, dedicated, sincere people, and I felt the old prejudices and indoctrinations in my head dying more rapidly now. It's a very exciting time of my life, and I'm beginning to feel my full potential for the first time. That's more or less where I stand now."

Perhaps nothing provokes the ire of gay activists more than the ac-cusation, by unsympathetic straights and even a few gays, that gay activists are "flaunting" their homosexuality. The model of the heterosexual nuclear family is all-pervasive, and the insistence on male-female coupling is learned at an early age. "Do you have a date?" "Did you get any nookie?" "Are you meeting any nice girls at college?" "When are you going to get

married?'' These questions, and the heterosexual model that is their foundation, are commonplace. If there ever was evidence of "flaunting" or "recruitment" or "proselytizing," this is it. In truth, this mere assumption of universal heterosexuality is very effective. Many gay men, ignoring or repressing their homosexual desires, embark on social lives embodying the heterosexual norm. Some men, no doubt, authentically feel heterosexual urges and act on them quite naturally. For other men, however, socializing and having sexual relations with women is largely a matter of facade in order to satisfy the demands of society. In the following group of quotations, gay men describe their sexual evolutions, each of them including sexual involvement with one or more women:

⚥ "When I came out it was the last step of a long and agonizing separation from a fairly good straight marriage which had reached a point where it served neither of our needs any longer. The separation involved many issues, a major one of which was my former wife's involvement in feminism and a side affair sexually which left me with full-time child care for our two babies, and almost no money or chance to earn any. My gayness was only a minor factor in this separation. Finally, however, desperate to have some activity or commitment outside the home (for I had truly become a house-husband if there ever was one, partly from my own lack of assertiveness and self-confusions), I contacted a university GLF group. Mind you, I had had only one homosexual experience, one year earlier, when I made this contact. But I walked into GLF and within two months I had bloomed into a person I felt more pride in than I had in ages. My closet was awful. I prolonged it as long as possible, forcing myself into straight marriages, once with a woman I scarcely knew and had only the most modest feelings towards, simply because I knew that if I let myself be alone and single I would end up being a 'homosexual,' which I perceived to be the worst of all possible fates. I never sought counseling, and kept my feelings of dread entirely to myself. When I met gay men or talked about them, I always projected a tone of pity: 'Oh, how sad that he can't hide it, or get it changed!' I have never had more than the most infrequent sexual fantasies involving women. However, my sexual life with my second wife was surprisingly good and for two years or more my homosexual fantasies went dormant. During the last years of that marriage, however, I frequently could only sustain sex with her by imagining she was a man and that my penis was in her ass rather than in her vagina. I could control my erection this way and prolong its duration so she always had full orgasm. Our sexual life, however, was reciprocal and I never felt it was my responsibility alone to satisfy her. We talked openly about our desires and inhibitions.''

⚥ "I had covert and unacknowledged homosexual experiences with friends in high school and with a roommate after college. After I got married, I had experiences once or twice a year until I was about 34. Their frequency increased over the next six years and began including baths, bars, etc. Then I had a brief affair in another city which was totally different from any previous experience—I fell in love for the first time. After I

separated from my wife as a result of this experience, I identified myself as gay and have been attempting to build up a group of gay friends. I lived with a lover for three months during the last year and decided not to do that again until I am very sure about the person. For now, I am open to gay experiences and go to bars about twice a week and have some pleasant times, but find that I do not yet feel a part of the 'gay community,' if there is one.''

&"I almost always realized I was different in some ways from other people—and I felt so damned unique! Because I was poor in sports, I sure felt marked and isolated! Then I was made to feel somehow special by a doting, worshipful mother who told me I was very special to her—typically, she was overprotective. This feeling of being special was further reinforced by the fact that nearly all the hired hands on our farm treated me very nicely—like a little prince.

"In college I had three male one-night stands and no sex with girls. These three sessions caused me much grief—I struggled to forget the fact that they had really happened. I would not accept the fact that I might be a (horror of horrors) homosexual.

"As far as my earlier years, I recall the time I was 7 or 8 harvesting hay, working with a 14-year-old orphan boy that my grandparents had for farm labor. He frightened me a trifle. He seemed somewhat ominous. He and I were on the barn floor alone one afternoon and he had me play the game of bitch dog and puppy. Yes, I was the puppy. He took off his overalls (that's all he had on) and I was to nibble and suck on his nipples. It seemed silly, but I did it. After a while, he told me to suck on his 'big nipple.' Eventually I did it a little bit. As I remember it, it felt good even the first time, but I also had a deep sense of shame and the feeling that I had committed some unforgivable sin, that I was ruined or besmirched for life and that it was a *terrible* secret of which I could never talk to anyone.

"I married in my mid-20s still struggling with the guilt of those three one-night stands. I thought that marriage would erase all gay desires and that I would somehow escape the guilt feelings (actually the gay urges and yearnings I was struggling with subconsciously and trying to suppress). Sex with my wife was not terribly exciting then—I was sexually immature, inexperienced, and she was a virgin.

"We reached a ho-hum stage after several years and several children. I was sent to a four-day seminar to Minneapolis. Tramping up Hennepin Ave. the first night, looking for some kind of excitement, I noticed one neon sign for Hennepin Baths with a big arrow pointing down some basement steps. I went in, paid my $3, checked my valuables, and was shown into this small room with a cot. I stripped, donned my towel, and started exploring the place. I sensed it was gay because of the rather extreme appearance of some of the men lounging around. I was excited, tense, and nervous. I asked someone where the steam room was and my voice was tight, my breath quick. I went into this small room, saw a lot of people just sitting. After I calmed down a bit, I went into another, larger steam room

with stepped seating. Again, a lot of men just sitting. After a bit everyone
trickled away, except for one young blond guy. He came and stood in front
of me, then slowly reached out and delicately ran the back of his finger nails
along the inside of my upper limbs, without touching my genitals. It made
my blood leap! I stammered an invitation for him to come to my room. I
went and dropped on the cot, awaiting his tap on my door. It never came!
Eventually, I went looking for him and brought him back. He was
blasé—quite a veteran of the place. In spite of this initiation, I spent every
free moment during that seminar at the baths. I just let my defenses down
and wallowed in sexuality. When I came back to Philly I found a way of
getting a membership card in the local gay bath (one has to be 'sponsored'
by a gay member) and have steadily developed sexually ever since, and now
that my wife has found out about my bisexuality, we have a glorious,
refreshing sex life, full of variety, spontaneity, and love, and I find that my
homosexual experiences pale by comparison. They were a sexual education,
a period of growth, but rather empty and unsatisfying. I still feel the need to
find a man now and then but I think ultimately I'll be able to drop it
altogether. I don't believe that old 'saw'—'once a homosexual always a
homosexual.' "

 ⚥ "While in the closet, I was certainly not one of them 'faggoty queers
over in the dark slimy corners of society.' Hell, no. So I became as macho as
I could to retain some integrity, fantasized about men—naked, muscular,
wrestling, working, sweaty, fucking women, men, or me. Lived in dorms,
barracks, etc., for ten years from age 14–24. Hid this and suppressed it and
spent lots of energy denying it.

 "Marry and it will go away. Well, I married, and I was still full of
those feelings. Fifteen years later changes began; I was 42 years old and the
kids were 11 and 13. The summer was spent in Europe with the family. In
Amsterdam, I cried at night in fear I would die without being loved by a
man. In October 1975, I told a psychologist friend, 'I think I'm gay.' On
December 5, 1976, I had my first gay trick—I got a blow job at the gay
cinema. I went there deliberately for that purpose (had been going to see the
shows for some months). Started with a new shrink on January 1, 1977,
continued to experiment in D.C. bars, gay cinema, cruising grounds. Joined
men's consciousness-raising group in February 1977. Wrote in my journal,
on March 6, 1977, 'I am gay.' Told my wife March 8. Felt whole and free
the first time March 28. We worked till July on staying together, when
tension and hostility began to get serious. I changed shrinks, she started
with one. We are now separated. I've learned fast. I have names and phone
numbers of more than forty men I've had sex with—six or eight are good
friends. I have another dozen good friends with whom I've not had sex. I
have learned to get fucked and fuck and all sorts of neat things. I even lust
for cock to suck and a year ago I was terrified of putting my mouth to one,
but wanted to do so. Not to brag, but I think this old dog (who really looks
only 32) has learned some neat new tricks from some pretty good teachers,
and I am so happy!!!"

❦"Right about the time I reached puberty, I had a couple of boy friends with whom I would engage in sex play as often as I dared—I reached puberty early and they really didn't know what we were doing, or at least that's what I thought. I had my first mutual sexual experience with a family friend when I was about 13 or so; it was still in the category of 'boys will be boys,' I suppose, but I knew it was more. My parents were very strict, so I really had no sex life while I was in high school, although I did have simultaneous crushes on a man and a woman I went to school with. Then when I went to college, I had my first adult experience with my roommate, who was straight, and then my second year of college I had a rather spectacular affair with a Greek Orthodox priest, and became overtly sexual. This was my bisexual phase—I had at the same time relationships with two men and three women. I slept with two different women once or twice apiece during this time, had sex with a man a couple of times, and all the while was madly in love with my straight roommate, who didn't want to have anything to do with me. Then I moved away and decided to forgo the bisexual shit and just be gay. I had a couple of brief affairs, and then met my current lover before long, and have been with him for almost three years, during which time I have had two sexual relationships and had sex with maybe thirty other men, most of them impersonal encounters."

❦"By about the age of 14–15, when my schoolmates were interested in fooling around with girls, I knew I was only interested in using them as dancing partners. I was much more attracted to the older boys, and my two closest friends turned out to be gay later as well. I have always been quite active sexually, and yet the only woman I have ever had sex with was my wife. We were close friends for six years before we married, and virtually from the beginning, I told her I was gay. That didn't seem to bother her too much, but later, when I was 25, we both really did believe that I had evolved into a heterosexual. Then for seven years, I was exclusively heterosexual, without even gay fantasies. Then, at the age of 31, when life at home got more and more impossible, I started seeking men, and I'd say that for one year I was bisexual. When I told my wife that I was having sex with men, then I'd say my straight sex with her got better than ever—really good. But she couldn't handle it, and the duality bugged me, and we decided to separate. From that day on, it has been exclusively men."

❦"Frankly, I think I was gay when I was born. At three, I was given a pencil and paper and drew men's genitals. I investigated 'little girls' in youth but was only interested in investigating 'little boys' and always the crushes I had were for men. At 17 I told my father I was gay and I wanted to change. At that time, Johns Hopkins announced in the New York papers a cure for homosexuality—a new hormone shot. I wanted it. My father, my mother, and the doctor all laughed at me but finally, on my insistence, I did go to a psychiatrist in the Medical Center, uptown Manhattan. And after several months going to him each Saturday, and hormone shots from my own doctor during the week, this happened: I was on the subway going to Penn Station when an older man made a pass at me and I almost fainted

with excitement and got off at the next subway stop to cool down. I decided then and there I was gay and that was that. I decided to live my life as best I could and be true to myself. I went home and told the family I was 'cured' and let it go at that. When I got back from three years in Africa during the war—and met my first real lover—the family found out. They took it well and it was an open subject for all of us until they all passed on. I have no hangups on anything of that nature. I did have three strong sexual affairs with women over the years but I always broke them off for everyone's good. Women often fall for me and get in too deep. I try to be nice and am always having to take a walk. It's flattering but it is also a pain in the ass.''

⚨ "I was 12 when I first had sex with another boy. I asked him to stick his dick in my ass as we were playing with each other. He did, and I dug it. I feel that I have progressed for the positive in the way I matured both physically and emotionally to this present point, except for a bad setback in my emotional development: I was out with a girlfriend and she said she would not have sex with me because I was queer and unable to do it. I reacted very badly to that statement, and got mad at her, so I took off all her clothing and screwed her. Then I turned her over and screwed her in the ass. I agreed to go to a state hospital for treatment so I would not have to go to prison for forceable rape. I know what I did was wrong but I still did it.''

⚨ "I have had gay needs since I was in high school. My first gay experiences were in college, and I really felt guilty about them. I certainly didn't think of myself as gay, or 'queer' as the term was. Although I had intermittent gay and straight sex from then on, it was not very frequent, as I thought all sex outside marriage was 'bad and wrong,' according to my upbringing. There were always many propositions of gay sex while I was in college and in the army, but I couldn't bring myself to act on them regularly, or even often. Finally, while I was living abroad, after my army days, I began to have more gay sex, but I still felt very guilty. When I returned to the U.S.A., I went to graduate school and I had more gay sex than straight. I began to feel more comfortable with it, but still a lot of guilt was there, and fear of being exposed or of insulting somebody by making improper advances. (How I hate myself for not pursuing one absolutely gorgeous 'hunky' student who, as I now look back, gave me every sign to come on to him. I was an instructor, he was one of my students.) After I got settled in Baltimore, which is not my hometown, I began to have quite regular gay sex with one friend and occasional sex with others. It began to bother me that I was thinking in terms of gay sex exclusively at this time, and because of this, I consciously cut down on the gay activities and turned to straight sex instead. I remember one real put-down at that time. I had a date with a very sharp-looking nurse. She had come to my apartment for dinner, one lovely spring evening. After we finished eating, I began to make advances, caressing her and making it pretty clear that I was horny as hell for her. Finally she told me that she just couldn't do it with me because she was a lesbian! But she did give me one of the nicest massages that I ever

had, so it wasn't a total loss. Soon after that, I began dating my wife. We finally lived together for a while and got married. I gave up gay sex. After our divorce, ten years later, I soon took up with my present girl friend, Joy, with whom I have lived for about seven years now. About two years ago, the old itch for gay sex began to reappear. By then, 'gay liberation' was in the air and the so-called sexual revolution of the '60s had already taken place. I felt much freer to express myself in ways which had earlier been fraught with fear and guilt.

"I do not feel sexually 'different' from others; in fact, I feel that most people could function bisexually if they needed to. I do feel more sexually active than most of my friends of my age, but it is not a topic of conversation that comes up often. We are all suffering from the conservatism of the 1930s, when we were children. Now, at the present time, I feel more at ease with myself than I have ever felt. I am able to relate to Joy according to her wants, and to go outside our relationship for gay sex when I want. My biggest problem is the friction caused by these gay adventures between Joy and myself, because she feels threatened by them. I know that a part of me needs some gay contacts and I am not fearful of seeking satisfaction. But I also don't want to cause her any more hurt than she has already suffered. Somehow, Joy simply will not accept the notion that my gay adventures are secondary to our relationship."

Sex with Women, Marriage, and Bisexuality

Whether due to societal pressures or their own inner feelings, most gay men experience some sexual contact with women, just as many "straight" men experience some sexual contact with other men. This ambiguous, as opposed to exclusive, nature of male sexuality was clearly indicated by Kinsey's famous studies. The gay men in the survey were asked about the *frequency of their sexual experiences with women, as well as their feelings about it*. The responses are indicated in the following two charts:

	ALWAYS	VERY FREQUENTLY	SOMEWHAT FREQUENTLY	SOMEWHAT INFREQUENTLY	VERY INFREQUENTLY	ONCE	NEVER
in the past	2	8	11	12	23	10	34%
currently	.5	2	3	4	10	1	78

	VERY POSITIVE	SOMEWHAT POSITIVE	NEUTRAL	SOMEWHAT NEGATIVE	VERY NEGATIVE	NOT SURE
your past experiences	13	21	25	15	21	6%
your current experience	11	11	32	9	24	13

Since 78% of the men are currently not having sex with women at all, it is hard to know what they meant when giving their feelings about current sexual experiences with women. One can, of course, feel positive or negative about not having sex with women at all. Perhaps the most striking figures in these charts are the ones showing how many of the men had sex with women in the past, yet do not have sex with women now. This presumably is a clear-cut indicator that while the overwhelming majority of the men (66%) tried sex with women at least once, somewhere in their sexual evolution they decided that they preferred sex with men. Negative feelings about sex with women result from many factors, including the inability to have an erection, the feeling that it is not exciting (even when 'performance' was all right), an understanding that sex with men is more exciting, or other factors.

The following is a selection of comments on sex with women, especially as compared to sex with men:

⚥ "I had only one sexual experience with a woman in my life. It was disastrous! I was 28 and she was 35, but sooo beautiful. She was a photographer's model in her earlier years, and I still have an old paperback classic novel on which her picture graces the cover as the fictional heroine of the title. We worked in the record department of an appliance store and got along famously. After work, we occasionally went to the cocktail lounge next door for a few martinis. One evening we had more than usual and wound up at her apartment. Her husband was out of town and her 6-year-old son had been put to bed. I knew what she had in mind and I felt that it was high time to prove to myself that I could 'do it' with a woman. I had had enough martinis to fill me with bravado, and what a beautiful woman I had for my first performance. It was hardly any time at all before we were on the floor, my pants down and her dress up; and I never had such a soft cock in my life. When she tried to ply it with her hand, it only shriveled all the more. And her pussy felt so mammoth; nothing at all like my lover's ass. While I was pumping away, trying to get an erection on the softest cock in the world, her little boy climbed out of bed and stood watching us. Well, that was it! She was furious and immediately put him to bed while I pulled up my pants. The rest sounds like a Woody Allen movie but I swear that it's true. I sat, finishing my drink, and waited for her to come out again. When

she didn't, I went into the bedroom and found that she had climbed into bed with her young son. She had been crying. I tried to console her, to apologize. 'No,' she said, 'I'm just no longer attractive.' 'You're the most beautiful woman I've ever seen,' I told her, and meant it. Finally, there was nothing else to say, and I left. I didn't know how I'd face her the next morning at work, but I did and she was there. Our first moments were strained, but then we decided to discuss the night before. 'I'm just old,' she said, 'and no longer attractive.' 'You know you're beautiful,' I said. 'I just had too much to drink. It happens sometimes.' I wasn't about to tell her what I really thought. She was finally convinced and our love-friendship lasted for many years after. We never mentioned that night again. As for me, I never again entertained the idea of going to bed with a woman to 'prove my manhood.' What I had proved was that I certainly wasn't a latent heterosexual."

⚤ "I have never had sexual experience with a woman and have absolutely no desire to have one. I most certainly do not hate women. I think that they are fine, enjoyable to work with, socialize with, but would never want to live with one, much less have sex with one."

⚤ "I'd no more be sexually intimate with a woman than I would with a reptile. *Utterly repulsive* idea. I've never even come *close* to sex with a woman."

⚤ "I have an active sexual relationship with a woman in my home city—when I'm there I see her, we make it; also we communicate infrequently while I am here in Toronto. I thoroughly enjoy sex with her, find her sexy, stimulating, intelligent, etc. It continued because there is no threat of having to settle down or commit myself to her. She makes no emotional demands on me."

⚤ "I was and am more free in having sex with women since it leans more towards the sensual side. I was in love with a woman once and she with me, but we both realized that in the long range it would not last since sooner or later I would bed down with a man. As for sex with women, it is not as physical, but at times I need and desire the softness of a woman and the gentleness they offer as a counterpoint to the hardness of a male."

⚤ "Sex with women is great, usually gives me a more sensational orgasm, if only because it takes so damned long! Don't like fishy pussy however, never have. I don't trick with women."

⚤ "I find women entirely too scheming to engage in a relationship with them, but have known women where my spirit was willing but the flesh was weak."

⚤ "Since I have begun practicing oral sex with my wife, my sexual life is far more satisfying than with men. We have no barriers to our sexuality—just as I have no barriers with males—but the difference is that we *love* each other and have twenty-two years of marriage behind us, with many memories."

⚤ "I generally prefer sex with a man. If you are going to get down to the actual physical feelings of sex, I find that a man is much better at sucking a

cock than a woman. This is probably because he knows what the sensation is like and thus knows how to perform. A man is also generally a better fuck because an asshole is much tighter than most pussies. Some say it's not as moist, but with proper lubrication or preparation this is no problem. And finally a man can do one thing a woman can't do, and that is fuck the other person. So really two men have a greater variety available to them than a man and a woman. I must admit that sex with either can be most enjoyable, and I do enjoy eating pussy. But all things being equal, give me a man.''

⚤ "Good God! I don't like the way women feel or smell, and I hate boobs. When I was 16 a woman raped me—and that was that. I resented it at the time and I still do. I could not be raped by a man.''

⚤ "Generally sex with women is too passive and they play the guilt thing up too much.''

⚤ "A woman and I came out to each other at approximately the same moment while we were making love.''

⚤ "My sex with women has been a lot more satisfying since I came out—the women I have slept with have known I'm gay and that eliminates a lot of my fears about being able to perform. (What a lousy word, 'perform,' is this a play?)''

⚤ "I tried sex with two whores in 1931 and could not get an erection. It was on a dare from the boys at work.''

⚤ "I am totally inexperienced in sex with women, and remain proud of that fact.''

⚤ "I was never sexually satisfied the years I was married and had no man.''

⚤ "The few times I have had sex with women, I was fantasizing the whole time that I was with a man, so it's almost like I've never slept with a woman. I'd like to say that I am open to sexual relationships with women, but I don't know if that would be honest, although I do have very close relationships with women.''

⚤ "Although I appreciate women's personalities and can even aesthetically appreciate a beautiful woman's body, I feel no eroticism for women. I once had a year-long relationship with a lesbian. During this time I often had sex with men, and only a few times with her. We even thought about the possibility of marriage, but we'd agreed we'd both continue having sex with our own sex. We both thought that heterosexual relations were perhaps preferable to masturbation, but not as good as homosexual relations. Sexually, we kissed, she sucked my cock, I sucked her breasts, and we fucked. I could not perform cunnilingus on her. I am *very* turned off by the female smell.''

⚤ "The vagina is a very special place. It feels different from any orifice a male affords, and I like it. If I could combine the ease I've often felt with women with the excitement I feel with men, I'd have it made.''

⚤ "My sole sexual experience with a woman was when she seduced me (characteristically) after I was drunk. I did not like the way she came on to me because she knew I was gay and considered me a conquest. I was very

turned off, afterward, when she told me she wanted a baby by a white man (she was black), and that the man she seduced me in front of (also black, in a room full of black people) had been putting the make on me. I felt I had been used. I remain open, however, to the possibility of having sex with a woman, but again, she would probably have to seduce me. (One lesbian once told me that I was the most passive male she had ever met.)"

♂"I've never really tried this. I do not seem to have sufficient erotic attraction to make an attempt."

While some men—such as the last one quoted above—assume they will not enjoy sex with a woman, or will not be able to "perform" sexually, others decide experientially that their only erotic energy is homosexual. For some gay men, however, there is an erotic capability, of varying intensity, toward women. Such men are sometimes called, or call themselves, bisexuals. Not all men who have sex with women consider themselves bisexual, since many of these men fully realize a homosexual preference and consider that preference to be a defining factor; they sleep with women, perhaps, for purposes other than sexual gratification.

Bisexuality is a controversial subject among gay men. First, the men were asked, *Have you considered or do you consider yourself bisexual?* In the past, 46% of the men considered themselves bisexual, while currently 20% of the men consider themselves bisexual. For some of these men, clearly, "bisexual" is a helpful or convenient label in the transition toward self-acceptance as homosexual. It might be argued, however, that some men assume exclusive homosexuality because of intolerance of bisexuality in the gay world.

Here are comments on bisexuality from men who consider themselves to be bisexual at present:

♂"I can relate to both men and women, and most of my life has been spent sexually as a straight. The first time I went down on a male was in Houston, Texas. After a long evening of trying to pick up a female, I staggered into the Pink Elephant Bar, back in 1954, and was picked up by a middle-aged man and went to a hotel room with him. Reason? I was horny. I enjoyed it but I was in the service and didn't want any hassles, so I stayed away from the gay scene for nearly twenty years. I was aware of the potential for homosexuality, but there was too many women and little motivation. I returned to gay activity after picking up a black drag queen in Shirley, Mass. (at the Mohawk), and tricking with her at the Coach House Inn on Route 2A.

"I have just returned from a week at P-town where I made it with several guys, but they might have been females if any young and attractive ones were interested. A lot of middle-aged guys are turning to homosexual relationships because they find it harder to make contact with young and appealing girls. We seem to find bisexuality natural and comfortable, and very often we are married and/or have been married, with kids, etc. A

further attraction for gay acts for older men is that they are rather kinky and few females want to participate in them. I must confess that I would not care to be entirely gay. I think that a fully gay lifestyle is difficult and very frustrating. As a bisexual, I feel no need to 'come out' and my employment and my relationship with my wife would be endangered by such a move. At the same time, I am sympathetic to those who do want to come out and have joined several area gay groups to lend support at least to gay rights, which I consider to be human rights. I am turned off by those who act too feminine in public unless they are obvious queens and wish to be treated like women.''

⚥ "As a practicing bisexual I consider sleeping with women to be just as normal as with men.''

⚥ "I still consider myself bi, but that's going bye-bye gradually.''

⚥ "As a bisexual, my sexuality operates on an overlapping bell-curve pattern. I have traditionally gone through a stage of liking both men and women, then rising on one curve to where I can't stand the thought of men and only want women, to the other pole of not being able to stand women and desiring only men. This once again slides to the overlapping stage and continues. This has often led to great frustration and confusion. Rather than being the best of both worlds as has often been suggested, it is more like straddling a fence.''

⚥ "Sometimes I wish I could live with wife and child in suburbia and then, dammit, this tremendously rich capacity I have to love a man. And let me ask you: why is it wrong? What makes it something to hide? How long must this nonsense go on? Hiding generation after generation? Won't someone tell someone it is a nice, pleasant, friendly thing to relate to another human being as a human being. Oh, I know you know the answers, so many of us do. Please don't forget those of us out here with families and wives and jobs that pay well, that we enjoy. Smile at us. Please understand us. We understand. Believe me, we understand. And in our way we are raising sons and daughters who will understand too. Don't you realize, we are the future. Please speak to me! I love you and wish you good fortune. Will I join you? Sorry, but I guess I must stay behind. I *am* sorry. I can't sign my name. I'm sorry and I'm crying. God bless you gentle people.''

⚥ "I consider myself to be bisexual, in that I have sex with both men and women. I attended one ten-week 'Bisexual Rap Group' over last summer, and I don't think it helped me get a clearer picture as to what bisexuality is. There were men and women in the group, with some basically promiscuous and some basically monogamous orientations for both sexes; and it just seemed that the only commonality that we had was that we are as different from each other as homosexuals or heterosexuals are different from each other.''

⚥ "I have grave doubts about the actual existence of bisexuality, but have run across two or three real bisexuals in my many sexual relationships. I think I come fairly close, but my strong preference is for homosexuality. I imagine this is true with most men: one or the other.''

⚣ "I find it somewhat difficult to go back and forth from one sex to the other. When I was secretly going to the 'baths,' I was afraid of bringing my wife home some venereal 'gift.' Maybe that's why I was reluctant to have sex with her very often. I think the possibility of infection for a married bisexual, whose wife doesn't know, is a very great fear."

⚣ "I suppose I could call myself a bisexual since I am capable of fucking with both men and women. I find bisexuality more confusing than anything else, however, and it complicates things enormously."

Only 12% of the men said that they had negative feelings about bisexual men. Yet there were many negative comments on the concept of bisexuality itself, perhaps due to the widespread use of the label "bisexual" as somehow better than "homosexual." The following comments on bisexuality—both negative and positive—reflect the range of opinions of the gay men participating in the survey:

⚣ "Bisexuality is a cop-out. If it comes down to a choice between the straight or the gay partner, I know who is going to get the shaft. Societal pressures to be straight are very strong and very hard to ignore. I would never become involved with a married or straight man. I'm not going to feed their needs and then get the shaft. Fuck them!"

⚣ "I sometimes wonder whether most men who consider themselves bisexual and/or live that way may never have discovered the full potential of a love-sex relationship with either sex and think that sex is just a matter of satisfying the cock and getting off one's load. My own definition of true bisexuality is that it exists only when a person is *equally transported* in ecstatic union in a sex experience with either sex."

⚣ "The usual question is, 'Wouldn't you rather be straight?' No way. But I do think it would be nice if I responded sexually to women. I think bisexuality would be best."

⚣ "I think too many times bisexuals are escaping the fact that they are really gay."

⚣ "I would like to be a bisexual, but the thought of having sex with a woman is so odious to me that I can't contemplate it. I was 28 before I didn't hate women on sight."

⚣ "I have occasionally fantasized about developing a lover relationship with a bi-guy who eventually got me into being able to make it with a woman."

⚣ "Often feel that bisexuals play off one sex against the other. A friend of mine once said, 'A male bisexual is a guy who treats his boy friends as poorly as he treats his girl friends.' I wonder . . ."

⚣ "I always find bisexuals to be very selfish. They want both worlds."

⚣ "Sometimes I feel bisexuals are the real elite of human beings, able to experience and to understand more than either straight straights or straight gays."

♂"I've known some 'bisexual' people who would be better described as 'horny bastards.' "

♂"I am very much in favor of bisexuality and an end to extremist labels. It doesn't matter that much to me what sex I'm with. I don't like queers any better than rednecks. They are both extreme."

♂"Frankly, I don't believe in bisexuality. I think those who call themselves bi's are kidding themselves and their friends. They are queers who want it both ways and are willing to play the game. Like me: my wife believes I am bisexual, calls me that. But I know I am totally homosexual, always have."

♂"I think that to define oneself as either purely gay or purely straight is a little bit sick. Both are preset restrictions we have which tell us how we can express love to the other half of the human race. The fact that most people seem biologically bound to one extreme or the other only indicates the depth of the illness. On the other hand, I don't like the term 'bisexual.' It means two kinds of sex relationships with two kinds of people. Instead, to the extent that one needs a label, I've adopted the term poly-amorous, meaning many kinds of love relationships with many kinds of people."

♂"I have a few friends who are bisexual, and frankly they 'bug' me. I become very turned off when they fuck a woman. I have one woman who lives next door to me and we go to the discos a lot. She always ends up picking up a gay man to go home with. I don't like it. How a gay man is not able to resist a woman I don't know."

Earlier in this chapter, several men refer to marriage relationships with women—some terminated in divorce or separation, some that are still ongoing. Of the men who participated in the survey, 7% reported they were married. Most of these men were living with their wives, and the wives were informed about the husband's sexuality. In only a few cases, the men said their homosexuality was a secret or that they weren't sure whether the wife knew or not. About 1% of the men reported that they were involved in "marriages of convenience," either to help them pass for straight or for other legalistic purposes such as inheritance, gifts, or immigration.

About 2% of the men said they were separated from their wives, and 9% were divorced. These men were asked *whether their homosexuality was a major factor in their separation or divorce,* and the replies are shown in this chart:

	YES	NO	NOT SURE
separated men	78	11	11%
divorced men	45	42	13

The men had various comments about their own marriage arrangements and about the institution of marriage itself. (Comments on homosexual marriage appear in Chapter 9.) The comments given here were made by men involved in marriage with women, as well as by men who have never married:

⚥"I have been married for nearly twenty years. It has been, to say the least, stormy. I think I have learned from it. I have two gorgeous sons, without whom there would have been no follow-up."

⚥"Marriage. Hetero? I think that after two people have lived together for fifteen or twenty years, bought a house together, furnished it, and had a kid, raised it for five to ten years, *then* they should consider getting married.

⚥"As far as a gay man marrying a hetero woman, I think this is a hypocritical goddam fucking rotten thing to do for all concerned. It cheats the woman, getting a fag husband. It cheats the statistics by adding to the 'hetero' population erroneously. It cheats a potential lover from marrying the gay, and in most cases, it is living a lie. Same goes for a gay woman marrying a hetero man. And parents who force such marriages should be sued for fucking up the lives of their children."

⚥"I'm sick of all the advantages that a 'married' couple has over another couple (either straight or gay). The legitimacy that society throws over married people is disgusting. And couples who live together only because they are going to get married eventually drive me crazy. What is it about this legal ceremony that makes everything okay? People just have too many hangups about fucking and they have to have society's permission to fuck; they don't want guilt.

"I've also seen too many cases where married people were given a job because they were married. Disgusting! And even some, where a person was given more for the same job, because he was 'married' (and what was worse, he hit the 'johns' more than I did—I felt like biting his cock off)."

⚥"I believe legal marriage to be chains on women."

⚥"Punishment for heteros."

⚥"Good for straights."

⚥"Its only value is in providing a structure for children, and it has become almost nonfunctional on this level."

⚥"Speaking as a cleric, I'd never preside at a wedding at which one partner was gay, even if the other partner knew of it. It's a real can of worms, no matter how accepting the straight partner is before the wedding."

⚥"I am currently married and am very happy and contented with life. Before marriage, I led a bisexual life with homosexuality predominating. My former male lover is also married, and our families are quite close. My wife knows of my gay past, but does not know that our friend was my lover. He has urged me to resume the physical side of our relationship, but I have refused. I am, as I said, very comfortable, happy, and secure in my marriage and I don't want to jeopardize it."

⚤"I am a man, 51 years old, and have a very happy life with a straight woman. We have been married twenty-six years now. I did not realize I was gay when I married, and it was perhaps six or seven years after we were married that I realized it. For some time, of course, I hid it and still do most of the time, as I have two grown children, and I would not like for them to ever know of it. But I told my wife three years ago, and she didn't mind, as she felt there was something wrong but couldn't put her finger on it. We are much happier now, and she allows me to be active as a gay man and she does as she likes. We love each other very much. We are both very careful and we still have sex together about four times a month, which she loves and I can tolerate."

⚤"My ideal dream marriage is where I meet a beautiful, intelligent bisexual woman with whom I fall deeply in love and we get married and swing (together and apart) and eventually have two kids (one of each)."

⚤"I am making life hell for my wife. I love her and hate what I have done to her."

⚤"My lover and I live with my wife and children as a temporary situation."

⚤"If I didn't have straight kids, I'd come out myself. Life is a lot easier than it was thirty-five years ago. We were pressured into marriage, etc. I get along okay with my wife. We fuck less. I'm more homo active in the last few years. I jerk off more. Sometimes I fuck my wife, come, get up, go in the bathroom, and jerk off with a male fantasy. I don't think any of my contemporaries think I'm gay at all—I can switch-hit, but it's *boys* I like! *Cocks* I love!"

⚤"Marriage—I'm *vehemently* opposed to it. I think when gays marry in order to obtain camouflage or to kid themselves it's pathetic and disgusting. I usually break off all ties and contact with gays I know who marry women."

⚤"I think that married men who come out and then leave their wives pose a possible conflict between gay men and feminists. Of course such men have the right to self-realization, but some men are very inconsiderate of their wives, especially where children are involved. I hate it at gay marches when people chant, 'Two four six eight, are you sure your husband's really straight?' This antagonistic attitude toward women who may actually be married to closet cases is very negative. Gay liberation should be promoting honesty and an open, loving community for men, women, and children."

Children

One of the purposes of marriage, ostensibly, is procreation, and the desire for family life is one of the factors that motivate some gay men to try marriage. The expectation of parents—the adults who most influence a young person—is that the family structure will be reproduced. Parents want their children to marry, then they want grandchildren. Of course, a growing

number of heterosexual couples remain childless, but often not without hassles from the older generation. So single people, gay people, gay couples, and childless straight couples all share a common opprobrium—all are looked at somewhat askance for their failure to produce children. In an overpopulated world, however, nonreproduction can be considered a blessing and some gay people have been known to argue that not having children is one of the positive contributions of gay people to the modern world.

On Earth Day in April 1970, for example, the Gay Liberation Front in New York put out a leaflet praising "all those homosexual women and men through history who in couples and small groups turned for warmth, sex and friendship to members of their own gender thereby providing the human race with an affirmative and joyous alternative to the problems of population explosion." There are even those gays who are militantly nonreproductive, using the hostile term "breeders" to refer to child-producing heterosexuals. The total picture, however, includes parents who came to terms with their gayness after marriage and procreation, gay men or women who are fully conscious of their gayness but who nonetheless have children (with or without benefit of marriage), and gay people involved in work situations where they spend at least as much time with children as most parents do.

Although it contradicts the facts, the idea that gay men "can't have children" is used to promote antigay prejudice. Anita Bryant has stated that because gays are childless, they have to "recruit" other people's children. Some people accuse gay men of being selfish because they do not share their lives (and their money?) with a wife and children. There is a popular notion among radicals in "third world liberation" movements, including blacks, Puerto Ricans, and Native Americans, that homosexuality among their people could lead to "race suicide" or that white people promote homosexuality as a form of genocide. These various accusations are founded in falsehood and reflect existing patriarchal attitudes. Of the gay men in the survey, 13% reported that they have their own children, which could well be considered a large percentage considering the myth that gay people "can't have children." Most of these men have one or two children, but there are a few with a larger number (up to six). One crucial point, furthermore, is that whether they are fathers or not, gay men generally like children. *Whether or not you have children,* the men were asked, *"What is your attitude, in general, toward children?* The responses were:

very positive	49%
somewhat positive	24
neutral	11
somewhat negative	11
very negative	5
not sure	1

The overwhelmingly positive attitudes come in part from gay men's appreciation of the nurturing, child-care role that is generally denied to men. It should also be taken into consideration that men, unlike women, do not suffer in their formative years from the constant pressures of the cult of future motherhood (as there is no parallel equation of fatherhood with self-worth). Despite exceptions, men helping to rear children are generally not burdened with as much of the drudgery as are women, and so kids can seem to be "more fun."

About 12% of the men reported that they participate in the rearing of children even though they are not their own biologically. This includes living in communal situations, being an uncle, babysitting, and working as day-care workers and teachers. Several men said they had foster children placed in their care by the courts. About 90% of the men involved with childrearing in this manner said they were satisfied with the arrangement.

For the overwhelming majority of gay men, however, being childless is the reality. The following chart indicates how the men without children feel about being childless:

very positive	29%
somewhat positive	12
neutral	28
somewhat negative	22
very negative	6
not sure	3

Here are a selection of comments from gay men who have children of their own, who work with children, or who spend time with them in other ways:

⚥"During the past two years I've had the pleasure of working with preschool children. From this experience I've learned that kids are the beautiful people, unspoiled by society and not yet corrupt. They're a delight to work with as they are open and honest and don't hide behind sarcasm and masked feelings. They're very real. To be loved by a child is indeed a very special thing. I believe that my being gay has given me an advantage over the nongay male as far as dealing with kids. I'm not afraid to pursue a traditionally female-oriented career, I don't care what people think. As a gay man, I'm more in touch with my emotions and I'm able to share my love and not be frightened of expressing it."

⚥"I like children. I borrow some from friends and relatives sometimes for a day. It is something I've at times regretted about the gay life—not being able to have children. Yet, I feel ambiguous; there are many things I can do now, not having kids, that I could never do if I had had some."

⚥"I have one son, 9 years old. I'm fortunate that his mother is so adept at teaching and raising him. I have very little patience and although I have progressed to see him differently than I used to and thoroughly enjoy him

when I see him now, my inability to relate to him at an earlier age would have been disastrous if he had been in my care only.''

⚥ "I'm fortunate. They are a delight and I know I am envied. My kids have more loving 'uncles' than they can deal with.''

Some of the men, those who are fathers and those who aren't, directed their comments on children toward the way they are raised in this society:

⚥ "Child-raising is not the little paradise society makes it out to be, and unless people are mature enough to unselfishly allow their children to go completely their own way rather than the parents' way, then those people should not be parents. Too many parents raise children as status symbols instead of as people.''

⚥ "There is the Cult of Children in our society that can be extremely oppressive for gays. The Cult states, (1) the most valuable (perhaps only valuable) thing you can do is to bring children into our society, (2) that gays, being essentially childless, envy the straights' childbearing qualities, and wish to prey on their children. I can't tell you how sick I am of being portrayed as a child molester; the last thing I'd want to do is molest or, for that matter, 'convert' a child. I feel sorry for children because they have absolutely no rights and are completely at the mercy of whatever adults are raising them, but my interest in children is minimal.''

⚥ "Children are mainly delightful, but it is maddening to see them destroyed by ignorant and insensitive parents.''

As part of divorce, many gay men yield custody to their wives, though on occasion a gay man wishes to obtain custody and his homosexuality becomes an issue in the court's decision. This type of custody conflict has not been as much of an issue for gay men as it has for gay women, since it is so much more common for mothers to receive custody, and antigay fathers have used lesbianism to contest the normal custody procedures in some cases. While 2% of gay fathers reported that custody has been an issue, 3% indicated problems with visiting rights. Sometimes, if the mother knows that the father is gay and she disapproves, she will insist that the father not reveal his homosexuality or that when he visits with the children there are no visible signs of a gay lifestyle present (for example, the father's lover may have to move out of the house while the visit is taking place). The following are comments made by gay fathers concerning visiting rights, custody and related issues:

⚥ "My wife has pulled the macho trip on me, insisting that the kids not meet my friends. She had the moral support of my own mother and I gave up in disgust.''

⚥ "I had constant battles with my in-laws, involving the sheriff. I finally let go and I feel good about me but I cry for my children. They've been taught so much hate.''

⚦"I have custody because their mother is a neurotic alcoholic, but the children live on a farm with my sister."

⚦"My wife is positive; she lets me see the kids whenever I want."

⚦"My wife knows about my gayness, but we have worked out a very good relationship with the children staying with me two or three days per week."

⚦"I have allowed my ex-wife's husband to legally adopt the children."

⚦"At first when my wife and I split, she insisted on keeping the kids because of the negative influence of having a gay father. But as the realities of nonstop responsibility for them set in, along with her own wishes for liberation, she began sharing responsibilities with me to the extent that today I have the kids as often or more than she."

⚦"She tried, and succeeded, in cutting me off from the children. But I saw them clandestinely and now that they are married and parents we have a very open and loving relationship. My ex-wife still doesn't like the idea."

⚦"My biggest personal agony of being homosexual is the loss of my children. I love children very much."

⚦"My three teenagers receive constant brainwashing to generate hatred towards me. I doubt if we will see each other for several years."

As this section was being compiled, the following very relevant item came in the mail from Scott (not his real name):

⚦"Last summer I picked up a copy of the gay male questionnaire and began filling it out. I never finished it and I am wondering if you are still taking them. If so, much has changed and I would need to do a new one. If not, I am enclosing a letter written by a woman I was having a relationship with. We had decided to have a baby and raise her together. This woman also had another child (4 years old) who was and is still relating to me as her father. When our infant was 2½ months old this woman left me with the children and has been threatening court action to take away my rights as a parent if I do not meet her demand to 'get straight.' As yet no court action has been initiated. She is in a very angry, confused space. Because of my sexuality, I have not seen my children since the end of February. It's a lonely spring."

And here is the letter written by Scott's woman friend to accompany his original questionnaire:

"I am a 24-year-old woman living with the man who is replying to this questionnaire. I'm writing this because I think I have some valid information that applies to it. I'm seven months pregnant. When I met Scott I was aware that he had had gay experiences in the past, but that's where I thought they were, in the past. I was three months pregnant when he told me that he wanted to start having gay experiences again. Being in the position that I was, I didn't feel that I had any choice but to 'grin and bear it, grit my teeth, and keep a stiff upper lip.' I was lulled into a false sense of security by his seeming inaction to put his request into practice. Then when I was five

months pregnant I walked in on him and a lover. Neither my relationship with him nor my pregnancy has been the same since. I feel a lot of anger, resentment, and bitterness about this whole thing. I did not get pregnant to 'trap him.' I got pregnant because he wanted a baby. And I feel it was dirty pool to dump all of this on me while I was pregnant. I still love Scott but between this and my pregnancy it's just about destroyed our relationship. Several times I have tried to reconcile myself to the fact that his gayness is an essential part of his make-up and I honestly feel that I could have succeeded if it hadn't come at a time in our relationship when I was particularly open and vulnerable to threat. I know that it's caused a lot of pain and loneliness for me. And it will probably cause more. I don't know where I'll go from here.''

Perhaps the letters from Scott and his woman friend should go without comment, but one is tempted to point out that they illustrate the volatile nature of the interrelationship between sexual freedom and sexual responsibility and how, when children are involved, a gay male perspective and a female perspective can be very different.

Being childless is the focus for many of the comments made by gay men about children. Many men apparently feel the ambiguity of it—childrearing is such an expense and a task that to be free of it is a blessing, but then again, having children can be fulfilling, and interesting.

⚤ "I married for children. My wife refused, having an abortion without my consent. She said that it would have ruined her career. I love children. I am a children's artist. My friends include many children. It would be hypocritical to say I entirely regret being childless, for I know children would interfere with my delightful, free gay lifestyle. But I would like to have known the parent/child relationship.''

⚤ "Straight people concerned with the problem of overpopulation ought to be happy there are gay people. Of course, some people need to continue having children, but I don't think heterosexuals are an endangered species.''

⚤ "Being childless allows me to maintain freedom and flexibility.''

⚤ "The greatest disappointment of my life is that I have not had children (in fact, this was one of the chief reasons we got married, but it was not to be), for I dearly love them, and the urge to reproduce and raise them, a form of immortality, has been strong with me.''

⚤ "Not being particularly fond of children, I have no qualms about being childless. All this talk of children being the door to immortality is, simply stated, bullshit.''

⚤ "I love children and would like one or two. How, God only knows. I haven't come to terms with being childless at all. Partly this relates to my being Jewish—I must propagate the race as well as me.''

⚤ "I love children. I don't know if I would ever want my own. But children come out of love for a woman and if I don't love a woman, I

wouldn't want her child. If men could produce children, then I probably would have one someday, but they don't, so I'll have to be satisfied with loving other people's children.''

⚥ "Children are required if the race of homo sapiens is to continue. I presume there will always be people who desire and who bear children (leaving aside the matter of test-tube birth). I see nothing terrible about a small portion of the world's population desiring to dally with their own sex—and even this does not certify that such people will not produce children from their own genes at some time or other. As for the matter of me and children, other than with certain, sweet specific exceptions, and without wanting to be classified as a child hater, I must confess to being of the opinion that a good percentage of all children I've ever encountered ought to be kept in a barrel and fed through the bunghole until they are of sufficient age to get along in and appreciate the world they are a part of. No, he finished off (grinding the topic into the floor), I do not see myself as a parent, and have no slightest twinge of sadness at the possibility of remaining childless.''

Some men hope to find ways in the future, including adoption, to have children:

⚥ "I like children and feel at times I would like to raise some or have the opportunity to be a father. I feel enraged about laws that prohibit me from adopting.''

⚥ "If faggots and dykes all had kids, what a wonderful opportunity to raise children free of antigay prejudice, though not necessarily gay themselves.''

⚥ "I think gays and lesbians should unite for purposes of reproduction so that gay lifestyles can acquire a broader base in the population.''

⚥ "I love my daughter (8 years old) and being with her. Have considered being a foster parent to gay children—a new area opening up.''

⚥ "Wish I could adopt one, but so fuckin' expensive. Maybe I should settle for a poodle?''

⚥ "I do not intend to remain childless because I really want to someday have a child and I do not mean just to father a child; rather I intend to play an important role in his upbringing, etc. How this is to be accomplished: I have not found a solution as yet although there are a number of directions I can take, such as having a child with a lesbian, one that would allow me to take part in the child's life (an equal sharing in the responsibilities and enjoyment would be the ideal solution); or mating with a straight woman who prefers to devote herself to her children and would not make demands on me as she would a husband.''

Telling Others—Another Aspect of Coming Out

In writing down their feelings about children, several of the men dealt with the issue of whether or not the children should be told about the

homosexuality of their parent or parents. If a gay person is a parent, in fact, hiding or revealing the gayness to the child is a decision that has to be made. The issue of children being aware of a parent's gayness, or the fact that the child will meet a parent's gay friends, can be a factor in child custody or visiting rights—as has already been mentioned. Openness with children, as with others, is a matter of consciousness as well as social attitudes. Here are some comments dealing specifically with children:

☿ "I have two beautiful children, ages 9 (a girl) and 7 (a boy). They are both blond and have blue eyes just like Mom and Dad. I love and care very much about them. I want them to grow up happy and do the things in life that they feel are important and that give them joy. Maybe someday if the time and attitudes are right I will be able to tell them of my gay life and share with them how happy I am and have been."

☿ "I don't feel that gays should raise their children in an *open* gay lifestyle. They should be free to choose their own sexuality without undue influence. Growing up is difficult enough without deliberately adding such a taboo-laden burden on a child."

☿ "Like any parent, I believe gay parents should be themselves and give time/energy to themselves. If gay parents hide their gayness from their kids, the kids are sure to feel the tension."

☿ "I recall one discussion with my 23-year-old son, who was worried about his masculinity. We sat up late at night talking and I finally said, 'As you probably know, I'm gay.' 'Yes,' he said, 'I've known for a long time.' I told him he'd find out whether he is homosexual when the time comes and I also said I thought his generation was more fortunate than mine in that they didn't have hangups about sex and morality—that they slept with whomever they were attracted to at the moment regardless of sex. Anyway, this is all too intimate to go into, but I do want you to know that at the end of our discussion he kissed me on the lips and said, 'Daddy, I want to thank you for being you!' I cried. I'd like to proclaim my homosexuality but I can't because it would hurt my wife and some of my children and would certainly hurt my business. So, alas, we must be practical."

The question of being open about one's homosexuality, including telling (or not telling) others directly or indirectly, is one that all gay men have to deal with. The question is not even a matter of "secrecy" versus "openness." There are many different approaches to dealing with this problem, which is undoubtedly one of the thorniest faced by gay people. Even in gay liberation circles, there are differing views on how to approach the topic.

The problem with this aspect of coming out is exacerbated by the fact that there is always a presumption of heterosexuality, unless a person visibly provides evidence to the contrary. The men were asked, *Do you feel that most people can tell instantly that you are gay?* Only 5% said yes, while 78% said no and 17% were not sure. Commenting on this question, the men

indicated that in the straight mind, instant recognition of homosexuality is related to "femme" behavior. Here are some comments the men made on the subject of instant recognition:

⚤ "I can't tell you who is or isn't, so why should they, I suppose."

⚤ "Fortunately I was blessed with a good masculine body and appearance."

⚤ "It would be better if they could tell instantly."

⚤ "In my mind I think I appear gay. Most of my straight friends say the opposite."

⚤ "I pass easily. However, I think that almost all gay men can spot one another any time."

⚤ "I have more problem in the other direction. For some reason, some people have thought I'm a cop. What a mind blower. To look at me you can no more tell whether I'm Republican or Democrat; the same goes for my being gay."

⚤ "As 'campus faggot' at my school I was known as gay by many people before they met me. However, when they do meet me I have had people deny my gayness. Once, when on a speaking engagement, I was asked if I grew a beard to disguise my homosexuality."

⚤ "I am often concerned about dressing and acting 'straight' enough so that people will not be able to tell instantly that I'm gay."

⚤ "My voice gives me away."

⚤ "Not unless I wear my earrings or some other outward stereotyped articles."

⚤ "I feel that I don't try to hide my preference for the male sex. And at my work (I work with eighty women), the camping sometimes comes out very easily. Also I don't try to play butch or act like anything that I am not. I also do not try to act femme or croon on and on about something. Actually, I think that people consider me strange before they consider me as a gay person."

⚤ "I was straight for so long, it's hard to break the habit."

⚤ "I have muscular dystrophy and am disabled so people don't expect me to be anything sexually."

⚤ "I don't feel that people can instantly tell that I am gay for two reasons. First, I am not a stereotyped queen, and am by and large straight-acting and -appearing when I'm not deliberately playing the fag. It usually takes an acquaintance some length of time to put the pieces together when it comes to my sexual proclivities. Second, there is the natural reluctance that straights have to label all but the very most obvious as homosexual; I find that sometimes I have to furnish photographs of myself engaged in sexual acts with another male for people to believe that I am what I say I am."

The last comment focuses on the invisibility of homosexuals. Ending this invisibility has been one of the goals of the gay liberation movement. It cannot be accomplished, however, without massive participation by the

nation's 20,000,000 gay men and women. Ending that invisibility is a political goal. It is not necessarily the personal goal for all gay men—quite the contrary, for at this time most gay men choose *not* to reveal their homosexuality to most other people. The men were asked *to indicate how many people know about their homosexuality in each of various categories.* Here are the responses:

	ALL (YES)	MOST	SOME	ONLY ONE	NONE (NO)	NOT SURE
gay male friends	87	9	2	0	.5	0%
lesbian friends	68	10	4	.5	10	7
straight friends	15	27	35	4	10	8
neighbors	4	12	27	2	31	24
employer	18	6	10	4	44	17
teacher	6	7	18	4	50	15
co-workers	16	10	31	6	26	13
schoolmates	8	9	37	2	33	10
your employees	12	4	13	3	54	14
mother	44	—	—	—	35	21
father	37	—	—	—	43	20
sisters and brothers	38	5	6	7	30	14
your children	7	1	.5	2	81	9
other relatives	5	8	21	6	42	18
other children	2	3	14	1	59	21

These statistics show that the majority of these gay men feel that the only safe place to be is with other gays. The statistics also reveal that most gay people believe they effectively do pass for straight, even with those very close to them such as parents, and even with people they spend many hours with such as employees, employers, teachers, and co-workers.

But the ways that gay people pass for straight often involve self-denial. At an early age, many gay men learn to squelch behavior patterns that are totally natural to them but are seen by others as "effeminate," "sissy," or otherwise socially unacceptable for a little boy. At a later age, men will relate to women in essentially dishonest ways in order to portray themselves as "normal" in others' eyes.

"Passing for straight" may also involve laughing at "queer jokes," being cold to others who are obviously gay, steering clear of conversations where Anita Bryant is being discussed, refraining from any socializing on the job even though the people are nice, etc. Where intimacy is increased— as with co-workers and straight friends—there are more cases where the homosexuality is not kept secret; but even in these two categories, only a small portion of gay men have totally open relationships. It seems, then, that secrecy must be important at least some of the time for virtually all gay

men. The following chart indicates replies to the question *In general, how important is it for you to keep your homosexuality a secret from each of the following?*

	VERY IMPORTANT	SOMEWHAT IMPORTANT	NEUTRAL	SOMEWHAT UNIMPORTANT	VERY UNIMPORTANT	NOT SURE
gay male friends	.5	1	6	4	87	0%
lesbian friends	1	.5	7	3	86	2
straight friends	13	20	13	16	36	2
neighbors	18	20	16	14	29	2
employer	27	22	13	8	28	3
teacher	16	13	25	8	33	5
co-workers	18	26	15	10	29	2
schoolmates	15	13	22	9	38	3
your employees	21	18	15	6	34	5
mother	22	14	10	5	45	4
father	24	13	11	5	45	3
sisters and brothers	15	14	13	8	47	3
your children	19	6	18	5	44	8
other relatives	19	20	15	11	29	5
other children	18	11	21	8	32	9

One alternative to secrecy is purposeful communication, though of course there is a huge middle ground which includes many relationships. The men were asked, *How important is it for you to purposely communicate the fact that you are gay to each of the following?*

	VERY IMPORTANT	SOMEWHAT IMPORTANT	NEUTRAL	SOMEWHAT UNIMPORTANT	VERY UNIMPORTANT	NOT SURE
gay male friends	51	18	14	4	13	1%
lesbian friends	41	17	20	4	16	2
straight friends	19	24	20	9	26	3

	VERY IMPORTANT	SOMEWHAT IMPORTANT	NEUTRAL	SOMEWHAT UNIMPORTANT	VERY UNIMPORTANT	NOT SURE
neighbors	7	8	30	12	40	3
employer	11	10	21	12	42	4
teacher	9	8	30	11	39	4
co-workers	12	14	21	13	37	3
schoolmates	10	14	26	11	36	3
your employees	11	7	25	11	44	3
mother	32	11	16	5	32	4
father	29	11	17	5	34	4
sisters and brothers	30	12	18	7	29	4
your children	18	7	27	4	39	7
other relatives	10	13	24	12	38	4
other children	8	8	28	9	38	8

Reluctance to communicate forthrightly the fact of one's gayness can be a matter of personality but it can also be a political issue; that is, it reflects gay men's fear of the reaction of others. A large percentage of people checked the "neutral" box in the preceding chart, indicating that they would rather "let it be" than specifically discuss their gayness. The chart below indicates responses to this question: *Of those who know you are gay or homosexual, what has been the reaction of each of the following to that fact?*

	VERY POSITIVE	SOMEWHAT POSITIVE	NEUTRAL	SOMEWHAT NEGATIVE	VERY NEGATIVE	NOT SURE
gay male friends	85	7	7	0	0	.5%
lesbian friends	74	8	13	1	0	4
straight friends	22	40	21	10	3	5
neighbors	7	16	41	6	4	25
employer	13	15	36	5	9	23
teacher	9	19	39	3	5	25
co-workers	16	24	34	6	3	16

	VERY POSITIVE	SOMEWHAT POSITIVE	NEUTRAL	SOMEWHAT NEGATIVE	VERY NEGATIVE	NOT SURE
schoolmates	9	24	34	7	5	21
your employees	13	10	43	7	5	23
mother	14	17	20	20	14	15
father	10	11	24	19	16	20
sisters and brothers	21	22	23	11	6	17
your children	9	9	37	1	5	39
other relatives	13	12	34	5	4	30
other children	9	7	42	2	2	37

The relatively small number of negative responses is striking, especially when compared with the large number of neutral responses. These figures seem to indicate that only a small portion of the people who have had to deal with the reality of a gay man in their lives have chosen to respond negatively. On the other hand, these men may be carefully choosing who they tell, assiduously avoiding telling a person whose personality make-up and opinions suggest that the response would be hostile. The statistics do indicate that if a person is careful, he can be "out" comfortably with most of the people who matter in his life. The highest scores for negative responses go to parents, siblings, and friends. In the case of parents, especially, this may be due in part to the widespread notion—fostered by generations of psychiatrists and psychologists—that parents are "to blame" for the homosexuality of their offspring. In these cases, negative response is likely to be a form of guilt which can only be eliminated, if at all, through education.

The question of telling or not telling others is practically a daily issue for gay people, especially these days when people discuss intimacies more openly and when gay-rights issues are frequently in the news. The men shared their experiences of communicating about their gayness to others (or, conversely, keeping it secret). The following statements concern experiences with and attitudes toward communicating about gayness by those who more or less keep it under wraps.

⚤ "Being in or out of the closet is not the consideration; it is a matter of feeling comfortable with your environment. I don't feel the need to tell everyone (including those at work) because I have a lot of gay friends to socialize with and value the 'straight' aspect of my life. I like the idea of 'passing' for straight and feel no need to tell people I'm gay."

⚤ "I am keeping my homosexuality secret from the men whom I work with. I have a blue-collar job and most of my co-workers are not well educated. 'Cocksucker' and 'fag' are common terms around the shop for whomever is disliked that day/week/month etc. There is a locker room where I work and any revelation of my sexuality would be grounds for my discharge because of the use of the locker room as a changing and shower room. I am not sure if these would be legal grounds or not but I am sure that the guys wouldn't enjoy my presence there if they knew."

⚤ "Men (straight) don't go around telling that they have fucked their wives or that they have had oral sex. I don't go around talking about my sexual activities. It is my business and it should be of no concern to anyone."

⚤ "I work to try to help clarify others' thinking when I feel this is possible. For example, in my college classes, we discuss the topic, and I attempt to make clear the issues, and as in all else in the college class situation, it is finally their choice to make, not mine. I don't feel that my saying I was a homosexual would add, but only be a red herring. If they do not accept homosexuality, they won't change because they know I am one. Change, if it comes, is a slow process and can't be somehow magically brought on by someone 'revealing' something to others. For me, I enjoy relating to persons who do not understand, are straight, and would be upset if they knew I was homosexual. Just as they would be upset if they knew certain other things (for example, my politics or religion—I reveal these only to those who I feel can interestingly understand and discuss the topic. Otherwise, we stay away from the topic.) So, I attempt to deal honestly with the subject when it comes up, but don't push it. I don't attempt to pretend to be straight by dating women, etc., and should they ask, I would honestly answer. If being 'in' the closet is what one is when one keeps one's sexual preferences to oneself, then that's where I am, I guess, in some people's eyes."

⚤ "Thus far I have admitted it to no one except other gays that I am gay. In one way I am still fighting it, but at this age there seems little chance of falling in love with and marrying a woman. When I was about 28 my mother found a letter from a gay friend; it made her feel bad and me worse. But nothing was said after that and whether she and my dad thought I had 'reformed' or they had accepted it, I do not know. She died four years ago, and with no one else do I ever discuss it. In fact, I deny it when accused, as I have been twice: by a school superintendent (who ultimately forced my resignation in 1963, thanks to two snoopy postal inspectors who had found a letter of mine with a chap they had investigated); and now, by the church where I am minister—one man has continued the issue until he got enough convinced that I must leave. At 49 and with no prospects that is not funny."

⚤ "My homosexuality is only secret on the job and perhaps I go over-board to guard against being found out there. I do ridiculous things like pinching secretaries' asses, throwing women in swimming pools at office

parties, etc. I'm thought of as a 'swinger' at work and I'm content with that image.''

⚥ "I dislike the dishonesty of presenting one face to the world and another to my gay acquaintances. However, I dislike much, much more the mindless abuse and resulting misery that comes with complete sexual revelations. Very little would be gained for the cause by my 'coming out.' The damage done to my parents and my wife and boys would be horrendous and far-reaching in their devastation. It would not be fair to them nor to myself. It is relatively easy for a single gay living in a big city to declare himself. It is impossible for a family and community man to let it be known to everyone that he is gay, even in 1977. At least that's my opinion.''

⚥ "I am still 'in the closet' in my employment environment because I have an important position (vice president of a major insurance firm) that would be jeopardized if my sexual preferences were known. Because of this, I live in a city other than where I work and live in a completely open way there with my lover.''

⚥ "My fear about being 'out' altogether publicly is a fear of not being loved and liked, and not getting an opportunity to use an education that I've acquired most painfully.''

⚥ "I've never been in a position to come out of the closet. Even now I'm a 'foster grandfather' to a couple of retarded boys at a regional center, and would be fired if my 'secret' came out. This need of living a lie has been somewhat depressing at times. When people are telling jokes on gays, or repeating some standard misconception, I've wanted to speak out but didn't quite dare. That is why I am so glad gay lib is gaining in its goal of obtaining civil rights. It must be becoming clear that we aren't *that* different!''

⚥ "Mother is quite ill and would react harshly, possibly terminally.''

⚥ "I don't want the hassles while I am still in college.''

⚥ "I don't feel that my homosexuality is anyone's business, unless I choose to make it so privately. It is a little like being a political conservative: it is anyone's right, but the preference of only a few. The difference is that I see no need to proselytize. Being gay, to put it another way, isn't much different than having red hair—not many people do, and it can be hidden most of the time if that is considered desirable, but the condition itself is wholly natural and not deserving of the amount of attention it usually is accorded.''

Even most of the people who generally keep their homosexuality a secret have told at least one or two carefully chosen friends or relatives. The decision to tell others is difficult, and most men keep it a secret until they have a modicum of independence and are certain they can handle the consequences. The men were asked, *At what age did you first tell anyone other than your sexual partners about your homosexuality?* The responses were:

15 and under	4%
16–19	28
20–25	41
26–30	13
31–40	10
41 +	3

Who does one tell? This is essentially a matter of trust and intimacy, in most cases, but all the more so when it is the first person *ever* who is being told. Those most frequently told for the first time were a member of the family (52%) or a friend (41%). The remainder shared their secret with a member of the clergy, a psychiatrist or other therapist, or a doctor. (About twice as many men felt they could share their secret with a sister rather than a brother.)

Since the advent of the gay liberation movement in mid–1969, telling others has been not only easier but more common. The men were asked *in what calendar year they first told another person about their homosexuality* (of course, these figures are also a reflection of the age of the respondents). This chart indicates the responses:

1929–45	4%
1946–68	36
1969–77	60

In any case, most gay men would probably agree that gay men have been more able to be open about themselves in the 1970s than at any other time in modern history.

Many of the men described their situations as mixed, where some people know while some don't—where openness and secrecy depend on circumstances. Some gay writers have referred to coming out as a process, and these comments, reflecting some of the ambiguity, doubts, concerns about privacy, and other "gray" areas, demonstrate that sense of process:

⚣ "I'm out of the closet to some extent, but not to my co-workers or most of my family. I still have a lot of straight friends. But it is eating on me from the inside, spurred on recently by Anita Bryant and her co-conspirators. I am daily gaining a gay identity, and my closet is getting more windows all the time. I told two more old friends this month."

⚣ "I have never felt obliged to tell other people I am gay. If they ask me I don't deny it. I suppose the civil service people who fired me in 1954 for being gay were the first to ask the question. At that time it never occurred to me that a gay person had any rights, so I went quietly, along with my partner. I didn't discover the existence of gay liberation until 1967 and have been interested in the movement ever since. I have written on the subject of gay rights in our area newspapers, so I expect my sexual orientation is no

secret to anybody who is interested. However, in my personal contacts I do not bring up the subject of homosexuality unless people express interest.''

⚥ "When I was younger and had been taught that homosexuality was 'abnormal,' I hid my sexual identity. More than that, I lived in terror that someone would find out. Yet, I was in the army in World War II. I served shoulder to shoulder alongside straights. And I served every bit as well. I earned the rank of corporal and received an honorable discharge. I went to college under the G.I. Bill of Rights and still hid my gay nature—I was no fool. I never disclosed my homosexuality for fear of hurting my parents. They might think they were responsible. Despite what psychiatrists say, they were not. Now that both of my parents are dead, I hide my nature from no one. My neigbors, friends, and associates and my boss know I'm not only gay but damn proud of it.''

⚥ "I haven't made any announcements. I admitted it to my grown children when I moved in with my lover. It has been difficult for them to accept the fact and him, but I feel they're coming around. I'd prefer to be out of the closet and am to a certain extent. I just don't advertise being gay, but go to gay bars and gay group meetings. I wish society in general would accept the gay lifestyle!''

⚥ "I'm out but not hanging out. I carry no signs except my lambda ring.''

⚥ "I never did have to tell my parents; somehow they knew and are very accepting; they just want me to be happy, healthy, and prosperous. My one brother and wife are supportive, my eldest brother would kill me if he knew, my sisters are supportive. I don't feel as though everyone has to know—I don't tell them my religion or race—I mean it's not a secret and if someone asks, I'll tell them.''

⚥ "My family knows but I have never told them. I think as long as I don't state the fact that I am gay, they are content with my life. This may be dishonest on my part, but if I can avoid hurting them by being silent I will gladly do so. Usually I don't tell anyone since it is none of their business. My present employer knows of my homosexuality and it doesn't bother him.''

⚥ "My parents had a private investigator tag on my ass for one week. They found out what they were probably afraid to ask me. They paid a pretty price for an answer which I could have given them free of charge.''

⚥ "I've told only a few straight friends that I was sure could handle it. Many would fall apart if I laid it on them.''

⚥ "I am not especially into telling people that I am gay—most of those who know are either friends or have direct knowledge. However, with the exception of work, which frequently involves working with students who are under my supervision, I do not go out of the way to hide the fact that I am gay. I think homosexuality should be neither flaunted nor hidden.''

⚥ "I have never told anyone that I am gay. I am not 'gay' or 'saved' or anything else. I am just a person and I like making love with men. I act like I am. When I talk in conversation I talk about what I am doing, who I made

love with, etc. When they figure out that I am gay then they notice it. But if I am in a situation in which sex is not relevant then it is not mentioned—not mine nor anyone else's. I worked for two years with a woman in a office with close daily contact without mentioning that when I made love with someone I meant it was a man. When she found out she was astounded. She said, 'But Jack, you never told me you were a homosexual!' And I replied, 'Well, Roz, you never told me you were a heterosexual either!' I am not 'gay' or 'queer' or 'deviant' or 'deceptive' or 'perverted' at all; I am completely straightforward and no one is going to pin a label on me which implies that I am not.''

♂ ''My friends know I'm gay, and I have some straight friends. My family knows I'm gay. I don't worry about anyone knowing. I don't put on any special acts for anyone. In a working situation, I am just me. I do what I am paid for and that's about it. No lies, no phony stories about girl dates, or pretending I go to hockey games, or laughing at boring sex jokes, none of that junk. What has my sexuality got to do with being on the job anyway? Nothing. If there is some guy in the area I'm turned on by, nobody'll ever know. It's got nothing to do with the job. I don't hide my sexual orientation, I just simply leave it out of situations where it isn't appropriate. What I dislike (what I feel so sorry about is more like it) in the closet cases is the horrible guilt, the waste, and the shame these ignorant frightened minds are living with. I realize that we all have different circumstances, and I just wish these poor drecks would come out of their closets, not only to find out that gay is as good as anything else, but to look around and try to understand about the prejudice and ignorance of society—and to know that changes are happening.''

♂ ''Virtually everyone knows I'm gay, with the noteworthy exceptions of my own relatives, and most of my family's friends, who are grimly dedicated to the cause of gentility and would not notice homosexuality if I sucked off a stable boy right in front of them. I don't like my family not knowing, yet I don't tell them because it is so obvious that they don't want to know.''

♂ ''When I told my parents my mother said it was a relief to know for sure and that I felt close enough to tell them. My father hugged me and I cried. This is another book. I dislike being in the closet in the business world. But why need they know? It is so much easier to have an anonymous social life.''

♂ ''I told my best friend in high school and he told me to try going out with girls. We were sophomores and I had a crush on him. When I was a senior, I told another friend and got the same advice. As a college freshman, I told my closest friends from high school and they all rejected me. Since that time, one of them has accepted it and we are close friends again. Since then, I haven't really had any problem, probably because I've been in a university community which tends to be liberal. I haven't had anyone close to me reject me because of it, but I am sure that many acquaintances would, if not reject me, place distance between themselves and me or view

me differently, in a worse light, because of it. At times I like keeping it a secret because it makes me special. There's an important part of me that can't be known unless I make it known. Being open, though, removes some of the guilt I felt when I thought I had to hide that from everyone or they'd reject me. Some who are out are too flamboyant. I know I should be proud I'm gay, and I am, but I don't feel everyone has to know my sexual orientation either. I feel sympathetic towards those in the closet and I understand why they feel that way. I would like to help them come out just a little, get to know other gay people at least.''

&"I have told only two straight people, but they have been very supportive, and my honesty seems to have strengthened rather than weakened our friendship. I look forward to telling more of my straight friends, and I expect the friendships to last. The years of lying finally welled up and forced me to come out. I do not like to lie to people I regard as my friends. If they change toward me, that's okay, as I have changed myself. Also, because I have made gay friends, the loss of a few straight friends wouldn't hurt as much as this damned hypocrisy. The only reason I haven't been totally honest with everyone yet is that most of my friends are at work, and I don't really want my employer to know.''

An increasing number of people are coming out in many ways, but telling relatives can be especially weighty. The following statements reflect experiences of people who have told family members about their gayness:

&"My mother asked me if I was gay and I told her. It was a very painful experience and I cried all day because I didn't want her to find out and was afraid she would reject me forever. She and I get along quite well now and she no longer hassles me about my friends or activities. I have introduced her to a lot of my friends and she seemed to like them. They are all very level-headed people and very straight-acting. Now that my mother knows about me I don't worry about anyone else, because I feel that the worst is over. I'm not sure if my father knows or not.''

&"I told my brother and he said, 'Mike, God loves you. I'll pray. Let's pray together.' My mother read a letter from a friend in which he asked if my parents knew I was gay. She cried that evening, saying, 'Oh, but I so always wanted a blond-haired, blue-eyed grandbaby.' (I'm blond, etc.) My father's first words over the phone were, 'You like to suck that cock, huh?' I paused a few seconds, taken aback a little, and then answered with a simple 'Yes.' ''

&"I have just recently told my family—my mother, who is 70 and from a very small town, and a straight brother and sister who are both married (and their spouses know too). All have taken it just great. I really can't believe it! The one thing: I told them in love as I wanted them to know me as I am in total. They accepted me in love . . . and I cry as I write this, because I am so thankful. I am a Baptist and a Christian and I feel that God loves

me and accepts me for who I am and I expect to meet Him face to face later on! I am *not* a religious fanatic but I *know* where I'm going.''

☿ "One of the highlights of my gay life was about four years ago. I was coming back with my cousin from a show I decided that since we were like brother and sister, I would tell her that I was gay. Her response was, 'Great, I'm a lesbian.' We were suddenly closer than ever. She has been the one to whom I have often turned when I needed someone to talk to about my own gay experience or lack of it.''

Most of the men included comments on coming out to their families in the broad context of coming out in many different settings to many different people. The following statements describe some of these varied experiences:

☿ "My first attempt at disclosing my gayness was to tell a close schoolfriend, who was a year or so older than I. His reaction was to hold me down while one of his girl friends kissed me, in the belief that a taste of 'the real thing' would soon put me on the right road! Needless to say, it didn't, and thereafter I was less willing to bandy my gayness about at random. I am sure my mother must know I'm gay, as I've always had close male friends, and have lived with three different men; if she ever asked me about it, I would tell her, but I have a distinct feeling that she does not want it put into words, and so I wouldn't force my gayness on her.''

☿ "I was lucky enough to be forced out of the closet only a few months after I came to terms with my gayness. Had I known just how much of a public homosexual I was to become, I probably would never have volunteered to run the school's gay center. I was, however, the only one willing to do it and eligible for college work-study funds for my work, so it fell to me. That led to speaking engagements, signing letters, taking crisis calls. I became, in short, the 'campus faggot.' Almost every time I went to a party somebody I'd never seen before would come up to me and ask questions about homosexuality. I've read gay poems at public readings, worn a shirt saying 'faggot revolution,' and generally been pretty open about it. I was threatened with nasty notes a couple of times, and denied several jobs because of my gay liberation activities. Still, I am very glad to be out, and could never hide my gayness again. Now, about the only people I don't tell are those to whom I'm applying for a job, and I resent not being able to put my gay liberation activities on a resumé.''

☿ "Most of the people I tell know me or respect me in some other capacity and accept my gayness as part of my total being. I did have one very difficult experience when I told two of my classes—juvenile delinquents at a boys' prison—that I am gay. They were almost all very hostile at first, some even threatening me and cursing me to my face, Although I was forced out of the institution eventually, coming out to my students proved to be a very worthwhile experience. Eventually all but two

of the twenty—all very aggressive, macho males—came around and allowed as how I could be that way if I wanted; it was all right with them. They saw that I was the same person as before they knew—the same person they had come to respect for his concern for their well-being, his fairness, his humor, commitment, abilities. The fact that I could come right out and tell them, seem to suffer no guilt or fear, even show some humor, was good for them and for me. Even though I lost the job, I'm glad I came out to them.''

⚭ "I live in a Quaker subculture with my lover. Most Quakers we know by now know that we are a couple. So we no longer have to tell anyone that we are gay. If we do, it's easy to do. We go to Quaker conferences and register as a couple and expect and demand to be treated as such. We have lots of support. Being a couple makes it more difficult to pass for being straight. I love being out of the closet. If someone can't handle it, they have the problem, not me. At one Quaker meeting, a young man asked if we were brothers. We just replied, 'No, we're lovers.' He took it in stride.''

⚭"Girls I have told like comparing our tastes in men, discussing their problems with men, or (in a few cases) take advantage of the situation to discuss their secret lesbianism.''

⚭ "One interesting experience coming out to a fellow employee happened a few months ago at a restaurant where I was a waiter. The coming-out incident involved an approximately 60-year-old bartender who I assumed knew that I was gay; after all, everyone else did, or at least I thought they did. This bartender kept pressing me for information about my sex life, asking me all sorts of questions about women. My responses were inevitably negative (I never lie), until finally he asked, 'What *are* you? *Dead*?!' and I replied, 'No . . . gay!' He flipped. I loved it. After that he maintained his respect for me and I maintained mine for him. He asked many questions, which I encouraged. We both learned from the experience.''

⚭"My sexuality is so important to me that I will change every other facet of my life to maintain it. I will not work for a man who does not accept me. I will not associate with anyone who will not accept me. In short, I won't put up with any shit over my gayness.''

⚭"The first person I told that I was gay was my brother. I was in the middle of a depression that had as part of its cause the fact that I had a crush on a straight person whom I could never tell. I was very upset, and my brother saw me that way, so he asked me what was bothering me, and I told him. He took it very well, and it did not affect our relationship in the least, except to make it even stronger. The next person I told was my mother, who was at the time watching the *Today* show with me. David Kopay was being interviewed, so I thought that it was an appropriate time to tell her I was gay. She wouldn't believe it at first, but after talking to her awhile, she did finally believe me, and accepted it very well. After I returned to college, she told my father, and he accepted it also. I am on very good terms with my parents still. The final group of people I told I was gay were the people in my dormitory house at college. I had written a letter to the Des Moines

Register about gay rights, and the day it appeared in the newspaper, I circled the article and set it in the house den. Later that day, I heard a massive group of shouts and screams and realized that they had seen the article. Most of them were horrified, and until I moved out of the dorm, I got obscene shouts hurled at me, my door kicked, and threats of physical violence. Several, however, remained on speaking terms with me and helped to prevent nasty confrontations.''

☼ "I first told a gay teacher friend of mine that I was gay, and he helped me to 'come out' by talking with me and introducing me to other gay people. I told my first straight friends about a year ago—no problem. I told my family three months ago. My parents are having a hard time adjusting but the siblings are not. Coming out was one of the most important and liberating experiences of my life! Keeping my gay identity a secret was a poison that pervaded every part of my life and has left me with many residual problems with which I must still deal.''

☼ "Women are almost invariably receptive and sympathetic; men are colder and more hostile.''

☼ "Recently I've confronted men in public twice when I've heard them downgrading 'fags' and though I did it with trepidation, I'm glad I did it. But I am paranoid about widespread homophobia and have depressing fantasies about being physically attacked, going to a detention camp, or being tortured or executed because of my sexual preference. On Memorial Day, 1976, I escaped a fag-beating by three teenagers in San Francisco. The experience was very degrading—even though I have no doubt that my attackers were really the sick ones. Although I believe in the slogan 'Gay and proud,' I have not overcome my discomfort at the scorn society heaps on me because I'm gay. Being in the closet is stifling and desperate. Being out of the closet makes one very vulnerable. I feel envy for those who are totally out and are able to survive and even thrive. I feel very threatened at the thought of being totally out—partly because I think it makes me a marked man, a target for abuse, perhaps even murder.''

☼ "I never want to go back into the closet again and feel uncomfortable when people *don't* know I'm gay. Even the guys at the straight gym where I work out know.''

☼ "Most of the people I've come out to have accepted me . . . not merely tolerated me, but really accepted me. I think people are not too down on gay men and women any more. No person I can think of has ever rejected me. Some straight people can, at worst, be patronizing or condescending. They find out you're gay and start all kinds of games. Such as:

" 'Some of my best friends are gay. I adore Tennessee Williams. Do you know so-and-so?' etc. ad nauseam.

" 'Won't you come to my cocktail party next week?'

" 'I've read *The Front Runner* and loved it.'

" 'I'm not gay myself but I think you have a right to do whatever you want in the privacy of your bedroom.'

" 'I can't get into having sex with another guy, but I don't mind a blow job once in a while. It's better than jerking off. Hey, if you're not busy later on tonight why don't you stop by my place?' "

⚭"One case I remember was the husband of a good friend; he was the very butch, silent type. When I told him, he sat back, stroked his beard, and after a while said, 'Yes, I can see how I could be turned on by a man.' I really loved him for saying that: he would go to the trouble to empathize with me for the sake of our friendship."

⚭"What I dislike about being out to straights is that occasionally I feel that the other person only relates to me in terms of my different sex life."

⚭"My lover and I were fortunately accepted as a couple by both our families. His had a little more trouble than mine since he was an only male with three sisters whereas I was one of four boys with but one sister. Funny—my favorite niece, when about age 5, decided he must be 'Aunt' S., as my other brothers had wives who were aunts to her. After we had been together about seven years, his father broke from his third wife and moved in with us. He didn't seem to mind that the two of us shared the same bed. Later, the father's latest heart-throb moved in! After about a year they established their own place. My own father was killed in the early '50s and my mother went to live with my sister and her husband and five children. That was a disaster. Mother would visit with us periodically for longer and longer extended stretches of time until in the mid-'60s she stayed permanently. Though I never discussed my sexuality with my mother, I understood she knew and accepted the nature of our relationship. Sometime after my lover died, she said I shouldn't spend the rest of my life with an old woman but should find companionship."

⚭"One major mistake was telling my longtime college roommate and his wife. I loved them both, and thought they loved me enough to understand. They didn't. One of the great disappointments in my life."

⚭"I first told my roommate in college that I was gay, in a very apologetic and teary conversation. At that time I was referred to the college shrink who tried to assure me that I could overcome these desires if I would only think of my intended sexual partners thirty years hence when they were physically unattractive. I never went back."

⚭"I've only told two girls at school and they've taken it okay. One has become a very good fag-hag friend. She goes to the bars with me."

⚭"My experience about telling people about my homosexuality has had many results, ranging from full acceptance to full rejection. I find that younger people are more accepting generally than older persons. I think that the first people I ever told I was gay were a group of college students. I was really apprehensive about the speaking engagement. But talking to individual students afterwards I felt better and positive as they could understand the problems of hiding my sexuality and the difficulties of being a 'social outcast.' They thanked me for being honest with them and for teaching them something they never knew before. Some are still my best friends today and are themselves telling other people about some positive

sides of homosexuality to their friends and families, thus helping others to accept homosexuals like myself and others in general. In daily life, with people I work with, I've never had to come right out and say I'm gay. They ask me if I date a girl, I say no. They ask where I've been dancing if I mention that the previous night I went to a disco, I say the name of it, being in this city or Boston, and they usually accept me the person knowing the discos are gay. Of course, there are those that snub me completely, but that's their problem. I don't shy away from them in the course of my work, but show them I'm not threatened by their inability to accept homosexuality, and I still treat them the same as I always have."

⚤ "I tell those I trust and care for that I'm gay. If it becomes relevant to tell others, I do so. If they don't like it, tough shit for them."

⚤ "My landlady knows, though she has never been told. She has been in my apartment to supervise repairmen, when I wasn't there. She has seen pin-up calendars and statues. I guess she doesn't care, as I have lived in the same apartment seventeen years, the first four with a lover."

⚤ "At 13, I told my parents. At 16, my best friend. The first experience was lousy; they were angry and hurt and tried to make me feel guilty. We have yet to resolve that. My best friend, a straight guy, was very supportive—he told me it was time I started dealing with the person I was. At 17, I came out in high school politically, with a letter to the editor. I formed a school gay rap group. I did lots of speaking and confronting. That experience was pretty exciting for 1971–72."

⚤ "Until recently I had always been semi-closeted. My parents and sister and several close nongay friends knew I was gay, and I certainly did not put on an act to convince others I was straight. I just never said anything about my sexuality at all. If anyone had asked, 'Are you gay?' I feel reasonably sure I would have said yes. But no one ever asked. I have been active in gay organizations for about six or seven years, but never up front. The night of the Dade County vote I dropped by the office of a local gay organization because I had been told that they were to be in direct contact with Miami and would know how things stood with the election results throughout the evening. Soon after I arrived, the TV cameras arrived. It wasn't until I sat watching the 10:00 news that I discovered they had used a close-up of my facial expressions during a sizable portion of their Dade County report. The next morning I went to work with a great deal of trepidation. Not only was I depressed about the election, but I honestly did not know what to expect from my co-workers, mostly younger women who might be described as 'liberal rednecks.'

"I was late. No one said a word. Good, they didn't see the news . . . or was I being avoided? Although the office is air-conditioned, I was perspiring profusely.

" 'Oh, by the way,' the assistant office manager said casually as she passed my desk about two hours later, 'I saw you on television last night. You really looked good.'

" 'Was that you on television last night?' another asked. Still another:

'Why didn't you tell us you were going to be on TV?' The general attitude seemed to be, 'Wow, someone I know was on television!' Being on television was the big topic of conversation, not being gay.

"In the weeks that have followed, I have come to view my coming out in a very positive manner. I am much more relaxed on the job, no more wondering or worrying. Any change in attitude toward me has not been noticeable. If anything, the women feel more comfortable with me; the whole atmosphere of my office relationships is more relaxed. Several have confided in me—'My sister is a lesbian and I'm having trouble understanding; can we talk about it?' Another: 'I think I may have a physical attraction toward other women and I don't know how to cope with my feelings.' Many of my co-workers have expressed verbal support for the rights of gay people. My sudden unplanned coming-out has given me new awareness and many opportunities . . . and it has changed some people who were just co-workers into people who are friends."

⚥"I'm only 19 now and I hope that by the time I am 30 I will be able to hold my head up naturally without having to force it up like I do now to show my pride and dignity for the person that I am and the lifestyle that I lead. I work in a battery factory where everyone knows that I am gay. My family and friends, my probation officers and teachers, and people I see at the places I frequent know me and know my lifestyle. Because of my openness and sincerity most people respect me. Sure the howls and catcalls are a daily routine, but they're part of the medicine, and a spoonful of sugar helps the medicine go down (*Mary Poppins*). I believe the American society will never function as a whole (to its fullest) until we have disintegrated all the barriers of subculture and unite to become one culture—ultimately, the Human Race."

The issues of closetry and blatancy are political issues dividing the gay community.

"Out of the closet!" was an early rallying cry of the gay liberation movement; it is heard less often now. "Closet case" is a term from old gay slang—often used with disdain—that has taken on new political meaning. In the name of gay unity, some feel that "closet case" is a dirty name that should no longer be used. Others continue to see "closet cases" as traitors of a sort.

The men were asked, *How do you feel about people who you perceive to be "in the closet"?* The responses were:

very positive	3%
somewhat positive	7
neutral	37
somewhat negative	36
very negative	12
not sure	5

A related question concerned people *who you perceive to be "blatantly gay."* Since blatancy can derive from outspoken political stance, or from mere physical appearance, these characteristics were separated for the purpose of compiling responses to the question. The responses are shown in the chart below:

	VERY POSITIVE	SOMEWHAT POSITIVE	NEUTRAL	SOMEWHAT NEGATIVE	VERY NEGATIVE	NOT SURE
those who are politically outspoken	46	25	16	7	5	1%
those who physically appear to be "obvious" homosexuals or lesbians	14	17	24	29	15	1

While only 10% of the gay men responding to the questions have positive views of "closet cases," there is a large group of "neutrals," testifying to a widespread feeling that others should not be judged. About half of the men hold negative attitudes toward closetry, attitudes doubtless related to gay political awareness. Politically outspoken gay people are admired by 71% compared to only 31% who have positive feelings about those who physically appear to be "obvious" homosexuals and lesbians. This discrepancy is due in part to the damage done by false stereotypes but it is also a reflection of hangups about sex roles discussed in Chapters 7 and 9. It is fitting, perhaps, that this chapter about personal growth close with a selection of mostly political statements on closetry versus blatancy:

⚦ "I don't believe in being blatant about it, but I do feel that we need to stand up for our rights as people. I don't believe in forcing anything on anyone, but I think we've got to come out of the closets to educate people to the fact we're just like them."

⚦ "I love queens. They take all the shit, they're brave people. The same for politicos."

⚦ "I dislike blatant homosexuality—those people who put on an act for the sake of shocking others and being in the spotlight. I have no feelings against feminine men or masculine women for whom this is a real part of their personality."

⚦ "As for people who are in the closet, well, I feel only pity. Life slips away too fast to spend it in a self-made prison. I can understand a married man's secretly seeking the sex that is his nature, especially if he has a family he wants to hold together. But how too sad."

☿"I am increasingly alienated from certain gay friends who feel that I am too outspoken, too political. Nothing gets me more angry than gay people who want to keep *me* in a closet because they're still hung up or worried about making money in some lousy job or business."

☿"Being in the closet is really up to the individual. I wouldn't openly express any gayness unless necessary. It probably is best to keep your sexual preference to yourself; you'll find a lot of people won't mind your sexual preference unless you try to press yourself onto them. Then you'll lose friends."

☿"I don't tell anyone. I prefer my life the way I have worked it out."

☿"Convincing the 'majority' that it is better to be homosexual and that 'gay is good' is both a lie and a political stupidity."

☿"Out-of-the closet gays bother me when they're flamboyant. Militants kind of scare me, but I'm glad they're there, and I wish I had the balls to do the same thing."

☿"Sometimes being out can be draining, because those who know and are straight seem to watch you a lot. I like people who are out of their closets because they are less tense and paranoid, more open."

☿"Too many homosexuals incur enmity and disapproval through their own fault by flaunting their homosexuality or behaving in an obnoxious manner."

☿"I admire people who are secure enough to act any way they choose, however outrageous it may seem. They are the revolutionaries."

☿"I must say that I get exasperated over men who will give the straight world the appearance they are straight and will put down the gay man, but then in the company of gay men will be the biggest queen in the bunch. I don't like the obvious double face and will have nothing to do with men who are out of the closet among their gay friends but are in the closet among the world."

☿"Some people are a little too militant for my taste. They don't bother me, but you really don't need to stand on the corner and tell people you suck cock. On the other hand, closet queens are an affront to me. I know several who put on the big act. They won't have anything to do with me or my friends because people might get the idea that they are gay if they associate with us. But I know for a fact that they drop their pants and bend over any time a good-looking stud gets it up. Honesty, I guess, is the thing I like. So, I'll take an upfront drag queen to a closet queen any day of the week."

☿"I feel that anyone who must closet themselves for their own protection should send contributions to gay-rights organizations."

☿"I had a lot of emotional problems with trying to keep my homosexuality a secret. Leading two lives and keeping secrets can lead to a paranoia or schizophrenia that frightened me when I realized I was making up lies for my straight friends or associates. The lies and stories just kept getting more complicated and more difficult to maintain."

☿"I wish all gays would come out—preferably all at once. We should set

up a national 'Out of the Closet' day or week, and have everyone tell their parents, friends, relatives, bosses, employees, etc. This would show the world our numbers and power—who and what we really are—regular people living our lives as we like to and proud of what we are.''

⚥ "I just find it difficult to respect gay people who refuse to come out even to their friends."

⚥ "I wish more professional people, more doctors, lawyers, college professors, et al. would come out in public, as my friend Howard Brown did a few years ago. What a different picture of homosexuals that would give the general public! I would include in this, of course, successful businessmen, executives and the like. As long as all of us are judged by drag queens and the waifs of Christopher Street, progress toward 'liberation' will be slow!"

⚥ "Some liberated gays are cool, they're straightforward and okay; others are just too swishy or flashy or flamboyant and they make me nervous."

⚥ "I feel all gays should come out for political, economic, social, and health reasons. Being closeted is the only way we can continue to be oppressed. Being out shows society: we are millions . . . we are just like all others . . . we are their sons and daughters . . . we are okay . . . we cannot be oppressed."

⚥ "Many gays whom I have met during the past two years have an exaggerated idea of the rejection which they suppose straights will give them if and when they come out. These gays seem to me to suffer from a case of bad self-image, lack of self-confidence and paranoia. They want to believe that they will be hurt by coming out and revel in the self-pity which such a belief provides. This I find quite sad to observe."

⚥ "I recently saw at the beach a heterosexual couple holding hands and another couple kissing, and I looked around and saw several gay couples I knew and thought to myself why the hell should heterosexual people be able to be open and others who are supposedly just as free and who can express themselves just as well be required to be secretive?"

⚥ "I dislike some people who are still in the closet—the paranoid ones, the ones who tell you a false first name and are afraid to tell you where they work."

⚥ "When I have an affair with a guy who is secretive, it makes me nervous and I feel put down. I usually try to help them deal with it, and encourage them to be more open. I suggest books. I introduce them to straight friends of mine who are open and accepting."

⚥ "People who tell everybody every half-hour that they're gay gross me out. Nor do I like people in the closet, worrying about others finding out. I try to tread a middle ground of not caring."

⚥ "I have hated closet queens as long as I can remember. By staying in the closet, every invisible queen contributes to the repression of others by not showing the numbers we have and thereby reinforcing the public image of weirdos and sex perverts. Closet queens are responsible for more mental

illness, problems ad nauseam, than all of the honest faggots, drag queens, flamboyants, and what-have-you combined.''

⚢ ''I bear a special resentment against right-wing closet cases who wave Bibles and the American flag—judges, politicians, priests, cardinals, senators, cops, preachers, scoutmasters, etc.—helping to foster a climate of hatred and intolerance and rigid sex-role distinctions while sneakily getting their gay sex on the side by buying hustlers or manipulating teenage boys or others under their control.''

⚢ ''As a teacher, I believe that the best reason for coming out is to educate those around us. One's homosexuality should never be used to shock or punish anyone, especially relatives. Recently, I was very pleased when I saw Malcolm Boyd on the Phil Donahue show. I thank God for people like him, Kopay, Matlovich, etc. Boyd mentioned that he had been approached by several high-placed clergymen who were afraid to leave the closet. I felt very sad about this, because if they did come out they would be doing us a great favor. I really do not understand how these clergymen can lead such dishonest lives and expect to be accepted by God.''

⚢ ''My closest year-round resident friends here on the island do not come to our gay rap group—still too terrified. It has caused much discussion, and I have begged and pleaded. But you can't reason with terror, so they stay in, and have their porno film festivals and the occasional drag parties.''

⚢ ''The only excitement to being in the closet is the very secrecy of it, the mischief of a secret club, or being what most people are afraid to be and being right there among those people without them knowing 'what' they are standing next to. I think some of the joy of homosexuality is its deviousness, but I ultimately prefer everything out in the open. I only dislike people in the closet if they 'scold' me for being out of it, but I do tend to look at them as somewhat pathetic. I only know a couple of closet cases who are actually very happy that way and that is all that ultimately matters to me—that people are happy wherever they're at. I have a hard time believing heterosexuals are really happy, though, not because of their sexuality per se, but because of what society has done with it and because they're bending to that treatment. The only time I dislike out-of-the-closet gays is usually when they're first coming out and it's such a relief that they do tend to 'parade' it. By 'parade' I only mean they run around saying 'I'm gay' to anybody anywhere without any sensitivity to the situation. Mentioning it in context with a conversation or event is not parading it. I do not, however, blame the people parading it as much as I blame our sick society for pressuring some people's happiness into being so awkward.''

⚢ ''Closet cases are often thorns in my side. Too often, excuses for remaining in the closet are limp and mere covers for apathy at best and cowardice at worst. Our visibility is our strongest weapon for battling hypocrisy and bigotry.''

5

Sex, Love, and Emotion

Frequency and Importance of Sex

Some of the detractors of lesbians and gay men feel that homosexuality is a "sin" because they think of gay lives only in terms of sexuality. To determine how active the participants in this survey are, respondents were asked two questions. The first is: *On the average, how often would you like to have sex?* Here's how the lesbians and gay men answered:

	Lesbians	Gay Men
more than once a day	6	10%
once a day	11	19
several times a week	60	58
once a week	16	9
several times a month	3	2
once a month	0	0
less frequently than once a month	0	0
never	1	0
not sure	4	1

The participants were also asked: *On the average, how often do you actually have sex?*

	Lesbians	Gay Men
more than once a day	1	2%
once a day	3	8
several times a week	37	39
once a week	19	15
several times a month	21	18
once a month	5	8
less frequently than once a month	11	7
never	1	1
not sure	2	5

The figures show that while 93% of the lesbians would like to have sex at least once a week, only 60% were actually having sex at this rate. At the same time, 97% of the gay men would like to have sex at least once a week while only 65% were having sex this frequently. Note, however, that some people complained that they got too much sex!

It should also be pointed out that in response to these questions some respondents may have included masturbation ("having sex with oneself"), though presumably most people conceptualized the questions (as we did) in terms of sex with a partner.

In any case, while a lot of respondents seemed to want more sex, the largest number of responses fell in the area from several times a week to several times a month. Obviously lesbians and gay men were not spending all their time in bed. And gay men did not have significantly more sex than lesbians. Like other people, most lesbians and gay men have jobs, many have children, and a good number of homosexuals spend a significant part of their lives in relationships or one relationship (see Chapters 8 and 9). Therefore, the answer to those who say that homosexuality is centered on sex is that the lives of gay people center on *love*. The love of homosexuals is for people of the same sex, and for those who claim that such love is "disgusting," "revolting," or "sick" we would respond that *hate*, not love, is sick, disgusting, and revolting! To paraphrase a song sung by lesbian singers Jade and Sarsaparilla, perversion is in the eye of the beholder!

Obviously, the love is in some part genital, and as one might deduce from responses in other chapters, there was an aversion on the part of some homosexuals to the genitals of members of the opposite sex. But a certain number of all people feel also negative about their own genitals. More often, homosexuality is a preference for one sex, rather than an aversion to the other.

To determine how important sex is to the respondents, they were asked several questions. One was: *How important is sex to you?*

	Lesbians	Gay men
very important	42	46%
somewhat important	49	47
neutral	5	4
somewhat unimportant	3	2
very unimportant	1	0
not sure	0	.5

Respondents were also asked: *Do you feel you place too much or too little importance on sex?*

	Lesbians	Gay Men
too much	10	25%
just right	73	62
too little	8	6
not sure	9	7

Finally: *Do you feel that others place too much or too little importance on sex?*

	Lesbians	Gay Men
too much	37	48%
just right	16	17
too little	10	10
not sure	37	24

Obviously, there is an interesting discrepancy here. While most felt that they placed the right emphasis on sex (although 15% more gay men feel they put *too much* emphasis on sex) few people felt that *others* place the right emphasis on sex. Many lesbians viewed this as a hangup, and as such this problem is discussed in Chapter 16. But other lesbians and gay men didn't feel that the discrepancy was their hangup, and they shared their feelings in the essay section, where they were asked *what the importance of sex is for them and for others.* Here are those feelings and experiences of lesbians and gay men. Lesbian responses are marked with a ♀ symbol, and gay male responses are marked with a ♂ symbol.

♀"Sex is important in my life because it is a way of loving people, of 'knowing them' in the biblical sense, of sharing, of fulfilling a relationship, of meeting someone new, of playing together, of giving off energy generated by doing something creative (other than sex) together and sealing the time of joy. On the other hand, if I were in a situation where I didn't like anyone or have a commitment, I could easily go into celibacy for quite a while and not miss sex, probably to the extent of not even masturbating; I have done this with no discomfort several times. As for the importance *others* place on sex and judging whether it is too much or too little, it's really none of my business and never will be. Only *misuse* of sex or misunderstanding about it bothers me, as the fundamentalist-religion-type guilt or vicious rape or using people sexually to 'prove something'—all of these are saddening, destructive, and not in humanity's interest."

♂"Does anyone get enough sex? I find the more sex I have, the more I want. I am satisfied with the occurrences of my sex life and take care to keep sex from taking away from my responsibilities. Living in the Castro Street area of San Francisco, I am really put off with what I have come to call 'The Professional Homosexual.' I find way too much sex, and time placed on sex, in this scene. I find it terrifying to think that sex is all a lot of those people have. Not wanting to sound a prude, as I do carry on myself, but just try and not get into the overdoing-it number."

♂"Sex is too important. I waste a lot of time looking, and never remain sexually active with the same partner for more than eight months (that was the longest affair) except my lover of the past eight years, and our sex life withered on the vine years ago. Some of my best friends started out as tricks, became affairs, and wound up as friends. Sometime I jerk off just to get my mind off sex for a while and do something else like the laundry or go to a movie or spend an evening with straight friends."

⚥ "Sex is extremely important in my life. I think I place too much importance because at times the sex urge really controls me and my thinking processes. I seem to be horny all the time, and driven to all sorts of machinations to satisfy the urge. There have been times when I didn't get involved with somebody because I didn't find him sexually attractive, even when he might have had insights and emotions to contribute that I could have used. Other times I've put up with real assholes, and played a lot of bullshit games just to get into bed with somebody who had a great physical appearance and nothing else. Sex is a tremendous, exciting thing in my life (at least when I'm scoring successfully), but it can enslave and degrade you."

⚥ "Sex is important to me. If I go beyond three days, on the average, without having sex, the desire to come becomes a disproportionate factor in my life. In my relationships with most other male gays, sex is the thing. Most often this results in one-night stands. There are a few partners where I had several sex acts over a stretch of time and I find that these can be especially rewarding. You get to know what they especially like, and they in turn learn the same for you. There are a few guys where sex has become decreasingly important and just friendship has grown in importance. I find it much easier to go places and do things with a gay friend because there is less need to watch what you say—or you can say what you want to say. Sex still is important, in that I feel a real need to have it somewhat frequently."

♀ "If everything is going well, sex is only a part of everything and is not more or less important. But when something is funky in our lifestyle or a job is bad or something, sex can be a proving ground for an injured ego and if the partner doesn't comply, it becomes an issue. All told, I believe sex is very important because it is a cleansing experience, reminds me of who I am: a sensuous beautiful woman. And it allows me to show the person love, just how much I love her."

♀ "I feel that sex is an extension of sensuality, which is an extension of our individual selves—alone or in a relationship. I am not exclusively a sexual being: my partner and I do not have an exclusively sexual relationship. Sexual acts, taken by themselves, do not have significance for me. It is only when they are part and parcel of a broader, more inclusive reality that they are meaningful. I find the emphasis on sexual acts demeaning and sexist, especially since women are usually the objects.

♀ "Sex is important to me—as is clean air, safety in the streets, a good job, a best friend, etc. Sex is one way I have of telling my partner how much I love her. It feels good and I like it, as part of our total friendship."

⚥ "Sex is important in my life, but not the be-all and end-all. Some guys I've gone with *seem* to place too great an importance on sex. I have and do use sex as a device to meet people, to get into places I want to get into, to obtain items and to make money. I do not believe that sex (gay or straight) is some sacred thing that should be reserved only for 'special' occasions. I do believe that sex should be looked upon as a very real part of human life and not something apart from our lives."

♀"I think that sometimes I put too much importance on the *lack* of sex in my life. This stems (or at least I think it does) from feeling that everybody else has a tremendous sex life and that that aspect of their lives is one of the more important aspects. This is a lot of bullshit, and I know it, but still, I feel less than adequate because of it. If only society didn't emphasize sex so much. Everywhere I turn I see reminders—commercials, ads, sex, sex, sex. It almost makes me feel that I'm not normal (of course, by *their* standards I'm not, but I'm just referring to sex in general here) because sex is not *the* outstanding motivation in my life."

♀ "Sex is quite important in my life—it's high on my list of priorities—a good job, good friends, good sex. I feel that I place the right amount of emphasis on sex for me. I think that people who place very little value on sex are missing a lot, but it's their business. I don't see how people can go for years without it, or perhaps a lifetime. I have gone several months without sex, but largely by my own choice, so I could get myself together in other ways."

♂"Sex is very important in my life. If I was really hungry and had to make a choice of a steak dinner or a cute young boy, I would take the youth or young male every time."

♂"Placing too much importance on sex makes us lose perspective on everything else. We become 'numbers' instead of people."

♂"Sex is the reason there are weekends. It's something to look forward to after the 9:00-to-5:00 workweek is done."

♂*"Absolutely the most important thing in my life!* It is impossible for anyone to place too much importance on sex. To me, sex is the way to express our joy in *all* of life. It's the way we celebrate life. You must first of all have something to celebrate, and then sex enriches and enhances all of the human experience."

♀ "Sex is important to me. I sometimes look forward all day to making love when I get home from work. The anticipation is sometimes more important than the reality. I also enjoy touching C. and I kiss probably one hundred times a day—most of these are just like pats on the shoulder, but they are possible because of our sexual relationship. It is very important to me to have someone near me who feels comfortable touching me and whom I can touch."

♀"I think about sex lots and lots and lots of times more than I actually do it, and I usually get very depressed when I think about it and about how I strike out. When I'm very subtle about it, nobody seems interested, and when I'm forward, people get grossed out and say stuff like 'Boy, you've got a one-track mind' or 'Is *that* all you ever think about?' They act like it's something too horrible to try to do with your woman friends. And of course one good friend said I needed to go to bed with a *lot* more women while another said I seem to have a compulsive need for it. So frankly, I'm very confused and am seriously contemplating being celibate and saying to hell with all this. I *less* seriously contemplate going 'straight' (at least it seems more clear-cut what *men* have in mind for you) except for (a) I've never

been 'straight' at any point in my life and (b) I hate men and am never feeling attracted to them.''

⚥"Being gay is central to my life right now, and sex is *the* major part of being gay. I feel I place too much importance on sex (and so do others) when I find I'd rather go out and cruise than do something more 'creative' or 'constructive'—like practice piano, read, etc. It's the All-American Guilt, I think.''

⚥"I like sex and lots of it. When people care (take responsibility for one another), sex is a deep and profound communication, even if the people aren't well acquainted. Sex is never between strangers, only between people who would like to be better acquainted.''

⚥"Sex is important in my life, because it relieves tension that builds up inside me. I say this out of experience. If I go without sex for two weeks, my mood changes. I have less patience. And I find I get pissed off at just or- dinary, little everyday things that seem to happen. But when I have sex regularly, everything is bright and sunny. I feel I place the right amount of importance on sex. I don't want it more than four times a week. When I have sex, I expect it to be good, like two people participating to their fullest. One-sided affairs score zero in my book. There are some people I know that place too much importance on sex. At least, that's what I think. By the way, they are always commenting on the size of some guy's cock or on how many times they've had sex, where, when, etc. They tell you right out, as if bragging. I have two friends who literally keep track of how often, with whom, and what size the guy's cock is.''

⚥"Sex is very important. In many ways it keeps me going even when other parts of my life fall apart. Very gradually I'm growing away from the religious training which caused me so much grief and I'm beginning to want, truly want, to be gay. I've submerged myself into work, booze, and television at different times only to come up lacking, but during this past year when I began to accept that this is the way that it is and I'd better get into it, sex is more comfortable.''

⚥ "I put too much emphasis, but you have to take into consideration that gay people meet each other this way by seeking sex partners. Relationships often develop from a successful sexual encounter, or at the least, a friend- ship. The physical attraction comes first, and since society has so limited normal meeting procedures, long-drawn-out courting rituals are shunned in place of the chance encounters—grabbing it while you can when you can. I love sex very much and feel there is no better way to get to know someone rapidly than hopping in bed with them the first chance I get. Older gays will tell you how sick they are of this kind of promiscuous behavior, but they behave no differently. Older gays tend to be more hypocritical.''

♀"Women must learn to free themselves sexually, economically, politically. There are so many inhibited women running around, and I am in some ways inhibited, but in general I am willing to try anything. I am not ashamed about my sexual feelings, and don't feel guilt. I just wish more women would feel free to experiment and be more open about their

sexuality. Sometimes feminism gets so puritanical and stifling! However, recently as I have been reaching out more, I have found some women who feel like I do.''

♀''I feel sex is like drugs—when you are used to a certain amount, you need it unless you go through a long, painful detox program. I have a great need for sex and find it necessary about three-five times a week. I don't like being so highly sexed and wish I could better control myself. It can be very annoying to have to find sex so frequently, but I generally have a few regular sex partners who are as highly sexed as I, so it's very convenient.''

♀''Sex becomes important when I'm without it (anxiously important) and is a pleasant accessory to a relationship when I can count on it. I hate that 'on the prowl' state when I appraise every woman I see sexually (I feel male).''

♂''I am a Taurus and physical attraction is wildly strong. Sex, I guess, is damned important in my life. I am always on the look and at times when I haven't connected, I will manipulate myself to ease the tension. Although I am always thinking, or often thinking, of sex and/or some one person, I don't think it is too much as far as I am concerned. It is the way I am and that's that.''

♂''Since coming out, since entering into serious relationships which last more than two hours, sex has become more and more a part of my thinking! I enjoy it more, I do it more, and I want it more. I can see the dangers of becoming obsessed with sex, and I could easily fall victim. Right now I rationalize it away by declaring that I am making up for lost time. Most of my friends are gay, which was not so a year and a half ago. As we travel together, usually gay spots (we are all members of the same black gay disco club), we go to Central Park on Sundays or each other's homes, a large time is spent inferring or discussing sexual relationships. I have begun to see tremendous dangers in all this gossiping—having been hurt by it and having used it myself—and I am beginning to withdraw, although sexual preoccupation is still strong on my mind. I am always cruising!''

As the above response—as well as many of the others—indicates, even many gay people who felt they place the right emphasis or felt that sex is rightly important to them also felt that sex has some or many drawbacks. Others felt that sex is not very important or unimportant either because of these or other drawbacks or because it simply had little place in their lives.

♀''Too many women that are gay play many sex games. They remind me of guys that try to see how many girls they can score with. Many women have had to realize all too quickly you can *get laid* by another woman as easily as you did by the men you dated. Too little value is put on sex. Someone else's emotional needs, personality, many things are going to be affected beyond their body when you have sex, and all too few lesbians have any responsibility about this.''

♀''I can take it or leave it. Everyone places too much importance on it. I

prefer a good emotional relationship. My technique is to first jump into bed with a person to gain the required 'intimacy.' Then, I can develop a relationship by either not sleeping with them or by phasing out sex. Of course, this does not include the infrequent torrid affairs which we must all get out of our systems once in a while.''

♂ ''Sex for sex's sake is unimportant to me—making love is important as it's emotional as well as sexual. I feel that emotions are an important factor. I don't like people to be viewed as sex objects—'find them, feel them, fuck them and forget them' is cold and unfriendly.''

♂ ''Generally I think people place too much importance on sex. However, it is possible to blame someone else for this considering the extent to which our society, particularly the media, emphasizes physical beauty and sex. If we don't look like the Winston men, then we are supposed to feel inferior.''

♂ ''I feel frustrated and angry that sex is expected so soon in gay relationships. Gay people seem to feel drawn, hop into bed the first night they talk or discover each other, share a lot, get suddenly close, then days or weeks later lose interest and move on to their next affair. Sex is *too* important. When I was celibate for a while, many people weren't interested in getting to know me. Then when you want to hold off on sex but continue a relationship, you are labeled 'hard to get.' When you decline the invitation to sex, you are rejecting the person. Sometimes I feel that we're all caught in a destructive but self-perpetuating system. When men feel lonely or alone, they are trained to desire others sexually. Men cope with loneliness by pretending to feel horny.''

♂ ''Though sex is important, I think there are a lot of other more important things, and that gay people will never have political power until they deemphasize sex and start being concerned about and paying more attention to what's going on in the wider human community.''

♀ ''I feel that many lesbians I know place too great an emphasis on sex. It makes sense to me that when you're first coming out, or during adolescence, or in women's groups, or something, when your consciousness is moving fast and furious, you go through a stage of being preoccupied with sexual technique, self-definition, etc. But I find that in the women's community (largely lesbian community) of which I was a part for several years until a recent move there was an alienating, pervasive preoccupation with 'smashing' monogamy, sleeping with lots of people, general talk about sex. In my view, it interferes with what I consider the crucial thing for women—to get a work identity together (whether 'career' or political or creative projects, something that expresses us as individuals and carves out a bit of power). It all feels to me like a replication of the trap/sphere women have always been in—the love, sex game that keeps women from the real world. It seems easier for women to redefine and essentially stay within that sphere in the name of revolutionary lesbian approaches to sexuality than to confront power and our individual and collective future. The community I'm talking about has group orgies all the time. Everyone is sleeping with

everyone else and then 'dealing' with it later ad nauseam. And nobody ever seems to get any work done. As you can tell, I feel very strongly on this subject.''

⚥ "I think that far too much emphasis is placed on sex in a gay male lifestyle, but it seems directly related to this unaccepting society at large and a proliferation of hangups from childhood conditioning. Sex very easily becomes the almighty panacea for many gay men's problems, anxieties, whatever, but I believe that we are really only using sex to satisfy the need for love and affection from other men and as a substitution for these things it is lacking. Thus the bar phenomenon becomes/remains an institution of gay lifestyles—not to mention the baths and public restrooms.

"In general a lack of nonsexual environments in which to meet and cultivate a relationship prior to sexual experience encourages or maintains a pattern of sexually focused relationships which have little other base from which to build and which have little promise for growth toward a more lasting and fulfilling relationship of substance on the 'whole person' level, although it does occur, albeit infrequently.

"This is not altogether a gay problem, however, as a straight woman friend pointed out recently that similar problems in building relationships exist despite the assumption of straight sexuality by others and the openness that is obviously allowed by 'society' among heterosexuals. The fact that a bar phenomenon exists for all segments of the population and the easy availability of sexual encounters tend to thwart the efforts of those seeking a more profound relationship.

"Since I am not openly gay at work and society is not together sexually, I spend a great deal of time fantasizing about sexual encounters with people I meet in the course of my work, some of whom I feel are potentially gay, which is also a waste of energy since I seldom see these people socially and do not feel it wise to verbally question their sexuality on the job. I would not be so prone to fantasize in the same way if I were able to date and ask for dates in the same way that heterosexual men would be allowed to in the same or similar circumstances.''

⚥ "Sex is not the most important thing in my life. It never has been nor is it ever likely to be so. I grew up in a bone- and mind-crushing atmosphere of Protestant work ethics and the abnegation of all forms of affection except the rare goodnight kiss or birthday squeeze. For years after I left home (at age 18), I fought to overcome this dreadful condition. And I *have* overcome it . . . to the extent that I am openly and freely affectionate among my contemporaries, my friends, my family (when and as they allow me to be, the misguided souls!), and even among acquaintances, and upon certain conditions being intuitively sensed, even affectionate towards virtual strangers (who look as if they could use a friendly hug and quick kiss of warmth/friendship). Therefore, *affection*—including demonstrations through words written and spoken, attitudes towards people, and actions—means a great deal to me. I am affectionate with many more people than I could ever hope to be sexually intimate with. I like 'sharing' myself

with other human beings. And I respond most openly and freely to affection directed towards me.

"As for the general idea of sex: yes, I think there is far too much emphasis placed on sex in today's world. But it wouldn't be today's world were sex relegated to furtive encounters. The average person is gripped, from birth, in a web of sexual messages, intrigues, and snares designed to keep him/her pacified all his/her days so that the 'real' (so-called) business of running the planet can be left to men and women who sneer at the concept of sex and find it unnecessary in their lives. (I do *not* include here people who have experienced the joys and sorrows of sex and for whatever reasons—philosophical, social, psychological, artistic, religious, etc.—have resolved to commit sex to no place in their lives). I refer to such people as would wield power—power being something the full usage of which inhibits the enjoyment of sex and sex being something which power may founder upon."

♀"Right now sex is not too important in my life. My relationships in the past have been with women who ended up wanting a much closer relationship to me than I to them, as I enjoy being with myself alone much more than most people. In those relationships I suffered a lack of time with myself and a subsequent loss of identity. I resented having to crawl out of my mood and thoughts to fulfill their needs when mine were so abandoned by me that my identity had slipped away."

♀"I think far too much importance is placed on romance and romantic relationships. I'd like to see the day come when we would have sex with our friends the way we have dinners with them or go to the movies with them: not fraught with implications. I think I'd be more into sex in that situation than I am now. As things are, I prefer to stay celibate than go through all the grotesque phases of infatuation just for the initial honeymoon period, exciting though it may be."

♂"I usually say I'd be much happier if sex didn't exist. It has been a major factor in the downfall of my relationship attempts. Part of the problem is my guilt about having sex with someone I care for. Anonymous sex is much less threatening because I won't see them again anyway."

♀"Too much importance is placed on sex itself; more should be placed on communication. I have never seen a couple with good communications who also had a sex problem."

♂"Sex is one of God's most beautiful gifts, but sex without love and without the love of God is empty."

♂"Sure, even at 56, I suppose I could make out in the city, but I have sacrificed sex for the joys of living on a beautiful island, away from the city with its attendent ugliness, crime, and hassle. Is the screwing you get worth the screwing you get? Not to me, so I settle for my fist. I would love to have a real love affair going here on the island, and I'm certainly open to it, but it simply hasn't happened. So I settle for what I've got."

♀"Now I have sworn to no longer have sex with anyone I do not love, women included. Perhaps my sexual appetite is lower than average, not

physiologically maybe, because ever since I have learned how to orgasm, I have been doing it every day, but emotionally. I live alone, am used to being alone, and have always been very independent of others (I have not lived with my family since I was 16), so I can generally satisfy my social needs with such things as conversation, joking, or even shallow flirting with friends, rather than actual biological sex. However, I do fantasize a lot, as sublimation, and I always long to meet someone to fall in love with.''

Emotional Involvement

This last respondent said that she can no longer have sex without emotional involvement. But are sex and love connected for gay people or are they two different and separate elements? To find out, three questions were asked of the respondents. The first was: *How important is emotional involvement with your partner?*

	Lesbians	Gay Men
very important	86	47%
somewhat important	11	36
neutral	2	9
somewhat unimportant	.5	6
very unimportant	1	2
not sure	.5	1

The second question: *When you have sex, how often does it include emotional involvement?*

	Lesbians	Gay Men
always	56	13%
very frequently	36	32
somewhat frequently	5	27
somewhat infrequently	1	17
very infrequently	2	10
once	.5	.5
never	0	1

The third question: *Have you ever been in love?*

	Lesbians	Gay Men
yes	94	93%
no	1	0
not sure	5	6

Part of this question also asked *how many times the respondents had been in love.* We got the following answers:

	Lesbians	Gay Men
once	16	22%
twice	28	25
3 times	24	26
4 times	12	10
5 times	7	6
6-10 times	7	4
11-20 times	2	3
21-30 times	.5	0
several, many times	4.5	5

These statistics from the subsample make it clear that almost all of the lesbians and gay men in the survey found emotion important and that sexual encounters often involved emotion. Most of the lesbians and gay men in the survey had been in love at least once, with twice or thrice being the most prevalent. One may also conclude from these statistics that emotion and love in a sexual situation were more important for lesbians than for gay men.

While it may seem that at this point in history, nothing new can be said about the importance of emotion in connection with sex or about the connection between sex and love or finally about love itself, our respondents got quite voluminous and even poetic on the subject. First they talked about the importance of emotion while having sex.

♀"Emotion is totally important to me sexually. Whether with a fond friend or an intense lover, emotion must be present. I don't have sex without feeling *something* for the other person."

♀"Emotion is very important to me now in sexual involvements. For a couple of years, I just 'screwed around' and got little real enjoyment out of it. A good feeling came out of it because I generally performed well, but the feeling was soon replaced by a very empty sensation. I turned down several opportunities after I got fed up with the whole scene, and decided that I wanted a total involvement with a single woman who was near my age, who was intelligent, and had herself together. It became important to me to have these things, and a married woman was practically throwing herself at me, but I simply wasn't interested any more. I met my present lover, and I get a good feeling just thinking about what we have together."

♂"Emotion is *very* important to me sexually. If all I wanted was an orgasm, I would be satisfied to masturbate, but I am not, definitely not! I have had sex with and without emotional involvements and tend to prefer being emotionally involved."

♂"Emotional involvement is very important to me for one main reason. As is true of many gays, I suspect, we have spent so much time denying our feelings that once we have finally begun to accept them, we find it difficult. I for one have a lot of trouble getting in touch with and keeping in touch with my feelings. I will cruise the bars as often as anyone else, but I am

ultimately looking for a fulfilling emotional relationship in which sex is also a natural part. I am capable of deep emotion but have not felt it for so long that I am becoming somewhat discouraged.''

⚥ "Emotion is the ground point for my sexual fulfillment. There must be something in terms of emotional involvement for me to feel satisfied. I admit to being very physically attracted to and aroused by men with whom I have no emotional relationship, but underneath any fantasies I have regarding the person sexually, I also carry an emotional bond or fantasy about how it would feel to have sexual experiences with a particular man if I knew that he cared about me a great deal and vice versa.''

♀ "Emotion is the great abstract place where we make or break love. Yes, I need emotion, rarely if ever having sex without it. I need to wake up next to someone whom I'd like to spend my waking hours with. Love and sex are just two steps in the same process. If I love you, I want to give you my trust, my tuna sandwich, my body. You will value my friendship and respond.''

♀ "When I first had sex, it was separate from emotion. It was fun, an exercise game, and felt great. I cared about pleasing the partner only to the extent that I would improve my sexual knowledge, ability, and reputation. When I fell in love, my life changed in ways very difficult to describe. I lived to see the light of approval in my lover's eye. I tried to please her, to share feelings, and 'I' no longer mattered. Now I don't enjoy sex with others as I used to. It's just a relief, not even a game.''

⚥ "Emotion is very important to me sexually, but I'm not looking to be involved with everyone I have sex with, so very frequently just a certain amount of emotion is as far as it should go. I don't like hypocrisy—it insults me emotionally and mentally. And I am very alert to what one could call emotions of the moment, those individuals who mutter and moan about love and romance while the sex is hot, and it's nothing more than that. Emotion shouldn't come cheap in our sexual lives.''

⚥ "Emotion is very important to me in sex. I often see someone who is very attractive to me. I would like to approach them, but I don't. This is because I find it very hard to have sex with a person I do not know. I have had times that I simply could not get aroused because I had not had time to get used to my partner. For this reason I very seldom pick up someone for sex. I feel that one of the saddest things about homosexual experience is that so often the act of sex is a frantic race to orgasm rather than an expression of deep emotion.''

♀ "After ten years of sex with men, mostly without emotional involvement, it's of the utmost importance to me now. When I was younger, I used sexual abuse (my own) as a form of punishment on myself. Now that I have a halfway healthy opinion of myself, I find I just can't get into sex without emotion. Even if I have casual sex with someone, I know them before I allow it, at least as acquaintances.''

♀ "I don't think anyone has come up with a definitive reason as to why, but it's clear to me that women connect sex and emotions far more than

erally; in fact, in my experience, lesbians do it the most and gay
t, with their prick-oriented encounter joints, baths, etc.
's not a question for me, or most of the dykes I know, of
e in love' with someone you sleep with. There is a fine line for
between friendship-love and sexual attraction, and I think that many
dyke communities evidence that—what I mean is you sleep with your
friends (or could if the opportunity came up). You are friends with your
lovers. This is recent, of course, coming out of the women's movement,
'sisterhood,' female bonding of recent years, etc. But what it means con-
cretely for me as a product of all that is that the only women I've slept with
over the past four years were good friends (although one woman is no
longer my friend, and the experience sort of destroyed our friendship), but
it doesn't mean that I would want to have a long love relationship with
those women or that I necessarily would sleep with them often. In some
cases, it was one-night, sort of fun experimental forays into a new level that
hasn't been repeated; in other cases, it's part, and not a very big or compelling part, of an ongoing friendship that has hints of flirtatiousness,
sexiness at the fringes. I don't do the bar pickup scene. So I would say that
some emotional involvement is necessary, but not necessarily heavy-duty
type.''

♉ "Wow! This is another whopper question. If you mean emotional
involvement as most people would generally take it, then, no. However, for
me, almost each encounter now is one in which I attempt, and succeed, to
tap into the other person's feelings and permit them to do the same for me.
Of course, there are times when I seek and find sexual release simply for the
sake of sexual release. But as I grow older and more secure in myself, I find
that sexual encounters are only satisfying to the fullest when I really get into
my partner's head—know a little about his feelings, talk over some personal
things. I've developed a knack for doing this and I have been very successful at it. Many past partners often call up just to talk. That's great too.
When such an encounter occurs, the sex is the icing on the cake; it's the
filling-out of the entire encounter.''

For other people, however, emotion was not very important for having
sex, and some people were confused about what role emotion plays, or they
could have sex with or without emotion.

♀ "I do not feel that there has to be terribly much connection between
love and sex, though I sort of feel that when I feel deeply close and special
and warm to a woman it feels like going to bed with her would be a natural
occurrence. I'm usually very hurt when they say they're not interested, and I
feel like I've done something gross just by bringing up the subject. I'm
feeling *swamped* with emotionally and spiritually intense and close
'platonic' relationships with women and would give anything for some
physical affection! But to them, I'm usually their one good, warm, and
loving nonsexual relationship and they often tell me how wonderful it is to

be so close to women in a nonphysical way. Frankly, I'm getting tired of it.''

♂ "I like sex both with and without emotion. It is a lot 'safer' and less painful psychologically to 'make it' without emotional contact. This is my most frequent type of sexual contact. I just meet someone, we get it on, and I split to someone else. If I get involved with an emotional exchange, it seems inevitable that I will have to contact that place deep within the personality which is totally empty, unsure, and void. The pain of contacting this place of death and loneliness in another human is debilitating and takes the shine off the most pleasurable sexual contact.''

♂ "I prefer sexual encounters without emotional involvement since I can be totally uninhibited with a stranger I might never see again. I do not rule out emotional attachment after initial encounters, and have developed such relationships.''

♂ "I have casual sex. I frequent a health club where many times no word is spoken. Those quickies where a man is quickly serviced. I also have a roadside park where there is generally a quick one. For me those serve a purpose, but I need the club as well. I'm affectionate and want to give and receive affection. I've been in love once. It was a devastating experience. I was jealous a lot, felt my lover did not pay me enough attention.''

♂ "I used to have more emotional involvement in my sex life, but after being 'burned' a few times, I am reluctant to invest much emotion any more, although it is always in the back of my mind. I would like to find a like-minded attractive person to have a romantic involvement with, but I fear that is wishful thinking on my part.''

♀ "I've never been emotionally involved with any of the women I've had sex with. It's not that I don't want it—I do, but it's always been a pick-up that nothing ever came of. Usually because I lose interest after we get it on because they're inexperienced and/or nervous and just don't turn me on. The first woman I slept with was dynamite in bed, but I just wasn't emotionally drawn to her at all.''

♂ "I need no emotional involvement. They can just line up.''

♀ "I enjoy sex with strangers—no emotional involvement—but find that I'm seldom free to go around experiencing this except between relationships, and there haven't been too many betweens. I also enjoy sex with my partner/lover who was one time the stranger.''

♀ "I have had sex purely for the sake of satisfying a deep, internal drive—momentary and to the point of satiation. I have also had sex with deep personal commitment. They were particular situations at particular times.''

♂ "I am a novice at emotional sexuality. Aside from the couple of real love relationships I've had—in which there was *heavy turbulence* in me—I generally relate to men on a level of thought rather than feeling. The *turbulence* was originally guilt over my sexual behavior, over 'cheating' on my wife and leaving my social role. That became a whirlpool—not of guilt—but of confusion over the appropriate, safe, nice, good, unselfish thing to

do. I am in a process of becoming emotionally clearer than I have ever been in my life. And simultaneously I stay *out* of relationships and sexually everything is stylized and impersonal.''

If emotion is important for some people but not important for others, what is the connection between sex and love? A variety of responses, including some one-liners, were given to this question.

♀ "Sex and love go together like peanut butter and jelly: Neither is good alone."

♂ "What a question! One can be in love with someone and never have sex with the person: One can have sex with a person and never be in love with him. For me, the highest, most complete expression of love is sex. Having sex with a person one loves is the closest one can get to that person. There are no more defenses, no barriers, and it also is the closest the two of them will get to God—the sexual experience with a lover is the most fulfilling human experience, and through it, one gains a tiny glimpse of God."

♂ "There is sex without love, and there is love without sex. The connection would probably hinge on the issue of *trust*. To love someone, most often is to imply to that person you trust them. To have sex in any sort of ultimate manner also implies a great degree of trust, which hopefully is shared and returned in like measure. Beyond that, anything I could say about the matter would sound trite at best and pedantic at worst."

♂ "I rather like Henry David Thoreau's observation (as interpreted by Jonathan Katz in his *Gay American History*) that friendship (love) without sensuality (sex) is trivialized and sensuality (sex) without friendship (love) is degraded."

♀ "Love makes sex unearthy."

♀ "I guess you could say that making love to someone you truly love can be called 'making love,' but making love to someone you don't love can be called just 'making.' "

♂ "The connection between love and sex has been aptly expressed at about 6 inches."

♂ "Giving the heart away is forever: Once it's gone, it's gone. But giving some of the prick away means nothing: It won't wear out."

Some people, however, offered lengthier views of all sorts on the connection between love and sex.

♀ "For me love and sex are intimately connected. Although I may not be in love with someone I have sex with initially, I generally must feel there is the potential for an emotional involvement between us before I am even interested in having sex. So much of sex for me involves demonstrations of affection (cuddling, holding, kissing) that I must feel a bond of affection between myself and my partners, before I am able to have sex with them."

♀ "Genital sex is one form of nonverbal communication, far along the continuum of behaviors which include eye contact, hugging, kissing, etc.

Different acts require different amounts of trust, and the level of trust needed for a particular act is different in each person. I need a whole lot of trust before I can engage in sex, and since I see trust as a major component of love, sex is to me one of the possible expressions of love—though not a necessary one.''

♀''The connection between sex and love is hard to pin down. I have felt great love but no sexual desire for certain friends and for relatives. And I have felt sexual desire but no love for sex partners. However, when love and sexual desire are combined in one person, then the world stands still.''

♂''Emotion and sex for me are inseparable. I have as yet to have sex with a total stranger for the sole purpose of engaging in sex. All of my partners, while not being lovers, have been friends or acquaintances prior to the time I had sex with them.''

♂''Sex is the only way to completely know and experience the inner being of another person. It's the key to love. Love without sex is just 'liking' somebody. Sex makes love happen. It's also good for your complexion.''

♀''Sex can be a tool in the growth of love. I experienced this by relating sexually to a friend that I had known for a number of years. We had been close but not really intimate. During the months we spent together as lovers we became very close emotionally. When the sexual aspect of the relationship ended, the closeness and love did not subside. Through sex, we had become better friends than ever before.''

♂''Love and sex to me are like intersecting circles. Each has an area into which the other does not intrude, and yet there is a space which is common to both. To me the ideal state of being in love is to remain (forever, if possible) within that area shared by the two circles. If the relationship moves out of that shared area, then it had better remain within the circle of love, because the circle of sex isn't likely to last indefinitely. Bodies age, physical relationships change, but love as a motive force transcends time and space itself.''

Loving and Not Loving

As a final question, the participants were asked *to describe the feelings of being in love, being loved, of wanting love, of not wanting love, of not being in love, or of not being loved.* Here are some of the stories of those who were in love and were loved.

♀''I am in love now. The feeling of being in love is very warm and filling. My stomach fills up. My boundaries seem to melt into her for a time. Energy flows through me. Intellectually and emotionally being in love is feeling that she is the most important person in my life, that I want her to feel happy and satisfied. I care what happens to her. I really want to be there and be needed when she's depressed, sad, scared. Being loved is a wonderful, secure feeling. She shares her life with me, cares about what happens to me every day, misses me when I'm gone, has fun with me, can be alone with herself when we're together, quiet. She is there for me when I

need her. Being in love can also mean that important differences can hang you up, and you feel they are insurmountable and you might want to split up and not be together again. When you're in love, you risk losing the other person and you need to realize that relationships need work in order to grow stronger and more intimate."

♀"I am always 'in love.' Feelings of infatuation come and go, but true feelings of love continue to grow with time. Of all the women that I have ever considered myself to be 'in love' with, I still love them all no matter what our relationship actually is or was. All love feelings are a natural high, and I cannot imagine being out of love."

♀"Certainly I've been in love, more than once, and currently with a man and a woman. My feelings of love and loving are different with each person, but I have to say that it always follows the pattern of them fitting into the spaces in me and making me feel whole and more than I am capable of being without their relationship to me. The wise Eastern concept of Yang and Yin applies, with the broken line within the circle having a different conformation for each love. I am extremely romantic and sentimental, and have been in love for so many years that it is hard to remember the feeling of not being loved by anyone at all. Losing a love or thinking I am losing a love throws me into great depression and introspection and creates physical disorders."

♂"My own personal definition of love says I have been in love five or six times. My stomach knows when I'm with them, at least until we have sex. I lose all composure when I smell anyone smelling like them or see anyone looking or behaving like them. Comparisons of 'love' with myself and those who are close to me become obsessive, and if the situation is so awkward that I cannot express my feelings for this other man, the obsession will drive me to do things I would never normally do. Blood pounding, a feverish daze, limp bones, it all is a very real part of these infatuations."

♂"I have been in love twice, once with a woman and with my friend at the moment. It is great and includes physical, emotional, and mental feelings. Without all three I am not in love. It is being with the person and having the same feelings when they are gone."

♂"I like to whisper, 'My lover,' and also hear it in return."

♂"I have been in love in such a way that I meant nothing to myself except insofar as I was recognized by the other person. Another kind of love has been the situation where I feel the other person's life is more important than my own. The latter feeling is, I think, superior and more satisfying."

♀"Being loved—3 feet off the ground, time rushing too fast and too slow. Locking eyes smile at my heart beating till I thought everyone would hear. Oh to relive those days—throwing our love back 'n' forth living our own special world and giving more to everyone. *Security* and a warm body next to a warm fire."

♀"I've been in love four times and am well on my way to number five, though she's already involved. When I am in love, there's just not enough I can do for the girl—her happiness is my happiness. I absolutely melt at the

sight of her—cow eyes like nothing else. And it's absolutely tremendous if the girl cares for me in return. I never get over the idea that the one I love should honest-to-God love me too."

♂ "Yes, I have been in love. I lived with a guy fifteen years my junior. It was a bumpy seven years, but I liked those times when we had a happiness of being together, entertaining friends—homosexual and heterosexual. I was happy in my work because I was happy in my home life. I could show affection, and I received the same. Sexually we hit it off, although I quite often spoiled things with premature ejaculation."

♀ "I've been in love twice. Loving is an ache. Loving makes you painfully and ecstatically aware of your essential oneness, the lost loneliness of being an individual, a human being, part of the human collective but still agonizingly and intensely alone because loving brings you into an incredible and overwhelmingly powerful realization of the *reality* of another human being. There is a moment in which the fragile assumption that someone else is a person as intricate as one's self becomes the stunning connection, a deepness so astonishing that it is the synthesis of all emotions: elation, fear, anticipation, apprehension. A moment of astonishing confusion and contradiction so loving hurts when it is most powerful because there is always the desire to be one with the other, which is painfully and obviously impossible. And there is always the fear of becoming lost in the other, of being overwhelmed by contact with and desire of that other person, that other self. Being loved is to know the intense beautiful joy of being affirmed as another human being, to experience contact on a level so personal that it implies universes, and yet it also means the same ambiguities, the same fears and potential injuries—all integral parts of the ecstasy."

♀ "Yes, I've been in love and feel so now. I met a man recently at the beach and feel it's been a love-at-first-sight kind of thing. I was very attracted upon seeing him and was more so after talking an hour. We've been seeing each other for a month and I've felt very high, also kind of manic-obsessed the whole time. I feel very good, high, relaxed when we're together. The sex is fabulous. I feel whole, somehow integrated with myself and with him. When we're apart, I worry it'll disappear, and he'll suddenly stop seeing me.

"It all amazes me as I decided long ago all this was an adolescent state and one I didn't really want any part of as I feel out of control completely. I can't control my emotional state and even some of my actions. I can seem to think of little else. However, right now I wouldn't end it for anything. I last felt this way about 2½ years ago, and that was the first time in ten or twelve years. I think what disturbs me most about this feeling is that it feels so unreal, so unbelievable, like an artificial high, which will definitely end. I hope there's something left when it's all over. Also, what could such feelings be based on when I've only just met him and don't really know him well? This all sounds trite and sophomoric, but you said you wanted to hear it. . . ."

♀ "Love is an extraordinarily emotional psychic phenomenon—thrilling

and totally absorbing when control and reason, despite my best intentions, fall aside. Fantasies of building a life together tumble in the mind with fears that it might not wash, that I won't meet expectations. It is wonderfully reassuring to be told by someone you love that he loves you too.''

♀ "I've been in love twice, deeply, passionately, cataclysmically. There's nothing like that feeling. It's the perfect internalized consummation of matter and emotion. It's timeless. I think all human beings need love and want love. Anyone who claims they don't is lying.''

♂ "I have been in love, but unfortunately I never realized the intensity of it until my lover passed away unexpectedly this May by committing suicide. I will say that I gave this man everything I knew to give while we were together. What I am saying is that it was a young relationship, and we had to learn from day to day about each other. I wasn't really too awfully willing to adapt my life around him, and I see now that he was almost totally dependent upon me. I never realized that the severe emotional problems he was disturbed with were that bad. It was beautiful, though. I liked to have someone there and am sure he did too. So naturally now I want to be loved and miss it. I can feel his love and want to give him mine, but there is no tangible way of doing it. In the newspaper after he passed away, I put an 'In Memoriam' which said, 'To love is to remember and I will never forget.' ''

♂ "Man has spent most of his existence trying to define/figure out/write about/sing about/ *analyze* love. If we could describe it correctly and fully, it would be *less than it is*. Knowing love is the most wonderful thing in the universe. Knowing exactly what love is would be the most terrible thing. Ignorance is bliss. Thank God we will never find out.''

Very frequently, the respondents wrote stories of not being loved— usually unrequited love. Many had also fallen in love with heterosexuals or otherwise unavailable people. Some of these were the same people who wrote the previously given poetic descriptions of love!

♀ "I think I was in love once. I was infatuated with one girl who looked like my physical ideal, and was desperate to be with her as often as she would let me. She was flattered by the attention and would sometimes let me kiss or even pet her—but only in public (she was an exhibitionist). The thing was, as I eventually learned, she was straight, but her boyfriend was bisexual, and to one-up him and make him jealous, she had this phony little affair with me. I finally learned the truth when she tried to neck with me in front of her boyfriend in a restaurant, and I walked out, upset. She came to my house occasionally, but we never slept together. After I walked out, my feeling for her was briefly hatred and rage, and I even imagined doing something as out of character as beating her up, but of course I never did. Oddly, I dreamed about her just a few nights ago, and woke up feeling peaceful. So perhaps it was love? It was definitely the most erotic experience I ever had, though it was limited to kissing.''

♀"My most intense feelings of being 'in love' involved being 'in love with love.' The objects were all women who were inaccessible, generally straight women, whom I loved from afar. Most were also before I came out and admitted to myself what these intense feelings were all about."

♂"I have been in love only once. It was with a straight guy in my high school class. However, he was not aware of it. I am positive that it was love, and not a crush, however, because I have known him for over 1½ years, and I still have feelings of love for him, even though I now rarely hear from him. I fell in love with him because of his warm personality, his kindness, his intelligence, his looks, and other qualities that I can't name. He was very friendly towards me for a while, but he is now uncomfortable around me because I think he realizes that I have some unusually strong feelings towards him."

♀"Yeah, I've been in love once. I'm not sure I ever care to be again because of the way I reacted to it. It was beautiful for almost three years, having someone who accepted me the way I was, enjoyed the same things, bought me things and let me buy her presents, who made me feel special and important and confident. I could go on and on, but let me get to the bad part. After all this happiness for the first time in my life, she started to fall out of love with me. Sex became less and less frequent. I kept giving but didn't get much back. Eventually, she finished me off by starting to date a dude, to bring him to our place, to stay away for weekends. And she expected me to try to cope with it. And the worst part is that I tried! I was so desperate that I stayed too long, loved too much, and generally put my self-respect aside. The love now borders between indifference and hate, now that she's declared herself straight, denied that I ever existed, moved out of my life. I think I consider love a masochistic practice right now, but I'm sure I'll be right back there before long. I just hope I have better luck and a clearer head the next time. I think I took too much shit because it was my first gay relationship, and I hear the first time is always the hardest."

♂"I've been in love three times, and it was terrible because I had this stupid penchant for straight men. The ironic thing was I wasn't falling for them out of masochism or self-destructive tendencies: I just didn't know any gay alternatives existed, or rather, I knew they existed *somewhere,* but due to my circumstances, they were so far out of my reach, sight, and general sphere of existence that they may as well have not existed at all. Thus I was stuck with loving men to whom it was impossible in every sense to reveal my feelings."

♀"I have been in love once, with a woman I was in a relationship with for over three years. I totally gave myself to her in that I was faithful, dedicated, etc., and determined the whole course of my life around hers, basically. She was married. I waited three years until she got it together to separate, at which time we started living together. When I was so 'in love' I did not question her inconsistencies, my sacrifices, and I guess I felt sort of noble, that our love was so strong, pure, good, that she was just so wonderful, that it was okay for me to give so much. The romantic interludes

were great, and for the longest time sex was romantic-myth quality. However, we only saw each other every three months or so on vacations because she was working in the East, and I was in school in the West. Distance worked. The challenge of her husband also worked, to intensify things. Further, this was in the early '70s, just as the women's movement was starting, and much before gay rights. We were quite closeted even from friends during most of our relationship. For a good while I felt secure and taken care of, and I associate that with being in love. I was also intellectually stimulated. However, in retrospect, I feel she was destructive to my ego, and that I gave up far too much of my power to her. I am bitter, and have not since allowed myself to give over that much power. I also question what romantic myths about love I have bought and which might be deeply conditioned, such that I'm not aware of their influence."

♂"I was in love, with a guy who wasn't attracted to me, but was my friend for many years. It was totally frustrating. He was my first gay friend also. Being in love was miserable. I thought about him all the time, I did everything with the thought of what he would think of it, and I wanted desperately for him to love me the way I loved him. I refused to accept the fact that he had other sexual relationships but would not have one with me. I fantasized about him all the time."

Finally, here are some comments of people who have not been in love.

♂"I think three or four of my friends 'love' me. It is not mutual, I must admit. I can walk out of their lives tomorrow if I want and not really miss them. I keep in close touch with them only because I've no one else to fill their gap should I split (at least right now). I'm sure I could make new contacts, but I fear the hurt I'll cause them. It's nice to know you are loved."

♂"I am afraid of real love. I know it will come someday. But I fear it. It takes me a long time to recover from crises. At middle age, just discovering love. Well, I wonder. I would be skeptical of anyone who said they loved me. Too many have done so already. I am sensitive, emotional, impulsive. Real love would hit me very hard. I am afraid of how I would/could handle it. It is almost a temptation of the devil with me now."

♀"I don't know if I've ever been in love. I think I was in love with the image of a couple of people, but time has shown those images to be false. I think love grows over a long period of time, but you can have a strong instant attraction to someone. I haven't really thought about the other aspects of love."

♂"I do not know if I have ever been in love. I have cared intensely for men and women who would make me throw up if they were to molest my body. Conversely, I have spent days in the sack really enjoying guys that I couldn't live with for a week. My own personal concept of being in love is being in lust, and I have been there many times. It seems that as soon as my potential partner is totally available to me, and there is a security between

us, this 'feeling' goes away, and I am no longer with the feeling. The initial feeling is replaced by resignation and eventually boredom, and then disgust, and divorce. As far as 'wanting' or 'giving' love, this is too far out for me to go into.''

♀"No, I have not been in love except for thirty minutes or a day at a time. Not being loved is hurtful. I'm amazingly strong to keep on living. Sometimes I wonder why bother, but then I'm amazingly strong. Love is also very frightening because I might not survive the breakups. Is there anyone for me to love anyway? And if someone loved (or has loved) me, maybe they just loved a fantasy they made up and I have to be careful not to disrupt it by bringing in that unwanted, unknown person, the real me.''

⚥ "I've had a few infatuations, but I've never been in love. I am not an unhappy person. I like myself, and I have an interesting and in many ways a generally fulfilling life. But I feel I've really missed out big on something, so far, by not being in love with someone and having the love returned. Part of me really balks at the thought because I am extremely independent, but another part would really like it. These two parts are always at odds.

Affection

In addition to sex and emotion, another important aspect of any kind of love is affection. The respondents were asked, *How often do you engage in a physical affection (hugging, cuddling, caressing, kissing) with each of the following?*

Lesbian responses:

	ALWAYS	VERY FREQUENTLY	SOMEWHAT FREQUENTLY	SOMEWHAT INFREQUENTLY	VERY INFREQUENTLY	ONCE	NEVER
lovers	75	21	3	1	0	.5	.5%
sex partners	64	23	8	3	.5	.5	2
lesbian friends	11	34	26	11	13	0	5
gay male friends	4	11	19	19	19	1	27
straight women	2	13	22	19	28	1	15
men in general	.5	4	9	13	43.5	1	28
parents	8	11	17	22	30	1	12
other relatives	5	6.5	13.5	17	37	2	20
children	6	20	21	15	24	.5	14

Gay male responses:

	ALWAYS	VERY FREQUENTLY	SOMEWHAT FREQUENTLY	SOMEWHAT INFREQUENTLY	VERY INFREQUENTLY	ONCE	NEVER
lovers	70	18	4	1	2	.5	5%
sex partner	39	43	12	3	3	0	1
gay friends	10	29	29	15	12	.5	5
straight men	1	3	10	13	33	3	39
women	5	12	19	21	29	1	14
parents	5	9	15	17	35	.5	19
other relatives	2	7	13	17	37	0	23
children	5	9	19	16	28	0	23

The respondents were also asked, *Whether or not you engage in physical affection with any of the following, indicate how you feel about the idea of physical affection with each of them.*
Lesbian responses:

	VERY POSITIVE	SOMEWHAT POSITIVE	NEUTRAL	SOMEWHAT NEGATIVE	VERY NEGATIVE	NOT SURE
lovers	99	.5	.5	0	.5	0%
sex partners	92	7	.5	0	1	0
lesbian friends	77	13	6	1	2	1
gay male friends	35	23	23	7	8	5
straight women	38	31	13	7	8	3
men in general	13	13	21	23	29	2
parents	38	30	18	7	5	3
other relatives	31	22	23	12	7	4
children	52	22	14	5	4	3

Gay male responses:

	VERY POSITIVE	SOMEWHAT POSITIVE	NEUTRAL	SOMEWHAT NEGATIVE	VERY NEGATIVE	NOT SURE
lovers	96	2	1	.5	.5	0%
sex partners	88	10	2	.5	0	0
gay friends	64	21	9	5	1	0
straight men	40	18	18	10	11	3
women	41	21	19	9	9	2
parents	42	20	22	8	6	2
other relatives	33	18	29	10	8	2
children	45	19	19	4	11	3

Several interesting facts emerged from these charts. First, it was apparent that in every comparable area, except for members of the opposite sex, the women were generally more affectionate than men. However, it is culturally acceptable for women to kiss other women, regardless of sexual preference, while it is not acceptable for men to kiss other men at all. Therefore, many of the differences shown in this chart are cultural rather than phenomena of gay people. In fact, gay men felt more positively than lesbians do about affection toward members of the opposite sex. Another interesting point is that the majority of both lesbians and gay men were positive about giving affection to children, although only a minority in practice gave affection to children on a frequent basis. Perhaps lesbians and gay men would like to be more affectionate toward children, but being aware of the myth of the homosexual child molester, they refrain from touching children at all. The charts show the way in which societal mores have hindered the expression of affection in gay people—and perhaps in all people.

Nevertheless, as all the comments in this chapter indicate, lesbians and gay men did spend a lot of time thinking about loving, being in love, not being in love, not being loved, and expressing affection toward others. Gay people, like all people, want happiness (or most do!), and love is thus a basic part of the homosexual experience.

6

Self-Image and the Socializing Process for Lesbians

Are Lesbians Instantly Identifiable?

Many heterosexuals and homosexuals subscribe to what Karla likes to call the "radar theory of homosexuality." This theory pretends that male homosexuals or lesbians can recognize each other immediately. As the story goes, put two homosexuals in a room of a thousand, and they will find each other out immediately. The theory is an elaborate version of "it takes one to know one" and is ultimately as silly, although many famous people, including Marcel Proust, the homosexual French novelist, heartily believed in it. In fact, he makes the analogy in *Sodom and Gomorrah* that homosexuals are recognizable to other homosexuals in the way that the Greek gods were recognizable only to other Greek gods unless they chose to reveal themselves to humans. Of course, this analogy to the Greek gods also reveals Proust's bias toward homosexuals! In another place in the same book, Proust gives a fine example of this theory when Morel (a homosexual) says to another homosexual in the book: "Take a look at the little blond woman who is selling those flowers you don't like. She is surely one who has a little female lover somewhere. And the old woman who's eating at the table in the back also. . . . Oh, in a second I can spot them. If we both walk in a crowd, you will see that I won't be mistaken twice."

Ah, if life were only so easy for gay men and lesbians! It is true that in a few large cities such as New York gay men in particular wear certain clothes (denims and leather) and wear handkerchiefs identifying them not only as homosexuals but also as participants in certain sexual acts depending on the color of the handkerchief (see Chapter 13). Also, a few lesbians and gay men sometimes do wear buttons or jewelry with symbols on them, such as the lambda (the Greek letter symbolizing strength through unity—originally the symbol of the Greek city-state of Sparta), pink triangles (replicas of the pink triangles homosexuals and lesbians were forced to wear in German concentration camps under Hitler), or double-female or double-male

biological sex symbols (♀ or ♂). These symbols are more readily identified by other gay men or lesbians (although a few savvy heterosexuals may also know their meaning).

And it also is true that sometimes lesbians and gay men can spot one another because of dress, demeanor, or speech, but although some homosexuals are "obvious," others are not. Because of unisex styles—with so many women wearing short hair, tailored suits, and so on—it is particularly hard for lesbians to spot other lesbians. When Diane Keaton wore ties in the movie *Annie Hall,* no one seemed to make the assumption that she was a lesbian. It is even difficult now to spot other lesbians and gay men through the use of lesbian or gay male slang. Much campy language, such as "the pits," has been brought into popular use by stars such as Bette Midler.

If lesbians are sometimes able to spot other lesbians more easily than straight people, it's for several reasons, not the least of which is that lesbians are looking for other lesbians, and heterosexuals often wish not to find or notice them. Because of this desire to meet other lesbians, a woman may notice slight speech innuendos such as reference to going out with a "person" instead of a "man."

The lesbians were asked, *Do you feel that most people can tell instantly that you are a lesbian?* Only 6% said yes, while 68% answered no and 27% were not sure. As one woman put it. "Don't be silly. I can't tell other lesbians are lesbians. How can *most people*, which would indicate *straight people*, tell I'm a lesbian?" Others were equally positive they are not identifiable.

♀ "My lesbian friends joke that I'll never look like a dyke even if I wear men's jeans and a Pendleton shirt because I look delicate and have retained 'femme' mannerisms. Men who don't know I'm a lesbian sometimes ask me out."

♀ "No. Most people are too wrapped up in themselves to notice other people, so I have to tell them."

♀ "No, I'm very small, very quiet. Many people seem to believe that lesbians are surly, *big* women."

♀ "No, I dress casually, and so does everyone else I come into contact with. I think most people assume you're heterosexual unless you dress so 'butch' it's obvious."

♀ "No, I receive as many whistles from straight men as I do stares from gay women on the streets."

♀ "No, while I always wear slacks, no make-up, and have aggressive body movements and posture, do not shave, and have short hair, I am basically 'feminine' in appearance (facial features, build, etc). Occasionally, though, I am mistaken for a boy."

♀ "I dislike role-playing and consider myself a woman who appreciates being a woman, therefore, who does not need or want crude 'category acceptance' from other homosexuals."

♀ "Since people can only tell instantly by clothes, looks, etc., and also since anything goes these days regarding clothes, general looks, behavior,

etc., it's hard to tell where *anyone's* at at a first glance. With me, people can only 'tell' by context, that is, who I hang out with and where, etc. Also I do 'image-fuck'—cross all the lines of acceptable dress and behavior, etc., depending on whom I'm image-fucking.''

A large group of women are not sure.

♀"I'm not sure. I wish I had the energy to dress more femininely, but I disapprove of clothes obsession and the expense of female clothes.''

♀"I dress in the fashion of the women of my college, which is very, very proletariat. Outside this college setting, people may suppose, upon my dress, that I am a lesbian, though they would suppose wrongly about others from my school who are straight.''

♀"I'm not sure. What does a gay person look like?''

♀"Not sure. I've dreaded this all my life, despite constant reassurance that I don't look 'suspicious.' ''

♀"Lesbians seem to think I'm a lesbian. Straight people don't seem to assume this unless they've seen me with my lover and noticed our way of interacting.''

♀"Others say I'm obvious. I feel as if I'm not.''

♀"Not sure. I am quite tall and in no way try to 'femininize' my appearance. I am occasionally called 'sir' to the surprise of myself and my friends. I assume it is my height that these people are responding to. I'm sure that I would never not recognize myself as a woman.''

♀"Not sure. I don't look traditionally feminine, but dykes tend to be invisible—that is, people just don't think 'such things' about women, me included.''

♀"I think about it somewhat. My long hair tends to make people not automatically assume. But I usually chew a toothpick in a rather 'tough' way and wear clothing that is relatively masculine in terms of the average person. So many people have guessed without knowing me.''

♀"A lesbian can often spot another woman. Straight people assume you are heterosexual unless you do something to offend them and then they look again.''

♀"I'm not sure. I do have some 'masculine' traits, but so do some straight women I know.''

As noted, though, 6% felt that people can instantly tell they are lesbians.

♀"Yes, it has been my experience in dealing with individuals who have very little 'consciousness' that they tend to think that any woman who professes to be a feminist is also a lesbian—that is, one and the same.''

♀"Yes, and I don't hide it.''

♀"Yes, I have short-cropped hair. The clothes I wear (jeans and T-shirt) are quite unfeminine, and that seems to make a difference. Also,

my behavior with men tells them: I don't flirt with them and don't take any shit from them.''

It is clear from these responses that most of the lesbians in the survey did not feel they are recognizable and that most of the lesbians (as heterosexuals do) identify an ''obvious lesbian'' as one who assumes a ''masculine role'' by either wearing men's clothes or by behaving in a ''masculine fashion.'' As pointed out in the chapter on lesbian relationships, most of the lesbians did *not* role-play either sexually or nonsexually. The majority, 59%, said that they had never role-played sexually and only 17% role-played sexually with any frequency. The majority, 56%, also said that they had never role-played nonsexually, and only 9% role-played nonsexually with any frequency (see Chapter 8 for more data).

When asked, *In general, how do you feel about the use of the categories or labels masculine/feminine, butch/femme?* most of the lesbians in the subsample were decidedly negative.

very positive	2%
somewhat positive	4
neutral	15
somewhat negative	29
very negative	49
not sure	2

In short, if lesbians are ''invisible'' it is because they do not fit the stereotype that many heterosexuals and homosexuals have of the ''boot-stomping, cigar-smoking butch.'' And most of the lesbians in the survey did not play the roles heterosexuals think they do. This fact is supported not only by the statistics but by the answers to one of the essay questions, which asked: *Do you consider yourself masculine (''butch'') or feminine (''femme''), or both, or neither? In what ways? Which characteristics, personality traits, activities, etc., do you identify as masculine or feminine? Do you think others identify you as masculine or feminine? How do you feel about these categories or labels, and what importance do these categories have to your self-identity?* The following comments indicate that most of the lesbians considered themselves neither masculine or feminine, or both masculine and feminine.

♀ ''I consider myself neither masculine or feminine, but I do exhibit 'masculine' characteristics to the extent that I may appear masculine, but never enough to be labeled 'butch.' I walk heavily and solidly, like a man. I'm very physical in my body language, down to earth. I'll sit more often with my left ankle crossed over my right leg, rather than cross my legs. Also I'm outspoken, not passive, but active and aggressive, not sexually, but just

in a general sense; in sports for example, I like strenuous activity and give my all. I'm honest, sometimes too blunt; in these areas I lack refinement—that feminine, gentle aspect. However, I like to wear a little make-up, jewelry, and I want my clothes to look neat and 'soft' in the sense that they would be attractive to see and touch, and I don't put on any airs with strangers, but I smile usually, and I'm warm and friendly, and very affectionate.

"I think that masculine characteristics are coldness, roughness, physical strength, self-assurance, aggressiveness, lack of diplomacy, tact, gentleness, tenderness, refinement, and also lack of self-consciousness. Men also show off, are arrogant, blunt, self-assertive, insensitive, tough, self-sufficient, independent (just a little bit), forceful. I also physically associate masculine with being heavier, more forceful in gait, a slouch or swagger, broad, strong shoulders, narrow hips, firm jaw, clearly defined contours, leanness as opposed to slimness or slenderness, muscular, substantial and solid movements and mannerisms, very short hair, hairy armpits, beards, mustaches, rougher skin, sexual assault, boxing, construction work, politics, irrational love of cars and reckless driving, drug-pushing, thievery, making gangs.

"Feminine characteristics are feebleness of mind and body, shallow-mindedness, cowardice, concern with trivia, subjectivity, emotionalism, oversensitivity, understanding, tenderness, warmth, thoughtfulness, dependency, passiveness, lack of strength and vitality, sacrificing (dirty word), irrational fears, lack of self-confidence, full of tact, diplomacy, passiveness, far more concerned with personal appearances. Feminine physical characteristics are an affected, cute walk, and opposite of the masculine characteristics I mentioned already plus soft buttocks, wider hips, longer hair. Feminine activities are shopping, knitting, sewing, raising children, house cleaning, washing clothes, volleyball, badminton, typing.

"All of these activities don't suggest that this is the way I think it 'ought' to be—it's just what I think of in association with those words 'masculine' and 'feminine.' I don't like these labels, because they are in some respects like judging a book by its cover—what you know are your own preconceived notions in relation to surface qualities you perceive in another—and it therefore makes your judgment of a person biased and often incorrect. Certainly we must classify this or that in identifying reality and organizing our thoughts, but the stigma attached to a 'masculine' woman or a 'feminine' man is an unnecessary evil. We are individuals to be judged according to what we are in our own personal worth, not our exterior appearances and the prejudice related to that, yet this is difficult to do, because I know that a more 'feminine' woman is attracted to me instead of a 'masculine' one, but on further thought there seems to be more to it than that. I think it's a whole person, the character, personality and body that makes the impression. For example, a woman can be masculine in her traits and mannerisms, and yet if I am attracted to her personality and character, then the former enhances her being, rather than the opposite."

♀ "I consider myself as a woman with both characteristics—masculine and feminine. I guess my ideas of masculinity and femininity generally correspond with those of society. I think others probably identify me as masculine. I think the labels are degrading and prejudicial, and they have no importance to my self-identity."

♀ "I consider myself neither butch or femme—somewhere in the middle. I enjoy sports which are masculine, I suppose, but I also enjoy cooking. I'm not domestic to any great degree. I'm aggressive, stubborn, and initiate relationships which are masculine traits. But I'm also very sensitive, romantic, soft-hearted, emotional, nurturant, and supportive. I usually play a passive role as far as power in relationships and tend to avoid disagreements or fights. This is a possible conflict in my personality as I can sense a great deal of suppression of resentment and aggression, which may be why I drink too much sometimes.

"I suppose the butch types see me as 'femme,' but the real femmes see me as a 'butch.' I don't know. I've always been against sex roles and labels and such and have never felt since I've come out that I was one extreme or the other. At least with Mary I didn't sense any role-playing at all. A butch I was involved with made me feel uncomfortably feminine and the feminine woman who was my most recent involvement made me feel uncomfortably masculine. I'm comfortable with neither extreme. If I had to choose, I'd select feeling too feminine, however."

♀ "Well, I suppose Anita Bryant would call me a bull dyke! My hair is real short and I've gotten pretty muscular and I've never worn make-up and I wear I guess what is called the unisex look (denims, cords, men's shirts, undershirts, vests, levi jackets, etc.) or the dykey look or whatever. And boots rather than platforms or pumps and don't carry a purse either. Frankly I feel really good and practical and efficient in these clothes. I feel good-looking too. I don't think it is being masculine, only to the extent that men have been able, up to this point, to dress in a way that is good and practical and efficient and comfortable. If you put a man in women's clothes, he doesn't look feminine, he looks stupid. Frankly, I think *women* in women's clothes look stupid too!

"I feel like I'm becoming more self-confident and sure of myself. (If you think I'm bad now, you should have seen me *years* ago! Believe me, I'm improving!) I go up the stairs two at a time (my legs are long) and go around with my hands in my pockets and sit with my legs apart and look people right in the eyes rather than looking down. And I cuss something awful. And I speak my mind. So to a lot of people, I guess they think I'm masculine and I hate being a woman and all that. I don't see it as masculine. To me, masculine is machismo, how men feel they have a right to put their penises anywhere they want to—that sort of thing. But I don't even know if I want to call it masculine. I don't feel like the words 'masculine' and 'feminine' are even valid in my vocabulary. They seem to me like mainly the socially accepted stereotypes for either sex. Probably from years of my Ma

saying, 'You should be more *feminine*,' and meaning put on a dress, wear lipstick, and stop swearing. I don't feel personally like they have any meaning for me as words or as concepts. If I'm anything, I'm dykey.''

♀"I suffered for years over whether I was masculine or feminine. I searched for answers, tried on definitions, suffered, cried. And then I discovered the simple concept of androgyny. And like Moses before me, I saw the light. I think there is no such thing as intrinsically masculine or feminine behavior—all human beings contain all things, mixed and mingled, mutated and marvelous. Freedom means never having to say, 'I'm butch' or 'I'm femme.' ''

♀"I don't consider myself as anything but myself. And I don't think that I ever have. I have a distrust of images, part of which is due to my Quakerism. We do not judge a person by his/her title, but by his/her self. I am myself, and if I must be put into a category then I am a lesbian/a woman. I am struggling to get away from putting other people into pigeonholes. And I think we tend to do this. He wears a suit and tie and therefore is a businessman. He could just as well be a secretary. She stays home all day; therefore, she is a wife/slave. But then again she could be a writer. I think we are slowly breaking away from these images, but it is difficult. I probably am seen as neither totally feminine nor butch. I dress in jeans, yet I have long hair. I like sports and taking care of my house. I am assertive and outgoing, but like to be taken care of. I like to think of myself as a beginning of the new and really working for the revolution.''

♀"I am neither butch nor femme. I am me, a whole woman. As a woman I can be attractive, weak, strong, assertive, warm, nurturing, intelligent, educated, successful, independent, dependent, loving, angry, frightened, courageous. There are no qualities which I any longer consider to be 'masculine' or 'feminine' except in a stereotypical sense. It's taken me a long time to get over the roles and classifications our culture has advocated. Fortunately, I had encouragement from my family to be an individual, and achieve what I wanted in my own right—I'm grateful for that.

"I have never been identified as masculine on the basis of physical traits, but I have been on the level of character traits—like strength, assertiveness, aggression, leadership, logic. And I don't consider those to be sex-linked characteristics.

"I get angry about the labels. All the positive characteristics are labeled 'masculine'; the undesirable ones labeled 'feminine.' That's garbage. I am glad we are finally beginning to publicize that these traits are not sex-linked because I think they have affected all of us and our own self-image. The women's movement has a lot of responsibility for that, and I'm proud to be a feminist. Prior to the women's movement, I used to feel somewhat apologetic for my good qualities, in a sense—not enough to try to hide them or to be different. I doubted, at times, my womanliness, and thought at times I was strange or alienated as a result. But feeling good about my own accomplishments, my own abilities, my own independence, my own success

was more important. It's only been in the last ten years that I have really come to feel integrated as a woman, proud and a part of (rather than apart from). I think I'm pretty neat and whole."

♀ "I consider myself masculine, most of the time. I dress in suits and masculine clothing. My short, curly hair, low voice, and my coolness and perfectly unemotional personality traits make others think of me as a masculine type. I don't care for labels, but they don't bother me that much either. I'm neutral here."

♀ "I am mostly femme, not butch, but I have played both roles with certain women. Others identify me as feminine. Masculine qualities in women are toughness, boldness, very strong sense of pride, but femmes can have that too. Dressing like a man or unisex clothes and doing male-related jobs are butch. Feminine attributes are a lot of softness, tenderness, ladylike behavior and dainty or womanly dressing and female-related jobs. I do not like categories or labels. We should never have anything to do with them, and these roles do not have a damn thing to do with my self-identity."

♀ "I consider myself 'butch' because of the way I feel. However, other people consider me 'femme' because of the way I look. I like contrast—for example, heavy, masculine-looking watch and band, wide, archaic-looking wedding band with feminine clothes or make-up and earrings with jeans and a T-shirt."

♀ "I am considered feminine. My nature is more passive and quiet rather than active and loud, more introverted than outgoing. However, I am easygoing but not easily abused, enjoy the active role in lovemaking almost as much as that of the passive. I feel large and am a powerful woman, muscular yet feminine in build. I feel I am a woman with attributes that tend to be more feminine—mostly related to introversion and passivity, but I make efforts towards a more outgoing-active orientation."

♀ "I consider myself butch. I feel I have a more masculine view of things in general. I find it extremely hard to cry. I constantly push myself physically and I am fairly aggressive. My job is a masculine one (construction worker), and my muscle development is definitely a socially masculine trait. I love to mother things, however. I think other people identify me as masculine, although I try to let my feminine side show too.

"I know lots of people object to these labels, but I don't. I feel calling myself 'butch' (or having someone call herself 'femme') identifies me with all the other lesbians who came before me who were into role-play only because there was no other way. In other words, I feel it ties me into gay history. Women who were 'butch-looking' or 'femme-looking' and unmarried years ago not only paved the way for us to be more free, but were strong and brave in the face of terrible opposition and social castigation. It's a way I have of saying I'm proud to be part of the lesbian culture—past and present."

Body Image

No matter how the lesbians behaved, most of the lesbians in the survey were generally positive about the way they looked. When asked, *How do you feel about each of the following aspects of your body?* most lesbians gave positive answers.

	VERY POSITIVE	SOMEWHAT POSITIVE	NEUTRAL	SOMEWHAT NEGATIVE	VERY NEGATIVE	NOT SURE
height	45	34	12	8	2	0%
weight	23	34	6	28	10	0
build	33	38	14	13	3	0
"looks" in general	28	55	10	5	2	.5
how people perceive your age	35	39	17	6	2	.5
facial hair	32	25	28	13	2	0
eyes	53	31	11	4	.5	0
nose	29	36	25	11	0	0
lips	44	33	19	4	1	0
complexion	31	35	15	16	3	0
head hair	49	36	10	3	2	0
body hair	39	26	25	7	3	0
breasts	37	39	12	8	3	0
legs	30	32	18	16	3	0
buttocks (ass)	25	32	22	17	4	.5
genitals	42	37	18	2	1	0

A chart as complex as this one is somewhat difficult to analyze. Two of its elements—breasts and female genitals—are further broken down and discussed in Chapter 10. The women were most positive about their eyes and head hair and least positive about their weight. Most complained about being overweight—the national American trauma—but a few women did complain that they are too thin. In commenting on how people perceive their age, more women were concerned about looking too young than about looking too old. No two lesbians seemed to look alike, if one looks at the descriptions. But here are a few samples of how lesbians described themselves.

♀ "I am attractive. I have a pixie-type quality. I am 5'2", 125 pounds. I would like to lose 10 pounds, and this is the most negative aspect of my appearance, which I still struggle with even though I try to confront looksism and the politics of fat. I have a 'cute' face, large green eyes, and I have a lively personality. I have always been fairly confident about my looks. I made it okay as a heterosexual, and now I want women to be attracted to me because of looks and strength. I relate closely to my breasts. They are just right, and I look at them quite often and caress them. I sometimes feel like a sex object, much less since 'coming out,' but I accepted that identity for fifteen years or so and it still comes up now and then. Basically I want to stay socially attractive so that I can enjoy the social privileges that brings. Also, I enjoy knowing I am a dyke by choice, not because I can't get a man."

♀ "I feel myself to be attractive, but uniquely so and it took a long time for me to become aware of this. Attractiveness has for such a long time been male-defined and been a measure of success and acceptability for women. Yet beauty is *so* elusive. Features are malleable—they change from era to era, from mood to mood. Every body type somewhere sometime was or is the epitome of beauty. But attractive is individual, is it not? Evocative? erotic? pleasant to view? intriguing? curious? All are attractive.

"I know my body to be highly sensual—internally and externally—that my contours and textures are exciting in the proper circumstances, and that knowledge *does* make me attractive. I've had both help and hindrance. I'm rather well-endowed with hair. I sport a fuzzy facial foliage: my finger-feast, a soft-brown goatee, grown to about 3 to 4 inches. I have no mustache or hint of one. It's very soft and curls like pubic hair and is not very thick. I enjoy it greatly although there have been years when I didn't. I have long hair—very fine but healthy and very reddish brown. I also have thick hair on my legs, which I enjoy, and *thick* pubic hair and wheels of hair around my nipples. I love it. It takes time for others to adjust, but my own enjoyment carries them over and they soon too can appreciate the textures and tactile possibilities.

"I also have fine bones in my hands and limbs—smallish frame, but not thin. I tend to heaviness, but well within my desired and most comfortable weight. I have strong arms and legs from dance and working in carpentry and bicycling, and I feel good about my body. My face would have been classic at the turn of the century (minus the beard). I have blue, blue eyes, a strong chin, oval face, lips tending to fullness, straight nose and teeth, high cheekbones: 'Handsome,' I'm told. That helps the others get used to the beard, I suppose. But I care more for how my body feels and functions."

♀ "For the most part I consider myself attractive. I am petite (5'2", 102 pounds) with short dark curly hair, olive complexion, and unexceptional features. I have been approximately the same size for about the last twenty years, and there have been times when I felt victimized by others' perception of my size. People have often called me 'skinny,' a hostility ('How would

you feel if I told you how fat you are?') as I do not feel at all complimented by it. Also, I feel that many people have difficulty attributing power and authority to people who are small of stature, and I am frustrated by this assumption of powerlessness. Nevertheless, I am more comfortable and pleased with my size and overall appearance at this point in my life than I have been for many years. I have concluded after many years of self-depreciation because of my size that others tend to see me as I perceive myself—far more than they see my objective body. If I appear to like my body from the way I hold it and present myself, others will see my positive body image rather than simply my body. This philosophy evolved only recently (in the past three years) after many years of struggling with my feelings about myself.

"At this point the only thing I would change about my body is the size of my breasts. I wish they were bigger. I do not feel I am a sex object, but have had the experience of realizing someone was making a judgment about my whole being on the basis of what my body looks like. I have a mixed reaction to this. When it's a man, I am enraged. When it's a woman, I feel complimented! How is that for a double standard?"

♀"If anyone doubts my attractiveness, I simply get up and dance. I can outdance anyone and drive up a stone wall's hormone level. My breasts are small, and my hips somewhat fat, but I am a *real* blonde. Others like my body. I'm cute and everyone just likes to cuddle me."

♀"I feel very positive most of the time about my body. I'm just really pleased with the way I 'turned out.' I think I inherited most of my good features from my father, who I think is very good-looking.

"I'm 5'9", which I think is a good height. I can reach just about everything I want with little trouble, yet I don't have much trouble buying clothes as a taller person would. I weigh 145 pounds. I used to weigh 140 in high school, but I don't think I was done growing yet. I have lost about 10 pounds in the last six months, and I feel so much better. I really like my build too. I like to take my clothes off and turn this way and that in front of a mirror to see how I'm 'put together.' I'm quite muscular, and I like to flex my muscles in different ways and watch them move. I'd like to see a film of myself running, so I could watch my leg muscles.

"People generally judge me to be still in high school although I'm 21. It doesn't bother me: I figure I'll stay younger-looking for a longer time that way. I don't like the idea of trying to look older than you are. It seems to me that the people who do suddenly find themselves in a mad rush to look younger than they are when they get older—usually with not-so-great results.

"My face is kind of peach fuzzy along the jawline, and that's okay. There are a couple of long blond hairs that grow out of one cheek, and I pull them out because someone eventually comes up and says, 'You have a hair on your face,' and thinking it's loose, they pull it and it smarts. There's a woman at work who has reddish-brown hair, and she has a mustache that I'm just wild about. I wish I had a blond one like it. But that's not possible.

I do pluck my eyebrows conservatively so that they arch a little. I used to pluck them more, but it got to be too time-consuming, and I didn't like them all grown out, so I compromised.

"My eyes are grayish with a little green around the pupil. I think they go well with the rest of me. I used to wish for very blue eyes, but I don't like the idea of contact lenses to do that as I have seen several women with fake blue eyes. My nose is small and upturned. I like it because it doesn't have a bump in it. The nostrils don't flare, and it doesn't overwhelm my face. It's just there. I used to despise my lips when I was younger, but I think most of that was due to my older sister calling me 'nigger lips.' I used to be very self-conscious about them and tried to hold them in as much as possible without being too conspicuous. Now I really like them because they are full and sensuous. My present lover and I are a good match in this respect, so I can really enjoy kissing. It's hard to kiss a thin-lipped person because I end up kissing half her face too.

"My complexion is really nice. My cheeks are rosy, and the skin is smooth. I have occasional blemish problems in the oily areas, but nothing too serious. It's just a reflection of my overall good health.

"My hair is medium brown with occasional reddish highlights. The hair is very thick, soft, and smooth. I like it short, so I can take care of it more easily. It's shiny and very healthy, and my lover says it smells nice. I love to have someone run their fingers through my hair.

"I used to depilate my body hair as much as possible because I thought it was yucky. I used to shave off the hair between my navel and my bush, and I'd shave in close around my bush in swimsuit weather so it wouldn't hang out. I tried to let my leg hair grow recently, but I didn't like it. So now I shave my legs about once a month, my armpits every couple of weeks, and let the rest *grow*. My bush hangs out of my swimsuit, and I don't care. In fact, I like to watch the water run through the hairs on my upper thigh when I get out of a swimming pool. It's really neat.

"My breasts are size 36B, which I think is a nice size for the rest of me. I certainly wouldn't want them any bigger. I sometimes wish I had bigger nipples because I think mine look girlish.

"My legs are the only thing that disappoint me a little, because the thighs look so big. I think they're getting smaller now that I'm running a lot. I took the pill for a while, so I have cellulite deposits in my thighs especially, but even some in my calves on close examination. I like the muscles though, and I like to watch my thigh muscles 'work' when I run. I think my ass is really neat, though. It's smooth and firm and makes for a nice line—looking from the side. The back view tends to be a little on the broad side but not too bad. When my lover plays with my ass, I go wild as it's quite sensitive.

"In summary, I'm just plain pleased with my body. The things I can't really change I've just learned to accept, such as the color of my eyes. I don't try to hold myself up to any 'ideal' images such as fashion models,

because I wouldn't be comfortable with that. I think it's *very* important for a woman to accept, love, respect, and be proud of her body, so she can unashamedly share it with others, and more importantly, share it with herself.''

♀ "I am attractive to some women. I am a vibrant, radiant, very strong, healthy, active, humorous, deep person. I feel fairly good about myself, but I'd like to lose 10 pounds from my hips. My eyes receive a lot of compliments because they are a very deep blue and are sparkling and expressive. I am muscular and have big hands, and I get my share of looks from gay women. I am short, though, and maybe too autonomous for some. But I am happy the way I am and my woman loves me fine.

"I think women like my muscles and my eyes and my smile. People usually think I'm younger because I'm short (5′3″). I know my athletic build is attractive. I have a blondish mustache which I don't particularly like, but which my friends ignore. It's not that noticeable. My lips are sort of thin, but I use them well. I have nice full breasts and strong legs. I think women often relate to my athleticness and to my musical talent. People I know are drawn more by the person than by my body.

"I know men fantasize about me and that bothers me. They're always staring at my bust and ass as I walk downtown to the office. That really bothers me. To women I don't think I'm a sex object at all.''

♀ "I like my own looks fairly well, but I *feel* very unattractive to other women. One woman came out and told me she thought I was very good-looking but in the next sentence she said she didn't want to go to bed with me. A woman I know told me a friend of hers told her she thought I was cute, so maybe there's hope for me yet. The last time I ever thought I looked 'pretty' was my high-school graduation picture in which I was a dyke impersonating a hippie-chick.

"Looks-wise I feel pretty good and strong-looking. I feel I look a lot stronger than I actually feel. I once drew a self-portrait as this big fierce-looking bull dyke and down in the corner of my left leg was huddling this scared little girl—guess who?

"I don't think others relate too favorably to my looks, or I haven't noticed any positive results from it if they do!''

♀ "I like myself. I have been proud of my body and try to keep it in shape. I have had people comment on my figure as very positive. Long legs, slender hips, small fanny, some think my eyes are very expressive. I have straight, good teeth, good posture, smile easily. My last lover (pretty sexy herself) said she thought I was sexy! I do not consider myself unattractive, but I am not beautiful. Old age takes its toll, but most people think I am my younger than my actual age, which is 67.''

There were some women who felt predominantly negative about their own appearance.

♀ "I think I'm plain and plump. What that probably really means to a stranger across a crowded room is: fat and ugly. But I always hope that those who know me will go for character and performance."

♀ "I am not a physically attractive woman. For a long time I didn't cope with my lesbianism because I thought only beautiful women should be gay so no one would say, 'Poor thing, no *man* would have her.' My experience has been that both men and women begin and end many a relationship on how you look. I accept this as life but spent many of my younger years crying, 'Why? Why?' My lover says I'm beautiful, and I say she's blind. The question of appearance is more than skin-deep. You are formed partly by how often people respond to you, and being an ugly in twentieth-century America is one hell of a bummer—certainly when you're seeking to be loved for your oh so precious, sensitive, loving, profound self and folks keep saying, 'Hey, you know any nice women you can introduce me to?' A touch of bitterness here—old wounds never heal. They just scar over.

"My profoundest desire (oh, sisters, forgive me!) is that once before I die I shall be regarded as a sex object, as opposed to being rejected as a sex object. This is gut level—not intellectual understanding about the oppression of being 'only a sex object.' Dig?"

♀ "I consider myself unattractive, but I have a pretty good personality. I don't get picked up or propositioned. People usually just like to talk to me. I am too overweight mainly. Men usually say things about my breasts and things like 'You'd be pretty if you lost weight.' Women don't insult me. Women say to my lover, 'Elaine, if you get tired of her, can I have all of her?' "

♀ "I think I am attractive from the neck *up*. I have been hugely overweight since my early teens so of course this has had a negative affect upon my experiences and my self-image."

♀ "Although I know that I am not ugly and have a pleasant appearance, I am not pleased with my looks. Part of this has to do with lack of confidence. As a teen I felt like a wallflower. I didn't have dates and always wanted a boy friend. I was not the cheerleader, cute type, so didn't attract boys. My personality wasn't able to make up for the looks. I suffered the usual teenage traumas. I reacted to all this with no knowledge about homosexuality. I couldn't make it as a straight teen. I needed love and emotional reinforcement and couldn't get it as a teen from boys. So I got my emotional reinforcement from girls. Still, this was not known as homosexual at the time. I do think this ties in with looks. I always wanted to be prettier so I could be like other girls and have boy friends, etc. I was always trying to change my hair, my complexion, my breast size, and I wasn't successful with make-up. The best way I looked was in tailored things. In college when I started to feel better about myself and the pressures of teenage dating subsided, I was able to feel attractive in my tailored look. It wasn't until I met my lover that I was able to let go of my controls and become feminine. A woman then unlocked the door to my

long-hidden and fought-against desires to be feminine and to be happy with my body, my looks, and myself. Ironic, isn't it? I feel men see me as a sex object, but I just don't relate to them on that level.''

♀"I think I'm intelligent and have a fairly pleasant personality. However, I do not consider myself very attractive physically. I am mainly too fat and that colors how I feel about all aspects of my appearance. Perhaps I'm projecting my own feelings about how fat people look, but I feel that it is the first and most important thing people notice about me. My face is okay, but it doesn't get much notice. I've just gotten the message about being fat too often to avoid thinking of it as the focus. I'm almost always either on a diet or feeling guilty about breaking a diet or about not being on one at all.

"M. tells me she thinks I'm 'cute,' and sometimes I almost believe her. In fact, the only way I can believe her is to divorce myself from my body altogether and pretend it's not there in the form it is. I guess I'm a little better than I used to be. In fact, I can sometimes forget about it for long periods of time. Then I only think about it when I try on clothes that are too small or try to do physical activities that exhaust me. And questions like this make me dwell on it and remember how I look.

"I think most people find my body as unattractive as I do. Maybe that's just a projection of my own feelings, but I've had enough feedback to know that's probably true. M. tells me it doesn't matter to her, but I think she'd like it better if I weighed less. There are some specific aspects that I think people find attractive in me—my eyes, for instance.''

Most negative lesbian self-images seemed to center on being overweight. There has been some movement on the part of lesbians, particularly in California, to combat what has been called "looksism," that is, defining beauty in stereotypical WASP American terms—slimness and other physical attributes. The anti-looksists point out the way that anti-fat attitudes damage women's self-image, and of course they also mention sexual and job discrimination against overweight women. However, from all the voices in this section, it seems that the anti-looksists will have to fight not only the American medical establishment, which holds that overweight is unhealthy, but also the opinions of many lesbians—even those who acknowledged the oppressive politics of fat—who took a dim view of their own overweight condition.

What Do Lesbians Want in Other Women?

Another fact which emerged from the above answers was that the women did not generally relate to one another as sex objects. Destroying sex objectification—that is, relating to a woman on the basis of her body or of

part of her body instead of relating to her as a whole person—is one of the goals of women's liberation. Women do not want to be regarded by men—or by other women—as sex objects. When talking about their bodies and about how others perceive their bodies, many of the women noted that men treat them as sex objects, but women do not. Here are some more observations on the way the lesbians felt men regard women and the way women regard other women.

♀ "Men treat me like a sex object. Not all, of course: there's brother and Dad, you know. My women friends rarely treat me as a sex object. They can see I'm intelligent and would be offended."

♀ "Others tend to relate to my 'personhood,' not my body, though my lover, when we're in bed, makes sweet and flattering comments about me physically. But she didn't fall in love with my body; she fell in love with me, and my body just happened to come along with the deal."

♀ "I used to feel like a sex object when I was with men, but not with women."

♀ "With my husband, yes. With my lover, no."

♀ "I sometimes feel that other lesbians relate to me as a quasi-man, which bothers me. If I hug someone like that, they kind of melt, like a hetero porn movie. With someone I know that's okay, but it can bring out mixed feelings in me, depending on the mood I'm in."

♀ "I've sometimes felt like a sex object only in bars, but never really seriously. Most women have more respect for one another as human beings—sex objects come from male eyes."

These sentiments were confirmed by the survey findings on what women want in other women. The majority of women in the survey looked for personality qualities and compatible views, not for blue eyes or blond hair. Looking at personal ads in newspapers like *The Village Voice, The Advocate,* or *Majority Report,* one can see that ads placed by gay men looking for other gay men usually stress physical qualities. A sample ad specifying looks and sexual acts might read: "Gay white male seeks same, uncut, 5'10" or taller, French active." Men not only treat women as sex objects but this behavior often carries over into the way that gay men treat other gay men. A personal ad from a lesbian might read: "Woman in her 50s seeks same to share music, theater, hiking. No smokers." The stress is on personality and mutual interests, although factors such as age and race were often of importance to the lesbians in the survey in terms of what they seek or avoid.

The lesbians were asked, *How important is each of the following in terms of what you look for or what you avoid when you seek a sex partner?*

	VERY IMPORTANT	SOMEWHAT IMPORTANT	NEUTRAL	SOMEWHAT UNIMPORTANT	VERY UNIMPORTANT	NOT SURE
age	12	57	13	10	8	0%
height	2	30	35	14	19	0
weight	10	51	20	12	7	0
build	9	48	23	11	9	0
"looks" in general	18	57	13	6	5	1
eyes	22	34	28	9	8	1
nose	2	20	52	12	12	1
lips	9	27	42	12	10	1
complexion	9	42	32	9	9	1
facial hair	9	27	40	13	9	2
head hair	12	35	32	11	10	1
body hair	5	21	46	16	11	2
breasts	11	32	35	12	8	1
legs	4	27	43	15	11	1
buttocks (ass)	7	25	42	13	11	1
hygiene, cleanliness or lack of it	65	29	3	1	1	0
clothing	10	46	26	10	8	1
race	9	19	36	12	19	5
social class	6	24	35	18	14	3
educational level	16	47	19	9	8	1
religion or spiritual orientation	10	27	35	10	16	2
political views	26	35	25	7	6	1
overall personality	74	23	1	2	0	1
masculinity/femininity butch/femme	10	27	30	8	22	3
intelligence	62	32	3	1	1	1

It is absolutely clear from this chart that the most important factors for the lesbians, even when looking for a sex partner, were personality (97% labeled it important), intelligence (94% felt it was important), and hygiene

(94% labeled hygiene important, and no one mentioned they were looking for a dirty person). A majority (61%) also felt that political views are important, as well as educational level (63%). Religion, social class, roles (masculine/feminine), and race were all relatively unimportant.

Analyzing how the lesbians felt about looks is more complex. A slight majority of the women did not relate to a certain physical type. This information was confirmed by answers to the question *How often do you relate to a certain "type"?* From the subsample, we got the following percentages.

always	6%
very frequently	15
somewhat frequently	26
somewhat infrequently	16
very infrequently	0
once	11
never	25

A substantial 47% related to a certain type with some frequency, but many who answered this question referred to their "type" as having a certain personality or political outlook rather than certain physical characteristics.

Looking at the physical characteristics some women did seek in a "type," one can see that "looks in general" was the most important, if vaguest, category, with 75% rating looks as important. The most important component seemed to be weight, with 61% rating it as being important (most stated they avoided obesity). General build, eyes, and clothes seemed to be the second most important component of looks, each with 57% or 56% of the women noting them as important. Complexion scored 49%, head hair scored 47%, and the rest seemed to be important only to smaller percentages of the lesbians, with the nose being the least important feature.

A very notable feature is age. In the subsample, 69% noted it as important. To determine what ages were favored, another question asked, *How often do you have sex with women or girls of the following ages?*

Age	ALWAYS	VERY FREQUENTLY	SOMEWHAT FREQUENTLY	SOMEWHAT INFREQUENTLY	VERY INFREQUENTLY	ONCE	NEVER
65+	.5	0	0	0	.5	0	99%
55–64	2	.5	0	0	.5	1	96

	ALWAYS	VERY FREQUENTLY	SOMEWHAT FREQUENTLY	SOMEWHAT INFREQUENTLY	VERY INFREQUENTLY	ONCE	NEVER
45–54	2	3	2	1	5	4	83
35–44	9	8	5	5	8	6	60
30–34	13	16	11	7	8	6	40
25–29	16	26	14	7	7	4	28
20–24	14	24	12	5	10	5	31
16–19	4	6	4	2	6	9	70
13–15	.5	1	.5	0	2	2	94
9–12	0	0	1	0	0	1	98
under 9	0	0	1	0	0	0	99

This chart seems to indicate that most of the lesbians had sex primarily with women aged 20 to 34. Women who fell into those age groups also made up the bulk of the survey (the average age of the lesbians in this survey was 29.6 years). The above figures were correlated with the age of the respondents to determine who was having sex with whom. Generally, women were having sex with those in the same age group, although there was a slight tendency for the lesbians to have sex with the next-youngest age group. This is particularly true of women aged 35–44, the majority of whom (56%) were having sex with women aged 30–34. The cross-correlations (too complicated to reprint here) also clearly showed that lesbians are *not* child molesters. Those having sex with lesbians under 19 in this survey were almost always themselves under 19. Thus anyone who still believes this bizarre myth about lesbians should examine her or his motives for wanting to believe such bigotry.

The tendency to choose slightly younger women could be attributed to one or more factors. The number of lesbians in the sample thins out as the age increases. If there are fewer older lesbians in the general population, then some older lesbians would have to seek younger sex partners out of necessity. The tendency to select slightly younger partners may also reflect the ageism of Western culture as a whole, especially in North America. One cannot conclusively accuse lesbians of ageism, since most of the lesbians felt positive about aging. When asked, *How do you feel about aging,* the majority, 53%, were definitely positive.

very positive	13%
somewhat positive	40

neutral	21
somewhat negative	16
very negative	5
not sure	5

Some women were ironically philosophical, asking, "What's the alternative to aging?" while other answers reflected a positive self-image.

Because of feeling positive about one's own age, and perhaps because many lesbians have heard that lesbians are either child molesters or are "seeking a mother substitute," most lesbians felt very negative about having sex with women who are either much younger or much older. The women were asked: *Whether or not you have sex with any of the following age groups, indicate how you feel about the idea of having sex with each of them.*

	VERY POSITIVE	SOMEWHAT POSITIVE	NEUTRAL	SOMEWHAT NEGATIVE	VERY NEGATIVE	NOT SURE
65 +	12	7	13	22	31	12%
55–64	17	9	17	22	26	10
45–54	30	15	19	15	14	8
35–44	52	21	15	5	3	4
30–34	66	21	10	1	1	1
25–29	70	17	9	2	2	1
20–24	56	20	9	10	6	0
16–19	14	20	11	25	29	1
13–15	2	4	6	15	69	4
9–12	1	1	.5	6	87	4
under 9	3	.5	0	4	87	2

As one might expect from actual sexual practice, the women were most positive about those women who fall within the age groups they actually had sex with. These were ages 20–44, with the most positive feelings being about ages 25–34 with 87% being positive. A large minority (45%) was positive about sex with those aged 45–54, but the feelings of those in the subsample became predominantly neutral and even negative about those over 65. 84% were negative about having sex with women 13–15, and 93% were negative about having sex with those 9–12, and 91% were negative about having sex with those under 9. It should be pointed out that when we

did further crosstabulations of this attitudes chart, we found that partners, those who were most favorable to having sex with those under 16 were themselves in the age group. Also, those who were most favorable to sex with older women were themselves older, although more younger women felt positive about sex with older women than did older women about sex with younger women.

To sum up this section on the question of age in a sex partner, here are some of the comments about it from our respondents.

♀ "I am 30 and would like to have a relationship with a woman older than myself—late 30s or early 40s preferably. But I'm having a rather streak of bad luck in meeting anyone who is interested in me and whom I'm interested in (of any age)."

♀ "I'm 28 and women within ten years either way seem to be the easiest to get along with."

♀ "Any woman under 18 is too young (I'm 32). She has not experienced life as yet and can't make a realistic decision."

♀ "My present lover is 32—eight years older than I. Another woman I was with briefly was 38. These are the sexiest women I know. I also feel quite positive about those in my own age group—and very negative about teens. They definitely have enough problems, and I don't want to be cast in the role of 'older woman/seducer.' And I am very negative about the idea of sex with young girls. It is inexcusable for anyone to take advantage of a child."

♀ "I'm 21. My experience has been with women in their late teens and early 20s. Age doesn't really matter to me in the range of 16–44. But I still feel negative about having sex with women much older than me. And I can't imagine having sex with girls under 12."

♀ "I feel horrified at the idea of sex between children and adults. Other than that I don't care about age but don't get to meet many women much older than me (I'm 37)."

♀ "I'm 24 and had a relationship with a woman ten years older, which took a lot of getting used to (she had a child, was married), but I do feel that the growth on both our parts and that one experience were invaluable."

♀ "I'm 37. I prefer young women because of their energy and habits."

♀ "I'm 23, and I don't think young girls would do anything for me emotionally. I'd have to be interested in someone 35–65 emotionally to be involved sexually."

♀ "I can't imagine making love to a woman old enough to be my grandmother, but the experience might be rewarding."

♀ "A very special woman of 16 (I was 25) loved me—and I her. After several months of discussion, we decided our physically loving one another would not have any negative ramifications. She is 20 now, and though we have not slept together in the last two years, we are still very close."

♀ "I'm 21, but I think having an experience or relationship with an older woman would be very rewarding, as has been my experience with a woman one year younger than I."

♀ "My partners have always been in my age group or slightly older. I wouldn't fool around with kids. It is too dangerous, and I don't have anything in common with them or much older women."

♀ "I feel negative towards older women. It has nothing to do with my attraction to them, but I'm intimidated by them. I'm 22, and they are my mother's age. Scary."

♀ "My preference is for a peer in age, all things being equal. My current lover is 14 years younger than I. It's her personality and the positive aspects of the relationship which attracted me. Usually, I would not seek anyone less or more than ten years in age difference."

♀ "I have felt sexual attraction for women in their 50s and 60s. I would not want to automatically rule out sex with a very young woman, but I would be concerned she understand the implications of what we were doing."

♀ "Under 9? You've got to be kidding!"

♀ "Young, innocent-looking children are a turn-on, but I think I would feel like a child molester if I followed through (ageism strikes again). I'm 16."

♀ "When I was 9–12 I had sex with girls my own age several times, so I answered yes for this."

♀ "I feel positive about all ages over 25. Someday we will have been all these ages."

Now that the important question of age has been discussed, here are some overall pictures of what lesbians want in a sex partner. The participants were not only asked to describe their "type" but also *to tell whether they relate only to a certain type and what they like or dislike about the idea of having a type.*

♀ "I prefer the 'Marilyn Monroe type.' Partly I guess this is the result of an inverted heterosexual conditioning, and partly just purely aesthetic criteria. Even when I was 14, I liked buxom women, and my favorite movie star was Elizabeth Taylor. The blonde fetishism is only two or three years old. I am not a blonde myself, though I was when I was little. Perhaps yellow hair symbolizes my lost childhood, my innocence. That's just a Freudian speculation. In my poetry and stories, I associate yellow hair with light, the sun, precious gold, etc. But I have in the past also been very interested in brunette girls. In fact, my blond thing is mostly sex-linked, because I would never sleep with a man who wasn't blond (perhaps this is because blond men have less body hair, and I detest body hair, especially in men). In women, I am not fixated on this one type. It is just my ideal. I like all women who are healthy-looking and pretty or interesting-looking. The only thing I actively avoid is a bad complexion—the face is the part of the body I like to caress most, and I cannot do this if the skin is bad. I can't bear pimples, warts, or moles either.

"I do relate to other types too. Only once did I meet my actual type, and that was a heterosexual girl who tricked me into having sex.

"The whole idea of 'types' reeks of sexism, fetishism, and sex-objectification, like men sitting in a locker room and discussing their girl friends in the minutest detail. People are people, not a collection of parts. On the other hand, no one calls great artists sexist for painting only certain types. People are works of art, and aestheticism is a valid attitude so long as it is not conceived to dehumanize the 'types' into pretty objects, or to denigrate those who do not qualify. And, of course, there are many people who are old, handicapped, or deformed, and it is just not their fault. Hitler made his first experiments in mass murder by gassing such people. Of course, they have the right to live, and living includes emotions, friendship, sex, the whole thing. So the aesthetic attitude excludes them. But I don't want to give up the aesthetic attitude either. Someday maybe we'll have it so that people are not born with any physical defects, and aging is slowed down. Anyway, so much for the flaws that are not anyone's fault, but most people have at least some control over how they look. In our society, women try desperately to look like men want them to, and men don't care how they look, which I think is the height of arrogance. People should set their own standards."

♀"I prefer sexy, beautiful women like myself. I like older women, Jewish women (not many gay ones around here for miles!). I like big women, but not obese, but rather overweight, taller and bigger than me. I adore long, long legs. I love red and blond pubic hair. I like Latin women of all shapes and sizes, except terribly skinny ones. If I can't find or have a woman I am visually, vocally, and physically attracted to, well, it's frustrating. But there are many, many other women to relate to. I avoid obesity, skinniness, obvious butches, and women trying to act butch."

♀"The type I prefer is an athletic, healthy woman who is self-confident without being conceited, and who is self-reliant and independent. She must have a strong character. I look at how a woman carries herself, and I like to see strength without roughness, aggressiveness, but not at anyone else's expense. I look for a sense of humor, a depth and philosophy that she may have. I look for a love of music, especially guitar. I like women who are feminists and lesbians. I like women who don't seek others for strength but who share their strength with others. I like strong muscular women who are lean but not skinny. I like a good, square build, medium height, dark hair and eyebrows, blue eyes (but as long as the eyes are sparkling and expressive I'm not picky), strong hands and jaw, a smooth low voice. I like strong thighs and small but womanly hips and buttocks. I like women who dress sharply—flannel shirts, jeans, Frye boots, crew-neck sweaters—unisex clothing. I like vests and suits on women. I like women who are intelligent and bright. I like women who are not malleable but who have strong characters and principles. I like women who are open and supportive of other women, but who don't wear their hearts on their sleeves. If you've

ever seen a picture of the singer Casse Culver, then you know what I like. Strength, independence, compassion, sensuality, alertness. I look for a nice full mouth that is moist and smiles easily and teases. I like womanly breasts, but not too big. I like a woman who cares about herself, who stands up for her beliefs, who seeks to right injustice. I look for sensitivity to my emotions and body, and a selfless love. I tend to avoid loud women, very tough and old women, conceited women, selfish and prideful women, fat women, skinny women, haughty women, shallow women, real feminine women (make-up, etc). I like women who are into camping, backpacking, sports, music. It all boils down to me loving the women who seem to epitomize the woman I am growing into.

"Actually I can relate to almost any woman who has some sense of acceptance for me as I am. I have a lot of compassion for women, so I'll talk to 'losers' who everyone else ignores. But as for attraction, I am fairly limited to the rather general type I have just described. Having a type I am attracted to is fine for fantasy's sake, but it's rare that that is any basis for starting a relationship."

♀ "The most important quality that any woman can have is her brains. If she is smart, not necessarily well educated, I will take the time to get to know her. Secondly, she must at least understand and hopefully share my politics. I am a full-time feminist. I find it very difficult to relate to non-feminist women. Hopefully, she will also be a lesbian, socialist, or anarchist. Then comes looks, which remain secondary. My perfect woman is one who looks like a woman (in the traditional sense). She has breasts that one can see; she has hips and a fine-featured face. She is usually thin, tall, and dresses in pants rather than dresses. She is clean, very healthy-looking and muscled. In other words, her good-looking body comes from good health rather than from cosmetics. All of this matters little, however. It seems that I can become attracted to any type as long as they are intelligent and we have something to talk about. Finding areas of mutual interest is not usually difficult as I have very varied interests."

♀ "I am afraid that I do have a type. My lovers have mostly not been far from this physical type: black or dark-brown hair (usually long), shorter than me, comparatively large breasts. They have invariably had either Taurus or Cancer rising, and either a planet or an important point within 3 degrees of 12 Taurus, where my Jupiter and Point of Fortune are. I am not attracted to wimmin whose Neptunes are in Libra, which means not more than ten years older or more than five years younger than me. I could never consider a relationship with a womon older or younger; it would never work out."

♀ "I hate admitting this, but I will. I do prefer a certain type: slim, attractive, more feminine-appearing than masculine-appearing. Also, I'm attracted to women who are intelligent, college-educated, lovers of reading, professionals. I avoid women who are a lot younger than I. And because of my long-term relationship with a woman nine years older, I have avoided older women too, because experience does make a difference. I don't

imagine I'll always feel this way though. I think I am an ageist. I have definite preferences for people who have tight bodies, small asses, small rather than huge breasts, nice eyes, little facial hair. Politics, education, sensitivity, honesty are all important. And a sense of humor too.''

♀ "My dream woman has glasses, not short hair, a little afraid of living, a little arrogant (but hiding it well under humbleness), intellectual, a sweet face, maybe a little aged, deep-looking. I like a lot of other types too—most types, especially New York-looking. Jewish or Italian, dark, sharp, a little hard, very sweet inside, also sophisticated and not too smily-sweet outside. I also like healthy California dykes.''

♀ "Judging from the women I have been attached to over the last ten years (though without sexual involvement until my present lover), the one quality which they seem to have had in common is a rather childlike naiveté, though most were close to my own age. Apart from that, they were of various sizes, shapes, colorings, etc. I did not realize that this was my 'type' until I had met and fallen in love with my current lover. On a friendly basis, I can relate to almost anyone—gay, straight, or in between. Sex is not important enough to me to worry about whether I can relate sexually. On one hand, having a certain type would seem to needlessly limit one; on the other hand, I suppose if you are put together in a certain way, it takes a certain 'type' on the part of another to fit in with you. There is, however, only one factor that really counts at all in the long run: I must be in love.''

♀ "When I look for a lover, I'm looking for a woman who is about my age, height, weight, and build. I like a woman who cares about her appearance. I tend to be partial to the more attractive women. I'm a lover of beauty, but it isn't a prerequisite. I don't demand that my lover be a ravishing beauty. If she is that's just fine, but I refuse to wake up every morning having to face some ugly old war horse appearing as if it just crawled off the battlefield. I'd rather not be in love at all than have that. The beauty I'm referring to is not the photogenic Miss U.S.A. but a woman who looks pleasant. One who takes care of her looks and has some poise.''

♀ "Yes, I have a type. There are no physical characteristics to this type. It's totally attitudinal. I am attracted to very 'in control' types of women. By that I mean they're outgoing in groups, opinionated, usually demonstrative about anger, and assertive. This is a butch type I'm referring to. I can tell by the way a woman walks if she's this type—the walk is assertive and confident in a 'masculine' way. I like to be courted and swept off my feet by my lover, and this type always does that to me. It's interesting to me that when I was straight, men like that made me sick!''

♀ "If I had to choose a type, it would be a femme woman. Not really 'femme' but down to earth and real. She must be from 20-44, medium height, built rather nice, not too fat and not too skinny (120-160), must be average or attractive (not really beautiful), no pimply skin, average facial and head hair. Breasts, legs, and buttocks must not be too big or skinny. She must be clean, and her clothes must be neat and clean. She can be of any race. It also does not matter which social class she is from, or what her

religion is. She must be intelligent to a certain extent and have a nice personality. No role-playing. I relate to all types of women, and I do not get upset if I do not find the right type. The above attributes that are especially important are age, personality, neatness, cleanliness, and intelligence."

♀ "The eyes are the most important. I can 'get lost' in someone's eyes. Legs are next on the list. I like an attractive woman, but that's really relative, isn't it? One thing I can't stand which you neglected on your list is teeth not properly cared for. The woman could be a real 'knockout' in every sense of the word, but if she neglects her teeth, I'm gone! Hygiene is the most important—I can't stand slobs. Body hair in quantity turns me off: who wants a gorilla? Race couldn't matter less although I *prefer* white women (I'm mulatto). Intelligence is *very, very* important."

♀ "Twenty years ago when I was 25, I didn't want an 'older' woman of 45. Now I am 45, and I certainly wouldn't be turned off by a 25-year old!"

♀ "The type of person I am most attracted to whether male or female, is the dark-complexioned, foreign-looking person."

♀ "I prefer a woman with dark hair and brown eyes. (I am blond myself—opposites attract.) When I don't find my 'type' I usually have calmer and more stable relationships. With my type, I have stormy but dynamic affairs. I think everyone has a type—the kind of person who turns your head on the street with whom you fall instantly in love. The important factors presently in my choosing a lover is to *avoid* my type. I need a calmer relationship."

♀ "I don't have a particular type that attracts me according to appearance. If any physical attribute is important, it probably is the person's eyes—warmth of expressions, etc. I am attracted to a person who is friendly, has a good sense of humor, a congenial temperament, is assertive rather than one who plays games and a person who is comfortable to be with. I would not become involved with anyone who is not comfortable with her lesbianism or someone who is a minor. I would like my lover to share my political views as a woman—that is, a woman should have choices and control over her own body and destiny."

♀ "I can't relate to this question. It seems geared to a male-defined mentality that habituates bars and looks for quick fucks. The only thing I can say here is that I don't like women (or men either for that matter, when I was into them) who are much taller than me. It makes me feel powerless, and out of control. I also don't like really skinny women. My ideal woman, although I certainly don't go looking for her, would actually look sort of like me—be a little plump, strong, and athletic, I have fantasized about having a lover with red hair, like I have, but none of it seems very real. It's sort of like my fantasy of parthenogenesis. If I were to ever have a baby, having one that looked just like me. But it's all part of what I see as a 'lesbian adolescence,' a fierce period of self-love that I'm going through as a relatively new dyke."

♀ "I don't think I'm attracted to any certain 'type.' It seems limiting. Generally I find overweight women attractive—something of a secret I've

felt embarrassed to admit to until recently. But I don't feel it's limiting—that is, I'm not attracted *only* to overweight women.''

♀"I really don't believe I have a type that I prefer sexually. But I don't find 'feminine' women who wear dresses and make-up and stockings in the least bit attractive. I don't even consider them real women. 'Real' women don't conform to a male standard of beauty. I've learned the hard way to avoid straight women. My only 'type' is lesbians who are comfortable being lesbians. All women in this category are beautiful to me; I would not turn down any of them. Of course, there are women, I suppose, who are only interested in women who are not fat or who look a certain way.

"Your question, 'What happens when you don't find your type?' makes it sound like I go out cruising every night for ladies to go home with. Wishful thinking! Frankly I know very few feminine-looking, male-identified women, so I guess there's no shortage of my type! As I said, I don't think I have a type. The list seems to be mainly directed to women who go only for blondes or Jewish noses or whatever, if such women ever exist.

"On a gut level, I dislike the idea of someone having a type. I'd hate to feel that I was crossed off somebody's list just because my boobs are too big or my legs are too hairy or whatever. It seems trivial to me, but then if some woman only gets aroused by small breasts, that's the way she is. It bothers me so many women tell me I don't appeal to them sexually. *I* could get warmed up to *any* reasonably 'together-looking woman' (that is, one who doesn't smell like rotten eggs or look like Farrah Fawcett-Majors).''

♀"I don't really have a type. I do find women with certain physical attributes more attractive than others. Physically, facial hair is the only thing that really turns me off. Cleanliness and neatness are very important, but I think it's realistic to expect something a person has control over (as opposed to height). Nonphysical traits are more important to me than physical ones, especially for relationships that are potentially long-term. I find it extremely difficult to tolerate political or religious extremists. I prefer someone who is as intelligent or more so than I (IQ 140), and comparably educated (college or more), because intelligent discourse is important to me. Ideally, a partner for me is sincere, considerate, has a sense of humor and some impetuosity. Physically, and this matters almost exclusively in a cruising situation when I'm just out to pick someone up, I tend to be attracted to tall, thin blondes. I don't fall to pieces if there are none around. Attractiveness comes in many shapes and sizes. I do not relate to nor am I attracted to overtly butch or femme types for their types. I judge each individual on her own attractiveness and try not to let dress or other aspects of role-playing interfere with my judgment of a person's character. Sometimes it is difficult to get behind the facade to see what's really there. For me the type is an ideal. It's not realistic to expect or demand the ideal. Each individual must be weighed on her own qualities. Tolerance is an important part of maturity, and variety is indeed the spice of life.''

♀"My first response to the question was a definite yes. I am very at-

tracted to light hair, light eyes, long, thin legs. However, my 'other woman' was quite short, and since I have come out I find myself more physically attracted to and aware of women around me. I thoroughly enjoy watching women, gay or straight, and I find that now as I see someone attractive I respond on a more physical level—not simply an aesthetic one. I also find myself finding more and more women attractive. Oh, I'm so loose! And I love it! So now, blonde, brunette, short or tall, I'd love them all!''

How and Where Lesbians Meet

Once a lesbian figures out who she is and what sort of woman she's interested in, the next problem or step is trying to find that other woman. Meeting another lesbian is not as easy as a torrid glance at another woman across a crowded room full of heterosexuals—not by a long shot, although that sort of thing may occasionally happen. Basically, lesbians are invisible—even to each other. It is the invisibility of lesbians and gay men which allows heterosexist society to persecute them because if society could see how many gay men and women there actually are, they would have to think twice about wanting homosexuals out of the army, the schools, and the police and fire departments. They might realize that a lot of classrooms would be empty without homosexuals. They would realize that gay people are not all that "queer." As the slogan goes: "We are everywhere!"

Despite the large numbers of lesbians and gay men in this country, it is often difficult for gay people to find one another. Gay men have always had more options than women because of their male privilege. Men can walk the streets of Greenwich Village late at night searching for a sex partner, whereas a lesbian might be afraid to be out then. As women, lesbians are vulnerable and thus they have traditionally been even more invisible than gay men—leading to the unproven assumption that there are more gay men than lesbians.

Because lesbians are women, and women have low economic status, lesbians have thus had fewer meeting places. Before the Stonewall riots in New York City in 1969 (when a group of angry lesbians and gay men resisted a police raid on a bar in Greenwich Village—an incident often called the starting point of the current gay liberation movement), there was one all-lesbian bar in New York City, perhaps because with less income, lesbians couldn't buy a lot of alcohol. That meant that they could either put up with verbal abuse from the organized crime-connected male bouncers, the overpriced, watered-down drinks, the orders to "drink up or get out," or face ostracism and isolation. The only alternative lesbian group at the time, Daughters of Bilitis, was boring and conservative in the eyes of many younger lesbians, and the West Side Discussion Group seemed a predominantly male organization then. Many women also remained trapped in heterosexual marriages and could not go out at all.

After the Stonewall riots, things vastly improved for lesbians socially, not only in New York City but all over the country. The Stonewall rebellion did not lead to the destruction of the bars but to their proliferation. Now

there must be over a dozen in New York City. The diverse women who were once all forced to socialize together regardless of race, religion, class, or attitude toward roles split in different directions. The affluent East Side New Yorkers had their bars, while the third-world women had theirs. Obviously liberation was not synonymous with cohesion.

In smaller cities and towns, the lesbian bar, which may also admit gay men, is still the focal point of much lesbian socializing. Some cities have none and thus lesbians may drive hundreds of miles to get to a bar if there is no social alternative.

Bars became the focal point for lesbian socializing because they were the only places that would admit lesbians as a group. This institution is not new by any means—Radclyffe Hall described early-twentieth-century bars in *The Well of Loneliness,* as did Colette in *The Pure and the Impure.* The lesbian bars, then as now, would gladly take gay money, and if they behaved as the owners (usually heterosexual) dictated, the lesbians could stay. They were so delighted that anyone would let them congregate that they gladly put up with what might be considered demeaning conditions. But even today in some lesbian bars in many cities, such as Cleveland, lesbians are not allowed to dance together because of order of the management or state laws.

In some smaller cities, the lesbian bar remains the focal point because there just aren't enough lesbians to support an alternative, such as a coffee house or restaurant. Or the lesbian (or lesbian/gay male combination) bar may deal with heterosexual workers or businessmen during the day or may be "gay" only one night per week.

In both small and large population centers, many alternatives sprang up after Stonewall. Now there are lesbian-owned restaurants, resorts, community centers, music festivals, coffee houses, karate schools, garages, education centers, university groups, and bookstores, to name but a few. Such alternatives have the advantage of providing income for members of the lesbian community instead of outsiders and they also provide alcohol-free environments, as do lesbian conferences and dances.

To find out how lesbians meet in the 1970s, the respondents were asked, *How often do you meet other lesbians in each of the following places?*

	ALWAYS	VERY FREQUENTLY	SOMEWHAT FREQUENTLY	SOMEWHAT INFREQUENTLY	VERY INFREQUENTLY	ONCE	NEVER
bars	10	18	16	19	19	2	15%
at work	1	6	13	19	30	6	25

	ALWAYS	VERY FREQUENTLY	SOMEWHAT FREQUENTLY	SOMEWHAT INFREQUENTLY	VERY INFREQUENTLY	ONCE	NEVER
at school	1	14	18	12	20	3	31
neighborhood	2	7	9	13	27	4	38
parties	9	29	20	15	15	2	10
gay dances (mixed men and women), other than bars	8	10	12	12	19	3	37
lesbian or all-women's dances, other than bars	12	16	18	10	16	6	22
social groups	8	26	21	18	14	1	13
political groups	10	23	19	10	9	1	29
through friends	17	42	20	10	4	3	5
gym, "Y," sports	3	7	7	11	18	1	53
church	3	3	2	3	5	2	82
personal ads	0	0	1	2	3	3	91

The lesbians were also asked, *Whether or not you meet other lesbians in any of these places, indicate how you feel about the idea of meeting lesbians in each of them.*

	VERY POSITIVE	SOMEWHAT POSITIVE	NEUTRAL	SOMEWHAT NEGATIVE	VERY NEGATIVE	NOT SURE
bars	28	23	21	18	9	1%
at work	50	23	18	6	2	1
at school	55	22	17	3	1	2
neighborhood	52	19	23	2	2	2
parties	55	28	13	1	1	1
gay dances (mixed men and women), other than bars	41	29	19	5	3	3
lesbian or all-women's dances, other than bars	53	32	8	4	2	1
social groups	64	22	11	.5	.5	2
political groups	60	19	15	1	2	2

	VERY POSITIVE	SOMEWHAT POSITIVE	NEUTRAL	SOMEWHAT NEGATIVE	VERY NEGATIVE	NOT SURE
through friends	72	19	8	0	.5	.5
gym, "Y," sports	50	16	27	0	3	5
church	28	8	28	9	17	11
personal ads	9	3	13	18	48	10

On a frequency basis, the lesbians most often (79%) met one another through friends. This method (along with parties—58%) is not a new way: lesbians have always met through other lesbians because, other than the bar there were no social institutions for meeting. The survey shows that only a minority met other lesbians at bars frequently (44%), and thus bars have slipped behind social groups (55%), political groups (52%), and lesbian dances (46%) as meeting places, although the bars were still way ahead of mixed gay male and lesbian dances (30%). As these other institutions continue to grow, one can expect their popularity also to increase. Despite the appearance of gay churches and synagogues, lesbians did not seem to be meeting one another there (only 8% on a frequent basis), and only 36% felt positive about meeting via church. The other area that lesbians were predominantly negative about was personal ads. Only 1% of lesbians met one another via personal ads on a frequent basis and only 12% felt positive about the idea of them.

As one would expect, since most of the lesbians met others through friends, they felt most positive (99%) about this alternative. After all, friends usually have common interests and provide a pleasant, nonsexual atmosphere for meeting. Parties are still popular too with 83% of lesbians meeting there.

The lesbians were almost equally positive about social groups (86%) and political groups (79%). Interestingly enough, the women also felt positively about places where they did not frequently meet other lesbians; for example, 81% felt positive about the neighborhood even though only 18% met in their neighborhood frequently. The lesbians were also positive about meeting others at school (77%) or at work (73%)—other infrequent meeting places in actuality. (See Chapter 18 for further comments on this discrepancy.) Gay dances (mixed) were the least popular of these, with a majority (70%) still positive, but less so than the other alternatives just mentioned.

The fact that 15% more lesbians felt positive about lesbian dances than gay male dances reflects a general attitude toward environment. The

lesbians were asked, *How much of your time do you spend in each of the following environments?*

	QUITE A LOT	SOME	VERY LITTLE	NONE AT ALL	NOT SURE
lesbians only	51	30	15	4	1%
women only (lesbians and straight women)	43	41	13	2	1
gay only (lesbians and male homosexuals mixed)	12	47	33	7	1
mixed straight and gay, men and women	27	29	31	10	3

The lesbians were also asked, *Whether or not you spend time in any of the following environments, how do you feel about each of them?*

	VERY POSITIVE	SOMEWHAT POSITIVE	NEUTRAL	SOMEWHAT NEGATIVE	VERY NEGATIVE	NOT SURE
lesbians only	76	16	3	2	3	1%
women only (lesbians and straight women)	65	24	6	3	2	1
gay only (lesbians and male homosexuals)	42	33	13	8	3	1
mixed straight and gay, men and women	25	26	18	17	9	5

The lesbians not only spent more time in lesbian-only or women-only environments, but they felt much more positively about these environments. This explains the 15% more lesbians who felt positive about lesbian dances than about mixed gay dances. In fact, the lesbians preferred to socialize with all women, be they gay or straight, than to socialize with gay men. They felt less positive about all-mixed environments (straight and gay), even though many women explained in comments that they spent more time in them because of work, school, family, and so forth.

One might even suppose from these figures that the lesbians in the survey were thinking of women's or lesbians' social and/or political groups when they gave their positive answers in those categories, although that is not clear. It is clear that the lesbians favored women's environments over gay male environments every time. Another question supports this fact. The lesbians were asked, *How important are the concepts of lesbian and/or gay community, and lesbian and/or gay culture to you?*

	VERY IMPORTANT	SOMEWHAT IMPORTANT	NEUTRAL	SOMEWHAT UNIMPORTANT	VERY UNIMPORTANT	NOT SURE
gay community	37	43	9	4	4	2%
lesbian community	64	25	5	1	2	3
gay culture	34	47	11	4	5	3
lesbian culture	62	24	7	1	2	3

Again, the lesbians felt much more positively about anything which is strictly lesbian-oriented rather than gay-oriented. Lesbians did socialize more with lesbians and straight women even though groups like the National Gay Task Force claim that the political ties of lesbians are with gay men. This fact is shown by the answers to the question *How often do you socialize with each of the following?*

	ALWAYS	VERY FREQUENTLY	SOMEWHAT FREQUENTLY	SOMEWHAT INFREQUENTLY	VERY INFREQUENTLY	ONCE	NEVER
lesbians	22	55	12	5	6	0	.5%
straight women	5	34	31	14	16	0	1
gay men	4	15	22	23	27	1	8
straight men	2	7	17	20	37	1	16
bisexual women	2	12	22	15	32	2	15
bisexual men	2	3	12	13	38	2	30

The lesbians were also asked, *How do you feel about each of the following?*

	VERY POSITIVE	SOMEWHAT POSITIVE	NEUTRAL	SOMEWHAT NEGATIVE	VERY NEGATIVE	NOT SURE
lesbians	85	11	2	.5	.5	0%
straight women	33	43	15	8	1	0
gay men	30	42	19	7	1	1
straight men	15	13	17	31	24	.5
bisexual women	23	28	23	15	5	6
bisexual men	18	20	27	16	13	6

In addition to showing that the lesbians did spend more time with straight women than with gay men, another interesting fact emerged: the lesbians felt most positive about other lesbians, and they felt no more positive about straight women than about gay men despite the fact that the lesbians in the subsample spent more time with the former. Of course, the lesbians were generally more positive about straight women and gay men (72–73%) compared to straight men (only 28% positive) and bisexuals (48% positive for bisexual women and 38% positive for bisexual men). Another interesting point is that the lesbians in the survey spent less time with bisexual women and felt more negative about them than about straight women. Bisexuality and feelings about it are discussed in more detail in Chapter 3.

The women were asked *How active (you do the "picking up") or passive (you get "picked up") are you in seeking a relationship or sex partner?*

very active	10%
somewhat active	28
equal	37
somewhat passive	10
very passive	7
not sure	9

The women were also asked *to tell about the process of meeting other lesbians and about being shy or outgoing:*

♀"I usually meet other lesbians through political work in the women's movement. I am outgoing and assertive in conversations, but shy away from openly stating my point of view in policy-making. I have an easy time inviting a woman out to dinner or to talk, but naturally feel uncomfortable

determining whether or not to initiate any sexual advances. I am never sure I want to or how they will be received. The bar scene and parties threaten me. I feel a lot of pressure in these situations to act a certain way: light, carefree, self-assured, and I can't act that way unless I am with friends, so bars and parties don't work for me as far as meeting new lovers. Political and social groups are best for me as I can meet and work with a woman and we can move towards a sexual relationship or not without the pressure of a bar or party environment. Meeting people through sports or through friends feels all right too. I feel comfortable getting to know a woman on another level before sex enters the relationship. This takes time (days, weeks, months), and so I prefer groups or activities such as working together to find a lover. This is a tough question, or is it that meeting other lesbians is a tough situation?''

♀"When I first was in the process of 'coming out' and meeting other lesbians, I was tremendously self-conscious. I felt totally frightened and inadequate. I was certain no woman would find me attractive. I was devastated by insecurity—all of which was especially difficult because it shot to hell my previously self-confident, assertive, and outgoing image of myself. I went through a period that I can only liken to adolescence—at the age of 31! It was difficult for me to relate comfortably to other women who were lesbians if they were strangers to me, so although I was really eager to get around and meet lots of women I would find myself tongue-tied and stuttering in social situations like parties and at women's bars. I was self-conscious on two levels: I was certain other women would find me physically and personally unattractive, and then, even if someone did like me, I was sure I would be an inadequate lover. I just wouldn't know what to do sexually. This whole period was one of the most painful of my life. It lasted an agonizing year or so at which point I finally began to meet more women and establish friendships with other lesbians I could identify with. I worked out this unsettling lack of belief in myself by recognizing that other lesbians were just like me—they were women too—and they too went through a painful coming-out time, and miracle of miracles, some of them liked me and thought I had my act together! It was at this point that I started feeling good enough about myself to really be open to another women's interest in me—and that's when I became involved with my current lover.''

♀"I'm probably most comfortable meeting other lesbians through mutual friends as opposed to the bar scene as I'm not into cruising, and I think a lot of bar women are. I should say I'm a novice to the singles scene, as my first relationship evolved ideally with her moving from co-worker to friend to close friend to lover over a period of time. I'm not by nature a shy person, once I've had a chance to observe a person for a while. Of course some women are easier to relate to than others.''

♀"I haven't as yet been to a gay meeting place, but have checked them out just last week. Being married is a drawback, but my lover and I have

talked about going, and I think it's great that one has a chance to meet other girls for friendship—if nothing else.''

♀ ''Unfortunately when it comes to meeting other lesbians, I'm insecure. No confidence. I meet gay women through feminist meetings or not at all. It's very limiting, especially out here in suburbia, but quality is better than quantity.''

♀ ''My brother taught me how to meet other gay women through visiting gay bars, social gatherings, etc. I was insecure at first, but soon it was easy.''

♀ ''I'm now in New York City and would like to meet other lesbians but I find it difficult. I need *friends,* not a lover, but I feel I may appear too anxious and come off seeming as if I'm 'after them.' Sometimes I feel secure, but too often I feel self-conscious, depending on how badly I want to be with someone.''

♀ ''Most of the time, I meet other lesbians on a strictly 'friendship' basis. They sense this and are not either afraid of me nor do they make sexual advances toward me. I don't make sexual advances toward other women, whether straight or gay, as I'm really not interested. The bar is probably the most important place with our Metropolitan Community Church and the Daughters of Bilitis (a lesbian group) the next in importance.''

♀ ''Here in Indianapolis, it's really sickening! Being kicked out of the only women's bar here is proving to be more of a disability than expected.''

♀ ''I'm quite shy. I'm intimidated by butch-type wimmin and don't like people to cruise me. The best way for me to meet other wimmin is to be introduced. I live in a rural area where there is one gay bar and not many gay wimmin. I don't know any at this moment. I wish I did, but I don't want to go to the bar alone. I don't like cruising. I think it's important to have places for lesbians to meet. I wish there were more dances. There aren't any groups here. I wish there were a wimmin's bookstore or coffee house or something that would make meeting other wimmin easier because the bar is a drag. I've had situations where I've felt a little uncomfortable with other lesbians. Most of the women I know wear jeans all the time and don't shave hair and so on. Well, I prefer a skirt and love to get very dressed up and wear lots of make-up. I feel like they don't approve of me doing that.''

♀ ''I am very involved in the women's movement in Montreal and find it quite easy to meet other women, be it at a gay bar, a gay dance, meetings, etc. I am not usually shy in meeting other women. As a matter of fact, while visiting Boston a few weeks ago, the women thought that I was being rather 'nervy' by just going up to a gay woman and talking with her. They asked, 'Do all women in Montreal do that?' How else, may I ask, are you supposed to do it?''

♀ ''I meet other lesbians mostly in the bars and through friends. I'm pretty gregarious and don't have much trouble meeting new people. I am sometimes a bit hesitant to introduce myself to women I find *extremely*

attractive. I get bowled over as it were, but I am usually able to overcome it. Most people think I'm 'charming,' and this sometimes gives people the idea that I am insincere or perpetually 'on the make.' This is not true, and it bothers me a bit.''

♀''Having been 'with someone' for twenty-seven years, I don't go looking for lovers or sex partners. But I like to socialize, and find other lesbians (and women) in organizations, and occasionally in bars. I personally feel a bar is a bad place to find anyone (hetero or homo) and don't recommend them to people. I think movement groups are best.''

♀''Most of the friends I have are gay, and I have met most through gay-organized groups, socials, consciousness-raising groups. I have never picked anyone up at a bar, though I have asked women to dance. I'm sure that if I were 'single,' I would be aggressive enough to initiate a relationship.''

♀''I have met most of the lesbians I know through women's retreats. I am a good talker (so my lovers tell me), so I attract people pretty easily but I am shy about presenting myself sexually. I think we need more, bigger, and better places for lesbians to congregate in safety. I love the places in New York City, although I have only been there in groups, not alone. I love the women's retreats.''

♀''Meeting lesbians? Unless you go to a bar here, it's next to impossible. And if by chance you do stumble upon a fellow woman-lover, you are so anxious to like each other that you're too tense to be real. Meeting lesbians can be disappointing. It's a hard thing to realize that just because two women share the same sexual preference, they may not have much in common, and possibly aren't compatible at all.''

♀''Generally, I think it is the sad state of our society that makes the most natural and almost only place to meet lesbians from your own community the bars. More recently I have met other lesbians at professional meetings when we find ourselves at feminist (women's) or gay caucuses.''

♀''I'm really confident in meeting other lesbians, but when it comes to who's going to make the first move sexually, I become very shy. I've never made sexual advances to someone when I wasn't sure if they were gay. I don't like meeting other lesbians in gay bars because I feel that bars promote alcoholism. I feel there should be other places for gay people to meet each other. Although I do go to bars, I go with friends and I've never really met people in bars other than those that were friends with the people that I was with. I've never gone to a bar alone, although I may do so in the near future. I've met a lot of lesbians at work and school. My first roommate in a college dorm was a radical lesbian. I also meet people at parties and political groups. I prefer that because they're usually people that I have something in common with.''

♀''I have never been to lesbian bars, dances, etc. But I expect to have some of these experiences in the near future through membership in the Dorian Group (a gay group). I have never had to consciously seek out

partners up to now. They just happened—someone you meet in a class, at work, anywhere. Being retired, moved to a new area, and a professional do not provide contacts that once were relatively available.''

♀ "I never thought about meeting other lesbians when I lived in New York. I had a wide circle of friends, and it simply occurred in the normal course of life. I met other lesbians through my business (I was a publishing executive), social contacts, friends. Rarely at bars. When I moved to La Jolla, there was a whole different situation. There was no real gay community. I did not run into other career-oriented women and had no circle to draw from. I discovered that I was very shy about making contacts and that I didn't know where to go to find other lesbians. Having been self-confident in a metropolitan atmosphere, I found myself feeling insecure in a different atmosphere where I didn't seem to know the rules—or how to learn them. It taught me a lot about myself and what I had taken for granted in a more open milieu.''

♀ "After coming out, I felt very unsure about my identity, so I went along to our local gay women's group in order to meet other lesbians. I met them at gay discos and doing gay switchboard. Otherwise my social life remained completely separate, except for making friends with one lesbian in the group, with whom I then had a sexual relationship. However, I've since dropped out of the group, which has no feminist consciousness, as my feminist friends have started to explore lesbianism and have come out. I've brought at least five women out, which is pleasing. It just seems that I was a bit further advanced in discovering my sexuality than they, so there was that intermediate period when I went to the group. Out of four lovers, only one had had sexual experience with a woman, so I'm getting quite used to telling hitherto straight women that I'm attracted to them. I feel that the potential of lesbian relationships to avoid patriarchal behavior and structuring is enormous, and for this reason I don't like to see lesbians being patriarchal towards each other. I view such things as courtship, cruising, and one-night stands as patriarchal. I think lesbians should be able to meet each other everywhere: in our own clubs (except not as ghettos, as they are at present) and at work, in family events, etc.''

This last respondent likes to 'bring out' straight women, which raised a sticky question for many lesbians. Should one make advances to straight women or not? On one hand, as the last respondent points out, many lesbians were at one time heterosexual. Many have brought each other out. On the other hand, the term "proselytizing"—a negative word to begin with since it often implies one is trying to convert away from one's original faith—is often cast at homosexuals. Heterosexuals think that since homosexuals don't reproduce themselves, they must "recruit"—conjuring up images of lesbians putting up recruiting stations in bus terminals to lure runaway heterosexuals. This also implies that those recruited have been brainwashed and without the "evil influence" would have remained

literally on the straight path. Most lesbians, when asked *if they make advances toward heterosexual women,* reacted negatively, possibly reflecting their knowledge of the "recruitment" charge. Others felt it is a positive thing. Here are a few opinions and experiences.

♀ "I have never made advances to anyone I wasn't sure was gay."

♀ "If a woman doesn't know I am interested in her when we meet, she knows soon enough. I have corrupted straight women."

♀ "Sexual advances for me usually come only after a friendship has been established."

♀ "I always make advances to women I like, whether or not I want to go to bed with them. I do it in such a way that if they're not gay, they don't even realize I'm doing it. They just think I'm being friendly, which I am. Once I made friends with a girl who turned out to be gay and then we had a relationship until I moved to another town."

♀ "I did this recently in a work situation with a woman I was sure was gay, but she turned out to be straight. She was not, of course, about to tell anyone as it would make her suspect (which it should have, as I am sure she was cruising me), and I continued working there for another year with no repercussions. In fact, I feel that for once I saw her behind all of her defenses and I think she respected my courage for taking a chance and asking for what I wanted."

♀ "If I feel attracted to a woman, I usually tell her so there's no mistake about my intentions. It's ruined a lot of friendships, but if my lesbianism bugs them that much, I wonder how much of a friend they were in the first place."

♀ "If I'm not sure they are gay, then I usually forget the whole thing, and it doesn't bother me. For me there's nothing worse than being hurt by a straight woman, so basically I avoid the situation all together."

♀ "I was very much in love/attracted to a woman I wasn't sure was gay. I courted her for months with attention, small gifts: shy and fearful was I. A torment of: is she or isn't she? Finally one night, alone in my apartment, the electricity failed! I kissed her and told her I loved her. She answered, cool and high, 'Oh, that's it, isn't it? Well, what are your intentions?' Intentions? That we'd walk hand in hand into the sunset, I suppose. I was so intimidated by her lack of response that I never brought the issue up again."

♀ "Straight women have always been terrifying but challenging. At least half of my lovers were 'straight' or believed themselves to be at the time we made love. At least half are now lesbians. I think perhaps the best method is to consider a woman gay until she tries it with you and doesn't like it. The worst that can happen is the ending of a sexually sterile friendship."

♀ "I haven't ever asked a straight woman because I'm not really self-confident. If I make a pass at someone, it's because I met them in a gay bar or through a mutual friend who has introduced us as gay. I've never been able to get the guts together to go after someone straight without taking three months to become friends, ask the person, and then try."

♀ "My only experience with a 'straight' woman sexually was when I was 20 and neither of us had ever experienced sex with another woman. I took the lead, and we both enjoyed it for several months. We are still acquainted after twenty-eight years and have never mentioned it since. She is now a grandmother and still with her husband. Last year I took my current lover to meet them. I have no idea whether or not she ever told her husband."

♀ "I had one experience with a nongay woman which cured me. I met her at a straight bar. She held my hand, played footsie with me, and ran her hand over my leg. In my apartment, I touched her hair and she threatened to call the cops. A policeman did show up after she left and he attempted, physically, to force me into sexual intercourse. He failed, thank God, but I've *never* touched another woman since whose sexual preferences were not known to me."

Such mixed sentiments were also revealed when the subject turned to cruising, one-night stands, and promiscuity. Adding up the negative sentiments about cruising places, such as the bars, among women, the influence of the women's liberation movement against treating other women as sexual objects and the fact that 80% of our lesbian respondents were currently in relationships leads to the conclusion that not too many lesbians "cruise." But what does cruising mean? Does it mean that one looks at other women on the street? Or does it mean going to a bar to look for a sex partner? And what does promiscuity mean? Is promiscuity having more than one sex partner at a time? more than two? more than five? more than you are comfortable with having yourself?

If cruising means that one picks up and goes home with a stranger, then the lesbians in this survey did not cruise. When asked, *How often do you go home to have sex with someone you have just met?* the majority had *never* gone home with a stranger, and only 9% cruised with any frequency. Here are the exact statistics.

always	1%
very frequently	2
somewhat frequently	6
somewhat infrequently	6
very infrequently	16
once	12
never	57

The lesbians were also asked *to give their feelings about going home with a stranger whether or not they do so.*

very positive	6%
somewhat positive	20
neutral	20
somewhat negative	30
very negative	21
not sure	4

Therefore it is apparent that not only did the lesbians not cruise but also that they were predominantly negative (51%) or neutral (20%) to the idea of cruising. Here are a few opinions about and experiences with cruising and one-night stands.

♀ "Great if you can get into it. I've often fantasized about how great it would be to live in a majority sexual culture like the heterosexual one where you could get laid for one night and perhaps never see the person again. Where you could flirt at any point or at any moment in your sexual life—in the classroom, at the job, in the store, in the laundromat, in the street. How wonderful! I feel I live in a very *deprived* sexual world/culture as in my daily life I don't know who is gay so I don't have sexual hopes toward anyone when I know them. Alas! I wish one *could* tell a lesbian by how she looked. And I wish the lesbian communities weren't so small and interwoven so that if you get involved with someone, everyone knows it. There isn't much mystery there. I'm tired of feeling asexual when I go to the bar or a gay party. I want to live in a gay community, neighborhood, gay town, etc., where I can feel sexual sitting on the front stoop, taking karate, and get turned on by the lesbian teller at the bank!"

♀ "Cruising is not something I ever did, and it would make me uncomfortable—I'm too much a product of my society in that way. One-night stands never really interested me, although I've had about three, but I prefer to know someone before going to bed. And good sex doesn't happen instantly: it takes time. As for promiscuity, I have no idea what you mean by the word. Often it is pejorative, and has as many connotations as users. I have had many relationships—both homosexual and heterosexual; I would probably have been classified as promiscuous by some standards. I don't consider myself or my sexuality in any negative way. Multiple relationships need not be promiscuous. Frankly, I think it's one's own business and as long as I am honest with myself and my partners, I have a positive feeling about myself."

♀ "I enjoy cruising, but do not believe in one-night stands. I want to have a few meetings (courtship) before I dive into bed with someone. I don't see someone having sex with just anyone. There should be more to sex than that."

♀ "I am sometimes turned on by cruising and one-nighters, but normally prefer to devote my energies to developing and nurturing my present and hopefully lifelong relationship."

♀ "I cruise with my eyes. I mean I'm always looking and sometimes when I'm with other gay women I yell things out of the car window at pretty women I see on the street, but as for any of it being a 'real' come on, no. I'm not a very promiscuous person. Sex really isn't that satisfying when it's done for the primary reason of getting you and your partner off. It's so much better if there's some kind of genuine love or affection for the other person."

♀ "I say what goes for you goes for you. Lesbians are as varied as any other group of people, and I see no reason why our lifestyles have to be similar. There's 18-year-old Kelly who's slept with every 'attractive' woman from here to Kansas, sings like an angel, is free as a spirit, brings love like a gift. There's 40-year-old Sarah whose lover of twenty years just walked out on her, and Sarah refuses to even go to parties to meet women. So it goes."

♀ "A married, male psychologist once said to me, 'If homosexuality serves the purpose of bringing people together and forming close, loving relationships, then I'm all for it.' I feel the same way. I don't approve of one-night stands, cruising, or of getting together with a woman for sex only. If other women can live that kind of life, that's fine, but I found that I need a one-and-only to share my life with, not just my body."

♀ "I don't like cruising and I don't do it. It just doesn't come naturally for me. I like courtship and find it one of the most wonderful times of falling in love. I often think of the courtship period later on when I am with a steady lover."

♀ "I generally feel negatively about 'cruising,' one-night stands, etc. I think it's too impersonal and dehumanizing and dangerous emotionally (and otherwise too perhaps)."

♀ "I enjoy the 'ceremony' of cruising myself but try to keep the first night to a conversation level only, which it usually turns out to be. I feel that if other people want to get involved with one-night stands, it's up to them. It's their bodies and their head space."

♀ "I maintain my 'everybody to their own' philosophy on the subjects of cruising and one-night stands. But deep down I really don't understand them. I guess I expect women to be better than men in that their relationships should involve not just the physical being. Of course, I'm speaking as one of the lucky ones who doesn't have to go through it. I think if I had to, I'd prefer masturbation to one-night stands."

♀ "In my opinion cruising only leads to cruising and nothing else. I feel free to be promiscuous, but only with someone else who is also fairly free. So usually I am not, and usually I don't get as much sex as I would like. If I feel that a woman is going to become dependent, or lay trips on me, or bad-mouth me for sleeping with her, I would rather not bother. I still have to feel an equality or similarity for the time concerned or I won't be getting anything out of it. And I won't go near a woman who is using sex as a power trip."

♀ "I think it's pretty 'macho' and reminds me too much of dudes. I don't

like meeting people in bars because they're not themselves with booze in them and neither am I.''

♀ "They're fine for a change. All those things are part of the gay culture, and as such should be recognized as valid and perfectly acceptable sexual mores. It certainly helps the application of new attitudes towards sex. I suppose it's really a reversal of all those years of traditional prudeness.''

Again, most lesbians prefer extended relationships to one-night stands or cruising, and details on this subject are found in Chapter 8. As should be clear by now, lesbianism is much more than a sexual preference, and therefore meeting other lesbians is a lot more than finding the right body.

7

Gay Men: Reaching Outward, Looking Inward

Despite the myths about pinky rings and secret signs, there is no simple easy formula which gay men follow in order to meet others so inclined. How an individual man will socialize with other gay men depends to a great extent on how much he is immersed in the gay scene, or as it is sometimes called, the gay subculture. This, in turn, may depend on his living situation (rural or urban), his marital status, his gay consciousness, and other factors. It is not simply a matter of saying that it's easier for gay men to meet each other inside the gay subculture—undoubtedly it *is* easier, but many men, by choice or due to circumstances, function apart from the gay world.

If one considers the connotations of the word "queer," one will have some idea of the dilemmas facing gay men in their social interactions. The sexual preferences of a gay man, especially if he is *not* bisexual, make him feel emphatically different no matter how much his other characteristics are harmonious with his usual surroundings. In hiding the fact that he is "queer" (or "different," to use a kinder word), and in doing whatever he does to act out his queerness, a gay man is likely to lead a fragmented life. The only way to ameliorate that sense of fragmentation, the only way to make one's life more integrated, is to immerse oneself in the gay subculture or to be totally open about one's homosexuality in the world at large. Neither of these choices is easily or even readily available, and the majority of gay men, even the majority of politically conscious men, have been unable to achieve this kind of integration. At the outset of the gay liberation movement, the oppressive aspects of the social lives of gay people were among the foremost concerns. One of the very first programs of the Gay Liberation Front in New York City, in late 1969, was to hold dances that would be an alternative to the bar atmosphere. It turned out that the people brought many of their old habits (including heavy cruising) to the "liberated" dances, and the alternative was not as successful as some had hoped. Indeed, while some gay activists continue to press for the creation of

alternatives, there are others who do not object to the social aspects of the gay subculture and merely wish to make the institutions of the subculture "classier," safer and more legal.

Whom Do Gay Men Socialize With?

In order to determine something about the social lives of gay men, the men were asked *how often they socialize with each of the following, and how they feel about each of them.* The responses are indicated in the charts:

	ALWAYS	VERY FREQUENTLY	SOMEWHAT FREQUENTLY	SOMEWHAT INFREQUENTLY	VERY INFREQUENTLY	ONCE	NEVER
gay men	18	55	18	5	3	0	1%
heterosexual men	5	31	28	19	15	0	2
lesbians	3	8	22	24	31	2	10
heterosexual women	7	30	27	19	13	0	3
bisexual men	3	12	23	24	25	2	11
bisexual women	2	7	16	24	30	1	21

	VERY POSITIVE	SOMEWHAT POSITIVE	NEUTRAL	SOMEWHAT NEGATIVE	VERY NEGATIVE	NOT SURE
gay men	83	14	3	0	0	0%
heterosexual men	43	27	18	9	3	0
lesbians	48	22	19	8	3	0
heterosexual women	44	28	21	5	3	0
bisexual men	45	27	13	7	5	4
bisexual women	38	21	22	9	5	5

From a strictly social point of view, these statistics indicate that the gay men are not inclined toward extreme segregation. In practice, the group that gay men are most separated from, perhaps ironically, is lesbians, but that may be a reflection of the fact that both gay men and lesbians frequently

socialize in their own special environments, while both play straight in straight settings. Significantly, there is no widespread dislike or negative feeling for any people based on their sexual orientation, quite the opposite result of polls of the general population which show widespread dislike for homosexuals. The existence of a separate gay world, then, is clearly the result of prejudice and the unwillingness of straight people generally to mix socially with gay people who are upfront and honest about their sexuality.

The men also indicated *how much of their time they spend in the various social environments,* and *how they feel about each of them.* These responses are shown in the next two charts.

	QUITE A LOT	SOME	VERY LITTLE	NONE AT ALL	NOT SURE
gay men only	44	39	15	2	0%
men only (gay and straight mixed)	17	40	31	10	1
gay only (lesbians and male homosexuals, mixed)	22	41	28	7	2
mixed straight and gay	28	38	24	6	2

	VERY POSITIVE	SOMEWHAT POSITIVE	NEUTRAL	SOMEWHAT NEGATIVE	VERY NEGATIVE	NOT SURE
gay men only	65	23	5	6	.5	0%
men only (gay and straight mixed)	38	30	18	11	2	1
gay only (lesbians and male homosexuals, mixed)	49	27	13	8	1	1
mixed straight and gay	49	29	15	5	3	.5

For pure enjoyment, relaxation, and ease of relating, gay men choose to be "with their own kind" a good deal of the time. Since negative attitudes toward mixed environments do not prevail, one can only assume that gay men avoid the mixed environments for practical reasons—either they feel rejected or alienated or they cannot meet one another with ease in mixed company.

To a certain extent, this division of the world into gay and straight is quite artificial. Of the men who answered this survey, with the words "Gay Male Questionnaire" in big type, many were married and 17% report that

they spend very little or no time socializing exclusively with gay men. One does not necessarily have to find other gay men only in those places where gay men congregate. This is undoubtedly one of the greatest challenges and dilemmas of the gay male lifestyle. One can seek out other gay men (or willing sex partners who may not describe themselves as "gay") just about anywhere—in that case, one risks exposure and the sometimes violent response of straight men. Those gay men who function socially in this manner usually have to play certain games, somehow assuring their partners that their masculinity is not being impugned. Or one can seek out friends and sex partners in the gay world, where other games are also played and where an intense sexual marketplace buzzes with commerce in which the merchandise is carefully scrutinized and sometimes rejected. Furthermore, there is a truly commercial marketplace of hustlers and johns.

Meeting Other Men

Elsewhere in this chapter, men comment in detail on such topics as the bars, the baths, anonymous sex, quickies, one-night stands, courtship, trade, and sex for money, but first here are some general comments or overviews about the process of meeting other men:

⚥"I'm not really comfortable with the whole idea of meeting men. I don't like the whole cruising scene in general because so many people (including myself, at times) become jaded, and sex loses the feeling of tenderness and intimacy that I consider important. Also, I'm not particularly aggressive so I find cruising situations difficult; I may stare at a man for a while but I usually wait for him to come up to me; I rarely make the first move; I'm very afraid of being rejected. The places I meet sex partners the most tend to be bars or the streets; I prefer the latter because sometimes I meet people who aren't into the bar scene and tend to be more interesting than people I meet in bars. I don't like the baths or parks because I don't like quickie sex; I think it's fine for those who are into it but I need more than genitals and orgasms. I like to talk to the partner, to have long-drawn-out sex in one of our homes. I do think that constant casual sex tends to burn people out, to make them treat each other like objects, and that upsets me. It's not really a gay phenomenon, in that this whole society is into quickie everything: quickie hamburgers, quickie therapy (est, Esalen), quickie sex, etc., but it seems even more caricatured in gay life where people fall in love in two days and out of love just as quickly, with little willingness to put effort into having meaningful intimacies. Whenever I find myself getting that way, I stop for a while until I regain a sense of what it is I want from my sexual and other relationships. In moderation, I think that casual sex, cruising, etc. are fine and healthy, but I object to the extreme fashion in which they're carried out (particularly in cities like San Francisco). This summer I was visiting my parents in a suburban, straight town, and it was a pleasure to walk down the street and not cruise/be cruised/be aware of sex all the time!"

⚥"I find meeting other men a pain in the ass. I detest bars and find this part of being gay the worst of all. There is practically nowhere to meet men who you know are gay. I am very timid about approaching anyone who I think might be straight, as I do not need the degradation, so there are few places where any opportunity exists for me to meet other gay men."

⚥"I like to meet gay men in a gay setting and feel rather self-confident to approach anyone, realizing rejection is a real factor. When rejected, to overcome my bad feeling of humiliation, I just say, 'His loss!' "

⚥"I have been having sexual relationships with men for over fifteen years and my overall impression of the behavior of gay men is fairly negative—with the exception of the last two or three years, during which time I notice an improvement in regard to kindness, openness, friendliness. I have had largely negative experiences meeting gay men in gay bars, gay men's centers, gay organizations. All of these have struck me as snobbish, youth- and body-oriented environments. I have had good experiences meeting men through gay classified ads: men were generally more sensitive, kind, and seeking relationships beyond just sex—less game-playing. I have also had casual sex with men in baths, parks, movie theaters, and restrooms and my feelings about these experiences are also very positive. Unexpectedly, I found more kindness, affection, and willingness to talk than among most men at gay liberation activities. Often, friendship or a love affair has grown out of these 'brief' encounters. Sometimes, perhaps often, these meetings are no more than a quick exchange of sexual pleasure, but they strike me as more honest than bars or gay organizational meetings."

⚥"I believe in 'auras.' With one, it is no trouble meeting other people. An aura has something to do with one's self-image and self-confidence. I find it most difficult to talk with a stranger but force myself to do it since no one will usually come up to me first. Besides, I like having the initiative in social situations. If we were all 'out' more fully, meeting each other wouldn't be such a problem. Then we could meet on the street or just about anywhere. As it is, we are afraid to show our colors so we resort to 'our' places where we know that the other customers are gay also. Gay bars are uptight and poor places to meet people; but they work and they have their place."

⚥"Meeting other men: I don't hardly. My self-image is shit. My come-on is always overwhelmed by my lust. The phrases 'Been in town long? Sure is dark/dull/quiet/noisy/in here. Do you work around here?' all are so phony that all I can think of is, 'You are gorgeous, how about letting me eat you?' When I use the latter line, I get some freaked-out answer that means no. I am insanely jealous of the people who can say (maybe mean) the bullshit lines that end up in the bedroom, lines that I simply cannot deal with.

"I cruised bars for four years, between the ages of 21 and 25, and made out so goddam seldom that I was frustrated out of my mind. Even if I would make out, it was so late and I was so tired and we would go to the dumbest place, like the couch in a third or fourth person's home, and have

others come home at 6:00 a.m. and wake us up and the whole thing was a crock of shit. Then I discovered the baths. Here I could come on the only way I knew—with my hands. A grasp of the skin totally circumvented the 'been in town long?' syndrome and said exactly what I wanted to say up front: 'Let's fuck!' My score went from none a week to fifteen a day and I virtually paid the rent on several bath houses for the next four years.''

⚥''I am usually in heat in a nongay atmosphere, like at the university, on the street, at a park, in public, etc. As soon as I go into an officially gay place (like a bar) I am half turned off, and after I have been there for fifteen minutes, I am totally turned off. Several times, I have been in heat during the day from looking at the gorgeous boys all day, have gone to the bar and left, not only without a trick, but also so turned off that I wonder why I went in the first place. To this end, I make the statement that I do not cruise. That does not mean that in a day, I don't see about twenty people that I would literally eat alive if I could figure out how to 'get' them in the first place. I know that if I could get any of these unknown strangers into my bed I could manipulate their bodies in such a way as to bring them pleasure, straight or gay. I would show them more respect and more physical pleasure than their hands or their girl friends. I simply cannot get to the first step, the come-on.''

⚥''I don't like meeting gays in places or situations where one usually picks up people: bars, baths, parks, gyms, etc. There's too much pressure for sex, so a love relationship is kind of stifled from the start. I like meeting people through friends, or in groups, where sex is not so much a prerequisite.''

⚥''I meet other men in various contexts, but primarily in the West Village on 'The Strip'—Christopher Street. I prefer the street or the pier to bars, although in winter I must rely on the bars. My confidence varies according to my moods and if I'm feeling depressed or down on myself for any number of reasons it's difficult for me to 'pursue.' Often I am pursued because of my looks, and it's easy for me to rely on my looks to attract people, hence I wait until I am noticed before I make any moves. Usually, however, I am rather direct, and if I'm attracted to someone, I have no qualms about approaching someone and telling them that I am attracted. I don't mean to sound glib about this. Only in the last two years have I summoned the confidence to be able to approach people and the confidence is only a result of due validation on the sexuality commodity market. Up until two years ago, I could never approach anyone. I would wait to be approached. Now that I understand the general etiquette of the gay world, and the general dynamics of life in the West Village, it's very easy for me.''

⚥''I think most of the ways gay people meet each other are atrocious. The primary emphasis on sex bothers me a lot. I don't believe that most gay men even give monogamy a chance. Promiscuity is conditioned or self-conditioned so early that it becomes 'normal.' I've met almost all the people I have dated in church—the Metropolitan Community Church or

otherwise. I am opposed to quickie sex, sex for money, and other expression which does not take into account knowing (in any meaningful way) the other person. Responsible sex must mean responsibility for the other, which is impossible if all the contact you have is their penis coming through a wall in the public restroom.''

⚥"Usually I begin by meeting another person's eyes and smiling. If he smiles back I introduce myself and talk to him, usually about what he does. I usually allow him to make the first move about sex. Sometimes if he is friendly I invite him to my house.''

⚥"Meeting other men is a mystery to me. I've just about concluded that it can't be done. Women are much easier to meet and get to know.''

⚥"I do not go to bars, baths, or any gay meeting places in my area. On vacations, I am a little more daring although I've not connected with a sexual partner very often.''

⚥"I have noticed that some guys (far too many, especially those 30 to 40) are afraid to approach another guy for fear of rejection. While I do not have sex with every guy who talks to me or dances with me, I do not make myself rude and rejecting.''

⚥"I usually advance on men in a joking manner. I joke enough that they take the hint if they're gay. If they don't, I tell them I'm only kidding and stop. It usually works.''

⚥"I rely too heavily on booze to loosen myself up to meet people. Once I cross this barrier, I find myself to be one of the most attentive listeners around.''

⚥"I have a great deal of difficulty in meeting other men. I am mainly afraid of rejection.''

⚥"I'm a seaman. And unlike other seamen, I don't have a girl, nor a guy, in every port. I make it when I can and wherever I can. I'm on an oil tanker and we're only in port for short stays, so it's always hit and run. I write books for my own enjoyment, and this replaces the sex I'm not getting.''

⚥"Meeting other men is often a terrifying experience. And the gay games many times create awkward dilemmas. For example, I don't like hurting people's feelings. If you're in a bar and you merely speak to someone they can make you feel obligated for the night. But if you try to avoid that game people think you're cold. I am reasonably good-looking. Yet no one has come up to me for as long as I can remember now. I always have to be the aggressive partner or I go home alone. They're scared of me, thinking I'm arrogant, and I'm terrified of them. An unending vicious circle.''

⚥"The most difficult thing for me to do is actually ask someone to sleep with me. Telling someone to whom I am attracted that I would like to have sex with him is like facing the firing squad.''

⚥"If I'm hitchhiking, I say something like, 'Haven't I seen you at the L&F sometime?' If they're straight they usually say, 'at the what?' And I

say, 'The Lost & Found, it's a restaurant in Southeast.' If they say they've never heard of it, I just drop it. Once a very hunky (oh, he was *so beautiful*) guy in a Corvette gave me a lift. When I got out of the car I said 'Thank you, you're really beautiful.' He just drove off. I've never done it with a 'straight.' ''

♂''If I see a man in a bar or at the beach or in some gay setting, and I think I want to make it with him, I usually approach him and say, 'I'd like to ask you a question.' Then, when I have his attention, I say, 'What's the chance of getting it on with you?' Reactions vary, and naturally I get plenty of rejections, but I succeed more than I fail. Sometimes I feel shy about doing what I do, but mostly I'm not too troubled. The gay leather-western bar is my main avenue of making contacts.''

♂''In my work I meet gay people, most always younger than myself. Sometimes a friendship develops, never a sexual encounter, but I think of my home as a place where gay people can come and relax and be natural. I probably have somewhat of an inferiority complex. My age is against me. I am too conservative, I'm sure. I was burned once in my job so I'm extremely careful. For one who seldom has sex with another man, I will take what comes along if it appeals to me physically. I wish there could be more than one-night stands and 'quickie sex' but I find no alternative. I'd be happy to have a friend whom I could go out to dinner with, maybe hold a hand under the table, go to a show, movie, or concert, go home for some love and end with joyful sex. Sort of a boy friend, not a lover.''

♂''I see and meet a lot of good-looking men at work I would like to have an affair with. Of course, I can't make an approach at work. I live my afterhours by myself. I am usually alone and very lonely. I don't go to dances or bars, etc. I have a very restricted social life where an acquaintance could be made. I would describe myself as shy when it comes to sex. In the last two months I have picked up some hitchhikers and wanted to touch them. I finally did and my first one was a rejection. The second one accepted my offer and we made love, and the third let me fondle his leg and penis but would not come home with me. He simply sat for 20 miles allowing me to fondle him and I enjoyed it. I was surprised to find other men having the same desire for physical contact as I. I wish I knew this a long time ago. I simply need more courage to carry out a pass. I did not and still do not know if they consider themselves gay.''

Places Where Gay Men Meet

In the previous statements, the men mention some of the many different places where they meet one another for friendship and/or sexual contact. The men were asked about many different places where they are likely to meet. In addition to the places listed below the men mentioned public transportation, the laundry, supermarket, coffee houses, library, museums, art institutes, hitchhiking, and "everywhere." *How often each of*

the places are used, and *the men's feeling about meeting men in the places (whether or not they meet other men there),* are reflected in the following charts:

	ALWAYS	VERY FREQUENTLY	SOMEWHAT FREQUENTLY	SOMEWHAT INFREQUENTLY	VERY INFREQUENTLY	ONCE	NEVER
bars	11	34	18	10	18	2	8%
at work	3	8	12	18	28	6	24
at school	2	9	10	14	26	5	35
neighborhood	2	8	14	13	30	4	28
parties	4	17	22	23	23	2	10
gay dances (other than bars)	6	9	11	13	23	4	36
social groups	4	15	19	16	24	4	18
political groups	2	10	11	9	20	4	47
through friends	6	32	28	15	14	1	6
resorts and beaches	2	9	13	17	23	4	32
gym, "Y," straight health club, sports	1	4	5	10	21	5	55
church	4	4	4	6	13	5	65
personal ads	1	4	4	6	12	9	64
public toilets	1	6	6	9	16	4	58
highway rest stops	1	3	3	6	11	6	70
baths	5	11	12	10	13	5	43
parks	2	7	9	12	20	5	46
streets	2	8	11	14	23	6	37
pornographic movie theaters	3	5	7	8	12	3	62

	VERY POSITIVE	SOMEWHAT POSITIVE	NEUTRAL	SOMEWHAT NEGATIVE	VERY NEGATIVE	NOT SURE
bars	40	27	20	11	2	1%
at work	41	22	20	6	8	2
at school	45	20	23	3	5	4

	VERY POSITIVE	SOMEWHAT POSITIVE	NEUTRAL	SOMEWHAT NEGATIVE	VERY NEGATIVE	NOT SURE
neighborhood	44	26	23	3	3	1
parties	54	28	14	1	2	.5
gay dances (other than bars)	48	24	19	3	3	3
social groups	52	26	16	2	1	3
political groups	46	20	24	4	3	4
through friends	66	23	10	.5	1	.5
resorts and beaches	44	29	22	2	2	1
gym, "Y," straight health club, sports	35	24	27	7	3	4
church	32	13	28	6	16	6
personal ads	15	16	22	23	21	3
public toilets	11	7	11	18	49	3
highway rest stops	13	10	16	18	40	3
baths	24	21	20	15	16	5
parks	20	20	23	16	19	2
streets	22	21	24	14	16	2
pornographic movie theaters	14	13	12	25	32	4

The most socially anonymous and least visible of these places—public toilets and highway rest stops—are, interestingly, among the least-used and engender the most negative feelings. Furthermore, the most normal public arenas where heterosexual socializing takes place—at work, at school, in the neighborhood, social groups—are thought of very positively by gay men, but used infrequently. Most often, men meet at bars, the baths, at parties, and through friends. What these all have in common is safety. Rejection can occur in any of these settings, but they do not involve possible exposure to straight society with the risks of violence, humiliation, and other consequences. These statistics indicate that the demands of the closet, a status imposed by the prejudices of straight society, compel many men to meet others in ways that are "safe," and prevents them from meeting others in the many other ways that they feel positive about.

The most popular and traditional gay meeting place is the gay bar. That alcohol loosens people up is undoubtedly a factor in the association of gay socializing, or any socializing, with bars. However, the owners of bars are in the business of selling liquor: by providing the gay clientele with a haven of sorts, they make a profit in the process. Despite the fact that the

statistics indicate overall positive feelings about meeting men at the bars, most of the men who wrote detailed experiences were decidedly negative. Perhaps the bars are looked at positively because men experience them as safe, convenient, and functional, but there are widespread feelings that the social interaction inside them is often unpleasant.

⚢"It would seem that the 'gay bar' is the hub of our social universe. Larger cities have more diversity, I am sure, but the typical image of a gay club or bar is some windowless little hole with nothing but the street number on the outside of the building, which often used to make me feel like looking furtively around me before going in, to make sure no one saw me enter. The gays who run these establishments seem unconcerned, generally, and would in all likelihood prefer to maintain the status quo. Until we can stand in the light of day like all other human beings, I can't see very much improvement in any of the aspects of the gay culture as expressed in its places of public gatherings."

⚢"Gay bars and gay parties are safest, and where I meet most of my gay friends. I prefer a bar or group where I know people, and would rather be introduced by mutual friends. However, I'm not one to be at a loss for words, and easily strike up conversation. The more interested I am in a person on sight, the harder it is for me to start anything. Liquor does loosen my tongue, and it takes quite a bit of it to impair my performance."

⚢"I go out religiously on Friday and Saturday night. I stay in town from 8:00 p.m. to 5:00 a.m., barring an early 'pick-up.' I go from bar to bar, beginning with a piano bar, then to a leather and denim bar, and finally to a disco. I move about, evaluating each bystander. If I see one I like, I get as close as possible to him. But here's where I'm all cockeyed (pardon the bad pun). I look, but don't touch, nor do I talk. My thought processes go like this: I want him sexually *but* I'm afraid of being too aggressive and also getting brusquely turned down. I also feel that conversation is hypocritical if sex is topmost on my mind. Meanwhile I'm downgrading myself for being backward. It's so much more convenient when the other guy makes the first move. I also feel insecure about my build and my less-than-stylish clothes, which doesn't do much for my 'act.' "

⚢"Bar experience—meeting another man begins long before I ever get to the bar. It starts with a 'psych-up.' Showering, I clean every area of my body and then carefully and strategically place cologne on my face, chest, legs, ears, and wrists. I carefully blow-dry my hair (and taking time to brush my pubic hair and beard or mustache if I have one at that time). I pick out an album to fit my mood and put it on and begin to get dressed. If I'm looking for class, I dress class; if I'm looking for butch, I dress butch. All the time I'm convincing myself I'm going to be the best-looking guy to walk into the bar tonight! From there it becomes a matter of endurance, of keeping the 'psych-up' until I meet someone. I am very shy and wait until someone introduces themselves to me or I am introduced by a mutual friend. I use subtle body language, like getting 'caught' wetting my lip or rubbing my crotch, as if I didn't think anyone else was watching."

♋"During my lifetime, most of my gay friends have come from meeting at a bar. By getting to know some of the bar people, you do get to know others by being introduced by mutual friends."

♋"I'll give you three 'meeting' experiences. In a bar, I looked around until I found an acceptable person. I casually walked up to him and started a conversation. I don't know what I said initially but it was painful, like 'Been here long?' We started what began as an awkward conversation which evolved into a reasonable exchange of pleasantries, found that we had a *few* things in common, and after three drinks and 2½ hours, he said, 'Been nice talking to you,' and *left*.

"I walked into a bar with two friends, a pair of eyes caught mine from 'across a crowded room.' They stayed on me. I walked over to meet them. I was hugged and kissed, introduced to everyone at the piano bar, and, as he played with my legs, he announced to everyone at the bar how we were going to 'go home and fuck.' After finishing this drink, he had another. After an hour or so, an unknown person walked in and they discussed putting the garbage out, the car, the cat, etc. I asked the unknown person who he was to find that he was Romeo's lover, and I asked him why the guy was coming on with me. He answered, 'When he gets a few drinks in him, he's like that; it doesn't mean anything.'

"I walked into a bar and saw Adonis. I said, 'I think you're beautiful; let's go home and have sex.' He laughed and turned his back on me."

♋"I guess I do have a problem meeting other men. The main reason is that I do not like to go to the bars. Oh, I do not say that I do not like to have a drink once in a while. I do. But if I go to a bar, so many of them have had too much to drink, and that turns me off."

♋"Although bars can be an exciting experience in meeting other gay men, generally I find it frustrating. I seem to leave bars frustrated and depressed more often than I do feeling elated."

♋"I enjoy being around other gay people but the bars frighten me, as do large crowds. I can't and don't relate well in such situations. I prefer small social engagements where people can get a chance to know each other as more than just a face and body in a group."

♋"Since neither of us are drinkers, we don't relate to bars too well. When we do go to show visiting friends, we go more as detached observers than for hard cruising."

♋"I especially hate the late hours that are kept by most gay men. I wish bars closed at 9:30 p.m. That way the last-minute rush would be about 9:00 and people would pair off and go home earlier and get to know one another before a fireplace, with a glass of wine (or a joint) and classical music, perhaps."

♋"I wish that I could meet someone in a bar and say no to sex and still remain friends. Bars are funny like that. When you say hello to someone you don't know, you're 'cruising,' even when you aren't necessarily doing so. Sometimes bars are too tense because of that."

♋"When I go to bars, it's rarely to cruise; I go with friends—we party,

dance, and leave. Sometimes I meet a sexual partner there. But bars are essentially places to be seen; their function is to be a smorgasbord, and some guys just like to pick and choose and take their time deciding; this involves more games than I care for.''

⚭''Thank god for discos and baths! There we can let our hair down, drop the straight pretensions, and be who we long to be and who we are. Once my lover was out of town. I went to Denver's best disco and a friend of mine asked, 'I know M. is out of town but wouldn't you feel safer at home?' I replied, 'It is a hell of a thing, but I feel safer here than any other place in the world.' ''

⚭''I've had a lot of relationships start in a bar or gay coffee house, and a lot of interesting one-night stands, and while there are the lonely and the alcoholics, there are also a lot of happy, healthy people in these places.''

⚭''No one I have met in a bar has become my friend—I think that speaks worlds for that meeting place.''

⚭''The gay bar is an institution. After all, where else are we to meet one another—church socials?''

⚭''When I was young I took a lot of chances, meeting men in toilets and bushes. In those days it wasn't as dangerous as it is today. Today, I prefer to meet men in the gay movement, the baths, the beach, at MCC [Metropolitan Community Church], or at work. I don't like bars: because I don't drink, I don't like all that smoke; I don't like drag shows; and I don't like music so damn loud you can't carry on a conversation.''

⚭''There are any number of ways to meet men in San Francisco, but perhaps for me the bars are the most common. In nine cases out of ten, I come across as the active aggressor. The idea of standing around waiting for someone to make a move towards me is not appealing, because there's no control. I have a pretty good image of myself so I'm usually able to come across as pretty self-confident. This is essential, because I think self-confidence is the most attractive quality that people pick up on (or, to put it differently, an obvious lack of confidence is the quickest way to strike out). I may offer to buy the man a drink, or just engage in conversation with him. If the vibrations are good and he's responding favorably to my appearance and how I come on, then I'll eventually make the pitch for him to come home with me. I have no use for bars as places of socializing, and would just as soon meet someone fast and leave.''

Other gay meeting situations run the gamut from furtive encounters in alleys and public restrooms to friendly rap sessions in recently established gay community centers. Even the meeting places most associated with anonymous quick sex can and do give birth to friendships and affairs, or at least a one-night stand in someone's bedroom. After the bars, perhaps the most institutionalized gay meeting place is the gay bath, made relatively famous in contemporary America by Bette Midler (who got her start as a singer in one), and in the play and movie *The Ritz*. Elsewhere in this book,

men refer to sexual experiences in the baths, and a few comments are included below, along with various statements and experiences concerning gay meeting places:

⚥"In our town there are four gay male bars and two steambaths, a trail in a park, and parts of two beaches. That's it. That's where 'we' are allowed to go and do our 'dirties' with heavy police/punk/state harassment. To say I'm now jaded is putting it mildly. I know the score. We are repressed and oppressed. And it stinks."

⚥"Best place I had for several years for meeting men was at Provincetown, Cape Cod, first as a vacationer and then for two years as a full-summer employee at a gay inn. Some are still among my closest friends."

⚥"In my 20s I spent much time—too much—writing to men whose letters and sometimes pictures were in such magazines as *Grecian Guild Pictorial.* Once I had a letter and picture published and got a good number of replies, but few of these I finally met and became friends."

⚥"I get most of my sex at the baths, because I find it quicker and in more variety there than anywhere else, and when I'm sated, it's so simple to just leave and go home, no stranger hanging around to bother me afterward."

⚥"There is something very happy, indeed, about meeting gay people in what are supposed to be straight contexts—work, school, etc. It reinforces the reality that we *are* part of the world and do not have to hide so much."

⚥"I know a truckdriver who visits occasionally. He's married and has several kids. His wife won't suck him off, which he really digs, so he comes to me. I met him in a subway restroom. I went down on him then and there. We got to talking afterward and he told me his story. I told him that he was welcome to come over any time he wanted to. He comes over and stays for about an hour. He just lies back and watches me suck him off. After he comes the first time he looks through some straight pornography I have, and I suck him off again. Then he calls his wife and tells her he's been working late and will be home shortly."

⚥"Why can't there be in New York City, for instance, a communal building where guys can go for all sorts of activities—like game rooms, lecture halls and classrooms, films, music, group and individual counseling, etc.? In a way the Gay Activists Alliance firehouse did some of that, but a place on a larger scale, well located, nicely furnished and well lit, would be fantastic."

⚥"Laguna Beach, California, has a gay beach where I have met many very nice men. Some of them are our best friends. When I lived in Dallas there was a place near downtown called the 'Circuit' where the 'boys' would drive around a three-block residential area and stop when they saw someone they wanted to meet."

⚥"Up to and including the present the only way I am sure that a homosexual I meet is God-fearing is that I meet him at the Dignity/Chicago's Mass for the Gay and Lesbian Community."

⚥"Truck stops are often interesting. At some rest stops you can be very

open and frank in your statements—'How is everything?' 'Is everything okay, or could you use a little personal attention?' Most guys indicate interest by showing their hard-on bulge in their pants and by the way they stand or sit.''

⚦"Places are important. This town needs more of them. We have one dreadful gay bar where I don't often go, a park that's too central to the town for any privacy, and highway rest areas that usually swing. I go to Montreal a lot; it's only 1½ hours away. There, I hit the parks, bars, streets, and have friends who introduce me to new people.''

⚦"Personal ads are awkward, since I must see the number before I can get off on him. All of the frustration of scheduling the big meet, and then we discover that we are each other's toads. I got my sixth lover from an ad, but it was an ad to rent my place, not to have sex.''

⚦"In my experience, being totally tearoom, meeting other men is simply a process of standing at a urinal until a willing partner comes along. I seldom make the first move, but wait for the 'sign' that he is willing to have sex with me.''

⚦"I have records of the baths I have been in and those that provided contacts. Of the 124 I have been in, only 32 led to nothing. These were mainly in foreign parts. I have also kept records of the Ys I have stayed in. Of the 186, I have missed in 37. It is very sad to see them passing from the scene. What is a young Christian to do?''

⚦"I find it much easier to meet people within some context, like a political meeting, class, someone's house for dinner. I never meet anyone at bars.''

In a brief reminiscence about an earlier period of his life, one man recalled various meeting places in New York City:

⚦"My favorite meeting places were: (1) the park (Central Park, mostly—I tried some others with little success); (2) the streets (very good, because I lived in the West 70s, even then a gay ghetto, not elegant but still closeted); (3) Washington Square Park and the Village; (4) the library restroom at Columbia University, my alma mater (the fact that I always carried my alumnus card rather protected me there—besides, they seemed indifferent to what was going on; my favorite ploy there was to write messages on slips of toilet paper and hand then under the cubicle or, even more daring, just hand them through the door from the outside to whoever was on the inside. The notes would usually read, 'Hi, what are you looking for? I like to get blown,' or to that effect. If they were interested I'd take them up to the eighth or ninth floors where there were individual men's rooms and the door could be locked from the inside); continuing the list, (5) some of the East Side bars. It was a gay student of mine who mentioned the Blue Parrot, Third Avenue and 54th St., and I went there from about age 27 on. In the summer of age 28, with the idea of a lover in mind, I went there regularly (occasionally trying some others in what was called the 'bird

circuit'—included the Golden Pheasant, Bob's, later Shorr's, etc.); it was for those days an excellent cruising spot, the 'hunted and the hunting' someone even said then; the long narrow front aisle allowed you to pick up your beer (even then I would nurse one beer for the whole evening) and move to the large square back room, dimly lit with blue lights (whence the name), and though there was no 'orgy' element in the modern sense, there was a good deal of freedom of conversation, quick propositions, etc. One Greek fellow I remember I met in a very different bar, the piss-elegant type where people did not openly cruise; I met him my first time there, but when I returned there later on (it was in the New Weston Hotel), I was finally asked to leave because of my openness!' "

Cruising, Promiscuity, Quickies, One-Night Stands

The Queen's Vernacular's definition of cruising, "to look for sex," is good enough, but Webster's four definitions—"to sail about touching at a series of ports," "to travel for the sake of traveling," "to go about the streets at random," and "to travel at the most efficient speed"—all express elements of what gay cruising is all about. (Webster's, in its prudish dishonesty, doesn't even give the definition "to look for sex," which is as legitimate a meaning as any of the others.) Perhaps the most interesting thing about cruising is that it can be idle and relaxed, like checking out the people while running errands or shopping, or extremely purposeful, like leaving home at 10:00 p.m. Saturday night with great hopes of coming back with a man. The following comments express a wide range of experiences and feelings about cruising:

♂"I spend a lot of time cruising. No matter what I'm doing, I'm always looking to meet new men. When my sole purpose is to make sexual contact, I make myself obviously available. I also frequent places where sexual contacts are easy to make."

♂"My own personal sexual manhunt is tinged with guilt. Why? Cruising in the parks are plenty of people who seem to seek sex for sex's sake, just for release and not for involvement. Many of the faces are the same, day after day or night after night. Do they feel guilty, too? They don't look it . . . but then, I doubt I do either. We're all just craving the same thing. But even the craving has more to it than just another body. There is always a pursuit for *the* body *and face* that 'turns one on.' It's more than just sex for its own sake; otherwise we'd take the first body that comes along and have sex. Even though no emotional involvement might be a part of this sexual cruising, there is still the pursuit of one's type."

♂"It fits with the historical and prehistorical habits of the male of the species: i.e. the prowl, the hunt, the chase, and, not always inevitably, the conquest. There are moments when the concept of cruising seems rather pathetic, but these reflections usually follow an incident of unsuccessful cruising when I berate myself for having wasted time better spent at some other 'pursuit.' "

⚤"Cruising is a fun game and some nice tricks result as well as lots of frustrations."

⚤"I think cruising is silly and undignified in some ways—seeing all that need expressed so unsubtly rather amuses and upsets me. Can't deal with it. Too much signaling and staring, too little talking."

⚤"I used to like cruising more than now—scenes and situations aren't as good as they used to be. Am sad to say it could be in part due to gay lib—too swishy, faggoty types have helped ruin rest areas."

⚤"Cruising, though it can be fun and at times adventurous, is basically dishonest game-playing in which there is no winner."

⚤"I feel very uncomfortable cruising. I find it difficult to do."

⚤"Cruising's fun, but I don't like people to cruise when I'm out with them."

⚤"My lover and I cruise together without intent of picking up. We enjoy looking at beauty and comparing notes."

⚤"Cruising is the greatest social activity in the world. Even many 'straight' people get a charge out of being cruised and will respond."

⚤"Cruising is simply not for me. I'm not a bar type, and the whole idea of standing around for hours, getting loaded, with the idea of making a score is to me a terrible waste of time. I'd much rather go to a baths, enjoy all the sensuousness of the water, steam, flesh—more direct and healthy, less time-consuming and drunk-making. For some reason the idea of picking someone up off the streets or any public place never occurs to me."

⚤"I find it disappointing and debasing what I'm expected to do to meet other gay men. I must go to a city where there is a gay bar. The nearest one is Denver, 240 miles away. There I play a game called 'cruising' that is a series of actions communicating your interests to other men there for the same reason. This quickly becomes an impersonal thing with people having sex without an emotional involvement and that's just a bad trip for me."

⚤"I feel sometimes that cruising is compulsive/obsessive. I feel I'm in heat twenty-four hours a day. Can't I see a handsome man without reacting sexually?"

Promiscuity is perhaps one of the more controversial aspects of gay male social patterns. If one follows Webster's definition of "promiscuous," all it takes is "having sex with more than one" sexual partner, but the usual implication of the term is *many partners* and *frequent sex*. Promiscuity is one of the "charges" that straights make to attack gay men, and gay men tend to answer in one of two ways—either by denying promiscuity and holding up as an example the many couples who have been together for years, or by accusing straights of being jealous and by celebrating the easy, relaxed sexuality that permits varied, frequent sexual expression.

Essential to promiscuous sexuality are two gay male institutions—the one-night stand and the quickie. Quickie sex can take place in a variety of settings—even in one's own bedroom with a lover—but usually it implies a

very brief stimulation to orgasm in such places as the baths, a back-room bar, public restrooms, cruisy areas of parks and beaches, and such special places as the old piers and truck parking areas of New York City's Lower West Side. The term "one-night stand" suggests a one-time encounter, but the implication of the term is something a bit more extended than a quickie, perhaps with the pair spending a night in bed. One measure of promiscuity, undoubtedly, is the number of sex partners one has in a given period of time. We asked the men *how many different sex partners they had in the past week, the past month, the past year, and in their lifetime.* The following charts indicate the responses:

Different sex partners in the past week:

none	26%
1	38
2	18
3	9
4	3
5	3
6	1
7+	2

Different sex partners in the past month:

none	11%
1	23
2	15
3	12
4	9
5	6
6	6
7–10	10
11–20	5
20–60	3

Different sex partners in the past year:

none	2%
1-10	39
11-25	19
26-50	10
51-75	3
"numerous" etc.	27

Different sex partners in lifetime:

none	1%
1-10	15
11-25	17
26-50	20
51-75	6
76-100	7
101-200	8
201-300	4
301-1,000	6
"thousands," "many," etc.	17

Where does one draw the line and say that certain people have been promiscuous, and others have not? What value judgment is implied by the term "promiscuous"? These questions are impossible to answer because they depend on subjective attitudes. The "lifetime" figures are especially problematic, because they must be considered in the context of how long a person has been a "practicing homosexual." In any case, more than half of these men have had fifty or fewer different sex partners in their entire lifetime, while nearly a fifth have had hundreds, even thousands of partners. Or, to look at the weekly figures, 64% had sex only once or not at all, while nearly a fifth experienced the pleasure of three or more different bodies. The men had strong opinions on what promiscuity means to them:

♂"Promiscuity is a heterosexual concept which is used to attack us. *But if you are speaking of the John Rechy type of promiscuity portrayed in City of Night and The Sexual Outlaw,* I find it dehumanizing, sexist, and ultimately damaging to the psyche. If you speak in terms of 'sexual freedom' and sharing of sensual experience, it can be a fine thing. I guess it all depends upon motives."

♂"I have trouble with the word 'promiscuity' because I really do not know what it means. Where is the line between infrequent or frequent sex and promiscuity? If I have sex three times a day and am very selective in the choice of mates, am I promiscuous or highly selective and super-horny?"

♂"Promiscuity is an individual thing; it means different things to different people. I feel if someone 'purposely' seeks *only* quickie sex, one-night stands, and has to keep score, has to have sex with someone different every day or several times each day, then that person is 'promiscuous' and is not very emotionally mature or stable."

♂"I was always shy, afraid to approach the wrong persons (straight), but during the course of my fifty-year 'career' I used all sorts of 'dangerous' places trying to make contacts—tearooms, gay sections of movie houses, steam baths, street cruising, etc., with the exception of gay bars (I don't drink), with all kinds of varying results. I've made my share of mistaken

judgment, even been 'busted' (the night I got out on bail I was back on 'Queen's Row,' the Boston Public Gardens), but most of my contacts were pleasurable, even if they resulted in 'quickies.' I wouldn't recommend my life of promiscuity to everyone, but it sure has suited me, and given me many memories.''

⚭ "Promiscuity is a straight problem not to be applied to gay people. It is a product of that thing we know as the 'family.' ''

⚭ "I believe my estimate of 4,000 sex partners to be very accurate. I have been actively gay since I was 13 (thirty-one years ago). An average of two or three new partners per week is not excessive, especially when one considers that I will have ten to twelve partners during one night at the baths.''

⚭ "I have had a problem relating to the high degree of promiscuity that the gay life seems to impose on me. I guess I have high ideals, but I'm striving *not* to be promiscuous. I must admit, though, that I am now. I was glad to find a statement in a frequently quoted Quaker book that spoke to my condition. Quakers often speak of the Light within the person—meaning everyone. This 'Light' is sort of love I guess, but it has different meanings to different Quakers. The book is *Christian Faith and Practice in the Experience of the Society of Friends* (London Yearly Meeting of the Religious Society of Friends, 1960). The passage comes from a section entitled 'Sexual Morality' and was written in 1959. The passage is: 'The Christian attitude to sex is based on a total view of man's nature, comprising body, mind and spirit; no relationship can be a right one that in any way casts a cloud over the Light within a person.' In other words, if the act does not cast a cloud over the Light within myself then it is not an immoral act. This means that I must be very sensitive to the Light within myself and 'monitor' it. I have spoken about this to other Quaker friends of mine, gay and straight, and they have appreciated my efforts to sort this out for myself.''

⚭ "I enjoyed a period of exceeding promiscuity when I was coming out in San Francisco. I discovered for the first time the freedom to be me, the freedom to meet lots of new men, the freedom to explore my sexuality, and it was a joyful thing. After a while it got old and I needed more than that, more depth. But at the time and in my personal history, it was a good thing. I suppose I see promiscuity as negative when it becomes desperate or jaded.''

⚭ "I'm very promiscuous in a gay setting, and almost cold in a straight setting.''

⚭ "Though it's very important for people to experience a wide variety of situations (single, lovers, monogamous, etc), and cruising is a lot of fun, I am angry that gay people in general seem to be so down on any kind of stability, think of it as a prison, and sometimes are so inconsiderate about other people's commitments as to try to break them up.''

⚭ "Promiscuity is a real gay sickness, and I admit to having caught the disease myself. But what alternative does a guy have? Celibacy? I've had enough of that.''

Here are the comments on quickie sex, which is a major factor in the phenomenal number of partners that some men have had:

&"Society has too many hangups about sex and makes 'quickie sex' into a bad thing, as if everything has to be the 'earth-moving' and romantic, etc. 'Quickie sex' etc. is fine if both people (or more) know what they are getting into and aren't expecting more. Honesty is really important, though."

&"Quickie sex is not for me. I think it's dehumanizing; in order for me to enjoy sex I've got to spend a minimum of a couple of hours. I'm not very orgasm-oriented and that's what quickies are all about."

&"I think most quick sex is fun and informative, but I get the feeling that not everyone I meet has a healthy outlook on what he is doing, as I feel I do. I meet many men, young and old, who obviously function for the most part in the straight world, and dip into the gay world of tearooms and porno houses for an hour or so and make no attempt to integrate. I meet many gay-identified men who have no other form of sex in their lives except quick sex, and who don't relate to people in other than a cruise."

&"Quickie sex—love it! I'd have quickie sex on an elevator between the first and second floors if I could."

&"There's a certain bar that has a back room with one *very* dim light. It tends to get packed with guys around midnight engaged in quickie sex. The room is steaming with body heat. The groans of orgasmic pleasure come from all over—otherwise, no other sounds to speak of. One really can't see his partner. Sucking is the prime activity, although some fucking goes on. It's a thrill once in a while, but I can't make a steady diet of it."

&"Sex for its own sake or sometimes for the sake of spending a night with someone rather than alone is fine with me. Sex, I believe, is both a physical and an emotional need and sometimes one needs to be satisfied without the other. I have experienced times when I just wanted to 'get my rocks off' regardless of the circumstances and then I have had times when I wanted a night-long companionship not necessarily with sex (even though that nearly always comes to pass). I have picked up guys that want to spend the night with me and even though we may have a sex session, they do not achieve orgasm, but instead have wanted to be held and kissed and hugged."

The basic ingredient in the institution of the one-night stand is going home with someone you've just met, whether after a few minutes or a few hours of conversation, even though there is at least a possibility that you will not see one another again or at least not sleep together again. The men were asked, *How often do you go home to have sex with someone you have just met?* The responses were:

always	5%
very frequently	23
somewhat frequently	22

somewhat infrequently	19
very infrequently	21
once	3
never	7

Clearly, then, the one-night stand is within the experience of an over-whelming majority of gay men. Asked for *their feelings about going home with a stranger,* the men gave these responses:

very positive	29%
somewhat positive	31
neutral	20
somewhat negative	14
very negative	5
not sure	1

The following are comments on the one-night stand:

⚢ "I like having sex with a stranger as a way of becoming intimate with each other. I like to become acquainted and feel good about the person first."

⚢ "It's possible to meet many interesting guys this way; after all, I met my lover during a one-night stand. I had over two years of happiness from what began as a one-night stand."

⚢ "One-night stands are inevitable. I don't like them, but getting to know someone well enough to know that you will want to see them again before you first sleep with them is unusual, and there is always the possibility that things will just not work out in bed."

⚢ "I receive virtually no pleasure from one-night stands. I need a deeper involvement with a person in order to enjoy sex."

⚢ "While I had no lover or serious possibility of one, one-night stands were fun and filled my physical need. I rarely go with someone knowing from the start that it will be only for one night. I usually pick someone who I think might turn out to be something more. It does not overly bother me that this is rarely the case. I have had a couple of one-night stands while I was seriously interested in other people and find that I generally feel shitty when I have done this even though there is no commitment as yet between us, and have decided not to do this again."

⚢ "In four years since coming out I've met hundreds of gay men, slept with many, most only once. I have *never* regretted an encounter. Many quickies have become true friends. I am very glad for all the good times."

⚢ "One-night stands are more desirable than 'quickie sex' but less so than sex with a friend or lover."

⚢ "We don't have to promise respect, love, or a house in the suburbs before we get to enjoy ourselves or others sexually. Relationships should last for the duration that love sustains them, not one minute more, not one

minute less. Therefore, if a 'relationship' lasts one night (and I have experienced one-night *relationships*), that's as long as it should last.''

Courtship

The term "courtship" conjures up rather medieval images of noblewomen and their suitors, but in modern times it has the implication of postponing sexual gratification while cementing affectional ties. Perhaps rare, but not unknown among gay men, courtship evoked a variety of comments:

&"Courtship is as important to me as to many 'straights.' I would really prefer to get to know a man well enough so that sex would seem natural when it came if it did. Too many people are in a rush to jump into bed and don't stop to think of the consequences that sex will have when trying to establish a personal relationship later on.''

&"Courtship is ridiculous. Why not meet people sexually as well as asexually from the beginning—come to know them holistically instead of putting part of them aside as more or less important when that part is ultimately what you're after?

&"Courtship is a nice concept but I don't think that contemporary lifestyles for gay men leave much room for it.''

&"I hate dating rituals that seem like elaborate avenues to bed. I'd much rather just go around the corner and get our rocks off than all this phone numbers and dinner and that bit. I guess I genuinely hate the idea of courtship, unless it is happening so slowly that I don't notice it for a long time or unless we completely abridge it. I can't tolerate that process; it seems to me so straight.''

&"To a certain degree, I wish that there were more courtship in gay life, since it gives one a chance to know someone else a little better before committing himself to a sexual situation.''

&"I'm a very outgoing homosexual and act towards straight men in much the same way straight men react to women. I literally court them and have been known to ask a nice-looking man when he gets off work and would he like to have a drink. The response to this is usually negative, but it is surprising how many men go for it.''

Sex with Straights, Trade

As this last quotation indicates, the division of men into gay and straight is actually quite artificial. While most gay men probably prefer the convenience and hassle-free aspects of seeking out sex partners in situations where one is reasonably sure that the other men are also gay, there are men who do not socialize in this manner. There are many reasons why some gay men choose to socialize among straight men, or, more precisely, men of unknown sexuality. For one, some men are turned on by the very idea of

straightness. This, of course, can lead to great frustration, and it also may have elements of neurotic self-hatred in that it is based on the idea that only heterosexual men are manly enough to be worthy of one's attention. But some men just may not wish to accept the ghettoization implied by the gay scene—they know intuitively that a very large percentage of men have at least some potential for homoerotic experience and they act on the strength of this intuition. The presumption in any nongay environment, of course, is that all people are heterosexual. Gay people know better, thus the button "How dare you presume I am heterosexual?" The gay man who socializes in mixed environments refuses to make assumptions about who or what a man might or might not prefer in bed. In fact, if anything such gay men assume that their sexual talents will be appreciated by *most* men. "Trade" is a gay slang term for a nonreciprocal sex partner—generally someone who lies there while receiving a blow job. The person who is "trade" usually claims to be straight, but one of the adages of the gay world is "Today's trade is tomorrow's competition." (Although the term "trade" has implications of commercial sex, that's not what the term means.) In the questionnaire the men were asked *to comment on their experience with trade and with making sexual advances toward men when not certain they are gay?* Here are some of the responses:

⛳"All my advances are with men/boys that I know are not gay, and 95% of the time I am successful with them. You learn the right time of night to drive around. After the bars close between 10:30 and 2:00 a.m. on weekends. The guys are looking for sex at this time of night and nine times out of ten they already know my car and are more than willing to get done."

⛳"I don't go after straight boys—if they are gay, they'll come out eventually, or if they don't, I don't care. It's their concern. I want someone who wants me—not someone who is in the throes of defending, excusing, or justifying himself while still being gratified."

⛳"If I see it and want it, I go after it. I've had sex mostly with men who considered themselves straight. No problems having sex with these men, very difficult to have a relationship."

⛳"As a rule, I never approach men I'm unsure about, although the first man I had sex with and fell in love with was straight. He would allow me to suck his cock, which I loved doing, but there was a lot of emotion to the act for me that wasn't there for him (or he wouldn't admit it if there was). He actually loved to have me suck him off, but he had religious conflicts about homosexuality and conditioning, etc. It was a very traumatic experience, so I don't intend to repeat it, ever."

⛳"Sex with straight men does not appeal to me. Approaching a man who is ostensibly straight is a bad idea in my opinion. Even with what we perceive as accepting signals, a man could be uninterested. I think that approaching straight men strengthens the belief that homosexuals prey, turning off straight men and perhaps creating a permanent negative attitude toward homosexuals—'A queer tried to pick me up once, but I set the cocksucker straight!' Straights know that gay 'areas' exist and if they are so

inclined they are free to take a walk on that wild side. (Straight men, though often attractive, would be bad sex.)''

⚥"I never approach men who I don't suspect as being gay for fear of embarrassing them or getting beat up for being a 'faggot.' I've had sex with two guys who claim to be straight. The sex was really hot, heavy, and good. It was afterwards that was demeaning to me since they both were insecure and feeling the need to affirm their heterosexuality. I didn't like nor appreciate the coldness toward me since I was the one who was a confirmed gay.''

⚥"I enjoy 'trade'—it starts with eye contact, they approach, some small talk, then they tell a 'dirty' joke with emphasis on the sexual aspect. I usually suggest going someplace—then, if it happens, it happens.''

⚥"This comprises the bulk of my sexual experiences, as I seek out 'straight' men—specifically truckdrivers, welders, blue-collar types in general. While it's necessary for me to play the part of the cocksucker initially, I have found a high level of reciprocity in such contacts and many of these contacts have not had the hangups about sex that many 'gay' men seem to have. This is part of the attraction of these types—you don't know if they're going to be just straight trade or if you are going to have an experience that is really satisfying for both partners.''

⚥"I have had trade. At one point in my life I was trade myself. Most of the experiences entailed quick blow jobs in a car, and in the plant locker room. I had one rather long-going relationship with a man. We worked at the same factory and I would often come home with him at night. His wife thought that we were staying up and getting stoned, listening to records. Instead we were in his music room having sex. He always maintained that he was straight, but near the end of the relationship (when I was applying pressure) he was conceding that he had a lot of latent gay feelings. I learned that he had had other sexual relationships with men and that his marriage was practically arranged by 'friends' who were trying to 'straighten' him out.''

⚥"I have had a number of experiences with 'bringing out' men who have lived straight, and it was always they who made the opening. Let me tell briefly about one man of this kind. He used Jimmy Carter's *Playboy* interview as the wedge that led to general talk about who should have the say about who does what sexually. As he learned that I had no conventional aversion to 'odd' sex, he became more specific: heterosexual oral sex. Finding that safe, he proceeded to gay male oral sex. As he went along this line, taking probably an hour, he asked me if a man had ever 'done that' to me. Yes. Have I ever done that to another man? Absolutely. What is it like? Etc. As I explained to him what certain kinds of men could make me feel about them, he felt safe enough to confide that I had attracted him, as other men had done in the past, but fear had always made it impossible to proceed. This man was unusual in that he became a willing and very good partner in cocksucking and for the two months that he was in town we were good sexual companions.''

♂"I have made advances to men in straight bars but only when extremely horny and after drinking quite a bit. I kind of study them out before approach, and never have been physically or verbally threatened as a result of such an advance, though disbelief is a common reaction. My tricking success rate in such situations is probably about 20%."

♂"I have a written history of my sex life from June 24, 1939, to the present. I gave Kinsey a copy when he interviewed me in 1953. I can read it over anytime and recall many of the incidents. So many were straight or drunk partners. The drunks seemed to know the score after we got started, and many of the straights were servicemen and some wanted a blow job."

♂"I find it thrilling to make a pass to someone I'm not sure about."

♂"Don't like to go after straight men—there are enough gays to go around."

♂"I have had a great many experiences with 'trade' in jails, the service, hitchhiking, and other places. I think your questionnaire reflects a middle-class conceptual bias and is largely irrelevant to these men, most of whom are working-class and have a wholly different definition of and understanding of homosexuality than you do."

♂"The change-of-heart kind that wants to beat or rob you as soon as he's got his nuts off after having a hell of a good time is really number one on my shit list and probably the main reason I no longer cruise much. I've had a couple of very bad experiences."

♂"On several trips to Puerto Rico I have made contacts in gay bars, which are now fairly out in the open. The *puertorriqueños* whom I have gone home with and whom I have had sex with in other places feel very strongly that as long as they only fuck they are not really gay. Only after they have fucked you will they allow themselves to be talked into being fucked. They will not admit the next morning that they have been fucked, and even if all else fails, they can blame it on the fact that they were drunk, even though they weren't."

♂"I have had a few sexual experiences with so-called straight men. One was in a situation where I was staying with a female friend for a night in another city. She has one large bed in a small trailer. She and I always sleep together, but never have sex (but we are very affectionate and close). We picked up a hitchhiker, who seemed friendly, etc. He ended up staying the night. He wanted sex with her but she didn't want it and fell asleep. I was lying next to him, horny as hell, and started massaging him. He pulled my head to his cock to suck. He got off on it but I was feeling weird about having sex in my friend's bed. So, I held back a bit, which communicated to him bad sex. Later he apologized for being into it, saying, 'I was really into sex with her; I'm not a faggot.' He was admittedly young—19."

♂"Being gay is like being in one huge, secret society which has its own secret codes. I've never outright 'made advances' to someone who I didn't know was gay, but I have had experiences first establishing the person's sexuality without outright asking. Like most gays, I have a radar system

that can often immediately diagnose someone as gay (even without the stereotype mannerisms) or straight. It's the area of gray in between that requires other resources. One example: on a trip to Athens, I noticed there was a very good-looking guy on the tour, traveling with his mother. My radar told me there was a distinct possibility he was gay. On one of the islands, I happened to run into him alone, and I engaged him in a conversation. I was not going to ask him outright whether he was gay or straight, of course, but I started throwing out the gay code words. I told him I was from San Francisco and watched his reaction. A straight might react with impersonal interest, but a gay, when hearing a single male comes from San Francisco, will look at you with new speculation. This guy did just that, and he said, carefully, and with a certain hidden significance, that he had visited San Francisco and had quite a good time. I replied that I liked being there, and that the night life and bars were a lot of fun. Again 'bars' is a code word. He replied that he had enjoyed the bars too, throwing the code word back at me. I asked him if he had made it out to Castro Street, which has an interesting night life. A straight person only tangentially familiar with San Francisco most likely would know nothing about Castro Street, but for a gay, it's a dead giveaway. This guy said yes, he had had a good time at Castro and had met some interesting people. Without outright saying it, we had established that we were both gay. We made a date to hit the Athens night life that night, and later, we got it on.''

The Personality Factor: Shy or Outgoing? Insecure or Self-Confident?

Whatever the person's preference for the type of social situation for meeting other men, how one functions is largely a matter of personality. The men were asked about this with this query: *How active (you do the "picking up") or passive (you get "picked up") are you in seeking a relationship or a sex partner?* The replies were:

very active	14%
somewhat active	42
neutral	21
somewhat passive	18
very passive	4
not sure	1

They were also asked *to tell in what ways they were shy or outgoing, insecure and/or self-confident.* Given that relatively few men described themselves as passive, while many comments focused on shyness, it seems that many gay men think of themselves as shy but by necessity work to overcome shyness, rather than allow shyness or lack of self-confidence to lead to a ruinous social life. The following comments focus on these aspects of personality as they come into play in gay male socializing:

♂"I'm a somewhat shy person and have always had a hard time starting a conversation with a stranger. If they start talking to me first, I'm okay. I am coming out of my shell as I get to know more about the gay life, as it's a never-ending lesson, and I learn something new every day. I have just become involved in my first 'rap group' and find this a very relaxing and fun time in my life, being able to communicate with other gay people and seeing all the joys and heartbreaks each of us goes through."

♂"If I see someone that I am extremely sexually attracted to I seldom, if ever, make the first move. I remain coy and aloof, shooting meaningful glances at my target, hoping all the while that my message will be intercepted and understood and that he will make the first move. Needless to say, I often end up going home alone."

♂"Perhaps one of my biggest hangups is apparently 'coming on' too strong to people I've just or only recently met. Maybe people aren't supposed to put so much up front so soon—but the appellation 'cool' almost always seems vaguely repugnant to me."

♂"I often spend an entire evening in a bar or disco without speaking to anyone but the bartender. I'm thought to be aloof, where I'm just shy. When I do make contact, I overdo it—mistake a casual acceptance for love. I'm financially well off—which is attractive, and I mistake interest in my money for real interest. A problem."

♂"I have overwhelming confidence in my acting ability—I'll do anything on stage and get away with it. I crumble in a bar scene. Gay men intimidate me. I wish I could wear a sign that said, 'I'm a mean cocksucker, take me home and give me a try.' "

♂"I am usually very aggressive in a friendly, hopefully nonthreatening, way—initiating a friendly conversation with someone who attracts me, and letting the conversation run its course; usually it culminates into a sexual invitation. I am very shy about getting to the issue of sex right away, without feeling that I have taken the person's measure first."

♂"I am shy and aloof, but if I see something I want, a man I want to meet, I go after him. That's how you get things in this world."

♂"I particularly dislike lying, dissembling, circumlocutions, and the whole bit. My most successful non-hustler nights have been with 'You're the most interesting guy in the place. Do you want to come home and have sex?' There have also been a hell of a lot of 'nos.' "

♂"In most instances I am very shy and awkward socially, and I can't cruise—I can't look into another person's direct gaze for a long period of time—it feels like I'm being poked in the eyes. This makes it very hard for me to meet men at gay bars."

♂"When I meet other men sexually, I am a vamp and a flirt, but stationary. If it is at all possible, I will get them to pick me up. So am I active in the picking-up process? I choose, and generally get, the man I want. But I make him pick me up. It is sexually stimulating to me to be picked up. But I definitely entice to the utmost of my capabilities."

♂"I'm very outgoing and aggressive in bars; friends tell me I'm like a

'shark in a pool of groupers.' My philosophy is that if I were to lean against a wall all night (like so many of the guys), I'd never get anywhere. Besides, I'm 39 and don't have the luxury of wasting time. (I'm still looking for 'Mr. Right' and the more guys I can meet, the better my chances of finding him.)''

⚥"I find that because I am tall, others expect me to make the first move, something I'm uncomfortable doing because I have a rather weak self-image.''

⚥"There have been plenty of times when I have cruised the shit out of someone, but not made any advances, only to find out later that they thought I was stuck up. I often feel that guys look at me and think, 'Why is he waiting there to be approached? He's certainly not the best-looking guy in the bar.' I am trying to get over my shyness and talk to more people, loosen up, and generally enjoy myself more at the bars whether or not I trick. Part of it is meeting friends so I have people to talk with. Sometimes, I look too hard and consequently don't enjoy myself and feel depressed if I don't meet someone.''

⚥"I am self-confident with straights—not gays. Gays seem to have more hangups. Gay men can be very boring at times—too much importance is placed on 'relationships.' ''

⚥"I am shy because (1) I think I'm ugly—this eliminates the faggots; (2) I have a good job and don't want to be arrested and lose my job—that eliminates the tearooms, parks, and other illegal things; (3) I am a lousy fighter, and a devout coward—that eliminates the butch numbers that might slug me in a come-on.''

Buying and Selling Sex

One way to take some of the emotional complications out of the process of meeting other men is through the purchase of sex. John Rechy's widely read novel *City of Night* offers an interesting portrait of the world of big-city hustlers. Boy prostitution has increasingly been a subject explored, usually with sensationalism or do-goodism, by the media and social science researchers. Male prostitutes meet their customers in a number of ways—on well-known streets and corners or other pick-up spots such as bus stations, through ads in gay or "underground" newspapers, through massage or escort services, as part of an organized call-boy service, even by advertising on bulletin boards in gay neighborhoods. Aside from out-and-out prostitution, some men will obtain sex by paying in ways other than money, such as dinner, theater, and a night out on the town. The most elaborate of such arrangements involve "kept" boys or men and their "sugar daddies," sometimes including live-in arrangements.

The men were asked *to indicate how often they have paid for sex with a man or boy,* and *whether or not they've paid, how they felt about the idea of paying for sex.* The charts show the responses:

	ALWAYS	VERY FREQUENTLY	SOMEWHAT FREQUENTLY	SOMEWHAT INFREQUENTLY	VERY INFREQUENTLY	ONCE	NEVER
with money	1	2	2	1	9	9	76%
in other ways	.5	1	3	8	11	4	72

	VERY POSITIVE	SOMEWHAT POSITIVE	NEUTRAL	SOMEWHAT NEGATIVE	VERY NEGATIVE	NOT SURE
with money	4	8	21	19	45	2%
in other ways	4	8	27	20	35	6

Although paying for sex is not very common, about one-fourth of the men have tried it at least once. Negative attitudes toward the commercialization of sex predominate, yet there are a few people who feel positively about the practice even though they don't engage in it. One might guess that they are afraid of violence, that they can't afford to pay, or perhaps that they find the idea of hustlers a turn-on but choose not to participate.

The men were also asked *how often they had been paid for sex,* and *whether or not they'd been paid, what their attitude was toward the idea of receiving money or other benefits for sex.* The charts show the responses:

	ALWAYS	VERY FREQUENTLY	SOMEWHAT FREQUENTLY	SOMEWHAT INFREQUENTLY	VERY INFREQUENTLY	ONCE	NEVER
with money	0	2	2	2	8	10	76%
in other ways	0	2	5	9	12	5	68

	VERY POSITIVE	SOMEWHAT POSITIVE	NEUTRAL	SOMEWHAT NEGATIVE	VERY NEGATIVE	NOT SURE
receiving money	6	9	20	16	48	2%
receiving other benefits	8	12	25	17	35	4

More men are positive about being paid than about paying. One is tempted to say that in a capitalist society any way to get money is all right, though from a traditional socialist point of view, the prostitute is being exploited and is hardly in an admirable position. Looking at the issue more psychologically, it is apparent that gay men in general are more inclined to show contempt for the john than for the hustler. In the popular mind, the customer pays for sex because he can't get it for free. Often, however, this is not true—you don't have to be wealthy to pay for sex occasionally, and men may choose to pay because hustlers are convenient, anonymous, and sexually appealing, with no cruising games necessary. Among men with money it may be that buying sex is just as easy and uncomplicated as buying anything else. As for the hustlers, some take money for sex because it alleviates the guilt associated with homosexuality; others have no problems with gay consciousness—hustling is just a job. Whether the job is freely chosen or whether it is an alternative to going hungry is another issue, especially for hustlers from very poor families, from black and Latin ghettos, and in foreign countries where they offer their bodies to affluent homosexual tourists. Some of these rob and beat their customers; definitions of victim and exploiter become blurred.

Several men offered some first hand experiences with paying for sex, and being paid:

⚦"I've paid for hustlers twice: once a street-corner pick-up who was too concerned with his image to be fun; and once with an agency 'model,' more expensive, but more fun. I've been paid twice, both times in situations where the 'client' assumed I was hustling and automatically pulled out money at the end; I refused the money the first time, and the guy got very insulted; the second time I was not as surprised, and accepted the $20 gratefully, as I was short on rent that month. I think prostitution (freely chosen) is perfectly legitimate, morally and economically: another area in which the legislators have their heads up their asses (but they have 'secretaries')."

⚦"I adore hustlers. I am and always have been quite willing to pay for sex. That way I get who I want and I get what I want and there are then no ties that bind. I have a telephone number in New York City who will provide me with exactly the kind of man I want who will do what I

want—and then leave. I've had hustlers come up here for a night, or two nights, and I think it is great!''

♂"I don't in the least mind paying a younger man who provides me with the pleasures I like, the companionship of a manly male. I cannot give them the attractions that would turn them on; they offer me their masculine charms, so in return I offer cash. I have at least three muscular very well-endowed 'call-boys' on my string at the moment. I do think they enjoy their parties with me; they seem to do so in every way. But I also know I wouldn't have them with me if I weren't paying for their time. I like my relationship with them as there is a mutual trust, they are clean, they come when I want them to and leave at my will, and they do with me what I enjoy. Having them with me is much preferable to the chance of being robbed, of not having a satisfactory relationship. In a curious way, with each of these three young men I have a continuing affectionate understanding relationship. They are tolerant, agreeable, and in each case most superlatively endowed with the characteristics that I adore. One is a tough southern hillbilly type, bartender in New York, and a body builder, who loves to fuck. One is an elegant, narcissistic hairy-bodied aesthete, who loves to be made love to as he looks in the mirror. The third is a black ballet dancer so extraordinarily endowed sexually he seems to have a third leg. Each I find amusing, companionable, and well worth what I have to pay. And all of that is handled gracefully and easily too. I have become quite fond of these gents. There are others, too, whom I've met and enjoyed. Sometimes I think the relationship with gentlemen-for-hire is better than casual pick-ups, which can be fraught with danger, social embarrassment, and often ultimate sexual frustration.''

♂"I've been paid before. I got out of it because I couldn't tolerate fats and trolls. Never could get it up. Usually got $30 to suck them off. Advertised in local weekly gay bar magazine. No streets or bars.''

♂"When I know a guy really needs a couple of bucks, I will give it to him, as a guise to help him. But I won't outright pay a hustler.''

♂"Sex for money played a big role in my earlier life, especially during the Depression and 1955–60 in the baths, since one could pay the masseur $5 and have him in your own room. The money angle doesn't bother me as it bothers others.''

♂"One boy took me to his divorced mother's house. She allowed me, for a fee, to undress and play and jerk him and rim his ass, and suck him, and kiss him, hug and caress him (while she watched, clapped, and approved of my success). He wet in my mouth and I rewarded his behavior by making him and her yell, 'Uncle! Stop! Enough!' ''

♂"My sex with others is mainly with young hustlers. I am, sadly, only attracted to young athletic men (an attempt to recapture youth?) and thus am forced to buy sex in order to minimize the time wasted in 'pursuit.' Frankly, most sex I have experienced has been unsatisfactory, even degrading, because there was no love, seldom affection, and often indifference or hostility 'twixt me and my partner.''

⚥"I once had sex for money through Rent-A-Man, out of Queens, N.Y. I didn't enjoy the sex, but liked the idea that I was getting paid money for it. I know that I'm not suited emotionally to being a prostitute. I don't like the work."

⚥"Sex for money is not regarded highly in gay circles as in straight as a general outward view projected by the community, yet I believe that as long as there are those (gay or straight) who are willing to pay, there will be those willing to sell. I am a male prostitute and I feel no different about selling my body for sex than selling my mind and body to a company at $150 a week to keep books or type or file. I have several marketable qualities and it so happens that my body for sex is the best-selling in the current market."

⚥"When in Amsterdam once, I was approached by a very tasteful young man, who was probably gay himself, but when he indicated, after the conversation had reached a certain point, that there would have to be a financial transaction if he came to my hotel room, I rather pompously replied, 'In London we don't expect to pay for sex,' he smiled sweetly, and replied, 'In that case, you should have stayed in London!'—a riposte which demolished me more effectively than anybody else has ever managed to do! I see nothing wrong in sex for money; I have only once paid (seeing a very tempting cock in a restroom, I handed over $2 for the privilege of sucking it!), but I feel that, for some people, paying may be a much less painful procedure than the hazards of cruising and possible rejection. Each to his own is my motto."

⚥"I paid for sex once in Washington, D.C. I did in mainly out of curiosity, using a phone number from the 'models' section of *The Advocate*. My general impression was that for me it was too obvious that the fellow was not really 'involved' in the 'goings-on,' though he was trying to act as if he was. This turned the session into basically a mechanical exercise."

Some men enjoy their sex-for-money experiences as much as any other sexual encounter; here is an experience described in detail as a "most pleasing sexual experience":

⚥"Two weeks ago I met a real cute blond-haired boy, aged 16 and wearing a pair of faded blue jeans which were skin-tight, and he really filled them out beautifully in the ass and the thigh area. I knew he was active in the gay area of life because some friends of mine spoke of him many times about their involvements with him and of his circumcised 8 inches.

"I took him home and began showing him some movies of youths his age and younger. It turned him on because in a few minutes his hand was by his fly and his stiff erection out and standing majestically. He began jacking off but I told him to stop because I wanted to nurse on his honker and would give him $20. He stopped and began stripping off all of his clothes including socks and shoes. He lay on his back on the bed in the room and continued watching the film. After a little while his legs began to spread apart and he said he could not wait any longer.

"I turned off the projector and crawled between his young and firm thighs and began kissing them upwards towards his nuts. As I kissed and licked his nuts he began moaning and squirming. His balls had a real fantastic aroma which I loved and could not seem to get enough of.

"He reached for my head and pulled it up toward his cock and it eased into my mouth. My tongue began to circle the head of his young cock and he began to heave upwards, driving it down my throat. He kept squirming around and I slipped my hands on his firm young ass cheeks and began caressing them. He must have gone through some sexual pleasure like never before because he shot out about seven gushes of teenage honey into my mouth and it was real sweet going down. That lasted about twenty minutes and was really exquisite for me because of his blond hair and sweet 16. Also because of his beautiful bow-shaped cock which was as hard as a rock.

"He then lay on his stomach for me and I caressed his nice firm ass cheeks and kissed them. Very gently I spread the cheeks and began smelling and licking between them. I wanted to put my tongue in his asshole but I could not. Too tight for that. After about twenty minutes of that we walked into the bathroom and I knelt down in front of him. His cock was soft and I slipped it in my mouth and he pissed real slowly so I could drink his nice sweet piss.

"He then dressed and I gave him $20 and he left, thanking me. Before he dressed I gave his cock and nuts some goodbye kisses until I see it again. He said that I would see him again next week. I sure hope so.

"Since I am 48 years old and only desire sex with boys and young adults I do have to pay almost all of the time. I should say that I do not regret paying for it because that is more fun for me than anything else in my life."

Opinions about commercial sex from nonparticipants were varied. Here is a sampling:

♂"Sex for money is fine since the parties are agreeable to it because it is folly to think that the most potent human urge will go without being commercialized."

♂"I am not interested in sex for money and cannot understand why people pay for it when there is so much around for free, unless they can't get it any other way—which most probably could."

♂"I have a rather low opinion of money to start with, and don't want it soiling sexual relationships in any way."

♂"If I felt I could charge money for sex, I think I would. If someone offered me money, I'd probably accept it—but I'm in no position to demand it."

♂"Sex for money is fine. There probably are people who are unable to have sex any other way. There may be some reason why the majority of men

would find them unattractive. So, if they're willing to pay and know exactly that that's all they're getting, then I say, 'More power to them.' This reminds me very much of Olivia de Havilland's portrayal of *The Heiress*. That movie changed my whole attitude about those who pay and those who operate for payment. As far as selling is concerned, I don't think that I could do that. It's not that I have anything against prostitution, it's just that I don't like to think that I have to do whatever is asked of me or else I won't get paid. It means that I have no control over the situation.''

⚥"Sex for money is an inexcusable breach of morality.''

⚥"Sex should not be a buy/sell commodity! One of my fantasies is to live to see the day when there is no market for prostitutes, either male or female (but that would take a revolution in the way society treats love, so I'm not too hopeful). I've never paid for sex but once was bribed/black-mailed into bed with gifts. One of the most negative experiences of my life.''

The Question of Attraction

An essential yet somewhat mysterious aspect of gay male social interaction is the entire question of attraction. What physical and nonphysical aspects of a man attract another man? How important are the various factors in making a man attractive (or unattractive)? Sometimes, a group of factors go together, and a person can be said to be a particular "type."

The men were asked *how often they relate to a certain "type."* The responses were:

always	7%
very frequently	41
somewhat frequently	31
somewhat infrequently	9
very infrequently	7
never	5

There's no doubt about it—an overwhelming majority of the gay men choose their partners according to a certain type or types. In order to determine what qualities are important, twenty-five different items were listed and the men were asked *to indicate how important each of them is, "in terms of what you look for or what you avoid."* Of course, the chart does not tell all: for example, a person checking "very important" for "facial hair, beard, mustache" might mean that a man with a beard or mustache is a big turn-on, or a big turn-off. For reasons of space, the questionnaire could not cover all the possibilities. Later on, the men describe some of the types that they look for. For now, here's the chart showing the importance of various characteristics:

	VERY IMPORTANT	SOMEWHAT IMPORTANT	NEUTRAL	SOMEWHAT UNIMPORTANT	VERY UNIMPORTANT	NOT SURE
age	22	55	11	8	4	0%
height	6	33	33	13	14	0
weight	29	54	9	5	3	0
build, physique	24	61	8	4	2	0
"looks" in general	34	56	7	1	2	0
eyes	21	30	36	5	8	1
nose	5	27	47	10	11	1
lips	8	31	43	8	9	1
complexion	15	48	26	7	5	.5
facial hair, beard, mustache	19	37	29	7	8	.5
head hair, baldness	20	40	26	7	7	.5
body hair	17	34	33	8	8	.5
buttocks (ass)	15	40	29	9	7	.5
penis size	11	35	30	13	10	1
circumcision	13	20	37	9	19	2
hygiene, cleanliness or lack of it	73	22	4	1	0	0
clothing	10	42	32	8	8	0
race	19	29	28	10	14	0
social class	6	24	35	15	20	.5
educational level	11	35	30	11	14	0
religion or spiritual orientation	3	18	37	12	30	.5
political views	7	20	38	13	22	1
overall personality	52	41	5	2	1	0
masculinity/femininity, butch/femme	30	41	20	3	5	1
intelligence	30	47	16	4	4	0

The most important item on the list is cleanliness, and judging from the comments that were submitted, someone who is dirty is the biggest turn-off of all. "Overall personality" was indicated as the next most important factor. Among the physical attributes most often described as important were weight, build/physique, facial hair, complexion, and looks in general. Other factors frequently rated as important were intelligence, masculinity/femininity, and age.

A complete listing of the various preferences expressed by the men in their answers would take many, many pages. Male beauty standards reflected in the media include at least some of the types appreciated by gay

men. While there may be some predominant types, virtually *any* characteristic is appreciated by *someone*. The following listing of types, peppered
with some brief statements concerning specific characteristics, offers some
idea of this range of preferences:

♂"I prefer jocks with brains or any man who combines virility with
intelligence. Generally clean-shaven men with or without long hair. A clean-
cut man is what I'm looking for basically. Someone who is neat without
being prissy. A good but not too heavy a physique with a nice crop of chest
hair. About 26 or older. He must be masculine and love dressing straight.
Preferably not too big or small in the hips. A clear complexion. A broad-
minded man with energy and some personal standards of excellence
(character). Preferably white. I don't care for freckled men."

♂"Perfection: 16, 5'8", 130 pounds, thin but muscular, blue-eyed,
handsome with a clear complexion, long curly blond hair, without facial
hair, round, tight ass cheeks, a short and thick cock, circumcised, clean,
dressed in levis and no shirt, with a smooth, hairless chest and large, round,
sensitive nipples, intelligent, agnostic, leftist, warm, funny, and masculine
(not in order of priority)."

♂"I only respond to a man who is at least fifteen years older than
myself. He also has to provide some kind of intellectual challenge to me. I
immediately, upon meeting someone in a sexual framework, start scoping
them out intellectually, teasing, and throwing out curious little intellectual
barbs for them to catch on. I don't know why this is important but it is. I
respond also to very precise physical features; very dark brown hair, taller
than myself, preferably dressed in sports clothing (as opposed to butch,
truckdriver regalia). He must be slightly overweight, but not obese, just a
moderate middle-age spread (this can vary slightly). Beyond this there is an
elusive quality that separates a man that fits this description from someone
that I would like. I term it, for lack of anything better, middle-age
cuteness."

♂"Fat people make me sick to just touch it and well another part of it is
that when ya try to fuck their ass you have one hell of a hard time trying to
get it in as ya have to find the hole through all that fucking fat."

♂"I find that most cute people are really fucked up in the head."

♂"Since foot fetishism is my favorite, I want feet clean and toenails
trimmed and cleaned. This is *very* important to me. I'm not especially eager
that partner be brainy or well educated. Being a Ph.D., I've come to dislike
them intensely and prefer a less bookish partner."

♂"I like all men. But I especially like *all man*. I am turned on by men
who are physically powerful. Muscular arms and chests are particularly
attractive to me. But these types are only my favorites. I have been attracted
to and have enjoyed sexual activity with men who do not match the above
description at all. I think personality is the one essential. I am not attracted
by dead-fish types. I like vibrant men. I am not attracted by bald men, and
never expect to have sex with one. As for what constitutes 'looks,' I
generally notice the face first. If the face is unattractive, I don't care how

strong or muscular the guy is. I just can't stand to gaze into the eyes of a homely face.''

♂"My type is a variation of the Montana mountain man fantasy: jeans, flannel or plaid shirt, a beard, an air of confidence, and good nature, masculinity, and unaffectedness. I can be attracted to totally different types, but this is undoubtedly my favorite. As far as specifics, I like dark, black, wavy hair, tan complexion, blue eyes, tall, lean, muscular frame, Caucasian, and especially having a good thick well-cropped beard. I like small, firm ass and large circumcised penis. Social class isn't too important, but intelligence is. I'm attracted to someone who is independent, dynamic, and thinks for himself, but who is also ready to learn new ideas and viewpoints.''

♂"Boy, do I have a type. Or, types. I suppose to be brief these may be referred to as 'Modified Robert Redford' (Type I) and 'Modified Burt Reynolds' (Type II). The two most important attributes I look for are a mustache *(obligatory)* and well-developed chest muscles. I cannot recall the last time I was turned on by someone who was not wearing jeans, except in a bath or on a beach or someplace where clothing or jeans were not in issue. Short hair is almost a necessity; at any rate, really long hair turns me off. I am not particularly partial to beards, unless they are very well trimmed, in spite of my mustache fetish. I avoid people in chic clothes and avoid flamboyant types and people who are not in shape ('no fats or fems' as the ads say). Also, I do not like shaven heads or baldness for no reason which I have been able to figure out. Type I people are very hard to come by but New York City is filled to the rafters with Type IIs, so I have little problems in finding someone.''

♂"My ideal lover (oh, where is he?). Mr. Right: good-looking, taller than me, slender, well built, dark straight hair, dark eyes, beautiful features, hairy chest, cute tight ass, large cock (not super large), educated at an elite eastern university, a professional or prospective professional with a good or potentially good income (at least $20,000-$30,000 a year), likes to fuck and get fucked, good social skills, not 'overly' intellectual or culturally sophisticated (in other words not obsessed with opera, classical music, art, or ballet), but moderately interested in these as well as more 'popular' areas such as commercial movies. Jewish, Italian, or a WASP who has been around Jews a lot and understands them. Emotionally sensitive and supportive. Shall I continue? Oh, not *at all* effeminate.''

♂"I am interested in quiet, somewhat effeminate males. Physically, I am most attracted to Mexican men, without facial hair, with dark skin and features.''

♂"Redheads—very clear, perfect skin, dark red/auburn hair that is full-bodied as opposed to kinky, orange hues.''

♂"I don't like redheads—I find their crotches have an odor different from other white men, and it is one I don't care for.''

♂"The strong silent butch types are a drag—mostly only concerned with who dares to approach them.''

⚛"The person I look for as a partner is the type who looks as if he swam, ran, played in sports, and was generally active. I also look for a quiet, gentle person. Let me say that I find the Richard (John-Boy) Thomas type of man very attractive."

⚛"I prefer a masculine guy that dresses with a 'soft' or casual look that is wholly masculine, not at all prissy, who speaks quietly and sincerely, and has eyes that match the voice!—who is gentle and appreciates beauty wherever it is. A man I wish was my lover had me over for dinner a week ago. At one point he led me to the window in his living room to show me the leaves that had fallen overnight—because he thought they were beautiful. This incident says more about my type than another page of writing would do."

⚛"I look for sensuous eyes and listen for a soft voice."

⚛"I notice body hair a lot. I like extremes, either very hairy or extremely smooth bodies."

⚛"I dig sweat. I like making it with someone who's showered in the morning, worked all day, and then goes out again all sweaty and musky."

⚛"I'll take what comes, but no nellies."

⚛"I cannot be attracted to the world's most handsomest man if he is a cynic."

⚛"I like 'jocks,' 'Camel filters men,' 'Marc Spitz swingers,' and 'tanned surfers with sun-bleached hair and broad, flat chests.' Also I find 'dark, mysterious women' and 'Jane Fonda type' hip women very attractive."

⚛"I look for persons who are much like myself both in manner, attitude, and physical characteristics."

⚛"I like dark, well-built men (Italians, Greeks, Spanish-Latino looking). Lots of men I've loved were handsome, flashing eyes, blue, brown, green, and generous mouths often with mustaches. Defined features, cheekbones, etc., with broad shoulders and fine, strong hairy chests. Nice asses and good legs and 7″-9″ cocks. I don't like 'muscle' men, body head trippers, or thin limp-wristed queens who look great in clothes and awful out of them. I also avoid anyone who looks like he doesn't like living in his body, i.e., dirty, fat, etc."

⚛"I love blacks. My life centers around blacks, I am turned on by a black man's body. I prefer a man in his 20s, average height and weight (maybe on the tall side), good-looking, with whom I can have fun and be serious."

⚛"Very little turns me completely off. If someone has a big cock I'll make it with him, no matter what the rest of him looks like."

⚛"I find a deep voice hypnotic."

⚛"I find people boring after a while if they haven't been exposed to the New York *Sunday Times,* Genet, theater, Truffaut, or Tchaikovsky. So many gays (as so many straights) do not read books (or only best sellers) and are not politically aware. They—one clique in particular—smoke pot or take acid and disco all night Friday and Saturday."

⚛"I unconsciously avoid black men. I don't find black men attractive,

and part of that may be some kind of racism, but I don't consciously think so.''

&"To name a few I find attractive: Jon Voight, James Olson, David Soul.''

&"I want what everyone else wants—an Adonis, a sexual athlete, a formidable intellect, a decathlon athlete, plus all the other good things rolled into one. However, I frequently settle for somewhat less. I do not like fats, fems, stupid people, compulsive talkers, nervous types.''

&"I think nice even white teeth are important. The way one holds his mouth also tells a lot about the personality of a person.''

&"I prefer someone who is not religious or at least not pushy about his religion.''

&"The gay world (in its mimicry of the straight) seems obsessed with 'types.' The muscle man, the straight-world images of the athlete, the marine, the construction worker . . . This view of people, however 'convenient,' is unimaginative, limiting, and seldom how things really are. I find myself trying to cultivate a taste away from a standardized type-mold response. Indeed, I find myself most attracted to people who don't seem to quite fit a mold—who seem 'different' or 'special'—people who don't really care about images and types.''

&"I do not care for overly 'pretty' or handsome guys, nor the musclebound kind either. They're usually duds in bed and only interested in hearing you gurgle over them.''

&"Hygiene is *the* most important. If there is any indication that a potential partner is not a practitioner of good hygiene habits, there is no way I will take that guy to bed.''

&"My ideal would be a very straight-looking man with a beard, mustache, and neat trim haircut.''

&"My type is almost any black man weighing less than 250.''

&"Yes, I very definitely do have a type, a very specific type. He is 5'9" to 6'2" tall, has blond hair and blue or green eyes. He weighs 150 to 165 pounds. He is fairly well built but not overly muscular. He is friendly, quiet (though not introverted), gentle, very intelligent, ambitious, from a good family, kind, well informed, creative, interested in people and ideas, is fairly masculine (but doesn't need to prove it), is well groomed, has pleasing features, clear eyes, good complexion, strong legs, muscular buttocks, little body hair (especially *not* a hairy chest or back), a 6" to 8" circumcised penis, a nice smile, good teeth. He is no older than 26 at the outside, and no younger than 18.''

&"I have a vast repertoire of types and discover more all the time. These are a few of them: (1) brawny truckdriver or serviceman, (2) tough/scared boy just coming out, (3) debonair, worldly older (30s, 40s) man, (4) these most of all—boys and men in whom I see some facet of myself: people who dress like me (a mix of 'Ivy League' and 'proletarian drag') and share my interests (movies, twentieth-century literature, German, opera, theater,

aesthetics, activism). I'm usually either not interested in sex, or, when aroused, not fussy. I can get off on 'making a present of myself' to an older, unattractive man.''

⚤"I relate usually to someone who appears to me to be 100% man. If anything about him tends to suggest some kind of 'weakness' about him I'll usually back off as gracefully as possible.''

⚤"I can't stand people with so much body hair they look like they are wearing rugs.''

⚤"I love Latins and refuse to go with blacks.''

⚤"As long as I don't know that a person is a racist, a sexist, etc., I can sleep with him based on sexual attraction alone. If I know for certain he's a pig, forget it.''

⚤"Intelligent, liberal, not into gay liberation, definitely masculine but not overly butch, tolerant personality, appreciation of rock and roll and most other music, art, and good times.''

⚤"His ideal age is around 18, but he can be older if he has a youthful, 'pretty' face. Height is unimportant. His weight should be a little on the light side for his height with nicely developed chest and legs. Eyes can be any color, I never think about the nose or lips—they will complement the pretty face. His complexion should be clear and I prefer no facial hair. His hair should be black, soft, shiny, and moderately long; the chest smooth and hairless. His buttocks will be small and firm, his penis will be 7″ or longer. If he is immaculately clean, and he will be as an ideal, he may be uncircumcised, but this is not *vital*. I want him to be scrupulously clean and sweet. Clothing is not important. I prefer that he be Caucasian, for no reason I can think of . . . if he is not, all right. The rest I can sort of lump together. I want him to be interesting, witty, nonathletic (not a sports nut), with a love of music, theater, good films, etc. His politics is not particularly important, although I would not welcome a rabble-rousing radical. I do not want a 'mincing fairy.' I would like to be able to appear in public with him and have people think, 'What a nice young man.' ''

⚤"My type is an androgynous male.''

⚤"A somewhat older, bearded, well-built, intelligent professional man is the ideal I suppose—but if all of these appear in an excruciatingly boring or obnoxious personality, I turn off.''

⚤"I tend to gravitate toward the more 'boyish' girls and 'girlish' boys. This is not to say effeminate acting, which turns me off, but the 'cute' boy type.

⚤"I prefer a so-called nonconformist not into money, material collections, nor too self-centered.''   ·

⚤"He must know and like to dance, which is very enjoyable to me in a bar or at home.''

⚤"I do not like alcoholics, dopers, or flagrant faggots.''

⚤"I will take anything with a good stiff prick.''

⚤"Upper-class men tend to intimidate me because they are always

wanting to pay, and since money is power, I feel dominated, which I dislike as much as I disliked being required to dominate women when I dated them.''

⚥''Nothing is worse than fat. Beer guts are unattractive and people who are overweight are repulsive to the point of being objects of pity.''

⚥''I am 6'3" tall. I find it awkward to have sex with a very short person (under 5'9").''

⚥''I am a white supremacist and a member of the National Socialist League. I do not have sex with anyone who is not Caucasian.''

⚥''I won't go with blacks no matter what, except black women once in a while.''

⚥''I would never spend the night with someone I thought was dull. The idea of having sex with someone with whom I'd have nothing to say bothers me. They must be able to spark my interest intellectually as well as physically. I am also a snob. I love beautiful hands, ones which are not callused or stubby, but long, tapered, and well-manicured. I think it beautiful.''

⚥''Jewish boys for some reason attract me more than any other race.''

⚥''Especially like straight-looking type, the fraternity type, beard and glasses can be a turn-on.''

⚥''I expect a fundamental decency in terms of regarding the value of human life and feelings.''

⚥''Must be able to discuss current events, art, design, some science.''

⚥''I am immediately attracted to bald men—for me there is something exceedingly 'sexy' about a bald head, or he should have a receding hairline.''

⚥''I find a hairy chest and forearms attractive. I do not usually find hairy backs attractive.''

⚥''I detest rich, upper-class, and businessman types. I can't stand religious fanatics or devotees. I hate rednecks and conservatives, Republicans, violent and insensitive people.''

⚥''I'm superstitious about eyes being windows on the soul. In different moods, shy or bold gazes turn me on.''

Some people are truly ''locked into'' their types; for others it is only a mild preference. What happens if a person doesn't find his type? How do the gay men feel about the entire process in which types play such a major role? Here are some responses to these questions:

⚥''Most guys (in fact, most people) seem to go through stages of having one particular type or another, but I think the healthier ones have outgrown their own limitations in this respect.''

⚥''I hate having a type. I like young straight men. I really hate not being able to relate to gay men better as sex partners.''

⚥''I wish my 'typing' weren't so strong, because I would like a lover, and I think I'm a little too picky for my own good. A couple of times I've

known guys who have very nice personalities (which is more important in the long run) but I didn't get involved because they weren't physically attractive.''

⚥"I'm afraid the butch men who really make my breathing cease momentarily are OMCD ('Out of my class, darling'). I never get my ideal man, so I settle for second best. Fear of rejection strikes again!''

⚥"I relate to lots of people. The type is an ideal. I once had sex with a skinny, 75-year-old man (he looked much younger) who was sensational.''

⚥"Ideally people would judge others on the basis of kindness and ability to love rather than on physical attributes over which no one has control. Unfortunately, and unfairly, the dark, 'butch,' mustached 'hunks' and the lithe, blond surfer boys have it made, while the rest of us suffer.''

⚥"Unfortunately, I am very impressed by looks. Unfortunate, for it denies me many sexual relationships which may be rewarding. But I am a graduate of 20th Century–Fox, which taught me as a youngster that prettiness equals happiness.''

⚥"I have no compunction about gravitating towards certain types of people. In my lifetime I have met people of all types, walks of life, backgrounds, persuasions, and proclivities; a number of them I was required to deal with closely. And many of them wouldn't otherwise interest me because our interests, etc., are too diverse. Given the option, which I currently have, I choose only to relate to and surround myself with people who 'uplift' me, with whom I may learn from, share things with and/or teach things to. And why not? I've already classified myself here as an elitist.''

⚥"What happens when I don't find my type? Silly question. There are hundreds of other kinds of beauty. If Burt Reynolds won't say yes, am I going to ignore Robert Redford? If I can't have Sean Connery, will I turn down Rudolf Nureyev? If Al Pacino is out of town, am I going to reject Gene Hackman?''

⚥"I don't know how to comment upon whether I 'like' the idea of having a certain 'type.' Is it something that one has a choice in? Astrologically, I'm ruled by the planet Venus, which means that I'm not happy unless I'm surrounded by beauty. I found out the astrological trait long after I realized the truth of it for myself through my own awareness.''

⚥"If it's okay for me to prefer men over women sexually, why isn't it just as okay for me to prefer men who are young and attractive? I'd like to overcome all such limitations, but it isn't that easy, and I also want to enjoy life.''

⚥"I have tried, and still do occasionally go to bed with people who do not fit my type, but whom I thought were just outstanding people. It doesn't work. I think that it even is destructive. I tend to feel slightly negative towards someone who I go to bed with who is not my type.''

⚥"Generally I only orientate towards my type and naturally end up going home alone. However, I have wanted men who seemed to be both butch and level-headed and good-looking. Fact is I'd rather go home and

masturbate than sleep with a man below my standards. Having a type seems inescapable. It would be terrific if these physical things weren't as important as they are. Sometimes, though, if you keep an open mind just about any type save the grotesque can surprisingly appeal to you.''

♂ "I frequently have sex with people nothing like my type. I don't really think it is romantic to have a 'type.' ''

♂ "Types are okay and I feel gays often choose types who are (a) very much like themselves, or (b) the opposite of their self-perception.''

♂ "There are few points on which I am willing to compromise. If I don't find my type, I generally sleep with no one. I have many times slept with people who deviated slightly from this model, and generally have regretted it, or simply not enjoyed it. It rather mystifies me as to why I am so specific in the type to which I am attracted. I find it rather inconvenient in that it limits the possibilities of getting involved with someone who meets the most important of these criteria, but for instance has black hair. I have *never* been sexually stimulated by anyone with black hair. Why? I really don't know. The personality characteristics I mentioned are really just as important as the physical characteristics in my ability to be sexually attracted to an individual.''

♂ "Having a type is fine provided you don't carry it to extremes. I have a friend who continually holds out for Mr. Right and in the process spends many long lonely nights alone.''

♂ "I think that the few people who go only with very specific types have hangups that they do not understand.''

♂ "I don't like being tied into a type, since it's usually physical or superficially mental in its determination, and one has the chance of missing out on meeting some really neat people who don't fall into a specific category. My current lover does not fit any of my types, and had I rejected him for that reason, I would have missed out on some rewarding years.''

♂ "I will only relate sexually with my type. I do relate verbally to almost anyone regardless of sex, race, creed, looks, age, etc.—dancing, drinking, playing pool, etc.''

The men in general seemed keenly aware that sexual attraction involved a complicated balance of physical and mental attributes, and by no means agreed on whether the entire process is rooted in practical, material reality or is more mystical and intangible in nature. A few men had no apologies for their tendency to seek out a type or types. Generally, the men saw the process of typing as an evil necessity at best, a nasty problem at worst, but nonetheless something very much a part of the day-to-day social interaction for most gay men.

Age

As indicated, one of the most important factors in determining sexual attraction between men is the question of age. Those concerned with analyz-

ing such matters have even coined a new word—"ageism." Since we live in a youth-oriented culture, it is no surprise to find youth particularly sought after in the gay world, and usually the term "ageism" is used to refer to social patterns in which older men are rejected in favor of younger. A richer definition of the term, however, might include any rigid preference based on age, including the scornful attitudes of adults who ignore the legal and emotional plight of minors and who often consider youths to be inconsequential or unmanly. The men were asked *how often they have sex with men and boys of the following ages, and, whether or not they have sex with any of the age groups, to indicate how they feel about the idea of having sex with each of them.* The two charts indicate the responses:

	ALWAYS	VERY FREQUENTLY	SOMEWHAT FREQUENTLY	SOMEWHAT INFREQUENTLY	VERY INFREQUENTLY	ONCE	NEVER
65+	0	0	0	.5	13	5	81%
55-64	0	0	1	3	20	7	68
45-54	.5	3	5	11	27	11	42
35-44	1	11	22	23	17	7	19
30-34	4	29	34	12	11	3	7
25-29	4	42	32	10	8	1	3
20-24	5	34	26	17	13	.5	4
16-19	2	6	11	13	31	8	27
13-15	0	1	1	1	11	9	77
9-12	0	0	0	1	2	4	93
under 9	0	0	0	1	2	1	96

	VERY POSITIVE	SOMEWHAT POSITIVE	NEUTRAL	SOMEWHAT NEGATIVE	VERY NEGATIVE	NOT SURE
65+	8	5	14	21	45	6%
55-64	9	7	19	23	37	5
45-54	16	16	21	23	20	4
35-44	32	32	21	9	5	1

	VERY POSITIVE	SOMEWHAT POSITIVE	NEUTRAL	SOMEWHAT NEGATIVE	VERY NEGATIVE	NOT SURE
30-34	59	25	11	3	1	1
25-29	70	20	8	1	.5	0
20-24	65	21	10	3	1	.5
16-19	38	23	12	14	12	2
13-15	11	8	8	15	51	5
9-12	4	1	3	5	77	7
under 9	3	2	2	3	82	7

At first glance, the statistics seem to indicate that the men in their 20s and early 30s are the most sought-after age group, but it must be taken into consideration that the majority of the men who participated in the survey are in their 20s and 30s. The youth orientation of gay men—which few gay men would deny—is nonetheless reflected in these statistics. Consider that roughly 16% of the sample is age 20-24, but 65% of the men have sex with people age 20-24. Again, while 24% of the sample is age 25-29, positive feelings about that age group are expressed by 90% of the men. In the men's comments on their type, words like "younger" and "boyish" and "in their 20s" appear with frequency. Most of the men appear with frequency. Most of the men appear to prefer partners their own age or slightly younger. A few have a definite attraction to older men, while teenagers are also a sought-after age group. In all, 77% of the men cite age as an important factor in choosing a partner, which means that most gay men are likely to feel very aware of their age. The comments on boy-love and aging later in this chapter shed more light on this topic.

It is worth noting that in the above charts one can see that on both the older and younger extremes there is much more positive feeling about sexual relations with those groups than there is actual sex in practice. This may mean simply that the men "feel good" intellectually about anyone having sex with anyone, whatever their own preferences. It could also indicate that many men are locked into certain set age-oriented fantasies, and don't function outside of those fantasies, even though they might like to. On the younger end of the spectrum, it may indicate a fear of the harsh legal consequences of sex with minors. The age preferences shown by these men clearly counteract Anita Bryant-style myths about homosexuals "recruiting" the youth. Although a small minority of men prefer sex with boys in their teens and, more rarely, even younger, most men avoid sex even with boys in their late teens. Here are a few comments on age differences:

⚨"I am friends with people of all ages, but I find I'm prejudiced sexually in favor of the youth and younger persons—say 15 to 35 years of age."

⚨"I can find older men attractive, and they are usually good company too; I tend to be put off by younger men, especially when their youth is apparent in their behavior—I find I have little in common with them, little to share that they can understand."

⚨"I am sure it is true that older, experienced men have a strong attraction for younger men. But two young men of the same age can have quite a ball."

Sex Between Men and Boys

Sex between men and boys, whether adolescent boys or prepubescent children, is one of the most sensitive topics that the gay male community has had to deal with. In part, the subject involves the whole question of childhood sexuality, which is covered in Chapter 4. But there are also legal and psychological factors. Can a child give consent, and if so how and at what age? Does a sexual relationship between a child and an adult harm the child? Is such sex 'good' or 'bad,' or does it depend on the circumstances and the ages or age difference? Do the men who engage in sex with children deserve the harsh punishment and general opprobrium they now experience in this society? These are not questions that can be answered satisfactorily in this book. However, it seems clear from the information gathered here that the myth that the homosexual is a "child molester," destined to snare innocent babes in order to recruit them into the sinister gay fraternity, has no basis in fact. What is a fact, however, is that some men love boys, and some boys love men, and sex between men and boys does occur. In Chapter 4, while describing childhood sexuality, some of the men recall incidents from their own childhood. Here, however, are some descriptions by men of sexual relationships that they have had, as adults, with adolescent boys and prepubescent boys:

⚨"My preference has always been for younger men, and I cannot recall ever having a 'crush' on anybody older than myself. As far as juvenile sexuality is concerned, and the thought of sex between young teenagers and adults, until recently I was very much against it, believing that a boy ought to be given plenty of time to 'find' himself before starting to have sex with men out of his own age bracket. However, my ideas underwent a drastic change as a result of the discovery that the 13-year-old living next door is definitely gay, and has been having sex since he was 8 (at which age he was the passive partner in anal intercourse—which is now his favorite form of sex). I allowed myself to talk to him about gay matters, trying to alert him to some of the dangers (e.g., VD, falling into the hands of a sadist, etc.), but had no intention whatever of engaging in sex with him. However, he took matters into his own hands by going into the bathroom and emerging stark naked, with a very appealing hard-on! Flesh being able to withstand only so much temptation, I cleared my conscience by telling myself that I

was not coercing him, and that he was, in fact, seducing me, and I proceeded to fellate him, to his obvious pleasure—an act that has been repeated several times since. My lover/roommate was similarly tempted, and fucked the boy, but then got cold feet and started saying how dangerous it all was (something I'd said from the beginning!), and has been rather cool to the boy lately, making excuses ('We're just eating'; 'I'm just watching TV') for not inviting the boy into the apartment when he rings the bell. I now feel sorry for the boy—although only 13, he has adult sexual urges in a child's body, and it is no comfort to him to be told he's too young, and that he ought to go home and jerk off. His parents are divorced, and he lives with his mother and sister, so does not have any adult male figure to relate to; I feel I can help him by listening to him, and trying to educate him about the pitfalls of gay life, but at the same time I really feel threatened—however strongly I feel about back-pedaling the sexual angle, if he feels horny and just peels off his clothes, I am lost! I positively swear that I have never once taken the initiative, or in any way urged him to have sex, yet if, say, his mother found out and chose to make trouble, in the eyes of the law all the guilt would be at my door! I don't know if he is an exception, or whether his aggressiveness is part of today's permissive society, but when I was 13, I could never have been that bold, even with somebody closer to my own age.''

⚥ ''One time I was visiting this couple of philosophical anarchists in their little cottage in the student district, so covered with ivy that nobody could see either in or out the window. They had a house guest, Paul, the 12-year-old son of a visiting folksinger. We got to rapping about poetry, all of us, even the kid. After a while the couple asked if I'd mind staying with the kid and answering the phone till they got back. I said, 'Sure, I'm not planning to go anywhere right now,' and they invited me to stay for a big spaghetti feed afterwards. When they left, the kid and I were rapping about Dylan Thomas. I showed him the 'Light breaks where no sun shines' poem and explained the sexual symbolism, which nobody had mentioned to him before, and it blew his mind. We were sitting side by side on the couch, the books on our laps. Right out of the blue, and completely casually, he said, 'You do fool around, don't you?' and gestured toward his crotch. This time it was my mind that was blown. I nodded and said, ''Sure, how'd you know?' He said, 'I just thought you might.' He started taking off his shirt and saying, 'Their bed's already messed up, they won't notice if we mess it up some more.' I followed him in, stripped, and was startled to realize that he was built more like 15 than like 12, and that what he most wanted—after we'd spent some time hugging and French kissing—was 69, though he didn't know the word for it. He never told me about his earlier sex life, but judging by how expert he was at sucking, he must have had plenty of experience and good teachers. He had long wavy brown hair which gleamed in the stray sunbeams which poked their way in among the ivy leaves; though this was years before the *Death in Venice* movie, he looked—color aside—rather like Tadziu, with the same kind of willowy dancer's grace.

Nothing effeminate, really, but gentle and without any hint of coarseness or roughness. Afterwards, when the couple came back, there we were once again, sitting side by side on the couch with books of poetry, the only difference being that my arm was around his shoulders. When the woman asked, 'You two been sittin' there the whole time?' Paul said, 'Well, not *quite*,' and we both chuckled; but not another word was said about it. Next time I got there, he had gone back with his folksinger mother to the other coast, and I never saw him again; but I've never forgotten him either. I wonder if he will read this and remember the incident.''

⚲"A 16-year-old was once staying with me because he was having a family problem—his family knew where he was and didn't care. None of them knew I was gay. The kid was with me for three weeks before sex happened—it sort of erupted spontaneously one night when he started out crying and telling me all of his trouble. Neither of us intended sex but it happened, and kept happening for about a month until I found a straight family that made a home for him to finish high school. His emotional attachment was awfully intense; it scared me. It's smoothed out since then and he's happy where he is (in New Jersey with some friends of mine who don't know I'm gay), but I think he had a lot of pain, and sex complicated the whole thing.''

⚲"I have filled out your questionnaire as honestly as I could in hopes that it will serve to inform the fearful uninformed, particularly in regards to young boys. My lover and I are into young boys 13-18 years old. I do not seek them; they come to us, and I am actively involved with many of them insofar as the social services, family courts, schools, probation departments, etc. are concerned. The boys are heavily into sex with us until about 18 or 19; then they drift away as they get heavier into girls and eventually marry. I am a godfather many times over. No boy has ever turned gay. Most if not all of the boys over the years have done nothing but benefit from their relationship with us. Many drop-outs and general fuck-ups were encouraged back to school, into good jobs, etc. These boys average about 400 a year from New York, Puerto Rico, Dominican Republic, and points in between. So by all means score me into your statistics so that we can prove Anita Bryant wrong. I have never forced or even talked a boy into sex.''

"Pedophilia" is the scientific term for this "love of children," so often called "molestation." Of course, there *is* such a thing as child molestation. In fact, in Chapter 4, where childhood sexuality is discussed, a few men recall unpleasant and even violent incidents, but on the whole such recollections from childhood are pleasant ones. Some men prefer to use the term "boy-love," or "pederasty" (after the Greek tradition), or even "intergenerational sex." While there are those who defend this kind of sexual contact, there are many who deeply and sincerely believe that it is wrong. There are also those who simply believe that considering the

widespread prejudice against homosexuals, it would be best if the topic went away, or that expedience demands that "responsible" elements in the gay community reject the "irresponsible" elements. The terms of gay slang dealing with this aspect of gay male socializing indicate some of the prevailing attitudes. "Chicken," a word for a boy or very young man, is certainly a dehumanizing term in which a youth is relegated to a piece of meat ("chicken," as compared to "beef"—slang for a masculine man). A "chicken queen"—also a negative term—is a man who likes young boys, while the term "chicken hawk" implies a predatory "chicken queen."

Here is a sampling of opinions on the topic of sex between men and boys:

☍"I do not believe that boyhood experimentation with either gender automatically pushes a boy either away from or toward the gay lifestyles. If sixteen years of social pressure hasn't made a boy straight, a few experiences with another boy or man in bed can't make him gay, any more than being pushed into bed with a woman will make a gay man straight. I believe this is something every boy has to make up his own mind about. I believe he should be free to seek experiences where he wishes to, though consent in either direction should be informed—he should know exactly what he is likely to get into. If his parents haven't honestly answered all his questions, and his schoolmates answer only with prejudice according to their religion and social class, than he will have to learn elsewhere, and where better than an older friend who can speak honestly, unprejudicedly, informedly?"

☍"I always hope that the kids I see are having as much fun as I had when I was a kid. I am attracted to teenagers but I feel strongly that adult men should stay away from them. For me they must be 18 or older—and preferably 20 and up. I don't want to exploit young teenagers and I feel that I would be if I had sex with them. I guess I feel that they are better off with their own age group. There were a couple of older men who had sex with me when I was a teenager and as I look back, I do not feel badly about it, but I do feel that I was exploited. I don't think it hurt me in any way—especially since I was already very sexually active with my peers. Had I not been, it might have been traumatic. But I wish I could in good conscience do it now. There are so many cute ones around. But for sure, I have no problem looking and not touching. Furthermore, young men from 18 to 20 can turn me on as much as teenagers and there I have no sense of exploitation."

☍"I've never understood why kids should be expected to wait for sex until they are 18, when most kids become sexually mature at 11 or 12 and even young kids can be sexual. My 3½-year-old boy is even sexual and is sometimes interested if I get a hard-on, but like all of his interests, it quickly fades when something else comes along. I am learning (somewhat easily) not to be freaked by his curiosity, to be very very open about sexuality and male/male strong affection and sex, as well as male/female affection. I am

admittedly soured when I hear of friends having sex with young men (12–16) because I fear for their own police-related safety. Americans are so freaked about their kids having sex with older faggots that fear turns to hate often.''

⚥ "Of course, violence and coercion should be punished, but many men are serving life terms for sex involving no violence and coercion.''

⚥ "I'm not very positive about sex between adults and children. I think in general that kids should be allowed to grow up free without any coercion (this includes other aspects such as forced religion, etc.) until they are old enough to sort things out for themselves. School is one of the worst offenders in molding kids' minds into ticky-tacky, and I don't approve of it one bit.''

⚥ "I agree with the ancient Greek custom of a boy's father introducing the boy to a friend of the father's that the boy may admire, for the purpose of staying with him awhile to be taught the sexual pleasures of manhood.''

⚥ "Most older gays have so many hangups and fears that they are incapable of helping youth. That may change now that the original gay liberationists from the late '60s become older. I certainly hope so. Youth really does need help saving themselves from a narrow-minded fear-laden straight community.''

⚥ "I have never met anyone under age 21 or so who was emotionally capable of handling sexual intimacy and feel very negative about seduction or involvement with them.''

⚥ "I think that sex between older men and young boys is a beautiful thing if the child wants it. Every boy at the age of 9 is aware of the joys of masturbation. At the age of 7 they reach the age of reason and therefore should decide for themselves. I feel they should not be forced.''

⚥ "I have known people living together with 40-year differences, but they love each other. I have known teens living with older men who could be their fathers or grandfathers, yet they all seem to be very happy and live together for years.''

⚥ "To most of my friends my tastes appear narrow and limited. I get put down for being a chicken queen. It's possible that I'm attracted to boys because sexually I'm still their age, having just recently come out; wanting to live the youth I missed, or something like that. I've never slept with anyone younger than 17. I am 26. I don't know if I will outgrow my taste for boys. I am often drawn to younger men of working-class or poor backgrounds, partly because they are more accessible than protected middle-class teenagers, partly because their directness complements my head-centered nature. But for a long-term relationship I imagine I would do better with someone with a professional-class background because of shared orientations.''

⚥ "How long will we boy-lovers have to wait? How long before we can walk honestly and proudly hand in hand with our young friends and not have to palm them off as our nephews or our stepsons? How long before we can free our loves from elements of furtiveness and conspiracy?''

Self-Image, Aging, Masculinity vs. Femininity

In the social life of a gay man, his own self-image is bound to be a major factor in how he functions. In the sexual marketplace, especially, physical appearance is given great importance. Self-image is a tricky matter, because it involves both objective and subjective criteria. A man may be slightly overweight, but if he is bouncy enough and projects a certain kind of personality, the extra weight may not be noticed. However, for some men a trait generally considered undesirable—such as extra weight—can result in an overall presentation of a man who is dumpy and miserable. To explore the question of self-image, the survey asked men *to tell how they feel about various aspects of their body.* This chart shows the responses:

	VERY POSITIVE	SOMEWHAT POSITIVE	NEUTRAL	SOMEWHAT NEGATIVE	VERY NEGATIVE	NOT SURE
height	47	33	12	8	0	0%
weight	27	37	9	24	3	0
build/physique	15	45	15	23	3	0
"looks" in general	23	50	17	10	1	0
how people perceive your age	31	39	19	9	1	0
facial hair, beard, mustache	31	36	22	8	0	2
eyes	40	37	19	3	0	1
nose	21	32	33	12	2	1
lips	26	36	32	5	.5	1
complexion	27	37	21	11	3	1
head hair, baldness	34	35	15	11	5	.5
body hair	27	33	27	12	1	.5
buttocks (ass)	25	35	23	13	2	.5
penis size	30	34	19	13	4	.5
circumcision	31	29	32	4	3	1

With the exception of weight and build, there are no prevalent areas in which any significant number of the men feel bad about their bodies, though of course some people have negative feelings in every area. The men were asked *to discuss in more detail their feelings about their bodies, ways in which they perceive of themselves as "attractive" or "unattractive," how others relate to their bodies or aspects of it.* More bluntly, the men were

asked, *Do you feel you are a sex object?* Many men offered specifics about the things they liked—i.e., their long, blond hair and green eyes—or the things they disliked—i.e., flabby body, receding hairline. Here are a number of statements on self-image, some rather complete, some just focusing on one or two aspects:

☺"I think I am fairly good-looking although I am not totally satisfied with my body. I love my face and hair. My body could be slightly meatier but it's okay in my own assessment. I do have a very distinctive look, strong features, longish hair, and a great smile. My clothes, or, rather, my presentation is generally West Village aesthetic—leather jacket, T-shirts, jeans or army pants, Adidas or work boots. It works well with my looks.

"I am always astounded by the extent to which others find me attractive. I am consistently told I am 'extraordinarily good-looking,' 'gorgeous,' etc. and although I think I am good-looking I am unable to see the 'extraordinary' beauty others see in me. I love hearing it, but I still don't see it, partly because I am simply not really my own type. Yes, I am a sex object. I am a Tadzioesque personage; I look young, and I am very aware of my sexuality and comfortable enough in my body to use it in the way I love, walk, dance. I have been called very 'seductive' in the way I walk, sit, etc. I love being a sex object in contexts where that is the sole measure of value—bars, streets, etc. I know that I am more than that in nonsexual contexts. People tell me that they are intimidated by my looks."

☺"I do not consider myself attractive, although I do not consider myself ugly either. I'm 22 years old and not fat or gross-looking. I guess I'm just average. People say I have nice eyes, but they usually say your eyes are beautiful if they can't find any other good-looking traits about you. I'm not popular and feel if I were an 'Adonis' I'd be more popular. I think gay men are very much into 'lookism'—evaluating the entire person by merit of their attractiveness. If you're not attractive, you're a loser."

☺"I consider myself attractive because I'm broad-shouldered, tall (6'), clear-skinned, big-chested, and have a masculine, well-formed face as well as a thick, curly-wavy head of dirty-blond hair. (I feel like a damn fool saying these things.) Presently I am in good shape but for a year I was overweight (212 pounds). Now I am 195. When I was overweight nobody would have anything to do with me. I felt like I was a piece of shit. I was so lonely. That made me realize how much of a commodity a queer is in a very crass and particular marketplace. It made me sick. I tend to take any praise or notice of whatever looks I now possess with a bitter grain of salt. It seems apparent to me that everybody in the gay world is a sex object more or less. Personalities count for very little. It is a dead end trip set up only for attractive commodities between the ages of 19 and 40. It is based wholly on physicalities."

☺ "I wear hairpieces and feel like I look awful without it on. I won't even answer my door without it being on, which is insane. Admittedly, I look quite older without the hairpiece (I am 27) yet certainly human. I am afraid

once people see me without the hairpiece they will dislike me or at least forget about getting any relationship going. I am also afraid the person will discover the hairpiece.''

♉"I've been bald since I was 21, but wore a hairpiece for the last seventeen years. Got tired of it and took it off one year ago. I do see that I am not as able to make pick-ups as easily, but I still get a lot of attention. Perhaps my shiny head makes me look 'virile.' ''

♉"I'm aggravated that I cannot grow facial hair. I love dark beards and mustaches. I shave what little beard and mustache I have. I've been told that my mustache makes me look like a used-car salesman.''

♉"I look at myself in the mirror and say, 'Christ, I wouldn't go to bed with *that,*' but I am constantly amazed at how well I make out at the baths, and the number of younger, very attractive guys that I have rather steady sex with.''

♉"I have recently lost a lot of weight. I was overweight all my life, and that fact has affected me greatly. I am recently developing some self-confidence, as I have lost all of the excess weight. For the first time in my life, I feel that I can be sexually attractive. The old habits are hard to give up though, and I am not yet able to look at myself as handsome.''

♉"I'm 6′4″ and love being tall. I hated it in grade school since I was always the tallest and had to sit in the back row.''

♉"I have had some problems in the past with people wanting me only because I am good-looking, and then not really caring after they've gotten what they wanted, and have at times deliberately dragged someone on conversationally because I knew what was going to happen, just to shoot them down when the question was thrown out. I've also hurt some nice people because I read their intentions wrong.''

♉"I don't think the boys who make it with me do it because they think I am good-looking. It's more often something like hero worship. I have been something of a celebrity in the circles where I find them, and they can find things to admire in me that don't relate to looks or athletics.''

♉"I have had and, I'm afraid, continue to have a low self-regard, concerning my appearance. Being called 'sissy' in school because I was not the least bit athletic didn't help. Not dating tended to ostracize me from social groups in the small high school. Today I look in a mirror or at a photograph and I don't see a face *I* would judge attractive. (Photographs are uniformly unflattering. I do sometimes catch an angle in the mirror that I like.) Even so, I am becoming aware—intellectually—that I am somewhat attractive. I can look back and see the signs, even see cases where I was actively pursued! Yet, emotionally, I don't believe. It still comes as a surprise when a guy I find attractive finds me attractive.''

♉"Sometimes, during masturbation, I see myself as though I were someone else. For just a few moments, the rush of the popper overpowers the logical power of my mind and I just see this form of a man standing opposite me: after a few moments, I realize that it is simply my own reflection, and I am overwhelmed by my admiration for the image—what a

handsome, attractive, and powerful figure it is I'm seeing. I realize then—without caring, finally—why many men are attracted to me. It is wonderful for me because I generally am a very very critical observer of myself, overanxious about the gaining of a pound, depressed if I cannot fulfill with vigor my exercise routine, impatient for better physical development, depressed—not much with the process of aging—with the 'flaws' of my physical structure. In moments of masturbation, I lose all those judgments and see myself as a stranger, just as a physical image, as a physique, as a face, as a stereotype, and I find myself very very compelling.''

⚣ ''When I was real young I had some tattoos put on. I hate these. I try to keep myself in body as feminine as I can, and I'd give anything to have a pussy rather than a cock.''

⚣ ''I have definitely felt myself to be a sex object. I used to have *bunches* of anger about it. Now I am clear on who made me a sex object, who keeps me a sex object: *me*. And that state comes with two effects: shit and glory. And the consequences, both the shit and the glory, are my own. I have long been aware of how other men's fantasies get laid over me like a cellophane costume through which I do appear, but not without alteration. When I used to hitchhike a lot, I could often see myself cast in the image of American Wonder Boy. Among other faggots, I often get cast as Strong Together Guy. When I get that hint real strongly that I am being cast as Something, my resistance goes up and I do whatever is necessary to break the set. Not always, but usually. When I get cast as Butch in someone's eyes or among a group of men, I will do outrageously effeminate stuff. When I get cast as Nice Gay Man, I will become my most perverse.''

⚣ ''I have never had a very positive image of myself. Like many people, I always wanted to be what I was not—better looking, curlier hair, whiter teeth, bigger cock. My teeth are a bit crooked (orthodontists were an unknown breed in England when I was growing up) and I've always been self-conscious of them, deliberately cultivating a closed-mouth smile and a rather mumbly kind of vocal delivery, to avoid too much display of teeth. I had a lot of trouble with acne and blackheads as a young man, and was self-conscious of that too and attempted to avoid close contact with people in strong light. I had a mild case of tuberculosis when I was 17, and had to rest for a year or so, and thereafter was forbidden strenuous exercise, so while most of my friends were developing nice chests through swimming or tennis, I was very aware of my own lack of muscle and 'build'—so after all those hangups it came as quite a surprise the first time I was told I was good-looking (perhaps that's not quite right; I think the word was 'distinguished,' which to an Englishman is almost preferable to mere good looks!). But in general, I have never felt I had much to offer in the purely physical sense, and that probably accounts for my hesitation in approaching people, for fear of rejection. By way of compensation for my perceived physical shortcomings, I have always tried to cultivate other qualities that I think are important: sincerity, honesty, considerateness, compassion or

sympathy, being a good listener, and generally minimizing the other person's faults in the way that I would hope mine were being excused. No, I don't feel I'm a sex object, but I do feel good when my lover (16 years younger) says I fuck better than anybody he's ever known!—and tells people that my cock gets harder than any others he's handled.''

⚥"I think I'm very good-looking and have no doubts about it; after all, I've been in two porno movies and look many years younger than I am. To me, such beauty is an aristocratic privilege and carries with it a sense of *noblesse oblige* (or what a girl friend calls the 'mercy fuck'), though this should not get out of hand. Beauty is one of the last natural aristocracies in America, where birth rather than skills or IQ reigns. I feel I am a sex object and think it's delightful. I have no regrets.''

⚥"I'm one of the people you take home from a bar as a last stab!!''

⚥"Three hundred and twenty pounds of love ain't many gays' idea of 'their ideal.' I have a pretty high self-image or self-esteem which I hold up to the public. I am a very sarcastic person. My size may cause this, or it may just be my personality regardless of size. My face is attractive. I think it is one of my strong points. I have a small cock, which embarrasses me. My large breasts have always made me feel strange. People can be cruel—'You need a bra,' etc. Maybe my cynicism is my defense mechanism to shelter my inner feelings. I feel happy and well adjusted.''

⚥"I have rather large nipples which some people don't like.''

⚥"Don't know what you mean about 'sex object'—such horseshit! Does a guy in his right mind want to be a non-sex object? If somebody digs me sexually, I consider it a groovy thing. Since the rest of me is also pretty much likable, I know I'm being appreciated in other areas as well. Sure, I've had an occasional guy 'use' me to get his rocks off, *but* I was 'using' *him,* too. And we both enjoyed ourselves/each other a whole lot!''

⚥"I do not consider myself attractive in the sex-symbol sense of the word, but I am also not a monster. I am overweight and tend to dress conservative. But I have a good personality and that helps. I feel when I do go into a gay bar that I am being rejected by all the rest, just by their eyes. I feel they are not interested in me because of my face etc. But with a straight trick, all he wants is a blow job, so I don't have to worry about that aspect.''

⚥"I think people like my ass—it gets grabbed quite frequently, even sometimes by people I don't know, which is embarrassing, but nevertheless good for ego-building.''

⚥"Probably the biggest thing going for me is my body, it's always in demand. But I have always felt that people use me or abuse me and I get little in return. I have a fantastic education and am very creative, but at a bar, who cares???''

⚥"Right now, I have the gay world by the balls, and I am pulling. I am 22; I look like I am 18. I am not gorgeous, but I think I am a little cuter than average. I can attract, basically the kind of man that I want to be attracted to me (that being an intelligent, older man).''

♂"My self-image began to deteriorate when I had to start wearing glasses. Later, after college, my hair began to thin rapidly and my self-image deteriorated further to the point where I felt I look unattractive. Kids are unmerciful when they have found a weakness and I lived with the appellation 'Four Eyes' for years. Many people seem to find baldness funny, and have mentioned bowling balls to me."

♂"I hated like hell being a sex object. The best way there was to guarantee that a man would never get next to me was to tell me what a 'pretty boy' I was or 'pretty chicken.' I'm a person, not a vessel to shoot semen into."

♂"My hands have long tapered fingers and are soft and well manicured. My family was once of consequence in Boston and certain ideas remain in the attitudes handed down to me, such as the way a gentleman takes care of his hands."

♂"I have great buns and do exercises to keep them tight."

♂"A lot of exploitation goes on at all levels. Lechery tends to make people crass and indifferent underneath whatever jovial, arid, bored, cynical exterior they show to the world. We are all trying to find permanence in impermanence (beauty, casual sex, fun). We want love but we want no rules or self-discipline or morals or commitment. We want the perfect trick and the perfect lover. Yet we don't come near the outrageously high standards we set for others either physically or psychologically. We are a spoiled narcissistic generation of mama's boys who suffer from the delusion that we are the heroes of novels we're writing. We're not ready for growing old. It scares us and we hide from it. We dehumanize each other with our lechery. We don't realize that if we are to be taken seriously as a minority we have to behave responsibly to ourselves first and then to others. Maybe God destroyed Sodom not for its sex but for its crassness."

This last writer somewhat angrily offers us a brief diatribe directed against gay men's insistence on youth and beauty and the "lechery" that dominates the social lives of many gay men. Central to this argument is a truism about aging—youth is not eternal—a theme explored perfectly by one of the world's most famous gay writers, Oscar Wilde, in his novel *The Picture of Dorian Gray*. The image of the "aging faggot," the stereotype of the "old auntie," straight people's questions about what gays are going to do in old age (conveniently ignoring the plight of the aged generally in this society)—these are actually weapons used to intimidate gay men. And yet aging is a reality to be confronted. The men were asked *How do you feel about aging?* The responses were:

very positive	12%
somewhat positive	28
neutral	23
somewhat negative	29

| very negative | 8 |
| not sure | 1 |

Given the specter of old age, and the premium on youth in the gay world, it is perhaps surprising that the responses aren't *more* negative.

Those who indicated positive or neutral attitudes—a substantial majority—accept aging as a fact of life, and perhaps this self-acceptance is closely related to the basic self-acceptance that is necessary for a gay lifestyle in the first place. Being gay is a bit scary, somewhat of an adventure, and for most people at the beginning it involves a sense of stepping out into the unknown. Much the same can be said about aging. Here are a selection of comments about aging, from gay men of all ages:

⚥"Aging? Who can avoid it? Why not make it a good, maybe even a happy process? Why not call it maturing, and forget the derogatory connotation? I am 69 and am busier than I ever was when employed, and (I hope) my life is perhaps even slightly more meaningful because I can do my own thing, not just someone else's."

⚥"I abhor getting middle-aged. I can't blame young men for usually shunning me. Aging is bad for anyone at all, but especially awful for gays."

⚥"Aging—hate it, but there it is, something I must face, accept, and learn to live with."

⚥"I prefer not to think about it; trying to fight it."

⚥"I feel hurt that my aging is so apparent that someone can reject me because I look my age. For several years I dyed my hair, even chest and pubic, to keep my white from showing, but for over a year now, I have let it be snow-white, or white and auburn. I still am very conscious of my age, and that is one of the things that make me so retiring when I cruise, or meet others."

⚥"I certainly used to be considered damned good-looking—as a youth I was quite accustomed to the deference given beauty (a Tyrone Power lookalike). Now, at 56, the hairline is receding, I'm very gray, and the eternally slim body has to be watched continuously or it turns very easily to flab. Getting old is a pain in the ass, but I guess the alternative is worse, so I live with what I've got. But I must admit to resentment of the lessening muscle tone, the thickening waist, and the other traits of advancing years. And in this youth-oriented gay society, I am made to feel my age. And I guess I am guilty too—I certainly would prefer to bed someone younger than I am."

⚥"I am quite conscious of the aging process and what it does to make me less attractive to others, men and women. I have considered cosmetic surgery (face lift) to improve my image, but I am afraid it would make me look freaky—that it would make it obvious to others that I am vain. I keep my body in relatively good shape—at least slender and in reasonably good muscle tone—and people still comment on my boyish appearance. But I am 42, and 42 is not 24 or even 35. I hate the psychological damage that this sort of upset does to me, but I can't seem to adjust. Like everybody else in

America, I want to be young; youth is where the thrills are. Or at least I would like to have the youth that remains with me more effectually recognized. A stereotype reaction, I fear, but one that I share with others my age and older. I derive some kind of comfort from knowing that I'm not alone in my responses or solutions.''

♀"I hope to age gracefully. It can be a beautiful process, experience.''

♀"Some of the best gay sex I've experienced has been with older men, 55–60, who were vigorous, passionate, in shape, and used a thinking technique—that is a varied, imaginative, lusty approach to sex, with no holds barred.''

♀"I dread getting older than 30. I dislike old grouchy men and I hope I never have to pay for sex when I'm old and ugly. I'd rather be celibate.''

♀"I inherited something from my mother—the ability to age well. At 50 I am tall, still don't have a great body, but there is no excess fat. I'm a long way from being gorgeous but I am considered an attractive mature man. I'm rather proud of being 50. A lot of my contemporaries—the good-looking guys I knew years ago—are frankly middle-aged and paunchy. They had it in their youth; now it's my turn.

"I feel very uncomfortable around elderly people and am ashamed of these feelings—trapped by the media blitz on youth.''

♀"I don't dread getting older. I'm looking forward to maturing more. I've studied gerontology quite a bit and have overcome a lot of the hangups that most go through later in life. As an openly *young* gay, I have forced myself to be self-actualized at an early age. As an old gay, I'll have plenty of good experience in handling loneliness and discrimination. Our society looks down upon homosexuality much more than on old age or old people. As a young gay who has a good track record in handling my gayness, I don't think I'll have any problem in handling a 'simple' thing like old age.''

♀"Gays should not be so hung up on youth. One thing about us leather people—we seem to respect older guys a helluva lot more than the rest of the gay population does, and rightly so. I have several good gay friends 50 and older.''

♀"I like the older gay men I meet; I like the care they take with their bodies and appearance, the warmth they develop in maintaining rapport with younger gay men; I see them as far more viable role models than older straight men taken as a group. I do not fear aging, and look forward to a long life. Turning 30 was like finally shucking off the last residues of adolescence. I feel totally in control of my life, and like it that way.''

♀"I feel that as age advances one should readjust one's lifestyle and expectations. Older gays sometimes make fools of themselves (sorry to be harsh) in young milieux. Perhaps the older gay could be more useful in a counseling, mentor role. I suspect young people like me find 50+ gays sexually upsetting (fear of unwanted advances makes me uneasy). This queasiness makes otherwise friendly relations difficult.''

♀"It seems that elderly gays are the most disliked or hated group. How often we hear, 'Oh, he is too old,' 'Who wants an old man?' etc. We are

slaves to a youth cult and we need not to be if we hope to have human rights for all.''

⚢'I'm not lonely now but I'm afraid I might become too old to attract a sex partner. I'm not so worried about having friends or companions—I worry about not having sex. It's a good thing I've learned to enjoy sucking cock because that's a sex activity you're never too old for.''

⚢"I try to keep learning new things, trying new activities, stay active and alive. Had my 48th birthday a few days ago, a big party, which was fun, with all kinds of people both straight and gay. We consumed a case of wine. I told people that I decided to celebrate my 26th this year—so what difference does aging make? Actually, I have noticed a little slowing down during the past few years. Now I only ejaculate once a day while when I was 20 I did it twice or more, in quick succession. Otherwise I feel very little different than when I was 26, even have some clothes from that time which still fit.''

⚢"I am hardly a youth 'faddist' and I generally deplore our society's obsession with youth. I have no illusions about getting old. However, this is a subject of much discomfort with me and I find myself sometimes avoiding it altogether. I am still young, active, and in perfect health. I guess I fear aging the most because I feel that I will be that much closer to the time when I have to look back and confront the meaninglessness of it all. I fear a breakdown in health. I can't imagine life with pain or affliction. I fear death more than any aspect of living consciousness. Death is the final and complete end to existence; I wish I could believe otherwise. I have predicted (playfully, sort of) my own death in some instant of total irony. (Hit by a train?) Subconsciously, I hope to defer the horror the subject brings to me. I view life accordingly. I live with guarded enthusiasm.''

⚢"The 'wisdom' we are supposed to get when we grow older sure doesn't compensate for lost youth. May I paraphrase Sophie Tucker, 'I've been young and I've been old. Young is better!' ''

⚢"Aging strikes fear in my heart. I worry about what I'll look like in a few years. And I hope that I have a lasting relationship with someone that will not be reliant upon looks, or age. I fear being old and alone.''

⚢"I feel uncomfortable when gays ignore older gay men in bars, etc. At times I make a point of talking to some of these 'older' gays as they are very interesting people, and gay life for them can be a cold lonely place, as they need friends as well as anyone else.''

⚢"When I'm dressed I see myself as a nice-looking man in his middle 50s. I feel quite confident that I have a pleasant and somewhat attractive personality and that this too gets communicated along with my being a nice-looking man. However, I know that most of the men I'm attracted to will not be attracted to me because they are either straight or I am too old. (I felt the same way about older men when I was younger, so I do understand.) It's a *great joy* when once in a while a younger man really finds me attractive. And it does happen often enough to keep my trying! Nude, I'm not very

great. I've never been athletic, therefore my body is soft and in no way muscular. On the other hand I'm blessed with a basically healthy and nicely formed body. I've tried hard to keep my weight down and am not over-weight. I've had some surgery (fifteen years ago) that left me with an in-cisional hernia, definite abdominal bulge, and badly spotted legs from varicose veins. So, nude I'm not much to behold. My legs are a bit tooth-picky. But to my amazement, I still find men who apparently find me at-tractive in dim lighting or broad daylight and appear to be turned on, touching, and affectionate. I am rarely a sex object, but when I am the pleasure and flattery of it will last me for days!''

♂"For fifty years (approximately), I led a fairly average life, 'un-dercover' as an active homosexual. I was promiscuous, using most of the usual haunts for acquiring partners. Most of them were 'temporary' or 'one-night stands,' a small number became good friends, visiting me frequently over a period of years (I lived in Boston for about twenty-five years). After I moved here to New London, I acquired a new group of acquaintances, but my 'cruising' has dropped to zero, and since I moved into this elderly housing project only a couple of my old 'steadies' visit me with any degree of regularity. Today, though I am interested in sex, I can do without 'partners,' though I wouldn't turn down a chance if it came along. I do masturbate to climax several times a week, believe it or not. I'm still 'in the closet,' but applaud those who have the courage to 'come out.' The necessity of leading a double life is humiliating and frustrating.''

Masculinity and Femininity as Aspects of Self-Image

Throughout this book, references have been made to the sex-role system based on heterosexual norms of masculinity and femininity. The question of sex roles—specific forms of behavior in sexual and social relations, based on traits considered masculine/feminine, butch/femme—is discussed at length in Chapter 9. But these roles, or to be more precise, the identities that go with them, are a vital part of self-image. It has been an assumption of the straight world that gay people see themselves in terms of these roles. When speaking in public before straight audiences, gay men sometimes sense that people are examining them carefully for certain traits that they can identify as "faggoty" or "effeminate," as if there is some visible clue to gay sexuality that can be discerned by a keen eye. This preoccupation with the outward signs of masculine/feminine behavior is not appreciated by the overwhelming majority of gay people, who would like to behave in whatever way is natural to them, without concern for the criteria of the sex-role system and such labels as "butch" and "femme." The men were asked, *In general, how do you feel about the use of the categories or labels masculine/feminine, butch/femme?*

These were the responses:

very positive	3%
somewhat positive	9
neutral	24
somewhat negative	33
very negative	28
not sure	2

The men were also asked *whether or not they apply these labels to themselves, on what basis, and to express their feelings and experiences with the entire butch/femme syndrome in terms of self-identity.* The short-answer part of the questionnaire did not provide space for this kind of characterization, but judging from the essay responses, a majority of the men describe themselves as having a mixture of masculine and feminine characteristics. Of the remaining men, a majority described themselves as "masculine," but in so doing many of the men specifically said that when they say "masculine," they include certain positive characteristics usually thought of as feminine. A few seemed adamant in their affirmation of "manliness." In any case, the semantic problems with this seem nearly insurmountable. Here are a few comments from men who accept the word masculine for themselves:

⚦"I consider myself masculine, but not 'butch.' Being 'butch' is a role you play where you hide your emotions, display no tenderness or affection, are always dominant, and go around dressed by a certain code whether leather drag, cowboy drag, marine drag, etc. I'm masculine in the sense that I'm a confident, aggressive person, I come across in a direct, honest manner. My gestures aren't 'extravagant,' but I don't force them to be contained. I can express tenderness and affection, but I do so actively, not passively. I try not to hide my feelings, but I also try not to let my feelings control me. That is basically how I define being masculine.

"Being feminine, as I see how society defines it, is being passive, gentle, emotional vs. intellectual, stressing relationships and the person rather than the physical attributes of that person, and having a desire to please the other person rather than demanding to be pleased yourself. Some of these traits I think are very attractive, and I try to incorporate them into my own personality. I don't like the way society has divided up these characteristics and given half to the men and half to the women. In my efforts to be masculine, I think I've over-intellectualized myself, can never allow myself the luxury of occasionally being passive, and find it difficult to establish a strong, ongoing relationship, which allegedly is a woman's forte."

⚦"I am very masculine, and that seems to be at a premium at the bars. I worked long and hard to avoid effeminacy in my younger years, to the extent that I have no real tendencies in that direction. My closeted state, therefore, seemed to cause my masculinity. I guess my extreme fear of discovery caused me to overdo it, as many formerly closeted males are

effeminate. Perhaps my long battle internally causes me not to like the external effeminacy I see.''

⚥ "My outward appearance is probably considered definitely masculine. I have been mistaken for straight many times. Although I do not actively cultivate a masculine persona, I am most aware of the special rewards one receives in this society for being masculine (and straight, and white and rich . . .). I have encountered standoffishness from more effeminate faggots. One recently suggested that I dress in drag (which I have never done) just to feel the feeling. I felt a bit threatened at first, but resolutely declined, adding that I prefer these dirty old sneakers to a pair of 4-inch heels. I recognize the oppression that stems from this society's strict guidelines for 'acceptable' masculine and feminine behavior. I want to see these standards smashed. I deplore these restrictive and dehumanizing 'categories,' but I also want to continue to be the person I feel is really 'me,' if indeed such a thing exists, and to continue to dress in the same old clothes, and to reject or ignore all notions to 'peg' me or penalize me at a quick glance.''

⚥ "If I had to choose between butch and femme I would pick butch every time, both for myself and my partner. After all, I am gay because I am male and like males. I am decidedly not female and I am not attracted in the slightest by males pretending (however slightly) to be female. Do not, however, think that this means I do not appreciate gentleness and sensitivity; I regard these as quite masculine characteristics—the opposite of the 'bitchiness' one finds in femme guys.''

⚥ "I am butch; others have told me I am. It is important to me to continue to be aggressive and to keep corporate executive mannerisms.''

⚥ "I am only 5′7″ so I cannot be the super big butch stud; so I guess I am a little butch stud. I think that most of my activities are masculine, both physically and characteristics. I dig sports, motorcycles, guns, fishing—things that femmes don't usually do (but some do, I hear). Most people would identify me as masculine, and that is important to me as a man.''

⚥ "I consider myself masculine but not butch. Being butch would be male impersonation. I hate, loath, detest, and despise butch guys whether gay or straight. I cannot conceive butch behavior as being natural, whereas effeminate behavior I can accept as natural. Butch behavior is willful troglodytism, willful stupidity, planned inhumanness, the ugliest manifestation of animate reality. Hitler was butch. Stalin was butch. McCarthy was butch. Nixon is butch. Reagan is butch. Murder is butch. Torture is butch. The CIA is butch. Have I made myself clear? Femme behavior can be vicious and destructive, demeaning to women and gay men. But I have found that many people gay and straight can be both femme and warm, loving, vivid, and lively human beings. I don't feel at all natural attempting femme behavior. I don't even dare parodying it for fear I might offend someone who is genuinely femme.''

⚥ "I consider myself masculine, though I think others identify me as feminine. I think I act feminine in the way that I would rather do stuff like

women do (cook, take care of flowers, wash clothes, etc.). I feel embarrassed to talk to other people when I feel they think I act feminine.''

♂''I am masculine! All ways—acting, appearing, etc. It is very important to me to be masculine, and I try to act like any macho straight does, not because I want to be straight but because the macho straight is the kind of guy I would enjoy having sex with.''

♂''I consider myself butch. Being 6′3″ and 240 pounds, I don't look like the average chick. Most people label me as masculine.''

♂''I do consider myself masculine. As an iron and steel worker I swing sledge hammers a lot and lift heavy products, which very few women would be able to do for eight hours per day.''

♂''I consider myself masculine and have a deep resonant voice. I walk tall and am not the body builder type but am manly in every way, I think. I look super best in a tux and am really a clothes horse. Blue and white compliment me and I wear a lot of that combination. Straight men sometimes stop me on the street to compliment me on my suit or how I am dressed. I go to the barber three times a week and seldom go anywhere without someone saying how beautiful my hair is. It is now gray and I tint it each time at the barber to keep it that way. I always loved gray hair and it does something for me, for sure. I would not want to be feminine—I want to be a man, and I am a man, only I am a man who likes men.''

♂''I consider myself masculine. I was born that way. I think you should be as you are—male or female—and stay that way. Pretending to be otherwise is what gives homosexuality (in public) a black eye.''

♂''I consider myself masculine. I act like a 60-year-old man, my life is geared to the heterosexual world. If I'm effeminate it is when I can tell about a recipe I made.''

♂''The assumption that all gays are fruits is one of the biggest stumbling blocks holding back gay liberation. The general public assumes that to be gay means to be unambitious and ineffective, etc. Every time I have come out to one of my straight friends, the first reaction has been, 'Gee, you don't act like it,' or 'I never would have guessed.' ''

♂''I relate to myself as masculine and feel I can do most anything I please, with respect for the rights of others. That is to say, I consider it ridiculous of anyone to tell me it's inappropriate for me to cook, sew, be passive, put up frilly curtains, etc. (feminine-action stereotypes)—all of which I sometimes do and enjoy. First and foremost, I am a human being, and will not deny my potential (at least not on clear days). I feel masculine mostly because of my body and the sympathetic vibrations I share with men. I feel I approach the world with a certain will and strength of determination. Passivity I relate to receptiveness, and see yielding as important as dominating in relating to people and environments, giving none of these general masculine/feminine values.

''Thinking this through a little deeper, I see I am using my own language here, or at least my own meanings. Your question seems to refer to cultural definitions of butch or effeminate roles, which don't relate much to

what's going on inside of me. Without considering my gender, my self-perception of my masculinity is the same as my self-perception of my humanness—determination to actualize as much of my potential, 'doing my own thing,' responding as the situation demands, these are experiences shared by everyone, showing the relative meaninglessness of masculine-feminine categories in my mind. Apart from gender, I don't even have a concept of femininity in my life.''

♂"I feel it is a gross insult to women to confuse being 'femme' with femininity. To me someone who is 'femme' is a self-indulgent, scatterbrained, silly, selfish, pouting, sneering, artificial, giddy, spiteful, self-centered, petty, scheming, gossipy gay being whose self image has been warped and shaped by an unfortunate family situation. They may be intelligent, they may be well-meaning, but underneath it all there is something missing—lack of consistency, a poor grasp of reality, a mechanical view of people as something to be exploited and used, even liked as far as they serve the self. I believe that a lack of faith in their own abilities, except to manipulate, mark many of them. On the whole I find them very shallow. I see no virtue in defending a warped version of traditional female stereotypes, which are in themselves highly questionable. To me masculinity is the capacity to take initiative, forgive wrongs, strive for high ideals, to take over leadership especially of one's own life first, to be wise and balanced and fair, to guard and respect the dignity and worth of others (even if they themselves don't), to give credit where credit is due, to be in an attitude of wanting to learn and understand, not assume you know it all.''

As the previous quotations indicate, there are many different ways to define "masculinity," and many men feel comfortable with the label, whether it's defined in traditional terms or in terms that are very much an individual expression. Only a few of the men defined themselves as fully or predominantly feminine:

♂"Straight and gays alike would probably consider me effeminate. However, I don't feel I'm a flaming faggot. I just like to camp a little, picking up a mannerism here and there from my sister queens. Biologically maleness/femaleness are the only distinctions I can really make. Beyond this, I feel we are all human, androgynous. 'Feminine' characteristics, such as compassion and understanding, seem very desirable to me.''

♂"I consider myself androgynous but when I am by myself or with close gay friends I am quite ''nelly'' or 'queenish.' Given my personality traits, I am called 'mother' by most of my close friends because I am always looking out for their safety and well-being—a regular Jewish mother. I really don't like labels because you are judging somebody by their looks not on their self or personality.''

♂"I am femme because of my young looks. I hate it and it has a definite effect on my personality.''

♂"Don't think I am butch or fem—a mixture, more fem than butch.

Like to bake (not cook), sew, crafts requiring careful detail, macrame, rug making, etc. Typist, writer, like animals, raise tropical fish, like flowers and plants, building (craft). I think others regard me as a feminine man (at work and such).''

While masculinity is prized in the gay male sexhunt, as previously shown in this chapter, many gay men retain a self-image that is a clear mixture of masculine and feminine characteristics. For some, this mixture is simply a natural reflection of a whole personality. For a few, it is a self-conscious attempt toward a goal of androgyny. Here is a sampling:

⚨"Against a contemporary image of stockiness and muscularity, I may appear more than a trifle feminine to some. They don't realize how wiry and resilient I am—like the willow that bends to the storm. My quality of empathy and deep-rooted emotionality can also be construed as feminine. I wouldn't change it for anything. I 'see' so much more than I sense many people do via these attributes. Basically, I consider that I am rather well in touch with my masculine and feminine components, far more so than many people are. They are part of *me*, and I have lived long enough to realize that my mold is 'set' and that these attributes are always going to be a part of me. I can't please all of the people all of the time (and wouldn't desire to if I could), and some people I'll never please any of the time. That's the way the cookie crumbles, so I go on and try to make the most of what attributes I *do* have.''

⚨"Masculine and feminine are attributes assigned by society. They are arbitrary, unrelated to fact and sources of oppression. Others perceive of me as masculine: I am not an 'obvious' gay. This is because, until age 32, I compensated for my knowing I was homosexual by acting super-macho. In other words, I fooled society into thinking I was straight by reinforcing all my 'masculine' attributes. I wouldn't do it that way again. I celebrate, today, my 'feminine' and my 'masculine' attributes. I celebrate the real me and shun society's labeling.''

⚨"I'm amused that sometimes with an hour in my life I'll be running big power tools, then immediately go to doing intricate beading on a costume or whipping up a French chapeau, then help a ballerina get made up, and most everyone else is having an equally varied set of work-life experiences.''

⚨"I am mostly masculine in my body movements and speech patterns. I have no trouble at all in passing. I take 'pride' in this emotionally, although intellectually I think the categories are sexist. My personality is more of a mixed bag. I can be 'hysterical' at times in a feminine way. I am very emotional and sensitive, all qualities labeled as feminine. I myself never felt totally 'masculine.' I am not often directly aggressive (though I'm getting better), and although I am very competitive, I always felt inadequate competing. I hate all team sports and only since coming out have I taken any pride in my body and using it physically (including sexually).''

⚨"I strive for androgyny. I don't look effeminate, i.e., I don't flame.

But I am gentle. I like that I sew and do other domestic things. I also like that I am a good carpenter. I really get off on being androgynous.''

♂"I consider myself to be masculine in appearance. I love to cook and write poetry. I enjoy the ballet, opera, and the symphony. All things which a majority of 'straight' society considers to be feminine. I feel that the time has come to reeducate people to the facts, that, outside of the action of giving birth, there is no exclusively feminine or masculine activity. I strongly resent the efforts of society to pigeonhole me. I'm basically a nonconformist and iconoclast.''

♂"I consider myself to be fairly androgynous. Although my apparel changes from time to time—flaming to more sedate, colorful to tailored, etc.—I wear an earring constantly, and often swish a bit, while my apparel is pretty neutral.''

♂"I'm neither butch nor femme. I'm a man who prefers sex with men over sex with women. I have no desire to be a member of the opposite sex, nor have I a desire to act or look like a woman. I may assume some roles that have traditionally been women's, but I like being a man. I seem to have maternal instincts; I like children. I'm very gentle. I do well with homemaking, cooking, cleaning, organizing, coordinating, indoor gardening. Some people think I'm feminine because of this. Also, I like classical music, folk music, theater, films, ballet (but I can't dance), museums. But no sports—again, because of this I don't fit the traditional masculine role, so people think I'm feminine. Yet, I am a masculine male. I like the company of women, and I like to sleep with them, but I prefer men, it's more fulfilling for me. I wish others could open their eyes, ears, hearts, selves, and see—and share.''

♂"Does the fact that I am soft-spoken, or that I like to arrange flowers, or that I enjoy watching ballet or modern dance, make me feminine, therefore I must be a homosexual? Does the fact that I enjoy doing heavy construction work, that I enjoy (and am good at) repairing and refinishing furniture, that I have a deep bass singing voice, or that I was happily married for fifteen years make me masculine, therefore I must be a heterosexual? What nonsense!''

♂"I would describe myself as butch-looking in the sense that I am not 'pretty,' I am not a modish dresser, and there is a certain solidity about my body and presence—none of this by my calculation; it is simply the way I am as a physical and mental person. Although an amateur ballet dancer, I am not a willowy type, more an André Eglevsky type. I think I am a sexy man in that I am very sensual, well hung, and nicely built, but I am not a sexy man in the beautiful-person sense. I think I am masculine in that I am strong as a person, assertive in areas of importance to me, able and willing to accept responsibility, and able to care for myself and others. I am independent, and love knowing that I make my own decisions. I am feminine in that I am loving, tender, gentle, expressive, and determined. To me, every whole person is both masculine and feminine. Parodies of super masculinity or femininity are just that—parodies, exaggerated, not whole. I

like my blend of masculine-feminine, and feel that because of it I am a much better, more giving person. I certainly have known straight men who had this blend, but I think it is more common for gay men—it is one of the reasons why I am happy to be gay.''

⚥"I consider myself equally oriented in both the masculine and feminine. For many years, and actually in all my years, I knew that I was rather feminine in my nature, and many times before I came out, I was told by people that I had a strong feminine way. They always termed it as 'sissy,' 'queer,' 'little-girl,' and the like. I knew this was true, but there was really very little I could do about it, and I thought that because I was a man, I should not further acting in this way too much. I never tried to act like a bully or tough, though, just continued in my same ways. The ways I knew I was effeminate were the way I carried my voice, a bit of a limp wrist, my playing with girls, never being athletically inclined, and very pacifistic. I always played with my sisters and was unashamedly a 'woman' whenever, and wore female clothes, played with dolls, paper dolls, basically always in a female role. I remember nothing being said by either my parents or sisters.

"It is rather well-defined in society what physical characteristics, personality traits, activities, etc. are identified with the masculine and feminine natures. Up until a year or more ago, I always thought you fell into those things expected of you, though it never dawned on me that I was not following these patterns myself. I always just acted like 'me,' although being pretty self-conscious a lot.

"Of course, I think that most people very strongly identify me with heavy feminine traits, but basically see me as a man. I love it because now I can be as nellie or campy as I want to, when I want to, with no regard to anyone. I simply don't hide it any more. While I feel every bit a man and like it, I prefer not to have labels on myself or anyone else. I am *just me,* I have never been any different, therefore, I know nothing different. I feel comfortable with myself, that's what's most important.''

⚥"I've always hated the terms 'butch' and 'femme.' While I was growing up I never enjoyed doing the things that 'normal' boys did. I hated sports and would rather read or draw and most of my closest friends were female. Not excelling in sports and being less than a jock in my outward actions resulted in my being the target for many of the older and bigger guys who were trying to prove their 'maleness.' As I refused to fight, this gave these macho morons even more delight. 'Let's torment queerbait.' I was continually being called 'fairy' and by a feminized version of my name. Growing up nonassertive in small-town Maine was sheer hell. The one thing that kept me going was that I was smarter and quicker than most of these people I encountered. I could come back with quick, curdling remarks. My quick wit allowed me to save face on many occasions.

"I hold no value on masculinity or femininity. Helpless women turn me off as quickly as do jockstrap men. My view of a real man is one who follows his inner dictates and doesn't try to impress the world with his manly ways. Seeing my father cry at my grandfather's funeral made more

of an impression on me than anything he'd done before. I felt real compassion for this man who I'd come so close to hating on so many occasions.

"I have many traits that I'm sure are viewed as feminine. But I'll not hide them, they are a part of me, part of my make-up. Realizing my gayness gave me enough insight into myself to be comfortable with *me*. I'm through trying to conform to society's image of a 'real man.' I really don't give a damn how people view me. If a person is comfortable with their own identity then they'll see me for what I am, not what I should be. I suffered through years of conflict and self-doubt because I wasn't capable of playing the role correctly. I spent years wrestling with myself trying to get to where I am now. If society can't deal with me the way I am, then that's their problem. I'm through with role-playing!"

The last quotation expresses some of the rebellious pride which is increasingly common among gay men. Previously confined to silence or a dismal ghetto, gay men are breaking out of silence, improving the quality of life in the ghetto, and at times functioning socially well beyond the restrictions imposed by a hostile straight society. Self-actualization for gay men is not easy, but neither is it easy for heterosexuals with their dating games, singles bars, parental pressures, and sex-role definitions of how to behave. Learning how to socialize in the context of homosexual desires, therefore, is one of the unique aspects of life gay men experience as they grow up and come out.

8

Lesbian Relationships
and Role-Playing

What Are Lesbian Relationships Like?

One of the persistent stereotypes about lesbians is that they remain in couples forever—no matter what. Part of the underpinning of the myth is that heterosexual men often choose to see lesbians as primarily "asexual" (after all, the men say to themselves, two women can't do much together). In addition, what women are traditionally supposed to desire from a relationship—intangibles such as security, devotion, and so on—would be doubled should two women team up.

Oddly enough, while combating this stereotype originating in heterosexual mythology, the lesbian simultaneously faces some hostile dogma, from self-avowed "radical" lesbians, about her relationships. These women, who represent a tiny fraction of the lesbian movement (let alone of lesbians in general), sometimes offhandedly condemn any couple relationship as "counterrevolutionary" or "exclusionary" simply because it is modeled on what they perceive as a heterosexual norm. These lesbians are correct in pointing out that the nuclear family has indeed been an instrument of oppression for gay people because they do not conform to the institution of the family and because the purpose of gay sex is not procreation. And they are also right in perceiving that the model could use a lot of improvement! Such women propose avant-garde alternatives to the old structure, usually communally oriented, which are important to consider, and for some to strive for. But practical consideration, the real world, rather than utopia governs most women's lives. Avant-garde or visionary action and theory can be useful only if they are not shoved down people's throats.

It may not be the "couple" that is oppressive, but the way in which the "couple" is institutionalized as a norm for everybody. Those lesbians who condemn anything connected with patriarchal society may, however, be throwing out the proverbial baby with the bathwater, since they are

301

alienating themselves from the majority of lesbians who want to be or who are in couple relationships. Perhaps the instinct to "couple" is "natural" since it is found in birds, such as the lesbian seagulls. Right or wrong, most lesbians approve of "relationships," and "commitment" was a word which came up often. In fact, 80% of the subsample said that they currently have a lover.

The women were asked *what is the longest time in the past or the present that they have been with one lesbian lover.* For past relationships, the shortest time given was one month, and the longest was twenty-three years. The average (mean) time of a "longest relationship" was thirty-eight months. Of those women in current relationships, the shortest time in a relationship was again one month and the longest was again twenty-three years. However, the average length of time for a current relationship was twenty-seven months.

Relationships are hard to categorize, since almost every one is unique, although later in this chapter common issues such as fidelity, concepts of "marriage," and so forth will be discussed. But first here's a look at some past and current relationships.

♀ "I am in a relationship with a woman five years older than I am. I am 28. I knew her when I was a kid and always liked her. After my marriage and separation, we met again and became lovers. We live together and are monogamous. Although I see women to whom I feel attracted, I do not feel that a passing sexual encounter is worth risking my relationship, and we both feel this way. We do *not* role-play, and there is equal give and take in both the bedroom and in other areas of our life. The thing I 'dislike' is not having enough time to myself—more work is needed in this area for both of us. If I were single again I'd probably go dancing a great deal—one thing I miss since my lover doesn't dance. And I guess I *could* go out alone to dance, but then one runs the risk of meeting women who want to meet you for more than dancing!"

♀ "I am with the only woman I've ever known. I had just turned 32 when we met, and I was living with a man. She's been gay since she was in her early 20s. I was at the end of my hippie phase. He and I supposedly had an 'open relationship,' and he had always sort of ridiculed me for not having tried a woman, so I was looking for an experiment/adventure.

"My woman lover and I would meet in the afternoons, and she would go out or work at night, and I would go home to my man lover. (It was a gourmet's delight of sex for me for a while there.) I was very much in love with my man, but as I got to know my woman more and more, I saw my man more and more clearly, and I was less and less able to play the roles he wanted me to. He wasn't able to handle me when I became honest, and I finally quit him. I moved in with a straight woman friend—a WASP like me, with two kids. I'd spend weekends and some weeknights with my lover. We did this for 2½ years until I moved in completely about six months ago. The lady whose home I moved out of is still a very good friend. I never

expected my relationship with this woman to last very long, but it is stronger now than ever. Sometimes I get very panicky about the thought of being a lesbian, but less now than I used to. We don't have other lovers. The idea is inconceivable to both of us. She has no use for men whatsoever. She won't give them any energy at all. I like some men. I occasionally get turned on to men I encounter in my work. Mostly I just enjoy the feelings, but I wouldn't act on those feelings. I don't find myself sexually turned on to other women, although I am very attracted to other women as people.

"She's more butch, and I am more femme. We're not into roles heavily, but I usually do more of the housework and cooking, and she's apt to change the fuses and tires. Occasionally we get into roles more heavily—sexually. But we switch roles at times too, during sex, or when she's sick and feeling fragile and young."

♀ "Presently I have two very deep relationships—one with a woman neighbor who is living with her boy friend, another with a woman I came out to last year at work (a former co-worker). Both relationships have been of about one year's duration. They are both very free relationships. We are not lovers, but do hold ourselves responsible for each other's well-being, and general happiness. These two relationships are extreme opposites. One is with a very sophisticated, educated, stable, and dominant woman. The other is with what could only be called a 'street' woman, very dependent, passive, and amiable. I feel very fulfilled in that I can act out my passive and aggressive self completely."

♀ "My past relationship was very strange, in that we were both straight at the time. We planned very easily and logically at one point or other to have sex. We eventually did, and the whole situation backfired. I dropped my man within a few weeks; she did not. I fell madly and helplessly 'in love' with her. I was willing to wait to see her when and if she could see me. This was about once a month with much turbulence in between. I did not know then that she was going through a great emotional and mental trauma about myself and her sexuality. All I knew was that I hurt and ached to be with her. We were both new at having sex with another woman, but it was very intense, and we both had multiple orgasms. I was much more emotionally involved than she was. She was also very secretive and did not want me to even stay overnight at her house. She was afraid of having her business out 'on the street' as my neighbors would find out or maybe her family. I never had sex outside the relationship for over one year. I felt a bond of fidelity to her that she did not feel except for her male lover.

"It finally became too much for me, and I decided to start seeing other women. That is how I met my present lover. We started out not having sex at all at first. I would sleep over and just hold her, and she would hold me. Then we started having sex almost every night and sometimes all weekend we'd stay in bed. Now it seems we are on a quality, not quantity, basis. It's down to a few times a week, once a night, but it is very good, warm, and satisfying. Our love seems to grow each day, and I hope it keeps doing so.

We live together mainly because it is best economically. Also we need to be together as we both love to hug and hold each other and cuddle quite a bit. We always make love, but we don't always have sex.

"I have had sex a few times with my ex-lover outside of my present relationship. At first I could not understand why, and I did not like doing it (although my current lover and I have an agreement that we would be able to do so if we wanted to, as long as we came 'home' to each other and no great emotional ties were involved). I now understand that I felt she needed someone and that I could make her feel good. She is hurting and alone and although I don't love her the way I did, I still feel a love for her. She knows it and has no illusions about why I come to see her. She says she will wait and see me if I can. I have had many opportunities to see her more often, but I don't do it because I feel she should try to find someone as good for her as I found someone who is good for me.

"Outside sex makes me feel a bit guilty as I know my present lover does not indulge. She did when I was away but not in the last 1½ years. If she also indulged, I'd feel better about it, and when she does start to see other women, I will feel less guilty. I do know I feel much more loving and affectionate after seeing my ex-lover. Maybe my ex-lover makes me appreciate what I have even more as she has nothing at all.

"What I like about having a lover is that we can depend on each other for emotional strength and we can share our good times together. What I don't like is the concessions you have to make to another person's lifestyle. When you live with someone, it can't be all *your* way."

♀ "I'm now living with my eighth lover. My first lover was at age 19 in boarding school. We had little sex and felt very guilty. My second lover was from ages 20 to 21. We lived in the college dorm, had much sex and less guilt, and accepted the fact of our sexual preferences. From ages 21 to 25 I lived with a woman with three children. We had sex two to three times a week for the first two to three years, and then once or twice a month for the last few years. It was a butch/femme relationship. From ages 25 to 27, I had another butch/femme relationship and had not very satisfying sex once a week. At 27 I had a relationship for six months, and we had great sex almost every night. It was my first equal sexual experience, but she was into free love. From ages 28 to 37 I had my longest relationship. I was deeply in love, but sexual acts stopped after three years. We remained together for another seven. She had some sexual hangups. I couldn't seem to overcome them. I felt dirty, unwanted, embarrassed to make sexual overtures. There was much heartache for both of us. From ages 37 to 38 I had a relationship with great sex, but I didn't really love her. I was still spending much energy getting over my previous lover. My current lover and I have been together almost a year. I am in love again and happy. We have sex once a week, but it's not too important. We don't keep track. All my other sexual encounters have been between relationships. I've had unspoken fidelity agreements with most partners."

♀ "My lover and I make love about once a week. I really never dreamed

that sex could be so good, especially after six years with the same woman. We live together and have lived together since about four months after we met. We have had, in the past, an open relationship where we could have affairs so long as they did not interfere with our sex life with each other. For a long time, these outside encounters seemed to enrich our relationship, since we had some sex problems. All of my outside sexual encounters were emotionally uninvolved until I met a woman with whom I became emotionally involved. This almost broke up our relationship; at that time it had gone on for 4½ years. I really couldn't get turned on by my lover. So I was ready to leave her and take up with this other woman. But I chose instead to try and work out the problems with my lover. I don't think I would try an open relationship again. For one reason, I don't need to any more. Once my lover and I solved our communication problems, our sexual problems just seemed to melt away. And for another, I don't think I am capable of having sex with others without somewhere along the line getting emotionally involved. So now we have agreed to remain faithful to each other.''

♀ "My current lover is a super person. She is away in Michigan (I live in Los Angeles) attending special summer classes to add to her sports ability. We haven't lived together basically because each of us is in rotten shape financially. When we are together in the same city, I see her all the time, and we spend a lot of time in bed. We also enjoy going to movies, concerts, plays, bars, and both of us like having a lot of people around. We get bored easily and are constantly doing new things to amuse ourselves, in and out of bed. She's into sports a great deal, which I'm just getting into. I'm into the arts (art history was my degree, with a job in a leading museum—and am also into painting and photography), and now she's getting involved in my area of the arts. It's a neat relationship. We have so much to share and give and grow with. My lover parties sometimes too much for me, and could use some mellowing out, but it's coming with time. I guess right now, I am more single than steady, which I like because I have a great deal of freedom. My lover/girl friend sometimes is a touch possessive. I like to be alone a lot, to work, to get things done, to truck around on my own. We both know I'm not ready for anything serious, or a commitment. It's an understanding she's living with, and so far, things are working out very well. I miss her! We have both had sex once or twice outside of our relationship, and compared notes about the whole thing, and we were both surprised about how bored we were with someone else! My lover and I agree we do work well together in bed. Often we wish we got along so well in 'reality'!''

♀ "I presently live with my lover and two other women. Our relationship is friendly and loving, and we share many interests and a car and have been discussing doing income-sharing among ourselves and other friends. We have sex two-three times average a week. (Sometimes two weeks will pass without making love. Sometimes we'll make love several times in a day.)

"Our relationship is comfortable and companionable, and includes in it our responsibility to struggle with each other over issues important to us.

My lover is from a working-class background, and my background is middle-class. Many class-related differences come up between us. We try and talk these out in the spirit of 'protecting and educating' each other and of helping each other change and grow.

"I like living with my lover, though we both feel strongly that we want to live with other women too, because we like living communally and don't want to get insular. I have some ambivalence about being in a couple. I enjoy the security and companionship, but also wish for more time to myself."

♀"Pam and I have known each other since eighth grade and have been lovers since eleventh grade—the first love for each of us. Since then our relationship has gone through many changes. At first, it was a secret, innocent time before our parents were aware of our relationship's new developments. Then we went through a year with many parental restrictions on our time together. That was followed by four years in college 600 miles apart. We fell out of love and back in again, with a lot of growing up for each of us in between. We each discovered women's and gay communities, and then came back together and shared what we had found. Now finally, after over five years, we are living together in our own apartment, and are learning to deal with this kind of intimacy. Our years of seeing each other only on rare occasions were ample opportunity for us to strengthen the nonsexual part of our relationship, and I feel we have as a result a strong base of honesty and the ability to communicate our needs. We have decided to keep ours an 'open' relationship, with outside relationships 'allowed.' Though it will take a lot of energy to deal openly with our emotions, it will in the end be easier and healthier than trying to hide or deny feelings we may have for other people.

"Since we have lived together, I have felt that I accomplish less on my own, and I am uncomfortable with that feeling. I need more time to myself, to do more of those things I used to do when all I had was myself: poetry, letters, drawing, reading. I fear the loss of my identity. However, we are working this issue out, and I feel good about the strength in our relationship which allows these kinds of feelings and needs to be expressed and remedied."

♀"After my husband came out of the closet a few years ago, and our marriage became open (more so than anyone else's we've met—to our personal knowledge and according to most people we consort with), a young girl of 17 (I'm 41) came into my life, literally, at the theater where I was directing *The Killing of Sister George*. I had gotten the directing assignment *despite* my 'lifestyle,' as viewed by some members of the board, which they had concluded was lesbian or bi because I showed open affection for some of the younger gals—not to mention most of the men—at the theater. I found this highly amusing, for I have always been a hugger-kisser-toucher, and in college was viewed with suspicion regarding one of my roommates and because of some of the male company I kept. Actually, lesbianism is something I had never considered indulging in at all, which is

all the more reason, I suppose, that falling in love with T. was such a bombshell of delight. All I can say is that something went 'click' and we adored each other, she falling first, I think, and me tumbling in afterward, unable to resist the glow and magnetism.

"I was very careful to wait until she was 18, and also, amusingly, to make sure that both of us didn't go into our first sexual encounter as 'virgins,' so I consented to a foursome involving my husband, a male lover, and his wife as a trial run. That was so terrific, especially finding that it was great to feel orgasm through touching another woman while she was responding to a man, that I resolved to say 'the hell with it' and *have* T. as soon as possible. Both of us being romantic and theatrical, I dressed in a gossamer yellow one-shouldered gown that needed one tug on a cord to fall away from my body and softly called her into my bedroom on the evening we had agreed to 'begin.' The expression of her face and the gasp of surprise I shall never forget, nor her wide-eyed wonder when she looked up from between my legs later and said, 'I can't believe I'm here at last,' for neither could I. Ever since, I have been her 'lady,' alternating with such appropriate accolades as 'bitch.'

"Of course, the romance has stayed, no matter how each of us has tried to deny or damage or buffet our love, and we are *we.* Since I have now moved to New York and she is in Maryland, we have sex much less often, but the quality and intensity when we do are 100% marvelous. We make each other stutter, get clumsy, turn to jelly, laugh, rejoice, create, share. It's a completely unexpected bonus to have met and fallen in love another *first* time, this with a woman.

"We don't live together, but we have discussed this. I have five children at home, parents who hate gays and would never understand even our lifestyle as a couple, and she still lives at home with her parents, who would be equally difficult. We each have to be where we are, for reasons of responsibilities and activities we are bound to. Also, we are probably too much alike to occupy the same space, and neither would want to change the direction and momentum of the other's life just now. We shall see what time and circumstance bring. It brought us love, after all!

"T. accepts my relationship with my husband (and he accepts gladly my being in love with T.), with other men, and with other women, the last, as long as it's done with *affection* and not as 'a piece of female ass!' I reciprocate, but even more freely, for she has her whole life ahead of her, and I am more concerned that she be happy than attached to me. We don't have to agree about fidelity—we just grow in our love. We have always tended to widen our circle of love and draw others in rather than being concerned with exclusivity. The more you love, the truer it is, the more it bubbles over joyously and can be shared."

♀ "Presently my lover and I have been together for a month and a half. We live in different towns, an hour and a half apart, so we see each other only on weekends. I wish we could be together more, but I'm leery of uprooting myself from this town, and everyone I know is here. I think she is

also wary of living together. We've both been hurt and are rather cautious. Neither of us has brought up the topic of moving in together. We have sex on the weekends—oh, about three to five times. Once we spent almost a whole day in bed. I feel very good about our sexual relationship. We started out kind of fumbling, but now we're really getting to know each other's body. We don't have sex outside the relationship. We haven't really talked about it, but I would feel very hurt if she made love to another woman, and I believe she feels the same way. She was dating another woman when we started going out, but has stopped.

"I like having a lover because she makes me feel special. I have been very lonely in my life, convinced that no one cared about me or that no one wanted me for anything more than an 'easy lay.' She helps me feel good about myself, though in no way is just having a lover a panacea. She is the right person for me."

♀"Six years ago at the age of 24, I admitted to myself that I was a lesbian. Previous to that point I had been continuously depressed as far back as I can remember. After that point, I have not been depressed since. Shortly after that personal coming-out I acquired a lover. We moved in together and had a relationship of a sexual nature for about six months. Then she wanted to change to a platonic relationship, and I agreed (being an agreeable person). But it was a very difficult transition for me. It took about a year of suppressed resentment to adjust, but we still live together, are best friends, and now I couldn't think of her in a sexual way if I tried. We plan to spend the rest of our lives together.

"About a year ago, I acquired another lover, whom I have no intention of living with, but care about very much. We are very good together physically, and I enjoy her affection and company. I love her. Each knows about the other, and I feel I am faithful to both in their respective ways. I have no desire to form other relationships."

♀"This is about a past relationship. We were together for about three months. This was the longest steady relationship I've had with another woman. We were introduced by mutual friends (a lesbian couple). We were very strongly attracted to one another physically from the very start. We had some interests in common and grew to like one another a great deal in a fairly short time (two or three weeks). Unfortunately we couldn't agree on some crucial issues (all nonsexual) and decided it would be best to be friends only. Most of our problems had to do with my coming out. I was just beginning to come out, and she thought I wasn't coming out fast enough or far enough. The situation created a great deal of tension in our relationship, and together with some other problems, began to pull us apart. We still see one another socially and are good friends, but we never sleep together."

Frequency of Sex in Relationships

As can be seen in some, but not all, of the above relationships, sex can be the item that makes or breaks a relationship, or sex can often become the

proving ground of love, as one woman so aptly put it in Chapter 5. The lesbian respondents were asked *how often they have sex in their relationships*. Some had sex daily, while others had no sex. The average amount of sex was about 8.5 times per month—or about twice a week. The lesbians were also asked about *the quality and intensity of their sexual relationship*. Here are the responses of the approximately 1% who have sex more than once a day, and the 4% who have sex once a day.

♀ "We fuck about eight times a week—that is really just a very rough estimate. I know that the longest we have ever gone without fucking is about six days. We fuck more often on weekends, often staying in bed till late afternoon on a Saturday or Sunday. Our sexual relationship is a joy and a revelation to me. I have never had a long or very close sexual relationship with anyone before. Our relationship has opened my head and my body to many new experiences sexually. I am especially happy about our mutual willingness to learn and expand ourselves. We are very open to new things. In the beginning of our relationship I was very concerned that I seemed to be the initiator in our fucking, but she has relaxed her head and now feels comfortable with being more sexually assertive than me. The intensity of our fucking still amazes me. It is ever new and joyful. I love to feel new things, and she allows me the freedom to let my body go. I love to watch her and feel her experience new things. I can't wait to find out what it will be like to fuck with her in ten years. I know it will be a joy."

♀ "With my present lover sex is about three times a day, but now that I get up every morning early for work we missed a week. We are both college students and many nights we are just too tired. We may make up for it on some weekends. We have sex morning or night. Our sexual relationship is very good."

♀ "When we are together, we have sex at least three separate times a day or night. Both quality and intensity are fantastic."

♀ "We have sex about once a day. Our intensity is somewhat lost many times because she has to go to work and so do I so that many spontaneous acts aren't so intense and spontaneous because we have to watch the clock (*don't take that literally*). My lover has always had problems having an orgasm and I feel that although I don't usually keep orgasm as a goal, I want her to have one, so I don't feel like I'm the only one who is having one, and also I want her to experience it too!"

Much more numerous—57%—were lesbians who had sex several times a week but not as often as daily.

♀ "We usually had sex at least three or four times a week and twice on Sunday in my past relationship. Our sex life was very good. We were communicative and considerate of each other's desires and fantasies. We tried anything we could think of and were quite open about our sexual relationship."

♀ "I am involved with the first person I fell deeply in love with—

someone with whom I have a strong, sane relationship. When we first got together, we had sex all day and all night—as often as we were together. There seemed to be a constant feeling of electric attraction between us. We've been together over one year. We spend two nights together and have sex between none and two times a week. I wish it were more, but I'm not assertive or aggressive enough. I often wait for her to start to make love with me. I feel that although we don't make love as often as I'd like, we have a very intense sexual relationship. We are attuned to each other and know what we like to do and are sensitive to each other's needs and to each other's body.''

♀ "We have sex several times a week. I feel very satisfied with the quantity and quality of it and only wish we had more privacy and less interrruption from her two children—ages 3 and 7.''

♀ "My lover Mary and I were friends about two years before we became lovers six months ago. For those years I did not see her in sexual terms. I was in a monogamous, living-together relationship with another woman. This monogamous relationship was not satisfying to me, and Mary has seen that so we are trying to keep our sexual relationship open. We have sex about two or three times a week. The tone of our lovemaking is romantic and passionate. I want more passion, more abandon, but I think that will come in time.''

♀ "I've been with the same woman for six years. At first we had sex every day. Now we only have it two or three times a week. It is very fulfilling, and we both always have climaxes.''

♀ "In the relationship between me and Ruby (not her real name), our definition of 'having sex' is rather hard to pin down. Maybe twice a week she will make love to me. Often and usually because I've expressed a desire for it, but she will *not* let me do anything physical to her, saying she's too tired or doesn't feel like it. She insists she gets perfectly satisfied just in being physical towards me, and I have no reason to doubt her. Our relationship is very honest in that she will *not* fake any desire if it's not there. Perhaps twice a month or possibly three we actually make love where we are physically pleasuring each other. Invariably it's on the weekends, which I find very depressing, but the thing is that Ruby is gone weekdays from before 6:00 in the morning to after 6:00 at night to work and rides the bus over three hours a day and so she *is* very tired on weekdays. I've just had part-time jobs recently or done my art work at home. So it's easy for *me* to be all full of energy.''

♀ "Right now Martha and I have sex a couple of times a week. I'm pretty sure she'd like it to be more often. I feel it's about right, but since I think she's not satisfied, I'd like to desire to have sex more often. I think that would bring our desires more into synch, if we had sex almost daily. I am almost always satisfied sexually when we make love, and when I'm not, it isn't that big a deal to me. I don't ever recall being left particularly tense so beyond that I don't have any big hangups about having an orgasm every

time. I don't know if she feels the same way, however, so I feel bad if I'm not sure that I have satisfied her.

"Also I consider more than just lovemaking to orgasm in thinking of our sexual relationship. Cuddling, hugging, kissing are really more important to me, and I really like that aspect of our relationship. She gives me lots of attention and tender loving care. I, on the other hand, am not always as good in those areas either, and may disappoint her when I don't respond as strongly or as often as she might like. That seemed to be more true a few months ago and maybe now we've hit a fairly compatible and satisfying level."

♀ "My lover and I have sex quite regularly three to five times a week. We enjoy being close that way as well as being close emotionally. We have a very honest relationship sexually and otherwise. We constantly strive to keep the excitement in our sex life and by and large, I feel we succeed. Our sex is intense sometimes, funny sometimes, cosmic sometimes, outrageously passionate sometimes. It's a lot of things. We are still pretty spontaneous in our initiation of sex. We'll have sex against the refrigerator, in bed, on the stairs, on the floor, in the woods—you name it!"

Some women (25%) had sex once a week, and others (8%) less often but "several" times a month:

♀ "Theoretically my lover and I have sex once a week, but all too often something interferes, so it ends up being only about twice a month. I'd like to make love a lot more often than this. I'd also like to try new things to add to the excitement. Thus, we intend to add massages with oil, and I'd also like to try making love in new places in addition to our bedroom. Otherwise, I am satisfied with the quality and intensity of our relationship. Our lovemaking is usually very passionate although I occasionally have difficulty getting turned on."

♀ "I've been with the same woman (my first woman lover) for over a year. We're deeply in love. We're good friends. We care for and take care of each other. Our relationship works because we make it work. We have sex, at the moment, about once a week. Our relationship has gone through different levels of sexual expression, sometimes where we made love every day, sometimes not at all. I think our sexual life reflects our emotional lives."

♀ "We now have sex about once a week after three years together. It was more frequent in the beginning, but the quality has now improved as far as I am concerned because of my relaxation and decrease in anxieties about orgasm. In the earlier part of our relationship, it was more intense but also, for me, more anxious."

♀ "My present lover and I do not have sex more than three times a month. I wish we would have it more often as I get frustrated when she is sleeping all the time."

♀ "I had a seventeen-year relationship of which the past seven years were sexually overt. We had sex every two weeks on the weekends. In my mind I was married for those seven years."

♀ "We live apart and in separate cities and get together at least once a month and have sex at least once a day when she stays over or I stay over. We've been together a short time—a few months—so our sexual relationship is progressing along with our emotional one. Both are getting better all the time. We—at least I—haven't had sex outside the relationship, but I think she and I would agree that it would be fine if we did."

♀ "In my past relationship and my first one with a woman, we had sex several times a week for a while, several times a day at first. After that it was a steady decline, until at the end of three years, it was down to about once a month or less frequently. The quality likewise diminished, as it dwindled from a mutual exchange to her getting me off so I'd shut up about it. When it was good, it was very, very good; but when it was one-sided, it was awful."

For a few women sex was not a part of their past or current relationship. (Celibacy outside of relationships is discussed later in this chapter.)

♀ "I am presently living with an old and dear friend. She has been heterosexual, and is now celibate. I love her very much and would like a sexual relationship with her if that were something she wanted. It isn't, for now anyway, and it probably never will be. At the moment, I am living celibately too. I have some sexual opportunities available to me, but I am so involved in this relationship emotionally that I haven't really wanted to confuse the issue. There are several reasons. First, I've tried it, and while I don't mind making love to someone under these circumstances, being the recipient is unrewarding as my thoughts and emotions are elsewhere. Second, it may complicate my relationship with the person I have sex with. Third, it may be emotionally unfair to the sex partner. Fourth, weighing all the factors, it doesn't seem worth it. I had a heterosexual fantasy recently— rare for me, and it hasn't happened in years. I figured out that at this point a man might provide sexual satisfaction that did not impinge on my emotions at all."

♀ "I am in love with a nun. Our relationship is mostly nonsexual by *her* choice. She allows myself and several other women to orally manipulate her breasts, but she goes no farther with anyone. We do not live together, and she will not leave the convent (she is the president of the community). Obviously she is not faithful to me, and I am not to her either, especially since she cannot satisfy my physical needs. I love her very much, but I wish I could find someone who can have a total relationship with me."

♀ "My present mate doesn't enjoy sex. I've been turned down so often I've stopped suggesting or instigating. I've lost some of my love for her, to the extent that when she has suggested sex, I can comply, but she can no longer satisfy me."

♀"It is hard to be specific about past relationships. The frequency of sex is usually much more often during the early part of the relationship, and then seems to level off, maybe to a pattern, or dependent upon circumstances, maybe frequent for a time, then less, etc. In one situation, three of us lived together for about thirteen years. One chose not to continue having sex."

♀"Sex is probably one of the least important aspects of my life right now. I have been gay for five years now and have been with one woman during that time. Because we are breaking up, we haven't had sex for quite a while, and I don't really miss it."

Living Together and Living Alone

Another important factor in a relationship is whether or not the couple live together. Among the respondents, 55% of the women said that they live together, usually citing as the reason the fact that they love each other or want to be together, although some women mentioned economic reasons or convenience. The major reasons for not living together were that the women often lived in different cities or states where they had family, school, and/or job ties, or one of the women lived in a dormitory, or one or both of the women were married, or one or both felt that they weren't ready yet or preferred living alone.

Here are some comments specifically about the pros and cons of living with a lover, from those who do:

♀"I presently live with my lover in an apartment. We have been living together for eleven months, we were lovers for about five months before we moved in. I choose to live with this woman because I want to share with her the daily hassles and joys of my life. I enjoy our living together, and it is a constantly changing and learning experience. I have grown immeasurably from our relationship and the constant contact with her has helped me learn about and from her."

♀"The thing I dislike about living together is the misunderstandings and disagreements we have which bring out the bad side of both of us. We really hate to fight, but I guess that at times it's unavoidable. Otherwise it's good to have someone to sleep next to at night and wake up to after a bad dream to share it with."

♀"Living together eliminates the anxiety of having to go to separate houses after a date. We also enjoy intelligent conversations with each other. We feel that we are the best sexual partners for each other, and we have an open relationship where we do not stifle each other."

♀"We live together because we have tried different alternatives and found living together to be the most satisfying. For eight months I held out because I needed privacy, etc., and for five of those months I was involved with another woman. We love being with each other always and can find privacy with each other as well. It provides more time and sharing."

♀"We've lived together for over three years and have gone from abject poverty to a comfortable (if uncertain) income—that is, 'security' in this

society. Actually, income-wise, I'm still impoverished so there is an element of economic necessity in our relationship. It *really* is hard to know how much we should support each other. *I* still lie awake worrying about paying my half of the rent (which is only $50) and think about how I am going to get the money. I do 90% of the cleaning and cooking since I'm home more of the time, and we both sort of agree I should get some of my way paid for, though it's hard to decide how to go about one's life when there are no role models. I *also* want to add that we *also* live together because we like to. It's very fine to be able to spend so much time and share so many experiences with someone you honestly love."

♀ "We live together because we both enjoy the companionship and sharing and because commuting romance and sex was tiring since we lived 50 miles apart."

♀ "We live together because we are both very busy women and if we had separate homes, we'd never see each other."

♀ "We do live together at present, but it is only because of financial reasons. We can't afford to each support a place of our own."

♀ "We have been living together for several months. I hadn't lived with anyone for about seven years (since college), so the idea appealed to me a lot more than I think it did to her. She resisted the idea when it was first mentioned because she had deliberately chosen to live by herself last year (for the first time ever, I think). However, since she was spending every night with me anyhow, it began to seem a little ridiculous to spend the time, energy, and money needed to live separately.

"Now when I'm not working and am home during the day, I have a lot more time and space to myself than she does. Perhaps when I begin working again, I will miss the privacy of living alone. However, I really enjoy living with someone and having the companionship and love that I had missed for so many years, so I think it's worth any loss of privacy. And I think we can each maintain enough separate activities to keep from feeling too much loss of individuality."

♀ "We live together because we want to share all aspects of our lives, including daily life. We are also considering ourselves to be a 'femile' (defined as two or more women who live in the same dwelling), and we live *very collectively*—we have a strong commitment to staying together as long as we can work out any problems that we may have."

Here are the comments of the large minority of lesbians in couples who didn't live with their lovers.

♀ "No, we don't live together. The important things in her life are in the city. I have lived in the suburbs for ten years and have two kids and I'm not ready to move. My kids would kill her off eventually, so it is in the best interests of our relationship not to live together."

♀ "I love having my own space right now. I've grown a lot by living alone. These circumstances will not remain static, however, since we en-

vision living closer and sharing more time together. It is comforting to have such a special lover, one who cares so deeply for me, one who is my best friend.''

♀"We don't live together because she left a three-year monogamous relationship after becoming involved with me, and isn't ready to 'settle down' again. We see each other about four times a week but only spend weekend nights together. That's because she doesn't want to feel homeless—like she's living in two places with her clothes scattered around both. Although I respect her feelings, I wish we spent more nights together. I like sleeping with her next to me, our bodies entwined. Although I wish we lived together, we have different needs for where to live. I want the city, and she wants the country. I also know that the way we work out space and time will be difficult if we live together since we relate very differently to them.''

♀"My lover needs a roommate, but my parents aren't ready for me to come out yet.''

♀"We did not live together because she was married and respectability to her was being a suburban housewife. I also had a female child to take care of who was my grandchild.''

♀"I don't live with either of my lovers because my previous experiences with living with lovers were extremely negative. When I had a lover for five years, we broke up drastically after living together for six months.''

♀"We do not live together currently but are talking about the possibility of doing so in the future. One of the things that concerns us about living together is that I have two cats whom I adore and whom she abhors. Second, we have different values about cleanliness that would cause us some conflict if we lived together. A third factor is that she has never lived alone, and we both feel it would be a maturing and strengthening experience for her to do so. Fourth, we disagree about *where* we should live. I would like to remain in my current home, which I love and have only recently moved into, and she feels (and from the point of view of *her* needs, I agree) it would be better for us to find a new place altogether that we can move into together and feel belongs to us both equally. Fifth, I have an intense need to be able to spend some time (if only one evening a week) completely alone—that is, without the company of a lover whose needs I must take into account. I have lived alone for over a year now and have during that year gotten in touch with this need. I know I can get irritable and irascible if not given the opportunity for periodic aloneness. Therefore, although we spend six nights out of seven together, we are continuing to live in separate houses and will do so until these issues are resolved.''

♀"We are not yet living together, but are looking for a house. I have not lived with anyone for fifteen years, so this was a major decision and is a comment on the depth of my commitment. Our relationship is only six months old. I wanted to make sure it was a positive, growing relationship, constructive for both of us, and that it was deep. I also wanted to be sure our basic values were close enough to prevent conflict in a living situation.''

Lesbian "Marriage"

Whether or not lesbians live together, society considers all lesbians (unless wed to men) "single" in the legal sense since lesbian couples do not have the right to file joint income tax returns, obtain insurance reductions on two cars, and so on. In some states lesbians as well as gay men have tried to challenge the laws which allow for marriage only between two members of opposite sexes. Others have tried to circumvent laws in states which have loopholes—for example, in Colorado the law did not clearly state that a marriage could only be between a man and a woman, and a number of lesbians and gay male couples were married because of a technical oversight.

Lesbians who want to get married wish to do so for a number of reasons. Some want the legal protection granted to heterosexual couples— joint income tax, protection against wills being contested, cheaper insurance. Others are primarily interested in the emotional benefits of a marriage. They believe that a marriage ceremony adds a feeling of more commitment to the relationship, that it shows family and friends the seriousness of that commitment, that it involves them in a tradition they admire but are excluded from.

Of the lesbian respondents, 40% consider or have considered themselves "married" to another woman. The majority, however, 51%, did not consider themselves ever "married," and another 10% were not sure. Only 6% of lesbians have ever had marriage ceremonies. These ceremonies are usually called "unions" and are performed primarily by gay churches, although there are some heterosexual churches which will perform same-sex ceremonies. Also, a few women stated that they had performed a ceremony themselves.

The respondents were asked, *Whether or not you are in or have been in a lesbian marriage, what is your attitude toward it?*

strongly favor	24%
somewhat favor	21
neutral	23
somewhat oppose	14
strongly oppose	14
not sure	5

It is obvious that while more people favor marriage than oppose it, the question is a semantic one as well as a political one, since so few lesbians had actually had a marriage ceremony. The small number of lesbians who have married one another is a bit surprising, considering that society has traditionally pressured women more than men to get married. In fact, the

words for a single woman, such as "spinster" or "old maid," all have negative connotations, while "bachelor," the word for a single man, is positive. Thus despite the fact that heterosexual and homosexual marriages are worlds apart legally, one might think that more lesbians might want to consider themselves married, if only for psychological satisfaction.

♀ "We haven't had a public marriage ceremony (and I'm not sure I want to), but we do plan to live together indefinitely. I somewhat favor it as long as there is no butch/femme role-playing. That defeats the idea of *women* in love with *women*."

♀ "We were married in December."

♀ "I'm not sure. I believe strongly in commitment, however that is expressed."

♀ "I've been married. It was done just between the two of us."

♀ "I'm neutral but feel we need to define new ideas for relationships, avoiding the usual roles, anchors, and claims."

♀ "I haven't had a lesbian marriage ceremony but would like to."

♀ "I consider myself married and that it is a lifelong commitment."

♀ "I want to be married. It infuriates me that the government has the right to say who a person can love. It's none of their business, and besides, who can it hurt? There are three reasons we would like to be married. First, to further express our commitment to each other. Second, for legal and financial reasons. Third, it's a violation of our basic human rights to be denied marriage. We could be married in the Metropolitan Community Church (a gay church), but being an atheist, that's not important to me. One thing that straight people are always holding against gays is their 'promiscuity.' And yet they won't let us get married. So what do they expect?"

♀ "Marriage is a great idea. I am totally for marriage. That's my scene. The ideal situation for me would be to live with a woman for a year or so, and if all is well, join our lives by marriage. If I felt I deeply loved someone and she felt the same way toward me, then marriage is absolutely in order."

♀ "Marriage is a funny word. I realized I had been married after I broke up with a lover of nine years. I think homosexual marriages should be made possible. Either that or only allow those heterosexuals who have children on the way to marry."

♀ "I'm for it! I was for it in the early '60s! But polygamous gay marriage is not practical and doesn't work well. Monogamy works best."

♀ "Gay marriage is fine for some people, terrible for others. I do feel it's the ace-in-the-hole that heterosexuality has over homosexuality. As a marriage counselor, I know that many marrieds would rather work on their marital problems than split, many times just due to legal hassles. With lesbians, getting out of a relationship is much easier, generally no kids to hassle with custody, and both parties are usually self-supporting."

♀ "I think it's okay for those who want it. Personally, I do not feel the need to go through any marriage ceremony because I think that for me to

subscribe to it is to go along with and sanction the Judeo-Christian system that has only served to perpetuate the very hatred and persecution and oppression that gays are trying to fight against.''

♀ "To me marriage implies at least some role-playing, no matter how the partners try to avoid that, and that's not for me personally.''

♀ "Marriage used to be my number-one goal, but I have now rejected the concept as well as that of monogamy.''

♀ "I personally think it's ridiculous to bind two people together if there's anything more than desire to be together keeping them together. It feels to me like just another one of the patriarchy's property-rights games. I know there are women in the Metropolitan Community Church who feel it's better to live together with a church ceremony, but the only women I know who had an MCC ceremony broke up shortly thereafter. I feel it would strain our relationship if for any reason we had it done, but we both do not believe in it.''

♀ "I once attended a wedding between two women at MCC where one was dressed in a bride's gown and the other woman wore a tuxedo and tails. Good old Troy Perry read the traditional ceremony but changed the gender of appropriate words. Afterwards, there was a reception in the basement of the church. There was a cake with a bride and groom on top, napkins with the names of the bride and 'groom,' and so on. Although I liked the two women involved in the ceremony, I felt shocked by their participation and belief in such a role-oriented system. I was humiliated to be present and to witness lesbians imitating some of the worst heterosexual role-playing, and I wished Rev. Perry had had the consciousness to talk those women out of it instead of marrying them and taking their money. I was totally torn between supporting the two women as individuals and wanting to tell the church where to get off.''

♀ "Marriage is a societal institution whose function is the preservation of property rights through the maintenance of clear patriarchal lineage. Both its nature and its function are oppressive to women. I no longer will attend, endorse, encourage, or support marriages.''

Role-Playing

Another question which often concerns couples—or any pair of women—is role-playing. One of the original goals of the gay liberation movement was to eradicate sex roles which were perceived by the gay liberationists as the basis for gay oppression. For example, many lesbians are perceived as such or persecuted because they do not conform to the standard models of "feminine" behavior. Similarly, many gay men have been persecuted because they are not macho enough.

In recent years, some heterosexuals, influenced by the women's liberation movement, which had attacked roles assigned to women before gay liberation even started, have also seen the ways in which the roles all people have been brought up in are demeaning and limiting. Although there

has been a breakdown of stereotypes and people are now more aware of women engaging in sports and men knitting, for example, progress has been slow and small. Many jobs, such as secretaries and construction workers, are still largely sex-defined, as are many other areas of life.

On a sexual level, role-playing means that the man is always the "aggressor," while the woman is "passive." The man is "on top" literally as well as figuratively. In lesbianism, this would mean that the "butch" takes on the man's role while the "femme" takes on the role of the woman.

Unlike the man, however, whose primary interest in sex is to please himself, the butch's primary preoccupation is to please the femme. Sometimes the butch will not even let the femme make love to her in return, for by doing so, the femme would affirm the womanhood the butch is trying so desperately to deny. While it is clear that the majority of lesbians do not role-play currently, there is no way to determine how many did so in the past. An extensive analysis of role-playing in lesbian culture and socializing can be found in Chapter 6.

When two people of the same gender choose to live together, they have several options. Either they can try to eliminate role-playing or they can live with one woman or man taking on the roles usually assigned to a member of the opposite sex. Some couples try to find some middle ground—that is, they role-play only in certain areas of their life.

The participants were asked, *How often do you "role-play" (butch/femme, masculine/feminine, husband/wife, dominant/submissive) in your relationship?*

	ALWAYS	VERY FREQUENTLY	SOMEWHAT FREQUENTLY	SOMEWHAT INFREQUENTLY	VERY INFREQUENTLY	ONCE	NEVER
sexually	1	7	9	7	15	2	59%
other than sexually	.5	1	8	10	23	.5	56

The women were also asked *whether they feel they are more physically active during sex than their partners.*

much more active	11%
a little more active	23
the same	47
a little less active	17
much less active	2

It is clear from these statistics that the majority of the lesbians did not role-play either sexually or other than sexually. Only about 17% played sexual roles with any frequency, and only a little over 9% played nonsexual roles. These statistics are interesting, since heterosexuals have often perceived lesbians as being committed to butch/femme (man/woman) roles and often wonder how lesbians have survived without them.

In the essay section of the questionnaire, the participants were asked *about role-playing, both sexual and nonsexual.* They were also asked *to tell who does what (if they are into roles) and to tell how they feel about it.* The respondents were also asked *what they like or dislike about role-playing in their relationships or in relationships they observe.* First, the majority, who did not assume roles, speak out.

♀"I have intensely negative feelings about role-playing among women. I see it as an imitation of heterosexist society. Traditionally gay couples have been tolerated if they fit the accepted pattern of a 'man/butch' and 'woman/femme.' It is the only framework in which straight society seems to be able to understand us, and this stereotype has been perpetuated. Actually I see very little obvious role-playing except among older, more traditional women. I think the women's movement has done a lot to help us see through role-playing in all aspects of our lives and in all segments of society."

♀"Subordinate/dominant relationships seem to me to be the root of tyranny in general."

♀"I don't like role-playing because it copies the traditional male/female relationship. I'm proud I'm a woman. And I love women, not pseudo-men."

♀"I don't feel there is any role-playing in any aspect of our relationship. We tease each other about it, but it isn't there in actuality. I revolt against the idea and do not feel that I would be at all comfortable in a relationship where it existed. I rebel against feeling dominated and am also too reticent in many areas to feel obliged to always take an aggressive role. I feel most comfortable when I can do whichever I feel like at the time and count on the other person to do the same (and I'm not just talking about sexually).

"It bothers me to see role-playing in others also. I feel these people are just falling into the roles society expects them to play and are reinforcing all the worst stereotypes. Lesbian relationships should allow all women to grow to their fullest potentials and allow all women to get out of their traditionally subordinate places."

♀"I strive to eliminate all vestiges of role-playing in my relationship with women, as the opportunity to do so is one of the major reasons I am a lesbian. My lover and I have constantly shifting roles that we fill in our relationship—we may each play the role of friend, confidante, sister, lover, mother, daughter, partner, nursemaid to the other depending on the needs of the moment. If ever I felt we were getting locked into any roles, especially

those of butch/femme, I would run screaming to the wilderness to escape from this relationship.''

♀ "Role-playing is an interesting subject. There are a lot of different views about it. I have done some role-playing in the past, both sexually and otherwise. But in the past year or so, my feelings have changed. I've equaled out quite a bit. I used to think certain types of actions would attract a lover, but I've found out differently now. My first relationship rather demanded that I drive the car, decide what to do, and pay for entertainment. I had to be strong and loving all the time. I never had time to break down or even be alone. That was okay at first, but it got to be a real drag after a while. Now I believe that role-playing, if any, should be left to the discretion of each relationship. I don't think any person should be too overbearing unless that's what the people involved choose for themselves.''

♀ "I dislike roles and role-playing. I myself enjoy being a woman. I like wearing dresses, make-up, and getting dressed up. I am not attracted to 'butch' types who try and look like men. If I wanted a man, I wouldn't be a lesbian. The girl I'm living with is the same way. I perhaps have a few more 'masculine' traits personality-wise. I am aggressive and more outspoken. Some lesbian friends consider this 'butch,' I suppose. I do not. I see it as a result of the way I was brought up and my relationships with my family. My lover considers herself 'butch,' but as far as I'm concerned she is very 'femme.' She tries to act butch but she is very quiet, gentle, and kind. She is very attractive and couldn't look butch no matter what she wore.''

♀ "I really don't know anyone who role-plays, thanks probably to feminism, except for two women in the gay documentary the people I work for are making, but they don't realize they're role-playing. 'I used to look just like a man,' says one woman who everybody thought, until then, was a man. It makes me nervous. Why duplicate a patriarchy?''

♀ "I have been a *feminist* since 1968. I'm dead set against role-playing for myself and others. Since I am older (in my 50s), I was 'butch' in experience prior to 1960, but *never* heavy butch. Just a wee bit more the aggressor, paying the way of my partner, for example. From 1960-64, there was more equality; actually I was a bit more femme with a partner who was more butch. Since 1964, I haven't engaged in role-playing. We are equal women together. I will not get involved with women who are into role-playing.''

♀ "I hate games! I hate role-playing! It's so ludicrous that certain lesbians, who despise men, become the exact replicas of them!''

♀ "I wouldn't say I role-play overtly, but who knows what one does subconsciously? I'm basically an aggressive/maternal woman; I tend to help or nurture in all my relationships. I can also be vulnerable and am, more so to my lover than to anyone. She's also aggressive/maternal, so the combination does not lend itself to role-playing between us. With us, as with many people we know, there's more of an interchange based on need

or situation. Nothing is predefined in our relationship. Basically I think roles are bullshit and stereotypical, freezing people into images they can't escape. No one is any *one* thing, man or woman. The greatest result of this so-called sexual revolution will be to disprove the heretofore divine sex right predetermination of role, in our society and in our world.''

The following are some stories from women who consciously role-played part of the time or all the time.

♀ "When our relationship was new, we really role-played. But somewhere along the line, I got my consciousness raised, and realized that I was embodying all the negative masculine traits and was a worse male chauvinist pig than the men I constantly railed about. So I got some books, started working on it, and have myself better under control now. We rarely play roles now, unless we are out in the bars here in Fort Worth, where most of the women role-play. I am a minister, and I feel that in order to relate to some of the 'superbutch' women, I have to play the butch role. My lover agrees, but we both know it's a game. Sexually, however, my 'type' is very feminine, and her type is very masculine. So sometimes we get into this in the bedroom—not often, however.''

♀ "Well, *I* don't feel like anything of the sort is going on, but my lover is very edgy about the concept. She works full-time and gets good pay (that is, for what we're used to!). I spend most of my time at home working on my art, so I do almost all the cooking and housework. I don't have a steady income, and she has sometimes had to pay my rent. But I don't feel like there's any of that 'butch-femme' business going on. It's a matter of logic. She has a degree and a good career job. All the jobs I've gotten were minimum-wage, waste-of-time jobs, and my art work is not too profitable, but I *do* want to spend some time at it and take some art classes for a degree next year. I'm perfectly happy doing the cooking and cleaning if it means I can be home with my art rather than drudging in a factory or serving up mashed potatoes or the other ways I've had to prostitute myself for money. But Ruby often says, 'It looks like we're getting into roles and it bothers me.' But I feel like *I* should be the one who would feel oppressed, like a 'housewife,' and I feel nothing of the sort. I even point out to her that technically, *I* am the butch since I have my hair short and wear men's clothes and big boots and am very 'openly' lesbian. (I was like this even *before* I became a 'housedyke.') I am technically a 'butch,' but I think very 'feminine' made-up women are absolutely repulsive and I sure don't feel any attraction for them. I like nice, dykey, strong women like myself.''

♀ "With one friend, I enjoyed play-acting—not so much sexual roles, but mainly acting out scenes from movies, or spouting sexual clichés for laughs. When I am with a younger girl, I like to act 'male'—that is, protect her, and I like it very much if she lets me buy drinks, etc. Once I was with a girl, and one of our mutual acquaintances (male) called her a 'slut.' I forget exactly why, but I sprang to her defense and threatened to beat him up (he out-

weighed me by 70 pounds), and forced him to apologize. I enjoyed this very much. What I like best about the 'male' or 'butch' role is the protective angle, even though I realize intellectually that this is a lot of sexist shit. I like role-playing in general when both sides know it is just a game, a parody of heterosexual relationships, not something to get trapped in. I hate anything that is done obsessively.''

♀ "This is a tough question for me because I've been so conflicted about it for so long. I'm a radical lesbian/feminist activist, and I'm very into sexual role-playing. It turns me on more than anything else sexually. My lover and I do switch back and forth most of the time, but no matter who's being made love to it's always in a very obviously role-playing way. Someone is a very controlling butch, the other of us various types of femme (seductive, aloof, slutty, sweet and innocent, etc.). When we do S&M, it's even more extreme role-playing. The way we do that is with one of us in an S-butch role, and one an M-femme. As I said, we take turns with the roles, but almost never have roleless sex. The reason this bothers me is I can't seem to make it synch with my politics. In fact, I'm aware of the general negative feeling in our community towards role-playing and most of us are too intimidated to be openly honest with each other about role-playing. This makes me feel like a part of me is always lying. My image and the reality of my sexuality don't match. My lover and I aren't into roles much outside of sex, except one playing area. Sometimes we pretend we're a het middle-American couple (who'd vote Republican), and call each other Charley and Lucille. There's no issue of power or control going on here, so I'm not sure I'd call it role-playing. This is a way we tease one another. For example, if we're in a department store and see a pink shower curtain with swans all over it, my lover would say, 'Hey, you'd like that, Lucille.' We also switch off who's Charley and who's Lucille.

"One thing that bothers me a lot is how much trashing there is in our community of 'Old Gay' lifestyles, when so many of us are doing the same things, and simply being secretive about them. I have myself trashed women who are still 'Old Gay,' and am aware it's a way of credentializing myself in the eyes of other feminists.''

Fidelity: Monogamy vs. Nonmonogamy

In addition to the question of role-playing, the issue of fidelity can be a tough one for many lesbians to handle. Lesbian relationships do span the entire spectrum on the fidelity issue, and many couples are completely monogamous while others are nonmonogamous only under certain conditions (for example, when one lover is out of town or only when the other relationship has no emotional ties), while still others are completely free about having lovers outside of the couple relationship. The number of those lesbians in the survey who were monogamous was probably about the same as the number of those who did not practice monogamy or who were against

it in principle. Some couples also changed from monogamy to non-monogamy and vice versa.

The following are charts of *the number of sex partners the lesbians had in the past week, the past month, the past year and in their lifetimes.*

Number of sex partners	last week	last month	last year
0	28%	18%	4%
1	68	64	34
2	3	12	24
3	1	2	11
4	1	2	10
5	0	.5	3
6	0	.5	4
7	0	0	3
8	0	0	2
9	0	0	2
10	0	.5	3
11-13	0	0	1

Number of sex partners	lifetime
0	.5%
1-10	62
11-25	24
26-50	11
50-300	1
Indefinite answer ("hundreds")	2

Here are some of the comments of women about monogamy and fidelity agreements.

♀ "I live with my lover now. We absolutely practice monogamy. It would kill us for the other to have other lovers. We are both jealous. We are currently seeing a lesbian therapist as a couple and individually to help with jealous feelings, especially over past lovers. My lover is very jealous over the fact that my past relationships were with men."

♀ "We do have a contract of fidelity, which I broke once, and it almost broke us up. I was unhappy about having this kind of commitment, of being tied down and boxed in. Now I can understand when other people feel this way. But, thanks to the 'other woman,' I've realized just what I've got. And as long as I'm with my lovely lady—you can tie me up, box me in, commit me to the hilt. She's what makes it worthwhile. She's the reason I love to come home. She's the reason I smile at work. And she makes me feel so good about myself. So now when I hear about serial monogamy, polygamy, group sex, being single, I smile and say, 'If you dig it, do it.' But really what I'm smiling about is that I'm sure about where I'm at and damned happy to be there."

♀ "We are not nonmonogamous any more, nor do we want any part of it. The other relationship almost destroyed us, and it was the existence of another love, not necessarily the sex. I'm not sure what agreement we would have had if five or six months of our relationship hadn't been uncomfortably nonmonogamous. I started being with this other woman when I was only one month into my present relationship, and it greatly affected how we related after that. We hadn't agreed to be nonmonogamous. Politically we felt we couldn't, and historically with other lovers it hadn't been a problem. We've since agreed to be monogamous because it works out better for our happiness and growth and allows a lot of freedom of sharing. We also are quite aware that these promises become outdated when and if one of us falls in love with someone. It won't matter that we 'promised' once, because falling in love isn't predictable. However, we have avoided a lot of potential conflicts by knowing that we've agreed completely to the idea of monogamy. It means we can be freer with our friends because they know it, too, and there aren't sexual tensions when we go to parties and such. We are open to one-night stands, sort of to fulfill fantasies and perhaps to boost the ego, but we haven't exercised this 'clause' yet. We've laughed about it having to be really worth it to miss one night of sleeping together."

♀ "We have each had sex with other people on special occasions. However, we try not to and generally have no desire to. We have an agreement of fidelity, which I think I imposed because I am afraid I might lose her."

♀ "We do not have sex outside our relationship. I don't think we exactly have an 'agreement' about that, but we each know that the other would be very hurt, and that it would destroy our relationship if one of us got *emotionally* involved with someone else. As far as I know, my lover has not had any outside sexual relationships since we started living together. I suppose I could accept a *casual* infidelity on her part, but since we both need lasting relationships, this is not likely to happen."

♀ "It is very hard for me to explore this because I have such mixed emotions. On the one hand, I can be very rational and 'mature' and say that as long as the two partners feel secure in that relationship as the primary one for each, it shouldn't matter if either or both have outside lovers. On the other hand, however, it's hard for me to imagine such a situation where one or the other isn't going to feel hurt, neglected, betrayed, etc. I think I basically feel that monogamy is the best and easiest type of approach. And it also seems to me that it takes a good deal of energy to maintain one relationship, so I doubt if I could maintain more than that and have quality in any of them."

♀ "I do not have sex outside of our relationship. Fidelity—actually I prefer the term 'monogamy'—is a learned behavior and both of us are struggling to understand our jealousy. Abstractly I can allow that her fucking with someone else is not a reflection on her loving me. It does not mean that she loves me less. I believe in freedom above all else and respect

her rights to her own body and behavior. *Nonetheless,* I would become sick with jealousy if I learned she was fucking outside our relationship. This is a hard thing for my head. I don't like it and am trying to overcome it.''

♀''I would like to have sex outside the relationship, but my lover cannot tolerate my doing so. I've had three outside flings which she has difficulty forgetting about. She's extremely jealous and insecure (especially since she is my first woman lover). We have an unspoken 'fidelity' agreement because she wants it that way. I think if she were strong enough to share, that freedom alone would give me the space to decide, and I would probably decide not to hurt her by going outside the relationship for sex. It's purely an adventurous experience for me anyway.''

♀''We do not have any agreements about fidelity, but it *feels* to me as if there are no restrictions. The reality is that at the moment it is monogamous, but a week from now it may not be. The feeling that our relationship is open seems to be more important than actually acting on it right now. I don't know how long this 'undefinition' can continue, but we are both aware of postponing facing it as long as possible.''

♀''We had an agreement about fidelity that I was not happy with. Basically, the situation was that if I wanted her, I had to be monogamous. It was a trade-off that seemed fair for a long time.''

In some relationships, one lover had sex outside the relationship, but the other lover did not.

♀''I do not have sex outside this relationship, but she is still distantly involved with another woman. We have not discussed sexual monogamy and do not have an agreement about it. This is partially because of her involvement with this woman, who lives in the West. I do not plan to become involved with another woman while I am involved with my present lover, but I also realize she cannot make that commitment to me right now.''

♀''I have sex outside the relationship, and we talk about it openly. So far it has had a positive effect. We both agree to be nonmonogamous and may or may not share our other sexual experiences. Mary has not had sex outside of our relationship but is considering it.''

♀''We are generally monogamous, but she is much more so than me. This is a toughie because in a sense we maintain a double standard because of the different places we are coming from in the relationship. She is ten years older than me, and would be satisfied with a monogamous relationship and has no desire to 'sleep around.' She was married and has a son, and came out about two years before I did, during which time she slept with several women, as well as had a very intense first lesbian relationship. So two things—her age, combined with the fact that she's had enough experience (in her view)—lead her to want a very monogamous lifestyle. I, on the other hand, am younger, more outgoing, less experienced with lesbian sexuality, and haven't had other relationships that were intense, so I

have a natural inclination to want to play around, although I should say that I don't want to leave her by any means. So after some struggling about this, we have worked it out that I can sleep with other women, if it's not in the same city (I travel for my job a lot). I did have one affair that lasted for three months in Chicago, but it made my lover too jealous and took up too much time worrying about and fighting about to really make it worth it (although it was magnificent, sexually). In the long run, I guess I just don't think that sex is as important as other things one can do with one's time, like work at learning new things, or whatever. But I do find I have a natural inclination to express my sexuality with others through dancing and talking.

"I would say that as long as I have my chance to explore these desires to sleep with other women and flirt at bars and whatever, that our relationship will last, as far as that big question goes. She respects my needs in those areas, and I understand where she's coming from. Although the double standard we live by is something some of our friends don't understand, it works for us."

♀ "I have had other sexual relationships outside of ours; my lover has not. We both claim to be nonmonogamous. She states she is not interested in having another sexual relationship, and if she wanted any more sexual activity, she would rather it be with me. I have sexual attractions for a few close friends, but knowing them and their circumstances, I have had no desire to be further involved with them. I told my lover the specifics about the one outside sexual relationship I did have, and this sharing helped our relationship more than anything else did. Once my lover knew where I was at in relation to her, she felt okay about these relationships. We both are ambivalent about all this, and I know no sure-fire answer (monogamy vs. nonmonogamy)."

In other couples, both parties were not monogamous.

♀ "I have sex with the woman I live with and with my other lover. Sex outside my relationship has been traumatic, but after one year of monogamy, I feel we have worked it out, and my partner and I have a solid, trusting relationship: We have been living together for thirteen years now. We are all friends. My lover lives with her partner and all of us are aware of the sexual relationships. My lover and I enjoy sex and unfortunately lack space and privacy a lot. Our relationship started with more emphasis on sex, but during the years it has developed into an intimate friendship including sex."

♀ "One-nighters are okay for each of us if nothing better comes along."

♀ "We both have sex outside of our relationship. We both feel it enriches our sex together and our own sexuality. I enjoy having my lover assert her sexual independence. I want her to always feel that she is with me because she wants to be, not because she is tied to me by demands—sexual or otherwise. I have never wanted to be sexually faithful to anyone. I hate people who make demands of sexual or emotional fidelity on me. No one

owns my body, and I don't own anyone else's. Just because I am deeply involved with my lover does not give me the right to own her sexuality. It has taken a lot of work to overcome our jealousies, but we don't hassle each other about our other lovers. We also aren't 'discreet'. We tell each other we want to sleep with 'so and so' (unless it just happens). If I say I don't want her to, or she says she has objections, then we don't have sex with that person. Otherwise, we do. Sometimes we share a lover in a three-way or separately. Not very often, though. The only other 'rule' we have is that we shouldn't be in bed with another lover when either one of us is going to come home and find us in bed. I enjoy our freedom and honesty very much. I feel no strings binding me, and so I stay, willingly, lovingly."

♀ "Ideally I would like to live with my lover, her 7-year-old girlchild, her husband, and my male lover. We have a very loving, compatible, pansexual quartet. All of us are happily nonmonogamous. I can't easily imagine a monogamous relationship holding up for very long. Sex with other people enriches our own relationship. I feel secure in her love, knowing that she sleeps freely with who she likes means she also chooses me. I always tell a lover/friend in advance that I am nonmonogamous and pansexual. A lover does not have to be pansexual, but she must be tolerant of my preferences, as I accept hers. I don't want a monogamous lover, however, since I feel that would be an inequality in the relationship. I like having a lover or lovers for sexuality, companionship, intellectual nurturing, and emotional sustenance."

♀ "We both have sex with other people. I have sex occasionally with my husband (more out of a sense of decency than desire). She has had sex from time to time with men, but never another woman. I tend to get a little upset about sex with anyone else. She says it's *only* sex and doesn't understand why there should be a problem if there's no emotional attachment. I confess to finding that a little hard to understand and cope with, but I'm grateful she's honest about her feelings and motivations."

♀ "We practiced 'qualified monogamy.' This means that we have a great commitment to each other and do not expect to leave each other for another woman. It also means that time spent alone with another woman whom one of us is sexually involved with is scheduled ahead of time. We don't want to live together and never know when we can count on being with each other. We also believe in spending more time with each other than alone with other women. We consider ourselves to be in a *primary relationship*, and we don't believe there is *time* or *energy* for two full-time (primary) relationships. Also we are both very secure in our love for each other."

Sexual Jealousy and Lovers' Quarrels

"Jealousy" is a word which came up often in the section where the participants were asked about monogamy. Often jealousy or lack of it determined whether the relationship was monogamous or not, although

other words such as "trust" and "security" were also mentioned. Jealousy has been a big topic of conversation within the lesbian community. Part of the problem, as Karla analyzed it once in an article on "Surviving Gay Coupledom," is that in a same-sex community every person is a potential sex partner (not just 50% as in male/female relationships). This factor is often aggravated by the small size of many local communities (except in large cities such as New York or Los Angeles). Having only small numbers of women to choose from often means that a lesbian has to break up an existing couple to find herself a partner. Thus, the lack of a pool of available women may create a tense situation in some instances. The following are some comments about and experiences with jealousy.

♀"When I first moved here, I had a tight friendship and relationship with two women. In fact, we were known as a family. Sometimes, though rarely, the three of us slept together or one would sleep with the other. There wasn't any jealousy between us, but the time came when one of us went to live with a house of women, and the two others felt a lot of resentment about that. Although I am still friends with both of them, the ill feelings never got resolved between the other two. Ironically, they were the ones to teach me about being upfront with feelings and thoughts.

"In another relationship I made a conscious effort to deal with possessiveness and jealousy which worked for a long time, but there was one woman and two men who were sexual threats to me. Over time I understood the other woman, but the jealousy I felt for the men was never resolved. I certainly wasn't into having a threesome with them."

♀"I read an article which stated that sexual jealousy is of biological origin, and I agree. It is inborn in animals as a way to protect the nest, and we are animals too."

♀"Sexual jealousy is one of the most common of human emotional maladies. Like warts, you don't like having them, but you can't get rid of them and they're bound to come back. I always founded my relationships on openness and honesty, so I haven't had any problems with sexual jealousy."

♀"Sexual jealousy and monogamy are problems in my life right now. It appears I have a lot of insecurity that surfaces when lovers (men only, not women!) are sleeping with somebody else, too. Actually this only applies presently to the man I lived with until a year ago. So I guess I'm insecure about someone in whom I invest a lot of feeling. I would like to achieve a life within an extended family someday, and I feel it will simply take a lot of time, trust, and loving people who *feel* trusting and loving to *me*. For now, I'm thankful that I can be loving and trusting with women I'm close to, and I have confidence and faith that I will be able to extend these feelings as time goes on."

♀"I think jealousy is synonymous with insecurity and emotional immaturity if carried to the extreme."

♀"I'm not a jealous person, and I don't see any positive aspects to

jealousy. If I love someone, I want them to have what they need, even if it isn't me, because they won't be giving me anything positive anyway if they are feeling tied down by me."

♀ "I have figured out a way of looking at jealousy that works. I have discovered that I only feel jealous when I am dissatisfied with my own relationship with the person in question. If I concentrate on building that relationship and making it the best it can be, I can forget about whatever her relationship is with the third person."

♀ "I've never been a very jealous person. For example, I think my lover is sleeping with someone else tonight and I'm hoping she's having a good time. As long as she keeps her priorities in order and her common sense of functioning well, what she does is fine with me."

♀ "Being in a nonmonogamous relationship in which I'm also not being monogamous, I guess I still feel a lot of it, though I don't quite know how to define it. What I feel is that when she's spending the night with someone else I figure that other person must be ten times better at it than me, and when she's talking to her other lover on the phone and laughing I suddenly feel that, shit, she hardly ever laughs with me any more. I can go on forever with examples, but it's hard to define the exact feeling. Inadequacy? Fear? Uncertainty? Not being appreciated? Taken for granted? I'm a great believer in laying it all on the line and talking about it when something hurts. I feel that 'talking about it' can probably cure everything—a little emotional penicillin!"

♀ "Sexual jealousy is tremendously corrosive to any relationship. The jealous one usually ends up by creating just what she wishes to avoid. I think that jealousy usually indicates a low sense of self-worth, and anyone who is excessively jealous needs to do some work on herself. I think the homosexual community often encourages jealousy, however. There is often a lot of interaction between those who are single and those who are in couples. The idea that jealousy is a sign of real loving and caring, however, is false. Yet many people get into that trap. Most of us have some jealousy in us, and most of it comes from our own insecurity and fear of rejection. Sexuality seems to be the focus, but that's not really where the problem originates, or needs to be solved."

Even in the best of relationships, quarrels or disagreements may arise. While most of the lesbians felt that verbal quarrels are not a bad thing and generally clear the air, at the same time most were against physical violence, and it seemed to be rare in the lesbian community. With wife-beating an international plague, one can readily see why lesbians prefer gentleness in other women. In any case, the following are some experiences with and feelings about lovers' quarrels.

♀ "I am quick-tempered and it's easy to verbally challenge my woman. But we quickly see the senselessness of arguing. We settle down and talk things out quietly. I think we're able to do this because we have such respect

for each other. We hardly ever fight, since it hurts us. We are more inclined to be so open that differences never arise. I would never use violence on my friends because I never want to hurt them. Unfortunately, I often will emotionally destroy them, but I have for the most part outgrown that malicious tendency. No, I'd never hit a lover.''

♀"Everyone argues or quarrels at times. A relationship is pretty sterile and unhealthy without our resolving our differences and negotiating. Violence is simply an indication to me that someone is either unable or unwilling to work through those differences. For me, a relationship would not survive much violence.''

♀"I think it's more prevalent in straight relationships. My husband blacked my eyes on numerous occasions. I've yet to experience this in my relationships with women.''

♀"Lovers' quarrels are necessary. They should not be deliberately avoided. Violence makes me nervous, but some small amount of it may be necessary to work out certain things—I don't know. Is violence a class issue?''

♀"I avoid confrontation whenever possible, but I guess it's sometimes healthy to get things out in the open. Unfortunately, this often results in people saying things they may not really mean in the heat of an argument, and the other is hurt needlessly. There have been very few times in my life when I've felt mad enough and frustrated enough to hit someone. I think that I'd be the most surprised person involved if I ever hit anyone. Unless there were special circumstances I can't foresee, I would not stay with someone who hit me, and I would not expect anyone else to put up with me hitting them.''

♀"I hate it when we quarrel, but we do. Violence scares me. We never hit each other or break things. To me, fighting verbally is violent enough. I really take it too seriously, I guess. I don't know how to quarrel very well.''

♀"Quarrels are difficult because the underlying cause is often hidden by the anger that emerges. My lover and I argue well sometimes because we are conscious of this, and after letting our anger out, we try to figure out what is really happening. Anger is an equally valid emotion as love. I cannot pretend that I do not hate sometimes if I say I love. We are taught to hide our anger as children. If I am pissed off, I want to shout and scream and be unreasonable and unfair and get it out. This is not always easy, as my lover has great difficulty expressing anger and often just becomes silent. This is frustrating and often increases my anger.''

♀"It's part of being in love. You have to balance out the good times with the bad. Violence is okay as long as it's confined to dishes and walls. When it comes to bodies, look out. Feelings have to be expressed; however, it's not good keeping violence inside.''

♀"I don't much like quarreling and I'm opposed to violence in any and all forms, at any and all times. I'm a confirmed pacifist who reared two pacifist sons. At the same time, two people cannot get close to each other without frustrations and anger arising, and I think it's far better to air anger

the moment it is felt. Too many people, especially women, seem deathly afraid of their own angers.''

♀ ''I lived with a lover for four years. At first it was fine, but then she wanted to keep me in the house. But I didn't want to give her up. On her birthday, she wanted to take me out to dinner, but I was sick. A quarrel ensued, and I shot her. She did not press charges and came to visit me at the jail every day until I got out. When I got out finally, we didn't go back together but we are still friends.''

♀ ''I've never quarreled so much with a lover as with my current woman lover. And there has been some violence. I guess I think fighting with a lover is inevitable, but I'm a bit dismayed at my own level of violence in those fights. I don't really hurt her, but I'm tempted to, and I have punched her a bit. (I'm stronger than her, so her impulses to hurt me, which are also there, have not been as realized as my own.) It seems that there is some deep, bitter competitiveness between women (at least the ones I know, myself included) that is exacerbated by our own powerlessness. We fight with each other rather than always being able to join in fighting our real enemies. It's all too easy to fall into, especially with our own unfortunate but unavoidable internalization of the woman-hating, self-hating of the society around us. And that seeps into personal relationships.''

♀ ''My lover has set up certain standards for my behavior. When I violate them, she hurts me. When I fight back, she becomes angrier and hurts me more. I resign myself. I know I should obey her and deserve to be hurt when I don't.''

Being Single

After reading the last few experiences with violence in relationships, having no lover may seem like a good alternative! In this section, the responses of women who did not have relationships or lovers will be discussed.

It should first be pointed out, as George Whitmore did so well in an article on living alone, in *After You're Out*, that being single or living alone is not the same thing as being lonely, that people are apt to be lonely even in a crowd (as the cliché would have it), and that even people who are in relationships are sometimes alone. Therefore, living alone or being alone—without a relationship—can be a positive or a negative experience depending on how one looks at it. Most people in this country are taught to believe that people who live alone are ''strange'' in the tradition of Emily Dickinson, for example. There is also the implication that one is alone because one has been rejected or cannot find a partner. Of course, this myth is based on the falsehood that everyone is looking for another person or that somehow we are ''incomplete'' until we find the missing half which will make us whole.

For a lesbian, living alone may have a doubly negative edge, since the myth of not being able to find a partner has particularly been directed at the

lesbian. Probably everyone has heard the comment that so-and-so "is a lesbian because she can't get a man." Of course, such a statement is extremely misogynistic because it represents women as second choices. Again, it's the attitude involved, and looking at the beautiful lesbians around, one might conclude equally falsely that a straight woman is one who can't get a woman!

Only 20% of lesbians did not have lovers currently. The following are some experiences and attitudes about being single.

♀ "Being single, I sometimes miss feeling there is someone for whom I am the most important person in the world. I miss the intensity, the oneness, the growth, having someone to take care of and to have take care of me. The advantages of being single are time, space, and not having to expend the enormous amounts of energy it takes to carry on a serious relationship. Right now, single is my choice."

♀ "I'm single now for the first time since I've come out, and I have mixed feelings about it. I miss the closeness, the security of a monogamous 'permanent relationship,' if two years could have been considered 'permanent.' I'm curious about the dating scene and I've met some interesting women I would like to get to know better. I don't miss the jealousy and the occasional boredom in a long-term relationship, but it is a familiar situation to me, and I need security, both for me and my daughter. I really don't know what it's like to be single yet, as I sort of still feel like I'm part of Mary. But it's passing."

♀ "I don't want a lover. I can't stand the idea of having someone around constantly—always having to sleep in the same bed with someone (or if not, each night having to explain to her why I don't want to be with her)—no privacy. I don't miss having sex with a partner available all the time, but I do very much long for a person to 'hang out' with during those free moments away from work (that is, the work that's important to me). I feel sad that people seem to hang out primarily with their 'lovers' and not with nonsexual pals."

♀ "I currently have no lover in my life. I am lonely sometimes; perhaps 'frequently' would be a better word. I hope that shall pass. I believe it will. But in the meantime I know that I am a lesbian and I don't know what else to do with that knowledge. Isn't there somewhere for me to go, just to meet people who think the same way I do? I'm not desperate for a lover. I can live without one. It is the reinforcement of other people that I lack. I am a strong woman. I am doing my best to be an independent woman. That is all I can do for myself right now. I wish I could do more."

♀ "I've never had a lover to whom I could give enough, could love enough. I haven't got a lover at present. I still love my former lover, and still love every woman I have ever loved, anyone who has allowed me to love her, has accepted my love. It wells within me to such a force sometimes that it is incomprehensible—when I would make love to a tree if it would accept it. Strange, no, I don't mean that in any kinky way. But if I can't have the presence of the women I love, I get overwhelmed, or if I can't find someone

to love, I release it as I can, in dance, in theater, in poems, in sound, in tactile response. I want a lover very much. I want to share, to explore, to grow with someone, to expand with and through someone, to give them joy and growth, to expand my perceptions. Of course, I want a lover. I want to give—give without holding. I can give to my former lover, but only partially, for I don't wish to unbalance her new relationship as I'm fond of the woman she loves. I can give to the straight woman I've lived with and loved for three years, but must restrain myself in many, many ways. I want to give without restraint, to cause joy, to love. What else can I say?''

♀"I don't actually have a lover any more, although I'm still living with my past lover. We don't really have a relationship. I would not like to have another lover (at least, not right now) because of the other person's demands for sex and also their intrusion in my life.''

♀ "I'm really not certain whether I want a lover. Lovers take energy, and I don't know if I have enough energy.''

♀"At this time I am not involved in a sexual relationship. I would like to be in one and am always looking. Being single, in particular living alone, has its advantages: privacy, time to myself, freedom, lack of commitments and obligations, etc.; but I think I would rather be involved in a close, intimate relationship with one primary person. One fringe benefit of being part of a couple is increased social opportunities with other couples. It would seem that most of my friends come in twos and as a single person I have too often been a third or a fifth wheel.''

♀"I don't think I'd want a lover. I've become accustomed to living alone and am quite selfish and set in my ways. I'm a very free and independent spirit. I'm also very involved with my career and evening education, which would really make a commitment at this point quite unfair.''

♀"I would like to have a lover right now, but when classes start again in September, it would be an added strain because of the many hours that must be devoted to homework. I don't know if it would be worth the price. Maybe I'd like to have a lover after I graduate. You see, obviously, it's not that important to me. Being single is lonely sometimes, but having a lover inevitably means emotional commitment to her, concern and worry about her, and the self-discipline to concentrate upon my other responsibilities when I would rather be with her.''

♀"If I had a lover, I would spend less time cruising, and perhaps I could devote more time and energy to other things.''

♀ "I would feel better having a lover, and I would feel much better if we could live together. I don't like being single, although I would rather be single than have a very possessive lover. I have many friends and outside interests to support me. I believe in sexual fidelity, but not complete dependence.''

♀"In the past, what I most disliked about lovers was that having an 'affair' was very time-consuming. My schedule would get disrupted, and I couldn't do the work I had planned to do. I am compulsive about my work and follow a rigid schedule, so that was always very upsetting to me. I lack

flexibility. Even if I ever have a permanent lover, I will need an agreement where I have my own private room so I can work without disruption.

"What I most dislike about being single is when I go out to a movie, and everyone else in the theater is sitting in pairs, and I feel left out. Then I wonder if this is because heterosexual society raises us to think in terms of pairing off, or if there is some natural need for one close mate."

Celibacy

Celibacy and being single are not necessarily the same thing. In some of the relationships discussed in this chapter the women involved said that they are celibate. On the other hand, some women who are technically "single" may be having a sex life with one or more partners.

Like being single, celibacy can either be positive or negative depending on one's attitude toward it. If celibacy has been forced on a person either because she can't find a sex partner, or because her lover refuses to have sex with her, or because she finds herself in some isolated situation, then a person may consider celibacy to be a negative state of affairs (or lack of affairs). But many women choose celibacy so that they can further discover and define themselves, or to experiment with relating to the world in strictly nonsexual terms. Such an experience can be very positive. Here are some of the experiences of the lesbians who say they never have sex, and of some lesbians who had been intentionally celibate in the past.

♀"I enjoy celibacy. (I do masturbate.) I think that politically it is the only way to be. You can put almost all your energy into politics."

♀"Learning about and experiencing celibacy has shown me I am much stronger than I thought, and that it is not necessarily something that will destroy me. At times I really enjoy and feel good about it. Sometimes I even choose to continue it when an opportunity comes up for a sexual encounter with a woman. But only lately, in the past few months, have I been able to do that. I am no longer afraid of it or bitter about it."

♀"My period of celibacy was a very rewarding period of my life. I found that all the energy I was devoting to sex could be rerouted, so to speak, to finding out who I was as a person and getting rid of all the negative images of myself people had pawned off on me and which I accepted in whole or part.

"The hardest part of my celibacy was when people—both men and women—questioned why I chose to be celibate. The feelings most people expressed were that you must be a real oddball or freak, or you were frigid (men), or you couldn't 'catch' anyone. Fortunately I had some friends who supported my choice."

♀"I've spent a lot of time being celibate and I like it. I haven't made love in two or three months."

♀"Celibacy is a very important concept to me, not just people being 'celibate' while they're waiting around for another lover, but a conscious commitment to being celibate because it enhances their lives. I've been

celibate (except for four sexual encounters) for over five years after having had a very active sexual life from age 14 on. I use the term to mean abstaining from sexual—romantic relationships with others, but not abstaining from sex totally. After spending years pursuing romances and using up most of my energy in sexual relationships, being celibate has been a tremendous relief. It's freed me to concentrate on work and making friends. The value of friendship has become more to me for the first time in my life."

♀"Celibacy is a most underrated state. I was celibate for three years between being straight and gay. It was a wonderful time. As a woman growing up, I felt defined by sex. It was wonderful to think about other things, to learn, to interact with everyone without sexual undertones. I got lots of support from my friends, strangely enough. They acted as if I were being very brave. People should try celibacy. It's gotten such bad press. It can be very enjoyable, help you clear away your sexual confusions, and you can concentrate on all the things there are in the world besides sex. My favorite thing is to be in a lesbian relationship, then celibacy, finally heterosexuality."

♀"I think celibacy is useful if you choose it or accept it as a temporary thing if circumstances bring it about. It can help you sort out your feelings about sex by giving you some thinking space. To me, it felt good to say no and feel comfortable with it rather than feeling guilty about turning somebody down if I didn't feel like having sex at the time."

♀"I am celibate very frequently. The women I sleep with I like or love in one way or another, and if there isn't anyone like that near then it's better to go without—unless of course I get drunk and forget about all the romantic aspects and rid myself of the state of celibacy."

♀ "Except for a couple of years out of my life. I've been celibate. It seems to contribute toward a more creative state of mind, probably because when I'm not celibate I spend most of my time thinking about my lover. Anyway, I enjoy the state of creativity but at the expense of some intermediate bouts of loneliness."

♀"As I consider fucking with men a counterrevolutionary act and an energy drain of women, I feel celibacy is the alternative for women who cannot or will not or don't want to act out their lesbianism. Celibacy is a positive action, a way of conserving energy to end oppression."

♀"My celibacy started out unintentionally and became intentional after a couple of weeks. I have been celibate for about six weeks now. I decided to do it so I could look at people nonsexually, which is new and unusual for me. I am lonely sometimes for lack of cuddling in bed, but mostly I am digging it for the different perspective I'm gaining."

♀"I think celibacy is a valid lifestyle. I know some women who choose to be celibate (some of us are at times celibate with no say in the matter, and that's a bummer, but survivable). I know a few 'lesbians' who call themselves 'celibate' (and I'm sure they are!) because they have become Christian, and it's a sin to experience good, healthy woman-love, but you're

okay if you keep it suppressed. I think this is really gross, and it disgusts me that good, strong women would kiss ass with some 'god' that says you're okay as long as you realize you're a horrible sinner and as long as you don't do these perverted acts with other women. I think Christianity is gross.''

♀ ''Celibacy is boring, but at least I have a certain amount of self-respect. But I'm beginning to think that may be too high a price to pay when judged against the loneliness.''

♀ ''I've been doing a lot of thinking about celibacy lately. It stinks. My lover expects me to be celibate, but although I love her very much, I'm always interested in other women.''

♀ ''I feel that celibacy is a rather restricted point of view. In my opinion, people with this idea have a fear of being hurt by others, never realizing that you get what you prepare for. People get hurt because they never protect themselves from it. They let their feelings just happen without realizing the real situation. If you say, 'I never want to get married or be tied down,' you are really saying, 'I can't handle a close relationship with other people.' That type of feeling restricts a person from ever being emotionally satisfied.''

♀ ''Celibacy has been my life for the most part—I would say it's hell!''

♀ ''I was celibate for about a year after college—there I had fucked around with men and wound up feeling much abused and worthless. Celibacy can be a valuable time of thinking things over, but not for me. I felt dissatisfied, desperate, like I needed a lover to prove my worth. Now, though I dislike celibacy, I would prefer it to rushing into a relationship were my lover and I to break up.''

♀ ''I am now celibate and I do not want to be, but I am. I think I must need to be celibate at this time in my life. I feel that celibacy is not a good thing, though, and the pressure in this society is on coupling.''

♀ ''Celibacy is ridiculous. I'm not a nun!''

♀ ''It's a terrible waste.''

It is easy to see that not all the lesbians agreed on celibacy or on any other aspects of relationships. But after all, lesbians aren't a homogeneous group; although nonlesbians sometimes mistakenly perceive gay women that way, lesbians have no intention of becoming so, apparently.

9

Gay Men: Couples, Singles, and the Butch/Femme Question

Male Couples

The couple is nearly as much an institution in gay life as it is in straight life. But for gay men, the process of forming a couple and staying together is by no means the same as it is for a man and a woman, married or not. "Wife" and "husband" have certain generally agreed-upon definitions in the society, and there are certain expectations about how heterosexual spouses will relate. Major assumptions about heterosexual couples are: first, they will live together; second, they will be sexually faithful to one another; third, they will bear children. Even so, if one gets to know a lot of married couples well, one will discover a great variety of patterns and behavior, often in violation of one or more of these norms. With gay male couples, it is hard to even suggest that there are norms of behavior. In reading through the many essays on relationships, it became clear that there were many many different definitions for the term "lover." A "lover" relationship for one couple would seem patently ridiculous to another pair of lovers, and vice versa. One might expect to find a clear pattern of "categories" emerging from the answers to the questions about lovers, boy friends, and relationships. In fact, no such pattern emerged, and this first group of answers reflects the incredible variety of responses that were sent in. Later in the chapter, four aspects of male-male relationships—living arrangements, sexual fidelity and jealousy, gay marriage, and roles—are explored in more detail. There is also a section in which men who are currently "single" or "unattached" (for lack of better words) describe their situation and their attitude toward it.

Of the men who responded to the survey, 46% said that they currently have a lover or boy friend. As with all the statistics, it is difficult to know if the subsample suggests an accurate figure for the gay male population generally. Those familiar with the gay male scene would say that 46% is not too low a figure for men with lovers or boy friends. It may be higher than

339

for the general gay male population because it may be easier for someone who has a lover to sit down and spend time with a questionnaire such as this one.

The men were also asked *what was the longest amount of time they were ever in a relationship with a lover, past or present.* Similarly, they were asked *to indicate the length of their current relationship,* if any. In both cases, the average length of a relationship was about two years, and the most frequent response given was also about two years.

One failure of the questionnaire was that it did not ask directly, "Have you ever had a lover or boy friend?" Since 30% of the men did not answer the question concerning the length of time of their past or present relationship, one can presume that a good number of those men have never had a lover or boy friend. Of those who did reply, several reported relationships lasting less than a month, while the longest relationship reported was in its thirty-seventh year. The following chart indicates responses to these questions:

	LONGEST RELATIONSHIP, PAST OR PRESENT	PRESENT RELATIONSHIP
less than a month	2	2%
1–6 months	20	26
7–12 months	16	14
1+ to 2 years	17	19
2+ to 3 years	12	8
3+ to 5 years	14	12
5+ to 10 years	12	14
10+ years	7	7

The men were asked to tell about any present or past relationship with a lover or boy friend, and it was suggested that they discuss the sexual relationship and the question of outside relationships and fidelity, as well as the pros and cons of having and/or not having a lover. One of the men, in declining to answer this question, said, "Your questions on relationships have very little to do with relationships." Presumably, he was objecting to the emphasis on the role of sexuality within the relationship which is implied by the questions. While it is true that the questions, indeed this entire survey, do focus on sexuality, many of the men in commenting on their relationships discussed other aspects, as expected. As this book was being prepared, the gay magazine *Christopher Street* published a unique portrait

of a gay love affair in which, interestingly enough, the sexual aspects of the relationship took on major proportions. While further exploration of gay relationships is needed, and while at least one book on gay male couples (by Charles Silverstein) is in the works, the following essays offer a good look at a complex subject:

☿"We have been 'married' about fourteen years, and presume it will last our lifetimes. We are known as a couple, and those who tend to treat us as if the other hardly existed are not considered friends. We live together but of a mutual desire to share what we know, do, like, dislike, etc., since we overlap on a majority of these things. We are both very into cooking and entertaining at home, traveling anywhere together, daily long walks and bike rides, movies and theater in general. We both like having a nice house and furnishings, and feel we have a very lovely home together. We are invited places as a couple, as 95% of those who know us know us as lovers, not just roommates, or whatever. . . .

"And, at the same time, I feel we are two distinct individuals with a lot in common, but each with his own pursuits. My lover is quite involved with his career and with his family, neither of which really involves me (nor do I wish them to). Except for the same periodicals, which we devour, we read totally different books. We have diametrically opposed views on many things, and sometimes can't stand each other's opinions. In sum, I think all I'm trying to say is that we are different with a common bond of wanting to be together, and finding those things we share in common, and use those things to strengthen our relationship.

"With all the outside sexual contacts we've made (and I think these have been without any guilt for the most part) our prime marriage comes before all else. I think we've gotten to the point that no matter what the temptation others might be for us, we are secure in the knowledge that we are and hope to remain for each other and our marriage first."

☿"My current lover and I have been together about three months. We usually have sex about once a week, and the intensity and quality of our sex is very high for the most part. It is a *sexual* relationship in the sense that sex is the predominantly binding factor. We like each other a great deal but our interests don't click. He's ten years older than me and he's a lot straighter in living and ideas—he doesn't get high and hardly drinks, whereas I smoke dope a lot and like wine a lot, too. He goes to church fairly regularly while I'm an agnostic. He likes classical and show music while I like blues, jazz, rock, and country. He likes living in the city while I can't stand the city and would rather be in the country. I could continue but I guess you get the picture by now. Yet, paradoxically, we respect each other for our divergent interests. We don't live together, of course, because of our different life patterns and ideas as well as the probability that it would really mess up our relationship if we did. There are a lot of things about my lover that get on my nerves with long exposure (I'm sure he feels the same about some of my thoughts and actions). I feel my lover is far more effeminate that I am in speech patterns and gestures, but I would never bring this up to him (and he

doesn't feel he is effeminate) because it would just make him self-conscious and uncomfortable, and it would be ridiculous (and impossible) for me or him to try and change anything so fundamental and intrinsic to his character. Yet I must admit it unnerves me to a degree, especially in public—but I keep my mouth shut. Not only is it best to leave well enough alone about it but I must also remind myself that he has every right to talk and gesticulate in any manner that suits him, and my wanting to change that is just another manifestation of a heterosexist value system I've internalized which condemns any way of behaving outside the sex-role norm. So that's why we don't live together. As for fidelity, I don't really feel any desire for other men at this point and neither does he (that doesn't mean I don't get horny when I see a nice-looking man on the street—it means I'm not making any attempts to actualize my fantasies for others outside of my relationship). I've told him if he wants to fuck other men, it's fine with me as long as he doesn't tell me about it. I think that made him uneasy because it probably planted a seed of suspicion in his mind as to whether I've been doing any outside screwing, but I haven't thus far, and won't as far as I know. The thing I like about having a lover is obvious: it's a steady piece of ass. It might not be love, but steady, mutually desired sex is nothing to be sneezed at. I'm 24 years old, and this is my first relationship. I mean, hell, my sex life before this hasn't exactly been like Jean Genet's. I went through some long, lonely dry times and now I feel very good about finally having a lover, with all of the realizations and self-evaluations that it brings. I realize I ain't no prize, and the fact that my lover and I don't look like we just walked out of a *Playgirl* centerfold or an ad in *The Advocate* affirms and testifies not only to our humanity but also to the constancy of sexual attraction and the renunciation of preconceived and self-defeating ideas about the 'ideal lover.' It's taught me a lot, and in the end, that's what I like most about it.''

⚥"I've been with my lover for seven years. We have sex nearly every day—often twice a day. Our sexual relationship is great. He once told me I was the best sex he'd ever had. Wow! Talk about an ego trip! I feel the same way about him. He's dynamite!

"We've both done considerable tricking and he had a prior lover, so we're not inexperienced. I was married for eight years as well.

"In our case it appears that the old line about love being better the second time around is valid. We've lived together for the past five years. Prior to that he was in college (living with a lover) and I was married. Living together is vital to our relationship. We really share. Separate digs would destroy us.

"Sex outside the relationship is confined to my occasional business trips and his quarterly trips to the midwest. While the cat's away the other cat . . .

"We enjoy threesomes and actively pursue them. He likes the baths, so we go four or five times a year. I don't care for them, but oddly, he wants me to go with him.

"The pressures on a gay couple are intense. The nature of gay life tends toward promiscuity. Bars are the main social centers. It's all but impossible not to be tempted sooner or later. A monogamous relationship is too inflexible and therefore too fragile. We are secure in our bond. The baths and three-ways plus the odd tricks when we're separated satisfy the wanderlust. We tell each other about our solo assignations. Frequently we turn each other on this way. If this sounds unusual, how many hetero couples do you know where one or the other doesn't sneak a little on the side? We pragmatically faced facts and got rid of the sneak."

⚣"For some time now, I have been having sexual relationships with this person who I would consider a lover. He is married. We do not live together but we see each other regularly on a social basis. Whenever we want to have sex, he is usually the one to suggest it. Until about a year ago, it was done on the average of once a week. For the past year I would say that we have engaged in sex no more than ten times. When the frequency declined I became jealous for I thought that he was having sex with another male. No proof. That doubt is still there but I have accepted it as a fact of our relationship. Maybe one day he will say to me this is the last time for there is someone else, or I do not love you any more. But until then, I just masturbate and have my fantasies."

⚣"When my lover and I decided to maintain an affectionate relationship without sex, and never to reveal to one another the existence of our 'private lives,' we were then able to have a happy life together. The first five years (*with* sex) were hell. The last twelve (without) have been wonderful, productive, and we have made real contributions to society. Actually, we make love a few times a year—and with great passion. Our friends don't understand! But we seem to outlast other couples."

⚣"Ex-lover department. Have had two. Number one lasted 1½ years and really fucked me around. That little bastard was the original shrew. He ended up taking me to the financial cleaners. I had his grave picked out before I came out of it. Then I led approximately three years in Los Angeles (1967–1970) of tricking around and enjoying it. Number two lover: have just recently broken up, after seven years. Too bad but I think it is/was one of those things which had to be done. I feel that 'lovers' *do not* have sex outside of the relationship. I've been told I have old-fashioned feelings. I do not have a lover at present, and would not like to have one for at least another three years. Mainly because a 'relationship' is too stifling at times. On the other hand, knowing that someone thinks of you as Mr. No. 1 in their life can make a lot of bumpy roads seem very smooth."

⚣"A relationship I had (am having?): with R. We have never lived in the same town, seldom in the same country, having traveled together in the Southeast and Mexico and Asia over the last six years. We've not seen each other now for two years, our longest separation by far. I have learned a great deal from R. about lifestyle (he was a hippie and I was a recently separated married fine-arts librarian). When we are together we do not have sex very often or regularly. One of the nice things about him is that he

doesn't have sex mixed up with rewards, symbolic communications, or love. I have known so many men who are compelled to have sex as soon as they lie down with me, or I assume as soon as they lie down with anyone. R. can just go to sleep. He may touch or may not touch. Touching does not mean fucking. He is hardly cosmic or spiritual or platonic about it; he is very mundane and candid and unanalytical about it. R. is interesting to me because of his compulsion to change, to travel, to explore new places and subjects; I have come to love him more as I realize that he also has deep resistance to these yearnings, that he has tensions, that he disguises anxieties and fears which he does have. We make a good pair in that I generally manifest the anxieties and tensions and harbor the impulses and ambitions. He brings out the adventurer and the rebel in me. We were last together for a few months in Southwest Asia, and I suppose we had sex about every five days. Sometimes it remains very very intense; the process has become quite abbreviated, since for me much of a sexual relationship with a man is passing through trust and resistance barriers in me. With R. we just fuck or don't fuck. Usually. Sometimes I still come up with a barrier.

"Even when we are together we do not expect sexual fidelity. We have had other lovers around; I have been lovers with R.s best friend, and it was simply another bond of our familial love among the three of us. It is a very expansive relationship without having a lot of apparent sentimentality about it. On many levels, R. seems rather cold; deep down he is very sweet: he describes it as his 'eternally teenage heart,' that I am his 'James Dean' who survived the crash enough to do the improbable and fall in love with R.

"Still, I don't describe myself as having a lover. I have had relationships in the last couple of years which were quite loving and deliberate and still I didn't think of them as lovers: one I thought of it as a possibility, felt we were headed in that direction. No longer, though. Nor do I want one very much. I like being left alone in the morning; I hate waking up with someone schlepping around; I like my time to drink my tea, do my exercises without self-consciousness, etc. Basically I think the reason I don't want a lover is that I am so self-conscious R. is the only lover I can even *imagine* feeling independent around; and I seriously doubt that that could manifest, either. I have children who 'need me.' I don't want anyone else 'needing' me. I meet few men who are interested in a relationship as sterile and cool as I would like. When I do they are as unlikely to pair up as me. So that seems settled."

♉ "I have had relationships of a serious nature with men whose political radicalism was somewhat like my own; those relationships have been laborious, difficult, turbulent, deadly, arduous, and disappointing. I don't think I can love men who are as idealistic as I am, who are as involved in analysis of things, who are as serious. It is like we are self-consuming: I see this process of ingesting ourselves, digesting ourselves, shitting ourselves out, eating the shit, digesting . . . I am clear that I will not do this pattern again!"

⚭ "I was introduced to Richard when he was 16; I was 22. And we saw each other a few times in about a month. Richard was what you could call a 'regular' of a friend of mine. Well, after about a month I fell head over heels in love with Richard. And we became very good friends. At first it was for just sex. It was always one-way sex. He didn't lay a hand on me, and never did. In fact, when I first was introduced to him, I was not very good at giving head, and he told me how to do it, what felt good and what did not. I owe all my success in this field to him. Anyway, we started hanging around together; we did everything together. He drove my car wherever we went. We went shopping, movies, even on vacations together. I knew his parents and they know me as a gay man. And we got along. This relationship went on for five years, and as we grew to know each other better, we did not need sex. We were more brothers than sex partners. I got enough sexual satisfaction just being with him, or when driving placing my hand on his leg as we traveled. Two years ago, he got married and it lasted one year. His wife knew I was gay and did not trust me. She thought we were still fooling around, which we had not done for several years. So she gave Richard an ultimatum: either break off our friendship or she would leave him, so we parted as friends, as I understand what was going on, and all I wanted was for him to be really happy. Well, they are divorced now, and he can't bear to face me because of the way he treated me before. But I have told him time and again in letters that it makes no difference to me what happened; he will always be my friend. Ever since that time, there have been others, two in particular, but not to take the place of Richard.

"About a year after this, I met Gary; he was also 16 at the time. I have what I like to call 'the Mother Hen instinct' and Gary needed a mother. He had no father; he was a bastard and his mother was a little on the mental side, and did not love him or care for him. It was late November when Gary came into my life, and all he had on that night was a jean jacket, and that is not enough to keep you warm in November. My heart went out to him, and from that moment on, I tried to get him a new winter coat. But he kept saying no. Finally during one bad snowstorm, I picked him up and forced him to K-Mart to buy a new coat. We saw each other for several years off and on until he moved a few months ago to Texas to look for work. Then Mike came into my life about that time. He also was 16. Gary would never take money; Mike will always take money, no matter what. He is so different from Gary and Richard, but he is so nice also. We can be friends also, besides sex partners.

"I try to have sex at least once a day, if not more. If I go out of the house I am always sure of getting at least two if not three tricks a night. Plus I have one regular who calls at 11:50 a.m. each day to see if he can be my lunch. It does wonders for the pocketbook, because I don't spend on food—saves money and my waistline too! He's so filling! No, I would not like a lover, because I become too possessive of another person. I would rather be a free spirit. I know I will end up sad and alone when I get older,

but who knows, I may change when I get old and find a lover that I can be happy with. For right now, friends are 100% more important than all the lovers in the world.''

⚤"At the moment I am having a relationship with a man who is seven years younger than me. At times the age difference bothers me, especially lately because I have not had much solitude and so I'm more sensitive than usual to his awkwardness with the gay scene and a certain lack of tolerance towards other people who don't fit his expectations. I hesitate to say that I 'love' him, as I have defined love, since the infatuation has dwindled as it always does eventually. But when I am excited by him, there is no question about the intensity of my feelings for him, his exuberance and his mannerisms, his body and lifestyle. It hurts when I think of losing him. Our main conflict tends to be his wanting to live on a farm while I want to be in the city, and at the moment, our growing lazy with each other and with our evenings. I want to have sex more frequently than he does (we have it maybe once or twice a week), but when we do have it, I get off on his huge balls and energy, and if he's up to doing a bondage trip, he does it the best of anybody I've done it with so far, at least for tightness if not complexity. He isn't really into it, though, nor is he into bestial wrestling, so I satisfy these needs with another man I see now and then.

"We don't live together because both of us need our periods of solitude and most of all a sense of independence. I never have been able to deal with roommates. My art suffers, and I become explosive in my moods after the second month of not having a space that is exclusively private when I need it. I probably need about 50% of my time to be totally alone.

"Although my 'lover' does not seem to be much into 'extramarital' sex personally, I am, and both of us are very adamant about giving each other the space to trick now and then, which is not to say we lack our streaks of jealousy. We just work to control them. I need a steady relationship where my emotional involvement can center when I'm not into being alone, but I also need the excitement and variety of tricking and meeting as many different faces as possible. My timidity, however, makes meeting people a slow process, and so I need a lot of time or freedom to do so. So far, none of this has impaired our relationship.

"I tend to fluctuate (according to my introverted/extroverted cycles) between wanting a lover and not wanting one. At the moment my need to be alone more is lowering my affection for my 'lover' and making me long for greater promiscuity (variety). Once that introversion is satisfied, I will be very much into my 'lover' again (the present one if we survive my present mood, a new one if we don't) and not as reserved about the relationship as I am feeling now. I don't want to lose my present 'lover' because we are very compatible in many ways, but I am having difficulty expressing my present needs, mostly because I fear he won't totally understand how I can still need him while also needing to totally get away from him for a while.

"I like having lovers because the more I have sex with somebody the more sensitive we become to each other's bodies, so the more pleasurable

the sex as long as it doesn't become a rut. I like being single because I am in better control of my life and freer to do what I want, when I want, and with whom I want.''

⚤''This is going to be extremely unusual, but here goes: I do have a lover but since he is in prison, we don't have sex at all physically, but have to exist on a rich diet of fantasy until he gets out. Yes, I do have sex with other people, men and women. So far, this has not affected the relationship. We have an agreement (I believe) to allow for sex with third parties, together and separately, so long as emotional primacy is maintained. This seems to me to be the only sensible arrangement for two males to make. What do I like about having a lover? It gives me security, adds another dimension to my identity, is an adventure, gets me to intimately know another unique human being, allows me to give love and to give myself.''

⚤''I met my present lover in 1944. We courted for about a year or more, then decided to live together. We lived together for seventeen years and then split up for four years and then resumed the relationship, but live separately. The four-year separation, with the help of a psychiatrist for him and a psychologist for me, gave us a chance to sow wild oats, reevaluate ourselves and the relationship. We felt that we had a great deal invested in time, and tried to salvage the relationship. Living separately, we have become more independent, more complete people and consequently better for each other.

''I have sex outside the relationship often only because our sexual needs are not identical in quantity. It is an unspoken arrangement—never discussed—and absolutely does not affect the relationship.

''We have sex on the average of twice a week. It is usually very intense and satisfying, although on occasion, as with any couple, we have a clinker or a no-show. But we also have a deep love for each other and a feeling that it is the two of us against the world and that we come first.''

⚤''At present I live with a man named Joe; we have lived together for four years in a small town of 300 people in the North Cascade Mountains. We have sex once or twice a week, and it is of high quality—more so if we go longer without it. We live together partly because we are the main support for each other's sexuality, living as we do in a heterosexual town (but we get support also from friends and neighbors).''

⚤''While in England, I fell in love with a young man exactly twenty-one years younger than I am. I brought him to this country, put him through college and through graduate school. Our love affair lasted ten or eleven years, and then the romance was over, but not our affectionate friendship. I still see him, and never a week goes by that he doesn't call me. When we meet and when he leaves, I always get a very warm and beautiful kiss but we do not have sex any more. Those days are gone. We do not live together. He has made his own life, and although he works in New York, he has his own home and circle of friends about an hour's drive from here. We both had outside sex even while we were romancing. Man is not monogamous.''

⚤''My lover and I met in high school in 1950. I was 16, he was 19. We

have been together ever since—twenty-seven years. We have sex once or twice a week; sometimes it's difficult for me without stimulants. We have lived together twenty-six years, i.e., since the first year. We do at times have sex outside the relationship. This has always been a problem. Maybe our long relationship is due to the fact that we have never resolved the problem. It's the best thing in the world to have someone to share the good times and the bad.''

⚢ "My lover is schizophrenic and very sexually repressed, and on top of that, I'm not the type of man he's attracted to. But we do love each other, and it's not sex, but all the other aspects of our relationship that have kept us together.''

⚢ "Three months before my 17th birthday I met a boy who had turned 16 only a month earlier. At that tender age we fell in love and decided to remain faithful. We considered our love to be like that of David and Jonathan, Damon and Pythias. Only later did we understand that our love also had another name. Except for an innocent indiscretion of the heart, he remained faithful (sexually) to me during all those twenty-five years of our life together. (His platonic affair occurred about three years after our initial meeting.) But shortly after our tenth year together I had a love affair with another boy. I don't think it would have happened if the new boy (my age) hadn't been so masculine, and if my lover hadn't started going in for drag. I loved them both and couldn't give either of them up. So I took to the bottle and began a decline which lasted about three years. After my lover fell asleep I would steal out of bed and go to the 'club.' Anyone who wanted to suck my cock needed only to ask. Eventually my lover gave me an ultimatum: if I didn't give up the bottle and my promiscuity, he would leave me. I agreed, and for most of the remaining twelve years of our life together, all was bliss. Then he became ill. I nursed him at home during the last weeks of his life because I wanted to be with him when he died and didn't want him to die in a hospital. I was taught how to give him injections against pain, and I didn't allow him to be in pain for a moment. When he died at 41, I was 42 and returned to the bottle. Soon after his death a gay friend (?) told me, meaning well (?), 'It's such a shame that you're in such a fix and don't even know how to cruise.' (!)

"The happy postscript to this brief biography is that my lover had worked with a wonderful man during those last fifteen years of his life who became a very close friend to both of us. He was twelve years our senior and we never once thought he was gay. Perhaps he didn't either until, after my lover's death, I confessed to him just how close F. and I really were. I soon realized that he was in love with me, and, after about a year's courtship, asked him if he would move in with me. He did, and we have been living together for the past five years. We will continue living together (faithfully) for as long as the other lives.''

⚢ "My lover comes over every weekend. We have sex two or three times. Sometimes it's good, sometimes not so good. We don't live together. We did live together for about a year in a studio apartment. Being that close for

that long was not a good thing, especially since we had only known each other for three weeks when we moved in together. I decided to move out when I got a job and could afford my own place. I like seeing him once a week, preferably on Saturday night, staying until Sunday afternoon. I like to be free the rest of the time. I have sex outside of our relationship.''

⚥"I live with my lover though we spend most of our time apart and have our own separate rooms. We generally have sex once or twice a week if he is not away for weeks at a time, which is not unusual. Our relationship is based on mutual respect and a real physical interest in each other. Our having sex is generally quite intense and our agreement is that third parties are welcome if mutually acceptable, but we never go our separate ways when we are together. When out of town and away from each other we consider 'fidelity' irrelevant. Also my lover is invariably interested in only younger boys (barely bar age or younger adolescents on boardwalks, etc.) and I feel no sense of competition with those boys. We have our jealousies, which we voice, as we discuss all our problems, so that in four years, third parties have presented no serious problems.''

⚥"The relationship between me and my lover does not fit some of your questions. Legally still married, but fully separated with a shared-custody agreement, my former wife and I have established for our two children dual households. This pattern of traveling every other day back and forth has been going on since the children were ages 3 and 2, so for all practical purposes dual households is their norm. For the same length of time, my lover has been a primary adult in their lives. Thus, my relationship with him from the beginning has really been a family-type structure, though very open. At one point we had a threesome relationship, and for six months last year we shared our large house with another faggot father and his 8-year-old son. Financially our life has been a struggle, and both my lover, former wife, and I place emotional satisfaction, open relationships, etc. as of more value than affluence and material acquisitions; as a result we put vast amounts of energy into all our relationships. Although my second straight marriage was a rich and good relationship, I have to say that my current gay relationship is more open, honest, and reciprocal than anything I had ever expected to experience. For the first two years, he and I rarely used the word 'love,' and refused to call ourselves lovers or even a couple. Careful to protect autonomy at every point, we wrote out frequent contracts and were as exact in describing the changing stages of our feelings as we could be. Within the last two years, however, we each have totally committed ourselves to each other. I feel a security when being held by him that is more final and intense than I've ever felt in my life. I trust him absolutely. We have arguments and fights, but these always feel somehow unreal, formal exercises signifying nothing. Physically I find him if anything more attractive now than ever before, often finding myself gazing at him and beginning to get aroused. Our relationship, affection, kissing, hugging, sleeping naked in the same bed—all are open to my children, who now understand at their ages what gayness is and why we take certain

precautions outside the house, such as with the parents of their school friends. The contracts we write usually pertain to household responsibilities, income earning, transporting the children to their mother's or to school, etc., rarely about our sexual commitments and autonomies. Once I carried on a two-month affair outside our relationship which entailed my staying over at this man's house one night a week; my lover was extremely supportive, as I shall be should he ever choose such an experience. Early in our relationship we were both prone to jealousy and possessiveness.''

⚥"When a sophomore through senior in high school, I had my first lover. We both dated girls who knew we were both gay, but liked our company. We'd always double-date them, drive them home first (in my mother's car), and the two of us would park on a country road and have sex. Unfortunately, since we both lived at home, this wasn't easily done more than twice a week. Occasionally we'd both go to downtown Chicago and pick someone up while cruising. Though I loved him, and still love him thirteen years later, at the end of the senior year in high school we went our separate ways—this was something I never doubted and only assumed, but he was quite shocked and hurt.''

⚥"I had one past lover relationship in which the guy thought of me as a possession—to use his words: 'My relationship with you is like a kid with a new toy at Christmas; after a while he gets tired of it.' That really burned me up. My current relationship is unusual, with my roommate. We are very close. He threatens me with a divorce jokingly, and we are always seen together, even in the bath house once a week, so a lot of people believe we are lovers.''

⚥"My situation is unusual. I am in love with a straight guy that is married. It all started over just friendship and fishing together. He gave in a few times and sex was all one-sided. He never participates but enjoys what I do to him. He told me all he can offer is friendship and I feel that I can no longer see him even on a friendship basis if there is no sex involved. He values my friendship to the degree that about once a month he gives in. We've had lengthy discussions concerning all this, however, and I fully understand and accept the fact that this is all our relationship will be—this is not enough sex for me. I'm really starving inside for love and sex. So . . . I got out and found another lover only to find that I cannot love him as I do No. 1. It is not fair to him (No. 2), so it was discontinued and he was really someone to fill in and take No. 1's place. Now, I am out looking and hoping, and eventually I will find my dream lover and get over No. 1. I fully believe that once you love someone you always will, to a degree. I really wish I could have No. 1, but I have told him how important it was for me to be last, for him to put wife and child first—of course he already knows and feels this.''

⚥"Past relationship (I haven't been in one for 1½ years). At first we had sex almost every night (I often found myself more turned on upon waking in the morning, but my lover hated to have sex in the morning so we rarely did). The sexual intensity died quickly, as it has in all my love relationships,

and I found this very disconcerting, since I consider sex to be an essential part of the relationship. After a while we were having sex two or three times a week, but it was only satisfying for me on rare occasions (like when very stoned). Usually I felt more like I was performing a 'wifely duty' as it were. I really understand how women have come, oftentimes, to feel that sex with their husbands is a chore and a bore.

"We never lived together (relationship lasted nine months); I've never lived with a lover. In this particular case, I felt that our lifestyles were too different; he was very sociable and always needed people around. I like a lot of quiet and privacy, and couldn't stand always being around people. Also, he wanted to have a lot of outside sex when we were living together and I found that distasteful; it was hard enough to deal with this issue when we weren't living together; it would be too painful for me if we were living together and he didn't come home at night. We both had sex outside the relationship. I was very threatened by it, particularly because he would often want to see his partners again. I had more sex with other people while I was involved with him than the total amount of sex I have now that I'm not with anyone; in some ways I think I wanted to make sure I had as much outside sex as he did so I wouldn't feel inferior. I think outside sex was especially problematic for me because I really wasn't in love with him and knew that if I met someone more attractive to me I probably would leave him; if I wasn't secure in my own feelings for him how could I possibly trust him?

"I was once involved in a monogamous relationship; there, too, the sexual intensity died quickly (though not as much as in the relationship I just described) and I always wanted outside sex; had we stayed together I think I could have worked it out (my lover didn't want any outside sex), because we really trusted each other). I don't think outside sex can work until you've been together long enough to have real trust for each other and a relationship based on something other than sex. My experience is that gay men tend to form quick sexual relationships which we think are love relationships; after a month or two we wake up and wonder just who the hell it is we've been carrying on with for the past while, and realize that the only basis for the relationship has been sex. If, on the other hand, a real intimacy develops, it is possible, as long as the primary relationship comes first, to have outside sex, I think, if it doesn't become a major part of one's life."

☎"I don't have a lover. At times I want to be with someone because I feel I'd like to share parts of myself that I don't with friends, that I'd like the security of having a lover, and because my sexual needs are often unmet because I'm not crazy about casual sex. On the other hand, I have a fear of becoming 'trapped' in a relationship (neurotic anxiety) and I still have fantasies of the ideal relationship, which is bullshit in reality, because there are no ideal relationships. I don't know if I'm at a point yet where I'm willing to sacrifice and compromise and work things out; I'm more there than I used to be but I'm probably not quite ready for a relationship yet."

☙ "It's great having one person to share your life with. Wish I could have a few."

☙ "My boy friend and I had sex every day for most of the six or eight weeks we were together. Now that the relationship has ended I can see that sex became a problem between us: my boy friend couldn't relax enough for me to fuck him (I am rather well endowed) and I couldn't let go enough for him to make me come, a situation I find myself in quite often. Since the initial basis of our relationship was sexual, when sex got complicated and I got more involved emotionally than he did, things fell apart."

☙ "Past relationship with lover—three years ago. Lasted 1½ years, during college, during which time we lived together (openly gay, in an all-male dorm). We still write letters, exchanging them every several weeks, and intend to continue our relationship someday. We split (reluctantly) because of career goals (my decision to finish college and his to attend a dance school on East Coast). We had sex at least every other day. It was perfectly satisfying to both of us—and seemed to get even better as our relationship progressed. We both felt that sexuality was an expression of a *deeper* closeness. Except for several instances, we did not have sex outside the relationship. We had an understanding that we would always be honest with each other. We were close to overcoming the feelings of jealousy that an outside relationship evoked in us, but neither of us could begin to overcome the fear that the outside relationship may become more important or exciting to our lover than we were. We were both aware of the element of risk, and that was always a threat; but neither of us thought it fair to deny the other their freedom of relationships with others, either. Although our fears were in vain, we both went through a trying period of time."

☙ "My present lover and I have been together now about eighteen months. The relationship is a very stable and very happy one, in which we share everything, including money, home, possessions, etc. It is as much a marriage as is possible without the legal ties encountered in straight marriage. If we could be married legally, we would be. We have sex usually on the average of two or three times a week. The quality is good and getting better the longer we are together. We live together because we are married in our eyes. I do not (and to my knowledge my lover does not) have sex outside the relationship. Neither of us feels the need for outside sex, at least at this point of a rather new marriage. We have an unspoken agreement on fidelity and both conform to it willingly. I like having a lover and always have. My previous lover and I had six years together. My personality and psyche seem to be that I do not function as well alone. I need and appreciate someone to share me and my life and its accomplishments and failures. It seems to be a necessity to my livelihood."

☙ "I had a lover I loved a whole lot—still love as a friend—and we slept together every night and had sex with decreasing frequency through the years and never lived together in the same place during the day except sometimes in the country. We loved holding each other. There was a lot of 'mother' in it. We worked together and that was good at first and later not

so good. I held on to the relationship too long, for security. It was painful to give up the idea of a 'marriage' but now it's over and that's not so painful, but it's a matter of getting used to myself alone without feeling sorry for myself, and even liking myself, and liking to be alone. But it can only develop out of my own sense of my own strength. An emotionally poor person has nothing to give.''

⚤"I have had one lover, for three years. It ended in December 1975. For the first year and a half, we had sex about five times a week. Thereafter, it lessened to three or four times a week. Our sexual relationship was quite boring after about six months, very mechanical. The whole relationship was bad—we were both insecure and jealous. We had promised fidelity but in fact we weren't very faithful and while we both knew that the other was tricking, we never admitted it. We lived together for the duration of the relationship and for six months after its dissolution. In fact, at this time we have a very good, close, nonsexual relationship and really love each other a lot.''

⚤"For the past 1½ years I am living with a former student of mine. He came to me, before we knew each of us was gay, when his mother put him out. After about two months we had the first evening of sex together. From then until about two months ago we averaged sex about once a week (sometimes several times a day, sometimes not for a couple of weeks—he is now in college away from home). He has always objected to the feelings I feel towards him and does not want us to consider ourselves lovers. We have always agreed that our relationship would be open and we try to be considerate of the other's feelings in seeing other people and having others sleep over. Sex has always been at his desire and he has stopped all sex between us for the past couple of months. I am his guardian, help support him. He signed the renewal of my apartment lease together with me, and we have just joined the National Gay Task Force together. Yet we do not socialize together, although we might go to the same place together. I drive him around a lot but we seldom go out together. We talk to each other a lot, for a long time we fought with each other, sometimes even violently and physically. I am very jealous of him and I have gone into fits when he has someone else over (getting drunk, playing loud sad music, sitting around in tears). Seldom have I had anyone over when he is home. I spoil him, clean up after him, buy him most of what he wants, am available for practically every beck and call, and I love him to death. He cares about me but his love for me is quite different. I would settle down with him, on whatever conditions we could agree on, and I would be most flexible, immediately, but he is young and adventuresome and in demand. We have always stated that as two free human beings we have no holds on one another nor could we put any. I have learned to compromise and submerge petty feelings and to mesh my life with his. I have to give him room without smothering him.''

⚤"I have lived with my lover for four years. He was the second gay person I met after coming out. Our relationship is very close and intense on all levels—sexual, emotional, intellectual, and spiritual. Our relationship

has not had a negative moment since it started, and I see no way that it can fail to go on as it has been, flying from one high to another. We have sex, on average, once a day, but sometimes as often as three times. Because we know each other's sexual turn-ons etc. so well (because we have discussed them so much together) we can share our fantasies for great sexual effect. We are very happy with the sexual intensity of our relationship. We live together. With a relationship as close as ours, we just can't get enough time together. Living together is the only way. We have no strong theoretical objections to outside sex (in the sense of one of us having sex with a third person without the other) because our relationship is too close, and we know each other too well, for jealousy, etc. to rear its head. We don't usually do it, though for lack of 'cruising' time and because the sex so obtained is so comparatively uninteresting. We put in a different category, however, having sex together with someone else in a three-(or more)some. We very much enjoy this, and regard it as a positive extension of our sex lives. We have almost identical sexual tastes and are turned on by exactly the same kinds of guys, so this can work out very well. Unfortunately, there is a lack of attractive, willing partners here. Most of our friends are very hung up about sex, and regard us as quite scandalous. Sharing my life with my lover is about the most important thing in the world to me.''

Sexuality Between Lovers

As the preceding portraits of relationships reveal, the importance of sexuality—and the success of it—within a relationship varies considerably. Some relationships endure even when sex wanes; others have sex as their cornerstone. Here are the figures on *how often the men have sex with their lovers:*

more than once a day	2%
once a day	9
several times a week	38
once or twice a week	40
less than once a week	11

Here are comments focusing on the sexual aspects of relationships, including compatibility as well as frequency:

♂"I have had the misfortune to have been united with my last lover (we finally split last month) for seven years. He was a good lover, but a horrible sex partner. I can't believe that I was as faithful to him as I was. He wouldn't suck my cock, and gagged those few times he attempted it. He allowed me to fuck him only very infrequently (never in the last four years) and only allowed me to suck his cock. He loved it and I loved his 7¼-inch cock. It was beautiful and fit my throat like it was made for it by a custom cock maker. That is about the only problem I've experienced with sex. Oh yes, there is one other little thing. I was sexually active prior to meeting him.

In fact I had sworn off masturbating as just a waste of good come. After becoming lovers, his need for frequent sex diminished, and my masturbation increased to about three times a week. Horrible.''

⚥"We had sex at least once a day at the beginning of our relationship and that tapered off to three or four times a week as we moved into the seventh or eighth month. During the last few months, when things were frequently tense between us, long periods of time went by without sexual activity. Our sexual relationship was fun and warm. There was not a tremendous depth of communication in it because my lover was not a particularly introspective or sensual person. I found it satisfying in most ways. However, on only two occasions during the relationship did he attempt to let me fuck him. The second time he began to enjoy it. The basic problem as we discussed it, however, was that he had real feelings about his masculinity being threatened by being fucked. It was not at all a large issue, but a minor disappointment to both of us. Our sexual relationship was basically good and when it began to pale it was not the quality of the sex but a reflection of the tension in our whole relationship.''

Living Arrangements

Of the men with lovers, 47% said they lived together, while 53% lived apart. Nearly all (93%) of the men who lived with their lovers explained this choice by saying "We want to" or "We love each other"; 1% said they lived together because they considered themselves "married"; and 6% cited financial reasons. As for those who lived apart from their lovers, these were the reasons given: 19% said they lived in different cities, 17% said it was simply the way they wanted to do it, 11% said something like "We need our own space," 11% said the relationship was too new, 10% said that one or both persons in the couple were married, 7% cited job reasons, and 5% cited financial reasons.

Whether or not to live together is an obvious choice for some couples, and a major conflict for others. Two men living together, especially if one or both of them are older than 25 or so, run the risk of being taken for "queer." For some men, then, not living together is an act of "discretion," in other words a response to the antigay pressures of the outside world, connected in some way to the fear of discovery. For some men, though the choice of not living together is one of the freedoms granted by the gay world which accepts the idea that lovers do not have to share the same house or the same room. Straight people often misinterpret gay lives because they do not realize that roommates don't have to be lovers, lovers don't have to be roommates, and groups of gay men living together don't have nightly orgies! Here are a few comments from people dealing with the issue of living arrangements:

⚥"After being together for four years, my lover decided that he could not continue to live in the city any longer. I could see *something* coming, yet I didn't know that it would manifest itself quite this way. I had felt our

relationship deteriorating over the previous year; in fact, he out-and-out left me for a few months, trying to blame me for his sense of alienation. He started some therapy during those months. He came back the kind of man I wanted very much to love.

"It was, though, quite apparent that he could not continue to develop a working relationship with himself unless he left the city. He moved to a small city (100,000) about 250 miles away, where he had some friends and was able to get a responsible job that helps his self-image greatly. We discussed this all, fairly completely, and agreed that after a year we could judge the results.

"Six months have now passed. In one sense, our relationship is more perfect than it had ever been before. We visit each other on the average of every other weekend. We have a marvelous time with each other. He no longer feels petrified by the city, and I find going out with him a great thrill. But I'm coming to the realization that in another six months, he's not coming back. I don't think he's realized it fully yet, but I think he has some idea of it, too. We talk now about a more distant future when we live together, but he only discusses it in a nonurban setting, and he understands that I cannot find that way of life yet a possibility for me. His family has lovely property in the far north—we've been there a number of times—and it is his dream that we live there. Yet I realize how cut off I, the person I am here and now, could feel in that situation. So our relationship has fallen into a holding pattern, and landing seems a long way off."

⚢"I'm still going out with the guy who 'took my virginity away' three years ago. He's twelve years older than I. We don't live together. I used to want to, but he lives with his parents for financial reasons, he says. I live on my own and make only one-third what he does, so I see this as a lie. It used to upset me, but now it doesn't because I don't want to live with him."

⚢"My lover and I lived together after we had been lovers for about four months. The time came when we felt really oppressed by the necessity of being apart which resulted from not sharing a home. We wanted to build our relationship more constantly, wanted to share the small and everyday moments that we were missing. We wanted to have a place we could fix up, make an expression of ourselves, have friends into. I had a roommate previously and he lived with family, so there was always a limit to our freedom when we were together before we moved in together."

⚢"Living together is vital to our relationship. We really share. Separate digs would destroy us."

⚢"We live together because we like each other a lot as people; we're compatible and we like sharing our whole lives, and we do so with a nice balance of dependence and independence."

⚢"We do not live together because, for one thing, I'm very hard to live with, and second, he has friends who are very homophobic and he doesn't want them to find out he's gay."

⚢"We do not live together because he and I live with our parents, and

because of economic reasons. We're both low-middle-class people, meaning we don't make enough money to own or rent an apartment or house.''

⚥"We live together because in San Francisco no one gives it a second thought, and it's cheaper than paying rent on two places.''

⚥"Mornings are very refreshing. More so than when I lived by myself. We got a place together that is better than either of us could afford alone. I first suggested living together, and he wasn't interested at first but finally became interested. Our musical interests are complementary and mutually instructive. Both of us are religious and neither likes TV or entertainment. Both of us have lots of friends and like to play the host to them. Also, we're both kind of sloppy because of lack of time to clean, cook, etc.''

⚥"I would like to see him more often and would like to live with him. However, he absolutely will not go along with living together, and will only stay together all night long on weekends. I do not think he would mind living with me if only he'd erase the paranoia of social oppression from his mind. He has a fear that if we were to live together his relatives and fellow employees, and employer, would jump to the conclusion that we are 'queer' and would retaliate. Although we are both young and many young single guys share apartments for economic reasons, he will not believe that his relatives and friends would go along with this reasoning.''

Fidelity, Monogamy, Jealousy

Adultery, like sodomy, is a punishable crime under biblical law. This "crime" has been passed down through the generations, codified in civil law, and presented as an official way of life. "Fooling around," or extramarital sex, as it is sometimes known, is nonetheless a well-known fact of life for heterosexuals. Under the double standard that reigns, it is more acceptable for men to seek outside liaisons than for women to do so. Likewise, it has been a common assumption that lesbian couples are more faithful than gay male couples. The issue of monogamy has been a major item of debate and discussion in lesbian-feminist circles, where monogamy has its proponents and opponents. Reading the gay male journals and literature, one gets the impression that monogamy isn't much of an issue, i.e., few men, even long-term lovers, advocate adherence to an ethic of 'one spouse, faithful forever.' There are, to be sure, some gay male couples who practice such strict fidelity, but statistics on precisely this topic were not gathered. The men in our survey were encouraged, however, to discuss their feelings and practices as they related to the issues of fidelity, monogamy, and jealousy. There are further comments on the issue of gay male promiscuity and social relations in Chapter 7. The previous statements by men about their relationships with lovers indicated some of the viewpoints and experiences with monogamy, fidelity, and jealousy, and here the men focus on these topics:

⚥"I/we have sex with someone outside of the relationship. It's no big

deal. A little change is needed every so often. There's no jealousy involved; that's what led to the break-up of my first two lovers and me. Maturity is a huge part in keeping a relationship going. I am approached more than my lover, but pick up on only about 5% of the propositions."

♂"Because of my lover's expressed 'need' for sex outside our relationship, I also do it (after much anger, hurt, upset, and a year each of therapy). I don't need it but I won't be faithful if he's going to fool around. Fidelity in spirit and feeling we agree on. Bodily we do not practice it but we are not promiscuous about it."

♂"When I begin to get emotionally involved with someone, I find it's a good idea for me to have sex with other people so I don't become obsessed."

♂"I feel that if two people swear fidelity, that they end up lying to each other because they trick on the side."

♂"Outside sex gives me the opportunity to appreciate my lover when sex with him begins to become 'routine.' Outside sex is also a wonderful way to boost a failing ego. We do have an agreement about 'fidelity.' We both travel frequently separately and have agreed that 'while the cat's away . . .' Lately this agreement has broadened to include clandestine sexual experiences with another. I think that we are both assured of the love of the other and trust has developed. We both had a long history of tricking before we met and realize that there was something about it that we enjoyed. Now that we are sure of the other's love, we have started to reconsider the importance of strict adherence to any sort of policy of fidelity. Of course words like the above have preceded many painful 'divorces.' I think we realize that we are playing with potential fire by relaxing our fidelity requirements. Jealousy is innate. We are entering this 'phase' cautiously and with a trust and love that should enable us to be warmed by this potential fire, rather than be consumed by it."

♂"Monogamy is a form of insecurity expressed chiefly by clutching at someone, and clutching most often leads to strangulation."

♂"I have some sex outside of the relationship but he doesn't know it and I feel guilty about it. Sex with others is not very satisfactory and I'm trying to stop. We don't really have an agreement about 'fidelity'—he says I'm 'free' but as I said I really don't want to run around. I'm afraid of VD and the possibility of bringing it home."

♂"We were strictly monogamous for the first three years, but have included three other friends in threesomes in the past year. The decision to do so was carefully considered and we both feel good about our new direction. We see it as a positive movement. Monogamy served a useful purpose when we first started living together, and though we have included others now, we don't see our relationship as being *completely* open now. We don't go out looking for new people to have sex with. If there is a friend we love, we are open to considering whether or not it would be best to express that love sexually."

♂"We both have had outside sex. For me, when my lover takes another

sex partner I get very hurt because I consider it a preference thing. He swears to me it's just a sex thing and that he's not involved nor does he plan to get involved. He feels the same thing is okay for me if I want it. Usually if I do, it's out of spite to hurt him and myself. I would like it better if neither of us has outside sex. It's not happened very often, maybe two or three times, but it's very threatening on my part no matter who's doing it. We have a commitment to be true to each other, and honest. I suppose faithful is more than just having sex with one person.''

⚣''We had an agreement about sex outside the relationship: if either of us tricked, we had to tell the other—this became destructive because we used it against each other. Sex outside the relationship truly diminished what we had within the relationship. It diffused our intimacy, our trust of each other. It became a tool or weapon of *anger* coming from within the relationship. I could write about this for hours but I haven't got the time.''

⚣''His jealousy of my relationships with (mostly) straight friends and relatives felt like a repressive smothering, and my jealousy of his other relationships brought out my anxieties and insecurities.''

⚣''Right now I am living with a man in his 20s who is absolutely mad about me. I love him but my feelings are not as intense as his. He is really quite jealous and if he knew I was playing around he would hit the ceiling and probably leave me. I would not flaunt my extra activities in front of him and go to great lengths to not hurt him in any way. It's just that I have gotten to be a whore, I guess, in my old age.''

⚣''We have come to agree that it's perfectly all right to have outside sexual relationships, although it is always a little scary, sometimes one or the other feels more vulnerable about it. We do have certain rules—that we will not have other relationships if the timing is not right. That is, if I'm feeling down or depressed or harried or needy, it would be inconsiderate of my lover to be pursuing another relationship, so he wouldn't. Also, we have to tell our outside partners that we have a lover, and we don't have sex with third parties while the other is in the house.''

⚣''Monogamy means having one spouse at a time, and what gays usually mean is the issue of having a lover and having sex with others. This is more appropriately labeled sexual exclusiveness or nonexclusiveness. I feel that this is an issue which too many couples fail to face, simply accepting a societal norm of exclusiveness without examining their own needs and reasons. Some couples grow best together when they remain exclusive, some grow best when they share with others in one or another form of nonexclusiveness. The basic requirement is that the agreement, whatever it is, be mutual, loving, and deeply examined.''

⚣''I could not be true in a monogamous contract with another gay male. Gayness and promiscuity go hand in hand, in my opinion. I'm always looking for new cocks, new personalities, new experiences and adventures, etc. One small part of this is that such cruising and subsequent conquests make me feel a part of the vast human 'family' and less insignificant and alone.''

&"Right now I'm having no sex outside my relationship. It's very monogamous. The one time I did 'cheat' I felt very very guilty. Why? I am not sure."

&"I have had a monogamous sexual relationship for the past ten years. While this may seem atypical of gays, I prefer it. I think sex with love is far superior to sex without. I have experienced both kinds. I am also quite a bit old-fashioned, due both to age and the fact that I am pretty much of a closet queen."

&"I like the monogamous relationships I have seen, and tend to feel that gay monogamous relationships are the best relationships of any I know."

&"For those able to accept monogamy's responsibilities and possibilities as a way of life, it is a potentially great joy and fulfillment. Our society's contemporary values, attitudes, and especially its hedonism work against many finding the fulfillment offered in this way of life."

&"Jealousy—ugh! The killer! More pain, problems, misunderstanding and general ill feeling come from sexual jealousy than anything else I know of. I used to be more patient about it, but now, when I see jealousy, I either get away or tell whoever not to be so goddam possessive!"

&"Some people think jealousy shows caring, but I think it's more of a possessive and selfish emotion and therefore destructive in most situations."

&"Sexual jealousy has not been a large question or problem for me. I have never involved myself with a lover who was terribly possessive, nor have I ever felt more than passing flashes of jealousy. I am very clear that whatever love exists between me and someone else is made by us and cannot be transferred elsewhere, expended elsewhere, or increased by love existing elsewhere. The men I live among are simply too clear and fraternal for heavy-duty jealousy."

&"As much as I find sexual jealousy 'impertinent' ideologically, I am one of the most sexually jealous people I know when I'm 'romantically' involved with someone. To be romantically attached is to have summoned that whole primal network of emotions one has had for one's family as one was growing up—hence, there is dependence, love, need, anger, affection, and ultimately a primal *attachment*. For me, that attachment is most threatened in the sexual arena. The gut fear is that my lover (past, present, or future lovers) will find someone more primally sexually exciting than me. I have been 'in love' with two men; as far as I can tell, the components which summon that host of feelings known as being 'in love' include a complete respect and admiration of who the person is (in terms of worldview, intellect, decency) and a driving sexual attraction to him at once. An equal attraction to body and mind. If my lover fucks with anyone else, it is a tangible symbol of the possibility of losing him, much more than if he has an intense three-hour dialogue with someone which might ultimately be more rewarding and more of a communication. In my three-year relationship, we both 'tricked' but there was a rule established by me that when we tricked, we told each other, to establish 'trust.' As long as we

weren't hiding anything from each other, it seemed safe. But I got jealous anyway. The most interesting experience I've had with jealousy was one night recently when the two men I've had long-term relationships with met at a party I was attending, and the two of them were instantly, electrically attracted to each other sexually and wanted to fuck. I had only recently ended the relationship with one of them, and so I was not fully resolved about my feelings for him, nor am I really resolved about my feelings for the first. I never experienced the level of anxiety and jealousy (and fear of total abandonment) as I did at the thought of the two of them fucking. I was afraid that they would fall in love with each other, afraid that each of them would find the other 'better sex' than each had found me to be. I demanded that they do not sleep together out of respect for me. I felt like I had no right to make that demand, but that I had to for emotional surcease. I don't believe anyone who says they don't experience jealousy. Either they've never been 'in love' or they are very 'repressed.' That is my belief. One can get past jealousy in one's life, but one has to experience it to be able to work through it and get past it."

Lovers' Quarrels (Including Violence)

With wife-beating emerging as one of the major social ills in contemporary society, it seemed logical to include the subject of lovers' quarrels and violence in the questionnaire. None of the men replying to the survey indicated that violence was a regular occurrence in their relationships and in response to the question on political values, "pacifist" was one of the most widely chosen labels. The following are indicative of the gay men's feelings on this subject:

♂"Disagreements, quarrels are part of any human relationship, but when they are violent or take place in public (that includes in front of friends) I see such quarreling as a signal that there is something not quite right with the relationship, particularly when such violent or public quarrels occur with some degree of regularity."

♂"My lover of six years—the very first—was a violent person and that is what eventually broke us up. Today I wouldn't tolerate it in any way. Life is too short. Scenes are stupid."

♂"Quarrels are essential. The object is to have good, creative, not playing-dirty fights. Anger is good to get out, necessary to get out. If you fight good with your mouths, and get it out when you're feeling it, you'll never get to fists."

♂"If you are mad enough to hit someone it is a great tension release to hit them, but I don't like to pursue a relationship until it reaches that point."

♂"Lovers' quarrels are as important in a real relationship as the affection within a relationship. They are part and parcel of the same fundamental feelings summoned by the nature of that kind of relationship. To love someone, to be romantically involved with someone, entails a whole

range of emotions—love, tenderness, need, anger, jealousy, hate, etc. Lovers who don't argue and who pride themselves on having a really smooth relationship have not dealt with the reality level of that kind of relationship demands.''

⚤''Replace lovers' quarrels with lovers' discussion. If that doesn't work, separate. There should never be violence.''

⚤''I am not a violent person and I would not accept a lover who became violent toward me, or others. I would simply walk away. Quarrels, if done in a mature fashion, can help clear the air, and help the persons involved understand each other. The question is only how will we learn to deal with them, and can we learn to accept them as part of life's joy and pain.''

⚤''Lovers' quarrels are healthy if fighting is to the point, not below the belt, and is nonviolent. An occasional slap or punch is all right if circumstances are extreme, but even then, violence, as always, is risky, both psychologically and physically.''

⚤''I had enough bickering in my family for two or three years so that any quarrels, let alone violent ones, are disgusting to me. They tend to continually evade the issue, explode around ridiculously unimportant matters, and are not worth all the time and energy involved. If anything, they are (like pain) a signal that something is wrong. When there are too many, then the relationship is sick. It is frustratingly true that lovers' quarrels do tend to solidify that love, but when it reaches the point of quarreling being the only or major 'glue' for that relationship, then it should break and seek more productive ground. Enactment of a good strong S&M fantasy might prove healthier, but then I'm biased.''

⚤''Often destructive but also often necessary. I have never been able to quarrel well with anyone but my lover. We have terribly violent fights but because he loves me, it's great afterwards. You get to let out all that tension and then make love afterwards.''

⚤''Fighting must occur in a relationship, or it will die. You may stay together without fighting, but the relationship slips away because no two people agree entirely on almost any subject. If you don't fight (express a contrary opinion), resentment builds and love dies. This does not extend to violence.''

⚤''I hate quarreling and I hate violence—there was plenty of both around the house when I was growing up. My lover is a more violent person, and sometimes he taunts me into yelling and screaming at him, just to see me get violently emotional. I know that he does this but it always makes me feel badly—to get to the point where I will yell and scream at him, I really have to build up a residue of hatred, and that doesn't easily go away.''

Gay Marriage

Chapter 4 included material about men involved in marriages with women, sex with women (as compared to sex with men), bisexuality, and

children. Marriage is an institution established by the church, and then the state, to sanctify heterosexual relationships. It has been shown, in feminist writings, that marriage was designed to prove and protect the male's ownership of wife and children. Marriage also connotes a permanent union since the marriage vows involve fidelity, and the ceremony implies a joyous celebration with friends and family. Some of the reasons people get married, therefore, are relevant to at least some gay men, and the question of homosexual marriage has been raised politically, if only tangentially, by the gay movement.

The specter of gay marriage has been raised by opponents of the Equal Rights Amendment, while in fact the gay movement has expended relatively little energy dealing with this subject. Gay churches have celebrated marriages or "holy unions," and the entire issue of homosexuality and the church inevitably grapples with the subject of marriage, since marrying people is one of the traditional tasks of the church. We asked the gay men, *Do you consider or have you considered yourself "married" to another man?* Of the respondents, 25% said yes, 66% no, and 9% not sure. Only 3% reported participating in a gay marriage ceremony. We also asked, *Whether or not you are in or have been in a gay marriage, what is your attitude toward it?* The responses were:

strongly favor	25%
somewhat favor	21
neutral	32
somewhat oppose	12
strongly oppose	9
not sure	2

Considering that nearly a third of the men are neutral, one can safely conclude that a majority of the men feel that there is something not quite relevant or appropriate about the idea of gay marriage. A few apparently perceive marriage as something okay for straights, but there were some vociferous declarations in opposition to all marriage, gay and straight. In asking the men to comment on marriage, furthermore, the questionnaire didn't specify straight or gay, so some of the following comments reflect general views on the subject:

⚥ "I consider myself very much attached to my lover but not necessarily 'married.' I believe our bonds are stronger than could ever be expressed by the term 'marriage.' "

⚥ "Marriage is a sham. A means for the state to intrude on private relationships. Don't legalize gay marriage—outlaw straight marriage! If I ever do it, it'll be as a tax break."

⚥ "Marriage should be restructured or abolished by the state."

⚥ "As for gay people getting married, why imitate such an outmoded institution? Private vows, rings—fine with me. But these public ceremonies (look, man, I'm getting married) drive me bananas. And finally, on the

monetary side, no one gave me any presents when I started living with Vincent, so if anyone invites me to a wedding just to get a present, he's out of luck."

⚥"Married for 1½ years. Before that, married for three years (both men).We live together in a monogamous relationship and were married in an Episcopal-type service. We consider our relationship of the same order as a heterosexual marriage, vows of fidelity and permanence. I am very happy and satisfied."

⚥"My other half, significant other, or whatever you want to call him, and I consider ourselves a couple, and are planning eventually on a Metropolitan Community Church Holy Union ceremony."

⚥"I've never understood gays who parody the worst aspects of straight society, but I also strongly believe in every person's right to the lifestyle of their choice, so long as no one is involuntarily hurt by it."

⚥"Marriage should be abolished. Permanent association between sexual partners should not be mandated by the state. And it isn't necessary for the bringing up of children, although love and stability are, as well as models from both sexes."

⚥"I've had a complete turnabout over the years about this topic. I used to be quite hostile about marriage as an institution. I now feel that the church and state, in denying us this institution, is denying us stability and respectability in our relationships. I think there are many ways of making commitments between people, but that marriage provides a useful code of conduct—it's all too easy to walk away from an arrangement when there's no committment instead of trying to work out problems. Finally, I wouldn't consider myself or other people as having succeeded as a human being until we have really tried to get to know, love, and live with another human being. It's too easy to brush off sex as a passing phase, a thing done with drink, etc. Living with another man or woman, and being honest about it, is what the gay lifestyle, in my opinion, is really about. That's really facing up to it."

⚥"I support marriage as a positive, stable force in society and as a means whereby society can be of support to a couple. However, marriage is corrupted by legalities and by religious sanctions to the point that it has become both too easily entered and too often a trap or a formality. I should like to see gay couples, who are presently free at least from the legalities, build the kinds of marriage bonds which set a renewed standard for creative contribution to society."

⚥"In a gay documentary movie I saw once, there was a scene of a lesbian marriage in a gay church. One of the women was wearing a white gown, the other a tuxedo. If that's what those two people want, fine, but in my view such things have nothing to do with gay liberation. I'd be embarrassed for my straight friends to see it."

⚥"When I find a lover, I would very much want a ceremony to announce our union. In this way, we would have a commitment to each other as an outgoing measure, and our friends could join in our happiness."

ॐ"The pressure for gay marriage is one of the most reactionary causes associated with gay liberation. It leaves me cold. "

ॐ"I approve of homosexual ceremonies equivalent to marriage, as a stabilizing factor, and would like to see it become acceptable to two gay partners to adopt children. I'm against hanging on to a marriage for convention's sake after all the love and consideration have gone from the relationship."

ॐ"The institution seems to be coming apart at the seams. I see no ultimate discordancies in two people (straight-straight, gay-gay, lesbian-lesbian, and other permutations) simply living together—and raising a family if they so choose. Why a civil and/or religious ceremony and a piece of paper should be so prized (if it still is) strikes me as, at least, blind obedience to convention and, at worst, a height of irrationality."

ॐ"Legal or institutionalized marriage should be outlawed; it is on the societal level one of the most oppressive sexist institutions going. Legal gay marriages as a political goal I think is a waste of time."

ॐ"We have both read and continue to refer to the O'Neils' *Open Marriage*, largely on my contention that there is no significant difference between straight and gay marriage. Relationships are relationships and people are people."

ॐ"Marriage is basically a promise/vow that friends make to support each other in a relationship. Most important, it involves a lot of friends, not just the two who are getting married. I think it is a great idea and should be revived for both gays and straights. One thing missing in our society is the whole concept of a promise, of a vow. The idea involves optimism about one's control over a long period of time over one's behavior patterns and is very healthy."

Role-Playing

Heterosexual role models, visible in the households where virtually all gay men grew up, initiated at birth with blue blankets for baby boys and pink ones for baby girls, and reinforced daily through such media as advertising, TV, the movies, and the senior prom, are a basic part of the human experience in modern society. As the women's liberation movement fiercely challenges the stifling roles that women have been placed in, a few men agree that roles are oppressive, but most men defend their positions of power with ferocity. This new examination of the old roles is the backdrop if not one of the main catalysts of the gay liberation movement and the general changing consciousness among gay men. Although gay men are seen as being in defiance of traditional male roles, there is simultaneously a sense in which at least some gay men join with other men in defending male turf and the male image. The comments on role-playing in relationships made by the men replying to the questionnaire indicate a critical attitude toward roles along with an acquiescence to them in some cases.

The men were asked, *How often do you "role-play" (butch/femme,*

masculine/feminine,   husband/wife,   dominant/submissive)   in   your relationships? A distinction can be made between role-playing with regard to sexual behavior and role-playing in such matters as social behavior, work, dress, mannerisms, etc. The following charts indicate the responses concerning frequency of role-playing and feelings about it:

	ALWAYS	VERY FREQUENTLY	SOMEWHAT FREQUENTLY	SOMEWHAT INFREQUENTLY	VERY INFREQUENTLY	ONCE	NEVER
sexually	4	8	12	13	21	1	42%
other than sexually	2	7	8	13	23	0	47

	VERY POSITIVE	SOMEWHAT POSITIVE	NEUTRAL	SOMEWHAT NEGATIVE	VERY NEGATIVE	NOT SURE
sexually	9	11	33	21	22	3%
other than sexually	5	8	28	23	32	3

While negative attitudes toward role-playing, and avoidance of it in practice, characterize about half of the men, it is also clear that there is not an overwhelming commitment to the destruction of role-playing. The men seemed genuinely interested in the topic, and it generated a variety of comments and experiences. No one involved in a strict husband/wife type of gay marriage arrangement sent in a detailed description of his situation, though there were men who indicated briefly that they played the roles of breadwinner or homemaker.

Some men expressed attitudes toward role-playing indicating comfort with, and enjoyment and appreciation of the process, or a negative response to the recent assault on role-playing with its emphasis on androgyny and sexual equality. Here are some of those responses reflecting positive attitudes and experiences with role-playing, social and sexual:

⚥"There seems to have arisen a belief in our society that there is something wrong with a dominant/passive relationship. Everyone today

should be 'equal.' That's terribly polite and marvelous in theory but the real world doesn't operate quite like that, whether among the human species or any other. I have a very dominant personality (I said dominant, not degrading), my lover is more towards the passive side. Our relationship tends to be well organized and very stable as a result. There is no constant tension for dominance of any given situation. This difference in personality traits simply is. We take care of one another using our own particular strengths. There is no lesser or greater person. The dominant/passive situation is organizational in nature only. For instance, our sex life, as well as many other areas of our lives, if analyzed in such terms, would result in no fixed pattern. I like sucking. He likes sucking. I like screwing; he likes screwing. I liked to be fucked; he likes to be fucked. This flexibility and stability makes your question of fidelity a sad, sad commentary on the whole homosexual lifestyle."

♂"I'm butch and I turn on to butch guys. Femme guys are sometimes fun to camp it up with in a gay bar, but they don't interest me sexually."

♂"I am told I am 'butch' and it pleases me, so I guess I play butch. But if I'm butch I think it's because I'm naturally that way; what I dislike about role-playing is the tendency to get into a role that isn't really *you*. The guy I'm having sex with these days thinks he's 'nelly,' but really he's quite masculine if he'd only admit it."

♂"If I'm butch it's because I've been influenced by straight men all my life practically. Even now for the sake of my job I have to appear straight. I don't like it but until I can feel secure in coming out at work, I'll play straight."

♂"I usually seem to fall into the husband role, although I personally don't hold to it much. This is possibly because of my generally dominant role in sex. Sometimes it would be so great to have someone else make all the decisions—provided I agree with them, of course. Or at least understand them. I must say, I am usually attracted to very gentle people, and do not find femme a turn-off. But maybe that is because I am a pacifist and abhor violence in any form. As for other people's role-playing in their relationships, I say whatever works is right."

♂"I have role-played in the past. With my high school football player—I was his 'little woman.' Of course I wanted him so bad I fell into the role. My *grande passion*. I wanted that knight in shining armor to sweep me off my feet, to subdue me, to conquer me. But in reality I was the dominant of the two, because I forcefully tried to will his desires and mine into actuality."

♂"I put a strong emphasis on roles, more sexually than nonsexually. But, and this is the distinctive part, I can feel perfectly comfortable in either set of roles: butch/masculine/husband, or femme/feminine/wife, but like to keep these roles clearly defined with any given person, rather than switching back and forth with the same person. I like the stability and clarity of it, the ease of prediction and minimal conflict it provides; the communications are so much easier, more familiar. It also allows people to get more deeply into their basic feelings."

♂"I feel I have a predominant, though not unalterable role, which is often passive. Butch/femme roles can usually be determined in a comparison with another person or group of people, and although I'm hardly the jock type I'm not a queen either. We all have both masculine and feminine aspects of our personalities, and these are evidenced in our varied actions, thoughts and ideas. Roles can be bad when they become ruts and therefore oppressive. We all have a predominant role in any situation, and as long as the role is not incompatible with that of a partner there is no reason to demand a change."

Many men affirmed their refusal to role-play and their opposition to the consciousness upon which role-playing is usually based. Here are some of those comments reflecting negative attitudes toward role-playing:

♂"I don't think I really engage in role-playing. I'm not hung up on my masculinity, and I don't try to play some exaggerated 'butch' role. (I may wear jeans and a flannel shirt to appear masculine, but that's as far as I go. I don't affect what I consider 'masculine' behavior.) As far as playing a femme role, the idea repels me, and I have no use for people who do play that role.

♂"I don't like role-playing because it's a phony hype. It also is a statement that the person is ashamed or disappointed with what he is and is trying to be something else. When a gay man butches it up, in effect he's saying that he believes the bullshit that being gay means being less than a man, and he has to compensate with all his butch drag and mannerisms. When a gay man 'femmes it up,' he's saying the same thing, that he believes that he is less than a man and has to act accordingly. I only feel comfortable with gay men who are comfortable with themselves, and like what they are (and thus don't feel compelled to act roles)."

♂"I especially dislike role-playing in public as it confirms straight society's stereotyped views of gays."

♂"No role-playing for me. Let's leave that to the heterosexuals."

♂"I never role-play in my relationships with other men to any extent. I treat gay acquaintances as equals. I dislike role-playing because it reinforces stereotypes that straight society has about gay people. Also, with one person playing a more dominant role than the other, inequalities can develop that would ruin the relationship, such as one person supplying all the monetary support. However, if role-playing is what a couple wants to do, and if they can adjust to it, then in some cases it may be beneficial to a relationship. I believe in couples' handling their relationships in their own way, and although I would personally not like to role-play, it doesn't bother me to see others do it."

♂"I am very conscious of role-playing in couples (I am single). I've found myself distancing myself from gay couples who are heavily into role-playing because I become acutely aware of injustices yet I feel it is 'none of

my business.' My best friends are other 'single' people, but I relate very well to couples, gay and straight, where role-playing is avoided or minimized."

⚘"Role-playing seems to me by nature to involve dominance and control, both of which make me feel uncomfortable."

⚘"We do not role-play. We are both men; what we do gives us physical pleasure as men. We have no fear of our own masculinity and/or femininity. These two characteristics are found in each person and to be a more emotionally rounded person we must experience all our feelings."

⚘"My lover and I don't usually role-play in the relationship except I am the more practical whereas he is the more idealistic. Sexually I tend to be a bit more of the femme because it's easier. He's 6'7" and I'm about 5'6". So with a small bedroom it's easier if he moves around rather than me trying to move him. (I hope that makes sense to you.) With other men, I also tend to be femme because I like butch men and since I am small and 'pretty' they no sooner get me in bed before they tell me to lie on my stomach. I dislike constantly being taken for femme, so sometimes I rebel and refuse politely, then screw them. Sometimes these butch guys are so surprised, they agree!! I dislike heavy role-playing where one guy does the washing and ironing always—usually only our older friends do this."

⚘"I don't role-play in our relationship nor with others. I don't like labels. I like men who act like men. Queens, drags, leather, and uniforms are my definition of roles. They're facades—people pretending to be something they're not. Who needs it? I want to know people for whom they are, not what they want to be. Most of it seems foolish. I walked into a leather bar in Omaha and while waiting for my drink overheard two motorcycle types, all done up in leather, chains, and studs, arguing heatedly over the proper ingredients for fondue!"

⚘"With my lover of three years, it was sexually role-defined—he was the aggressor—he fucked me and insisted that he hated getting fucked. This pissed me off on a really primal level for those three years. Although he was dominant sexually, he also performed most of the 'wifely' duties domestically. This was where the role definitions balanced out. He was the 'husband' sexually and I was the 'husband' in the rest of the relationship. I hated this imbalance of power—I wanted 'total' equality but since I didn't get it sexually, I withheld my responsibilities in other aspects of the relationship. I did not want a heterosexually defined relationship, but I'm realizing that it's very difficult to extend the boundaries of role definitions."

⚘"No, I don't role-play. It is a betrayal to mock heterosexuals in a homosexual lifestyle. That is one way by which we can easily liberate ourselves, and it outrages me that some gay people still involve themselves in the same old tired heterosexual master-slave relationships. Yes, I usually do the dishes, but because I like to and he doesn't. And he usually cooks, but because he's good at it, although I'm learning to with his help. I don't consider that role-playing: it's just practicality. In bed and elsewhere we are

equal parts of the relationship. We, as gay people, have a special opportunity to be creative with our relationships and with our lives. Why copy the dying, oppressive heterosexual stereotype?''

For many of the men, the issue was more than just being involved in roles or not. Some of the complexities, subtleties, and ambiguities of the issue characterized their comments, including the suggestion that role-playing was okay under some circumstances, and not okay under others. Here are some of these statements:

⚨''I have seen gay relationships as a unique opportunity to do away with prescribed roles, proving that relationships can oftentimes work *better* without them. But unfortunately, we are bombarded with role caricatures every day paraded before us as heroes, setting up barriers of power and status. And in gay life, role consciousness seems to play an even more upfront part in defining these barriers. From the pages of *The Advocate* to the masks and poses of the faddist 'leathersex scene.' It is particularly aggravating because gays (and blacks before them) continue to emulate straight values. Although I generally dress in a very casual manner, I am aware that my overall 'look' is that of another straight hippie type. I feel caught in a bind of sorts. Between my recognition of all the 'special rewards' the society gives straightness and masculinity and my own felt need to 'be myself.' I struggle day to day with ongoing consciousness raising. The gay movement and the women's movement especially have helped me be aware of my own need for self-improvement in the area of feminist politics.

''Role-playing during actual sex may be a different matter. I am speaking specifically of created roles as in an S&M setup. For some people, active role situations (reversals, variations, etc.) may very well be thereapeutic, good for the soul, cleansing . . . and perhaps a good way to break down rigid barriers of all kinds. I seek this myself. Though most of my experiments in constructed role situations have been less than comfortable. Perhaps I need more actual experience.''

⚨''I like to get fucked. If you call that role-playing, then I role-play. I certainly do not ever feel like a woman/wife, or whatever. I don't think any of my tricks or lovers have ever felt I was submissive to them in any sense other than sexually. I have been conditioned against role-playing by my upbringing. My parents' relationship is one of perfect equality, and they always said that dominant/submissive marriage relationships were symptomatic of bad breeding and low social status, something never to be encountered in 'good families.' ''

⚨''I don't exactly disapprove of it, but I think those with strong desires to role-play should think about it a lot.''

⚨''I don't play any role. I am my lover's wife and I love being his wife.''

⚨''I do role-play, but hate myself for it. I see it as being inequality, and the equality is what I like about gay life. I see myself as a slightly macho

nonsexist male who happens to like to cook as well as go running and hiking. I really hate it when I get thrust into a housewife role.''

⚧"I see nothing wrong with role-playing if it's confined to the bedroom. To 'play house,' though, one man as the husband, the other as wife, is in my own mind bad. I guess because I've seen so many bad straight marriages where the wife stays at home and stagnates. The whole thing reeks of sexism.''

⚧"To some extent I do role-play. I usually project a masculine role. My lover alternates between projecting a masculine role and a role that is not so much feminine as perhaps merely nonmasculine, androgynous. I find that much of my sexual interest is centered around masculine images, boots, leather, being tough. Also, much of my sexual interest is a reaction to societal values and conditioning, knowing that men aren't supposed to do what I do and that I'm going to do it anyway. There can be no mistake about it, I am a man doing this. On an intellectual level, however, I realize that there are some very negative aspects to this behavior. I have been greatly influenced by feminism and have been working hard to try and integrate the feminine aspects of my personality into a meaningful sexual expression. I have been mostly successful in this effort.''

⚧"I don't role-play, wouldn't know how to. I am a programmed male and part of that programming is to give my partner satisfaction too. I think the ideal relationship is for both to take turns being active-passive. I do like guys who are queens and who like to do things to you, but I relate to them as women. Too macho types don't turn me on. I like honesty in people.''

⚧"When I go to a gay bar or to visit gay friends, I often assume a somewhat femme role. Sexually, I have never role-played because that is the place to take off the masks, not to put them on.''

⚧"I don't consciously role-play, but I am comfortable 'playing housewife.' I have no qualms about cooking, I enjoy cleaning and keeping a neat apartment, and I certainly do not feel any less masculine because of those feelings. I also love to watch college football games, swim, and water ski. Along the same lines, I do not feel that makes me any more butch than any one else. I do not like placing butch/femme labels on any of my actions or those of others. I fully believe in letting each person express himself or herself in that way that is most natural to them. Sometimes I like to design women's clothes, I often like to design homes and buildings since I was initially an architecture major, and I like to dabble at painting. I love music and play both the piano and organ. This is all a part of me, but has nothing to do, as far as I'm concerned, with role-playing. The biggest role I do play is that of teacher by week, and then I can be totally myself during the weekend.''

⚧"I am what is called a 'top man' but I do not see myself role-playing at all. I think my feminine side is secondary but not hidden or repressed. I am gentle but masculine in manner. I do not like aping women; it is neither masculine nor feminine but artificial and hollow.''

⚦"You'd do us all a big service if you could tell the world why men who despise women will then act like women and why women who hate men act like men. Why don't we simply look at our physical equipment and act like our sex? The bland grotesqueness of unisex which we're still trying to be sold by fashion designers and 'today' psychologists is doing so much more harm than good. And it is for that reason that I will not aid you in generating labels and categories. Some things cannot be defined by a mere list of words."

In one of the above quotations, one man refers to his role as a schoolteacher. Indeed, there are many roles that one can play other than the strictly butch/femme ones. Such roles can be based on authority and experience (such as the teacher) or on such matters as age and money. The following are a few comments showing gay men's experience with other roles, giving an added depth to this discussion of role-playing:

⚦"My lover and I do not role-play in the strictest sense. We share all household duties and sexual roles; it's a very egalitarian relationship. However, I do find myself sometimes falling into a certain role pattern when I am with older men (my lover is eleven years older than I), which is that I am very quiet and observant and act like the stereotyped 'cute young kid'—it makes me feel very uncomfortable, because it's not me, but I fall into it a lot."

⚦"I don't necessarily role-play in my relationships with other men sexually or nonsexually. I am a physician, and my profession very often involuntarily causes a reaction in others which puts me in a certain position, often a very false one, where they role-play. It is often difficult for even an open-minded person to accept me as me without the bag of my professional role. I try to keep my professional role out of the way, but this is a very hard thing to do because most of the people I meet already know what my profession is. I am rather shy around other people, especially straight men, in social situations. To that extent, I sometimes suppress my natural way of expressing myself and role-play. I do not like this."

⚦"It seems that nearly all the people with whom I've lived in a gay relationship, since I've been out this time, have used me as a 'sugar daddy,' though I cannot really complain, I guess. A friend, who is a psychotherapist, told me once, 'You cannot be used, unless you are also using.' This made me look, and anytime that I have paid for sex with meals or lodging, or favors, it has been because the other individual was satisfying my sexual needs by screwing me, or being available for whatever I needed for my own satisfaction. I really do not approve of paying for sex, but sometimes I have the feeling that I may have to continue in my practice of taking people in because of my increasing age. It really gets difficult here, at least, to find partners when one's hair starts graying."

⚦"I agree that I often appear to be the doting parent figure for my lovers, but that can be both butch and femme."

♂"I dislike seeing gays playing the role assigned by society—that of an ineffectual pervert."

♂"I role-play in that most of my friends are straight and I pretend to be the 'he-man' type, even to the point of pretending to have had sexual experiences with women in order to carry out the role."

♂"With the 13-year-old boy friend I had, I suppose I was a father or big-brother figure, and I suppose unavoidably he was a son or little-brother figure to me. In my last affair—I don't think there was role-playing: he interested me in tennis (but that's good exercise and that's very practical), and I interested him in classical music (and that is enriching to the soul, and if it is our goal to live a balanced life, I guess that's practical too). Athletics vs. arts I only consider masculine/feminine in a Jungian way."

♂"I don't role-play consciously, but I guess we all do. I'm not exactly John Wayne, but I've never considered myself effeminate, though I probably am. I have a very deep voice (result of years of training) and have played all sorts of roles on stage, so never think about role-playing much. I am comfortable with what I am and how I act. If there is ever any role-playing it would be as gay man making love to a straight man. I like straight men and am quite happy to suck their cocks, but I never feel feminine. Years ago I had a lover (we were both young) who liked to play games. We'd do elaborate sex scenes and since I was an actor I got all the good parts. Sometimes I'd be a rough construction worker and I'd tear his clothes off (he kept a supply of old clothes) and 'rape' him. Sometimes I was the 'rapee.' I'd be swishy queens, elegant movie actors, predatory teachers. I rather enjoyed it all, for a while, but it got old. He never did get over it and I'll bet he's still doing it. If a guy really wanted some role-playing, I'd do it, but it is not my thing."

The strictly sexual aspects of role-playing provide a very interesting opportunity to consider the relationship between biology and consciousness. Obviously, there are some men, gay and straight, who perceive of the anus as a substitute vagina during the act of ass-fucking. To a certain extent, it is impossible for the sexual acts that gay men engage in to be completely divorced from the more widely accepted and better-known act of heterosexual intercourse. However, there is a sense in which the analogies can be exaggerated, and the specialness of male-male sex overlooked or denied. In this group of comments, the men comment on various aspects of sexual role-playing:

♂"No, I don't role-play. Taking a hot fuck doesn't make me a woman or a wife or mistress etc. I always think of us as two guys getting it on. From age 18-25 I *was* into roles, and, because of my preference for being fucked, regarded myself as 'femme.' "

♂"Other than liking to be the recipient of the other person's climax or orgasm, I do not role-play in sex."

♂"I love to be the female, cuz I love to be overpowered, for someone to be domineering with me. He likes being masculine cuz he can."

♂"In all the longer relationships I have had, although I have generally done most of the fucking, there always seem to have been days when I was tired, or feeling very relaxed after a couple of glasses of wine, when it has seemed quite natural for me to welcome my partner's assuming the active role for a change, and I would not feel that it was really a partnership if I refused to allow that reversal of the usual pattern."

♂"When I first started having sex I was restricted to passivity out of ignorance. It did not occur to me for a couple of years, I believe, that I was capable of fucking. After I found out that I could, I began to about 50% of the time, and since then I have had the greatest joy when no roles were played—you fuck me and I'll fuck you. That seems to make the most sense, and I am glad to see that most gay men nowadays seem to take that view. Years ago we used to hear gay men say, 'Oh, I never let anyone fuck me,' as if they lost status in that event. This is rarely said nowadays, I think. In San Francisco, many of the men dress in rather butch attire (logger shirts, marine fatigues, boots), but many are doubtless quite willing fuckees."

♂"I am a man who loves men, even femmes. As an 8-year-old I was very willing sex partner to a 14-year-old half-brother who cast me as the wife. He'd lie on top of me, rub off (though seldom or never to climax) while talking about what my father and mother did in bed, and conclude with my having a mock labor and delivery of about one second's duration. Some trip."

♂"The closest thing that I would consider to be role-playing is when my lover and me engage in anal intercourse. I always let him insert his penis in my anus. Otherwise we treat each other as equals. Maybe my lover does not let me fuck him because he dreads pain, or is afraid of being considered gay. I don't know; I can only speculate."

♂"Role-playing in an S&M relationship or encounter is essential. It fulfills fantasies and dreams, and releases feelings and tensions like no other sex act."

♂"I don't believe, even in a lover relationship, that just because you get fucked you're the wife. Hogwash! This attitude is denigrating . . . destructive."

♂"I think the only time I role-play is when I'm in the mood to be fucked, then I do some different things, like a cat who wags her tail in your face when she's in heat. I become stereotypically female seductive (thanks for the lesson, Joey Heatherton)."

♂"I am masculine even though I like to be fucked."

♂"I try not to play roles, although my physical appearance and bearing occasionally force me into a 'butch' role."

♂"I was visiting a bath in Washington, D.C., last December. There was a strikingly good-looking blond about 21 years old who was understandably

a center of attraction in the orgy area. He was as much 'my type' as anyone could be and I took a turn swinging on his crank and really grooving on his masculinity. A short while later, in a bunk area, he indicated he wanted me to fuck him. Well, I just couldn't get it up firm enough to achieve penetration! It was purely mental: *I* couldn't fuck *him;* it was backwards. For me to enter him would have been desecration.''

⚥"I despise those macho types that state very arrogantly, 'I don't get fucked,' which translated means, 'I'm going to defeat you by screwing you. I'm a real man; you're a faggot.' Any woman probably knows this type. Such ignorance of the joys of the body and mind deserve to be lost to them.''

Camping It Up

One special variety of role-playing is what in gay slang is called "camping it up." The word "camping," according to *The Queen's Vernacular,* was originally a sixteenth-century English theatrical term referring to young men wearing the costume of women in a play, since at that time men played all the roles, including women. A man who is camping it up is acting like a stereotypical faggot or queen—there is an implication of effeminacy but it usually involves poking fun (at oneself or others), humor (perhaps sarcastic), and great wit. It is usually done with a sense of bawdy fun, most often exclusively in the presence of homosexuals. Although *The Queen's Vernacular* states that camp is "one of the most famous and used of all homosexual slang words," quite a few of the men replying to the questionnaire indicated that they did not know the word. It is, in fact, a word one is likely to pick up from a circle of well-educated gay friends or in literary circles. The men were asked *how often they camp it up or watch others do it,* and were also asked *how they feel about the idea of camping it up.* The following charts show the responses:

	ALWAYS	VERY FREQUENTLY	SOMEWHAT FREQUENTLY	SOMEWHAT INFREQUENTLY	VERY INFREQUENTLY	ONCE	NEVER
camp it up	1	6	17	24	31	1	19%
watch others camp it up	3	12	27	26	26	1	7

	VERY POSITIVE	SOMEWHAT POSITIVE	NEUTRAL	SOMEWHAT NEGATIVE	VERY NEGATIVE	NOT SURE
camp it up	16	23	25	19	15	3%
watch others camp it up	16	23	31	19	9	2

Several men referred to camping it up in response to the question about roles:

⚥"I do not role-play sexually, but I do sometimes camp it up or act swishy as a comedy sort of thing. For the most part the image I like to convey, because it is me, is that of an ordinary, masculine sort of guy without being macho. Role-playing on an occasional basis can be entertaining but care must be taken that it doesn't become habitual or you damage your *self*-image."

⚥"I don't role-play sexually, but I often camp it up and act 'feminine.' This is not an imitation of real women, just copying other queens. I do have an affinity for southern-belle accents, which I have been known to use in public (i.e., straight environment). I could never be butch. I haven't got the build or the gait for it. I find husband-wife roles distasteful."

The fact that so many more people like to watch campy behavior and feel positively about it than actually do it themselves is probably a reflection of the fact that campy behavior is a femme role. Leather queens can be camp, too, but only when they talk and move in a campy way, and then the humor is in part the juxtaposition of the masculine clothing with effeminate speech or mannerisms. Some campy humor is actually quite vicious, often explicitly racist and sexist. Those characteristics, or its extreme crudity, can be a turn-off, depending on one's mood and personality. Sylvia Sydney is a drag queen who camps it up regularly on stage in Boston. Some of the comments he makes about blacks and women (especially lesbians) are laughed at or blandly tolerated in the context of the drag show. His shows have been called "oppressive," and if he weren't in a role on a stage, the racist and sexist remarks probably wouldn't be tolerated at all. This particular drag queen plays the role of "foul-mouthed bitch." In general, drag shows, where campy humor is combined with female impersonators doing original vocals or lip-synch with popular records, allow gay men to express their version of old-fashioned femme roles. *Attitudes of gay men toward drag shows for entertainment* generally follow feelings about camping it up, as the following chart shows:

very positive	6%
somewhat positive	10
neutral	30
somewhat negative	28
very negative	24
not sure	2

Some men who indicated that they did not like transvestites (see Chapter 13 specified that they did enjoy drag shows. Perhaps the raised stage is a convenient barrier to unwanted communication. There are many people, gay and straight, who have enjoyed drag shows but who would not really feel comfortable having one of the entertainers over for dinner! In fact, Craig Russell, the female impersonator and star of the movie *Outrageous!* told an interviewer for Boston's *Gay Community News* that his fame did not improve his social life. Many lesbians have expressed negative attitudes toward drag queens and drag shows (see Chapter 12).

Being Single

A majority of the men (54%) said that they did not now have a lover. As should be obvious from the descriptions of lover relations earlier in this chapter, the gay male world is not divided into monogamous couples and promiscuous singles. There are men in couples who have very little sex and 'unattached' men who trick all of the time—and vice versa. A couple arrangement tends to offer steady sexual contact, but it also includes involvement which is nonsexual, in varying proportions. Most of the men who are unattached have decidedly ambivalent attitudes toward their status—that is, they feel that being single has great advantages and great drawbacks. The drive toward coupling seems nearly universal, however. There were a few men who criticized the couple orientation of society in general, and the gay world in particular:

⚤"Yes, I would like to have a lover. It would make me feel better about myself to see that someone else was willing to invest much of their time and feelings in me. Plus, I love being helpful and supportive of someone whom I trust and can be with whenever I need to. I know it isn't realistic to expect a long-term relationship since so few of my friends/relatives have had good ones. Yet the society has told me to want one and I can't escape the media pressure to have one. Couples make me feel worse about being single than I would otherwise. Couples on ads or in real-life encounters both make me feel left out of some experience. It's nice to be alone at times; with close friends and activities one can survive singleness. At the moment I have little of either diversion."

⚤"I am very much a 'loner'—I refer to myself as a hermit in society. I do not rule out a relationship, but given my independence it's unlikely. One of the main detriments to a straight existence, as I see it, is the extremely tight

coupling (legal, etc.) in heterosexual marriage. I see some of the same problems in gay 'marriage.' "

One single man, apparently involved in a lifestyle of brief sexual encounters, simply wrote, "Never having had a relationship of more than a few hours, I am unprepared to answer questions in this section." There were a number of men who seemed either resigned or committed to a lifestyle in which having a male lover is nowhere on the horizon:

⚥"Being married in a conservative area I never have had a lover and am in no position to have one. I might like to have someone I could screw whenever I felt like it, so long as such a relationship didn't interfere with my normal life patterns."

⚥"I've never had any lover, partly because I'd risk my job if I lived openly with a male. Also I suppose I'm selfish and want everything my own way and it would be hard to share a household with a lover. Or with anyone."

⚥"I have lived by myself so long that I don't believe I could live with another person, male or female. I am too used to being alone. I don't mind an overnight guest (especially if there is sex involved) but I am used to reading while I eat and doing things my way."

⚥"At the present time I have no lover. I've had several: one lasted ten years. But I've learned something: I'm basically a loner. I enjoy living alone and prefer good 'friends' to lovers. One of my friends I've known for thirty-two years, another for twenty-six; the woman I make love to I've known for twenty-two years. Lovers are too 'hot' to last. Friends last forever."

⚥"The greatest sadness of my life is that I have never had a lasting relationship with either a male or female. I have come to the feeling that I am repulsive to both sexes even though I am not ugly."

⚥"I really prefer my present set-up of having several people who have my phone number for whenever they want to, while at the same time I am free to indulge myself with whatever opportunities come up such as one-night stands, toilet quickies, gay baths, threesomes, etc."

⚥"I have given up hope of finding someone to intimately share my life with and I feel that society has cheated me of the mated happiness that is practically forced on heterosexuals. I seek only to live in peace. I do achieve some satisfaction from just being a friend to several very decent young homosexual men who, when tired of taking on the world, come to my house where they know they can completely be their true selves. It is very much love, very little sex, but it pleases me to think my advice and experience might help them avoid some of the pitfalls of being gay in an alien and hostile society."

Most single men, however, seem to have a long-range view that having a lover would be a nice thing. Some are actively looking for one, some have

no special expectations or hopes, some are enveloped by a feeling of desperation and loneliness. There is also an awareness of the positive aspects of not having a lover:

⚥"I have not had more than three or four 'lovers' in my adult life and all ended in a frustrating separation for one reason or another. Probably my only ongoing sex relationship was one with my best friend from third grade through high school. I searched and longed for a lover from high school until about my middle 40s. At that time I had a long talk with myself and consciously *gave up* looking for that one man that I could love. This was the beginning of newer and happier days for me. With my expectations vastly lowered I was much happier with whatever pleasant sex encounters I had. I would still love to happen onto that special man, but I in no way look for or expect it. Thus I'm free from what was for years a sort of destructive illusion, i.e., that I would someday meet *the guy* and live happily ever after. I'm so glad I got rid of that fantasy."

⚥"I have not been involved in any extensive gay love experiences. I have always thought how great it would be to find a person that I could really be involved with. Up until a year or so ago, I wanted very much to be able to get married and have a family. I realized I was gay, but sort of hoped that the right woman could 'straighten me out.' Now I realize that that is not going to happen. I guess that this past year has been one of really coming to grips with my gayness. Now more than ever, I would like to become involved with another man."

⚥"I believe that sex is a lot better when you care about the person, and that it actually should be secondary to this caring. But various things get in the way of my forming a relationship: (1) I'm extremely independent, and the idea of being 'answerable' to somebody else is hard to swallow; (2) I set really high (perhaps unrealistically high) standards for a potential lover to meet; and (3) San Francisco is a big candy store. Everybody is pissing and moaning about looking for a lover, for 'Mr. Right,' but playing around is so easy that there's no real motivation to make a relationship last. Most relationships involve paring down your ideal fantasies to reality. In San Francisco, if reality doesn't match fantasy (which it never does), you can easily (somewhat) find someone else who will live your fantasy until you bump again against reality."

⚥"I no longer consider myself as a single person waiting for the time I'll be living with someone. Being alone is not a state of transition. I have accepted my aloneness."

⚥"I want a lover very much. I want to know that experience in my lifetime. I've never had one and regret that."

⚥"Single life is nice as far as having your privacy is concerned but there are times when it does get to be too lonely."

⚥"Once I yearned for a lover; having had a few, I get along quite well on my own. Perhaps it is the function of aging, but the petty compromising and game-playing can be wearing after a while, and one does wonder if the rewards (?) are worth it. Independence is valuable to me. Perhaps my fault

has been that of consideration; it is usually I who bends to the will of another, at my own inconvenience, and it isn't often more than accommodating the selfishness of another to buy tranquillity. What's that worth? Not much, probably.''

♂"Being alone is the worst thing about not having a lover. And any occasional sex is just a physical act that often leaves me feeling worse after coming.''

♂"Yes, I would like to have a lover, but I would not disturb my nice, orderly single life to establish a life with another man unless the odds were overwhelming that it was important enough to endure. I would much rather be alone than have another person around who was okay to have sex with but not really vital to my life.''

♂"Although I've adjusted to a 'single' life fairly well, I would like a love relationship very much. The only things I don't like about single life is the loneliness that can occur at times, and the stigma society places upon a single person ('Why can't you get a lover?')''

♂"Being single is more hassle than it's worth. True, my independence is just about complete, but when I'm feeling down it takes a lot of scraping around to find a sympathetic ear and supportive or critical voice. I've become very good at pulling myself out of despondency, but not good enough for my consistent well-being. I need help, and I need to give help, too. Being single doesn't do much for those needs. On the other hand, being single certainly helps one avoid the thousand petty annoyances another person can inflict on one. Either living single or living with a lover (whether in the same place or not) is agreeable in theory to me, but I've got a lot more experience with the former. In a few more years I may not need the latter.''

♂"I don't have a lover but would like to have one. I think that my whole enjoyment of life, my perception of its beauty and wonder, is heightened by the participation in a loving relationship: music sounds better when I am with someone I love, food tastes better, snow is whiter, the spring sunshine feels warmer, I sleep better, get up happier, and am more productive in my work . . . etc.''

♂"After my experience with my lover breaking off our relationship, I became a very bitter person. I don't think I'll be able to 'fall in love' so easily again. That affair ended more than six months ago and nothing has developed in my life. The experience was very painful for me. I was extremely demoralized, depressed, and pondered suicide. I don't know if I'll ever get a lover; maybe I'll be single the rest of my life.''

♂"I don't have a lover now and sometimes I feel that I really *need* one. Yet I'm aware that a lover can't be *sought*. I'm beginning to appreciate some things about being single: I enjoy the freedom to plan and schedule my own time. I appreciate the alone times, the private space, the freedom to plan the future, the freedom to be compulsive and inconsistent, the freedom to choose relationships and how to express them without having to always consider my lover's feelings, the freedom to be celibate or have sex, the space to get to know and explore myself without always having to relate to a

significant other, the freedom to choose relationships or none. I've finally realized that being single is a decision, a decision I affirm each time I limit the scope of a relationship. As I take responsibility for my singleness, it becomes more of a deliberate, positive experience.''

Celibacy

The question of celibacy has been widely discussed among feminists, but not so much among gay men. Some women have written about how they choose celibacy—a period of time without sexual relations—as something better than relating to men (especially after new feminist awareness). After any difficulty with sexual relationships, some feminists have observed, celibacy may be a good way "to get your head together." One can only assume from the comments offered by the men in the survey that celibacy is not so widely practiced or respected among gay men. In the aftermath of a break-up, for example, at least some of the men would choose wild promiscuity rather than celibacy. According to an archaic definition, celibacy simply means "not married" (when sex meant marriage!), but nowadays the term is understood usually to mean a period of time without sexual relations, voluntarily or involuntarily. Some people (notably priests and monks) practice celibacy for spiritual reasons. It can also be a reaction to negative feelings about promiscuity, which is in a sense also a "spiritual" reason. Celibacy can also result from extreme passivity, because a "marriage" relationship has reached some sort of stasis, because a person lives in a rural area far from easy gay sexual outlets, because an individual is not successful in the sexual marketplace for any number of reasons, or because a person is in the closet. In their comments, most men seem to assume that celibacy is voluntary, however. A significant portion of the comments on celibacy specifically concerned church-oriented celibacy:

⚣"As I was a vowed celibate for 24½ years, I feel I can speak with some authority on the subject. I believe it is an unnatural state, as we are all sexual beings. Very few can live celibate lives and be, at the same time, well-adjusted people. I have seen a lot of sexism develop in priests as a result of their celibacy. For a person who has not voluntarily vowed him/herself to celibacy, therefore, it is an even more unnatural state. The Catholic Church and almost all the other Christian churches apparently do not consider this when they tell homosexuals that they may not express their sexual bent. On the one hand, the churches tell homosexuals that they are sinning if they have homosex, but on the other, they offer no alternative to their homosexuals.''

⚣"A topic about which I have thought considerably, but one which is still far from a solution. Though I've managed to come to a point of relative celibacy, and feel I have really grown to see its value and its potential in the last three years, I still have a lot of trouble being celibate. I have consciously chosen to be in a religious order (and left a wonderful lover for it), but I've never really thought I made a mistake. My real values in life are living in a

community (many of whom are gay, but with whom I do not normally have any sexual relations), preaching, and living the Gospel. I could have done much of that in a lover relationship, but I choose to forgo that to make myself more free to pursue this. I see this life as incompatible with having a lover (though occasionally someone tries it), and am finding real fulfillment here, in a religious community, and without a lover. We share a great deal of intimacy here, of course—emotional intimacy—especially with others who are gay. But together we've tried to help each other to be celibate— since it's the value we've chosen—in order to better do this work, which I feel demands celibacy because of its non-8:00-to-5:00 nature. If you're going to preach, counsel, and be there when people need you, you have to make that your first priority, and I simply couldn't divide my time fairly between this work and a lover. So I'm happy here—but I would not want that happiness to be construed as a rejection of a lover relationship. I was very happy with mine, and I think it led me to realize that this was what I really wanted. It was hard for my lover and I to break up, but he's managed to accept it pretty well.

"I feel deep pain for those people who are alienated from the Church because of their homosexuality or gayness. They need not be. Of course, the Church does not yet admit of a grace-filled lover relationship, but we're moving in that direction as soon as we are able to overcome our moral hangups about sex in general. I want very much to be able to show God's love to those gays who because of their guilt have prevented themselves from feeling it. Love is love is love is love, and gay love, if it is love, is just as holy as God himself."

⚤"I was in a monastic order for about a year, but left when I became sexually active with another Brother. I came to realize that his dedication was greater than mine and I had to leave before our love was discovered, which I am sure would have ruined his life. This was one of the most difficult things I ever did in my life, because we loved each other so completely."

⚤"I was a monk. It's okay and I don't denigrate sublimation for the sake of heightened religious experience. However, it can and has driven some people crazy. One should be very careful—and know damn well why one is sublimating."

⚤"I practiced celibacy for thirty years of my life. It's a means of social control imposed by the church on clerics. Get your workers to give up sex and you have them by the balls."

⚤"I once became interested in a guy who wanted to become a priest. We had sex together several times until one night he told me that he thought that our sex was hindering his ability to serve the Church. He felt he should remain completely celibate. I was hurt because I am also a religious person and felt that he was using God as an excuse to get out of a friendship that he felt guilty about."

⚤"Celibacy is not for me. If someone else chooses it, all right. I do tend to be condemnatory of clergy from those churches which require it in clergy and who yet have very sexual lives. However, one good friend who is a

Catholic priest told me that the vow was a means to an end—it allowed him to be a priest, so he could take the vow, knowing it would never be followed: certainly, 'intent' is necessary in any sacrament or vow."

The other comments on celibacy indicated widespread abhorrence of the idea, with occasional glimmerings of positive feelings about it:

⚤"I am opposed to celibacy. I am celibate most of the time and hate it!"

⚤"It's something I call self-punishment."

⚤"Celibacy is the pits. I was celibate for ten years, from when I first had gay feelings at 12 until my first gay experience at 22. It was the most frustrating, joyless period of my life."

⚤"Being that I have lived celibate for the greater part of my life, I can speak more to this than possibly any other subject. It's harmful, mentally shattering, and for the most part, unnecessary. My opinion only. I feel as if I have wasted many good years of my life by not having an active sex life. I'm sure this is why I have the difficulties that I do now. I go through short periods of celibacy (a week or two), but this is only because I can't find any action, or rather I don't want to."

⚤"Celibacy is self-love. I've learned from people who are celibate that it can be fulfilling. They seem happy and healthy."

⚤"Celibacy is fine if you can cope. I couldn't."

⚤"It seems like a very romantic choice, and dreadful if not consciously chosen. I like it for periods of time, not too long ones."

⚤"I have great experience with this since I came out. I seldom have sex—really don't seem to feel the lack, though. And I still go to the bar, dances, parties, dinners a lot—anywhere to be with a group of gay people. And I don't seem to be cruising—just want to be where I feel comfortable."

⚤"When I had a six-month bout with scabies, I didn't have sex for the duration, and although I missed it at first, I became familiar with celibacy and directed that sexual energy elsewhere. While I would be the last to encourage anyone to practice celibacy (or scabies, for that matter), I do think that there are facets of life which call for more attention than sex."

⚤"Celibacy is ridiculous and unhealthy as is anything that deprives individuals of the joy of feeling good about their bodies."

⚤"If by celibacy you mean sexual abstinence, I think that such behavior is unnatural and should be frowned upon by society. Sexual interaction is a part of the totality of all human interaction and it should be encouraged rather than discouraged. To abstain from sexual relations is to abstain from society and thwarts growth. When you have sex with someone you both benefit, you know a considerable bit more about a person's personality after you've been in bed with them, and to be concise, you're just a better person. One last thing that I might say about celibacy is an experience my ex-wife once had. She was nursing a man who was in his 50s and had to give him a bath. When she went to wash his genitals, she discovered that he was quite small, in fact, he almost went in instead of out. He summed up his demise simply: 'If you don't use it, you lose it.' So I've been trying hard not to lose it ever since."

10

Lesbian Sexual Experiences

Orgasm

Lesbians are often asked with great curiosity or even hostility, "What do you people do, anyway?" The implication of the question is that lesbians cannot function without a penis. In the past, some of this phallocentricity was based on the myth of the vaginal orgasm—that is, that the "real" orgasm occurred in the vagina. The other orgasm, the "clitoral orgasm," was a sign of "immaturity," according to Freud and other male psychologists who obviously had a vested interest in seeing their own penises as the focus of "true" adult sexuality. Lesbians were thus women who had "failed to develop" from the clitoral to the vaginal orgasm. According to more recent sex research, there is no such thing as a vaginal orgasm as distinct from the clitoral orgasm. In fact, the vagina has few nerve endings, and most sexual nerves are centered in the clitoris.

In an ironic way, the tables have really been turned on heterosexuals. Books such as *The Hite Report* by Shere Hite and other studies have shown that only a minority of women have orgasm through penis/vagina contact. Lesbians might indeed ask, "What do you heterosexuals do with a penis, anyway?" since the penis seems to be a most ineffective organ for female orgasm! On the other hand, lesbians have long been aware that the clitoris is the center of the female sexual universe, and lesbian sexuality focuses on the clitoris. As a result, perhaps, lesbians have a much higher rate of orgasm than their heterosexual counterparts, and achieving orgasm is an important part of sexual contact for lesbians. The women were asked, *How important is it for you and for your partners to achieve orgasm during sex?*

385

	VERY IMPORTANT	SOMEWHAT IMPORTANT	NEUTRAL	SOMEWHAT UNIMPORTANT	VERY UNIMPORTANT	NOT SURE
you achieve an orgasm	49	42	6	2	1	0%
partner achieves an orgasm	62	32	4	.5	.5	1
partner achieves multiple orgasm	13	24	34	14	12	3

It seems that during sex women place more emphasis on their partner's achieving orgasm than on having an orgasm themselves. Probably this is a sign of true consideration, but lesbians also feel this way because they generally have no trouble achieving orgasm themselves and therefore focus on their partner's pleasure:

	ALWAYS	VERY FREQUENTLY	SOMEWHAT FREQUENTLY	SOMEWHAT INFREQUENTLY	VERY INFREQUENTLY	ONCE	NEVER
you have an orgasm	37	44	8	3	3	1	4%
you have multiple orgasms	5	24	17	16	16	5	18
you fake orgasm	0	2	2	4	25	15	51

The authors did not ask too many questions about the female orgasm, mainly because they felt this area had been well documented in previous sex research. Here are a few comments regarding orgasm:

♀ "Orgasm is very, very important. Otherwise, it's like eating [food], and not swallowing it—I feel dissatisfied. I almost always have an orgasm, unless the phone rings or the house catches fire!"

♀ "I usually do have one, but when I don't it's okay."

♀ "I feel terrible about faking orgasm, but it seemed the easiest way out the one time I did it."

♀ "How could you look them in the eyes afterwards if you thought you had to fake an orgasm?"

♀ "Never! never! never! fake orgasm."

Other comments regarding orgasms can be found in Chapter 16, where those women who felt that not having an orgasm is a "hangup" discuss their feelings. Orgasm during masturbation is discussed in Chapter 14. This chapter deals primarily with pleasing sexual experiences, and some women did have such experiences without one or both partners having an orgasm, as this example indicates:

♀ "I have only one lover, feel completely 'married' to her, expect to stay married to her until one of us dies, and every time we are together it is great.

"Except when we are away on trips, we have our bedtime dates during the day as we're both married to men and live apart. We undress, climb into bed, begin with general body contact, hugging, kissing, usually talking and laughing throughout. Ordinarily, though this varies frequently, I will make love to her first: kiss her face, throat, shoulders, breasts, etc., suck the nipples while she is lying on her back and I am astride her. I rise up to kiss her again on the mouth and lower myself to kiss her navel or hip bones, depending on moods and whether we are talking, etc. We often use a pillow under the hips to elevate the pubic area. In time I am low enough to kneel between her spread legs to fondle, kiss, and suck the clitoral area and clitoris. My lover doesn't care much for manual stimulation and does not want anything at all in her vagina—says she wishes she could sew it up. She is warm, affectionate, freely physical, but unfortunately has always been nonorgasmic, but we're working on it.

"We then reverse positions, and the same occurs. We usually spend two to three hours in bed at one session. I'll go down on her twice usually, and she'll do the same. We have also tried 69, both side by side or one under, one on top. That is great too. We spend time lying on each other just to be close, will often wind up sitting facing each other talking, joking, etc., which is emotionally so satisfying—how can it be put into words? Important factors are that her touch is so soft and gentle, the most marvelous touch in the world. No clothing at all is of course a must. The only sounds are our talking, laughing, etc. We draw the drapes but can see each other clearly enough."

Manual Stimulation

For the vast majority of lesbians, however, orgasm was a part of the pleasing sexual experience for both partners. Most used a variety of techniques for sexual satisfaction including manual stimulation, tribadism, and cunnilingus. There were also some other methods used by a minority of lesbians, and these can be found in Chapter 12.

It is difficult to categorize pleasing sexual experiences by specific acts, since it seems that most lesbians engage in combinations of them. For simplicity, the sexual experiences in this chapter are divided according to the *primary* method by which orgasm is achieved in the experiences mentioned. Thus, even if a lesbian performs oral sex and tribadism, if the orgasm is obtained by manual stimulation, then that experience will be found under this last category.

In fact, manual stimulation, despite the emphasis in lesbian sex manuals on oral sex, was still the most popular method of achieving orgasm during sex. The lesbian respondents were asked, *On the average, how often do your sexual experiences involve any of the following aspects of manual stimulation ("mutual masturbation")?*

	ALWAYS	VERY FREQUENTLY	SOMEWHAT FREQUENTLY	SOMEWHAT INFREQUENTLY	VERY INFREQUENTLY	ONCE	NEVER
partner stimulates your clitoris/clitoral area	64	21	6	4	3	1	1%
partner stimulates your vaginal area	49	29	7	9	3	0	3
partner stimulates your anus	3	9	14	14	25	7	27
partner stimulates herself	3	5	12	13	27	3	36
you stimulate your partner's clitoris/clitoral area	66	22	7	1	1	1	2
you stimulate your partner's vaginal area	50	26	12	5	3	0	4
you stimulate your partner's anus	5	9	11	12	20	8	34
you stimulate yourself	5	7	10	16	23	5	35
any of these to the point of orgasm	40	39	10	3	4	1	3

Since most aspects of mutual masturbation are so successful and pleasing, most respondents of course felt positively about them. Lesbian respondents were asked, *Whether or not you engage in any of the following aspects of manual stimulation, how do you feel about each of them?*

	VERY POSITIVE	SOMEWHAT POSITIVE	NEUTRAL	SOMEWHAT NEGATIVE	VERY NEGATIVE	NOT SURE
partner stimulates your clitoris/clitoral area	90	7	1.5	0	1.5	0%
partner stimulates your vaginal area	81	7.5	7	3	1.5	0
partner stimulates your anus	26	22	13	20	15	5
partner stimulates herself	42	20	17	10	5	5
you stimulate your partner's clitoris/clitoral area	92	6	1	1	0	0
you stimulate your partner's vaginal area	86	8	4	1	1	0
you stimulate your partner's anus	32	20	13	16	14	6
you stimulate yourself	37	20	17	13	8	5
any of these to the point of orgasm	88	7	3	1	1	0

Several conclusions can be drawn from these statistics. It is apparent that the most popular method of mutual masturbation involves stimulation of the clitoris or clitoral area only. Vaginal stimulation is less prevalent, and anal stimulation is practiced regularly only by a minority. Also, a sexual partner does not stimulate herself regularly during sex with another woman. In all categories women felt more positively about each act than the frequency of actual participation indicates. These figures may signify either that more women would like to do more of these acts or do them more frequently, or they may indicate approval of these acts for others. In any event, here are some pleasing sexual experiences in which manual stimulation is the *main* method for achieving orgasm, which almost all the respondents can achieve with some form of manual stimulation.

♀ "My lover called me at work to invite herself into my bed (we live together/separate bedrooms). This was something to look forward to. The phone call was exciting me—an affirmation of her wanting me. I came home, closed the house up for the night, and went to my bed. She was waiting in bed for me. I undressed for her, lay on top of the bed linens wearing a spaghetti string T-shirt, she under the covers in pajamas. We talked and kissed for a short while, caressing each other's face and neck, and I stroked her arms, her breast, through her pajama top. She invited me to come in under the covers. Our light remained on.

"We lay facing each other side by side, kissed, enjoying soul kisses that

turn both of us on. I moved on top of her, continued soul-kissing her, her arms and legs stroking my back and legs, and my legs straddling hers, then directly on top of hers. I spent a while moistening her by rubbing my body in a sort of circular motion against her thighs, then against her thighs and pelvic bone. When we both were getting wet, I began to rub our clitoral areas together. Mine was a circular motion and her motions were in response to mine. We are a very good fit (I'm 5'1'' and she's 5'7''—both of medium build). The rubbing of clitoral areas is extremely stimulating. Our heads moved to the side, she kissing my shoulder and neck as we moved on each other. My tongue lightly licked the framework of her ear and entered her ear spaces. We moved back to look at each other, and then soul-kissed. My eyes close when I kiss her. She spends time opening her eyes to watch me. I know this. It doesn't bother me, and the awareness of the fact that she may be watching my movements excites me, makes me feel incredibly sexy, and I think inspires my sexy look while 'making out.'

"Her fingers are reaching for my mound—first her hands up over my back and down and then coming between us from the front of my thighs and down. We are both breathing heavily. Our breath is warm on each other and our kisses very wet. I lift my body lightly so she can stimulate my clitoris and turn us again on our side. Our arms—first hers in front and then mine in front—apply added pressure and increase the pleasure on our bodies. She moves me onto my back as we continue to rub each other's vaginal area. She kisses my breasts, and wets them with her mouth. She enters me with two fingers. I have switched fingers and am using my thumb to enter her, which excites her. There is a lot of affectionate talk as she gently moves inside me. 'You feel so good.' I agree. My body arches, and her head and back arch away from me as excitement continues to peak. We are still both in each other, me now with several fingers inside with the others massaging her clitoral-vaginal area. She comes to straddle on top of me. My legs lift so that I am open. She uses them to apply pressure to her own buttocks. We start to pace each other in movements and speed, one mimicking the other's actions. Clitoral stimulation, then entering, then many gentle exploratory touches, then varied with deep thrusts as the vaginal walls hold tight and throb. My free hand reaches out and pulls her down on me as my own body rises to meet her climaxes. She turns the entire situation to where she is on her back. My protestation of 'I can't stand it' does not in the least give her any indication that I want to end. I spread her wetness all over the inside of her thighs with strong hand strokes. Her hand is lost inside me as I enter her again as she pleads for me to do so. We give verbal affirmations: 'Yes,' and we call each other's names. We have more climaxes, unbelievable climaxes.

"We settle exhausted and stroke the full length of each other's body. Our kisses exclaim satisfaction. I massage her breast with my wet hands, and we hug face to face, and rub our clitoral areas. At this point we are so sensitive that it triggers another climax. This excites us again and, exhausted, we are both calling for more with our mouths, our hands, our

whole bodies. We make love again and in manually stimulating me, she touches what to me is like a funny bone. I go crazy laughing, saying that I'm being tickled. The laugh I'm making is different from any laughing I have ever experienced. I'm being too tickled, and I plead for her to stop (I have stopped stimulating her). She slows down and removes her fingers and in that time I've begun to rise. She asks me where I'm going. I tell her nowhere and move to her other side and turn her over on her stomach with one hand, stroking her back and applying pressure to her buttocks. With the other hand, I stimulate her clitoris slowly, making her extremely wet. Her eyes are closed. I enter her and bring her to climax by thrusting my fingers deeply into her and using the palm of my hand for pressure on her clitoris. Her body is squirming, rubbing against the bed. I straddle one of her thighs just below the pelvic bone and stimulate myself by rubbing against her. Her arms are back reaching for me and stroking the leg nearest her. I use my thigh between her leg for more pressure. We have more climaxes. She says she's exhausted. We settle down and exclaim satisfaction. She brings the covers up from the end of the bed, lies back, and opens her arms to me. We hold each other and say each other's name. We have been making love for three hours. She snaps off the light after we agree that we need rest after she kids me that my face and even my ears are red. She turns away from me as I at first cleft my body to fit behind hers, but then in agreement we lie side by side because our bodies are still so warm and wet and no sleep will ever come about that way. We kiss soul kisses and hold each other for a while to express the love we feel and then before we know it, we are asleep.''

♀ "It was a chilly, spring evening; the only light was from a gas heater which made the small cabin-like room rosy and warm. My lover and I were lying on the sagging double bed, fully clothed, holding each other casually, thinking about nothing, not talking. Suddenly the embrace became very close, and she began kissing me very gently on the neck and face. She was above me and began kissing me deeply. I could feel her whole body tensing with desire. I responded by holding her very tightly and raising and separating my legs so that one of her thighs was pressed against my sex and my leg was against her sex. She became very forceful—kissing roughly and taking my clothes off at the same time. I began undressing her. It was graceful, somehow. We were naked and she was still above me, kissing and nibbling at my breasts. I was running my fingernails along her back and kissing her hair and shoulders and neck. We were both very aroused, and she rolled over on her side. She thrust her fingers into my vagina, and I reached hers. It got all complicated with legs over shoulders and kisses along every available area and ups and downs. I was biting and sucking and so was she. I reached orgasm (a good, strong one) from her hand on my and in my vagina and clitoris, and she did too. It was really like having transcended the mechanics of sex—real passion, lust, as opposed to kindness or mild pleasure. After, we held each other very closely for a long time, and she said, 'It looks like we can make it for another year, doesn't it?' Somehow desire had become the vow of love.''

♀ "We usually start by hugging and deep kissing for any length of time, or we decide in advance and then take our clothes off. My partner caresses my abdomen and sides and breasts while I lie on my back. I close my eyes and let her kiss me and lick and caress me. I move my pelvis a little, and I caress her shoulders and neck with my hands for about one-three minutes. She kisses my breasts and sucks on my nipples. I breathe and sigh a lot. Also, she caresses my thighs and more lightly my mons a few times. She puts down her fingers inside my labia and strokes moisture from my vagina up to my clitoris. She stops kissing me and lies with her head on my shoulder—my arm under her neck. She strokes beside my clitoris gently for about thirty seconds. I breathe harder and move my pelvis more. She moves faster as time goes on, usually in rhythm with my quickening breathing. Sometimes it takes longer than others, but usually after about one-three minutes (sometimes five or more) I come closer to orgasm and breathe and moan faster. She strokes faster and harder, depending on what I tell her (giving suggestions such as 'faster' or 'a little harder' or 'a little more to the center'). Orgasm comes anywhere from ten seconds to one or two minutes after this. I moan deeply and clutch my arms around her shoulder, pulling her tightly to me, stopping her hand with my other hand when my orgasm is over. Then I sigh and we smile and hug and kiss and giggle. Often we just lie there talking for a few minutes, or we switch places (so we can both use our right hands), and I kiss her on the mouth and caress her abdomen and thighs and pubic area for about the same length of time as above. (She does not like her breast stimulated, which I often wish I could do.) Our position is much the same—my head on her shoulder with her arm under my head. I put my fingers inside her labia and gently stroke the skin over the clitoris around in circles, not touching the clitoris directly for one-three minutes. She begins to breathe faster, and I stroke faster and more firmly, still in circles. The length of time until she reaches orgasm varies from one to five minutes or more.

♀ "First we remove our clothes and stretch out on a blanket on the rug in front of the fire, with a record on the stereo (Holly Near, Chris Williamson, Meg Christian, etc.). We usually begin with total body hugs and very long kisses and lots of appreciative noises. I feel an excitement in my pubic area, in my clitoris. At some point we do any of the following: She first gently sucks and then bites softly and then harder my nipples. The currents of electricity spread through my body until I scream with delight and agony. It builds and builds until I have an orgasm.

"She bites my neck, shoulders, and back, working down to my buttocks. The sensations go from tickling to exquisite pleasure. When I am ready to scream, she slips one finger into my anus and two into my vagina deep inside so that her fingers massage the tip of my uterus. I 'come' with a long, screaming exciting orgasm that goes on and on. Sometimes she kisses, licks, sucks my clitoris. That is wildly exciting too.

"Now what I do to her and how it makes me feel: Whenever I touch her anywhere, I feel sensations in the same part of my body, so making love

to her is like making love to myself. I also suck, bite on her breasts as she gets more and more excited. I love it. She makes lots of noise and that is exciting. At the same time I feel a tingling in my own breasts. The first time she had an orgasm through her breasts, I came too from the excitement of it. It had been happening to me for quite a while, but she didn't think it could happen to her.

"I also love to curl up next to her with my head between her legs while she strokes me. I suck on her clitoris or finger it. At some point I put my fingers inside her both vaginally and in her anus. As her excitement builds, mine does too, and at some point I wrap my legs around her, rubbing my vagina against her body (can't tell what part—sorry!) and when she comes as we hug and cry, I often come too.

"There is so much more that I could add. Our lovemaking is extensive, experimental, and long. Sometimes we nap in between, and then we wake up and go on. We each have several orgasms in different ways at different times. We never aim for mutual orgasm, but it sometimes occurs. We have found that at some point in 69 one of us becomes too excited to continue stimulating the other. Yet since we find making love so exciting, the one who goes on being active sometimes comes too."

♀"My experience began when we were walking on campus, where touching is not common between women, and we began touching. Everything was very subtle, and we pretended not to look at each other! I started squeezing her ass a little, and she rubbed my thighs with her hand. We went to the car and drove home. An exciting part of this was that we both had classes in an hour. (It didn't work—it took three!) My room was outside the campus and as soon as we got in the gate I started taking off my shirt. The sun was hot and my hair felt good on my back as I heard Teri say, 'Mmmm, woman.' I started taking off my pants when I got to my bed, and she pulled them off me, rubbing her naked breasts against my back. I hadn't seen her take off her shirt, and it was a pleasant surprise. I drew in my breath with a gasp and turned to meet her. She smiled slightly and nuzzled my neck, working her way down to my breasts, which she rubbed and sucked. I felt a rush all up and down my body and a feeling in my stomach like the kind you get on a roller coaster. My cunt was hot, and I could feel its wetness on my thighs. I held her head in my hands and kissed her neck, softly, then more strongly with passion. I pulled away from her as a tease and lay down on the bed on my back with my legs spread apart. Her reaction is always important to me, adding to my excitement. Sometimes she will smile coyly and tease me with her fingers on my belly. This time she drew her head back and moaned as if she couldn't wait to eat me. I could feel her cunt was hot as she knelt on the bed, straddling my legs. She was wet, and moved slightly back and forth so her cunt was rubbing against my knees. She started stroking my breasts with her hands slowly and then bent down so her breasts would rub on my belly, soft as kitten fur. We were smiling at each other, and every time I thought of how much I loved her, my body would ripple with a physical rush of feeling, tingling strongly. She

said, 'I love you,' and lay her full length on top of me, her leg between mine, and kissed me slowly and tenderly. We started moving rhythmically, and with our tongues made an allusion to tonguing each other's clitorises (hereinafter abbreviated 'clit'), teasing in and out, building subtly in force until our tongues were deep inside each other's mouths, pushing strongly as we do at the end of cunnilingus when one of us is about to come. I slipped my hand down Teri's back and we kissed circling until I was squeezing her ass. Then as we broke away from our kiss, she lifted her pelvis, and I slipped my hand under until I reached her vagina. I like to have different 'techniques' or stages blend and overlap so that it's all very fluid. Teri wasn't really expecting my finger on her vagina entrance and was still reacting to the kiss. She smiled, and then closed her eyes and moaned deeply and loudly as I thrust my middle finger into her as far as it would go. She was so wet and tight that she came within thirty seconds, and we both laughed, surprised. She rolled around a little, straddling my thigh as she felt the 'contractions' that follow orgasm, and started sliding down me until her face was at my cunt. She pulled my cunt hair nearest my clit with her teeth, and I felt the heat of her breath warm my cunt, heat my whole body. I was moving back and forth, waiting for her tongue on me. She darted in little movements with her tongue on my clit until I begged her to 'eat' me, which she did marvelously. Sometimes I like very concentrated tonguing on a small area, depending on how excited I am. This time I wanted her to tongue me all over and around my clit, which she sensed without my saying. I gazed out my window, where the sun poured in and I could see trees, and felt beautiful. When I started 'losing it,' meaning the sexual feeling sometimes lessens after she starts eating me, I fantasized about her and other experiences we've had. I came, hard, moaning loudly as she kept her tongue on me. I came again and again, and the last time (as soon as I could move) I turned her over and went down on her passionately. I ate her fast and strong, and she came several times. Afterwards, we lay in each other's arms, stroking each other's bodies affectionately. We talked about our lovemaking, what parts we liked best, what new things we'd like to try. This heated us up, and we made love again.

"It was beautiful. It makes me realize again how attuned I am to Teri, that our lovemaking is just how I've always wanted to make love with someone. The right ingredients are there, and I know I probably can't make love with a woman without being strongly affected emotionally in a loving way. The emotional security is most important to me and that's why the rest can follow."

Here are some additional comments about the joys and problems of manual stimulation. One should remember that a small percentage of the respondents were negative to all aspects of mutual masturbation.

♀"Manual stimulation has always been the correct way to make love for me. It has always been the cleanest and most simple method for me. For a

very long time, I never thought of sex other than through manual stimulation, nor did I believe there was any other way.''

♀ "Our love life would be zilch without this. Both my lover and I really get off on manual stimulation of the clitoris. So far, neither one of us has had an orgasm any other way while together. I usually like to start manual stimulation when I feel my lover can't get any more aroused through kissing and caressing. If I start too soon, then it doesn't work as well.''

♀ "I prefer this above all. I find it easiest to do, have more control. I prefer doing it to my partner first as it is an energy spender and afterwards, I just prefer to lie next to my partner and rest awhile until she begins to do it to me. (By the way, I hate the term 'do it,' but that's all I can think of right now.)''

♀ "Internal manual stimulation I don't find particularly stimulating in itself, but I find it very satisfying in combination with oral stimulation, in instances when I want to feel my partner in me, or when I have the sensation of wanting to be filled up. I am stimulated by penetrating my partners as well, and some of the most exciting sexual experiences I have had have involved prolonged manual fucking of another woman. I think some of my pleasure comes from the power I feel while doing this. There is no denying that this is a significant part of it for me (unfortunately or not). I am turned on by rough sex to some extent anyway, and manual fucking is a great way to get into that if both partners are aware of what's going on. In some instances I have penetrated another woman anally with some pleasure, but I have never particularly enjoyed having this done to me.''

♀ "I enjoy this method best because I almost always orgasm and it allows my lover's head to be close to mine so we can kiss and look into each other's eyes, while being aroused. I also enjoy tremendously when she manually stimulates me while watching my clitoris and telling me about the genital changes during sex. My partner also enjoys manual stimulation and always orgasms, but she really prefers oral sex so I perform oral sex about three-quarters of the time since she prefers it, and I really enjoy doing it.''

♀ "Manual stimulation is better than cunnilingus when the clit is too sensitive for the tongue. It takes some time before a partner can learn the best ways to stimulate manually, so it gets better as time goes on.''

♀ "Manual stimulation is my preference. My body can be directed anywhere by this method, and offers me the most satisfaction. The worst drawback is that I can enjoy it for long periods of time, which makes it hard on my partner's wrist and fingers. Unfortunately, this is also my favorite method of making love, which usually isn't sufficient for others.''

♀ "I love manually stimulating someone. It gives me almost always an incredible feeling of closeness. With my lover it sometimes feels as though we are cosmically connected beyond our bodies. It sometimes gives me a feeling of oneness with her, an intensity beyond words.''

♀ "Being a drummer, I am able to play sixty-four notes with my fingers very lightly over her hole and on her clitoris. This gives her an orgasm all the time (vibrator effect).''

♀ "I like it, but my lover thinks it's inferior to other things, so we don't do it much."

♀ "A hand just doesn't compare to a warm wet mouth, but coming is nice in any form. Sometimes we'll stimulate each other manually for an additional orgasm after having had oral sex."

♀ "I don't care much for manual stimulation. I find it rather boring and something I'd rather reserve for masturbating. There are so many other things to do with another person. I don't think this is one of them. It leaves something to be desired and doesn't require the movement and complete body action I like. It's the general passivity and lack of movement I don't like about this. However, when I do it, I like for someone to do it sneakily, to slowly open my pants, and put her hand down. When I do it, I like to do it in the same way."

♀ "Manual stimulation feels very good, but I am seldom completely satisfied by this. I am more inclined to use and want external manual stimulation as a preliminary stimulation, or in conjunction with oral stimulation. The feeling of both fingers and tongue stimulating my entire genital area simultaneously is tremendously exciting. I feel as if I'm being taken from all sides."

♀ "I am not turned on by vaginal penetration, even by a woman's fingers. Even the anticipation of this tends to make me tense involuntarily."

Cunnilingus

Cunnilingus, also known as oral sex, "eating" or "eating out," and "going down," as well as other terms, was the second most prevalent form of sex between two lesbians. The lesbian respondents were asked, *On the average, how often do you engage in each of the following aspects of cunnilingus (oral sex, clitoral or vaginal)? Check one for each item.*

	ALWAYS	VERY FREQUENTLY	SOMEWHAT FREQUENTLY	SOMEWHAT INFREQUENTLY	VERY INFREQUENTLY	ONCE	NEVER
doing it to your partner	25	32	14	9	12	2	6%
having it done to you	22	34	16	10	11	2	5
you have an orgasm	31	29	11	6	7	2	15
your partner has an orgasm	29	35	10	6	5	2	14
simultaneous ("69")	3	5	9	16	32	13	22
orgasm during "69"	8	7	7	11	18	6	43

As with manual stimulation, most respondents felt positively about most aspects of oral sex. They were asked, *Whether or not you engage in any of the following aspects of oral sex, indicate how you feel about the idea of each of them.*

	VERY POSITIVE	SOMEWHAT POSITIVE	NEUTRAL	SOMEWHAT NEGATIVE	VERY NEGATIVE	NOT SURE
doing it to your partner	74	14	3	6	3	1%
having it done to you	79	11	6	2	2	0
you have an orgasm	85	7	5	1	2	0
your partner has an orgasm	86	8	3	1	1	1
simultaneous ("69")	42	23	18	10	3	3
orgasm during "69"	54	14	19	4	3	6

Several observations can be made from the statistics in these charts. First, even though oral sex was a bit less popular than manual stimulation, still a large majority (70-72%) gave or received oral sex on a frequent basis. Also, a large majority of lesbians (71-74%) were able to achieve orgasm in this fashion most of the time. Simultaneous oral sex was neither as frequent nor as popular as nonsimultaneous oral sex, maybe because it resulted in orgasm for only 22% on a frequent basis. Many women stated that simultaneous oral sex is confusing. In any case, here are some pleasing sexual experiences in which oral sex is the primary method for achieving orgasm.

♀"We started off drinking wine together and talking. We hadn't seen each other for a week, so there was a lot to say. We were sitting on her bed, and as we ran out of things to say, we began kissing and hugging, long deep kisses, stroking each other's clothed bodies with our hands, and pressing together, rubbing my thigh gently around her clitoral area. We got more excited and reached under each other's clothes, and quickly took them all off. I felt warm and calm for a moment as we hugged and felt two excited bodies coming together, skin to skin. We kissed more and stroked each other's backs, buttocks, legs; we kissed each other's necks and shoulders, and our hands were playing around the buttocks and thighs. We each moved our legs apart and were fingering each other's vulva, playfully, reaching for the clitoris. I moved on top of her, my leg rubbing roughly against her vulva, and she lifted her leg a little so that she could rub against me as I moved forward and back. All this time we were kissing, deep soul kisses, and I was licking her ear, or sucking the skin on her neck and shoulders. I stroked her strongly with my hand, from her leg all the way up

her front. After a while I came off her and used my fingers to stimulate her more. Her vulva was wet then, and I let my fingers run around in it, feeling the slight stinging where I had cut myself. I found her clitoris and flicked my fingers over it, while kissing her breasts, sucking her nipples, sinking my face into her stomach. I kissed her pubic hair, and the tops of her thighs, playing around with my tongue, and gradually approached her vulva. I licked her lips and slowly licked her clitoris. She gave a little jerk, so I knew I'd arrived. Slowly I moved my tongue around, getting used to the warm wet feel and the taste of her. I began to quicken, my tongue giving varied short strokes instead of long straight ones. My favorite is to flick it from side to side very quickly. Now my fingers were exploring too, finding her vagina and entering her, moving around inside, feeling the tip of her cervix and the walls of the vagina. She was responding, moving her pelvis round and round as my tongue went back and forth and my fingers went in and out. With each thrust I felt her anus, and my little finger entered her gently there. As she got nearer to orgasm, I took my fingers out and buried my face in her vulva, all wet and sticky, and moved with her, holding onto her legs (none of the rest of me was in contact with her body) and licking and sucking all over. We were both moving strong and fast; my tongue went into her vagina, then back to her clitoris, then back again to the vagina, and I didn't let up until she came. Then all was quiet, and I kissed her clitoris and her lips and her buttocks and thighs all over many times. At length I rested my head on her stomach and lay still.''

♀"I'm in the large, light-green tile shower at my lover's house. It's summer in Hollywood. There's a thick breeze through palm trees postcard-framed by the bathroom window. It's morning, and I'm up before she is, feeling content. At the beginning of my second chorus of 'Your Cheatin' Heart,' she opens the shower door, her long, black hair wound up in a towel on top of her head, howling along with me (she is tone-deaf and not ashamed of it). She steps in with an offer to soap my back, which she proceeds to do, slowly and with her hands. I gently back her up against the shower wall, and we rub our slick bodies together. I get my hands soapy and pass them firmly up and down her thighs (and around to her butt as far as I can reach from our back-to-front position) and between her legs. Her arms encircle me, and she strokes one nipple with each hand. We both emit slow moans, and an occasional, 'I love you.' 'Oh ya?' the other responds, which exchange is ended by more fervent soapy strokes. I turn around and take her face in my hands. She takes my lower back in hers, and we French-kiss. I run my tongue from below her ear to her breast and encircle her nipple with it. We kiss again. She puts her tongue in my ear and slides one thigh between my legs and into my crotch. She lifts my hair from my shoulders and runs her tongue along my neck, where her mouth settles (her face settles) as our fingers find each other's clitorises from behind. We continue, with variations in kissing, until the hot water runs out. We turn the water off, and I reel back around facing her and take one of her breasts in my mouth as my hands press her to me. I kneel and slide one hand up inside her thigh

to her vaginal area, which I caress, and then find her clitoris by gentle exploration with my tongue. I do that for a while. It gets cold there in the shower, so we get out and dry each other off. As I sit on the edge of the bathtub, she unexpectedly kneels on the rug and quickly brings me to orgasm with her tongue.''

♀ "It was late summer, very hot and dry. Toward evening we went to visit a friend we hadn't seen in several months. Upon arriving at our friend's new house, we were amazed at the plushness of it: thick carpeting in soft brown and rust shades, enormous rooms, gold and green velvet curtains, heavy, polished furniture, exquisitely framed photographs, lighting that gave a soft glow to everything.

"It was past dinnertime but not yet dark (it being summer in Phoenix). I guess you could say it was almost dusk. We decided to go for a swim. The pool was huge, and the water not at all chilly. Our friend said it was okay to swim nude, since no one was expected home and the neighbors could not see over the fence. We all three played in the water awhile, diving, somersaulting, racing. Then our friend had to answer the ringing telephone. My lover was floating on one of those plastic rafts made for pool lounging. I swam over and kissed her. There was something special about that kiss—the water, the time of day, the incense, the happiness, the sensuous surroundings—all combined to make it electrifying and urgent. I pulled her off the raft and held her with my arms in the water, kissing her mouth, neck, ears, and tits. I moved to the steps and put one knee up to support her ass and with my free hand started massaging her clit while she kissed and sucked my tits. Right then our friend came back outside, having finished with her phone call. My lover and I nearly drowned in our haste to pull apart before our friend saw what was going on. But we were both incredibly turned on, and were both trying to think of a way to get rid of our friend for a while. We didn't want to leave, as we still wanted to visit with her, and besides we'd just got there. We just wanted her to disappear for a while. Instead, she came and sat at the edge of the pool and dangled her legs in. My lover, having much better manners than I do, got out and sat beside her and talked with her. I amused myself by swimming back and forth across the pool, touching and teasing my own clit when I was sure they couldn't see me, and swimming underwater to my lover and sucking on her toes for a second before popping up and splashing them both. Once when our friend went inside to get us all something to drink, I popped up from the water right in front of my lover, pushed her knees apart and started licking and sucking her cunt—in and out of her vagina, back to her clit, a nibble on the tender inside thigh, back again, etc., etc. My lover, leaning back on her arms, was scared to death we'd be caught, but just couldn't bring herself to tell me to stop. When I heard the sliding glass door open, I stopped and dove back underwater, leaving my lover to deal with it as best she could. I don't think our friend saw us, because it was almost dark by then. In fact, it had started to get chilly, so we decided to go inside. We didn't dress, as it was a novelty to be nude, and we all wanted to sit nude on the soft, fuzzy couches and

chairs. I think our friend knew something was up by then, as my lover and I could hardly keep our hands off each other and our longing looks were evident. We were careful not to touch any place that would be too intimate in front of someone else—not wanting to embarrass our friend or ourselves. We sat on a couch, each with an arm around the other, and there was plenty of 'accidental' touching—a nipple grazed my arm, fingers caressed my thigh, a soft tit crushed against my side, a whisper of lips on my shoulder. Once, I leaned across my lover to get something from the end table on the other side of her, and my mouth was inches away from her cunt. The smell was overwhelming and I hesitated, wondering what my lover's and our friend's reaction would be if I leaned a little farther and simply kissed the triangle of hair showing. My lover obviously knew what was going through my head, as she very casually, not missing a step of the conversation, covered herself with her hand, thereby letting me know it would not be a good thing to do. Our friend kept getting up and leaving the room (she *must* have been aware of all that sexual energy and the fact that we were both preoccupied with each other), and every time she left the room I would frantically rush my fingers to my lover's cunt, and she to mine. And we would just as frantically pull apart at the very last possible second before our friend returned. Finally our friend went off to take a shower, and I moved to the floor and sitting between my lover's legs, kissed and sucked and fingered and licked her cunt, and she came and came and came. (And we hoped no one would notice the wet spot on the edge of the couch!) Our friend appeared before my lover had a chance to return my treatment. We all decided to go to the bar and go dancing for a while. I spent about two hours trying, in every possible moment, to touch my lover in as many places as possible. *Finally* we went home, where my lover and I had a mutual, uninterrupted lovemaking night that lasted for hours.''

♀ ''If we make love on a weekend when we're both off the next day, I like to take a little speed and drink wine beforehand. It heightens our sensations and lengthens the time we spend making love with each other. We'll share a bottle of wine, and this loosens us up because I'm a little inhibited about my body (old Catholics die hard). In bed we'll lie naked against each other, and I'll put my knee between her legs, lightly touching her pubic hair. I'll put my tongue in her mouth, doing everything slowly, then lightly suck her tongue, her lower lip, kiss her face and neck. We'll do this for a long time, and all the while we'll stroke each other—back, arms, sides. I'll touch her breasts, press them softly, then kiss my way down to them. I love to suck her breasts and rub my tongue over her nipples. She likes it when I flick my tongue rapidly back and forth across her nipples. At this point she usually begins to breathe hard, and I press my knee up against her crotch firmly—she's all wet and slippery by now, and that first touch of her clitoris is a real rush. She holds her breath a moment and holds me tight against her—God, she feels so good, so soft and wet and warm. With my hand I barely touch her down there, and she opens her legs, and the lips are parted. I slide my hand lightly across her vulva. She moans, and I slide down between her legs. I

kiss and lick her belly and her thighs, biting them lightly. I like to nuzzle the hair between her legs and move my lips against her vagina and kiss and lick her there. She's very aroused and presses against my mouth and begins to move her whole body in a sort of rhythm. I know she doesn't want to wait much longer. I form my lips in an O around her clitoris and suck. If she pushes against me, she wants me to do it harder. Sometimes I'll move my head in a circular motion, pressing the softest part of my lips against her clitoris, and sometimes I use the flat part of my tongue. Once we begin a rhythm we don't break it. I apply more and more pressure with my mouth until she comes, and when she does I feel a rush too—not genital, but an emotional rush. When she orgasms, she moans loudly and shudders, and at that moment I grip her buttocks tightly. And then we both sort of melt. I lay my head there between her legs and against her crotch, and we just lie very still there a moment, and then I kiss her wet, soft genitals and climb up to her embrace. We hold each other very tightly and very still at this moment. I feel such wholeness with her at this time. It's very emotional and sometimes we even cry—a happy crying. I love her so much, and at this moment when we're holding each other I feel suspended in time and space.''

♀ "We lay on top of each other kissing deeply and stroking each other. Then I started to touch her breasts—softly enveloping my hand around the roundness of her, then focusing on stimulating her nipple. I became more excited and moved my lower body on top of her. After a while I needed to suck her breasts and to gently stroke the outside of her vagina. I love to nestle my head between her breasts, whispering, 'I love you,' and moaning. I was kissing her chest and touching her vagina with my index finger, moving it from the lips of her vagina up to her clitoris and slowly back down to the opening of her vagina. I put some of my weight on my knees so that she too could rub my vaginal area and kiss my breasts. I felt warm, wonderful, and full, and could feel those feelings from her. We sensed that we were both very excited. I was almost dizzy. She moved her lower body up to my head and moved her head down to my vagina. She was on top of me with her stomach down. I was under her on my back.

"I nestled my face into her vagina, holding my hands on her buttocks, stroking her from waist to ass. She was licking my vagina, moving her tongue back and forth over my clitoris. I love to smell her vagina, and started to blow it gently, and to move my index finger up and down over her clitoris—very gently—like a tickle. She was hot and wet—I put my finger into her vagina and moved it out to her clitoris. She moaned. I put my finger deep into her vagina, and began to lick her clitoris—soft at first and then harder. Her clitoris hardened under my tongue. Simultaneously her vagina began to pulsate, and her clitoris moved back and forth as she came. She moaned and moved her body away from my tongue. I withdrew my finger, held her tightly with my arms around her buttocks and kissed her thighs.

"She began to stimulate my clitoris. I would get very high and move fast—bringing her head up and down between my legs. Then I would slow

down and relax—then I would move again and get higher. After a while, I asked her to put her finger inside me. I immediately began to push down on it as she continued to suck at my clitoris. I felt very excited and stayed at that level until I finally let go and broke through to orgasm. Once I came, I wanted her finger to remain inside me, and her lips to stay at my clitoris. We lay like that for a while. Then she moved around to be on top of me, but head to head. We hugged and kissed—the smell of sex all over the both of us. We lay like that together, feeling warm and close and then became excited again. We kissed passionately and moved all over each other rhythmically. Then I felt I wanted to make love to her again. I got up on top of her, kissed her breasts, and then sucked one while touching the other. After a few minutes I stroked her stomach and lightly kissed her all over her stomach, thighs, between her legs. I then got down to her vagina and licked her labia, played with her pubic hair with my fingers and tongue. Then I licked and sucked her clitoris while stroking the rest of her vagina with my finger. She came immediately. I could feel the pulsations and contractions throughout her body. She opened up her arms to me, and I moved up to be cuddled and kissed by her. We lay quietly for a while, and then we both started kissing and hugging each other. She began to kiss my ears, neck, breasts, and moved her head down to my vagina. She pressed against me with her palm, causing me to press the lower part of my body against her hand. I felt dizzy again. She took her index finger and moved my pubic hair to either side of my vagina. Then she moved her whole body down away from my head and torso and down between my legs. She looked at my vagina for a while and then started to stimulate it with her tongue. I moved my body back and forth against her head. My stomach filled up with warmth. I began to move faster and faster as my whole body tensed. I came and felt like a 'poof' of warm sensual liquid had exploded through my body filling every one of my cells with a tingly feeling and a smile. She moved back up into my arms. We stroked each other's heads, chests, arms, smiled at each other before we dropped off to sleep.''

The following are some additional experiences, and feelings about cunnilingus:

♀''I love going down on my lover. She is so vulnerable and trusting and womanly then. I love it when she asks me to go down on her. The anticipation as I slowly go down on her body is so exciting.''

♀''I love to have this done to me because somehow it is given to *me* for *my* pleasure. It excites me to just think about having it. Physically it's always perfect, and I always reach a long, soft, strong orgasm. (This sounds like a tissue commercial!) I can't imagine it as a pleasure for the one doing it. I will eat my lover because I want her to experience this intense pleasure, not because the act itself excites me. It's the one sexual act I always desired and took years to get the courage to do—or let it be done.''

♀''I love what I have heard men refer to as 'pussy farts.' If a woman's

cunt passes air while I am performing cunnilingus on her, I feel that she is relaxed and enjoying it and this excites me *very much*."

♀"Cunnilingus by far is the most exciting experience for a woman. Women can do it much better than men, simply out of perseverance."

♀"I love to drink another woman, to feel her skin and muscles contract, her wetness change. I like to touch the inside of her vagina with my tongue, and little else in this world has so much meaning for me. Until I made love with another woman this way, I truly did not know what 'making love' meant. I especially like the time, long before orgasm, when I feel free to roam about and smell and taste and bite and know her."

♀"I love the feeling of the clitoris becoming hard in my mouth, and I like to feel her thighs become tensed. Oral sex is very fine!"

♀"Cunnilingus is one of the most beautiful sexual experiences. It feels gentle, loving, and irresistibly orgiastic."

♀"I usually like to stimulate my lover's genitals with light strokes, staying on her clitoris a bit longer than on the other areas. I kiss her genitals as if I were kissing her face, and then I use a sucking motion all over. As I concentrate on stimulating her clitoris and she reaches for my hair, I become as stimulated as if she were going down on me. Many times when she is performing cunnilingus on me I get an insatiable urge in my mouth to do it to her, so I tell her to turn around so that we can both do it. In a 69 position, it feels as if I were going down on myself."

♀"I am quite turned on by oral sex, both giving and receiving. I think this is the most intimate way women can make love with one another. The feel of my mouth on another woman's genitals is very sensuous, the wetness and feeling her harden as she becomes excited. I like having another woman go down on me for the same reasons. I would also include rimming here. I love having it done to me, and I like doing this to my partner. The one thing I don't like about going down on someone or being gone down on is that there is relatively little upper body contact when orgasm occurs. (And although 69 is very pleasurable, I don't seem to have the dual concentration necessary to reach orgasm.) Sometimes the situation has been resolved by having my partner get on top of me after I have had an orgasm through oral sex and rub her genitals or pubic bone against my genitals. Then often I can come several more times, and I am physically closer to her. I also like to do this to my partners—depending on how we are constructed, if it will work. But generally oral sex in all its variations is exciting and very satisfying to me."

♀"I enjoy the idea of having her wrap her legs around my head and her being able to see me making love to her. I like kissing and feel this is the ultimate kiss."

♀"When I am doing it to someone and am down on her, I feel warmth and glad and passionate. When she comes, I feel a sense of power and control. When she is down on me, I love the feeling, but I also feel lonely because she is between my legs and not beside me."

♀"Oral sex gives me the best orgasms. The mouth is capable of so much

more variety than the hands or other parts of the body—licking, sucking, flicking back and forth, up and down. It can produce air current—and it comes with a built-in source of lubrication. What more can you ask for?''

♀ "The idea of a woman lying between my legs, it's so erotic. Just the thought of it now makes me wet. The reality is mind-blowing.''

There were others who found either giving or receiving oral sex unpleasurable, and there were also those who found all aspects of oral sex dissatisfying.

♀ "Oral sex is okay—quite nice really, but not as a steady diet. It's sort of like butterscotch sundaes—too much and you'd get sick of it.''

♀ "I have *always* enjoyed performing orally on both men and women, but used to feel/be embarrassed to have it done to me, except when he/she really enjoyed it. I felt too slow in reaching orgasm. My current partner has done more to relax me in bed so I enjoy it and my own reactions more than with anyone else in the twenty-four years of active (more or less) genital sex that preceded this partner.''

♀ "I like this though I never get off on it enough to have an orgasm. The person who is my sex partner doesn't like it and won't even let me do it to her. So I don't experience it.''

♀ "I've had it performed on me twice. It's a neat feeling, but I don't like to climax that way because it means I can't have my arms around my partner. I've never done it to anyone else and the thought of it still repels me.''

♀ "I do not really like oral sex. I do not like the smells of unwashed genitals, either mine or my lover's. Clean genitals are not unpleasant and on occasion we have oral sex, but these are special times. My lover is usually the initiator, and I am the recipient. If I am relaxed, I enjoy it. And if the mood is right, I am the initiator.''

♀ "I am sometimes more reluctant to do this to my partner than to have it done. However, it's more the anticipation than the actual doing that gives me a problem. Once I am into the act of using my tongue on her and sucking her, I really like to do it.''

♀ "I have a hard time performing oral sex for several reasons. I love the taste and smell and warmth, but can't get past the pubic hairs. They make me gag and panic to get them out of my mouth. Twice it caused me to throw up. I'm still trying to find a way around this. Also my first lover had a hangup about her body and was ashamed for me to perform oral sex on her. One of the few times I tried, she fell asleep on me; the other time, my husband walked in on us. All in all, I've had pretty bad luck with it and will probably avoid it unless it's important to my lover. I very much enjoy having it performed on me, but hate to take without giving in return.''

♀ "Giving someone else pleasure through cunnilingus is cool (a mildly positive feeling), but I ran into the same problem with it that I did with fellatio: After a while, I feel like my throat is closing up and like I can barely

breathe. I had thought it was from having a long prick crammed down my throat but obviously it's not from the fullness since I get the same feeling from cunnilingus. What a thought to have in the middle of making love: 'Oh my god, I'm going to suffocate to death at somebody's crotch!' Great.''

♀"I am not into oral sex. I still get uncomfortable with the idea of my mouth tasting vaginal juices. The idea of sex being dirty is fading for me, though.''

♀"I have *never* done *oral sex* or *analingus* and probably will never be able to bring myself to do them, no matter how I loved my partner. These two acts are repulsive to me.''

There is a further discussion of oral sex in Chapter 16 where those women who listed the inability to perform oral sex as a "hangup" discuss their feelings and experiences.

Tribadism

Although tribadism (rubbing one's genitals against some part of one's partner's body) was also practiced frequently by a large majority of lesbian respondents, it was the least popular of the three primary methods for having an orgasm in lesbian sexual experience. The lesbian participants were asked, *How often do you engage in any of the following aspects of tribadism?*

	ALWAYS	VERY FREQUENTLY	SOMEWHAT FREQUENTLY	SOMEWHAT INFREQUENTLY	VERY INFREQUENTLY	ONCE	NEVER
lying on top of partner	15	36	26	10	8	0	5%
partner lies on top of you	13	35	23	16	9	0	5
rub against each other's thighs	19	30	23	10	10	1	7
you rub on partner's pelvic bone	8	20	17	17	19	1	19
partner rubs on your pelvic bone	8	19	18	19	18	2	17
you rub on partner's pubic bone	11	23	20	18	14	1	13
partner rubs on your pubic bone	9	21	22	20	14	2	11
rub clitoral areas together	9	13	15	20	21	4	18
other (specify)	8	20	12	0	0	4	56
any of these to the point of orgasm	10	18	8	11	16	7	30

As with the previous acts described in this chapter, most of the lesbian participants felt positively towards tribadism. We asked, *Whether or not you engage in any of the following aspects of tribadism (rubbing), indicate how you feel about the idea of each of them.*

	VERY POSITIVE	SOMEWHAT POSITIVE	NEUTRAL	SOMEWHAT NEGATIVE	VERY NEGATIVE	NOT SURE
lying on top of partner	70	22	4	3	1	0%
partner lies on top of you	69	23	4	3	1	0
rub against each other's thighs	64	20	13	2	1	0
you rub on partner's pelvic bone	51	19	22	5	2	1
partner rubs on your pelvic bone	53	21	20	3	2	1
you rub on partner's pubic bone	54	25	17	2	1	1
partner rubs on your pubic bone	56	23	15	3	1	1
rub clitoral areas together	59	21	16	2	1	1
other (specify)	36	20	28	0	8	8
any of these to the point of orgasm	70	14	11	1	2	3

Again, several statements can be made about these statistics. It should be pointed out that over 10% of the subsample checked "other" for both parts of this question. Other parts of the body which lesbians mentioned rubbing against are: all over, buttocks, back, legs, front, breasts, knees, arms, and elbows. One might also say that the first three categories—either lying on top of one's partner or under one's partner while rubbing against the partner's thighs—were by far the most popular methods on a frequent basis. Even though orgasm was achieved through tribadism only a little over a third of the time with any frequency, the method was still popular and almost all lesbians felt positively or neutral about rubbing genitals against a partner. The authors did not receive many answers in which orgasm by means of rubbing constituted the most pleasing sexual experience; however, tribadism was often part of a pleasing experience in which orgasm was achieved by one of the two methods previously discussed in this chapter. In any event, here are a few pleasing experiences in which orgasm is obtained by tribadism:

♀ We sit on the bed and begin to take off each other's clothes, slowly and sensuously. I am more aggressive about this than she is, meaning that I usually initiate this process, and carry it through from start to finish. Then I take off whatever of my own clothes she hasn't already taken off. I kiss her a lot, laying her gently down on the bed on her back. She is hugging me, and

I kiss her and stroke her body, which is now naked (except for maybe socks which we always laugh at forgetting to take off). We rock back and forth, me on top, or half on top, rhythmically moving, which turns us both on. I rub her breasts and finger her nipples until they are erect. Then I touch her clitoris and go a ways inside her vagina, then out again and rub my hand around her ass and inside of her thighs. Then she touches me, usually sucks my nipples, and kisses me. Then I lie on top of her, with my Venus mound just below hers, putting pressure on her genital area. I move, up, down, around, pushing against her, and meanwhile stroking her body and kissing her neck or mouth. She likes me to kiss her hard as she gets close to orgasm. She moans, with her eyes closed (that turns me on a lot). Usually it doesn't take very long for her to come. She has one long orgasm; then it's my turn. A common way she makes love to me is to stroke my breasts and legs, and then when I'm turned on, she performs cunnilingus while lying on top of me, so I grab her ass and press it against me while she is licking my clit. We move back and forth, again in rhythm.

"Generally, we both like gentleness, with a little more rough pushing, as we get closer to coming. We like privacy, and dark or light—it doesn't matter. We make love in so many different ways that describing one common way seems inadequate. I would say that lesbian sexuality for me, as opposed to hetero sex, which I experienced plenty of before I came out, is slower, more sexy, sensuous, varied. Both my lover and I like just about everything. We both prefer to come with the other person applying some pressure on top of our bodies, though we can both come ourselves being on top of the other. Usually we take about one half to one hour."

♀ "She and I had gone to bed tired after such a hectic day. We wound up around each other, sheltered from the cold February night. Her back and bottom were pressed against my breasts and legs respectively. My arms were under her neck and waist. Lazily rolling herself over, she stroked my hair. We lightly touched lips to cheeks, noses, and then our lips and our tongues together. I moaned lightly, feeling turned on, feeling exhausted. We lay there not moving. My eyes and mind slowly moved open and shut, drowsing and smelling her next to me. Hooking onto the inevitable, I touched the inside of her thigh and my fingertips played lightly on her and felt her respond and stir in my arms. She took my face in her hands and rolled toward me, looked at me, and kissed me while playing with my hair. My hand, which had been tucked between her thighs, moved to grab her ass as we kissed deep and long. My clitoris made herself known. Her hand seemed aware too. She stroked lightly, a finger or two bringing moistness from cunt to clitoris. My body went electric, pressing close to hers and feeling delicious with and for her, and me too. At some point I pulled her onto me. We lay there with our lips, legs, fingers, together like one entity. I moved my leg between hers and began moving to stimulate her, and her leg provided the same for me. We moved as if in a trance. This lovemaking was new to both of us. The spontaneous, adventuresome, almost sleepy quality turned it into a long, languorous, and mystical transcendent closeness we

had not experienced before. I have experienced that kind of 'delicious sex' before, although perhaps not so completely. She felt like a part of me, me of her. Coming did not feel important or even imminent until it happened. More, the feeling of warmth, both physically, emotionally, and the completeness within the experience were overwhelming.''

Here are some more comments, experiences, and feelings about rubbing:

♀ "Many times after orally stimulating my lover's genitals, we engage in tribadism. We don't have much trouble positioning ourselves. I rub my nipple over her genitals and press my breast over them to feel the warm moisture. She does the same to me, and it feels great.''

♀ "I enjoy the feeling of a woman of about my same size and weight lying on top of me. I enjoy the feeling of weight and pressure as our bodies press together. It is not as good if I am the one on top. I also enjoy the feeling of my lover's knee or upper leg pressed into my crotch.''

♀ "My lover is very fond of this and likes to lie on top of me in the heterosexual missionary position and have me rub my pussy against hers. She usually reaches orgasm in this manner. I do not. However, I enjoy the act, probably because of the pleasure she derives.''

♀ "I have brought a lady to climax by stimulating her with my breast bone. I have also experienced a lady using her head between my legs as stimulation. Another friend loves to ride my pelvis. Stimulation can be accomplished with many different parts of the body.''

♀ "For a long time, I didn't do much of this. Lately, I have been doing it more. I used to feel shy about it because it seemed kind of aggressive and selfish, but as I've gotten more comfortable about my sexuality, I've started to do this more and like it a lot. One thing I've discovered is that the longer I have been in a lesbian relationship, the more I learn that I have more and different desires. I think when I was a heterosexual, I hardly ever asked myself how I wanted things to be and so now I am only just learning gradually. The things that made me shy about rubbing myself against her were that I was active in seeking sexual pleasure while she was just there, while cunnilingus, kissing, touching, etc., seemed more mutual because one person was actively creating sexual pleasure for the other. But now I am getting more comfortable with bigger variations on both our parts about activity and passivity and alternating.''

♀ "I love being as near to my lover as often as I can and in this way we almost become one.''

♀ "I love it. The complete (or almost complete) body contact, the face-to-face communication, and the mutuality make it, really, my favorite mode of sex. And it's handy. You really don't have to take your clothes off, although it is better if you do. I've worn through perfectly good jeans, not to mention knees, on the rough gravel by railroad tracks at the full moon,

embarrassed relatives in the kitchen, have embarrassed drive-in movie goers, and if the Goddess wills, I'll collapse my deathbed before I go. I'm usually active, but I don't have anything against being passive. The best part is seeing my lover's breasts hanging free.''

♀ "Tribadism is one of my favorite acts. I like the movement, the sub-missiveness and dominance that can take place. I especially like to 'play' where I'll throw my partner on the bed or vice-versa and jump on top of her and begin pumping. It is nice when my partner plays a very innocent, un-willing role, saying, 'No, please don't,' and fights me somewhat by moving from side to side. It can make me feel very overpowering at times, and I enjoy it.''

♀ "Tribadism and manual stimulation are fine and exciting, but ultimately rougher than I like.''

♀ "I like to be on top like a man would be and fantasize that I am a man, but so does my lover, so there is a little bit of a conflict here.''

♀ "I love the feeling of tribadism. I get very excited very easily and sometimes come quickly. I sometimes feel embarrassed about this because my partner rarely comes during tribadism. In a sense I feel most vulnerable when I get so excited in this way, yet I also think that on some level I must be afraid that I'd better come now because I won't be able to later when we are more intimate with each other.''

♀ "When she lies on top of me, our bodies seem to be like perfectly matched pieces of a puzzle. Our genitals touch, our entire bodies are in contact. Energy flows between us. It's absolutely the closest we can get.''

♀ "I had never come into contact with this until meeting my current lover. She comes by lying over my thigh and pressing her clitoris against me. I can't come that way at all, and I'm very envious, since she has no trouble and can come almost instantly when she wants to. The best part about it is that we can embrace each other and kiss and caress while we make love. I enjoy the feeling of her whole body against me and the rhythm of our movements. If I could come the same way, it would be great.''

♀ "I used to orgasm with my lover by having her thigh between my leg while I was making love to her, but she felt deprived of making love to me so I stopped doing it. When I was younger—before I 'came out'—this was the only way I'd orgasm with men. Both of us with our clothes on—him on top, of course.''

♀ "I haven't really tried this as far as rubbing clitorises together, although my roommate has and is always raving that my other roommate and I should learn. But it sounds fantastic, and I will eventually learn, I'm sure—really I can't wait.''

♀ "Rubbing our genitals together is stimulating, and a pleasant feeling, but I find it impossible to reach orgasm this way.''

♀ "Tribadism is somewhat boring to me. I've done it a little, nearly always along with other methods. I once had an orgasm that way. It mostly reminds me of being a teenager and getting a cheap thrill without being

touched or touching with the hands. I've done it dancing in gay bars when I've had a little too much to drink, but seems silly in private where so much else is possible.''

♀"My lover and I just aren't built for this. We tried once for twenty minutes to get together and wound up laughing hysterically at the positions we were getting ourselves into.''

♀"I've never really tried it, and I doubt if it would work for me, and especially for my partner. I have no desire to try it.''

It is ironic in a way that tribadism among lesbians as a primary form of sexual expression was the least popular of the three discussed in this chapter, since historically tribadism was almost synonymous with lesbianism. In fact, the word "tribade" means "lesbian," although this word has gone out of fashion. The word has indeed become so removed from lesbian experience that when trying the questionnaire out on test groups, the authors discovered that few lesbians recognized the word by itself, although most knew what the act was after it had been described and said they had done it.

Oral sex (whether heterosexual or homosexual) is a rather recent development in society on a popular basis. Part of the increase may be due to a general increase in bathing and cleanliness, the latter factor being one which many lesbians mentioned in deciding whether or not to perform oral sex. Or oral sex may merely be a matter of changing fashion or greater awareness of possibilities.

The authors did not do cross-correlations between age and sex acts because we did not feel that there would be space to analyze such data in this book, but a look at the questionnaires indicated that oral sex was more prevalent among younger women and tribadism was more prevalent among older women, although some younger women did tribadism and some older women performed oral sex. There were no strict divisions, but one 82-year-old respondent explained it in this way:

♀"I was a bit surprised myself at how scarce my sexual *activity* had been, when it seems to me I've spent my life (before seventy, let's say) perpetually *in love*. I have also limited my methods of sexual expression to comparatively few, certainly without protest from my partners. Perhaps my enthusiasm made up for my lack of gymnastics? I honestly *did* mark every microscopic square of my questionnaire—as long as they were all the *truth*! Sorry if it looked so barren, but 'my generation' was comparatively restrained in what they let themselves do—no cunnilingus for example or '69.' But what we *did do*, we did *con amore!* (*And* I had a very fair number of partners too!) I hope I don't skimp your statistics. Good luck with the enterprise. I hope I see the results. No matter what it costs, I'll pay up gladly!''

Kissing

No matter what technique was used to obtain orgasm, almost all lesbians were enthusiastic about kissing as an important component of a pleasing sexual experience (or important for affection too, without necessarily having sex). Participants were asked, *On the average, how often do you engage in the following aspects of kissing?*

	ALWAYS	VERY FREQUENTLY	SOMEWHAT FREQUENTLY	SOMEWHAT INFREQUENTLY	VERY INFREQUENTLY	ONCE	NEVER
kiss on lips only	39	28	9	8	12	0	4%
get kissed on lips only	37	28	10	8	14	0	3
soul kiss (deep kiss, French kiss)	49	33	10	3	3	1	1
partner soul kisses you	47	32	11	4	3	1	1
you refuse to kiss partner	0	1	2	3	23	2	68
partner refuses to kiss you	0	1	3	1	22	5	68

The respondents were also asked, *Whether or not you engage in the following aspects of kissing, indicate how you feel about the idea of each of them.*

	VERY POSITIVE	SOMEWHAT POSITIVE	NEUTRAL	SOMEWHAT NEGATIVE	VERY NEGATIVE	NOT SURE
kiss on lips only	67	13	8	5	8	0%
get kissed on lips only	66	13	9	4	8	0
soul kiss	89	7	1	2	0	1
partner soul kisses you	88	7	2	1	1	1
you refuse to kiss partner	4	2	5	12	69	8
partner refuses to kiss you	3	1	5	11	73	8

We all know from our own experience that lesbians love to kiss, and these statistics seem to back that up. The favorite form of kissing seems to be soul or French kissing with almost equal numbers kissing into the partner's mouth as being kissed in the mouth (so-called "active" and "passive"). One surprising figure is that a large number of lesbians have refused to kiss sex partners somewhat infrequently or their partners have refused to kiss them somewhat infrequently. One woman explained that she would not kiss someone when she had chapped lips or dental work. People also objected to bad breath. At the same time lesbians were overwhelmingly negative about the idea of refusing to kiss someone or being refused a kiss. But perhaps the refusal was based on some lesbians' only liking certain kinds of people or kisses, although almost everyone likes some form of kissing. Here are some experiences and feelings about kissing.

♀"I love kissing, from the lightest touching of lips together to the crushing, passionate French kisses. I also love to kiss my lover all around the face and neck, with a few soft-mouth bites or a flick of my tongue. I abhor being licked all over. One time a woman tried that, and I thought, 'Yech, if I wanted that, I'd get a dog.' Kissing is a very essential turn-on for me, and it's really important to me that my lover is a good kisser. The above-mentioned woman kissed me briefly once, and that was all. She just wanted sex, and that turned me off. I never saw her again."

♀"I like to kiss my partner all over the neck and shoulders and breasts. I *do* like 'soul-kissing,' especially if my partner has a small mouth and is aggressive with her tongue and lips. This is an area where I'd rather be passive than aggressive. I used to dislike soul-kissing exceedingly—too messy. I still don't enjoy it with men, which leads me to believe there is a large emotional component in my enjoyment of it. I always wipe my mouth afterwards, which has gotten to be quite a joke."

♀"I love kissing. I can get more out of kissing sometimes than 'coming,' 'completing the act,' etc. It's the most tender and personal of all sexual acts, I think. I usually am more afraid to kiss someone new than I am to go down on her because it is so tender and reveals a lot of deep feeling."

♀ "I enjoy feeling a woman above or beneath me—roughly, strongly, all motion, and deep breathing, deep kissing. It is powerful. I am almost afraid of that power. It is here in this way of making love that I am most confronted with my confusion about my true sexual politics—the confusion between power and sex—the hint of dominance and submission. Although I reject the heterosexist, capitalistic frame for love, I guess on some level there are strange connections between sex and power in me."

♀"Yeah! Keep kissing! I love kissing! Lips, lips, lips! Kiss and hug, kiss and hug! Smack your sweetie on the mug!"

♀ "We do this a lot, although it is not often of a real passionate nature when not connected with lovemaking. I am not real turned on by French kissing and don't concentrate on it too much as preliminary lovemaking."

♀ "Kissing is terrific. The mouth is so sensitive. It's a wonderful way to

touch and to be touched all over. I like it to be gentle; I don't care for lip-crushing kisses. I enjoy soul kissing very much also, but it must be active. I can't stand it when someone sticks their tongue in my mouth and just leaves it there.''

♀ "Kissing is one of my favorite things, and probably most sensuous. I like to get into French kissing slowly, with sudden, wild bursts of it. Then I like to just sort of half kiss—to take my partner's wet lips between mine and very lightly suck them. Then we just rub our wet lips together, sometimes lightly pressing our tongues between each other's lips.''

♀ "Kissing is my favorite thing. It feels very close to me, soft and wonderful. I could kiss for hours and have been extremely frustrated by women who aren't good kissers or who don't like to kiss. Once I became totally repulsed by a woman because she didn't kiss well. I like long, soft, passionate kisses. I like playing with tongues. I love to kiss and to be kissed. I kiss standing up, sitting, lying down—all the time.''

♀ "I used to get involved in all kinds of exotic tongue techniques, but I find that the emotions, the commitment, the love, and trust I feel for her make a kiss a moving experience. One night we were lying in bed after a long and exhausting day. I was lying against her shoulder while we talked in the dark. When I leaned over to kiss her goodnight, as our lips touched, it was like an electric current running between us. Our mouths were pressed together gently with just our tongue tips touching, and we stayed that way without moving for ages, while wave after wave of—what, emotion? love? arousal? I don't have a label—an intense awakened awareness with all senses receptive, but with no urgency to *do* anything but that—swept over both of us. If I could have stopped time at that moment, I would have done so.''

♀ "The majority of women I've been with are good kissers. They don't drool and slobber or mash your teeth or scratch your face with whisker stubble as men do.''

♀ "I hate a lot of tongue stuff—ugh. I like very soft repeated kisses—with mouth parted a little but tongue staying inside—or maybe touching the lips occasionally.''

Stimulation of Other Parts of the Body

In addition to stimulation of the lips and tongue in the act of kissing, the women liked to be stimulated in other areas for a completely satisfying sexual experience. After all, sex between two women does not merely consist of a kiss and then genital contact, as one can readily see from reading any of the experiences in this chapter. To determine which parts of the body were most important for a pleasing sexual experience, two questions were asked. The first was: *On the average, how important for your satisfaction is the stimulation of each of the following parts of your body by your partner?*

	VERY IMPORTANT	SOMEWHAT IMPORTANT	NEUTRAL	SOMEWHAT UNIMPORTANT	VERY UNIMPORTANT	NOT SURE
your clitoris	87	10	2	1	0	0%
your clitoral area	83	14	1	1	1	0
outer vaginal area	47	40	8	3	2	0
vagina	43	36	18	1	3	0
pubic bone, mons Veneris	18	38	26	8	9	1
breasts	55	31	8	4	2	1
ears, neck, toes	24	53	10	4	7	2
anus	5	20	21	8	41	4

The second question was: *On the average, how important for your satisfaction is it for you to stimulate each of the following parts of your partner's body?*

	VERY IMPORTANT	SOMEWHAT IMPORTANT	NEUTRAL	SOMEWHAT UNIMPORTANT	VERY UNIMPORTANT	NOT SURE
clitoris	81	16	1	1	1	0%
clitoral area	81	16	1	1	1	0
outer vaginal area	61	32	3	2	1	1
vagina	55	31	9	3	2	1
pubic bone, mons Veneris	28	29	27	8	8	1
breasts	67	28	4	1	0	0
ears, neck, toes	38	42	11	4	4	1
anus	11	14	22	8	40	5

A similar question asked: *How much does what you do to your partner "turn you on"?*

Quite a lot	78%
Some	19

Very little	2
None	0
Not sure	1

In almost all areas, except for the clitoris, the women felt that it is more important to stimulate parts of their partner's body than their own. This difference shows up in the "very important" column all the way down after the entry for "clitoris." Women felt it is important to stimulate all areas mentioned except the anus. Admitted, it was probably an error on the part of the authors to lump ears, neck, and toes together for space reasons, but women must have found at least one of these areas important because they were consistently checked. We also asked women for "other" areas they wanted stimulated or to be stimulated. These areas were not added to the computerized data, but some mentioned were: all over, nowhere, neck, shoulders, arms, hands, back, buttocks, stomach, thighs, calf, feet, knees, pelvis, nipples. Here are some comments.

♀ "I like to be generally massaged and like to touch or caress all over."

♀ "I get more satisfaction from stimulating my partner than being stimulated myself."

♀ "The clitoris is where it's at for me!"

♀ "I like to kiss and massage buttocks."

♀ "It's hard to break down into parts. I love/am attracted to her *entire* body."

♀ "Sensuality is very important to me, with or without sex. Stroking the whole body (giving and receiving) is more important than anything else, including orgasm."

♀ "I cannot be stimulated vaginally. I still have too much of a hymen."

♀ "The only thing that's important to my satisfaction is that I satisfy and/or 'turn my partner on.' "

♀ "It's really all in my head, and she has to do very little. *After* lovemaking, however, I like my body touched and stroked all over. Again, *after* I come, it's very important to touch my partner's body all over, but before and during it's very unimportant. I guess the foreplay really becomes unimportant."

Breasts

The fact that the clitoris was more important for stimulation than the vagina shows up in almost all of the satisfying sexual experiences. Vaginal stimulation was found with clitoral stimulation but rarely alone. Aside from these two areas, the most important area for stimulation was the breasts. When asked *how important the breasts are in looking for a sex partner,* the lesbians responded:

very important	11%
somewhat important	32
neutral	35

somewhat unimportant	12
very unimportant	8
not sure	1

Therefore, almost half believed that the size, shape, and feel of a partner's breast are very meaningful. When asked *how they felt about their own breasts,* the lesbians answered:

very positive	37%
somewhat positive	39
neutral	12
somewhat negative	8
very negative	3
not sure	0

One of the essay questions asked about breasts. Most lesbians were enthusiastic about having their breasts stimulated, and every type of breast seemed to have some aficionados. The women were also asked *to comment on the size, appearance, and feel of their own and others' breasts.*

♀ "My breasts are very soft—not your average heterosexual male turn-on. Small breasts are nice, and large ones are great to bury your face in and kiss or touch with your hands. I just like breasts in general, perhaps smaller ones a shade better."

♀ "I love breasts of all sizes and shapes. I have only recently come to this attitude, however. It has taken me a long time to accept my own breasts as 'normal' just because they are not the breasts of your usual late-blooming 17-year-old as portrayed by *Seventeen* magazine. My breasts are slightly more 'mature.' They sag a great deal, are somewhat flabby, change shape a lot depending on what position I'm in. This is normal, but I didn't know that for a very long time. Even now I'm still a little uneasy about my breasts, and I sometimes find myself wishing to be smaller and firmer. But then my girlfriend wishes she was more like me. I think we've all been brainwashed to be dissatisfied about our breasts. Another way for society to keep us from self-acceptance."

♀ "I love my breasts. I think they're beautiful. I would like to have sex with a woman whose breasts were small and firm like mine. I'd like to do to her breasts all the things I like having done to mine. But I have a strong dislike for large breasts, especially if they're floppy. They feel mushy to me and unresponsive."

♀ "I wish my breasts were bigger, just a bit, and have never gotten over the high school teasing prevalent in a patriarchal society that worships size and rewards women for physical appearance. I like my nipples a lot. Breast size isn't really important to me in others, but I do admit to having a preference for soft nipples that are rather puffy instead of huge and/or pointed."

♀ "I enjoy breasts. I like them semi-large. My first lover had small ones and was self-conscious of them. She rarely let me touch them. My second

lover had large ones and said they hurt when I caressed them (I was always gentle). My current lover has moderate-sized breasts, and we both enjoy each other's breasts. We are the same size almost.''

♀''I dislike the large size of my breasts. I don't much like other people's either. My current lover has okay ones, but we have both agreed the world would be better off without them.''

♀''I like the look and feel of my own breasts, except for the hair on them! On other women, I am very pleased with all shapes and feels of breasts. I really like small, roundish ones best, probably because my first lover was like that. I think one tends to fixate on first experiences.''

♀''I feel great about the size and appearance of my own breasts. I enjoy having my breasts sucked second most to having orgasm. I would prefer medium to large breasts on a lover and enjoy centering much of lovemaking around breasts.''

♀''I love breasts, especially my own. They are very sensitive, and I go crazy if someone rubs or kisses or especially sucks on them. I feel I come close to orgasm this way. I love feeling other breasts and kissing and sucking on nipples!''

♀''I am not what would be termed a 'breast person.' What I am trying to say is I really couldn't care less what my lover's breasts are like.''

♀''I like breasts a lot—big ones, small ones, firm ones, almost all breasts. My own don't seem as neat to me. Mine have hair around them, and that seems repulsive to me. I have a great deal of body and facial hair and have had some electrolysis treatments. My mother received male hormones as a treatment for acne when she was a teenager. She was 19 when I was born. I think I got some too. Anyway, I am trying to change my negative feeling about that being unfeminine and ugly, but it is difficult to change lifelong feelings.''

♀''I really love my breasts. My nipples stay erect most of the time, and the breasts themselves are not what I would call large, but are slightly above average. Call me a victim of this mammary-centered society. They are a very important erogenous zone, and I can have an orgasm when they are sucked. As it is, I very much enjoy any stimulation there, and look forward to nursing a daughter.

''My lover's are quite large, and it really turns me on. Her nipples are not as responsive as mine, but I call it a challenge. One thing I really like is for us to suck each other's breasts at the same time. This leads to cunnilingus usually. Also we like to surprise each other by taking off our bras—which we both wear because we need them—when the other isn't looking, and touching our bare breasts to the other's back or arm. This leads to confusion in the kitchen.''

♀''I do and always have felt badly about my breasts. I am a 34B, on the small side. I remember my mother trying to get me to wear padded bras, and then I wanted to wear them because I was ashamed of my size. I felt, and sometimes feel, like less of a woman. If there was one thing I'd change about myself, it'd be to increase my breast size. On other women I am very

turned on by larger breasts and get turned on by looking at gay or straight women's breasts, even under clothing. I am very attentive to my lover's breasts, which are large 36C. I recall even as a youngster being attracted to breasts and wanting to touch them.''

♀"I am not a breast person. I have double D breasts and have always been the recipient of 'compliments' from men about that part of my anatomy. I never felt it was any of my doing to be so endowed and never felt complimented by the comments. Fortunately, my lover is also well-endowed, and also doesn't see any particular value in large breasts, so for the first time, I don't feel that a piece of property caught me my lover.''

♀"I enjoy the feeling of another's breasts against mine. Erect nipples are beautiful. Besides sexual pleasure, breasts provide such comfort, warmth, security. No, I don't have a mother fixation. Wouldn't you rather lay your head on a pillow than a rock?''

♀"I prefer large breasts. Fat is very luxuriant. It has no purpose but warmth and sheer sensuality. One of my lovers has very soft, large breasts like a silk comforter stuffed with goosedown that belonged to my grandmother. Maybe it's the lust for the mother, or maybe for the mother-Goddess archetype, but I always feel blissfully safe and warm and childlike when snuggled up to sleep with my head on her breast.''

Breasts very often seemed to be a case of "the grass is always greener . . .'' Small-breasted women wanted large breasts and vice-versa. Maybe if women could trade for a week. . . .

Menstruation and Female Genitals

There are other factors which often affect sex. One of the main ones is menstruation. Again, there was division. Many women found their period a delight while others found it a bother. Some women found that menstruation interfered with sex and some found that they were more aroused during menstruation. In general, the lesbians seemed to be more positive about menstruation than heterosexual women. Part of this positive feeling was due to the fact that lesbians are much more positive in general about female genitals. After all, female genitals are the center of sexual pleasure for lesbians, and most lesbians haven't bought the myth of the mainstream culture that female genitals are "smelly,'' or "fishy,'' or unclean. To determine how lesbian respondents felt about female genitals, the participants were asked: *How do you feel about the following aspects of female genitals?*

	VERY POSITIVE	SOMEWHAT POSITIVE	NEUTRAL	SOMEWHAT NEGATIVE	VERY NEGATIVE	NOT SURE
smell of your own	52	27	12	7	2	1%
feel of your own	71	20	7.5	.5	.5	.5
appearance of your own	52	26	16	4	1	1
smell of others	50	31	9	7	1	3
feel of others	80	13	4	1	0	2
appearance of others	65	20	12	2	0	1
taste of others	54	24	9	6	2	5

As with breasts, the women were generally more positive about the feel and appearance of others' genitals, although they were only very slightly more positive about the smell of other women's genitals.

♀ I think women's genitals are really neat, especially the smell. It really turns me on when I have my lover's scent on my fingers and a plain old peanut-butter sandwich never tasted so good! I had a hard time learning to like my own genitals, but that was mainly because I didn't bother to look at them and find out what was where. I feel very positive about them now. I don't douche except after my period, nor do I use 'hygiene' sprays. I'm healthy so my vag takes care of itself. I was really excited when I got a speculum and saw a part of me that I had never seen before. I wrote one of my friends and told her about it. She probably thinks I'm losing my marbles or working too hard, but I don't care. I have a right to see my own cervix. I like the way I feel—my clitoris is a good size, so I can stimulate it easily. I like to pull gently on my labia minor and touch my perineum."

♀ "I had never felt so turned on toward a woman's genitals until my first woman lover. Now, just the thought of a moist, dripping pubic area is *very* erotic. I like my scent too."

♀ "I love the natural smell, salty taste, and smooth moist slippery feel. I never paid much attention to the appearance until I saw a special slide-show presentation by Bay Area artist Tee Corinne. She showed close-up color photos of the genitals of dozens of women. I was amazed at the infinite beauty and variety in size, shape and color. They were as individual as faces, but since we have no set social standards of beauty for women's genitals, all were equally beautiful."

♀"Female genitals have become central to me. I love the smell and taste of my own and others. I would love to use a little of both for my scrambled eggs every morning."

♀"I think women's genitals are very beautiful—they're like flowers and so delicate. They're too lovely to waste on men!"

♀"Learning to be 'cunt positive' was a difficult thing for me and probably many other women within our repressive society. The first time I went down on a woman I was afraid that I was doing it all wrong, that she would know I was doing it all wrong, or that I would throw up or burp or just do something dumb. My current lover and I made a concerted effort to learn about our cunts. We looked at them closely and asked each other how we felt about them. I read *Our Bodies, Ourselves* in order to learn more about my cunt. It was very good, down-to-earth, and very cunt-positive. Now I love cunts. My lover's is soft and fragrant. Her clit is beautiful, especially when she is excited, because it becomes very red and swollen. I enjoy the taste. I like my cunt. I dig licking my come off my lover's fingers or mouth and tasting myself."

♀"I think my own are great. My labia minora are more prominent than most wimmin's I've seen, and my clit is slightly larger. My cunt is a nice shade of maroon, and I do like it. I love the feel of my labia minora— they're like sponge almost, and very easy to feel because they sort of extend between my labia majora, like I suppose an African woman's might be— that is, a womon who had had them stimulated quite a bit. Only mine are natural and I'm mostly Caucasian anyway.

"I love the smell of wimmin, especially when aroused, and even just myself can turn me on. And of course I love other wimmin's cunts—I wouldn't be a dyke if I didn't. The smell and taste turn me on. I hate any kind of disguise of them. Wimmin's cunts are all so different. I enjoy the variety. I don't have any preferences, though. However, I had one lover who was almost childlike in that her cunt was very undeveloped, and I didn't like that—it was like making love to a kid, because she had very little pubic hair, and her clit was small and her labia minora were almost nonexistent."

♀"I think female genitals are enormously interesting in their complexity. They are wonderful to explore. Taste, smell, and feel are very pleasant to me. Cleanliness is *extremely* important in this. I *don't,* however, approve of the use of 'feminine deodorants.' I think they are unhealthy, unnecessary, and symptomatic of society's oppression of women and its trying to convince us that we are inferior and unpleasant in our sexuality (as well as other ways)."

♀"Sometimes I think my genitals look silly, and at other times I think they're astoundingly beautiful."

♀"I never hope to run across an apter image than that of Rita Mae Brown's *Rubyfruit Jungle.* There is a secret garden thrill about a woman's

genitals of which I gladly partake, as well as offer in love and friendship to some very special women. The smell, which men have variously compared to tuna fish and caviar, evokes in me lust rather than analogies.''

Some women were more neutral, or have mixed feelings or are even negative to female genitals.

♀ ''I'm not too crazy about smells yet, but I haven't had much chance to get used to them. I never liked the smell of men's genitals much or the looks of them for that matter. Women's bodies in general seem more pleasant and refined, and I like my own body. The actual genitals still look as shocking to me today as they did when I was a child, and first masturbated while looking at my genitals in a mirror. They seem red and swollen and flappy, as if they were *internal* organs. I feel this way about penises as well.''

♀ ''Sometimes my lover tastes bad—I think it is what we eat.''

♀ ''Female genitals have taken some getting used to. I've been aware of 'structures' for years, but have never been too well acquainted with my own. I call that area my 'dark continent'—largely unexplored. I don't mind the smell when it comes down to just smelling, but it puts me off sometimes to touch my genitals as a result. I'm always amazed that it doesn't bother other women—my smell, that is. It always seems stronger than anyone else's. Appearance-wise, I see genitals at work all the time, and I guess I'm kind of neutral there. I find the feel of genitals very strange and comparable only to the mouth in terms of warmth and wetness. Genitals alternately fascinate and repel me in terms of touch.''

♀ ''Basically I like, am interested in, enjoy female genitals—both in reality and imagery. They fascinate me. However, I have negative feelings about my own. I'm too big, too messy, too smelly. I feel this is a hangup left over from my hetero experience and my homo life is curing me of these feelings, which I think are irrational.''

♀ ''I am not turned on by all female genitals (which is probably a good thing, since I am a nurse). I *demand* that my lover always take a bath before we have sex. I also ask that she doesn't use powders, etc.''

♀ ''I disagree with many feminists' feelings about body odors in general. Genitals just *are*—I don't attribute to them any fantastic acclaim. An unclean genital is just that—unclean. Call me prudish, but I also don't appreciate nonuse of deodorant. After lovemaking the smell of bodies can be pleasing, but sweat from no use of deodorants is just bad. I prefer the clean, shaven look and feel for myself and for my lover.''

♀ ''I have no specific feelings about female genitals. The sight does not repel or stimulate particularly. I enjoy feeling other people's genitals and am really neutral about my own. I'm not sure about the smell of others or the taste. Sometimes I think they are a bit distasteful.''

♀ ''I'm not crazy about genitals as genitals. They often smell 'bad' and

even seem a little ugly to me. But as they are the doorway to such pleasure, I have become fond of genitals and feel tender towards them.''

♀"If I'm enamored at the moment, every particle of the other person, every element (every odor, feel, and smell), is delightful. If I'm temporarily disinterested, genital smell is smelly, genital feel is slimy like okra (which I hate), and genitals bear absolutely no resemblance to Georgia O'Keeffe's paintings.''

♀"The only time I feel God is a man is when I survey female genitals—pretty they ain't! Esthetically, they're a joke. Try to imagine a *Martha* Washington monument as a sexual symbol. It's a hysterically funny picture! However, Lord knows, there's no more appropriate place to locate it than beside George's in the D.C. swamp by the Potomac! My own smell I often regard as a nuisance, for my nose and mucous membranes are super-sensitive to odors and foreign substances, respectively. Being close to gay men, I know the female smell widens the distance between the genders for them. The term *fish* bothers me to the extreme, mostly because it's so damn accurate.''

♀"I do not really get turned on by female genitals of themselves. I have always thought mine were repulsive and I guess I feel that way in general. If I were in love, I am sure I would feel more positively toward my lover's most personal areas. I especially dislike pubic and anal areas of all human bodies. I hate hair anywhere on anyone—male or female—other than the hair on people's heads.''

Perhaps because so many lesbians had positive feelings about their genitals, they also had positive feelings about menstruation. Again, it is difficult for lesbians—indeed, for any woman—to have positive feelings about menstruation when society has labeled it "the curse," "the plague," and some religions, such as Orthodox Judaism, even consider menstruating women "unclean," requiring a ritual bath. Many lesbians have reversed the constant negative message of male, heterosexist society and feel positively about every aspect of the body, including menstruation, and they do not see it as an obstacle to having a pleasing sexual experience with another woman or as something unpleasant to circumvent during sex. Here are some feelings about menstruation and how it affects the sex life of the lesbian respondents.

♀"I feel very positively about menstruation and have never been uptight about making love during my period. One time when I was making love to my lover I was going down on her and had my fingers in her, and when I drew them out, they were covered in blood. I tasted my fingers, and the blood was salty and warm. My feelings were positive, and my lover wasn't freaked out because of my attitude.''

♀"I'm not at all modest about menstruation. I use a natural sponge instead of a tampon and enjoy showing my friends how to use it and how to rinse out the blood. But I don't like having periods. I get moderate cramps

each time and find it all a great inconvenience. Having sex while I'm having my period has never bothered me. My sexual energy cycles don't seem to be related to my menstrual cycle at all.''

♀''When I first started my relationship with my first lover, I was very shy about menstruation. But by now, that is all over. We make love when we have our periods, though it may be somewhat less than average. We also do cunnilingus at this time, which I was shy about at first. (I have read about women drinking each other's menstrual blood, which I am definitely *not* into, however.) I think I want sex more right before my period. Sometimes if I am tired on the first day of my period I am not too interested in sex. My lover wants sex *more* during her period, and she gets those horrible, paralyzing cramps. I hardly ever feel any pain, though sometimes I get tired and irritable. She also likes to be massaged and touched more during menstruation, which I do to her.''

♀''Menstruation increases horniness, never detracts. Sometimes it's a pain and I don't like taking care of it, but it's not a problem with sex.''

♀''I am one of the few people I know who likes bleeding as an art. Mainly, I think, I like my body and find myself amazed at the workings of my body. I like my body and my physical energy almost all the time. Bleeding brings heightened physical awareness, life energy flowing.

''The first time I crouched on the grass and bled was an experience that was very spiritual, and I felt more stoned than any chemical I could have taken in. The energy was me in union with the earth. All energy was in a state of flux and yet very constant. I like very much being a woman, and menstruation is an integral part of my being, physically necessary, internalized since age ten with my first 'period' emotionally and spiritually not accepted until fifteen years later—a long time coming of age.''

♀''Menstruation is okay. It does not seriously affect our sex life. In fact, we maintain that there is nothing like a couple of good strong orgasms to get the old blood flowing. In the past it was an excuse for me not to engage in sex with the men, but that does not happen now.''

♀''Menstruation is a sanitation problem, nothing more. I'm annoyed when I stain another pair of underpants, but I don't regard menstruation itself as any great calamity, especially since the invention of tampons. In any case, for years I had no period, and today, though I have one, it only lasts one or two days. The only time menstruation ever screwed up my sex life was when I had my first chance to engage in a lesbian orgy, and I was having my period.''

♀''I feel very positive about menstruation. I like to catch the blood in a diaphragm or sponge and give it to my plants, taste it, make offerings of it to the Goddess on my altar. The blood is such a rich, strong color. I like feeling in harmony with the moon and the earth. I feel very negative about premenstrual tension. Then I feel out of control with my emotions. Menstruation doesn't change my love for giving or receiving cunnilingus.''

♀''I get *very* horny during my period. I don't particularly like the taste of blood (I don't like to suck my finger when I prick it with a needle either)

but am not averse to going down on B. when she is menstruating. She's comfortable with menstruation also. Once we were lying on my couch naked at opposite ends with our legs apart, just laughing and talking and facing each other. Our tampon strings were hanging out, and we made a joke about tying them together or having a tug of war.''

♀"Having borne six children—only two planned—I tend to welcome my period. I hate my husband's (and others') term 'got the rag on,' which makes me feel dirty and degraded, and I do feel the odor, especially at the beginning and end of each period, is unnecessarily obnoxious. The blood itself I rejoice in, for like pain and pleasure, it tells me I am alive and healthy and functioning as I should. It also represents a great feminine potential and links me to time and eternity. Often it arrives at the most inconvenient times in my life and often because it responds to my tension or excitement it comes early or late, so I have learned to have a sense of humor about it and an acceptance of it, for my period has an unpredictable 'feminine' responsive 'mind of its own.' I also still feel young because it occurs, and wonder how menopause will affect my self-concept.''

♀"I feel quite positive. I like the smell and the idea that blood is food. I have sex during my period but always keep the tampon in. It just means that there is no vaginal penetration, which is fine by me. There's plenty else to do. I wouldn't mind making love without a tampon, but I think it would take time to adjust to making love with my lover while she had a period and didn't use a tampon. A couple of articles I read in *The Lesbian Reader* really enlightened my attitudes about menstrual blood.''

The majority of lesbian respondents, however, were still somewhat or very negative to menstruation. Many called it "a pain in the ass," "a bother," "messy," "a nuisance," "a drag," or "a waste," since many lesbians do not intend to have children. Others were negative about menstruation because they become physically ill before or during menstruation, and this has often affected their attitude. Here are some neutral and negative feelings about menstruation:

♀"I usually don't like to have sex while menstruating. I just don't feel sexy. I'm a little inhibited too. I don't feel revulsion but am turned off by the potential messiness.''

♀"I consider menstruation a natural bodily function. I would still hesitate about having sex during my period, however. I'd be afraid that it would bother my partner. I might also be afraid of staining the sheets (left over from early adolescence when mother scolded me for blood on the sheets).''

♀"I have such painful cramps I've wished I never had to deal with my period. It doesn't really affect my sex life: orgasms help my cramps.''

♀"The best way to sum up my feelings about menstruation is that it's a drag! I know that I have twenty-five days of no worries, but I really dread those six or seven days of blood. I use that term because it's like I'm going

through a war. My body smells, I get fatter (just what I need!), I have cramps, but most of all I hate the inconvenience. I haven't yet learned how to insert a tampon, so I have to use those fucking pads. And the first couple of days, I've got to carry around enough for at least one each hour. What a drag it is to always have to run to the bathroom to change them, and oh, shit, if I have a one-and-a-half-hour class, what a mess! Does that seem fair? I say no, and I'm only 20 and have started to think about having a hysterectomy. After all, I'm gay and two women can't produce a child very easily (at least the last I heard). But then I got to thinking I was too young—maybe in five or ten years I'll want to marry a man and have a child by him. Then I remind myself that I don't enjoy life *that* much. The way I feel now, I want to live for at least another two or three years, maybe even till I'm 25 or 26. But I can't imagine living beyond that age, so why not go ahead with the operation? Very simple: money.''

♀"I have some real feelings of resentment about menstruation. It's a great inconvenience, demeaning, and I consider it part of the shit that is dumped on women. As I have little sex life, there is not that much effect. I don't like to be made love to when I'm menstruating, though my current lover is assuring me that it is my hangup and does not affect her.''

♀"Menstruation is an abomination. Yech! It affects my sex life because I don't like to finger-fuck during my period or eat pussy. Tribadism is okay though.''

♀"To me having my period is a big pain in the crotch. It always comes when I'm on the road playing in the band. I get cramps, headaches, stomachaches, backaches, and constantly feel pressure on my crotch. It makes things real hard to deal with musically as well as emotionally. I'm real down when I get it. If it could be stopped without a hysterectomy or pregnancy, I'd do it. My period would definitely affect my sex life (if I had one). I wouldn't let a woman touch my genitals if I had it. I would feel really self-conscious because of the mess and smell the blood makes.''

♀"I have much trouble with my period. I have been to the doctor a lot for it. I am on medication for the immense pain I suffer for the first three days of my period. You can see why I find it negative. I have no sex during my period as I am in so much pain I miss work and can hardly eat. The doctor is trying new medicines on me. She is really trying to help—I sure hope something will!''

♀"Sometimes I get dizzy spells and cramps. Sometimes we still have oral sex during our periods. It depends on how heavy the periods are. My cramps are sometimes so bad I can't breathe, so this discomfort often limits my desire for sex. I have some prescription pills for this, but they make me drowsy. I don't smoke pot a lot, but I do have a few healthy live pot plants, and I've found that smoking or eating some fresh pot helps my cramps! I heard Queen Victoria did this, and it really works!''

Some women who are no longer menstruating also expressed their feelings on the subject.

♀"I disliked menstruation from the day it started. The discomfort, nuisance, and feeling of insecurity (usually a long, heavy, flow) were a true living 'curse.' I had minimal problems during menopause, other than a period of hemorrhaging, but the day it all stopped was one of rejoicing. It did affect my sex life some—usually no sex during my period."

♀"*Yech*! I had a hysterectomy at age 28 and *love* the freedom from periods. I had trouble with my periods all my life and was glad to get rid of them. If I had one question to ask God when I see God, I'll ask why, if God had all power, would He/She make women with such a monthly mess. I think I could have found a better way to shed the eggs! No problem with our sex life, though. We go ahead and make love through my lover's period."

♀"I'm happy to say I'm in menopause. I have not menstruated for four years. It is a joy to have it done and over with. I had difficulty making love with a menstruating woman or accepting full lovemaking while menstruating myself. It was contradictory because I was always horny as hell one day before and on the first day."

♀"Menstruation had never been any kind of problem to me, but I'm now 52 and would just as soon knock it off. It affects my sex life only in that I would not go to bed with my lover while I'm menstruating, but that is of no particular consequence."

Where Lesbians Have Sex

Aside from the lesbians' attitudes about female genitals and menstruation, still other factors affected the pleasing sexual experiences of those lesbians who answered the questionnaire. Of course, the environment had a lot to do with sex. As one can see from the experiences already given in this chapter, some lesbians preferred dim lighting while others preferred darkness or daylight. Taste in music also varied from classical to strictly lesbian tunes. Some lesbians liked the television on during sex. For many, talking was an important part of sex—all the time or either before, during, or after. Participants were asked a few specific questions regarding conditions under which they have sex. Unfortunately, it was not possible to ask questions about every possible factor, but one question asked was: *On the average, how often do you have sex in each of the following places?*

	ALWAYS	VERY FREQUENTLY	SOMEWHAT FREQUENTLY	SOMEWHAT INFREQUENTLY	ONCE	NEVER
your home	30	56	5	4	3	1%
your partner's home	21	53	7	5	6	7

	ALWAYS	VERY FREQUENTLY	SOMEWHAT FREQUENTLY	SOMEWHAT INFREQUENTLY	ONCE	NEVER
a friend's home	0	5	8	15	27	45
car	0	2	4	10	18	66
van or camper	0	3	5	9	12	72
tent	0	3	5	12	16	64
motel or hotel	0	2	13	19	31	35
secluded woods or fields	0	1	6	10	18	65
barn or farm building	0	.5	1	3	6.5	89

Respondents were also asked, *Whether or not you have sex in any of these places, indicate how you feel about the idea of having sex in each of them.*

	VERY POSITIVE	SOMEWHAT POSITIVE	NEUTRAL	SOMEWHAT NEGATIVE	VERY NEGATIVE	NOT SURE
your home	95	1.5	1.5	1.5	1	.5%
your partner's home	88	7	3	1	.5	.5
a friend's home	37	25	22	13	2	1
car	24	13	17	22	23	1
van or camper	47	20	22	6	3	2
tent	53	22	14	4	5	2
motel or hotel	61	21	10	5	2	1
secluded woods or fields	57	21	9	6	6	1
barn or farm building	42	19	17	8	10	4

In the subsample, seven respondents mentioned having sex on the beach, one in a cemetery, one in a dormitory, two at work, one in a theater, and one in a bar. Most felt positively about these experiences, except for the lesbian who had had sex in a theater. Aside from these places, which were put down as "others," it is obvious that the most frequent places of sex were the respondent's home or the home of the respondent's partner.

Motels or hotels ranked slightly above a friend's house for actual sex and was much more positively thought about in general. Also, the lesbians were very positive about the idea of sex in most of the places mentioned even if they did not have sex in those places. The following is a motel story:

♀ "My funniest sexual experience happened with my present lover. We were at a music symposium in San Diego and were looking for a motel to stay at. We hadn't made reservations so were stuck looking for a motel at 5:00 p.m. on a Saturday afternoon in June. After looking for three hours, we passed by a motel that we had seen before with a 'No Vacancy' sign on that now had a vacancy. My lover (of just a month then) went into the office to find out about the room. She came back out and told me that the room was $30. Well, I couldn't believe it because the motel was just a plain old motel. But she went on to tell me that they showed X-rated films over the TV and that was why it was so expensive. I told her we had better take it because it was obvious that we would probably not find another place.

"So we took the room. This room was too much. It had plush red carpeting, a white bedspread, and red light bulbs in the hanging lamps by the bed. We were really surprised since neither of us had seen anything like this before, but were both kind of excited. While my lover was downstairs getting our suitcases, I decided I had better check out the movies, since we were paying for them. I'll have to admit, even though the movies were pretty gross, I was getting excited. Anyway, to make a long story short, we ended up making love all night while watching ourselves in an overhead mirror and watching the X-rated movies."

Whether or not they actually did have sex in the places listed, the lesbians felt positive about many places on the list. Some of this discrepancy is clarified by two other questions, which were asked of the lesbian respondents. One was, *While having sex, how important is privacy?*

very important	86%
somewhat important	12
neutral	0
somewhat unimportant	1
very unimportant	1
not sure	1

Another question asked, *How often do you spend the whole night with your sex partner?*

always	53%
very frequently	35
somewhat frequently	6
somewhat infrequently	3
very infrequently	1
once	1
never	3

Analyzing these two questions, one can readily see that both privacy and spending the entire night with one's sex partner were important to the lesbians who answered this questionnaire. One might conclude, therefore, that although the *idea* of having sex in a barn, the woods, a tent, or a camper might be appealing, these places in actuality have the drawback that they often lack privacy (there was one case in 1967 in Michigan where two lesbians were caught making love while camping and were sent to jail for three years!), and some of them do not allow the participants to spend the night.

In addition, women made comments on the issue of privacy during sex, and here are some of them:

♀ "Privacy is a must. That's why I marked 'never' for tent in the other question. My lover doesn't feel it's private enough."

♀ "Other people in close proximity make me less able to be verbal."

♀ "Two is enough."

♀ "I could not do it without privacy."

♀ "I prefer to be alone with my lover where we won't be interrupted and where we can both make as much noise as we want. It was difficult when we were in my apartment as the walls are paper-thin and I'm a bit nervous about the neighbors' hearing us."

♀ "Safety is important. I cannot forget that society on the whole sees lesbian sex as wrong and has violent reactions."

♀ "Privacy is terrific! Love it! Also a cut-off switch on the phone is lovely."

♀ "God! . . . remembering making love with my parents downstairs and making love in a single bed with my college roommate (very straight) 10 feet away. Privacy is very important!"

♀ "There's nothing like worrying your lover's father will burst in at 3:00 a.m. if you have a door that doesn't lock."

♀ "We had sex at my mother's house. I found it hard to really enjoy the experience for fear she would walk in. (We were on a couch.)"

For a minority, either privacy was not very important, or the prospect of getting caught sometimes made an interesting *fantasy* for some lesbians. In fact, some of the respondents had fantasies in which someone walks in while they are masturbating. These fantasies are included in Chapter 14. Here are some comments lesbians wrote on the attraction of a lack of privacy.

♀ "I'm turned on by the thought of possibly getting 'caught' yet turned off at the thought of somebody listening."

♀ "I fantasize about exhibiting ourselves."

♀ "I would like someone to photograph the lovemaking."

♀ "I have fantasies of semi-public sex, but in reality I very self-righteously close all the curtains, afraid that men will break in and rape us if they see."

♀ "We made love in a room with seven women sleeping and to whom we

were both connected. We were the only two making love, but it was a very supportive context."

♀ "I live with friends and lovers, so privacy is not a common occurrence."

♀ "I had a lover whose 5-year-old daughter used to walk in while we were having sex to demand a glass of water or to ask us to look at something she was doing. Once she announced she wanted to take off her clothes, get into bed, and make love too. This is the only situation in which lack of privacy has really bothered me—her walking in was an instant turn-off—as I've made love before where people could watch or usually hear. However, in this instance, I made my lover build a door, one with a good lock!"

♀ "While living in a college house, my lover and I were constantly interrupted by a couple of good friends, who did not live with us. We were somewhat amused at their fascination with our sexual lives."

The following are some responses to the question on how often the participant spends the entire night with her lover. Many respondents simply said that they always spend the night with their lovers because they live together, but there are other responses:

♀ "I always would stay the whole night if it were my choice."

♀ "Either I go to my lover's home for the weekend or she comes to my apartment. I love to sleep and wake up in her arms—though she teases me about grinding my teeth while I sleep. In the past I have had to leave, or my partner has, right after making love. I hate that! No chance to just relax and enjoy the closeness of her."

♀ "I like company as well as sex."

♀ "I prefer spending the night: affection, talking, sleeping, etc. are important parts of my relationships. Sex alone, without affection and sharing, is rarely appealing.

♀ "It seems 'cheaper' to 'have sex and run.' I like cuddling after sex."

♀ "I usually want to continue the contact I feel after making love. With men in the past I often would have liked my partner to leave! This hasn't been my experience with women."

♀ "Why go home when you're feeling so loved and good?"

♀ "It's hard not to spend the night with my lover when we have only one bed in the house!"

♀ "Sleeping together and talking in bed are as delightful as making love, so there's no point in missing out on it."

♀ "It's very important for me to wake up with the woman I've had sex with. There's a certain closeness to be found in this, whereas if I am to have sex with a woman and then leave (or she leaves), it seems to me to place much more emphasis on the physical and sexual aspect of lovemaking than the emotional. The emotional aspect is becoming increasingly more important to me."

♀ "I'm not even going to consider going to bed with someone I don't want to wake up with."

Other people did not spend the entire night with their partners. A common factor often mentioned was that one partner had to go home to parents or children.

♀ "My lover often has to go home to her mother."

♀ "My regular lover and I live together, but my other lover lives with her lover, so therefore it is variable whether we spend the night."

♀ "I usually like to sleep with the woman I've made love with. After orgasm, I'm too tired to move on. However, sometimes I like to be left alone afterwards."

♀ "I infrequently spend the night with my lover. It's easier to plod home late than try to wake up in the morning. I'm semi-nocturnal."

♀ "I'm an insomniac! I can't sleep with someone else. While she is *sleeping,* I usually am reading or painting."

♀ "Sometimes I need to sleep alone to replenish and nurture my own energy."

♀ "I like sleeping alone better. It's easier to remember my dreams and I have more room."

Drugs and Sex

Certain drugs are used in connection with sex, and one can see from the stories in this chapter that marijuana, alcohol, and amphetamines were part of pleasing sexual experiences. The respondents were asked, *How often do you use the following in association with sex?*

	ALWAYS	VERY FREQUENTLY	SOMEWHAT FREQUENTLY	SOMEWHAT INFREQUENTLY	VERY INFREQUENTLY	ONCE	NEVER
alcohol	1	8	20	23	24	2	22%
marijuana	3	10	16	14	21	4	32
psychedelics (LSD, mushrooms, mescaline)	.5	0	1	1.5	10	4	84
"uppers" (speed, amphetamine)	.5	1	1.5	1.5	5	1.5	90
Quaaludes	.5	.5	.5	1.5	4	1.5	91.5
"downers" (barbiturates, tranquilizers)	.5	.5	1	2	3	2	91
heroin	.5	0	.5	0	2	.5	96.5
cocaine	.5	.5	0	2	7	2	88
amyl nitrite ("poppers," "aroma")	.5	1	.5	2	4	6	87

Respondents were also asked, *Whether or not you use any of the following, how do you feel about their use in association with sex?"*

	VERY POSITIVE	SOMEWHAT POSITIVE	NEUTRAL	SOMEWHAT NEGATIVE	VERY NEGATIVE	NOT SURE
alcohol	6	26	28	21	17	2%
marijuana	23	23	25	10	16	3
psychedelics (LSD, mushrooms, mescaline)	5	9	14	9	52	10
"uppers" (speed, amphetamine)	1	4	13	10	62	9
Quaaludes	4	3	10	9	60	13
"downers" (barbiturates, tranquilizers)	1	2	10	13	65	9
heroin	1	1	6	5	77	10
cocaine	9	11	11	6	51	12
amyl nitrite ("poppers," "aroma")	4	5	14	6	58	13

A third question asked: *Have you ever refused to have sex with a partner because*

	YES	NO
she used any of these?	17	83%
she would not join you in the use of any of these?	2	98

It should be noted that under this general category of "drugs" associated with sex, each question provided space for participants to list "other drugs." The lesbian respondents showed that they used a broad definition for such drugs, which included tobacco, aspirin, caffeine, glue, and music. It is clear from the last question that many more lesbians had refused to have sex with another woman because of her use of drugs than others had refused to have sex with them because they would not participate in the use of drugs. When refusing to have sex because her partner used "drugs," lesbians most often mentioned alcohol. Another fact which emerged from these statistics is that while more lesbians have never tried marijuana than have never tried alcohol in relation to sex (although a solid 22% has never tried the latter), marijuana seemed to be used on an absolutely equally frequent basis (both are used 29% of the time with some frequency). The next most popular drug used in connection with sex was psychedelics, with cocaine next. But none of these—or the others on the list—was used with any frequency, and hard drugs, such as heroin, seemed

to be almost totally avoided in the lesbian community in association with sex. The respondents offered the following comments on drugs in general and in connection with sex:

♀ "Except for alcohol (which I don't like), I have done and will do *any* of the others whether in connection with sex or just because. But in moderation because I don't have the extra money and because it's hard to find good dope!"

♀ "Speed dries me out, making sex more than unpleasant. P.S.: We happen to have some Quaaludes so we are going to try that out tonight."

♀ "I smoke pot and drink alcohol very frequently, but not just because I'm going to have sex."

♀ "I use tobacco, caffeine, and sometimes alcohol. I get high on the woman I love—who needs drugs?"

♀ "Marijuana is a part of my life and every person I know. I've been too busy and wrapped up in politics to do other drugs since 1970. Drugs aren't a big deal."

♀ "Except for smoking, I dislike the use of drugs."

♀ "I am very much into drugs. My lover shares my extreme fondness for grass, but discourages my use of downers and speed. She does allow me to use hallucinogens as long as she is present. I'm a dedicated and long-time drug abuser. I hate reality."

♀ "Marijuana in moderate amounts turns me on and greatly increases the pleasure of lovemaking, especially my sense of touch—both touching and being touched. Getting too stoned is a definite turn-off and my sex urge goes to zero. I would like to try cocaine once, but have no interest in any other drugs."

♀ "Grass is a very positive thing for me to do. It is relaxing and opening and lots of fun. The concept of drugs as a negative thing is dependent upon functionalism as the necessity for sanity. States of consciousness vary according to situations, and drugs are not the only inducement to changes. Drug use and mind expansion are discouraged because they do not keep one functioning within the cultural norms and institutions. As a function of racism and classism they are used to keep the oppressed classes quiet. It is necessary to take control of drug use from the state so that it can become a tool for personal growth."

♀ "One time I was tripping on psychedelics, and this woman who I had been having an affair with (who was also tripping) was massaging my scalp as I sat on the floor leaning up against her legs. She gave me a tremendous orgasm just with the massage. My head had an afterglow for about three days after that."

Many more women expressed negative or neutral feelings, especially about hard drugs.

♀ "I'm against all drugs. I'm only barely willing to use penicillin and aspirin, and not too often either. I cannot relate to people who are always in

some altered state, whatever the substance involved. For one thing, I can't tell who or what they really are. Occasional use of small amounts of alcohol or marijuana is okay, but dependence on those things (or any others) for relaxation or enjoyment is not."

♀ "I'm not for the really heavy drugs for *anybody*. I know too many sisters who've been really messed up by them. Such a waste of our spirit and strength! The lesser ones, okay, if someone really has to have them to get by, except for tobacco smoking, which I think is obnoxious. I don't use any drugs, not even aspirin, and I don't smoke anything or drink anything stronger than herb tea. You couldn't believe how many of my *sisters* feel really threatened by this, like they think I'm trying to lay some big superiority trip on them. I just don't want to mess up my lovely person! A woman who I love very much wants to try to get me 'loaded' all the time or wants me to try smoking a joint if she's got one, etc. I really resent this."

♀ "As a sober alcoholic I am averse to drinking and drug-taking."

♀ "I'm on an alcoholics program and have refused to have sex with people who drink."

♀ "Maryjane is a drug that I escaped with for a good seven years, smoking several joints a day every day for this period of time, and being constantly high. Recently I quit using it, and I have been truly high since. I was just drifting for a large part of the time. I was trying to escape myself, my responsibilities, the ways that others viewed me. It didn't do me any good. Sure, it didn't do any physical harm, and I wasn't 'addicted,' but it was no easy job quitting either. You are always about 2 feet away from dealing with other people when you are high. Drugs can be very useful learning tools, but they can be habit-forming too. I wish that some of the women and men who I see around me using maryjane to excess would get off their butts and do something positive instead."

♀ "I have been involved as a user and presently am a counselor in the drug subculture. I have seen a good number of gay men and women use drugs and alcohol to block out their bad feelings about being gay. I think for the most part drug use is a dangerous thing. So is alcohol abuse."

♀ "I've tried lots of drugs, from bad to worse. I want nothing to do with drugs or anyone who uses them."

♀ "I avoid drugs like the plague. I almost became an alcoholic at 15 or 16 and would have become a pill popper if I hadn't had the will power and good sense not to. I can't deal with people who are heavily into drugs. I had a friend who OD'd on pills once and I knew it would happen. I kept telling her this, but she didn't listen."

♀ "The only thing I'm hooked on is the nitrous oxide my dentist gives me. I wish I could get it over the counter!"

♀ "Most drugs are a waste of time. I've tried them all at one distracted time or another, and there's little point in using them. Try natural highs."

Summary

If love (or sex) is a many-splendored thing, it is certainly also a very complex thing, with many, many variables. Some researchers have spent a lifetime investigating the components of sexuality, and nothing is conclusive yet!

Nevertheless, one might agree that the true test of a good sex life is whether or not the person feels that her sex life is satisfactory. We asked, *On the average, how do you feel about the quality of the sexual experiences you have with women (without reference to how often you have sex)?*

completely satisfied	41%
very satisfied	43
somewhat satisfied	11
neutral	1
somewhat dissatisfied	4
very dissatisfied	1
completely dissatisfied	0
not sure	0

In brief, about 95% of lesbians felt satisfaction about their sex life. The pleasing experiences in this chapter are testimony to this fact, and one might venture to say that one could hardly find a more satisfied group of people anywhere, of any kind. Perhaps there is a great deal of truth to the bumper sticker which reads, "Lesbians make the best lovers."

Gay Male Sexuality

For the gay male, sex is above all a source of fun, pleasure, recreation, and communication. There may be fears, guilt, hangups, traumas, frustrations, and the emotional turmoil of relationships, but the enjoyment of the experience is at the root of gay male sexuality. Spiritual values, including romantic love, may be a factor, of course, but the pleasurable sensation of male-male sex is what makes men return to it again and again. This simple, biological fact of nature is often overlooked.

It is this fact, however, that brings gay men into conflict with the heterosexual world. First, although heterosexuals may "enjoy" sex, its justification is too often connected to the idea of procreation. Second, in the traditional heterosexual model, there is a strict role sytem that is usually followed: man on top, woman on bottom; male active, woman passive; male insertor, woman receptor. The assumption has been that the man's pleasure is primary, that the woman's job is to "please" her man. A woman who focuses on her own pleasure is called by such names as "tramp," "slut," "nymphomaniac," and "shameless hussy." It is assumed that a man can and will use lusty language and show exuberance about the sexual experience, while words like "demure," "virginal," "chaste," and "prudish" are almost always used to define women.

In other words, in human sexuality, it is thought that there is a male role and a female role. Although this heterosexual role model is by now imbedded deep within the human psyche, there is no good reason for two people, regardless of gender, to follow that model. Ironically, in male-male relations, there are pairs who do follow such predetermined roles, with one playing "man" and the other playing "woman," and for such pairs, as for any other two people, the model may be more or less useful and pleasing. The survey indicates that strictly-adhered-to butch-femme role-playing is no longer very common (see Chapter 9). In general, it can be said that gay men violate the sex-role system, simply because homosexual acts are seen as "unmanly." This violation can be uptight and reluctant; it can be lusty, angry, and defiant. In a role-free relationship, no one person's pleasure is

primary and each man gives pleasure to the other. At any given moment, for a particular pair of men, there will be one on the top, one on bottom; one active, one passive; one insertor, one receptor. A few minutes later, or the next day, those very roles may be reversed.

Gay men are influenced by both masculine and feminine socializing, but divorced of the trappings of the heterosexual system, these characteristics become not masculine or feminine but merely human. Unfortunately, straight society doesn't see it this way, and the gay man's defiance of the traditional male role, as innocent and healthful as it may seem to some, provokes an outpouring of anger and hatred from the straight man. This sexual root of homophobia often goes unrecognized. The straight man hates the male homosexual because he cannot bear the idea of a man on bottom, a man who is passive, a man who is the receptor, a man who is giving, yielding, caring, emotional—this violates his entire notion of manhood as it threatens his system of rule and control. A commitment to androgyny is by no means universal among gay men, but most evidence, including this survey, points to an increasing respect for the man who embodies both masculine and feminine characteristics.

Affection

The sharing of sexual pleasure between two men is the common denominator of the gay male experience, and the purpose of this chapter is to discuss the specifics of that experience. In the questionnaire, gay men were asked *to describe a very pleasing love-making experience . . . with a sex partner or lover,* and the responses to this question were often the longest of the written essays sent to us. While the description of a particular sexual experience usually focused on certain sexual acts, and usually included orgasm for both partners, the men indicated that overall affection is very important in their lovemaking. We asked the men *how often they engaged in physical affection ("hugging, cuddling, caressing, kissing") with their lovers and sex partners*, and these were the responses:

	ALWAYS	VERY FREQUENTLY	SOMEWHAT FREQUENTLY	SOMEWHAT INFREQUENTLY	VERY INFREQUENTLY	ONCE	NEVER
lovers	70	18	4	1	2	.5	5%
sex partners	39	43	12	3	3	0	1

The figure of 5% who "never" are affectionate with their lovers, especially compared to only 1% for sex partners, seems strange. Perhaps men who have never had lovers checked the box for "never"—otherwise the figure just doesn't make sense. The men were also asked about *the idea of physical affection, regardless of the actual experience,* and these responses show the nearly universal importance given to affection:

	VERY POSITIVE	SOMEWHAT POSITIVE	NEUTRAL	SOMEWHAT NEGATIVE	VERY NEGATIVE	NOT SURE
lovers	96	2	1	.5	0	.5%
sex partners	88	10	2	.5	0	0

Stimulation of Parts of the Body

General comments about lovemaking experiences often included reference to affection and "foreplay," a term generally used for stimulation of the body prior to any act that leads to orgasm. Manual stimulation, favored by some men as a way to have orgasm, was nearly universal as a form of preorgasmic sex play. The acts of touching and holding were often mentioned. At one New England college, the men call their sex-education course "Holes and Poles," but for these gay men the all-over stimulation and emotional satisfaction connected with affection is an important aspect, quite beyond the "holes and poles." As for focusing on erogenous zones, the men were asked, *On the average, how important for your satisfaction is the stimulation of each of the following parts of your body by your partner?* These are the responses:

	VERY IMPORTANT	SOMEWHAT IMPORTANT	NEUTRAL	SOMEWHAT UNIMPORTANT	VERY UNIMPORTANT	NOT SURE
penis	85	12	2	.5	0	0%
testicles (balls)	38	39	15	4	3	0
anus	24	32	20	10	13	1
prostate gland (inside rectum)	16	22	21	13	23	6

	VERY IMPORTANT	SOMEWHAT IMPORTANT	NEUTRAL	SOMEWHAT UNIMPORTANT	VERY UNIMPORTANT	NOT SURE
ass	26	34	18	10	11	1
nipples	24	35	20	6	12	1
ears, neck, toes	22	41	21	8	6	2

In a parallel question, the men were asked, *How important for your satisfaction is it for you to stimulate each of the following parts of your partner's body?*

	VERY IMPORTANT	SOMEWHAT IMPORTANT	NEUTRAL	SOMEWHAT UNIMPORTANT	VERY UNIMPORTANT	NOT SURE
penis	81	15	3	0	0	1%
testicles (balls)	46	32	17	2	2	1
anus	23	32	21	9	12	2
prostate gland (inside rectum)	14	21	28	11	20	6
ass	30	32	20	8	8	2
nipples	30	37	21	5	7	1
ears, neck, toes	28	37	23	5	5	1

Many men indicated that they want to give and receive stimulation "all over," and others specified other body parts, including mouth and lips, head and hair, chest, back, thighs, underarms, hands, and perineum (the space between the scrotum and the anus).

Comments about most of these pleasure-centers are dispersed throughout this chapter, but here are a few comments about specific areas of anatomy that are not used in intercourse:

♂"If the other guy likes his ears sucked, I'm happy to do it, but I don't like my ears sucked at all. Kissed and touched, yes, but *not* wet and sucked."

♂"Probably the most sensitive part of my body is my ears. These can, if treated properly, turn me on more than any other spot on my body."

♂"I enjoy having my tits rubbed more than having my cock rubbed, and only a combo of the two will bring me to orgasm."

♂"Nipple stimulation doesn't do anything for me. I can't understand why so many guys make such a big thing out of it."

♂"For some reason, my balls don't like to be played with too much or they ache a little bit."

♂"Testicles somewhat painful to touch, unless done very lightly; nipples not at all sensitive, penis sucking by partner not particularly desired."

Mutuality and Compatibility

The men indicated that mutuality in sex is important to them. The previous two charts show that most men derive satisfaction from both receiving and giving stimulation. The men were also asked, *On the average during sex, do you feel that you are more physically active than your partner?* The replies were:

much more active	14%
a little more active	29
the same	39
a little less active	15
much less active	3

Giving pleasure is an important turn-on for an overwhelming majority of the men. Asked, *How much does what you do to your partner "turn you on"?* the men replied as follows:

quite a lot	70%
some	25
very little	3
not sure	2

Sexual incompatibility can be an issue for sharp conflict. At times, disagreement over a particular act will lead to the termination of a sexual encounter. The men were asked, *How often has a sexual encounter been terminated because you would not perform a particular sexual act your partner wanted?* and the replies were:

very frequently	2%
somewhat frequently	4
somewhat infrequently	11
very infrequently	35
once	11
never	38

They were also asked, *How often has a sexual encounter been ter-minated because your partner would not perform a particular sexual act you wanted?* The replies were:

very frequently	1%
somewhat frequently	3
somewhat infrequently	8
very infrequently	30
once	4
never	53

Only a handful of men have this type of problem in bed on a regular basis. Most can usually work something out with a partner to the mutual satisfaction of both people. There are those occasions, however, when the specifics of sexual acts can lead to unresolvable conflicts, but even those are readily solved by separation and the search for a more compatible partner.

When asked to describe a "pleasing sexual experience," the majority recalled a favorite situation with much rapture and many specifics, but some men found it difficult to focus on a particular experience. Furthermore, some of the responses were so wide-ranging in their inclusion of various sexual acts that they defied categorization. Here are some general comments about pleasing experiences and the importance of affection and body stimulation, including some individual accounts of love-making reflecting a variety of attitudes and moods:

⚥ "Those pleasing lovemaking experiences that I've had have not been distinguished so much by what was done, but rather by the degree of intimacy attained, and duration. A feeling of caring, knowing that my partner actually cares about me as a person rather than a sex object, is paramount to success, success being gratification. Gratification is mental rather than physical, meaning that it is not necessary that either of us achieve orgasm, but that we are secure in the knowledge that we have given and received pleasure, that the experience was pleasing. This is done primarily by communicating, by verbally relating past experiences, sharing fears and desires not in regard to the sexual act, but about life in general. During this time, a variety of sexual activities will have been engaged in, whatever is agreed upon mutually. Role-playing is not desirable, since it only erects barriers to discovering one another. It is my belief that the whole person must be involved in a sexual act for it to be pleasing."

⚥ "There is no real *one* most pleasing experience, but I find the few memorable times were spent with men who took their time (and urged me to do the same) in becoming knowledgeable about sensitivities. Gently strok-ing, caressing, tonguing, sucking, nibbling all over the body—noting heightened awareness/sensitivity. Not concentrating on orgasm or even self-fulfillment but rather pleasing the other and taking turns of doing and receiving has been the height of pleasure. There are no specific movements or positions. Gentleness is very important—but be careful not to let a soft

caress turn into an agonizing tickle at the wrong time. Quiet music (folk or classical) and soft or colored lighting are also very nice. Sometimes we would drink a little to relax our muscles and smoke some grass. But if I'm too tired, I fall asleep.''

⚥ "Almost all my lovemaking experiences are 'pleasing.' Start with touching, kissing. Everything feels good. How long does it take? It all depends. Sometimes a few minutes, sometimes an hour. We have rough ones and gentle ones, all positions. I don't like this question.''

⚥ "My sex experiences are based mainly on knowing these people and possibly having a relationship. I do not go too much for just having sex, especially with a stranger. I like foreplay, kissing (French-style), and then tenderly exploring my friend's body—eventually going to the 69 position and then sitting on each other, rubbing our cocks together, lubricating with oil. Sometimes we come in the 69 position and sometimes in this sitting position, depending on how much foreplay was done and how turned on we both are. We usually come together. Sometimes I do something to please my friend when it really does not do very much for me. I like to satisfy my friend. I don't like bright lights; I like lighting sort of dim, but I do like to see my friend's body.''

⚥ "My most recent extremely pleasing lovemaking experience was with my lover/partner. I will call him Jim for the purpose of this survey. This last weekend he and I were spending the weekend with gay friends in Hollywood and we got back late or rather early a.m. to their apartment with no one else home. We continued to drink wine as we had all day and had a very nice sharing conversation about our relationship. I felt very good and the atmosphere was just super. We were alone and for some reason Jim had on only a bath towel, yet I was still fully clothed. We were listening to a very sexy, sensual record album and began necking on the couch where we had been sitting and talking. We were soon on the floor with Jim's suggestion that I take off my clothes also. I got up and restarted the album and turned on the gas fireplace. And we proceeded to have a most interesting and pleasing session of lovemaking. The atmosphere was just right. The music. The wine. The fire. Being on the floor. I love to kiss and deep kiss. I sucked Jim's tongue as usual. He always seems to like it. He loves to get fucked with his legs and feet in the air. I penetrated him and we moved to the feel and motion of the music. I love it all and like to make it last as long as possible every time I have sex. Ultimate orgasm is not always that important. But I did come during this session. It was great. But we had to stop very abruptly, since our friends returned home and surprised us on the floor all intertwined with each other in front of the fire. We have had some of our best sex sessions away from home. Especially once near the beach with the waves crashing outside below us. It was the first time that I had been able to take Jim's cock in the anus. I finally managed this by sitting on it, with him flat on his back. I have a hard time taking it in the anus. But I'm working on it. If I can just get over the initial pain and relax (sometimes on liquor) or

with the help of a sex partner who will be patient and not rush me, I can do it and indeed love it. It makes me feel very complete and sends waves of vibrations and emotions to every nerve end in my body.''

♂ "My most pleasing sexual experience is for my partner to allow me to help him undress slowly and then to allow me to view his nude body. Then I like for him to allow me to touch any part of his body that is desirable to me at that moment and to allow me to kiss it. He may do the same thing to me, if he so desires. I love the smell of a clean male body and I greatly enjoy smelling the different anatomical areas of my partner. I enjoy kissing and being kissed.

"I believe it was an ancient, male-chauvinist, Greek writer who said that a woman could support any weight—if it was put upon her by a man! I identify with this idea tremendously. I love for my partner to lie on top of me (as we face each other) so that I can feel his full weight crushing me. As far as I'm concerned, he can remain in this position as long as he wishes to—so long as he allows me to kiss him, to gently rub my hands up and down his back, and to part his buns and run my fingers through the crack. Pure heaven! I love hairy men, and those that have a dark shadow on their jaws drive me wild. For some unexplainable, fetishistic reason I tend to associate hairiness with masculinity. I especially love for my partner to rub his cheeks (facial) against mine so that I can feel his beard stubble scratching my skin. (By the way, I'm pretty hairy myself and I also have a dark shadow on my jaws.)''

♂ "I feel too much emphasis is placed on genital sexuality and too little on whole-body sexuality, which is, to me, far more important. Also, what I want depends on my mood and my partner.''

♂ "The hands themselves are often really important to me. A person who knows how to touch his partner can touch you anywhere and make it feel great.''

♂ "The more I like a person the more I like to do.''

♂ "I really get turned on when a guy rubs his hard-on against my neck and face. Then to feel his hairy balls touch lightly on my nose, eyelids, and neck is really great.''

♂ "I like my partner to stimulate any part of my body, as long as they don't try to fuck me.''

♂ "Hugging and cuddling are the most important things for me. I think just spending an evening hugging and kissing before a fireplace, with good music (classical) in the background—followed by the contact of naked bodies—is the most beautiful thing in life. Orgasm is great, but I've had beautiful sexual experiences where orgasm was a minor event—several times no orgasm at all.''

♂ "I love to be nude in bed with the other person nude. Much caressing and stroking. Very often I enjoy giving the other person a full sensual massage with warm scented oil, and I'm delighted when this is reciprocated, but it must be a gentle massage, no hard muscle-probing. I love to kiss my partner on the neck, ears, chest. Mouth kissing doesn't do a lot for me, but

I'll do it and somewhat enjoy it if it turns my partner on. I love to pet and feel my partner's ass, and love to have my own petted and caressed. I love to fondle his cock and suck on it, and vice versa. Balls do not do much for me, and my own must be handled very gently. In fact, gentle is the word in my lovemaking. No room for pain or discomfort, or even such action as to make one sweaty or exhausted. My favorite way to achieve orgasm is inserting my penis between his legs and fucking, slowly and pleasurably, using either saliva or oil as a lubricant. I love this to be reciprocated. If my partner wants to be fucked in the ass and he is clean, etc., I happily accommodate, but never try to get someone to let me fuck him. It's only if he wants to be fucked that I really enjoy it. I don't like to be fucked in the ass at all. I lose my erection and unless the penis is very very short and small, it hurts! I'm pretty sure this is psychological, but so far I have not been willing to overcome my negative feelings about it. Fellatio is something I enjoy doing for the other guy if it turns him on, and I enjoy being done, if it turns him on. In quickie situations like a theater or toilet, I can respond with gusto to a blow job. In the comfort and privacy of my own bed, I prefer more body contact, caressing, etc. A rewarding sex session has to last at least twenty minutes and better a half-hour or hour. I enjoy the massage and the caressing so much. It's also nice to be active awhile and then let the other guy be active. Nice just to lie there and be pleasured, and vice versa."

&"In general, the specific 'acts' in lovemaking are not that important to me; just these things: that the lovemaking be as 'rough' as it can without actually causing any physical pain, that the music, if any, be soft but rhythmic and fast. Lighting: pink, purple, orange lights are the most stimulating. Clothing: prefer to start with all clothes *on* rather than naked. Anal intercourse and 69 most preferred."

&"It is hard to single out one pleasant experience when after a while reality and fantasy mix. I have been living with my roommate for one and a half years and we have had sex together so many times that I would be unable to reconstruct the times and incidents. I do know that I have never experienced such exhilaration as having sex with him. The highlights which compose those pleasing aspects have all taken place but if all of them occurred together or not is not easy for me to remember any more. The beginning highlight is my emotional feelings and inner commitment to my roommate. It is the emotional feeling and trust which allows me to be completely free and to experience. The longer we involve ourselves in both the foreplay and the actual sex the greater my enjoyment. Oftentimes we might begin with play-fighting (pillow fights, water fights, mild wrestling) or me giving him a massage."

&"Most of my lovemaking begins by exploring my partner, moving my hand over his body with special attention to his cock. We then may kiss and hug, lying side-by-side or on top of one another, intermingling arms and legs until we are completely aroused. We will then blow one another, he generally doing it first, and we then take turns. Only in very special cases when we are both especially turned on do I care to do 69. From an especially

attractive partner I would enjoy quite a lot of roughness as I have a strong
S&M streak that I have never fully explored and seldom satisfy, yet it is
there just below the surface. I do not care to be fucked in the ass except on
very special occasions by very special people. Generally I suck off or beat
off my partner—I seldom come myself no matter how horny I am or how
much my partner turns me on. If there is time, I like to stay and cuddle or
fall asleep in his arms after sex is over. I seem to prefer a mixture of
roughness and gentleness and try to be as active or passive as my partner
desires. Generally, the more attracted I am, the more mutually satisfied we
both become."

    Romantic factors can be a major aspect of what makes an experience
"very pleasant." Here, an "incurable romantic" describes one such time:
    ♂"I think probably the most pleasing lovemaking experience I've ever
had was about three summers ago. It was not with a lover, but a sex partner
for the evening. I was at Ogunquit Beach, having just come out, still un-
jaded and excited about my newly discovered sense of identity. I was talking
to a friend who was visiting, when someone came up behind me and asked
for a match, in French. I turned around and it was instant infatuation with
this tall, blond, mustached Quebecois. We went back to his hotel room and
made love. We just stood there soul-kissing at first. When I turned around
to pick up his keys, he embraced me from behind, and slowly began undressing me, all the while tonguing every part of me that was freshly exposed—neck, nipples, navel, feet. It was all done so slowly and deliberately
that I was getting turned on to the point where I thought I'd burst. Unable
to wait, I began undressing him. He smelled faintly of musk oil and san-
dalwood. His silk shirt was smooth and cool, and that contrasted with the
feel of old blue jeans was a knockout. We climbed into bed and Roger and I
began some of the deepest soul kisses I've ever engaged in. Once again, the
traveling over my body began. I'd never had my toes sucked before, and it
was a different and wonderful sensation; meanwhile his fingers were going
lightly up and down my spine, a feeling that's like a fuse for me.
Responding, I left no area unexplored, his erect nipples, his flat stomach,
till I got down to his cock. It had to be the most perfectly sculptured one I'd
ever seen, long and good-sized but not too much, and shaped perfectly. I
went down on him, being unable to control myself, burying myself in his
groin, my hand feeling up and down that lithe body. Roger was moaning in
French, as was I, which shocked me since I had always been quiet and
reserved with my bed speech. Suddenly with a quick feat of acrobatics
Roger switched positions and began sucking my cock, slowly, then quickly,
alternating rhythms. I held back as long as I could and finally exploded in
his mouth. After two weeks of celibacy I could not contain myself and
exploded, intensifying the orgasm with a torrent of French. I was tingly all
over and my mind was in seventh heaven. Oddly enough, this was
prolonged for several minutes when Roger lay on top of me, grasping me

with intense passion, rough but pleasant, and began rubbing himself against me and my already sensitive cock, until he came. We both lay back exhausted until we woke up in time to see the sunrise over the ocean. Looking back on this experience (I'd forgotten all about it until now), I can only get turned on all over again. Roger was like a white knight. Having just come out at 22, being shy and unwilling to say no because I didn't want to hurt anyone's feelings, I had had some pretty bad sexual experiences until Roger came along. He was sort of the fulfillment of some medieval romantic fantasy for me. French being my first language and being a Francophile at the time, it was like being made love to by some Norman prince. But more, for once I had met someone who preferred *making love* to *having sex,* someone who could get off on two or three hours of foreplay instead of a two-minute quickie, someone who was agile in bed, passionate and tender but not so tender as to lie there like a log, someone who got off on quiet sunrises and early-morning coffee. That morning was a continuation of 'heaven' for me. We barely spoke at sunrise, just held hands and smiled at one another. Even at coffee, it was basically a silent, shared communication. Of course the experience was a one-night thing. Roger went back to Quebec that morning and I back home to my parents. In those early days, I always thought if I slept with a man we would become lovers overnight. So when Roger left I went home and cut a fresh rose from the garden and played Mozart for hours on the piano, wrote some poetry and went for a long walk along the edge of the salt marshes. I was an incurable romantic in those days. Now I no longer expect or desire this 'glorified fantasy' which is so very 'straight,' especially after seeing straight relationships. If it did exist, I probably would desire it, but three years later I find myself a bit more realistic. I cannot fault myself for that experience; it was the first time that I was truly in touch with and expressed my deepest feelings, feelings that three years later I would like to recover, being somewhat jaded at this point. Perhaps I am still an incurable romantic, but I guess I don't know. I'm sure if I had to relive that experience over again, I would.''

Male Genitals, Penis Size, and Circumcision

Gay men have overwhelmingly positive feelings about male genitals, their own and others. Although there are major hangups and inadequacies, real or imagined, especially in the area of circumcision and size, cocks and balls are considered a joy to behold, to touch and to be touched. The positive feeling about male genitals is one of the advantages that gay men experience from living in a male-dominated culture. This can be tricky, however. The point comes when too much interest in male genitals on the part of a man is seen as "queer." There is also the risk that worship of the phallus can turn into hatred of women. The following chart indicates *the feelings about male genitals* (their own and others) expressed in the questionnaires:

	VERY POSITIVE	SOMEWHAT POSITIVE	NEUTRAL	SOMEWHAT NEGATIVE	VERY NEGATIVE	NOT SURE
smell of your own	39	19	30	5	2	6%
feel of your own	64	23	12	1	0	0
appearance of your own	47	34	12	6	1	0
size of your own	39	32	16	9	3	0
smell of others	33	30	24	8	4	1
feel of others	69	24	6	0	0	0
appearance of others	57	33	10	0	0	0
size of others	46	31	22	0	0	1
taste of others	47	25	20	5	3	1

The men expressed many points of view about the various aspects of genitals. The question of penis size and circumcision evoked more comments than anything else, and some of those have been selected out later in this section. But first, here are a few general comments about male genitals:

⚤ "I love cocks and balls—all sizes, shapes, and degrees of hardness, in clothes or out, just watching them, or when they become part of my body. I like big cocks for some things, small cocks for some things, and I love mine. From various comments I guess others find mine okay, too. One thing I like that may be a bit different. I like to take both of a man's balls (and cock, too, if it'll fit) into my mouth at the same time. A real feeling of intimacy and powerful control."

⚤ "I've never made much of a fetish of cocks (never even look at them in the high school locker room—am I an anomaly?). I like them and all, but a beautiful face turns me on a lot more; I could never be turned on to a cock if I weren't turned on to the rest of the body. Size is of no importance except big ones intimidate me if I'm getting fucked (huge ones, that is). I think uncircumcised ones look rather hideous, particularly when flaccid, but I'd never turn one down for that reason. My own cock is just fine, no big deal one way or the other. I love the smell and taste of cock and balls."

⚤ "Cocks must be clean, have a clean smell. I think any cock above 6 inches is appealing to me. I admit the bigger the more turned on I am. But when in love it doesn't matter. I like a nice firm thick cock. I like circumcised cock. I like lots of pubic hair. Also big balls turn me on."

⚤ "I like to roll balls around in my fingers—to me they symbolize male power!"

⚤ "I go to the Y regularly for exercise, and never fail to be aroused by the sight of so many exposed cocks. I love to watch someone attractive undress while I speculate about his penis size, shape, circumcision, etc., and then,

once he is stripped, see how right or wrong I was. Although I am circumcised, as are probably four-fifths of my sexual partners, I am fascinated
by an uncircumcised cock—probably just because it is infrequent. I love to
manipulate a loose foreskin, and slide and stretch it in every possible way.
Sometimes I wish I were not circumcised so I could always have a ready
foreskin to play with. Most all my friends are Jewish and find a foreskin
downright offensive.''

⚬"There is still a part of me which is as equally repelled by men's
genitals as I am attracted. That little part of the society at large which is still
in me judging, saying I'm dirty that this isn't okay. At the same time, I
really want physical affection from men, but the parts I focus on are their
eyes, hair, mouth, and body.''

⚬"I am rather self-conscious and uncomfortable about the appearance
of my own genitals.''

⚬"I always check out pee partners, and have an enormous picture
collection. Don't dig sweaty or dirty cocks, or deformed heads. One guy I
know has poor blood circulation in the head, which is like chicken-gizzard
blue, with rough folds of bright red around the crown. Ugliest damned cock
I ever saw. Another guy (black) has a whole row of little fibrous tendrils
about 1/16th inch long around the crown edge. Very strange to feel them
with my lips. Two guys I know had lousy circumcisions, and a strap or strip
of the head flesh extends down into the shaft. This doesn't turn me off, but
it is not attractive. Another black guy I know has about 2 inches wide by
over 9 inches, and midway down the shaft it turns almost 90 degrees to the
right. Have to blow him from the side, because when it's up it's so tough
and rigid it can't be straightened out—forget about getting that one up my
ass.''

⚬"The normal sweating and oil given off by a dick attract me. I don't
mind a slightly smelly prick, but realize some people do. I do like to get
head from young innocent boys when my dick is slightly dirty, just smelling
good. I guess that is a carryover from my sex-is-dirty days.''

⚬"An odd-shaped one, such as a 'hooked' one, is not very appealing.''

⚬"I am insecure about my own genitals because the cock (5¾") seems
too small and the balls are proportionate. Also when relaxed my penis gets
quite small and does not project through my trousers the way some men's
do. This feeling of inadequacy prevents me from competing in the ass-
fucking arena—a source of no end of unhappiness, despair, and ultimately
loneliness.''

⚬"How do I feel about male genitals? Whoo-ee. Alpha and omega.''

⚬"I have a lot of difficulty with uncircumcised cocks. Being Jewish, I
associate them with uncleanness, as well as with paganness. I haven't
thought too much about balls. Generally I like them whatever way they
come. The strangest cock I've ever seen was on someone with whom I had a
two-month-long affair. He was over 6 feet tall (we looked like Mutt and
Jeff), and his cock was shaped like a semicircle. It was very thin. He had the
hugest balls I've ever seen and when he fucked me they would swing below

and hit my ass, which was a feeling I adored. Sometimes I get into considering my cock as a friend and I give him a name."

&"I don't find male genitals particularly attractive. They may be essential for sex, and feel good (my own or to grope), but I don't think they look pretty, bare."

&"I came to realize I was homosexual first through my strong appeal to male genitalia."

&"I like pubic hair, usually, to be fine and soft, so that the overall feeling or sensation of the genitalia is one of richness, comfort, and soft texture, even when the penis is turgid."

&"I'm always aware of my own sex sitting there in my pants/shorts/trunks. I like my own cock a lot, my balls, too, especially when they're tight and horny and I haven't had sex or jerked off for a couple of days. Sometimes I like to dance naked at home and watch my dick and balls swing back and forth and slap against my belly. It's my best friend. Sometimes I like to sniff my balls. I like the smell of nuts, mine and others. I don't like the smell of piss, though, on mine or the other guy's cock. I like the feel of them, too, both erect and just there."

&"Smooth shafts are more appealing to me than veiny ones, and a simple curvature up, when erect, is nicer than those that stand out in peculiar directions."

&"I recently had sex with a 14-year-old boy for the first time, and I was amazed at the smooth feel of his hairless balls."

&"I consider myself a feminist male, but I am angry at the way some feminist writing expresses negative views of male genitals. I know that some women have been fucked over by men, but as a gay man I don't want to have to feel guilty or bad about loving my own genitals or male genitals in general. On the other hand, I also get angry at gay men who show signs of disgust when the subject of female genitals is brought up. I agree with Walt Whitman that all parts of the body, male and female, are beautiful and wonderful."

&"It amazes me how gay men can be sexist about women smelling like 'fish,' when the male genitals are odor-producing, too. The smell doesn't appeal to me but is less distasteful than the product of orgasm."

&"I especially enjoy heavily veined cocks. I enjoy cocks which resemble my own; I always feel like my cock is brothers/friends with a similar one in size and shape. I don't much mind 'funky' smells, but I *hate* any treatment which is supposed to improve the smell, like lotions, powders, cologne. That truly disgusts me. I assume immediately that the person hates his cock."

&"I find male genitals humdrum in themselves as shapes or symbols. I like the immediate contact with an erection, but find the genitals most exciting when covered by bathing trunks or the like where some mystery as to their actuality remains."

&"I feel that testicles are ugly, and asses too, especially when they are

craggy and irregular as mine have become. Still, the sensations and smells on the surface of testicles are beautiful.''

⚤ ''I like my own cock very much, probably because of the compliments. I'm 7¼" uncircumcised, but straight and smooth. Many people have said, 'Beautiful, just beautiful.' I agree! Others: I like medium to large cocks, circumcised or not, 6" to 9". I like straight cocks, not bent or twisted, or curved up or down greatly. I like thick as opposed to thin cocks. I don't like poorly circumcised cocks, with ridges or scores, and don't like 'pink' cocks. I like clean cocks and men. I am turned off by smells, BO and smegma.''

⚤ ''I am in awe of male genitals. In a way I almost feel a divinity about them.''

No less a literary figure than Lillian Hellman has dealt, if only briefly, with the question of penis size. In a section of her memoir *Pentimento,* dealing with her theater days, Hellman recalls the night the director Herman Shumlin went to talk to Tallulah Bankhead about taking a part in one of Hellman's plays. Bankhead asked that the consultation take place while she was in bed with a bottle and John Emery, an actor boy friend. As Shumlin rose to go, Hellman recalls, ''Tallulah said, 'Wait a minute, darling, just a minute. I have something to show you.' She threw aside the sheets, pointing down at the naked, miserable Emery, and said, 'Just tell me, darling, if you've ever seen a prick that big.' '' Hellman adds: ''I still have a diary entry, written a few days later, asking myself whether talk about the size of the male organ isn't a homosexual preoccupation: if things aren't too bad in other ways I doubt if any woman cares very much. Almost certainly Tallulah didn't care about the size or the function: it was the stylish, *épater* palaver of the day.''

Well, penis size probably is a ''homosexual preoccupation,'' though more precisely it probably is a male preoccupation, for there is a sense in which *all* men check each other out for penis size. Culturally speaking, big cocks are akin to big muscles and big guns. But for some gay men, it may just be a matter of aesthetics. The survey did not specifically ask whether the men preferred large penises or not, but judging from some of the comments, big cocks are often but not always considered the priceless treasures or prize endowments that their owners may think. Here, then, are the comments on size:

⚤ ''They say that there are two kinds of gay men: size queens and liars.''

⚤ ''Male genitals—the bigger the better. My adolescent lovers had enormous cocks for their ages. I was spoiled. I am a 'size queen'! I prefer clean genitals but can't afford to be choosy. My cock is small. Soft, it disappears below mounds of fat. When hard it's about 3 or 4 inches. Maybe this has a lot to do with my sexual preferences, but I have known I was anally oriented since I was a very young child. I have always enjoyed inserting things into my ass.''

♂"I prefer a smaller, thinner penis on a partner—6 inches at most—because of sucking ease (also easier to get fucked by it!). Balls that fit comfortably in my mouth are better than giants. You can save all the 'size queen' dudes for the gay porno magazines—I never want them for partners."

♂"I won't let a small cock fuck me. The stabbing and choppy motions are painful. It is much easier to take a large cock."

♂"I've never had a size complex. I'm large and my penis has given me pleasure, no argument. For myself, I would rather have a lover about 4″ to 5″. I can suck it or get fucked by it without choking or feeling like my guts are being ripped out. Size is a visual fantasy; the reality of accommodating 7″ is quite another thing. Cocks are the central symbol of what I love—my own sex. I adore them—feel, smell, taste, sight. I am enraptured by them."

♂"Those that I've found are turned on to me just because of my size usually turn me off."

♂"I am an uncircumcised male. I am always shy about the size of my cock when flaccid and unsheathed. When I am naked in front of others I usually pull back the foreskin, exposing the head. This manual contact usually is enough to make my cock lengthen somewhat and in any case, in my opinion, it looks better—more like a circumcised cock, which is the norm. However, when erect, I have a quite handsome 7½″ cock with a beautiful, healthy head on it. My balls are a good handful and I feel quite good about my male equipment."

♂"I know this is a stereotype—but on the average the black men I have had sex with have larger cocks than the white men."

♂"I am often told my penis is of gigantic size. This does not make me feel good because I do not care to screw (fuck); I love *getting* fucked."

♂"Some real large cocks do not ever get really hard, and I like a cock to become good and hard for real sex fun."

♂"I am always amazed when my partner, who might be very well hung, will mention that I have a very nice cock. My ego swells like mad. Of course, there is one advantage in having a cock on the small side. No one ever says, 'You're not going to stick that monster in me!' "

♂"When I see a man (he doesn't have to be gay), I always think—how big?"

♂"Since adolescence, I've felt that I was 'underendowed' and experienced great embarrassment in locker rooms, at the doctor's office, etc. I always feared the thought of having to disrobe in front of a group of my peers, and my particular fear was of a mass disrobing during army physicals. I have learned that I am really unendowed in relation to other men, but I've learned to live with it. I know that I still can sexually satisfy other men, but I still feel some insecurity when with a sexual partner with a much larger penis."

♂"To me size is very important, and I really envy big size since I am only

average, and I spend a lot of fantasy energy imagining myself to be enormous and have a beautiful body, etc. I am very unhappy with the average size of my dick and balls; I would like them to be enormous, even to the point of grotesque.''

♂"I am not a size queen, but I must say I can't get very excited over a teeny-weeny.''

♂"I am very size-conscious—the bigger, the better. I once had an experience with someone who had had silicone injections. It looked nice through jeans but was grotesque naked—the head was extremely small in comparison to the girth. I am somewhat disturbed with my own penis, which is long enough but is very thin and has a very pronounced downward bend when erect. My testes are much larger than average and bigger than those of almost everyone I've met, for which I am glad. Large, heavy testes seem to turn some people on.''

♂"Why should a man who was born with a larger penis receive special treatment or admiration? The tremendous emphasis placed on size causes men to feel insecure.''

Circumcision—the surgical removal of the foreskin—is one of the most rigorously obeyed laws of the Jewish people. It is also required by other religions, and despite disagreement has become widely accepted as a health measure by Western medicine. The continuing debate over circumcision is by no means a gay-male issue, but gay men, so enthralled with the phallus, have strong views on the subject. Here are some of them, starting with a first-person account of adult circumcision:

♂"For my first 21 years I felt a little bit more different than my peers, because I was uncircumcised. I discovered this fairly early in life, having seen other kids and adults, and found myself in another minority other than my semi-conscious homosexuality.

"Later the difference was aggravated by one of my seventh-grade classmates yelling across the locker room, 'Hey,———, who sharpened yours? It was very funny to my classmates, but crushing enough to make me self-conscious about undressing around others, and launch me on a lifelong 'head count' of who isn't and who is circumcised.

"While still attending high school, I discovered the best way to make my survey was by viewing men through glory holes and stall-door jambs. This satisfied my voyeuristic curiosities and was and remains a great turn-on for me.

"At age 18, I tuned in, turned on, and came out. I started going to gay bars during the time I was running around the country. Once in Philadelphia, and very short of cash, I decided to hustle a few bucks, since I was unable to collect enough spare change. I sold myself to a particularly unattractive john who promised to pay me $20 for each time I was able to come. We went around the corner to a seedy hotel, where he paid for a

room for the night or whatever. Upon reaching the room I dashed to the bathroom to be sure I was completely clean (it seems that even as careful as I was there could always be a slight trace of smegma).

"He examined my penis with a displeased expression, took a few swipes, then stared as my erection disappeared. He finally said he had changed his mind. I suspected he had and was trying to beat me out of the cash. I really didn't understand the sudden change, being very inexperienced with both hustling and the gay scene. Naively, I suggested that possibly our horoscope signs were incompatible, to which he replied, 'Yeah, I only like signs that are circumcised.'

"At age 21, I encountered what I thought to be the first love of my life—a beautifully tanned Adonis. He was very gracious about using either my mouth or ass, but always managed to avoid going anywhere near my penis. One evening during a passionate session, I suggested to him that I would like him to go down on me. The suggestion was greeted with a very loud and surprisingly final 'No.' No explanation was necessary—I had been here before. I left very quietly.

"I had decided that I really didn't like being different physically from what I had approximated to be 99 44/100% of America. I made an appointment with a surgeon in another town. I had to keep this embarrassment a secret. He scheduled to operate a week later; I could hardly wait.

"At the hospital (I've since learned it could have been an office operation), I was prepped by an orderly, given a shot of Demerol, and floated via stretcher to the operating room. They slipped off my hospital smock and gave me a very pleasant armful of sodium pentathol, and next thing I knew I was being wheeled back to recover. I had finally done it, and I couldn't wait to see the results.

"It had apparently been through an ordeal, because it was very swollen and purple with black stitches around the incision, kind of a junior Frankenstein. I knew it would heal and become even more normal than before. I was finally relieved of my hangup.

"About two weeks later, it completely healed, although a little more pink than usual. I was finally normal. I thought I had kept a pretty good secret, but when I got home I received a call from an acquaintance congratulating me on my loss. He was also uncircumcised and had decided to go ahead and also have the operation. He also had been hung up for years about it. It was the strange beginning of a friendship.

"I had some difficulty adjusting to my newly exposed head, but the period of adjustment was short compared to the years I had been emotionally uncomfortable. I still feel I made the right decision. I'm glad I was able to make the decision for myself. I do find it easier to maintain. I find sex just as pleasurable as before, maybe even more comfortable. I still have no preference for circumcised or uncircumcised partners. I'm glad I'm circumcised even though I've run into people who 'don't like guys who are cut.' Such is the irony of our penis-centered cuture."

☞"In performance, I prefer the circumcised one, as the uncut is usually more sensitive, and more easily hurt by rough play. Thus I find myself being more careful with the uncut and this distracts from the freedom of fun."

☞"Being circumcised is a must for me; uncircumcised pricks turn me cold. I just like that German-helmet-looking head running around in my mouth."

☞"I had a late circumcision and the scar is not too aesthetically pleasing."

☞"In reference to circumcision, I am very negative about this being done without the male making this decision for himself. This meaning that it should not be done at birth. The mother should never make this decision and the father in most cases does not know the pros and cons of circumcision. And in most cases the doctor does not know much more. Most people do not understand what the skin can add to a man's life; if he is into masturbation this is a great aid."

☞"Circumcision is a subject which I have firm opinions on—it is totally unnecessary except for a very few congenital conditions which exist. I prefer uncircumcised penises, but have found relatively few due to the predilections of our medical fraternity."

☞"Uncircumcised cocks really turn me on. I never saw one until I was in high school and our football coach was uncut. I made it with him several times and we never needed any lubricant when he fucked me. It was so hot, and I dig uncut cocks a lot now!"

☞"I'll admit that although I'm circumcised, I wish that I still had my foreskin. For me, an uncircumcised man's penis is particularly attractive; it seems to me more 'natural'; there is something extra to play with and enjoy. When I meet a really pleasant man who is uncircumcised, then I compliment him and tell him he's lucky. Uncircumcised men are usually quite surprised by this because they tell me they have often met with rejection or a negative response from men who object to a foreskin. As long as personal hygiene is observed, why should a circumcised man complain if his partner is 'uncut'? This is another kind of oppressive behavior gay men should try to eliminate."

Blow Jobs/Fellatio/Cocksucking/French Culture

A Boston-based gay-male newspaper, *Fag Rag*, once published an article entitled "Cocksucking as an Act of Revolution," and the author, Charley Shively, then went on to write a series of articles discussing the revolutionary dimensions of gay male sexuality. "Cocksucker" is one of the nasty words that men call each other in this society, and years ago it was one of the words that got comedian Lenny Bruce arrested for obscenity. "It sucks!" is current hip jargon for something disagreeable, and this usage is probably just an extension of the taboo against cocksucking. "Fellatio" is a word of Latin origin that scientists have used as their fancy synonym for

sucking cock, and no one seems to know why blow jobs are called blow jobs.

"French culture" is an old-fashioned phrase used for cocksucking, generally not much in use these days except occasionally in personal ads. Curiously, "French active" designates the insertor, even though the cocksucker ("French passive") may be doing all the work! Whether this practice is especially common in France is beyond the scope of this research. So much for the semantics.

The survey shows that an overwhelming majority of the gay men are inveterate cocksuckers, and as many like getting a good blow job. The following chart indicates *the frequency of the gay men's experiences with various aspects of fellatio,* followed by a chart indicating *feelings about them, regardless of participation.*

	ALWAYS	VERY FREQUENTLY	SOMEWHAT FREQUENTLY	SOMEWHAT INFREQUENTLY	VERY INFREQUENTLY	ONCE	NEVER
sucking your partner's cock	39	35	14	5	6	.5	2%
getting your cock sucked	26	46	17	8	3	0	.5
coming in your partner's mouth	7	31	26	15	15	2	3
partner coming in your mouth	10	30	25	12	15	3	5
swallowing partner's come	24	23	18	11	12	3	9
partner swallows your come	14	30	23	13	13	2	5
simultaneous sucking ("69")	5	20	25	25	18	3	4
simultaneous orgasm during "69"	3	4	9	18	33	6	27

	VERY POSITIVE	SOMEWHAT POSITIVE	NEUTRAL	SOMEWHAT NEGATIVE	VERY NEGATIVE	NOT SURE
sucking your partner's cock	73	16	5	3	1	0%
getting your cock sucked	78	14	7	2	0	0
coming in your partner's mouth	64	16	15	2	2	0
partner coming in your mouth	55	21	10	7	6	.5
swallowing partner's come	50	20	13	7	9	1

	VERY POSITIVE	SOMEWHAT POSITIVE	NEUTRAL	SOMEWHAT NEGATIVE	VERY NEGATIVE	NOT SURE
partner swallows your come	56	15	24	3	2	1
simultaneous sucking ("69")	51	20	17	7	3	1
simultaneous orgasm during "69"	49	16	24	4	4	3

For many people, as the statistics indicate, oral sex is not seen as the final goal. Later in this chapter, people's experiences with anal intercourse and manual stimulation indicate that often oral sex is used as incidental foreplay and the actual orgasm occurs by other means. However, for about half of the respondents, oral sex is a preferred method of coming, when compared to other sexual acts, as can be seen in the tables in this chapter. The following group of "very pleasing" experiences have in common the use of oral sex as the main sexual focus. Appreciation of the phallus itself is an important aspect of cocksucking. It may be significant that two of the experiences were first or youthful ones. Many men indicated that oral sex was preferred by them in their earlier years of homosexual life, before developing a preference for anal sex, though of course there are those who always prefer oral sex. Some of these experiences indicate that even when most of the erotic energy is in oral sex, the actual stimulation for orgasm is supplied by other means (usually the hand), but the experiences are included because of the oral focus:

&"My first and most pleasant lovemaking experience was when I was in the army during World War II. I was only a corporal, but I was always being assigned duty with this very good-looking captain. One day we were ordered to go to Brussels to pick up some rivets being made for the engineers. We were to spend the night in Liége, and we obtained separate rooms in a hotel there.

"The night was so cold, and so was my room, that I shivered under what covers I had. Then the captain came in. He asked me if I was comfortable, and I told him I was freezing. He said that he was also and said that he knew it was against regulations, but he suggested with such adverse conditions that we might be warmer sleeping together. The thought excited me, but I was afraid at the same time. I was only 20.

"Anyway, he stripped to his shorts and climbed in with me. I became very excited. My penis became very stiff. I wanted so much to reach over and fondle his crotch, but was still afraid.

"I guess he sensed my tenseness—he reached down and felt my hand with his. Then he turned facing me, and suddenly I was aware of his penis and testicles against my hand. It drove me wild, and I threw caution to the

wind. I started fondling his genitals and felt them become stiff in my hand. He gave a little groan and the next thing I knew he was on top of me. He pulled his shorts off and so did I. I wrapped my arms around him and we rubbed wildly against each other—cock against cock, balls against balls. I kissed him square on the mouth—a deep sensuous French kissing. I could feel the sticky viscous prostate fluid [sic] getting my penis sticky. Never had I wanted a man so much as I did this one. Emboldened by our lovemaking, I told him I loved him. He responded by nibbling on my ear and hoarsely gasping in my ear, 'Please suck me off—you're driving me wild.' With that, he rolled off me onto his back. I tongued and kissed every square inch of him down to his very stiff penis, which I joyfully took in my mouth. The taste of his penis flesh was fresh and clean. My fingers encircled his cock, as I have done with all men I have sucked. Then I love it when the cock swells almost to bursting and suddenly I feel the semen rushing through the urethra and then exploding into my mouth. It turns me on to hear him groan and breathe hard as he ejaculates into my mouth. The captain's semen was very thick and copious and smooth-tasting. Some men's semen tastes very bitter, but not my captain's. I savored every drop. After that, every time we got together, we had sex. We both loved each other, but because of the army, we had to hide it.

"There are many men in the services this way, and I feel that if sexual freedom in private were allowed in the service, there would be no fear of blackmail for secrets—they (the enemy) would have to find some other way. Also the old fig that the troops would be demoralized is a bunch of hogwash, because only those who desired to do so would participate."

⚥ "This very pleasing lovemaking experience happened not too long ago in Vermont. This is important because being in northern Vermont enhances every minute and every experience of every day. It was the first night I had spent with a person who is now a very close friend. I had just occupied a room in a college dorm when he came up, telling me that he had lived in the room previous to me. He was looking for a poster. It wasn't there, but we began to talk. We talked for about three hours and it was beautiful, as if we were finally brought together to meet in person, although our souls had known each other before. He needed a place to stay, so I told him he could get a mattress from downstairs and sleep once more in his old room. He thought that was great. During all this time there was no seduction going on—just enjoyment of each other's company and newness. When it was time to go to bed I realized he didn't have a sleeping bag, at which point I told him that he could share my bed if he wanted. Still at this point, no seduction. We didn't know if the other was gay. So, we both got completely undressed and went to bed. It was a single twin-size mattress. The light from the moon and the stars was illuminating the room. There was a serenity in the air. We were both very pleased to have met and for having talked for three hours. He is very kind and loving. I try to be that way, too. Slowly, we explored the sexuality of the other. We both lay flat on our backs, fingers and toes oh-so-gently brushing the other and then resting next to the other's

skin. Meeting no rebuff or retreat, more than just the fingertips and toe tips was put to the other person. And then knees, or calves, or thighs. But always gently—aggressive and tender, assured yet tentative at the same time. My hand went to his beautiful straight blond hair. I caressed him. He reached out to me—took my other hand. We embraced. I was on the bottom, he on top. My hairy chest to his hairless one. My arms around him, his at my face. Genitals to genitals. Legs entangled. A deep, probing kiss— what a moment! It seemed to last for a very long time. How happy we both were—happy and alive! We'd look at each other often and smile. I'd lick him, his neck and ears; he loved to have me lick his ears. He was on the bottom. I over him, on my knees, I'd lick his chest and under his arms. I love to lick armpits, except when the person uses underarm deodorant. Often, I'd return to his face, to kiss his mouth. What beautiful kissing we had! I'd lick his face and go back to his chest and then lower and lower, to his groin and thighs. I'd lick his genitals and then go to his legs and feet. Then come back up his legs and lick his ass and anus. What a beautiful ass he had! Oh, how fortunate we were to have the moonlight shining in through the three big windows. And I worked my way back to his genitals. I sucked his cock and balls. I used my hand with my mouth still over his penis. I took it way down my throat. He came. We were both esctatic. He pulled me back up so he could kiss my mouth—a long sweet, probing kiss. He rolled me onto my back, kissed and licked me here and there (my tits, my navel, the space between my scrotum and my anus, my anus), and went to my genitals. He sucked my cock and balls lovingly and very quickly I came and came and came. And then I pulled him back up to my mouth and once more kissed in that beautiful way which we found with each other. We rested and lay in each other's arms, me on the bottom again, he on top, always caressing each other, bringing each other manually to orgasm again. Resting, caressing, and then 69-ing and coming for the third orgasm, this one simultaneously. How satiated we were—how good we felt! How well we slept that night! The windows were open, the breeze was blowing. What a feeling of being alive!''

    ☯ "I will now describe a very pleasing lovemaking experience that happened to me recently. I met a young man, aged 24 but younger-looking, in a bar. I went over to him and said, 'What is a cute thing like you doing by yourself?' He looked around and said, 'Who? Me?' After that I sat down next to him and talked. We went to another bar and I bought him a drink. Then we went to his house.

    "This guy really turned me on. He was incredibly handsome. I'm not boasting, but he was one of the nicest partners I had in my entire life. He was rather quiet and shy. He was no closet case, though, because he had just graduated college in Maine and was active in the Wilde-Stein club up there. I'm almost always turned on by guys with some body hair, particularly some hair on the chest, but this one was almost hairless. He was French, Scotch, and American Indian background.

    "We went into his bedroom and started kissing and hugging. My

excited hands started to caress and stroke his entire body. Then I put my hands under his shirt and massaged his slender but well-built torso. My fingers played with his nipples. I gently lifted his shirt off his back. We were now lying in bed, still French-kissing and fondling each other. My eager hands first groped his stiffening cock through his pants. It was unbearably delightful. Then I reached under his pants and grabbed his erection. I gently pulled his pants off while he pulled my shirt off and was kissing my chest. Naked, we both hugged and held each other. It was bliss; he was so tender and so gentle.

"I took the first initiative and lowered my head towards his crotch. His beautifully perfect cock was extremely hard and stiff. I took my tongue and ran it from the base to the tip. Then I tongued his sex organ horizontally. After it was well lubricated, I put the whole thing in my mouth (total ecstasy!) and started to give him a blow job. He was not too big, about 5″ or 6″, so I was able to swallow the entire thing. He started to groan and grabbed my penis. Soon we got into a 69 position and we sucked each other off. I came first, I was very excited. After I came I devoted about ten minutes or so until he came. Besides sucking him, I also used my fingers by sucking him and masturbating him at the same time. He finally came, and I gladly swallowed his come. Before I swallowed I let his come stay in my mouth a moment or two so I could fully taste this essence of him. I was thrilled beyond belief."

The men expressed a variety of attitudes and experiences relating to blow jobs:

♯"Fellatio—in my view, the quintessential sexual love act. It is a coalescence of feelings, it is artwork in action, each act is its own masterpiece, it is a joining of body and emotion, it is poetry of human existence."

♯"Not one of my favorite acts (I prefer eating food.)"

♯"Would rather suck a cock than eat a meal."

♯"I seem to enjoy it when performed on me but I find it somewhat difficult to do the reverse on my partner."

♯"I love to give a blow job but don't care if it does not happen to me."

♯"I used to see a man who would take out his false teeth and suck me with his gums and I loved it."

♯"I'm pretty picky. I like lots of pressure but no teeth. Not that many of the guys who do me can do it well."

♯"Can really get into doing it to a guy if he shows signs (words, groans, squirming, etc.) that he is enjoying it."

♯"I would never give a blow job to someone who is not highly attractive to me."

♯"I enjoy swallowing a man's semen only if I like the man. I feel that by swallowing his semen he becomes a part of me. He becomes part of my bloodstream and goes with me wherever I go."

☯"I worry that I'm not doing a good job and—with a few memorable exceptions—blow jobs don't turn me on that much. I usually take a long time to come and worry that the man doing me is getting tired."

☯"I love the guy to force his cock down my throat when he's going to come, and the more of a load he's got the better. You haven't included 'face-fucking,' which is somewhat the same but lying down—with the fucker doing like push-ups. This is also a lot of fun."

☯"I like teeth (gently) crosswise on my cock. Sort of 'corn-on-the cob' style. I tend not to suck cock. People want my ass so much, they usually come by fucking me. So I tend to be out of practice and hence don't do it."

☯"Blowing someone without my dentures is a turn-on. With very young boys the taste of sperm is sweetish and pleasant; as they grow older there are brackish and bitter overtones, but everyone's tastes different."

☯"Come is like wine to me."

☯"I regard cocksucking as distasteful, though I used to do it when I was new to gay sex in order to accommodate a partner. Now I usually please myself and find some way to avoid sucking a partner's cock."

☯"I don't like the taste of come, and can't understand why my partner would; therefore even if he wants me to come in his mouth, I have a hard time doing so."

☯"Most guys do not really know how to suck cock. (Thus, the old joke: 'Suck, you bastard, suck; it's only *called* a blow job!') Most of the time, it feels so soothing, instead of stimulating, that I go soft and have often fallen asleep because of the relaxation produced."

☯"Very negative opinions; have thrown up twice."

☯"I like sucking on a soft cock, flattening it against the top of my mouth and my tongue, rolling it around, sucking it deep into my throat. Then feeling it getting hard, growing bigger, filling my mouth. I like to feel my sex partner thrusting his cock deep into my throat."

☯"I tend to concentrate on the tip and head of a penis. I do not like to take it deep, and have no interest in trying to swallow the whole thing."

☯"I will perform fellatio on my lover but just cannot bring myself to take sperm into my mouth."

☯"I love the feel of sperm shooting into my mouth. I especially enjoy the *idea* of someone coming in my mouth."

☯"I love the sensation of a full mouth of warm throbbing flesh ready to shoot and the piston action of a good-sized cock head reaming my throat. I like to use the saliva technique and slide my thumb and forefinger tightly along his wet cock shaft with each thrust of my mouth over his cock head."

☯"The ultimate is to 69 and climax at the same time."

☯"I do not enjoy the practice of 69 because it is distracting to suck someone while he is sucking me. Also, it is easier to get bit."

☯"I don't like to be 'force-fucked in the mouth' by a man with a large penis. It makes me gag and makes me feel like I'm being raped or forced."

☯"In all modesty I'm very good at it. Once at an orgy of approximately

thirty-five people I had nine of them standing in line waiting a turn, and at a movie theater which shows fuck-films and has a lot of carrying on in the audience, I sucked off thirteen guys, one after another.''

⚭''I react negatively when someone sucks me off and then leaves to spit out my come, so I usually swallow my partner's come if he comes.''

⚭''My wife doesn't do it well—too small a mouth, not relaxed enough.''

⚭''I remember the first time I ever had my penis sucked off, many years ago. It was in the bus depot in Calgary. There was a whole row of toilets. I went into one, and there was a big hole in the wall and a guy in the next one. I put my big hard penis through the hole and suddenly there was this real nice feeling going through my cock. I thought at first that he was jacking me off; then I realized that he was sucking on it. It was such a beautiful feeling and suddenly I was shooting into his mouth. That was my first experience and it was beautiful.''

⚭''If I have a number that can't come right away or can't come at all, it's okay by me; I just love to suck and suck and suck. Ninety-nine percent of the time I suck so-called straight kids between 14 and 19. I feel that I am there to give pleasure to them, and nothing in return. I get my sexual gratification doing them.''

⚭''A blow job is a sadomasochistic turn-on for me. I feel superior to the one doing it to me, and I feel like a slave to the one I do it to. The cock itself doesn't turn me on; the getting down on my knees before a beautiful male to serve him does turn me on.''

⚭''Cocksucking I enjoy most in anonymous sex situations (like backroom bars). For me, more than any other form of gay male sex, cocksucking (where I do the sucking) is a form of sex I use to express my feelings about power, as well as the 'dirtiness' of sex. I love being on my knees in front of someone bigger than me while he jams my face into his crotch, stuffing his cock all the way down my throat, feeding me a popper and whispering, 'Suck my cock.' Perhaps because I associate cocksucking with something 'dirty,' and because for me it means, on some level, being powerless (identifying with the aggressor?), it is not something I get into very much with lovers or people I feel affectionate towards.''

⚭''I sometimes have the desire to suck my own cock. I've even had dreams where I was able to do it. Since I can't, really, though, the next best thing is to suck someone's else's. When I suck I would like to be able to get my lips all the way down around the base of the cock, but I haven't learned to 'deep-throat' yet, though I've practiced with a hot dog on a fork.''

⚭''I really get off on cocksucking. I love it. I feel bad about some men who won't let me suck their cock (rare, but it has happened). I also like to take the scrotum in my mouth and to savor the shape and size and texture of each testis separately. I like to have one ball in my mouth and the rest of the scrotum out of my mouth, and to pull away and see how this works. In some cases, it will hurt my partner, and then I stop. But some men like the intensity of the sensation up to a peak point, and that is fun to achieve

together. About cocksucking, I especially like to suck up and down the shaft, and to try to slip my tongue in and out of the urethral opening.''

⚥"One characteristic of me sexually is that I come an unusually large quantity; I enjoy that many men notice and comment and enjoy this trait.''

⚥"I often like to have a lot of control over the person's head with my hands, forearms, thighs; I seldom feel mean but like to feel controlling.''

⚥"Fellatio is my primary source of guilt in lovemaking since I intensely dislike touching the genitals of another man (except through clothing), and do not want to fellate anyone unless I am drunk and they are very 'butch.' It seems to be 'legit' for me to do things under the threat of physical harm— someone 'butch' could beat me, etc., if I didn't do what he said so I'm not voluntarily doing these 'bad things' and the guilt is removed.''

⚥"My partner, entirely nude, must submit to fellatio in utter passivity, while I remain fully clothed, refusing any reciprocal action except kissing. Ergo, I am never in full body contact with my partner at any time. My own release is obtained through masturbation, after I have blown my partner to an ingested climax and separated from him. I never masturbate in his presence. I am 100% oral, my sexual expression being exclusively fellatio.''

⚥"I enjoy the excitement of having all five senses so very directly involved with the phenomenally powerful and awesome experience of male orgasm when I go down on a guy.''

A number of men commented on how their attitudes about blow jobs have changed over time:

⚥"There was a time when I felt guilty over my preference to be blown rather than to blow. Then I discovered there is this whole crew of men who actually preferred to blow.''

⚥"Initially I wouldn't let anybody come in my mouth. Now I love eating my partner's come.''

⚥"I have had to teach myself, with a good lover's patient help and advice, to be a good cocksucker. Now I love it, but when we started together I found prolonged sucking tedious and my jaw muscles ached. I worked too hard, and we both got uptight. Now I love it, and can deep-throat suck for long stretches, and the feeling of security and protection that comes while I'm sucking especially when he caresses and directs my head, is so intense I occasionally almost cry from the joy of it.''

⚥"When I was a teenager and in my twenties I couldn't abide cocksucking, either to do it, or to tolerate someone doing it to me. I've now accepted it as a part of sex, but rarely as an end in itself.''

⚥"When I first came out, I didn't like performing fellatio, but now I wouldn't give it up for anything.''

⚥"A few years ago I would not do most things, blow jobs especially, because I thought it was 'disgusting.' This was connected with my being ashamed of being gay. That's all changed now.''

⚥"I find I can take the come of people better now than I did at first. No one *loves* the taste of come!"

Anal Intercourse/Butt-Fucking/Greek Culture

In the Commonwealth of Massachusetts (as in some other states), the union of the penis and the anus is known as "the abominable and detestable crime against nature." Reading the responses to the questionnaire, it is clear that there are innumerable men who find nothing but delight in anal inter-course, while its popularity at this time and throughout recorded human history would seem to imply that it has the blessing of Mother Nature no matter what some nervous priests, ministers, rabbis, gurus, and lawmakers might have to say. Also referred to by such names as "ass-fucking," "butt-fucking," "cornholing," and the old gay slang "browning," anal inter-course is a frequent choice of sexual pleasure for about half of the men in our survey, though it is assiduously avoided by many. The following chart indicates *how frequently the men participate in various aspects of ass-fucking:*

	ALWAYS	VERY FREQUENTLY	SOMEWHAT FREQUENTLY	SOMEWHAT INFREQUENTLY	VERY INFREQUENTLY	ONCE	NEVER
fucking your partner	3	20	24	18	21	5	9%
getting fucked	5	21	16	15	21	8	13
coming inside your partner	17	18	18	13	19	4	12
partner coming inside you	18	19	14	11	16	5	17
come while being fucked (without manipulating yourself)	1	3	5	6	20	7	59
come while being fucked (with manipulation)	9	13	12	11	18	4	33

Good feelings about the various aspects of anal intercourse are widespread, but hardly universal. Over a fifth of the men avoid this act, and a similar number have some negative feelings about it. Later in this chapter, gay men discuss their problems with anal intercourse, and the subject is also brought up by some men in chapter 17, devoted to hangups. The following chart indicates responses to the question, *Whether or not you engage in any of the following, indicate how you feel about each of them:*

	VERY POSITIVE	SOMEWHAT POSITIVE	NEUTRAL	SOMEWHAT NEGATIVE	VERY NEGATIVE	NOT SURE
fucking your partner	51	23	12	8	5	1%
getting fucked	42	20	7	13	16	1
coming inside your partner	60	18	11	6	4	1
partner coming inside you	57	15	10	7	11	2
come while being fucked (without manipulating yourself)	46	13	17	5	11	8
come while being fucked (with manipulation)	48	18	17	4	11	3

The following group of statements are from men whose pleasing sexual experience includes anal intercourse. These essays show the variety of experiences, including the focus of energy on the sex act itself, or, conversely, emphasis on the relationship, feelings about the partner, or simply the set of circumstances surrounding the encounter:

⚣"I'll try to describe an actual experience with my lover. The setting is the apartment we share together. Lovemaking begins on the verbal level, affection, appreciation of each other; interest in having sex is expressed in words. Soon we're lying in bed, still clothed, kissing and embracing. Then we help each other out of our clothes—and lie naked in each other's arms, kissing and rubbing our bodies against each other, groin to groin, so that our cocks touch and rub against each other. Each man reaches with a free hand for his partner's cock, and we gently masturbate one another. Then I turn my partner on his back and sit astride his thighs, rubbing our cocks together, using lots of spit for lubrication. Holding our cocks together with one hand, I lean forward and we kiss for a while; I continue rubbing our cocks with my hand. Then I lean back and move lower down on my partner's body and gently lick and suck his cock and balls. Soon he pushes me gently aside, turns me on my back and does the same to me (sits over me rubbing our cocks together, then sucks my cock for a while). Everything described so far takes about fifteen to twenty minutes.

"Soon we shift into a 69 position. Each man lies with one leg raised, bent at the knee; the other leg is flat on the bed, flexed so that each partner can rest his head on the other man's thigh while sucking. Also this position gives good exposure and availability to cock and balls. We stay in the 69 position, licking and sucking for about ten or fifteen more minutes. Both of us consider oral sex to be more a form of foreplay than a means of reaching orgasm.

"When we disengage from the 69 position, one of us asks the other, 'Want to fuck?' and we reach for the lubricant. Most of the time we use KY, occasionally Vaseline. We lie loosely in each other's arms, each with one hand free, and start loosening up each other's asshole with finger-fucking. We usually finger-fuck each other simultaneously, but the man who is going to get fucked first, usually me, gets more attention. First the outer rim of the asshole is rubbed with KY, then a finger is gently inserted and moved slowly until the asshole is loosened up. The finger is withdrawn, more lubricant applied, and the finger is inserted as deeply as it will comfortably go. Then the whole procedure is repeated, this time with two fingers. When two fingers can be inserted comfortably, my ass is ready for my lover's cock. I lie on my side, and with my hand I guide his cock into me. (Previously I have lubricated his cock with KY and masturbated it gently until his hard-on is good and stiff.) When my lover's cock is inside me, I relax, concentrate on the good feelings, and he starts fucking me, gently. He works his cock in deep, turns me over on my stomach, and fucks me for a while in that position. Then we disengage, put more lubricant in my asshole and on his cock, and I lie on my back, a towel underneath me, my legs up, knees bent, my feet resting on his shoulders. He reinserts his cock—by now my asshole is really loosened up and he can do anything he wants to with me. This is the part of getting fucked I enjoy the most: with his cock in me, my lover can lean forward and kiss me, and play with my nipples, cock, and balls. He fucks me slowly and rhythmically, and I like to feel him as deep inside me as possible as long as he does not thrust too hard. The speed of his thrusts increases as he reaches his climax. We cling together, kissing and moaning. Slowly we disengage, kiss some more, then lie together quietly.

"After we've rested for a while, my lover begins to play with my cock again until it is hard and I play some more with his asshole. When his asshole is good and loose, we lie on our sides and I enter him. Then I begin to fuck him gently, and sex proceeds as I described it above, with changes of position: first lying on our sides, then with my lover lying on his belly with me on top of him, finally with my lover lying on his back, knees and legs up, his feet on my shoulders. When this final position is reached, I am careful not to fuck my lover too hard or thrust into him too deeply, which he can find painful. In fact, when I am nearing my climax, I don't insert my cock up to the hilt, I keep it in about halfway (half its length) in my lover's asshole, and use short—not deep—quick thrusts as I come off. I like being able to look at my lover's face while I fuck him in the knees-up position, and see the changing expressions on his face; also enjoy playing with his nipples, cock, and balls. Looking at my lover while I am approaching climax and moving my body to give pleasure to us both is my favorite part of fucking. I can never make up my mind which I enjoy more—fucking or being fucked. It's like giving presents at Christmas and getting them at the same time.

"When my lover and I fuck each other, we usually take about thirty to

forty minutes. So the whole experience of love-making takes about 1½ hours or more. We enjoy making love in the morning or afternoon when possible; if we make love at night, there is usually a light on in the next room. Part of the pleasure is visual.

"I enjoy all the aspects of lovemaking in the session I have described but enjoy fucking and getting fucked the most, because it is so intense and intimate. After the 'sex' is over, we like to lie together quietly, sometimes kissing and embracing, resting. A beautiful experience."

⚥"One very pleasing experience which comes to mind happened a couple of years ago while I was going to the University of California at Davis. I met a man named Jose. One day we went riding our bicycles out into the countryside around the little college town of Davis, taking a picnic lunch. Several miles out we found a large field of tall grass of some sort. We pushed the bikes out into the middle of it, spread out the blanket, took off our clothes, and made the picnic. In a little while we were just sunning and sunning. We brought a jar of coconut oil, which became warm and creamy. When I bask in the sun it gets me very 'horny' all over my body as if the whole thing is a big penis getting erogenous. I think Jose is the same way, because soon we were putting the coconut oil all over each other and had the biggest erections ever. I got on top of Jose and started rubbing our bodies together, then kissing him and rubbing his body with my hands. He is rubbing me with his hands and twisting his hand around my cock. If he twists his hand sideways around the head it feels particularly good. I get both of our cocks together in my one hand and start thrusting against his while squeezing them together. Jose is moaning and rolling around on the blanket. He looks like Krishna (we went to the Krishna Temple together and danced to Krishna a lot at that time) and my heart feels like I will absorb him completely in all his beauty. After a bit I lean over to kiss him and guide his cock toward my asshole while kissing him. By this time we are so oily that it slips right in with no struggle or pain at all. I start rotating my hips and pulling up and down on his cock. Then I push myself up with my arms so that Jose can grasp my cock with his hand. He knows that I will start thrusting into his hand as if fucking and at the same time contracting my asshole with pleasure and pumping him all the more so as to get all the good feelings on my prostate from having his big cock rubbing and jabbing against it. Suddenly he gets all excited and wants to roll over so that he can get into fucking better (sometimes it is difficult to get into fucking uphill with a big weight sitting on you—to do it really pleasurably you have to pull the person forward to kiss you and then place your feet flat on the ground with the knees up so that you can push off with the feet to get leverage for the pelvic thrusts and hold the partner's hips in your hands so you can adjust them properly for you to pull back and thrust into them efficiently to bring off the orgasm.)

"We roll over carefully so as not to come uncoupled, I put my legs over his shoulders, cross the feet behind him, and pull him forward so as to kiss him. I put my two hands on my back and push upward so as to brace myself

for fucking and also so that he will have a good leverage for fucking (I learned this from doing the shoulder stand in a yoga class I took). Soon he is fucking away and forgets all about kissing. His eyes are closed and I know he is fantasizing and really getting into the sensations. He holds me by the sides and is thrusting, thrusting, thrusting like riding a horse galloping across the fields. I am moving too, rotating round and round and pulling down so that the head of his penis will come almost out and I can squeeze down with the anal muscles and grab on it. I begin to feel as if the sun itself has come inside my body and is glowing and shining all through me. I notice that come is running and dripping and shooting out of my penis as it flops against my belly so big and hard—I want to bend my head up and suck it (if I only could). Jose begins to make all sorts of noises and I notice that tears are popping out of his eyes and they fall all over me and mix with the come that is already all over my chest by now. Jose starts having orgasm and cries, 'Aargh, aargh,' begins trembling and shaking all over and throws himself on me hugging and moaning. I put my legs down and hold him around the waist with them. He leaves his penis in and we lie very still. The universe suddenly seems extremely quiet (as if my ears forgot how to hear) but little by little I again notice the grasses and hear small noises as they move slightly in the spring breeze. Nothing seems real. I feel as if I walked into a picture and all the trees and grasses, the distant houses are paper cutouts which someone has made on purpose to create this picture. I try to make it seem real but the intensity of our experience and the depth of abandon to sensation has been too much; I cannot believe that I am part and parcel of this thing. It seems like the crust on bread—an outer surface only—while underlying that are all these dimensions of intensity. Jose is all wet with sweat and is more slippery now than a noodle. I touch him and slowly he opens his eyes and looks at me. We communicate something but it is so deep that it touches a different dimension of human exchange than love—it is a sort of worship; an awe; an uncertainty as of madness at this possibility for such intensity and abandon.''

♁ "A prominent male whore—for men—in New York named Michael had attracted me all during the period when I was being kept by a very wealthy man, studying ballet, and appearing in some Broadway shows, but I could never get anywhere with Michael; didn't have the money and apparently was not attractive enough for him to sleep with me without money. Comes London, June, 1937; the Coronation of George VI. We—about fifteen people or so—were invited to an apartment that had windows overlooking the route of march. Everyone who was going to look at the parade the next day, including those of us who were (like many others) invited to an apartment along the route, had to be inside the police cordons by midnight the night before. So there we were; very little drinking, some wonderful conversation, a card game, etc., until finally everyone conked out, on sofas, the floor, wherever. I was aware that Michael was one of the guests, but only chatted with him casually. Sleep. The next morning, all at the windows to see the crowds, back into the apartment to eat scrambled

eggs and grilled tomatoes. Finally, the moment; the gold coach is coming! We all rushed to the windows again, as we had been doing all along to watch the parade: those gorgeous guardsmen, empire types, etc. As the gold coach was coming along, with George VI, newly crowned, his wife Elizabeth, and the daughters (the current E II R, and the wicked Margaret Rose, then a baby), I was leaning way out. I felt a hand close over mine, which was gripping the window sill. I looked slowly, thinking it was probably one of the creepy types that so often pursued me in those days. *No!* It was Michael! He didn't say anything at all, just looked with those enormous dark, dark eyes. It was an assent, anyway. Later when the parade was all over, he simply walked out, knowing that I would walk out with him. (I was a ballet student at Sadler's Wells at the time, and of course we had the day off, as did all of London and the whole country and empire.)

"We walked around awhile, glad to stretch after a night cooped up in the apartment. Then we went over to Buckingham Palace, where George VI, Elizabeth, and the two princesses were making regular appearances on the balcony, like those little figures that come out to tell the weather in those little houses. They would all wave regularly, palm upward in the manner of Dowager Queen Mary, who was also on the balcony with them.

"I climbed up on the monstrous statue of Queen Victoria which stands squarely in front of Buckingham Palace to get a better look. When I came down, with Michael's arms helping me, he suggested we go to the house of his then lover, a very wealthy long lanky Englishman named Peter something or other, who had gone to Switzerland to escape the crowds of the coronation. We did. Michael had the maid draw a bath for me, hot, perfumed with a lime essence, and Sybaritic in the extreme. He then bathed, and when he got out, there were lamb chops with a little Bordeaux waiting on trays in the bedroom. Huge double bed, thick, thick carpets, servants coming and going silently. Finally, after we had eaten we got into bed and slept a little while. Soon Michael's hands started exploring. Soon I had an erection and so did he. Skillfully, without seeming to manipulate, although he was, he raised my legs up over my chest, inserted his good-sized penis into my anus, and started fucking me. Very slowly at first. Soon I was up in the air—that is, lying on my back but with my whole ass up, so that he was on his knees, and doing a superb job of fucking me. Then, he started going down on me at the same time. I had, for one of the few times in my life, maintained an erection while being fucked. Michael was able to continue to penetrate me deeply, and at the same time suck me completely, taking all of my rather large prick into his mouth and throat. He kept this up, somehow caressing my whole body at the same time, until we both exploded into orgasm, almost simultaneously. I know the simultaneous orgasm is largely a myth, but it happened then. It was absolutely indescribable: glorious, incredible, after those two or three years of wanting this guy, and then having him do such a thorough job of pleasing me, himself, and any servants looking through the keyhole, although I expect there were similar shenanigans going on belowstairs.

"I ran into Michael on the street in New York two or three years later, and we tried to repeat the experience: it didn't work. Length of time, you ask: I have absolutely no idea; an eternity, a moment, but it is in me forever."

⚤ "For most of 1969, I lived in Lindos on the island of Rhodes. Lindos was a village of, perhaps, 600 persons, fifty of them non-Greek nationals; the remainder of the inhabitants drawn from eight countries around the world. I was one of seven Americans living there, having gone there to be apart from urban life (read New York City), to reorganize my life, examine priorities, do some creative thinking and work on ideas dear to me. I was on retreat and, as 'fooling around' with the Greek locals was strictly verboten, I expected to be celibate. I wasn't counting on Bill.

"Call him 'Botticelli Bill,' as someone did. My age (24), eastern-Canadian born and raised, an individual searcher like myself, arriving to live in Lindos about the same time I did. It took us a couple of months to actually get to know one another, and to discover a mutual attraction. A poet, Bill possessed a swimmer's body, slightly taller than my 6-foot height, smooth-skinned, tousled, taffy-yellow hair, heavy-lidded unremarkably blue eyes, curious of mind, sensitive and sensible; an Aquarius.

"We gravitated to each other almost accidentally, with me making the initial, embarrassed overtures. We were both eligible bachelors in the eyes of the non-Greek women, but we were not drawn to any of them (a fact which necessitated—in Bill's eyes—our keeping our time and activities to ourselves, as gossip travels quickly in such a setting and would surely have caused storms in chai cups had it been generally known; it *was* known to a few of our closest friends, all of whom approved of the pairing). After the initial breakthrough, we spent many days and most nights together with him keeping his house and I keeping mine, some few hundred yards distant from each other. Our liaison was to continue for three full and glorious months, until pressures finally exploded and Bill felt it necessary to quit Lindos for other places. As the only two 'gay' non-Greeks around, we were eventually ripe for scorn and ridicule, a fact which I wish Bill could have dismissed.

"Lindos was one of those magical spots of the world. A cluster of one- and two-story white-washed stone houses nestled in a crescent-shaped valley on the eastward coast of the island. An established archaeological preserve, the predominant feature of the town was its acropolis: a sudden upsurge of stone on the seaside of the village, some 350 feet high and flat-topped, dropping off almost sheerly to the sea. On top, the remains of a temple to Diana and surrounding it a mélange: Byzantine chapel, and Romanesque and medieval fortifications erected during the second and third Crusades—exotic, Arthurian, cross-culturally magical *in extremis*.

"One morning, early, early in April, Bill and I and a blanket made our way around that eastward face of the acropolis, along a narrow path across the cliff, out of sight of any humanity. At a point where the path widened by 8 feet, we laid our blanket. Above us only cloudless blue skies and birdsongs wafted by a breeze. Behind us the tips of the remaining columns

to Diana and the battlements surrounding them, 140 feet below. Below, another 200 feet, rocks against which pounded the surf of the Aegean, blue upon blue upon foam. In the distance as the sun rose above us, a storm could be seen making its way across the open water towards Turkey and its snow-capped summits in the distance (perhaps 12 miles). Around us a carpet of anemones shaded with every possible hue but green, a fragile, lone note of the Greek 'spring'; perhaps a few pellet goat droppings. Beneath us and our blanket all the rocks of Greece and the thin soil covering them. Primitive, basic, poetic, God-blessed and -blasted, an almost arid Eden. Precarious but not dangerous, a trifle rough on our bodies, but our own 'space' as long as we inhabited it . . . which we did for three hours or longer.

"I was Bill's first lover, and he was mine. For all his beauty and intelligence and sensitivity, he was uncertain as to his sexuality. He had had only a single sexual experience with a woman, and none before with men. Yet he took to sex, gay sex, as if it was part of his genetic heritage. What he didn't intuitively 'know,' he learned quickly. Quite pleasantly amazing. What I did, he liked. What he did, I liked. No toys, no aids—where would we have found them had we wanted any?—just we two and our 'pallet.'

"And so, as always, we kissed, deeply and lightly, here and there. All over. Two tongues probed every orifice, explored and re-explored. We nuzzled and caressed and hugged, and held. His smooth surfaces and my hairy body rubbed against each other. Neither of us was so much athletic as welcomely demonstrative. We couldn't have become too rambunctious, as there was no room for that.

"We took turns lying back on the blanket while the other sprawled, belly down, and sucked cock. My Piscean nature included a 69 position in all of this, but neither of us came. Twisting legs around head and shoulders, we could manage some analingus mutually. The excitement to each of us, because we were who we were and were with who we were with, stimulated the secretion of more than enough saliva to lubricate both our bodies. It was all either of us needed. And eventually, as these things may go, we fucked.

"It happened, as it almost never had before or since, that our cocks were virtually the same size, shape, and coloration. My olfactory nerves have never been acute and I cannot recall what particular odor his cock gave off (only that his sweat in the 70-degree air smelled sweet, and glistened on his chest and back). I do recall that his penis length was untouched by body hairs; they remained 'two dimensional' nesting his scrotal sack. Like mine, his cock was more narrow towards the base, widening as it approached the head. His large cockhead was redder than mine, and my cock is distinguished by a brown 'birthmark' (or whatever) which covers half its length from the base. At extension, we were both something over 7 inches long. But enough of that.

"We fucked.

"I fucked him and he fucked me. I can't recall who performed first; it never made any difference to us then. Each of our lower intestinal tracts

and sphincter muscles had long since become accustomed to easy
penetration, so entrance wasn't difficult. We each took advantage of all the
usual positions—stomach to stomach with legs over the partner's shoulders,
dog-style up, and belly to back on the flat, standing with the lower body
braced against the rocky incline and the other person holding him around
the waist for traction. Our fucking was never more than playful. Neither of
us cared to practice 'rough sex' on the other—at most, there might have
been some pseudo-wrestling (but not *this* time). Basically it was rhythmic
and steady—in and out and in—changing positions, with mutual consent,
for better leverage, for a different purchase. Eyes open, mouths kissing
whatever part of the other's anatomy happened to be in closest proximity;
speaking softly, offering gentle directions, laughing, giggling, uttering
endearments, licking off errant trickles of sweat.

"We didn't come at the same time. It might have been *too* 'cosmic.' As
it was, he came inside me once and I did the same with him. And each of us
manually stimulated the other (or self-stimulated) to come onto ourselves or
each other. No semen was wasted that I can recall. What fell on a body was
either licked up or wiped up and swallowed; half for Bill and half for me.
We shared it all—the semen, the fucking, the kisses and caresses, the
tenderness, the unions—all of it.

"At the end of it, once Time had resumed its more familiar flow, we
donned what little clothing we had to wear and made our way back to
'civilization' single-file along the trail. The anemones still bloomed
delightfully, the bird breezes still sung to us, and only the changed position
of the sun indicated that our union had been other than a matter of minutes
or years. We smiled and talked, and shared a vile Greek-tobacco cigarette.

"To us, virtually every physical union was an expression of mutually
shared love for each other and for ourselves, each was a defiant gesture
towards provinciality and the bigotry of adamant heterosexuals (though, to
the best of my knowledge, neither of us could be termed misogynistic), each
experience was a poetic, artistic, aesthetic expression of our freedom as
human beings, as men who loved one another. Of course Time and the
vagaries of memory may be playing tricks on me (that, and Idealization, are
always mutables), but I seem to recall the experience as clearly as if it
happened only an hour ago. I certainly recall it as one of the most—if not
the most—blissful, halcyon, pertinent, and undeniably key love/sex
moments in my entire life—a statement before Existence and Eternity,
naked among the Elements, of who I am, and who Bill is/was, and what
makes Life so important to me. Without such moments of Love, life is a
mathematical equation—completely logical, utterly rational, and devoid of
the wavelets, epicenters and anomalies which make us *human*."

⚤"A very pleasant lovemaking experience with my lover R. It is on a
weekend, so we are both relaxed from the tensions of work, which tend to
make us more desperate. We have maybe bathed beforehand so our skins
are soft and more alert to touch. Light is coming in through the big windows in my room and a cool breeze through the little window above my

mattress, which is directly on the rug. We probably haven't smoked any dope because if we do usually we react so differently that we end up miscommunicating. R. always wants to get right down on the bed naked but I like to grab him while he's still standing, clothed. I hug him and squeeze him so his chest and mine press against each other and our stomachs do the same. Somehow this simple act always fills me with joy. I feel covered and protected in my most vulnerable areas. We probably won't kiss unless we haven't had sex in days, in which case we're so hungry for each other's bodies that we plunge into each other's mouths. In any case, I move down and undo R.'s belt while he's standing, and reveal his bulging underwear. I kiss his smooth thighs even though I know it probably tickles him more than pleases him; it pleases *me*. I rub my hand over his smooth, slightly lax stomach, and over that bulge in the underwear, and without waiting much longer I open the package and there is that beautiful tool, bulging as always and pretty stiff, a delightful sight as always. I lick it up and down with my lips and tongue and grabbing R.'s ass, I swallow it whole. It is such a pleasurable sensation to have R.'s cock in my mouth, to feel it transform from juicy-soft to rod-stiff; I run my tongue and lips up and down and swallow it till I almost gag. It's hard to believe I used to be so squeamish about cocksucking; I would only do it as a 'favor.' Now it's hard to keep my mouth off the thing. Meanwhile R. might caress me lightly. I like when he does so because it shows he's thinking of me, but I also like when he doesn't caress me at all because I enjoy the fantasy of being his servant, of servicing him. He is always very silent during lovemaking, not even any heavy breathing, except maybe when he comes. I assume it's because of all those years in the tearooms, and other furtive situations. I sort of wish he would be a little more expressive by words or sounds or breathing, but I wouldn't want him to do it to please me. I'd want him to do it so that he could open up his own body channels, which have been in some ways closed to sex despite his sexual-athlete status.

"By this time R. has moved us to the bed—he's had enough standing up and enough cocksucking for the moment. At this point he takes over the initiative, usually for the rest of the time. First he'll start to undress me, which I will hastily complete. Then he will pay me some attention, like suck my cock a little and comment on how huge it's gotten. (Even though I don't have a big cock by conventional standards, R., who in fantasy is a size queen, always makes me feel quite huge by this time.) Or he'll rub my ass and my asshole and comment on what a nice ass I have. His compliments are always the same, and yet always made as if he'd just discovered what a nice ass I have or how big my cock has become. I am always flattered. At this point R. would like to get right down to fucking—he's pretty phallically concentrated. Sometimes I'll go along, sometimes I'll draw things out by trying to rub him some more, kiss him, suck his cock. We could get into some pretty heavy kissing. Usually he puts his tongue into my mouth. Occasionally we reverse, but he doesn't seem to like it as much. We twirl our mouths and lips around—one thing we never have been with each other

is self-conscious. The passion dominates, and if a kiss gets too sloppy, so what? I like to kiss his neck and snuggle into it like a small child. I like to kiss his huge biceps, because they're beautiful. And his firm breasts and dark nipples. Certainly by this time R. has had enough playing around and starts to grease up—a little KY on my hole, a lot on his pole. I like to lie stomach-down on the bed at this point so he can enter in the basic missionary position. It's the most comfortable, and despite my hemorrhoids he usually pops in there with no pain (any more).

"At this point he usually wiggles it around inside me, deeper and deeper, which gives me chills of pleasure. If R. is impassive, I am perhaps over-demonstrative. I pant, I breathe heavily, I tremble, I moan and sigh. I like to do all these things and I can barely stop myself even if I try. R. seems to accept my displays, although maybe he thinks them a bit excessive. At this point R. gets into his love of fucking and enjoys directing a little fucking scene which includes a wide variety of positions. His imagination is limitless and always expanding to something new, and I am his willing accomplice: doggy style, me on top, sideways, at right angles, backwards, over a chair, over a banister, we do it all. Finally comes the big thrust to conclusion. R. chooses his favorite pose of the moment and starts thrusting, usually so hard that his thighs and pelvis slap against the back of my legs and buttocks. He tends to tense up and become hard all throughout his body. I enjoy the thrusting, even if my hemorrhoids hurt, in which case I enjoy the thrusting and try to ignore the pain, which has become less over the years. I do a kind of yoga breath, one to each thrust—I did it originally to soften the pain but now I can't undo the breath and I like it, as my participation. Then R. comes, usually with a slight whimper, and I feel really high—the pleasure has several components: I vicariously enjoy his pleasure, I often come a little when he stops, and my asshole is relieved that the thrusting is over. R. collapses on top of me with his full weight. I love that feeling of his weight pressing down on my chest and stomach. I like his childlike exhaustion, and I stroke his hair or body lightly.

"Sometimes at this point we will both fall asleep. Anyway we usually lie together for a while and then R. will jerk me off. Actually it would probably be more pleasurable if we did this immediately while he was still big and I was still hot, but usually we wait awhile. And I enjoy his exhaustion—I know after coming myself I don't feel much like attending to anyone else. So when R. is ready, we roll over so we're both on our backs; he's still inside me and I'm on top of him at an angle. He greases me with some mineral oil. And jacks me off with his hand, or sometimes I do it myself and he rubs my stomach. I come pretty quickly, partly because of all the previous arousal and partly because of years of masturbation. It's funny—emotionally R.'s orgasm is much more important and real to me than my own, yet I enjoy my own orgasm and can get very hurt if I feel it is not attended to. But I wouldn't mind getting fucked a few times before coming myself—it suits my slave fantasy. Or R. pumps my shaft and I spurt

all over my chest, sighing loudly. Afterwards I usually say something in words, however banal, like 'That was nice,' or 'I love you,' just to establish communication and see if we're on the same wavelength.

"Sometimes I fuck R., but this is a controversial subject for me. First of all we only do it when R. announces he's ready for an intrusion—I never initiate explorations the way he does. This is partly because R. claims that his hemorrhoids usually prevent him from pleasurable penetrability, but also partly from my own lack of aggressiveness. I must admit I don't entirely believe R.—I think his lack of enjoyment of being fucked is as much psychological as physical; I know in my own case it took quite a while before I really enjoyed being fucked. To his credit R. does try to please me—about once every month or two, and he puts on a brave facade of enjoying it, though he makes it clear I shouldn't take too long, nor pound him the way he does me. Once I'm in and he's loosened up, he seems to really enjoy it, especially if he's doing the wiggling and not me. Even as a bottom man he likes to be in control. All this collides with my own lack of intrusiveness to make me feel a little jealous of his top position in our sex life. Even though, as he tells me, a good fuck is hard to find. So if I fuck him, I usually come quickly, not being used to such intense pleasures, and having trained myself to do so in other situations.

"We both enjoy our sex life together. It is a strong bond between us and from the start R. and I hit it off sexually. Our sex life varies from pleasant to incredible and there have hardly ever been any unpleasant times, even if our patterns are somewhat unbalanced as described above."

Anal intercourse, while it is an ancient and venerable sexual expression, brings forth a wide variety of responses from participants and non-participants. The comments from the gay men involved different physical, psychological, and even political aspects, including the question of pain, positions, queasiness about shit, dominance/submission, and masculinity/femininity. Some men categorized their problems with anal sexuality as a "hangup," and those responses appear elsewhere, in Chapter 17. But here are more general comments concerning anal intercourse:

♂"It's great, if there is a certain amount of affection involved in it. I neither need nor want to be merely pumped—it would be a bore and I'd have to fake my pleasure. It's happened. So, speaking from the receiving end, it all depends on how it's done. I also will dig the whole fuck a lot better if my partner has rimmed me first, then lubricates me in a horny way, before he penetrates me. As for fucking my partner, mixed feelings. More often than I care to remember, I come much too quickly. The tightness of the ass and the heat of the asshole gets to me far too fast, and I've almost had to apologize for some one-two-stroke fuckjobs. I have a very 'responsive' cock head, and the foreskin rolling up and down the length of

my dick inside someone's asshole brings me off far sooner than either my partner or I want.''

♂"I will take a dick up my ass to please a partner but it doesn't give me any particular pleasure. I don't ass-fuck, doesn't appeal at all.''

♂"I can only be fucked if they are not too thick and I am a little drunk. I especially like to fuck married men and will only let myself be fucked by someone I consider as masculine as myself.''

♂"Getting fucked does not make me feel like a woman in the least bit. And when I fuck another man I don't feel superior to him, in as far as 'I fucked you, so I'm more of a man than you are!' ''

♂"I thoroughly believe that getting fucked in the ass is the most therapeutic technique known to man. When someone can completely relax their asshole and really get into being fucked, you can be sure that there is very little of tension or anxiety being held there (or anywhere else in the body or personality).''

♂"The stimulation of my prostate is less important to me than the sensation of entering and moving in my anus.''

♂"I love *both* fucking and being fucked, as part of the *same* sexual interlude, but I've had some difficulties finding like-minded partners.''

♂"A lot of times I want to fuck someone but I just can't figure out what cues are appropriate to communicate my desire, and other times I want someone to fuck me but again I can't find out how to get them to make the move toward it. Sometimes I try to get into it with someone and they move away from it with apologies as if they feel really sexually inadequate because they aren't skilled in getting fucked. But I know that it feels good with some men, and there is pain with others. I carry a little bottle of oil and lotion mixed together with me so I can oil the penis up well. I can't believe that so many men will try to jab it in a dry ass. Why cause pain? There must be a tremendous level of ignorance or inconsideration among gay men. When I fuck someone I always make sure that everything I ever learned that caused me pain is avoided. I take it slow until the ass relaxes, grease up my cock well, masturbate the other guy's cock until it is quivering with desire and therefore giving the sensations in his ass the impressions of extreme eroticism rather than pain.''

♂"I have very little patience with persons who are into power or fear the loss of manhood to the extent that they must always be the fucker and never the fuckee.''

♂"Do not want to be screwed and have never been. I enjoy the dominance of screwing but am not sure why. My friends tell me that it is an imitation of heterosexuality, which I do not accept.''

♂"I am extremely fond of this, especially when I am the recipient. An erect penis thrusting against the sensitive nerve endings of the anus fulfills and satisfies. The most comfortable and sensuous position is face to face, my legs around the neck of my partner. In this way, more depth is attained and more sensitive areas are exposed for stimulation. Looking into the eyes of someone who means a lot to you while he is fucking you is like looking

into his soul. All defenses and walls are dropped—only love, passion, and kindness are seen."

⚭"I was a homosexual for eight years before I let anyone fuck me, had a mental block against it. Even though I've learned to enjoy it occasionally, it is still not my favorite. I'd say it's a last choice. But fucking someone else ranks second in my choices. I like to spread them wide open on their backs while I stand on the floor and roughly fuck them, taking my dick all the way out and all the way in in a fast and furious manner. Since very few little darlings can stand this treatment, I seldom get a chance to do this. I would not do this that way unless the passive partner absolutely enjoyed it."

⚭"My rectal area was damaged last fall by a misadventure with a too large tool which was plunged in with such force that it ruptured my sphincter muscle and forced me to have an operation which has left the area sore and tender, which sort of leaves out rectal play now and for an unknown period into the future."

⚭"A poor substitute for intercourse with a woman—I have done that, and if I wanted to fuck, I would find a girl. Also, it represents a much easier road to VD."

⚭"On one occasion, about a year ago, when I withdrew, my penis was covered with excrement. I'm still trying to get over this experience and haven't done it since."

⚭"I've been ass-fucked many times and always the initial penetration is painful. We always lubricate, so after the pain subsides, it's quite a pleasure."

⚭"I am revolted by any activity, photos, films, or pornography which relates to the anus or its environs, including the buttocks—which I regard as the sole anatomical miscalculation on the part of the Creator. (I strongly suspect that gays who are into ass-fucking are not homosexual at all, but, rather, closet heteros.)"

⚭"I suspect that women are better for penetration and that the male form will never be what it always promises to be."

⚭"I've never fucked or been fucked. Once you get inside the rectum, there's shit there, possibly, and I don't want to be involved with it."

⚭"Unless I know something about my partner, I always use a condom for anal intercourse."

⚭"I really don't like using lubricants—too messy."

⚭"I enjoy fucking guys, especially young men, age 15–18. To me, it feels dominating to be fucked, though not dominating when I fuck someone. I enjoy the feeling of being dominated."

⚭"I think that fucking and, more important, being fucked is the single sexual experience that is the most important link between gay men and women."

⚭"I quite bluntly enjoy the pain/pleasure principle of fucking and do enjoy the mild look of pain on the person's face while he is being screwed."

⚭"At the moment before orgasm, my lover stops fucking and drives his cock as deep as he can and holds it in; I use my sphincter to clutch and grab

this orgasming cock, so that the climax is usually a double climax in that he comes, and I have what I call an anal orgasm with deep spasms and heavy twitching of my whole body. I do not come with semen, however.''

♂ "I particularly enjoy withdrawing right to the head, stimulating the glans by several short strokes right at the sphincter, then suddenly plunging in as far as I can go.''

♂ "I love to do it, but it takes a lot of getting ready before I can take it up the ass myself. I like to clean myself out with an enema first, then get rimmed and finger-fucked, and unless the guy is small I need some lotion or oil or KY. If the guy is really big I want a drink first, or a joint, or I want to use a popper when he's ready to go in. Once I get past all my preliminaries, I try hard to make it good by squeezing tight on his cock with my muscles, moving around a lot, reaching back to fondle his balls, etc.''

♂ "The thing I like best about being fucked is the feeling of the guy lying on top of me, feeling his full weight on me.''

♂ "Generally, I fuck strangers and get fucked by boy friends. It is a distinction I am not altogether happy with but has evolved out of a very clear sense of a need to protect myself, of a history of feeling ripped off and related to on the basis of looks, of being attractive. I am not very much into getting fucked right now, at this period. There have been periods of real exquisite pleasure in receptive anal sex, both from lovers and from tricks. At the moment anal reception on my part is involved with playing out male roles, experiments and games on being fucked and feeling very male about it. I don't know what 'feeling male' means aside from *not* feeling 'feminized.' ''

From many of the written responses, it seems that fucking is something that many gay men 'come out' to long after their first gay sexual encounters, or they change their attitude toward the roles in the act.

♂ "When I first started making love with men I sucked them off and got fucked sometimes but I found that I was unable to fuck another man in the ass. My cock would just go down and get too soft before I could get it in. I think that I felt that I just couldn't dominate another man's masculinity in that way. However, I knew how pleasing it was to me and how very satisfying getting fucked could be if the one fucking took it easy and knew what he was doing (which meant in most cases that *he* had been fucked enough to know how to do it right—but later on I learned how to guide them so they didn't hurt me), and just couldn't understand why I couldn't do that to a man who wanted it. Things came to a head in a peculiar fashion one night when I met a really hot 19-year-old in a bar. As it turns out I was somewhat older than him and he took me for a real butch number. I, on the other hand, was so enamored of him that I never even considered the sex aspect of things when he insisted on coming home with me. He was hung so beautifully that I was in love with his penis from the moment I got my hands

on it, and he, for his part, no sooner got me raving hard than he wanted it crammed up his ass. This was certainly the moment for truth: I tried getting him to fuck me instead and he gave it a try but his penis just wouldn't stay hard enough to get in. Imagine! He had the same trouble as me in this respect (except that I wasn't crazed over being fucked and this guy definitely was that). Finally he got tiffed because I was laughing at the twist of justice in the affair and said I could just take him home if I wasn't going to fuck him. Well, I wasn't about to let this masterpiece slip away, so I managed to cram my dick in him somehow and fucked till my eyeballs were hanging out. From that time on, I have enjoyed fucking, and believe it or not I never had any more trouble with not keeping hard enough to fuck some man in the ass.''

⚥"For some years following my coming out, I considered that if a person began as a 'bottom man,' he remained as a bottom man throughout his life. Call it naiveté. Call it insecurity. Call it a preference. But it happens that I did not fuck another man until I was approaching my mid-20s. Following that, there was a 'retaliation' period when I did nothing else. I'd discovered a new game, and earnestly desired to master it. And master it I did.''

⚥"The first time I positively enjoyed anal intercourse, being fucked, that is, was when my partner was a man with whom I was in love. Once having reached that stage of enjoyment, I have found my enjoyment of the act increasing largely without regard to being in love with my partner or not. I always, of course, enjoyed fucking, since in the active role there are not the initial problems of pain and discomfort to overcome.''

⚥"I have become more and more interested in being the passive partner in anal intercourse, ever since I realized that it was not unmanly.''

⚥"Anal intercourse is very exciting for me. I have only engaged in doing it over the past year, and it seems to be getting better and better. Two years ago I would not allow anyone to fuck me. However, I would enjoy fucking them. I soon began to realize that denying my partner the right to fuck me, while being anxious to fuck him, was quite a selfish attitude, even though I did not mean to be that way. The simple matter was that I feared the pain it would cause me due to my inexperience. After much discussion with gay friends about the pain (both real and imaginary), I consciously set out to experience being fucked and learning how to enjoy it. The first few times were painful and I did not enjoy it whatsoever. However, I performed it with a lover who I trusted would not hurt me intentionally. It was his patience and trustworthiness that helped me realize that even though I was being fucked, I would always be in a position to control the pain by withdrawing if it became too intense (just by asking him to stop). I did withdraw several times over a period of time; however, I persisted in trying it so that each time the intercourse was allowed a greater length of time until I arrived at the point where he ejaculated inside of me. I tried it a few more times and his manual stimulation of my cock first superseded the pain, then

even brought me to ejaculation at the same time he was fucking me. Now that I learned to relax while he fucked me, I began to enjoy it. Now I still have some pain upon insertion into me, but it is far less in intensity than it was in the past, and it is of short duration, after which I begin to feel enjoyment and arousal. A lot of it depends on my partner and his stimulation of me before and during the intercourse. Some of my best orgasms occur when I ejaculate by manual stimulation while my partner is ejaculating in my anus during intercourse. Of course, my greatest passion is to actively fuck my partner and will always remain so. I prefer my partner to either lie motionless or, better yet, to move just slightly with my thrusts into him. However, I do not like him to move wildly with his hips while I fuck him as this sometimes puts too much stress on my cock so that it is rubbed too hard and is irritated.''

Manual Stimulation

As the preceding sections on various sexual acts indicate, gay men rely on their hands to stimulate both their partners and themselves. Chapter 15 deals with masturbation, and most men have lots of experience using their hands to provide this ''solitary pleasure,'' as it is sometimes called. During sex with a partner, manual stimulation is important, too, as indicated in the following charts showing both *frequency of and feelings about manual stimulation:*

	ALWAYS	VERY FREQUENTLY	SOMEWHAT FREQUENTLY	SOMEWHAT INFREQUENTLY	VERY INFREQUENTLY	ONCE	NEVER
masturbating your partner	17	31	24	15	10	0	2%
your partner masturbates you	16	32	23	17	10	0	2
simultaneous masturbation	11	28	22	21	13	1	5
rubbing your cocks together manually	10	22	27	20	17	1	3
you masturbate yourself	11	25	23	18	16	2	6
partner masturbates himself	5	18	23	23	24	2	5
any of these to the point of orgasm	20	31	22	13	11	0	3

	VERY POSITIVE	SOMEWHAT POSITIVE	NEUTRAL	SOMEWHAT NEGATIVE	VERY NEGATIVE	NOT SURE
masturbating your partner	59	24	13	4	1	0%
your partner masturbates you	59	26	11	3	1	0
simultaneous masturbation	57	23	16	3	1	0
rubbing your cocks together manually	52	24	19	4	1	.5
you masturbate yourself	44	21	18	13	4	0
partner masturbates himself	39	22	21	14	4	.5
any of these to the point of orgasm	58	23	13	5	2	0

Manual stimulation is not so complicated a topic as anal intercourse or oral sex, though some men categorize it as somehow "less" than the "real thing." It is difficult to know for sure how many men rely on manual stimulation as a favorite form of sexual experience. Relatively few of the essay questions about "pleasing experiences" focused on manual stimulation, and the high percentages in the charts do not necessarily indicate the popularity of J/O scenes. For example, during anal intercourse, men who are being fucked very frequently stimulate themselves manually, or are stimulated by their partners, to the point of orgasm. It is possible that men included manual stimulation *during other acts* in their responses to these questions. The essays below reveal two major aspects of sex involving mutual masturbation—first, the importance of the visual or voyeuristic experience; second, the choice of manual stimulation as an "old reliable," when other sexual acts don't seem to be working:

♂"I am heavy into masturbation, the so-called J/O scene, and I do a *great* deal of masturbating by myself, complete with fantasies, smoking grass, sniffing poppers, etc. Naturally, I participate in other forms of sexual activities (I am bisexual), but it's J/O that really turns me on. I have several buddies with whom I get into J/O sessions, sometimes just two of us, sometimes as a whole group. The whole J/O scene, it seems to me, is based on the 'maleness' of the situations (i.e., this is something you can do only with other guys) and the very male notion of watching. I think all J/O guys are voyeurs at heart.

"As I've indicated, there are several guys I do this with, but one in particular, my best friend, is really a special J/O buddy. We aren't 'lovers'—we do not live together and, as a matter of fact, each of us has

other emotional commitments: I with my woman and he with his lover. Nevertheless, our scene is a very special one. Our evenings usually begin by having a drink, either on my terrace (in good weather) or in front of the fire. We talk while we drink, catch up on gossip, etc., and then we smoke a joint, sometimes two. Pretty soon we are feeling very good, and somehow our conversation takes on a tone of unfamiliarity, as if we've met only recently. Soon—and remember, we are still speaking of many things and not about sex—we are stroking our cocks through our pants, but pretending to do it surreptitiously, pretending that we don't want the other to know we do it. Pretty soon, one of us asks the other, 'You're one, aren't you?' and the other plays dumb for a while. Nevertheless, the sex begins to build, and the pressure is being applied. The idea is that there is some sort of awful thing going to happen if one admits to being 'one' and the other isn't. And of course 'one' means 'masturbator.' When we finally bring it out in the open that we are both masturbators, it is as if we were members of some special secret society of masturbators, a very exclusive group of men, and that it is a privilege to be a masturbator.

"Soon we go into the bedroom, which is heavily mirrored, and we take off our clothes. We watch ourselves masturbate in the mirrors, and we watch one another, and it is a very groovy turn-on experience. I use grease on my cock when I masturbate, usually Vaseline or Crisco; he does not. We neck a little, but very little. Our scene is not kissing but masturbating. We talk a great deal about masturbating, about how much fun it is, how we love to do it. We also talk about other people we know and wonder if they masturbate and, if they do, how they do it. We're both in businesses where we come into contact with famous people and sometimes, when we know them, we have sex with them, and both of us like to talk about getting famous people turned on to the J/O scene. It seems important that people we admire be classed as masturbators.

"When we begin to feel as if we are going to come, we get closer together. Sometimes we lie down on the bed and shoot off on ourselves, and other times we'll stand in front of a mirror and shoot the come onto the surface of the mirror. Another favorite thing—which he enjoys very much—is for me to lie on my back and for him to stand or kneel over me and come all over my body. After we've come, we usually embrace, kiss, rub our bodies together, mingling the come, and we frequently fall asleep this way. It is a very satisfying scene.

"I have very positive feelings about this whole scene. It is a very pleasant turn-on for both my buddy and me."

⚥ "My typical sexual experiences vary greatly from year to year. I can remember periods of all fellatio and lots of 69; periods of mainly anal (active) sex; periods of mainly masturbation. I'm in a mainly masturbation period now. But amazingly, every time I've had sex with my lover of one year, it's different—different fantasies (or none), different positions, different feelings mentally and physically. Typical might be: starting lying next to each other; 'playful' conversation; lover initiates with grab for

penis, 'What's this?'; then hugging, fondling; then either one gets on top of the other, or one grabs baby oil and applies it, or both lie on sides and hug; then some mutual masturbation, lying side by side, one on top of the other, crosslegged face to face, or one sitting astride the other, or lying on sides face to back, soon one (usually me) gets near to coming and initiates further positions; comes; then concentrates on making the other come. Coming is facilitated for both by body-stroking, kissing, sometimes touching testicles, ass, or nipples; sometimes touching beneath testicles near anus or actually touching anus. I always have different fantasies; mostly about fucking in the ass, sometimes about being fucked in the ass; or about watching other men do this; sometimes narrative fantasies of uniformed soldiers being dutifully stimulated in semi-undress by nurses manually or by boys anally; fantasies include verbal abuse or cool objective requests, but in reality I only pant and grunt and writhe, as does lover. Sometimes verbal play includes humorously impersonal requests and descriptions: 'Excuse me, sir, but I believe this will be effective in relieving your sexual tensions.'

"Ejaculation is particularly exciting, and I like to feel the semen shooting onto my belly and chest, or vice versa, onto his. After I have come, I sometimes feel impatient trying to make him come, since in this current relationship I am the fast one, he the slow one, contrary to my usual pattern where I am the slow one. But then I resolve to be patient, and sometimes he intervenes and helps masturbate himself or rubs against my belly or chest, which is exciting for me. Sex is always preceded and followed by polite kisses and hugs, sometimes by very moving avowals of love, though these sometimes make me feel embarrassed and are more likely to come from the other party, being silently reciprocated by me. Sometimes I actually pray during sex, concerned that my underlying feelings will come through somehow to the partner through the vehicle of sex. Leg, arm, head positions, etc., are unbelievably varied; sometimes I discover after orgasm that I am extremely uncomfortable. There is usually some laughter afterwards, and a towel is retrieved, usually by the other partner. I myself like to wallow in the sweat and semen as long as possible. This pattern is quite different from those of other periods in my life."

৬"This happened last night after I got off work past midnight. Half a glass of wine left by a patron at the restaurant where I work, off to a diner for breakfast. Driving home I pass down the gay street in town. I met a man on the street and we decided to return to his apartment, where after about an hour's worth of conversation and smoking we had sex. We started first feeling each other's bodies sitting on the couch, clothes on. After only a few minutes we got up, turning the couch into a bed. We both undressed ourselves and lay down on our backs and proceeded to feel each other with our hands. He had a hairy chest, which felt soft and warm and sexy. Down, feeling thighs, then balls and cock, stimulating an erection. Getting further into things I began to lick his body quite gently with my tongue, first his nipples and then slowly down the chest while fondling his genitals. Then I began to lick the inner thighs around his balls (he is flat on his back, me

kneeling beside and above him, my head between his legs). This area seemed to greatly excite him, which he verbalized, so I continued licking in this area for five to ten minutes (although remembering time periods is hard . . . I wasn't much interested in that, but the whole thing must have been 1-1½ hours). I was getting more excited and then lay on top of him butting my cock on his body and licking his neck. I tried kissing him, but this seemed to bring little response from him. Shortly, I moved and lay beside him, using my hand to feel his chest. He began feeling my cock and he said he liked the size of mine. This eventually led into a decision that he was into a very gentle sensitive stimulation and that if I played it slow and let him do the inserting it would make him very hot for me to fuck him. We proceeded in this direction for about ½ hour: we got a bottle of Intensive Care and oiled up each other's cocks, getting each other very hard. My hands were roaming his body up the chest and down to the anus, playing for some time this way. Eventually I got up and kneeled between his legs. His legs went up and we placed my cock to his ass. I was attempting to go very extremely slow, letting him push against me, to insert, but the position was difficult to maintain as my body was a bit worn from 9½ hours of rather physical work. So I likely applied too much pressure to insert and was likely a bit painful, to him, so we ceased attempting to fuck and rested both on our backs. We had about a ten-minute conversation about the sex we were having and his strong request for extreme gentleness. It was too involved to try and verbalize, but I wanted to say that it was one of those rare times you really get into an aspect of a person very deeply and very quickly and know that you'll retain a fond memory of him for some time to come, whether or not you see him again. To finish the sex, we mutually masturbated, heavily oiled up. He came first and we watched it fall all over his chest. Then I got up, kneeled over him, and jerked myself off again onto his chest. A great time was had by all."

In commenting on manual stimulation, the men indicated it is pleasurable enough, and convenient, but often not comparable to other acts:

♂"I like this act. It's a turn-on to see another guy get into his own body. I don't have many opportunities to do this but I fantasize about it a lot."

♂"Manual stimulation with a partner is a waste of time when you have a mouth and tongue."

♂"I often enjoy sitting on my partner or having him sit on me, in such a way that we can jerk off rubbing our cocks together."

♂"I like jerking a guy off actually more than being jerked off. I like to feel a stiff cock in my hand. The problem with being jerked off is sometimes my partner does it too hard and too fast, too rough."

♂"It will do in a pinch. I enjoy watching a man beat off because of the 'intrusiveness' of my presence. Masturbation is usually a solitary act and viewing someone doing this is an entry into the person's privacy, bordering

on acknowledged voyeurism. I enjoy being watched for the same reason.''

♂♂ "Oddly enough, this is the only way I can ejaculate (come). However, I readily get a hard-on from a variety of stimuli. The final stimulation must be by my hand.''

♂♂ "I enjoy manual stimulation but only in combination with fellatio; otherwise, it seems very impersonal—often the hand seems to get detached from the mind.''

♂♂ "I don't much like jacking other people off—seems like an invasion of privacy.''

♂♂ "Always feel a little cheated when somebody comes by hand (his or mine), because I'd rather take the load in my mouth. Sometimes I'll J/O a pest just to get him off so he'll leave me alone.''

♂♂ "Still enjoy it, but it seems to be a last resort most times, either with someone and either of you is not quite turned on, or it's your third time, and you are exhausted, or you have been out of circulation for a week or two and are just horny.''

♂♂ "My first sexual experiences were with my brother, who wanted to fuck me. Even at the tender age of 13, I had the sense to say he could only do it to me if I could then do it to him, so that ended that attempt on my virgin rear! Instead, he used to put his penis between my legs, and I'd grip it while he moved it back and forth (his being uncircumcised made this easier) until he came between my legs. He'd then scoop up his come and use it as a lubricant while masturbating me, and I found this very exciting. Now it would seem rather an elementary form of sexual activity—though I still do find it exciting for my partner to shoot his come over my penis and then masturbate me.''

♂♂ "Lying side by side, fondling each other's cocks while kissing is one of my favorite things to do. I could do it for hours. And it permits fondling other parts of our bodies as well. Sitting between each other's legs so that we can rub our cocks together is very stimulating, and it allows for kissing and stroking too. Rubbing cocks together is very intimate and extremely erotic. Lying on your back with your partner's head on your chest, his legs around one of yours so that he can rub his cock against your leg while he plays with your cock—this is another one of my favorites.''

♂♂ "I love masturbating myself while watching my partner masturbate himself. I love placing a partner in different poses and masturbating myself. I love masturbating a partner to orgasm. I enjoy doing this with a lover when we have less energy. I remember one particularly pleasant experience in the steamroom of the baths.''

♂♂ "Jacking off has been a real passion with me for the last few years, after joining a group called J/O Buddies, which sent me this questionnaire. Watching a guy masturbate, showing off his cock, strutting around, talking about his erect cock, moaning and groaning, jacking off in outfits from rubber to blue jeans to construction or western drag, are all turn-ons for me. I like to see another guy who is really getting off on having me watch him and encourage him to bring himself to climax. Watching a guy get an

erection through his blue jeans or seeing an erect cock in a pair of tight underwear, jockstrap, or bathing suit gives me instant erection. One time while watching a particularly handsome guy with a nice body and a sizable, fat cock do his thing, I stood mesmerized and eventually, after fifteen or twenty minutes, I had an orgasm without even touching my own cock. I think that evening I really became interested intensely in the whole area of masturbation by myself and with others, and began to communicate via letters and share experiences and ideas with other guys who liked the same.''

Rubbing/Frottage

In gay slang, it's called "collegiate fucking" and the "Princeton rub." The implications of the terms are clear—they reflect sexual immaturity appropriate to college boys who have not yet fully come out. Body-to-body rubbing is a source of pleasure nonetheless to many, though not a particularly favorite way to have orgasm, as indicated in the following charts showing frequency and feelings about rubbing. The men were asked, *On the average, how often do you engage in placing your body against your partner's body so that your penises rub together?* and *Whether or not you engage in any of the following aspects of rubbing, indicate how you feel about the idea of each of them.*

	ALWAYS	VERY FREQUENTLY	SOMEWHAT FREQUENTLY	SOMEWHAT INFREQUENTLY	VERY INFREQUENTLY	ONCE	NEVER
with you lying on top	17	40	21	11	9	0	2%
partner lies on top of you	15	41	23	12	7	0	2
either of these to the point of orgasm	4	11	13	19	26	5	21

	VERY POSITIVE	SOMEWHAT POSITIVE	NEUTRAL	SOMEWHAT NEGATIVE	VERY NEGATIVE	NOT SURE
with you lying on top	59	20	19	2	2	0%
partner lies on top of you	59	22	17	1	1	0

	VERY POSITIVE	SOMEWHAT POSITIVE	NEUTRAL	SOMEWHAT NEGATIVE	VERY NEGATIVE	NOT SURE
either of these to the point of orgasm	49	17	23	5	3	3

Since the men seem to have a generally positive feeling about reaching orgasm through rubbing, yet accomplish it with relative infrequency, it may be that the stimulation is inadequate or that the sexual dynamic simply moves most men on to other acts for orgasm. Here is an experience:

⚥"Brad and I were best friends and roommates in Livingston Hall, a Columbia University dormitory, where we had sex almost every night for about two years. We loved each other very much, yet we pretended to be nothing more than good friends. We were true closet cases—neither of us knew other gay people and we didn't even think of ourselves as gay. On a typical night, I'd take a shower early and go to bed. Later, after studying more, Brad would go off to the shower, and I'd lie in my bunk bed (upper) with a hard-on, waiting for him to come back. He came back, turned off the light, and climbed into the lower bunk. We lay there in silence for a while. Then I casually let my arm flop down over the side of the bed. In a minute (it seemed like an hour) Brad would touch my hand. We played with each other's hands for a few minutes. Nine times out of ten, I would climb down into his bunk, though when he climbed up to mine, it was heaven. We kissed furiously. Sometimes we sucked each other's cocks. Usually, I would lie on top and grind away, it felt so good. I could come almost immediately, so I constantly asked him if he was close. When he said he was close, we intensely kissed and embraced and just the right amount of rubbing would bring us both off. We used a towel to wipe up the come, and we always wondered whether the Irish housemaids who cleaned our rooms ever noticed the stiffly stained towels. While we were having sex, I always asked, 'Does it feel good?' When he said yes, as he always did, it made me very happy. I think it was the closest we ever got to talking about our love. I still like rubbing, but sometimes I think that it, like that college affair, is a little pathetic."

The following are additional comments about rubbing:

⚥"I can't tell you how much I love the feel of his body against mine, legs entwined around legs, torsos fused, cocks rubbing together."

⚥"Personally I think it's a clumsy way of making love; it somehow seems to be an attempt to imitate heterosexual lovemaking."

⚤"I often fantasize that someone lying on top of me and humping away is actually penetrating me, even impregnating me."

⚤"What a waste of hot sperm."

⚤"The sound of pubic hair grinding against pubic hair sounds exciting."

⚤"This seems sort of natural to me—for the longest time I didn't think that this was homosexual activity. My older brother used to do this with me from the time I was 12 until I was 18 or 19."

⚤"I don't look at it as a sex act in itself, but rather as part of the total stimulation of the body during intercourse."

⚤"Rubbing of genitals against my partner is what I prefer most—the warmth, the effortlessness of it. Body contact is what I like most and is occasionally enough in itself to induce orgasm."

⚤"If my partner has no body hair, I can shoot my rocks very quickly this way."

⚤"Yes, good stuff, to orgasm if possible because I love smearing come all over tummies, chests, whatever else presents itself to frenzied imagination. Not many other guys I've been with seem to share my come-bathing propensities, however. A pity, that."

⚤"I like to be on top, partly because I'm a little guy and big guys smother me."

⚤"Child play and not satisfying."

⚤"Great upon *first* bodily contact in a prone position. The sensation of a warm body against mine with an awakening vital cock pressed against mine is a tremendous stimulus."

⚤"Rubbing of genitals against partner is a rare art. I can't get off that way usually, but I really enjoy lying back and letting someone else do it who can."

Finger-Fucking

Many of the sexual experiences on the previous pages show that insertion of the finger is a rather common incidental form of stimulation, or a prelude to anal intercourse. Fist-fucking is covered in Chapter 13. The following charts indicate the men's responses to questions concerning *frequency and feelings about finger-fucking:*

	ALWAYS	VERY FREQUENTLY	SOMEWHAT FREQUENTLY	SOMEWHAT INFREQUENTLY	VERY INFREQUENTLY	ONCE	NEVER
you insert finger(s)	4	15	19	18	26	4	13%
partner inserts finger(s)	2	12	20	25	23	5	13

	ALWAYS	VERY FREQUENTLY	SOMEWHAT FREQUENTLY	SOMEWHAT INFREQUENTLY	VERY INFREQUENTLY	ONCE	NEVER
you come while being finger-fucked	2	4	9	9	18	4	55
partner comes while you finger-fuck him	2	4	6	13	20	3	52
you touch partner's anus, but don't insert	9	21	24	17	17	1	11
partner touches your anus, but doesn't insert	7	18	27	18	19	1	10

	VERY POSITIVE	SOMEWHAT POSITIVE	NEUTRAL	SOMEWHAT NEGATIVE	VERY NEGATIVE	NOT SURE
you insert finger(s)	32	22	20	12	11	3%
partner inserts finger(s)	33	24	14	14	13	2
you come while being finger-fucked	30	21	18	10	15	6
partner comes while you finger-fuck him	31	18	20	12	13	6
you touch partner's anus, but don't insert	30	26	24	9	8	2
partner touches your anus, but doesn't insert	31	27	24	8	8	3

There were no detailed descriptions of a sexual encounter that focused on finger-fucking. However, the men offered various comments and points of view:

⚨"As long as it's only one finger, it's great. It adds a whole new dimension to fellatio or manual stimulation, and usually makes me come in half the time."

⚨"I sometimes do it to myself but don't like having it done to me or

doing it to someone else. Maybe I'm uptight about other people's assholes.''

⚭ "Had an infection in my rectum once, caused by a fingernail, and told myself if they don't want to put their penises there they can damn well keep their fingers out also.''

⚭ "I like to finger-fuck my partner because I know it gives him pleasure but I do not like to be finger-fucked because I am afraid I would not be clean enough.''

⚭ "I hate getting finger-fucked. I like doing it as I blow someone. When they come and I feel the prostate getting tighter and tighter until it starts pumping, well, it's just a real big turn-on.''

⚭ "For some reason it always hurts when it's done to me. I never do it to anyone; it never occurs to me.''

⚭ "Useless. Either don't bother with it, or jam a shaft up the guy.''

⚭ "Finger-fucking can be very pleasurable, but only with someone who knows how to be gentle and knows how to stimulate the prostate.''

⚭ "I much prefer a cock but sometimes will use my finger when I'm in the mood to masturbate alone. I'm too cheap to buy a dildo.''

⚭ "I like fingers to get me ready for fucking. I often instruct my partner—first one finger, then two, then three. But no more than three. Oil is a must. I like to use a small mirror to watch his finger(s) touching the smooth pink skin of my asshole—shiny, oiled, and very sensual.''

⚭ "This is very exciting while 69-ing, foreplay, or as an added stimulation while masturbating. Often I do it when I want more tongue depth during analingus: I slide my index fingers in and gently spread the anus in order to insert my tongue between them.''

Analingus/"Rimming"

Stimulation of the anus with the lips and tongue, popularly known as "rimming" (sometimes "reaming"), is one of the more controversial gay male sex acts. Aficionados appreciate the special contact between the smooth, sensitive skin of these two orifices, while detractors are thinking not about these sensual factors but rather about shit and its microbes. Only a minority practice this with any frequency, and most of the men seem to agree it is a question of weighing the pleasure against the risk of disease, or unpleasant tastes and odors. For some, rimming is unabashed fun; for most, however, it is simply an unclean act to be avoided. The following chart indicates the *frequency with which men experience rimming*, followed by a chart showing *feelings about the act*:

	ALWAYS	VERY FREQUENTLY	SOMEWHAT FREQUENTLY	SOMEWHAT INFREQUENTLY	VERY INFREQUENTLY	ONCE	NEVER
rimming your partner	4	13	11	16	20	7	30%
being rimmed	2	11	16	25	27	7	13

	VERY POSITIVE	SOMEWHAT POSITIVE	NEUTRAL	SOMEWHAT NEGATIVE	VERY NEGATIVE	NOT SURE
rimming your partner	23	20	10	15	29	3%
being rimmed	36	22	16	10	13	2

This subject seemed to engender rather strong expressions of opinion. On the negative side, words such as "horrible," "disgusting," "ridiculous," and "revolting" were used. But rimming seems to have its fans. Here are some of the comments:

⚢"Let me explain to you why rimming turns me on so much. It has to do with a fanciful theory (or rationalization) that I've conceived. To me a man's most guarded possession, or greatest secret, is his asshole. He keeps it hidden much more than his penis and will only allow certain lucky individuals a glimpse of it on special occasions, and mostly by accident. I feel that when a man has learned to trust you and has developed a real love for you, this man wants to share himself with you completely. He wants to give himself to you; he wants to share with you his greatest secret. So, in a sense he says, 'Here is my asshole. This is my most precious possession. I lower my defenses and give it to you. Take it; it is yours. Kiss it; love it; do with it whatever you please. I love you so much that I trust you completely. It is the secret entrance into my soul. Enter and you will know the real me.' "

⚥"I enjoy being rimmed. At times I can really become absorbed in rimming, like that was *the* act. I like the pungent smell of many men's asses. I only rim when I am sleeping with someone or lying down for extended sexual encounter. I occasionally get rimmed where I go for stand-up sex. I like that, the feeling of being served."

⚥"I have a real disgust regarding excrement. This makes this activity very rare for me—I will do it only if it is with a sex partner I especially like and I am really turned on. My reaction when it is done to me is usually disgust rather than erotic."

⚥"In the bedroom, I lie on my back, with my legs bent at the knee, and the trick sits on my chest, his back resting against my knees. This places his ass right in my face. I place a small pillow under my head and can eat till my heart's content. I have used this a lot with certain tricks—they can watch stag movies and get eaten at the same time and they love it."

⚥"From a very young age my mother and my nose taught me that assholes and their products are 'not nice.' Later in life, I was taught by the city health department that hepatitis is an 'ass to mouth' disease. Therefore, it is particularly difficult to intellectually put myself into rimming or being rimmed. However, at age 24, I met the grossest, horniest, hairiest fruit I ever knew and he flipped me ass over tincups and tongued out my virgin hole like a pussycat. I was so hornied up, that I did a modified 69 reciprocation and since that time, some fourteen years ago, I can say that the fantasizing of a rim job by the right person can get me to spring a hard-on any time. In terms of doing it, the odds are far less. I have to go through a lot of 'clearing factors' before I go for the hole. First, does the person seem 'healthy'? Second, how is his hygiene? Third, when did he (we) take a bath? Last, am I motivated to do this particular act with *this* person? In more specific terms: if dinner is spread before you, is it appetizing? If someone is lying under you spreading cheeks does the *sight* of this combined with the four prerequisites add up to a pie-eating job? If so, go. Numerically, out of 1,500 tricks, I have rimmed perhaps ten. As far as receiving a rimming, that is an exact reversal of the four requirements, above. If I am in good health, clean, bathed, etc. and someone is motivated, it's cool; if I feel dirty, I will have a fit. I have been eaten out about ten times, but not necessarily reciprocally."

⚥"I have done it on boys with hairless asses who are clean and whom I want to greatly excite."

⚥"I can't imagine getting in bed naked with another man without licking his ass."

⚥"There is a great feeling not only from the tongue but also from the hair of the head on your ass and back."

⚥"The hairier the asshole, the more I will enjoy doing it, the longer I will want to do it. As for being rimmed by another person: any time, any place, and just about anyone. But I'm still waiting for someone to come along with a truly incredible tongue to really get up into my hole."

⚥"It tickles me and I'm likely to lose my erection."

⚥ "More so than fellatio even, it breaks a very strong societal taboo, and much of the excitement comes from that, in addition to the fact that it feels so good. Although it can be strenuous for the tongue, I find excitement in gently spreading the cheeks of the ass (a part of the male anatomy which is very sensuous) and slowly wetting and loosening the anus enough to insert my tongue an inch or so. It is one of the few acts that I would describe as being truly exquisite."

Some men indicated that their feelings about this act changed considerably over time:

⚥ "I thought rimming was one of the most bestial of acts—now I think it is the ultimate intimacy."

⚥ "Rimming seemed repugnant for a while. All the weight of dirt, and squeamishness about excrement, is centered there. But the ass is so lovely and sensitive, and with careful washing can be as sweet as a rose. So lately I've been rimming as well. One way of really 'getting into' a desirable guy is to bury your face between his buttocks. (When I slept with women one of my favorite things was to bury my face between their breasts. I think I would write a scholarly work on what might be considered a Freudian displacement—woman/man, breasts/buttocks—but I would write it tongue-in-cheek, so to speak.) Yes, there are dangers of hepatitis with rimming, so all you gay guys should wash your asses and use a strong mouthwash, and choose guys who don't look yellow. I personally can't imagine giving up this pleasant practice."

⚥ "I remember years ago when I first came out, there was an old queen who claimed that eating assholes was his specialty. I was somewhat shocked and really didn't believe him. It was first done to me about two years ago, and I believe that I came off having it done. Recently I have started doing this to my lovers and enjoy doing it when the guy is clean and attractive."

⚥ "I was once very positive about analingus, both as a recipient and as a performer. However, a nine-month battle with amebiasis has eliminated analingus from my repertory in either role."

Kissing

This is one of the most universal of human experiences, and gay men are no exception. Along with holding hands, kissing is one of the few ways in which the straight world has had to deal with the physical aspects of homosexuality, as a growing number of gay people openly kiss in public as straights do. There is an especially memorable moment in the film *Sunday, Bloody Sunday,* when Peter Finch, playing a homosexual Jewish doctor, kisses Murray Head, the handsome young bisexual sculptor—memorable because it is one of the rare moments where homosexuality is explicitly shown on the screen. The men in the survey expressed strong feelings about kissing, including negative feelings about those men who won't kiss. It

seems apparent that unwillingness to kiss is related either to being in the closet or to the absence of emotional involvement, sometimes in combination. The following charts indicate *frequency of kissing and feelings about it:*

	ALWAYS	VERY FREQUENTLY	SOMEWHAT FREQUENTLY	SOMEWHAT INFREQUENTLY	VERY INFREQUENTLY	ONCE	NEVER
kiss on lips only	20	27	14	11	23	1	6%
get kissed on lips only	17	27	15	12	22	1	5
soul kiss (deep kiss, French kiss)	35	44	10	5	4	1	1
partner soul kisses you	32	43	12	5	4	1	3
you refuse to kiss partner	1	2	2	10	27	5	55
partner refuses to kiss you	1	1	4	10	38	10	37

	VERY POSITIVE	SOMEWHAT POSITIVE	NEUTRAL	SOMEWHAT NEGATIVE	VERY NEGATIVE	NOT SURE
kiss on lips only	43	22	18	9	7	1%
get kissed on lips only	42	22	18	10	7	1
soul kiss (deep kiss, French kiss)	80	12	4	2	1	1
partner soul kisses you	78	12	5	2	3	.5
you refuse to kiss partner	2	1	12	15	64	5
partner refuses to kiss you	2	1	10	15	66	5

Here are comments about kissing:

⚥"There are a million different kinds of kisses, and I love them all, except the one that says 'kiss off.' I have kissed and had kissed every cubic centimeter of the body, and all of the orifices as far as can be reached. I really get off on the guy that knows how to kiss, how to analyze my needs with his tongue. For me the most important kiss is the long, exploratory ones during the first few minutes of greeting each other. Or in the random three or four minutes before climax, or immediately after he has taken my semen in his mouth, or in the warm 'afterglow' or cuddling period (quick

pecks or long, prolonged soul kissing). Occasionally prolonged and accentuated sessions of rimming are the thing—one of the most exciting kisses in the book (or out of it)."

⚢"Kissing is really important to me and I can't relate to a man who won't kiss or won't allow you to kiss him. As a matter of fact, in a few instances when a friend of mine and I haven't been able to engage in sex for whatever reason, we have limited ourselves to kissing each other passionately for a long time and I have found this quite satisfactory. His taste lingers on my lips and I feel the warmth of his breath on my cheeks long after he's gone. I know all this sounds very romantic—and perhaps you would prefer that I remain in the realm of reality—but it's no use: I'm a hopeless romantic."

⚢"Okay as hello/goodbye and show of affection to my lover. Not an important part of sex ritual except in a very few cases."

⚢"Mostly a bore, except in a few dazzling instances. It can be a highly erotic act and I am intrigued with the inside of the mouth. I loathe casual kissing. I usually avoid kissing even my most intimate friends. I hate a casual kiss as much as I hate a handshake."

⚢"Most of the more radical gay men I know, including me, have replaced the handshake with a kiss. Sometimes this seems so nice, but at other times it seems phony and dogmatic."

⚢"Kissing is a necessary part of foreplay, but I do not like cheap display of emotions where it is a meaningless act, as it lessens its value to me. I enjoy Frenching when it does not become sloppy. Enjoy kissing back and neck while screwing."

⚢"Something I save for women. I have negative emotional reaction to kissing a man. Note also class difference in kissing behavior; generally deep kissing is avoided by working-class men."

⚢"Kissing for any length of time is only important to me if there is some major emotional pairing going on. If this involvement is not present I usually prefer not to kiss at all."

⚢"I love to French-kiss, but I must admit, when dealing with so-called straight numbers, they don't like kissing. They will fuck you and suck your cock, but it's 'queer' to kiss another man. You figure that one out."

⚢"I love to kiss and be kissed and licked all over my body. At first I would never kiss anyone or let them kiss me. When I am being sucked I don't let them kiss me afterwards."

⚢"I have never kissed a guy, but I would really like to. I have dreamed about this many many times. I think it would feel very very erotic."

⚢"I almost never have sex without kissing. I've met a few people who liked to kiss much more than I do, and I get bored with that after a while."

⚢"Kissing on the lips only is for my sister and nelly queens and other gays I don't like. I have never been able to understand someone who will rim and suck but will not kiss or share a toothbrush."

⚢"It used to seem more a man-lady activity. But I realize how it makes the man-to-man relationships more intimate and fulfilling."

⚤"I feel that anyone who can't or won't kiss their sex partner on the mouth is really not getting into it—they are only interested in cock, balls, and ass, not the person attached to them."

⚤"Kissing is wonderful, especially when it intensifies with the passion. I don't like to find a tongue down my throat just when I'm warming up, nor do I like a face bath at any point of lovemaking. Kissing I find a very skillful method of stimulation and practice it as an art myself. Wish more men did."

⚤"I can't stand people with tight, narrow lips. I prefer nondrinkers and nonsmokers. I have also discovered that a freshly brushed mouth is unnatural—turns me off."

⚤"Reserved for those for whom I have a very strong attraction over long periods of time. I am willing to fellate a stranger, but not kiss him (odd?).

⚤"I like little pecks on the cheek as a kiss of friendship."

⚤"For some reason, my lover does not like kissing me. As he is black and I am white he prefers the characteristic thickness of lips of blacks."

⚤"I love kissing on the lips, gently as well as deeply, less so with someone who smokes, and more so with someone with full lips, a black person for instance. I am white."

Drugs

The use of certain natural or chemical substances to enhance the sexual experience, or to encourage it, is fairly common, as indicated by the men who casually refer to "having a drink," "getting stoned," or "doing poppers" in the sexual experiences described earlier in this chapter. The men were asked, *How often do you use the following in association with sex?* and *Whether or not you use any of the following, how do you feel about their use in association with sex?* The charts indicate the responses:

	ALWAYS	VERY FREQUENTLY	SOMEWHAT FREQUENTLY	SOMEWHAT INFREQUENTLY	VERY INFREQUENTLY	ONCE	NEVER
alcohol	2	18	24	17	20	1	19%
marijuana	3	13	16	12	15	5	36
psychedelics (LSD, mushrooms, mescaline)	.5	1	1	5	12	5	75
uppers (speed, amphetamine)	.5	0	1	3	12	3	81
Quaaludes	.5	.5	2	3	6	4	84

	ALWAYS	VERY FREQUENTLY	SOMEWHAT FREQUENTLY	SOMEWHAT INFREQUENTLY	VERY INFREQUENTLY	ONCE	NEVER
"downers" (barbiturates, tranquilizers)	.5	.5	1	2	8	2	85
heroin	0	0	0	0	2	1	97
cocaine	.5	0	1	4	6	5	83
amyl nitrite ("poppers," "aroma")	3	9	9	8	17	9	46

	VERY POSITIVE	SOMEWHAT POSITIVE	NEUTRAL	SOMEWHAT NEGATIVE	VERY NEGATIVE	NOT SURE
alcohol	9	21	30	20	18	1%
marijuana	19	27	23	11	19	2
psychedelics (LSD, mushrooms, mescaline)	7	8	15	11	53	7
"uppers" (speed, amphetamines)	3	3	15	11	60	9
Quaaludes	4	4	13	8	61	10
"downers" (barbiturates, tranquilizers)	2	2	12	11	63	9
heroin	1	0	6	4	81	8
cocaine	9	8	11	6	55	10
amyl nitrite ("poppers," "aroma")	12	16	18	14	34	6

Negative attitudes toward drugs prevail, and the figures are sharply negative in reference to hard drugs. Alcohol, it would seem, is appreciated because it makes some people uninhibited, while pot and poppers can affect bodily sensation. One might say that gay men are pragmatic about their use, and avoidance, of drugs, though the danger of alcohol and poppers is only beginning to be discussed.

Some men have strong views about drug use, both positive and negative. Asked, *Have you ever refused to have sex with a partner because of*

drug use, 29% said yes, mostly where the partner was using alcohol. Asked if they *refused to have sex with a partner because he would not join you in the use of any of these*, 3% said yes, mostly in reference to poppers.

A few men focused on their drug use in describing a pleasing sexual experience, and others had other comments concerning drug use:

⚢ "Marijuana acts as an aphrodisiac on me. I remember once we smoked one joint nude in bed before getting down to business. We petted heavily, David being the aggressor, and on top. This involved biting, kissing, caressing, intertwining of limbs, rolling, light wrestling. David would pin my arms over my head and bite my armpits, sometimes hard. Occasionally we would stop, muttering, 'My God, that is heavy,' smoke another joint and continue. This went on for three hours with absolutely no exaggeration. Finally, being aroused to a nearly unbearable fever pitch I told David I wanted to be fucked, to which he replied, 'You're going to be.' "

⚢ "I will describe my most unexpected and delightful sexual experience. One night at Ritch Street Baths it was very late in the orgy room. I had only been in the baths four times before and felt really naive and unsure about things. Nothing much seemed to be happening and I felt that all the action for the night was over; yet I felt really unsatisfied, having been fucked a couple of times but not gotten into anything to satiate me. I was leaning up against the wall with my towel on and just watching the men go by and mess around here and there. Suddenly I noticed a beautifully built guy standing in the middle of the room with his towel slung over his shoulder. Looking at this body, I gasped in awe at his sheer beauty. He was a body-builder type with perfect muscles on chest, legs, arms—everywhere was breathtaking, not the least of which was his fabulous penis and balls, which were plainly visible even in the dimmest light. He was just standing there staring straight at me. I could only watch him, helpless in the face of his beauty.

"He came to me and touched me, ever so slowly working his hands over my entire body. 'Oh God, I hope I'm ready for this,' I thought as he started rubbing his penis against mine, getting hornier and hornier. I put my hands on his body and felt his fabulous shape. It was a deep-set drama coming true for me—a living fantasy. I expected him to throw me on that round thing they had in there and fuck me with the big brutal dick of his at any moment and I only hoped I could take it without disconcerting the perfection of his image, when suddenly he spun around in my hands and planted his hard well-formed ass squarely on my cock. I had never fucked anyone standing up: in fact I had never even thought of that position before, much less fantasized fucking a god of physical beauty. He seemed intent on me fucking him gloriously and before I knew it I was holding his pelvis in my hands as if it were a ripe peach and pumping the shit out of his glorious ass. Suddenly he came up with one of those bullet things that has amyl in it, took a long drag off it, and put it to my nose. I had never used amyl before and was dead set against it. I hated the sound of poppers and especially the smell and was sure that the stuff did lasting brain damage but at that moment I thought, 'Anything for you—one time couldn't possibly

do any appreciable amount of damage,' and took a strong sniff of it. The effect was almost instantaneous. For someone who has never used amyl before the first time is surely surprising but under the special circumstances for me at that time, it was utterly overwhelming. I immediately went into a fantasy world where multiple layers of the unconscious were made available for generating associations and meanings. Innuendoes of cosmic meanings manifested and I seemed to be fucking among the astral bodies of the gods. My penis grew in my perception to marvelous dimensions and the ass I was fucking seemed endlessly long and lined with membranes of lavender and turquoise colors and seemed to be composed of multiple layers of silk and satin and velvet with a life of its own pulling and milking my cock in a dimension of supranormal sensation. My head opened up through the top and I reached out and pulled white lights from all around me into my body and shoved them up his beautiful ass until I was running with them and suddenly I was coming and coming. I grabbed him under the arms around the chest by the shoulders and just shot all my load into him.

"He was very sweet but he just left as if that were the sort of thing that happened all the time. I collapsed slowly into the arms of an older man who had been standing beside me the whole time feeling my body as I fucked. I cried on his shoulder; I wasn't aware that such deep levels of release were possible. He held me quietly until I pulled myself together and left."

♂ "I think amyl and the various substitutes stink. I consider myself 'liberated,' and I've tripped on LSD nearly a hundred times, but I wouldn't touch poppers. I think someday it's going to come out that poppers are very dangerous. I think the companies that sell the stuff are run by rip-off artists who don't give a damn about the faggots who sniff their products."

♂ "Drug use is a big thing in gay culture. I feel that drug use is a form of escapism that people use, as they are not dealing with things within themselves."

♂ "When I do sex, I want nothing to interfere with the purity of two bodies interacting."

♂ "For the sake of social grace, I'd never refuse to share a joint with a partner."

♂ "I have taken acid, mescaline, cocaine, marijuana for years. In that period I have received two B.S. degrees (was top graduate in one of them) and I graduated with distinction from law school. It has not had any adverse effects upon my performance of my job, nor my mental capabilities. In fact it has benefited my mind in that I can perceive many things that I would have just let gone by had I not been under the influence of drugs. I believe in 'Better Living Through Chemistry.' Drug users certainly are not the 'vermin of society' as described by Spiro Agnew and the Nixon Administration. Why the government continues to perpetuate the persecution of millions of drug users in America is beyond me. All that should be required is that the drugs sold are of good quality and purity, and also people should be educated on the proper use and effects of drugs. After that the choice should be up to the individual."

Where Do You Have Sex?

One of the expressions in our society for having sex is "going to bed," but in fact you don't have to go to bed in order to have sex. Another euphemism is "sleeping together," when often there isn't much sleeping going on, and in some cases the sexual encounter isn't accompanied by "sleeping together" at all. It is generally well known that male homosexuals often perform sex outside of the home. John Rechy's books, especially *Numbers* and *The Sexual Outlaw,* document the lives of the sex hunters of city streets and parks. The use of public toilets for cruising and sex is so well known that a technical book sponsored by Cornell University and entitled *The Bath Room* includes a whole section discussing the homosexual issue in the design of modern public restrooms! Sociologist Laud Humphreys has done a special study (*Tearoom Trade*) of the men who frequent public toilets, or tearooms as they are called in gay male slang. Psychiatrists have on occasion suggested that men choose public places because they find the danger attractive. Most contemporary gay writers, however, indicate that sex in public places is chosen for its convenience and its anonymity or both, and a few have even suggested that there is something revolutionary about both promiscuity and public sex.

In fact, privacy is favored by a majority of gay men, as indicated by the following charts showing *the places the men chose to have sex.* The first chart shows responses to the question about *frequency*; the second shows response to the question *Whether or not you use any of these places for sex, how do you feel about the idea of having sex in each of these places?*" In addition to the fifteen places listed, the men referred to other places, including a boat, a plane, on a motorcycle, a church, a state mental hospital, a museum, on a ski slope, in a swimming pool, in a youth hostel (with twenty other guys in the room), in a church choir loft, in alleys and behind buildings, in the stairwell of a large apartment house, on a roof, in unused rooms on university campuses, "at work," "at school," and in cemeteries.

	ALWAYS	VERY FREQUENTLY	SOMEWHAT FREQUENTLY	SOMEWHAT INFREQUENTLY	VERY INFREQUENTLY	ONCE	NEVER
your home	9	56	13	8	8	1	5%
your partner's home	6	44	24	10	12	.5	4
a friend's home	1	8	9	16	34	7	24

	ALWAYS	VERY FREQUENTLY	SOMEWHAT FREQUENTLY	SOMEWHAT INFREQUENTLY	VERY INFREQUENTLY	ONCE	NEVER
gay bath	1	11	8	15	19	6	40
beach	0	1	3	8	19	14	54
park, "bushes"	.5	3	6	10	20	11	51
public rest room	1	4	5	7	16	8	59
car	1	3	3	13	40	14	26
van or camper	1	2	.2	5	16	12	62
tent	0	1	3	7	17	11	61
motel or hotel	1	4	10	16	41	9	20
bar	0	1	2	4	20	8	66
secluded woods or field	1	2	7	11	30	13	35
barn or farm building	0	1	2	5	14	5	73
peep show, pornographic movie house	0	3	6	9	15	8	59

	VERY POSITIVE	SOMEWHAT POSITIVE	NEUTRAL	SOMEWHAT NEGATIVE	VERY NEGATIVE	NOT SURE
your home	85	9	3	2	1	0%
your partner's home	77	18	14	12	0	0
a friend's house	42	22	20	10	5	2
gay bath	29	18	20	16	12	4
beach	29	23	20	13	11	4
park, "bushes"	15	11	16	23	32	2
public rest room	8	8	10	15	57	3
car	13	17	28	27	12	2
van or camper	24	28	32	9	5	2
tent	30	28	30	6	5	2
motel or hotel	35	33	26	4	2	0
bar	8	9	18	21	40	4
secluded woods or field	41	27	18	5	7	2
barn or farm building	32	23	27	5	9	4
peep show, pornographic movie house	12	13	12	21	40	3

Significantly, a majority of the men have never had sex in such public places as public toilets, peep shows, and bars, and these places are generally thought of in negative terms. Nonetheless, many men simply do not have sex in what is the most preferred, and presumably the most logical, place—their own home—and this may be due to the reality of being in the closet or lacking privacy. This is especially true for teenagers, a group which is underrepresented in our sample in any case. Even men who live alone can be reluctant to bring sex partners home, for fear of robbery, discovery by nosy neighbors or relatives, etc. On the other hand, it won't do to say that sex in public places is simply due to "oppression." Many men feel quite enthusiastic about so-called public sex (most of this sex takes place out of anyone's view). There were many, in fact, who checked "very positive" for every possible place.

The men were asked *how they feel about the issue of privacy and the danger or possibility of violence.* The question, unfortunately, was not clearly worded, substantially negating its value for statistics. However, the comments offered by the men indicate that an overwhelming majority prefer privacy in most cases and abhor danger or the possibility of violence. Under certain circumstances—at the baths, for example—lack of privacy is accepted by some men. And undoubtedly there are those who derive pleasure and excitement from the risky aspects of public or semi-public sex.

Here are some comments from men concerning the questions of privacy, danger, and the possibility of violence in sexual settings:

&"I did toilets, especially glory holes. Rest areas are great but many in Michigan have been raided, and I've almost been picked up twice by the cops. The danger has decreased my enjoyment and made me more uptight than I used to be, and consequently, I don't get 'into it' like I used to."

&"Sex is most enjoyable when I can be completely free from fear of someone else walking in on me."

&"I very much prefer privacy—I feel this is a very personal thing between two people—emotional and physical."

&"I would not like to be 'caught' having sex by unprepared heterosexuals. However, in a semipublic place where other gays are there doing it, it doesn't bother me."

&"I occasionally enjoy the 'orgy room' in the steam baths."

&"It depends on the situation. I enjoy watching and being watched at times."

&"I think sex is the only natural response man has—and it should be the most accepted and common thing in our life. It should be the most natural act seen in public."

&"I was arrested in a Los Angeles park once, got out of the habit fast."

&"At a gay bath, fifty nude men may be in the same room I'm in, but since we're all there undisturbed by straight gawkers or police, I consider that to be a private situation."

&"I have noticed that I reach orgasm much more rapidly in public areas (rest rooms, bars), where there is a chance of discovery, but I have no

conscious desire to be caught. I always try to pick places where there will be a time to cover up if someone else appears.''

☿''When I used to cruise the Rambles in New York's Central Park, I was not attracted by the possibility of violence. Rather, I was so horny I threw caution to the winds. I think toilets are stinky, but I feel that sex outdoors is very lyrical, and I can remember some very pleasant encounters in such places as the Judy Garland Memorial Park in Cherry Grove on Fire Island, N.Y., the tropical bushes of Dania Beach, Fla., the Bird Sanctuary, Cambridge, Mass., etc.''

☿''I like privacy and security; however, I have pulled some daring maneuvers and have been very lucky. Examples: on a church hay ride, back seat of family car with other passengers in front, in a military barracks, in a church camp, in a tent with other people.''

☿''I am definitely the type of person who prefers a nice cozy room with a lighted hearth that promotes security and comfort. If my mind is on fearing the arrival of outsiders I cannot concentrate on sex.''

Sex in unusual settings brings back strong memories to some men, some of them very pleasing. In response to the question about funny, scary, or unusual experiences, a number of men referred to incidents that took place in locales other than the bedroom. Here are a number of incidents and experiences where a non-bedroom location contributed to the situation and made it special:

☿''I was on a train trip to last about five or six hours. On this Friday, the train was filled. There were a few single seats in my car. One attractive slender guy of about 25 years caught my eye. I was invited to share the empty seat and did. We engaged in some trivia and the other guy 'fell asleep.' I read and later he seemed to stretch out, asleep, and he touched my leg with his. I didn't know how to respond and so I didn't. About ten minutes later he seemed to fall more deeply asleep and he rested his head on my shoulder and snuggled it! In broad daylight, I was somewhat embarrassed and didn't know how to respond. So I pretended to fall asleep to 'play it cool.' I still wasn't sure what was happening, because I normally wouldn't even fantasize this. Maybe another ten minutes passed and I felt a finger stroke my arm that was crossed. Even people walking in the aisle didn't see this. At this point I was sure of all signals and so I could or could not respond. So respond I did by simply stroking his arm in like fashion. This continued for about ten minutes with me getting very hard. The train made a stop and so we talked for about an hour. He was intelligent and had a college degree, too, so we talked on many subjects, but mostly about being gay. I remember that the body language was beautiful in our talk. We then decided that a drink was in order and proceeded to the bar, but he wanted to stop off in the men's lounge. We checked to make sure that no one was there and proceeded to kiss up a storm. I kept my ass jammed against the door to save anyone embarrassment. I didn't feel comfortable

with my surroundings, daylight and the shade open on the window when we stopped at a station, since I didn't want to get arrested, so we adjusted ourselves to go to the bar. I noticed a very nice erection getting placed in an unnoticeable position before we left. We kept on grabbing one another on the way to the bar when no one was around. We had a drink and decided to carry it to the dome seats. But we stopped in the men's room first and kissed again. This time he kissed even more erotically and on the ear and neck, which made me go crazy! In nothing flat he had my pants down and was blowing me. I was very apprehensive about this, keeping my bare ass against the door to prevent someone's entry. I pulled him up and undid his fly also. He was cut and had about 7 inches of beautiful cock. He also had a slight crotch odor that really turned me on. I sucked him, stroking his balls with my hand, alternately grabbing his tight ass cheeks and legs. I would have liked to fuck him, but that was out of the question due to the danger of someone else coming in. Being uptight about this anyway I must have painfully sucked him hard because he reacted like he was being hurt slightly. He came with loud groans. He then continued to suck me. This was pleasant to watch and I too came in torrents. I would not in ten lifetimes have ever done something like this, but it was so spontaneous and erotic. I wonder about a 747!''

⚥"One of the most erotic experiences ('lovemaking'?) I had was in a wooden john in a wayside park. I was fantasizing about a brochure containing pix of 'barnyard sex.' I was sitting on the john (I love to see a guy sitting with his legs spread and beating a hot, throbbing cock, especially on a toilet). A hunky, butch blond young man came in with tears in his jeans and took out a long, hot piece of meat, about 9½ inches. He sucked me and I sucked him (lots of come). So I was heading back to Grand Rapids, Mich., and stopped at the new rest area which parallels the one I was in. He was there and we went in the woods and sucked each other again—I came twice again and the last time when he was sucking me he shot his load in his hand and then I licked it into my mouth.

"Another time in New Jersey, I met two 'rough-trade' types at a rest area. Went on a deserted road—the one wasn't so rough, but the other kept calling me 'motherfucker.' But what huge cocks and big loads, and built like brick shithouses.''

⚥"In 1974, I was a student at Western Washington State College in Bellingham. I was in the process of coming out but was very uneasy about letting anyone know I was gay. I held a job in the college library and for weeks had noticed a man who also worked in the library. He was, and is, an incredibly open person, full of love and life. I always wanted to talk to him since I knew no gay people at school and I knew he was gay. One day I started hanging around his department asking contrived questions about things he was supposed to be of assistance with. We got talking about our desire to want to spend the night in a library. Since it was getting near closing time he convinced me, which wasn't hard, to hide in the stacks until the library was locked up (also his job). When the lights were going off I

was squeezed between the dictionaries with thoughts of 'What am I doing?' 'Why am I doing this?' etc. When the library was all shut up he came for me, called his liberal boss, and told her that he and a friend were sleeping in the library and she was to wake us up at opening time since she was there first. We both then explored the whole dark building, which was very exciting in itself. (I've really always wanted to spend the night in a library.) We went to visit our favorite sections, mine being Asian history, his being reference. We sat in the old foyer and read, or he did. My mind was racing, 'Why are we reading? . . . Maybe I've made a mistake . . . he's not gay . . . I'm trapped in a locked library with a heterosexual. Oh God.' Well, as time went on, he announced it was time for bed. We searched for a place to sleep and found one in reference, his favorite place. We were kneeling down and talking small talk when he broke off and put his hand on my knee, very softly stroking it. He told me he was gay and liked me. I was so relieved, I told him I too was gay, and so began a sexual encounter. I've never forgotten nor ever will, I hope.''

⚥"The scariest experience I had was when I was still an inexperienced kid of 15. I was in a theater toilet with a glory hole, and a cop walked in standing next to the glory hole to urinate. When he finished, he started to massage his penis into hardness and stuck it through the hole. I was so horny I took his penis into my mouth. He promptly pulled it out and ordered me to go with him. He took me in his squad car and lectured me, and finally told me that I should not seek out sex partners in public places like that in such an obvious manner. He advised me to do my propositioning in other than public areas, and that he understood the gay life. He then drove me to a secluded area and let me finish sucking him off. I was really excited about sucking a policeman's cock and tasting his come, but the lesson remained with me.''

⚥"The funniest sexual act I ever had was when I had sex with a man in my car parked in a farmer's corn field. During the act, it rained, and when it was over, the car was stuck in the mud. It was funny, the both of us asking this farmer for help: 'What were you guys doing parked there in the first place?' ''

⚥"At a series of salons in San Francisco, on three consecutive evenings I kept seeing this unhandsome but very magnetic man. His attraction to me was obvious, but his lover was possessive. The third night, tight, I went with him into the bathroom and leaned him over the edge of the bathtub and fucked him for a long, long time. We were both very amused with ourselves and were having lots of fun; our indiscretion was quite outrageous, we were laughing about something, and suddenly I was having an orgasm that started from the soles of my feet and rose like a tidal wave. I was very noisy. He was talking dirty very loud. We left the bathroom together. The people at the salon cheered for us as we emerged. Startled, we blushed, split up, and have never seen each other again. His lover didn't seem pissed. I got VD.''

⚥"I had been on a long trip with a friend with whom in the past I had

had an affair. During the time away from home, we had been sleeping together and enjoying it very much. We were having fun together. On the way home, we were on a very, very long stretch of desert, flatness for miles, with an endless blue sky overhead and the sun shining hotly. He was driving and we had suddenly began absently fondling each other as we drove and talked. And suddenly, there I was doing what I had on occasion fantasized about, blowing him while he drove. It was both unusual and funny, because as he came he found his foot pressing the accelerator and he came going about 90 miles an hour. He and I have enjoyed the memory of that a number of times since.''

&''Funny—being screwed on an air mattress on a lake, and just before he was to come, we fell into the water.''

&''My scariest sexual encounter was on a Greyhound bus somewhere in the early-morning hours on the western Nebraska plain. Another man and I had discovered each other early on during a three-day cross-country journey and had been sitting together consistently. The first night we went into the toilet to smoke dope and kiss a bit but nothing more. The second night, we pretended to fall asleep and crumple over onto each other's shoulders. As the night wore on this half-asleep, half-awake activity became more elaborate with groping, occasional furtive kisses, and reaching into each other's clothes. There was a heavy burly cowboy type who was sitting across the aisle several seats ahead of us and who had been pestering young women the whole trip and drinking whiskey, but who also seemed to be asleep at this point—suddenly he leaped from his seat and wheeled back at us, pounding with his fists. I was on the window seat and ducked down so he only managed to pound the seat; my partner was by the aisle and received at least one blow in his face. A tooth cut through his lip and he was bleeding profusely. He ran up to the driver, who did nothing except to tell him to sit in the front seat for the rest of the trip, which he did at night, but not during the day. I changed seats, too, but I did not sit with him, and was not able to sleep any more that night.''

&''This experience was between me (age 28, attractive, youthful-looking, slim, nice build, long hair) and my partner, Dan (age 24, factory construction worker, attractive, hunky, medium hair). Met at Man's Country Baths, Chicago. We were instantly attracted to each other. Man's Country has a disco on premises. We went into the large disco music hall, and gathered several floor pillows. Under the flashing lights and disco music, off to the side of the room, we laid out several pillows to create a bed. (It is popular to fuck in the disco music hall.) Our entire sexual experience lasted about four hours, of hot, vigorous, energetic sex. He then called into work—took the evening off, so that we might continue. We continued sex for about twenty-four hours, on and off.''

&''Recently at a gay cinema, I was standing in the back when a mustachioed man 30–40 years old stood next to me. We were looking at each other's flies more than at the movie for a few minutes when we began,

furtively at first, groping each other. When he reached around to the seat of my pants, my groping became more intense. I unzipped his fly and groveled through his jockey shorts till I came upon his cock. He suggested we sit down together, whereupon little by little, tauntingly and teasingly, he removed my jeans while I separated his ass from his jeans and underpants. We were stroking and caressing each other's bodies, with his head on my shoulder or lips on my lips and hands exploring tummies, and thighs and crotch and ass. We played around there in the theater seats for at least fifteen minutes when it became time to go into the areaway near the water cooler and the door to the men's room. There's an understanding among this particular theater's clientele that the areaway is where you 'do it.' The lighting is dim but the space is heavily trafficked. So many theatergoers need a drink of water or a trip to the toilet! While standing there with my newfound friend, we were able to take off all of each other's clothes and get into affectionate embraces. Passersby often stopped and groped us, but we seemed lost in each other. First, gradually I got on my knees and took his cock head into my mouth—a perfect fit. I grooved on it while playing with his balls and he reached down and caressed my head and ears. He gently pulled me up by the shoulders so he could get down on me and tongue my cock and then my balls while making stray passes at my tits. We exchanged this gentle and tender affection for almost an hour. I became aware of several people watching. That was exciting. I decided for our finale I would come first so he could have the final pleasure last. After we came, we both stood there in the aisle, naked, sweating, hugging for what seemed a long time. We got dressed and kissed and left each other. I tried to find him in the crowd and maybe he was looking for me, but we got away from each other. I thought he left. So I left and just as I drove away I saw him come out of the theater. I stopped, waited to see if he wanted to meet me. But he just smiled and waved, and that was my last sight of him.''

⚥ "Once my lover and I were in the desert and we were going at it hot and heavy out in the sun and he wanted to be fucked and sat his ass on a cactus plant. I couldn't help laughing and he didn't see the humor in the situation for several weeks.''

⚥ "Once I got picked up by two truck drivers while hitchhiking, and we found a way to discover that we were all gay, and so we made it in the cab of this big rig tooling up Interstate 95 between Richmond and Baltimore in a blizzard a few years ago. Weird.''

⚥ "My scariest sexual experience was when I was 18 and hitchhiking near Honesdale, Pa., late at night, and after hundreds of cars passed me by, one stopped and the guy said, 'I'll take you anywhere you want to go if you let me blow you.' Well, I was really scared. I didn't know what he would do if I said yes and what if I said no. I pretended not to know what he meant by 'blow you.' He explained, and I figured, 'Well, I really need the ride, so why not risk it?' And we rode off the side of the road and he blew me right there and then took me where I wanted to go.''

Even when sex takes place in a bedroom or other private place, it is not necessarily the occasion for sleeping together. The men were asked, *How often do you spend the whole night with your sex partner?* The replies were:

always	13%
very frequently	45
somewhat frequently	16
somewhat infrequently	12
very infrequently	11
once	.5
never	3

Following are comments on why or why not:

⚥ "Most men I meet turn out to be married and therefore have other responsibilities."

⚥ "I'd love to do it, but at times someone gets expectations of a love that won't develop and who wants to get hurt? Baths avoid this but also avoid the chance to develop intimacy."

⚥ "I like to like the guy I'm with and prefer to be able to spend some time together. It's nice to have sex again in the morning or middle of the night."

⚥ "Don't stay . . . feel they would be disappointed in the morning."

⚥ "Unless I am very horny, I do not like to blow and go. I enjoy making a night of it and getting emotionally involved."

⚥ "Cuddling follows sex like a rainbow after rain."

⚥ "My young lover lives with his family. My older lover is a doctor and he works as a surgeon—too many demands on him."

⚥ "Have never been asked. Have never asked. Would love to."

⚥ "Spending the night invests the encounter with greater human warmth."

⚥ "I don't like people hurrying off after sex. I'm not an accu-jack."

⚥ "Too much flack from my wife if I don't come home."

⚥ "Most of my sex has been with pickups. Spending the night involves waking up the next morning and dealing with each other nonsexually."

⚥ "Because I have sex with people I know and like. The intimacy of falling asleep with someone is part of what sex is about for me."

12

The Specialized Tastes of a Few Lesbians

In the past few years the gay male and lesbian media have printed a number of stories by and about lesbians and gay men who are coming out of "second closets"—the lesbians who have hidden their sexual practices from others because what they do in bed varies from the vast majority of lesbians discussed in Chapter 10. These lesbians often feel like "freaks" within the community because they are into sadomasochism or some form of sex which the "average" lesbian considers "kinky," or even repellent.

The gay and feminist media are to be commended for their fearless coverage of areas often considered beyond the pale of acceptability when at times it must be tempting to them to present gay people as the same as heterosexuals except that gays' sex partners are of the same sex. Perhaps some homosexuals realize, deep down, that heterosexuals often consider gay people to be the freaks, or downright disgusting. Therefore, not wishing to perpetuate or transfer onto others the oppression gays have too often been the victims of, gay newspapers and magazines extend to the minority groups within the community the right to speak which gay people have often been denied in the heterosexual community at large.

In the same manner, this chapter will provide a forum for people who are into minority sexual practices. If there is a danger in presenting aspects of sexuality which appear to be bizarre, there is a greater danger in covering them up. The danger here is only that the straight reader who is looking for the most unusual or "queerest" lesbian of all will take this chapter out of context and make generalizations, when the statistics accompanying each section show the low frequency of such lifestyles within the lesbian community. The other extreme or danger would be to whitewash these lifestyles by dragging in statistics to prove that heterosexuals engage in these practices at least as frequently as homosexuals. To do so is to be defensive and at the same time to subtly put down those who engage in alternative lifestyles. This chapter reports the findings about various alternative lifestyles.

Sadomasochism, Bondage and Discipline, Humiliation, "Talking Dirty," and Fist-Fucking

These five activities immediately elicit hostile words and feelings from most lesbians who answered the survey. They felt that sexual activity should be a matter of pleasure, not pain, and that humiliation is something lesbians get enough of in the straight world. The overwhelming majority of lesbians were negative to these activities. When asked, *Whether or not you experience any of the following, indicate how you feel about the idea of each of them,* the women gave the following answers:

	VERY POSITIVE	SOMEWHAT POSITIVE	NEUTRAL	SOMEWHAT NEGATIVE	VERY NEGATIVE	NOT SURE
sadomasochism	2	7	7	13	68	4%
bondage and discipline	4	7	6	11	65	7
humiliation	1	1	4	5	85	4
"talking dirty"	7	18	21	14	35	6
fist-fucking	3	5	11	9	59	12

As one can readily see, there were slight variations in feelings about these acts, which may be due to confusion. Many women confessed that they do not know the difference between some of them. The most misunderstood term seemed to be "talking dirty," a fact which may account for more positive feelings about this practice. Many women thought it means saying something like, "Hey, honey, do you want to fuck tonight?" They did not understand that talking dirty, for some people, is a sexual act in itself. According to Dr. Charles Silverstein and Edmund White, authors of *The Joy of Gay Sex,* talking dirty "creates the act as it describes it." Talking dirty can also be "occasional bursts of four-letter words or the unwinding of an elaborate fantasy." Other women did not understand the differences between sadomasochism and bondage and discipline (sometimes called bondage and dominance). As defined in *The Queens' Vernacular: A Gay Lexicon* by Bruce Rodgers, S&M is "sexual pleasure derived from fetishes, pain, torture, domination, etc. The forms of S&M range from very mild fantasies (wearing of uniforms, for example) all the way to heavy extremes." B&D is "sexual excitement related to binding and/or being bound in various positions with different types of binders (rope, handcuffs, leather thongs, etc.). Forcing to perform and/or performing a variety of demeaning and comtemptible actions for sexual satisfaction." Humiliation is a situation where one person is forced to grovel or perform servile acts or is

called demeaning names. Finally, some women were not sure if fist-fucking (which entails thrusting the entire fist up the rectum or vagina) included "finger-fucking" or penetration of the vagina by more than one finger.

Perhaps the authors should have included some definitions of these terms, but frankly lack of space prevented this. In addition, the authors were inclined to believe that those who were into them would understand what they mean, while those who weren't could answer "not sure," or not answer at all. The authors reasoned that people who engaged in these practices know the distinctions, just as most lesbians are more likely to know what the terms "butch" and "femme" mean than heterosexuals are.

Most lesbians did understand the terminology enough to react with decisive hostility, as shown in the chart and the comments. In the short-answer section of the questionnaire, many summed up their reaction with one-word comments such as: "Yuck!" "Disgusting!" "Revolting!" "Sick!" "Counter-revolutionary!" "Anti-woman!" "Male!" "Yech!" "Ugh!" and so on. Some people, however, offered further comment:

♀ "I have never done these nor do I care to try—I *hate* them and the idea of them because they automatically put one person on a lower level. I could not love or respect someone who I was not on a par with. I couldn't do this to a person and I wouldn't allow it to be imposed on me."

♀ "I have never done any of them except 'talking dirty' on a few occasions. None of them appeal to me. I *hate* the idea of S&M, bondage, and humiliation. When I make love to my lover, that's what I want to do, make love to her, not tie her up or treat her as a thing. We are equals in bed, two women who love each other."

♀ "I have had no experience with the practices listed, and I can see no reason to start now. Such activities may be essential to stimulate some people, but if so, I would be inclined to think that these people are emotionally disturbed."

♀ "I have had no experience with any of these things. Most seem to be based on exploitation and degradation and have no relevance to my ideas of loving sex."

♀ "No experience and no interest in acquiring any, except that I've found out what fist-fucking is, and found I have done that because I have small hands, and some of the women I've known had lots of room when they were turned on. In general, I don't want anything done to me that hurts. And I don't want to to anything that hurts and the difference between pain and pleasure is crystal-clear to me. I've never run into anyone who wanted to be hurt, but I think it would turn me off."

♀ "I don't like humiliation. My mother used to employ humiliation as a form of discipline, which I detested then and I think it would carry over. Fist-fucking sounds good in theory, but seems to have the potential for being extremely painful. I've never tried it, so I don't know."

♀ "I'm glad I don't have to get my kicks that way. Good old-fashioned lovemaking is good enough for me. Any sex act is fine in the privacy of one's home and as long as neither partner is forced or hurt in any way. I just don't happen to enjoy kinky sex. In fact, it really turns me off."

♀ "This question seems to have been written from a male viewpoint, although I will wait and see what your results show. Maybe more women are into this stuff than I imagine. Anyway, I think the idea of S&M and B&D is horrible. What in the world for? If you are in bed with someone you love, why hurt them or be hurt? The point of making love, for me, is tenderness, vulnerability, emotional warmth that are part of it. It is beyond me how anyone would want to break that down with pain. All that goes for humiliation too. What for? I like it when sex makes us feel better about ourselves and each other, which it can. Women face enough humiliation in the real world. 'Talking dirty,' if that means using words like 'fuck,' 'piss,' 'shit,' and so on, I use them, but not particularly during sex, and it certainly doesn't turn me on. As for fist-fucking, I like the skin around the entrance of my vagina to be rubbed and stroked but don't care one way or the other for something being inside. A fist sounds like way too much. I guess I wouldn't object to doing this to my lover if she would like it but so far it has never come up."

♀ "I feel that these are all symptoms of a serious inequality in a relationship. I don't understand how anyone could find humiliation exciting."

♀ "I'm agin' all of these things, and if you had any more, I'd be agin' them too!"

A few people expressed more of a "live and let live" attitude.

♀ "My feelings on those things are that if you want to do it, fine. Just don't force me into anything I don't want. Talking dirty, B&D, and threesomes are okay if you don't put undue emphasis on them in the relationship."

♀ "Most of them I would hate for myself, but if someone else wants to do them, I suppose that's their business. I cannot understand how dykes could get into sadomasochism. It's so male-oriented. Most of that stuff is male-oriented in my opinion."

A small percentage of lesbians were into sadomasochism, bondage and discipline, humiliation, fist-fucking, and talking dirty. Since cross-tabulations were not done in these areas, it is not certain whether it is mostly the same lesbians who are into all five categories. However, this was how the women responded when asked *how often their sexual experiences include these acts.*

	ALWAYS	VERY FREQUENTLY	SOMEWHAT FREQUENTLY	SOMEWHAT INFREQUENTLY	VERY INFREQUENTLY	ONCE	NEVER
sadomasochism	.5	0	2	3	8	2	85%
bondage & discipline	.5	1	1	4	6	1	87

	ALWAYS	VERY FREQUENTLY	SOMEWHAT FREQUENTLY	SOMEWHAT INFREQUENTLY	VERY INFREQUENTLY	ONCE	NEVER
humiliation	.5	1	.5	.5	2	.5	95
"talking dirty"	.5	5	5	8.5	16	1	64
fist-fucking	.5	1	2	0	.3	4	88.5

Here are some of the experiences and comments of those who participated in alternative sex practices. It should be noted that some of these experiences were included in response to the essay question which asked the participant to describe a pleasing lovemaking experience.

♀ "My last lover and I used to do a lot of theatrical B&D together. I was always passive since she was unwilling to play both roles. We could caress and play together for a while. Then she would tell me to lie on my stomach while she scrounged up scarves and belts to tie me with. One time she picked up a man's hat we happened to have in the room plus a lovely meerschaum pipe I had given her for Christmas. After some giggling and slapping, she managed to tie me face down on the bed. Then she began hitting me with the belt, mostly making loud slapping sounds but not hurting me very much. Later she entered me with her hands. (We were also in the habit of using zucchini, carrots, and occasional wine bottles.) But the moment I remember most is lifting my head to see her kneeling over me, belt in hand, with that hat and pipe. She is a delightfully androgynous person, and 'butch' apparel always looks rather charmingly boyish on her—her softness is still unavoidable. We usually played together like this for an hour or so, sometimes waking the roommates with the belt sounds and my screams of delight."

♀ "Sadomasochism is okay between two consenting adults. It goes well with B&D, and I enjoy the combination occasionally as an erotic, artistic, and emotional sharing experience. I am more sadistic than masochistic. I enjoy tying someone up on occasion, but I cannot bear being tied. Masks are okay if I'm wearing them. I enjoy S&M and B&D with men occasionally and with them I play a slave or whatever. I enjoy humiliating men because most of my life they seem to have been intent upon humiliating me. Perhaps I'm being a bad sport, but . . ."

♀ "I have had a few experiences with S&M. I have had my lover beat me with a belt and carve a cross into my back with a knife. I would like a nun to beat me, but she refuses. I enjoy it once in a while, but it is only pleasurable with someone I love. I haven't tried B&D really, but I'd like to. I like sexual humiliation and talking dirty."

♀ "Last summer for the first time I acknowledged that S&M intrigued

me. I came from a Catholic background where sex had never been discussed. All that I knew about it I learned for myself and all that I had ever heard about S&M was in sleazy novels or in dirty jokes. It was one of those perversions that seedy people did in back alleys. When my lover and I first started fucking, everything was exciting, and the freedom I found in fucking helped to loosen my head. I was able to admit that I frequently had S&M fantasies. We talked about it a little. We were both embarrassed. The thoughts lay dormant, and then a few months later when we had become more open with each other, she asked me to tie her up. We were unsure, but we knew we wanted to try it. I tied her arms to the closet door and the radiator post. She looked great with her arms stretched out and her muscles very taut. I kissed and licked her all over and went down on her. I loved it. She would try to move up to lessen the tightness on her arms, and I would pull her back down by the hips so that she was stretched to the maximum. Afterwards, we were very open about discussing it and how we felt about it. In the beginning I felt guilty, my upbringing coming out. I told her that I wasn't sure I wanted to feel the feelings I felt while she was tied. I wasn't sure I wanted those feelings in connection with her. She told me she liked it a lot and described the feeling of helplessness. I felt strong and powerful; the idea of having so much control was intoxicating. I gradually became more comfortable with tying her and soon told her that I wanted to be tied too. When she did it, it was beautiful. I had no control over what my body was going to feel next. She could control tempo and the extent of anything that we did. Sudden anal penetration when tied can send me up the wall. It is by far one of the most exciting things I have ever done.

"Despite how good each of us felt about tying, actually trying to hit one another put us through the same difficult pattern of overcoming guilt. We both have now, and I love it. Our S&M activities have increased in frequency, but they are not the primary sexual activity we share. We always try to maintain an openness about discussing it and how it feels and why we like it. This is a developing thing for us, and I am enjoying it very much. The implications I get from the term 'humiliation' are all negative; my sexual life with my lover is a positive reaffirming thing. Humiliation is not a part of it."

♀ "I love S&M. I am a masochist and enjoy the feeling of powerlessness, degradation, and humiliation. I like being humiliated. I love the feeling of being a sex object and having my desires ignored, as I know my lover is actually striving to meet my desires."

♀ "I've done light bondage with one of my lovers a few times. She tied me up and made love to me, sometimes putting objects in my vagina. I like to beg to eat her."

♀ "I've had very little experience with S&M, limited mainly to spanking at crucial moments during lovemaking. I'm very interested in it but don't know anyone else interested who would trust me enough or that I trust enough to play around with it. I think setting limits ahead of time would be very important."

♀ "I sometimes enjoy getting spanked (lightly) near my genital area but have only once had this done (feel a little guilty about asking for this). I have never performed any sadistic act on anyone else (and don't desire to), although I do think a little pain in sex sometimes feels good. I once had my lover tie me down with legs spread apart and manipulate my clitoris manually followed by an electric vibrator on my clitoris until orgasm. It was great. No lover has ever asked me to bind her. Humiliation is a real turn-off for me, and talking dirty doesn't do much for me or my lovers."

A few other comments on sadomasochism and bondage and discipline included comments on hickeys, clawing of backs, or rough sex. Generally hickeys do not qualify as sadism, although it might depend on how long your teeth are or how hard you bite! The division between back clawing and rough sex being pleasurable or painful may be a rather thin line. Like these acts, fist-fucking may be considered painful or pleasurable depending on who is doing it and how. Most lesbians, again, felt negative about this act.

♀ "Fist-fucking sounds like S&M on a hard-core level. Yuck! A sure way to develop hemorrhoids or anal warts."

♀ "No way! That's for masochistic gay men! It is utterly dangerous! Hemorrhoids, tissue falling out, colostomies, intestinal diseases! No appeal. I like to shit and that's it!"

♀ "I can just barely deal with a finger in my anus."

♀ "First of all, nobody's fist would possibly fit in me, and it sounds really unpleasant. I *did* go to bed with a woman who wanted a sort of violent penetration like that (she was used to going to bed with men), and I wouldn't do it. I did gentler things to her. She was nonorgasmic, at least at that point in time. Small wonder, if *that's* what she was used to!"

Despite these negative feelings, some lesbians did engage in vaginal fist-fucking, and here's how they feel about it. (None of the lesbians described any first-hand experience with anal fist-fucking.)

♀ "I got into fist-fucking with one lover and loved it. We worked into it slowly, and it was a peak emotional experience. I felt so incredibly full of her; it was as if we had merged our bodies and souls. And when she (or I) took her fist out, it was as if I was giving birth to her. Really neat. But it isn't something I could do with every lover. It took a lot of time, trust, and love."

♀ "I personally enjoy fist-fucking both ways, in a passionate way. I love the feeling of a woman I'm in bed with being inside of me. One experience I particularly enjoyed was with a lover who was lying on her back and I was straddling her torso. She penetrated my vagina with her entire hand, with the help of KY jelly, and I moved up and down on her arm. She was able to push it in as far as her wrist and forearm. I *loved* it. I enjoy being made love to more than doing it. I like it rough when I'm excited, and gentle af-

terwards. During this experience, my lover was holding my breasts with her hand as I leaned against it, while I moved my body up and down on her hand. All the elements were present to make it an extremely exciting session.

"I get off on this more than anything else. I must say, at this point, that I've never been to bed with a man, and I never intend to. I've never had any sexual desire for a man. I like the feeling of a *woman* being inside of me. I have to have emotional involvement to get off on anything, and I've never felt anything for a man but total indifference."

Despite some confusion over the meaning of the term the consensus was generally negative about talking dirty no matter how the women defined it. Most of the remarks about talking dirty are included with those on sadomasochism, but some women specifically referred to this practice.

♀ "Talking dirty is like pornography. Usually it has some kind of sexist approach. It's like what 'I'm going to do *to* you,' not what 'I'd like to do *with* you.' As such it doesn't excite me too much."

♀ "I'm not sure what classifies as 'talking dirty,' but I do get on a lot by talking during sex. I like to say and hear such things as 'Take me,' 'I want you,' etc. But most of my talk is about how good I feel or she feels and how she looks."

♀ "Men have burned me out on 'talking dirty' for the most part. I prefer a more emotional approach, although I have done this."

♀ "Once a lover screamed 'rat filth' and my orgasm went away."

♀ "Most 'dirty' words are also sexist words—that is, anti-woman. They should be eliminated from vocabulary completely, not given an erotic element."

On the other hand, some women found talking dirty an exciting part of sex.

♀ "I am Brazilian. In Portuguese the word for 'cunt' is very, very heavy. When I was a child, it was the absolute dirty word. This has had a long-lasting negative effect on me. Lately, with age and the women's movement, this word has become more acceptable and some women say it normally. I can't do this yet. I still feel very uncomfortable with that word. The result of this is that it turns me on immensely! I love to be in bed with a woman and say to her: "Oh, your cunt is so wet. What a delicious cunt you have." And she is turned on too, because being my age, she went through the same. I want to make it clear that it's not the English word that turns me on, but the Portuguese word, the forbidden word of my childhood. And when I masturbate, I say this word mentally a lot.

"I think this is ridiculous, but what can I do? I'm not too harsh on myself. I like to give myself pleasure, and if this is the way I enjoy it most, let it be like this. What I think is that I have to *act this all out,* to really do with a woman what I do only in my imagination, and I'm sure after a couple of times the magic of that word will wear off and I'll feel much healthier."

♀"The term itself is a moral judgment—if you mean saying swear words that refer to the body. I like to say exciting words that are societally 'daring' and enjoy it when someone says them to me."

♀"My ex-lover liked me to 'talk dirty' to her. It kinda turned me on too!"

♀"A couple of times I've experienced this in a pleasant sort of way, like with my woman lover growling, 'Oh, woman, your cunt is so juicy and slushy,' and found it kind of exciting. But I wouldn't have liked, say, being called a bitch or something."

♀"I just recently found out that we can both get very turned on by describing to each other what we would like to do. This is lots of fun."

♀"Talking dirty turns me on, I guess, because it's very aggressive, somewhat humiliating, and just very sexy."

Urination, Defecation, and Enemas

If people felt confused about what talking dirty is, they were even more confused about urination ("water sports"), defecation ("scat"), and enemas. "Isn't that a medical procedure?" asked one woman incredulously about the last. Women often used the same expletives as for sadomasochism, bondage and discipline, and humiliation, but added words like: "Filthy!" "Unsanitary!" "Are you kidding?" "Why???" "Messy!" Here's how the statistics on these feelings broke down.

	VERY POSITIVE	SOMEWHAT POSITIVE	NEUTRAL	SOMEWHAT NEGATIVE	VERY NEGATIVE	NOT SURE
urination	2	1	7	7	77	7%
defecation	1	0	3	2	89	5
enemas	.5	1	8	4	79.5	7

And here's how some of these feelings were verbally expressed.

♀ "I've heard of males doing this, and the first thing that comes to my mind is, who cleans it up? Or do they do it in the bathroom? I know males like to watch each other piss, but I don't see why. It seems dirty, in the sense of unsanitary, if they touch it without washing afterwards."

♀ "My previous lover did water sports *to* me after a long time of trying to get me to say yes. Well, she did it and I didn't feel anything but grossed out! (Took a shower!)"

♀"I've pissed on four men who paid me! Both urination and defecation are cover-ups for wanting to get hit and humiliated. It is a symbol of

humiliation. A regression to infancy. I've never shit on a man, but I'd love to *throw* shit at the assholes on the street and everywhere I meet them! Enemas are also sublimation for direct verbal and physical confrontation with an authoritative-parental figure—a mother or father fantasy. Maybe even guilty incest feelings, conscious or unconscious.''

♀ "I've never had an enema, not even for medicinal purposes, so I can't say.''

♀ "Sometimes reading about men getting enemas turns me on. Mostly, however, I tend to think of them in medicinal terms.''

Very few women were into these practices; in fact, enemas and defecation involved too small a percentage to be calculated.

	ALWAYS	VERY FREQUENTLY	SOMEWHAT FREQUENTLY	SOMEWHAT INFREQUENTLY	VERY INFREQUENTLY	ONCE	NEVER
urination	0	.5	.5	.5	3.5	2	93%
defecation	0	0	.5	0	.5	0	99
enemas	0	0	0	0	.5	.5	99

Those who participated in these acts contributed these thoughts on the subjects.

♀ "I enjoy it to the extent of urinating or having my genitals urinated on. However, my lover isn't into it, so I only do it with other partners when it happens. I don't really miss not doing it a lot.''

♀ "I have tried urination because of partner's fascination and am neutral or slightly positive about it except for being cold and wet and having to clean up afterwards.''

♀ "I was having a bath with my lover (you *didn't* put mutual bathing in your list of exotic delights—shame on you!) and we were playing with the sponge and trickling warm water on each other's legs and found it a pleasant sensation and thought maybe that's why people get off on being peed on. I don't know if it's just for the sensual pleasure or for a humiliation sort of thing. If it's the latter, I'm against it (for me).''

♀ "Urination is nice to do once in a while.''

No women told stories of defecation, but a few reported giving enemas to one another as a sexual act.

♀"Enemas are pretty sexy, but awfully messy. They're okay to do once in a while and I have done it."

♀"I adore enemas—giving and especially taking them. I have no idea how this state of affairs came about. It just exists like my green eyes and brown hair. I don't see it as perverted (unusual, yes; perverted, no) but others do, so I never mention it or ask for an enema, except with my 'enema pal' whom I met through ads in a magazine, either mine or answering others' ads. My fondest wish is to meet a woman who is also into enemas—many fantasies about that. I have brought up the subject in an oblique sort of fashion with B., but she said, 'Yech,' when I mentioned the word 'enema.' "

Analingus/"Rimming"

Although analingus ("rimming," oral/anal contact), unlike urination, defecation, and enemas, usually does not involve either humiliation or fetishism, half of the lesbian respondents were still negative to the idea of it.

The women were asked, *How often do you engage in either of the following aspects of analingus ("rimming"—stimulation of the anus with the lips and tongue)?*

	ALWAYS	VERY FREQUENTLY	SOMEWHAT FREQUENTLY	SOMEWHAT INFREQUENTLY	VERY INFREQUENTLY	ONCE	NEVER
rimming your partner	2	3	4	7	12	6	68%
being rimmed	2	1	5	6	15	6	65

The women were also asked, *Whether or not you engage in analingus, how do you feel about either of these?*

	VERY POSITIVE	SOMEWHAT POSITIVE	NEUTRAL	SOMEWHAT NEGATIVE	VERY NEGATIVE	NOT SURE
rimming your partner	13	10	18	23	28	8%
being rimmed	14	13	17	19	26	10

Therefore, only 8-9% of lesbians engaged in rimming on a frequent basis. The majority, 65-68%, had never engaged in rimming at all. Over half of the women were against rimming, with 51% feeling negative, and slightly under half (45%) were averse to being rimmed. The following are some experiences and feelings about rimming.

♀"I'm uncomfortable with this for two reasons: fear of infection and fear of harming the anus and having hemorrhoid problems. Light stimulation of a clean anus with clean fingers (not inserted or if inserted, not deeply and not if it hurts) is okay and I find it stimulating. I do this to myself occasionally."

♀"I don't like analingus. I had it once and didn't like it. Perhaps here too I've been trained by society to think my anus is dirty or 'untouchable,' but I don't think that's the reason. I simply didn't care for the way it felt. I don't know if I would refuse to do it to someone else or not. I've never been asked to. I think it would depend on the person I was with. I would probably be more likely to do it to someone I know and care about than a casual encounter (pickup)."

♀"I'll be honest. Until I got this questionnaire, I'd never even thought of it. Didn't even know it existed. I know the anus is an erotic area, and I know it feels good to insert a finger, but licking it? No thank you. That's one act I consider to be 'dirty'—that is, unclean."

♀"I don't find anal sex as disgusting since I escaped a straight marriage where my husband would wait until I was drunk as hell and proceed to indulge himself in it, so to speak."

♀"No, it's unhealthy. Those sensitive tissues are only used for one thing and one thing only. An asshole is an asshole. It has only one function for me."

♀"This may sound rather chauvinistic, but I prefer having it done to me than to do it to someone."

♀"I have only done this once with a partner, but my masturbation techniques involve a lot of anal stimulation. I love doing it to someone, and I love having it done for me; any anal stimulation combined with clitoral stimulation raises the intensity of my orgasms several notches higher. Doing it to someone either with a tongue or a finger is an incredibly intimate experience, and gives me a sense of incredible closeness to my partner. It seems like you're being allowed into the depths of someone's most intimate self. Perhaps I enjoy having it done because it is a submissive kind of role—you are at your partner's mercy, and you are, very literally, vulnerable to pain, Because it combines all of those aspects—the forbidden, hidden part of the body, the possibility of pain, an opening of oneself to one's lover—it's a really powerful technique."

♀"I dearly love analingus. My lady isn't too keen on receiving this, although I enjoy doing it to her. The tight feel and smell of her anus is a stimulus to me. She does this to me often, and I enjoy the feeling of being totally loved."

♀ "Analingus is exciting. My anus is very sensitive and erogenous. I have always liked to stimulate my anus when masturbating, and analingus is exquisite. Part of the excitement is possibly that it feels slightly naughty, but it is a very pleasurable sensation, and I love to do it to my lover also."

♀ "Analingus to me is part of a very prolonged and involved session of cunnilingus. I can't consider it as a sexual act in itself. When I go down on a womon, and we're in the mood to make it a lengthy and intricate experience, of course I'm going to lick her ass. It is close and usually it will turn her on more than she already is. Also my lovers are clean wimmin, and I do enjoy touching each part of them. Analingus is a large part of lovemaking. Usually, we have already made love many times. She is resting, lying face down. I massage her back (backs are terribly erotic to me) and while keeping my hands on her, trace the line of her spine with my tongue. I don't do this directly from neck to tailbone, but work downward in stages. When I reach the area just below the waist, most wimmin are responding, even if they haven't before. When I reach the deep crease of their asses, I get excited because I know I'm near their cunts. But I linger, running my tongue over their asses until I'm ready to get back to the crease itself. Many wimmin have told me that they hadn't known how sensual this can be. When my tongue reaches her asshole, I usually move around and on it in a circular motion until the muscle relaxes and then try to penetrate it. My saliva serves as a lubricant and I very often insert a finger. My present lover doesn't particularly like this, but previous lovers have. I leave my finger there as I do cunnilingus."

Sex with Animals

If a dog is man's best friend, can he/she be woman's best lover? No, for even those who did have sexual relations with their pets felt that they are second best to another woman. One interesting fact about bestiality among lesbians is that the sexual involvement with the animal (and in one case reptiles) did not involve intercourse but usually involved the animal performing oral sexual acts on the woman. In answer to the question, *On the average, how often do your sexual experiences include sex with animals (bestiality)?* the responses in the subsample break down as follows:

always	0%
very frequently	0
somewhat frequently	1
somewhat infrequently	1
very infrequently	2
once	2
never	94

When the respondents were asked, *Whether or not you experience bestiality, how do you feel about the idea of it?* they answered:

very positive	0%
somewhat positive	4
neutral	13
somewhat negative	69
very negative	6
not sure	6

♀ "Sex with animals is horrid. I find that totally *repulsive.* I love my cat. This kind of behavior would be preying on that poor little animal. I *totally* and *strongly* disapprove of this *misuse* of animals. They are our little friends, not creatures to be humped. They must also be respected."

♀ "I had a lover who had a trained cat. The idea was never too appealing. I love dogs and would probably like to own one, but she would sleep beside my bed and give me moral support, not sleep with me."

♀ "Makes wonderful fantasies but bothers me greatly in reality. Obviously love is not involved. I don't like to see people brought down to the level of mere bestiality."

♀ "Bestiality that is with a cat or dog that you love sounds okay—you mean, not anything having to do with a penis—but rubbing and licking with a friend/animal is fine. However, I wouldn't do it. Basically it sounds uninteresting."

♀ "No appeal whatsoever. That's how VD was *started!* By stupid jerk-off-macho-pricks fucking horses and sheep! I had a man tell me once that he knew of a man who fucked a sheep and said that the sheep was the only animal in the world that had a vagina that was equivalent to a human female vagina!"

People who did have sex with animals had it for various reasons, with the common denominator being that the animal usually started the sexual contact.

♀ "The only bestiality I have experienced involves a few encounters I've had with some friends' boa constrictor and python. These snakes are very affectionate and sensitive to moods of people they're crawling on. They are all soft flickering tongue and warm, gliding, powerful muscle. They feel terrific, and one of them is fond of licking vulvas, I presume because of the salty smell or taste, but maybe she gets off on vicarious pleasure. Snakes are not intelligent, but they are very empathetic with human vibrations. The only bestiality I would approve of would have to involve not only consenting adult animals but animals initiating a sexual-sensual activity. One of my favorite fantasies is to make love to a dolphin in the ocean."

♀ "About half of the time I masturbate I start out by having my dog eat me out. Since I don't have much opportunity to experience cunnilingus from lovers and since it feels *so so* good, I make do with what there is. I feel a little bit bad about it; 'bestiality' seems sick, but I don't have much of a guilt complex, so I don't worry about it much. One related and interesting

thing is that since my dog gives me so much pleasure, once or twice I wanted to give her (yes, I prefer females in all forms!) the same type of pleasure. I failed. (How the hell do you turn dogs on?) But still, I think of her, in a way, as a lover, more than anything. It is she that I run to when there's nowhere else to go. When I need the soft, warm feel of life, I go to her after all else fails. No, I'm not obsessed with her, but late at night when my friends aren't around to bitch off on, she's closer to 'real' than a teddy bear or biting my nails, right? God, I'm getting defensive—needlessly, I hope.''

♀"I lived with my oldest sister and her husband, and I trained their dog to go down on me. It was pretty nice, but she'd bite me every once in a while, so I didn't do it very often. I once had a little dog that I tried to train to do the same, but he wasn't as good, so I gave up. I dislike the idea of having sex with a big dog though.''

♀"I have had a very positive experience with bestiality. I live with a female dog who is very sensual and enjoys having her genital and anal area scratched and rubbed. Recently I have found a way of stroking that can get her very excited, and I enjoy sharing this with her. She is very close to my lover and is growing closer with me. When we fuck, she often comes up on the bed and will lick our asses or cunts. Once when my lover tied me and was going down on me, she stopped and let Sam eat me. It was great!''

Clothing Fetishes, Foot Fetishes, and Transvestism

Another minority group consists of those who participated in clothing or foot fetishes. Although some lesbians who answered would have liked to believe that these acts, as well as the ones previously covered in this chapter, are male-only, the truth is that any act, with feasibility taken into account, probably occurs within any given sexual group or gender.

It goes without saying that most of the lesbians were not into clothing fetishes. In fact, most definitely preferred their lovers to wear no clothing at all during sex! "Clothing fetishism" refers to being turned on by a certain type of garment, such as a shoe, or a black leather jacket. "Foot fetishism" is being turned on by the foot itself.

As about the practices in the above sections, the lesbians were negative about fetishes.

	VERY POSITIVE	SOMEWHAT POSITIVE	NEUTRAL	SOMEWHAT NEGATIVE	VERY NEGATIVE	NOT SURE
clothing fetishism	3	5	27	10	45	10%
foot fetishism	3	4	27	9	45	12

Two facts emerged clearly from these statistics. First, the statistics for clothing fetishism almost perfectly matched those for foot fetishism. This shows that there was a clear feeling among the respondents that these two acts are very similar. Second, there was much less hostility to fetishes than to previous acts with a slight majority (55%) feeling negative while a significant 27% moved into the neutral column. Most lesbians who expressed separate feelings about fetishes dismissed them as "harmless," while they definitely felt that S&M, B&D, etc. can be harmful. As one woman joked about foot fetishism: "If the shoe fits, wear it." Other reactions are:

♀"Clothing fetishes sound perverted to me. I think I don't understand foot fetishes either, but my lover loves feet. So I just sit back and giggle at her."

♀"Does clothing fetishism mean dressing up in costumes or rolling around in someone's clothes? Either way I am not too interested. I don't exactly know what foot fetishism is, but I can't think of anything people could do with their feet that wouldn't seem okay to me. On the other hand, I don't seem to have done anything like this so I must not be too interested."

♀" 'Male sexuality' and I don't know why. Repulsive to me physically but also intellectually intriguing. I am unwilling to relegate 'perversions' to 'closets' devoid of understanding."

♀"If clothing or foot fetishes turn you on, okay."

♀"Clothing fetishes just seem like such a gimmick for sex. The concept seems unappealing to me, although I've never run into it personally. My ex-husband had a foot fetish, which mainly made me nervous, but didn't do anything for me."

Here's the percentage of women who participated in clothing fetishism or foot fetishism.

	ALWAYS	VERY FREQUENTLY	SOMEWHAT FREQUENTLY	SOMEWHAT INFREQUENTLY	VERY INFREQUENTLY	ONCE	NEVER
clothing fetishism	.5	.5	1	2	5	2	89%
foot fetishism	.5	0	1	2	5	1.5	90

And here are the comments of those women who were sexually excited by certain items of clothing or by feet.

♀"I must admit that wearing men's underwear and a dildo sometimes really gets me excited, but my mate doesn't like me to do so because it reminds her (negatively) of her ex-husband."

♀"Once I met a gay man who liked to make love with men dressed in sweatshirts, and I think I would like that too. Also, sometimes it is neat to stroke a vagina, first through nylon underpants, then directly, then indirectly again."

♀"I love clothing fetishes. Wearing costumes is fun."

♀"My lover loves to watch me masturbate. I never thought I'd do it, but I put on a real show for her. And she has all these erotic photographs of me—really raunchy, I think, like spreading my labia while wearing a mean expression and one of these 'John Lennon' caps. My photographs of her are quite different. My favorite is the one where she's wearing a long white dress and sitting very demurely with a bouquet of violets—very, very Renée Vivien! Of course we pose each other for these photographs. I would feel a bit strange except we can't be with each other constantly."

♀"I enjoy the smell of leather and the feeling of control, but not all that much to want it as a regular thing."

♀"I think worn denim is sexy, but there aren't any particular garments I'm turned on to."

♀"I find those eighteenth-century cleavage-plus outfits like in *Tom Jones* luscious!"

♀"I really get into feet, but have a problem since my lover is very ticklish in her feet. We are working on gradual desensitization, though, and I now can hold her feet and kiss them carefully. No genital contact with feet, though, and that's okay. I'd just like to be able to touch my lover's feet more."

♀"My lover and I used to suck on each other's toes."

It is also possible to wear certain clothing (or remove clothing!) to attract a certain type of sex partner. Clothing can act as a kind of "signal" to another person to indicate what one's sexual preference might be. Gay men take this signaling to its farthest extreme when they wear certain color handkerchiefs in the left or right rear pocket of their pants to signal to others exactly what sex act they are into giving or receiving. For example, a yellow handkerchief on the left rear pocket might signal that a man is into performing water sports on someone else. Although lesbians do not go to this extreme, it is true that certain types of clothing, say "butch drag," may indicate to a potential sex partner what that woman may be like in bed.

Again, very few lesbians wore particular items of clothing to attract sex partners, nor did their sex partners wear any specific sort of clothing to attract them. In answer to the question *How often, in connection with attracting sex partners, do you wear any of the following items?* the women offered the following response:

	ALWAYS	VERY FREQUENTLY	SOMEWHAT FREQUENTLY	SOMEWHAT INFREQUENTLY	VERY INFREQUENTLY	ONCE	NEVER
skirts and/or dresses	.5	4.5	7	8	16	1	63%
unisex clothing, blue jeans, etc.	35	40	7	3	4	0	12
drag butch clothing	1	.5	2.5	5.5	18	2	70.5
make-up	5	10	7	5	11	.5	60.5
cigars, pipes	0	.5	2.5	1	6	1	89.5

The following chart shows *how women feel about each of them, whether or not they wear them:*

	VERY POSITIVE	SOMEWHAT POSITIVE	NEUTRAL	SOMEWHAT NEGATIVE	VERY NEGATIVE	NOT SURE
skirts and/or dresses	16	16	35.5	17	15	.5%
unisex clothing, blue jeans, etc.	62	21	13	.5	3	.5
drag butch clothing	6	18	25	20	28	3
make-up	12	13	25	21	28	1
cigars, pipes	4	8	36	15	34	3

A similar question asked, *How often do sex partners wear any of the following items?* The response:

	ALWAYS	VERY FREQUENTLY	SOMEWHAT FREQUENTLY	SOMEWHAT INFREQUENTLY	VERY INFREQUENTLY	ONCE	NEVER
skirts and/or dresses	1	7	11	17	26	3	35%
unisex clothing, blue jeans, etc.	37	50	6	3	1	0	3

	ALWAYS	VERY FREQUENTLY	SOMEWHAT FREQUENTLY	SOMEWHAT INFREQUENTLY	VERY INFREQUENTLY	ONCE	NEVER
drag butch clothing	1	4	7	10	15	1	63
make-up	4	10	12	11	22	2	41
cigars, pipes	1	2	3	7	11	5	72

When asked about *how they feel about the idea of a sex partner using these items,* lesbians responded:

	VERY POSITIVE	SOMEWHAT POSITIVE	NEUTRAL	SOMEWHAT NEGATIVE	VERY NEGATIVE	NOT SURE
skirts and/or dresses	22	17	37	12	9	2%
unisex clothing, blue jeans, etc.	64	18	15	1	1	1
drag butch clothing	5	18	20	17	35	4
make-up	13	16	27	22	21	1
cigars, pipes	3	9	34	20	31	4

This question also asked women *to specify other items they wear or like their sex partners to wear.* Some of the answers include revealing clothing (usually low-cut blouses), earrings, silk underwear, leather, and boots. Many women specified that they wore the items mentioned all the time (especially unisex clothing) so that they did not think of these clothes in sexual terms.

Several patterns emerged from these charts. It was apparent that lesbians did not engage in a double standard regarding clothing; in other words, most of the lesbians seemed to wear the same sort of clothing (usually unisex) as their sex partners or lovers. Also, the myth of the drag butch sporting a cigar or pipe can be laid in its grave, we hope forever. A striking 71% have *never* worn butch clothing, and a trifling 4% wore butch clothing with any frequency. Women did, however, go out a bit more frequently (12%) with women who wore butch clothing and who sported cigars or pipes (6%). On the other end of the clothing spectrum, the skirt

and dress also seemed to be unpopular, with a large 63% never wearing
skirts and again fewer (35%) never having gone out with women who wore
them. Women did feel much more positively about skirts for themselves
(32%) or others (39%) than for drag butch clothing for themselves (24%) or
others (23%). With only 21% being at all negative toward skirts and/or
dresses, the lesbians who stated they are "afraid" to wear them might be
unduly intimidated. Still, the jokes about the movement uniform being blue
jeans and a T-shirt are based on truth. See Chapter 8 on roles.

♀ "I wear tight, bright blouses, lesbian/feminist 'uniform' clothing like
plaid workshirts. I like European hippie-style clothes on other women."

♀ "I'm uncomfortable with roles in any relationship and feel that certain
types of clothes (butch clothing and make-up to a lesser extent) seem to set a
precedent to a relationship. I project how I see the person—how they
dress—to how I think they would relate sexually."

♀ "Jeans or pants are not only more comfortable and safer and more
convenient, but sexier too. I like soft shirts, but go braless only in private,
with lovers or in a strictly lesbian space."

♀ "I dress to be comfortable, not to attract sex partners. I dressed 'to
kill' when I was straight. People should wear light clothes in summer. The
women I know don't put too much importance on attire in regard to the
attraction of sex partners. Neither do I."

♀ "A person should wear whatever they feel comfortable wearing."

♀ "Too many gay women make themselves unattractive."

♀ "Nice soft fabrics that help illumine a partner's attractiveness are nice.
I like attractive clothes and jewelry."

♀ "I enjoy fashionable clothing including skirts, platform shoes, make-
up as well as jeans, and T-shirts. My moods are mine, those of a *woman*. I
hate pseudo-males."

♀ "I'm somewhat negative to cigars and pipes. I'm not into roles at all.
Cigars and pipes are a personal preference. I wouldn't mind cigars (not fat
ones), if they weren't intended to look 'butch.' "

♀ "I like women who look like women."

♀ "I wear unisex clothing, I guess, because it's comfortable, not
necessarily to attract women. However, I wouldn't wear a dress to a bar,
but I would wear one to work."

The trend toward unisex clothing, of course, reflects current styles.
Years ago the exact same clothing, say men's jeans and a workshirt, would
have been considered "drag butch" or "cross-dressing." Today women in
men's clothing do not attract any notice, and some lesbians who self-
consciously dress in what they view as men's clothing complained that no
one can tell any more that they're transvestites. Even straight women now
sport three-piece suits and ties!

Males who dress in female clothing stand out much more, since most

men in North America have not adopted skirts and dresses as attire. Many lesbians feel that men in women's clothing are either outlandishly feminine, portray everything women's liberation is battling against (as in the helpless, dizzy woman), or exploit women for entertainment purposes (see Chapter 13).

Transsexualism

Even more controversial than the subject of men dressing as women is the question of men who become women—that is, male-to-female transsexualism. There are some rare instances of female-to-male transsexualism, but the phenomenon is primarily male-to-female. For lesbians, this has become an issue, as it seems there are a number of men who have become women through surgery and now define themselves as lesbians. So, the controversy rages over whether these people are "real" women or "real" lesbians. The entire world became aware of all this controversy when Dr. Richard Raskind became Dr. Renée Richards and fought for the right to play tennis as a woman.

While Dr. Richards' sexual proclivities have not been made known, a similar but less publicized controversy has raged within the lesbian/feminist community around a male-to-female transsexual working for Olivia Records, a women's recording company. Since Olivia hires only women, some women feel that the transsexual should not be hired because she is not a "real woman," because she grew up with male privilege which gave her expertise in sound recording, and so on. Those who support her say that the operation permanently removed male privilege and that transsexuals are people born into the wrong body. Here are some feelings about transsexualism as reported in our survey:

♀"I support an individual's right to change her or his sex if she so desires. I make no claims about whether people can, in fact, be 'born into the wrong body.' But I feel very strongly about this point: Men that have become surgical females should not be allowed into all-women's space. They have been reared as men, and have men's experiences. They will act like men—that is, selfish, pig-headed, condescending, pricklike, etc. For example, I recently attended the Second Michigan Women's Music festival. It was simply mind-blowing to be among so many women, never having to be afraid to look over your shoulder because of pricks. Then, I heard that at least two transsexual men were present. One of these 'men' is with Olivia Records! I think this is ridiculous. I don't think that just because a man has his prick voluntarily cut off he should be allowed to witness women in their natural state, naked, free, enjoying music and the Goddess.

"While the women were on stage performing music, one of these 'men' jumped up on the stage, seized a microphone, and began singing in the middle of an instrumental. I was disgusted. 'He' was very drunk, had no respect for the women on stage, and acted just like a man, trying to get into

the spotlight. This person was obviously no sister of mine. He had no right to invade our space with his prick-consciousness.''

♀"I think it's a form of medieval torture. To say a woman has a man's mind is somewhat like the theory of spontaneous generation. I know three male-to-female transsexuals and two are lesbians. The lesbians are still homosexuals only now they're women with women and the straight one is still doing what she always did, only her genitals are socially acceptable. A woman's mouth on a man's dick is socially acceptable—a man's mouth on a man's dick is wrong. Jesus—it's just *too, too* dumb. And here are these people chopping off their dicks and tits because the medical profession has them convinced that their mind has a sex. I always thought the human brain was neuter until it got programmed with 'male' or 'female' thoughts.''

♀"Transsexualism seems so terribly extreme to me. For women, it seems particularly so, since the constructed penis is not a sexually functional organ. I can't imagine playing around with my body chemistry, hormonal changes, etc., but even more, I can't imagine what an incredible adjustment it must be on a social and emotional level. I am not opposed to it. I can't know what others' feelings are—but they must be extreme to be willing to go through all of that. I think they need a great deal of support.''

♀"I know some males who have gotten neutered, and I can't say I think too highly of them. I do admire their taste, but really they are not wimmin, don't act like wimmin, and aren't wimmin, and will never be in this life. As for the other, it is not for me to deal with. I am neither the Goddess, nor Her aspects of Kali, Medusa, or Hecate the Tearer of Flesh.''

♀"It must be a hard thing to have to live with. I'd like to believe it doesn't bother me at all, but I couldn't go to bed with a woman who had been a man. The thought of reconstructed genitals gags me.''

♀"I don't like the idea of a woman who once was a man; can't imagine why a woman would want to become a man.''

♀"Transsexualism is stupid. Plumbing is irrelevant. A person can do most things he/she wants with determination, regardless of sexual apparatus.''

♀"I feel that transsexuals are victims of the ridiculous sex-role system in our culture. If individuals were simply allowed to be themselves, without regard to biological sex, I don't think the phenomenon would exist.''

♀"I think transsexuals are probably the most misunderstood group of people in the world, in part because it is only recently that such operations have been possible. I don't understand how it is that the body of one sex could be coupled with the sensibilities of the other, but that is no reason for me to condemn or judge those who feel strongly enough that he or she is not right inside, and has the desire and means to change sex physically. Then I support that decision, and accept that person in her or his new identity.''

♀"Would you force a dog to live in a bird cage? Transsexualism should be as accepted as eyeshadow or an appendectomy.''

♀"Not long ago, if I could have taken a pill that would have made me a

man, I would have done it. Even now, I sometimes feel an urge in this direction. But mostly, I wouldn't want to walk around in a hairy, sweaty body with a penis hanging down in front of me. I feel genuine sympathy for those who need to undergo this operation, and understand why they do it, especially men. Maybe it's a human right to choose one's sex?''

♀"I am just learning about it. My lover thinks she might be a transsexual. We are exploring it.''

These last two women were the only ones who wanted to become men or knew someone who wanted to. In fact, most transsexualism is male-to-female, which destroys the myth that lesbians really want to be men and have penises. We did, however, have a response from one male-to-female transsexual who is now a lesbian:

♀"I am a transsexual, male-to-female. I began to cross-dress at 9. I decided to become a woman at 18, took hormones at 19, started living as a woman at 20, and had my operation at 22. I am 22, almost 23 now.

"Ordinarily, I would not have filled out such a survey. However, I have never read anything in transsexual literature about transsexuals who led gay lives after their operation. It seems to be that certain people (like Dr. Deujamia) would like to imply that gays and transsexuals are different shades of the same scale, when they are not.

"I have met two other lesbian transsexuals, and have heard of others. The only reference in literature on transsexuals I have read concerning a man wanting to be a lesbian insinuated he wanted to be a very butch woman and therefore wanted no hormones! That was never the case of any lesbian transsexuals I had heard of! All of us wanted to be women, considered ourselves women, and did everything we could (hormones, electrolysis, sometimes implants) to appear to be women. But we were attracted to other women. That we were attracted to women did not make us any more a man than it makes other lesbians men, but some of the straight world would like to think that. Since I am truly a woman and a lesbian, don't discriminate against me by not placing any of my answers in your book where they apply.''

Prostitution

Having sex with another woman for money probably seems absurd to many lesbians, yet some women reported that they did so. In fact, there is a bar in New York City where male pimps are currently doing a brisk trade by selling lesbian prostitutes to the other women in the bar. When asked, *How often have you paid for sex with a woman with money or in other ways?* the lesbians gave the following replies:

	ALWAYS	VERY FREQUENTLY	SOMEWHAT FREQUENTLY	SOMEWHAT INFREQUENTLY	VERY INFREQUENTLY	ONCE	NEVER
with money	.5	0	0	0	0	2	98%
in other ways	3	0	2	2	3	0	91

When asked *how they feel about the idea of paying for sex, whether or not they have paid for sex,* women were generally negative.

	VERY POSITIVE	SOMEWHAT POSITIVE	NEUTRAL	SOMEWHAT NEGATIVE	VERY NEGATIVE	NOT SURE
with money	2	4	7	10	69	7%
in other ways	5	6	10	12	61	6

Of course the corresponding question is *whether one has been paid for sex with money or in other ways.*

	ALWAYS	VERY FREQUENTLY	SOMEWHAT FREQUENTLY	SOMEWHAT INFREQUENTLY	VERY INFREQUENTLY	ONCE	NEVER
with money	0	1	1	1	1	5	91%
in other ways	2	2	1	1	9	1	85

The women were also asked *how they felt about the idea of being paid for sex, whether or not they had actually been paid.*

	VERY POSITIVE	SOMEWHAT POSITIVE	NEUTRAL	SOMEWHAT NEGATIVE	VERY NEGATIVE	NOT SURE
with money	3	3	11	8	71	4%
in other ways	4	4	11	11	64	5

While one might expect that the women might have felt more positively about being paid than about paying, the figures were almost equally negative, showing that lesbians generally had a high consciousness about the drawbacks of sex for money.

Feminist groups have held speakouts on prostitution in several cities, and the survey sample reflected a good knowledge of how women pay for or are paid for sex in ways other than money. Some of the items women mentioned paying or being paid with included drinks and/or dinner, presents, movies, entertainment, rent, food bills, trips, clothes, time/companionship. Women also mentioned paying in "blood, guts, and emotion," love and affection, giving up autonomy, and other sorts of obligations. Some women contributed longer comments on experiences and feelings about paying for sex or being paid for sex.

♀"The economic power of another woman should play no part in my sexual experience."

♀"There ain't no such thing as a free lunch. Sometimes I've been coerced by a dinner."

♀"Sex is something I freely give, usually to someone I feel very close to. Paying or being paid for it makes it into a transaction and detracts from the spirit of love involved."

♀"I feel negative with women, positive with men. What else are men good for?"

♀"It's sad that has to happen, but better to buy than to do without if those are the options open to you."

♀"I'm not sure. It's always been easier to spot someone else's game than my own."

♀"Women are not property to be bought and sold."

♀"Sex is more important and enjoyable given freely and mutually."

♀"I hate the suggestion or idea of it."

♀"Neutral. It would be nice to arrange massage or tradework for someone for threesomes who wouldn't be emotionally involved."

♀"At one point in my life I was a whore. I didn't get paid money, but I took dinners, dances, hotel rooms, etc."

♀"I used to sleep with my employer (while on duty), who was a bisexual."

♀"There are a few women I'd probably contemplate just about anything for."

♀"I would like to try it (pay for sex) once in my lifetime."

♀"I would pay if I wanted sex and that was the most logical, convenient way, but I would pay with *money* only. I have been taken out to the movies, dinner, entertainment, and given presents."

♀"Prostitution is one of the more oppressive institutions of the patriarchy. Right up there with electroshock for political prisoners, though I have fantasies about prostitution."

♀"Politically negative, sexually titillating."

Threesomes and Orgies

A substantial minority of lesbians (38%) had tried threesomes, that is, having sex with two other people. Only about 16% had been involved in orgies.

	ALWAYS	VERY FREQUENTLY	SOMEWHAT FREQUENTLY	SOMEWHAT INFREQUENTLY	VERY INFREQUENTLY	ONCE	NEVER
threesomes	0	1	2	6	10	18	62%
orgies	0	0	1	4	5	8	84

Whether or not the women had tried threesomes or orgies, they felt more positively about these than about most of the other alternatives mentioned in this chapter.

	VERY POSITIVE	SOMEWHAT POSITIVE	NEUTRAL	SOMEWHAT NEGATIVE	VERY NEGATIVE	NOT SURE
threesomes	12	22	24	13	21	7%
orgies	7	17	19	18	29	9

In both categories, there was a fairly large number of women who fall into the "very infrequently" or "once" category. These figures would indicate that women who tried these abandoned them because they found them unsatisfactory or difficult to arrange. Women were about equally divided positively and negatively about threesomes and were more negative about orgies. Again, the lack of overwhelming negativity may have been due to the fact that the women viewed these activities as harmless, but there were other experiences and reactions:

♀"I was involved in a threesome once, and that was a mistake. I am a one-woman lover, and I thought I should be more liberal, so I tried it. I didn't like it, but it did teach me to be more satisfied and content with my conservative lifestyle."

♀"Threesomes are okay for those who can handle them. I never tried a threesome, because on the few occasions that the possibility presented itself, it was clear that one of the three was going to end up on the short end of the stick eventually—so it was too risky. (I would not mind participating in a threesome as a voyeur, however. I guess that would remove the responsibility from my shoulders.) Group sex is much safer, I think, even though the one time I participated in it I ended up continuing with one woman after a while."

♀"I enjoy three-ways. I've had numerous three-ways with two men (one gay and one straight), with a man and a woman (closet cases), and four that I can remember with two women. Straight orgies are *boring*. This could only work with dear and close friends. None of my straight and dear friends can handle an orgy, let alone a three-way."

♀"Threesomes are fine for other wimmin, but I personally cannot relax enough as I'm always worried if the attention to each is equally distributed. I don't want to feel uncomfortable, have any other wimmin feel that way. Perhaps this is one of my sexual hangups. I really don't know."

♀"I'm too jealous for a threesome! Very rarely does this work. When it does, it's fine. Orgies are too unemotional, boring, usually not very erotically sophisticated scenes."

♀"Previously I have engaged in this, but at this point in my life I can focus on only one person sexually. Also threesomes are too confusing to me. I don't like too many things being done to me at once!"

♀"I'm too shy. I'd never do it. I have trouble doing it with one woman in the privacy of my own home, let alone with an audience."

♀"I don't think I'd object to an orgy if the situation presented itself; as a matter of fact, I always used to fantasize about the possibility if I were in a group of congenial women. (Probably a lot of them had the same silent fantasy. We should have spoken up!) Once I *was* in a group where a couple of the women said, 'Lets all get together.' Things were sort of seesawing back and forth between maybes, but I was new to the sexual aspect of lesbianism (though I'd identified as one for as long as I can remember) and I felt threatened and scared and was one of the more vocal dissenters. I should have shut up and tried it!"

Some women have tried threesomes and orgies and have liked them.

♀"I once found myself in bed with my lover and a former lover of hers. We were all good friends, so everything just came naturally. I found it very exciting to have a woman going down on you and caressing your thighs and another woman is nibbling at your neck and breasts, etc.! And never quite knowing whose arm or leg it is made it very fun and intriguing too. I was the only one of us new to such activity.

"I more recently found myself in bed with my lover and her *current* other lover (who I was not well acquainted with). The situation behind that was it was my birthday so we decided to have all our dyke friends for a party at the one lesbian bar in our town. Who was there but a woman I was very much in love with, in a very unrequited way, for over a year, and she was there with her new lover and she was rather drunk and she was 'dancing dirty' with me in a way that was getting me *very* excited. My lover and *her* current heart-throb left early and I and most everyone else (including my great futile love of my life) stayed until closing. So I went on home and was rather disappointed to see my lover and her lover both there. I sure wanted my loving! Since my lover's lover had to be on this side of town in the morning, we decided why not stay over and we all got into bed. I had told *my* lover about my plight, so she suggested we do something about it. And *her* lover sort of joined in with some caresses and kisses here and there. It was really lovely. But then the two of them got involved with each other, and I was mostly a spectator, though it was a very nice experience. So that's a torrid tale of three-way sex!"

♀"I have had some experience with a threesome with a man and wife. The woman and I were all over each other, and her husband just lay there and let his wife go down on him. I tried to have intercourse with him, and he went limp. It would seem to me that one person would be left out at one time or another because when two people get rolling, they don't want to stop. It was an okay experience, but I don't think I'd do it again."

♀"I tried a threesome once with my former male friend and my present female mate. I really enjoyed it when it did occur, but was afraid to really get too much into it with her because of anticipated reaction from the male friend. I think this experience helped me build up to my present relationship. I had never made it with a woman before. In the 'threesome' situation, all I did with her was mostly gentle stroking, mostly of breasts and some rubbing of genital area and some stroking in general."

♀"Threesomes and groups are something we do occasionally. I like the *idea,* but the structured emphasis on performance usually turns me off when we do it. Spontaneous threesomes or groups, however, have been very enjoyable on the rare occasions when they happened."

♀"I've been in an orgy with five people. This was nice. I might be very inhibited with a room full of strangers, though."

♀"My partner and I got into an orgy once with two gay guys and one straight guy. It was lots of fun, but very unfulfilling sexually and emotionally."

♀"I've had many positive experiences with orgies. All of the ones I've been to have been mixed—gay, straight, and bi men and women. Most of them were arranged through groups which deal in this sort of activity. There are several things that I like about orgies. For me, they are a good way of meeting a woman and getting through the sexual part of getting to know her right off the bat, because usually I can be very shy about asking a woman to go to bed with me, and sometimes a relationship just won't happen because neither of us asks. During an orgy everyone is there for sex, and there seems to be no need to ask—things happen spontaneously. Also, one feels freer to ask because if a woman isn't interested, there are at least ten other women around who probably are, so one never feels rejected.

"I know people object to orgies because they think they must be very programmed or place too much emphasis on 'performance.' However, the orgies I've been to have been very sensual, with lots of people giving each other massages, supporting (quietly and with gentle touches) those who are making love, enjoying the warm vibes. People who go to orgies are generally more sexually 'liberated' and aren't hung up if you are into women only. They respect your right to say no (if not, they are removed!) and your right not to have any sex at all if you choose not to.

"People also think that orgies are impersonal. I think they are in the sense that sometimes if you get tangled up with a group of people, you don't know who is who. On the other hand, they are not anonymous like male fuck bars or baths. I've developed two strong relationships with women I've met at orgies. I went out with one for four years and with another for one year, and I'm still good friends with both."

Incest and Forced Sex

Incest and rape generally seemed associated in the minds of the lesbians who answered this questionnaire. And it is a fact that most incest is between older males and young girls, and this fact probably led most lesbians to feel negatively on the subject.

♀"Incest exists in a much higher incidence than most of us would like to think. I am generally opposed—particularly where it is a question of an adult and a child. That is a situation without knowing consent, which I object to in any sexual situation. The only reason we make such an issue, however, when it occurs within a family situation is that it violates one of our basic societal taboos."

♀"Usually this means rape by fathers, which I think is horrible. On the other hand, sex between two children with no coercion would be okay. Now that we're grown, I sometimes feel attracted to my sister."

♀"Incest is disgusting."

♀"Parent-child incest is criminal and anti-child, but I think there are cases where sibling interest can be interesting and rewarding. (All kids do it anyway.) My older sister and I used to play sex games when we were little,

and I once had a sexual experience with my brother (not intercourse), which I thought was fun, and he wasn't complaining either.''

♀"It's a taboo necessary to maintain patriarchal family stability. I oppose the taboo and would love to have the freedom to fuck with my sisters, but know that it is impossible.''

♀"I was lucky to never experience incest in any way. I think it's a very scary, humiliating experience for a child and so the taboos against incest are necessary to protect children. I'm not so sure that the taboos make as much sense when two adults are involved. I personally have no desire to engage in sexual activities with any of my relatives, male or female.''

♀"No experience with this, but I think that people who do this to children need help in a bad way.''

♀"I understand how this can happen, but I could never bring myself to participate. It is repulsive to me.''

♀"If incest weren't such a taboo, I would love to make love to my baby brother, who is now 19 already! And my 21-year-old sister, for that matter. The taboo was created by society by men who didn't want their female mates getting pregnant by their mutual male offspring. Men have been fucking daughters forever! Incest is a culture shock. It is not warped or brain-damaging. If women were totally equal to men, they would be seducing their sons. Incest will continue. It happens freely in African and Oriental societies. So be it. It is natural.''

♀"Incest is out for me, as is any sort of approach to my children's friends; it confuses roles, and is selfish. Perhaps in some cases, this is not so, but I think the taboos here ought to stay until society as a whole is less repressive in accepting the new sexuality in general. I think the trauma should not be as great today as in past centuries, but again, in most incest cases, there is more force or compulsion or selfishness on the part of one person, and sex should be mutual.''

♀"I believe wholeheartedly that incest is a delightful thing. When you grow up with a family member (whether blood-related or not), you very often develop similar tastes, values, assumptions, etc. You share race and class background. You are likely to have good rapport unless there's been a lot of tension in your family. It makes sense that you would feel sexual toward this person and also very comfortable being around her/him. Why not have sex together? The taboo against it is not necessary.''

♀"I like reading about it in pornography. Any combination turns me on.''

♀"Not bad with members of the same sex. Who could love you more than family? But I doubt I could do it.''

Since the question did not ask specifically about female-female incest, we received stories of all sorts of combinations. However, considering the number of total respondents, these answers represented a small percentage.

Most women were negative about their incestuous experiences with males but positive about their experiences with females.

♀"Well, the type of incest that I have experienced is also called rape. My older brother has made seven attempts and succeeded only once. To me it is a very repulsive concept, which is due to the adverse experiences I've had. The time he succeeded was after he knew I'm a lesbian. He thought he was going to 'cure' me. When I told him I chose to be a lesbian and I have no intentions of changing, he only became disgusted with me."

♀"I have never seen nor known of an example of mother and son, but incest is too common an occurrence among male relatives and female children. I know it is a highly damaging experience. My older brother, though only a child himself, penetrated me when I was 4. For years nothing was said, and for years it brought me feelings of guilt, confusion, and resentment. Finally, I was able to speak about it—to put it in the realm of a childhood experience. But the idea of its being done against my will has remained a significant ethic."

♀"I was helped along my sexual path by an older brother. We did about everything imaginable including cunnilingus, fellatio, and intercourse. I don't know exactly how old I was, but I think about 8 or 9. Anyway, I always knew more about sex than I suppose most other kids my age."

♀"I was pretty turned on at an early age but felt exploited by my brother and his friends. I jerked my brother off a lot. I still resent my brother a lot but also feel childhood sexual inclinations are very real. Most girls get ripped off by brothers or friends and really don't get to explore their early sexual feelings. I think this area is pretty much of a taboo as far as research and understanding are concerned. My mother caught my brother and me in the outhouse together but didn't say a word to me. Maybe to him."

♀"I had incestuous feelings about my father throughout my childhood. When I was 17, he made a pass at me. I felt very ambivalent about it, but refused. I'm glad I refused and glad it didn't happen sooner, when I was younger and might have said yes. At the time I felt responsible for his advances, as I knew I had often secretly wished to have a sexual relationship with him, even though when the possibility was offered I didn't want to. I also felt betrayed, as I thought that as the adult he should be responsible, and not allow it to happen. I now think all children have incestuous feelings and that adults should be responsible for not stimulating them or allowing them to be acted out. Any other course puts too much responsibility on the child and involves adults and children in a tangle of complicated and complicating feelings."

♀"My first honest-to-goodness relationship with a woman came about when I was 20. She was 65 or older. (I don't really know and I didn't ask.) She's my father's cousin, and I've always liked her since I was about 5 years old. She visited very seldom, but I was always impressed with her. I lived away from the town she's in, also my hometown, and one time when I was visiting, I just decided to go and see her and find out if she 'was or wasn't'

as I knew she had never been married. It was about 9:30 p.m. when I got to her house, and I went to the door. When she answered, I introduced myself and she let me in. We talked about what I had been doing since I graduated (she came to the house one time in my senior year). There were a lot of awkward pauses in the conversation, and our eyes would lock on each other's. Then I'd start on some other subject. This went on for a couple of hours, and then we finally switched around until we were sitting on her couch together. The conversation got stuck again and she said, 'Whatcha thinkin' about?' I said, 'You.' She sighed and said she thought so. She said she and I could never be lovers, and that it was no kind of life to lead, etc. I persisted, writing letters, and visiting her when I went to her town. We finally kissed and hugged, talked and went out to dinner occasionally. It was really a hassle, though, because she was a hard-core closet-case lesbian and she didn't want me to come over too often or we couldn't go see a movie or go out too much because 'someone might see us.' We had quite a romance though, as we'd send each other mushy cards and letters, and she was a great letter writer. Of course, I had to destroy every last one at her request. Our lover relationship came to an end because the second time we went to bed, I tried to go down on her, and she wouldn't let me, so I let it go for the time being. I wrote her and asked her if she disliked cunnilingus, and I told her it was my favorite thing to do for someone. She wrote back a *very* stinging letter attacking my generation because of its 'anything goes' attitude toward sex, and she thought that cunnilingus is disgusting and dirty, that it made her cheap. She went on to say that she could hardly bear the thought of kissing me if I had done that to someone else. I was really taken aback, and we fought through the mail and over the phone for quite a while. We had a couple of reconciliations and a couple more fights, and now we're good friends.''

Of course, incest with children brings up the question of consent. One of the myths about lesbians is that they molest other women, especially female children. Only 6% had ever had sex with young women aged 13-15, under 2% had had sex with children 9-12, and under 1% had had sex with children under 9. When cross-tabulated with the actual age of the respondents, it became clear that most of these women were also young (see Chapter 6). Since some of the respondents were as young as 14, the sex partners of these young women may have been even younger. In conclusion, the incidence of lesbian child molestation was almost nonexistent.

The question of molesting children brings up the question of consent itself, for all of the acts discussed so far in this chapter require two or more consenting adults. If lesbians did not molest children, did they force other women into any sex acts? To find out, lesbians were asked, *How often has a sexual encounter been terminated because . . .*

	ALWAYS	VERY FREQUENTLY	SOMEWHAT FREQUENTLY	SOMEWHAT INFREQUENTLY	VERY INFREQUENTLY	ONCE	NEVER
you would not perform a particular sexual act your partner wanted	1	.5	.5	0	8	4	86%
your partner would not perform a particular sexual act you wanted	.5	1	2	.5	8	5	83

A similar question asked, *Have you ever forced another women to have sex with you against her will?* Less than 2% answered yes. To a corresponding question, *Have you ever been forced by another woman to have sex against your will?* 7% answered that they had. The most common frequency of forced sex mentioned for each question was once or twice, but a few women reported being forced more frequently than that.

♀"I started to force a woman to have sex with me who had already had sex with me willingly before. It was because of an argument we had, but when she got mad at me and furious with me, I felt humiliated and let her go without actually forcing her to have sex with me."

♀"My lover wasn't feeling emotionally happy, and I feel that I forced her a few times during two months, even though I didn't like doing it to either of us."

♀"My lover is dying of a blood disease, and once I think she took out some hostilities on me in bed. She threw me down, tore off my clothes (almost literally), and despite my pleading for her to slow down, she started fist-fucking me so hard I couldn't even catch my breath. I kept gasping, 'Stop, stop,' but she went wild. She tried to force me to be very rough with her, but I wouldn't. I was so confused and it was all happening too fast. I just started crying and fell asleep exhausted; and we haven't really discussed that incident."

♀"I have been psychologically coerced."

This last comment relates probably what the majority of those who answered yes to both questions were thinking. Feminists, having explored the question of rape, feel that the term includes the broadest possible in-

terpretation. In other words, if you aren't totally willing to have sex, you are being forced. Other yes answers may have resulted in not understanding the question.

♀"It sounds exciting if you mean 'force' in the sense of mild or playful coercion. Not real violence."

♀"There were times when I was still in the closet when I devotedly hoped someone would drag me out. I know a few women who seem to wish I would take the initiative."

♀"Although I would never force someone to have sex with me, there's a certain attraction to having someone force me, although not in a rape-type situation. More of a fantasy—'coy refusal' (on my part)—and gradually being forced, secretly wanting to, but getting into a very submissive role. Definitely *not* all the time—perhaps just once."

The confusion evidenced by these responses was probably due to the fact that the word "force" instead of the word "rape" was used in the questionnaire. Technically the authors were not sure whether the word "rape" could be applied to a woman forcing another woman to have sex. In any event, some of the answers did come close enough to anyone's definition of rape, which sadly shows that even lesbians have not created a perfect environment. Most women obviously identified with the victim. A few, apparently, identified with the perpetrator. Only 7% have had first-hand experience with lesbian force. More had experiences where one or the other would not perform a certain act, but the sexual encounter was then terminated, which did not indicate rape but perhaps rather indicated sexual incompatibility. In rape, on the other hand, the sexual experience is not terminated because of force on the part of one sex partner. It should go without saying that most lesbians were overwhelmingly negative to the idea of force. The writers asked, *Whether or not you have done either of the following, indicate how you feel about the idea of each of them:*

	VERY POSITIVE	SOMEWHAT POSITIVE	NEUTRAL	SOMEWHAT NEGATIVE	VERY NEGATIVE	NOT SURE
forcing someone to have sex with you	0	2	1	5	91	1%
being forced to have sex against your will	1	1	2	6	87	2

♀"Force offends me, turns me off. I need to feel wanted and enjoyed tenderly."

♀"I refuse to be forced into anything, especially sex. It would not only turn me off, but it would make me hostile."

♀"No one forces me to do anything I don't want to. I'm a Scorpio!"

♀ *"No! No!* A thousand times no! Though I might feel very hurt by someone's refusal, though I might be persistent in my appeals to them, I would never force them to have sex with me. And though I hate violence, anyone who forces me would do well to get out of town before I recover and come after them."

♀ "Isn't that politically incorrect?"

♀ "After having been raped five months ago by a man, it's a scary idea to think about."

♀ "Perhaps people may think that it relieves them of the responsibility for their acts when they are 'forced' to have sex with a woman against their will. I don't think it is physically possible to do that unless you actually want to; therefore, it must be fantasy."

♀ "It plays into my pattern of having been a victim of sexual abuse in my childhood. It would be easy to be a victim. It would be revenge *(wrongly directed)* to use that power on someone else."

♀ "It is equivalent to rape or sexual assault. It violates personal and social integrity."

♀ 'If the two of you aren't willing, why bother? I like to know my partner wants me."

♀ "I'm somewhat positive about forcing. I like the feeling of sexual power."

♀ "I feel guilty about wanting to force other women. I am overwhelmed by differences in sexual appetites."

Sexual Aids: Toys, Oils, and Pornography

The previous sections of this chapter discussed alternative methods of sex which usually did not require apparatus, aside from some equipment used in connection with sadomasochism and bondage and discipline. This section deals with toys such as dildos and vibrators used by lesbians in connection with sex, as well as oils and pornography. A discussion of these items used in connection with masturbation can be found in Chapter 14.

The lesbians were asked, *On the average during sex with another woman, how often do you use the following items—hand-held dildo, strap-on dildo, battery vibrator, electric vibrator, oils, pornography?* Both hand-held dildos and strap-on dildos are usually "penis imitations" and come in various sizes. The main difference is that the strap-on dildo, because it can be worn exactly where a penis would normally stick out, gives more of an impression of a woman having a penis. Also, some strap-on dildos are constructed so that the wearer also gets some clitoral stimulation. A hand-held dildo can be made to look exactly like a penis, but today, simple household objects, particularly the bottle containers of men's deodorants and colognes, look so much like dildos that they might be included here. Battery vibrators tend to be shaped like a penis, whereas electric vibrators are for clitoral stimulation, not penetration, and therefore are not phallic in shape.

It is a popular myth that lesbians use strap-on dildos in connection with sex. This myth was created largely because heterosexual men cannot conceive of a woman having enjoyable sex without the insertion of a penis. (Better to have an imitation than to ignore it!) However, as one can see from the chart below, regular use of the strap-on dildo was almost nonexistent, and the others were used only by a small minority.

	ALWAYS	VERY FREQUENTLY	SOMEWHAT FREQUENTLY	SOMEWHAT INFREQUENTLY	VERY INFREQUENTLY	ONCE	NEVER
hand-held dildo	.5	.5	2	3	6	6	82%
strap-on dildo	0	0	0	1	3	3	93
battery vibrator	.5	1	1	5	10	8	73.5
electric vibrator	1	2	5	5	6	4	77
oils	1	4	5	10	17	2	60
pornography	0	.5	4	6.5	13	5	71

As with other "minority" practices, most lesbians were decidedly hostile to some of these implements. As one might expect, lesbians were most hostile to the idea of the strap-on dildo, because they were aware of the myths and resented their persistence.

	VERY POSITIVE	SOMEWHAT POSITIVE	NEUTRAL	SOMEWHAT NEGATIVE	VERY NEGATIVE	NOT SURE
hand-held dildo	6	11	16	20	39	8%
strap-on dildo	5	7	14	17	50	7
battery vibrator	9	25	25	14	20	7
electric vibrator	14	17	21	16	23	8
oils	29	24	29	4	9	6
pornography	9	19	22	15	24	11

♀"I don't like the idea of using a dildo, largely because it seems a lot of people think we use them. Perhaps straight people think one can't enjoy a

fulfilling sex life without a penis or a reasonable facsimile. I think that idea is absolutely ridiculous.''

♀ "Any woman who needs a dildo to achieve sexual satisfaction can find plenty of live ones walking the streets."

♀ "I hate dildos. I've never used one, but the idea of wimmin making love with other wimmin and using dildos upsets me very much. It's too much like fucking a man. It's like you want a cock."

♀ "I've never used a dildo, or even seen one. I suspect that men invented them wondering how else women could get it together."

♀ "I dislike the strap-on dildo because it feels too much like an imitation of a prick. I used a hand-held dildo while masturbating in my heterosexual days, but not since."

♀ "Dildos are best for fags."

♀ "These things are all fun and interesting but are not vital for a good sexual experience."

♀ "I guess 'toys' are okay as long as they don't become *the object of one's affection* after a while. If I have a relationship again, I might try some. I don't think they would ever become of prime importance to me and our sex life together. Only the woman I would be sharing it with should be *important*."

♀ "We've never used one, but some gay men we know say they're going to give us a dildo for a wedding present, and I'll have to reserve judgment until then."

♀ "I have never used a dildo or had one used on me, but I have no particular aversion to them. They just seem fake and impersonal."

For those women who used dildos (hand-held or strap-on) most found them pleasurable and some related stories of dildo use in answer to the first essay question—in other words, a dildo was part of their most pleasurable experience.

♀ "When my lover and I are about to make love she gets very seductive-looking and warm and puts herself in a position where her breasts are very alluring. We are sitting on the bed, and I start to kiss her on the mouth, which feels like warm honey, smooth and sweet. Our tongues tease each other and get more and more serious until we are really kissing deep in each other's mouth.

"Then we lie down and she lies on top of me and starts to rub. Either her legs are spread over mine or our legs are hers/mine/hers/mine. We still have our clothes on. She starts to talk to me about our fantasies (being in the back seat of a car when we were 16 and getting fucked, etc.), and she rubs and I rub too. Then she starts to get really turned on, especially because when she is on top she feels like a man fucking me, and I play along with this. Then we take off our clothes, and I go on top of her and start to kiss her deeply and touch her breasts. I start to kiss lower and lower until I

come to her pubic hair, and she spreads her legs very wide, and I separate the mat of hair with my tongue and start to go over her clitoris gently at first. Then I insert a dildo that we have, and she loves it. She is in ecstasy as I use my tongue harder and harder.''

♀"I've never used a dildo on myself but did so with one partner because this gave her much pleasure, and I would try to please any partner in any way.''

♀"I used a dildo a couple of times, but fingers are warmer and more intimate. We might like a strap-on dildo for shared fantasy once in a while, but not often enough to justify the expense.''

♀"I really enjoy the use of some toys, particularly the dildo and to a lesser degree pornographic books (as 'foreplay'), vibrators, and bondage-type toys (cords, etc.). I have been a feminist since I was 14. I came out at age 19, and I am very politically aware. I am very active in lesbian politics and women's movement activities. I point this out because most of the lesbians I've talked to think that women who like dildos are either hulking, crew-cut butches or fading femmes. I am neither. I am a strong, intelligent, aware lesbian, forced into a second closet by some of my sexual behavior. I have had six lovers as a lesbian (not including one-nighters), and out of that total, three of my lovers have used dildos, I have used the dildo with one lover, one lover requested that we buy a dildo (I was, unfortunately, too shy at this point), and the subject never came up with the other two. I think this reveals that many more lesbians use dildos than is commonly admitted by lesbians en masse.

"Using a dildo (or having it used 'on' one) is *not* the same as wanting to *be* a man or wanting to *have* a man. I am not at all interested in fucking men, but I am interested in the extreme sexual pleasure I get from the use of the dildo. I am angered that I cannot admit this to women, for fear that they will attack my politics and my psyche. My sexual pleasure has always centered about my vagina. Oral sex does little for me (usually) unless it is accompanied by manual stimulation to my vagina. 'Finger-fucking' is extremely pleasurable and was my favorite sexual pastime till I discovered the joys of the dildo. Sadly, I find many women either ignore my vagina or seem afraid to penetrate me. They concentrate on the clit to the exclusion of anything else, and are often amazed when I tell them what I prefer.

"In conclusion, I have two things to say: (1) Lesbians, don't be so afraid of seeming masculine that you ignore your own and others' sexuality. After all, reasoning by analogy, any clothes that I wear are womanly because I am a woman. My belt is a woman's belt; my boots are women's boots. Similarly, my use of a dildo is a part of women's sexuality, since I use it. It does not make me masculine in any way. (2) Sisters, let's stop oppressing each other's sexuality. Until all the votes are in, you can't tell me what I'm doing is perverted. When you do you sound just like the Man. So let's not put ourselves and our sisters in second closets.''

♀"I have experienced a hand-held dildo and found it most enjoyable as much as I hate admitting it! But it isn't necessary and I can be perfectly

satisfied without it. It really is somewhat out of the ordinary to use a dildo but when I am under the influence of alcohol I crave vaginal penetration that wide and deep.''

♀''My lover uses a dildo on me infrequently, but I do not look at it because the sight of or the representation of male genitals makes me sick.''

♀''For a while I used dildos—actually 'experimented' is a better word. I was in this sexuality group and two of the women said they used candles, carrots, hot dogs, etc. so I tried them all except for hot dogs (I don't eat them) and I've decided I like fingers best.''

♀''Although I like the 'natural' ways best, I find dildos fun sometimes as it feels good to be full. Usually they add a kind of unfleshlike uncomfortableness after a while, however. So I don't very often use one. I found them exciting the first few times I used them (with a lover usually), but that wore off and I now prefer making love with hands, mouth, etc.''

When it comes to vibrators, only a minority were definitely hostile and a large number of the women moved from being negative to being neutral or positive, even though only about 10% more used vibrators during sex. Perhaps this difference appeared because vibrators have not received bad press among lesbians, nor are they part of male stereotyping about lesbians. Also, vibrators, especially electric ones, are a more recent development.

♀''I have never liked the idea of using a vibrator, although I don't believe that you'll get 'hooked' on them.''

♀''I have used a vibrator once and found it most unsatisfactory and inhuman, and would never do it again.''

♀''Vibrators are okay if women really need them to come, but I am very afraid of electricity, and the thought of sticking 100 volts or whatever into my vagina turns me pale. So I've never used that.''

♀''These probably feel real good. I know because I can create a vibrator with my fingers (I'm a drummer!). So I say vibrators must be okay. I could do without them, but I'd try it at least once.''

♀''I'd worry about getting dependent on a vibrator. I've heard of that happening.''

Although vibrators are used more frequently for masturbation (see Chapter 14), here are some experiences women have had with them during sex; again, some of these answers described a most pleasing experience.

♀''We kiss for about ten minutes, maybe longer, then my lover rolls over on her back and I move on top of her. I begin kissing her neck and shoulders, as well as her face and her mouth, meanwhile caressing her head, shoulders, her fingers, and blowing in her ears. As I do this, I am aware of the taste of different parts of her body, sometimes salty, sometimes sweet, and the texture of her hair underneath my tongue. I work my way down to

her breasts, making sure my stomach is pressed against her genitals (her legs are spread apart). I suck her breasts and play with her nipples with my mouth and my fingers, squeezing them gently and hard, sometimes rubbing my teeth against the tip of her erect nipples. She gets very excited when I stimulate her nipples, and my breathing gets heavier too. I think I probably spend from five to ten minutes on her breasts. During this time, she runs her fingers up and down my back and arms, kisses my ears, squeezes different parts of me, and moves the upper part of her body, arching her back. From this point on I am always aware of the fact that I am very turned on and very relaxed and excited at the same time. From her breasts I move down to her stomach, licking and kissing and sucking and squeezing. I include her sides and her legs, spending a lot of time kissing her thighs, running my tongue up and down her legs, kissing her behind the knees. I like to bite her gently on her inner thighs and breathe my hot breath onto her genitals, smelling the musky sweet smell of her. I try to put off directly stimulating her genitals until she seems really excited, either moaning or moving around a lot. Then I start by licking long, slow licks from her vagina to the top of her clitoris, using my tongue to separate the inner lips from the outer. I lick her for about ten minutes (this time estimation seems silly!), mostly until my neck or tongue gets tired. I spend a lot of that time stimulating her clitoris directly and indirectly. Because she is very slow to orgasm, I usually get tired before she comes, so I lie down next to her after we kiss a little, and she uses an electric vibrator to bring herself to orgasm. During this time, I suck her nipples or hold her. She usually has an orgasm within a couple of minutes with the vibrator, and goes on to have three or four. Sometimes I put one or two fingers inside her and move them around rhythmically. I enjoy feeling her contract and expand. When she is satisfied, she turns off the vibrator, and we hug and kiss and look at each other and talk, and then she starts to make love to me.''

♀''We both begin by undressing each other, kissing and stroking each newly unveiled part until we are both naked. We hold and press against each other, especially genital area against genital area and intense French kissing. We then suck breasts, manipulate each other's clitoris and do 69. This is followed by much friction and rubbing genitals with each other upside down—I rub my clitoris against her anus. Finally, we bring each other to orgasm via an electric vibrator. We end with much caressing and fall asleep in each other's arms.''

♀''Once I got a woman off with my Swedish vibrator massager with a long cord and two speeds. That was the first time she had ever had an orgasm with another human being.''

♀''The vibrator plays an active part in my sex life with partners, since the orgasms with it are intense and in a category of their own.''

♀''I feel great about all toys listed—especially vibrators. I had my first orgasm with a vibrator, and it is almost always (95% of the time) used in my current sexual relationship to bring me (and my partner) to orgasm. I feel

perfectly fine about this and do not see it as 'wrong,' 'unnatural,' or due to a bad sexual relationship.''

♀"While having sex with a partner, I sometimes use the vibrator sort of sandwiched between us. The vibrator is for clitoral stimulation: it is not insertable. I've never used a dildo and the thought of it turns me off.''

♀"On occasion I have used a vibrator with a partner, but just for a kick.''

When it comes to oils for sex, a majority of the lesbians seemed to be positive. Here are some feelings and experiences with oils, which can be used for massage purposes or for lubrication of the genital area.

♀"I've used Kama Sutra oil occasionally, and like it a lot.''

♀"We use oils for lubricating our cunts when we use manual stimulation on each other. Sometimes we also use flavored oils (I like chocolate mint, and she likes lemon) when we do cunnilingus because we like the different flavors.''

♀"Oils are nice and sensual when the situation is nice and sensual—they are part of a larger trip. I am very turned on by textures, smells, and scents and so when the situation is right oils are pleasurable to use. The right situation (for me) is when my partner and I have time for a long, sensual lovemaking session, and can get into many side trips. I would say that when two people are really hot for each other and can't wait to get to bed (or wherever), oils would be a waste.''

♀"We once used lotion as part of massage (she used it on me), which led to a very pleasant session of lovemaking—without the massage ever getting finished. With a previous partner we used a lotion once which proved to be very sticky and uncomfortable and led to a quick shower.''

♀"My lover and I have recently begun to use one of those lotions that get hot when one blows on it. I find that very stimulating. We also plan to try using oils and giving each other massages, and I think that, too, should be very pleasing.''

♀"I use KY jelly which makes sex really nice.''

♀"I adore for a woman to rub, wipe, smear, fondle, soothe, knead my body with her hands full of oil, etc.''

♀"Once in a while we will rub an ice cube on each other's cunts for the freezing sensation. We have also used Vicks Vaporub on our cunts for the tingly sensation and neat smell during mutual masturbation.''

♀"I have in the past used 'love oil' . . . it gets the area hot and tastes yummy so it's fun.''

This last mention of eating or licking oil off a partner's body brings up one area neglected in the questionnaire—eating food off a lover's body. A few women mentioned it anyway. A favorite seems to be whipped cream, but there are others.

♀"We have sprayed whipping cream on each other and licked it off . . . and lined popcorn all along each other's body and sensually eaten it off. We have also tried body painting."

♀"I used to put candies up my lover's vagina and she'd do it to me. It makes eating pussy a whole new thing, but it's just a variety really."

♀"My lover and I love to feed each other. We get something luscious like strawberries and whipped cream or eclairs. First, we feed each other small bites and take time to taste, chew, enjoy the eating and the watching each other. Then, one of us with her mouth full kisses the other. I feed her that way. It is very exciting to be fed strawberries and whipped cream from your lover's tongue. Then as we get into body sex, we put blobs of it on each other's bodies and eat it off. It feels wonderful when the cold of it lands on my warm body and then when her tongue licks and sucks it off. I don't know if others do this."

♀"Eating coffee yogurt off my partner's breasts and her doing the same to me. Licking wine off my lover's body. I have recently discovered the joy of mixing food and sex, not only eating food off my lover's body but also taking food breaks between sex. I also have recently experienced eating slowly and sensuously makes me eat less, and I am losing weight."

Other lovers reported passing food from mouth to mouth or sometimes liquids. Maybe two *can* eat for the price of one.

The last area to be covered under the heading of alternative sex styles for lesbians is using pornography during sex. Once again, the lesbian respondents were slightly more negative than positive about using pornography but not decidedly so.

♀"I used to read pornography, but I've become so turned off by the way women are portrayed."

♀"I have nothing against pornography, just don't like to depend on artificial aids to reach orgasm."

♀"I am turned on by some porno, and I wish there were more of it geared for gay women. It took me a long time to admit that some porno excited me, but now I feel okay about it. I don't *need* it; it simply adds variety or an extra dimension to lovemaking from time to time."

♀"Pornography always left me let-down, 'soiled-feeling,' and eventually it got dull."

♀"Pornography tends to turn me off rather than on. Some erotic pictures *do* turn me on, but I'm not sure where erotic art becomes pornographic—perhaps that is best judged according to its effect on an individual. For me the line would be drawn at the point where the pictures began to disgust me rather than excite me."

♀"I sometimes fantasize about pornography. I used to read pornography I'd find in people's homes where I'd babysit when I was a

teenager. Getting excited by it led me to discover my clitoris and how to masturbate! I used to look forward to babysitting certain families, especially after I learned to masturbate! Pornography itself, though, the idea of using women's bodies to sell magazines and reinforce and perpetuate our sexist society, angers me. It also angers me that pornography can still excite me.''

♀ "I don't like porno. I can't get behind gay male outrage at the indictment of Larry Flynt, the publisher of *Hustler*. I think pornography promotes the objectification of women and also violence against women. I can't imagine lesbian pornography, only lesbian erotica.''

♀ "I think pornography should be against the law, especially the kind that debases women or exploits children. The ACLU will never collect a dime from me to protect the so-called 'democratic rights' of pornographers. Pornographers are exactly the same as pimps. So long as women are oppressed or need money, they will offer their services, but that doesn't excuse men who take advantage of them to make themselves rich off women's degradation. Besides, after Flynt and Reems and those types were arrested, the more traditional men's magazines such as *Playboy* et al. really started toning down their stuff and even coming on as converted feminists, at times. So it's good to shake up the flesh peddlers every now and then.''

♀ "Pornography is made for males by males, and I find it repulsive. The expressions on those wimmin's faces sicken me, and the grotesque positions embarrass me. Why would two wimmin lie in bed and look at pictures when they could touch each other? Pornographic 'literature' is even worse. I can't stand bad writing.''

♀ "Pornography can be very stimulating but in general is very boring.''

♀ "I would love to read some really good lesbian porn.''

♀ "I like pornography although I sometimes feel I shouldn't and it's wrong. (I've never found any good lesbian pornography.)''

♀ "I've written pornography for my lover but have never run across any good stuff by women about women. The other stuff I don't find exciting.''

♀ "We don't use porn as an actual sexual aid—just read some porn to get horny.''

♀ "I am turned on by reading heavily sexual material. I had one lover who was open-minded as I am and with whom I shared my 'shameful secrets.' We spent hours and days in bed, commencing often with reading passages from porn aloud to each other, and leading up to 'regular sex,' and using the dildo and the vibrator.''

For those women who have now made it to the end of this chapter, you may not have done everything a lesbian can do with another lesbian, but you certainly have read about everything!

13

Erotic Variations of Some Gay Men

What Is Kinky?

According to *Webster's Seventh New Collegiate Dictionary*, a kink is "a short tight twist or a curl," as a kink in a rope or kinky hair. The dictionary offers as synonyms "eccentricity," "quirk," and "whim." A kink is also defined as "a clever or unusual way of doing something" or as "an imperfection likely to cause difficulties in the operation of something."

Whether kinky sex is eccentric, quirky, clever, or unusual, or an imperfect way of doing it, is bound to be a matter of opinion. There are even problems with segregating certain sexual practices into a separate chapter, and as compilers we recognize this. But presumably even the most militant proponents of sadomasochism will agree with us that it is the preference of a minority, and certainly our statistics bear that out. The minority status of these "out of the ordinary" preferences and practices, then, is what places them in this chapter.

Many gay men, not only those who participate in these activities, have feelings and opinions about them, and these are also reflected in the information we gathered. Attitudes toward sexual minorities also reflect the debates on sexual politics that occur in sectors of the gay community, and they also are related to attitudes in the surrounding heterosexual culture.

"Kinky," then, is a word that is used advisedly, for with it often comes a kind of grudging appreciation for the one who is living the more extraordinary sexual life. But, as we shall also see, there is a good measure of disgust, disapproval and rejection present in many gay men's responses to the less usual forms of sexual expression. (Note that in this chapter we deal essentially with varieties of male sexual acts. Minority sexual practices involving special relationships, including incest, celibacy, bisexuality, and boy-love are covered elsewhere in the book.)

In his classic "Gay Manifesto," originally published in 1969 and reprinted in *Out of the Closets: Voices of Gay Liberation,* Carl Wittman de-

clared that sadomasochism "when consensual can be described as a highly artistic endeavor, a ballet the constraints of which are the thresholds of pain and pleasure." He also states that certain acts, seen as "perversions" by some, "can be reflections of neurotic or self-hating patterns."

Barroom conversations, the gay media, and the porn industry have made many gay men aware of a significant presence of sexual expression that involves various aspects of dominance and submission. In New York City, participants in S&M and B&D have even organized a group, the Eulenspiegel Society, which meets regularly and holds forums and rap groups. Erotic material designed to stimulate men along these lines has become more widespread, seemingly indicating the popularity of S&M and curiosity about it. Several moviemakers, notably Fred Halstead of Los Angeles, have achieved renown with S&M pornography. In 1971, Halstead appeared personally at a preview showing of two of his films; Stuart Byron, the gay film critic, did Halstead's publicity and invited many gay activists, male and female, to the showing on the grounds that the films were relevant to gay liberation. While some in the audience appreciated the films, others were shocked and outraged at the suggestion that such imagery of humiliation had anything to do with gay liberation. For example, in *L.A. Plays Itself,* Halstead's boy friend Joey grovels at his master's feet and licks his boots; in *Sex Garage,* a gay man has his head shoved in a toilet bowl by a straight man. More recently, *Blueboy* published an S&M photo-essay portraying such extreme behavior as bloody self-mutilation and the insertion of burning matches into the urethra (neither of these specific acts was mentioned by any respondents). The respondents to the survey indicated that titillation and curiosity and fantasizing about S&M are more widespread than the actual practice of it.

S&M has become a matter for political debate, but some of its most outspoken proponents turn out not to be snarling ogres but sensitive poets, pacifists, and anarchists. Boston's *Gay Community News* even published an interview with a black man who plays a slave role to a white lover in an S&M relationship, yet maintains he is fully committed to the political ideals of racial equality.

Gut-level repudiation of relationships based on dominance/submission, as well as carefully reasoned political arguments dealing with the moral aspects of power-related consensual sexual acts, have also been expressed in the gay and lesbian media. Both the frank appreciation of and the staunch opposition to such sexuality—and the various shades in between—were expressed, with lesbians voicing their ideas in the previous chapter and gay men speaking out here.

The following chart indicates *the frequency of certain sexual practices* among the gay male respondents:

	ALWAYS	VERY FREQUENTLY	SOMEWHAT FREQUENTLY	SOMEWHAT INFREQUENTLY	VERY INFREQUENTLY	ONCE	NEVER
sadomasochism (S&M)	1	3	6	8	13	7	63%
bondage and discipline B&D)	.5	3	4	4	10	6	73
humiliation	.5	1	3	3	11	3	78
"talking dirty"	1	4	10	15	23	5	42
urination ("water sports")	.5	.5	2	4	7	9	77
defecation ("scat")	0	.5	0	0	2	2	96
enemas	1	0	1	.5	4	4	89
fist-fucking	2	1	2	3	10	6	78
sex with animals (bestiality)	0	0	0	.5	6	7	87
foot fetishism	1	1	2	3	11	6	76
jock straps, underwear	1	5	6	11	19	5	54
boots, leather	.5	2	3	6	9	3	75
other clothing fetishes	1	3	4	3	11	3	76

Whether or not these statistics accurately reflect the frequency of these preferences in the overall gay male population is something we cannot know for sure. It does indicate that the practices are not as widespread as suggested by media interest, themes in pornography, current gay jokes and banter, or the use of masculine-fantasy clothing. On the other hand, sadomasochistic sexual expression is frequently practiced by 10% of the respondents, and that is a significant minority of gay men. If experimentation (doing it once) is taken into account, many of these practices have been experienced by large numbers of men. Nonparticipants are not necessarily horrified by these practices, even though negative feelings are expressed by a majority in most cases. There remains a residue of curiosity and fantasizing—with perhaps some discomfort or fear that keeps some men "in the closet" as far as certain practices. This choice may be based not on repression but on intelligent, carefully reasoned thought; some may see such reluctance simply as "unliberated." In any case, attitudes toward these same practices tend to show more positive feelings than the percentage of participants would indicate. Here's the chart showing *feelings toward these acts, regardless of whether or not a person participates in them:*

	VERY POSITIVE	SOMEWHAT POSITIVE	NEUTRAL	SOMEWHAT NEGATIVE	VERY NEGATIVE	NOT SURE
sadomasochism (S&M)	4	10	13	19	48	4%
bondage and discipline (B&D)	5	10	12	17	52	5
humiliation	3	5	9	11	68	4
"talking dirty"	8	18	30	13	28	4
urination ("water sports")	4	8	13	12	59	3
defecation ("scat")	1	1	5	7	82	4
enemas	2	5	13	12	63	6
fist-fucking	3	8	11	14	59	4
sex with animals (bestiality)	2	4	13	9	68	3
foot fetishism	5	6	32	14	37	7
jock straps, underwear	14	20	32	10	21	2
boots, leather	7	12	27	19	31	4
other clothing fetishes	7	6	35	12	31	8

"To each his own" and similar sayings were used by many people to reflect an attitude toward dominance/submission that could best be described as liberal or tolerant. Many of the participants were enthusiastic and unabashed in revealing their experiences, but these "kinky" preferences were frequently cited by men in response to our question about what things they keep secret. The felt need for secrecy is a response to the negative attitudes found not only in the straight world but in the gay world as well.

Sadomasochism, Bondage and Discipline, Humiliation

Many people chose to comment generally on the entire list of practices shown in the chart, but in this first group of quotations, the focus is on sadomasochism, bondage and discipline, and humiliation. Some of these include other acts, such as fist-fucking, but clearly the context of the fist-fucking is sadomasochistic. Other people involved in fist-fucking see the act differently, so there's a separate section on it later in this chapter. The previous chapter about lesbians includes some definitions, but terms like "sadomasochism" are difficult to define, and the "experts" in this field have their own arguments about the nuances and differences. The responses to the survey illustrate that much of the terminology involved in defining the various dominant/submissive relationships is hopelessly intertwined. There is no space here for a full catalog of or an analysis of the various permutations and combinations (i.e., a scene involving water sports where a

person is tied up and also whipped, versus a scene involving water sports where the participants abhor any hint of S&M or B&D). At best this section indicates some of the experiences and feelings of the respondents.

Some of the following quotations are extracted from people's essays on their "most pleasing" sexual experience, but most are in response to a request for comments on the specific practices listed in the previous chart:

♂"I am into mild discipline. I have a lover whom I do not live with (we are 100 miles apart) but whom I see fairly frequently. Our relationship has been going on for over eighteen months and we have established a pattern which we both enjoy. I always go to his place, and when I arrive he will meet me at the front door and will be very stern and will immediately order me to take my pants and jockeys down and lie over a large leather chair he has in his den. He will then proceed to spank me very hard with his hand while I lie over the chair. I try to get away but he holds me down and continues to spank me. He will then stop and order me to get upstairs to the bedroom. I will go up and then strip completely naked. He has laid out on the bed a strap, hairbrush, wooden paddle, and on occasion a small whip. He follows me upstairs after a few minutes (enough time to allow me to strip) and he will then sit on the edge of the bed and will order me to lie over his lap as a little boy and will then use the strap on my ass. I must count the straps and it usually is 100. He will then allow me to lie on the bed and he will then strip. He is pretty well hung and he always gets an erection when he spanks me. He will tell me to watch him as he takes off his pants and his jockeys and when he has his shorts off he always tells me, 'See what you have done to me,' as he reveals his enormous erection. I try to fondle it, but he tells me that I don't deserve to be allowed such a pleasure. He will then usually take the hairbrush and give me some more. I, however, get myself in a position so that I can touch his erection and play with it, and go down on him. Our spanking is really only foreplay—I enjoy being spanked—I am honest to admit it—and he enjoys spanking. Soon we have left the spanking behind and we cuddle close. I love to play with his cock and he spreads his legs wide so that I have full access to it. He will reach down and play with mine. I have learned that he enjoys having the skin and hair under his balls fondled and played with—it drives him crazy to have someone feel him there and he just gets harder. We play with each other's tits and playfully pull the hair around the tits. This could go on for hours and generally does. We both are in our late 40s and age has begun to take its toll in that we do not stay hard as long as we used to so he will tell me to fetch him the strap and he will give me some more which causes him to erect hard again and turns me on. We will have kissed and licked each other and fondled and cuddled each other considerably. We suck each other and it will end that we either suck each other to climax or we will jerk off—it makes little difference to us. In some cases we will not even climax during our whole session and it does not bother us that we don't."

♂"I like S&M and of course spanking. My first experience with spanking was when my dad spanked me. One day he spanked me with a belt and I was

wearing corduroy pants. I guess I had an erection, must have been about 13 years old. Maybe in looking for other men to spank me, I am seeking out a father image as my dad has been dead for twenty-one years."

⚢"I met this man in a gay bar. We went to my place and went to bed. I laid on top of him French-kissing for a few minutes, then I started chewing on his ear, then ran my tongue down his neck to his chest. He put his hands down in the back of my pants and played with my ass. After a minute or so, I took off his shirt and he took mine off and caressed each other from neck to cock. Then we removed our pants and boots. We lay down in the bed; this time I was on the bottom. He chewed on my chest, then on my stomach, then on my cock. I rolled him over and did the same. Then I tied him down to the bed by a rope attached to each corner of the bed. I slapped him a good one on the waist and he moaned as if he loved it. So I gave him more of it. Then I tied his feet together and rolled him over on his stomach and started to fist-fuck him. He took it almost a foot or so, then I fucked him for a while, and came on his ass and back. Then I untied him, and he attacked me. He tied my hands together and then my feet, beat on me with a belt. Then fist-fucked me and then sucked me off. I just loved this experience. After that night, I dated this man for six months."

⚢"I have a lot of ambivalence about these. On the one hand, I think people should do whatever feels good as long as there's mutual consent and respect. On the other hand, on a gut level I don't feel it's healthy for people to abuse each other in these ways, that it's basically degrading and reflects serious personality problems, and that one can't feel good about one's self if one makes a fetish of engaging in these. I have a sense that a lot of these activities result from gay men being so burned out by having so many sexual partners that they can't feel anything unless it's totally intense and outlandish. I just can't see a community of men who love each other getting off on fist-fucking each other and eating each other's shit; it goes against my whole impression of what feminism means to me. In my own experience, I've engaged in some minor S&M with a long-term lover (spanking, pinching, scratching heavily to the point of pain) with us interchanging roles, and really enjoyed it. I ended up with someone who 'talked dirty' to me and found that, although I was sexually turned on by him, afterwards I felt degraded and revolted at myself for allowing it."

⚢"Much of my sex with others is on the fringe of S&M and I always play the top role. I have developed a rather large stable of Ms who come to me for this type of sex. I am not a true sadist. I am much more responsive to the needs of the M. I don't enjoy inflicting pain *per se,* but will do it if it is part of the turn-on for the other person. I enjoy having someone in bondage, building him up over a lengthy period of time with masturbating him almost to the point of orgasm, fucking him with my cock or dildos, forcing him to suck cock or rim my ass, playing with any erogenous parts of his body, applying whatever pressure or pain to his nipples that will evoke the strongest sexual reaction, etc."

⚢"I love a rough fuck—either giving or getting. I love being forced

down on someone's cock—or vice versa—all if I am in the right mood. I also have space for gentleness. I like people who talk dirty to me, but I can't yet do it back.''

⚥ "As a psychiatrist I know that these practices point toward unresolved traumas from early childhood. They are, if connected with physical abuse or self-destruction, sick."

⚥ "The scariest sexual encounter was my first with a guy into S&M. I walked into his bedroom, saw handcuffs, whips, ropes, etc., and having heard that S&M was a heavy pain scene, I wanted out and fast, as I hate pain and don't like hurting anyone else. I really panicked. However, he was a remarkable guy and put me at ease and explained a lot about S&M that I was misinformed about and learned that it can be a 'game' played between two men with complete respect for the feelings of the other, and their needs. It was educational and enjoyable after all."

⚥ "Once I answered a rather strange ad about an apartment to share, and after this man showed me the apartment, he got me to hang around, feeling more and more suspicious. Finally he gave me some ridiculous cock-and-bull story about he wanted to shoot a short film about a burglar who gets caught; this gave him an excuse to tie me up, see. Then he got me lying across the bed with my ass in the air and tried to spank me. As soon as it hurt I told him to stop, and he did; then he jacked me off, which he was extremely good at. I went along with the whole thing because I wanted to see what he wanted. The whole thing was a bit weird."

⚥ "There are certain aspects of S&M which I am very much attracted to. I like the idea of an intense, physically 'gripping' sexual experience. A mental as well as physical orgasm. I am turned on to the idea of pain, physical bondage—fulfillment through suffering. However, I have been unable to realize most of my fantasies based on this theme. I am very much turned off by the 'leather scene' and all its tired trappings. The costumes, the heavy macho flavorings, its very 'straightness.' I don't fit in at all. Outside of this scene (even in San Francisco) it is very hard to make good contact for S&M or specialty 'scenes.' ''

⚥ "I enjoy an 'S&M blowing' (where I move his head back and forth over my prick) and an 'in and out' laying, the best. This latter is described as inserting into the asshole, then withdrawing fully or almost so, then ramming it in again and again; I find others enjoy this done to them as much as I like doing it. I am also *very* turned on by the combination, which only a few will do: he sucks me, I lay him (not to orgasm), he sucks me *immediately* again, that is, without interruption by washing, and so on, alternate sucking and getting fucked, at my command; I finally come in one orifice or the other. It's best if he's tied over the table."

⚥ "The thought of being a slave turns me on, the thought of pain at another's hands turns me on. Reports of torture turn me on. Never really have done it."

⚥ "I drew the line at anything that draws blood or produces scars."

⚥ "Sadomasochism is definitely a part of me, although the S&M is to a

fairly moderate degree. I do not enjoy blood or mutilation but find a certain degree of pain very arousing, and from past experiences have found I have a higher pain threshold than many. I enjoy the 'challenge' of overcoming my pain and struggling against my bondage until I have exhausted whoever is binding me. The tighter and more complicated they bind me, the better. Discipline, however, is too close to humiliation, and I don't like either one. Whether I am the dominator or the dominated, I enjoy S&M-bondage as a mutual struggle more than a thorough subjugation. Rope is my main fetish. My first sexual arousal was while climbing ropes in gym glass, and my first ejaculation was while playing and being tied up as if crucified.''

⚥"I'm inclined to think that S&M and B&D are pathological. The very guys who get their rocks off submitting in sexual situations are likely to be those who are perfect bastards at work and in their social relationships, and generally sexist, often misogynist, as well. S&M is also linked in my mind with fascism as are boots and leather and other kinds of extreme masculine clothing—what John Rechy calls 'male impersonation.' Yet I am prepared to take people individually for judgment rather than lumping them together for group condemnation and so I hesitate to sweepingly denounce all S&M, B&D, denim and leather people as fascistic and sexist.''

⚥"I love to lie on my stomach on a bed or the floor and have my ass spanked or whipped with a belt till my ass is red and hot, then have a hand and arm shoved up my ass to the elbow or farther. I also love to drink piss and eat ass. I like rough sex with lots of amyl and some good rock or disco music in the background.''

⚥"Sadomasochism—a difficult moral and political question. I find it personally unacceptable within my sexual life. For others, I am torn between my desire to see total freedom in sex between consenting people (not only adults), and my desire to see human suffering and pain eliminated. I believe it should be tolerated, but not approved, and that it would disappear with the establishment of a more human and humane society.''

⚥"I agree with John Rechy in his book *The Sexual Outlaw* concerning S&M. I think it is a negative force in which the neurotic shame/guilt factors are strengthened rather than liberated. This also applies to humiliation.''

⚥"Have never done S&M and don't want to. The hyperbutch men who seem to engage in this are fascinating to me in the abstract but not enough to be tempting.''

⚥"I am opposed to S&M on religious grounds. I believe that human bodies ultimately belong to God, and that an individual does not have the right to harm a human body, or to permit his own body to be harmed in any way.''

⚥"I don't enjoy pain, immediately lose my erection with pain.''

⚥"S&M and B&D are too close to reality for comfort, because I have been arrested and handcuffed for real and have contemplated the possibility of physical abuse by a policeman.''

⚥"Can one really call these people homosexuals or gays, that is, part of a really gay lifestyle? Where is the love and the caring? No, they are either

having problems or are sick or just want to shock people. I do not class them as gay people. I have never met a person who was into any of those acts.''

⚥''I may *enjoy* a particular act, humiliation for example, but not approve of what it suggests in my personality, and I may try to arrive at a point where I don't desire that act any more—or come to grips with my wanting it. I wish I knew why I liked certain things—repressed experiences? political climate? rebellion? I really haven't a clue.''

⚥''I have only experienced humiliation once. It involved a big rough trick at a friend's house. He sat on my head and made me rim him against my will (he was not clean), and as I rimmed him I had to tell him I was his little piggy and go oink oink. It turns me on when a trick calls me a little cocksucker or some other such name.''

⚥''I'd like to humiliate someone closeted who's smug and thinks he's straight. I can think of all kinds of things I'd do or say, and situations that I'd enjoy.''

⚥''I like to be humiliated sometimes, i.e., have a leash and collar around my neck and be led around the house.''

⚥''I do wish these people would stay in the closet with this part of their lives.''

⚥''Cocksucking seems like a form of humiliation to me. I fantasize about being humiliated, but when I feel humiliated, and have an orgasm, I feel terrible afterward.''

⚥''Humiliation—isn't there enough of that from straight society and the state?''

⚥''The two times I have done something approaching an S&M scene, I became bored. It seemed like acting to me. One time I was whipped and another time I hit and stepped on someone wearing a uniform. For me, though, it is really psychological S&M I like. Uniforms help a little (i.e., leather jacket, jockstrap). What it really is about is power and aggression—either directly or through identification with a masochist.''

⚥''B&D is something I would definitely try. Even as a very little boy I felt sexual excitement at being tied up or tying someone up when we played cowboys and Indians. I think it also goes along with my rape fantasies.''

⚥''I am intrigued with being tied up and massaged or possibly tickled to the point of extreme titillation. Also have been interested in being paddled until pink to see what effect this has as to my arousal and emotions sexually. (Have no need to be paddled as a means of punishment—I feel good about sex.) I've never tried B&D except to pick up a belt lying on a bunk beside a naked guy in 'the baths' and obligingly swat his ass—moderately. I felt sorry for them—needing this means for arousal. I was not turned on doing it.''

⚥''I like bondage for the dramatics part. But nothing like chains or rope. I just simply love to be tied, legs outstretched and arms across a bed. With neckties around each wrist and ankle, to the bed frame. Everything else about these acts just makes me sick.''

One man who is not personally into B&D describes the evolution of his sexual relationship with a lover who is:

⚥"I suppose five years ago I would have had trouble even reading the list, much less commenting on it. Yet I've come to see these acts as alternatives for some, for others a means of expression that is the only satisfaction. I suppose that my personal experiences with most of these things are almost nonexistent. The only one I can really discuss is B&D.

"After an extremely drunken New Year's Day round of parties, my lover of then one year and I dragged home somehow and went to bed. Somehow making love that night turned quite a bit more uninhibited than it usually was, and he asked that I tie him up. As I remember, I was drunken enough to think it was quite logical (an interesting twist on 'Christ-was-I-drunk-last-night'). He explained that he'd never done it and had always wanted to.

"Time went on, and we refined it, always with him as the bound person. It became quite an intellectual pastime for us, trying to think of new things to try, yet both always aware that it was pretty much a role-playing game. We explored his fantasies, and I tried to live them out with him as best I could. He went so far as to install permanent eyes in his bathroom walls to secure the ropes. For a few months, it was thrilling because it was so wicked; it was the sort of thing I'd only read about.

"I discovered that I really wasn't finding much satisfaction in it, though. Whatever I was getting was the satisfaction that he was having a good time fulfilling his fantasies, and my needs were becoming more and more secondary. I remember seeing him trussed up, blindfolded, and I thought, 'How fucking autistic.' It seemed to me that any act between two lovers must an act of love, and this wasn't. It all seemed like some purely masturbatory fantasy in which I was nothing more than a tool. We managed to go on a time-sharing basis, equal time satisfying my needs (making love on a bed) and his.

"Whether for a joke or not I will never know, but one year for Christmas he gave me my own set of manacles to tie him up. I never have thought that I was able to hide my sense of outrage at his spending that much money (those things do cost a damn lot, I learned) and calling it a Christmas present for *me*.

"I'm happy to say that we've been able to grow into meeting both his needs and mine much more successfully. It's not a major thing in our life. Months go past without even a reference to it. Yet when his need must be filled, as his lover I am the one to fill it.

"I've tried to guess what it would mean to our relationship if B&D were the only form of lovemaking open to us, if that were the *only* way to satisfy my lover. I suspect I wouldn't be able to deal with it for very long. I have a high need for affection. I guess I can't really understand what anyone can find in lovemaking that honestly expresses no real interplay between two unique people. S&M still strikes me (no pun intended) as theater, as does B&D. A small sense of being in the theater is fine, I guess,

but being an actor night after night must be hell. Where does the slave type be real if not in bed?''

Talking Dirty

The simple use of frank language to describe sexual acts or parts of the body is not uncommon. Indeed, those who find it difficult to pronounce words like ''fuck,'' ''suck,'' and ''cock'' or to say ''I'm coming!'' etc. are probably rare nowadays. For some people, however, ''talking dirty'' is elevated to a special erotic place. The survey indicates that 15% of the men ''talk dirty'' frequently, while more than half have tried it at least once. Nearly half, however, have negative feelings about it. The term itself is somewhat ambiguous and may not have been clearly understood by all, however. There were many different experiences and attitudes reflected in the comments of the gay men toward ''talking dirty'':

⚥''Dirty talk can add some thrills to getting it on, and I love to do it. 'Fuck that ass, stud-fucker! . . . Really ram it in and make me feel it . . . gimme all the cock you got!' ''

⚥''Dirty talk is different from sexy talk and good natural sex noises. I associate dirty talk with low intelligence and lack of education.''

⚥''Dirty talk can add to the experience if it's done well. If it's not done well, I am prone to bursting into giggles at the absurdity of it.''

⚥''Two years ago while I was staying at the Y while between apartments, there was this young kid (20) and his lover (35) that came into my room. While the kid sucked me off his lover talked dirty and I got into that. Certain whites I can get into talking dirty to as they suck on my stiff black cock.''

⚥''Talking dirty—always do it under the influence of poppers. Adds excitement by bringing out the basic animalism of the act.''

⚥''Once I was asked to talk dirty and rough while I fucked a man. I didn't get anything out of the experience but he did. His eyes almost bulged out of his head.''

⚥''Talking dirty can be fun, especially when both persons understand the inherently innocent nature of the talk. I've done that with some frequency and had it done (under the same conditions) to me, and liked it. It becomes intolerable when a note creeps into my partner's voice indicating he is quite serious about it all, when he actually means whatever salacious or degrading comment he utters. Then I put a stop to it until we can reexamine our ground rules.''

⚥''I feel that if a person has to talk dirty he must also think sex is dirty and I don't think so. I think sex is beautiful and should not be put into the gutter.''

Urination, Defecation, Enemas

With the holes for elimination of body waste also connected with genital organs and erogenous zones it is certainly no wonder that there can

be, for some, connection between sexual acts and acts of elimination. Many respondents described these acts with words such as "degenerate," "aberrant," and "unhealthy." Nonetheless, water sports, scat, and enemas remain a sexual turn-on for a very small minority. Here, respondents indicate enthusiasm, revulsion, and other views for these sex practices:

⚣ "Water sports—*yes yes yes!!* My favorite thing of all is piss. I like partner to piss his pants. I like the smell of piss. Like to piss my own pants . . . like to feel and put face in crotch of partner while he's pissing or after he's done so. Like to drink it outside of his underwear, levis, etc. as he pisses. Here, I'm more submissive than dominant in that I would prefer to be pissed on than to piss on somebody else. I like the warmth and wetness. I like wearing rubber to hold in the warmth (as in a wetsuit). I like to wet the bed but especially for the partner to do so. I like wet diapers, wet levis, wet rubber, and wet leather especially—self and partner. Like him to lie on me and piss his pants. Like outdoor piss scenes where there's a chance someone might see. Like self and/or partner to piss on floor, furniture, etc. *Not* especially turned on by bathtub piss scenes—like a warm, soft, enclosed place like a sleeping bag. Would rather be kissed and feeling him up while he pisses than to have him standing over me and pissing in my face, etc., but I do like him to piss on my boots."

⚣ "Defecation (scat)—I think the two main reasons I haven't gotten into this more than I have is that I don't like the smell and because of having to clean up the mess afterwards. I have not gotten into actually eating the shit out of the guy's ass yet, although I have tasted it with my tongue."

⚣ "I've been taking enemas since I was ten years old. I used enemas as a means of masturbating, especially when I did not have other sexual outlets. If I go out where I might get sexually involved with someone, I usually take an enema before showering. There was really only one time that I was involved with enemas with another person. I answered an enema ad and went in to visit the guy. We had two sessions on different occasions where we gave each other enemas and messed around with other sexual stimulation. It was okay but this particular guy was a bit uptight to be able to relate to. Years ago when they were more available and popular, I used to get colonic irrigations from physical therapists. I made up my own colonic irrigation device for use at home. After I left my wife, I went heavily into the enema bit for a while. I sent away for a 6-quart bag, colon tubes, fancy nozzles, etc. The enema thing is principally something that I have done by myself. If another person is available I would just as soon fuck or make love rather than play with the enemas."

⚣ "I'm sorry to use this word, but I think urination as a form of sex is sick. Anybody who does this must hate and loathe himself to a high degree to want to subject himself to this."

⚣ "I have always thought that water sports would be fun to try but only as a Golden Shower type thing. Ingestion for me or my partner is not exciting for me. A fantasy is to face each other in the bathtub with nothing but

jeans on and to piss into the jeans after mutual insertion through the flies as a prelude to a shower and sex."

⚥ "I have never been involved in scat but the thought is exciting and sexually arousing."

⚥ "Once, right after I came out, I was taking a shower with a 16-year-old boy, and by way of joking he pissed on me. It was very much of a turn-on for me. I never saw him again, so I couldn't ask him to pee on me again, but to this day I get turned on by talk of pissing and pornography of pissing and fantasize about a young good-looking stud pissing all over me. I have never experienced scat nor do I want to. The thought of it revolts me."

⚥ "If there is such a thing as perversion in the gay sex world, I guess urination and defecation are it. Yuk! I have drunk my own piss before—it didn't do anything for me but make me piss some more."

⚥ "My most unusual experience was with a man who wanted to watch me shit and eat it, lick the shit out of my ass, etc. As I was fucking him he encouraged me to talk about how I was fucking shit and how good, warm, brown, and smelly it was. After I came he licked off the shit and come from my dick. It's not the sort of action I look for but with that particular guy, because he got off on it so much, I got off on it." '

⚥ "Enemas—nothing about it seems exciting to me. I really don't see the point. Medically it doesn't seem wise to repeatedly tamper with the colonic 'ecosystem.' "

⚥ "I think piss and shit stink."

⚥ "When I first learned of urination, I thought it was weird, couldn't understand it. Now I can understand how some people, probably due to some unusual childhood experience, could find it very exciting. I've had men who requested me to urinate in their mouths and claimed it was a sexual jolt to them. While I was fellating a black healthy stud he announced suddenly he had to urinate and before I could release his cock he shot a strong spurt of urine in my mouth. To my surprise, I found it pleasant and stimulating. He went and relieved himself, came back, and I resumed my blow job with renewed interest. (I've since learned that urine is sterile.)"

Fist-Fucking

Perhaps the most impossible-sounding of all sex acts practiced by gay men, fist-fucking is experienced regularly by one out of every twenty of respondents to the survey, though three-fourths of the men respond negatively to the idea of it. Yes, it is possible for a man to insert his fist and forearm into the rectum of another man. Though this is described as pleasurable by some men, medical doctors interviewed by the gay press have repeatedly warned of the danger of this act and cite their experience treating men for perforated colons, which sometimes lead to colostomies and even death. Nonetheless, fist-fucking has its enthusiasts, who call themselves members of the FFA, Fist-Fuckers of America. Many of the respondents

commented on the act in strongly negative terms, with particular reference to its danger. A few took the familiar "to each his own" attitude, and there were a few comments from participants:

⚥ "I think that compared to most people I could be categorized as a warm, affectionate, and fairly intense person. I have always loved to touch and be touched, cuddle, kiss, and to fully share myself with a sexual partner. I have always had a strong anal orientation (enjoyed getting fucked) but in the past few years, this has led to the addition of fist-fucking as a regular part of my sexual activity. For me, this activity has nothing to do with the S&M activities with which it is usually linked. Instead, I have found it to be a fantastic extension of the activity I've always enjoyed (and continue to). In trying to 'explain' this, I can only say that fist-fucking seems to me to be the most intimate, caring, and, yes, *loving* sexual experience that I've enjoyed; with the two partners entwined and feeling each other in a level of intensity that I haven't found in any other activity. Done properly, there is *no* pain—rather the incredible pleasure of having another person deep inside you (or, as I love going both ways, the feeling of being inside one's partner and providing him with that same pleasure).

"To emphasize the intensity of the pleasure, intimacy, and beauty of it (I should mention that I like mirrors so that I can see the physical beauty of it, too), I should emphasize that I have always enjoyed doing it most when I am cold *sober*—no drugs, alcohol, poppers, etc.—and have made the greatest achievements (would you believe, to the elbow) most easily when waking up after a good night's sleep! The contrary is also true: I cannot even get a few fingers in if I have drunk or smoked enough to lose a good sense of exactly what is going on."

⚥ "I fist-fucked a couple of people from time to time. Then I met and fell in love with this man who liked to be fist-fucked. Before C., I just thought of fist-fucking as a kinky, jaded, sort of boring thing to do. But with C., from the very beginning, fist-fucking him was a sensuous and intimate way of sharing. My hand is quite limber and collapses very far for a man my size, so fist-fucking is easy for me. The feeling of being inside C., practically to my elbow without hurting him, experiencing his organs, feeling his heart beat from inside him, feeling his pulse, feeling my own pulse in my cock, knowing that instead of his feeling my throbbing inside him I was feeling his, it was really wonderful, and I have a new respect for fist-fucking and look forward to more intimate experiences. The idea of fist-fucking because it is chic or butch still bores me and is not sexually exciting at all."

⚥ "I will not fist-fuck. It just seems repulsive to me."

⚥ "I have observed fist-fucking in New York bars with amazement and interest but have no interest in participating in any way."

⚥ "Like anything else, great if you like it. Someone did it to me once and tore some tissue in the rectum; the pain for three weeks was excruciating."

⚥ "I have participated in fist-fucking from both ends. It has been done to me twice after a lot of liquor and poppers. I have done it to others about eight times—the first was twenty years ago when it was entirely unknown. I

do not approve of the practice because I believe it to be extremely dangerous if not deadly."

⚣"I witnessed a fist-fucking session once which turned me on, but I am not about to agree to being on the receiving end of a fist-fuck, probably because I fear physical damage, but I think I might enjoy fist-fucking some hairy ass if it wanted it."

Bestiality

Very little has been written about bestiality and gay men. Charley Shively wrote an article for *Fag Rag* entitled "Bestiality as an Act of Revolution," but people looking for information on how to make it with a dog must have been sorely disappointed, as the article was a rather philosophical treatise on the carnality of animals and of men. Judging from the questionnaires, sex with animals occurs primarily during youth when a "warm body" is desired and the most available one may just happen to belong to another species. Sexual stimulation by or with an animal, including pets and farm animals, was within the experience of only a few men, with 13% having tried it at least once. But it was not a frequent contemporary pleasure for any. Here are some experiences with and comments on the subject:

⚣"The neighbors (straight) have a black Labrador retriever that fucks me (when I can get him alone, of course, which isn't too often). We (I?) almost got caught by them, so have to be very careful."

⚣"I had a dog named Comanche. I would pull down my pants and get on my hands and knees. Then I would get his two front legs and put them on my back. I then would reach back and get his cock and put it at the entrance of my asshole. I would pull the foreskin back and scoot my rump back on the naked bone. Then I would begin jacking him off. When he begins hunching, his bone would push farther in the hole and then I would lean forward and let him bang me. After he was finished and his hard-on had gone down we would repeat the same procedure. I would do this for about five times. By then I was so hot I masturbated myself."

⚣"I have no opinion on sex with animals, never having done it or heard about it from anyone I know, though I saw a film of a dog fucking a woman and it looked like she was hating it (it was a very exploitative film)."

⚣"My first sexual experience besides masturbation was when I was 12, with a cow—not bad, but boys are better."

⚣"Sex with animals is for horny farm boys out of the 1950s."

⚣"I've had a dog lick my cock and balls and drink my cum a couple of times, but it's not worth the trouble for me."

⚣"I experimented with this while in high school. I used to finger-fuck a little girl dog next door while she was in heat and she used to like it. It turned me on too and sometimes I would masturbate while I did it. I also used to lay her on my crotch and stomach and rub her back and forth on me till I shot off. This too felt good. I've also masturbated male dogs and a few

times let them fuck my ass. I remember I was really scared about getting
caught but it was a real turn-on. I wouldn't do it again now as I have no
interest, but I'm glad I experimented. I still get turned on when I watch
horses get hard-ons, but I don't know what I'd do with a horse.
Nonetheless, it makes a nice fantasy.''

⚥ "Bestiality just isn't relevant to me. I need a psychic interplay of sorts,
not to say pets don't have marvelous personalities.''

⚥ "Sex with animals: not interested, although as a boy on a farm here in
Florida, a cousin and I used to fuck a horse, female! Mostly, we would
experiment with how deep her vaginal canal went by putting our arms down
in it. I could insert mine all the way to the armpit. We did it only once or
twice and lost interest. He then started working me over: I was 10 or 11, and
he was a little older, had a huge prick, and finally managed to penetrate me
anally, which seemed a lot more interesting than fucking around with
horses.''

⚥ "Sex with animals—not for me. Repulsive when I think about it.''

⚥ "Sex with animals is great when there is no one else. Living on a farm
can be lovely; I've fucked many cows and had calves suck me off.''

Foot Fetishism

Although some people ignore the feet altogether while otherwise
caressing a partner's entire body, others pay casual attention to them, much
the way one might caress a knee or an arm. For certain people, the foot is a
focus for their most intense erotic energy. About one-fourth of respondents
indicated that foot fetishism played a part in their sexual interactions at
least once, but half have negative feelings about it.

⚥ "While I have engaged in almost every type of sex and am very
uninhibited, my experiences in foot fetishism have been extraordinarily
gratifying and correspondingly embarrassing. There is not too much (if any)
'fetishism liberation' around. Also, although people may be very liberal in
some issues, they can be just as narrow on other issues. I have done
numerous forms of foot fetishism, and have gotten enormous pleasure from
it. However, I have frequently gotten many negative reactions, if only, I
believe, from the 'unusual' nature of it. Perhaps you can suggest ways to
further liberate ourselves and others in areas related to homosexuality, but
more esoteric, exotic, atypical, and 'kinky.' ''

⚥ "I love feet. I follow men in the street just to get a look at their feet.
The way the heel lifts and swings in at each step turns me on.

"Toes are like little cocks. Once you slick them all up with sucking, and
lick the soles in long strokes, you can get three or four in your mouth at
once. I lick along the top of the foot, sticking my tongue between the toes,
and love feeling both feet against my face, soles and toes, while I slowly jerk
him off and play with myself. And I love the way toes clench and spread in
my hand when a guy I'm sucking starts to come. There's no softer skin on
the body to kiss than along the instep.

"Feet can be butch and muscular, with square, blunt toes, hairy on top; or slender and white with high arches and slender toes; or have rounded toes set close.

"I look forward to summer, when guys go barefoot or wear sandals. Clogs give you a glimpse of the sole and show the heel.

"In a sauna once, I sucked and licked every inch of a blond guy's feet, twice each foot, while he lay back with his eyes closed and slowly played with his cock. Then I sucked him off. I had never sucked and licked feet before that, although I had often wanted to.

" 'Bare feet,' 'barefoot,' 'toes,' 'sole,' 'heel,' 'sock,' 'feet'—even these words turn me on, as do 'shoes' and 'sneakers,' 'Adidas' and 'boots.' Feet turn me on more than asses and almost as much as cocks.''

⚥ "When I am making love I want to caress that person with my hands and tongue him all over the body, except the feet."

⚥ "I find feet usually dirty if not ugly, from the result of shoes and resultant misshapenness—calluses, corns, etc. They turn me off unless perfect."

⚥ "I've had a fetish for male feet nearly all my life. I can remember being attracted to a boy's feet when I was in kindergarten. This particular weakness of mine has been the prime cause of my self-hatred which has only recently begun to abate (beginning about five years ago, very slowly since then), to where I now am beginning to feel very mildly positive about this troublesome aspect of me. As you can tell from my choice of words, though, I'm far closer to neutral than positive. To be specific about a subject distasteful to most people, I'm most strongly attracted to male feet of size 10 or above on males between 15 and 25. Over 25 and they usually become too heavily calloused to qualify as 'prime.' Under 15 they are usually too small to be top quality for me. I refuse to speak much further on this topic since it discomforts me greatly even now to think my lover might find out and reject me. I have learned to do without this fetish by becoming interested in other parts of the body more commonly appreciated; by becoming interested in the whole person; and by fantasizing when necessary. All of my fantasizing, by the way, does not involve my fetish."

⚥ "I enjoy having my feet massaged and toes sucked."

⚥ "I have gotten into feet as a humiliation thing. In high school, I used to challenge friends to toe-biting contests. Whoever could bite the other's toe first wins. Obviously, this was sex-play in disguise."

⚥ "I love feet because they're different on everyone. Feet need love, too. I love to love someone's feet, let them know they're beautiful. I love sucking toes. It makes me feel like I have five small cocks in my mouth waiting to come off and choke me to death with sperm. Love those toes."

Boots, Leather, Jocks, Underwear, and Other Clothing Fetishes

Many people said they liked their sex partners best of all when naked. Disrobing is often an important part of a sexual encounter, and it is only

natural that partial states of undress have special erotic meaning. For some people, about 10%, particular items of clothing assume special sexual power. Even when not elevated to the importance of a fetish, clothing can play an important role in enhancing or detracting from sexual attractiveness, though for some people clothing is quite unimportant. Clothing was described as an important factor in their choice of a sex partner by 52% of the respondents. When asked *how often they like sex partners who wear certain items,* the respondents indicated the following:

	ALWAYS	VERY FREQUENTLY	SOMEWHAT FREQUENTLY	SOMEWHAT INFREQUENTLY	VERY INFREQUENTLY	ONCE	NEVER
"very masculine" clothing, uniforms	7	20	17	14	16	1	25%
colorful, stylish or unisex clothing	6	20	23	18	11	.5	22
blue jeans	13	48	18	8	3	0	10

Asked *how they feel about sex partners using these garments, whether or not they actually use them,* the respondents said:

	VERY POSITIVE	SOMEWHAT POSITIVE	NEUTRAL	SOMEWHAT NEGATIVE	VERY NEGATIVE	NOT SURE
"very masculine" clothing, uniforms	22	31	23	12	11	1%
colorful, stylish or unisex clothing	19	33	28	11	8	2
blue jeans	44	34	15	1	2	1

At least some respondents accept the adage that "clothing makes the man." We asked participants in the survey *how often they themselves, in connection with attracting sex partners, use certain kinds of clothing.* Here are the responses:

	ALWAYS	VERY FREQUENTLY	SOMEWHAT FREQUENTLY	SOMEWHAT INFREQUENTLY	VERY INFREQUENTLY	ONCE	NEVER
"very masculine" clothing, uniforms	3	13	11	9	13	.5	52%
colorful, stylish or unisex clothing	3	15	20	13	15	1	34
blue jeans	12	45	18	7	5	.5	13

Asked *how they feel about wearing certain items, whether or not they actually do,* the responses were as follows.

	VERY POSITIVE	SOMEWHAT POSITIVE	NEUTRAL	SOMEWHAT NEGATIVE	VERY NEGATIVE	NOT SURE
"very masculine," clothing, uniforms	23	25	25	15	10	2%
colorful, stylish or unisex clothing	20	29	31	8	10	2
blue jeans	48	30	17	1	2	1

Interest in women's clothing and fabrics associated with women is discussed later in this chapter. Among the other items of clothing mentioned were jean shorts, swim trunks, short shorts, tank tops, T-shirts, and bikinis. Clothing as a fetish and the use of clothing to attract others sexually are perhaps separate items, but they do overlap. Here are some detailed comments on both aspects:

⚥"In the D.C. Eagle one night I was talking with a man with whom I've had a nodding acquaintance when he asked me why I wasn't wearing boots. I replied that I most often wore tennis shoes as I was wearing then. He corrected me; 'Not tennis shoes—chucks.' I told him they were Converse all-star tennis shoes and he explained that they are called 'chucks'—Chuck Connors signature basketball shoes. Oh! We talked further, I invited him home, we sat around for a short while, and he caressed my legs, then ankles, and playfully untied my shoes. I read this as the signal to go upstairs, which we did. He carried my sneakers.

"I got undressed and helped him undress down to his 'slim-guy' jockey shorts. He flopped on the bed, and I followed him and started to embrace him when I noticed that he was clutching my tennis shoes. He explained he had this little 'thing' about 'chucks' and asked my indulgence. I was surprised and amused, so I explained my little fascination with his beautiful jockey shorts. Somehow we made it. With one sneaker over his mouth and nose and one held up as an object for his glazed stare and his underpants draped over my head and face we managed to jerk each other off. We traded—sneakers for jockey shorts—even-steven."

⚥ "I like to dress like a hot stud—boots, jeans, wide belt, jacket, and get wet with all these clothes on and fuck or masturbate."

⚥ "In one of the very few threesomes I've been in, one guy and I had a satisfying climax and the third man just couldn't get off. I asked repeatedly what I could do for him and yet all my different positions, pressures, and angles 'failed.' Finally he said, 'Put on the boots.' I had this gorgeous pair of pointy, hand-tooled cowboy boots. Soon as I put them on, he grabbed my feet, jammed them between his legs, and vigorously bounced them up and down on his genitals. He was moaning and whispering, 'These fucking boots . . .' and he reached orgasm in about two minutes. I thought it was real funny, but tried not to laugh."

⚥ "Boots and leather turn me on. They're sexy-looking. If I'm really hot I'll like a guy's leather jacket. I suppose with the right guy I could be 'persuaded' to lick his boots, but as of yet it's never happened."

⚥ "Black leather is one of my biggest turn-ons—I own several pieces of leather clothing and also leather boots. Like it on myself and partner. Cowboy boots a turn-on too, but don't own any myself. I like lace-up steel-toe black leather workboots with ripple soles. I also like levis very much—myself and partner. Especially dig the button-fly straight-leg type of levis, faded or new. I own two leather vests, one M-C jacket, the above-described work boots, a leather pullover shirt, bikini jockey shorts, studded belt, and pair of tie-front leather pants. Another clothing fetish is rubber pants—both self and partner—especially bikini-style jockey shorts and especially black rubber. I like dirty, pissy clothes especially."

⚥ "Boots and leather—usually these 'super-male' poseurs have BO and very little masculinity and lack a great deal in humanness."

⚥ "I am sometimes attracted to leathermen but see behind it and feel uncomfortable in my attraction. When I am lucid, I think they're funny."

⚥ "Boots and uniforms turn me off—one year of college ROTC led me to see through the masculinist shams of militarism, and influenced me to become a conscientious objector during Vietnam."

⚥ "Military uniforms turn me on because I associate them with young, good-looking, clean-cut men. It's no fetish, just a preference for 'butch' or straight-appearing men. I don't go into exaggerated masculinity, and often like sensitive-looking men; but straight-looking guys like college students absolutely turn me on."

⚥ "The smell of a man's dirty socks is the biggest turn-on for me. If I

have a guy sucking me off (and he's *good*), plus a pair of his socks to sniff on, I'll pop off like Vesuvius.''

♂ "Nazi uniforms have a certain warm spot in my heart."

♂ "While long johns are arousing, in a tactile and visual way, jockstraps are the only underwear that is visually very arousing to me. Leather is a very strong fetish. I love seeing it, feeling it, wearing it, and smelling it. The more leather the better, as long as it's not very stylish. I also am very aroused by thick socks especially if they've been worn a lot, and by feet. Lithe men in dancing tights (especially wool ones) are just as, if not more, arousing as men dressed in leather pants and boots or moccasins.''

♂ "I'd like to wear jocks all the time or else no underwear. Also like to smell sweaty old jocks.''

♂ "Jocks and underwear—these really don't do anything for me. I'm strictly neutral on this subject, except that really skimpy colored briefs turn me off as being stereotypically 'faggy.' ''

♂ "I had a mail correspondence with a man I met through a sex ad. We exchanged cassette tapes of masturbation scenes, exchanged jock straps and underwear in the mail, and generally got into lots of kinky scenes together. It was a tremendous turn-on, even though I didn't even know what the guy looked like. He had a sexy voice, though. It was also a period of sexual enlightenment for me. I was able to explore some of my fantasies through the anonymity of the U.S. mails.''

♂ "I love bikini underwear, and the mysteriousness of what's behind those little pants. Naturally I have a large and lovely array of underwear.''

♂ "I often wear the jocks of my athletic brother.''

♂ "Jockstraps remind me of the jock that I wasn't when I was in high school, and am becoming now. I'm a belated jock and I like jockstraps. I like coverings of all kinds if they enhance the hidden sexuality. I refer you to *The Denial of Death* and the chapter on fetishism for why I like 'veils' over skin—leather or socks or jeans, etc.''

♂ "I find Castro Street drag—plaid shirts, blue jeans, brogans—attractive.''

♂ "I have a strong fetish for business suits.''

♂ "I wear a lot of secondhand clothing—depending on what it costs and whether it fits.''

♂ "I like T-shirts with suggestive messages or buttons on regular shirts that only other gays would understand, while socializing with straights, too.''

♂ "It is more important who is in the shorts.''

♂ "I enjoy the sight of men in western clothing, mild leather, and in jockstraps or underwear but cannot be bothered with such impedimenta while having sex. I prefer my sex partners naked.''

♂ "I own a dozen or more styles of boots—motorcycle, Wellingtons, cowboy (with spurs), construction, etc. Leather—yeah: MC jackets, bike chaps, gloves, belts, body harness, bike cap, codpiece, short pants, arm bands . . .''

⚢ "I have never even seen a jockstrap in my life."

⚢ "I like white underwear on a well-built, tanned guy."

⚢ "Jocks and jockey shorts—I incorporate these items into my masturbation and sometimes into sex with partners, either by wearing them on my hips or over my head so I can sniff them or by sucking on my partner's pouch while he fills them."

⚢ "I sometimes like having sex partly dressed, especially when my partner is wearing jeans."

⚢ "Clothing doesn't turn me on except as a symbol, and I frankly find a well-cut three-piece suit sets off a handsome man at least as well as leather."

⚢ "The Paul Bunyan outfit of flannel shirt and jeans is my particular fantasy."

⚢ "I dislike clothing fetishes. Whether gender-fuck, drag queen or leather drag, they all seem to say the·same thing to me; I'm not a person, I'm a hallucination and demand to be noticed because only my clothing makes me worth noticing."

⚢ "My overall all-time erotic stimulant is silk, PJs or silk robes. I really dig virile athletic-type men in these garments. I feel there is nothing 'abnormal' about this fetish of mine."

⚢ "If the clothing is masculine I like it. I had been somewhat turned off to fetishes for women's underwear and stockings, although I did see a color photo of a man wearing stockings, a garter belt, and panties, with a big hard-on sticking out of it all. The incongruity of this image I did find interesting."

⚢ "I like people who dress for themselves and not to impress others—no ego-involvement kind of people."

⚢ "I wear what I perceive to be a good bar costume or pick-up outfit."

⚢ "I prefer wearing clothing that is conservative and conforms to straight society."

Sometimes special items of clothing indicate a sexual preference, and in major gay male centers, especially New York and San Francisco, there is an elaborate handkerchief and keys code to indicate preferences in such areas as S&M, urination, defecation, cock size, and sexual acts. The respondents were asked, *How often do you or your partner wear something that indicates you prefer a particular sexual act?* The replies were:

always	2%
very frequently	6
somewhat frequently	7
somewhat infrequently	7
very infrequently	14
once	2
never	62

Asked *how they felt about this practice,* the men reported:

very positive	13%
somewhat positive	11
neutral	33
somewhat negative	17
very negative	21
not sure	6

Here are some comments on this aspect of sexuality:

⚣ "You New Yorkers must be pretty hard-up to be concerned about costumes."

⚣ "Wearing something to plan sex is somewhat negative since it can become a game or a restrictive statement."

⚣ "As far as wearing particular pieces of clothing, I guess it's all right but somehow seems to be blatant advertising."

Transvestism, Transsexualism

One of straight society's most popular misconceptions about homosexual men is that they are suffering from gender confusion, that they want to be women. In a rigid sex-role system, such as the one that most Americans live in, it is not surprising that some men rebel against the demands of the system and adopt various characteristics usually ascribed to the female gender.

The division into masculine and feminine includes personality traits and behavior, but it also includes gestures, posture, and the area of clothing and body adornment. In Chapters 7 and 9, respondents discuss roles and the masculine/feminine dichotomy in detail. Here, participants in the survey offer their experiences with and feelings about cross-dressing and sex-change surgery.

The men were asked *how often, in connection with attracting sex partners, they wear certain apparel or items usually associated with women.* The following two charts indicate *frequency of the gay men's use of these items,* as well as *their feelings about them, whether or not they use them.*

	ALWAYS	VERY FREQUENTLY	SOMEWHAT FREQUENTLY	SOMEWHAT INFREQUENTLY	VERY INFREQUENTLY	ONCE	NEVER
women's clothing	0	0	0	.5	2	1	96%
make-up	0	1	1	2	7	2	88

	ALWAYS	VERY FREQUENTLY	SOMEWHAT FREQUENTLY	SOMEWHAT INFREQUENTLY	VERY INFREQUENTLY	ONCE	NEVER
jewelry	4	5	7	8	13	0	64
handbag, purse, etc.	0	1	.5	1	3	.5	94

	VERY POSITIVE	SOMEWHAT POSITIVE	NEUTRAL	SOMEWHAT NEGATIVE	VERY NEGATIVE	NOT SURE
women's clothing	3	4	20	15	55	3%
make-up	4	8	20	17	48	3
jewelry	12	14	30	10	32	2
handbag, purse, etc.	3	7	22	13	51	3

We also asked *how often the gay men like sex partners who, in connection with sex, use these items,* and also, *whether or not their sex partners use them, what their feelings are about the use of them:*

	ALWAYS	VERY FREQUENTLY	SOMEWHAT FREQUENTLY	SOMEWHAT INFREQUENTLY	VERY INFREQUENTLY	ONCE	NEVER
women's clothing	0	0	1	2	10	2	84%
make-up	1	2	3	4	17	3	72
jewelry	2	6	11	9	15	1	55
handbag, purse, etc.	1	2	3	7	13	2	74

	VERY POSITIVE	SOMEWHAT POSITIVE	NEUTRAL	SOMEWHAT NEGATIVE	VERY NEGATIVE	NOT SURE
women's clothing	3	2	15	15	64	2%
make-up	4	4	19	15	55	2
jewelry	7	12	29	12	38	2
handbag, purse, etc.	3	5	22	14	54	1

Asked simply *how they feel about male transvestites or drag queens,* the men indicated primarily negative attitudes:

very positive	6%
somewhat positive	10
neutral	30
somewhat negative	28
very negative	25
not sure	2

The issue is not strictly one of garments, however, as the issue of cross-dressing by men has been made political. Drag queens have spoken out against the discrimination they experience from the gay community and from society at large. On the other hand, feminists have accused drag queens of mocking women (see Chapter 12). Some of these debates start with clothing but end up dealing with consciousness about masculinity/femininity, and these issues are covered in Chapters 7 and 9. Here are some comments on the issues of transvestism, transsexualism, and the use of clothing and adornment generally ascribed to women:

⚭"In terms of ornamentation, I had my ear pierced many years ago, before it became a fad. (I had traveled around the Horn and across the International Date Line, and felt that such was my 'due.') I have kept some stud or hoop in my ear ever since then—much to the dismay of family members. Except when someone comments on it, I rarely think about the ear ornament—it is so much a part of me (and always will be, most likely). I also sometimes sport a thin silver chain around my neck, on the order of a choker. When inquiries have been raised, I've admitted it indicates no special sexual significance, and have never found anyone who knew what it meant, if it 'means' anything. Otherwise, while I may admire jewelry on others, my monies have gone to things other than ornamentation (partially

due to the fact I can never find any sort of wrist band, bracelet, necklace, pins, pendants, etc. which attract me enough to want to purchase them)."

⚭"When I was coming out, finding my sexual identity, I wore leotards, fur coats, and mascara. I had sex in that attire, but that was really an aspect of the '60s."

⚭"If the other guy is wearing women's-type outfit, it detracts from his sex appeal to me (I still like him and feel excited, but my dick doesn't respond much)."

⚭"I think transvestism is a bad parody of the female. It seems to me that drag is a method some men use to 'get back' at women. That's the only explanation I can give myself for the outrageous way they portray women."

⚭"Transvestism is something I can't understand and frankly am tempted to term a 'sickness' just as straights so often term gayness a sickness. I wish I could get away from this categorizing, but there it is."

⚭"I feel bound to state that I do not castigate gays who feel impelled to be exhibitionist, who carry on as 'screaming queens,' dress ultra-flamboyantly, use make-up, etc. I think I understand why they do as they do. It's true that I don't find them attractive—I am attracted to *men,* not pseudo-girls! But that is irrelevant. My point is that I believe it would be helpful to the cause of gay liberation if they could restrict extreme appearance and behavior to private gatherings, gay bars, drag balls, gay enclaves such as Cherry Grove, and the like."

⚭"Transvestism is for the birds. I'm proud to be male—even if you are male, you can be screwed up the ass, and it won't make you 'fe-male.' "

⚭"Transvestism can be a real burden for many men. I have known only one true transvestite, and he was one of the most aware, intelligent people I have ever met, who suffered greatly in his relations with his wife and family due to his need to wear women's clothing. The end appearance of many male transvestites is unimportant, I think; it is the sensation of wearing women's clothing that provides the stimulation needed."

⚭"I think back very affectionately about Sylvia Lee Rivera, Marcia Johnson, Bubbles Rose Marie, Nova, and the other drags I met in the early days of gay liberation in New York."

⚭"My most unusual experience was picking up a straight guy that wore pantyhose. He likes to have you rip out the crotch, basically raping him, by fucking him very hard through the hole you rip. He likes his ass slapped all the time that he is doing it. He was very good-looking, well built, and from New Jersey originally, if that means anything. I have seen him a couple of times. He has two children, his penis is 7½ inches long and quite fat. He repairs and programs computers."

⚭"I have one straight construction worker friend that wears a red slip with black lace a lot. He loves to get my cock in his ass while he is wearing it."

⚭"One time, I put an end to sex because this guy was playing mind games with me, and wanted me to wear his wife's panties so he could 'rub

my dick through them.' I thought if he couldn't accept the fact he was in bed with another man without having him wear panties, then I surely could not waste my time by merely covering up my maleness and letting him pretend I was his wife. If he wanted a woman that badly I felt he should go to his wife or find a pick-up. If I had gone along, I would have felt I was selling myself out as well as him.''

&⚥ ''Once a guy came back in the room dressed as a woman. I ran away.''

&⚥ ''Being a transvestite, I've experienced a lot of isolation and confusion in my life. I knew I was a TV before I knew I was gay. My first gay lover brought me out, but he always was trying to make me 'butch.' The terms 'butch' and 'femme' don't mean anything to me. I look very masculine and men who are attracted to me dislike drag queens and TVs. When I share what I like to do it turns people off. Most people, gay and straight, think TVs are drag queens and female impersonators and crazy, sick people. Tripp, in *The Homosexual Matrix,* was the clearest in his description of transvestism. Many writers on the subject are uninformed. My experience of other TVs is that of secrecy and trying to hide their identity. I refuse to remove all my body hair and I was told that I couldn't do drag with hairy legs. So there is status and exclusion among TVs. I sincerely hope when you cover this chapter in your book you present a clear picture of transvestism.''

&⚥ ''I feel uncomfortable around most TVs. They don't create real lives; they seem to act out the 1950s.''

&⚥ ''I think transvestism is based in sexism and I don't feel comfortable with it unless there is no attempt made to give an illusion of being someone of the other sex, but it is a parody of gender polarization. Then it can be a powerful statement, but again there is the danger that satirists become the satire. I have witnessed men who act no differently from the bitchy, campy traditional drag queens, but when confronted, claim that they are doing it to 'make the roles, the women's names, the dress meaningless.' I believe the Fort Hill Faggots do this . . . I am very very skeptical of their feminist consciousness when they manifest it in this manner.''

&⚥ ''After seeing the movie *Outrageous!*, I can't help but feel that drag is great. I mean, if male and female 'roles' are just that, then drag is just as legitimate as me dressing up as a lumberjack to go to Chaps—it's all the same. People threatened by it (superbutch gay men, some lesbians, etc.) are the problem, not the transvestites.''

&⚥ ''I do gender-fuck. I feel the same *inside* the dress as I feel in jeans. I enjoy watching how dramatically everything *outside* changes. The power of a few items of apparel is truly mindboggling. Drag to convince annoys me.''

&⚥ ''I express my femininity and find a great release in transvestism, especially since I look good in drag. I have several times sat at a bar in drag and have had lesbians try to pick me up. I like the looks on their faces when I start talking to them.''

&⚥ ''Drag queens were never really a group I had to mentally deal with before, that is, until a move to south Florida. There I made it a point to

introduce myself to a few. The ones with the radical concept of what they were doing were most intriguing and truthfully among the most interesting people I've ever met in my life.''

⚥"The people who do it all seem so hostile and unhappy.''

⚥"I have gone to bed with some—the dress comes off, you know, and the meat is the same underneath.''

⚥"If I am to be honest, I have wondered if I could dress in women's clothes and pull it off. I have thought about the freedom I might have wearing a skirt. Most men who cross-dress exaggerate hair-do's and make-up, etc. I don't like that. Also I don't want to be a woman. I want to be a man. But it might be fun to try cross-dressing sometime. I guess that's why God made Halloween.''

⚥"Imitating oppressive roles is a drag, but wearing frills can be fun.''

⚥"Transvestism is a threat to my masculinity, so obviously I am negative on it. But, just as I don't want to be condemned by straights for practicing homosexuality, neither will I condemn those who get their jollies by dressing in the garb of the opposite sex.''

⚥"The few queens I do know look better in drag than they do in person, so maybe that's why they do it. You just never know what the right pretty dress and a little make-up can do.''

⚥"I don't understand it. It makes me uncomfortable. I never met a transvestite (and I know many) who I have thought was well centered or together . . .''

⚥"It's fun to watch. I would have done it except I've been macho too many years. Did it as a 10-year-old, though.''

⚥"My lover is a drag queen, but really more of a drug queen. I love his *other* characteristics.''

⚥"When I first came out I had a brief interest in cross-dressing. My experimentation was limited to parading around the house in front of my lover in a dress a friend had given to me. My lover wasn't particularly turned on to it and neither was I. I was also into some aspects of scag drag, make-up, earrings, very unisexual, yet zapping gender-fuck for the straights at the time that's where the city was at politically. I feel cross-dressing is essential for the developing of a society that has no sexist bias.''

⚥"When I was first married, I used to prance around the bedroom and found it rather sexy in a funny/comic way to wear her underwear, but I did it mainly to please her because she is a lesbian.''

⚥"I am a rejected transsexual. I've applied for and have been refused a gender reassignment. I've prayed to God and to the Devil to be female in deed—I've offered my soul in exchange for a female body. Out of necessity many transvestites have had to unite with gay friends in order to have friends at all. We're the least understood of all minority groups. Anyone interested in writing about transvestism may write to P.O. Box 141, Reading, Mass. 01867.''

⚥"I've considered transsexualism myself, would reconsider before doing it because the operation is irreversible. Don't see anything wrong with it.''

⚥ "If someone wants to change his or her sex, that's their business. I just get pissed off at straights who think that all gays wish they were the opposite sex."

⚥ "I don't understand it. Doctors are making a haul."

⚥ "Renée Richards is a very brave woman."

⚥ "Most transsexual cases I have known have been homophobic enough that I suspect it is a denial of homosexuality rather than an affirmation of gender identity. I think it has a lot to do with role identity rather than gender identity. The transsexuality specialist surgeon I knew was such a crazed, liberal, sexist pig, he only confirmed my worst suspicion about the role nature of transsexuality."

⚥ "I like my penis and the pleasure it gives me too much to consider cutting it off. I like living in a man's world too much to give it up. That's what transsexualism means to me."

⚥ "Sex-change surgery—yes, definitely, for those who want it and need it. It's too bad that the media exploit it, though. Sex change is no joke."

⚥ "A major issue I can't understand is why, after the surgery and hormones and all, transsexuals tend to ally themselves with the rougher, more vulgar element of the gay society. Hustlers, pimps, that kind of thing. If I were going to go through all that torment and pain and frustration and time and money, you can be sure I'd end up with guys of class on my side and not the pimps et al. Why go through all that just to denigrate one's self after completing the transition? I can't figure it out. I have personally known two changes here in Rochester and both were disastrous, one leading to a murder death. Such a waste."

⚥ "I wonder on a medical level what it does in terms of the potential long-term repercussions physically. The operation hasn't been around long enough to study the effects (of forty or fifty years) physically. I'm curious about this."

Toys, Pornography, Oils

The first dildo was probably a stick, a bone, or a phallic-shaped stone inserted and enjoyed by prehistoric man or woman. The genre has been perfected, and in modern American consumption society the items euphemistically known as "marital aids" fill whole catalogs and entire stores. Pornography is a major publishing and distribution industry involving huge sums of money, often with the participation of organized crime. For gay men, pornography is also an important source of reflection of fantasy and is actually quite popular. It is also controversial, involving such issues as the First Amendment, the concerns of puritanical religious crusaders, and recently the opposition of feminist-minded men and women who see it as a purveyor of roles, violence, and degradation. Oils and lotions are important lubricants in anal intercourse, but they also can enhance the appearance or aroma of the body or otherwise serve as an erotic aid. The use of toys, porn, and oils during masturbation is discussed in

Chapter 15. The charts below indicate *how often the respondents used these items during sex,* and *how they feel about them whether they use them or not:*

	ALWAYS	VERY FREQUENTLY	SOMEWHAT FREQUENTLY	SOMEWHAT INFREQUENTLY	VERY INFREQUENTLY	ONCE	NEVER
hand-held dildo (penis imitation)	0	2	1	6	11	6	75%
strap-on dildo	0	0	.5	.5	3	2	94
vibrator	0	.5	1	4	14	8	74
accu-jack	0	.5	0	1	2	2	94
cock ring	.5	5	5	6	17	8	59
nipple clamp	.5	1	2	3	5	2	87
oils	6	14	10	15	16	6	33
pornography	2	5	10	11	21	7	44

	VERY POSITIVE	SOMEWHAT POSITIVE	NEUTRAL	SOMEWHAT NEGATIVE	VERY NEGATIVE	NOT SURE
hand-held dildo	9	12	26	15	31	7%
strap-on dildo	5	6	23	18	40	8
vibrator	10	18	32	14	22	5
accu-jack	9	13	27	15	25	11
cock ring	12	19	27	12	21	8
nipple clamp	5	9	13	17	50	8
oils	33	26	24	4	8	5
pornography	20	29	28	8	10	4

Other objects mentioned in responses to this question include many of the items already covered under clothing fetishes; specific materials such as rubber, satin, silk, leather, nylon; various edibles including chocolate syrup, vegetables, fruit, honey, and whipped cream; mirrors; belts, ropes, collar, leash, mask, butt plug (a dildo that remains in place for hours),

parachute harness, and a toilet seat on legs. One man referred to "verbal pornography," which was covered under the subject "talking dirty."

These statistics indicate that many men who have positive feelings about toys have never had occasion to experience their use, or are shy about using them. The most noticeable discrepancy is in the category of "oils"; many men who recognize the positive attributes of oils nonetheless don't use them. The question was somewhat ambiguous in that it did not make a distinction between oils and other substances used primarily as a lubricant (such as KY surgical jelly or Vaseline petroleum jelly). In general, mechanical sex aids do not seem to be very popular. The first group of comments focuses on dildos, other toys and oils:

"I like the feeling of a dildo. I like to walk around with it inside. I have a friend who has a dildo which straps on and after I have it on we go out somewhere and it's fun to know something other people don't."

"Dildos are not a turn-on for me; I will use them on a partner if he wishes—but always a bit reluctantly, as I feel that a big dildo will stretch the rectum and lessen the sensation I get when I fuck him. My current lover is the only person I've allowed to use a dildo on me, because it excites him to see it go into my anus, but I don't really get anything from it."

"Recently purchased a Jac Pac and I think I still prefer masturbating to the Jac Pac."

"I rarely think about using extra sexual devices. It seems a little frightening to me, something like mechanized sex. An accu-jack reminds me of science fiction. Nipple clamps seem bizarre. I don't see the point in viewing pornography while having sex with someone in person. It is admitting that the partner is not furnishing enough stimulation. There is something pathetic about those pictures."

"A young Vietnamese boy who was the barber I went to in Vietnam used to turn me on intentionally with a hand-held vibrator he used to give all his customers a rubdown with. Since that time many years ago it's had a fascination for me. I've never used one but expect that it would be very nice."

"I like toys. The toy I'd most like to have if I had room for it is a swing on a wood frame. The swing's seat is leather-covered and has a dildo attached to it. I'm not into vibrators. Dildos—I like them black leather. I like black leather handcuffs, both the fleece-lined and rubber-lined. I dig whips and black leather paddles, but especially studded belts. Oils—I like '3-in-1' oil, the smell. . . . I like rubber sheets, baby bottles, and pacifiers. Chains turn me on too . . . enema equipment . . . I'd like to get a butt plug, especially one I've seen that attached to a pair of leather briefs. The studded belt and rubber sheets are basic necessities for my sex life."

"I like oil as a lubricant—coconut oil, almond oil, wheat-germ oil— massage as well as rubbing over genitals, and making it easier to rub genitals against one another's bodies."

"I have always been fascinated with 'toys' but in actual fact they

disgust me. The exception is toys that I myself have made—dildos, vibrators, etc., improvised at home. But I feel guilty about these and soon destroy them. The only toy I allow myself with others is a prophylactic. Someday my feelings may change."

⚥"Toys seem a bit sleazy."

⚥"I used a dildo a few times to get myself ready to take it up the ass, but it doesn't do anything for me."

⚥"Pornography is fun. Toys are for the people in the pornography, not for me."

⚥"I have no use for toys that are used for sex. They are inanimate objects and cannot transfer feelings to another person. The jackoff machine might give pleasure—I don't know. Pornography (soft-core), i.e., centerfolds of nude people, with hard-ons, people fucking, sucking, kissing—enjoying sex with love (not violence, S&M, etc.)—this kind of pornography is beautiful and essential to a person who does not have regular sex life, such as me, stuck out here 60 miles from any kind of sex. My bedroom walls are covered with centerfolds from *Playgirl* and *Mandate* magazines."

⚥"I have a terror of dildos, the result of being raped with a foot-long, 4-inch-wide one, which resulted in lengthy medical complications. I start to shiver and faint when I even see dildos in a porn shop. Pornography can be very arousing, but usually isn't, due to poor photography, poor writing, and uninspiring models."

⚥"My wife tried to use a dildo-vibrator up my rectum when our sex life began to decline. It's definitely not the same as a throbbing prick, is it?"

⚥"Cock rings initially add excitement to the situation (bondage?); they also build confidence that I can and will maintain an erection, lessening worry as to 'how I'm doing.' Nipple clamps (clothespins of varying tensions) are very exciting on nipples and also good to feel nipping at buttocks, inside of my thighs, and balls."

⚥"Oils, such as baby oil, did feel good one time. I mean this guy just spread baby oil all over him and me, and I got off on it. Sliding all over each other."

⚥"I think it would be fun to have a dildo to use on myself when I didn't have the real thing, but I have a fear that if I would die suddenly or have an accident and be hospitalized, someone would find it and I would be 'found out,' even after I was dead."

⚥"The dildos which I have seen look so repulsive that I cannot imagine getting any fun out of them, although I sometimes put the end of a broomstick, well greased, up the ass and find it very nice."

⚥"Toys? When you have a *man* to play with, dear, what *can* you want with toys? Dildos, I just can't understand at all. I mean if it isn't alive what use is it? Save the money and use a zucchini or something, though I can't see that either. I find cock rings irritating, though understandable. A man who uses one is telling me that I'm not exciting enough, he needs help, or he can't get it up. Oils might be nice once in a while, though I've never used

any, except of course to fuck with. Ditto porn. People who wear nipple clamps must like it; when people squeeze my tits it just hurts.''

The subject of pornography provided comments from users and nonusers. Some of the men described how they use it sexually, while others comment on pornography as a political and social issue. While some men were enthusiastic about the pleasure they get from using pornography, a number of men expressed a variety of objections.

☿ "Pornography is very important in my sex life. I like porn in all media—photos, films, stories, drawings, etc. I prefer soft-core to hard (i.e., I find soft-core more stimulating). I am not turned on much at all by what I call 'clinical' porn—the extreme hard-core variety where all shadows have been eliminated so as to leave nothing to the imagination. I don't think my imagination needs that much help.''

☿ "I have recently seen both a photographic essay and a pen-and-ink drawing essay which were sold as porn but which conveyed so much more a projection of feelings, responses, and intimacy than even the most positively imaged porn, that I felt a kind of aesthetic response which turned into arousal. These two essays in my mind had done what I've always asserted is possible and that is to use pornography as an artistic medium.''

☿ "Pornography has been around for a long time now. The only pornography which I would specifically take exception to, and would see rooted out and abolished (fat chance), would be that in which someone is an unwilling participant. If pornography didn't exist, we'd probably all be secretly inventing our own private forms.''

☿ "Very few films are 'heavy' enough for me—most S&M films I've seen seem faked to me. I've written my own 80-page fantasy novel, strictly for my own pleasure.''

☿ "I enjoy pornography a great deal and have a small collection of my own. If I'd been rich or if I were now, I would have bought a lot of it. On an erotic level, I find sexy pictures (especially of young guys) a turn-on and that's that. However, I am aware that the porno industry is full of devious types who exploit and rip people off. I always bristle with momentary guilt when I fork over $10 for some magazine. Or $30 for a movie.''

☿ "I enjoy all forms of pornography but I do not like to see it displayed in public where young people are exposed to it. It should be a real private thing and I think that we here in San Francisco have too much of it. I'm for closing most of the bookstores; after all, they all carry the same material.''

☿ "I don't think that violence in porn should ever be allowed, as well as the exploitation of the helpless, and in that I include the young. But I think all other porn should be sold freely, carefully categorized so that people's sensibilities are not offended.''

☿ "I like pornography if it's arty, but find that my main interest is in imagining what it would feel like to be the actors (models?). Freaky, huh?''

⚣"Pornography (movies and magazines) is virtually my entire sex life as I have no partner and don't foresee ever having one."

⚣"I don't buy it. I do a lot of browsing. Pornography does humanity a grave disservice by depicting sex without any emotion or feelings, failing to convey the ecstasy that is possible between two people who care about each other as total personalities. A lot of gays never grow beyond this narrow crippled view of sex."

⚣"I hate the way so much pornography depicts the models as 'straight.' Gay men really put themselves down when they need to think that the guy in the picture is 'straight" in order to be aroused. That kind of porn should be boycotted."

⚣"Tasteful, suggestive (Colt, Target) I like, but 99% of porn I've seen is laughable, not erotic."

⚣"Porn is healthy, but kiddie porn is wrong on principle. To be honest, I saw a gay kiddie porn flick recently, my first, and I turned on. But I'm not happy about it."

⚣"Pornography is very stimulating and may help in getting rid of many problems, like being shy and self-conscious, etc. It is also quite educational, I think."

⚣"At the age of 10 or so I discovered—believe it or not—Bernard MacFadden's *Physical Culture.* It was Depression and I had to sneak into the drugstore to glance through the mags. The underwear ads in the Montgomery Ward and Sears catalogs were a little help."

⚣"I usually initiate our love encounters by discreetly placing some magazines featuring male bodies or explicit acts (*Playgirl* is a good example) in my bedroom or nearby to get him in the mood."

⚣"I love pornography. I've even done some, both being the principal and being on the other side of the lens. There is a certain degree of safety in watching two other men fuck and fantasizing myself into the situation. I have a copy of the film I was in and watch it occasionally; I can't exactly say that I am proud I did it, but seeing the film and knowing that there are other men out there beating off while I go through my performance for the zillionth time provides a great deal of satisfaction."

⚣"What I most resent about porn is the way it depicts healthy, spiritually uplifting acts as violent/dirty/objectified/disgusting. I also have to wonder whether this kind of porn could be a factor in a man's decision to rape (a violent/dirty/objectified/disgusting act). Again, if there were no strictures against 'obscenity' I think there would be a movement toward nonobscene erotica and the market for porn would be transformed into art."

⚣"Pornography should be totally legalized as it is in most northern European countries. What I don't like is the wealth that is accumulated by the publishers and distributors."

⚣"I enjoy pornography, since I am in the closet. It provides a release for me when my tearoom is closed for the winter."

⚤ "What is pornography? Pictures or words of sex? I love pornography! Pictures or words of brutality? In that definition, I hate pornography!''

⚤ "Pornography I am not interested in; indeed, I agree with straights that it's sick.''

⚤ "I feel pornography is a valid form of entertainment and I'm opposed to all attempts to eliminate it or modify it. The negative attitude surrounding pornography is just another example of our society's sexual neuroses. As long as those who don't like it don't have to see it, they have no right preventing others from doing so. They don't have to look.''

Threesomes and Orgies

Sexual relationships usually involve two people, but the idea of more than two people having sex seems to be exciting to many men. More than three-fourths of the men in the survey have experienced it at least once. The following chart indicates *how often respondents experience threesomes and orgies,* following by a chart indicating *their feelings about multiple-partner sex:*

	ALWAYS	VERY FREQUENTLY	SOMEWHAT FREQUENTLY	SOMEWHAT INFREQUENTLY	VERY INFREQUENTLY	ONCE	NEVER
threesomes	1	5	10	20	32	9	24%
orgies or group sex	1	4	6	16	24	8	42

	VERY POSITIVE	SOMEWHAT POSITIVE	NEUTRAL	SOMEWHAT NEGATIVE	VERY NEGATIVE	NOT SURE
threesomes	26	35	19	9	8	2%
orgies or group sex	23	30	21	12	11	3

In Chapter 9, several men describe how they use threesomes to spice up their sex lives with their lovers. Here are some more general comments and experiences with threesomes:

⚒ "Threesomes are beautiful. My lover and I have never indulged in them, possibly because I'm younger and more physically fit, and it would be unpleasant for us both if a third party turned his attention predominantly towards me in my lover's presence. There should be an etiquette to threesomes; if two lovers invite a third to play, both lovers should concentrate on the third party, and the third party should attend equally to both hosts. Secret affinities should be explored one-to-one later. This leaves no one out in the cold. It takes a kind of saint to see his lover wrapped up in a twosome that began as a threesome, and for said saint to sit back and jerk off or toddle off to read a book. (I've heard of it happening, however.) The threesomes I've engaged in have gone splendidly; everybody knew the etiquette."

⚒ "The three of us meet in my dorm room, and proceed to kiss and gradually to undress one another. We hesitate as soon as we have each other's shirts off. We stop again when only our undershorts remain, taking time to explore one another's bodies with hands and tongues. We move to the bed and lie down, then tease each other's cocks, tickling them with tongue and fingers, finally with each of us on his side, emerging into three-sided 69—slowly at first, then with increasing passion. Once we have come, we kiss, much more slowly and deeply, then Lito rolls onto his stomach, Warren mounts him from the rear, and I mount Warren, trying to keep Lito excited by playing with his cock. We try to be gentle and considerate with one another. We prefer lights on. Feelings: magnificent—simultaneous sex with highly proficient partners."

⚒ "Often I have been picked up by two lovers and had a wildly good time."

⚒ "My lover and I tried a threesome once with a friend. We liked it better between ourselves since including another person added the task of learning new pleasure points for him."

⚒ "Threesomes—three is a crowd."

⚒ "Threesomes are okay but I don't like pairing off, and never do it myself, although I have been in a few that have, with strong feelings toward resentment afterwards."

⚒ "I've done threesomes and I like it, if everyone's 'vibrations' (for want of a better word) are in tune. In each of the threesomes I've been involved in, I've always been 'the ham in the sandwich,' so to speak. Unless two guys are romantically involved with each other I think sex-for-sex's-sake really ought to involve three or more people as often as possible."

The following are "pleasing experiences" involving unusual sorts of three-way sex encounters. The first features anal intercourse involving two penises penetrating at the same time; the second involves sex with two men and a woman:

⚒ "One very pleasing sexual experience was with a sexual partner *and* my

lover. My lover had invited him home and we both found him very desirable (having been together almost four years we knew each other's preferences). The most pleasing aspect of this encounter was when my lover and I fucked him at the same time. While it was difficult, we did accomplish it—to everyone's pleasure. My lover and I sat facing each other, legs over each other, so our cocks were together. Our new friend crouched over us and straddled us both and sat on my dick first (as I am the larger) and then took some poppers and sat on my lover's dick at the same time. It was great and he loved it, as did we. Obviously to keep in him we had to remain fairly still, but he didn't. He moved up and down at will and as deeply as he could stand. We were also able to masturbate him while fucking him and he obtained orgasm that way. We reached orgasm while fucking him. This was in 1975, and I never had a more pleasing sexual encounter since.''

⚥ "About a year and a half ago I had the great fortune of making love with two people I love most. Bob and I had known each other for about a year and had become very close; Mary and I had been having a very intense emotional and physical relationship for about five months. Bob and Mary had known each other almost as long as she and I had. We had talked about having a three-way many times; none of us participated in male-female group sex, but Bob and I had had all-male group sex. Mary had participated in no group sex at all and had never made love with a female. Also, Bob was living with a woman at the time. Mary was 26, Bob was 24, and I was 39.

"This particular night we had gone to a party and had ended the evening at my house at about midnight and until dawn we made love, then slept a couple of hours and made love again. The experience was very intense for all of us.

"We began with Mary in the middle of the bed; we had music, probably Dan Fogelberg or Judy Collins. It started slow and easy, touching and kissing, exploring and tasting; we also smoked a couple of joints during this time (we'd been smoking earlier, too). Most of the night is hazy but there are a couple of things I do remember. Mary was lying on her back; I was fucking her and Bob was fucking me. Mary had her legs around my waist and Bob was holding us both. I remember that Mary and I had orgasms but I don't remember if Bob came. For me it was extremely extremely pleasurable. I really dig being fucked while fucking. I rested awhile as Bob sucked Mary's clitoris. He particularly likes cunnilingus.

"Sometime later, just before we slept, we all came at the same time. I was fucking Mary, and Bob was masturbating while watching and touching us. Mary was vocalizing at tremendous pitch—it was intense as hell and we came together. Our energies were pretty much spent and we lay as close together as we could get. I remember that just before I dozed off, I flashed that if I died right then it would be okay. I had experienced perfection.''

Commenting on orgies, Allen Ginsberg, the gay poet, once said, "It's an important human experience to relate to yourself and others as a hunk of

meat sometimes.'' Ginsberg called it "one holy divine yoga of losing ego,'' and said that experiencing "orgiastic anonymity'' can be a valuable lesson "as long as you don't get trapped into that all the time as a single level of consciousness—as some queens do.'' Orgies for gay men take place regularly in the baths, in certain back-room bars (with virtually no lighting), and sometimes in outdoor cruising spots at parks and beaches. They can also be organized or spontaneous events in people's homes. Here are some of the comments on orgies:

⚥"Orgies can be wonderful. I used to attend a weekly one in the Boston area, usually able to avoid the participants I didn't find attractive. That's the thing about orgies—ideally they should include a bunch of men who are almost all mutually turned on. It's not fun to reject others or be rejected, and that can be avoided by a well planned orgy.''

⚥"I once went to an orgy that included gay men, lesbians, and so-called liberated straights. One horny straight guy had a great time screwing a married woman under the careful supervision of her husband, two lesbians found each other and fell madly in love and had a million orgasms, but for the rest of us it wasn't terribly exciting. The atmosphere was friendly, however.''

⚥"I like being the center of attention at orgy bars.''

⚥"I enjoy sex with any number of people. I know what you mean by threesomes and orgies, but my definition is different. As a rule I never pick up less than two tricks at a time, sometimes more. A friend's house is used with more than four or six. We gather up in his bedroom and put on stag movies, and he and I start sucking to see who can get the most fastest. I usually win, because he has to change the movies, ha ha ha . . . I do have one brother act, as we call them. The one brother, 23, gets sucked, fucked, and rimmed, by me, while the other brother watches and beats off. I never get to touch the brother. He says he doesn't like to get his cock sucked but he gets off on watching his brother get fucked.''

⚥"The only group I have been in was about seven of us in our teens. We masturbated to see who would shoot first and how much.''

⚥"I morally object to orgies because of my religious beliefs.''

⚥"I can see how orgies would be innocent enough, but for me they would ride roughshod over my need for privacy and one-to-one communication, so I view them dimly.''

⚥"Orgies—l'amour, the merrier. When I was really swinging in New York, I used to host one every Saturday night, and they were legendary. Between fifteen and twenty-five people, but everyone had to participate. No onlookers. Great fun and totally free. That was right after my divorce, and when I was sampling the joys of freedom. Later, I settled down with a lover.''

⚥"I don't have one 'lover' or even a number of people who are my 'lover' in the usual sense of the word. I have a circle of close friends and it is my expectation that I will have close relationships and sex with many of my friends, in various combinations. It is like an extended marriage, but not a

marriage. At times I have sex with this one or that one. At other times, we have sex in groups. Once, I came in and found two folks making love in the living room and two more on the other side of the same room making love. I joined one couple, and the other couple joined us, and so we had five people sucking and fucking and kissing together. This is always wonderful. Sometimes, we have had anal intercourse in rows of four or five to see how it would feel. I feel fine about it. When we get together and do sex in large groups, I feel we are breaking down barriers that others have put up. I feel that we are finding ways to relate that come organically from our needs, rather than from some television-Amerikan role model set out in front of us. We like to go bowling together; we like to dance in groups; we like to get stoned together; we like to go swimming together; we like to be all together; so who says we should only have sex in twos? So we don't! We experiment with having sex in groups. Politically, I suppose it is positive. But politics isn't important here. It just feels great, so we do it over and over. I love doing sex all together. I also find that I am less uptight about 'performance' when we are all sharing sex than when I am just one-on-one with one lover.''

♂"Once in New York, where I had an apartment on Riverside Drive, with a large circular terrace overlooking the Hudson River, I took a group of friends, including my then lover and a couple of other people I either had, or wanted to, sleep with (bad grammar there, but I can't get out of it) back to the apartment after a day at the World War II bare-ass beach (Point Lookout, beyond Jones Beach on Long Island's South Shore). I made a big pitcher of white wine and soda, and we all sipped away. When we moved the party out to the terrace, it began to turn into an orgy, totally unplanned. Gene, my lover, and I went into a 69, and soon found our respective asses being penetrated by someone. So here we were a foursome sandwich, with Gene and I in the middle sucking each other off, which was pleasant, and each of us being fucked by a good friend. Here again, all four of us came damned close to simultaneous orgasm: at least it was within seconds of each other. An explosive, unforgettable experience.''

Rape and the Question of Consent

In recent years, several state statutes dealing with rape have, for the first time, included male-male rape. Historically, rape laws were passed by men as a means to protect "their women," that is, "their property." The imposition of sex without consent between men, sometimes involving a weapon, is not nearly so common as heterosexual rape, if only because the status of the woman as the "weaker" sex is more institutionalized. But the identification of some men as weaker than others is not that difficult; indeed, labels like "faggot" and "sissy" and "queer" contain within them notions of weakness.

Male-male rape is a topic that has been virtually untouched by the gay media, except in articles about men in prison, and in those articles the

assumption always is that the rapist is not gay but a frustrated heterosexual. In fact, many men have been raped or forced to have sex (especially when younger and inexperienced), and while rape is not commonplace, these statistics indicate it occurs with alarming frequency in the gay male community. In addition to real-life rape situations, rape as a subject for fantasy is not unusual (see Chapter 15), though fantasy and reality are by no means the same. Some respondents indicated, however, a close correlation between rape and rape fantasies, and it is possible that psychodramatic rape scenes are reflected in the statistics, though these would seem substantially different from a situation in which real violence or the threat of real violence play a role in nonconsensual sex. Some of the quotations indicate that for some respondents the term "rape" included play-acting, persuasion, or a situation that ended up as consensual. Some men noted that rape could refer to the forcing of a specific sexual act, i.e., anal sex, in an otherwise consensual encounter. A very liberal definition of the term "rape" might well include anything that happens sexually without explicit consent.

Indicating *their experience with rape,* 18% said they had been raped and 82% said they had not.

Of those who had been raped, 62% experienced it once, 15% twice, 8% three times, 6% four times, 8% five times, and 2% "several times." There were several men who filled out the survey who might be called "rapists," or who at least stated they had forced others to have sex with them; 4% said they had raped or forced another man. Most of these men did not indicate whether they did this frequently or not, or whether the rape was truly forced and violent or rather a fantasy enactment. Questioned about *their feelings about raping or getting raped,* the respondents indicated the following:

	VERY POSITIVE	SOMEWHAT POSITIVE	NEUTRAL	SOMEWHAT NEGATIVE	VERY NEGATIVE	NOT SURE
forcing someone to have sex	3	5	4	11	76	1%
being forced to have sex	2	3	5	10	79	2

There were a number of experiences and comments concerning rape, attempted rape, and forced sex:

&"I was raped by a hetero-macho fucked-up faggot who convincingly posed as a gay man. Very violent."

&"The fantasy may be very exciting, but any situation even approaching reality provokes a very negative reaction."

♂"I forced a person to have sex with me and I'm now in a state hospital."

♂"I myself enjoy being raped if I like the looks of the guy. But I don't like to force myself on anyone."

♂"If the cock is cut and a good size it could be enjoyable in spite of being forced."

♂"Rape is a terrible experience for the one who's raped. It's a very negative idea to me to force sex. I admit I enjoy reading about it though. Single or gang rape is a very stimulating subject to read about, and teenage, military, prison, whatever gangbangs give me a hard-on. Recently an item appeared in the newspaper that a forest ranger had been abducted and raped. I wish they'd given more detailed information, like by whom, etc. It sounds like a sexy choice of victim. Rape of females is a completely negative idea to me in contrast to being stimulated by reading of homosexual rape."

♂"I was walking home late one night and I had to pass by a bunch of blacks, who were sitting on their porch. As I passed a girl (black) called me and I stopped. She called me to come up on the porch, and I did. Well, three or four of the guys held me and took all my clothes off. One of the girls said, 'Hey you guys, fuck him.' So that night I think I got fucked over twenty times and sucked all their peters the same, and I had to suck all the girls' pussies and assholes and even while I was getting fucked the girls would squat over my face and piss in my mouth making me drink it, or they would just piss all over me. The guys would piss in my mouth while I was sucking them off. I still don't know how many cocks I had in me that night, or how many cunts I had to suck, but what really got me was I never came once or even got to fuck any of them so I went on home, but I stopped in an alley to jack off."

♂"My scariest experience was with an ex-convict who thought he was going to rape me. I fought back and nearly didn't win. We were wrestling around on the floor and I managed to kick him in the chest, which threw him off me long enough to find a weapon—a stainless-steel letter opener. I hit him very hard with it against his chest hoping to find the space between his ribs and into his heart. I didn't but the force of it threw him backward and as he came up on his knees I sliced it across his throat. There was enough of a cutting edge to draw blood and scare him and I marched him at letter-opener-point out of the building. I have wanted to kill people in the abstract before but it was never real until then. The moment of going for his heart taught me that I can be coldly willing to kill another person. Not very good news."

♂"Two muggers waiting in the elevator forced me into my apartment, bound me, gagged me, and began to taunt me. 'Faggot! Would you suck my cock? Would you like dick up your ass?' I was terrified they would rape me, so I play-acted a heart attack, which frightened them off."

♂"I personally cannot get behind sex where my partner(s) is (are) not willing. Even in S&M and B&D situations I've been in, there was, of course, a tacit understanding that both parties were there for the same thing and

that, for the most part, any 'forced' sex was an enactment of a fantasy. The line between fantasy and reality here is very important.''

⚥ "At age 19, I was arrested by someone claiming to be a police officer who threatened to take me to jail if I didn't cooperate. It was a traumatic experience and I know now that if I hadn't been young and naive I wouldn't have submitted to such a gross personal violation.''

⚥ "I was raped as a child and forced to have sex a few years ago. Two of the most negative traumas of my life. Rape probably kept me in the closet a lot longer.''

⚥ "Occasionally rape refers to a specific activity after general agreement for sex is reached (e.g., one partner doesn't want to get fucked).''

⚥ "I was raped by a former 'boy friend' who happened to be horny at 2:00 a.m. and still had the key to my apartment. It was an act of disgusting brutality and typical of the American male philosophy of the domination of the weaker.''

⚥ "Using forceful persuasion on straight guys—getting them to reciprocate a blow job—is extremely rewarding.''

⚥ "The scariest experience I ever had was when I went home with an ordinary man who turned out to be a sadist. When I told him I wasn't into S&M he raped me with a huge dildo, hit me, forced me to inhale amyl nitrite, and threatened to gouge my eyes out. The experience was bizarre in another way: my rapist, I am now convinced, did not believe he was raping me. I think he believed my protests were all part of 'the game.' At least when it was over, he acted quite natural, with no indication that he realized I was in a state of horror and revulsion. I've been infinitely more cautious about sex with strangers since this experience.''

⚥ "I had someone pull a knife purportedly to heighten sexual pleasure, at which time I incapacitated him and left.''

⚥ "My most unusual and traumatic experience occurred when I was quite young. I'd gone to the Lundine Baths in Boston, was really quite inexperienced and naive. I was raped by seven or eight men, older than myself. At least, they held me down, as each took turns. I can't say I screamed for help, though I begged them for mercy, to go slowly and be more gentle. They were not in the least caring. They'd got themselves a chicken and silently and methodically they broke me in. It hurt at first but I got used to it, and now it is a rather exciting memory. At the time, I think it was frightening, perhaps because they all seemed so determined and so silent, none of them responding to my pleas to take it easy.''

⚥ "Scariest experience? That's easy. Getting gang-raped sixty times in two days by blacks in a big-city jail. I was afraid for my life.''

⚥ "I was dragged up a stairway and raped when I was about 12 years old, way before puberty—probably set my coming out back two years. I was petrified, and extremely upset. I couldn't understand what was happening, although I had the idea that whatever it was it was something that did not happen to males. As a result I kept that secret inside myself for about four years.''

⚭"A young man in Houston found my phone number on the wall of a public rest room and called me up. We quickly decided we were compatible, but my warped mind went wild over the anonymity of the situation. I proposed the following, and this is how our many encounters over the next several months went. The other man, known only as RV1, left his back door unlocked and went to bed, and I came over and raped him. I left without him ever seeing me (this relationship went on for several months and he never saw me). The encounters got more and more bizarre and imaginative. Once I played on his stereo a record of twenty minutes of howling wolves while I fucked him savagely, scratching his back with my fingernails."

⚭"Once with my ex-lover, we were wrestling in the nude and he got me in a hold with my face in his crotch that I couldn't get out of. He told me that I couldn't get away until I blew him. I did, of course. It was the closest thing to being forced into sex that I've ever had, and I still have occasional fantasies about it. The fact that he had complete control was the big turn-on."

⚭"The act of rape is an insult to the process of love."

Keeping It Secret

Many of the sexual practices discussed in this chapter, as has been shown, are not looked upon very favorably by a majority, even in the gay community. For this reason, many people who may be openly gay are not open about these sexual preferences. In response to a question about what aspects of their sex lives they keep secret, many men commented on their unusual predilections:

⚭"I'm ashamed of my tendency towards transvestism."

⚭"I think I could go for a highly passive role and even be an M but only in fantasy. My self-respect could never permit me to go this route in bed. It's a real hangup with me."

⚭"I could get into drag if I had the right body for it, but I am very tall and masculine-looking."

⚭"I'm not exactly secret, but I'm not really always open about my S&M tendencies. Allen Young's negative comments have been an influence on this as well as many of the negative comments by much of the gay left. I don't like not being open, but I also don't want to always justify my sexuality to my gay left brothers."

⚭"Bestiality—fucking a heifer."

⚭"That I've had one experience with a pet dog."

⚭"Receive a lot of gay magazines—pornographic and others. Have fear of family finding out although I now live alone. I've never told a straight person I was gay other than a psychiatrist."

⚭"Slight masochistic tendencies I do not speak of too openly—result of bourgeois upbringing.

⚭"S&M, B&D—I anticipate a put-down."

⚭"I am a closet bondage freak. I enjoy being tied up and often

masturbate this way. I've only been honest enough to tell one partner and the reality did not live up to the fantasy, although he was very supportive. Sometimes I'm guilty about bondage and then feel guilty about being ashamed."

⚥"I'm somewhat secretive about S&M to nongays because it requires more explanation than I care to bother with."

⚥"I don't widely publicize that I can enjoy water sports and scat. These I do only with like-minded guys."

⚥"Leather, because it's too kinky for most of my friends (gay or straight) to accept."

14

Lesbian Fantasies and
Self-Pleasuring

An Overview

Fantasies make the life of many people more enjoyable. All people have probably fantasized or day-dreamed at one time or another about "what life would be like if . . ." Or they may have gone over pleasurable experiences, and relived them in their imaginations.

Fantasies probably play a more important part in the life of women than in the life of men in general because women have been kept by men in the role of *dreamer* rather than of *actor*. They have been cast as the Sleeping Beauty or Snow White who waits passively for Prince Charming to come. They have been programmed to look pretty and wait for "Mr. Right" to come along to take care of their problems. Mr. Right is always idealized and perfect, as compared to women's helpless and imperfect selves.

Fantasy did play an important part in the masturbatory life of the lesbians who answered the questionnaire. They were asked, *How often do you fantasize during masturbation?*

always	35%
very frequently	30
somewhat frequently	12
somewhat infrequently	6
very infrequently	9
once	0
never	8

The respondents were then asked, *Whether or not you fantasize, how do you feel about the idea of fantasizing?*

very positive	63%
somewhat positive	23

neutral	11
somewhat negative	1
very negative	1
not sure	1

It is significant, though, that most of the lesbians did not transform this programmed dream into one about an imaginary "Ms. Right." In addition, very few of the lesbians fantasized about real female media stars. This lack of star worship is probably due to the fact that the media present lesbians with very few strong women worthy of adoration or emulation.

In addition to the fact that very few media personalities are interesting to them, lesbians also know that they have, in the final analysis, only themselves to depend on for economic support. They do not have the legal or economic protection of marriage, and the women they meet are most likely to be in the same income bracket—at the bottom of the world's economic ladder.

Personality Fantasies

One of the appealing features of dreams is that they do take people where they cannot go in real life, and a small percentage of those who answered the question on fantasies did mention specific media figures, including Farrah Fawcett-Majors, Audrey Hepburn, Mary Tyler Moore, Joan Baez, and Bonnie Raitt. One man, Mick Jagger, was also mentioned once. The only personalities included from the lesbian movement were one mention each of Rita Mae Brown and Karla Jay! About Rita Mae Brown, a woman wrote:

♀"My fantasy is always or most always about Rita Mae Brown. I've read her books and I like what she has to say. I met her once and can't seem to get her out of my mind. To be delicate—I'd like to do everything and anything with her."

Another woman wrote about her fantasy about Emmylou Harris:

♀"My fantasy about Emmylou was this: Somewhat sketchy is my memory, but I drove to her house in Bel Air. I got in the big gate, but the guard would not let me in the house to see her. I was frustrated over my attempts to explain to the guard that I was expected, but he was adamant in not allowing me to even speak to Emmylou. As I began to cry and get very upset, she finally came out to see about the hassle and waved the guard away very exasperatedly. She invited me in. The house was beautiful, yet funky. She took my hand and led me straight to her bedroom, which was messy but nicely furnished and well decorated. I went to bed with her and was very excited but there was no sex. I was engulfed with love and devotion for her, but she used me for that one night and that was all. I remember feeling crushed when my dream ended."

Current, Past, and "Future" Lovers

The most common masturbatory fantasy was one in which a lesbian fantasizes about her current or previous lover. Here are some examples:

♀"If I fantasize during masturbation, it is always about a woman with whom I'm involved or with whom I want to be involved. Generally, it is my making love to a woman, *never* being made love to."

♀"Most often I fantasize about the person I love when I can't be with her. People without fantasy are *boring.*"

♀"I fantasize penetrating partner rectally using one finger. Always works."

♀"My fantasies are rarely a complete story with beginning and end, but are mostly just flashes of scenes, positions, etc. Lately my fantasies are simply a mental reliving of a recent sexual experience. My latest fantasy (and one which I hope will happen soon) is simply myself lying on my back, giving oral sex to my lover, who is 'sitting' on me.

"Lots of my fantasies involve my lover 'offering' herself to me—i.e., cupping a breast and holding it out to me; propping a pillow under her rear and holding herself 'open' for me. . . . Such actions, when they actually occur, simply melt me. I become overwhelmed with the vulnerability of the position the person puts herself into. I have, on occasion, made such 'offerings' of myself, but obviously only when I was fairly sure I would not be rejected. The trust level must be high, I think, for this to happen. Such actions occupy a large part of my fantasy life."

Variations included exotic places, as in the following fantasy:

♀"My favorite fantasy with my lover is we're on this deserted island, all alone, and we're making love several times a day and night. We never put on clothes at all, as we both love to be naked together."

Here's another variation in which the respondent imagines several of her lovers making love to each other without her participation:

♀"Because I am still attracted to lovers of other years and new women but cannot sustain a sexual relationship which would be satisfying to any of them, I have encouraged several to get to know each other with fairly happy results, and one of my most successful fantasies is staging their lovemaking with each other, knowing as much as I do about their sexual tastes. Part of the pleasure is recalling to me of my own pleasure with each of them. I sometimes put myself into the scene but almost always am an observer because my fantasies seem to need to be grounded in what is actually

possible. The particular pleasure of the observer is to be able to see an act one is usually too involved in to be able to enjoy the shapes of bodies, the marvelous abandon and inventiveness of sexual appetite, and if one observes two women one finds attractive and has experienced long hours of lovemaking, the pleasure is intense.''

♀"Once or twice I've fantasized about watching two friends of mine (who are not, by the bye, lovers) have sex, and found this very exciting, oddly enough, although I haven't been part of a *ménage à trois*. Those fantasies have not involved any imagined participation on my part, but rather just an arousing fantasy about how these two women might make love with one another.''

One woman fantasized about both her male and female lovers:

♀"My fantasy during masturbation is always about one of two people—my male ex-lover or my female ex-lover. They were the two people I loved best in my life. With the male I fantasize us reliving an actual lovemaking experience. The female one is always the way I wish we had been—on the beach at night with her going down on me very gently.''

The second most common fantasy was about an imagined or potential lover, or about someone who was the object of a ''crush.''

♀"My favorite and most common fantasy during masturbation is one where I make love with a girl I know from my hometown. She is everything I'm looking for in a lover, and we have a lot in common. She is quite the foxy chick, too. Anyway the fantasy is like this. We are lovers living together here in my apartment. We decide to make love with each other and do. We both enjoy it very much and love each other very much.

"My feeling about this fantasy is merely one of self-enlightenment. I think it's more a desire to have this situation come true than a fantasy for entertainment or whatever.''

♀"I tried to pick up a woman in May, and ever since I've been thinking about her. She has very pleading, large eyes.''

♀"One favorite is that I'm busy doing something around the apartment when someone I know but whom I'm not expecting enters the apartment unannounced. She comes up behind me and starts feeling my body. I just stand there, not resisting and not helping. She pulls off my shirt, but remains behind, fondling my breasts, then unfastening my jeans and letting them drop to the floor. She then moves a little to the side, bringing her hand up between my legs. One hand stays with my breasts as she brings me to climax with the other hand. Then she slips out and I never see her.''

♀"My fantasies are nearly all about women who are sexually unavailable to me, especially straight women, but also gay women who are not in-

terested because of another attachment or some other reason. I just imagine having sex with them, nothing elaborate.''

♀"I usually try to visualize some woman to whom I am currently attracted and I run a whole scenario through my head and often think of myself as being on an outing with this woman. We are walking in the woods on a clear, warm day. We have a picnic and talk and really feel close emotionally and spiritually. We look into one another's eyes and she is prompted to reach out her hand and touch my face and stroke my hair. I lift my face to look at hers, and in tears, find our lips on one another's, and we are embracing and caressing each other. Then my mind 'hops' to us on a blanket in these woods or a little clearing. We are both naked now, and as my mind continues to see us making love I begin to physically run my hands over my body as I fantasize her doing. I usually embrace my pillow and pretend that is the lover. From there I get into masturbating because I am usually aroused by then. I have good feelings about fantasy because it is all I've ever really had. I hope I can make it a reality one day soon.''

S&M and Rape Fantasies

Other types of fantasy are less common. Among them are fantasies involving sadomasochism, bondage and discipline, or rape. Several points emerged from these fantasies. First, the women who had these fantasies were not necessarily the same women who were actually involved in S&M or B&D, and the women who wrote these fantasies usually also explained that they did not participate in these activities in their actual sex lives. They pointed out—correctly—that fantasies are not the same as reality, and having a rape fantasy, for example, is not the same thing as wishing to be raped. Moreover, all the women in these fantasies played the part of the victim/masochist/slave and not one was the master/sadist/rapist.

♀"One of my favorites is being handcuffed by a woman and told to 'come here' as she sits on my pillow couch. On the end table she has Vaseline, a rubber glove, and a paddle. She is also wearing a dildo, inside her pants. I come over, with hands handcuffed behind my back, facing her. She opens the snap and zipper of my pants and tells me to bend over her knee. I do this. She reaches with her left hand under me, down in my pants, and stimulates my clit as I'm bent over her. With her right hand she pulls down my pants and begins paddling me, yelling obscenities, thereby pressing me on and off her left hand in front. She then gets rougher and rougher, puts on the rubber glove, lubricates it, and penetrates me anally, still stimulating my clitoris with her left hand. She yells at me to 'move faster' to the fucking and her language gets more and more aggressive until finally she tells me to get on top of the back pillow which is down on the seat part of the couch. As I crawl with hands handcuffed up onto the pillow with the top portion of my body in a bent-over position, she keeps her fingers in

my anus, almost using that to push me up over the pillow. She then quickly pulls my pants all the way off, spreads my buttocks, and whips out her dildo, fucking me violently while using abusive language and also with her hands extended around me, stimulating my clit.''

♀"I am walking through the woods, and suddenly get attacked by a band of women athletes, who take me into their cottage and molest me. Usually I fantasize that one of the women sits on me facing my face and makes me lick her to orgasm. In a variant of this, I have to lick her while she is having her period. For some reason I am the victim in all my scenarios, although I can, at will, transfer my point of view to that of the attackers.

"As to my feelings, fantasies are God's gift to men and women, because you can do literally *anything* you want in the privacy of your own brain. But sometimes I worry that mine are so untender, although in real life I am very gentle. I think the reason is not that I really want to be in a victim situation, but that when you are stimulating yourself, you sometimes have to remove the responsibility from yourself: it is not I, but these fantasy creatures, who are creating my orgasm. When I fantasize, I lose all sense of my right hand, which is actually doing all the work. It has become something apart from and independent of my body. Without this voluntary self-alienation, I cannot come.''

♀"My masturbation fantasies are invariably masochistic. They involve a woman (whose part I play, although she is not myself) who is sexually abused by men, and through men, by animals. They involve a great deal of humiliation and pain, and never enjoyment. I have never understood why I have these fantasies, but have gone through many changes in my attitudes toward them. When I was young, I was very ashamed of masturbating (though nobody had said outright it was wrong), and every time I 'gave in' it was an admission of vile weakness. I blamed all sorts of external occurrences on these lapses of self-control. Gradually I came to claim the act as my own sexual right (after I had become involved with a woman, and had become more sexually aware), though I was still uncomfortable with the content of the fantasy. I tried to invent more 'politically correct' fantasies, but none of them worked for me. Now I feel that my fantasies are merely a means for me to get the sexual satisfaction I want from masturbation; they are the only methods that work, and as long as I realize that their content is not indicative of some secret desire to be raped, they don't bother me. It's taken me a long time to get to the point of accepting my fantasies, since there is not much support, even in women's culture, for masochistic fantasies—but I feel strongly that they are right with me.''

♀"I really hate S&M. My masturbation fantasies, however, are along the lines of exhibitionism and being manipulated sexually by others for their pleasure (and mine) without really doing anything.''

♀"I imagine that I am back in junior high school and am forced to wear a machine attached to my clitoris that constantly stimulates me while in class. At any moment I will be forced to climax in front of my classmates, and must try to control myself so as not to disturb the class.''

Exhibitionism

These last two fantasies lead us to the next category, which is one where the respondent fantasizes that she is being seen while having sex or masturbating.

♀"I am walking across a campus at night with someone I know. As we're walking and talking, she reaches over and unbuttons my shirt, just letting it hang open. Nothing more happens until someone walks past and notices this. Next she unsnaps and unzips my pants, then sticks her hand into the front of my pants, pushing the open shirt aside with her arm to expose a breast. We then walk until someone notices this and reacts quite violently. It usually never needs to go any further than that."

♀"During masturbation my fantasies center on exhibitionism. Generally people who I don't know watch me perform."

♀"Occasionally I imagine a stranger walking in while I'm masturbating (male or female, it doesn't matter) or someone looking in a window."

Fantasies About Men

A few women fantasized having sex with men. Again, fantasy is not the same as reality, and the respondent was not necessarily a bisexual or a latent heterosexual.

♀"I feel guilty about the theme material of my fantasy because it seems a betrayal of my chosen life, but I understand why I have the need for this fantasy, and it's a deep need because the fantasy has gone on for several years with just minor changes in plot/background.

"I have a large studio, where I paint, sculpt. A man, another artist, is watching me work (sometimes I am modeling for him, but usually I'm working). The man is physically very large, bearded, obviously masculine. As I work, I become very aware that I am exciting him. I continue to work, pretending I don't notice. Somehow the transition is made (I skip thinking *how*), and we are in bed. He has a huge erection, and obviously wants me but is eating me. Just as he has given me an orgasm, *I let* him enter me and have a second huge orgasm. The only thing I have against fantasy is that mine are so *obvious*!"

♀"My fantasy involves replaying scenes of making love with my male ex-lover, even though in real life I felt somehow pornographic and objectified. I fantasize that I am turning him on by moving seductively, slowly taking my clothes off, driving him crazy—watching him start to writhe about in front of me, moaning and reaching for me, grabbing my waist (things which I find mildly disgusting in real life). All the while, I'm laughing to myself, as I know I have complete power over him. He needs me, but I don't need him. I am a lesbian, and women are far more beautiful to me. Male sexuality is exciting, but icky. Then I undo my shirt and move my breasts against his

bare chest. He becomes more and more helpless and animallike, panting and salivating. I rip his pants off and make him stand away from me, his penis in a large erection. He is getting desperate as I sway and writhe naked in front of him, moving my pelvis around and hugging and stroking myself in a very sensual sort of dance (that I really needed to do when masturbating at age 20 or so). He cannot stand it any more and starts grasping his own penis frantically as I lie in front of him, rotating my pelvis so he can see my genitals. I am feeling sensuous, powerful, ecstatic, especially to see him so helpless and desperate. Finally, he grabs my waist and rigorously thrusts his penis into my vagina. It feels huge, and his abdomen presses on my clitoris. He thrusts hard, rhythmically, and uncontrollably while I enjoy the feeling of my clitoris being stimulated. Finally I come while he grunts and makes desperate animal noises in his throat. He comes only when I do: my orgasm releases him.''

♀"Strangely enough many of my fantasies during masturbation involve men. Nothing wild—just making love with a stranger. It *is* puzzling, however, because I've never made love with a stranger or a man.''

In a variation of this fantasy, the respondent became the man in the fantasy. Again, none of the respondents expressed a desire to become a man in real life.

♀"My fantasies occur in the morning when I am half-awake—wet dreams, so to speak. My most common fantasy is to be having sex with a woman as a woman and then change to a man and orgasm. Once the man is present, I become a woman again but he is still there. I'm into threesomes! In any case, I can change sex at will and feel that I have had the experience of a man in social and sexual roles through my fantasies. In my fantasies, I am never screwed by a man when I am a woman.''

♀"My basic sex or masturbation fantasies remain unchanged since my first hetero encounters years ago. I'm in the back of a cab. An attractive young man enters. He has an erection. He asks if he can make love to me. I agree. He does so quickly and leaves. I play either the man or the woman with variations on the theme. Or I'm at an elegant party dancing in a long black gown. Several men are talking in the corner. One challenges his friends by telling them he will make love to that woman, standing up, dancing in the center of the room. He does. I play either part.''

In a variation of this, the respondent simply imagined having a penis:

♀"When I'm masturbating, I spend a lot of time stimulating my clitoris with a vibrator. After I'm already pretty turned on, I like to pretend that my clitoris is a penis and that I'm stroking up and down the shaft of it with my vibrator. Just the thought of having my clitoris as big as a penis and stimulating it myself really excites me a lot. I just keep this image in my mind until I orgasm. Sometimes I get into visualizing this 'penis' of mine

growing, and that excites me too. I've never 'ejaculated' or anything like that. Sometimes I like to pretend I'm a man (I watched a man friend masturbate and he got very frenzied), and that somehow adds to the excitement. I'm a little embarrassed about this fantasy. You're the first I've told anyone. It seems not in keeping with my political feelings, but I do enjoy it.''

In another variation, a lesbian fantasized about sex between two or three men in the subway:

♀"My favorite fantasy during sex doesn't involve me; in fact, it doesn't even involve women. A businessman in his 40s is sitting on the subway and reading the newspaper. He feels a passenger standing in the aisle brush against his shoulder. Since the subway is crowded, he thinks nothing of it, even when his shoulder is brushed again and again. But gradually he realizes that there is a rhythm in the 'accidental' brushings, that, in fact, something is being rubbed back and forth across his shoulder. He feels embarrassed and excited; sweat prickles under his arms. He steals a glance to the left of his newspaper. It is a man in a tailored suit, the coat hanging open, his pants pushed out like a little tent by his erect penis, which is still rubbing back and forth.

"The seated man feels a shock through his body, ending in his penis, which instantly is engorged and erect, pressing against his briefs. 'No, no,' he thinks. 'This can't be happening.' But it is and with an inward groan he reaches his right hand under the newspaper and closes it around his throbbing member. He had hoped this would quiet the throbbing, but he feels his penis growing larger in his hand, and he starts to stroke it, trying not to move his arm much, trying to conceal his hand with the newspaper.

"But the stranger sees, and his movements increase in tempo and in pressure; the man can hear the stranger's breathing quicken. Then he hears a zipper being carefully unzipped, and feels a fresh throb in his own penis as he realizes he wants to get it free of his pants. He cautiously reaches up and unzips his trousers, reaching into the warmth to grasp himself and rub. But it's not enough; he frees his member from his briefs and it stands straight up in the air, the tip touching his newspaper. He can tell by this time that the stranger also has his sticking out of his pants, and the two rub as energetically as they can without attracting the notice of the other passengers.

"If I haven't come by this time, I have the stranger take the seated man's other hand and put it on his cock, or I have the seated man turn his head and take the stranger's cock into his mouth. Sometimes another passenger seated beside him senses what is going on and reaches over and starts stroking it too. It is all done in silence, except for the seated man's inward groans of disbelief and pleasure, almost against his will. He had thought he was immune to a homosexual attraction; it is much more arousing than he had ever imagined. He comes, the stranger comes, the

other passenger comes, all with little convulsive shudders. They stay near each other in companionable silence for the rest of the subway ride.''

Miscellaneous Fantasies

It should be noted that the fantasies of many women combined elements of all or most of the above categories either in one fantasy or in several different fantasies. In addition, many women had fantasies which fit none of the above categories:

♀"Cunts become very large and purple in my mind. If I try not to think about them, they become as big as me.''

♀ "My favorite fantasy is having a room full of erotic-looking women all stimulating me in some way to the point of orgasm. I would love an orgy!''

♀"My fantasy usually involves climbing up a mountain or the outside of a building as my tension increases. Climax usually involves an explosion of sorts, with stars.''

♀"Before I 'came out,' my main fantasy had to do with the love scene from *The Sheik*.''

♀"Since I was a teenager, I have recurrent dreams of wearing a Kotex all day and eventually orgasming from the rubbing. I also fantasize about being a goddess, being gently loved by attendants, male or female.''

No Fantasy

About 8% of the lesbians did not fantasize at all:

♀"I don't fantasize about actual sexual experiences—not that I wouldn't like to—it's against my upbringing.''

♀"I don't need it.''

♀ "I don't fantasize. I sort of wish I did. My friends have such interesting fantasies. When I masturbate, I kind of put the real world out of my mind, and think of waves or rhythms, but not a real picture of anything.''

Fantasizing During Sex

Looking at fantasies, one can well imagine why the people who don't fantasize were a bit envious of those who do! The only limit of fantasies seems to be the limit of the imagination itself—but that takes in a lot of territory. More lesbians, however, fantasized during masturbation than during sex. The women were asked, *How often do you fantasize during sex with a partner?*

always	7%
very frequently	16
somewhat frequently	18
somewhat infrequently	17

very infrequently	26
once	1
never	16

The lesbians were also asked, *Whether or not you fantasize during sex with a partner, how do you feel about the idea of it?*

very positive	33%
somewhat positive	23
neutral	21
somewhat negative	16
very negative	5
not sure	1

♀"I am not sure I have a definite feeling or opinion about fantasizing during sex with a partner. This is part of a learning process I am going through. I am trying to integrate in my head my beliefs in the freedom of any type of enjoyment and a feeling that if she is fantasizing it may mean that I am not good enough, that imagination is better than reality. This is difficult."

♀"Sometimes when I make love to her, I think of how it must feel or I think of how she has just made love to me (or will make love to me), and I get very excited. Fantasies are okay, but while making love, it's more important for me to think of the real woman next to me and what's happening right then."

♀"During sex, I'm usually thinking of academia and intellectual trivia. That is a problem."

Frequency of Masturbation

Now that the nature of the fantasies that usually accompany masturbation has been examined, we can deal with the survey results on masturbation itself. The lesbians were asked, *On the average, how often do you masturbate?*

more than once a day	2%
once a day	4
several times a week	28
once a week	15
several times a month	17
once a month	8
less frequently than once a month	16
never	6
not sure	3

The lesbians were also asked about *the frequency of orgasm and multiple orgasm during masturbation and about the importance of orgasming during masturbation.*

	ALWAYS	VERY FREQUENTLY	SOMEWHAT FREQUENTLY	SOMEWHAT INFREQUENTLY	VERY INFREQUENTLY	ONCE	NEVER
orgasm	52	28	7	2	5	0	6%
multiple orgasm	6	18	13	15	18	2	29

Importance of orgasm:

very important	63%
somewhat important	23
neutral	9
somewhat unimportant	2
very unimportant	2
not sure	1

As one might expect, orgasm was more important for the lesbians during masturbation than during sex (see Chapter 10 for orgasm during sex).

♀"Masturbation is fine. As an early adolescent and for the past forty years I have masturbated approximately once a week or more when I have no regular sex partner. Rarely when I'm into a satisfying, intimate relationship which includes living together."

♀"I masturbate an average of once a month or so—usually in bunches— that is, not at all for a long time and then for a week or so I'll have high sexual energy and have sex with myself three or four times, and then not again for a while."

♀"I don't masturbate very often now that I have a partner. I would guess maybe once a month and then usually when I'm home alone and have read or seen something that excites me. Before I had a partner, I would masturbate often—several times a week during one period."

♀"Recently I started to make love to myself. I masturbate every other day. Sometimes I do it very fast and don't pay much attention to anything but my vagina and clitoris."

♀"I generally masturbate once a day. Masturbation beats the daylights out of nothing—and the way things have been going lately, that's about the only alternative."

♀"I still don't masturbate, but I've talked about it with my lover and one of my best friends who is straight. I *never* used to talk about masturbating—my friends and I talked about everything sexual but that. I'm opening up so much about sex now that I'm talking about it."

♀"I have seldom masturbated in my whole lifespan. Probably the most was when I was a teenager. When I got married, for the full time of the twenty-plus years I don't think I masturbated at all. I have an idea that maybe it was because I didn't find my sex life that fantastic—it was orgasmic all the time, but it was not deeply satisfying in an emotional sense. In retrospect I find that when my lover/spouse and I are now separated I do occasionally masturbate and even think of her in a general sense in the process. I suspect that reflects very positively on our relationship."

How long the masturbation process took varied as much as how often the women did it. The women who answered the survey spent from several seconds to a full day masturbating. Some never timed it.

♀"It takes from ten seconds to an hour, depending on how fancy I want to be and on my menstrual cycle."

♀"Generally I masturbate once a day, and it takes three to ten minutes."

♀"It takes maybe fifteen to twenty seconds."

♀"It takes anywhere from a couple of minutes to several hours."

♀"I masturbate for several hours at a time."

♀"It takes between ten and twenty minutes, depending on how horny I am."

♀"My favorite way to masturbate is when I have the whole day to myself."

Masturbation Techniques

Although the vast majority of lesbians reported masturbating in bed, other favorites were the bathroom (masturbating with water, a technique which will be discussed), and all other locales in the house. Lesbians also reported masturbating in the office, in class, in Greyhound buses, in the library, in automobiles—virtually anywhere!

The techniques also varied greatly, but lesbians generally masturbate in much the same way as heterosexual women. The masturbatory practices of these women (including some lesbians) have been wonderfully and accurately documented in great detail in *The Hite Report,* by Shere Hite, and because the survey found no significant differences, this part will be rather brief. The reader is invited to refer to *The Hite Report* for additional accounts and more specific breakdown of methodology.

The primary method of masturbation was for the lesbian to lie on her back and stimulate her clitoris with her fingers.

♀"I lie on my back, close my eyes, clear my head, and start very slowly by touching my breasts, stroking my own body everywhere, and then finally

my clit. I rub it back and forth very fast until I come. I like to savor it, and take time over it. I always have at least three orgasms (the others around ten seconds after the first is through), and often up to around seven. I could keep going, but my right hand gets tired—although I'm trying to train my left hand, which seems still, after all these years, too weak or un-controlled.''

♀"I lie on my back. I masturbate by (optional) first touching my nip-ples—manipulating them with my hands. And then I use two fingers to manipulate my clitoris with. I use very rapid back-and-forth motions, while still playing with my nipple. I generally have an orgasm in one to two minutes.''

♀"I lie on my bed or on the floor, and most often I'm naked, though sometimes I may be wearing a shirt. I don't touch much of my body except for my clitoral area, and I almost never stick my fingers into my vagina. Since I tend to be a little 'dry,' I often lick my fingers, and then start to rub my clitoral area. I spread my legs apart, often with my knees bent, sometimes waving my legs in the air! I rub slowly, gently in circles at first, and increase the speed and pressure as I get closer to orgasm. Masturbation feels good.''

♀"I lie on my back and stimulate the general clitoral area with my right hand. My legs are apart, sometimes knees up. I run through one of my fantasies as I do it. My vagina does not usually provide enough lubrication, so I get spit on my fingers and rub it in. I also like to suck on my fingers just after they have come out of my crotch!''

♀"The most *common* way for me to do it myself is I'll lie on the bed or sofa to get real comfortable, either take everything off (if I had any clothes on to begin with) or maybe just take off my boots and loosen my belt if I'm wearing something I feel good about. I'll do it whenever I'm alone and feel like it, or even if I'm in bed with my lover, she'll join in, kissing and caressing me, though I prefer to do it alone (since that's the idea behind it). *Maybe* deep breathing and pleasant meditation, of pretty pastoral places and nice women, though I don't often fantasize. I like to look at my genitals in a small mirror and see how they look (what color). Watching me caressing myself and playing can be very exciting. I like to run my hands over my stomach and legs. I have a lot of body hair: it's very silky-soft hair. I get off on the idea of doing this just for myself, not on the fact that I'll pretend it's someone else. If I've gotten moist enough, I might put my fingers into my vagina, but I usually don't get enough juices flowing until my first orgasm. The best way for me to have one is to lie on my back and be naked so I can see all of my body. I'll press with my fingertips, all four, usually on the part that folds over my clitoris (it's covered with a lot of extra folds of skin, not directly exposed, which is probably why it took so long for me to learn to masturbate or even to think that the possibility exists). It's very sensitive, too sensitive, really, if I pull all this skin back to expose it. I'll use small circles or vibrating motions with my hand. Sometimes I'll

slack off on purpose and build up the feeling again, and finally I'll let myself have an orgasm, and oh, it's so nice.''

♀"If I am in bed, I like it dark. Sometimes I precede it by reading something erotic, and then I put the light out and create my own fantasy. The longer I hold off, the more profound the climax I have. I lie naked on my back and caress my body in a light tickling manner. I stimulate my nipples, then my thighs, and finally my clitoris. I use my hand or fingers. I spend the longest time with my clitoris, bringing myself just short of orgasm, then stopping and making myself relax, then starting over again. After doing this two or three times, I go all the way with a tremendous, high-pitched orgasm. It's really great.''

In a variety of this method, the lesbian stimulated both her clitoris and her vagina, and less frequently, the anus.

♀"When I masturbate, I start with my jeans on for a while gently fondling my crotch. Something about it feeling different through fabric. . . . When I start getting aroused, I strip down and very slowly start rubbing my hand around the clitoral area, being careful not to touch the clitoris. As my fantasy progresses, I insert several fingers into the vaginal area, being careful to move slowly, stopping now and then to prolong it. I usually enjoy spending several hours fantasizing and masturbating, keeping myself just below climax. When I decide to come, I stimulate the clitoris while just barely moving the other hand within the vagina. As I come, I let one finger stretch to just barely probe the anus and immediately climax. I keep the other hand in the vagina, because as the muscle starts contracting with the climax, the sensation in the vagina sets off a different-level climax and so does the anus. If my patience lasts to this point, I get three climaxes all at once.''

♀"I masturbate with my right hand. Usually I rub my genitals some and then stimulate my clitoris in circular motions, and move my legs in and out (knees drawn up, then stretched out). When I come, if I'm alone, I sigh a lot and my vagina opens up wide, sometimes makes noises, and I've developed a rather exact rhythm for myself, so that within ten to twenty minutes I can have fifteen or twenty orgasms of varying intensities. I get real wet, sometimes put a finger or two in my vagina. Sometimes I can get right up and do something else, sometimes just lie there.''

♀"I masturbate in many different ways. Usually I'm lying down, most of the time on my back but sometimes on my stomach, and I rub my clitoris and labia, often stimulating my vaginal area, less often my anus. I like to run my fingers over the whole area, applying greater and lesser pressure. I rub my mons Veneris with the fleshy part of my palm. As I do so, I become aroused and begin to stimulate my clitoris, not by rubbing, which makes me very sore, but by placing my index and second finger on the head and shaft and rhythmically and rapidly increasing pressure until I reach orgasm. (This

takes only a few minutes, often less than two.) Sometimes I use baby oil and spread it lightly over the entire area.''

More rarely, some lesbians masturbated by lying on their backs and stimulating only the vagina.

♀ "I quietly lie in bed, and think about S&M. Sometimes I get up without doing anything, or just put my finger in my cunt for a few seconds to get a small orgasm. I rub my breasts a lot and suck on my fingers. Also I suck on other areas like the inside of my lips, the pillow, my arm, the wrinkly, bulgy place that forms between a thumb and first finger when the thumb is closed.''

The second most generally common method was for the woman to masturbate on her stomach.

♀ "I love to masturbate. For many years, when I was a child I used a stuffed toy and rubbed against it, with my face down on the pillow and my left leg bent up and open, my right leg remaining straight. I still use this position on occasion, using my hand to rotate around and around my vulva and clitoris. After the stuffed toy, I evolved to using my hand with fingers together rubbing my vulva. I then progressed to touching my nipples and using fingers inside and stroking my clitoris with one finger or two.''

♀ "I've been masturbating at least since I was 7, and probably before that. Up until a couple of years ago, I always masturbated in the same way—lying down, on my stomach, using both hands to stimulate my clitoral area.''

Another method involved using no hands at all, and can be done in various positions.

♀ "I masturbate with my legs; lying on my back is my favorite position. But almost any position in which my legs are together at the top is acceptable. Environment is not important, as long as I'm alone. I usually cross my right leg over my left and bend it at the knee. I move my right leg so that the top of my thigh hits my clitoris very gently, while I rhythmically tighten and release the muscles in my vagina. I have orgasm about 90% of the time and it usually takes around three minutes.''

♀ "I fantasize or just decide to masturbate if I am bored or have free time. I take my clothes off or all but my shirt and sit down in a soft chair and cross my legs and move rhythmically and squeeze my vaginal area muscles. Often I stroke my breasts or the material over them or squeeze my nipples gently.''

♀ "I cross my legs and sort of press my thighs together in a kind of rhythm. I can do it sitting on a chair behind a desk if no one is paying too

much attention and can masturbate in offices, etc. I usually have an orgasm in one or two minutes. I usually keep doing it, though, for ten minutes or so.''

Aids for Masturbating

Another popular method was masturbating with water from a bathtub or shower.

♀"I masturbate by lying under the running water from the bathtub faucet. I just wait and the water feels so good flowing on my genitals. Then I get a tickly feeling and my body feels hot. The feeling on my clitoris is so good that I begin to move a little and then it gets better and better until I climax. I enjoy the moment with all my body, and then I lie in the tub awhile until I am completely relaxed.''

♀"I have a length of surgical hose attached to the faucet in the bathtub. When the water in the tub is deep enough to cover my genitals (this prevents splashing and also helps to distribute the sensation), I aim a stream (fairly hard) of warm water around my clitoral area, especially right above the clitoris. My legs are usually together when I do this. The hand that holds the hose is enough to separate the upper thighs to make the genitals accessible. It takes four or five minutes to climax in this way, and I usually have five orgasms.''

♀"When I masturbate now, I use one of those hair-washing hoses with the spray head taken off. I sit on the drainboard of the kitchen sink with my feet in the sink and direct the water onto my clitoris. I usually just spray the water on my clit at first until I get stuck on a plateau, and then I either rest or stimulate myself rectally while still playing the water on my clitoris.''

♀"I usually masturbate in a whirlpool with a jet stream. It's incredibly fast and intense—otherwise in a bathtub with legs up. Water seems important to me.''

Although water seemed to be the most common stimulus outside of one's own hands, some women mentioned that a disadvantage in some households is that the hot water can run out before one orgasms! For this reason, perhaps, and also for the sheer pleasure of it, lesbians seem to be turning to the electric vibrator. The electric vibrator has the advantage of never running out of steam (although one lesbian reported that her scariest experience was when her electric vibrator shorted!), and also it is not viewed by lesbians as a "penis substitute" since the vibrators which have recently been created primarily for use by women are not in the shape of a phallus. They are usually rounded and not intended for penetration, since the manufacturers realized, once Freud's myth of the vaginal orgasm was disproved, that the clitoris is the main organ in the orgasm process.

When the women were asked *how often they use an electrical vibrator in connection with masturbation*, they gave the following answers:

always	3%
very frequently	7
somewhat frequently	5
somewhat infrequently	4
very infrequently	4
once	4
never	73

Thus, while technology seems to have taken a giant step over the hand and the water faucet, most of the lesbians still had not tried this method. Those who had were enthusiastic.

♀"I never masturbated at all until I was in my 20s, partly out of ignorance and partly out of the fear of its not being 'nice.' My early attempts were boring and unsuccessful, very discouraging. Then I invested in an electric vibrator and presto . . . 100% instant orgasms! With the vibrator I can come in less than five minutes by direct stimulation of the clitoral area. The vibrator is so intense and powerful that I find it necessary to use the lowest speed and sometimes place a small towel between my body and the machine. Speed, however, is not the object. I have learned that quality orgasms are built up gradually. I like to take my time, turning the vibrator off from time to time for a few seconds' rest. This way the orgasm builds up in ever-increasing degrees of pleasure. The longer I can keep this up the better the orgasm. I usually spend about a half-hour in this way. Multiple orgasms are possible if I allow myself time to rest a few minutes before touching my clitoris after an orgasm. It's usually too sensitive to begin again immediately, even without the vibrator."

♀"With my vibrator, I lie on my back and place the edge of the vibrator to the right side of my clitoris. I should explain here that I use a different attachment here than the ball—the one with the rim is much better. I masturbate almost daily. Without a vibrator, I come two or three times within a half-hour. With my vibrator, I come eight times within a half-hour—this causes physiological havoc but I love it."

♀"I use an electric vibrator. It's a rather awkward hand-held model with several plastic tips that slide over a short metal decal on the vibrator. I usually masturbate when I get home. I get undressed, get into bed, find a nice quiet station on the radio, turn off the light. I lie on my back, legs fairly well apart. The vibrator is held with the rubber attachment between my index and third fingers. With it on, I gently stimulate the mons area, sometimes pulling the pubic hair gently. My biggest problem is making it last and not having an orgasm too quickly. When I'm ready, I gently touch my clitoris, usually to one side or the other, applying gradually more pressure until I reach orgasm. Very nice and never fails unless I've just got too much other stuff on my mind."

Fewer women reported *using a battery-operated vibrator on a frequent basis in connection with masturbation.*

always	1%
very frequently	1
somewhat frequently	5
somewhat infrequently	7
very infrequently	10
once	5
never	71

Perhaps the unpopularity of the battery vibrator stems from the fact that they are usually penis-shaped. As reported in Chapter 12, where dildos were discussed in connection with sex, most lesbians felt negatively about the use of the dildo, or of phallic objects in general. However, some lesbians did use a hand-held dildo in connection with masturbation.

always	0%
very frequently	2
somewhat frequently	3
somewhat infrequently	8
very infrequently	6
once	3
never	78

It should be noted that some of those lesbians who do use dildos did not think of them as penis substitutes. In fact, *Loving Women* by the Nomadic Sisters made the astute remark that to many lesbians a penis is a dildo substitute! Here's how one woman masturbates with a homemade "dildo."

♀"I have never been able to get it on using my fingers, so I've always used a dildo of sorts. In the past I've used hot dogs, carrots, bananas, the handles of various household items, and so forth. For the past year or two I have settled on a very effective, empty bottle of roll-on deodorant, which has a perfect size and shape to bring me to the peak. I do *not* think of this as a penis nor do I fantasize that it is one. I fantasize that it is my lover's hand or whatever, and I go from there.

"I usually like to lay my pillow on top of me because the touch and pressure of it on my breasts and on the whole front of my body is very sensuous to me. I hold it with one hand or stroke it as if it were my lover's back and shoulders, etc. I sometimes run my free hand on my breast to stimulate my nipples to erections. This really turns me on. Then I part the lips of my genitals and sometimes touch myself briefly and then I place the 'dildo' in between the lips. I spread my legs and run the smooth tip of the dildo down to the entrance to the vagina. I rotate it, push and pull it on the entrance until I get the fluids flowing. I then move the whole action from

the vagina entrance to the end of the lips at the top. I continue this several times, running back and forth the length of the whole 'crack' till the whole area is well lubricated. This feels good, and I really get turned on by the actual sounds of the suction of the fluid and the lips as the dildo passes over it all. If I have lots of time and feel especially sexual, I then try to enter my vagina with the dildo. I like the feel of a full vagina toward the end and I rotate it within the vagina and get really excited and wet inside too. Then I usually withdraw this instrument and insert a smaller one, which I leave there while I go back to my clitoral area with the deodorant bottle and stimulate myself to orgasm.

"With this object inserted in the vagina I find that I don't have to take so long or squeeze my legs together so much. All the while I am still fantasizing that I am with a lover. As I near orgasm, I sometimes stop and hold off and spread my legs and relax and then go the last few strokes without any straining. This way I feel the orgasm deeply, intensely, and it comes in waves, ever stronger, and I find myself gripping the pillow or the edge of the mattress and the squeezing of my fingers seems to be simultaneous with the vaginal contractions. If I'm sure no one can hear me, I let myself moan and make noises freely. I don't stop the stroking of the clitoral area at the onset of orgasm but rather I try to remember to keep breathing in a rhythmic manner and to stroke gently in long thrusts past my clitoris. This prolongs the orgasm as long as possible.

"If I am really into it, I then am ready to go on to more orgasms rather easily. After this initial one, I find the clitoris very sensitive, so now all I have to do is rub on the area from *outside* the lips, so that the lips are doing the actual contact. I can go on to as many as nine, ten, or more orgasms this way. However, the quality and intensity go down with each one and the legs and muscles get sore if I go too long."

Other women reported masturbating with insertable objects, such as candles, Tampax, cigar containers, bananas, and vegetables such as carrots, zucchini, and celery. Some lesbians also rubbed against (but did not insert) pillows, stuffed animals, chairs, clothing, and just about anything else. An old adage might be slightly reworded to say that pleasure is the mother of invention! Pornography was also used in connection with masturbation, and as one might suspect pornography was used more frequently than in connection with sex with a partner. The lesbians were asked *how often they use pornography in connection with masturbation.*

always	0%
very frequently	5
somewhat frequently	10
somewhat infrequently	9
very infrequently	19
once	5
never	53

Again the majority of the subsample never used it, and only 15% used pornography on a frequent basis. Favorite masturbatory material included *My Secret Garden* by Nancy Friday (which is a book about fantasies), *The Lesbian Next Door, Playboy* magazine (and other similar magazines), and erotic novels.

♀"The easiest way for me to become sexually excited is by looking at pictures of women in *Playboy*. I look at breasts more than at genital areas. I don't enjoy more hard-core pornography. I can also imagine *Playboy* pictures."

♀"I like reading sexy books while I masturbate."

Additional comments on pornography and other sexual aids appear in Chapter 12.

Feelings About Masturbation

Different types of lighting, including soft light or candlelight, enhanced masturbation for some women, although other women preferred to masturbate in bright daylight. Many of the lesbians also used music or incense. But no matter how, when, or where a lesbian masturbated, almost all agreed that it's terrific. The primary negative feeling expressed about masturbation was that it is second best to sex. The women were asked, *How do you feel about masturbation?*

very positive	62%
somewhat positive	22
neutral	10
somewhat negative	5
very negative	1
not sure	0

Here are some reactions to masturbation—*how it feels, how the lesbians feel about it, and how these feelings have changed over time.*

♀"I would go so far as to say that masturbation has been the most important aspect of sexuality for me in terms of connecting my sexual identity to some overall, central identity. Until I was 18, despite hearing about vibrators and such, I really never believed that women masturbated to orgasm (my love of water aside when I was little enough to fit under the tap in my parents' bathroom). I was a freshman in college, and had my first fucking boyfriend. And I read the Ann Koedt pamphlet, 'The Myth of the Vaginal Orgasm,' which I didn't believe for a minute since I had had orgasm with fucking since the very first time I did it. So I decided to experiment with clitoral stimulation, and it turned my head around! It made fucking pale in comparison, and all of a sudden I had no desire to have intercourse with my boy friend, and I wanted to masturbate by myself all the time. At that time, probably representative of my tentative sexuality."

♀"In the past I have hated myself for masturbating because I was a

fanatically fundamentalist religious person. So the act was considered as fornication; therefore a sin, etc. I thought I was the only one who did it: a *sickie*. Now, my life has turned around too, and so has the whole world, *for the better*! It's a wonderful thing to me now and a great pleasure, although solitary.''

♀''Orgasm during masturbation feels like waves of warm water washing over me combined with the feeling of riding a galloping horse, or a horse with wings. I've always felt good about making love to myself, though a while ago I thought it was just compensation for not being able to find a woman sex partner. Of course, I've only done it since I was 19 and was reasonably together in my head, and so didn't develop any hangups about it along with my other adolescent neuroses. I have no qualms about it. It's like self-affirming what miraculous powers we ourselves are in control of, and I've done my best, so far, to get over all my previous self-hatred. I'm a perfectly great little ole dyke. I've held together through all sorts of horrors and now I actually love myself, so why not let things come naturally from my great love and lead to lovemaking? I was my first lover, and don't we feel something special for a first lover?''

♀''Somehow lesbian masturbation seems self-affirming and male masturbation disgusts me. I didn't masturbate until I was 19, and I was thrilled with the implicit self-sufficiency and the indulgence. Before that, I associated masturbation with men (although I knew women did it) via Portnoy.''

♀''In the past eight years my attitudes have changed from feeling it's something to do when you're lonely and miserable or when you're frustrated to feeling that it's a wonderful, beautiful way I can do something special for myself.''

♀''I feel that people should be taught and encouraged to masturbate. Maybe they would avoid getting into trouble sexually with others (probably naive!). This is a special bug of mine in regard to retarded people and others who don't have other ways of getting sexual satisfaction.''

♀''Masturbation is very important to me. I want to be self-reliant. It calms me down when I am tense and it is better than Valium.''

♀''I don't have any specific feelings about it now, and I can't remember it being any different.''

♀''I discovered the water trick as a young child—maybe I was 9 or 10— and I knew better than to tell my parents about it, probably because I had learned that anything to do with the genital area was 'bad.' I used to associate masturbation with being bad. I sort of tried to make a bargain with God or something: if I don't do it any more, don't make me menstruate any more. Neither one of us lived up to her end of the bargain! I still feel a bit embarrassed discussing masturbation, and it's something that my lover and I mention only rarely.''

♀''When I was very young, I thought masturbation a bad no-no. I kept promising myself to stop but never did (ages 9 through 16). Later it became the only way I could orgasm and keep what sanity I had in a very confused

painful time (ages 17 through 25). Now it's nice, good, okay, sometimes a special treat, sometimes a humid relief."

♀ "I like masturbating, but it usually leaves me feeling empty when I just roll over and go to sleep. It's almost like going to the bathroom—just a form of relief. I only do it about once a month if and when I haven't had sex for a while."

♀ "I have ambivalent feelings about masturbation still, despite years of attempts at feeling it's okay."

♀ "I find masturbation boring and have only done it when my sexual need was great, and there was no available partner."

Thus, masturbation for lesbians, as well as for all women, seems to have come out of its closet, or perhaps it might be better to say out from under the covers! Almost everyone has done it and most are enjoying it thoroughly. If you would like more information about masturbation for women, the authors would particularly recommend Betty Dodson's *Liberating Masturbation.*

The Erotic Imagination and Masturbation of Gay Men

Defining Fantasy: An Overview

Fantasies involving sex are merely a specialized variety of fantasy. The ability to imagine or pretend is the essence of fantasizing, and it is closely related to the creative impulse. For many gay men, fantasizing at a young age helps in the process of escape from the demands of parents and traditional role patterns. The men who responded to the survey spoke positively about the process of fantasizing:

♂"Fantasies have always been important to me, as I would suspect they are to most men and especially gay men. We spend years masturbating (many of us) before we find a partner to share sex with. I was in my 20s before I came out and had a rich and elaborate fantasy structure to support my solitary sexual exploits."

♂ "My *non*sexual fantasy life is prodigious and inspiring. I consider it one of my greatest nonmaterial assets and one of my most basic 'curses' as an individual. (There were times when I had to fight my fantasy life and keep it from overwhelming my everyday life. A submergence in fantasy, coupled with ridiculous fears of becoming orphaned, and the onset of epileptic seizures saw me hospitalized for four months in 1961—an excessive surrendering to whim which has never been repeated.) Consequently, my feelings about fantasies in general and fantasies as a factor in the lives of others is, basically, very positive. I consider that a decent dollop of fantasy as the sidekick of imagination is extremely healthy. I approve of it just as I am occasionally moved to pity people who possess no sense of imagination whatsoever (based on the external evidence I perceive)."

During sex with a partner, fantasy is often used to add stimulation. The respondents indicated *how often they fantasize during sex with a partner:*

always	9%
very frequently	19
somewhat frequently	19
somewhat infrequently	19

very infrequently	22
once	.5
never	12

When asked about *their feelings about such fantasizing* the men indicated the following:

very positive	34%
somewhat positive	22
neutral	26
somewhat negative	11
very negative	5
not sure	2

One man who fantasizes during sex with a partner describes his attitudes this way:

⚥"Yes, I always fantasize. The most common ones are past experiences where I transpose some very fine lover in place of some dull partner I might be stuck with—then I really take off. I always fantasize the person ejaculating because that was one of the most unusual aspects of a former lover named Terry, who had the most copious ejaculate—vigorously expressed—it could go to 12 feet! Nothing to that kid! And I can make a mountain out of a molehill (the molehill I'm in bed with) by just thinking of him.''

From the point of view of the "molehill," however, comes this observation:

⚥"I get 'turned off' if my partner makes me aware of his fantasies of being with someone else when I'm there with him.''

Sometimes, a fleeting fantasy is needed to bring on orgasm:

⚥"I usually only fantasize at the last moments before coming, then some image usually of a past casual encounter flashes before my eyes. I am white, and most often this image-flash includes some black man I have had sex with. Usually, the flash is the opposite of what I am engaged in. If I am being sucked, then I fantasize sucking the fantasy man. If I am fucking, then I fantasize being fucked, etc. With one exception, I rarely fantasize at all while I am being fucked: my attention is completely riveted on my anal sphincter, and prostate sensation. During masturbation I rarely fantasize at all. I usually involve myself in an elaborate narcissistic self-exploration, often using mirrors, and often immediately after strenuous physical exertion so my muscles are glowing and pumped up with blood.''

For even more men, however, fantasizing accompanies masturbation, where it is indeed a major factor in those "solitary sexual exploits.''

Judging from people's comments on fantasies, furthermore, they seem to play a more vital role in masturbation than they do in sex with a partner. A sex partner may fit a "fantasy type," and this may be seen as fantasizing, but the mental working out of an elaborate fantasy story or situation is more easily accomplished during masturbation. The men indicated *how often they fantasize during masturbation:*

always	61%
very frequently	21
somewhat frequently	10
somewhat infrequently	4
very infrequently	3
once	0
never	2

There is virtually no negative *feeling about fantasizing during masturbation.* A "very positive" outlook on this is reported by 75%, while 16% feel somewhat positive, 8% neutral, and 1% not sure.

Recalling the Past

Fantasies tend to fall into several categories. Many men said they recalled past experiences, and one man commented that "this isn't so much fantasizing, I guess, as remembering." Bringing the past image to mind nonetheless involves the use of imagination, and surely it qualifies as fantasizing.

♂"Occasionally I'll go back in my fantasies as far as high school days, especially my favorite friend and sex-play mate from third grade through high school. He had a fine body and a gorgeous cock and we got together frequently for years. It really hurt when he began going straight our senior year in high school."

♂"When I first came out I lived in Atlanta, Ga. One night I was in a bar there and a gorgeous dark-haired dude with a mustache picked me up and we went to my place to fuck. The next morning he got up to take a shower and ran off to work. From my bed you could see into the bathroom. I sat up in bed and watched him dry himself and then shave. While he shaved I could see his dick hang over the edge of the sink and his hairy body was outlined beautifully with the lighting. So when I masturbate I remember that time and come with great satisfaction. I regret at times I ever met him because soon after our 'affair' I moved to Dallas, with his great disapproval. He had fallen in love with me and we slept together for three weeks before I left. I know I hurt him terribly but there was nothing I could do about it. But he would be pleased knowing I think of him at least once a week."

♂"As I write this, I'm fantasizing about a guy I met this weekend. Or rather, reencountered. We met first in a gay bookstore, and had a quickie in

a film booth, and didn't see each other till last Thursday at a disco. A photographer from New York was coming to Philly to photograph some guys, and I thought he'd make a splendid addition to our group. We spent the weekend at an old Quaker homestead, posing nude and seminude around the barn and fields (tractors, haylofts, pitchforks, chickens, horses—it was great fun), and giving each other a helping hand and tongue to get our pricks big enough to photograph. He's a gorgeous guy, and he's coming over this afternoon, and my head is full of images from the farm.''

Making an Experience Sexual

Fantasies are often used to extend a real experience devoid of sex into an explicitly sexual scene. As one man said, such fantasies "involve some elaboration on or extension of a real experience into a more explicitly sexual scene than it originally appeared in real life.'' For him, "swimming pools and locker rooms and gang showers have always played a big role—both in providing visual material and potential sexual or sexually loaded situations.'' There were many examples of nonsexual situations made sexual in the fantasy; the first of these is a bit long, but typical of fantasies that involve reaching into the past:

⚥"I am returning from the beach to my villa wearing my bikini and sandals. I walk through the forest and come to a glade full of moss and filtered with sunlight. Standing in the middle is Chuck, clad in a towel. Physically, Chuck was beautiful in the most masculine sense. He was 6'3" and weighed 192 pounds. He had blond hair and deep-green eyes and a body not to be believed. He had a deep tan, his chest clear of hair with just a slight amount below the navel before turning into a full pubic area. He smiles and I walk over; we don't speak but he just reaches out, holds me, and gently kisses me. He fondles my groin and I his, then pulls down my bikini and I take off his towel. He has a nice cock that matches his body and we fondle each other's cock and balls. He kneels and gently sucks me into his mouth. This continues until he pulls off and lies on his back with his legs raised. I kneel between them and push my cock gently into his ass, lean forward and kiss him as we begin our rhythm. We continue slowly and gently until I shoot in his ass and he comes over our bodies. After, we just lie in each other's arms and gently kiss and caress, knowing we will do this often.

"I served in Italy and Chuck was a sailor and I in the Air Force, but all us Americans shared the same barracks. So Chuck and I saw each other in the showers, around the barracks, etc. Another friend and I got a secluded villa with a wood and a beach. Chuck and another sailor also moved out of the barracks later on. After I left Italy a friend wrote and said he met Chuck at a party for gays and Chuck asked about me. He said he always wanted to approach me, but thought I was straight. I had the same problem. So as a result of our desire not to get kicked out of the service we both missed a

fantastic chance to enrich our lives. Chuck wrote me and asked if he could visit me after he got out of the service, and I said that would be great. About three months later my friend wrote and said Chuck had been killed in an auto accident, so that ended it in real life, but in my fantasy Chuck and I can make love forever, always the best and always with the greatest ease and love.''

♂ ''I often fantasize some cute young men I've met or seen that day. I usually fantasize entering them anally, in different positions. I fantasize weird positions—ones I could never act out, like entering someone and screwing them while they stand on their head.''

♂ ''I'm in a store trying on jeans, and the salesperson feels my crotch and ass to see how the jeans fit. After I've tried on several pairs he follows me into the dressing room and fucks me on the floor. Most of my fantasies are about me getting fucked, though in reality I don't always like getting fucked.''

♂ ''One of my favorites is remembering back to the locker room of my small school, remembering the various cocks on the boys. Three I remember especially. Larry was 6'4" and a real ornery sort—great at basketball and really hung—at least 6½-7" soft. He always stood on the bench in front of his locker longer than necessary, telling dirty jokes and showing off. Larry is married now, and is a Lutheran minister. His tall, lean, basketball-type body remains my ideal preference in sex partners. Ron's locker was right next to Larry's, and he was really hung, too. A natural athlete with a beautiful ass. His cock was big and had a lot of fatty tissue around the head, which was very large. Dennis had a hairy body, and was the only un-circumcised boy in the school. He was hung well, and it was the kind of cock that is never less than half-hard, with the tip of the head always sticking out from the foreskin. These really are the first cocks I was ex-tremely interested in. I didn't realize it at the time, and would never have done anything about it if I did, being in a small, conservative town in Nebraska. Strangely enough, I rarely fantasize about any of the many sex partners I've had during the past two years, but mostly about the ones that I've seen that I have not been intimate with.''

♂ ''When I was a kid, I used to play with my sister and her doll house. Therein lived a family called the Morgans with three sons (and a daughter). When I began beating off at age 15 I thought of the imaginary family and the three boys and the age that they would be if they were real . . . This imaginary family grew up also and now they are hunky college students.''

♂ ''Various situations—often missed opportunities—occur to me during masturbation. One incident in particular often comes to mind. That is an occasion when I took a walk in the woods with one of my students. At some point as twilight came upon us, we sat down to rest awhile. The student put his arm around me and announced that he never felt 'that way' about a teacher before. I understood and was aroused almost to orgasm. However, being the good and faithful teacher, I maintained my calm and did not reveal my real feelings. This memory always excites me.''

Celebrities, Porn Stars

Celebrity figures and specific pornography stars play a part in the fantasies of relatively few adult men, though movie and TV actors and comic-book heroes also form the basis for many childhood and teenage crushes (see Chapter 4). Among the personalities mentioned as part of masturbatory fantasies were Superboy, Parker Stevenson, Richard Chamberlain, Donnie Osmond, David Cassidy, Shaun Cassidy, Jan-Michael Vincent, Robert Redford, Jack Wrangler, Burt Reynolds, Charlton Heston, and Dennis Weaver. Here are a couple of typical celebrity fantasies:

⚥ "Burt Reynolds or Charlton Heston sitting on my face. He's sitting in a position so I can see his cock and balls while I'm rimming him. While I'm doing this, Dennis Weaver sucks him off and I jack off."

⚥ "Rumor has it here in Green Bay that David Cassidy has a real big honker on him and he really sends me climbing the walls."

Other men look at pornographic magazines and imagine they are having sex with the people pictured therein. Among the specific pornographic products mentioned are Target Studios, *In Touch* magazine, *Colt* magazine, and Tom of Finland drawings.

Here are a few fantasies that evolve from this type of media stimulus:

⚥ "When I fantasize, it's usually about some scene from one of the porno movies I have, in which I substitute one of the characters for myself or in which I am the voyeur."

⚥ "When I fantasize I usually imagine I'm with someone who really turns me on, e.g., the current *Playgirl* discovery, and we are totally alone with soft lights, music, and mirrors, and we are having the most exciting lovemaking ever with multiple orgasms, flashing lights, and the whole trip."

⚥ "I use the 'masseurs and models' ads in *The Advocate* . . . If I were in New York and had $40 to spare, it would, after all, be a possibility. So rather than fantasize about something that is an impossibility, I would rather think of something that *may* happen."

Additional comments on pornography appear later in this chapter as well as in Chapter 12.

Boys and Youth

This society often emphasizes youth, and there is a close connection between youth and beauty, youth and romance. Many of the men, as discussed in Chapter 4, first experienced sexual feelings for their boyhood friends, feelings that were often repressed or acted upon only furtively. It

should not be surprising, then, that many men focus their fantasies on boy-love or lost youth. Here is what some of them had to say about their youth-oriented fantasies:

⚥"The fantasies I have are almost exclusively affectional as opposed to 'heavy.' In my dreams (I am into Jungian dream analysis) there is an occasional and recurrent boy figure who probably symbolizes lost innocence and idealized perfection, perhaps a backward projection of myself."

⚥"My favorite fantasy involves a boy I grew up with when I lived on a farm in Missouri. . . . I remember him the way he was when he was 16 or so."

⚥"One of my favorite fantasies is a young boy aged 14 to 16 lying on a bed completely bare-ass. He is lying on his back and his legs are spread wide. I am between his legs and caressing his thighs and balls with a feather. In my other hand I have a vibrator, which I also move around his balls. He has a beautiful erection which is hard and red and is throbbing and moving around. Through all of this he is moaning and squirming around. He begins to beg me to suck him off but I refuse because I enjoy watching him in his state of heat and intense arousal. Drops of perspiration appear on his balls and I ease forward and lick the sweat off with my tongue. He throws his crotch area upward violently and I witness his cock spurting and spurting out the young cream onto his stomach. I move forward and slowly lick all of the honey up with my tongue and slowly let it ease down my throat."

⚥"I am 43 years old and I fantasize as I masturbate. I fancy myself as a good-looking 14-year-old boy being seduced by an older man. Sometimes it is a coach and his young player, sometimes a Scout master and his Scout in a tent, sometimes a jailer and his young prisoner, sometimes an uncle with his nephew at a ski lodge. This is imaginary, but I do like 'chickens.' "

⚥"My favorite one is recalling the many times I had sex with a beautiful 17-year-old, hairless, smooth-bodied, muscled with beautiful buns; just writing about it has given me a hard-on. I am very thankful to him as he has helped me get my rocks off many times and will continue to do so for a long time to come."

Special Settings and Turn-Ons

For some men, fantasies involve a specific situation—a natural setting, an all-male setting, a particular masculine type, or straight men.

⚥"My most common fantasy is one of fucking a beautiful surfer man out in the open on a gay beach."

⚥"My most active fantasies seem to be situations where my partner and I are playing super-masculine roles, as telephone linemen, policemen, construction workers, etc. I also imagine sometimes that the act is occurring in an all-male environment, gas station, factory, the steel mill."

⚥"Fantasy is of basketball players—the satin shorts, the body size, their thighs, long legs, etc."

⚥"Fantasies involve young boys or young servicemen, usually in restrooms, while I masturbate for them and vice versa."

⚥"I fantasize mainly about sex in various places—locker rooms, mountains, barns, etc. With this goes fantasy about well-built males—jocks or cowboys."

⚥"I fantasize about sex and making love with straight friends; and my mind jumps from friend to friend during course of masturbation, fantasizing about three or four friends in one episode."

⚥"[My fantasy person] could be fantasized as a sea-captain. I may have to go down to his cabin and the captain takes out his big dick and has me go down on him."

⚥"I can think of only one frequent fantasy which doesn't come directly from my sex life. I've no idea where it comes from or why I find it so sexy. Here it is: I am a cabin boy on a ship. Young, blond, slender. Large blue eyes with long lashes. The ship's eight officers are playing poker in the lounge. I am the prize. The one who wins gets to spend the night with me. I must do whatever he wants. I'm very turned on by this. Sometimes I go around the table, hugging and kissing each officer, hoping I'll bring him luck. Sometimes I wait quietly, hoping against hope the winner will be the dark mysterious man across the table. He's never so much as looked at me so I'm sure he's not interested—but still he's playing poker. Sometimes while waiting I go off to give the unattractive ship's captain his nightly massage and blow job. Sometimes I get fucked by the slobby ship's cook. He throws me down on a sack of flour. When we're through I'm all covered with white."

⚥"My fantasies take me outside on a hillside under blue sky making passionate love. Sometimes we're at sea on a sailboat moving with the movements of the waves. We carried out my fantasy on a hillside overlooking a freeway. Never reached orgasm so fast in my life. I like the thrill of the possibility of being caught in the act, but hope it never happens."

⚥"I guess my favorite is myself and another guy horseback riding and camping along a stream in the wilderness, setting up camp, cooking a meal, stripping and washing up in the stream, settling back in front of a fire, relaxing, enjoying the company of each other and slowly getting into exploring each other's body and ending up with each fucking the other and sucking the other and continuing throughout the night under a warm starlit night."

⚥"Trade. Sucking truck drivers, motorcycle riders, football players—all of these I fantasize about when jerking off."

⚥"My most common fantasy is that of sex with a policeman. I fantasize about him coming to my house in his uniform and of my helping him to undress, but there is no S&M slant to my fantasy. I prefer tenderness to roughness, anytime. Once undressed, my policeman becomes very tender and loving. We kiss and he allows me to cuddle him. In the end he goes to sleep in my arms and I kiss his forehead as he sleeps."

⚥"Mainly I see my lover being fucked by hairy, bearded men with enormous cocks driving him crazy, even hurting him."

⚥"I'll relate a recent fantasy. A young man (who is what I would want to be: mild-mannered, intelligent, attractive, gay) is on his way home from college, presumably on vacation. Initially, he accepts a ride home from the captain of the baseball team. Through some intelligent talking and much good fortune he is able to be so bold as to grope the college jock and initiate mutual masturbation. The sex scene primarily takes place off the road in this guy's dune buggy. Incidentally, the entire story takes place in the U.S. Southwest. After spending the night at the jock's family's ranch, a ranch-hand transports our hero, on horseback, albeit just about no luggage, from ranch to highway. The ranchhand, unlike the jock, is brunette, not blond, hairy-chested, as opposed to smooth, and wanting to get fucked, hence another sex scene for our hero. Shortly thereafter, he is picked up by two truckers and aptly fucked (I am getting an erection telling you about this, but you asked for it). The truckers drop our lad off somewhere up the road at a service-station junction. The station is naturally empty save for one sleeping attendant dressed in one of those one-piece outfits with the zipper that runs from gullet to groin. Of course the zipper is just about that low, and is lowered, once the attendant wakes and our hero talks him into a blow job. Knowing the proclivities of our central figure and a local farmer who shortly stops by, the attendant gladly hands the boy over to the farmer, who has sex with him in the back of his truck. The story continues in the same light with the farmer's brother, a cyclist, a policeman, a sailor, and a businessman until the boy is safely home."

Large penises, black men, incest, and group scenes (sometimes in combination) are other repeated themes:

⚥"If masturbating, I fantasize that I am getting fucked by a huge dick. If using a dildo, the fantasy is that much stronger."

⚥"During masturbation, I think of sucking a cock about 9 or 10 inches long while another man is screwing me in the asshole and while they are doing that another real handsome guy is under me sucking me off while I jerk him off with a free hand. We are usually in a fancy apartment. This is imaginary but I wish it were real."

⚥"I daydream about being hung and having a beautiful body."

⚥"My favorite fantasy is to be with two muscular well-endowed black men—as one is fucking me with his big black cock, his friend is in front with me sucking his black ass. When the fucker shoots his load they trade places and start again. Most of my fantasies have fucking and rimming."

⚥"Fantasy during masturbation—being forced to suck on an enormous black dick—or being forcibly screwed by a big black buck—split-open stuff."

⚥"My fantasy during masturbation is seducing Tarzan. I have a tribe of black boys who capture him and tie him, arms spread between two trees.

His body is rubbed with an erotic oil. Everyone drinks an aphrodisiac drink and dances around a fire. Tarzan's body is being touched and organs rubbed, bringing him to a frenzy. When he is going mad with desire I suck him off.''

⚥"In one fantasy, I am a father teaching a teenage son to masturbate, explaining to him how important it is, how good it can be, etc. (P.S.: I don't do this with my real teenage sons—one has made subtle overtures but I turned them, on each occasion, into objective intellectual discussion, about masturbation as part of the total sexual experience. As teenagers their minds are not yet made up and I do not want to influence them *in any way* which might harm my future relationships with them.)''

⚥"I often fantasize about my father, or about other fathers and sons, or brothers. I do not fantasize about my two brothers, though.''

⚥"I'm in a gay bath and six or seven humpy studs are sucking each other off. I get down in the middle of them, and when they start to come they shoot all over me and lick the cum off my body.''

⚥"I have often had a fantasy involving hordes of men having an orgy with me as their prime objective. Like the 'kissing booth' seen at any state fair, I've fantasized about setting up my own sort of booth for sucking and fucking. No money is involved; I'm doing it solely because of the volume of sex available.''

⚥"I often fantasize about doing 'surveys' or 'sexual studies' which require great numbers of attractive young men lining up to get blown. These usually involve some academic environment. I'm very professional about the interviews, etc., but am always anxious to get on with the actual 'testing.' '' (Note: This is not Allen Young's fantasy.)

A few men reported that they or their partners had sexual fantasies involving women, but none said that they imagined themselves as the woman in a sexual act:

⚥"My fantasies are of women having multiple orgasms and very muscular men with huge penises screwing them.''

⚥"I jacked off for Joey Heatheron a lot, and girls or guys I see or know in person. I fantasize I'm eating dick or pussy mostly.''

⚥"My fantasies sometimes include women—fantasy women, nobody I know, whereas some of the men are actual real people. . . . Some fantasies are merely mind-flashes, like having this enormous penis and women coming at me one by one to ride on it, fucking me until I can't give any more cream.''

⚥"I never fantasize while making love with another man. I was very hurt once when a man I had just given a blow job confessed that he had been fantasizing about Marilyn Monroe.''

One man added this note to his comments on fantasies:

⚥"When I have sex with my wife I do not think about gay sex at all.''

Dominance and Submission

A large number of fantasies involve dominance and submission, including rape, gang rape, sadism and masochism, bondage, and related acts. Presumably, many more men have fantasies in this line than actually practice such acts. In the majority of these fantasies, the person with the fantasy imagines himself in the submissive or masochistic role, but quite a few men have dominance fantasies, and many are "switchables." Some of the men indicate their feelings about these fantasies, but most simply stated them without comment:

♂"My most common fantasy during sex or masturbation: being humiliated by another guy, usually someone tall, slim, and well built who I had seen during the day. I imagine being told to strip, to crawl on my belly, to kiss his boots or shoes, to give a horsie ride to the guy, to suck cock. I imagine getting slapped, or put on a leash and walked around the streets. I imagine being put in a cage (sometimes I'll project the uniform of a cop or a Nazi on my fantasy object).

"I enjoy my fantasies, but I think that they are extremely perverse. I believe that they are sick fantasies stemming from a poor self-image, from a childhood in which I was always the worst in sports, could always be beaten up by anybody, and in which that was the only way that I would have contact with other males."

♂"I have had fantasies of both forcing people to have sex and of being forced myself. Usually it is the latter and falls into one of two types: (a) a group of three or four truckdrivers rape me in a truck stop; (b) I am bound and roughly raped orally and anally by eight to ten huge black studs."

♂"I fantasize men wrestling each other or me, crushing me in heavy muscular arms, forcing me and raping me but then loving me tender."

♂"I developed a fantasy of being roasted and eaten when I masturbated. Later it was elaborated with fantasies of trials, sentencing, being stripped and bound in tightbuck (the fetal position) and turned slowly over a fire. I would like to play a part in such a scene if it was a show but not in reality as the pain of fire is the most horrifying to me."

♂"Ever since a very early age I have enjoyed viewing the bodies of men and boys. I always kept a record of every man and boy I had seen. This list supplied me with hours of enjoyment especially after school shower scenes became a part of my life. I would imagine (and still do) myself usually being used (sexually) by these guys I went to school with. I would even write stories about how some of the toughest guys in school would get me alone (in an apartment, a park, a restroom after school, etc.) and force me to submit to all sorts of sex acts. I would refer to these stories frequently."

♂"My major wish, I guess, is to be possessed, taken charge of, by a Stanley Kowalski-type brute. Someone who would stalk right up to me and

grab hold of me and make passionate love to me, not quite against my will. (P.S.: I masturbated immediately after completing this question.)''

♂ "Masturbation fantasy: a superhero like Superman being exposed to powerful rays or kryptonite which weaken him. He is then assaulted and sucked off to exhaustion or forced to masturbate for his captors until he is completely drained. Also, the victim may be a policeman or possibly Tarzan. Newspaper accounts of policemen being assaulted or shot excite me, although I do not consciously desire such things in reality—it is all in my imagination.''

♂ "My most common fantasies involve 'butch' men with cigars or cigarettes in their mouths who force me to fellate them or grab me and do almost anything in the sexual repertoire. Very rarely is it anyone I know— usually men in commercial ads for little cigars or porn flicks. I hate smoking and avoid even meeting smokers so it may be phallic?''

♂ "My most common fantasy is about being forced to service five really good-looking guys in a car as we drive around. They are verbally abusive but really turned on and do not hurt me physically.''

♂ "I fantasize being tied over an ant hill, thrown in with snakes, many people made to shit on my body, to have darts thrown at me, to be whipped unmercifully, to have my skin ripped off piece by piece—this scares me so I scream when we come. I love fantasies.''

♂ "I get home, undress, and then I'm surprised to find the guy is into S&M. He ties my hands behind my back, forces me to my knees, and nearly gags me with this huge cock. Then he ties me up in bed and just about fucks me to death, pinching my nipples and commanding me. Other times, I'm out driving and I get stopped by this big hunk of a state trooper who gives me a choice of a ticket or doing him a favor, which ends up to be in the woods on my knees blowing him. Other times, though, my fantasies are quite mild, just beautiful sex with a past lover. The one thing I could never quite figure out is why my fantasies about bondage, cops, etc. are never acted on. In reality I would never let anyone tie me up, and I don't like rough sex.''

♂ "I fantasize about good-looking guys. One favorite fantasy I have is living in the dorms at college where I go and have a really straight and handsome roommate. He is uptight, but one night he is so horny that he comes over to my bed and I suck him off. I also fantasize that I am the czar of Imperial Russia and oversexed like Catherine the Great. I have literally battalions of young soldiers whose sole purpose is to sleep with me. If I'm horny while strolling down a corridor in the palace, I have the complete power to force a soldier standing guard to go down on me and then me on him. They have no say; I am the czar and they must cater to my every whim. I am ashamed of these fantasies and never admitted them to anyone. Not even in the men's sexuality workshop at a gay conference I attended. I think they're silly, but they help me fall asleep.''

♂ "I always seem to fantasize some situation where I am in command (though not in a sadistic sense). I may fantasize having a houseboy, or being

a big executive with young assistants, or being super-rich with my own masseur—but always I am involved with young, good-looking, and very willing men, whose mission in life is to minister to my needs (often more than one ministrant at a time).''

"Uncatalogued" Fantasies

Some fantasies didn't easily fall into any category. Here are a few of them.

⚭''I once had a fantasy of being fucked by a large dog and on another occasion of being fucked by a lion, the latter fantasy stemming from an ad I saw in a newspaper for a bar in San Francisco.''

⚭''Basically, my masturbatory fantasies are amorphous. Frequently they amount to a kaleidoscopic patchwork (something like a TV commercial run amok and reduced to its barest constituent frames of celluloid). These frames, sometimes of tanned men's body, sometimes of isolated portions of anatomy (a hand, a penis, a nipple, facial hair, navel, lips), flash by at dizzying speed.''

⚭''Favorite fantasy: self-destructive situations, especially with an indifferent audience. Death made casual. Also, getting on my motorcycle gear and shooting off in my pants from sheer excess of energy. I have written a book of creative writing on these themes, and can't create here.''

⚭''I love to fantasize about a man or boy with just underwear on, and not being able to see what they've got, and I orgasm just at the point that they pull down their pants.''

⚭''I pretend I am an infant, lying in bed clad only in a diaper and a knitted cap. I suck a pacifier, hold a rattle, kick my legs, and wave my arms. 'Daddy' comes in to examine his little boy. He unpins my diaper and examines my entire body. I lie still now. I watch his every move, intent on seeing what he will do, and his movements are all slow and deliberate. He first rubs my still-sore navel with salve. Then he carefully rubs the head of my newly circumcised penis with baby oil. Next he pushes up my legs and thoroughly cleans and oils my anus. Then he takes my temperature rectally. Next he salves the rectum, ass cheeks, and between my legs, followed by a powdering of same area. Lastly, a clean diaper is pinned on.

''Sometimes the scene shifts and I am a patient lying nude on an examining table in a doctor's office. A doctor enters and performs a thorough examination of the urogenital area. Again, I lie still and watch every move.

''This is all imaginary. I don't think I would actually want it to happen.''

⚭''I have two main fantasies during masturbation. One is typical for gay men I suppose. It's a version of a tall, dark, handsome, muscular, hairy-chested 'hunk' doing some sort of athletic activity. But the other one is a fantasy that I've not been able to share easily by explaining it to friends. It involves a vision of an imaginary young, white male of no particular face,

but who is enormously fat. The fatter the better. The bigness and roundness of his belly is most important. I fantasize him at a public eating contest. His belly is getting bigger and bigger. I'm in the crowd of 'watchers' watching his belly grow by the minute. My fantasy involves no actual sexual contact at all. He is fully clothed the whole time. But buttons on his shirt begin to pop. Then, once he becomes fully 'swelled,' then I visualize him having difficulty getting through doors and other tight places. Perhaps he is in a little bit of pain, too, from overeating. He also complains of aggravation of not being able to get through the tight places. His clothes are too tight and splitting.

"This fantasy, which I've had since childhood, is one that will get me off real fast. But I have never *experienced* my fantasy. I think I would like to experience my 'fat man' someday, though. Perhaps he is so fat that he can't even reach his own genitals around his fat belly."

Those Who Don't Fantasize

Although fantasizing is very common, and although most people are pleased with the process of fantasizing, there are some people who don't fantasize. Here are some comments from them:

⚥"I don't fantasize during masturbation and I have only had one wet dream in my whole life."

⚥"I find that I am losing the ability to mentally fantasize, to dream. I blame the use of pornography. I think pornography has caused me to look outside myself for fantasy. I am giving it up."

⚥"When I masturbate I don't think of anything except the sensation, how I feel. I know most men have fantasies, but I don't. Maybe that means I'm a realist. I sympathize with fantasies. In fact, I put an ad in a men's mag which goes pretty much as follows: Do you have fantasies of beating Daddy's ass, fucking the prof who failed you in French, pissing on your priest, or making your boss eat your ass? If so, elderly white-haired gentleman, who longs to meet rugged man who is queer for white hair, etc. Well, that's enough of that. I did get some good answers, and one of the answerers I continue to see regularly. We play naughty games: I'm Daddy and he's Baby."

Overview of Masturbation

In Mart Crowley's play *Boys in the Band,* Michael says this about masturbation: "You certainly don't have to look your best." Several men cited that quotation in order to express their views about masturbation. Many men, however, are much more enthusiastic about it, and it is a source of great pleasure in their lives.

Masturbation is the greatest common denominator among the men who participated in this survey. Ninety-one percent of the men do it at least

once a month. Asked *how often they masturbate,* the men gave the following replies:

more than once a day	6%
once a day	17
several times a week	42
once a week	15
several times a month	10
once a month	3
less frequently than once a month	5
never	1
not sure	1

For some men, masturbation is a simple "jerking off," a fairly quick businesslike process designed to relieve sexual tension. For others, it is an elaborate theatrical presentation, with but a single actor, but no speaking parts, and usually no audience. Sex researchers have reported that most men have been masturbating since the onset of puberty, and many men date their enjoyment of the solitary pleasure to much earlier in childhood. A few didn't learn until later. Masturbation is enjoyed by men of all ages, by those with or without lovers, and it is practiced in the morning, during the day, and at night. For some men, masturbation is accompanied by the fantasies discussed earlier in this chapter, or involves the use of pornography or other stimuli, while for others masturbation is truly a form of self-love enhanced by mirrors, bright lights, oils, marijuana or poppers, and a favorite musical selection.

Orgasm is the focus for men in masturbation, even more so than in sex with a partner, the statistics show. But orgasm is by no means always the end result in orgasm. Asked, *How important is having orgasms to you during masturbation?* the men responded:

very important	82%
somewhat important	14
neutral	3
somewhat unimportant	1
not sure	.5

Men do not always have orgasm during masturbation, though it was not determined whether this was due to ceasing the self-stimulation or because of difficulty in coming. The figures for reaching orgasm during masturbation may appear to be somewhat low, and this may be due to a misreading of the question. The men were asked, *How often do you have one or more orgasms during masturbation?* but possibly some men thought the question asked how often they had "more than one" orgasm. In any case, the figures obtained were:

always	51%
very frequently	24
somewhat frequently	5
somewhat infrequently	6
very infrequently	10
once	1
never	3

Techniques

Concerning "techniques," the most common method is to stroke the penis with the hand, but many men also use their hands to stimulate other parts of the body, especially the nipples, anus, and testicles. Inserting the penis in a pillow or otherwise rubbing against another surface is also common, and many men report that they vary from one technique to another.

⚣"I usually like to be lying down when I masturbate. First, I develop a fantasy to think about, or recall a pleasant past sexual experience. This has a great deal to do with the erotic sensations of all forms of sex. I slowly caress my penis as my erection becomes firmer. With my other hand I play with the nipples on my chest. I have a large cushion or pillow between my legs that serves to apply pressure to the inside of my thighs. As the one hand continues to stroke my penis, the other kneads my lower abdomen and down to the pelvic area around the base of my penis. Gently massaging my testicles, I then raise my pelvis as one finger penetrates my anus to further stimulate me. Now that I am totally primed, I climax and ejaculate all over my abdomen. I relax and lie there letting the good feelings and sensations wash over my whole body."

⚣"I use two fingers and thumb, don't use a full hand. When I'm alone, I'm not at all comfortable unless I'm standing up."

⚣"Generally, when I masturbate, I'm lying in bed on my back—I take my penis in my right hand and rub it up and down until ejaculation occurs—often in ten or fifteen minutes. It's usually dark, so I don't use pornography. Even though I'm 67, it occurs three or four times a week."

⚣"I occasionally masturbate lying down, holding a mirror above me with one hand. I like to do this with my feet and knees above me, as though getting fucked, thinking about how I look to the men who fuck me. (Quite a lot of narcissism in me!) I often caress my belly. I occasionally smell my armpits. I like the reflected images of me straining in masturbation, seeing the veins in my forehead, shoulders, forearms, neck, chest, and belly distend. Therefore I also use and enjoy poppers with my masturbation. I love the coloring they bring up in my chest and neck and face."

⚣"At first, my cock feels generally warm, and it starts to feel good. Then after a few minutes, I can feel a quantum jump from general good feeling to suborgasmic level, and this goes on for a while, and then I can tell

we are moving into orgasm city. At this point, I generally slow down the strokes on my cock, and try to dwell more in the world of my mind and fantasies. I think more about the shape of the body of the man of whom I am thinking, or I try to think more fully and slowly of the particular experience I am reliving. I try to slow it down and experience it all more completely. I am trying to savor it all in my mind. I am thinking of the time I was spending the night with my friend Ed, or I am thinking about the fantastic body of a teammate of mine from locker-room days in college, or I think about a man I met on the street the other morning. In any case, as I get closer to orgasm, I concentrate less on the physical act of stroking my cock, and more and more on the mental element of savoring the experience. The orgasm is now a vicarious one, a substitute for what I would be able to experience if the man were here now, or if we were actually doing now what I am thinking about. The hard physical cock rubbing at first is to get into the suborgasmic range, but once there, I like to maintain it with a moderate amount of slow stroking, and get more and more into the warm mental recollections or fantasies. Finally, I want to come, and I concentrate a little more on feeling the actual hand on my actual cock, and thinking also of the man or experience on my mind, and I soon can feel orgasm coming on, and I go with it. There comes just a moment in which I know that it is here, but not yet for another split second. There is nothing I can do to stop it now, and in expectation of that, I usually find that my toes curl up, and my breath comes up short. If I am alone, I will make noises, moan, gasp, cry out, or whatever. I will thrash around on the bed, or raise my legs in the air, or curve my back, or whatever. I will feel each thrust of my musculature, and each spurt forth of my come, and I will accentuate it with hip thrusts. Finally, the last spurt of come will have been and gone, and then there is the delicious end-of-the-orgasm orgasm, in which I strike my cock more and more, and out come the last drops of come, and the feeling at the end of the orgasm is the best part of it all. When this is over, I am a little disappointed that it's all over, but I smile and think of how nice it has been.''

⚥ "One day I was taking a walk down a country road when I came to a neighbor's land up the hill with a nice clearing. It was late fall, the woods being colorful and crisp. I shed my clothes, dancing in the meadow, feeling the cold air caressing my skin. Going to a large maple tree, I wrapped my legs and arms around it, hugging it, pressing softly close to it, slightly rotating my hips to feel my hard cock against hard bark. Picking up my T-shirt, pressing it to the tree so it clung, lightly brushing the backside of my erect cock up and down, I tickled and teased my growing excitement. Periodically I would back away to stretch and look at my body and cock, feeling the excitement in my body and mind. Leaning back, holding the tree with one arm and tensed legs, bent at the knee, I tickled my balls and felt my thighs, ass, legs, chest, and crotch. Skipping and jumping away I dug my straight hard cock as it bounced up and down slapping my legs and stomach. I then stopped under a pine tree at the edge of the woods where moss covered the ground. I dug a small trench the size of my cock with a

hole for my balls. Spitting into the trench, I rubbed it around to make it slightly muddy. I slowly lowered myself into the ground, giving support with my arms to lift myself higher as I rocked back and forth so that I could watch my cock going up and down in the trench. I loved the way the tip of my cock head would sometimes fold under, the hole open and close as if it were breathing. By this time every nerve in my body was in spasms and my cock was like a tree, erect and timeless. I would stop as I felt orgasm in my balls creeping to the peak, listening to my heart beat, the wind blow, and the trees groan. Settling to a natural rhythm the feelings flowed and in a prickly flushed rush cum sprayed and spilled and seeped into the earth as my sounds and sighs spilled to the sky from my upturned head.''

⚥"Usually with my right hand. Baby oil. A finger or two of my left hand inserted in my rectum and massaging my prostate gland. Lying on my back on the bed. It takes three to five minutes.''

⚥"I usually masturbate with my hands, oiled with lotion or oil. Both hands are used in long strokes, spiraling down the cock, sometimes stroking from middle toward both ends simultaneously. The double stretch pull tension is wonderful. Brushing my nipples with bedspread fabric or with the inside of my upper arms is delightful, especially when I arch or stretch my back to full extension.''

⚥"I always use saliva as lubricant. I use my right hand, sliding back and forth over the end half of my penis, not pulling the skin. I am especially sensitive around the corona on the top of the penis. Sometimes I'll watch myself in a mirror. Lately I have more often been getting into an 'active' position where I will thrust into my hand. I do not fantasize. I just think about what I'm doing and how enjoyable it is.''

⚥"I masturbate in the common way by grasping my penis in my right hand and jerking back and forth to ejaculation. I sometimes lie on my back rubbing my belly and chest area, fantasizing a man on top of me. I raise my leg into the air and insert my middle finger into my anus, fantasizing it is a man's penis.''

⚥"I try to take as long as possible and try to reach the plateau phase where I try to keep myself in tension as long as I can before ejaculating.''

⚥"I masturbate alone, usually as a break from other things (reading, watching TV, typing, resting, etc.). I masturbate standing because I find an erect position offers the most freedom of movement. Most frequently, I masturbate in front of a mirror. I use my saliva as a lubricant. Working mainly with my right hand (though I may switch hands), I begin kneading and manipulating my penis while the free hand brushes over my upper torso, playing with my nipples and body hair, and always returning to fondle my scrotum (which I often hold in a tight circular grasp and pull somewhat gently down and back towards my anus). My right hand works in the usual fashion (thumb in front, four fingers along the underside of my cock), sometimes moving slowly, sometimes quickening the pace. While my hands are busy, I stare at myself in the mirror, flexing and tensing the muscles of my arms, neck, chest, and legs, and watching my body change

shape before me. This may go on for as long as ten minutes before I decide I'm indulging myself (and have just about had enough of a good thing), and quicken the strokes for another quarter-minute—and ejaculate.''

&"I stimulate my breasts. I have actually, on occasion, even climaxed in an orgasm without touching my penis, but merely stimulating my nipples, but that was when I was in my early 20s, not now. I like the frenzy I can summon by smoking grass and taking poppers.''

&"Masturbation. Less than when I was younger. Sometimes not to the point of ejaculation (I feel I want to save the energy). I like to do it outdoors in the woods, or indoors on a bed with lots of cream and pornography. I'm uncut so my technique is adapted to that condition. Up and down, you know, and gentle stimulation of the head under the skin covering. Sometimes finger pressure on the prostate from the outside, sometimes finger in the asshole. Sometimes a mirror. Sometimes in a rocker on a cabin porch. Depends. I try to do it only when I'm liking myself.''

&"I usually masturbate in the shower. ('So that's why he has been taking such long showers' says my roommate!) Soap can do wonders. I touch and stroke and rub other parts of my body. My chest, stomach, nipples, the genital area and inside my thighs. I have become very tactile since being gay. I like to move my entire body.''

&"There is perhaps no way of playing with my cock that I have not tried at one time or another—I have a good imagination. There are variations in grip, speed of stroke, length of stroke, etc. Sensations range from a delicate tickling to warm glowing feelings to the deep burning urgency just before coming. There seems to be no wrong way to touch a cock (except when it causes pain, which I am not into). Warming up should not be ignored. I like to smoke grass first because it heightens awareness of the sensations and makes the whole experience much more pleasurable. Grass also has an effect on the erotic sensitivity of the mind which enhances the physical sensations and makes the fantasies more vivid.''

&"There are certain strokes that excite me more than others. The basic stroke—the fist around the shaft of the cock and moving up and down—is what I call a 'college boy' stroke, the way everybody learns to masturbate. I also have a second stroke which is beautiful—I put my hand around behind my cock and instead of stroking up and down I rub the greased palm of my hand around the big head of my cock. This is extremely pleasurable and, using this stroke, I can stretch my masturbating out to a long, long scene— all the while enjoying the fantasies from inside my head. I like to stretch it out, to get to the various plateaus and stay there for a long time before I go on to the next. There are certain levels, and I know exactly what each means, and I enjoy experiencing them to the fullest extent I can. Then, after so long, I feel myself going toward the edge of coming, and this is where the control becomes important. I'm very good with my control and can usually keep this going for quite a long time, riding this wonderful edge between coming and not coming. Sometimes the jism starts to slide out on its own (not spurting yet, just sliding out the slit at the end of my cock), but I'm

enough in control that I can hold back and delay the big O, the final thrust of the orgasm. When I finally decide—in my mind—to release my orgasm, the rush begins and I release my cum from deep within my body. The orgasm is always just spectacular, never a disappointment, and I am always totally exhausted following. I forgot to detail when I sniff the poppers. I can't tell you what it does, for I don't know, but it feels wonderful and, it seems for me, the feeling is centered right inside my cock head. I love it, and the sniffing becomes more frequent as I approach orgasm. I always program myself to have a good long sniff just before I release my orgasm, and the intensity is such that it nearly takes the top of my head off. Which, of course, I love.''

⚥"I generally masturbate by thrusting my cock backwards and forwards between two pillows, in simulation of the action of fucking, till I feel I am getting close to orgasm, when I will roll over on my back and finish by hand—though a few times a year, I will use either a rubber or a small plastic bag over my cock and continue with the pillow action right to orgasm.''

Some people use their own special techniques. One man reported holding his penis with his right hand and rubbing it against his left wrist. Another presses his penis downward and rubs it along his thigh. Here are some other variations:

⚥"To masturbate, I have to be in bed or a hot bathtub. I lie back in the bed or water, and I get a hard-on, and I rub my cock between my legs, holding onto my ankles with my hands to move my legs back and forth.''

⚥"A favorite masturbation movement of mine is to tuck my testicles up into my body cavity and bend my penis between my legs, curving it toward my rectum. As I close my legs together this action holds my penis out of sight and I lie on my stomach rubbing the area at the base of my penis, which is really the area where my balls are up in my body cavity, against a bed or on the floor or whatever I can rub against. I fantasize on being entered and providing my body as a depository for an imagined partner to release his orgasm.''

⚥"How do I masturbate? Let me count the ways. My favorite is to rub my cock on the sheets of my waterbed while looking through some good hardcover porno books. Also a fast hand job can be fun with hard-rock music turned up loud and a strobe light or jacking off while sitting (or attempting to sit) on a hot iron, thistle, or other stimulating item. A cock ring is almost always used. It makes the climax take longer and much more intense. I have had jack-off sessions that have gone on for hours before finally coming. But the average time is ten to fifteen minutes.''

⚥"One variation is to push my flaccid penis between my thighs, and to use solely their pulsing as stimulation, without using my hands. I developed this variation so I could masturbate in school without anyone knowing.''

⚥"My favorite way to masturbate is to lie in a shower tub and just let the

water run on my penis until I come (but there's a drought now so I don't do that much, and when I do I hold the shower spray so that it doesn't use too much water). I can just come with the spray of the water, I don't have to touch myself otherwise."

♂"I almost always masturbate by lying face down on a bed or the floor (or sometimes another body, male or female) and rub my penis and body against the other horizontal surface. Some slightly rough surface is exciting, and I almost always caress my nipples at the same time, as well as the whole of my chest and arms."

It's Done in Many Places

While most people masturbate in bed, quite a few do it in the toilet, and in many other locales, sometimes purposely exhibiting themselves:

♂"Some situation or fantasy will often trigger a desire to masturbate, and I have done it in about every imaginable place—johns, parks, beaches, buses, trains, airplanes, in the car, at rest stops, every room of the house, porn theaters and bookstores, the woods, my sleeping bag, bed, locker room, swimming pool, shower, steam rooms, and sun roofs."

♂"One way I use sometimes but not very often on the highway: unzip my pants, pull out my cock, and lubricate my right hand with saliva. As I drive with my left hand, I squeeze, pull, and rub my cock with my right. (Extra bonus—pull up alongside a trucker or a male van driver and watch their expressions. One guy stopped his truck, then sucked me off.) Highway masturbation usually doesn't end with climax—at least not while the car is moving. I might stop on a side road to finish, though."

♂"I am fascinated by exhibitionism and may at times stand near an open window, perhaps watching people outside working in the yard, or watching the people at the bus stop. I feel some sense of power knowing that my body, being in that state of stimulation and contortion, is something that has a real shock value; it is as if I have a power of exposure, the decision is mine whether I actually expose myself. I know how much control I have over people's feelings if I actually did expose myself. Yet I have never exposed myself during masturbation and probably never will."

♂ "When I masturbate in front of my window, I hope a man comes by and sees me. When that happens I get very excited. Never has a man got angry who has seen me."

Aids for Masturbating

Some men desire more elaborate stimulation during masturbation, calling on the help of assorted "toys," oil, and/or pornography. We asked the men *how often they use these items in connection with masturbation,* and the following chart indicates the responses:

	ALWAYS	VERY FREQUENTLY	SOMEWHAT FREQUENTLY	SOMEWHAT INFREQUENTLY	VERY INFREQUENTLY	ONCE	NEVER
hand-held dildo	.5	2	3	5	13	3	73%
strap-on dildo	0	0	0	1	1	0	98
vibrator	.5	1	2	3	16	3	74
accu-jack	0	.5	.5	1	1	1	95
cock ring	1	2	4	7	7	4	74
nipple clamp	0	0	1	1	3	2	93
oils	7	12	10	11	17	2	41
pornography	6	24	20	16	17	1	16

While all of the items are used by at least some of the respondents, pornography is frequently used by half of the men. The following comments are a selection of statements about masturbation with toys, oil, and pornography; other comments on these items appear in Chapter 13.

⚣ "Possibly once a month I get on a real kick and have a three-or four-hour session. I had such a one last Saturday night. About 7:00 smoked some grass, got out my dildo collection, douched, used a tight cock-and-ball restraint, greased my cock with Vaseline, dragged out most of my porno material, sat on dildos, used them to fuck my ass while masturbating, used plenty of amyl, achieved something I have recently found I can accomplish, which is to fuck my ass so that the prostate is massaged and I build up and up until I have an orgasm without ejaculation. It's fantastic! All of the feeling of coming, but only a few drops oozing out, the sexual desire continues almost unabated. I had four of these during a four-hour session before I finally masturbated to a complete climax (and almost collapsed)."

⚣ "With experience and age, refinements have been added: pressing behind my balls, playing with my balls, vibrator in the ass or (rarely) a finger, carrot, banana, or rubber dildo. Rarely I've added a jockstrap or swim briefs to jack off into. I've put on boots to feed a fantasy and once or twice licked boots while pumping myself."

⚣ "I like to watch my collection of 'home movies' in which a young man jacks off; I usually time my orgasm to match his."

⚣ "I look at the pictures I've collected of Parker Stevenson and start to imagine that he is present in my room."

⚣ "When I masturbate I always make a drawing to hold my attention, sometimes three drawings in a series of a plot of action."

♉"I usually masturbate with oil. I try to create the most sensual atmosphere possible, whether by candlelight or in an open meadow."

♉"Hello, rubber dildo, friend of mine. And I wait until they are gone and then in deeper, deeper. Can I do it. Hurting. Yes. *Yes*. Biggest head . . . your fullness is constant. And you there—larger, with the vibrator, makes me smile. Little battery keeps you running making tomorrow relax. Open my asshole. Fill my mouth. Double-ended bendable up and down and in until I tremble, plastic member, make my life a little 'gay.' Wife returning. Hide the cock. Wipe the Vaseline and blot the cum. Don't regret it. Wish for the moment when the pulsating cock was his."

♉"I am more stimulated by the soft-cock nudes in *Playgirl* than the photos in the gay sex magazines. Reproductions of erotic art, especially the Japanese, are more stimulating than either. I have also masturbated while reading a book entitled *The Cradle of Erotica* by Allen Edwardes and R. E. L. Masters."

♉"Sometimes I'll use pornography, but not regularly . . . close-up shots of someone sucking a big hairy cock, or close-ups of a thick cock halfway into a hairy asshole."

♉"I strip and stand in front of the mirror while masturbating, but then I start looking at preselected pornography laid out on my bed. I might pause from time to time to turn a page or get another brochure out. I fantasize having sex with the men I'm looking at, that the cock I'm stroking is not mine, but theirs. I animate the pictures in my mind and flesh them out, and try to imagine their skin against mine, or what their cock and balls would feel like, or taste like. . . . I'm standing in front of the mirror beating off, grooving on the narcissism, and my body. I then begin to direct my attention to the porno lovingly laid out on my bed of all my favorite porno stars (Al Parker, Stoner, Roger, an occasional Bruno, for nostalgia's sake, or a Gordon Grant, or maybe someone not quite as flashy or well known) and the fantasizing kicks into gear. As I feel the orgasm coming I lock intently on one picture, and as I'm shooting, I press down on a nerve in my scrotum that I know from experience greatly intensifies the orgasm. I then fall back on my bed, arch my back, stretch my legs, and contract my abdomen to milk every little sensation I can out of the orgasm."

♉"The most exciting 'toy' I ever used came from an article in a gay magazine, *Queen's Quarterly,* I think. The writer was proposing various ways of 'jazzing up' masturbation, and recommended the purchase of a ripe cantaloupe, which was to be heated for twenty minutes or so in the oven, to give it some interior warmth; one end was then to be punched out, and the cock was to be inserted with a fucking motion, I did all this, and it was one of the greatest sensations I have ever had—I got melon seeds and juice all over the bathroom, but got my rocks off in a way I don't think I've ever equaled."

♉"In high school I would take an enema whenever I was left alone in the house long enough. I used to take the enemas either lying down or sitting on

the toilet. When I was young I would usually come when I felt the warmth and pressure of the water inside of me. I usually would come without any stimulation of my penis. In my late teens I masturbated almost daily. . . . Since I have separated from my wife, I have used dildos, vibrators, and a butt plug. I sometimes use these when I masturbate.''

♂ "I get high on grass. Get out porno magazines. I set the mirror at the end of the bed between my legs. Make sure there's plenty of light. I lie there looking at myself, checking out my own feet, my whole body. I put on a metal cock ring (which I prefer to use any time I have sex). Pop some amyl up my nose. Feel the rush as I watch my cock rise. Wet my cock down with baby oil. Watch it glisten as I stroke it to full erection. An erotic exchange of self-indulgence with my own reflection in the mirror. I tie a strap around my balls, then pull down applying pressure. Watch my cock stand straight up. Visual fireworks. More amyl. More fireworks. Check out the boys posing so unashamedly with hard-ons in the magazines. I bring myself right up to the point of orgasm, then hold it. Sweet torture. Up again, hold. Lovely sight. Tits clamped hard in pain (ah, but it feels delicious) with clothespins. Heavy pressure on my balls. Long hit of amyl. Pumping to the final release. Eyes darting from page to page, to the mirror, down to my feet and toes, rigid, straining, almost shaking uncontrollably. I come in a moment of indescribable joy and freedom. I look at myself spent and wasted before the mirror. Cum on my chest, cock softening but still throbbing. Tits red and still noticeably pinched. Alone and fulfilled.''

♂ "I masturbate by hand, often using Vaseline. I stimulate my balls with the elastic waistband of jockey shorts. Also, I do it in the shower using a spray attachment. Sometimes I do it standing up, but more often lying on the bed looking at pictures or films. A vibrator is often used to produce deep and often-repeated orgasms of the most intense variety. Along with pictures, I indulge my S&M fantasies, projecting them on the pictures.''

♂ "I usually masturbate, standing, over the sink, with pornography, by my own hand. At rare times, I have used dildos, vibrators, and vacuum cleaner, and, as a teenager, anything that felt good.''

♂ "I like putting my left finger, and then a hot dog, in my ass. When I think I'm nearing climax I start to release the hot dog. With my anus muscles, and a little help of my hand, I make the hot dog end pop in and out, in and out. Then I let it come out halfway and grab it. The motion increases, I start beating faster. I push the hot dog in and out faster and harder. And then I shoot. I've gotten stronger orgasms now with the hot dogs and am considering getting a dildo. Oh, by the way, I release the hot dog completely when I shoot.''

♂ "I put lots of lotion or oil on my right hand and start fucking it as if it were a hot ass. As I get into it I put my feet far apart and squat down while fucking. My leg muscles seem to be amazingly strong at this point and really love getting into the act. Then I get a dildo or vibrator all greased up and start fucking it into my asshole, fantasizing some big-dicked fucker is pumping the shit out of me while I am fucking some other dude in the ass.

All sorts of archaic rape, bondage, and prison-type gangbang scenes push themselves through my mind in quick succession and then I am coming and shooting all over the place, jerk the dildo out, and the mountain of agony/ecstasy having passed I am possessed by a momentary feeling of wanting to smash the thing or anything else, then I clean off any mess on me and fall on the waterbed laughing and quivering with release while sinking slowly into a languishing relaxation so deep that I almost lose consciousness for a while. I come slowly back to the surface after about ten minutes, like a swimmer approaching the surface of water from a deep dive. The external environment seems to embrace me gently as if it were a velvet cloak. Everything in the apartment seems soft and glowing with happiness.''

⚣''I have tried using a carrot twice but it isn't much fun, so I don't think I'd like toys or dildos.''

⚣''I ordinarily masturbate with a hand vibrator. Most frequently I do it fully clothed, having wrapped a small towel or washcloth around my penis; sometimes I use a rubber. The reason for remaining clothed is that application of the vibrator to a couple of layers of cloth does two things: the vibrations are muted somewhat, making the experience more controllable, and the vibrations are spread, particularly by levi denim material, to include gentle, simultaneous stimulation of the testicles along with the shaft and head of the penis.''

⚣''I usually use some sort of bondage toy. The only other aid I use infrequently is not actually pornography but pictures from various muscle magazines, particularly those of the teenage contestants and winners. When I use bondage toys, I use handcuffs, leg irons, chains, leather cuffs, and straps, usually not all at once, and sometimes underwear or swimsuits. And along with this, I almost always use baby oil. Generally it takes place on the living-room floor. I place restraints on my ankles and sometimes fasten them to something like a table, chair, wall, or eye hook in the floor. With other straps or chains, I restrain one arm and sometimes the chest or neck to whatever is handy. This leaves the other hand free to apply oil and stimulate the penis, thighs, abdominal muscles, chest, and biceps.''

⚣''In 1972 I started using rubber vaginas. At present I'm waiting for an order for an electric cocksucker and a vibrator sheath with rectal vibrator attached.''

⚣''I get an empty toilet paper core which I've saved (a paper-towel core or aluminum-foil core is even better), and my (legitimate) hand-held massager. While still reading my gay porn I place the paper core around my cock. Still reading, I manipulate the paper core around my cock until I can stand it no longer. Then I plug in my massager/vibrator, place it at the top of the paper core, and switch on the motor. The pleasure is tremendous! By alternately switching the mechanism from on to off and back again, I can usually delay my climax for ten to fifteen minutes. When I feel I can stand it no longer and decide to climax, the pleasure is almost unendurable.''

⚣''Lately I have found it helpful to insert a 1-inch-diameter wooden handle of a toilet plunger up my rectum as an aid to help me ejaculate.''

   While the questionnaire covered some of the more commonly known
objects used in masturbation, some men chose their own very special
substances or items to enhance the autoerotic experience. Here are some of
the comments on these special stimuli:

⚭ "I masturbate about once a day, on rubber sheets, dressed in a diver's
suit, and tend to enjoy it, but this too is getting to be a bore, almost as if it
were a necessity and not a pleasure."

⚭ "I slip into a pair of socks and work boots. Wrap a pair of socks
around the cock and slip it into a pair of guy's heels. Pull the shoe back and
forth over the cock until I come."

⚭ "I've always enjoyed lying on my belly, cock pointed toward feet,
masturbating with blue jeans on tightly, creaming jeans and inside of left
leg."

⚭ "I have a real soft pillow and I put a satin pillowcase over it. Get
myself hard and sprinkle a little bit of baby powder on my dick to make it
slide easier. While I'm pumping in and out, I have to grab my balls and I
feel myself. I usually bite myself on my arms, giving myself a hickey."

⚭ "I turn on to my own feet in a pair of sheer black nylon socks. I use
mirrors and a bright light to accentuate their sheerness."

⚭ "I have a fetish that comes into play only during masturbation, and
that is for heavy wool sweaters, of which I own many. I love the feel of
rough wool against my bare skin during sexual excitement, and love the
sensation of rubbing a heavy sweater between my legs and against my balls
and penis, usually while wearing one or several sweaters. Sometimes I
completely wrap my genitals in a sweater, which I then slowly rub over the
head and shaft of my cock, and my balls, but all the while keeping the
genitals inside their wool 'diaper.' The sensation drives me wild, and is
about the best feeling I ever experienced in sex.

   "I have several sweater 'costumes'—letter and tennis sweaters for
'jock,' Shetland crew-necks for 'Joe College,' bulky fisherman knits for
'outdoorsman,' cashmere V-necks for 'man-about-town,' army and navy
surplus sweaters for 'serviceman.' Sweaters are an integral part of my
masturbation about 75% of the time. If I have trouble coming otherwise, a
favorite sweater rubbed and stroked along the penis will usually do the
trick.

   "I am very turned on by men in sweaters in magazine ads and on the
street, and sometimes fantasize about a recent man in a sweater that I've
seen while jerking off.

   "However, I have never mentioned this fetish to anyone, and never
incorporate it into sex with a partner. Once I have a partner, he always turns
me on more than any sweater would."

⚭ "By now you should be familiar with my silk PJ fetish. I take a shower
(I have a shower massage device), then after I dry myself I splash on Aramis
cologne. I then massage my cock with Nivea cream, just enough to
lubricate, for I enjoy the musky cock odor too much to hide it. Then I put

on my silkiest nylon PJs. Because of the expense I seldom wear my real silk PJs and then nylon seems to do the trick. Then I put on the Stones if I'm in the hard-rock mood or Donovan if I'm in the soft and feminine mood on the stereo. Then I dance, letting my hard cock throb and pulse in my silky pants, then I dance into my room and stand in front of a triple-reflection mirror and dance, my cock throbbing in my yellow silk PJs, my hot blow stick pops out, I grasp it in my hand and give one-two-three-four fast jerks, then one-two-three-four-five-six real fast jerks, or until I feel the pre-cum surging in my balls and at the base of my cock. Then I stop and see and watch my cock throbbing. I turn round and round and round, shaking my ass and torso, the silken PJs are swishing and swishing, over my asshole, buttocks, and baby, I'm hot as a fucking whore, I'm really hot and horny, and pre-cum is flowing out of my shining cock head, my fucking, sucking blow stick is giving me more joy, I'm ecstatic with lust and sexual stimulation. I pull my silk PJ pants down far enough so I can shove a small Joy-Gel greased rubber dildo up my asshole. When it's up there I continue to writhe my body in pleasure. Yet I don't want to come—not yet. I'm a faggot, and a silky sexpot, and I love it. . . . I'm in my silk PJs. I'm going to beat my meat. . . .''

High Technology Masturbation

In this age of technology, some men exchange tape recordings to provide masturbatory fantasies for distant partners, often men they've never met. The telephone can be used in a similar way; a disembodied voice can provide the stimulus for masturbation, whether the conversation is explicitly sexual or not. The respondents were asked *how often they engaged in masturbation during a phone call:*

very frequently	.5%
somewhat frequently	4
somewhat infrequently	5
very infrequently	14
once	10
never	67

Whether or not they had experienced telephone J/O, the men were asked to indicate their feelings about it:

very positive	8%
somewhat positive	16
neutral	35
somewhat negative	11
very negative	22
not sure	8

Here are some comments about telephone J/O:

⚤ "Masturbation during a phone call doesn't do a thing for me."

⚤ "Having answered a gay hot line for several years I could think of nothing duller than a phone call for masturbation."

⚤ "Have had bad experiences with this, having people use me over the phone to get their rocks off and I do not appreciate it at all."

⚤ "A stranger did that to me, and when I realized what he wanted and what was happening, I was glad to talk him into his climax. It was his nickel. But it would never occur to me."

⚤ "A persistent experience a couple of years ago showed me I could be very turned on by a seductive voice on the other end of the phone making sexually suggestive—not lewd—conversation. I enjoyed it, and was sorry when the mysterious caller stopped his calls. Sometimes I think I'd like to place such calls, too, to see if I can turn some others on, but never have."

⚤ "When I do this I'm usually talking to my lover and know that we want to be able to be together to make love so we talk to each other and jack off and talk about it at the time."

⚤ "Masturbation during a phone call is pleasurable because I never tell the person on the other end what I'm doing. Sometimes it might be someone who's straight that won't go to bed with me, or an ex-lover who's too far away."

⚤ "Phone sex is great and I belong to a J/O club with lists of guys given out for all members to call others with and 'get off' over 'the wire.' (I love you, Ma Bell!)"

Music

Music can be an aid to masturbation, though several respondents said they found it "distracting," and many prefer absolute silence. Here are a few comments about music:

⚤ "Sometimes I select the music very carefully, sometimes I just turn on the radio and listen to whatever is on. But in my life I have jacked off to just about every kind of music there is. Classical music of every style period. All varieties of rock, pop, jazz. Even music of exotic cultures—India, Japan, Bali. Some people like to jack off in time to the music, which can be fun, but I prefer to go at my own pace and use the music as an erotic background."

⚤ "I usually tune a rock station on the radio (WNEW-FM, to be specific)."

⚤ "Music sometimes is used, sometimes as a 'timer' to see if I can control all the rushes and near-climaxes until a certain moment."

⚤ "During the period of my second marriage's breakdown, the months preceding coming out, I was home a lot in the evenings and evolved very elaborate masturbation situations. Starting with a very hot bath, then smoking dope, I would end up putting some large-scale romantic symphony (Mahler, Sibelius, Prokofiev) on the stereo very loud, and slowly stimulate

both anus and penis, trying to coordinate my orgasm with the musical climax. One night, I was so stoned I decided to lie on the bed instead of the living-room floor where I usually went through this ritual. The symphony was the Sibelius No. 2. I lay naked with a sheet over me. During the last movement I grew very erect, my penis lifting the sheet up into a tent. I lay perfectly still, hands folded behind my head, and while the music built to its climax, I built too. Believe it or not, exactly as the stereo crashed its full volume of brass and percussion through the house, I orgasmed.''

Among the other music specifically mentioned was Donna Sumner singing ''Love to Love You''; ''Tommy,'' the rock opera by The Who; ''usually something soft and Baroque''; plus others cited elsewhere in the chapter. One man said this:

⚥''I don't beat off with music in the background, because it can break the attention and concentration I need to make the fantasies flesh out. Besides it would be a real bummer if I came just as a pimple-cream commercial on the radio was being broadcast.''

What to Do with the Come

Quite a few men recall their prepuberty days of ''dry'' masturbation, when orgasm came but no semen. But ejaculation and thus semen, is an essential reality in adult male masturbation. People's attitude toward the semen varied greatly, and many commented on what they do with it or how they feel about it.

⚥''Once in a while, I let myself go and let it spill on my stomach. If it looks like a good load (thick, white, and all of that), then I may taste it. Then I wipe myself off.''

⚥''When I'm about ready to come I do a lot of yelling, 'I'm coming, I'm coming,' and watch my come splash on my stomach. After a few seconds I rub my semen into my skin.''

⚥''Never bother to clean up the sperm. Never have.''

⚥''I feel the shower affords a very sanitary and logical place for fucking oneself. Pecker tracks in the bed are not my idea of glamorous.''

⚥''Once I've come, usually onto the floor, I become very businesslike. I clean up the remains, wash my hands, stretch, and return to whatever I was previously doing.''

⚥''The moments of ejaculating are euphoric. If I can let out sounds of strain, and tensions, similar to those of actual pain, I find that there is no letdown when the ejaculation is complete. I also often like to pull my clothes together and make no attempt to wipe myself off, and do not find the semen repulsive or 'dirty.' I also like the idea of coming on newly laundered underwear because it seems like a kind of violation, although I have no propensity toward dirty clothing as such.''

⚥"Masturbation is almost always with me rubbing up and down against the floor or bed while I look at pornography. This is enjoyable to me since I don't have to touch my penis or really feel the semen on the rest of my body. I suppose I fear the semen squirting since it might get on my face."

⚥"At climax I grasp the cock below the head with the thumb on top and the bottom with fingers, to guide the come into a container. Who needs the mess?"

⚥"Sometimes I turn myself upside down, with my groin over my face, and shoot into my mouth and swallow it. Other times I'll put a sock over my cock to catch the semen."

⚥"The other day I did a bunch of dance exercises (I take dance), felt loose and horny, pulled on a jockstrap, wore a jean jacket and cutoffs and leather boots. I lay on my back, then pulled my legs over my head and shoulders. My cock was just above my face. I pulled my cutoffs away and lubed my asshole, stuck my finger way up, my other hand pulling at my prick. I came all over my face and hair, trying to drink as much juice as I could. It was bitter, didn't taste that great."

⚥"Outdoors—in the woods—there is a special feeling of eroticism there. A feeling of naturalness, at-oneness with nature, an innocent creature of this planet enjoying being alive and in touch with other living creatures, a special awareness of the Life Force which is very deeply and fundamentally erotic. There is a special satisfaction in leaving my cum to rot and decay, to be reabsorbed into the life cycle and returned in some unknown form."

⚥"I arrange something to catch the ejaculate. Paper towels on the rug, or a Kleenex in the other hand, or a Kleenex rolled up inside a small plastic bag which I place around the penis. This may sound prissy and fastidious, but it's not; the alternatives are a stained rug, which is a pain, or doing it in the john, which makes it impossible to arrange my porn around me."

⚥"Climax comes fairly quickly, and I catch the cum in my left palm. I eat that (delicious)."

⚥"I never use a towel or wash up afterward, but prefer to roll over on my stomach and feel the liquid squish about as it quickly cools."

By the way, many men noted that shortly after ejaculation, they had to urinate.

Attitudes Toward Masturbation

Although masturbation is a source of joy for most people (having overcome predominant repressive attitudes in their youth), there are those who have negative feelings about the practice.

Several men indicated that their masturbation was one of the aspects of their sexuality that they keep secret from others.

⚥"I would not want to hurt my lover's feelings. He might feel inadequate if he knew I masturbated occasionally."

⚥"I am secretive about how frequently I masturbate (almost daily) because I don't feel that society (even our gay society) finds daily masturbation normal or healthy."

⚥"I feel inhibited about speaking about my masturbation. I think I have residual guilt feelings from childhood."

The men were asked *how they felt about masturbation,* and these were the responses:

very positive	58%
somewhat positive	25
neutral	11
somewhat negative	5
very negative	.5

Here are other comments concerning gay men's feelings about masturbation and how those feelings have changed over time:

⚥"I feel it is one of the healthiest leisure-time activities available, and think it is about time it came out of the closet a bit more. I have always felt good about it in myself, even during the most extreme antimasturbation periods of my rather conservative Catholic upbringing. Something that feels that good can't be all bad."

⚥"I like the feelings, but long for physical contact with another man, and this can be painful. As for my changing feelings about masturbation, when I first started I was guilty as hell about it, and remained so for many many years. Then, when I was married and in the closet, I accepted it as such, but felt guilty for not being a husband sexually to my wife. And I masturbated a hell of a lot in those days. Since coming out, I have masturbated very infrequently for some reason, and do it when I do it rather matter-of-factly, simply to avoid the inconvenience of being horny when there's no sex in view."

⚥"I used to feel guilty (mortal sin, 'impurity'). Now I just worry occasionally whether I don't do it too often, just idly."

⚥"It feels fantastic, exciting, relaxing—and during some moods and crises in my life, properly punishing."

⚥"I look forward to it as my special time with myself, in no way as a deficiency in my relationship with my lover. He and I usually tell each other about our masturbation sessions, much as we would tell about any other enjoyable event experienced while not together."

⚥"I couldn't get into masturbation as much as I do if I felt at odds with it, and I wouldn't be as sensitive to other people's bodies if I had not explored my own body as much as I did and do."

⚥"I have always felt good about masturbation. I don't remember how I learned about it but I know I was 'doing it' before I knew it ever had a name."

⚥"I have been masturbating since about age 11 or 12 and am not blind yet. However, I am starting to squint."

♂"I love masturbating, and prefer it to having sex with other people unless I really like them."

♂"I have wondered if in getting so used to sex alone I have killed the motivation to engage another in a relationship."

♂"In general I think masturbation is a great sexual gift and unappreciated and underrated by too many people. It should be celebrated and encouraged, not condemned or downgraded. I never felt particularly guilty about masturbation, though I did have a real scare the first time I had an orgasm. I was probably 11 or 12; I had been playing pleasurably with myself for a long time and always stimulated myself short of the orgasm. When I finally lost control and it came crashing through I was really terrified. But since I didn't die and nothing really bad happened I continued to masturbate and gradually figured out that orgasm was just the particularly pleasurable end to that activity that I had previously been engaging in and the problem was pretty much laid to rest."

♂"I belong to two masturbation clubs. J/O Buddies meets in sporadic and different-size groups. It's very informal but the people I've met have all been nice and the groups I've attended have been a real turn-on. TelePals is a phone organization for those occasions when I feel lazy or just into the fantasy trip. Masturbation is now and has always been my favorite sex. It is unabashed self-love, self-fulfillment."

♂"I never felt guilty about masturbation, though of course as a kid I feared being caught. My wife caught me jerking off once (in ten years of marriage) and cried for a week. She masturbated but was shocked that I did. Hmm."

♂"Any night that I can't go to sleep, I use masturbation as a means of relaxation; sometimes wake up and do it in the middle of the night."

♂"I love to masturbate. I started doing it when I was in about the third or fourth grade, and although I was a celibate (Catholic priest) for 24½ years, I did quite a bit of it during the latter part of that term and do it now almost every day unless I'm having sex with someone else. When I was an adolescent, of course, I felt very, very guilty about masturbation. I was convinced that I was going to be buried in the deepest pit of hell for all eternity for it; I thought I was damned and that no one else in the whole world was as evil as I was. I didn't begin to overcome my hangups on it until I began to lose my faith in the Church's teachings and my belief in God, and until a couple or three priest-counselors who were quite sensible on the subject began to loosen me up a bit."

♂"It was one of my few real pleasures about growing up. I think that my masturbation might have been my only link to gay sex (or a gay consciousness) for almost eight years when I had no sex contact whatsoever. When I was a teen I used to drive way out in the country, find some remote spot, then strip and run naked in the night. And then jerk off. More than any sense of danger, my real turn-on was the feeling of total freedom. Today I still find masturbation to be my best sexual release."

♂"It feels good while I am masturbating, but when it is over it feels like a

waste, very pointless and ungratifying. A very empty feeling."

⚥ "J/O is the most satisfying of most of my sexual experiences. With the aroma at the end it becomes a religious experience—I melt with God."

⚥ "When I was in my teens, I thought I was doing wrong, much as I loved it, and couldn't desist—to the extent that I had myself circumcised in the vain hope it would 'cure me.' "

⚥ "I have grown from being a guilty altar boy to becoming a lascivious self-stimulating man."

⚥ "The whole process hurts me psychologically—heavy guilt feelings."

⚥ "I was very guilty about masturbating when I was an adolescent until I discovered through reading that everyone did it (I could hardly believe it). Later I felt guilty because I used masturbation as an escape from everything and I feared that I wasn't progressing sexually (having experiences) because I was masturbating instead. Also, I felt guilty about the homosexual nature of my fantasies while masturbating. All of that has passed, of course."

⚥ "Masturbation is usually very unsatisfying; I don't feel any release from sexual tension afterward. The climax itself is very 'low-level' and the come usually flows or drips rather than shoots; I always miss the presence and contact with another person."

⚥ "I find that masturbation calms my nerves. I'm not a coffee drinker, but I find that I can't start the day without my daily dose of masturbation."

⚥ "I now prefer to call it 'pleasuring' myself."

⚥ "Thank God for mother fist and her five lovely daughters."

⚥ "I would rather masturbate than do anything else."

⚥ "I know that when I get very old, I will still get my kicks."

⚥ "If I'm frustrated and I finish masturbating, I'm usually more frustrated and depressed than before. I don't like masturbating that much, and I never tell anyone about it or admit it to anyone. It is extremely private, the most private thing a person can do. I get a charge by making other guys admit they jerk off, particularly if they are straight. Masturbation itself feels very good, but having an orgasm with someone else is always more rewarding."

⚥ "I have grown more positive about it with time. I used to think masturbation was the last resort of desperate lonely people and no one else."

⚥ "I don't particularly enjoy masturbation any more. I used to, as a teenager. But now it seems tepid compared to the ecstasy of interpersonal contact."

⚥ "I get a kick out of beating off, but I would certainly not want to be married to my hand. Give me a good old corn-fed, red-white-and-blue country boy with a dick between his legs and I'll show him why there are only two types of people in this world—those that are gay and those that wish they were."

⚥ "I consider it a very normal thing to do, or even talk about, so it's a little weird to me that only now are we reading about it, are people discussing it in print and in person."

16

Hangups and Handicaps: The Lesbian Experience

♀"Does she really want to make love? Does she just want to cuddle and go to sleep? Will she think me sex-obsessed if I proceed? Does she want to be doing this? Is she enjoying what I'm doing? Should I ask her what she wants me to do? (Shouldn't I know by now?) Is she doing this to me just because I did it to her? Does she think I'm doing this to her just because she did it to me? (Well, I'm *not*!) Is she cold? Will she think me puritanical if I pull the blankets over us (I'm freezing)? Why isn't she telling me what else I can do? Why isn't she moaning and writhing? Does she find me unimaginative?''

This woman amusingly poses questions to herself which reflect the all too serious and real sexual performance problems, anxieties, and hangups of lesbians. Although most of the women who answered this survey did not state they had any sexual problems or handicaps or said they had overcome them over time, that does not mean that we should ignore the problems of those who do have these problems, dismiss them as politically incorrect, or tell the women who have such problems to have their consciousnesses raised.

The reader may think that no one would treat problems so callously, but the sad reality is that the sex manuals available to lesbians take this very approach. For example, some lesbian sex manuals take the approach that if a lesbian is not inclined to perform oral sex, it is because she does not know the correct manner of doing it. They offer some tips, which may indeed help some women who think that oral sex is disgusting or who just can't bring themselves to try it, but for others, such an assumption that knowing is doing may cause shame, guilt, or even worse a rejection of sexuality itself because the women will feel that they aren't 'normal lesbians'! Very few women said their problem was that they don't know *how* to perform oral sex:

♀"The one time that I tried to perform cunnilingus on a woman I got so scared that I gagged, and shook like a leaf. I couldn't do it. Now I feel like

655

I'm ready to try again. It's been over a year since that happened. I think that a warm, aggressive woman would do the trick for me. If she could show me how to do all of these sex procedures, I'd be less scared."

Almost all the women with aversions to oral sex felt negative things about the act itself. These feelings, as well as negative reactions to other specific sexual acts, are described in Chapter 10. This chapter will focus primarily on performance difficulties in general, as well as anxieties or "hangups."

Problems with Orgasms

One area of performance difficulty was in achieving orgasm during sex or in achieving orgasm within what the respondent considers a reasonable amount of time. Again, current sex manuals, such as the *Joy of Lesbian Sex* by Dr. Emily Sisley and Bertha Harris, have aggravated the problem rather than alleviated it, mainly by spreading unproven myth as fact. Their book flatly states that "Lesbians *always* reach orgasm in their lovemaking" (P. 165; emphasis theirs). According to this survey, however, that is not true. During sex, 4% never had an orgasm and 7% had orgasms once or infrequently. During masturbation, 6% of the respondents have never had an orgasm, 5% had an orgasm once, 2% had orgasms very infrequently, and 7% had orgasms somewhat infrequently. In short, one-tenth to one-fifth of lesbians had orgasms infrequently or not at all. Misinformation about the universality of lesbian orgasms, as put forth by Sisley and Harris, probably with the best political intentions, could again cause a woman to conclude that because she does not have orgasms she must not be a lesbian. *Loving Women* is better in this regard, since it does not assume that all lesbians have orgasms, but does recognize that orgasm is one of the goals of sex.

Since sex manuals tell you how to do it, they also spend a maximum amount of time on positions to do it in, and a minimum amount of time on sexuality as an act of communication. Sexuality, for many lesbians at least, is a physical way of expressing affection or love for another woman, and if lesbians cannot communicate their desires, fears, and preferences any problems are likely to get worse, not better. In sum, the sex-manual approach to nonorgasm, which Karla prefers to call "preorgasmic" (as some books do), is often one of suggesting a better position to achieve orgasm in or a better technique rather than better communication. While technique improvements probably never hurt anyone, *The Gay Report* is meant to serve as a forum for communication; therefore, this chapter will give women who have sexual difficulties space to openly discuss them, and where women have found solutions, they will be offered. Here are some comments of women who did not have orgasms during sex or who had difficulty in orgasming during sex.

♀"I always have trouble with having an orgasm when my partner tries to get me to have one. I have never been orgasmic with anyone without

stimulating myself at one time or another. I never have trouble when I masturbate.''

♀"It's *very hard* for me to have orgasms with other people. When I masturbate, I always come. I don't know why I can't seem to come when other people stimulate me. It takes me a long time, and I feel like they don't want to eat me for that long or something. Once I made myself come. I felt embarrassed sort of, but I was glad I did it. I just wish I could come with somebody else stimulating me. I guess I feel inadequate about not coming. If I'm madly in love with someone, I don't make love for orgasms, but I wish I could just hop into bed with someone and have fun—a light fling, have an orgasm, etc., and laugh, but I don't, so . . .''

♀"Sometimes, often in fact, I find myself on the edge of orgasm and can go no further. It's very frustrating.''

♀"I find it difficult to have an orgasm, mostly because I have to be completely relaxed and trusting the other person. However, I'm not constantly trying for one because they aren't the be-all and end-all of a sexual experience.''

♀ "I have had almost a total mental block against men. With women I feel secure, but I still have difficulty in reaching orgasm. My overuse of the vibrator has probably burnt out much of my response. I think it's a mental problem of trust also.''

♀"I have had a problem achieving orgasm with a partner, though I can have them easily and readily by masturbation. I think this is due to lack of experience (I have only been a 'practicing' lesbian a short time), lack of long-term relationships, and by not being assertive enough in communicating my likes and dislikes to my lovers. Since they have been far more experienced than I, I have hesitated to tell them 'how to' make love for fear they would be offended.''

Some of the women who have trouble achieving orgasm have analyzed their problems and offer some insight as to what has helped them overcome them:

♀"There have been times when it takes an hour or more for me to achieve orgasm and that causes frustration for both my lover and myself. Usually we'll just come back to it at a later time and . . . it works.''

♀"I need an incredible amount of hard, clitoral stimulation for a long time (twenty minutes to one-half hour) in order to orgasm, no matter how much into it or turned on unless I use a vibrator or water stream.''

♀"When I first started relating sexually to people, I was insecure about my ability to have an orgasm. But after I had had one, I began to relax, feel I am not particularly hung up, and now I do what I like and don't do what I don't like.''

♀"My big hangup was that I never had orgasms till about three months ago. When I was becoming sexually mature, the 'Sexual Revolution' was

on. I was a prude, always have been, still am, and it looked to me like women were throwing themselves away and becoming total whores. So I was disgusted and always believed I was not a carnal person: I wrote poetry, cared about the state of the world, and so on, so hedonism was completely alien to me. Just glancing at the magazines on the newsstands, it looked like the entire world was just one big meat market. I thought there were very few of us intellectuals left—the others were just studs and chicks. I never even masturbated, and I hated all carnality. Around this same time, I became anorexic, and this state lasted for many years. I realize now (without therapy) that my anorexia was an unconscious attempt to starve away my sexuality. My breasts shrank to the size they were when I was 12, my uterus shrank (I stopped having periods for about three years, and the gynecologist said my uterus was unusually small, and I would not be able to have children). I guess by putting myself in this state I was destroying my female attributes, which I identified with 'femininity.' When I recognized my lesbianism, it was a great relief, but that still did not cure either my anorexia or my frigidity. For this to occur, I still had to got through a series of intellectual and emotional experiences. Eventually I accepted my sexuality and my gender. I recovered from my anorexia first, and then, much later, my frigidity.

"The latter occurred about three months ago, when I read *The Hite Report*. When I read it, I recognized myself in some of the women who rationalized away their frigidity as if being frigid and asexual made you more spiritual. I also reasoned that a woman who could not come was equal to a man who could not ejaculate, and if I were a man, I would die if I were 'impotent,' so why be proud of my own impotence? So I decided I would have an orgasm if it killed me, and I began to practice every day. Within two weeks I had my first orgasm, and since then I have not had any problems. I now feel more complete and no longer have a shameful secret to hide. I can start new relationships, knowing I am no longer 'impotent.' "

♀"I find that, although I am very sexually responsive at least once during sex, the time it takes is (by comparison with all the women I've had sex with) unusually long. I reach a kind of plateau and stay there, very aroused and sensitized, for a long time. Since this is not true when I masturbate, I think it's probably related to the trouble I had in acknowledging my sexuality to begin with. When I first recognized my feelings for women were also sexual, I freaked out badly, and for three years I tried very hard to be heterosexual—which failed, thank God. Unfortunately, those experiences still affect my sexual response to other people, the dynamics of sharing sex, so to speak. This has improved greatly recently, especially because I was involved in a fairly long-term relationship with a woman I trusted very much, and being able to relax made a significant difference."

Other Performance Anxieties and Difficulties

Aside from the specific performance problem of having an orgasm, women expressed many other "performance anxieties."

♀"I get very caught up in performance concerns of a partner and become a 'spectator,' which blocks my sexual enjoyment and spontaneity. I'm worried that I won't be able to do the things she likes properly and she won't have an orgasm. Or I worry about whether she is bored with doing things to me that I like. The best, most spontaneous experiences I've had in years were two times when I was stoned and just got lost in the experience. It was great for me because I just let the other person stimulate me and enjoyed it without caring what she was experiencing, but I wish I had also been able to get into stimulating her in return and really been excited by that too. I've always tended to feel lazy toward the sexual partner."

♀"It is often hard for me to dare to play an active role, to dare to try something. I always think that I will be offending or hurting my partner, even if she is hurting me! I have a history of not being able to reach orgasm with a partner. Now as I push past my blocks about taking an active role (I think I'm overcoming insecurity) I find myself much more apt to orgasm myself. Also, I found myself extremely uptight about masturbating in front of my partner. After repeated tries, I felt less and less inhibited, and finally she did too, and we finished with a most enjoyable sex experience."

♀"I am probably overly concerned with whether or not my partner has an orgasm. This has definitely gotten in the way from time to time. (It doesn't bother me so much if I don't have one, but then I usually do.) On the occasions when my partner has not had an orgasm, I have felt very bad, questioned my sexual competence (the whole detestable male 'performance' trip). Not having an orgasm has never seemed to bother my partner particularly, but her not having one has bothered me quite a bit. It also bothers me when I make love with a woman who does not respond vocally (verbally) or physically move much, even though she may be feeling very intensely."

♀"I think one of my hangups is that my sexual needs are too genitally oriented. I like orgasm—aim for it both alone and with others and in the same vein have acquired a rather 'male' performance ethic that can lead me to be disappointed in a partner if she is not satisfied, and certainly disappointed if my needs aren't met. I am saddened by people's silence in bed. Personally I find it difficult to be patient enough. I am enough of a romantic to want to learn about someone sexually in a nonverbal way, but enough of me grew up in the 'instant intimacy' age to want to cut through the fumbling and find out about her sexual likes verbally."

♀"I do not like it when my women complain about my lovemaking

techniques. I like to want them to feel good, so if they do not I feel even worse.''

♀''I feel very vulnerable during sex (not a *bad* thing) so must feel secure with my partner. When I'm not secure, I prefer to make love to her, not have her make love to me. My previous lover withheld sex from me quite a lot as punishment and told me I sexually repulsed her when she was in a bad mood. Consequently, I'm very sensitive about whether my partner wants to make love or not.''

♀''I feel that through being raised and conditioned in a heterosexual lifestyle (I've been married to a man), I've come to put more importance on pleasing my partner than myself.''

♀''One problem I've noticed with lesbian sexuality is I never seem to get a comfortable flow of who makes love to who. When I first came out, I was sure there was some kind of lesbian 'etiquette' about this. Five years later I find I still worry about whether or not I'm making love to my lover enough. It's almost like scorekeeping . . . whose turn is it, etc. I have talked to a few women about this and apparently it's a common problem. Mostly the anxiety for me comes with my feeling I should be as aggressive as my lovers are, and I'm usually not. It always seems like there's a moment in every sexual encounter when we decide somehow who will be made love to first and how. I never had this problem with heterosexuality. This is the only thing I miss about being straight. Also because there's no clarity about what will happen when we make love, sometimes we end up with *nothing* happening because both of us are being passive. Then we both feel frustrated and disappointed.''

♀''Because of butch/femme role-playing in the late '50s, and early '60s, I refused to let women make love to me as I did to them. What a fool. Consequently I wasted many years not knowing what it felt like to be passive or enjoy mutual cunnilingus. I still have a few leftover anxieties about the passive role and therefore am usually the aggressor sexually.''

Not all lesbians had qualms about their own lovemaking being inadequate. Several complained that their main sexual problem is that their lovers are inadequate.

♀''I have had considerable difficulties because I seem to run into many women with limited skill and experience, and different preferences. Coupled with my inability to communicate, I would get trapped in unsatisfying relationships. For example, I enjoy vaginal penetration, and yet the majority of women whom I have been with have not desired this themselves, and so have not understood my own desire for it. I feel general pressure in the vagina which is not released except by stimulation. I don't reach orgasm this way, but it provides for a much more complete orgasm when coupled with clitoral stimulation.''

♀''I have run into lots of anxieties, hangups, compulsions, blocks, etc., but they always belonged to the other party. I have not yet encountered a

partner as comfortable with sex and as enthusiastic about frequency as I am, although my later experiences have been better than my earlier ones (seventeen years of practicing lesbianism).''

♀"The only frustration I have experienced in regard to sexual relationships was a short involvement with a woman who would caress me to the point of orgasm, get tired of the effort, turn over, and go to sleep. Needless to say, I spent a few sleepless nights.''

♀"Sometimes (not often) I take a long time to come. I don't mind. I feel excited and good but sometimes my partner will be puzzled.''

♀"My first lover was very repressed and could not express her wants or needs. She was used to a man fucking her and doing what 'he' wanted. Every time I asked what she wanted, she'd come back with 'I want it all' or 'Do what you want.' Thus every one of our sexual encounters was up to me. This can be very trying and nerve-racking. There are things that I'd like to do, but I don't know if she will be able to accept them. She likes everything I've done to her, but it makes me tense up when I am suddenly given the decision as to what we are going to do. The quality of her skill as a sex partner was also and still is limited. I can express my wants and needs, and usually vary from day to day, but I must be careful she does not get too rough or hurt me. I also tighten up when I feel it's going to be painful and have a hard time coming. I really wish she could learn to be a gentle woman.''

Communication Barriers

This last woman's complaint as well as many of the others echo again what seems to be the root of most of the problems: communication (including trust, which is the foundation of communication). The women were asked, *How often do you ask your partner for what you want done to you?*

always	7%
very frequently	19
somewhat frequently	32
somewhat infrequently	25
very infrequently	12
once	0
never	5

Thus, for a total of 42% of lesbians, communication during sex was a problem the majority of the time. Some of the women who answered this particular question realized that lack of communication was at the root of the problem.

♀"I guess I'm as inhibited about sex as the next person. My present lover is the first person who I've had anal sex with, although I'd done it in masturbation before. I just couldn't bring myself to do it to someone else, in case she thought it disgusting. I have problems too suggesting what I like.

I'd been wanting to do the 69 position for ages before we actually did it. I'm hung up by the idea that everything's spontaneous so you don't have to talk about it, and you certainly don't plan it.''

♀"I began with a major hangup which is a product of our culture, the difficulty of talking about sexuality or specific acts. Took me lots of time in therapy to break through that one.''

♀"Most of my hangups are in the area of talking about sex and asking for what I want.''

♀"I worry about having to guess what she would like because she doesn't like to say. I try to tell her what I would like and sometimes that's okay, but lots of times she just doesn't listen. I guess this is because she sees it as criticism and so turns off listening before I am finished.''

♀"I feel I am too reluctant in talking about sex, so I am never certain that I am really pleasing the other person. Also I am not good at indicating to the other what I want. We don't talk enough about what is happening. I guess I'm afraid it will interfere with the spontaneity plus I'm afraid I'll feel sad if I learn I'm not actually satisfying her and vice versa.''

♀"With my first partner, we occasionally had times when things just didn't go right. I couldn't tell her what I wanted and she couldn't guess. And I would feel very inadequate.''

♀"I sometimes feel I can't tell my lover everything I would like to do and have done because I know she would find some things repulsive.''

Getting the Right Amount of Sex

Another communication problem between lovers is often one of perception. One lover may believe that she wants more or less sex than her lover and feels badly because of the perceived difference. The lesbians were asked, *Do you feel that you place too much or too little importance on sex?*

too much	10%
just right	73
too little	8
not sure	9

A corresponding question asked, *Do you feel that others place too much or too little importance on sex?*

too much	37%
just right	16
too little	10
not sure	37

Thus, while most of the lesbians in the subsample thought they want the right amount of sex, they thought only a minority of other lesbians want the right amount!

♀"Sex is a relatively minor part of my personal life, and I often find it personally offensive that so many people (especially straight men) place so much emphasis on it for their own happiness in life. I believe that is misplaced. My lover and I often go through long periods of time without sex because I lose my sexual interest. It's usually because of work or school or both, which sap my energy and dominate my time. By the end of the day, I'm too weary to want anything sexual. My lover is extremely patient through it all because we're always touching, kissing, holding, and caressing each other anyway."

♀"It seems to me that I periodically lose my sex drive for a period of time lasting from three weeks to three months or so. This happened with men; in fact, it was even worse. In fact, I don't think I ever had a sex drive with men, but I used to go through celibate times back then. But since I've been a lesbian—say three years or so, two years of which have been in a tight relationship with one woman—it's different in that I may still masturbate occasionally, if less than usual, and will make love to her, if a little grudgingly, but it is still definitely a loss of desire to have sex. It's like it evaporates from my life. I can't really figure it out. I used to think it was because I was gay but hadn't really come out, and now I don't know. Sometimes I think it's a kind of rebellion against my upbringing: my mother tried to train me to be very sexually alluring to men, to think about sex a lot, to make it very central in my life. So sometimes I think I'm rebelling against that training. And sometimes I think it's because it's so goddam hard to survive and grow, and learn how to work well as a woman in this society that I can't handle everything at once, so I just go on low idle, so to speak, sexually, while I'm under pressure about work or political projects I'm involved in, although there isn't always a correlation between very tense times in my life and this phenomenon.

"I'm just now coming out of one of these sort of asexual periods that lasted about two months. I felt a bit guilty about it, but my lover was very good about it (it was the longest one since we've been together). By the way, a lot of women I know have these times, though some seem to try to repress it and force themselves to be sexual. I've spoken to at least seven or eight women, mostly lesbians, who've felt this way and thought that they were the only ones in the world."

♀"I feel that I am not in need of sex as much as she is, so I don't think I'm satisfying her enough."

♀"For many years, I believed myself 'undersexed,' since my lovers almost invariably wanted more sex than I did. More recently I've begun to want sex more myself, and that anxiety has evaporated."

For one woman, her sexual needs varied from wanting little sex to wanting a lot of sex.

♀"I find it very difficult to maintain any intense sexual relationship when I am deep in creative work, and a book can involve my attention for

up to two years. The low-key sexual temperament of the woman I live with is, therefore, through long stretches, exactly in harmony with my own needs. But a great deal of the energy I invest in work becomes sexual energy when I am finished with a long project. For weeks or even months, I want a relationship which is intensely sexual and emotionally absorbing. It serves both as compensation for the long isolation of work and as a source of energy for new work. When I was younger, this pattern created great conflict between me and the woman I live with and hardship on any lover who would have to deal with an intense involvement with the promise of nothing but abandonment. As attitudes toward sexuality have shifted, the woman I live with is less threatened either by a sense of failure to meet my needs or loss of a basically important relationship, and there are more women who enjoy sexual involvement without feeling the need of commitment to every partner, and I therefore feel less guilty than I used to.''

Then there were those who always feel they want too much sex or more sex than their partners.

♀''I wish my lover and I had sex more often. This is gonna be a problem the longer we are together. I know she is perfect for me in every other way. I hope we can solve this because we are planning on getting married and going to Europe for our honeymoon.''

♀''My basic problem is that I usually want/need sex more than the person I am with.''

♀''I have a greater desire for sex than most women I know. Sometimes I want to continue making love until I am totally worn out (and my partner too).''

♀''I think the only thing that really bugs me is that we used to have sex almost daily, sometimes for many, many hours at a time, but now we're too busy!''

♀''I would like to have sex more frequently, but there never seems to be enough time.''

Perhaps worse than wanting too much sex or too little sex is not being able to get sex at all—that is, not being able to find any or enough sex partners for any number of reasons.

♀''I've had trouble finding sex partners. All of my partners to date have been pick-ups, usually people I would not even consider falling in love with. The people I have loved have been unwilling to have sex with me, for one reason or another. I've had more men than women even though I found out I was a lesbian while still a virgin. I *know* I'm a lesbian, but in order to have any sex life at all I still have to go to men. I don't like that. It's been one of my major problems. Still is, in fact.''

♀''I truly would like to have a lover and live happily ever after. Or at least for a year or two. If I had sex with one lover once a week I would be in

heaven forever! As it is, I masturbate about three times in two-week periods, try and sometimes succeed at getting at least one woman sex partner a month.''

♀"I guess my biggest problem is that I'd like to have more women sex partners than I've had in my first four years of 'active' lesbianism (two partners), but somehow, I never seem to get it across to other women. I've got a number of really close, special relationships with women, which to me seems only natural that we could share lovemaking as just another of our good experiences, but I've been turned down by all of them. Some even seemed offended at the idea! I feel like there must be something very unappealing in me! I'm not ugly or crude or anything. I'm *not* too forward. I've always had the feeling that if I asked a woman to go to bed with me, she'd be disgusted, which is a leftover from when I was a miserable, suicidal teenage dyke in a world I *knew* was 100% straight! Even one of the women I loved who was offended at the idea of me being sexually attracted to her said she thought I needed to have experience with a lot more women. (I somehow felt very emotionally ripped off at that statement coming from her.) I even wanted to go to a lesbian 'cruise bar' to see if I could engage in a 'pick-up.' But the places here are very couple-oriented. I don't know any good 'opening lines,' either. This all makes me very depressed and it sounds like every other lesbian in the country is having 500 times more fun than me (which my logical self says is a bunch of baloney!). I feel like a real turkey! I also feel like if the opportunity ever did present itself that someone wanted to go to bed with me, I'd drop everything no matter *what* time of the month it was or even if I had the world's worst case of vaginitis or had just got off work and felt like shit and no matter how rank this person smelled. I don't know if that makes me desperate or just nondiscriminating. It's probably also offensive to any woman who *is* interested in me that I have this air about me. It probably turns them off. But that *is* how I feel. Sometimes it really burns me up to hear lesbians talking about how hard it is to form 'platonic' friendships with sisters, like being a dyke is just one big bounce from bed to bed! It *sure* ain't that way here, though I kind of wish it was! Is it that I'm obsessed with sex to the point that I even want to do it with my very close and dear women friends, or is it that *they* are so hung up about it they just can't accept lovemaking as something that just can come naturally and beautifully between women who care a lot for each other? That's how *I* always thought it would be, before I got into the 'real' lesbian world, though somewhere back in my memory, it still stays.''

Guilt and Miscellaneous Problems

Another problem is that for every lesbian who is having trouble getting sex, there is another lesbian who feels guilty about having it!

♀"Early in my lesbianism, I had problems with guilt about my sexual enjoyment, but I went right on enjoying it!''

♀"The only hangup I have is that I feel guilty right now when I have sex

with women. You see, I still love my first lover, M., but she doesn't like me to hang around her, so that puts me into a very poor position."

♀"I felt guilty about my heterosexual experiences because it had been specifically forbidden, but no one had told me not to have homosexual sex, so the guilt was less. It was about equal to my guilt about masturbation. It was sex so I 'knew' it was improper, but it wasn't 'bad,' just embarrassing and secret. It wasn't going to make me 'pregnant' and 'in trouble.' "

Aside from guilt, several women felt that their sexual enjoyment was limited to certain environmental conditions:

♀"I must have privacy during lovemaking and no bright lights. A dim room is very nice. It's not that I have to make love in the dark, but areas of bright light really distract me and I sometimes have to put a pillow over my face to blot out a patch of sunlight shining through a chink in a curtain. I tend to find that bright light hurts my eyes anyway, so it may be related to that."

♀"I love to look at my lover's body, but I prefer to make love in the dark (or at least semidark) because my self-image is a little low, and I feel self-conscious when I am looked at."

♀"The only thing I hate is having sex with lights on. I find it almost impossible."

♀"In the beginning of our relationship I would not take my clothes off. I had never trusted or loved anyone enough to be at ease in the nude. Now it's beautiful."

Then there was one woman who complained about the age gap among lesbians.

♀"Since I'm 41, and many of my partners are younger, I hate hearing about the age gap, and I try not to throw it back in the form of experience, but often the younger crew imposes this hangup on me. Afterwards, I get quite different comments, but it's a problem that will no doubt get more acute with every year; I note in my own questionnaire that I went to 'neutral' at 65 + myself!"

Finally there were a few miscellaneous problems, related by only one or two lesbians who responded.

♀"I had one hangup; I am a very wet partner, so when the sheets got wet, I would sometimes feel silly or ashamed. But my current lover likes it, and now I think it's very sensual."

♀"I had a very serious 'hangup' where sex was concerned a few months back due to a rape experience over a year ago. This is how my 8-month-old son was conceived originally. I am getting better now because of the real love I feel for my lover. She is very understanding and helpful concerning

this horrible ordeal. This experience had a real bearing on our sex life because as you can imagine I was frightened to death whenever anyone touched me sexually.''

♀ "Masturbation is my only hangup. I do it, but feel it is private and don't discuss it.''

As the reader certainly understands by now, many lesbians have things that they are ashamed of, embarrassed by, blocked about, hung up over, terrified of, or angry at, and most of all they think they are the only ones having that problem. And isolation is probably the worst part of a hangup, because when you find out so many others have the same problem, you realize that it might not be a hangup after all. It was such a realization, when several women got together and discovered that they were not the only ones in the world who hated housework, that helped to start women's liberation. Perhaps this sharing of problems may help those who have these problems to be more open about them. After all, a friend of yours may very well have the same problem. In communicating the problem, you may be able to overcome it, or maybe a friend can suggest or has found a solution, as some of the women here have found some solutions. The survey showed that 48% of lesbians are secretive about some aspect of their sex lives. One of those keeping a secret may be someone you assume is totally "liberated"! The only way to find out is to ask!

Handicaps and Physical Disabilities

A handicap or physical disability is often in the eye of the beholder. For example, blind people rightly believe that they can function as well as sighted people. In the same vein, many liberal heterosexuals view lesbianism as a "handicap"—that is, some form of hindrance to their success in the world. Perhaps that makes lesbians a bit more understanding of other people who are considered disabled in the eyes of society.

Since the authors could not afford to print this questionnaire in braille, surely that factor did prohibit more blind people from answering the questions, although there was some response from blind lesbians. In that sense, being blind and a lesbian can be a handicap. Perhaps few materials are available for the blind lesbian, although now there is a lesbian/feminist braille magazine, and some gay books such as *Out of the Closets* were recorded for the blind.

Lesbian events, however, do have the added disadvantage that they often do not have facilities for the physically disabled or for the elderly. Women's centers and coffee houses often lack ramps for wheelchairs or elevators if the women's center (as is the one in New York City, for example) is more than one story high. Some progress has been made, however. At the Gay Pride Rally in New York in June 1977 the rally coordinators provided interpreters for deaf mutes. They translated

everything into sign language. There is now also a national organization for gay deaf mutes as well as a national conference. Perhaps these developments bode better times for the disabled among gay people. Further developments will probably be possible, thanks to the predominantly positive feelings of lesbians towards the disabled.

♀"Physical handicaps aren't important. I don't love someone for how they look."

♀"Big deal. Everyone is handicapped in some way, whether emotionally or physically, whether they admit it or not. I have a dear friend who is in a wheelchair for life, and just because she sits down all the time is absolutely no reason for me to shirk her."

♀"I'm beginning to pay attention to the problem of body image and the assumptions made that everyone is 'normal.' I myself am not disabled and consequently don't pay attention to the hundreds of ways disabled people are kept down. Although sexual prejudice against disabled people is present in most nondisabled people, I feel that a disabled lesbian is more likely to find friends and lovers among lesbians because women care much more than men do about a person's inner self and find beauty in a great variety of exteriors."

♀"Going along with the youth cult is the physically perfect cult. As usual, people who are 'physically handicapped' (whatever that means) are social outcasts. I have never had a relationship (on a sexual as well as friendship basis) with a 'physically handicapped' woman, but I can't see any reason not to have one."

♀"I work with handicapped people. In most people I like, the handicap is only a small part of that total person."

♀"I have never been attracted to a person with a physical handicap, but then I've met only *very* few lesbians with handicaps. I danced with a blind woman once, and I got over my 'protectiveness' to her when she turned out to be better at it than *I* was! I've shown a 'protectiveness' to such people, and I would like to get over it. I don't believe in falling all over myself to help such a person. The disabled people I know really resent having everybody in the world assuming they can't cope with things."

A few women stated that they are even attracted to handicapped people.

♀"I have always had an attraction for physically handicapped people. I kept clippings about such people hidden in a box in my bedroom and would lock myself in my room and look at them for hours. I remember having distinctly sexual feelings about them. (I wrote one younger 'poster boy' expressing my love and my wish to correspond. However, most of the clippings were of women.) It would be no barrier for me to get involved with someone with a handicap and might even tend to make them more attractive."

Two women who have been in relationships with handicapped people shared their experiences with us.

♀"I am fortunate in that my body is in good working order. I am not put off by people with handicaps. I really do look for the person—the mind and heart—and not how they look or function. In fact, my current lover is visually handicapped—legally blind. But she is the most beautiful, sensitive woman, and her 'limitations' rarely come to mind. Another friend of mine is deaf. I think everyone is handicapped in some way which may not be openly apparent. We are all imperfect and lacking. Some people's handicaps are physical, some are mental/emotional. My friend may not be able to see flowers and the moon or street signs, but she sees into me and others' hearts. I most certainly believe that just because someone has a handicap that is visible that doesn't mean they're any less of a person. True worth comes from the heart."

♀"My husband was physically handicapped. I loved him and things were okay between us, but it used to bother me when people stared at us. After we were divorced, several insensitive people asked if I had left him because he was handicapped. (The answer was no.) I understand a lot of the problems handicapped people have are due to oppression, not their own physical limitations."

A few people were negative toward people with handicaps.

♀"I don't think I could go with someone physically handicapped."

♀"I've been paid to have sex with 'handicaps.' It was curious and interesting. I met a lesbian in New York with a glass eye. I felt sorry for her. She was quite unappealing."

♀"I would prefer someone who is in the same physical shape as I am."

♀"I know some deaf people and find them hard to deal with, because they don't communicate in the detailed way I must have. Blindness doesn't affect me like that, although I would certainly miss experiencing visual things, especially reading. I have a good friend who is a paraplegic, and she seems to function fine, but then she's very intelligent. But if we had to fight, I mean really defend ourselves, what could she do? We must, those of us who plan daughters, see that those who could not function in primitive society are aborted or killed in early childhood. This may sound cruel to one who does not believe in reincarnation, but it is not."

♀"I believe in euthanasia if a person cannot live a fairly productive life. I don't mean to imply that someone who is blind should be killed, only someone who is a vegetable or a hopeless paraplegic."

Unfortunately, perhaps because it might be difficult for a paraplegic to answer the questionnaire, there were no responses from lesbians who have

such a handicap. Here are some firsthand experiences from women who have other handicaps.

♀"My physical handicaps (lousy words) do slow me down, but have never ruled out any sexual activity. I have (among other things) an artificial bladder which requires gentle treatment and will not tolerate excess pressure or strain upon it. But these minor adjustments have never bothered my sexual partners, though I was rather self-conscious at first."

♀"Tribadism is painful for me due to a rape by the American medical establishment. I've got a bald spot on my pubic hair and lots of scar tissue that is very tender, and the wrong sort of pressure can be excruciatingly painful. So I give it, but rarely receive it."

♀"The main problem for each of us has been the sometimes limited movement that comes from having sacroiliac problems. I used to feel pretty uptight, not able to let go and just let her be in charge of my body. That circumstance was mutual. We decided that it was because each of us had spent too long (over forty years collectively) with men, and we never did trust them to be sensitive or responsible about our satisfaction. This has pretty much dissipated, so the anxiety business is infrequent."

♀"Because I have arthritis, this ailment presents a problem during sex in that I can't tell exactly how much pressure I am putting on my sex partner's clitoral area. The arthritis has also limited my hand movements, but some cooperation and communication with my partner overcomes most of this."

♀"Although I have some vision, it is extremely limited. I am usually faced with wearing bottle-thick glasses to bed or not being able to see my sex partner. (I think it was a shock the first time I was doing cunnilingus and realized that I could no longer see her face, but I've since gotten used to that aspect of it.) Not being able to see her face slightly decreases some of the pleasure of sex. After all, I do like to see her pleasure as well as feel it. My lack of vision is only a major problem if a woman isn't vocal. For example, if she is totally silent, I can't tell sometimes whether it is because she has had an orgasm and wants me to stop or whether it is because I am not doing something in a pleasing way. Discussing this problem and asking women to vocally help me has alleviated this difficulty."

The major complaint in this section was from women who are overweight and feel that their obesity is a problem in obtaining a sex partner. Among lesbians, particularly on the West Coast, there has been sort of a Fat Liberation Front, which has alerted people to the sorts of discrimination faced by overweight individuals. They have pointed out the discrimination against lesbians on these grounds and labeled it "looksism." In fact, they are right. After avoiding unclean women, most lesbians avoided overweight individuals, a fact which demonstrates perhaps, that lesbians are not totally immune to the standards of the heterosexual society. Overweight lesbians feel this.

♀"I have socio-psychological and psychosexual setbacks, and hangups, caused by my being overweight."

♀"Extra weight makes a good horse work harder to win; this, in itself, is not a bad thing. Society has toward this, as everything else, a fucked attitude."

♀"Now that I have 'come out' in the past two years or so and still have not had much to do with women, I feel strongly that it is because of my grossly obese situation. This only leads to my further negative self-image and depression. I would be especially interested in the results of your survey regarding this question. Lesbian/feminist friends tell me that weight doesn't matter, and that it is a 'male standard,' etc. I think lesbians reject fat women just as much as men do."

In Chapter 6 weight is discussed further in relation to finding a sex partner.

Venereal Disease and Health Problems

Venereal disease doesn't appear to be a problem among lesbians. In fact, lesbians have about the lowest rate in the country for venereal disease. Part of the reason for this is that most venereal infections cannot live in contact with air, and therefore, lesbian sex acts usually do not involve a situation conducive to the spread of venereal disease. Another blessing of lesbianism! In the survey no lesbians reported that they had had syphilis; 1.3% reported that they had had gonorrhea at least once, but many of those stated that they had gotten them from men, not women! As for lesser conditions, 12.6% had had lice ("crabs") and 3.3% had had scabies, another, smaller insect parasite. Yet about 10% to 20% reported that frequently the fear of venereal disease influenced their choice of a sex partner, the sexual acts they engaged in and/or how often they had sex; therefore, one may conclude that the fear of venereal disease was more prevalent among lesbians than the disease itself.

The survey did not ask whether women had gotten herpes, vaginitis, trichomoniasis, or monilla infections from sexual contact with other women. It is possible to get these diseases in this way, and then they are indeed venereal diseases. But the authors thought that to ask such a question would be confusing, since there are other ways to get these ailments, including using a lover's (or stranger's) towel or washcloth. And some of them, like herpes, seem to generate spontaneously when a woman is in poor health. Indeed, these diseases do not seem to be well understood. Anyway, under "other" venereal disease, women did volunteer that they had gotten these diseases from same-sex contact.

Less than 1% reported getting herpes, 1% reported getting monilla, 1% getting vaginitis, 1% reported getting trich. Even for these diseases, the percentages are rather tiny, and one can conclude that in general lesbians have healthy fun together.

17

Anxieties and Ailments:
The Gay Male Experience

Many of those who have chosen to stand against gay people like to say that there's nothing gay about being gay. Presumably, much of what appears throughout this book will express the joy and the naturalness, yes, the gaiety, of gay life. But only the Pollyannas among us would try to claim that everything is carefree bliss for gay men. Now, not all of the problems gay men have are due to the fag-beaters and the Anita Bryants and the rip-off headshrinkers—for that, see Chapter 18, which deals with oppression. Gay men do have serious problems in their sexual and social lives, and though these problems are often rooted in the way sex is structured in society, it is not particularly helpful to tell people to wait until "the revolution" to solve their problems. Open discussion of such problems may be a start toward understanding and solving them.

The men were asked one long question which one respondent described as a "blockbuster." The question was this:

Relate any feelings and experiences concerning anxieties, "hang-ups," compulsions, blocks, repressions, special needs, handicaps, problems with sexual performance or functioning, problems with the frequency of sex or the quality or skill of your sex partners, that you have had in regard to your general sex life or specific sexual acts.

Replies to this question form the bulk of this chapter.

It is impossible to divorce the question of sexual functioning from the expectations that people have. Those expectations are in part premised on concepts and ideas learned in the general culture. In its crudest form, sex for men in this society is "getting a hard-on and sticking it in a pussy and shoving it in and out until you get your rocks off." This is the prevailing concept of male sexuality that young boys learn, whether they are gay or straight. But that concept is straight, and straight male definitions can be seen as limiting for gay men desiring to express themselves more freely. This is not a matter of mere substitution of another hole for "pussy." Much of

what is called "sexual dysfunctioning" by sex doctors can be simply an unwillingness or inability to fit into the mythology of straight male sexuality, which is so heavily centered on cock and orgasm. It is true that for a man, whether gay or straight, sexual functioning with a partner is presumed to involve erection, contact and stimulation, and orgasm with ejaculation. Nor is there necessarily anything wrong with this pattern. But it is a presumption—it is not a necessity and it is not a universal occurrence. In Chapter 11 many of the respondents describe their enjoyment of full body sensuality and such acts as holding, stroking, caressing, and kissing, none of which are centered in the genitals. Such attitudes, much in tune with feminist writing on sexuality, suggest that cock-centeredness is not necessary or even good. Of course, for most men the cock is a source of great pleasure, and its stimulation, especially during erection, is one of the most important aspects of sexual communication. The point, perhaps, is that departure from traditional cock-and-orgasm sexuality does not have to be seen as "failure," as it so often is labeled. There are other expectations which can be equally tyrannical. For example, the participation in certain specific sexual acts may be presumed, and some men may expect others to take part in (and accept the norms of) the "gay scene." These issues are explored in this chapter.

Whether or not a person's ideas or experiences constitute a "hangup" or a problem is bound to be a matter of opinion. For some people, obviously, homosexuality itself might be considered a hangup, though most of our respondents see it as an appropriate form of sexual communication for them. In this chapter, however, it is the respondents themselves who indicate that certain aspects of their lives as gay people cause problems. It is in that spirit of introspection, self-criticism, and inward-looking concern that this material is presented here. Many respondents said simply that they had no hangups. Lucky them, and yet, who's to say? Maybe their hangup is that they can't admit to hangups!

Orgasm

Let's start at the "end," with orgasm. Orgasm, sometimes known as "the big O," can be a problem. Respondents indicate overwhelmingly that *orgasm is important* to them, as follows:

very important	55%
somewhat important	36
neutral	4
somewhat unimportant	4
very unimportant	1

However, quite a few men have trouble reaching orgasm, or can reach orgasm only in a certain way.

The men were asked *how often they have one or more orgasms during sex with a partner,* and the responses were:

always	26%
very frequently	42
somewhat frequently	14
somewhat infrequently	7
very infrequently	7
once	2
never	2

There is some possibility that some men were confused by the question's use of the phrase "one or more orgasms"—possibly some men thought it meant "more than one." In any case, sex *without* orgasm, while not too frequent, was not a bizarre or unknown occurrence, and it is seen as a problem by some men.

Comments on orgasm came from men who have trouble reaching it as well as from men who feel there is too much emphasis placed on it:

⚣"I have trouble coming to orgasm, so I usually don't, and some of my partners think of it as their fault. I may be too used to masturbation or possibly 'hung up.' I don't know and I can't understand it."

⚣"Since I am a 'professional call-boy' I find that I may have difficulty in performance in my personal sex life. This usually takes the form of not being able to achieve orgasm easily, if at all."

⚣ "I have trouble coming with someone else. It always takes me a long time to come even when I masturbate, but then I can control it—I know what fantasy will turn me on. With others, sometimes it takes ages. Usually I have to jerk myself off at some time during sex. One lover I had really knew how to suck me just right—I never had any trouble, but I'll be damned if I know what he did. Sometimes it's easier for me to come if the guy I'm with finger-fucks me for a while before sucking me. It seems to relax me."

⚣"I do feel that I have some sort of mental block about orgasm. It takes me much longer than anyone I know to reach orgasm. Except through a glory hole. I do not enjoy the idea of a glory hole, but it is one of the ways that a 'straight' guy can perform sexual acts without being identified. I personally wish that I could get off as easy when with a person."

⚣"My main hangup is that I cannot 'let myself go'—I spend too much time thinking about the mechanics of sex. Therefore, I usually do not enjoy the sex very much and I usually don't come. In order to really relate to a person sexually, I need to trust him and know that he loves me."

⚣"I've talked with a few people about this, but mostly I keep it secret. I've come only twice during sex, and until I was 26, had never been able to come during masturbation. I made that breakthrough while working with a bioenergetics therapist, and it was a big step for me. I'm still not to the

point where I can come during sex and prefer it when my sex partners don't worry about it. I prefer not talking about it because I feel like a freak when I do.''

⚤''I have a problem of either not being able to maintain an erection with another person, or at least of not reaching a climax with another person, and this is a problem virtually every time I make love. It is definitely tied to anxiety, but I can't tell just what the anxiety is. For one thing, also, the pleasure I get from *giving* pleasure to my partner is not a genital pleasure, although it is certainly sexual. I feel very satisfied just giving pleasure, without having an orgasm myself. Yet I feel this disappoints my partners quite often. There is no doubt that my partners love the things I do for them in bed—they've made that clear—but I think they'd feel even better if they were not ever so slightly put down by not being able to bring me off.''

⚤''I have the problem of retarded ejaculation and most of the time I must masturbate myself to climax, even with a sex partner. This troubles me and I am working with a clinical psychologist using hypnosis to try to change this.''

⚤ ''I have one strong block to my sexual life: I know that after an orgasm it will take some considerable time to recover and be able to continue with my sexual activities, so I hold back an orgasm, but many times when this is done, later an orgasm becomes impossible. This is very frustrating.''

⚤''The most important problem I have had is that of taking a very long time to come. I always feel that I am tiring my partner out and it has only been with my present lover that I feel safe in letting him keep masturbating or sucking me—I don't feel I have to offer to take over and do it myself. I think I am getting quicker just through doing it more often and through being able to relax with my partner.''

⚤''As I have gotten older I find that the frequency of orgasm has diminished somewhat. When young, I always could have more than one orgasm within a short time. Always had one or more per day. Now I find that I seldom have more than one a day, and often only one every other day. (Except one time recently when I had three in a row, one without being erect, which I would have thought impossible, but found that it isn't.) Also the intensity of most orgasms now at 48 years is less than I remember when I was 30 or (if my memory is clear) when I was 20.''

Occasionally, the emphasis on orgasm leads men to fake it.

⚤''I feel very uptight when having sex with a partner. I feel I have to 'perform' and this makes me very inhibited. It's *very* hard for me to come and also embarrassing when I don't. I usually have to fake it.''

As indicated in the preceding quotation, some men do fake orgasm, although faking orgasm is much more difficult for men than it is for women. Asked *how often they fake orgasm,* the men reported as follows:

very frequently	1%
somewhat frequently	1
somewhat infrequently	7
very infrequently	29
once	11
never	51

The respondents were also asked, *How important is it to you whether your partner has orgasm during sex with you?* and the replies were:

very important	53%
somewhat important	38
neutral	6
somewhat unimportant	2
very unimportant	1

Responses in Chapter 11 about sex acts reflect this overwhelming importance placed on the partner's orgasm, and in some cases pleasure is obtained from the ejaculation and the seminal fluid itself. But there were also some critical comments on the entire orgasm emphasis:

⚥"Sometimes my partners are too 'come-oriented.' I'd rather take time to heighten the experience. Sex is a human not just genital act. I guess in furtiveness, we sometimes concentrate on the climax rather than the more important communicative preludes."

⚥"Many years ago I came to the realization that the process of lovemaking was far more fulfilling and enjoyable (and longer-lasting) than the moment of ejaculation. If he can't come but enjoyed the process, we made it; if I can't come but enjoyed the process, I made it."

⚥"My only possible kind of problem is that I like to and am able to climax quite a number of times in an evening, and many partners are not able to, or worse yet, immediately after their orgasm they become very uninterested in sex. I am interested and am able to go on—and want to. Finding a matching partner is sometimes very difficult in this regard."

⚥"If I had to think of a hangup about sex that I have, I guess probably, it's an ego problem, meaning that it upsets me if my partner does not have orgasm. I guess it's a feeling that I could not satisfy my partner."

⚥"I had a lover who had trouble coming. He had to masturbate himself for twenty minutes or more before he came. This did not bother me because I love him."

Coming too soon, or premature ejaculation, is a problem faced by some of the men, as follows:

very frequently	1%
somewhat frequently	1
somewhat infrequently	7
very infrequently	29
once	11
never	51

Although premature ejaculation isn't a very common occurrence, it does seem to be a source of anxiety for some men. The men were asked, *How concerned are you about premature ejaculation in yourself and in your partner?* and the responses were:

	VERY CONCERNED	SOMEWHAT CONCERNED	NEUTRAL	SOMEWHAT UNCONCERNED	VERY UNCONCERNED	NOT SURE
in yourself	10	18	17	9	46	2%
in your partner	4	16	26	13	37	2

The men offered the following observations on premature ejaculation:

⚧ "My main problem is that all too often I come immediately! Just one thrust up an ass and I shoot. The same through a glory hole."

⚧ "I've tried different systems of control but none works for me."

⚧ "I am extremely hung up about my smallness and my premature ejaculations. For so long I hid in a closet, only frequenting parks for quick releases, that I didn't experience, and thereby perfect, what I am learning now. The more I accept my sexuality and my sexual preferences, the more I experience, the more my hangups are becoming resolved."

⚧ "I feel my problem of premature ejaculation is caused directly by the masturbatory practices of my youth. I never used lubricant, just held it and went as quickly as I could to be sure I wouldn't get caught. I now have started to masturbate using lubricants and bringing myself close to orgasm and then letting off for a while to become used to having something glide over my penis. I am teaching myself that slow is fun."

⚧ "When I was more closety and less comfortable with anal intercourse, I used to come as soon as I penetrated my partner. I had my own theory about why I responded that way: I thought I came right away in order to get it over with because I was afraid of hurting my partner. But coming too soon always bothered me, and I disappointed many partners who were excited about getting fucked by my big cock."

Impotence and Erection

Difficulty with achieving or maintaining erection, usually called "impotence," was another problem gay men referred to in discussing their hangups. In his essay "Refusing to be a Man," published in the anthology *For Men Against Sexism* (Times Change Press), John Stoltenberg states that "what's called 'impotence' is another internalization of a perverse system of male-dominant cultural values." He suggests that men are trained to feel that a limp penis is useless, asserting that erections are closely related to fantasies of "penetration and violence." Thus, it may be that there is an overemphasis on erections, and indeed many men do strive to enjoy the sensual experience with another man without such an emphasis on genital "performance." It may also be that men do not get erect because they do not really want to. Perhaps there is an *expectation* of erection, on the part of another person or even on the part of society, but not getting erect in such a case should not be called impotence. Of course, it is also true that many men report that their own erection and their partner's erection are essential aspects of a pleasurable sexual encounter—indeed, this is the prevailing view. Here are a number of comments about erections and impotence:

⚥"I had problems maintaining erections with women from age 22–26. Went to counseling, was put on behavior-modification program of masturbating to *Playboy* centerfolds and porno mags of women. Found it not very helpful. Was 'cured' by finding partners (at first female and later male too) with whom I lost the performance anxiety which was related to my problem."

⚥"On numerous occasions I have had considerable difficulty in getting and maintaining an erection. This has been the source of much embarrassment and frustration. I am trying to discover what it is that makes it a problem. I avoid any kind of public sex primarily because I know ahead of time that I will probably be unable to get hard. Sometimes I am able to pinpoint what is turning me off, so to speak. Like something my partner may or may not be doing. Or some outside distraction. At other times, my penis seems to turn off by itself, even if my head is still very much turned on. I'm not sure why I have this problem, nor do I think it is particularly urgent. My best guess is that my anxiety about whether I like the person I'm with as a person causes the problem."

⚥"I had one experience where I couldn't get hard. I think it was due to the simple fact that the guy I was with was too good a friend of mine."

⚥"My major obstacle has been in feeling bad when I can't perform sexually—am impotent. This I find deeply embarrassing. However, I pretty much know when and why it happens to me. It stops once I get to know someone. But sometimes the fear of it assaults me during sex, and then I get anxious."

⚥"The tranquilizer Mellaril has stopped most of my hard-ons and coming. I took it for five or six years, forced on me; I used to fight over it, and I hate Mellaril."

⚥"The impotency problem that I still have started about four years before I left my wife. She was going through menopause and we were spending most of our time together arguing and drinking. I believe that the last good sex we had was in 1972 and we separated in 1976. After the fighting I would still be angry with her when we went to bed and be in no mood for sex even when she wanted it. She harassed and degraded me about the impotency, which of course made it worse. By impotency, I mean not having a stiff enough erection for penetration. Since I left my wife I have had sex with men only. Last April I was with a man to whom I was really attracted and still impotent. It was then that I started looking into doing something about it. I sought counseling through a newspaper ad, and ended up spending one hour a week for six weeks with a psychiatric social worker. He thought that my excessive drinking might be the cause of the impotency. I attended some meetings of a gay alcoholic group and finally determined that the drinking was related to my nonacceptance of myself as a homosexual. I have now cut way down on the drinking and the impotency problem has improved somewhat but is still not satisfactory. I had also tried one of these 'Erecto' creams that are advertised. That was completely useless and I got my money back. My next step is to go to a urologist to find out if there are any physical causes of the problem. If there are no physical causes, I'll have to cope with psychological causes or else get used to the problem."

⚥"I find it difficult to function properly unless I know the person quite well and feel a genuine affection for them. Nine times out of ten, when I go to bed with a person I've only known for a few hours I find it difficult if not impossible to get an erection. If I know the person well, I'll be hard before I can get undressed."

⚥"One thing I have noticed about others (and no longer blame myself for) is the inability of many people to keep an erection, and even to come. Thank God I almost never have had either problem with myself. I would tend to think it was me, or my lack of stimulating these partners, that was the cause. But lots of gossiping and checking notes, etc., has brought me to the point of knowing that 90% of these instances are not caused by me (or by me alone)."

Anal Sex and Other Problems

Some people report problems with specific sexual acts, especially anal intercourse. These problems can include "going soft," pain, or just general aversion. As we have seen in Chapter 11 many people have strong preferences about the sexual acts they like and dislike, but for some, the feeling goes beyond a mere preference to become a problem fraught with

emotional or physiological difficulty. Some of these problems are easily traced to cultural inhibitions and hangups related to bodily functions. For some men, the idea of anal intercourse brings with it considerable baggage from heterosexual relations, and so the act can involve an individual's concerns about masculine and feminine identity. Some of these concerns about sex and roles are discussed in Chapter 7 and 9.

Quite a few men say that to be on receiving end of anal intercourse hurts them. It is undeniably true that for many men, such pain is due to psychological hangups which prevent them from relaxing. But sometimes, it does just plain hurt! And for some men it may hurt *most of the time* despite their best efforts at consciousness-raising and relaxation. Unfortunately, virtually all of the gay male sex manuals, including *Loving Men, Men Loving Men,* and *The Joy of Gay Sex,* place a great deal of emphasis on anal intercourse, stressing the variety of positions, and implying that if the person is relaxed enough, it will feel good. Such a simplistic view is not fair to the many men who have trouble with this act.

There were even some men who indicated difficulty with anal sex when asked about what aspects of their sex lives they keep secret:

⚥"I have difficulty in engaging in anal intercourse and find it difficult to experiment or admit openly that I cannot engage in anal intercourse easily."

⚥"I prefer passive anal. I like to think that preference is no indication of or reflection on my masculinity, but . . ."

⚥"I've never had intercourse because I'm scared to death of it."

Here are more comments concerning anal intercourse as a source of anxiety:

⚥"I fantasize a lot about being fucked but can't actually do it; a frustration."

⚥"Not enough 'masculine' males can or want to get fucked."

⚥"I wish I felt freer to explore anal sex by being rougher and fucking people I like, not just people I find unattractive or stupid; also that I felt freer to be fucked and could enjoy it without it hurting."

⚥"Sometimes I go soft when raving hard and partner is ready and willing to let me fuck him."

⚥"Sometimes I really like getting fucked, but sometimes it hurts, and when it does hurt I just bear the pain and wait for my partner to finish. I wish I could assert myself and tell him to stop, but I'm afraid he'll think I'm just trying to be butch, and I'm afraid he'll be frustrated or disappointed if I interrupt him."

⚥"I have a bit of a block about getting fucked. This is because of a man who tried to fuck me dry once and who was very thick. It hurt so much; ever since I've had a problem. I think it's the head of the penis that does this. If I've had a beer or a joint or poppers, then it's okay."

⚥"It took me a long time, and a special course (in San Francisco) in anal

relaxation, before I enjoyed being screwed. I used to think anal acts were dirty, but as I have had more experience, those feelings dropped away. (Old toilet-training programming.)''

⚤ "I never liked to be fucked either with a finger or a cock until my lover slowly conditioned my ass to accept his finger, fingers, and cock with minimal pain. I know his love would not cause me physical hurt so with him I can trust and relax.''

⚤ "So many of the sexual partners I have had seem to be preoccupied with fucking. I can't understand why they don't fuck women if that is all they desire.''

⚤ "I will let only my lover fuck me. He alone can have that pleasure.''

⚤ "I guess I have a block about fucking someone else. I can fuck for a short time but will not climax and after a while will go limp. I feel sort of bad about that because most men I know like to get fucked and I want mutual satisfaction, and I don't want my partner to think that he does not turn me on—that's the idea he could get.''

⚤ "I am quite big and had the experience of people telling me very bluntly they couldn't take me (even though I'm gentle), which has tended to make me apprehensive about doing it even when they want me to. I lose my erection. With a lover, though, it's different.''

⚤ "I experience impotence when actively fucking a man's ass. I've gone to a special sex-therapist-psychiatrist for a couple of years and I got nowhere. I never found out where my aversion is, or what it is. The psychiatrist was not gay-oriented and could only suggest that I find someone with whom I could relax and everything would be all right. Because of this great inferiority of mine, I seem to be unwilling to have intimate physical contact with people whom I like; therefore the chances of finding an understanding partner become more and more remote. I tend to isolate myself, seek anonymous impersonal sex, experience loneliness—and often despair with all of life.''

Oral sex seems less problematical for people. But there were a few comments concerning problems in this realm.

⚤ "The only thing that still bothers me about specific sexual acts is that I really do not like to swallow come. I find it very distasteful and wonder why.''

⚤ "I have trouble 69-ing because I can't stay hard while sucking someone else's cock, unless I am on my knees in front of him, in a subservient way.''

⚤ "A prolonged blow job can be very tiring if the receiver is a slow comer. Also I am quite content to get my own rocks off, along with a little stimulation from my partner, but my partner often feels inadequate because he couldn't suck me off, etc., to a climax. Perhaps a problem also is I'm trying too hard to make my partner believe he is doing a good job, so I fail to really enjoy what's going on.''

⚥"I'm reluctant to let 'just anyone' blow me; I have been chewed and gnawed by too many amateurs, and I do *not* like it."

⚥"I hate the sensation of someone stimulating the meatus (piss slit) of my penis. I always stop them to explain to them not to do it, but I find it hard to explain and I'm afraid they'll think I am uptight or inappreciative of their efforts."

⚥"I have a pretty sensitive gag reflex and it frequently interferes with me being able to bring a partner to orgasm by sucking his cock, particularly if it's very large."

⚥"I like to suck but don't like to be fucked in the mouth. That has happened at times."

Lack of Communication

As can be seen from some of the previous comments, many men indicate that lack of communication—either their own or their partners'—is a source of problems. Some people are insecure generally. Some want reassurance that they are doing the right thing. Some feel uncomfortable because they are not more versatile. Some feel annoyed because their partner isn't doing something right, or won't perform a certain act. Often, anxiety occurs unnecessarily, while of course there are times when a real problem is causing dissatisfaction and open communication is necessary.

It may just be a matter of asking for what you want, or saying no to what you don't want. Sometimes, a sexual situation can be planned in advance by overt questioning. The men were asked, *How often do you determine what is going to happen sexually in advance with someone you have just met by asking him certain questions?* and these were the replies:

always	2%
very frequently	9
somewhat frequently	16
somewhat infrequently	17
very infrequently	28
once	2
never	25

A certain shyness or the belief that spontaneity is better seems to inhibit people from asking such questions, because the feelings about it are rather positive:

very positive	21%
somewhat positive	21
neutral	29
somewhat negative	17
very negative	9
not sure	2

As for communication in general, the men were asked *how often they ask their partner for what they want done to them,* and they gave these replies:

always	4%
very frequently	17
somewhat frequently	29
somewhat infrequently	29
very infrequently	17
never	4

This indicates that clear communication about wants and needs occurs infrequently for more than half of the men.

General Satisfaction

Are gay men satisfied with their sexual partners? Well, mostly yes, but not everyone. The men indicated the following feelings about the quality of the sexual experience they have with other men:

completely satisfied	13%
very satisfied	48
somewhat satisfied	30
neutral	1
somewhat dissatisfied	8
very dissatisfied	.5
not sure	.5

The total percentage on the "dissatisfied" side, including "not sures," is 9%. Here are some comments relevant to communication, satisfaction, and getting (or not getting) what you want:

⚥"When I am in bed with someone, I am very quiet and my partners believe that I am not enjoying myself when I really am. I am just naturally quiet."

⚥"Sometimes I'm more in the mood for mere physical contact (cuddling and hugging) and get annoyed that people are in such a hurry to get their rocks off."

⚥"I'm turned off by young beauties who will lie back and contribute nothing and expect you to drool over their youth and good looks—that's an emotional desert. (I seek interaction and always talk with my sex partners.)"

⚥"Among my pet peeves: gross narcissism and/or 'preening' on the part of a partner; the person who 'plays' at being hard to get or who desires to change the rules between meeting and disrobing; the person who 'only

does one thing,' however well that may be done; the enormous cock with no mind or body attached.''

⚤ "For the first year or two that I was out I felt very inadequate sexually. While I found sex to be incredibly pleasurable and sensual (and thought that my partners felt the same way) I was very concerned about my technique, being afraid that I didn't know how to do things right. While this was, to some degree, based on reality, a lot of it seems, in retrospect, to have been general feelings of insecurity about my competence as a man, in general, since I still feel sexually inadequate at times, with no real basis in fact. I think it connects to deep-rooted feelings of not being 'masculine' enough, connected to having been terrible at athletics when I was growing up. In fact, I'm objectively rather masculine, and consciously feel comfortable with my 'feminine' parts, but I think being gay for me is, on a deeper level, a feeling of having failed as a man. It's something I'm conscious of and am trying to work beyond, but I think it's there for a lot of us.''

⚤ "Most of my partners tend to be much too rough in their stimulation; I can respond to the most delicate of touches and prefer that to rougher manhandling.''

⚤ "Openness of discussion about just what feels good during sex is an important matter that is often a problem for my partners to talk about.''

⚤ "Sometimes I get uptight about the sexual encounter because I at the time am solely interesting in 'doing' (sucking, masturbating partner and seeing him come) and am not interested in being touched or sucked. I usually terminate the encounter because I don't think it is fair to either of us.''

⚤ "I have no trouble functioning, but sometimes I wish my partners would display more 'turn-on'—most of them lie there passively while I do all the work.''

⚤ "My special needs include intimacy, comfort, support, reassurance. I'm usually the one who feels unskilled.''

⚤ "I'd like to have more adventurous sex. More costumes, play-acting, and toys. But I'm too shy to ask my lover and too scared to go to bars supposedly catering to this. I don't want it as a lifestyle and don't want to be taken advantage of.''

⚤ "I need accompanying affection to even achieve an erection.''

⚤ "I dislike getting into a sexual scene with someone and then discovering that he is not into J/O, or looks down on it, or insists on fucking, or sucking, only, or some such situation. I don't like scenes where I have to give in to the other's demands—I prefer my own kind of sex. I wish I didn't feel so strongly about this, but I do. When I'm with a guy and he makes it clear he is not interested in any masturbation activity, I somehow feel he is putting me down, which I cannot accept.''

⚤ "I have problems with sexual skill of some partners as I have to continually ask at times if this or that feels good to them—he sighs in response so I don't know if partner is being pleased. I feel that they are not

allowing themselves to respond and be in touch with feelings (perhaps old macho image that men don't show emotions, which I feel is a bunch of bull). A real man in touch with himself and his feelings is more of a man than one who represses his feelings and emotions.''

⚣ "People seem more compulsive and 'hungry' now. They go straight into sex without foreplay. I remember differently when I was younger (I'm 32). Maybe it's my age but I think drugs has a lot to do with it. This compulsive behavior cuts down on the skill of lovemaking.''

⚣ "I find being affectionate very erotic and consequently there have been times when I've frightened tricks away in the middle of having sex. They misinterpret my affection as romantic.''

⚣ "If I'm in bed with someone and they force me to do something I freeze up, start sweating and having hot flashes, and pass out.''

Frequency of Sex

Frequency of sex is another issue raised by men in response to the question about the problematical side of gay life, though this issue is also explored in Chapter 5. For some, the issue was not exactly lack of sex, but discomfort with the sexual pressures often present in the urban gay community, a feeling of revulsion for "too much sex." Some people may naturally have smaller or larger sexual appetites. Others had sex infrequently because they experience rejection in the youth-and-beauty-oriented sexual marketplace, because of poor self-image or shyness, or the inability or unwillingness to deal with the expectations of the traditional gay social scene. Some of the comments were from men who found themselves in a situation with a lover where sexual needs were different. Here are some comments on frequency of sex and the gay social norms as a source of problems:

⚣ "My sexual appetite seems much greater than my lover's. He is very responsive to pressures and tensions at work, or to any minor physical ills (headache or cold, for example), and the least thing seems to put sex out of his mind. I never try to force him when he's not in the mood, but I do feel that it's 'all in his head' and that he ought to make an effort to respond more often. As a consequence of his frequent 'don't feel like it' moods, I masturbate more than I would wish to do, and—perhaps more of a threat to our relationship—I spend time in restrooms and porno movie houses seeking the action that I feel I am denied at home.''

⚣ "I wish we could have sex more often but our major problem is that he is not sure if he is gay or straight and after sex with me he feels very guilty. Usually our 'sex' is limited to kissing and stroking, just being physically close.''

⚣ "Frequency—the older I get the less I get.''

⚣ "I always have had a hangup about my body. I have a layer of fat so that no matter how hard I work out I can never have the definition that I dream would be wonderful to have. If I sit slouched over it looks like I have

tits, and when I worked up enough courage to ask a doctor about the possibility of plastic surgery he said it was mostly muscle and that type of operation would be impractical.''

&"The only hangup I have would be that of inferiority feelings about the size of my cock, and of growing old and losing my sexual charm, etc. While I am physically larger than the national average, try to tell my mind that! This, I believe, is largely due to looking at that fucking porn! They always pick hung guys that put everyone else to shame, and on top of the visuals, constantly lie about size.''

&"It has been about ten months since I last had sex. The problem is that I make very little effort to find sexual partners and have very high standards, as well as a certain type that appeals to me, as well as being very introverted in these situations, and hence uncomfortable and insecure. I tend to leave bars or clubs as soon as I get bored, which is usually fairly soon, and almost always before I meet anyone who I like. I have been very busy for the past year, and have found it easy to immerse myself in work and forget about sex.''

&"My problem is my shyness. I don't drink, smoke, or use drugs. Since I don't frequent bars, baths, or public toilets, I have a heck of a time meeting men, and consequently, I feel lonely a great part of the time. I am more inclined towards quiet evenings at home reading and listening to music.''

&"Evidently I am sufficiently repressed to do without a companion in this area of my life. I have lived alone for more than twenty years, and alone seems to be that way I will remain. (But for fantasy and imagination I would be either insane or dead by now!)''

&"Some of my sexual patterns are compulsive—definitely. I work in downtown Philadelphia where there are several choice spots for quick anonymous sex (a downstairs two-stall restaurant toilet where the dividing panel has been ripped out and left out; a remote department-store toilet with two noisy doors, where there is a time delay between the time the first door opens and someone enters through the second—consequently people kneel and slide their cocks under the stalls and there is enough time to retreat when someone hits the first door, etc.). I find when I am frustrated on the job, or for some unknown reasons just discouraged or depressed, I am drawn to one of these potentially dangerous places for the excitement of flirting with danger and the momentary exhilarating feeling I can get from sex, the feeling that I'm alive and despite my problems that I can just go 'fuck it all!' ''

&"Compulsion: role issues, thinking about roles to the point of interference with my pleasure. I am preoccupied with how I seem to others, how I appear, how I look. Rather than how I feel in sex. This comes from a long life as a pretty boy, then handsome man. It comes from having a professional model for a mother. It comes from looking for all validation from external sources for the first twenty-five years of my life. It is a huge injury to myself which I can repair only slowly.''

&"Another kind of hangup is about Saturday night. I feel that I simply

must be doing something terrific on Saturday night. Other nights, I don't much mind if nothing turns up. Saturday blank makes me begin to feel lonely and unloved, which is, in affection, simply not the truth. I seem to equate love with sex on Saturday night.''

&"When being approached or propositioned, I cannot directly say no because I don't want to hurt the other person. At first I ended up going with someone I didn't want to be with, then I would just slip away. I wish, though, that I could meet someone in a bar and say no, and still remain friends.''

&"I have had occasion to become a compulsive cocksucker. There have been days when all I wanted to do was to suck cock after cock after cock. Rather than be frustrated over this, I've gone out and done it.''

&"I had had 'impersonal' sex with three different 'pick-ups' and after each come to the same conclusion, that for me, sex is an act of caring and will always remain so. I am a compulsive cocksucker (mentally) and whenever I see another good-looking male I fantasize what it would be like to get him into bed. I am deeply emotional, or better phrased, I have deep emotions, and think this has always been a handicap in dealing with sex for the sake of sex.''

Closet Anxieties

Several men indicated anxieties stemming from the problem of being in the closet and/or the illegality of homosexuality:

&"My main anxiety is getting caught by the police in a public restroom plus the possibility of my children discovering I am gay.''

&"I have anxieties that my homosexuality will be discovered by fellow workers and that I will lose my job or have such intense pressures put on me under other disguises that I may have to resign. I fear the rejection by friends and that I might experience public ridicule. I fear the government might conduct an investigation to identify all homosexuals through the FBI or CIA. I feel very inhibited about my homosexuality. When I do occasionally manage some physical approach, my heart is pounding and my anxiety level is very great.''

&"The only requirement I have of my sexual partners is that they feel relatively secure in being gay themselves. I once met a religious chap who told me he would like to have sex with me, but that it would be sinful. We didn't have sex. I thought it was my good deed to help him resist that temptation for the day.''

Physical Handicaps

We specifically questioned people about handicaps, and a few respondents identified themselves as handicapped or indicated feelings and experiences with handicapped gays. In the past few years, handicapped people throughout America have been organizing to improve their status as

an "oppressed minority." In the previous chapter, on lesbian problems and handicaps, Karla Jay made a few observations about handicapped people and the gay community, many of which are also relevant to gay men. Here are some comments from gay men about handicaps:

⚤"I have no sexual experiences with physically 'handicapped' people. Intellectually I know their handicap shouldn't matter, but emotionally it shuts me off and it would become extremely difficult for me to function sexually with them. One of my lovers was deaf mute and I was really into him (enough to learn sign language) but he had fits of paranoia tantrums I could no longer handle after a month of our living together, so I broke it off. I never thought of him as being handicapped before now. Handicaps that shut me off sexually are deformities, amputations, and cripples. I probably would have trouble with a blind person because I have a thing about my own eyes and I do feel uncomfortable being a 'crutch' for somebody. I'm very intense on self-reliance."

⚤"Since the age of 22, I have had to wear a prosthesis (artificial leg) and this has made me self-conscious, but only once in forty-five years has a man felt it or seen it, asked about it and then refused to go ahead with sex as we had planned. When I meet someone whom I hope to cultivate as a friend and maybe a lover, I tell him about this fact early in our relationship, certainly before we undress for bed!!"

⚤"I've been to bed with men that have a club foot. This doesn't bother me. It's the overall person that counts."

⚤"I would love to care for a physically handicapped person. Could learn to love him and help with his problems. The main thing—love, tender loving care, understanding, patience."

⚤"If you're handicapped, you're handicapped, but don't snivel about it."

⚤"Small cocks are a physical handicap—I can handle that handicap and deaf mutes, no others."

⚤"If you're asking if stumps turn me on, the answer is no. On the other hand, if a beautiful man had one leg, but had other qualities which turned me on, I don't think I would let the one leg get in the way."

⚤"I've mentioned my artificial leg. Cause of some embarrassment? Undoubtedly, particularly at first. Cause of some inconvenience—of course. Cause of some physical pain, and also psychological—yes. But I am so much more important than my lower left leg that I have not and cannot let this interfere with my life! When I see blind people walking alone on the city streets, when I see people in motorized wheelchairs going about their business, I realize how lucky I am with only my minor 'handicap'!"

⚤"Often thought gay men ought to spend more time at VA hospitals cheering up the gay vets—one way or another. Lots of limbless guys there who are terribly lonely and needn't be. Topic for my future."

⚤"I'd never have sex with anyone in any way mutilated or handicapped. Appalling thought."

⚤"My closest friend and current roommate (straight) is a victim of polio

and walks with crutches. I have become aware of my inability to see him as a sex object. I am painfully aware of the repulsion his tiny, thin, undeveloped legs bring to my eyes. I want to smash these types of barriers. I want to realize the beauty in human imperfection. I want to get past the gut reaction.''

&"I feel sorry for the people who have any of these problems.''

&"Until 1970 I was able to function sexually without very many qualms at all. In that year I had an operation which left me half deaf, and now I hear less well in my good ear. Obviously not being able to hear has made it most unsettling and difficult for me when I go to the baths, as I am unable to pick up on verbal cues and I very much miss those sweet nothings that people used to whisper to me before, during, and after. Very much.''

&"One of my major lovers, who happened to be worth about $36,000,000 was a spastic paralytic. We had pretty good sex, and he was a devoted lover. I have also slept with a deaf guy in a Turkish bath—it was marvelous, no need to make silly small talk, just get down to business.''

&"One time I was visiting friends, and they had a guest who had the hots for me. I wasn't particularly interested, but he pressured the issue, and we ended up in the bedroom. When he took off his clothes, I noticed (noticed is not strong enough—freaked out) that he had a burn from his belly button to his neck. The whole front of him was a giant burn (scab?). We did attain orgasm, but it was an incredibly awkward situation.''

&"I had a stroke at age 44 which left my left arm and hand spastic due to brain damage. Exactly at the point of orgasm, not always but quite often, my left arm straightens out stiffly in a reflex action which I cannot control except to ask my partner to duck or put pressure on my left arm. It's quite wild the first time a person is with me, so I usually tell them about it in advance and I'm careful about positioning my left arm away from partner.''

Other health factors present problems for some gay men in terms of sex:

&"When erect, my foreskin goes all the way back so that one wouldn't realize that I had not been circumcised. However, the skin underneath the corona usually cracks open, something like a hacked lip. This is painful, but not enough to spoil anything. I have asked the doctor about this and all he could tell me was to make sure that I washed thoroughly with soap and water afterwards.''

&"My hemorrhoids are a handicap when it comes to being fucked.''

&"My hemorrhoids and pilonidal cyst have been especially bad the last four years. From time to time, the swelling is at a minimum and I can be fucked, but I do experience some anxiety and feeling of inadequacy around it. My lover, however, has been especially supportive and understanding around this problem, so that it doesn't dominate my sexual life.''

&"When I was 19 I had a urinary-tract problem and a resulting atrophy

of my left testicle. At times I feel inadequate, even though it has no effect on my sexual functioning. It's a feeling of not being a 'whole person.' ''

♂"I cannot get fucked. I have had amebiasis, colitis, and hemorrhoids, and anything stuck up there hurts like hell. This makes me more uptight about picking up people, since many people assume that fucking is part of the deal. If I'm about to go home with someone, I have to make it clear that fucking is out."

Venereal Disease

Venereal disease has reached epidemic proportions in the United States, and while gay women have few worries on this score, VD is a major source of concern for the gay male community. In recent years, public clinics in major cities have improved their attitude toward their gay clients, and many staff members of these clinics have learned to take a natural, forthright approach to such "touchy" areas as the need for a throat or rectal culture for gonorrhea. However, many gay men suffer from inadequate treatment, due to their own ignorance or fears, or due to the ignorance of health professionals. In the early years of the gay movement, some activists objected to the idea that venereal disease is more prevalent among male homosexuals. Presumably, the VD "accusation" was being used as a weapon against gay people. However, gay men cannot afford to worry about their "reputation" when in fact people are transmitting diseases through sexual contact at a rapid rate. Gay men's concern must be education, prevention, treatment, and perhaps someday immunization. In addition to syphilis and gonorrhea, the gay male community has experienced outbreaks of ailments such as hepatitis (a liver infection) and amebiasis, shigellosis, and giardiasis (intestinal parasites). These diseases are often present in the digestive tract, and since bits of fecal matter may be incidental to gay male sexual acts, the possibility of transmission is increased. Information about VD is available in several recent gay books including *After You're Out, Men Loving Men,* and *The Joy of Gay Sex,* and at many VD clinics.

The following chart indicates frequency of VD for gay men responding to our questionnaire:

	NEVER	ONCE	TWICE	3 TIMES	MORE THAN 3 TIMES	NOT SURE
syphilis ("siff")	86	9	3	0	0	2%
gonorrhea ("clap," "drip")	59	14	8	7	10	2
warts	81	13	3	0	1	3

	NEVER	ONCE	TWICE	3 TIMES	MORE THAN 3 TIMES	NOT SURE
herpes	87	5	1	.5	3	4
hepatitis (from sex)	87	10	0	0	0	3
nonspecific urethritis (NSU)	67	15	6	2	5	4
lice ("crabs")	28	20	11	14	24	1
scabies	74	15	5	1	.5	4

Regular checkups are important in the determining of VD. A few years ago, experts in the venereal-disease field recommended checkups every six months, but many clinics now recommend every three months for people who are sexually active with many partners. Of course, once a year or even less might seem appropriate for someone with a lover and few or no outside sexual contacts, but since one can't be sure about a lover's sex habits, the six-month checkup is probably a good rule of thumb for most. *How often do people actually go for checkups?*

every three months	17%
every six months	23
once a year	18
less frequently than once a year	22
never	20

VD checkups are available in cities throughout the U.S. in clinics financed in part by the United States Public Health Service. These clinics are free of charge, though sometimes donations are accepted. Law requires that names of contacts be given. These are held confidential; the contact is notified but your name is not mentioned. It is only common courtesy, of course, to notify any sex partner if you come down with VD, though if the contact has been anonymous, such notification is simply not possible.

In some cities, "free clinics," institutions founded in the 1960s or inspired by 1960s health activism, also offer VD clinics, some of them with gay personnel. Private physicians and any hospital outpatient clinic also offer VD care, but in these cases, there is a charge for treatment. The *Gayellow Pages,* a gay reference book (Box 292, New York, N.Y. 10014), has listings of gay community centers and gay hotlines which can give information about various clinics and private doctors who are accustomed to dealing with a gay clientele. Asked *where they go for VD checkups,* the respondents reported the following:

regular doctor	30%
another doctor	4
a public clinic	39
a gay clinic	15
other	12

Most people are satisfied with the way they are treated during VD checkups, though there can be problems, including dirty looks, brusque attitudes, violent thrusting of culture sticks or needles, or perhaps worst of all ignorance concerning most gay men's needs for rectal and/or throat cultures for gonorrhea. The respondents, questioned about *the way they feel about their treatment during VD checkups,* gave the following responses:

very positive	41%
somewhat positive	23
neutral	20
somewhat negative	11
very negative	1
not sure	5

The following chart shows *how often the fear of VD influences the sex lives of the gay men in the survey:*

	ALWAYS	VERY FREQUENTLY	SOMEWHAT FREQUENTLY	SOMEWHAT INFREQUENTLY	VERY INFREQUENTLY	ONCE	NEVER
your choice of sex partner	14	14	19	12	20	1	22%
sexual acts you engage in	11	15	18	10	18	1	28
how often you have sex	6	5	10	11	24	1	43

If nothing else, these figures suggest that the reality of venereal disease is engraved on the minds of most gay men. It is a fact of life for the gay male community that is understood by a majority of the community. Yet about one-quarter of the men show a complete disregard or lack of knowledge about VD and VD risks. Since the sample overrepresents well-educated gay men, one can only assume that the overall percentage of unaware people in the community is even higher than this. Of course, there are a few men who get carried away with fear and paranoia, and are hardly

able to enjoy sex due to irrational fears of disease. It is important to point out that venereal diseases are curable, and the many people who do come down with VD at one time or another get cured and go about their lives, sexual and otherwise. While awareness and precaution are necessary, there is no need for dread or sexual abstention.

The following are some comments men made concerning venereal disease:

⚥"I used to have a terrible fear of venereal disease, and for that reason would only masturbate others, and when I saw the ease with which others put cocks to mouth, I was astonished and envious. I still fear venereal disease. I always carry either a mouthwash like Cepacol or something with alcohol in it, *not* booze, with the hope that it will kill germs, or a bar of soap, or both, and I wash my mouth out with soap suds, gargle, rewash, wash my hands, etc. I am very unenlightened about contracting venereal disease orally and I wish someone would make all of the possibilities and preventions explicitly clear."

⚥"In 1973 I came down with a sore throat after a sexual encounter. I did not associate the two, but I went immediately to my physician, who gave me antibiotics for the sore throat. Later in the week when I told the doctor that my sex partner just prior to the sore throat had gonorrhea he guessed that the antibiotics took care of it.

"During the following two months, I began to experience vague arthritic pains. After that my eye became inflamed from an internal infection. The eye doctor sent me back to the internist to see why my eyes would not clear up. Weekly and then twice a week I was at the doctor's office. The arthritic pains became severely crippling. I was becoming very ill. None of the team of MDs could figure it out. Finally six long months later I broke out in blisters (lesions, they called them). I had a generalized gonorrheal infection. I was hospitalized for over a week and fed penicillin intravenously around the clock.

"Some of the members of my family and some of my co-workers including my employer found out that I had VD. It's still terribly embarrassing. I'm still somewhat crippled on cold damp days. I went into a state of emotional shock and am just recently experimenting with sex again. I'm still very angry, however. All the trouble could have been avoided if, one, I had not had the sexual encounter, or two, the first physician, who knew then that I was gay, had asked a very simple question, or later in the week, given me the proper medication, not one that would mask the symptoms until the infection was throughout my body. He was too embarrassed to treat a gay man for a gay man's problem."

⚥ "One time at the baths, I was about to fuck a guy and he handed me a condom to put on. I thought it was a bit strange, and it turned me off a little, but I realized that the danger of VD at the baths is real, and so I put on the condom and fucked him that way. It was all right, but I think I'd rather take my chances. I don't go to the baths very often."

⚥ "Never having had VD, it never crosses my mind."

⚥ "My main fear is getting hepatitis from rimming."

⚥ "I have anal sex less frequently than before due to fear of hepatitis and other shit-related maladies."

⚥ "I claim to have a natural immunity to VD."

⚥ "A hard cock knoweth not fear."

⚥ "I usually try to find out how often my sex partners switch partners to indicate the probability of VD being contacted by them."

⚥ "I know that some people in the baths like to get fucked by a dozen guys in one night. If I suspect my partner is one of those, forget it!"

⚥ "I enjoy sex and do not let the fear of VD ruin any sexual experiences."

⚥ "I take the after-sex precautions and hopefully minimize the risk."

Miscellaneous Problems

This chapter was set aside to deal with some of the problems and hangups in gay men's lives. Quite a lot of territory was covered, and here are a few "miscellaneous" items that didn't quite seem to fit anywhere else:

⚥ "The idea of making a virgin his first time is sometimes a blocker."

⚥ "I have the hangup of not being able to control my bowel movements while participating in fist-fucking."

⚥ "The most powerful repression (and the least conscious) is that toward women. I used to be much worse: I shuddered at a woman's touch. Now I can at least think about having sex with women. Yet I still downgrade women's bodies, having set up the male's proportions as the 'norm' or 'ideal.' I must learn to value women on their own terms."

⚥ "I was raped once and which also involved the man's trained dog. It was an ugly experience and I hold my legs quite tightly together ever since."

⚥ "I find it impossible to transfer my sexual fantasies into reality as they are so elaborate. This hampers my ability to make love. I'm not that eager to have sex as a result."

⚥ "I like to make love in the open (i.e., grass, bushes, etc.). This causes a fair degree of paranoia for both myself and my sex partners, due to exposure."

⚥ "I am very hung up about urinating in public, and I find it difficult to release my urinary sphincter muscles in a public lavatory. I am embarrassed about this. I wonder if this is a not uncommon thing among men in general or among gay men. I worry that this is part of the same hangup I have with anal sex. I feel that this is undesirable, and that I should be able to 'correct' this 'condition.' I am worried that I shouldn't be thinking that it is a 'condition' anyway."

⚥ "When it is warm, I have found that my balls hang lower and that I can usually come a lot more when it is warm. That is the reason why I am in Arizona (and getting drunk, too). The weather here, compared to the rest of the nation, is very good. From weather reports it looks bad all over, except for Arizona and southern California."

18

Prejudice and Pride, Oppression and Liberation

It is impossible to think about the oppression of lesbians and gay men without first considering that the very concept of oppression depends on the existence of power, authority, and status. That homosexuals are an "out" group in this society is obvious enough. Labels like "queer" and "pervert" illustrate the contempt in which gay people are held. Some of the initial gay liberation slogans—"Gay is good," "Say it loud, gay is proud!"—show in an almost simplistic fashion early efforts to cast off the "chains of oppression."

Children perhaps first learn the word "oppression" in grade school music class: "Oppressed so hard, they could not stand, let my people go!" That song—a Negro spiritual about Jews in Egypt—focuses on slavery as oppression. Cruelty, abuse of power, and the lack of freedom—the essential elements in slavery—have all been part of the gay experience at one time or another. The history of the persecution of homosexuals has only recently begun to be seriously and carefully dealt with, and gay people are beginning to learn about the horrible violence suffered by "sodomites," "witches," and "deviants" under the Spanish Inquisition, in Puritan New England, in Nazi Germany, in Stalinist Russia, and in other situations and eras. Despite Anita Bryant and sodomy laws, the U.S. and Canada in the 1970s are not the same as Nazi Germany, but an awareness of history is crucial to the survival of gay people. Today, an organized movement involving thousands of lesbians and gay men confronts and challenges those powers, authorities, hierarchies, and structures which denigrate and demean gay people. In addition to organized activities, there is a simultaneous change in consciousness. This pattern of movement and consciousness-raising adds up to a resistance to oppression. In this chapter, gay people share their experiences in the areas of oppression and liberation.

In the chart below, the figures indicate the responses by lesbians and

697

gay men to this question: *Do you ever or have you ever experienced any of the following in connection with your homosexuality?*

	QUITE A LOT		SOME		VERY LITTLE		ONCE		NOT AT ALL		NOT SURE	
	♀	♂	♀	♂	♀	♂	♀	♂	♀	♂	♀	♂
harassment	8	5	33	32	21	29	7	8	30	23	1	3%
loss of job	2	1	2	3	0	1	5	7	84	81	7	7
forced to move	1	.5	1	2	1	1	6	4	89	91	1	2
arrest	0	1	.5	2	1	1	.5	8	98	87	0	1
blackmail or threat of blackmail	1	0	2	1	1	1	5	11	90	86	.5	2
physical abuse	1	1	6	5	3	8	4	13	85	72	.5	1
verbal abuse, name-calling	8	7	31	28	19	33	13	9	30	21	0	1
robbery	0	1	.5	4	.5	3	1	14	95	77	3	2
shakedown	0	.5	2	2	1	1	0	7	97	88	.5	1
shame, guilt	9	15	21	22	16	19	3	4	50	38	1	1
fear of discovery	13	22	41	32	20	21	6	3	20	22	0	1

While the more extreme forms of persecution—loss of job, arrest, physical abuse, etc.—have been experienced by a comparatively low percentage of the respondents, these experiences are common enough to be part of the backdrop of the contemporary gay experience. It is important to realize that relatively few gay people experience these problems because most go to such great pains to hide their homosexuality. Those who do experience open persecution are often those who are overt about their homosexuality or who have had the misfortune of having their homosexuality discovered unexpectedly. While only a small percentage of the lesbians and gay men have experienced discrimination in housing and employment, for example, most gay people understand that such discrimination would be widespread if more gay people were out of the closet. Gay people are forced to hide the truth about their lives or, if they insist on being open, to hold menial, safe jobs and live in ghettos. There are few exceptions—even in so-called "safe" fields, such as in the arts, there are many gay men who play at being straight in order to further their careers. Some straight people looking at these statistics may say, "Why all the fuss about civil rights?" But a game is being played here, and the rules of the game say that gay people must be second-class citizens—scared, discreet, dissembling, and self-hating—in order to work and to obtain shelter. The hiding and secrecy discussed earlier in this book, and the fear of discovery reported by a majority in the preceding chart, are evidence of the vulnerability experienced by gay people. Those few who have suffered extreme persecution—and all gay people know they exist—serve a social

function of teaching other gay people what the limits are. In other words, what the average citizen expects in terms of the behavior of other civilized people is *not* what the upfront gay citizen can expect. Occasionally the "oppression" experienced by gay people, moreover, is self-inflicted oppression, a kind of self-defense against societal attitudes. An excellent discussion of gay self-oppression appears in the pamphlet "With Downcast Gays," available from the Pink Triangle Press, Box 639, Station A, Toronto, Ontario, Canada M5W 1G2.

Harassment, Verbal and Physical Abuse

Invisibility protects gay people most of the time from the most outrageous and violent kinds of abuse, but harassment is reported to occur at least some of the time by around 40% of the gay men and lesbians. Reports of beatings and even murders are frequent enough that this threat of violence compels many gay men and lesbians to exercise caution. For example, many of the gay people said that they would like to be openly affectionate with lovers and friends but refrain from expressing themselves due to the fear of such violence and harassment. (See Chapter 5 for statistics on affection.) Here are some comments from men and women concerning their experiences with harassment, name-calling, and physical abuse:

♂"I have been ostracized, harassed, hassled, and abused by countless individual heterosexuals (and closet queens) over the years, simply because I am unabashedly gay. Police stop me frequently for no reason at all. I've been beaten by an off-duty Los Angeles Police Department officer because he didn't like the way I walk. One homophobe tried to murder me when I was 17 and I was saved only by the intervention of the homophobe's female cousin, who begged him to take pity on me and let me off with a beating. An ex-convict tried to rape me, also when I was 17, and was dragged off at the last minute by his buddies, who feared being caught by the police (I was in a public place). Going through the file kept on me by the South Pasadena School Department, I found entry after entry on my 'problem' from teachers who feared that my penchant for art and aversion to sports might be indicators of incipient 'sexual identity problems.' I have far fewer problems with homophobia now that I am an adult. It is not that adults are less homophobic than adolescents and children, but they don't show their homophobia so blatantly, and so I find it easier to ignore homophobia now."

♀"When I was a drag-dyke, I got a lot of verbal abuse from straight men, some condescension from gay men (I still get condescension from some faggots who want women to stay in 'their place' as defined by hetero-male society), and I got into fist fights sometimes with straight men. I almost got beaten up by a cop, but managed to escape only verbally abused. I still get mad at the attitude some faggots have about butch women being either inferior or outrageous."

♂"No overt oppression yet, except being robbed and held hostage at

gunpoint for about a half-hour outside a gay bar. Whenever I walk arm in arm or hand in hand with a man, people laugh and talk, but I guess that's natural. I've become more conservative and withdrawn in expressing and revealing my gayness in public because of public reaction and because of lack of a strong support group, and because of some bad experiences (i.e., verbal abuse, getting bricks thrown at me, etc.)''

⚥"I am very openly affectionate in public. People stare and comment but it has stopped affecting me too much. They need it. I feel repressed as a homosexual (and *human*) as long as there is bigotry. Not to mention the laws.''

⚥"Lately I've been oppressed by straight punks that have hassled me and many other gays. I now have to take cabs to my favorite bars whereas before, for five years in this city, I would walk and/or take buses— anywhere, anytime—now it's just not safe any more. There's a chance a gay could be hassled these days even in broad daylight. It's all because of Bryant in my opinion. I do not think it's right that straights can walk around holding hands, kissing in public, etc., and we gays feel it's not a good idea to do so.''

♀"This happened a few weeks ago: There were three couples of us riding around and we decided to eat breakfast. Now, we were not drinking or carrying on with each other, but three of the girls were dressed in drag butch and the other three of us in shorts and tops. We all had shoes on. Well, we stood outside a few minutes and decided what we wanted to eat and then went inside. Would you believe it?—they refused to seat or serve us. I was so embarrassed! This had never happened to us before. Some of the others wanted to press the issue, but we didn't. I don't know if anything could have been done.''

♀"Men used to hassle me when I wouldn't date them. I always got the question, 'What are you, a dyke or something?' Now, I'd say, 'Yes I am, you asshole.' ''

♀"Once after a lesbian-feminist concert/lecture, some 'Christians' were picketing and yelling obscenities to the 'faggots' and 'bull dykes.' I felt sick to my stomach and really *afraid*. The picketers were so full of *hatred*.''

♀"I had a guy peeping in the window of one apartment I lived in many years ago from the rooftop of another building. I called the police, and I kept my blinds down thereafter for fear someone else would go on top of that roof (the only way they could view us). I was with a couple of masculine-looking gay women once and when we stopped to empty some things from the car some young guys started calling us names—dykes, etc. It made me angry that they could take such open offense against us.''

⚥"The first time I approached a peer for sex was as a college sophomore. He was my roommate and we spent all our leisure time together. We had cut classes to go swimming in a sand pit outside town alone and naked, which we had done on several occasions. After swimming we began chasing each other over the sand piles and rolling in the sand, waving to the passing cars on the expressway about a mile away on the

horizon. We were having lots of fun. Then we began to wrestle and grope. I suddenly asked him if I could kiss his penis and if he would kiss mine. Instantly, he began beating me up in earnest. I was rather bruised for days. I did not come out sexually until I was 28; this experience drove me into a really deep closet, and I went through two heterosexual marriages before coming out."

♂"I've been humiliated—followed down the street by jeering youngsters."

♂"The worst oppression I've ever experienced personally involved a rock being tossed through the window of the gay center while I was using it as a crash pad. I was overwhelmed by the pain in my psyche which I experienced when I looked at all the glass on the floor."

♀"I have been extremely oppressed because of my sexual preferences. I have had rocks thrown at me and my car, my tires slashed and my lover molested. I am currently facing five years' imprisonment because of retaliating against five men who followed my lover and me all over town and attempted to do us bodily harm. Because of harassment, I have become more militant and more involved in the gay movement. This militancy has caused more harassment. It seems to be a vicious circle."

♂ "Once I wasn't permitted to skate with a partner of my choice at a roller rink and was asked via the public address system to leave . . . pretty humiliating."

♂"In high school I was harassed to the point where it affected my studies and I was so afraid that I would do almost anything not to have to go to school. This went on in classes as well as between classes for almost four years. Some of the teachers knew about it and allowed it. Sometimes I was slapped or pushed or hit but the verbal harassment was worse than anything else. I was so paranoid that I would walk or drive miles out of my way to avoid any one of the people who harassed me—even outside of school."

♂"I always get beat up in school."

♂"I've only encountered name-calling a few times—once by a group of frustrated straight girls as they came out of a popular bar which had recently turned completely gay."

♂ "A couple of times, when going to or coming from 'known gay places,' especially when with friends, people have shouted things like 'Hi, faggots' or something more negative. This has caused me to have a certain amount of anger and fear."

♀"I've been oppressed as a lesbian by name-calling, harassment, humiliation. This in a girls' dormitory and at a work center when my lover and I met. It was the most cruel time we've had to go through."

Police Persecution, Robbery, and the Law

Gay men are more vulnerable to certain types of situations than are lesbians because of their different social patterns (see Chapters 6 and 7). Men involved with casual sex with strangers, cruising in public places, and

picking up hustlers can, if they are not extremely cautious and lucky, experience robbery, extortion, and/or violence, even murder. Gay women also report incidents of police harassment and brutality, and in most states the so-called sodomy laws governing "unnatural sex acts" relate to lesbian sexuality as well as gay male sexuality (and often certain forms of heterosexual relations such as anal and oral sex). Gay men (and more rarely lesbians) are actually jailed for sexual acts, but the criminality of gay sex is a factor in gay people's lives even when the laws are not enforced. Most of the following comments on this aspect of gay oppression are from gay men, but the illegality of homosexuality is a factor in the lives of all gay people.

⚥"Calumet City, Illinois, summer 1969—I had met a person in a bar and neither of us had any place to go, so we went out to a spot he knew about and proceeded to do it in the car. Within a half-hour we were in jail being booked for 'sexual deviancy,' in spite of the fact that we were a million miles from anywhere and very much in private. I had been partying all day, so by the time that this happened, I was fairly loose with what I was telling the police (insisting that they treat us like people, not like hardened criminals, insisting that they not call us 'queers,' and the like), and I suppose in retrospect it's surprising that we're both not still there. The desk sergeant came into my cell (they had separated us, drat the luck), and asked if I thought that my partner would be interested in attending their upcoming dance (in drag? thought I), and for the price of two tickets, $22, coincidentally the same amount of paper money we were carrying between us, we were set off into the night with the stern admonition to use a motel the next time. While it was going on and immediately after we were released, I thought that the experience was funny. In the clear cold light of morning, it took on an entirely different perspective when the impact of what could have happened had we not had a 'cooperative' jailer hit."

⚥"Most of the police harassment in this area takes place just before election time. Having been caught up in this 'political game,' I know it to be true. Rather than be intimidated like this, I quickly learned to stand up for my legal rights. The police know that the homosexual is an 'easy target,' because few of us want to risk the potential publicity and embarrassment. After seeing how other lives have been ruined in this manner, I protested my innocence and fought to be vindicated, which I was."

♀"For most of my life, each time I have made love with the woman I am in love with, I have also committed a 'crime' according to our laws, and I know I could be sent to prison. I can never show any affection toward her in public. I must even run and hide someplace to hold her hand. To us what we share is the most beautiful thing in the world, but to most of society it is an abomination or at best a 'sickness' of some kind."

♀"One time I was going to a party (it was about 2:00 a.m.) with two friends. All three of us were in the front seat—the others were dressed butch and I was dressed femme. We had all had some to drink but not enough to be arrested. A police car stopped us. At first he asked us what we were

♀ "Since I teach in a public school, it's necessary that I'm in the closet at work. Parents are not ready for gay teachers ('Save Our Children'); neither are most school boards. I stopped teaching for two years, partly because I couldn't deal with playing straight and working for a system which oppresses me. Now I feel more able to deal with this conflict, although it's difficult."

♂ "My homosexuality inhibited me from pursuing a career in the church for a long time. Finally I decided that I was gay and Christian—both of these were constants in my life, so they couldn't be evil. So I acted upon it. I was evicted from my apartment two months ago for being gay (the city gay rights ordinance didn't cover my living situation)."

♀ "I have two degrees, yet I am paid shit and am in the secretarial ghetto where I stay. I can't get ahead because it is presumed I will meet a man, get married, and leave the labor market."

♂ "On one job I was ridiculed and made the butt of jokes until I retaliated by losing my head and temper over something minor, resulting in my dismissal. On another job, I was kept on, after a suspended sentence, known only to a couple of top men, supposedly. Eventually, however, I was falsely accused of 'indecent advances' and 'allowed' to resign."

♂ "I'm a teacher. Obviously I cannot be open about my sexuality or lifestyle. When in teacher training, a gay professor told me to be careful that the head of the department not know that I attended the gay students' union, or 'I'd be washed out of the program.' I have been told by landlords that 'we don't rent to two men.' I have lied and claimed I was married or divorced to get housing."

♂ "I was fired from my job I held for thirteen years (engineering management) because I am homosexual. They discovered this when a letter to the editor I wrote decrying oppression was published in the local newspaper. I was denied renewal of my lease because I am homosexual. I was able to keep my job as long as I lied. At age 34, I started a gay group in Kalamazoo, Mich. It was for two years a force for good and a beacon of light for oppressed gays. I lived totally openly. As a result, I lost my job and my apartment. I'd do it again."

♂ "I joined the government for a secure, anonymous job but I will never be a GS-15 because of the background investigation. Housing, of course, is a fundamental item in my social life. Redneck, spying neighbors have always made things unpleasant."

♂ "I live in a town of about 200 people. I work in a city of about 5,000. I live in fear that someone will find out that I am gay. I am an elementary school teacher. I am not exceptional, perhaps, but I am a good teacher. I love my work with a passion and would be lost away from the classroom and children. It enrages me that some repressed person can stand up and say that a gay person should not teach. I am professional in my work. I avoid any involvement with my students that would be construed as sexual, although I am very close to my students. I want to actively seek other homosexuals in this area but I have to be painfully careful. One false move

could lead to a disgrace to my family, who could never accept such a thing. My career would be destroyed.''

♀"I got rejected from the nunnery and kicked out of the United States Marine Corps, lost four jobs, and got put out of an apartment. Since 1962, I've owned my own home and worked for myself. It encouraged me to stand on my own two feet and be independent. I was angry and still am.''

♂"I had to turn down a job offer which was conditional on my agreement to take a lie-detector test, because I was afraid they would ask The Question. It's hard to know the psychological ramifications of being afraid of discovery on my on-the-job performance, so I'll refrain from commenting beyond the statement that I think it's had some adverse effects.''

♂"For the second time in my life I have lost my job for no other reason than my being gay. And both times this was covered up and slanderous lies about my professional performance were used as reasons, thus making it extremely difficult to find new employment. I am angry about the oppression, but I am proud to be gay and I will survive and become successful.''

♂"I am a professor of history at a small, private Catholic college. I am a competent, respected member of my profession who has written one book, edited a book, and completed numerous articles for scholarly journals. I will finish a major monograph in draft this next week. I am in the closet because I fear that exposure of my sexual orientation would cost me my job and the respect of many of my fellow professionals.''

♂"I feel oppressed in the forcing by society of me to live in a large city or in a secluded rural area. I cannot live where I want with my lover. Suburbia would not have us. We are forced to live in a large city where we will be lost. Any intrusion into suburbia by two males living together would be seen as that, an intrusion. I don't think that we would be allowed to live comfortably or afforded the same courtesies that a straight couple would receive if they moved to the suburbs. Legislation alone is not enough to banish this 'fear' which we are met with. Positive education may create a more accepting environment for the homosexual in suburban areas. I see the yards and homes in the suburbs and think that I might like living there rather than in the noise and confusion of the city or the isolation of the country, but I know that most of the residents there have fled the city and all that the city means, homosexuals included.''

♂"In several of the major apartment complexes around this area, two men may not share a one-bedroom apartment together, but two women can.''

♀"Being discovered by my employer is one of my greater fears. I have every reason to believe, because of my employer's policies, that I would be immediately discharged from my job despite nineteen years of an unblemished work record.''

♀"I am oppressed as a lesbian because my employer's discovery of this fact would mean certain job termination for me. This especially angers me

because there are males who also teach at my school (all female) and their lecherous tendencies towards the students are looked on as normal, whereas if my gay associations became known I would probably be suspected of foul play. (I've never had a sexual encounter with one of my students.) My fear of discovery is always with me and has caused me to choose housing far from work to protect my secret."

♂ "When I was a Philco Techrep with the air force, I took one of the airmen into confidence. Within a week, the office of CID was on my ass, tearing up my bedroom for evidence. They claimed that I had propositioned this kid (which I hadn't), and found letters in my personal effects that would incriminate me. I was kicked off base, out of the air force, and out of the Philco Corp. in forty-eight hours. It took me three years to get back up to the pay scale that I knew when I was at Philco."

♂ "Yes, I feel that I have been oppressed. I was fired from a classified agency in the U.S. Department of Defense in 1954 by reason of homosexuality, and had lived in apprehension of that dismissal for several years before the blow fell. Afterwards, I resolved that I would never again accept employment where that sort of experience could be repeated. Accordingly I never applied for teaching positions (although that was what I was trained for), and refused them when offered. In our present employment, my partner and I are self-employed contractors doing translation work. Most of our work (probably all of it) is for the U.S. government, but we are not government employees. We own our own home, and in general are no longer subject to fears of reprisals if the fact that we are gay is known."

♀ "At present, I work for a woman who knows I am a lesbian. This is the first time I've ever worked in a situation where I was officially out. It is very nice, but she is leaving, and I am very apprehensive about what the new boss will be like. I think because of these fears, confirmed by experience, I have limited myself in pursuing a career. I haven't wanted work to become too important to me when it can so easily be taken away from me. I am not sure how much of the discrimination I fear and have experienced is directed at women and how much at lesbians. I used to feel it primarily as being directed at lesbians, but now I'm not sure."

Fear of Discovery

Lesbians and gay men fear discovery for many reasons, some of them contained in the previous groups of quotations. This fear can influence a gay person's life in many ways, as the following statements attest:

♀ "When I first became a lesbian at 18, I was horrified at the thought of anyone finding out. I dated men as a front. Now, I don't flaunt my lesbianism, but the fear is not as strong. I am tired of lies and deceit."

♂ "The fear of being discovered has colored my whole life. I often wonder what I'd have been without it. I took school, jobs, place of residence always with that thought in mind. If I could have not cared,

would I have been a dancer? A dress designer? Would I have lived in the Village, Laguna? Why am I proud of being able to pass?''

♂"My major was psychology, and we were always being 'tested' to find out this about you, that about you, and I was none too comfortable about the fact that these tests could pick up homosexuality as well as anything else.''

♂"Fear of discovery has made most of us excellent actors and very cautious.''

♂"The fear of discovery led me to be very distant from others, form no friendships—for fear of what they'd discover.''

♀"I don't feel I can be completely open. I have had to deny my lesbianism in court. I would probably lose my custody if I did not. My children at present do not have hesitant or uncomfortable feelings about the women I see, but they are selective about their own friends' exposure to them. While I do not feel I can continue to do the kind of work I want to do if I was open and actively political, I do find that there is a level of acceptance as long as it is never talked about—although it often is clear that most people know I am a lesbian.''

♀"The main oppression I've suffered came from a dyke and the only reason I was vulnerable was that my lover was still very much in the closet. She threatened both exposure and physical harm to my lover if I fought back. I like being out now so that no one can pull that again.''

♀"I am inhibited in going to bars and lesbian bookstores, for fear of being caught.''

Shame, Guilt, Self-Hatred, Isolation, Self-Oppression

The oppressive reality of archaic laws and overt discrimination is relatively easy for all to understand, but only gay people themselves can know the damage caused by the prevailing negative attitudes and the enforced invisibility which cause so many to feel alone and unworthy. This psychological warfare waged against gay people takes a heavy toll. Here are some comments:

♀"Most of my life I repressed my homosexuality. This involved a lot of guilt feelings of unworthiness to the point of suicide and not wanting to live. Whether a person responds to their homosexuality or not, they still know it is there and they still know that our society thinks so little of a homosexual that he can be beat up, robbed, or murdered and the law will not worry about it too much. We have been considered lower than murderers and rapists; and many of us are law-abiding citizens who contribute to our society.''

♀"The toll in shame and guilt has been great and immeasurable. I suffered in this manner an inordinate amount, because I was raised in the country by very narrow, opinionated parents and where there were few others to observe or model oneself after. I was taught by implication, innuendo, and also forthrightly that homosexuality was far, far out, practiced

only by slimy, desperate characters, loathsome to behold. 'They' were the bottom of the totem pole. I was also told that I was someone very special (meaning good). I was treated like a little prince by the hired hands and smothered with motherly 'love.' Hence, I had a hell of a time accepting my homosexuality.''

♂ "I feel that society says to the gay person: 'All right, don't tell us about your life. We'll let you work if we don't have to know. We won't enforce the laws against you if you stay in your place. If you'll lie to us, we'll snicker behind your back and be generous—you can live.' And I feel that in accepting these terms, the gay person damages his spirit (soul, if you will). He loses the most valuable thing that any person can have—*self-respect*.''

♀ "I've never been aware of being personally despised or reviled, but I knew others had experienced it and I suffered a lot of anticipatory fear around it. I suppose I still do, since I'm generally shy among strangers unless I consciously put my smile on and fight it. My own experience with guilt and shame has been, really, the awareness that 'normal' people would probably *expect* me to feel guilty and ashamed and this has sometimes caused me to question my 'sanity.' I would say that 'fear of suffering' has inhibited my enjoyment of life and my self-confidence in every situation, even though it mostly proved an unfounded fear.''

♂ "I am a young physician who didn't have sexual experience until I was 28 because of my own homophobia. I only had sexual experience with women until I was 32 but I felt I couldn't marry unless I knew for sure that I wasn't gay. I regret the pain and guilt that I put myself through from age 11 to age 32. I have always been my own worst oppressor. My own homophobia has been the worst thing I have experienced in my life. It has been the source of my insecurity and inferiority feelings. I hope I will be less miserable as a gay person than I was as a homophobic self-detractor. I see that others brought up in the same homophobic culture gave themselves a lot less grief than I did.''

♀ "I repressed my gay orientation until I was 21 years old, although I had been sexually attracted to women since I was 10. As a result of this repression, I was neurotic, nearly an alcoholic, and at one time a speed freak. Since I have admitted the truth to myself and others, I have given up a life that could have led to an early death, went back to school, did very well, and am presently in graduate school for psychology. That repression damn near destroyed me, though.''

♂ "Although I have not been overtly oppressed because of my homosexuality, I resent our society for oppressing others. I know boys who come to me for one-night stands, a chance to release some of their built-up desires. They are gay at heart, but society has oppressed them so long and so deeply that they themselves fight their gayness and when I find them I cry in my heart over a society that twists a person's heart and sexuality so greatly. I even know one man in prison who can't keep away from dicks. He has to have one now and then, but the experience fucks with his mind so much that he has gone out and deliberately murdered another of his fellow beings just

to show everyone that dick sucker or not, he is still a man. I see things like that and I hate. I hate the circumstances that produced a monster like that. I have become so full of hatred for society at large for fucking with my brothers and sisters in gayness that of late I wish for separatism.''

♂''I couldn't date guys in junior high or talk about feelings with anyone. I was filled with loneliness and self-hate.''

♀''I do not like the way society oppresses gays. I am insecure or paranoid enough that I don't care to be openly gay. I don't really care about being discovered so much as I'm concerned with what people think of me (or what *I think* they think of me, which is worse). I feel that because of my paronoia about being gay, I've withdrawn from the world, society, which is something I no longer want to do. Therefore, I've decided not to be gay any more and to get back into the world. Over the years, my values have changed.''

♀''The only really bad experiences I had were being thrown out of school and socially ostracized. These events at the time made me feel guilt— now I feel anger.''

♀''The fact that I didn't come out—even to myself—until I was 29 or 30, and that I suffered silently for so long, speaks for itself. We are oppressed, from the first breath that we take in the delivery room when they assign you a blue or pink identification bracelet, etc., and thus confine you to a set standard of role expectations. It never ceases. The shame and guilt is what I personally suffered from most.''

♂''I've been in the closet most of my life, and still am to some degree. I haven't physically been oppressed, thus, by housing or employment discrimination. But I have been warped and thoroughly fucked over by the ugly, destructive forces of guilt, shame, terror, loneliness, isolation, bitterness, and rage that I've had to undergo because of my gayness. I have spent years of my life hating myself and considering myself some kind of a freak, because of the vicious ignorant crap that has been crammed down my throat about homosexuality. I have had to fight tooth and nail for every degree of self-respect and self-love I now have, and the homophobic forces out there are still trying to grind my face back into the dirt. I am currently ghettoized in San Francisco, and to some degree shunted away from the rest of society. The homophobia that is drilled into everybody's minds has made me fear that I would lose the love and support of my family and straight friends if they knew of my gayness, and has forced me to be a hypocrite and a play-actor in my relations with them. I think I'm very much a victim of societal oppression, and it pisses me off royally.''

♀''Most of the oppression I suffered as a lesbian came from my own head—my own fears of rejection, etc. Granted that there are some realities in nonacceptance from society in general, from employers, etc. But it is our acceptance of society's standards which is our largest enemy. I have never lost a job, been refused housing, schooling, or social status as a result of my lesbianism—I have excluded myself from a lot of things, however, as a result of my own fears, or feelings of shame.''

Miscellaneous Attitudes, Experiences, and Incidents

In discussing the subject of oppression, the lesbians and gay men came up with a variety of comments:

♀"Anita Bryant licked the homosexuals in Miami. Maybe she could come and lick me if she gets the time! Seriously, though, I think she is an extremely dangerous person. She is saying that some Americans have constitutional rights and some Americans don't. Freedom of religion is a constitutional right in the U.S. and Canada, and Anita is trying to impose her literal, Bible-thumping, narrow-minded Christianity on all of us. She would make her brand of religion compulsory, and deny human rights to those who object to it. Would she rather homosexuals were working, productive citizens, or would she rather be supporting us on welfare or in jail with her tax money?"

♂"I hope eventually I will be able to openly admit my sexuality. I am a drag queen, and I would like to be able to come out of my house in drag, get in my car, and go to a gay bar without having to sneak in and out with neighbors making a big to-do over it."

♀"I am oppressed because 'Christians' claim we are unfit as mothers and responsible members of society. I happen to know several lesbian mothers who have shown more interest in their kids than the average housewife whose mind is on zero or soaps most of the day. I've known lesbian mothers who felt they failed when their kids went straight. They'll legalize pot before they legalize homosexuality. All I can say is thank goodness for people like Lily T. and others who are giving positive reinforcement to gays.

♂"I still feel fearful sometimes making love in my own apartment. But I used not to let any gay-oriented books, etc., lie in plain view, whereas now I do. So maybe other areas will ease up as well, as time goes on."

♂"I resent straight humor which ridicules gay people."

♂"I feel I am oppressed by macho gays for whom boy-love is defined as a crime."

♂"I have never felt any particular fear of my gayness being discovered by anybody, with the possible exception of Uncle Sam, who might be moved to deport me back to England if my sexual habits came to his attention."

♀"My major oppression as a lesbian really had little to do with my homosexuality, but a lot to do with being a woman. We, as women, have all been oppressed in our society, in subtle as well as obvious ways. Women have been second-class citizens, financially, socially, educationally, in careers, etc. There have been all kinds of oppressions which I need hardly elaborate here, since the women's movement has done it in volumes."

♀"I feel that I am oppressed as a lesbian mostly in my straight job. While other women are talking about what they and their boy friends did

during the weekend or what problems they may be having, I cannot discuss my lover or any problems that we may be having with anyone (except for one woman). I cannot walk down the street hand in hand with my lover for fear of harassment. These may appear to be very petty but they are very important to me."

⚨"Upon telling co-workers, problems arise because nongays often *expect* gays to *be* certain ways (faggots are natural disco dancers, etc.), or they say, 'Well, you are straighter than a lot of the queens I know, so it is okay,' which brings on feelings of self-guilt that I'm not as sissy-identified as I might be. Perhaps one of the worst forms of harassment is around our child. In these days of enlightenment, faggots are perhaps acceptable but still shouldn't be raising children. Oftentimes, in many different situations, it's not the harassing things people say that hurt—it's the things they are thinking and want to say but don't that bring on the tense vibes."

⚨"My sexual interests in porno are being denied me by this city and country. I have had six gay adult porno films confiscated by the local Canadian customs people, and three magazines 'stolen' by the postal authorities. I know straight porno movies are never confiscated."

⚨"I am oppressed when it is necessary for gay people to have to start a Christian church of their own."

⚨"I really resent the public school system for not teaching young gays anything about their sexuality. I really ruined most of my early years because I was just too afraid to have sex with another guy."

⚨"I resent people's regarding gay people as freaks, and I resent the too-close association of gay with S&M and other aberrant behavior."

♀"I just got back from the state International Women's Year conference where 'we' won over the Phyllis Schlafly–Anita Bryant ladies. Seeing these fascist women made me infuriated and horribly ill. I ended up in bed for two days with a high fever and cramps. All women are *not* our sisters!"

♀"Anita and her dear victory devastated my brain. That's oppression. Also, I've had enough of goddam guys saying, 'Yeah, I understand your gayness, but I don't accept it. What you need is The Right Prick to give you all you need. And, by the way, here I am.' Always, it's The Right Prick that I need! Damn them all, the bastards!"

⚨"The second-class citizenship every open gay has to endure is intolerable. We're consigned to exploitative bars, baths, restaurants, etc., which even if they're gay-run don't noticeably deviate from the noise, cheapness, and darkness in which we're supposed to thrive—and do, despite the mind-numbing stupidity of it all. The press and electronic media remain as closed to us as to Native Americans or Chicanos. We're inadequately protected, if at all, by civil rights laws, police, and judiciary. Our feelings and lives are not allowed in the schools or academia. Every honest artistic expression we have is ignored, demeaned, or trivialized. Our political and social ideas are belittled or co-opted."

♀"It's been obnoxious to me in theater to have only heterosexual parts

to play and putting up with heterosexual displays of affection all around you when people would be shocked if you so much as held hands with a woman publicly. I resent not being able to be 'out' at work. In my neighborhood (a white working-class neighborhood), where I am popular with the children and enjoy being around them, I have to be super-careful about showing my sexual identity. If my neighbors knew, I've no doubt they would try to drive me out.''

♀"I've been oppressed by thinking I was heterosexual for such a long time; by orienting my life around men; by society's expectations of me to get married and have a family and support a man; by being channeled into 'feminine' skills and studies; by my parents' rejection of me because of my lesbianism; by people thinking I'm 'funny' and other women being afraid I'm going to rape them or something (this applies particularly to the women at work); and countless other ways. I've never told an employer I'm a lesbian until after I've got the job. And at the moment I have to be very careful because of the immigration—if I left the country and they found out I was a dyke, they wouldn't let me back in.''

♂"Today I stopped at the newsstand. I picked up two magazines. *High Fidelity* remains on the car seat for the rest of the day; *Blueboy* goes under the car seat.''

♀"I have felt oppressed from listening to people condemn homosexuals as perverts and queers, and as being women who only want to be men or can't get a man. All the subtleties of our society that uphold its male dominance oppress me.''

♀"Yes, I know I've been oppressed along with all other gay people who do not dare to hold hands with their lovers walking along the street. When I can't bring my lover to a faculty party open to spouses of faculty, when I can't joyously and loudly proclaim to co-workers that my lover and I just celebrated our ninth anniversary or discuss truthfully what we did over the weekend—then I know we are oppressed. I feel angry when I see straight people doing a lot of heavy 'making out' in public. I wouldn't be that uninhibited even if gay relationships were accepted fully in this society—but I want to feel free to give a hug and a kiss in public without being nervous about it.''

♀"I am oppressed and enraged when others cannot see the person I am beyond my sexuality.''

♂"In high school I was thought of as a 'fairy' because my best friend (and secret love) was much braver and upfront about his sexual preferences. It was hell for me and I wonder how I survived.''

♂"I believe that the basis for the oppression of gay people is in the bourgeois nuclear family, one of the cornerstones of capitalism. It is not that straight people are 'naturally' prejudiced against gay people. There is a reason for it. The nuclear family must be maintained if capitalism is to be maintained. A labor force must be produced and homosexuality is contradictory to that. There is a certain level of 'acceptance' that gay people

may be able to get under capitalism—some concessions, in other words. But as gay people we will only get so much, the same as with any other oppressed group. Our liberation will only come with socialism.''

♂ "I've been oppressed by having to spend much valuable time fighting for rights others have and take for granted.''

♂ "The worst oppression I feel as a gay person comes from other gay males. No matter where one looks in the gay 'community,' there seem to be only two accepted modes of expression. One is the promiscuous sexual life exemplified by the bars and baths. The other is a sad mockery of the heterosexual ideal of monogamous marriage, with a house in the suburbs and a station wagon and a dog and a cat as surrogate children. There is little or no acceptance in the gay world for deviance from these two patterns; but I find the first repulsive and the second insipid. I am tired to the point of anger of being stared at and clucked over by my fellow gays because my ideals of human relationship are based on intellectual and emotional sharing rather than sex and/or economics.''

♀ "Most of my oppression as a lesbian has come from my straight sisters in the women's movement. I feel much pressure from them to be closeted . . . to just not ever mention it.''

♂ "My lover and I are constantly being verbally harassed on the street. I have been physically assaulted for dancing with a man in a straight disco. I was almost destroyed as an adolescent because of guilt, shame, and fear of being thought 'queer.' Indirectly, I am oppressed because of the lack of gay role models I had in growing up. I am oppressed because in this 'heterosexual dictatorship,' as Gore Vidal so aptly labels it, everyone is assumed straight unless stated otherwise. I am oppressed because Anita Bryant and her ilk are spreading the news that I am a child rapist unfit for human consideration. I am oppressed because sisters and brothers are being murdered and lobotomized, losing their jobs and apartments (or not getting them in the first place), being sent to prison and then raped in them because they are gay. I am oppressed (we are all oppressed) because of the masculine-feminine dichotomy imposed upon our personalities from birth. I am oppressed (we are all oppressed) by the violence and greed of monopolistic capitalism in which everyone is dehumanized.''

♀ "Of course I am oppressed as a lesbian! I wasted a good ten years of my life in depression and anxiety, and I am not free to go where I please and to express my preference in the open like heterosexuals can. There is a gay ghetto just like there are black or poor ghettos. Outside of these city areas, people are still being harassed and arrested for being outside the norm, for even being thought to be a 'queer.' Ultimately I think this is a positive thing because I have learned to fight for everything I've got, and now I won't give up my principles to 'make it' because I can see through the hollowness of 'making it.' Because I have been forced into a situation of seeing reality, I feel that I can relate to other oppressed people, and there are so many people who are oppressed for so many different reasons. I can see through

people's guises, and won't let them use me just to discard me later. In other words, I have no stake in the dreams of the middle-class world that I was brought up in. I wouldn't anyway, because I am a woman, and women, rich, middle-class, or poor, don't have no stake in a nothing! But being gay was the vehicle for my realizing this, and also for escaping the trap of marriage.''

Those Who Don't Feel Oppressed

A small number of gay men and lesbians stated that they did not experience oppression, or at least that their homosexuality was not an obstacle in certain specific settings. Here are some of their comments:

♀"Don't feel oppressed in any way, as a woman, wife, mother, lesbian, or whatever.''

♀"I can't say that I, personally, have been oppressed because I was a lesbian, although I am well aware of the so-called disadvantages in being one. I think a lot of the recent societal changes brought about by gay liberation have altered middle America's viewpoint so we can lead 'normal' lives, not as the ogres or child molesters of oral tradition and popular historical literature. Since it's easier for others to accept us, it's easier for us to accept ourselves, survive and integrate naturally. When I was young a lesbian was a freak; now being a lesbian is fashionable, even somewhat chic.''

♂"I am not aware of ever fearing being discovered. I have simply known that being homosexual was one of a number of things on which I and the apparent majority in our society do not agree. And I understand, as a mature person, that's also a part of life. For example, I think war and killing is a terrible thing. But, I understand I live in a society that practices both, for some very realistic reasons at times. So, I must on the one hand be true to my ideals, but, also not pass some kind of 'holier than thou' judgment either. I, as a mature adult, accept that there are others different from me. That's fine, that is their right, as it is my right to live as I have chosen, and as I have felt best.

"I cannot say I have felt 'oppressed' because of my homosexual feelings, just different.

"I simply take responsibility for my sexual feelings, and for myself in acting with regard to those feelings. I understand that if I'm going to live with others I must accept them for what they are, and what they are not. If they do not want to accept homosexuality as a valid lifestyle, then that's their business, and not my problem. I simply must decide how to relate to them and to their problem.

"Much of the talk I hear from gays about deing oppressed is really coming from persons who are immature and unable to face life's realities. I find them often attempting in this way to escape from having to face some truths about themselves they have not wanted to face. If they can keep

talking about their 'problems' with society and straights, they don't have to face certain uncomfortable truths about themselves. They typically are persons who are unwilling to accept responsibility for their own lives, and especially their own failures. It is much more easily done to blame society for my failures, rather than look within myself, and try to find what's really wrong.''

♀"I really don't feel that I've ever been oppressed as a lesbian or suffered any abuse. I've been careful who I've told, but those people have been really accepting.''

♀"I do not feel oppressed as a lesbian, because I do not feel it imperative to flaunt my sexuality. When I take a job I do not wear a badge on my sleeve and demand that people accept me. What I do after work is my own business.''

♂"I don't think of myself as being or having been oppressed, but I think that in general my perception of society at large as being intolerant of homosexuals has led to me having less respect for society at large and having little motivation for achievement in society.''

♀"I've never been physically or even verbally harassed on the street, and I am in the habit of being affectionately demonstrative in public.''

♂"I don't really believe I've been oppressed as a homosexual. Yes, I was arrested a few times (twice fined, once case dismissed) for cruising in a public place, but after all, I violated the law, and it never bothered me. I do not believe that my homosexuality, or the fear of being discovered, was ever a factor in employment, schooling, housing, social status, or other. But I am cognizant of the fact that I have been more fortunate than many many (perhaps hundreds of thousands) others.''

♂"I do not feel I have been oppressed. The open acceptance of gay life in this city, even by the police, has prevented me from feeling any way but good. I have never been put upon by anyone.''

♂"I don't feel oppressed directly, but I probably would if I were a 'liberationist' and insisted on proclaiming myself loudly and needlessly. I simply don't have any problems because of sexual preference.''

♀"I have not been oppressed as a lesbian, but then I am married, so have a facade; bi, so have an alternative; not publicly 'out,' so have protective cover. I am sure that I would be oppressed if these were not so, or if my parents knew. Also, I need to find a vacation spot where T. and I can go and be openly together so I guess I feel awkward there. I am probably more oppressed because I have six children; i.e., 'Are you Catholic?' 'Isn't that too many?' 'Are you sure you can work and take care of them?' (I held two jobs for three years.)''

♂"I have no fear of being discovered for I feel that many straight people have thought it for so long that it doesn't matter. During the years from 1926 to 1971 when I was with my lover we were never discriminated against in housing or employment or social status. We found during the years of

our living together that we were able to rent apartments, bought a home, and never encountered any discrimination.''

Prison

As noted in the introduction to this book, it was impossible to effectively distribute the questionnaires to prisoners. There are no figures available on the proportion of lesbians and gay men in the prison population, but since the beginnings of the gay movement, activists have focused on the plight of the gay prisoner. In men's prisons, the openly gay prisoner is at the bottom of the prison hierarchy and is often a victim of exploitation and rape. In women's prisons, the situation is different; lesbianism can be an outlet for sisterly support among female prisoners, but relationships are often broken up and stereotypical femininity is promoted by the authorities. In both men's and women's prisons, violence with sexual overtones occurs, although it is only in the men's prisons that gang rapes, knifings, and murders are practically a way of life. In 1978, under pressure from gay organizations, federal prison authorities were ordered to stop using the term "homosexual rape," since more often than not homosexual prisoners (or prisoners who happen to be younger, smaller, effeminate, or sexually desirable) are the victims of rape perpetrated by heterosexual males who see their victims as surrogate females. For gay people, prison life brings with it additional layers of oppression. The gay men and the lesbians commented on the question of sex in prison:

♀"Prisons should be reformed so inmates can have wives, husbands, lovers visit and enjoy sexual privileges. The current system is inhuman, unhealthy, breeds animals and social pariahs.''

♀"TV and newspapers are my only source of information. From them I get a feeling of fright of being gang-raped in a prison, but somehow I think that that's the exception, not the rule. Propaganda strikes again! Actually, I don't have enough information to make a judgment.''

♀"I am going to prison and fear the stories I hear. I doubt I can remain celibate, so I suppose I'll find a big, mean dyke and try to play her femme.''

♂ "About four years ago, I was arrested for counterfeit charges by the U.S. Secret Service. It was very serious and I was scared. I miraculously was spared from being sentenced and spent very little time in jail, but I wasn't always so cocksure that I wasn't going to be. During the months I was being tried, probably my greatest fear, besides being taken out of society, was the fact that I would most likely be sexually assaulted by the men in prison, federal prison at that. I kept thinking I knew I liked men and would most likely enjoy it immensely, but I didn't like the idea of being raped and forced to be a homosexual. I sometimes think or fantasize about the men in prison and how 'hot' it would be to be around all men, and especially those

who are 'straight,' and to be able to fuck and suck and kiss them (saying this turns me on).''

⚥ "If sex is denied in prison, the logic would extend to denying other basic human needs, such as for oxygen, water, and food. How barbarian to deny this need!''

⚥ "Sex in prison should be on a basis of freedom and respect, not forced and unnatural, and not forbidden. With *good* sex, prisoners could be helped in their rehabilitation more than by a lot of other activities or therapy.''

♀ "I am opposed to the existence of prisons; however, while they exist I support women who are in them and any efforts they make to get mutual support, understanding, comfort, etc., with their sisters who are prisoners. Lesbianism in prison is not an outlet for sex that is forgotten once one gets back to the 'real' world of heterosexuality. It is an obvious example of the ability of women to relate to and support other women in a physical way while they are in a totally oppressive situation.''

♀ "Having been in one of this country's juvenile correctional institutions I have a lot of feelings about the double messages received by the women inside. I also have a lot of feelings about the way the movements (both women's and gay) have seen fit to do nothing more than hold a few workshops on the subject at conferences instead of going into the prisons and letting the women do their own talking.''

⚥ "When I was away in a state juvenile institution at age 13½, I got involved with some of the other girls who were locked up with me. None of these involvements were for any longer than a few months. I was there for three years and the powers that be thought I had been rehabilitated enough to be paroled so I could start college. During this whole period my sexuality was questioned always with the feeling that I was 'going through a phase' even after I told them it was no phase!''

⚥ "This is where a lot of people discover that they aren't completely straight and supports my own theories about bisexuality. Sure, it's situational, but a lot of those relationships are much more than sexual and many of them continue after prison. A lot of the men I have sex with were exposed to male sex in prison; they're no longer in prison, are happily married, have families, etc., but still enjoy getting it on with another guy.''

⚥ "I know little about sex in prison but I do know that I have corresponded twice with prisoners and got burned twice. The second one cost me a lot of money and caused me a lot of trouble, and for several months I lived in constant fear. No way should a gay person correspond with someone in prison: I learned the hard way!''

⚥ "I used to do some work with Arizona prisoners who were gay. A few stayed with me when they first came outside. That was usually quite weird because they did not seem to follow the niceties of a relationship, and often related to me as though I were a woman—one in particular. But this had much to do, I suspect, with very, very different class and regional backgrounds.''

Influence of Religion

Biblical dogma forbidding homosexuality and the day-to-day antigay actions of organized Judeo-Christianity have made many gay people aware of the religious roots of homophobia. Eastern religions, such as the Hare Krishna cults, also preach against and prohibit homosexuality. Some religions are more liberal, and gay caucuses have been formed in some churches. Many gay people abandon the religions with which they were raised, choosing instead atheism, agnosticism, or various forms of free-flowing spirituality, including, particularly for women, Wicce or Dianic teachings (see appendix). Lesbian-feminists, especially, are vehement in refusing to participate in religions committed to patriarchy and a male god. Some gays, however, are trying to reclaim the Judeo-Christian heritage from homophobia, reinterpreting the Bible and promoting the "good parts" of the heritage. Here are some comments on the influence of religion on people's sexuality:

⚤ "Religion is not very important to me. I go to church only because my lover plays the organ there. I go to be with him. I often think that devoted churchgoers are the most unchristian people around. In fact, after a long time of reading many books, I am not certain whether Christianity has had a positive effect on the world or not. I am certain that over the centuries countless thousands of lives have been destroyed, ruined, or merely made unhappy, all in the name of religion."

♀ "My religious upbringing (Catholic) squashed my sexuality. I learned that I could be a madonna or a whore, a wife and mother (in that order, of course) or a sinner. No middle ground, No allowance for variation. I hate the Catholic hierarchy—how I ever escaped I don't really know."

♀ "The Jewish religion (and I've had twenty-five years of it) treats women like shit. And when you confront an Orthodox person with this second-class treatment, the men *and women* will tell you that the woman has a very honored place—in the home, under the management of a husband."

♀ "Even though I don't go to church any more, my Catholic upbringing has made a permanent dent in my thin skin. I went to Catholic schools from kindergarten through college, and that's hard to wipe out!"

♀ "I was raised in a small Mormon community in Idaho. Outwardly everyone was a 'good' person. But a lot of women got pregnant before marriage, there were dirty old men around. My father's friend made a pass at me; he was about 65 and I was a teenager. In my age group there was a lot of sex play at a very early age."

♀ "The Catholic Church has done more harm to the human race than cancer."

⚤ "Recently I have built up a deep abiding loathing for the Christian church. I realize I'm being unfair, because not all churches are hate

mongers. Still, whenever I see a plea for fascism, or a smear against me and my gayness, or a string of vicious lies and hate, it always seems to come from the Christian church, or in the name of Christianity and decency. After the Dade County fiasco, a friend of mine put a sign on his desk at work saying, 'If you're Christian, please take your hatred somewhere else.' That pretty much sums up my feelings.''

⚥"My religion was very helpful in enabling me to accept myself as I was and to accept others with their differences. Anita Bryant's 'Kill a Queer for Christ' notwithstanding, the Christianity I was raised in was one of love.''

⚥"I am very religious. I believe in the message of Jesus and am a conservative not unlike Anita Bryant except I feel Jesus' atonement was for *all,* including gays!! The influence extends to how I live my life and sex life. That is why I hardly ever trick. And feel I shouldn't, really. Jesus didn't die just to give us a sex smorgasbord like someone would have us believe. Also that is why I never go home with a Satanist, witch, heavy dealer of astrology (all Devil's Domain), or drug user.''

⚥"As a devout Roman Catholic who enthusiastically embraced the Church and her teachings I learned that I was wicked and to be despised among men. My longings, when I permitted them to surface, were to perform acts 'which cry to heaven for vengeance.' I have gotten truly *fucked up* in the name of Christ.''

♀"I just want to make a plug for Metropolitan Community Church. No other church deals with sexuality at all—gay or not. I am grateful to MCC and would not probably be a Christian today without it—no other church wants me.''

♀"I did not have a strong Christian background and was not influenced in my selection of lifestyles. I am upset by the Anita Bryant Christianity that is attacking lately. I think the Golden Rule, which is repeated in every major religion of the world, is more indicative of what any God wants from human behavior.''

♀"I object strenuously to that morality code which places sex as a procreation function, without joy and beauty and life and fun.''

♀"What bothers me is when people have to go laboriously through the Bible and the original translations to find one certain word or comma or whatever that says that maybe God does *not* hate your guts forever and people get into long arguments over, say, what is the translation of 'know' in the Sodom and Gomorrah story and were they really queer or just inhospitable? If someone comes from such a strong tradition that they just can't give up Christianity and the Bible, then of course, the MCC has its purpose in comforting them, but I gave up the idea of crawling to some male God on my belly begging for forgiveness!''

⚥"I was reared in a fundamentalist Christian doctrine, which imbued me with the conviction that all natural body functions are, categorically, unclean; and that the naked human body in particular is an obscenity.''

⚥"I'm Jewish, and was brought up with Judaism as a heritage and not a dogma, so it has not had a formidable affect on my sexuality.''

⚥"The Metropolitan Community Church is one of the most powerful molders of my gay sexuality and is by far my greatest motivator in life."

⚥"I am a practicing Catholic whose sexual orientation doesn't get in the way. I worked this all out years ago, and though the Pope would have a stroke, it gets me by. I think I'm pretty well adjusted in all phases of my life. Let me be blunt: sucking a cock Saturday night and going to Communion Sunday morning doesn't seem out of line to me. Maybe I'm fooling myself, but I honestly believe that God won't mind."

⚥"If I had my way, the inventors of organized religion and their followers would all be whisked away to Jupiter. All of the aspects of sex—homo, birth control, abortion—have some church-founded group acting in some 'return to the Dark Ages' role. Forbidding abortion. Opposing birth control. Fucking over gays. I despise the Christian and Catholic churches. I was raised an atheist and goddam glad of it. I have counseled gay Catholics who are so fucked up they are suicidal."

⚥"I think all religions are the products of some individual somewhere out to make a buck. I try not to be bitter about my experience with the church if only because resentment causes me to get hemorrhoids, which get in the way when I fuck."

⚥"I am increasingly convinced that it is only those people who are on fire with love of God who ever really experience the fullness of sexual ecstasy."

⚥"Religion and sexuality seem to be linked in some mysterious way for me, as they are with most of the Catholics and former Catholics I've met. Catholicism is a very sexy religion."

⚥"My Christianity is very influential in my coming out. I think Christianity and gay liberation—and other liberation movements—have the same goal, to allow a person to become fully liberated and authentic. My sexual liberation, personal identity, and Christianity are inextricably bound together. I have received much more prejudice in being Christian in the gay community than in being gay in my Christian community (although I realize that the church is full of gay baiters)."

⚥"I am now a Taoist and have found its concepts of androgyny compatible with my life and my being. My choice was influenced by my sexuality."

⚥"My scariest experience was when, by error, I picked up some Southern Baptist minister who dug the sex, then insisted we pray; I listened to him denounce me (!) for being a seducer. I was afraid this idiot would really go off the deep end. He fled when I told him I was a Jew and that he had swallowed the come of a Jew—he gagged and ran screaming into the night, babbling Bible quotes. Too bad, he was great sex until he shot."

Psychiatry, "Curing" Homosexuality, Therapy

With the rise of modern Western science, the prevailing anti-homosexual views have been largely reinterpreted so that homosexuality

came to be seen as a "sickness" instead of a "sin." Instead of priests and ministers who preached against homosexuality, there were psychiatrists who spoke of curing it. Although some of these men had humane intentions, many of them developed cruel techniques, including violent electroshock aversion therapy and even lobotomy. Psychiatrists helped to maintain an atmosphere in which homosexuals were looked upon as "sickies." In 1973, the American Psychiatric Association removed homosexuality from its list of diseases, but the profession remains filled with antigay psychiatrists who continue to encourage gay people to come to them for "cures." In fact, no psychiatrist has ever shown that he can cure anyone of homosexuality; usually what passes for a cured patient is someone who, through conditioned self-loathing, manages to repress homosexual yearnings while functioning sexually with a partner of the other gender.

The lesbians and gay men participating in the survey were asked, *Have you ever gone to a psychiatrist or psychologist to be "cured" of your homosexuality?* The result: 20% of the gay men and 8% of the lesbians said that they had gone to a therapist to be cured. For the men who participated in such therapy, the average amount of time was a year and a half, with one man reporting he's spent ten years trying to be "cured." Of the women seeking a "cure," the average amount of time was 11½ months, and the longest time spent was four years.

While seeking a "cure" for homosexuality is perhaps what many think of when discussing the relationship between therapy and homosexuality, many gay people seek help from therapists with the other aspects of their lives. Many gay people are themselves attracted to the field of psychology, and liberal trends in the profession have opened it up to gay people as individuals as well as to newer schools of therapy that are not antigay. The respondents were asked *if they were currently seeing a therapist, psychiatrist, or psychologist "for any reason,"* and 12% of the men and 18% of the women said that they were.

Among the reasons given by the gay men currently seeing therapists were the following: "mild anxiety," "relationship problems with my lover," "to help me understand and appreciate myself more," "to aid my wife and myself to adjust to an unconventional lifestyle," "depression after separation from lover," "paranoid schizophrenia," "self-destructive tendencies," "general adolescent problems such as fighting with parents, loneliness, periods of depression," "general life reassessment evaluation . . . the desire to do so came out of career and emotional boredom." One man said that he spent three weeks at a Masters and Johnson clinic and "learned how to fuck for $1,500." A few men reported experience with court-ordered psychiatric help or being compelled to see a psychiatrist by their parents.

The men were asked *how they feel about their experience(s) in therapy,* and the responses are shown in the following chart:

	VERY POSITIVE	SOMEWHAT POSITIVE	NEUTRAL	SOMEWHAT NEGATIVE	VERY NEGATIVE	NOT SURE
straight therapist	26	22	15	16	19	3%
gay therapist	31	24	20	5	4	17
don't know sexuality of therapist	17	9	38	8	4	25

It seems clear from the statistics that a gay therapist was more likely to evoke positive feelings in a gay client.

Among the reasons lesbians were seeing therapists are the following: "depression, adjustment, probably being in U.S. and away from my partner," "effects of rape, and generally just wanting to be more assertive and less defenseless," "to be a more complete 'me,' " "self-discovery and couples issues," "to undo relationship patterns carried over from survival needs as child/teen, especially control, withdrawal, going numb and sadistic behavior," "to learn to relate to people better, to get rid of my hangups and negative outlooks, to be able to relate sexually and interpersonally in a lover relationship if I find it," "difficulty maintaining my independence in relationships in the past (either men or women), lost my sense of self, who *I* was," "general life stresses, coping with work, sex, etc." One woman reported seeing a priest for counseling, noting: "The Church's rigid *official* stance causes me fear and some self-doubt. I started seeing him to work on my apparent *lack* of regret. But now it's to continue to grow in self-actualization." Another said she was in therapy because "I am not emotionally strong, have had breakdowns, need support and therapy and counseling."

The lesbians were also asked *how they feel about their experience(s) in therapy,* and the responses are shown on the following chart:

	VERY POSITIVE	SOMEWHAT POSITIVE	NEUTRAL	SOMEWHAT NEGATIVE	VERY NEGATIVE	NOT SURE
straight therapist	25	17	15	15	24	4%
lesbian therapist	44	23	8	4	1	18

	VERY POSITIVE	SOMEWHAT POSITIVE	NEUTRAL	SOMEWHAT NEGATIVE	VERY NEGATIVE	NOT SURE
feminist therapist	49	21	9	2	2	17
don't know sexuality of therapist	5	5	32	7	17	34

The influence of politics and sexuality on the therapy experience seems to be borne out by these statistics. The lesbians had more positive feelings—and few negative ones—for lesbian and feminist therapists.

Negative feelings about experiences in therapy can be a result of the circumstances leading to the therapy itself—such as being compelled to go by parents or the courts—or they can result from dissatisfaction with the therapist. The following are some comments from people with a generally unfavorable point of view regarding their therapy experience, or a negative attitude generally toward therapy's role in society:

♀"I went through three years of graduate school, training to become a psychotherapist. When the women's movement came along, I took a look at what I was doing and quit. I am *very very* leery of what therapists do to people and I think people should be extremely cautious when they seek 'help' for any reason. But I do know personally of a few (two or three) counselors who are both socialists and feminists and *also* are *highly* skilled in facilitating self-discovery and change without second-guessing and reading meanings into people's feelings and without trying to defuse their anger. It is possible to find such people and they are badly needed, but they are very, very rare."

♂"I wasted approximately four years plus with psychiatry trying to be 'cured.' What a waste of time and money! When my therapist left town to take a government position, his instruction to his successor was that I should return to my wife. Hell, I'd never left her. (I later read in *Time* magazine he opened a sex clinic with his wife.) The new therapist asked me if I had any securities—that he would accept that for payment—and that if I was interested in family therapy he was equipped to do that. That's when I pulled out! If I ever went into therapy again, which I doubt, I would seek out a gay therapist, one who could help me understand and better accept my gayness, one who hopefully would be more candid and honest from the beginning."

♂"I am aware of one psychiatrist here in San Francisco who I would love to see investigated. Bruce, my man who passed away, had him as a doctor, and he did him little good, except give him stronger drugs, and stronger drugs, and finally he just used them to kill himself. Bruce had problems,

and while I helped him as much as I could, I don't claim to know everything, and he could have had a doctor who might have helped him. I was working on getting him to change doctors. I know that this doctor seems to have a great many patients who are all on Supplemental Security Income (SSI), and are gay, and all of whom have a 'little pharmacy' at home from all the drugs he gives them. No one, but no one, needs as many different pills as this guy doles out. I have met at least four men who go to this doctor and all have the same symptoms. As far as I can see, they are receiving no concrete assistance in their chronic depressive states. I am truly sorry that my man had to be a martyr in this wild fight for human rights and mental sanity in this world.''

⚢"A therapist can't do anything for me I can't do for myself.''

⚢"The shrink I went to listened to me for eight weeks, saying *nothing,* and then said that I wasn't sick enough to need *further* treatment. Since he had said nothing for eight weeks, I had to agree that I didn't need 'further' treatment.''

⚢"I'm against therapy. If it helps, okay, but it seems to seldom do much good. I've got friends who've been in therapy for twenty years and they are as crazy now as they were then, maybe worse. Don't, I say, throw the baby out with the bath water, but where therapy is concerned, I've never been able to find the baby.''

⚢"I will just tell you about the shrink I went to for fourteen years, who was gay and who would never tell me so. I did not know he was gay until years after when I found out that he made a contribution to help the gay activists involved with the APA ruling on homosexuality. He was black and I guess because I was in love with him I met a black girl (at his encouragement). That, of course, did not get me to first base—so I met a guy named Rafael, who for the first time in life, loved me and whom I loved. Dr. K. said that if you continue seeing Rafael you will have to come to see me twice a week instead of once a week (and since I was very poor at the time that was impossible—also I was very dependent on him emotionally). So I broke up with Rafael after just about a week. I still cry when I think of it. Dr. K. has moved to another city, and I feel like writing him and telling him what a bastard he was. I don't think I could ever forgive him.''

⚢"To the best of my knowledge my first experience was when I was 4 or 5 years old. A lot of trauma followed that incident that has blurred my recollection of it. I know there was another boy involved who I was deeply in love with and he always wore good clothes and a clean white shirt and bowtie—the bowtie is a fetish that has stuck with me to this day. After this first sexual experience at age 4 or 5, my parents made bloody sure I would never remember the incident. Some 'treatment' was given to me to sublimate this sexual experience. A lot of family hatred and hysterics preceded these treatments. The whole thing is very confused. I only remember disjointed scraps which allow me to guess at the rest. In my teens, I started masturbating heavily. The trouble was that my fantasies were not about sex at all but of violence done to creatures who had the bodies of men

but had rooster heads. They were tuxedoed and bowtied and were bound and tied and violently murdered in a methodical manner. How the hell that ever got into my mind I can only suppose goes back to my mysterious sexual initiation or more likely the efforts of the man my mother took me to, to 'deprogram' me.''

♂"Since I have had extensive therapy (about 200 sessions in psychoanalysis and about 100 sessions in non-psychoanalysis), with the main intent of 'changing,' I have much to say about this. First, I do not believe that any therapist can really change a person's sexual orientation after about age 20, in spite of many many claims to the contrary. Therapists who attempt to do so, viewing homosexuality as a 'sickness' or 'disease' or as a form of immaturity, are doing no service for homophiles. Such therapists are still around and *their* view must be changed. They unfortunately have been brainwashed by the spirit of our time, which is homophobic, irrational, and tradition-bound by mores centuries old, based mostly on Biblical myths which only a very few enlightened persons understand. All too often the therapist is only inculcating (no matter how subtle he may be) his own heterosexual prejudices which he feels comfortable with. Right now we are going through a big transition in which homophiles have for the first time in history openly challenged orthodox psychiatric opinion. Nothing but good can come from such challenges. Homosexuality is not in and by itself a sickness. Many gays, however, do act frequently in ways (nonsexual) that may rightly be seen as 'sick' or rather abnormal. The real causes for this kind of behavior, however, stem from the oppressive society in which they live, the masks they must wear, the deep-rooted sense of inferiority they simply feel because they are branded as 'different.' ''

♀"I've been fortunate, in my 'out' years (these past four) to have enough 'together' sisters whom I can talk things over with when things bother me. I've always *extremely* distrusted therapists, ever since talking with sneaky counselors in junior high who always asked nosy questions and made me feel *real* uncomfortable. I've never been to one, but I've heard a lot of horror stories from friends (and read *Women and Madness*) that sound as though the therapist is more messed up than the patient.''

Some people had very positive feelings about therapy, however, often based on successful experiences. Here are some comments:

♀"I have nothing but 'raves' for therapy. If not for this help I dare not think where I might be now. For lesbians, a lesbian/feminist is the best choice and next best is a woman therapist who is feminist although hetero. Since this may not be within the realm of possibility for many I still think a hetero run-of-the-mill therapist is better than just no help at all. I started with one and if not for her I might never have found my way this far.''

♀"I'm into therapy now for the first time. I needed help to take the disintegration of the three-year relationship and needed some support. I like

what it's doing as far as getting me in touch with myself and maybe helping me learn not to set myself up so badly the next time.''

♀ ''I played around with bio-energetics and hypnotherapy and I think that many people have turned to radical and so-called radical therapies in a backlash against the churches and religions of the West. And non-church freaks like myself have found a unity, humanity, and spiritualism in psychological-sociological groups.''

♀ ''I had some therapy and found it to be of benefit. I also went through est, which I found to be of benefit. I know there are some therapists who are old-fashioned and would wish that women would have a therapist as groovy as mine was. She is gay, bright, and not the nonrelating kind of therapist. I think the nonrelating therapists keep people from growing up as fast as they could. I would really recommend est to many people. It gave me a philosophy and put many things into perspective that even therapy didn't. I think a person would get more out of therapy if they took est. Then they could utilize the therapy better.''

♀ ''I think therapy can really help someone get to know themselves and what's right for them. I went to a straight male therapist for 3½ years. He was very open to my gayness, and didn't consider it a problem for me. I was in my own little world when I started therapy, but now I can relate a lot, and love, and care, and touch. I never could do these things before. (I couldn't say 'touch,' 'kiss,' 'sex,' 'vagina,' or 'breasts' without getting headaches and a queasy feeling.) In conclusion, I owe the way I am now to the *help* that my therapist gave me. He helped me grow up.''

Some people had both bad and good experiences in therapy. Many suggest that the success of therapy depends on the therapist, that there are good ones and bad ones. Some viewpoints are characterized by ambivalence. Here are some of these comments:

♂ ''If a gay needs therapy, he's wasting his time unless he sees a gay counselor or psychiatrist. There is no way a hetero can begin to relate to us, on that level.''

♀ ''Can be really good or really bad, depending on the therapist. I've been in therapy twice—both straight therapists, one male and one female. I related better to the female therapist, but both therapists believed that homosexuality was a viable lifestyle. Any therapist who tries to 'cure' homosexuality is doing a great disservice.''

♀ ''Last night for the first time I read a journal called *Radical Therapy*. It was good. The premise was that therapy meant change and their purpose was to explore the possibilities. Therapy as it exists now is too often a tool for adjustment. It is used to keep people functional. It is sexist. Where I live there is a Women's Therapy Collective. I have not worked with them, but there seems to be an openness to change and a respect for the client that is unusual if not impossible with traditional male therapists.''

♂ ''I can't for a moment question the value of therapy provided it's done

by a person who's committed to helping another person accept himself *the way he is* rather than the way the therapist thinks he should be. I have seen instances where the person going for therapy becomes unhappier and develops additional problems. A friend was told by his psychiatrist that he was a sociopath, and he came to me in tears. I managed to convince him that all people are sociopaths to some degree. I resent the feeling that some therapists have that everyone must fit into some classification, and by handing out labels to put on people, they can contribute to the problem rather than help the person with it. I also have a great personal prejudice against psychiatrists, which doesn't help things."

⚥"I spent years in conventional Freudian-oriented therapy trying to change my homosexuality, of which I was terribly guilty and ashamed (pre-gay-lib days). As far as accepting myself as gay, gay lib was the best possible therapy. On the other hand (and in spite of Arthur Janov's antigay bias), I made tremendous changes with the help of a talented therapist using Primal Therapy. It is absolutely possible to re-feel (or feel for the first time) childhood traumatic incidents and thus understand how adult patterns have formed. I understood for the first time really how I came to have so much fear and compulsive activity in my life, have become a more feeling human being in the present, and have made more human relationships and done more new activity as a result of this therapy. Also, by the way, this was the first time I did any extended crying since childhood—something men are certainly not trained to do. I absolutely believe this is a revolutionary therapeutic tool for anyone feeling blocked—i.e., not feeling. It is far more powerful, in my experience, than any amount of talking or intellectualizing ever was for me. This includes consciousness-raising groups, so-called radical therapy groups, and gestalt and bio-energetic work."

Suicide

It used to be, not very long ago, that suicide or any form of death was the appropriate way to take care of a gay character in a work of literature. While such works of literature managed to ignore the lives of lesbians and gay men who found ways to love and to survive, it is unfortunately true that suicide has been, and still is, a response of some gay people to the realities of this world. The respondents were asked, *Have you ever attempted or seriously contemplated suicide?* and yes answers were given by 40% of the men and 39% of the women; 53% of the men and 33% of the women who had attempted suicide said it was related to their homosexuality. In addition to their own experiences seriously contemplating or attempting suicide, many gay people live with the specter of suicide and suicide attempts involving friends, lovers, and acquaintances. Suicide is a major cause of death in the U.S., Canada, and several Western European nations, and it would be ridiculous to suggest that only gay people commit suicide or have suicidal feelings. But there is no doubt that suicide and attempted suicide are frequent responses of gay people to the difficulties of the gay experience in a

hostile society. It has been suggested that psychiatrists, clergy, and others who insist on characterizing gays as sick and sinful are responsible for driving many gay people to suicide. It is a form of violent oppression resulting from isolation, discrimination, and the problems of survival. Here are some comments:

♀"I have seriously considered suicide, and feebly attempted it. At this point in my life I feel that there is always some hope, some chance that things will get better. In just this past six months I went through a period when I was very depressed and wondered what the point of it all was. But I hung in there and now I'm the happiest I have ever been. I am not against suicide. I don't view it is a sin or a cop-out. Sometimes it is tragic because it is unnecessary. But if the person is suffering so much, they may be more peaceful apart from this world."

♂ "During my first years of coming out I considered suicide often enough not to be frightened by it. I knew how I would do it. There were times that acknowledging my homosexuality was so painful that suicide seemed an alternative. No more; I want to live and I want to live gay."

♀"This is the most basic of freedoms, the most personal of acts, and for those reasons the state and its institutions (i.e., church, psychiatry, etc.) seek to control and discourage it. They project it as insane or sinful or pitiful. Suicide is the ultimate in noncollaboration."

♂ "I shall indeed resort to suicide as soon as my father dies. (To do so while he is alive would be to saddle him with a great sorrow.) I think *any* gay over age 45 or 50 should kill himself, as he has almost no chance for sex, aside from buying it from male prostitutes."

♂ "I worked in a suicide-prevention center for two years, and as an MCC minister have coped with a number of suicidal crises since that time. I am convinced that in most cases suicide occurs when a person becomes so immersed in a crisis that they can't see out, and that caring and supportive intervention at that point (or ideally far earlier) can help them to find reality once more. I believe that society participates by its oppression in encouraging the suicides of many gay people."

♀"In my personal life I have been extremely depressed at times. Especially so because of my inability to lose my tremendous poundage and the way in which this condition makes it nearly improbable for me to have a lover. I can get very despondent if I dwell on it, so I try not to. I have felt there is no way out and no hope for me at times, but so far I have chosen to stick it out in hopes of that 'miracle just around the corner.' "

♂ "Suicide I consider a viable alternative for a person who has reached the end. I think our society is silly and puerile to try to save suicides by chasing after them on bridges and up skyscrapers. Let the poor suckers jump. Often, I'm convinced they don't really want to commit suicide but are crying out for help; if we quit chasing after them, they'd come down off their pinnacle and walk into the counselor's office instead."

♀"I am fascinated by the idea of suicide, although I've never had the inclination to do it, except once in adolescence. Theoretically, it's a valid

thing—if you want to die, go ahead. But my second lover has tried to commit suicide twice in her life, and when I think of her doing such a thing it makes me very apprehensive.''

♂ "My suicide attempt occurred at age 24, during the time I was having trouble deciding whether to commit myself to a fully open gay lifestyle (with long-term lover, etc.) or whether to continue some semblance of fulfilling my parents' wishes to be whatever it is parents think they can be 'proud of.' After attempt was made and aborted, I decided it was more important that *I* be proud rather than parents—their loss, my gain!''

♀ "I once contemplated suicide very seriously, actually got into the tub with a razor, but I didn't do anything with it. It had a lot to do with a man I was with leaving me for another woman. When I say I played straight, I played straight! I practically had myself convinced.''

♂ "I have lived in total fear of my company, friends, or family learning of my homosexuality. I have lived with complete guilt related to my actions. In late 1973 I attempted suicide by drowning. I did not have the guts to keep my head below water, but learned that I am a strong endurance swimmer. Fortified with brandy, I started swimming straight out at 2:00 a.m. When the sun came up I was still far enough out that I could not see 40-story buildings on the coast. I got back at 8:00 a.m. and spent two weeks in a psychiatric ward.''

♂ "What for? Even when depressed I find things, almost always, in living that I can enjoy—though it may be a simple cup of coffee. Maybe when I'm 80, dying of cancer and can't take care of myself any longer. Probably, however, the human race will commit mass suicide first.''

♀ "I tried twice during college to no avail. I'm glad now that I wasn't successful. I'll never isolate myself so extremely again as to breed that reaction.''

♂ "I made a feeble attempt once when I didn't even understand my own homosexuality but was suffering from feelings of unworthiness because of it. My own mother committed suicide, which I came to understand after a while. It is not the way to go. One thing about having tried suicide, there is no place to go but up!''

♂ "I believe that there are cases when suicide is a person's sanest and most responsible choice; these suicides are usually well planned and always successful. However, suicide attempts which fail and fail repeatedly are either desperate cries for help, or techniques for manipulating and punishing others; in both cases some sort of crisis-intervention help is probably appropriate. I believe, as my therapist friends all claim, that probably 80–90% of all suicide attempts have some gay-related element to them; in other words, suicide is one manifestation of homophobic social values. But successful suicides are rarely due to gayness itself but other and permanent problems.''

♀ "I thought about it a lot when I was an adolescent dyke and sometimes really wanted to do it because I thought my being here was all a big mistake. But then I realized *that's* what all the straight people wanted—for us misfits

to just quietly off ourselves. So I decided to teach them a lesson and go on living. Besides, I was scared to do it. That was good judgment on my part and I'm glad I'm still here. I don't ever give it more than a second thought, and am no longer 'half in love with easeful death.' (I memorized Keats' 'Nightingale' when I was 17, and to remember it still makes me tremble and cry and think about a handful of white pills. That's an association I'd like to lose, but I'm afraid it will be with me always!)''

Responding to Oppression Through Politics

Until the advent of the contemporary gay liberation movement, only a few rare individuals would have suggested that there is any connection between politics and homosexuality. Now, gay liberation and gay rights are serious issues to be contended with by the major political parties, by the left, by the women's movement, even by conservatives.

The respondents were asked, *How would you describe yourself politically?* The list of political labels provided in the questionnaire covered a broad spectrum, and the respondents were told to check as many as they wished. The figures below indicate what percentage of the people for each gender checked that box. A few of the categories of special interest to women appeared only on the lesbian questionnaire.

	LESBIANS	GAY MEN
Democrat	24%	33%
Republican	3	11
independent	28	30
conservative	2	9
liberal	33	44
moderate	8	14
radical	33	16
apolitical	4	7
anarchist	9	6
socialist	21	18
feminist	21	22
women's liberationist	38	—
matriarchist	13	—
separatist	11	—
dyke separatist	7	—
pacifist	23	28
"third world" liberationist	2	5
libertarian	10	19
environmentalist	35	34
revolutionary	16	11
humanist	44	45
gay liberationist	44	44

Among the other political identifications suggested by the lesbians for themselves were "communist," "Leninist," "individualist," "prostitute lib," "woman-identified woman," "historic preservationist," "concerned, but not politically oriented," "paranoid schizophrenic," "passive anarchist," "art liberationist," "union activist," and others.

Other labels chosen by gay men included "Christian," "vegetarian," "independent utopian," "Marxist-Leninist," "monarchist, male chauvinist," "monarchist under the Queen of England," and others.

A significant portion of the gay population has accepted the concept of working politically to improve the status of gay people. There is no space in this book for a history, even a capsule history, of what lesbian and gay male political activists have attempted—and accomplished—in the past ten years. Gay people's presence in the political arena is being felt, and political action is one method (by no means the only one) by which gay men and lesbians have responded to oppression. That political presence has included lobbying for gay rights laws, campaigning for individuals in favor of gay rights, the election of openly gay and lesbian candidates to public office, gay caucuses in unions and other groups, petition campaigns, letter-writing campaigns, boycotts, demonstrations, pickets, zaps, sit-ins, attempting to influence the mass media of communication, the development of alternative independent gay and lesbian media, and so on. Of course, not all gay people are involved in such efforts, though the number of gay people who are politically involved has been steadily increasing and the gay political movement has become more diverse in terms of its participants and its ideas.

Detailed information was sought about the respondents' political involvements, especially regarding gay liberation and lesbian liberation. The gay liberation movement, in its current form, was launched in 1969 as a result of the Stonewall riot. On that occasion, lesbians and gay men attending the Stonewall Inn, a popular dancing bar on Christopher Street in New York's Greenwich Village, fought back against police who were raiding the bar. New York's Gay Liberation Front was born in the aftermath of the Stonewall riots, and before long similar organizations were founded in many large cities, on college campuses, and eventually in smaller cities as well.

Earlier efforts to organize on behalf of gay people were initiated in the 1950s and 1960s, especially in New York, San Francisco, Los Angeles, and Washington, D.C. Among the groups involved in this earlier political effort—usually referred to as the homophile movement—were the Daughters of Bilitis, the Mattachine Society, One, Inc., and the Society for Individual Rights (SIR). The post-Stonewall movement represented a quantum leap, however, in terms of spirit, attitude, sheer numbers of participants, and the impact on society.

A few of the respondents indicated that they heard about organized gay activity in the days of the homophile movement, but most became aware of the ideas of gay liberation in the post-Stonewall era. Several indicated that

they recalled hearing about the Stonewall riots at the time they occurred. Asked where they first heard about the movement, both the men and the women mentioned every imaginable means of communication. These included TV, radio, local newspapers, underground newspapers, national newsweeklies, gay periodicals, women's centers, the peace movement, conversations with friends, "rumors," gay organizations, gay demonstrations, posters, and so on. One person first heard about gay liberation from an antigay preacher!

Civil rights legislation has become one of the major focuses of the gay movement in the past few years. While some cities have passed such protective legislation, others have refused to do so, while in many the issue has never come before municipal government. Similar legislation has been introduced in the United States House of Representatives and in several state and provincial legislatures, but such legislation has so far floundered in committee or been easily defeated, with one exception—the Province of Quebec. On a local level, some local governments have repealed gay rights laws through the process of referendum. Anita Bryant's antigay campaign began first as opposition to Dade County's proposed gay rights bill, and then, once the bill was passed, it became the "Save Our Children" campaign which led to the law's repeal in a 1977 referendum. St. Paul, Minn., Wichita, Kans., and Eugene, Ore., repealed their gay rights laws through the referendum process several months after the Dade County referendum. Gay activists have attempted without success to obtain judicial and/or legislative action in other areas, such as repeal of so-called "sodomy laws" or "crime against nature" statutes outlawing homosexual acts, even among "consenting adults in private." But the civil rights legislation to prohibit discrimination in housing, employment, and public accommodation, with its implicit demands for "equal rights" as guaranteed by the Constitution, remains the focus of gay activity in the legal arena.

The respondents were asked, *Do you feel that the repeal of laws against homosexual and lesbian acts and/or the enactment of anti-discrimination in your state, neighboring state (or province), or nationally, will make your life better?* These were the responses:

	LESBIANS	GAY MEN
quite a lot	41%	43%
some	42	39
very little	8	12
none at all	4	3
not sure	5	3

When asked, *How much have you worked for such reform(s)?* they gave the following responses:

	LESBIANS	GAY MEN
quite a lot	11%	12%
some	38	37
very little	29	31
none at all	20	20
not sure	2	0

Opponents of gay rights legislation frequently state that such laws are not necessary, that discrimination does not exist, that sodomy laws are not enforced, etc. It is clear that the gay men and lesbians in this survey, with only about a tenth of them heavily involved in gay rights campaigns, are supportive of such laws.

The gay liberation movement entails much more than working for these legislative reforms. The movement is committed to changing attitudes, to improving communication and community among gay people, to combating stereotypes and lies in the media, to providing social alternatives, offering support systems, dealing with alcoholism and other problems, reaching out to isolated gay people, and educating misinformed straight people. In addition, lesbians have in many places formed their own organizations, largely a result of their dissatisfaction with the consciousness and behavior of the men in mixed groups.

The respondents were asked *to what extent they have become involved with gay liberation and lesbian liberation.* The chart shows the responses:

	GAY LIBERATION		LESBIAN LIBERATION
	LESBIANS	GAY MEN	LESBIANS ONLY
quite a lot	15%	21%	31%
some	39	31	36
very little	33	27	20
none at all	13	19	12
not sure	.5	1	2

About a third of the lesbians and nearly half of the men have not actively participated in the gay and lesbian movements. Our sample is probably weighted somewhat in favor of gay activism—since primary distribution of the questionnaires was through gay and lesbian organizations—so one can presume that a significant portion of the gay

population has remained aloof from these political efforts. Undoubtedly, this is closely related to the fears and dangers discussed previously in this book. On the other hand, the percentage of lesbians and gay men involved in gay politics is higher than the percentage of straight people involved in politics generally. For gay people, leading an open gay life or perhaps going to a gay church is seen as political, while no one would say that a straight person who is open about his or her family life and attends Sunday services is necessarily "political." One might also note that more women were involved in lesbian issues than gay issues—for example, custody for lesbian mothers and creation of "women only" spaces, as opposed to protest against police harassment of gay baths or cruising areas. Many lesbians also focus their energy in the women's movement.

The respondents were asked *to indicate how they feel about gay liberation (mixed male and female efforts) and lesbian liberation (independent lesbian efforts)*. These were the replies:

	GAY LIBERATION (MIXED)		LESBIAN LIBERATION	
	LESBIANS	GAY MEN	LESBIANS	GAY MEN
very positive	60%	72%	73%	39%
somewhat positive	29	20	15	20
neutral	8	6	4	20
somewhat negative	2	1	3	14
very negative	1	1	2	7
not sure	1	0	2	1

These efforts by gay men and lesbians to organize and work on behalf of the gay community in the name of gay liberation and lesbian liberation seem to have the overwhelming support of at least this sample of gay people. But the statistics do indicate some of the tensions between gay men and gay women. Although the women are willing to express good feelings about both the mixed efforts and the independent lesbian efforts, a significant portion of the men—more than half—are unwilling to give their wholehearted support to an independent lesbian movement. One out of every five men is negatively inclined toward lesbian efforts to organize separately. On the other hand, 40% of the lesbians are less than "very positive" about the mixed gay movement. This antipathy between gay women and gay men is a constant factor, though not an overwhelming one, in the life of politically minded gay people. Some of the issues behind the antipathy are explored later in this chapter; on a deeper level, however, the differences between gay men and lesbians (as well as the similarities) can be discovered throughout this book.

The respondents were asked to discuss their political ideas in more detail, specifically, *How does your homosexuality interact with your politics, if at all, including any involvement you may have with other political groups or movements? Tell about your experiences with gay liberation (or lesbian liberation); what have you liked or disliked about such experiences? How has feminism or the women's movement had an impact, on or changed your sexual practices, values, or identity?* Replies to these questions covered a lot of ground. The first group of responses is from lesbians and gay men who identify with the Republican Party or otherwise express political views that would be considered conservative.

⚦"Politically I am conservative. My homosexuality may have made me this way in part, because conservatism is usually found among people who feel that they have had to win their livelihood the hard way and that therefore it is possible for others to rely on themselves too. This is in fact the way I feel. I am optimistic about people being left to themselves with a minimum of welfare and external legal help. Also, since I grew up with an enormous threat of remaining dependent, clinging to my mother and father as a social cripple (common among homosexuals, in my experience), I am aware that paternalization is not an answer to people's needs. So I oppose socialism and excessive welfare, and I am for individual enterprise and initiative. At the same time, in order to feel part of a society which rejects me, or rejects my sexual behavior at least, I have had to dig deep to find out what they and I share in common. The common ground is certain religious values such as the dignity of the individual, individual freedom, and the symbolic unity of people through a higher body, such as the Church, or, in Buddhism, the movement toward enlightenment. I can see these values where they've been preserved in society, and I appreciate them more than do straights. I oppose some social changes which might make people forget these values. In addition, I feel I am a member of the group of gay people who are teaching this country something about freedom. I've marched in gay parades and felt the power of voluntary association. So I don't oppose voluntary association even if particular groups are against gays or against other things I like. I'd like to see a country where everything is voluntary groups; where you can move if you don't like the place you're living in, where you can get in touch with others who share your values. I would much rather fight it out with other voluntary associations and individuals than have either them or me dictate legislation. I'm against laws more or less."

♀"I'm slightly more conservative than liberal. However, as I get older, I'm getting more liberal. I am all for gay liberation, but my profession keeps me busy so I have no time to give my support except *vocally*."

⚦"Politically I'm a Republican, conservative. I'm opposed to women's lib, women priests in my church, changing our prayer book, but strongly favoring rights for gays, ordination of gay men to the priesthood. I admire and respect those who fight for gay rights. I do not like the obvious types of

homosexuals in the front ranks. They can hurt more than help. A masculine man can put the cause over better than an effeminate person.''

♂''Politically I'm very right-wing. I think politicians are the *most* despicable, lowest form of life that we have on earth. Real parasites.''

♀''I'm a lifelong conservative Republican who thinks the present parties should be realigned. So far, coming out has not affected my political views. I do feel that women should be equally paid for equal work, but I think ERA will be misused if passed. I do not align with the feminist movements, and my favorite squelch for several years to *men* who want to discuss it is, 'No, I don't want to be equal . . . why should I step *down*?' ''

♂''I am profoundly skeptical about left-wing politics and liberals in general, though my opinion of garden-variety U.S. Republicans is scarcely higher. I am a capitalist. My main criticism of American conservatives is that they are hypocrites: they say they support limited government, but then rush out to sign petitions against pornography, gay teachers, and the repeal of sodomy laws. I don't like to see governments trying to change the distribution of wealth or trying to change people's lifestyles as long as they aren't infringing on the rights of others.''

♀''I'm a rugged individualist, want a constitutional monarchy, free enterprise; I'm a capitalist, a libertarian, not an extremist; I want the law to protect every individual rather than the majority, and my lesbianism has not been a part of it, or any political group I've encountered.''

The following group of comments are from people who stressed their support of the Democratic Party:

♂''Politically, I am a staunch Democrat, having deviated only once, when I voted for Thomas Dewey in 1948, and that only because he was sexually more attractive than Harry Truman. I regretted it right after casting the vote, and have ever since. Harry is one of the great ones.''

♀ ''I vote independent but lean toward the Democrats. I admire the ideal of communism but not the actuality, so I'm not involved in it. I write my senator a lot and read a little about legislation and watch the news. I'm not very active, however, in organizations. I do write letters of protest or commendation and also sign petitions *after* I read them.''

♂''I am a Democrat because I am Negro and Roman Catholic. I am just now becoming aware of homosexuality and politics (no opinion yet).''

♂ ''I am a devoted Democrat and a friend of the Kennedys. They know I am gay, and there's no problems.''

♀''Politically I am a Democrat. I will vote for anyone I find out is supportive of gay people. I was involved slightly with the women's movement for a while and helped start a gay women's magazine. But there was some nastiness I didn't feel I wanted to be around. The women seemed to be so contrived and there were a couple who made cracks to me about my working for the 'establishment.' I make a good living, and I am not about

to give that up to wear tennis shoes all the time and complain about being oppressed. Such whining got tiring. Anyway, I feel the women's movement has done some great things. I hope the gay movement will do the same."

♂"Politically I am a liberal Democrat or independent. My homosexuality interacts integrally with my politics. I am interested in the decriminalization of homosexuality and the securing of gay rights; in the protection of abortion rights; promotion of contraception and family planning; abolition of all forms of censorship; legalization of prostitution; etc. I am co-chairman of our local chapter of the American Civil Liberties Union and an active member of the Abortion Rights Association of Illinois. I am a member of the gay students organization at our neighboring university, and would like to see it politically active, but in recent months it has been rather moribund."

♀"I'm a liberal, usually vote Democrat, am for ERA, am anti-Anita Bryant (of course), belong to the National Organization for Women, the American Civil Liberties Union, and the National Gay Task Force. I dislike the local gay center politics, which are aimed at revolutionary socialism with accent on Chicano/Third World liberation."

♂"I am a registered Democrat. Politically I will support the best person and especially those persons who are open about supporting gay rights legislation."

♂"Politically I am a liberal who belongs to the Democratic Party. I was a Republican until the Nixon thing and changed then. Though I have written the White House for specifics as to how President Carter will provide us with more human rights, Ms. Costanza has chosen to ignore my request for specifics although she did reply that the President was for 'human rights for everyone.' Every time I meet a candidate, for whatever office, state, city or federal, I ask his or her views on gay rights, and if the answer is appropriate, I vote for them; otherwise, I do not. This answer alone will sway my vote entirely."

♂"I am a Democrat politically, leaning toward socialism. I work with the poor and I see many changes needed. Sex has little to do with politics but I'd vote for a gay guy."

♀"I am a liberal Democrat. I'm not as politically active as I used to be but many of the lesbians I'm meeting now are politically active and I find myself fascinated and willing to participate in their concerns."

Here are some comments on politics from people describing themselves as liberals or moderates:

♀"I would describe myself as a political moderate. Because of my great love of the outdoors I have been somewhat involved with environmentalist movements for many years. I have been more of an interested observer than an activist in the women's lib movement."

♂"I am a liberal pacifist; I am professionally and personally involved in environmentalism and historic preservation. I run with a similarly liberal

group of people. I have relatives who are politicians. In the course of time, I have been active against the Vietnam War, and I have been involved via my profession in the whole area of geodesic domes and alternative technologies. In all of this sexuality per se has mattered little. I do not consider myself a gay activist, even though in a recent controversy here in Seattle (concerning a TV editorial on a station owned by the Mormon Church), I wrote letters to various public officials in opposition to rescinding the freedom-of-sexual-preference laws on the books here. I find really activist gays entirely too dogmatic; and they are hostile toward me in many cases because of my bisexuality, which they consider a cop-out toward a more clearly definable political stance.''

⚥ ''I was always a Trudeau fan, since he said in 1969, 'The nation has no place in the bedrooms'; he legalized consenting adults the right to have sex with someone of the same gender, in private. But in the past several years, Trudeau has done very little, either for gays or the stimulation of the economy. The national New Democratic Party have indicated that they're in favor of gay rights and changes in the criminal code, so the next chance I get to vote, it's NDP for me.''

⚥''I'm still moderate, leaning towards the left. I don't trust radical rhetoric, nor do I think that they have any grasp on how to realistically improve the system. However, I have deep, angry aversion to the political right and their God and the nuclear-family fascism. As I see this threat grow, I've become increasingly more liberal. I would never vote Republican for anything, as those conservative pricks are our greatest enemies, next to the Bible thumpers. My homosexuality, and the oppression I've received because of it, has made me more politically aware of other forms of discrimination. I think it has made me a more politically sensitive person.''

♀''Until May of 1977 I was an ultraconservative, though I had attended the gay convention in Texas, but I looked with disdain on most liberal economic policies not affecting lesbianism. Anita Bryant changed all that. I don't think I can ever again vote for a conservative candidate—the conservatives are the ones who are trying to legislate against us, and if they could get their way, they would take away *all* our rights, seize our property, jail us without trial, deny us the right to vote, etc. If we don't unite with other minorities, Bryantism will spread and deal us a lot of misery. We desperately need to form a coalition of all minorities and vote together on everything.''

⚥''Politically I am a cynical, iconoclastic, disbelieving, mistrusting hater of almost everything involved in it. I don't like the government having their beak in my stack of shit at all. I am for the complete wipeout of all victimless-crime statutes across the board. The issue of homosexuality should not even be a legalistic issue. I am diametrically opposed to the views of such self-appointed guardians of the morals as Anita Bryant, Phyllis Schlafly, Morton Hill, Billy Graham, Ernest van de Haag, Richard M. Nixon & company, Simon Leis, Jr., Larry Parrish, and many many others.

On the other hand, I tend to agree basically with the editorials of the liberals like *Playboy* philosophy, Larry Flynt, Al Goldstein, Ralph Ginsberg, William Burroughs, Gore Vidal, etc. Homosexuality undoubtedly has some bearing on my opinions, being in a repressed minority and all. I can sympathize with the plight of the blacks and Jews, etc., and particularly the American Indians who I grew up with and live around, there being many Indian reservations in this state! There is no such thing as a gay liberation movement in this state, so I have had no experience with same.''

♀"I am not a radical lesbian. I am a woman-loving, socially active, ladylike lesbian.''

♀"I am a moderate liberal. I supported and worked for George McGovern and the anti-Vietnam War movement. My gayness, as a secret, was not an issue at that time.''

♀"I think that I'm a liberal who believes that everyone should have the right to live as she/he chooses ('as long as it doesn't hurt anyone else'), without interference from 'the state' or from other people.''

♂"I am a radical-liberal, strongly influenced by feminist thought. I'm sure that my own experience of being a homosexual alien in a straight white male culture influenced my involvement in the movement for racial equality and later in the antiwar movement. At present my political life is limited to voting in elections.''

The Stonewall riots occurred when the New Left and the antiwar movement were at their height. Much of the early outreach of gay activists was oriented toward the left and the counterculture through underground newspapers, which were generally receptive, and there has been an important interplay between the left and gay liberation. The following statements are from lesbians and gay men who identified themselves politically with anarchism, socialism, or other aspects of left politics:

♂"Politically, I am a radical socialist. This interacts with my gay politics in that I believe gay liberation should not be a singular objective, but part of a far-reaching social, economic, and political revolution. I was a member of the Communist Party of Canada, but left because it was extremely antigay.''

♂"Politically, I am a leftist, presently active mainly in food coops and gay rights struggles. My gayness is very important to all this: part of a total reevaluation of our society and struggle towards making a new society. At the same time, I perhaps am not strictly speaking a political activist. I'm trying to integrate these long-range political goals with a personal life for myself. So, when I was first coming out, most of my energies were focused on my personal life, my relationships, etc. I did a lot of talking with my friends about feminism, sexuality, drugs, etc., but only in a very private personal way. It's only been in the last few years that I've been more active politically. This has been both satisfying and frustrating. I am bothered by how few feminist/socialist gay men there are, and I am continually

struggling against my fellow gay friends. I accept this, and try to look at it 'realistically,' but it is difficult. Part of the problem might be due to my current living situation, in Texas.''

♀"I am a platonic socialist-humanist and vicarious Marxist revolutionary. But my only political involvement is with the lesbian group in my community. I like the gay liberation group, except the raps are sometimes boring. My experience of oppression is all spiritual and vicarious, but is enough to make me identify with all oppressed groups. Often, though, other oppressed groups and people care only about their own oppression, and not about that of others, and I find this upsetting. Lately I have become convinced that human dignity is the ultimate goal of our species. By dignity I mean the intrinsic dignity of useful activity, creation, intellectual and emotional freedom, material progress, etc. and the sacredness of the individual life. Every kind of oppression, from a parent slapping a child, all the way to genocide, is simply the attempt to put boundary lines around the infinite human soul: 'Thus far shall you go and no farther!' But we always have to go farther.''

♀"I am a socialist-feminist. I do not work actively at gay liberation stuff—rather I work it into all of my other political activity. It is a big part of my political work and analysis. The connections are all there— patriarchy, capitalism, violence against women, sexism, racism.''

♂"I consider gay liberation as part of the class struggle but not the main part. Most of my friends are left and hetero. I hope some day to be more 'out' with them but I don't feel an urgent need to talk about sex with everyone. I am uncomfortable with gay people who see sexuality as primary and ignore the broader struggle for social change. While the left is to be criticized for its failures, sexual politics is not the answer for me.''

♂"I'm a libertarian anarchist, deeply feminist and as deeply committed to children's rights. I believe in economic socialism, i.e., worker ownership of the means of production and social distribution of the profits of enterprise. My homosexuality has influenced my anarchism by making me skeptical not just of the wisdom and fairness of majority rule but of the advisability of any and all laws, especially when they are made to apply to a large, heterogeneous population.''

♂"I guess I'm kind of an 'anarcho-libertarian.' I've read a lot about Emma Goldman and admire her. I am turned off by the 'straight white male new left' and do not consider myself a socialist.''

♂"I'm a collectivist rather than a libertarian, and believe in cooperation among small groups of people to achieve community goals.''

♀"I would describe myself as a radical-revolutionary. I am an ex-Young Democrat turned revolutionary. I believe the only solution to our problems is for lesbians to arm themselves and fight; we can expect no help from the males—they're still on top.''

♂"I'm a radical. I could get into making bombs in a dark cellar someplace. I work within the system, trying to get gay rights legislation passed. But I don't feel meek.''

♂"I am like a volcano, filled with hot molten political lava just ready at any time to spew out. While I am not a member of the Socialist Workers Party, I feel as though if I were in a larger city I would be very active in that organization. The SWP appears to be the only political party willing to accept an upfront stand on gay issues. Not only do they take such a stand but it is a very pro-gay position."

♂"Politically I am a communist. I am also oppressed as a worker. As a communist I do see that there is gay oppression and that it's rooted in capitalism. Regarding the communist movement and homosexuality, many new 'communist' groups are so antigay that it's disgusting. As you know, many organizations and 'parties' see gayness as 'bourgeois decadence.' We know this is wrong and from my experience, and knowing people in the Boston area, I feel optimistic about defeating such a fucked-up idea. I devote much of my effort to fighting against antigay chauvinism in the movement and everywhere in general. I realize things haven't been great for openly gay people in most socialist countries, but that won't make me blindly oppose socialism. I know gay people will continue to fight for their liberation—everywhere—and we have always existed alongside straight people and we will never go away. *Venceremos!*"

♂"Raised conservative, I became a liberal Democrat as soon as I learned what the major parties really stood for. I became thoroughly radicalized by the Vietnam War, a by-product of which was my exposure to radical literature that also reinforced my acceptance of my homosexuality. My gayness is a powerful reinforcer of my radicalism, although I do believe in trying to work within the system. (Most people who want to destroy the system have no idea what they want to replace it with.)"

♀"I'm a growing socialist with heavy capitalist, moneyed upbringing. I don't like to be around women doing a power-tripping, capitalist, men-imitating trip at all. It's very depressing to me. My own direction is to learn more skills, be financially independent and more active in the world while staying in touch with the underlying feminist principle in myself—letting it all come out in dance, theater, dance/theater pieces, and as I become more known, and make more money, keeping my socialist nonexploitative values at the fore of my life. I don't want to be a part of capitalism. Gay/lesbian liberation and feminism are the only two movements I work for politically. I find most political people aren't very supportive of artists (even those with the same values), which saddens me and makes me less active then I would be if this were not so. At the last school I taught at, I saw this clearly. There were the political radical lesbians and the artistic radical lesbians, and they were totally split and hostile to each other. So, as an artist, I stay away from those hostile vibes when I feel them."

♀"Politically at this point I'm an anarchist. I have been through the nonviolent movement, gay liberation, gay women's liberation, women's liberation, separatism, Marxism-Leninism-Stalinism, Marxism-Leninism-Trotskyism. I think being gay and somewhat political is what attracted me

to gay liberation. At the time I was involved (1970) it consisted mostly of men with a few women. The other women had split off to form their own group, which was hard to find. My opinion and all was respected. In fact we were needed for the women's viewpoint. Later I found gay women's liberation. The movement seemed to last a short time before it dispersed into other activities or none at all. I can't even remember what was discussed at the meetings. The gay women of Berkeley turned basically into a social unit. Lacking for something to do, I joined the women's health collective and went through a short period of separatism. Then I got involved with a lover who was into a big group here, and then a Marxist-Leninist group. Of course that only lasted a few months before I got kicked out and she converted. I did a lot of studying and decided Trotskyism is where it was at. But as of late, I think anarchism, a real government of the workers, is where it's at. Not with some yokels who took over in Russia at the right moment mouthing the sentiments of the workers and then disbanding the workers' councils, the very basis of the revolution. My interest in radical politics has always been with me since before I was a lesbian. Being a lesbian and a woman helped me to understand, and the analysis of the early women's movement (socialist), of society, and of the general climate of Berkeley brought me to believe that revolution is the only way things are gonna change."

♀"You're asking me to label myself—to say in a few words what should be done in many pages of description and explanation. Please be aware of how misleading this could be. Referring back to the list of labels, I'll give the following explanation: radical—unwilling to accept tokenism (or any 'ism') in any form; anarchist—Sartre, Russell, Locke, Marx; feminist—when I'm free, my brother will be free; women's liberationist—patriarchal power must be destroyed; libertarian—there is no source for authority of one person or group over another; humanist—humanity is the finest event of the cosmos . . . it must be free to grow; gay liberation—out of the closet and into the streets . . . now!!; existentialist mystic—autonomy, in the *true* image of the cosmic Will."

The Impact of Feminism

The movement of women struggling for equality, including a clear critique of the sex-role stereotype system, has been of special importance to lesbians—many of whom have been in its front ranks. Gay men, also, have learned from and responded to feminism—though many gay men reject feminism. The following group of quotations from lesbians express an essentially positive attitude toward feminism:

♀ "If it weren't for the women's movement, I would be locked up in my marriage forever. I feel that being involved has helped me come to grips with many things—it has also reopened my mind, which was closing at a rapid rate."

♀"By being a lesbian I am more directly concerned with women's issues, because in many ways they will benefit me more than straight women with husbands to fall back on."

♀"The women's movement has definitely changed the course of my life. Owning a feminist bookstore is something I never would've done without the women's movement! I suspect I never would've discovered lesbianism without the women's movement."

♀"The women's movement helped me and my identity as a black single gay woman in this racist, sexist society. I learned women also had played a large part in the history of the world."

♀"First it made me realize my anger, realize *what* I had been angry about all those years. I learned the courage to speak out about what bothered me. I have experienced a new and very supportive bonding with some other women and with some of the female members of my own family. Feminism did not change my sexual practices, but it did teach me to value them. My sensitivity to the plight(s) of other women everywhere has intensified tremendously, and I have reached the point now where I see feminism as part of a much larger and much needed social reorganization."

♀"I was raised by a feminist, was feminist by nature from birth, and while I aligned myself with the movement in time I don't think it has exerted much influence on me."

♀"Feminism has not changed my values, identity, or sexual practices. It has merely reinforced them and given me profound comfort and hope."

♀"Feminism totally changed my life. It changed my sexual iden-tification, helped me learn to like people and have friends, led me to discover my interest in the arts which had been submerged for years, helped me to understand oppression in general because of consciousness of my own oppression, and on and on."

♀"The growth of feminism and my growing awareness and acceptance of my lesbianism were intertwined. As I was evolving into a feminist and learning to accept myself as a woman, I was at the same time gradually coming to accept my lesbianism. It may be trite to repeat that 'feminism is the theory and lesbianism is the practice,' but I feel that it is true. I cannot conceive of one without the other."

♀"There has been no force in my life as potent as the women's movement. It has been my strength and my hope, my source of un-derstanding about myself. So I *wasn't* strange in high school when I wanted to join the all-boys projectionist club and learn about movie equipment! So my yearnings to play baseball instead of watching behind a chain-link fence weren't ridiculous! Hey, I don't have to feel bad about wanting to fully explore and participate in my world, or feel guilty because I'm angry at restraints! Those discoveries at age 17 unbound me and provided the im-petus to explore myself further, to trust myself and my feelings a lot more, and to go as far as I could in whatever direction I wanted to go. Thank you, women's lib! I could give up anything in my life, but not you."

♀"The feminist movement has had tremendous impact on my identity

and values, primarily by raising my consciousness to my own subordination because I am a woman. I am becoming aware of the centuries of second-class citizenship relegated to women. I see all the injustices and I seek to fight them. I have come to accept myself and not want to be a man because I know now that women can be strong and independent and aggressive. I have found the freedom to be a woman and not have that mean I am something less than a man. I feel good about my sexuality and that I need not look solely to men for my sex but that I can look to myself and to women. I am proud to be a woman because now I feel the freedom to be whatever I want and not to feel guilty because 'most girls don't feel that way.' I have been enlightened and encouraged through my readings by feminists. I have also found support for my rights to love whom I will. It's very exciting for me.''

♀ "The women's movement helped me a lot. It gave me the pride of being a woman and a lesbian. It gave me a feminist consciousness. I'm thankful to all the sisters who were and are more active in the movement, who produced all the newspapers, magazines, videotapes, books, etc., that opened my mind to the feminist viewpoint. Thanks to them, I'm a much happier and healthier person. Some landmarks were: Simone de Beauvoir's *Second Sex,* my Bible at age 14; *Our Bodies, Ourselves*—beautiful!; Betty Dodson's book on masturbation, and *The Yes Book of Masturbation*—truly liberating; some radical lesbian papers from New York, such as *Clit*—very true, pointed statements; videotapes by Norma Pontes and Rita Moreira, documentaries about lesbian mothers, lesbian love, a woman who rebuilt her apartment all by herself, the Women's Day March in New York, etc.''

♀ "My lesbianism is my politics. The basic class struggle is between women and men. The sexual division of labor was the first and it remains as the most exploitative. I did not become a lesbian because of my political feelings, but my politics evolved from my lesbianism. I am an anarchist feminist. For me this means a destruction of the existent patriarchal power structure and a belief that people, unfettered by artificially imposed behavior, will seek and find a means of cooperation that suits their needs. For the present, that is, before the revolution (although I believe revolution is an ongoing process), I believe that women must recognize that they are at war with men. Recognition of your oppressor is the first step towards ending your oppression. Fucking with men is collaboration with the enemy!''

♀ "I become a stronger and stronger feminist in all I do. I don't hate men but find less reason to interact with them, and want nothing from them.''

♀ "I am a lesbian-feminist. I see the need to have a new society by dismantling patriarchal capitalism. I have become very disillusioned with the current left movement. It gives lip service to feminism and is generally antigay. I do not feel good about the reformist gay male movement. I think lesbians are more radical, but I think many have retreated into culture and women's businesses instead of working on real change. I think the

development of women's culture is good, but I get depressed because of our overall powerlessness at present.''

♀"Feminism made me very angry. Without it, I'd probably still be sitting in a skirt behind a typewriter and fetching coffee for my 'master.' It has made me think of myself as a capable, strong human being who can do anything that I really want to, has made me a more fulfilled person, and has expanded my horizons.''

♀"I personally feel more in tune with the feminist movement than I do with the gay rights movement, because my first source of identity lies in my femaleness, and tied in with it very closely is my sexuality. But to me, my sexuality is more of a political expression than it is sexual. 'Woman' as a concept is just as exciting to me as women in bed, and it's much more important.

♀"I have always been a feminist, and the women's movement has made it possible for me to say so without being called a dyke by people to whom that is still a dirty word. That is a great gain from my point of view. The same reactionaries may oppose everything I believe in, but it is no longer automatically all right and respectable for them to do so, and automatically suspect for any woman to push for equality of treatment. I find this helpful on committees, at school board meetings, in employment interviews, in dealing with my daughter's school, and all sorts of interactions with 'the rest of the world'—in all those places where I am not 'out' and don't intend to be if it isn't necessary (at any rate, I want to choose when and where and with whom I am 'out'). My values haven't changed, but my relations with straight women have improved since theirs have. And this is good because I feel myself as a woman first and foremost.''

Some of the lesbians show ambivalent or mixed attitudes toward feminism, or feel it is irrelevant to them:

♀"I used to hate feminism; now I am continually surprised by men's attitudes toward women. I think women's lib gets self-righteous sometimes and overcritical of other women, but basically it acts as a light in the darkness.''

♀"I believe that feminism saved my life literally. It gave me a view and understanding that all the pain wasn't just mine due to my failures. It helped me come out sexually. But it has its price—I feel very alienated from men and many women. I'm sometimes too weak for all of the things I see happening.''

♀"Feminism is nonapplicable to me. However, I'm glad that women in general are standing up for themselves more. I always did.''

♀"It has no bearing on me at all.''

Some of the lesbians have strong criticisms of the feminist movement, a few rejecting it altogether, personally or politically. Here are their comments:

♀"I'm not a feminist. I'm a humanist. Women, like other oppressed groups, need their own liberation movement, but it must be linked up to the struggles of others. Too many feminists are egotistic and care only about the needs of their sex, and will not struggle on behalf of others. Dyke separatism is even more ridiculous than feminism, because we lesbians are only a tiny percentage of the world's population, and you can't just throw millions of people out the window."

♀"The women's movement has done nothing for me. I think it freed up a lot of women, though. And I think it laid a heavy burden on a lot of other women by refusing to accept that some women do not want to be liberated. They should have a right not to be. I think radical feminists and separatists are sick and are doing more to harm the gay movement than anyone."

♀"It's complete nonsense to say that the woman is the slave of the man. It's the opposite, I would say! The man has to get up at 6:00 in the morning, every day, and earns a salary for ten people. And the woman could stay at home, give orders to her servants, drink a homemade cup of coffee with her friends, sit in the garden, etc. Cooking and looking after the children—is that slavery? Nonsense! And all those electrical machines in her house, which she gets for nothing from her husband! And nursing her husband and children night and day—is that slavery? Taking it away from her is real murder and discrimination against the woman. This is a fact of the creation of nature, a law of nature, which nobody ever will be able to change. When I am together with lesbians, I often think I am an outcast, because I am a woman, who loves women, and I don't love those 'guys' who call themselves feminists. I think that not they, but I am the person who has *courage*! It is me, who is not afraid to show that she is a real woman who loves women. It is me who has the courage to stay beautiful and feminine in this world of madness, where everybody follows blindly (they pretend doing the opposite!), by dressing themselves in jeans, all uniform, expressing no individuality."

♀"Some women's groups seem to be hung up on getting away from traditional forms of leadership and trying to share leadership (often as a collective). Maybe because we haven't had a lot of practice in using these new forms, they just don't seem as effective in getting things done."

♀"Most feminists are a group of bitter hostile women; I can't get very involved with the movement because these women thrive on and spread depression. They have reason enough, but I just want to be happy."

♀"I don't like working with straight women *at all*!"

The gay men expressed various points of view concerning the women's liberation movement and the effect of feminism on their lives. Here is a sampling of comments from men who saw feminism in a positive light:

♂"Feminism was an enlightening phenomenon for me as well as the culture. As simply and concisely as possible, it alleviated the pressure of

having to be a stereotypically stoic male for me. It liberated me from prescribed behavior, and it opened up the world of free feeling emotion.''

⚭"The women's movement has made me think . . . change . . . and hope. I like women; I don't think many straight men do.''

⚭"Involvement with my wife in feminism (NOW) helped me come out. I do not approve of the racism and sexism among gay males.''

⚭"I have come to perceive clearly how my oppression as a faggot is just one branch of the huge tree of sexual oppression. The roots and trunk of this tree are the oppression of women. My oppression as a faggot is just a symptom of the basic issue.''

⚭"Feminism has helped me primarily by its challenge of sex-stereotyped roles. I'd say I agree with the basic idea and most specific demands of the women's lib movement. However, I'm afraid my sympathy for women doesn't translate into concrete terms. I rarely have any contact with the opposite sex.

"I question, thus, the sincerity of my feeling for womankind. I think that only when I can relate to women as whole, real people (including sexual beings), only then can I be genuinely a lover of women.

"I'm haunted by the idea that for many, if not all, gays, their/our sexual orientation could be a flight from women. Fear and hatred—misogyny—are these stereotypic or real among homosexual men?

"I admit that I myself have had in addition to an antisexual upbringing, a few unhappy experiences (personal, not sexual) with women. I was teased and never taken seriously as an admirer. (I was younger: that had an effect.) Girls thought I was 'cute,' but that's about all.''

⚭"The women's movement has made me aware of my own sexism, which as a male worshipper I had in spades. In a very convoluted way I gradually became aware that my sexism had something to do with my own negative self-image.''

⚭"I never thought much about feminism or lesbians, until I became good friends with one at school/work. Women (gay) seem to be much more political, and while I don't claim to understand it all, I would like to know more about how they feel and what they want. My lesbian friend has made me consider the idea that the U.S. may be imperialistic, and if this is the case, then there are things to be aware of and changed. I have a dyke bookstore across the street from my home, and while I used to dislike this, I now find it somewhat of a comfort. I support them, go into the store sometimes, although there isn't much for me there, and realize that this store provides an invaluable service to the lesbians and feminists of the San Francisco Bay Area.''

⚭"I think feminism has liberated men, too. Guys are no longer afraid to dress neatly and use such products as hair spray.''

⚭"Feminism has caused me to say 'woman' in the place of 'girl' or 'chick.' ''

⚭"I think I've always been a feminist and I don't think the women's movement has particularly affected me. I've always thought that women

were onto something that men were missing, that their consciousness was ahead of men's (and, I'm realizing, ahead of most gay men, who are often as antifeminist as straights), so feminism has been nothing new to me, except that I've come to see it in a political light, whereas I used to view it more psychologically.''

♂"I was raised in a working-class home. Dad went out and worked. Mom took care of the kids and worked at home. The same was true for every couple in our church. Some women had part-time jobs, some were nurses or teachers or hairdressers. None were ministers or elders or deacons. Women weren't allowed to be. The Bible said so. That was the line. Eve made Adam sin. It was her punishment.

"I was the oldest son, the firstborn. All my parents' hopes were pinned on me. I was to adapt and win a middle-class share in Canadian society. My sisters were told what was expected of them: get married to a Christian man and raise babies and have grandchildren. I got away with murder because I was the eldest. I had the family name. My sisters had to help my mom. I studied and fucked around in my room. I got my own room; they didn't. I got all of the advantages my poor family could give. My sisters had it harder. They had to figure it out themselves.

"Anyway, raised as a male, I was very suspicious of feminists, and have never felt comfortable around any—till just last month. I'm starting to meet some lesbian feminists socially and all the media nonsense is so much crap. I understood what they were saying intellectually, but my maleness felt threatened. I'm just starting to understand what they're saying now with the rest of my being.''

♂"I am an ardent follower of the women's movement and although I have no desire to fuck a woman, I respect and love them greatly. I cannot conceive of a world without women. Women have played a very important role in my life and continue to do so. The women's movement has made me aware of what a gay male chauvinist pig I really was. God bless women!''

♂"I've always felt, implicitly, pro-feminist, as I hated the image of women's place put forth in this society. (Passive women bring out my closet misogyny.) I have always respected independent women, so the emergence of the feminist movement confirmed a lot of my own feelings as one who had been harassed and taunted as a child as 'sissy' and 'queer.' ''

♂"In addition to being a homosexual, I'm a pacifist and a feminist. I'm sure these are closely linked but I don't know how to put it in words. These are three of the highest expressions of human spirituality. They are all tied in with our creativity. Consider the gay shaman in native cultures.''

♂"If it hadn't been for the women's movement, I doubt that there would have been a gay movement; at least, not yet.''

♂"All too often I am met with the fact that what many feminist women (most *all* actually) state about gay men being as sexist as their straight counterparts is true. I truly believe that women are still horribly oppressed by all men regardless of sexuality. I do not remove myself from some complicity, but I do try to gain a more feminist consciousness. This leads to

forming friendship with more women than men. This makes for an ironic situation where my sexual attraction is toward men, but my best friends are mostly women.

"I believe that feminism is the most important and influential facet of my life's diamond. What most men (straight and some gay men) react to inevitably is a man who is like a woman. Homophobia is a reaction to men who are like women. Some gay men bristle under this charge and consider it an insult. Again, I hesitate to use the terms, but I embrace my 'femininity' equally with my 'masculinity.' "

⚥ "Feminism is something I have supported all my life without really understanding the word. The women's movement caught on with me since I am one who has been consistently pushed into sex roles. My homosexuality is something which is reinforced by my feminism, since I realize that I reject the same roles as many women involved with feminism do."

⚥ "All of my friends are lesbians or feminists, and I feel alienated from male homosexuals who seem to have taken over traditional oppressive male values and roles as their 'liberation.' Now that Nazi garb is the standard gay male drag I see no difference between gay and straight males. I am one of those 'feminists trapped in a faggot's body.' "

⚥ "The women's movement is encouraging to me. Women always accept homosexuals faster than men, and homosexuals and women have a lot in common as far as oppression goes. We can identify more easily."

While most men were positive in their comments about feminism, some were neutral, indifferent, ambivalent, or overtly hostile. Here is an assortment of their statements:

⚥ "I am a little ambivalent on the women's lib movement. I'm all for them in their fight against being treated as an inferior subspecies of human. I'm all for ERA and all. Where I *do* disagree is in the super-feminists castrating attitudes and vocalizations. They, like so many other groups, go completely to extremes. I don't like manhaters or womanhaters of either sex. Finding out that Gloria Steinem was associated with the CIA (which I loathe) was enough to turn me off on her anyway. I also don't feel that the country ought to get into tokenism with women as they have with the Negroes. I don't feel women ought to get into the real muscular activities just to fill a quota. I'm slightly chauvinistic in my attitudes in that I feel women should be in dresses and in the home, but this is a bad attitude in these times and I attempt to change my attitudes when I feel they are outdated. Still and all, while I desire equal pay for equal work, and an end to discrimination for *anyone,* I still like my chicks to look and act like chicks. I would feel threatened by a bull-dyke in leather pants and a castrating attitude."

⚥ "Women go their way and I go mine. I sympathize, but don't mix. I did go to some lesbian meetings in 1955–56, since they had some fine speakers."

┃"I'm not pro-feminist. I think that all women, except lesbians, belong in the home raising kids. Obviously lesbians can't be asked to do that, and I do expect to see them leading the life of the liberated women. But heterosexual women I think have no place outside the home."

┃"The women's movement, for the most part, strikes me as being as absurd as gay lib. Neither is realistic, and both achieve points negatively, by exaggeration."

┃"I'm not too interested in the women's movement, but I do hope they overcome their oppression. Women don't usually go to the bars or bushes, so I don't know what outlets they have. I work with a lot of bitchy women, so don't care much for women in general."

┃"At the moment I am feeling fucked over by feminism. It is very easy for me to shout intellectual feminist values, but doing so, though it has created lots of conflicts, hasn't really changed my attitudes. Right now, what I think I did was introject another whole set of 'shoulds' that are impossible to live up to. For example: I am not supposed to equate getting fucked with being feminine and therefore bad. Well, sometimes I do do that, and yelling at myself isn't going to help me change. Also, what I really think was the evil thing I did was use feminism as a new excuse to deny my own need to be aggressive, competitive, and powerful, because, after all, that's what white men had done for centuries and they fucked up the world, and I don't want to be another bad white male who women will hate. Bullshit. I do. I've only realized in the last few weeks that maybe I can be competitive and power-hungry without stepping on women's toes per se as women. Who knows?"

┃"I'm not keen on tough women's movements any more than I am keen on screaming faggots romping the streets making a display of themselves."

┃"The feminist movement has made women in this country too competitive with men. They are trying to line up to the song, 'Anything you can do, I can do better.' Life is not meant to be one big competition. It is made up of learning to get along and compromising when necessary. Feminists won't compromise—they just 'want.' "

┃"The women's movement has done more to drive men into other men's arms than any single thing I know of. The thesis of Andy Warhol's *Women in Revolt* said it best: 'Women's liberation is not a struggle for equality but an effort to replace a patriarchy with a matriarchy.' I like women who are women (and I don't mean bozos; I love intelligent women), not women who have adopted male traits. As a matter of fact, I think it would be wonderful to be a sex object . . . at least then I'd know there were two sexes."

┃"Although I am sympathetic to the feminist movement, it is not my movement and I can't use much energy for it. I got along much better with lesbians before feminism became a strong issue with them. I know they have to overstate the case to get attention, but I'm weary of the rhetoric. I feel they forget that gay men *also* suffer at the hands of straight male society, and if some little queen digs doing drag, he shouldn't be put down for it. Women have been dragging as men since World War II—I know, I was

there. It really pisses me off to have a lesbian-feminist trash a drag while she's wearing blue jeans with a fly in front she got from the army-navy store.''

The Gay Liberation Movement

More than half of the lesbians and gay men responding to the survey have had at least some involvement in the gay liberation movement. That movement, furthermore, has had an impact on the lives of all gay people. Experiencing gay liberation as a participant, or as a gay observer, varies a great deal from individual to individual, depending on his or her situation. In the quotations below, lesbians and gay men describe their experiences with and feelings about gay liberation, indicating the things they have liked and disliked about the movement:

♀''I try to do what little I can from my isolated location by being in two lesbian rap groups. We do some activist things and some intergroup consciousness-raising. We send out letters to various places where it will do the most good, to protest antigay policies and activities such as Anita Bryant's crusade in Florida. We leave signs advertising our groups in clubs and bars on their bulletin boards. We give support and encouragement to one another and a sense of family and community.''

♂''I marched in the Boston (1975) Gay Pride March. I had just come out and was terrified but it turned out to be a very marvelous 'high.' I go to symposiums and other such events whenever I can. All this isn't much but with all of us doing our little things—maybe it will add up to a lot of power to change things. I loved all of my experiences with gay liberationists. Proud to be some little part of it!''

♂''I recently participated in a demonstration in Chicago when Anita appeared here. I felt very positive about myself and about the demonstration. The media was present and I risked exposure and my job by marching but I think that it's about time the silent minority is heard. Gay liberation at my college, if anything, turned me off. The speakers were always so typically gay. One time, I believed that many were not listening to the speaker, dismissing him as just 'a fag.' What he had to say was painfully minced out and he seemed pathetic. I realize now that he was very brave and that I wasn't or else I would have been speaking and appearing 'typically straight.' I feared the gay liberationists at my school because I did not want to have to become like them (effeminate) to satisfy my sexual desire.''

♂''I read what I can about gay activists but cannot come out of the closet now because I have no income save what I earn, and that depends upon appearing straight. I would like to contribute to their efforts, especially the air force man fighting his expulsion, but I have never seen any address to which money could be sent. I feel that too many of the acknowledged leaders are far-out types, especially women, that turn off the average person and hinder rather than help the cause. Men in neat conservative suits and

haircuts could do much more for the cause than these long-haired sloppy antagonizing characters.''

♀"The influence of my involvement in the gay movement upon my own coming-out has been very positive, and at this point in my life I would find it very difficult, if not impossible, to have a serious (or perhaps even superficial) relationship with a woman who was not an 'enlightened' feminist and who was not reasonably open about her lesbianism. The political issues that concern me most, and that I am most inclined to act upon in some way, usually involve sexual/minority discrimination and issues relating specifically to feminist concerns.''

♂"If it hadn't been for the National Gay Task Force, we probably wouldn't yet be seeing such honest treatments of gays on network television. Recently I watched *Alexander: The Other Side of Dawn,* and thought the gay aspects of the story were brilliant.''

♂"During my senior year in college I was so-called 'president' of the campus gay student group. At first I identified with this label, seeing myself as responsible for singlehandedly liberating all the gays in my community. The other gay people were encouraging me to fulfill their need for a figurehead-spokesperson, as many of them could not or would not come out, and the deference they paid me was a positive stroke to the masculinity I have never quite measured up to, but subconsciously desired. Later on in the year I realized what was going on, particularly as the others' dependency on me increased and I found myself saddled with most of the work. I spent the rest of my 'term of office' trying to get people to refer to me as coordinator, which implies working with input from others, as well as taking responsibility for liberating themselves and finding their own strengths and capabilities. I doubt I was enormously successful, but I'm now convinced I don't want to control other people, no matter how benevolent I may think I am.''

♂"I loved gay liberation very, very much when I was among those founding it, forging it—there was great brotherhood, spirit, intelligence: we all wanted something new. It still serves that function for some people just coming into it, but it is also weighted down by a lot of people who are gay, but are only opportunists and leaped onto gay liberation as a way to make money, make a reputation, or make a few more tricks. I'm very disillusioned with groups now and feel that 'liberation' and 'group' are antithetical terms.''

♂"I am pissed about the gay community's blissful lack of concern about what is going on in the country and in the world, and about what people are doing to help secure their rights. I think sometimes the artificiality and comfort of gay bars are a big escape from facing up to problems, and that nothing will really get accomplished until we get away from them sometimes.''

♂"Gay lib groups tend to falter because it is always a few who do all the work and when they tire of it and leave, the group dissipates. The best thing

about them is the group feeling there and the chance to meet other gay people outside of a sexual atmosphere.''

⚥"As for the gay liberation movement I feel that while the nellies have a right to live and enjoy life as the rest of us, still I don't think that cavorting in public in drag, displaying gay actions in demonstrations, etc. helps those who are fighting for gay liberation. So many hundreds of thousands of gay men are very inconspicuous and suffer for the nellies, who mean well, and have a right to live as well as the next one, but the public has not accepted us yet and actions speak louder than words many times.''

⚥"What I dislike—intensely!—about my experiences with gay liberation has been the woolly-headedly complacent assumption by so many people that they were revolutionary just for being gay, and against the system, without their having to do anything except live their own lives in a revolutionary way. Gay separatism is not revolutionary in itself, but only as a weapon to build the strength of gay revolutionaries.''

⚥"My gayness is the basis from which I work in all political movements. All oppressed peoples would do well to work together on common issues, but there is also a need for some degree of separatism which is conducive to added support and strength. I have worked in the movement for about four years. At first it was a fine thing: gay liberation was *fun* and exhilarating. For the past year, however, I've been feeling co-opted. The movement has taken a definite moderate, reformist turn and there are too many 'stars' supposedly speaking for us all.''

⚥"The gays in Canada are much more 'in the closet' than those in the U.S.—more indifferent, etc.''

♀"I have been involved in feminism for the last five years and have recently become involved in some groups working for gay rights. There are obvious visibility problems in being upfront for gay rights but my biggest problem is dealing with gay men. Some of them are really into hating women and are really not feminists.''

⚥"My only experience about gay liberation is through reading *Gaytimes* and watching TV. *Gaytimes* has articles that have made me happy and all of that. On TV I saw Anita Bryant. She had a pie put in her face. That wasn't fair. The lady has a right to her own opinion. Straights and gays alike should sit down and talk things over, and possibly make a compromise (if it is possible, at all, which I doubt that it is) between the two sets of people.''

⚥"Until a year ago, I was active in Gay Academic Union and in Gay Media Coalition, and my ex-lover did a gay radio show on WBAI which I helped to conceive. I now work for a gay counseling center called Identity House. My homosexuality interacted with my politics insofar as I needed the political support of theory and activism to help me come to terms with my own sexuality via consciousness-raising groups and general theoretical support systems and activity to assure myself that being gay was okay. I now realize that the gay movement was essential in its time, but too many people believed in 'gay pride' as a dogma, myself included at the time. I now realize that the only political function of the gay movement is to rally

for civil rights and any political activity I might now undertake for gays would be solely from the angle of civil rights. I need not identify with any group at this point in a binding generalization of sharing the same sexuality.''

♀"I feel a stronger and stronger need to be with lesbians and a greater and greater split with my straight world. I feel more and more the need to be active politically and am starting locally with feminist groups that exist here. But I know what I really want is to be part of lesbian liberation and I know that will come eventually. I am currently trying to write some books for children explaining lesbianism. If they are ever published they will certainly be a political statement and since I know from my own experience that none exist, an important one.''

♂"My only experience with gay liberation was a demonstration in 1976, when several hundred gays marched through the streets of Montreal, eventually ending up in a park rally. I thought the behavior of some of the demonstrators was definitely detrimental to the cause—laughing at straight bystanders, obscene gestures, etc. I felt somewhat sick about it. I'm not sure I want to be part of a demonstration like that again. On the whole, the demonstrators behaved properly, though many acted as if it was an outdoor party.''

♂"I was involved in the campus gay group for three years—one as president, 1½ as treasurer. The only real problem was the lack of involvement on the part of others. The campus was much too apathetic. But I got to know myself and learned a lot from the experience. I was very happy to leave it as a result of the apathy, but I also needed to explore my needs apart from the group. Anita Bryant has tapped the strength that is hidden inside gay people and I think (I hope) that she will organize gay people unlike anything she could have imagined. I think her vindictive cause is what was needed to destroy much of the apathy that has arisen.''

♂"I really think gay liberation is a positive thing; I feel though, at least here, that it has ceased to become political and has degenerated into do-nothing 'court' systems which are, to be sure, extremely poor political institutions. The idea of empress and emperor! I feel a little angry at such an institution, when it spends oodles of money in 'balls' instead of free dances (or at least reasonably priced), coffee houses, encounter groups, collectives, etc.''

♂"I think gay parades and marches and picketing do us more harm than good. I think we must move by persuasion in legislative matters, use to the greatest possible extent recourse to the law and the courts. We need a 'responsible' image, not a lavender one.''

♀"I have not been terribly active in the gay liberation movement per se, though I and members of the organization I belong to attend rallies and sometimes are on planning committees for gay events. I have given talks and written a couple of articles for the left press on lesbianism and socialism. The only thing I have disliked about gay liberation is that some of the men really hate women and defend such things as grown men having sex

with little boys as part of liberation. But they are not all like that. Oh, yes, and some lesbians get very purist, but that is waning right now. And even the purist lesbians have had some wonderful insights, so it's hard for me to get too down on them even though they make it difficult to work with them politically. The best experience with gay liberation was a big gay rights march a few months ago. The men were all nice and none were dressed up as women, and there were large numbers of women there and the press and police were even being sympathetic."

⚥"Being an out homosexual means I'm rejecting everything our society stands for. They say, 'Just hide, just shut up, we'll reward you with a nice gay bar, wouldn't you like that? You know, your kind love to dance and dress up and listen to disco. Just keep it quiet. Or else.' Well, I don't want to. Not any more. I've got nothing to lose, because my class background and sexuality keep me out of the big power/bucks/dames routine. What has changed me? My experience, the education of other gays, and the gay liberation movement."

♀"I see legislative reform as necessary and I'm glad other people are willing to spend the time at it because I'm certainly not. Legislative reform is just that—*reform*. I'm in this for revolution—radical social change in the ways that people relate to each other, radical economic change, radical ecological changes . . ."

⚥"My work in the gay caucus in my church has been about the most emotionally filling part of my life."

♀"Gay and lesbian liberation is the only way we can survive!"

⚥"I went to gay lib meetings, but I just listened and didn't take part. I was a member of the Society of Individual Rights (SIR), and as such was considered conservative, as SIR is said to be full of old fogeys. That didn't bother me. But I have admired youth fighting and sticking up against police at Stonewall."

⚥"I am very political and a gay rights activist in the Chicago area. There is a lot about gay liberation I don't like, i.e., sexism and racism. White males talk a lot of nonsense because they haven't felt real oppression as a black or even as a woman. If they could feel real oppression then maybe they would have a better understanding of what they are fighting for."

⚥"I found gay liberation very helpful in the beginning to strengthen my pride and gay identity, but eventually dropped it because of (a) the tendency of gay leaders to be anti-psychiatric, and to honestly believe that slogans can replace psychiatry in personal growth, which they cannot; (b) the tendency toward cynicism, which is not helpful to anyone and more than usually covered an unwillingness to get involved with people as any more than political or sexual objects; (c) the anti-spiritual drive of the movement, which I feel is destructive and shortsighted; and (d) most importantly, the inability of gay people in political movements to be firm with themselves, about tasks to be accomplished, or honest about personal self-criticism. I finally began to find the inability of gay groups to start meetings on time, to stick to an agenda, to perform even such simple tasks as getting coffee

together highly annoying, and when I began to realize that this is due to the incredibly unstable emotional states of most of the participants, I dropped out altogether.''

♀ ''My being a lesbian has only naturally gotten me involved in the women's movement and especially lesbian liberation. I am a member of Powerhouse Gallery—the only women-run and -financed art gallery in Canada (pity!)—and will be the next president of Gay Women of Montreal (a radical lesbian/feminist group). I find the lesbian liberation community very small here compared to what I have seen in Boston and even Provincetown. We need newfound energy.''

♂ ''I am quite militant as a gay person. I have decided I will not be at all intimidated by prospective loss of jobs or whatever. If I show intimidation, I will be caving in to the hateful majority and that will just keep gay people down. I and we must stand up and be counted. I am not ashamed of being gay and I will not let anyone push me around.''

♂ ''Since Dade County, I have been actively involved in an organization designed to inform the public about homosexuality. I've enjoyed working in this group tremendously, because of the intelligent, dynamic people I've met, and the work that I've done so far. However, while working with this group, I became aware for the first time how self-destructive the gay community can be. There have evolved intensely bitter feuds and accusations from various other gay groups directed at this group and at each other. People have been mired down in squabbles and ego-tripping, to the degree that a major part of the group's resources and time has been spent handling the flak thrown at us from other gays. This strikes me as being so stupid, and it disturbs me that instead of uniting to fight the enemy outside, gays don't seem capable of even working together without turning on each other.''

♀ ''I was involved for a while with a political, mostly male gay group. There are no organized lesbian groups in this city. I felt really good in this group, got a good awareness of what was going on in the world. I would like to join a lesbian group, but they all meet a distance from here and I have no car. There's no public transportation that can get me there in under two hours and I don't like spending all night on a bus.''

♀ ''My brief encounter with lesbian liberation was very distasteful to me. The women made me feel like lesbians were a secret society and you needed a passkey. This group was very young, beautiful, upper-middle-class, playing at blue workshirts, boots, freedom, but were paralyzed when a *real* butch working-class dyke arrived in her best Sunday drag in very real pain looking for some assurance/companionship.''

♂ ''I have done volunteer work for a number of gay organizations here in New York City. My experiences with gay liberation have been that few people are doing most of the work with little support from the general gay population, in terms of money or time. Open a new back-room bar and there will be a line. Ask these same people to contribute to the movement and they suddenly become poor. The National Gay Task Force boasts a

membership of 3,000. Considering there is supposed to be something like 20,000,000 gays in this country, I think that is a pathetically small figure. Perhaps gays don't feel as much oppression as movement leaders see. Perhaps they are too scared and/or guilty about being gay to support the movement.''

♀"I'm not a public lesbian in the political sense, although I am a member of the lesbian caucus of my professional organizations. My lover/spouse is, too, and works on a task force in her organization. The sense of solidarity is good about the experiences of joining a caucus.''

♀"I consider myself a political lesbian—I want to be free of male oppression; the base of male oppression is our socially enforced sexual subjugation. I work in women's health care and consider this political involvement—I have tried to work more closely with the movement, but have run out of steam. We are so critical of ourselves in our movement towards freedom—I have experienced infighting and trashing so I keep my distance now.''

♀"The movement needs all kinds. It needs people to be open and force the issue, and it needs others who have established themselves successfully and who at some time can say, 'I've worked here ten years and you never knew I was gay; I've done a good job and never did any of the things you're frightened of me about.' This will prove a point more than riots and forcing the right to kiss in public. Personally I can't stand open displays of heterosexuality, so I certainly am not going to like it in homosexuals either.''

♂"Once we picked up a guy at a gay bar one night. He returned early in the morning with four others and robbed us. We had them arrested. He charged us with rape. We live in a small town. We were a celebrated case. Our neighbors and other straights were splendid (he turned out to be straight) and rallied to our cause in every way they could. They went to jail. The case against us was dropped. But that shaped my life. I worked for the Mattachine for many years. We made many 'breakthroughs.' It was a most satisfactory experience.''

♂"I've had trouble working with gay and women's groups because of the infighting between men and women and lesbians and straight women and separatists and nonseparatists. I feel that gay men, lesbians, and women share a lot of common problems and those things that we have in common we should work for together and those things that we don't have in common we should work for separately.''

Lesbian Separatism

As the previous quotation indicates, separate organization by lesbians is a definite reality that the gay movement has had to deal with. The overwhelming majority of the lesbians and the gay men in the survey expressed the view that both mixed lesbian–gay male and lesbians-only organizing are worthwhile. About a fifth of the men, and only one-

twentieth of the women, expressed negative views toward such independent organization for lesbians. Full lesbian separatism, however, implies much more than separate organizations. It advocates not working with men and heterosexual women and preferably not dealing with them at all in day-to-day life. Only 11% of the women described themselves as "separatists," but such consciousness among lesbians may be higher, as many separatists declined to participate in this survey (see Chapter 19). Here are comments on the issue of separatism, and the general question of lesbians and gay men working together politically:

♀"I consider myself a dyke separatist. The only people who make sense at all to me are lesbians. Men in the movement think they know everything about everything (including lesbians), and they try to run everything. They do a bloody rotten job of it too!"

♀"I think that the lesbian movement suffers some from its separatism. Strong unity in the whole gay community would, I think, do a great deal of good a great deal faster. One does not need to see working with men as regression to our former dependence on men. We can see it as cooperation, which is a good thing and unhappily a scarce thing everywhere."

♂"Lesbian separatism has hurt me, as I feel oppressed by separatists who define all males as exploiters, sexists, and potential rapists, just as much as by macho rednecks who define all gays as criminals, and these separatists are depriving themselves of help I and other gays could give."

♀"I identify with lesbian separatist politics, though sometimes they seem too extreme for me to feel 100% comfortable. Like, I think male children *can* have a place in a woman's society."

♀"My feelings toward men rather than my lesbianism are what have influenced which groups I'm willing to work with. I find it very frustrating and obnoxious to work in groups with men, which is why I haven't had any interest in gay liberation. I feel gay men are like straight men in their approach to sexuality (objectifying the partner, being concerned with sexual prowess at other people's expense, etc.)."

♂"I somewhat resent the lesbian separatist movement because, in a very real way, I feel deprived of the experience of knowing and learning from lesbians."

♀"I wish more women would get involved in gay liberation as well as lesbian liberation because we as women just have to get out there and make our voices heard. Lesbian liberation can easily become a means of withdrawing, like a private social club, thus losing the very real and necessary power that it promises. First we must work within our own group, but it is also necessary to communicate the ideas and demands reached in this group to the world at large. The power of gay liberation will come from its being an integrated group, sexually, racially, and in terms of different ages and different types of people. Otherwise it's just going to be as oppressive to us as women as everything else is. But I feel that enough gay men are open to feminist ideas that if women don't become involved then it will be our own fault if gay liberation becomes a solely male thing. It hurts me when I see so

many lesbians being so unequivocally man-hating. I have gotten support from gay and straight men, and I have learned a lot about being independent and strong from men. After all, they are taught these things all their lives; many skills I must learn from men because these skills have been withheld from women. We would all have much fuller existences if men would be willing to learn from women and women from men, as well as within our own groups. I see this beginning to happen.''

♀''There is really only one aspect of lesbian politics which bothers me—the area of separatism. At first, I was mistrustful of it, but now that I understand it, I think it is sheer nonsense and reverse bigotry and narrowmindedness. I wonder if it doesn't stem from a sense of insecurity—saying that men are so terrible that it puts women to feeling even more superior. Some men *are* terrible, but some men are good people too and I can't see condemning the entire population! It is as fruitless as the stage I went through where I thought *all lesbians had to be* wonderful people. There are some pretty rotten lesbians, too, but that's just because people are people, and being a man doesn't make you bad or being a lesbian doesn't make you Wonder Woman. I could go on but all I can really say is that when the great mother Goddess comes for me, I'll go with her to lesbian loveland even if her chauffeur is male!''

♀''I'm a lesbian feminist; I could do without all but 1% of men. My continuing awareness of oppression makes me want to do without men. For me they are useless. They are so blind to their oppressive ways that they require too much energy.''

♀''I am thinking of moving to some place with a larger and more active lesbian community, ideally one that is working towards total separatism.''

♀''I don't like separatist politics and I have been ostracized by a group of lesbians who apparently viewed me as part of the 'opposition.' ''

♀''My lover and I relate to lots of gay men and they can't understand separatism. They want to relate to women in a healthy manner, not like many straight men do . . . and they can't understand why they aren't allowed to. I am ashamed of how separatists behave and react. The biggest shame was in Chicago when they had a conference and male children weren't allowed to attend. That's sick and is only one step before killing male children. Attitudes like that are a detriment to the movement. There are gay male groups in Chicago which have begged women to join them for the sake of the movement, but the women won't have any part of it. Then they sit back on their butts and bitch that no one hands them the world on a silver platter. The reason they don't get anywhere is that they have no leadership skills and won't utilize available ones. They cut off their noses to spite their faces. When my lover and I first began looking for social contacts in Chicago, we went to places like the women's center. It was an unfriendly place that left the impression that if we were not willing to be openly gay, deny men, for my lover to leave her husband, and stop dressing up and to wear the 'uniform' of the women, then we were not welcome. Women's bars were as bad. We started going to men's bars because people there were

friendly to us and we had and have far more gay male friends than women. I believe many men were beginning to get fed up with separatist ideas, and I don't blame them. My lover and I have done a lot to repair the damage done by separatists in Chicago. There is a large community of gay males and females who can relate and work together successfully. I would not attend an all-woman function, nor would I support one. I think women wanting to have a Lesbian Pride Week apart from the Gay Pride Week and refusing to participate in the latter are doing more harm to the movement than the claptrap espoused by Anita Bryant."

♀"I sympathize with lesbian separatists but am too easily bored by rhetoric to work as a separatist myself. I need to feel part of the real world. I am not as morally outraged by separatist narrowness as I sometimes feel I should be. Occasionally I feel it is bigotry; other times I'm caught up in group spirit and feel fortunate to be included. I have too much of a need to belong."

⚥"I've had several disagreeable experiences with lesbians and I'd just as soon let them hit each other over the heads till death rather than get mixed up with them again. They're a pain and a nuisance. And I can very well do without them. I don't frequent bars where they are patrons and will not work on committees nor social groups where they are active. Ultimately, they mean trouble. They seem to have this built-in thing about everyone is out to get them, that they have to be so fucking strong. If they continue on the way they're going, everyone *will* be out to get them. They're a pain in the ass."

♀"I consider myself a matriarchist but not a dyke separatist. Gay males can be just as feminist as we; I've known several who are."

The Apolitical and Antipolitical Stance

A small portion of the gay men, and an even smaller portion of the lesbians, were completely inactive politically. They ascribe this stance to an apolitical bent, to disillusionment with the political process, and to opposition to the idea of gay liberation. Here are some of their comments:

⚥"I'm not interested much in politics in general, nor am I involved with gay liberation. Too much importance is put on sex in the issue and it comes across not so much as being equal, but who is better and what is better. Although it's important for us to have equality under the law, and I certainly want that, I feel that we as a community have a lot of cleaning up to do to prove to society that we are deserving of those rights. Last year I was at a political party given for a man running for supervisor in San Francisco. It was a gay affair, and being a politician, he wooed them on the gay issues. I was struck by the silliness of voting for somebody because their sexual preference was the same as mine. These things do not belong in our political system and the sooner Anita Bryant and militant homosexuals are forgotten, the better off we'll all be."

♀"My lesbianism does not reflect in my politics. I am not involved in

politics of any kind. I think to some extent forcing the issue of gay rights could be a mistake. It's one thing for the straight world to live side by side with gays; it's another to acknowledge it.''

♀"I'd rather be working on a painting, or reading an art journal than be at a peace march or rally or something.''

♂"The gay cause is not a just one or one that Congress or society can legally accept. For one's sexuality is his or her own private business; and should not be flaunted before our lawmakers or the President. It's none of their concern what another chooses to do at the gay baths or in the confines of their own home. There isn't any need for anarchy, sexual revolution, women's liberation, civil rights, gay rights, or any other 'movement' for that matter, because America and its people always have been and always will be free! The fact is our younger generation of today is a restless one, much too much so for its own good. They're ruining the country with all of this 'do your own thing' idea in a permissive society whereby there is a complete breakdown in family life structure, and the parents don't care. Families aren't as close as they once were; and how often some of us long for happier times when we loved our parents and respected our elders.''

♀"I'm too chicken, too apathetic to be involved with gay lib. Too contented with my own lot—smug's the word, I know!''

♀"I can't get into the gay liberation scene because the men fuck it up as usual. They give gays a bad name by dressing in drag (which I resent) and acting like fairies. Men are all alike, gay and straight—oppressive. Many lesbians bother me because they aren't feminists and they oppress themselves. They role-play just like the straights do—it's depressing.''

♂"I know I should join the gay activists, and stand by their courageous acts, but I feel too vulnerable as far as job security, social rejection, etc. I guess I will reap the benefits those courageous souls provide for me through their personal sacrifices.''

♂"Gay liberation, like most movements, attracts a lunatic fringe who usually succeed in alienating those whom they are trying to win over to their point of view. I'm as liberated as I wish. I don't need them.''

♂"I think homosexuals have a right to demand proper treatment, but I am now too old to fight. I live out in the country in a beautiful home with many beautiful friends, both gay and straight. I just can't get involved.''

♂"I dislike sexual acts and preferences used as a basis for a political movement. To me gay liberation is little different than organization of a 'flashers liberation.' Gay lib people that I've met are too into trying to do what straight people do—house, insurance, marriage, etc.—how droll.''

♀"I have never been much involved in politics. I have focused on my personal life as the place to put my energies and hope for satisfaction. I do consider myself interested in moral and ethical issues, a liberal. I vote, and I do my best to find lesser-of-evils to vote for.''

♂"I have attended the local club for liberation and found it boring. Most of the persons I would not care to know on a social basis. It all reminded me

of a relative whose husband had to attend AA. She said that she didn't see why they didn't all just go out and get drunk, it was so dreary.''

⚥ ''After voting for the loser all my life, spending four years actively involved in the gay movement, to no avail, my political orientation is burned out.''

Gay Community and Gay Culture

The creation of separate community and culture has been one response of lesbians and gay men to the relative isolation they experience and to oppressive conditions fostered by the heterosexual male-dominated culture. Whether such efforts are significant or progressive forces in the lives of most gays is a matter of debate and discussion. The respondents were asked *how much their homosexuality, gayness, or lesbianism is "something other than a sexual orientation."* These were the responses:

	LESBIANS	GAY MEN
quite a lot	76	41%
some	16	24
very little	4	15
none at all	1	8
not sure	2	11

A majority of both male and female respondents recognize the existence of a gay or lesbian sensibility or culture or community—something beyond the mere question of same-sex sexual acts—but according to the above statistics the recognition of this is stronger among the women. This may be due to the fact that a portion of the gay men function successfully as men in their careers and see their homosexuality as merely a sexual difference. Lesbians are more often rebelling against the norms presented to them as women, so are more inclined to see their lesbianism as a multilayered concept, perhaps summed up in the phrase coined in 1970 by New York's Radicalesbians—''woman-identified woman.''

The lesbians and gay men were also asked *how important the concepts of gay and lesbian community and gay and lesbian culture are to them.* The chart shows the responses:

	⚥ GAY COMMUNITY	⚤ GAY COMMUNITY	⚥ GAY CULTURE	⚤ GAY CULTURE	⚤ LESBIAN COMMUNITY	⚤ LESBIAN CULTURE
very important	47	37	41	34	64	62
somewhat important	32	43	30	43	25	24

	GAY COMMUNITY		GAY CULTURE		LESBIAN COMMUNITY	LESBIAN CULTURE
	♂	♀	♂	♀	♀	♀
neutral	13	9	17	11	5	7
somewhat unimportant	3	4	5	4	1	1
very unimportant	4	4	5	5	2	2
not sure	1	3	2	3	3	4

The following are some of the comments made by the respondents regarding gay community, gay culture, and what homosexuality means to them:

♂"The concept of gay community and gay culture appeals to me rather strongly. My one fear about the concept is that we may become so interested in it that we lose sight of the rest of the world, and become, therefore, separated from it to the extent that things can happen there that will be destructive and oppressive to gays. The total community needs to be aware of gay values, gay styles, gay work, gay culture, and gay activities (they would be surprised at how innocuous much of our life really is). But somehow we need to be able to integrate that community and culture (while maintaining it for us) into the rest of the community. People need to be able to pass us on the street, recognize us, and accept us just as they do things for red-headed, brown-eyed, and dark-skinned heteros. Our contributions to the community at large need to be seen and recognized, and recognized as unmistakably gay contributions."

♀"My lesbianism gives me a beautiful identity. I'm so into women—our art, culture, rights, music, everything, and I love it."

♀"At this point I am very proud of who and what I am and my feelings toward the very term 'lesbian' have taken on a whole different aspect. Where once I was negative and ashamed of the whole idea and the name, I am now aware and informed of the true meaning and history behind the word 'lesbianism.' "

♀"I feel very *special* and lucky to be a lesbian. I am still very excited about it; I only wish I didn't feel so alienated in this predominantly straight culture that I am not immersed in a stronger, more pervasive gay culture. Sexually and affectionally, I can be fulfilled in the gay world. Creatively and intellectually, I encounter a total lack of mirrors both in sister gay people and in gay society."

♂"Gayness is social, intellectual, aesthetic (male beauty), political, spiritual—pretty much permeating my life."

♂"It's a lifestyle, and a topic for my constant education of the public."

♂"It's an attitude—one of the benefits of seeing America from the outside."

♂ "My gayness is in my sexual preference, not my lifestyle or behavior. I live in a straight world and abide by those rules."

♂ "My sexual orientation is part of my character in terms of politics and religion. It has been an image or a cause that I can identify with. It also has been a tool for creating friendships not only with gay men and women, but with straight women. My gayness has been a part of my ethnicity. It has forced me to reevaluate my life. It has been a force that has forced me to either destroy me or to really make something strong out of myself."

♂ "Are there people who think we should segregate ourselves? Seems to me this is counter to the eventual goal we should work towards, namely full acceptance and integration in the society of human beings. Using the term 'gay culture' similarly implies that there's something different about us (other than our sexual preference). I don't happen to believe that we are, so how can there be a separate gay culture? The implications of the question are dreadful."

♂ "As far as I'm concerned there is not really a gay community", so any efforts in that direction are superficial and unreal. No society can stand independent without propagating itself. Obviously, a homosexual or homosexual community cannot do this. Also, if I limited myself to gays, I would be shutting out a lot of experiences I could not otherwise have. The only actual way in which gays resemble one another is their sexual preference."

♂ "It is apparent to me that some homosexual men decline to become part of the gay community. Some immerse themselves in it. The remainder go to that community some of the time and participate in it for social, sexual, or intellectual reasons. I subscribe to many gay periodicals and relate to the community in that manner. However, I am a 'country faggot,' and I reject the gay community's insistence on urban lifestyles."

♂ " 'Autonomous gay culture,' insofar as it exists, is an adaptation gay people (mostly men) have used to give themselves the strength to live in a hostile straight world, and keep on going out to work for the Man. It's specific to our oppressed situation, and the reverse of the way out from it."

♀ "One time a group of us feminists, mostly lesbians, but some straight feminists, decided to start a woman-run bar and restaurant in Burlington, Vt., where I was living until I moved to Chicago. Pretty soon, it became clear that most of the lesbians involved in the project were more interested in creating a lesbian bar, and wanted to allocate space for a pool room, etc., while myself, a few other dykes, and all the straight women wanted to combine the bar/restaurant with a women's center—there was none at that time. Our priorities were establishing a functioning, financially feasible restaurant that would support a feminist project. The separatist lesbians' priority was entirely a dyke space for women—they were impractical, idealistic, and out to create and preserve a cultural space, not connect the project to any political work. It was very discouraging, to feel split: I like to play pool, too, to go to women's bars, etc., but I just thought it wasn't as important (or financially feasible) as a women's center, along with the

business. The emphasis on cultural stuff, a kind of retreat from confronting systematic power, bothers me about the lesbian separatist movement. On the other hand, I love women's culture, music especially, and we need it— we need both things.''

♂"While I am doubtful about the idea of a workable gay community, since too many people with too little in common are included, I strongly support the concept of a gay culture, a gay artistic/philosophical heritage dating from Plato through all times—a heritage of idealistic, somewhat alienated, romantic creativity. Too few people today appreciate that culture—our society in general is so shallow, so unaware of roots, so doped up, so narcissistic, that I feel as alienated from other gays who are ignorant of their heritage as I do from straights who seek to deny that heritage.''

What's in a Name?

Perhaps the greatest single signpost of community has been the insistence by most homosexual people in recent years on the use of their own names—gay, lesbian, and, for an earlier generation, homophile—instead of the clinical "homosexual." The appropriation of the word "gay" by gay people—as irksome as it is for some straights—has been a cornerstone of self-determination. Its use in the title of this book—compared with the use of the word "homosexual" by most researchers—is a reflection of that self-determination as exercised by the authors. Of course, it is ultimately a matter of opinion which names are appropriate, and the respondents were asked, *In general which word do you consider the most appropriate (best) word to be used for male homosexuals and lesbians?* Two of the listed words—"faggot" and "dyke"—were not included in the original questionnaire, though a significant number of respondents volunteered them and it was probably an error in judgment on the part of the authors not to list them in the first place. Here are the responses:

	LESBIANS	GAY MEN
homosexual	2%	11%
female homosexual	.5	—
lesbian	63	—
gay woman	17	—
gay	13	51
gay man	—	30
homophile	1	5
faggot	—	3
dyke	4	—

Other names suggested by women were "sister," "Amazon," "woman," "radical lesbian/feminist," and "woman-identified woman."

Other names suggested by men were "homoerotic man," "Uranian," "person," "man," and "human homo sapiens." Here are some comments concerning this nomenclature controversy:

♂ "What is the need for a word—most become derogatory."

♀ "I am not comfortable being placed in any category, when it deals with my personal sex life."

♀ "None of the terms suits me. No word presently exists which adequately describes the emotional and spiritual bond that women-oriented women have for one another."

♀ "I prefer 'gay woman.' 'Lesbian' has an awful lot of negative connotations, while 'gay' is a much more positively accepted word."

♀ " 'Homosexual' and 'gay' always mean *men*; only 'lesbian' means *woman*."

♂ "I wish there were a better word than 'gay.' 'Queer' won't do. 'Homophile' is pretentious, and 'homosexual' has a derogatory sense."

♂ "I like 'faggot,' but only to be used by gays."

♂ "Man, male, or human being—there are no homosexuals, only homosexual acts, feelings, and desires."

♂ "How about 'lucky'? (Sorry, today was Gay Pride March and I'm still high.)"

The Choice of Residence

In his "Gay Manifesto," Carl Wittman writes: "We are refugees from Amerika. So we came to the ghetto—and as other ghettos, it has its negative and positive aspects." Wittman characterizes San Francisco as a "refugee camp for homosexuals," but he notes that "refugee camps are better than what preceded them, or people would never come." The city of San Francisco probably has the largest identifiable community of gay men in the world. New York's Greenwich Village and other New York neighborhoods have high concentrations of gay population. Boston's South End and Back Bay neighborhoods, Houston's Montrose section, Chicago's Lincoln Park area—these and many other sections have visible gay male communities. The gay neighborhood is predominantly a gay male phenomenon, however, and it demonstrates the superior economic condition of gay males as compared to lesbians. The gay neighborhood is also essentially an urban phenomenon, and it is one reason many gays choose urban living. There have also been concentrations of gay-owned property (again, primarily male) in such seaside communities as Fire Island, N.Y.; Provincetown, Mass.; Key West, Fla.; and Laguna Beach, Calif. Here are some of the comments on the question of gay neighborhoods, as well as on urban versus rural living:

♂ "I love where I live. The West Village is like the college campus of the gay world. It is becoming more and more of a community. Half the time I hang out on Christopher Street, it's to socialize, hang out with friends and acquaintances, people I know I'll run into. The community has been

strengthened and somewhat allied by the nature of certain occasions of harassment by local neighborhood kids who beat up 'faggots.' Bars have formed groups of patrolling gay men for self-protection. If there is any trouble on or near Christopher Street, any group of gay men standing around will immediately help out. I don't think I could live anywhere else than New York City, preferably downtown, primarily for two reasons. One is the general intensity and cultural excitement of New York, and also because of the gay community, which has been a great help in making me comfortable with my sexuality and making me feel part of a neighborhood.''

♂"For the first time, I live in a neighborhood with lots of gay people on the street. Two gay bars within two blocks. The Haight-Ashbury district of San Francisco is one of the nicest neighborhoods in the country—wide diversification, a real sense of community, and an acceptance of almost any lifestyle. Being gay here is a lot easier than any previous place of residence."

♀"Certainly there is a much higher acceptance of alternate lifestyles in large cities, and homosexual contacts (not simply sexual) are much easier. I was shocked at the conservative bigotry of the San Diego area—after living in San Francisco and New York, it felt like a giant step backward into an archaic civilization. This made me aware of the advantages of a liberal community."

♀"More than half the apartments in my building are occupied by lesbians. It's great!"

♀"I hope someday to live in a complete lesbian community, self-supporting as far as possible, with farms, pasture, free land, and villages. In fact, I would like to see our beautiful Earth lived on and loved by dykes only."

♀"Residence is one of the most important factors in the gay life. Greenwich Village, mine, is the best place in the world to be gay! Wouldn't be caught dead out of the 'urbs' because in some places they probably still tar and feather dykes."

♀"It's hard to live a gay lifestyle in a straight neighborhood. You end up isolating yourself from your neighbors. I'd like to live in a gay community, city, state, or nation!"

♀"I have recently moved to a very liberal neighborhood with a large proportion of gays. I would definitely choose this kind of supportive neighborhood over a heterosexual family-oriented neighborhood. The only other choice might be a *very private* ranch in the desert."

♂"I seem to have found that the world is split into two types of residential area—(1) the type where the grass is mowed, the homes cared for, and the lifestyles respectable, and in general a very pleasant place to live; (2) a scroungy, poorly maintained, theft-ridden, prostitute-run area, where people can 'be themselves,' and where Mexicans, faggots, niggers, and the likes can intermingle and be comfortable—except for being robbed, beat up, and the likes. It seems that anywhere the fruit is 'accepted,' it is the

bottom-of-the-barrel acceptance. Before the fag is accepted in an area, they have dropped the rules on burglary, rape, murder, robbery, and whatever else you please. San Francisco is an example of this. A friend of mine lived in Piedmont (dahling). He maintained his property, paid his bills, worked hard, and all of that. He liked to have friends come over and have pot parties in the privacy of his living room. A neighbor with a telescope monitored his front door and set up a raid of his premises. The guy now lives in the cruddiest nigger flats of West Oakland and is happier, even though his place gets ripped off twice a year.''

♂''Being a rural person, I've long felt alienated, having to live in cities to be with a supportive gay and straight community. Last year we took the risk of living rurally—many miles from any 'gay' city. And the risk has been well worth it. In the Northwest at least, one need not live in Seattle to find other gay people and very supportive and friendly straight people. They're all over—farmers, townsfolk, fishermen, etc. Taking that risk has shown me that I'll never have to live in a city again, except by my own choice. It's not as bad for a faggot in the boondocks as we are led to believe.''

♀''In Toronto there is the usual 'gay ghetto' downtown where one is charged exorbitant rent for living in a gay neighborhood. Also, there is an older neighborhood to the west of the city core and ghetto where a large number of lesbian collectives and coops have sprung up to avoid the heavy rents. The myth that lesbian nation is dead in the suburbs has been shattered by a lesbian mother and her lover who have started a suburban gay group.

''When I lived in the ghetto, more than half of my building was gay, the remainder being other social outcasts and 'undesirables.' I lived with two gay women and a gay man.

''I now live in a quiet residential area that was once WASP heterosexual but is rapidly becoming gay and multicultural. Yes, we are everywhere! There are four lesbian couples and three single lesbians including myself on my street, living in four low-rise apartment buildings.

''There are several gay farms to the east and north of Toronto, and the women who live there want to get away from the gay scene and rat race of the city.

''There is the usual problem for the rural lesbian of isolation in the country or coming to the city with all its pressures but with the presence of other gay women. I hope the rural movement gathers strength. At the fifth annual gay conference in Saskatoon, the rural gays had a lot to say about their feelings of isolation from the urban community, but wanted to remain in the country and try and build up a communications network.''

♂''The topic is integration versus ghetto. I prefer integration even though it's tougher. First of all, the ghetto makes you forget what society is really like, and you lose the motivation to push for change. Second, if everyone is in the ghetto, who will be the positive gay model for young people trying to come to grips with their identities in cowtown?''

♀''Rural areas (to live in) depress me. In general I think they become

terribly restrictive. I prefer urban areas (with their own restrictions, I suppose); there is a wider variety of people, and more of a potential for experience.''

♀''I live in the woods and countryside here in New Hampshire. I love country life but am sorry that I did not come out when I was younger and living in the greater Boston area. It would have been easier to get out and meet more women. I feel isolated here. I have to travel many miles to see lesbian pals once a week or so. No bars here at all. No groups to attend nearby.''

♀''I live in a middle-sized town, near a college. I don't know my neighbors well, they don't know me. The idea of a lesbian collective appeals to me. I live alone presently, and I'd like to live with others who shared my lifestyle, so that we could give each other support.''

♀''I would *love* to live in a gay neighborhood. Gay block parties, gay neighbors, gay volleyball games, gay joggers! I'd love it!''

♂''I'm opposed to ghettos of all kinds. I would not like to live in a retirement village, a gay neighborhood, etc. Where I live we have several real mixed neighborhoods and I like that. I once lived on a street that housed several gay couples (male and female), several large families, Spanish Americans, Anglos, some very poor people and some very rich. That was a nice place to live.''

♂''Do you mean gay ghettos? Should people live in areas according to their sexuality? This hardly seems like a step forward!''

♂''I am very in favor of gay communities, wherever. I am anxious for the day when large cities, San Francisco, for example, are totally controlled by gays.''

♂''Especially as a Negro, I know 'segregation' is not good, and banning voluntary 'segregation' is not good either.''

♀ ''I live in New York because it is easier to be gay and know gays. When I think of getting a house I think of areas where there will be some gay population and some community ease about the gay people being there.''

♀ ''I live in an urban environment with three women's houses on our street and more in the neighborhood, although it wasn't that way when I moved here. It's nice to have someone close to socialize with. As for living in the country, although it's something I would like to do, I still see it as a privilege. If you have the money or know someone who does, then you can move to the country.''

♀''I live in the city now, because it's near the university I'm going to, but I'd prefer living in the country with a bunch of women! I grew up in a semirural area and in the last two or three years went to the country a couple of times for a week or so and felt like I was *home*. I would *not* live in the country if there were just a few of us and we were isolated and oppressed by our straight neighbors. I'd want a sizable community, and a location not *too* far from a nonconservative population center. I need space to get away from all the garbage of this male-dominated society.''

♂ ''We live in a rural area, having moved here in part to escape the urban

gay ghetto. We love it here, and you should see our flowers and our organically grown vegetables! We are completely out to the 'counterculture' types, but tend toward discretion with the 'locals.' Quite a few of them know we're gay, and there've been no problems. We've met a few local gays, but they are so closeted, so scared, or so unsophisticated (I know that sounds snobbish, but it's true), that it turns out that our closest friends are straight 'country freaks' who also used to live in cities. We are seen as outsiders by the native people even before they know about our sexuality, and it's hard to figure out ways to reach out to local people, especially the young gays who are forced to play straight. I would like to try to form a gay organization, even though it's scary, but part of the problem is that some of my gay friends here think we shouldn't go looking for trouble, so it's not just up to me. But I think that if gay people who understand gay liberation don't start something for gay people, the local 'native' gays might not do it for another ten years, if ever!''

⚜"All homosexuals should live together completely separated from straights.''

⚜ "I have lived nearly all my life in large cities, and feel that a gay person is able to live a much freer life in a large city than when subject to the scrutiny and pressures of a rural or small-town community. I approve in theory of the idea of gay neighborhoods, as I think that it is then easier to nurture gay cultural and community projects—but in practice, having lived a couple of years in New York's Greenwich Village, I think that the continual, visible presence of gay neighbors when you walk the street or go out to shop can make 'cruising' the be-all and end-all of your life. When I lived in Greenwich Village, even going half a block to buy a pound of tomatoes meant there was at least a 50% chance that I wouldn't return to the apartment alone! I now live in a fairly sedate residential area, but within easy reach of known gay areas where I can go for visual stimulation or some hard action when the mood takes, me, without the continual temptation that was present while I lived in the Village, and I think that is the lifestyle that I would recommend.''

⚜"I don't prefer an all-gay environment; I prefer a very diverse environment. I think that the human race will not be healthy until everyone has a country place and a city place to go to.''

The Bottom Line— Self-Acceptance

Judging from the predominant response of the straight world to homosexuality, one can readily conclude that in the eyes of straight people, gay people would all be better off straight. While it should be obvious by now to any straight reader that gay people's lives are not without problems, it should be just as obvious that these problems are not necessarily more overwhelming than the problems that straight people have to solve—just different. And despite all of the criticisms they have of the gay liberation movement, gay men and lesbians agree that one crucial accomplishment of

that movement has been in the area of self-acceptance for gay people—combating self-hatred and self-oppression, and moving beyond that to celebration, growth, and creativity.

Straight society's negative attitude toward homosexuality, and the presumption that that attitude is shared, has led psychiatrists to the notion of a "cure" for homosexuality. Earlier in this book, respondents refer to experiences with those cures. But what if the cure were a simple "magic" pill? The respondents were asked *If you could take a pill to make you straight, would you do it?*

These were the responses:

	LESBIANS	GAY MEN
yes	0%	6%
no	95	77
not sure	5	17

The degree of self-acceptance among lesbians is notably higher in our sample, with not a single woman in the subsample expressing the desire for a "straight pill" (though surely such women do exist).

The fact that nearly a quarter of the gay men (and a smaller portion of the lesbians) are not 100% comfortable with their sexuality should not be surprising, given the steady barrage of straight propaganda most gay people experience. The degree of self-acceptance is undoubtedly much higher than would have been found a decade earlier, but the victories won by the gay movement in the area of consciousness are by no means complete. Also, some people may have what they feel to be legitimate reasons for wishing that their sexual preference were different. But the fact remains that there is no magic pill, or other cure, and probably the research and medical efforts directed toward finding such a cure do much more harm than good, by perpetrating the notion of homosexuality as something awful.

To explore this question of self-acceptance, the questionnaire asked, *How do you feel now about your homosexuality? How have these feelings changed over time? What has influenced these feelings and any changes in them?*

Only a handful of the lesbians and gay men showed marked dissatisfaction with their lives as gay people:

♀"If I could be straight, I would change without hesitation. Since I am a lesbian, I am stuck in a life of unhappiness, unacceptance, and disapproval by society, religion, etc."

♂"I find homosexuality a very depressing thing, because you are a minority in society and you have to live with that. The 'straights' have almost complete control over what shape your life will be in the future and also whether they'll let you conduct yourself sexually in their city. Notice that I said 'their' city—as a matter of fact, if they wanted to probably quite

legally they could run you out of town. My feelings have not changed over the period of time I've been out, but perhaps in the years to come they will."

⚥"I wish I were not homosexual, but since I am I have to make the best of it, and adjust the best I can. My own sense of oppression for the past several years comes not from the larger society but from gay society. I have a long time ago personally experienced societal oppression—arrest, entrapment, blackmail. But in recent years, despite some personal growth through consciousness-raising group participation and becoming active in the gay movement while living in New York City, my self-image as a gay person has been shaken. I tend to avoid the usual 'make-out' places, like bars, because one is judged on the basis of physical appearance and I do not measure up—or at least can't compete with the majority of youthful and physically attractive men. In a nutshell, and to be very honest and frank, I am embittered. I have pretty much resigned myself to celibacy—I have given up an attempt to find a lover because the search has been painful and humiliating. A person can stand just so much rejection. I used the word 'resigned.' It's a choice made because otherwise my mental health could suffer. I suppose my lack of 'success' as a gay person is the greatest disappointment of my life. Professionally I am very successful, and respected. In the gay world, I am a flop. And I have indeed tried. The gay movement is for the younger generation. However, it seems to me it is built on very shaky ground when physical attraction and sexual expression itself is the basis. Actually, this is not quite what I mean. Obviously the right to sexual expression is basic. What about those for whom it is not possible—because of age, appearance, etc.? It seems to me the gay movement needs a massive amount of consciousness-raising. Another point—the needs of the 'older' gay man do not receive enough attention. And one becomes 'older' rather quickly in gay society."

Some of the respondents express their feelings about their homosexuality with ambivalence, doubt, confusion, and uncertainty, or they are beset by some of the problems. Here are some responses reflecting such mixed feelings:

♀"I feel ambivalent. Usually I feel good about it, but many times I wonder if I'm not just copping out and not dealing with a possible fear of men."

⚥"I feel fine about homosexuality overall; I *do* wish I'd been born in an epoch or a nation when and where it's approved. In short, I *don't* feel guilty about gay sex, but I *do* feel inconvenienced by it in this country and this century. Moreover, I feel *devastated* to be past the age of sexual attractiveness. If I were 20 years old, I'd be as happy as a pig in mud."

⚥"I can accept my being homosexual. It's just a part of who I am. It might be easier to deal with life in our society if I weren't, just as it might seem easier to live if I had a million dollars. And so I say if I could take a

pill to change I would, just as I would take the million dollars. Both would change my life, and I'm not sure whether it would be all to the good, but, I guess, just off the top of my head I'd now say I'd give both a try if they were available. But, who knows? I've not been terribly 'unhappy' as a homosexual. And I've seen some very unhappy straights, so . . . I accept being a homosexual, and live with it, and find joy in it. The only real regret I can speak of in my life to this point is that had I been better educated sexually earlier, I would have arranged to be living today in a more metropolitan area, where I could better express this part of my life.''

♀''I feel *much more* confident after coming out. My personality has improved itself, and since my parents found out we seem to have more of a mutual understanding between us. Although I'm now out, my fear of being discovered by the rest of society is tremendous, I guess because I know that society doesn't accept it, and because that makes me feel guilty at times. I have friends that don't care who knows, but that's just *not* convenient in my type of lifestyle. Some of my friends even show their lesbianism in public—*wow*!—that takes a *lot* of guts!''

♂''I sometimes wish that I weren't gay, but those times come further and further apart, and are usually the result of getting fed up with all the games I see other people playing, and seeing myself getting sucked into playing them as well. But I wonder . . . would being straight be any easier?''

♂''I feel fairly good now. I think I would feel better if my gay feelings found expression in a fairly solid relationship. Once in a while I feel mixed up, because I am still attracted to women, too, and it just seems hard to see how it all might work out.''

♂''I enjoy my homosexuality, but I don't like the 'butch drag' intolerance that's around these days. In my day, we were somewhat intolerant of 'nellie queens,' but we didn't hurt their feelings or make them feel they weren't legitimate members of the gay community. Now there's a lot of In Group/Out Group stuff on the gay scene. I dislike it and it saddens me. I also kind of resent the fact that so many gay activist leaders and other 'authorities' are people who were straight as recently as eight years ago, and they take it upon themselves to lecture me/us about what it means to be gay! I was gay before some of them were even *born*!''

♂''I feel pretty good about being gay. At times it feels wonderful, such as on Gay Freedom Day, or during a gay cultural event. I still have some homophobic feelings, sometimes around gay men who seem to make 'camp' and bitchiness the focus of their lives, sometimes in gay bars (we can be uncaring toward each other), sometimes during sex.''

♂''Early I told myself I wasn't homosexual, merely using males as a substitute for the females I didn't have. Once I admitted my homosexuality to myself, I tried every way to stop it I could think of—confession and prayer included. Finding nothing worked, I decided I might as well give in and enjoy it. It isn't a life one chooses; there are too many disadvantages, but I've learned to live with it—and I'm not sorry.''

♀''I am in a state of flux about my lesbianism at present. For the last 2½

years, I have felt secure, solid, and healthy, but secrecy takes its toll. I wonder sometimes now if 'they' aren't right, if I am really fucked up or immature. I wonder if I am being idealistic in assuming I can live this way forever and never be hurt because I'm gay. Right now I'm a student, so no one is too interested in my personal life. What about ten years from now? Will I ever lose a job because of it? How will I feel when my sisters and brothers bring home their husbands, wives, and children, who cheerily ask me when I'm going to get married? Will they ever take my child from me if I decide to have one? I want the privileges granted freely to heterosexuals. I want to be able to walk into a gay bar without enduring snickers and giggles from a group of passing adolescents. I want to take my lover home and say, 'Mom, this is the woman of my dreams, I'm in love, I'm so happy, aren't you happy for me?' I want to walk down the street holding my lover's hand as unconsciously as men and women do every day. Can I live a life without all these things? If I'm in love I can, because that matters most of all. But being in love doesn't take away all these other hurts.

"Another interesting change I am observing in myself is that I am liking men more. I don't know why—it may be because I'm running into older men now rather than goofy adolescents and college macho-jocks. It is partially due, I'm sure, to the fact that the feminist movement has had a tremendous impact on many men. I'm running into some real softies, men who are warm and fuzzy and sensitive, who don't need to put on shows or always be strong. I like that, and I'm trusting that kind of man more than I've ever trusted men before. Strangely enough, the idea of getting involved with a man is threatening because it shakes the lesbian identity I've strived for for so long. I consider myself bisexual in the ideal world, but in the real world that's a tough place to be. People need identities, anchors, communities—and bisexuality is a limbo. Another artifact of our rigid, labeling, categorizing society. Everyone has to fit somewhere or you don't fit at all."

♂ "Let me answer by clarifying my response to the straight-pill hypothesis. Gay rights are worth fighting for and I would do so even if I turned straight. Some say, you wouldn't have to risk it then and could cop out. I'm not that type and I fight againt racism even though nigger-haters abound, and I support the United Farm Workers in spite of agribusiness and police. I would probably be just as unstable and single if I were hetero but I did have two good chances with females that didn't work out because I couldn't have a physical rapport. The main reason I probably would go straight is to salvage the grief and conflict it has caused my relatives. Also, society has done permanent damage to my self-image in its antigay bullshit. It may seem a cop-out, but in scary environs, oppression can kill. Being gay is as normal and can be great, but we do live in a world of bigotry. I would not choose to be something others hate and since I'm already hated for my race, religion, political views, etc., there are times I don't mind the added bigotry gays get, but usually I could do much better without it."

♀ "I feel great about my lesbianism. The only bad feeling I've ever had about lesbianism is the thought of the extreme frustration of loving straight

women and not being able to express it. I've dealt with that so much and it makes me so sad.''

♀"I would prefer to be bisexual, but I don't think I'd want to be heterosexual in this culture, because it's male-dominated. But being gay isn't too sweet either. It's not a misfortune to be born gay, it's a misfortune to be born into a culture which condemns it. I'm gay, I've accepted it, and I'm going to make the most of it. That's the best I can do.''

♂ "A month or two ago I was wondering if homosexuality was good or bad or what, because I am a Christian and it bothers me on moral and biblical grounds. I guess I accept it and feel good about it, although I still have my doubts at times. When I first started dealing with my sexuality intellectually, I felt very guilty and felt it was something bad, sick, perverted. In college, I was very gay lib. Now, I've toned down and am starting to question it again. What influenced these changes was my own feeling that it was not the awful thing everyone said it was. The recent doubts have been caused by my return to my church and questioning the Bible and myself on this issue.''

♂ "I still—three years after coming out—retain mixed feelings about my homosexuality. I often enjoy my sex, and I enjoy my body and others' sexually. I have grown a lot in the past three years. Yet, being out has not been all positive. Although I can enjoy and savor my homosexuality as a personal experience at times, I have found that there is much in the gay world or 'gay community'—as there is in any community I have belonged to—much that I dislike. Furthermore, living in this society day to day and not receiving any official validation from it has not made it easy to rid myself of all of the negative stereotypes I swallowed that led to my self-hate. On a bad day, it is easy for me to revert and feel 'abnormal' or 'perverted' or to believe that my life would be perfect if only I would and could get married, have two kids, and live forever after in my castle in the suburbs (with two cars, of course). I have recently become aware that one of the reasons I have not yet fallen in love—mad, passionate love—with another man is that to do so would mean that I must admit to myself, 'I am a cocksucker and I love it!'—and to admit it to the world.''

♀"I feel great about being a lesbian. Every so often, when I see how some very rare women manage to be themselves and have stable, hetero lifestyles, I feel a twinge of jealousy because it's so easy for them to integrate into the world and be accepted and live out their lives, but then I know even more deeply that I can't do that, that I tried it, that I was always angry and unfulfilled and felt out of place.''

Joyful celebration of lesbianism and gayness characterized most of the replies to this question. Here are some of the myriad ways that gay men and lesbians describe their feelings of self-esteem:

♀"I feel good about my lesbianism. I am comfortable with it. I do not feel and never have felt guilty about it.''

♭ "Even at age 14, when I realized that I marched to a different drummer, I held on to the good image I had of my sex life and gave up everything. I came from a rich family and was set up for life if I would have given up homosexuality. When my stepfather died he left an estate of over $2,000,000, of which I never received a cent, but would have if I would have stayed 'straight,' married, and accepted the role my family had wanted. I do not resent this at all. I would give up $5,000,000 tomorrow rather than compromise my sexuality."

♭ "Once homosexuality was a source of shame and guilt and fear for me. Then it was a source of ferment and upheaval; and under its urging, I rebelled and broke away from a traditional upbringing. Gayness has made me a new and better person, more humane and loving in some ways, certainly more cosmopolitan and intellectually sophisticated (tolerant). It has led, however, to spiritual chaos and emptiness, to agnosticism. Gayness never meant 'be *proud* of your homosexuality,' merely don't be ashamed of it. What I am proud of is the liberating, stimulating, mind-expanding *effects* of my coming to grips with my sexual orientation.

"Today, I aspire to bisexuality. I feel that to love women as well as men would be a further expansion of my horizons. Once I worried about why I was gay. This means: What thwarted me, where did I go astray? Today, I can say that yes, perhaps my gayness was the product of an antisexual upbringing, but from that original 'misfortune' has come untold good. I would not *give up* my gayness; I ask only to add to it an appreciation of women. I can even hope for a distant time when bisexuality would prevail in society. This means a radically different world, I guess."

♭ "I feel that my homosexuality is a natural, God-given thing. Like all gifts of God, it must be used and expressed, but not abused. There is a responsibility attached to its use—a responsibility to use it for good."

♭ "I feel very good about my homosexuality because I can relate to life better from a gay viewpoint. I feel free and secure. A big influence on my life has been to move away from old childhood surroundings and meeting new people."

♭ "I am an Ivy-league-educated WASP male, from a polite, upper-middle-class southern family. That background, like my gayness, has created certain artificial barriers in my relationships with other people, who tend to want to deal with me as the representative of a category rather than as an individual. My background has also made my life as a gay man somewhat more difficult, since it is that much more difficult for me to find a partner who shares many of my interests and who is not intimidated by many of the things I supposedly represent. On the other hand, my gayness has probably been my greatest asset in helping me to realize and develop my own humanity and to perceive the humanity in other people. The gay people I have known and loved have only their sexual orientation in common, and my participation in their more democratic society has brought me into contact with a diversity of people that I would never have known otherwise. They have forced me to come to terms with my own sexuality and with my

deep capacity for love and affection—areas for hangups from my conventional background with which I might never have dealt had I been straight. Most importantly, because of the conventional hangups of others, I find myself in the incongruous position of being a member of an oppressed minority. As a member of the gay minority, I am able to empathize with others, such as blacks and women, who are the victims of unjust social labeling. Being gay has not been without its price, but I rejoice in the greater participation in human experience which being gay has brought me.''

♀ "I am grateful each day that I had the courage to find my own way along a dark unmapped road to lesbianism. I look at my married sister, brother, and friends and pity them, for I feel they are not happy as they could be. Not just because they are straight, but because of the way they have been socialized, the way they must live their lives, the things that marriage does to most people. For some people, marriage is the best and only way to live. Unfortunately, these people have convinced the majority of this, so everyone thinks they must marry and have children in order to be happy. Marriage is not for everyone, but still young people cannot wait to join their peers so they won't feel left out. More people should postpone marriage, get out into the world and find out if that is what they really want. When I first realized that I was a lesbian, I was very unhappy and now I realize that I might have fallen into the marriage trap, thinking it a cure. I consider myself very lucky to have had the strength to find out what is right for me. I first had to realize that I hated to be tied down and dominated. This helped me to say no to two marriage proposals (I tried at 20 years old to go straight).''

♀ "I feel the pride—the love of self and all other wimmin—the emergence of self. I have come from this 'Miss Goody Two Shoes' of my high school to (and I quote) a 'flaming radical lesbian' here. The outward changes are apparent and mostly political, until I've found myself awfully close to the separatists' camp. But inside, there's been a slow, warm recognition of my love of wimmin (individuals and as a nation) and acceptance of myself. (I'm not nearly as mean and tough as I talk politically.) Change was brought about by myself, my feminist friends (who gave so generously of their love and support and knowledge), the books I've read, the songs I've sung. It's been reinforced by experiences and friends. It is. And I'm glad. Praise the Goddess.''

♀ "I feel very positive about my lesbianism. Today I look upon it as an alternate lifestyle, not a sickness or a weakness or a shame. I'm proud of what I have come through, and of the understanding and depth it has brought me. Early in my homosexuality, I felt ashamed; I'd bought the psychiatric 'sick' concept, and felt that I was probably not a 'whole' person. I felt handicapped. It has taken a great deal of time and work to change those old feelings into positive ones. The greatest influences on that change are my experiences in therapy and analysis—which helped me to begin to accept myself, to be able to evaluate myself as a person, and to see my relationship to society. The women's movement and the gay movement are

the other major influences which helped me to change and to accept. They have put into perspective the societal influences which had created my negative feelings. I have been able to make a 180-degree turn with my feelings. And that's a joy.''

⚥ "I feel very good about my homosexuality. It is what I am, I like myself, I like my life. I have never had any real problems over it after the initial shock of realizing that I was gay and would never be anything else. I honestly mean it when I say I wouldn't take the famous pill if it were offered. I have no interest in women as sex partners. I don't like children as such (though I've helped raise two and am devoted to several kids I know, but I never think of them as children—they are just small men and women). I feel very deeply for people who cannot adjust to their gayness. I feel, but I do not understand it really. They have my sympathy but not my empathy. I wish I could tell them all how great it is to be happy with yourself—straight or gay. I also believe—and doctors and psychiatrists will never convince me otherwise—that I was gay before I started remembering and that nothing would have ever made me straight. I also believe that nothing will make a straight man gay. He may play around, but he'll never convert, just as I won't. Anita Bryant, et al., base their whole campaign on the conversion theory. Hogwash! Also, my mother did not make me gay. She's a terrific person and we've always had a good relationship. My father was a very strong person and my best friend. I loved him and eleven years after his death I still miss him so much I cry sometimes (I'm crying now). And that's why my mother must never have to face my homosexuality. She'd think it was all her fault and it wasn't. Let me add something here which really doesn't fit. I know that homosexuality is abhorrent to my family, but when I was a child they knew I was 'different.' I don't think they knew how or why, but they knew. And because of it they did things for me because they knew I wasn't going to be like the other boys. They let me take dancing and art classes and go to the touring shows from Broadway which they knew were what we called *risqué*. They encouraged my wild ideas and never tried to force me into baseball games and other sports. They were supportive at all times—and if that is what made me gay, tough shit. Nobody ever had better parents (the same goes for my sister, who is absolutely terrific, and I'm crazy about my brother-in-law, too). There, I had to say that. Everyone is always blaming their family. Phooey. I take full responsibility.

"Sure my feelings have changed, not my feelings so much as how I handle them. I always had gay pride; now I can say so out loud.''

⚥ "If I had had a choice in the beginning, I would have chosen to be gay. My personal philosophy is that homosexuality could be the hope of the world. It seems to me that being gay involves being capable of loving another man, of feeling something for him that precludes the desire to destroy him. Since war is basically competitive in nature, involving the heterosexual maxim of competition, wouldn't it be better for us all if two men could make love to each other instead of raping the other with gunfire?''

♂"I feel great about my homosexuality now and do not try to hide it from any one any more. I used to feel a little uncomfortable about certain people knowing that I was gay. But when a friend of mine (Robert Hillsborough) was murdered by four straight men I really came out of the closet. Not that I was in the closet that much, but when that happened I stood up and said, 'I have had enough!' "

♀"It feels great being a lesbian. It's *me*! I'm very positive about my orientation and people like Elaine Noble and Rita Mae Brown and Kate Millett have helped me gain a positive image."

♀"I feel more than ever that the oppression of women can't end until women have a sexual option or options other than heterosexuality. So I'm very glad to be living in 1977 in a lesbian/feminist community where I can exercise that option."

♂"I feel very proud being gay—just as proud and good as any straight person—perhaps better as I am not hung up on sex as many straights are. When I realized what homosexuality was and that I was a homosexual I tried to deny it to myself. Finding that I couldn't, and bright enough to know how persecuted gays were then (early '60s), I avoided getting into gay life. I also used to think that gays were all queens and into drag, which turned me off, and I wanted to have nothing to do with them. Once I came out and started going to gay bars I quickly found out that I was wrong and I loved it. It took me quite a while to get to like queens. Experience and getting to know them changed my mind completely."

♂"I am happy with my homosexuality. I am not 'proud' because I believe that I had little if anything to do with my being this, so I have not 'accomplished something' to be 'proud' of. However, I am not ashamed of it. The changes in my acceptance of myself as a homosexual are, more than anything else, an almost inevitable maturation, rather than a dramatic upheaval or an overt challenge to the straight society."

♂"I am very comfortable about being gay now, but this came about only in the last seven years. It was seven years ago that my lover and I discovered that he had bone cancer. I decided that I would spend every minute with him that was left to us. I told my boss that I would have to quit my job, and explained why. Being an understanding, beautiful man, he told me that my job would still be open whenever I wanted to come back. I took a cot to F.'s hospital room and literally lived there with him, coming home only to shower and check the mail. I listened impassively to snide remarks from a few of the nurses, and didn't feel the least bit intimidated. I no longer felt ashamed of my love for another man; instead, I felt extremely proud of it. I suppose I was also proud of my newfound courage to face 'the enemy' and stand my ground. After his death all of our gay friends came to the funeral parlor for the visitation. I embraced each of them as they entered, and none seemed embarrassed. I always knew that I could give my life for F., but I didn't know that I could come out of the closet for him. I only wish that I wouldn't have had to pay such a heavy price to find that out."

♀"I am so proud of finding myself that I want to shout it from the

housetops: 'I'm a lesbian and I'm happy.' I wouldn't hide it for nothing or no one, although I rarely advertise it. (I used to wear the button all the time, but I usually don't now.) I feel sorry for the people in the closet, for whatever reason they're there.''

♀"I feel very contented about my lesbianism because I tried so many different things, and I finally found out what feels best. When I first started thinking about loving women, I felt panicky, and I had to get rid of those feelings at any price. I used to seek guidance, and I would get very negative responses, and I used to depend a lot on others for decisions. As time went on and I had more experiences with women, and positive input regarding those experiences, I began to feel more comfortable with loving women. Now I feel very comfortable with the sex life I have chosen, and I feel it is a conscious choice. Through reading *Lesbian/Woman* and *Sappho Was a Right-On Woman* and subscribing to the *Wishing Well*, I don't feel like a lone 'freak.' Lately, I'd been feeling unlovable, and I was withdrawing from people again. I talked to someone well-versed in Transactional Analysis about my inability to get along, and she said that I had to open up, that we're all convinced that we have a 'rotten' place in us that we have to hide from others, but if people open up to each other, they find that they have a lot of 'rotten' things in common. This helped me accept myself even more. This woman also said that one may think you're an awful person, when in reality most people may think nothing of it (what you're hiding). I didn't even hint about my lesbianism, and I didn't let her know what I've been hiding. I thought that her advice was applicable, though, and I'll keep it in mind always.''

♂"My feelings about my sexuality have changed for the better as I once thought that to be homosexual was to be dirty, but by learning about myself and others I find that there is nothing wrong with being gay. The most important factor in my change is a homophile club called the Atascadero Gay Encounter. This club is a part of the treatment program here at Atascadero State Hospital and is for gay men who have problems with self-image and understanding their sexuality. There is also a group for homosexual social skills where we who don't know how learn cruising and how to act like a respectable homosexual.''

♂"I feel very positive; would not change if possible; feeling has changed with maturing and being in an 'outside' position—being able to step back and view all my relatives' petty straight entanglements: divorces, kids, squabbles, and in general the whole big Jewish family structure. No way do I want a part in that. My gayness is what saved me from it. I am artistic, intelligent, free-thinking, sensitive, and *aware* because of it—or maybe because I'm all these, the bonus of being gay went along with them!''

♂"My homosexuality has enriched my life and I would not want to change. I had some very considerable inhibitions to overcome initially. My father was a Baptist minister, and later in army and civil service employment I was prevented by inhibitions and apprehensions from realizing my sexual identity. My coming out was attended by a certain amount of

panic and guilt. If there had been a gay press and gay organizations then, things would have been much simpler.''

♀''After 1½ years of being out I've become relaxed and happy about myself. Whereas I used to suffer from a low-grade to deep depression all the time, I actually feel content and happy with my life. I've met many friends who have similar interests to mine and continue to meet more and more professional women who are also lesbians. For the first time in my life I am in a relationship that feels good and solid; one which I continue to work on with my lover.''

♀''I used to accept the view that there was something wrong with me, and that I needed to explain how I got this way. Now I feel that I'm fine, and I wish more other people were, straight or gay. I used to think that if my daughter grew up straight, that would represent 'success.' Now I don't care if she is straight, or gay, or bisexual, or a Carmelite—as long as she is okay and happy.''

♀''Being a lesbian is comfortable. Since coming out, I've found a lot of answers for things that didn't seem right before or had no explanation. I don't have to try to fit in the straight world any more, because now I know who I am and only wish I would have found out years earlier. The more lesbians I meet and get to know, the happier I am about being one. I think I get more blatant and more comfortable with each year. The changes seem to be in my attitude towards myself more than any outside influence, although being surrounded by a supportive women's community instead of being isolated in a relationship with just one other person for feedback is a definite plus.''

♂''Gay liberation has been of great help to me. I read a great deal about homosexuality (two dozen books in the last year). The black movement and women's lib had a profound effect on me. And sleeping with blacks and women has taught me something about myself.''

♀''I've begun to accept myself as God created me: one unique combination of heredity, personality, and genes existing in this time and space, never to be created again exactly the same. Of all the times to be a lesbian, this is the most positive, decisive, and creative. I've grown as a person but being a lesbian and *living* as a lesbian has changed my perception of my work. As an artist it has given me distinct advantages: greater flexibility, a deeper understanding of myself and others, insight and maturity, a need to be honest, and to root out and touch that center in my work. Basically, what's influenced me most is the strength of my relationship with my lover, how that's grown and changed and come through so many obstacles and confrontations, stronger and more vital. I've drawn from that, I've learned from that, I've become a better human being working through that.''

♀''I am very happy and contented being a lesbian. Whenever the question comes up—'Would you prefer being heterosexual?'—my immediate response is always, 'No.' I think that comes from being happy, pleased with myself as a total person, and not wanting to be any different—in most respects. I feel fulfilled within myself. This has changed

over the years, certainly, due to life experiences, as well as therapy. Coming to accept yourself and your values as a separate individual is a process, and coming from a very dominant, opinionated, rigid family, it has taken me some time. Being a lesbian is one part of a more total acceptance. I do also think that the current openness in the gay movement has helped as well as much reading of gay literature for positive reinforcement.''

♀ "Lesbianism is so obviously wonderful.''

♀ "I feel great about my lesbianism, very positive. At first, during coming out, I was really ashamed because I thought I had to do and be everything that the stereotypes said I should, and I read many negative books before I found the positive material. My brothers (I have four) and my closest friends at the time of my realization helped me, and continue to be closest to me and support me. They didn't believe I was what those books said, and encouraged me to do whatever I pleased to be happy and to be strong. I had to teach them lots of things at first, but now they stand behind my right to be homosexual. And realize it is a conscious choice.''

♂ "I like being gay and would be no other way. It took many years to reach this point. The new attitudes have helped greatly and also being in the San Francisco Bay Area. Having good friends is also a big help.''

♂ "I feel very confirmed, relaxed, and at peace with my homosexuality. I don't feel I'm unusual, perverse, or any of the other labels. My guilt in my teens has given way to a true enjoyment and appreciation of male-male sex, of companionship and love. I can think of nothing more I want from life than the love of a man *I* love.''

♂ "I feel very good about being gay, especially since everywhere I turn, I find that it is something I have in common with great people in history. Almost all of the artists I admired when I was a child were gay, though I didn't discover this till later. I feel it is a badge of distinction, of specialness; I really have an elitist view of it, though I also am very aware that the gay scene attracts some really untogether people.''

♀ "I feel good. I don't feel 'different' any longer as I did when I was growing up. I have learned that I have a lot to learn but so has everyone else. My daughter and her friends have probably contributed more to my changes and my family's than any other factor. She is now 26 and was adolescent in the '60s—which opened up a whole new range of attitudes and ideas to our family, especially my father and myself. I explained to her about my interest in women as well as men when she was 11 or 12 in case she might have some of the same feelings. I didn't want her to feel as different as I had. She has several friends who are lesbians and many who are straight women, none of whom seem 'hung up' on heterosexuality even when it is their preference. Her husband accepts my lover and myself as much as he accepted my male lover and myself. He thinks we're weird, but our sexuality isn't the main issue. Since I have been in this relationship sexuality has finally settled into being just one small but important part of my life, not a primary concern.''

♀ "I feel good about being a lesbian—it is probably the first time in my

life I really feel at peace. It's been a long journey and twelve years of marriage have taken a toll on my physical and mental health. My positive feelings have been a result of the support I have received from lesbian/feminist friends. I am still aware that I have to behave in a guarded fashion on my job but I am free to express myself in my support groups of lesbians and straight feminists.''

♀"I'm a lesbian by choice and proud of it. There is nothing anyone can do or say that would make me want to change. I am much happier realizing that I am gay. I am not straight and don't have any desire to pretend I am. It's a real pain putting on a straight front. My biggest influence has been the gay liberation movement. My experience with love has also been a great influence. When I knew another two women lovers it was thrilling for me. Having people to share my ideas of and about homosexuality is reinforcing. It was fun sharing experiences concerning our lesbian relationships. After that, I became interested in what goes on with the gay liberation movement. I also watched a talk show one night where gays were expressing their feelings and experiences. They did a good job of killing some of those ridiculous myths about homosexuality.''

♂"I prefer being gay to being straight. I would never even want to become straight even if it were possible. I think, along with Elaine Noble, that it is a gift. Of course, not in all cases, but I think many gay people develop more sensitivity than straights because of oppression. (I'm not Jewish, but could this also partly explain why Jews have contributed far more to culture than their numbers warrant?) I have more freedom than straights notwithstanding my oppression. I don't have a wife, mortgage, and four kids to support for twenty years. I am able to travel, read extensively, and develop my interests. I am able to explore more facets of life than the average straight. I have never felt any guilt about my homosexuality from the earliest times.''

♂"Once while speaking before a class on 'deviant psychology,' I was asked, if given the chance to take a pill and become instantly straight, would I take the pill. My answer then, and now, to such a question would be an unhesitating 'No!' By being a male in this macho society, one is forced into a confining, restricting, and unnatural role. The male child is raised to exhibit 'manly traits,' to act like a big boy. Pity the poor boy who cries; he is told to act like a soldier, that it doesn't really hurt, that only sissies cry. By the time· he is an adult he is one well-programmed robot. Society says this is the way a 'real man' acts. Being a gay male, a 'deviant from normal society,' has given me the opportunity to examine and question those roles and expectations I was taught were right. I had never been very comfortable with most of them so I decided to say 'Fuck it!' and follow my own dictates. It was as if a weight had been lifted from my back. For years I had been consciously and subconsciously trying to deny my needs and force myself into that tight little mold. But no more!''

♀"How do I feel about my lesbianism? Damn proud. It's a feeling of

being ahead of everybody in getting in on the ground floor of something good.''

♀''I think being a lesbian is the most wonderful thing that has happened to me. It has given me a lot of strength, given me an identity that is my own. It has provided a basis for my politics, given me a platform to live around. It has given me a very different viewpoint from which to observe society. I've felt this way about my 'difference' ever since the first time I looked in the mirror and said, 'That person is a lesbian.' I love the feeling of selfhood I've gotten from it. I hope I never lose it.''

These expressions of pride, joy, celebration, gratitude, and relaxed self-acceptance should serve to undo what is probably the most pervasive and insistent myth about homosexuality—that people who experience it are destined to be miserable and unhappy. For many gay people, this self-acceptance is like the proverbial light at the end of the tunnel. If it were a different kind of world, however, there would be no tunnel at all, and that is one of the goals of lesbians and gay men.

19

Feedback: Comments on the Survey

Praise, Enthusiasm, Joy, and Other Positive Reactions

Of course, most of the people who answered the survey were overwhelmingly enthusiastic about it. After all, if the survey totally disgusted them or annoyed them, they could simply tear it up or burn it; no one forced people to answer the questionnaire or to continue working on it once they had begun.

If the authors had not expected a predominantly positive response, they never would have undertaken the project to begin with. Yet, we must immodestly admit that the praise was more extensive than we expected. In addition to the initial enthusiastic response of people from all over the United States and Canada who agreed to help distribute the questionnaires, the authors also received many thank-yous scribbled on the backs and corners of the questionnaires, additional thank-you notes sent later, and much gracious praise when we specifically asked for feedback at the end of the questionnaire.

It must be said that we have been very grateful for the praise, encouragement, and support of so many anonymous people who answered the questionnaires. It was this support and trust which in part kept the authors going through months of poring over massive piles of material. And Karla and Allen also remembered how respondents mentioned over and over again the need for such a survey of gay people and by gay people.

But the purpose of this chapter is not just for the authors to pat themselves on the back. It is also to present criticisms and other comments the lesbians and gay men contributed to this survey. Since the response has been so favorable, the authors would first like to present comments from lesbians and gay men which demonstrate what those who responded learned from and felt about the survey.

♀"This is one the most thorough questionnaires I've ever seen. It's been a real turn-on. I hope you can organize such a conglomeration into a published work before I die of old age."

787

♂"I must say, that as an avid survey-hater (I hate surveys more than the average person, I think), this has been admittedly the best survey I've ever done. You leave no stones unturned in the sexuality sections and leave space enough in the other sections for one to answer thoroughly. I'm very impressed and pleased and wish you luck. Thank you for the opportunity."

♀"This questionnaire was a learning experience for me as well as for you. I've never thought of all my experiences as an entirety—as required in such questions as 'What was the scariest/funniest. . . ?' The question led me to search among my many experiences and see them all together instead of in separate bits and pieces. I found it a very welcome way of expressing myself. I guess the length of my answers and the time I've given it say a lot for the oppression I and all lesbians experience. It's like, finally, someone's interested in what a lesbian really is—finally a chance to express oneself, and for a worthwhile reason. Finally a chance to hopefully add to others' understanding of lesbianism."

♂"I am fairly well impressed with your questionnaire, although I didn't like your tendency to overcategorize (that is, restrict your alternatives) and at times I felt that I was being led to a certain answer. Writing about my sexual experiences has always been a turn-on for me, and some of the more detailed descriptions I've written almost led me to orgasm (in fact, I found it easier to write after I'd masturbated).

"When I first started to fill the questionnaire out, I did get a little angry about what I looked at as an invasion of my privacy. I had to sit myself down and tell myself that I did agree to answer it, and if I saw it as an invasion, then I could stop at any point. Also, this is the first chance I have ever had to reflect over my entire sexual history, and some parts were quite revealing, particularly recalling my sexual attitudes and practices in childhood and how they've evolved to being part of who I am today. It's really quite a thrilling experience!

"I congratulate you on your work. It is important that society recognize homosexuality as an alternate lifestyle rather than a thorn in its side, and information and education projects such as this are a good step in providing awareness. I thank you for the opportunity to participate."

♀"I liked answering this—it took me about eight hours! But it was well worth it. I appreciate the opportunity of expressing my feelings at length. I especially like to answer the questions about roles and about bisexuality, because having to think carefully about them made me understand my changing processes better. Writing about my hangups turned me on. I got excited and almost got up and went to masturbate. Maybe I'll do this now. Also answering the questions about doing specific sex acts turned me on. I feel good after answering because I know that telling the truth about my life and my feelings can only help other people who are going to put the book together, and eventually the women who will read the book. Right on, people! Keep up the good work. *All I said is absolutely true.*"

♂"Thank you—I took a good look at myself. I thought all the way through it. I reflected on my own life, on my future. One thing even

changed in the ten days I've taken to write the various pages—I went to the baths for the first time and was very carnal in the sauna! I'm growing and changing. I should take this 'test' again in a year! Thank you again for your help and positive approach!''

♀''Thank goodness there is, at last, a questionnaire such as this. Most such information about gay people, both men and women, seems to come from psychiatric reports and police records. No wonder we have such a bad image. This type of questionnaire coming from lesbians who are not in mental institutions, jails, or under psychiatric care should give a much truer picture than has ever before been known.

''I am a gay person, a lesbian. My feelings of love, sex, and affection are oriented towards other lesbians. I am as much a part of this nation as any other person who exists. A vast variety of people make up our great nation, which was founded over 200 years ago on the basis of equality and freedom for all of its citizens. Every citizen must protect these rights. Because of my sexual orientation, and only because of my sexual orientation, I have never been able to enjoy the equality and freedom that most of our citizens do. Many laws exist that oppress me. Many false ideas about me exist that condemn me. In the common interests of the freedom of our nation, I ask each citizen to take a few minutes to think about homosexuality and endeavor to sort fact from myth.''

♂''I love your questionnaire. I am a writer (part-time) and relate to the written word. I also believe that writing is the greatest therapeutic device known to man. When a famous love affair of mine broke up after twenty years, I saved my sanity by keeping a diary and writing all my thoughts. This questionnaire has made me think about a lot of things I always took for granted. If it is of no use to you in your survey, rest assured that it has been a great help to me. I can't wait to read the book. Since this is anonymous and you want the whole truth, I must confess that at one point I had to stop writing and go jack off. It was fun. The whole thing made me feel good, and not just sexually. It also gave me a better idea of what I was all about—and I thought I already knew. Who knows, I may sashay down to the local gay bar tonight and pick up a hunky stud. I probably won't, but the idea is there.''

♀''Answering the survey made me feel not just more positive about my lesbianism, but gave me the desire to become more politically involved with other gay/lesbian organizations. Thank you for the time, energy, and concern that you have given and are yet to give, in making this survey a completed effort.''

♂''Best wishes for your success! I truly hope the information provided you gives us a chance to show the reader we are really 'just like the boy next door' because we *are* the boy/man next door and only happen to love someone of the same sex. Otherwise, our hopes and dreams and aspirations and livelihood are just the same as theirs. Our straight counterparts are alike in every respect—except who they happen to go to bed with.''

♀''This questionnaire stirred old thoughts and feelings, made me

consciously acknowledge things that had up until now only been floating around in my head, and has been a great catharsis. I love talking about myself! Also, I'm willing to share more or expand on any of this if you'd like, but I'm tired right now. I guess I'm thinking that you won't get many answers from small-town lesbians (North Dakota especially) and I could expand on my views of the lesbian community as I experienced it there."

⚥ "This questionnaire is excellent. It is very inclusive, and the questions are good and insightful. I did this questionnaire more for my own purposes than for your purposes. For me, it was a review of my own sexual history. I was angry only with the length and extent of the questionnaire and only because it was demanding of my time. I also think a lot of people who should answer it won't because of the amount of time it takes. I didn't answer it as thoroughly as I could have because of the time element, but it has been valuable to me for a review of myself. A friend of mine, by the way, asked if I designed it since I often ask the same kinds of questions of friends or tricks or lovers. Good luck with the results and compilations of information."

⚥ "I have enjoyed this questionnaire greatly and feel that I have gained new insights into myself and the whole subject of human sexuality. It has seemed like a panoramic review of my life to date. Some of it has not been pleasant to bring back to memory, yet much of it has. Although I have 'written volumes,' I have had to do it hurriedly because I did it at work whenever I could spare the time rather than complete it at home and upset my wife with these enclosed soul baring revelations. We have reached a new intimacy and honesty and our relationship has never been better, yet there are some personal facts one should never reveal to anyone (that you care about) but that can only be told anonymously in this manner. I am saddened also by the anonymity and also feel reluctant to 'cut this off' and mail it. I wish I could meet with you, the reader, and get your reactions to this, my very personal profile, and answer your questions. I have written all these things down as if confessing them to a trusted friend. I look upon you as a friend, even though I know I will never meet you.

"When I finished Part I, I felt like mailing it in and ignoring the essay part. I couldn't seem to write down the intimate details of the first question and get started, so I skipped it and started writing on the second question. I still figured I would skip most of the questions and dispose of it very quickly. As I wrote—and wrote—I found I had the desire to answer all questions, and it had a particular allure to me. I couldn't seem to stop pouring out my soul on paper. I suppose I was benefiting from the therapeutic effects of a thorough confession.

"All those who put this questionnaire together knew what they were doing. It is very incisive and thorough. Some of you really know 'the scene.' I know your published results will be enlightening and beneficial to your future readers and I look forward to your publication."

♀ "Wow, I sure didn't mean to take all this space, but I'm very opinionated. I think it was very well written—that is, the questions in the

essay part, since writing on one topic led very naturally to the next one, and I didn't have to reorganize my thoughts too much.''

♂"This questionnaire is 'the best.' Every secret I have ever felt was worth keeping is revealed—gladly. Reading was an education and a trip. Sometimes I laughed; sometimes I cried—and I can cry if I want to—and sometimes I became sentimental and nostalgic. The multiple-choice section was easy to fill in, though very often I had to stop and think. I am not sure whether I would take a pill to make me straight. It took me several hours to fill out the essay questions. I surely didn't notice but you covered a lot of territory. This questionnaire will remain one of the most significant records of my life (I've made a copy), probably the most significant. Thank you for the opportunity to participate. This survey has helped to make me prouder.''

♀"I would not have spent a whole afternoon pounding away at the typewriter putting out nine single-spaced pages if I didn't think this was a good questionnaire! (It's a bit redundant in places, but it's very good.) I think your project is important and long overdue. The whole thing is very thought-provoking. I rarely have occasion to think about my lesbianism so fully and so carefully.''

♂"I liked the questionnaire. It helped me orient my thoughts about what I like and dislike in the gay world. I still am unsure about some of my 'ratings' because I think that it depends upon the other person, whether I like to 'fuck him' or 'get fucked.' Those questions made me stop and think.

"I also think I could never allow anyone to read my answers if they knew me, although I think that whoever *does* read my answers may think I'm stuck up or categorize me as a perfect example of 'something'—that's my only hesitation in mailing it in. Or I feel that maybe my experiences or descriptions are so commonplace that they will be thrown in the 'reject pile' after ten seconds of preliminary perusing! Nevertheless, I enjoyed putting into words things that had been in my mind, but which I had never put down on paper.''

♀"I started this survey about a month ago, maybe even longer. I know that in the last couple of weeks a lot has happened that would affect the way I might answer some of the questions, so I didn't read them over before I started to answer this question. I figured I would let the answers stand as they are: I answered honestly.

"It's hard to pin down how I feel about the survey. It was one of the most informative things I have done in a long time because I kept finding out new things about myself and my lover. I have enjoyed answering it. I don't think there was enough interest in the political feelings of the wimmin answering. Admittedly some wimmin might shy away from revealing too much about their political beliefs through the U.S. mails. Answering almost all of the survey turned me on. It was a truly great sexual experience because it was unusual in that it was entirely in my head. I allowed my head to spend long periods of time considering the questions: that felt good and free. Thank you: I used this survey to help my head a lot. I hope you get the

pleasure out of reading that I got out of writing it. And I finally figured out what fist-fucking is after I saw the Timex ad in the *National Lampoon*.''

♂ "This questionnaire could probably be the best thing for homosexuality since *The Kinsey Report*. By thoughtfully answering the questions, I have learned a great deal about myself and I have come to love myself a little bit more because of it. For this I am grateful. I did not answer the section on relationships because I didn't have much to contribute—maybe later. This part made me feel bad. The question on cocksucking and jocks and jockey shorts made me feel excited. The question on coming out and acceptance made me feel good—'Lord God Almighty, free at last!' Through this questionnaire I have accepted my sexuality more than I could have hoped. It has taken me a month or more of reading the questions, thinking about the answers, and then jotting them down. I'm beginning to know that happiness is a way of traveling. These questions and answers have helped me. I truly hope they can help others. My best wishes to the reader—you know me better than anyone else on earth. I think I love you.''

♀ "I enjoyed your questionnaire. It made me face the fact that my sex life with my partner has deteriorated. We discussed this. She is also filling out your questionnaire, and we will try to get our life together better in that aspect. Otherwise, we are very happy living as a gay couple. Thanks!''

♂ "I think your questionnaire is one of the best I have ever participated in, as evidence of which I have spent these five full days at it (especially over refinement of my answers to Part II). One thing that particularly appeals to me is the fact that, unlike most surveys that I have participated in, you have avoided questions related to the age-old subject of the 'causes' of homosexuality—such things as 'Was your father domineering?' or 'Was your mother domineering?' Such questions are related to highly speculative theories and are completely boring and unimportant, especially to anyone like me who is convinced that it is caused by my genes, thus innate, or if influenced by environmental conditions or happenings these during gestation, birth, or the very early years of childhood—and so what? There I was and here I am!''

♀ "I enjoyed filling out this questionnaire. It seemed to touch on most areas and also gave the opportunity to discuss some things in depth. It made me think about several things that I hadn't really given much thought to before. It was good to try to organize my thoughts about them and put them on paper. I was turned on by the questions asking for details on sexual acts, and I felt good talking about how far I've come in my self-acceptance. It makes me angry to think about the ways society oppresses gays.

"M. and I read each other's answers, and this seemed to be good for us both. We were able to gain some insights in areas we hadn't discussed before and this may perhaps lead to a little more openness in discussing sexual matters. I have made a carbon of my answers so I can look back at them later and see if I've changed my opinions. I have respect for the work

of Karla Jay and Allen Young. I met Allen at a Gay Activists Alliance Conference in Washington, D.C., and like his feminist viewpoint, so I felt positive about making a contribution to their work. I'm looking forward to seeing the results.''

♀"I think it's about time we were allowed to define ourselves for others rather than have so-called 'experts' do it. I hope people will see that there is a great variety among us, just as in the general population. We share common problems related to our homosexuality, and ones that just about everyone has—what am I going to do with my life, what color am I going to paint my living room, or should I buy Right Guard or Ban? I sure did get turned on recounting my past experiences with women. I feel good that I finally finished this, as I've had it about a month and half now.''

♂"In closing, I would like to say, thanks for letting me tell my story. Pass the word along that not all homosexuals are boy-rapists, child molesters, sadomasochists, murderers. There are some human beings too!''

Constructive Criticism, Gripes, Hesitations, Fears

Some people, although enthusiastic, offered criticisms of the questionnaire—which they were encouraged to do. The most repeated criticism of the questionnaire was that it was too long.

♂"My general reaction is summed up with the words, 'too long!' I completed it because I had gotten started into it and didn't want to leave it unfinished. I suspect many who might contribute some interesting and important things will not tackle it or stop long before completing it, for the reason they feel it is too long. I feel there are a number of ways some careful work could have streamlined this questionnaire. You should have consulted sociological researchers who know how to develop this kind of thing.''

♀"I think it's too long. I've spent about six hours on it and still haven't answered it fully enough. Normally I wouldn't have the time, but I'm on a long vacation at the moment and rose to the challenge of overcoming my inhibitions and writing specifically about sex. I also think that this written section restricts answers only to the articulate. That particularly applies to the first question, where I had real problems of vocabulary, and I imagine someone with less education than me would find it near impossible to be specific, which is a judgment more of society than of you.''

♂"Sorry I don't have the time to answer all your questions. You are like the man who wrote on the piss-house wall: 'I want 13 inches.' Someone answered him: 'You want too much.' Much love to you and good luck.''

♀"The questionnaire took me three days. I almost ripped it up in Part I, as you can see from the condition of the pages! I felt like screaming, *'It is too long!'* Do you know what it is like to dredge your brain and your soul for answers like these? Some of my answers are incoherent; some incomplete. It is just too much to ask of any individual. I wish you luck, but I don't know how many can *endure* this questionnaire.''

Another common criticism was that the questionnaire focused too much on sex. The authors agree somewhat with this criticism, but we also feel like the person who yells, "Sex," and then says, "Now that I have your attention. . . ." Certainly starting off with sexual questions did grab the attention of many, although the authors realized that practically any approach or opening would turn off some people. Anyway, here are some comments of people who felt there was too much emphasis on sex in the questionnaire.

♂ "Your questionnaire seemed to overemphasize the physical side of being sexually gay. I think you might be of better service to gay people if you delved into attitudes and feelings rather than the physical positions or ointments used during sex. Also, I think you omitted any real and deep sort of questions about people who happen to be living with a lover. I should think their answers might be more meaningful than from those who may not have ever had a lover, but only brief washroom encounters, or who only visit the 'tearoom.' Answering some of the questions did not turn me on. Some of it made me feel like the answers were none of your business except for cheap-thrill purposes."

♀ "Though I enjoy well-written pornography, I am bored when I try to write it, so a number of the questions in Part II seem to me too tedious to deal with. Positions and parts of bodies, techniques, seem of very little interest in themselves, a dulling of the sense of sexuality I have had. It has never been part of my pleasure to want to recount a sexual experience, though to relive it as part of a masturbation fantasy can be very pleasant, even to share it again with a lover by writing it in a letter. My desire to be 'useful,' to add to information about lesbian sexuality, is in conflict with some need to protect the wonder of my sexual life, the intense happiness of fulfilled desire. Just as it is hard for most people to analyze a poem and leave their pleasure in it intact, so to try to analyze lovemaking can seem to leave out the essence of it. I feel dutiful about the questionnaire and reluctant."

♀ "As I have been doing this survey, I have found my feelings of being turned off now have become anger. You do not stress how much two people could care/love each other, but rather stress what your scorecard reads! At first, I was not answering questions because I was not sure of my feelings or did not have experiences in the various categories, but the more I've gotten into this survey the more I have elected *not* to answer some of the questions that I feel are no one else's business except that of me and my mate. I also find your neutral terms offensive. You never mention terms such as 'mate' or 'spouse.' Third, when you deal with the question of orgasm, you deal with numbers and positions, not with something that is important such as touching between two people who care can be as rewarding with or without an orgasm and without the need or feeling that the person who did not reach an orgasm has to masturbate. You should have also asked questions about day-to-day problems, friction, etc., and about nonverbal communication."

♂ "I believe you have concentrated far too much on the merely physical

in your questionnaire. While it is refreshing to see you so frank, I think you are one-sided. We all know how to suck cock, fuck, etc., but very few of us know how to make a relationship click. You could contribute to making gay relations more human, not so physical.''

♀"I was offended by this questionnaire. With my head set to find out about myself as a lesbian, or to explore that topic, I was disappointed to find that most of the questions did not pertain to me, lesbian though I am. The offense, however, comes by way of the feeling that the 'meat market' orientation of the questionnaire is in fact the very root of most of the prejudice against gays. I am sure this is a valid characterization of some small group of gays (and straights)—a primary focus of their lives. As such, I'm sure it is scientifically worthy of study, but not, I think, politically worthy. I neither deny nor am offended by explicitness regarding my sex life, but I resent explicitness being equated with objectivity, materialism, and list-making. For instance, instead of scaling from always to never, you might use the options: (1) would never consider this; (2) all right for others but not for me; (3) have in the past, not now; (4) sometimes; (5) usually. Being scientific about a questionnaire does not necessarily mean being insensitive to the way people think.

"Also the sex-techniques section might have been done with drawings—the meaning of the words when devoid of emotional content as they are in the questionnaire is changed. It is naive to think meaning resides in syllables alone. Drawings might incorporate the emotional impact essential to the meanings of these items.''

♂"I almost threw away the questionnaire after I began to read through it. I think it is prurient and largely meaningless. If we are eager to convince people that what we do in the bedroom (or elsewhere) and with whom (or what) is largely irrelevant, then why this preoccupation with those precise issues?''

There was also a spectrum of other complaints, constructive criticism, and negative feelings.

♀"This questionnaire was very nosy.''

♀"This questionnaire was too voyeuristic.''

♂"Honest surveys dealing with intimate sexuality can only be done in personal interviews.''

♂"At first I thought this questionnaire was a great idea. But over the days that I spent on it, I began to wonder. The biggest doubt came over me when I read a review of another book, in *QQ Magazine.* In it the reviewer was unable to determine for whom the book was intended. It was ridiculous if for gays, and full of too many stereotypes if to inform nongays. I am beginning to think that the book which will result from these questionnaires may be used for heterosexual proof-texting. 'See, I told you that is what they were like . . . they say so themselves!' Of course, there is no way to control who reads a book, and there probably shouldn't be.''

♀"I dunno. Is this questionnaire written by faggots? It seems literal, narrow, too much emphasis on what parts of the body are used, very little on love. It seems to see things as absolutes, not as circles, changing-type things. It didn't mention varying types of orgasms—a male perception. It didn't mention aloneness, which I'm sure is a thing that happens to lesbians more than other people. I think it tempts people to lie. I know when I filled out the multiple-choice part, I made believe I was an active lesbian."

♂"This questionnaire reminds me of some exams I've taken. It becomes tedious and to break the monotony I became flippant, although not unserious."

♀"Your questions are basically good, but several questions were asked more than once, and were irrelevant, and also I *hate* the term 'lesbian.' "

♂"The questionnaire is far too long and repetitive, and I'm even sorrier to say, not very well written. That is, not very well planned. I found in answering it that I was naturally led into saying things in my answers to the second part that you didn't explicitly ask for until later. Shotgun-style, not very well organized. Neither part seemed to me really *pertinent* in the sense of asking me questions that really helped me formulate my thinking. In the first part I found the multiple-choice format maddeningly vague, and I think the use of uniform choices for the answers for each question is unnecessarily constricting. Of course, no one forced me to answer the whole bloody, great, long thing, but it's taken me months, on and off, and surely at least ten hours total of my time to answer all of Part II. I think you'd have done much better to ask for optional comments, or ask amplificatory questions tied to each (or some of) the multiple-choice part, and then ask a few much better-written and selected essay-type questions. Also you didn't include a deadline, and if after I've done all this work, mine gets in too late to be tabulated, I'll be pissed (if I find out)."

♀"I thought the questionnaire to be very inclusive, except that being (pardon the expression) an old hand at masturbation, I found that section rather skimpy."

♀"This questionnaire depressed me because N. and I have a lousy sex life."

♂"I feel that somehow the romantic aspect of this questionnaire has been down-pedaled. Granted you ask if I have been in love, but somehow the whole thing seems to be slanted more toward physical, sexual activities. I personally don't have these particular feelings, but how about things like walks along the beach; romantic feelings; the look of the lights across the Delaware River (Johnny, Philadelphia, 1962); sharing the interests of your friend (he likes art and flowers; I like machinery); the employment and interest interactions of potential lovers; reasons for divorce; the lengths of marriages and why they broke up. In other words, all of the nonhomosexual aspects of gay life. I feel that homosexuals are really not that different from heteros, and it is only the fact that they (not we) are all bunched up in a separate world that makes them think they are different. I would dig a bunch of questions that bring out how nondifferent the lives of

gays are when the sex activity is left out. My straight and gay friends are of all nationalities, religions, politics. I respect that many of these questions *were* asked, but not enough.''

♀"The questions made me angry. I resent having my privacy so totally disrupted. I resent having to think about these things when I need the time to relax with my daughter. I resent having to fight this way for the right to my existence.''

♂"The comment in the introduction about the study being 'non-scientific' sort of turned me off. I would *prefer* that the data I submit be handled by social scientists.''

♂"I resent your insistence on anonymity. I think the answerer should be given the option of remaining anonymous, but that decision should be his and not yours. There could well be particular opinions or experiences which are of special interest for the purposes of your book, but which really need clarification or additional detail—and by insisting on anonymity, you preclude any such follow-up.''

♀"I was confused by some of the questions in the short-answer section that asked how you feel about something, even if you did not do it. I wasn't sure if the question was how did I feel about these things for *myself* or for *other* people. There are many things *I* don't care to do, but don't care who else does; on the other hand, there are things I'm against no matter who does them. I'm afraid I wasn't very consistent in the sense in which I answered these questions sometimes for myself, sometimes for others (mostly the latter), or all mixed together. You should have made it clear which you wanted, or included separate categories for both.''

♂"The great fallacy of surveys of this kind is that the surveyors only receive the written word. The inflections, gestures, speech mannerisms all are lost, and these, more times than not, offer more information as to feelings, opinions, and true orientation than the words themselves. I trust you have the ability to scan the words and eke out the real meaning behind them. No answer can be given in strict verbal terms. As humans, we just don't act in that manner. I trust you realize this deficiency and will adjust your compilations with that fact in mind.''

♀"The only problem I had with this questionnaire was the intrinsic assumption of more than one lesbian lover. I'm hung up sometimes on what 'makes' me a lesbian. I have no interest in men physically, except to hug or kiss close friends. I find pictures or descriptions of intercourse revolting. Yet I kept feeling that maybe I shouldn't be answering your questionnaire because it assumed so much more experience than I had. Some of that is just a hangover from the days of being very promiscuous, and it's hard to throw away that identity. I was a very active and experimental heterosexual, and I am a very monogamous novice lesbian. They don't go together very well in my head.''

A few people did not answer the essay section at all, and sent along explanations of why they felt they could not do so.

♀"Your series of questions in Part II of the survey are devastating to think of answering in written form—taped answers might be more feasible."

♂"I feel that I have neither the time nor the inclination to answer the questions in the second part, especially since most of the section is just a repeat of former questions. I got the feeling that Part II is not so much a survey as it is an effort to gather pornographic material. Part II would also require several more hours, which I do not have to spare."

♀"I think that your survey is of sex without emotional involvement and I don't think there is any such thing so I didn't answer Part II. Men may do it, but they are empty plugs anyway. Women only think we're doing it when we need to not feel our own aliveness. Man's world has kicked life out of us and made us feel like death (deadness) is 'normal' and 'good.' As lesbians, we are saying 'No' to the ethic of violence and are remembering the real one of women. *This* is lesbian sexuality because a whole self is not cut up into parts. Do not be a voyeur of my spirit—join me in working and living. Make new truths, yes. But make them from living, not from statistics or behavior, please."

In addition to those who would not answer Part II, a small group of self-avowed 'lesbian separatists' (lesbians who will have nothing to do with any men or straight women) refused to answer this questionnaire, and in fact, even attacked Karla for working with a man on this questionnaire. They also objected to the fact that lesbian and gay male sexuality would be portrayed in one book, and that "pricks" would be allowed to buy the book. They also accused Karla of inviting men into lesbians' bedrooms and of giving information to the "enemy." In total about five letters of this nature were received.

All the letters were personally answered by Karla, and in fact, she tried to discuss the matter with a group of women in Northampton, Mass., who signed one letter, but they did not take her up on her offer. Here are some excerpts from one of Karla's replies:

"Thank you for your letter and for keeping your disagreements with my work to a sisterly tone. I understand and respect your work and have a lot of sympathy as well as empathy for lesbian separatism. However, for every letter like yours that I've gotten, I've received literally a hundred letters overjoyed at the questionnaires, from women thrilled at having an opportunity to communicate with other lesbians about sexuality and other important matters, excited at the knowledge they've gained about lesbians in general and themselves in particular, through participating in the questionnaire. All over the country, women, as did the women in your group, are discussing the questionnaire, are discussing sex seriously for the first time (often people write it's the first time they've discussed sex with their lovers!). If all my work does is to aid this communication, I feel all my effort so far has done a lot of good. Also, this overwhelmingly positive

response convinces me that this book will be needed, enjoyed, and appreciated by the overwhelming majority of lesbians. I know lesbian separatists won't answer the questionnaire, but however valid your views, you represent a minority.

"While you think that the book will invite straight men into our bedrooms, you should realize that having gay men in the book might actually *discourage* that type of straight man from reading the book because they will be 'turned off' by gay men. Also, since this book will represent the actual experiences of lesbians, rather than the macho fantasies of straight men, they won't find it exciting. And let me finally point out that even were this book all-lesbian, and put out by a lesbian press, straight men could still buy it. When I was in a lesbian bookstore, I saw *only* men buying *Loving Women* (a lesbian sex manual for lesbians).

"As I said, I feel very encouraged by the positive responses of the lesbians everywhere to this book idea. If I could show you their letters without breaking promised anonymity, I would. I take your criticism in good spirit, although, of course, I wish you and your sisters felt differently. In fact, I encourage you to answer the questionnaires—especially the essay questions about sex and politics, so that your opinions can be printed in the book, which is really a forum for all sorts of opinions. Please consider that option. As I said, I sympathize with your viewpoint, and am willing to publish your objections and your philosophy. I also understand what might seem to be the contradictions of your including them in such a book."

A brief debate about the questionnaire also appeared in the letters page of *The Lesbian Connection,* a lesbian newsletter, after some of the "contact dykes" (women in various states who make their addresses known to traveling lesbians) received copies of the questionnaires. They attacked the questionnaire as "offensive," and questioned where the profits would go. Much to Karla's surprise, several women wrote defending her in the next issue (Karla has on occasion been attacked in the press, but she is not used to being defended!). An unsigned letter in *The Lesbian Connection* from Syracuse replied in part: "Who gives a shit who publishes it? The important thing is that it *will* be published. I get more than a little tired of people who *expect* to share in the results of others' work. Why should Karla Jay pass out her profits, if any, which come from her work? The point is, she's a gay woman who's doing lots of alternative things which will ultimately help and benefit all of us. I applaud her energy, her ability, and her sense of responsibility to herself and the gay community. I consider myself lucky that she and other women do the work from which I can learn. If you can't or won't take the time to do the survey, give it to someone who can or will. Then don't complain when the results do not reflect your viewpoint, lifestyle, or philosophy."

Stacey Franchild of *The Albatross* collective (a New Jersey-based lesbian satire magazine) also wrote *The Lesbian Connection* in part: "It (the survey) helped us to focus on many of the problems in the lesbian community and in ourselves. We trust that Karla will use the information to the

advantage of the lesbian community (and she has done more than enough to earn our trust), and while we, too, would prefer to see anything relating to our lives published by lesbians, we also know that sometimes this is not yet possible. Time given to further our knowledge of ourselves and to educate interested others is never wasted, and the questionnaire provided ample opportunity for criticism and requested additional feedback and information—so how can we fault the compilers for leaving out questions when we are unwilling to assist her in her efforts? We have been fed misinformation by the straight world about 'what lesbians do' for a very long time and we need as much lesbian representation as we can get—Karla is not a 'creep' but rather a dedicated lesbian woman who has worked long and hard for us, and this is a fine opportunity to repay some of her efforts. . . . If the questions are offensive to you, then it will be a learning experience to examine your attitudes as to why questions about our sexuality should be offensive.''

Allen too received his share of criticism, mostly based on questions about the methodology, which the authors have explained in the first chapter of this book.

Suggestions for Additional Topics

Although one lesbian wrote, ''If anyone can find something you've left out, she should be given a prize,'' a number of people came up with questions the authors either hadn't thought of or hadn't included for reasons or space or priority. While we cannot answer all of the questions here, some of the answers can be found by reading other gay male and lesbian books and periodicals. We are also confident that gay male and lesbian writers will be producing more books in the future. A good source for information is the *Gayellow Pages* (Box 292, Village Station, New York, N.Y. 10014), which lists periodicals, mail-order book services, bookstores, businesses, services, and so on.

♂''You should have included some questions about how we feel about gay community, gay arts and letters, gay publications (not as bad as they could be despite general lack of intelligence). The thing that rankles my ass is the disgusting puerility of most gay entertainment, not to speak of its sedulous aping of black entertainment, and always the worst of it. You just can't know how sick I am of goddam disco music and stupid stage plays like *The Faggot* and revivals of *The Boys in the Band*. As far as I can see, the gay influence on the arts is primarily insipid.''

♀''I would like to see questions such as: 'Do you resent men?' 'Have you been raped by a man?' 'Do you think the way you were raised is responsible for your being a lesbian?' 'Is there a choice in whether to be gay or straight?' ''

♂ ''I feel that you have omitted dealing with the pain of getting fucked in the ass.''

♀"I would like to see more information on nonfeminist practices, especially in lovemaking that I know are carried out in relationships. I would also like to see more on lesbian mothers and on gay rights for women, not just men."

♂"One aspect you never asked about that I consider very important is *gay spirituality*—that elusive, almost mystical spirituality we can share as gay people—a certain awareness of spiritual dimensions that is more available to us, somehow, some way."

♀"While you list a lot of faggot stuff, habits and outlook, there is no question about *communication,* whether or not emotion is involved. Even among straight women, how we talk to each other is a major key to how we *can* relate! As long as we talk diapers and TV soaps and PTA, we will not liberate ourselves. In that respect, the women's movement has been very effective. Also, how lovers talk to each other is indicative of how they love. Also there should be specific questions regarding the success or lack of it and preference regarding 69, or mutual oral sex, for most sex writings are either fuzzy on this or treat it too lightly. I have yet to achieve success here because I can't get into giving and taking at the same time with a female, so T. and I leave it alone mostly. Does emotional involvement make a difference here? I have not been able to check it out, but I would think that the less I cared for a person, the more successful I would be, either because I was trying to *please* rather than *love* another, and because I would be less reveling in their feelings for me. This is true for me in orgies versus one-on-one with a male, for instance. Also you do not address ERA or abortion directly in the political section; whether or not you intend to bear children, as a woman I think you have a view on the implications of both these law structures, present and future. I oppose ERA because it is too vague and I think it will be misused. I definitely support abortion (and sought one myself for my sixth and last child, which I do not regret per se as a quest, but am glad to know her as a person now) because I think children should be wanted and that the woman is more important than one potential life."

♀"I'd like to see a question on whether you were born a lesbian. If not, how did you arrive at becoming a lesbian? I explained mine: I was born bisexual. The way men are helped turn me into a lesbian."

♂"I'd like more information on what is needed to make a primary ongoing relationship work well. Please advise."

♀"Aside from bars, how does one meet other lesbians? Do you know?"

♂"Where are all the good men?"

♀"Where are other rural lesbians?"

♂"I would like to see more on gay marriages. Most gays are, I believe, relating to wives and children. Also there is not enough on overcoming fears of self-acceptance of one's gayness, difficulties in finding partners, information on gay therapy, loneliness, etc."

♀"As a lesbian, I would like more information on fantasies and on power relationships and sex."

⚦"I am interested in what straights think of gays and their lifestyle. I have a stack of clippings a foot high from twenty years of gay articles in straight papers."

♀"I would like to see more on lesbians in the army and in private schools. (Incidentally, I went to a private school for a few years and didn't find a surplus of gay women there, unfortunately!)"

⚦"Omitted question: 'What are the advantages of being gay?' David Loovis recites some in *Gay Spirit* that I pretty much agree with, but to me the most important is being a male-lover in a male world. Although women are gaining greater equality, at present I can enjoy voyeuristically watching sports events, and in general moving in male society while more or less perpetually cruising."

⚦"I would like more information on nonmonogamous relationships and how those involved work them out."

♀"We need a national list of the brands of orange juice containing Florida orange juice, so we can boycott them."

⚦"I would have liked to see more on voyeurism and exhibitionism. Also more on trends in 'pop sex'—how do they change, how are they different from 'high sex,' who invents them?"

♀"I would like to see more about lesbian experiences with doctors, especially gynecologists and obstetricians. I found a female gyn that I feel great about. I've never felt better about a doctor. I would also like to see more on attitudes about bras. Also more on occurrences and attitudes and affects of being 'missexed'—having people think you are the sex you're not."

⚦"I would like more information on the idea of interrelationships between gay men and women and why there seems to be such a dislike for the women by so many gay men. They are cutting off a great part of life by excluding females and their ideas and companionship."

♀"Other questions: 'How important do you consider moments that don't always lead to sex, such as hugging, cuddling, discussion of current events, others?' 'How often do you wish a partner gave you more time to yourself?' 'Would you find it difficult to accept if your lover/partner asked you for more time alone?' "

⚦"I would like to know if the figure 10% of the population being gay is not erroneous. I've felt all my life it should have been higher."

♀"There is one area that I have not seen explored or discussed in print, namely the cause, effect, frequency, and significance, if any, of *splits*. It is possible that gay-community splits are more frequent or different than in nongay society, but it might be interesting to learn some of the specifics. There are some very long-lived relationships, too, but what are some of the dynamics involved with those who split once—or many times? What is the average 'recovery' time, and how is it handled, emotionally?"

⚦"I would like to have more information on how to unblock past ex-

periences that have possibly hampered my being gay and also how to get more enjoyment from sexual relations. How to be a conscious gay man. How to deal with lesbians more effectively. How to relate the problems and/or situations of life to being gay.''

♀"I think that you could have included more questions about parents and parents' reactions and attitudes. A person's environmental and cultural background, were they brought up to think that homosexuality was bad, wrong, or sinful, etc. or were they told that it is a normal lifestyle? I was taught that gay people are normal.''

♂"I'd like to know why we are gay.''

♀"Other questions: 'What would you do if your lover became an invalid?' 'What would you do if, for some reason, your friend became financially dependent on you?' 'What would you do if for some reason, such as sickness, it was impossible to have a proper sex life for a long time?' 'Do you think that you really love her? Does this mean that you would devote your whole life to her?' ''

♀"I'd like to see more about older gays—40 and over.''

♀"I'd like to see what other lesbians are doing politically. How do they view separatism? In an ideal world would there be categories of sexuality (gay/bi/straight)?''

♀"I'd like to find out more about the prison situation—I've always wondered what was true and what wasn't.''

♀"I would like more information on lesbian communities now in existence and how they are getting along. I would like to know what matriarchies have been in the past and are in existence today. I would like to know about cleaving and how two women can have children together. I also want to be informed on the gay rights process and which states are making headway and how.''

♀"I'd like more information on platonic lesbian relationships and on lesbian celibacy.''

♀"Other questions: 'Do you compete against other women for a woman? Whether you do or not, how do you feel about competing?' 'Do you read lesbian publications and/or listen to lesbian records? Which ones?' I do all I can!''

As the writers of some of these questions will have seen by now, many *are* answered in this book. For others it might take an encyclopedia to deal with them effectively. However, any gay person who would like to answer these questions and/or all or any parts of the survey printed in this book is invited to participate in this undertaking for future books. (The authors will also try to include in future works questionnaires that arrived too late for this book.) Finally, we welcome feedback on any part of this book from any reader, whether homosexual or heterosexual. The authors will try their

utmost to answer any and all letters, if the writer requests us to. Please enclose a self-addressed stamped envelope. Anonymous comments or responses to the surveys are also welcome.

All queries, comments, and answers to the questionnaires or to the questions in this section should be addressed to: Survey, P.O. Box 98, Orange, Mass. 01364.

Appendix
A Profile of the Respondents

The following charts show the socio-demographic factors for all the respondents who answered the questions. Most of the charts list the actual number of respondents, not percentages. Since not all respondents answered every question, the total for each chart may be different. In addition, if a respondent did not answer enough questions in the socio-demographic section, his or her responses were not tabulated. These figures are based on a total of 962 lesbian questionnaires and 4,329 gay male questionnaires. The gay male statistics include socio-demographic information from the abridged *Blueboy* magazine questionnaires, even though *Blueboy* respondents were not used for the statistical sample reflected in the other tables in *The Gay Report*. It was determined that the men who responded to the *Blueboy* questionnaire did not differ in any substantial way from the men who sent in the other questionnaires. However, some of the socio-demographic questions were not included in the *Blueboy* questionnaire, and these are indicated in this appendix by means of an asterisk (*).

TABLE 1
Residence of Respondents

United States and Territories	Lesbians	Gay Men
Alabama	0	13
Alaska	2	10
Arizona	11	37
Arkansas	4	12
California	191	641
Colorado	9	64
Connecticut	12	59

Delaware	2	5
District of Columbia	17	67
Florida	20	131
Georgia	6	50
Hawaii	2	27
Idaho	3	5
Illinois	25	207
Indiana	6	62
Iowa	7	39
Kansas	5	40
Kentucky	4	22
Louisiana	2	65
Maine	12	38
Maryland	19	62
Massachusetts	72	229
Michigan	17	152
Minnesota	18	73
Mississippi	0	10
Missouri	12	53
Montana	2	11
Nebraska	1	11
Nevada	0	11
New Hampshire	8	18
New Jersey	24	96
New Mexico	7	26
New York	136	574
North Carolina	11	54
North Dakota	1	4
Ohio	15	98
Oklahoma	5	31
Oregon	14	46
Pennsylvania	57	209
Puerto Rico	0	5
Rhode Island	9	19
South Carolina	2	27
South Dakota	0	9
Tennessee	5	27
Texas	33	184
Utah	0	8
Vermont	4	21
Virginia	21	78
Virgin Islands	0	6
Washington	13	72

West Virginia	0	17
Wisconsin	27	63

Canada

Alberta	0	26
British Columbia	15	68
Manitoba	0	4
Newfoundland	1	0
Nova Scotia	0	7
Ontario	15	140
Quebec	2	77
Saskatchewan	1	5
"Canadian"	1	2

Other

Europe and Caribbean	0	19
Africa and Asia	3	3

TABLE 2
*Size of Respondents' Community**

Note: This question is evidently based on the perception of the respondent. For example, if the respondent lives in a state where there are few cities, she or he may perceive her or his own city as being large whereas in actual population the city might technically be considered medium-sized or even small.

	Lesbians		Gay Men	
rural or small town	119	(13%)	189	(11%)
small city	132	(14%)	200	(11%)
medium-sized city	147	(16%)	294	(16%)
large city	164	(18%)	265	(15%)
major metropolitan area	287	(31%)	704	(39%)
suburb	75	(8%)	154	(9%)

TABLE 3
Number of Respondents Who Lived in Major Metropolitan Areas

	Lesbians	Gay Men
Atlanta	3	33
Boston	45	124

Chicago	15	152
Dallas	3	42
Denver	6	41
Detroit	5	54
Houston	17	42
Los Angeles	57	179
Miami	4	27
Minneapolis	10	55
Montreal	2	55
New Orleans	0	37
New York	98	405
Philadelphia	26	84
Pittsburgh	12	44
San Francisco	41	214
Seattle	5	44
Toronto	13	86
Vancouver	5	47
Washington	16	66
Winnipeg	1	5

TABLE 4
Age of Respondents

	Lesbians	Gay Men
14 years	1	1
15	0	1
16	4	8
17	5	16
18	9	35
19	20	66
20	32	102
21	34	150
22	47	152
23	51	188
24	58	151
25	70	219
26	61	207
27	46	191
28	59	204
29	51	211
30	76	217
31	39	155
32	42	178
33	31	151

34	28	135
35	21	138
36	18	131
37	22	118
38	10	93
39	12	82
40	10	101
41	14	60
42	11	86
43	11	65
44	5	51
45	10	86
46	6	52
47	3	63
48	5	52
49	2	28
50	4	51
51	1	44
52	3	28
53	3	25
54	0	25
55	2	25
56	2	21
57	0	25
58	2	14
59	2	11
60	3	19
61	0	9
62	1	11
63	0	7
64	1	7
65	0	12
66	0	1
67	1	6
68	0	2
69	0	1
70	0	4
73	0	2
74	0	3
76	0	1
78	0	1
82	1	0
Average Age	29.7	30.7

TABLE 5
Respondents' Race or Ethnic Group

	Lesbians		Gay Men	
black	11	(1%)	93	(2%)
Oriental	2	(.2%)	20	(.5%)
Spanish American	15	(1.6%)	54	(1%)
white/Caucasian	758	(82%)	3444	(81%)
WASP	98	(11%)	422	(10%)
**Jewish	3	(0%)	215	(5%)
American Indian	2	(.2%)	11	(.3%)
other	11	(1%)	3	(0%)

**See also Table 6 on religious affiliations.

TABLE 6
Religious Affiliation of Respondents

Religious Upbringing	Lesbians	Gay Men
Baptist	53	282
Born Again Christian	0	1
Catholic, Roman	200	1346
Christian Scientist	5	25
Eastern (including Buddhism)	1	2
Episcopal/Anglican	53	243
Jewish (orthodox)	4	7
Jewish (other)	120	235
Lutheran	30	195
Methodist	69	293
Mormon	2	29
Pentacostal/Fundamentalist	23	102
Presbyterian	37	159
Quaker	11	13
Unitarian/Universalist	14	26
other	16	85
Christian (no denomination specified)	13	91
Protestant (no sect specified)	175	868
personal	1	1
agnostic	9	11
atheist	19	15
none	63	139

Current Religion	Lesbians	Gay Men
Baptist	5	74
Born Again Christian	2	3
Catholic, Roman	41	526
Christian Scientist	0	9
Church of Our Beloved Disciple	0	1
Eastern (including Buddhism)	25	88
Episcopal/Anglican	15	188
Humanist	4	27
Jewish (Orthodox)	1	1
Jewish (other)	34	105
Lutheran	10	60
Methodist	3	75
Metropolitan Community Church	26	102
Mormon	0	8
Pentacostal/Fundamentalist	2	27
Presbyterian	0	52
Quaker	13	18
Unitarian/Universalist	13	52
Wicca, Dianic, mystical/feminist	66	0
other	27	163
Christian (no denomination specified)	19	114
Protestant (no sect specified)	11	201
personal	104	151
agnostic	49	228
atheist	54	147
none	329	1352

TABLE 7
Educational Background of Respondents

	Lesbians		Gay Men	
some grade school	0	(0%)	7	(.2%)
completed grade school	2	(0%)	14	(.3%)
completed 9, 10, or 11 grades	19	(2%)	86	(2%)
completed 12 grades	56	(6%)	367	(9%)
some college	262	(28%)	1251	(29%)
college graduate	210	(22%)	816	(19%)
some graduate school	152	(16%)	629	(15%)
graduate degree	250	(26%)	1131	(26%)

TABLE 8
Income Level of Respondents

	Lesbians		Gay Men	
Under $5,000	340	(36%)	664	(16%)
Between $5,000 and $9,999	268	(29%)	830	(20%)
Between $10,000 and $14,999	184	(20%)	1034	(24%)
Between $15,000 and $24,999	121	(13%)	1074	(25%)
$25,000 or more	15	(2%)	552	(13%)
not sure	11	(2%)	72	(2%)

TABLE 9
Occupation of Respondents

Note: In this table, people are listed by primary occupation only. For example, if a woman is a student but also works as a waitress, she would be listed only as a student.

	Lesbians	Gay Men
Gay Industry		
employed by gay community organization	10	10
employed by gay bar or bath	0	7
employed in other gay business	2	7
work for gay male or lesbian paper	4	6
owner of a gay business	0	4
Arts		
writer	25	53
artist	5	30
musician	1	36
actor or actress	2	32
commercial artist	0	72
photographer	13	13
dancer	1	12
Academic		
college or university teacher	34	134
high school teacher (grades 7–12)	17	50

grammar school teacher	10	23
teacher (level not specified)	31	195
librarian	14	57
other academic-related work (registrar, housing officer, etc.)	17	46
student	195	437
researcher	14	24
scientist	4	28

Health-related Work

medical doctor	1	30
doctor—other (dental, etc.)	3	12
nurse (all levels), physician's assistant	40	55
other medical (medical secretary, x-ray technician, dental assistant, etc.)	24	72
therapist—occupational, physical	10	12
therapist—mental (psychiatrist, psychologist)	41	53
health administrator	3	15

Other "professional"

attorney/lawyer	7	51
other legal (legal aide, etc.)	4	15
engineering, drafting	1	54
clergy—gay-related	3	9
clergy—nongay-related	1	41
editor, producer (publishing, journalist; TV producer, director, or writer)	12	122
community worker (VISTA, etc.)	10	42
architect	0	33

Business

managerial	31	465
accounting	19	91
computer-related	15	81
sales	18	186
clerical (mail clerk, secretary, file clerk)	37	200
advertising (all levels except clerical)	17	57

Government

elected offficial	0	0
high-level political appointment	0	3

other government	8	125
fire department	1	3
police department	1	10
probation or parole	4	1
social worker	38	44
military, member of armed forces	10	25

Industrial Work

general factory work	11	70
skilled factory work (including welders, printers)	17	83

Other

entertainer—specifically gay	0	10
entertainer—not specifically gay	6	9
maintenance worker, custodial, delivery, security, driver, household technician	10	93
service worker (cook, waiter or waitress, restaurant host or hostess, bellboy)	21	157
auto work (mechanic, parts person, bodywork)	3	8
self-employed—nongay business	38	306
carpenter, plumber	7	19
parenting, "housewife"	5	2
hair stylist	0	57
unemployed	41	62
welfare	2	3
retired	4	56

TABLE 10
*Respondents' Relatives Who Are Lesbians or Gay Men**

	Lesbians	Gay Men
mother	7	9
father	6	29
sister	50	90
brother	48	237
grandparent	1	1
cousin, female	33	99
cousin, male	39	197
cousin, sex not specified	61	570

other relative, female	45	78
other relative, male	31	265
other relative, sex not specified	2	0
daughter	0	7
son	0	6
spouse	0	2

TABLE 11
*Respondents' Number of Sisters**

	Lesbians		Gay Men	
1	349	(60%)	666	(57%)
2	162	(28%)	331	(28%)
3	41	(7%)	101	(9%)
4	21	(4%)	53	(5%)
5	8	(1%)	13	(1%)
6 or more	4	(1%)	3	(.3%)

TABLE 12
*Respondents' Number of Brothers**

	Lesbians		Gay Men	
1	366	(56%)	668	(55%)
2	187	(29%)	318	(26%)
3	63	(10%)	144	(12%)
4	24	(4%)	52	(4%)
5	6	(1%)	17	(1%)
6 or more	7	(1%)	15	(1%)

TABLE 13
Respondents' Source of Questionnaire

	Lesbians	Gay Men
friend	194	317
ordered it from Karla Jay or Allen Young	72	188
community center	28	111
political bookstore	16	6
feminist or other political group	18	5

march or conference	62	106
women's center	45	0
lesbian group	33	0
lesbian/feminist bookstore	84	1
lesbian/feminist paper	129	7
lesbian bar	20	1
other lesbian/feminist business	6	0
gay group	101	399
gay bookstore (general—not lesbian)	34	145
gay newspaper	17	273
gay bar	14	93
gay bath	6	13
other gay business	4	97
Blueboy Magazine	0	2462